Third edition

Goldmine's
Price Guide to
COLLECTIBLE RECORD ALBUMS
1949-1989
By Neal Umphred

4

Published by

 krause
publications

700 E. State Street • Iola, WI 54990-0001
Telephone: 715/445-2214

Library of Congress catalog Number: 89-83584
ISBN: 0-87341-241-9
Printed in the Untied States of America

Contents

Acknowledgments...8

Foreward to the 3rd Edition..10

Another LP Price Guide: The Intro...16

    Page Breakdown..18

    Grading the Records..24

    Record Collecting Abbreviations..................................29

    Pricing the Records...30

    Shrink-wrap, Cover Stickers & Bonus Photos................35

From ⌐ 'de-Channel Stereo To Multi-Channel Mono..............37

    Early Stereo 1958-1963..37

    Late Mono...40

    Key to Abbreviations..43

Other Audiophile Treasures..44

Beatles Originals Vs. Counterfeits..47

The World's Most Valuable Album...53

The 100 Most Valuable U.S. Albums......................................55

The Godfather Of Soul At 33 1/3 RPM....................................66

The Big Sound Of The Cars..69

Record Company Label Directory..75

Record Listings A - Z..96

Various Artists Compilations / Soundtracks..........................736

Late Additions..767

Appendices

Selling Your Albums *By Perry Cox*......................................769

The Uncommon Stereo Beatles *By John Christensen*.............772

Collecting Country 'n Western Albums *By Joe Goldmark*........778

Are You Ready For Glam. ... Yet? *By Dave Thompson*............783

Acetates & Test Pressings *By Christopher Chatman*..............785

Collecting Original Cover Art *By Christopher Chatman*...........788

Collecting Gold & Platinum Record Awards *By Christopher Chatman*
....791

Bibliography..797

And The Outro: An Author's Bio (Sort Of)..............................799

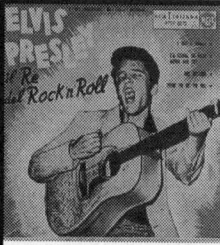

8

Acknowledgments

Thanks to the various discographies that have appeared in Goldmine by other writers and discographers over the past eighteen months; to the Goldmine readers who took the time to correspond with additions, corrections and suggestions; to my liaisons at Krause, Mary Sieber and Pat Klug; to editors Jeff Tamarkin at Goldmine, Ned Hammad at Pulse, and—especially—freelance editor and heartthrob Ingrid Seversen. This book would not be possible without the contributions of time and information from:

George Bigelow
Everett, WA

Stephen Braitman
Amourous Archives
San Francisco, CA

Ben Brown
Raleigh, NC

Cory Carrier
Salt Lake City, UT

Christopher Chatman
Beyond Records
Los Angeles, CA

John Christensen
Renton, WA

William Cristiano
Annapolis, MD

Charlie Cross
Backstreets
Seattle, WA

John DeBlaiso
Renton, WA

Chuck DeMean
Neptoon Records
Vancouver, BC, Canada

Mark Erbach
Whittier, CA

Charlie Essmeier
Retro Records
Salt Lake City, UT

Norman Feinberg
Blue Chip Records
South Salem, NY

Joe Goldmark
San Francisco, CA

Thomas Grosh
Very English & Rolling Stone
Lancaster, PA

Brian Guiberson
Seattle, WA

M. K. Hammour
Paris, France

Rick Haney
Calendula Records
Seattle, WA

Jon Hardgrove
The Carburetor Shop
Eldon, MO

Rich Haupt
Rockadelic Records
Dallas, TX

David Holder
Indianapolis, IN

Kerry Hopkins
Falls Church, VA

Ernest A. Huber, Jr.
Clifton, NJ

Ashley Johnson
Corpus Christi, TX

Gary Johnson
Rockaway Records
Los Angeles, CA

John C. Knapp
Rockville Centre, NY

Joseph Kusbel
Hammond, IN

Jeff Levy
On The Radio Broadcasting
Santa Monica, CA

Viktor Lindner
Salzburg, Austria

Barry Margolis
Hoboken, NJ

Gary Moreland
Auburn, WA

Kim Nott
San Francisco, CA

Stu Osborn
Kirkland, WA

Bill Paquin
13th Floor Records
Stockton, NJ

Walter Piotrowski
Always Elvis
Canton, MI

Simon Postbrief
Brooklyn, NY

Richie Ranno
River Edge, NJ

Rich Rockford
Vancouver, BC, Canada

Rick Ross
Thousand Oaks, CA

Bill Shonk
Jazz Grooveyard
Issaquah, WA

Neal Skok
Redmond, WA

Rod Sweetland
Sacramento, CA

Kate Turney
Newport News, VA

Todd Van Sittert
Phoenix, AZ

Tom Ventris
Long Beach, CA

Barry Wickham
Terra Linda, CA

Foreword to the 3rd Edition

In the past few years there has been a big change in the record collecting scene as one record after another exchanges hands for considerably higher sums, many attaining prices deemed improbable by otherwise astute observers. A Near Mint *Introducing The Beatles* stereo "ad-back" sold for $10,000, as did a white label promo of *Hear The Beatles Tell All*. And while it is certainly the prime pieces that are fetching the big bucks, they are not necessarily in the primest *(sic)* of conditions. A copy of the radio spots promo for the *Yellow Submarine* movie sold for $1,500 even though it was graded VG- by the seller!

It seems the purchaser of the latter had spent too many years searching for a copy in collectible condition (VG+ or better) and felt it was time to buy the first one that came his way. Which is the reasoning behind many purchases. After all, if you, as a collector, have spent more than a decade hunting for a key item for your collection, all the while assuming that *you will find it in nice shape at an affordable price* (the goal—and, too often, the delusion—of every collector of anything), at some point the realization that such a goal may not be as attainable as first surmised will probably occur. Which brings me to my redundant but sagely advice: *When you are offered a record for which you have been actively searching for more than five years, do not argue with the price. . . pay it.* The corollary to this bit of wisdom would be: If you don't, you may not see it again for another five years, *and* it will cost even more.

Of course, the big news since the previous edition of this book is that the album listed as the most valuable in that edition has been supplanted by a "new" discovery. . . Columbia CL-1986, the mono version of *The Freewheelin' Bob Dylan* pressed with several subsequently deleted tracks (refer to the accompanying article, "The World's Most Valuable Album," for more info), was listed with a suggested Near Mint value of $8,000-12,000. While it has retained this value, a stereo copy of the album (CS-8786) was found and sold for more than $12,000 in VG condition. It is listed here for the first time with a suggested Near Mint value of $15,000-25,000.

Bear in mind that the price that anyone will buy (or sell) an item for is often linked closely with the geographic and economic environment he or she is living in. A collector in New York City *should expect to pay more* for a given item than a collector from Wilkes-Barre, PA. After all, the Manhattan collector pays more for rent, a restaurant dinner, a slice of pizza, or tickets to the Mets and Yankees, because a New York City resident will be paid commensurately more for his job. Similarly, just as a dealer takes for granted that he or she will pay less for records when stocking his or her shop in Wilkes-Barre, the dealer should also expect to sell them for less *in the same market.*

So, the dealer should use this guide as just that. . . a guide. Basically, if you only find that this book helps point out the relatively rare pieces from the more common items, *even if you don't believe that you can get those prices in your market*, then the book is of value. Of course, for the collector, what may be of paramount importance is not the prices but the discographies themselves.

I believe that the more accurate, encompassing and detailed this book is the better it serves every one involved. For the dealer who is concerned that he or she may no longer be able to pick up good records for a [pitiful] fraction of their value—and as precarious an existence as wheeling and dealing in collectibles can be, that is certainly a justifiable fear—I maintain that while you will almost certainly find the instances of buying $100 records for a buck are diminished by the existence of this book, that the verification of the true market value of collectible vinyl *by this book* encourages more and more people to spend their hard-earned money on otherwise dubious investments. That is, the advantage you lose in those buys are more than compensated for by being able to service a broader market, a more educated clientele.

Should this sound like a snow job, bear in mind that in virtually every other field of collecting the price guide(s) recognized by the collectors in that field have helped the dealers enormously. One has only to turn his or her attention to what comic books and sports cards have become. Both were once regarded as "lowly" as records—lower, really—and both have left records far behind as a volatile, fluid place of business and, yes, fun.

Amassing the data necessary for this and other price guides takes years and, even after thumbing through countless books, magazines, fanzines, discographies, etc., much of the most important information remains elusive. That is because the collectors and dealers privy to this knowledge tend to guard it religiously, often in the belief that ignorance best serves their own needs. And an unwary owner of a truly rare record *can* be duped, especially if the information is either not in the price guide or, perhaps worse, is entered erroneously. My job is not to tout myself as an authority in any given field but, rather, to seek out the real authorities and convince them to share this knowledge.

The acknowledgements page that precedes this Foreword lists those collectors and dealers who were instrumental in the compilation and accuracy of this book; the contribution of each is valued and necessary if this guide is to be a growing concern. But. . . there are several individuals who performed above and beyond the call of duty in specific areas and they must be addressed separately. So, to those who have shared some of that previously hermetically sealed knowledge, special thanks to Rich Rockford for surf and car vocal records, especially The Beach Boys; Jon Hardgrove for car records, especially the non-music LPs; William Cristiano for straightening out the confusing discographies of The Fugs and The Holy Modal Rounders; Joe Goldmark for country 'n western and steel guitar albums; and Ashley Johnson for the extensive listing of private pressings.

For the new stereo data in this book I need to thank Barry Margolis, John Christensen and Ernie Huber. Norman Feinberg stepped in and shared two decades worth of experience buying and selling truly rare rock'n roll and rhythm'n blues albums from the '50s; the listings for these albums differ radically in this book from the listings the reader will find in any other such publication. And extra-specials to my constant source of updates, insights and recommendations, Rockaway's Gary Johnson.

The majority of the photos in this edition were taken by John Christensen from the collection of George Bigelow. Additional photos come from the collections of Ben Brown, Gary Moreland, Mr. Christensen himself, and the author. Should the reader be interested in submitting photos of albums for consideration, please follow this advice: Use a 35 MM camera with 400 ASA (or

27° ISO) black & white film (Tri-X appears to work best) at 1/125th-of-a-second shutter speed (or faster) to prevent blurring. Shoot the covers from directly above— *not at an angle*— on a pure white backdrop allowing as much of the cover to fill the frame as possible without cutting off the edges of the album. Set at least two table lamps with non-glare bulbs on either side of the cover and, holding the camera with a *masterful* hand or use a tripod, making sure that there is as little glare as possible on the cover. Often this entails removing plastic bags or shrinkwrap, which may not be desirable.

Any and all photos should be addressed to me, Box 40116, Bellevue, WA, USA 98015. For those wishing to contribute corrections, additions or suggestions for future editions, please don't hesitate to write me. While I can't promise that each and every letter will get a personal response in the mail, I do assure you that every bit of data is entered into the computer and every suggestion given consideration.

Portions of the text, including the articles on Beatles counterfeits, James Brown, the world's most valuable album, early stereo and late mono originally appeared in my "Avid Collector" column in *Pulse!* magazine. Published by Tower Records/Video, *Pulse!* is a monthly (except January) magazine devoting 100 pages to every aspect of the music business, primarily what's currently happening in rock, country, jazz, classical, blues, folk, world music, etc. *Pulse!* is complimentary from any Tower Records. Should you not have one near you, subscriptions are available for $19.95 (one year, third class) or $39.95 (one year, first class). Otherwise, call them at 916-373-2450 for information on a local magazine retailer that may carry the newsstand edition.

Readers familiar with the previous editions will notice that several vocalists are missing. Simply, those artists who are uniquely and exclusively jazz vocalists were deleted as their catalogs appear in *Goldmine's Price Guide To Collectible Jazz Album* (Neal Umphred, 1992) which contains 400 pages with nearly 15,000 listings in a format identical to this book. (Should you be unable to locate this book through a local source, it is available from the publisher; look for ads in this book.) Those vocalists who dabbled in both jazz and pop remain in this book. Note that the prices that are changed here on those remaining take precedence over the prices listed in the jazz guide.

Otherwise, for those who have followed my work in the *Goldmine* price guides, the essence of the introduction remains the same although there are some pertinent changes. I'd suggest the reader read on. . .

Neal Umphred,
March 1, 1993

Another LP Price Guide: The Intro. . .

This book is not the bible for record collectors; it is not the blue book of vinyl junkies; *and* it is certainly not the "official" price guide for anything. Nor does this book reflect *my opinions* of what *your records* are worth. The prices here are an attempt *to document what collectible records are worth on the open collectors market* with the prices quoted an attempt to reflect the broad differences in markets from region to region, state to state, and city to city. While attention was given to the foreign market, this is an *American price guide* that will be purchased *mostly* by American collectors, therefore I did not allow the effects of the weakened American dollar to unduly affect the pricing.

As for the fluctuations in the market, well, for those readers who expect values to rise automatically, the collectibles market is not all that different from the commodities market or the stock exchange, and *everyone* knows the wild fluctuations that occur there. So, while most prices do remain stable, or rise gradually, some rise dramatically while others actually go down. Value is established almost solely by supply and demand: Prices go up when the current demand is greater than the available supply; prices go down when the available supply is greater than the current demand.

Any number of factors can cause prices to rise or decline. The most dramatic leveller is probably the warehouse find, where boxes of a supposedly rare record turn up in sufficient quantities to meet the immediate demand, driving its value down for the near future. On the most mundane of levels, the value of a fairly common, out of print album can decline when that album is released as a compact disc, although the drop is usually temporary. When the supply dropped on the market in the wake of the record's digitalized debut is exhausted, the record will often return to its earlier value.

Each book has boundaries (size, page count, etc.) in which the author or editor must work. The more these boundaries can be defined, the more likely it is that the individual goals will be met. As most collectible records are the older ones, and that is where the main center of interest lies, I have centered the listings on those artists who started their careers in the '50s and '60s, with select artists from the last twenty years. The expanded size of this edition has allowed greater leeway in choosing what to include. You will find thousands of new titles in all fields, especially folk, psych, country, and rock 'n roll.

This book makes no attempt at completeness; rather, the reader will find more than 25,000 listings that cover, more or less the most collectible records in the business and those records most in need of attention at this point in time. While the discographies of many artists are complete, for others they are obviously incomplete. This approach is not meant as an artistic judgement on my behalf but rather an economical one. There *are* going to be instances where the information here is incomplete or wrong; it is almost unimaginable for any book listing tens of thousands of records not to make some errors. These may range in nature from common typographical errors, to transferring erroneous data from a flawed source, to incomplete research (missing catalog numbers, incorrect values assigned to records).

Although the scope of this book is wide ranging in terms of domestic releases, it does not begin to detail the staggering variety of collectible records from around the world. In most countries an album need sell only 100,000 copies to qualify for gold status, one-fifth the minimum for an American release. In effect this means that hit LPs in many countries are "rare" by American standards. The likelihood of their turning up here years later is remote. While those Americans who actively collect foreign records are relatively few, the even smaller amount of the truly rare pieces makes competition intense.

A rare and desirable rock 'n roll album from the '50s from such major markets as Canada, England or France in VG condition will regularly sell for hundreds of dollars, as near mint ones may not exist at this point in time! Imports since 1970 are more common and command reasonable prices. The attraction of these records are self-evident upon examination: In terms of the variety of releases and the quality of both the pressing and the appearance, the United States takes a back seat to many other countries.

It is difficult to view a collection of foreign records and not feel the desire to plunge right into a whole new field of collecting, one that is as rewarding and far more aesthetic than merely collecting domestic releases. Some dealers make a point of keeping large inventories of the more desirable recent releases. At the time, there is no reliable source for pricing and comparative shopping is nearly impossible. If the reader chooses to get into this aspect of the hobby, he or she will have to contact other fans and collectors and learn from scratch.

Page Breakdown

Artists are listed alphabetically using a single artist's last name first while the first important word in a group's name is the basis for their listing. When an artist's name is followed by another name in brackets, it means that the artist has recorded under two names. If the two names are similar, the records are listed together under the first name. For instance, "CHICAGO [CHICAGO TRANSIT AUTHORITY]," tells the reader that albums listed under either of those two names can be found under that one listing.

For the sake of usefulness, certain artists who started out as members of a group and who then rose to dominate the group have all of the recordings listed under the individual artist's usually better known name. For instance, while The Midnighters originally recorded under the group's name, the bulk of their material was recorded under the name Hank Ballard & The Midnighters, under which all of their recordings are grouped in this book. Similarly, the Crickets first album is listed under Buddy Holly; the Stone Poneys under Linda Ronstadt; etc.

References are kept to a minimum and refer the reader to another artist when the artist or group in question is named in the title of an album or is inseparably linked with the recording. Listing references for artists who appeared on other artist's recording is a book in itself. Should the reader desire one, the 3rd edition of Terry Hounsome and Tim Chambre's Rock Record (Blandford Press, 1987) is recommended, with thousands upon thousands of listings of who played on what, when, and where!

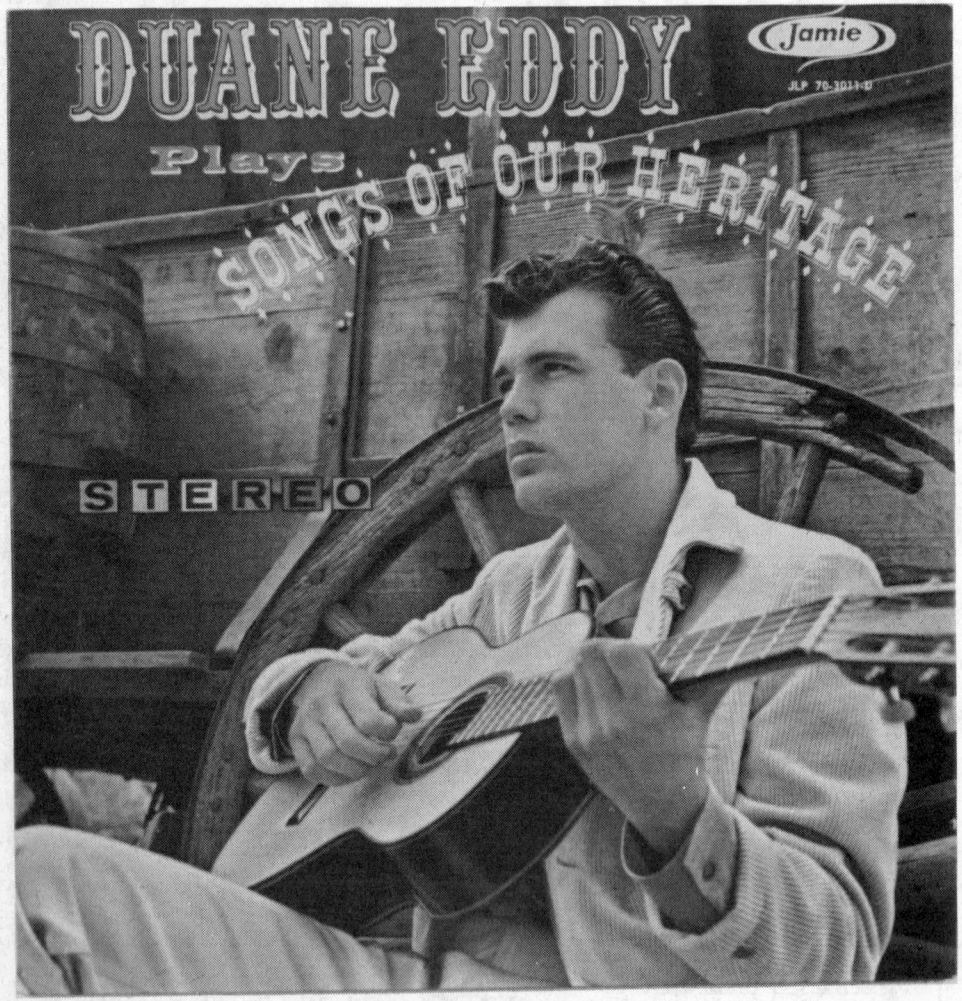

Duane Eddy's Songs Of Our Heritage was issued in a gatefold cover (i.e., the cover opens like a book) with a large full-color poster of Eddy attached to the inside cover. This poster was to be cut (along the dotted line) and opened and affixed to the fan's wall. Needless to say, finding copies of this album with the poster intact after three decades is not easy. Jamie also issued stereo copies of this album on both blue and red vinyl, also on the endangered species list.

The records are listed chronologically by label, interrupted by sound-track appearances. I have used fairly standard alphabetization throughout; there should be no real surprises for anyone familiar with an encyclopedia. Necessary notes are usually listed in italics in parentheses below the appropriate section or selections. Following is an example from the Duane Eddy listing:

Label/Catalogue #		Title	Year	VG+	NM
EDDY, DUANE					
Jamie JLP-3000	(M)	**Have "Twangy" Guitar-Will Travel**	1958	30.00	75.00
Jamie JLPS-3000	(S)	**Have "Twangy" Guitar-Will Travel**	1958	100.00	250.00
		(Yellow label. The title on the cover is in white print. "Lonesome Road," "I Almost Lost My Mind," "Three-30-Blues," "Detour," "Anytime" and "Loving You" are in true stereo.)			
Jamie JLPM-3011	(M)	**Songs Of Our Heritage** *(Gatefold cover)*	1960	26.00	65.00
Jamie JLPS-3011	(S)	**Songs Of Our Heritage** *(Gatefold cover)*	1960	34.00	85.00
Jamie JLPS-3011	(S)	**Songs Of Our Heritage** *(Blue vinyl)*	1960	80.00	200.00
Jamie JLPS-3011	(S)	**Songs Of Our Heritage** *(Red vinyl)*	1960	80.00	200.00
Jamie JLPM-3011	(M)	**Songs Of Our Heritage** *(Standard cover)*	1961	12.00	30.00
Jamie JLPS-3011	(S)	**Songs Of Our Heritage** *(Standard cover)*	1961	16.00	40.00
		— Original Jamie albums above have gold & white labels.—			

The first column indicates the label and catalog number. The second features a key notation for the record's sound: an "M" denotes a monaural recording, while an "S" means the record is stereo. An "E" indicates that the stereo effect of the album has been electronically created while a "P" indicates a partially stereo record (while most of the tracks *are* stereo, one or more are either mono or electronic stereo). "Q" indicates quadraphonic. Finally, "DJ" means that the record is a promotional disc, either uniquely promo or a promo label variation of the commercial title, which will be listed directly beneath it. Promos in the '50s and '60s should be assumed to be mono; those from the '70s on, stereo.

The record's title is the middle column; specific notes short enough to place on the same line follow. In this case, the existence of two different colored vinyl versions of Jamie 3011 are noted. These are followed by the regular first pressing on black vinyl, in this case issued in a fold-open gatefold cover. Subsequent releases, also listed, have standard single sleeve covers. This is followed by the year of release. The final two columns, the prices, are for records in the two most "collectible" conditions, very-good-plus (VG+) and near-mint (NM), and are dealt with at length below.

For those artists who achieved a long lasting popularity that saw their recordings repeatedly reissued I have attempted to list brief notations about particular records. *Notes indented beneath an album and enclosed in parentheses refer only to the title under which it is listed,* unless, of course, the note says otherwise. These may refer to that record's particular label or any other aspect that requires attention. In the example above, the note "(Yellow label. The title on the cover is in white print. . .)" refers only to Jamie 3000, *Have "Twangy" Guitar-Will Travel.* In this particular note there are two parts, the second referring specifically to the stereo release.

Notes that are centered and open (i.e., lacking parentheses) refer to two or more titles and are almost exclusively dealing with label specifications. These notes always include the qualifier "above" in their statements! As in the case of the above example which begins "Original Jamie albums above" the note applies to *all of the albums above it.*

There are several other parenthetical notes that are used on the same line as the title (space allowing): "No cover" indicates a record issued in a plain, unmarked cardboard sleeve (usually privately printed albums). Most soundtrack albums are listed as "Soundtrack;" in some cases, the abbreviation "Sdtk" was used. Similarly, while it was unnecessary to denote titles by specialist labels (Mobile Fidelity, Nautilus, Direct Disk) as half-speed masters, major labels that dipped into the audiophile field with such product are noted as "Half-speed master" (or simply "Half-speed"). Other peculiarities (colored vinyl, white label promos, etc.) are also noted in parentheses with the title.

Grading the Records

When purchasing a record at a show or through the mail (or even many stores) the buyer does not get to listen to it. For that reason, records are usually graded by visual standards, not aural. Unfortunately, this method relies on the subjectivity of the grader's eyes— or viewpoint— and the fact that records do not always play as good— or bad— as they look. For this reason *records almost always look better when selling than when buying.* Of course, the arguments against play-grading are similar: the subjectivity of the listener is also a factor, a factor that is multiplied by the type of equipment the grader is playing the record on to form his or her judgement. So, for the sake of convenience and necessity, visual grading is the standard by which almost all dealers and collectors work.

When grading a disc, *grade the overall wear of the vinyl.* A record advertised as "NM" or "VG" should tell the prospective buyer the shape of the playable vinyl. Common sense should be used: un-played records that are warped cannot be Mint. When defining the grades, it is difficult to describe several without discussing certain defects and/or the way the disc plays; these are included to help define the grade, not to cause confusion. Such defects as stickers on the label or tape on the jacket should be addressed separately with abbreviated notations. A reliable set of these notations have been developed over the years covering virtually every type of defect that can occur to a record or its cover; a list of most of the more common abbreviations and their meanings follow the grading definitions below.

Visual grading is most important in mail-order transactions where a buyer doesn't see his purchase until his check has cleared the bank. Grading needs to be as accurate as possible. The aim of grading is to make the buyer visualize the record and not be disappointed when that record arrives! A record that is accurately graded should play the same (or better) than the grading. In-person deals do not require a grade of any sort; if you are holding a record that has obviously been played a hundred times, you don't need a grade to determine whether or not you are going to purchase that disc.

Always grade records under a good, steady light. A 100 watt light bulb in a common desk-lamp will do an adequate job; most major defects will jump out and allow you to make a reasonably accurate assessment. Grading a record using light from the ceiling or from deflected sunlight entering the window will often "hide" paper scuffs, discoloration, groove wear and even some fingerprints. Remember, mistakes in grading are a problem all dealers and collectors are prone to make. Do not condemn a dealer for one mistake; but, when the mistake is the norm, find someone else to buy your records from. . .

Retro Records

Specializes in Audiophile Pressings: Original Master Recordings
SuperDiscs — Super Disks — Half-Speeds — Quiex II
& other collectables.

 **Charlie Essmeier**
PO Box 1327, Salt lake City, UT
Phone/Fax: 801-575-6413 (6 PM - 11 PM Mountain Time)

Collector of '60s and '70s garage-beat-folk-psych-prog LPs
and EPs and 45s w/PSs from Europe, Japan and Australia.
Wants to buy-sell-trade.

Ashley Johnson
344 Naples, Corpus Christi, TX 78404
512-888-5188 (No collect calls)

International Steel Guitar Discography
by Joe Goldmark

New Edition Ready in October 1993! $10 postpaid.
Lists every known steel guitar instrumental on vinyl, tape and CD.

Joe Goldmark, 2259 14th Avenue, San Francisco, CA 94116

13th Floor Records

Buy, Sell, Trade '60s Punk, Psychedelia, Pop.
Music from 1964 to the present. Private LP and 45 pressings wanted.

 **William Paquin, proprietor**
P.O. Box 129, Stockton, NJ 08559-0129
Phone: 609-397-3702

Mint. A Mint (M) record should appear to have just left the manufacturer without any handling; that is, it should appear perfect! No scuffs or scratches, blotches or stains, labels or writing, tears or splits; nothing. And age has nothing to do with it; *the same standards for Mint apply to a 10" soundtrack from 1954 as they do to a heavy metal album from 1989!* There are no sliding values for Mint.

A Mint album cover should appear to have never have had a record in it; no ring-wear, dog-eared corners, writing, seam-splits. I define ring-wear as any imprint on the cover from the record that it formerly held. *Any* imprint. To many dealers and collectors the ink has to be worn off for them to recognize ring-wear and grade a cover down. Uh-uh. Mint means perfect and nothing else.

Near Mint. A record that is otherwise Mint but has one or two tiny, inconsequential flaws that do not affect the play is Near Mint (NM) and should command 85-95% of the Mint price. For many, Near Mint and Mint-Minus mean the same thing; for the sake of this article, they are interchangeable. When dealing with a seller that discriminates between the two grades, inquire as to what the dealer means when he calls one record M- and another NM. Many dealers and collectors take the position that any used (opened) record cannot be verified as Mint so they use M- to describe what appears to be a perfect record that has been opened. Covers should still be close to perfect with minor signs of wear or age just becoming evident: slight ring-wear, minor denting to a corner, or writing on the cover should all be noted properly.

Many records *are available* in Near Mint/Mint condition, although these are generally more recent and the prices are nominal. That is, most dealers set a minimum price on the records they sell in their store, usually dollars ($3.99-4.99), just for normal, everyday, all-too-readily-available records. Whether they are un-played or "merely" near mint the price will be the same: it wouldn't be worth the dealer's time to stock the single unless that minimum price was met.

Sometimes referred to as "Excellent," a *Very Good Plus* (VG+) record has been handled and played either infrequently or very carefully. That is, an item obviously not perfect, but not *too* far from it. On a disc, this could mean that there are light paper scuffs from sliding in and out of a sleeve or the vinyl may have lost some— *not all*— of its original luster. A slight scratch that did not affect play in an otherwise nearly Mint disc would be acceptably VG+ for most collectors; a scratch of any sort that audibly clicked throughout the music would not be acceptable. Always list the flaws in a VG+ record or cover.

As a rule of thumb, a VG+ item is worth 50%, or one-half, of the Near Mint value, although this ratio varies with the rarity of the item. That is, a record that is fairly common in NM/M condition has little real value in VG+ to most collectors; consequently 25-35% may be more appropriate. On the other hand, truly rare records will fetch 75% in VG+. (By rare, I am referring to items in which the supply is merely a fraction of the demand and the record sells for hundreds of dollars. . .) On covers, some wear from storage is acceptable, especially light wear that does not affect the beauty of the artwork. Again, listing the flaws when selling is safest.

Very Good (VG) records will display visible signs of handling and play-ing, such as loss of vinyl luster, light surface scratches, groove wear, and spindle trails from countless spins on the turntable. A VG record looks like it will have some audible surface noise when it is played, although any such noise should not

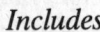

overwhelm the musical experience. VG records should appear to have been well-played although well-loved by a responsible owner. Gouges in the plating from slapping the disc down onto the spindle, rips in the label from pulling stickers formerly affixed, maple syrups spilt in the grooves by partying roomates, etc., are all unacceptable.

As more and more collectors spend more and more money on their acquisitions, the lower limits of acceptability for an item to be admitted into their collection rises. That is, to many collectors, a record in VG condition is not acceptable unless the item is truly rare and virtually unavailable in any other condition! And then, only if the price is scaled appropriately to match the condition. Used but not abused might sum up this grade. A VG record should command approximately 20-30% of the Near Mint price.

This is a difficult grade when discussing paper goods. Like a disc, usually a cover is VG when a variety of problems are evident: ring wear, seam splits, bent corners, loss of gloss on the photo, stains, etc. An aggravated combination of two of these problems— never all of them— would likely cause a sleeve to be graded VG.

Good ("G") in record collecting parlance all too often means a beat, trashed, take-it-to-the-flea-market frisbee. Good should mean that the record is well-played with any number of defects that collectors normally shy away from, such as an almost complete loss of surface sheen, aggravating surface noise, etc. Still, the purchaser, knowing full well that he or she is buying a Good record, should be able to take it home, slap it onto the turntable and have a good time listening to it. Records that do not provide this most fundamental requirement are just no good. A Good record should command 10-15% of the Near Mint price.

A Good cover has seen considerable handling over a course of years and displays the obvious signs: ring-wear on the cover; some seam-splitting, particularly along the bottom, which would receive the brunt of the record's sliding in and out; corners may be dog-eared to a light degree; an infatuated owner may have written his or her name somewhere; etc. If a record or cover is beneath your contempt, it is not in "G" condition; look below for the appropriate grade.

Any record or cover that does not qualify for the above "Good" grading should be seen as **Poor**. A "P" record should command 0-5% of the Mint price. Make a friend and give any "P" record away as a freebee to anyone who expresses interest in it. . .

Finally, it should always be borne in mind that visual evidence can be deceiving: the quality of the vinyl and the plating make all the difference in the world. A record properly manufactured with a high quality plating may look VG+ and play Near Mint; this is particularly true of records from the '50s through the mid '60s, when print runs were dramatically smaller, vinyl was fresher and more care was paid to the entire procedure. Records from this period are a better investment in VG+ condition than the more recent American product. In fact, many 45s from the '50s can be purchased in VG condition at reasonable prices and will play far better than the price paid would indicate. A record manufactured from recycled vinyl with poor plating (too many from the past 15 years) may look Mint and play VG. Still, most dealers do not have the time to listen to each item in their inventory, so visual standards remain.

Record Collecting Abbreviations

Listed here are several common abbreviations used when advertising to describe flaws and their locations on a record or cover. Different collectors/dealers have different ways of using these abbreviations; some capitalize them ("DJ"), some use periods after each letter ("n.a.p.") and some use a slash ("c/o"). Those defects marked with an asterisk (*) should *always be listed* when advertising an item for sale or auction.

cc	cut corner*
co	cut out*
coh	cut-out hole*
c-33	compact-33 1/3 rpm single or EP
cvr	cover
dj	disc jockey, or promotional, copy
imp	import
ips	inches per second
lbl	label
lp	12" 33 1/3 rpm long playing album
mo	mono, or monaural
nap	(does) not affect play
ol	on label
org	original
pln cvr	plain paper jacket (no picture or titles)
promo	promotional copy
re	reissue
reel	reel to reel tape
repro	reproduction, or counterfeit
2nd pr	second pressing
slt wrp	slight warp*
sm	saw mark (a cut-out mark)*
sm splt	seam split*
sol	sticker on the label*
sr	slight ring-wear on the front cover*
ss	still sealed
stkr	sticker
10"	10" 33 1/3 rpm album
t&ts	(disc jockey) title & timing strip
toc	tape on the cover*
tol	tape on the label*
ts	taped seams*
wlp	white label promo
wol	writing on the label*

Pricing the Records

"Yo! Just because one person paid — — — for a record doesn't mean that's what the record's *really* worth. . ." This is the remark I hear most often concerning the [presumed] excessively high values assigned to a record in one of my books. And, for the most part, I agree with the sentiments in this observation. . . most of the time. Not only do I generally *not* consider an extreme price paid for a fairly common record but the reader will note that I tend to take a rather conservative tack (those who know me personally might say I have a jaundiced view) when navigating the values of the more recent "collectibles" or artists. For instance, there was a time not too long ago when anything bearing Debbie Harry's likeness was an instant sale (including some bootlegs featuring DH's lovely face superimposed upon some rather, er, raunchy scenes). Or who can forget the great Police vogue that followed? And Bruce collectors have long paid excessive prices for new promos that have gained little in value since their release.

Certainly I try not to let such phenomenon have an undue effect on the values assigned. But. . . when the only copy of a record that has been offered for sale or auction on the open market for several years sells above and beyond anyone's wildest imaginations, when that sale is the only documented sale of that item in recent memory (and likely to be the only one for some time), then that sale, by definition, *must* have a bearing on the value assigned that record. And, as the opening paragraphs of the Foreword to this book illustrates, four figure sales for collectible records have become common. So, when the reader pages through this book and succumbs to "sticker shock" when coming upon a truly rare (and desirable) record, please bear in mind. . .

. . .the prices in this book attempt to document what records are worth *on the current market*. What that means to you, the average reader, is that these prices reflect more or less *what you should expect to pay to acquire a record that you desire*. Should you, a collector, choose to sell your records, the chances are good that, unless you run an ad in *Goldmine* or rent a table at a major show, *you will not see these prices being paid for your records*. Certainly, if you want to sell them to a dealer, you won't even come close. (Unfortunately, record dealers are not known for paying the most reasonable of rates for their inventory. In fact, if they entered any other business and tried to run it the way they run a record business, they'd be collecting food stamps within the year.)

If you will pardon my redundancy: This book is not the work of one person; it does not reflect my opinions of what your records are worth. Instead, I solicited the assistance of many collectors and dealers whom I have known for several years, both personally and professionally. Each dealer and collector was requested to provide *current values based on recent sales or purchases*, not transactions from years ago.

The records listed here are taken from a variety of printed sources plus the input of the contributors. This input and a constant scrutiny of the set-sale and auctions placed in the pages of *Goldmine* also played a part in the make-up of this book. I strived for a sense of internal consistency with the pricing so that the book as a whole works as a guideline for each region of the country to use as on outline for their own market. *Every item in this book has been scrutinized by several contributors*. The values that were decided upon represent a ball park value that takes into account each of the prices submitted by those contributors.

The prices quoted are for opened copies in either VG+ or NM condition. I use a scale that evaluates the Very Good Plus, or Excellent, condition record as a sliding percentage of the NM value as little as 40% and as much as 66%. VG prices are, for easy reference, approximately one-half (50%) of the listed VG+ value. The normal rule of thumb for pricing is that the cover makes up 40-50% of the value and the record 50-60%, although there are exceptions to this rule.

Important: For most used records the reader using this guide should start with the first, lower price and work his or her way up to a reasonable estimate. Most used records are not Near Mint and the reader is advised not to delude him/herself that the high price applies to each and every record found.

The prices quoted reflect the market during the period in which this book was assembled; *I cannot guarantee that they will remain the same for any length of time following the publication of this book.* In fact, price guides tend to have a direct—and often immediate—effect on the very market they attempt to chronicle. That is, the release of the new information from such a book into the general market can influence what collectors collect and, consequently, what prices are paid. Thus, prices listed here may be made obsolete *by their very listing,* especially when the listing offers new information or information that contradicts previously published information.

Okay—We've arrived at a point where my opinion of what your records are worth *does* come into play. . . There are some records that can be found in lesser conditions but are apparently impossible to find in Near Mint. In those cases no figure was assigned to the NM price column but a suggested range was noted parenthetically beneath the title. This is not to imply that the record is worth either the highest or the lowest of the values but rather that this range is a reasonable assessment of the discrepancies in the submitted values, the anecdotal transactions over the past and the opinions of the contributors who wheel and deal in the specific area covering the specific title. Using The Beatles as an example:

BEATLES, THE

Vee Jay SR-1062	(P)	**Introducing The Beatles** ("Ad back")	1963	**3,000.00**	Rare

*(Includes "Love Me Do" and "P.S. I Love You." The back cover has
ads for 25 other Vee Jay albums. Near Mint stereo copies have
a suggested value of $6,000-10,000.)*

As noted in the price column, the reader's attention is referred to the note, which gives an estimated NM value of $6,000 to $10,000. What this means is that a seller with a near mint copy might consider asking $10,000 for the album but should not be upset if "forced" to accept a mere $6,000. Conversely, while a buyer might win this record for as little as $6,000 he should not be surprised to find the bidding escalate to the $10,000 range. The same title in lesser condition should cut the estimated range appropriately: a VG+ copy would have a range of approximately $3,600-6,000; a VG copy ranges from $1,800-3,000.

The reader will find several of these records in the listings with a parenthetical note claiming the album is "Rare and generally sold in VG or less condition" and then giving three prices for the album: VG, VG+ and the nearly nonexistent NM. When this occurs, the reader should assume that the best he or she is ever likely to see (barring a miracle) is a clean VG copy sans major defects. That is, even hoping for a VG+ copy at this point may be delusive. . .

Bear in my that these are my suggestions, not dictates. They also apply to records that meet the standards of grading espoused by this book, sold on the open, competitive market, and, generally, by dealers or collectors with some reputation for accuracy and honesty. Instances where these records sell for less (or more) will occur— do occur.

The *average* dealer or collector is often years (at least months) behind the reality of the market when it comes to the specialized knowledge of truly rare records, mainly because they are so rare that few, if anyone, ever sees them for sale at any price. For example, the prices that are quoted for early '50s rhythm 'n blues 10" LPs may appear preposterous to a '60s British Invasion specialist; but r 'n b collectors know that certain titles are difficult to find at any price! *The more knowledgeable you are, the more useful and informative this book will be,* if only that the informed reader will be better able to assimilate the information and make use of it on a day to day basis.

Many collectors have expressed concern over the effects the overseas buyer has had on American records. The continued slump in America's ability to cope with honest competition (versus the collusion of the domestic market in general) may have glutted the coffers of the multi-national corporations that bend our elected officials' ears. This slump has also led to a weakened dollar and, thus, the ability of the European and Japanese collector to outbid the American collector. To ignore these events would be both futile and counter-productive. Thus, a reasonably common item that goes for a bigger dollar overseas is not unduly affected because the foreign collectors only purchase a fraction of the copies put up for sale each year!

But. . . a record that turns up infrequently (only a few times a year), and invariably leaves the country to an overseas collector who bids two or three times what American collectors believe the record is "really" worth, then those prices *do* determine the value of those records. I would, in effect, be doing you, the user of this book, a disservice were I to choose any other option. *The average American collector needs to know what he or she should expect to have to bid to win a truly rare and desirable record in an open auction on the open market.* Please bear in mind that many of the records listed here, especially those with three figure values, will sell for considerably more overseas than here. It is worth noting that there are many jazz albums (a field not covered in this book) that consistently sell to affluent Japanese collectors for $1,000, none of which are even offered to American collectors by the knowledgeable jazz dealer.

And then, of course, there are the budget labels. . . Many labels sprang up over the years that specialized in leasing masters of previously released material, usually of artists who were no longer hot, and all too often issuing albums in the cheapest possible manner: poor mastering, poor pressings on low grade vinyl, etc. These labels include Crown, Diplomat, Grand Prix, Guest Star, Spin-o-rama, Wyncote, and the undisputed king of low budget labels in America, Pickwick. While some of these labels did collect important material— Crown began by issuing great R&B— most of them issued albums of less than collectible consequence. Spingboard seemed to flood the department stores of America with a slew of new titles in the first few years of the '70s, many compiling sides that had not previously appeared on albums and which have become modestly collectible. Needless to say, most of the albums have little value and are almost impossible to sell, even sealed, for more than a few bucks. Most are *not* listed here unless they are of some importance.

Shrink-wrap, Cover Stickers & Bonus Photos

Please note that the prices quoted are for opened copies in either VG+ or NM condition. In many cases collectors are willing to pay a premium for still-sealed copies. Depending on the age and desirability of the record, the premium may be a modest 10% above the NM price to 50% above it; in the case of certain items, the increase would be dramatically greater. Sealed copies of Beatles albums on Capitol are worth three or four times the NM price listed in these pages. Albums with a sticker on the shrink-wrap advertising an enclosed bonus or calling attention to a hit single generally command a premium above and beyond what plain shrink-wrap would generate. While this could be a modest 10% for common albums or less collectible artists, it can double the price of a rare record or desirable name, such as the Beatles or Elvis.

While most titles on budget labels are repackages of old material leased from other labels and have very little value, in the latter part of the '60s, Crown Records released a couple of original titles of psych exploitation -- The Firebirds' Light My Fire *and The 31 Flavors'* Hair *(pictured here) -- both of which are very hard to find and are only beginning to attract collectors.*

Even more important is the practice of applying stickers directly to the cover. While dozens of Presley albums came with stickers on the shrink wrap, only a few carried a sticker on the cover and each of these is considerably more valuable than its corresponding number without the sticker. The first such album was *A Date With Elvis*, an album prepared while Elvis was in the U.S. Army in 1958-59. Nowhere on this album are the list of song titles and the possibility exists that this was to have been held as Elvis' "new" album should RCA be able to get Elvis into the studio while he was still in the service. The prepared sleeve *was* used for a compilation of earlier, released recordings and RCA applied a red sticker with the song titles directly to the front cover.

A year later the jacket for Elvis' first album of new recordings after leaving the Army was prepared while Elvis was still active. As RCA could not have known the album's contents, *Elvis Is Back!* was prepared without song titles printed on the cover. When Elvis was whisked into RCA's Nashville studios for four days in March and April, 1960, enough material for three singles and an album was completed. When the contents of the LP were decided, RCA again applied a sticker with the song titles to the cover. (Later pressings of both albums have the contents printed on the cover.)

Capitol also took to applying stickers to covers calling attention to a big hit or something of note on the LP, including several Beach Boys and Kingston Trio albums (although they could not be identified in time for this volume). And, while they certainly require a premium, they are not in the league of the Presley items above. Of a different concern is the recently documented existence of the Beatles' first Apple album, *The Beatles*, with at least two different possible stickers attached to the otherwise blank white covers. One sticker, nine inches in length and a garishly translucent red, noted the album's song titles and other pertinent data. A copy in VG+ condition recently sold for $300. A second sticker, a more modest four inches in length, also exists. Given the nature of the album's pristine graphics, I would assume these stickers were applied to copies sent to radio stations so that programmers would know what they were receiving.

As for still-sealed albums: First, shrink-wrapping albums at the factory was not a common practice until the early to mid-'60s. A label as large as Capitol was using the fact that their albums were "poly-wrapped in the factory" as late as

January 1964 as a selling point to the consumer. Should you be offered an album from the '50s or early '60s still sealed in shrink-wrap, think twice. Generally, a dealer cannot be held responsible for what is inside a sealed jacket. For example, during Elvis' career RCA often printed far more covers than records on the initial run (it saved money) and subsequently used the covers until they ran out. It is rather common to find second and third pressing records in first pressing covers. Consequently, Elvis collectors are not as obsessed with sealed copies and would rather see an opened Mint copy than take a chance on a sealed one.

There is also the practice of re-sealing albums. This was done over the years by the record companies and by firms specializing in remainders (I don't remember anyone calling them cut-outs in the '60s). Prior to the sales boom of the mid '70s, the industry had a very loose policy regarding returns; many of us over "thirtysomething" grew up able to test a purchase out on the store's turntable before taking it home. (*And* were often able to return records that we just plain didn't like. Of course, those were pre-corporate days when retail operations were independently owned and operated, and the proprietor knew most of his customers and catered to their needs).

When purchasing a valuable sealed collectible at a shop or show, pay for the record *with the mutual understanding* that you will open it *immediately after purchase, in front of the dealer,* and if the record inside is not what it should be, *you may return it on the spot.* Do not purchase a sealed record, leave, and return later claiming that you got the wrong record or a damaged copy. Naturally, very few dealers will offer a refund in such a case. On a less savory note, there are more than a few dealers and shops that do their own shrink-wrapping.

Companies often included a "bonus photo" to special albums or deluxe packagings. This practice became gospel with RCA's release of the [generally godawful] Elvis soundtracks of the '60s. These bonuses are noted when known throughout the listings. Should the reader have an album with such a bonus that is not listed, he or she should certainly consider the photo to be a desirable acquisition worth more than the album without such a photo.

In the mid '60s, record companies began printing on the covers of select albums a black circular notification of the title's being awarded a "Gold Record Award Audited And Certified By RIAA." This was, no doubt, meant to impress upon prospective purchasers the fact that so many others had already bought the album that perhaps he or she should also add this to his or her collection. . . For the most part these stickers were added to the album *after it had sold the required amount* (and for more on that, please refer to the article on RIAA Gold & Platinum Records in the appendices of this book). So, excepting those albums that were certified Gold based on advance orders, it must be assumed that copies of an album bearing this seal are, in fact, technical second pressings and that technical first pressings exist without the seal.

The importance of this cannot be underestimated: Finding copies of Ray Charles' classic *Modern Sounds In Country & Western* or any of The Mamas & The Papas' first three albums without this seal can be frustrating. While it was not possible to document the many cases where this seal denotes a second pressing, the reader should be aware of this (and, of course, with the readers' cooperation, future editions will carry more data distinguishing first and second pressings).

From Wide-Channel Stereo To Multi-Channel Mono

During the early years of stereo, approximately 1957-1963 (in England, true stereo recording and mixing was not the norm until 1967-68!), much of the best rock 'n roll, rhythm 'n blues and country 'n western recordings were done under less than state-of-the-art conditions and the technicians involved in making the master tapes were far more adept in mixing down to mono than creating a good stereo two-track. Conversely, by the early 1970s the ability, or sensibility, to mix multi-track recordings down to a single mono track had been "lost" by the majority of the engineers and producers of popular recordings.

Similarly, *today's* technicians have lost the means to mix contemporary multi-tracks (24, 48, 64, ad infinitum) down into the popular stereo of the '60s, known affectionately as "wide channel" stereo due to the distinct placement of the individual sounds in the two channels. Consequently, when a CD version of a popular '50s or '60s recording is remixed, the listening experience for the older fan can be downright shocking! While the track *may* be cleaned up and the dynamics expanded, the new mix can be disconcertingly different from the original. The wide channel stereo sound is often gone, replaced by the more natural, less affecting mix (often referred to as "multi-channel mono") with which today's engineers are familiar.

Original wide-channel stereo recordings made no attempt at reality but went for effect. The placement of individual instruments in the two separate channels made for a more involving listening experience, essentially inviting the brain to participate in completing the mix-down from the widely disparate signals emanating from the two speakers. Collectors of this type of technology pursue the best examples of it, not necessarily concentrating on the particular type of music involved.

Early Stereo 1958-1963

While two track recordings were made through the mid '50s, very few rock, blues or country records were cut in stereo. Consequently, early albums in true stereo are rare and highly desirable. *The Teddy Bears Sing!* (Imperial LPS-12067, 1959) is a legendary stereo album, long commanding big bucks. Featuring neophyte Phil Spector as one of the Teddys, the clean, wide open sound makes this desirable as a rock 'n roll rarity, as a stereo album and as a Spector artifact.

When stereo masters have been lost, which has happened frequently, original stereo pressings become even more valuable. The first rock 'n roll to contain true stereo recordings, Duane Eddy's *Have "Twangy" Guitar—Will Travel* (Jamie JLPS-3000, 1958), was originally issued with the title on the front cover in white letters. Jamie re-issued the album with the title in red letters, presenting a much more visibly arresting product on the racks. Within a few years, the stereo masters were lost! So, while Eddy's first album has been available in rechanneled stereo for thirty years, the early pressings remain among the most sought-after stereo albums of the '50s.

Long collected as one of the earliest stereo pop/rock albums, The Teddy Bears Sing! *features the nascent talents of one Phil Spector as singer, songwriter and arranger, and Carol Kleinbard, who later made a splash during the surf era as Carol Connors. 1961's* A Lot Of Dominos *is one of only two albums issued in stereo during Fats' fifteen-year stay with Imperial.*

Apparently unknown to the artist, both of Del Shannon's first two albums *Runaway* (Big Top 3003, 1961) and *Little Town Flirt* (1308, 1963) were issued in stereo in mono covers, sometimes stamped "Stereo" and sometimes unmarked. *Little Town Flirt* even carries a mono label and must be played to ascertain whether or not it is mono or stereo! While these records are of modest artistic achievement and rudimentary stereo, they continue to escalate in value due not only to their rarity (which existed on the day of their release) but the fact that the stereo master tapes have long since vanished.

At the other end of the audiophile spectrum are Roy Orbison's first two albums for Monument, *Lonely And Blue* (14002, 1961) and *Crying* (14007, 1962), considered by many to be among the very finest pop/rock stereo albums ever made. In this case, the extraordinary sound, impeccably produced by Fred Foster and magically mixed by Bill Porter, and the gorgeous performances more than justify the records' reps. In between these extremes are Fats Domino's two lonely stereo releases for Imperial, *A Lot Of Dominos* (12066, 1960) and *Let The Four Winds Blow* (12073, 1961) both issued on black labels with silver print and among the Fat Man's rarest LPs.

In some cases, mere economics can affect a record's rarity. Due to the incredible mix-up that the Chicago-based rhythm 'n blues label Vee Jay went through in the '60s (a time when even having The Beatles on the label couldn't save them), many of their albums had virtually nonexistent stereo press runs. Gene Chandler's *Duke Of Earl* (Vee Jay SR-1040, 1962) appears to have undergone a mass of variations, both legitimate and not, and is virtually impossible to find in stereo. When boxes of supposedly stereo copies of *Duke Of Earl* found their way onto the market, the discs inside proved to be mono, leading many to believe they were illegal reproductions.

When the British Invasion was in full swing, many of the tapes that were sent here for the American market were dramatically altered by American engineers, often adding over-generous echo and/or reverb to fill in the "hole" left by the cleaner British separation. Most U.S. fans grew up hearing a very different set of recordings than what their cross-Atlantic counterparts were listening to (or, for that matter, what the artists *intended* them to hear). This was so common that an attempt to list the tracks/albums affected would take up pages; suffice to say that virtually everyone— including the Beatles— suffered under this system.

When imports became common in many parts of the U.S. in the early '70s, listeners were often astounded at hearing the differences between the original U.K. versions of albums such as *Aftermath* or *Revolver*, where the lack of echo made both Jagger's and Lennon's voices decidedly English, an effect softened by the American tinkering.

The joys of two channel listening are not merely confined to rock music fans; to some extent the interest lies in both country and rhythm 'n blues, which is, admittedly, not as strong but has been growing in the past few years. In the field of classical music collecting, stereo specialists have become so rampant as to all but dominate the field. The pursuit of such proven labels as RCA Victor's "Living Stereo" (with a "shaded dog," of course) and Mercury's "Living Presence" originals has moved whole runs of titles into the $100 range while leaving their mono counterparts as used record store staples. About the only field where this is not the rule is with jazz collecting, where the serious listener tends to prefer the unencumbered straight to tape mono sound over the often doctored stereo effect.

Late Mono 1967-1968

The practice of issuing new albums in both monaural and stereo was phased out of the American market by 1968. Many of the mono albums from mid 1967 through '68 are very rare *and* valuable. Just as stereo copies of Elvis' first few albums from 1960 are worth considerably more than the monos, the reverse is true for his albums from this period. The mono version of 1967's *Clambake* (RCA Victor LPM-3893) is currently worth nearly four times the stereo version (LSP-3893). But this pales in comparison to his 1968 albums: *Elvis' Gold Records, Volume 4* (LPM-3921) and *Speedway* (LPM-3989), are worth $1,000 while the black label stereos fetch $40!

Several West Coast bands have highly collectable mono albums from this period: At one time or another, every member of Jefferson Airplane has expressed his or her disgust with the distracting echo and distortion of the stereo *Surrealistic Pillow*. But the mono mix (RCA Victor LPM-3766, 1967) is devoid of most of this echo and a more accurate reflection of the band's intentions (*and* a better listening experience). Similarly, *The Grateful Dead* (Warner Bros. W-1689, 1967) is far more potent a mix than the readily available stereo version and a must-own for Dead Heads.

The Doors (Elektra EKL-4007, 1967) is a must for Morrison aficionados. Seems that when Jimbo recorded the album's closer, "The End," he was still tingling from the previous night's acid experience (No, dear, there are no such things as "flashbacks") and was a bit more uninhibited than usual. At the song's climax, where he rants "Father, I want to kill you" and the band goes into its raga rave-up, there comes a point where Morrison can be heard chanting "Kill, kill, kill." He followed this with a muttered "Fuck, fuck, fuck," which was buried in the stereo mix but can be discerned on the more up-front mono mix.

Sgt. Pepper's Lonely Heart's Club Band (Capitol MAL-1653, 1967), while a cornerstone of multi-track recording and still a lot of fun to hear on head-phones, has its adherents as a monaural experience. The dub-downs from the multi-tracks to mono were supervised by producer and fifth Beatle George Martin, usually with the group, while the stereo mix-downs were left to the engineer. No less an authority than John Lennon maintained that "You haven't heard *Sgt. Pepper* if you haven't heard it in mono." Unfortunately, by 1967, few of the group's fans were interested in mono, making *Pepper* and *Magical Mystery Tour* (Capitol MAL-2835) among the rarest commercially issued Beatles albums on Capitol.

Some labels continued to release promotional albums in mono after phasing it out commercially. Jimi Hendrix's *Electric Ladyland* (Reprise 2R-6307, 1968) is the most valuable mono promo, valued at $800; Reprise also issued *Ladyland* as a stereo white label promo, currently worth $125. Other collectable white label promos include The Who's *Magic Bus* (Decca DL-5064, 1968), which garners some of its value due to the fact that several of the tracks on the stereo versions are messily rechanneled, and 1969's *Tommy* (Decca DXW-7205).

Monomania is not restricted to "important" albums by "major" artists: While earlier albums by The Monkees are garage-sale staples, *The Birds, The Bees & The Monkees* (Colgems COM-109, 1968) is the rarest commercially issued album by the post-fab four. Both *Steppenwolf* and *Steppenwolf The Second* (D-50029 and D-50037, 1968) are rare and sought after. Several country artists recording for RCA Victor had albums issued in mono in late 1968 and these are starting to attract attention from completists in that field.

Two of 1967's more sought-after monaural albums: Surrealistic Pillow is burdened with some of the most reverberant echo in pop history. While this is still evident on the mono mix, it is noticeably diminished, making the listening experience more rewarding. The Doors is also cleaner in mono, but more important is the fact that an important part of the one track's performance that was buried in the stereo mix can be heard on the mono album.

Unfortunately, in many cases, when purchasing a rare late mono album all one is acquiring is a rarity. By the middle of 1967 many companies simply had their engineers take the two track stereo masters and dub them down into a single track instead of preparing a properly mixed mono master. Because of this, many of these albums are decidedly inferior to their stereo counterparts, producing an unbalanced, muddy sound. While many a Byrds collector has avidly sought the very rare mono version of *The Notorious Byrd Brothers*, they are often disappointed if they were hoping for a different mix similar to that of the group's previous *Younger Than Yesterday*.

Considering the unlikelihood of the mono mixes of any these LPs making it onto CD (although EMI/Capitol's issuing the Beatles complete catalog in mono *and* stereo is not only not out of the question, it is recommended), it becomes all the more desirable to own and hear the truly classic albums of the psychedelic '60s the way the bands wanted you to hear them (and none of these LPs have climbed into the stratosphere with Elvis. . . yet.)

This article is *not* about albums issued *only* in mono after 1968. Continuing with Presley, the soundtrack to his '68 TV Special, *Elvis* (RCA Victor LPM-4088) consisted primarily of mono tracks from the now legendary "Burbank sessions" that were recorded live before a miniscule [and select] audience in June. While several tracks do appear in stereo, RCA wisely applied their mono "LPM" prefix to the album. After the demise of mono, many of the majors appeared to rethink their position on the practise of "electronically rechanneling" mono masters into a horrid phony stereo. By the '70s archival material was surfacing in original mono for the first time in years. RCA again was notable with Elvis' *Sun Sessions* in 1975, compiling for the first time what many historians consider to be the most important body of rock 'n roll music ever recorded.

Many important albums were issued in mono abroad after the American label had discontinued the practice. These range from such obvious classics as 1968's *The Beatles* and *Beggar's Banquet* (which is far more dynamic and powerful in mono) through 1969's *Let It Bleed, The Kinks Are The Village Green Preservation Society* and several prominent non-Beatles Apple titles. The collector interested in pursuing foreign pressings such as these is advised to expect a precarious but interesting pursuit.

Then there is the quadramania of the early '70s. Quadraphonic (a different signal emanating from four different channels and requiring separate electronic components to decode the signals) pressings are attractive for a variety of reasons, scarcity being the most obvious. But of far more interest is the fact that many quads have radically different, and sometimes superior, mixes to the original stereo. The best known instance is *Sly & The Family Stone's Greatest Hits:* The stereo album contains three singles— "Everybody Is A Star," "Hot Fun In The Summertime," and "Thank You (Falletinme Be Mice Elf Again)"— in fake stereo. When their engineers mastered the quadraphonic album, they dug up the original multi-tracks and issued all of the tracks in four channel sound, the closest approximation of stereo that collectors have found of the aforementioned trio! Jefferson Airplane's *Volunteers* is also notable for including at least four tracks with alternate takes or mixes. These remained unavailable to the general public until the recent release of the compact disc boxed set *Jefferson Airplane Loves You.*

Key to Abbreviations

(DJ)   The price is for a disc jockey, or promotional, copy. Traditionally these have white labels with black print—which remain the most popular with collectors although some companies have used other colors or variations on their standard label with "For Promotional Use" or "Audition Copy" added to the label *at the record's manufacturing*. Stock copies with promotional notices stamped or affixed to the cover or the label after the fact are not included in this category. While these records certainly have some value, they are not in the same league as manufactured promos.

(M)   The price is for a monaural (one signal emanating from both speakers) record, manufactured almost exclusively from inception through the late '50s and in tandem with stereo through the demise of mono in 1968.

(S)   The price is for a stereo (two separate, individual signals, one emanating from each speaker) album, issued in tandem with monaural from the late '50s through the demise of vinyl in the late '80s.

(E)   The price is for a record which has its stereo effects electronically created by engineers after the fact from the original monophonic signal. The most common form is projecting the mono signal with boosted highs from one speaker and the same mono signal with boosted bass in the other. Echo, phasing and time delays are also used. Known as "rechanneled stereo," these are generally frowned upon and normally only collected by completists.

(P)   The price is for a record that is stereo overall but may contain one or more tracks (usually singles recorded in mono) in either rechanneled stereo or in mono.

(Q)   The price is for a quadraphonic album (four separate signals emanating from four separate speakers requiring special playback equipment: a quadraphonic pre-amp and four speakers), in vogue in the early '70s. As the quad signal was mixed from the stereo multi-tracks, these albums are sought after for the often very different—and sometimes superior—mix and the occasional instance where the quad album contains true stereo tracks that exist in rechanneled stereo on the album's stereo counterpart.

Other Audiophile Treasures

One interesting facet of record collecting shuns the emulation of individual artists or styles in favor of, for lack of a more appropriate term, the recording's overall sound. These collectors are concerned with an accurate recreation of the musical event as it originally occurred in its natural environment. Many of these listeners place a primary emphasis on "sound field" recordings, those that, by use of the most appropriate equipment in the proper environment, with mikes properly placed and, most importantly, no post-recording manipulation of the signal, come closest to achieving the idealized sound presentation. Needless to say, most of this is not applicable to popular music, where the very opposite is the case: Most pop recordings since the mid-'60s have been recorded in the sterile environment of the studio, often in bits and pieces, with the use of over-dubbing, compression, etc., often grossly over-using the medium to manipulate the message.

Originally dubbed "golden ears," these hobbyists emerging from early hi-fi were not simply satisfied with whatever technology was available on a mass-produced basis for a reasonable price. These hobbyists pursued a more perfect medium, through the selection of the correct gear, the placement of speakers, the "tweaking" of each and every facet of their equipment and the environment in which it was enjoyed. Often perceived as obsessed by the more relaxed majority, many of the innovations now taken for granted, both in the hardware (the electronics and other playback equipment) and the software (the records, etc.), can be traced directly to the interventions, insights and perseverance of these pioneers.

In record collecting, the term "audiophile" is generally applied to those who specialize in high-quality recordings on high-quality vinyl. While every album *could have* been an audiophile pressing, few were and the standard of quality, especially in the amount of pressings done from each stamper to the quality of the vinyl used, dropped during the '70s. It was also quite normal for the major companies to finish up the making of an album—after the recording and post-production technical work is complete—by cutting a master lacquer disc in a matter of hours. From these are produced "mothers" and from them the "stampers" from which the records are actually pressed.

In a high volume business with a name star, the stampers can be used well past the point of their being able to reproduce the extremes in the highs and lows from the master. In fact, the industry's disregard for their customers and, of course, the apparent lack of discrimination *of* their customers, led to enormous quantities of noticeably inferior records flooding the American retail racks. Some sources claim that as much as 75-80% of the press run of Michael Jackson's *Thriller* were shipped defective. . . and the company knew and could not care less!

The vogue for half-speed mastered albums was ushered in by Mobile Fidelity Sound Laboratories at the end of the '70s and lasted, more or less, through the early years of the "digital revolution" of the '80s. As the general level of quality of American manufactured records dropped like the proverbial SAT scores, this enterprising company stepped in and leased master tapes from the original companies, manufacturing high quality records with a correspondingly high price (most of us paid as much as $20 per album way back then). Eventually, several other small companies followed suit and a mini-industry serving the perceived needs of a dedicated few blossomed. Mobile Fidelity's "Original Master Recording" series utilized a mastering process whereby the master lacquer was cut at 16 2/3 RPM rather than the industry standard of 33 1/3 (hence, half-speed mastered). This allowed the cutting of the grooves twice as much time to capture each nuance of the analogue recording.

Other steps—special mastering equipment including custom designed cutting heads, amplifiers, etc.—were taken to ensure accuracy but the most important to collectors was the shipping of the stampers to Japan where the albums were pressed on virgin vinyl by JVC (actually, they were pressed on that company's trademark "Super Vinyl"). This not only ensured a more faithful reproduction of the sound but allowed the user to play the disc repeatedly with less fear of damaging the grooves. Each album was pressed with a maximum number of 5,000 copies from each of the four stampers taken from the "mother," at which point the stampers were destroyed. Thus each disc was a "limited edition" of such noticeably superior quality that left many a listener speechless upon first hearing.

Other labels, such as Sheffield Lab, Wilson Audio and Reference Recordings, also specialized in audiophile pressings but their main output was jazz and classical and therefore outside the perimeters of this volume. The Nautilus label half-speed "SuperDiscs" were less successful on the market than MFSL and consequently their titles are a bit harder to find, although the demand is not as great from the collectors. Other collectible audiophile labels exist outside the boundaries of the increasingly xenophobic U.S., such as Cube (Germany), Vertigo (U.K.), CBS (Canada, Germany and Japan), Nimbus (U.K.) and A&M (Canada). While these pressings are outside the scope of this book, these companies' products are often available domestically and sought out by audiophiles.

Among the major labels, CBS poured out a number of their Columbia and Epic catalog in this format, but these were done in relatively small printings, did not fare well on the retail racks and thus, the demand for certain titles is increasing. The actual pressings themselves, from inception through mastering and pressing, were qualitatively far behind the smaller companies, leaving a great deal to be desired. When the relative failure of this line was obvious, rather than simply delete the titles and make them available to cut-out bins nationwide, CBS simply recalled them and recycled the vinyl for future use, making many of the CBS titles difficult indeed to track down. Thus their value as collectibles outstrips their value as vehicles for a truly pleasing listening experience. Collectors are continually discovering "new" CBS titles in this format; there are rumors of a couple of McCartneys and Aerosmiths, a Billy Joel. . .

While the prices for audiophile oriented collectibles will continue to rise steadily if not always dramatically, the rest of the market is volatile, with dramatic rises and declines in values, sometimes seemingly overnight, as a "new" piece is discovered, pursued and purchased. The prices on many items listed in this book have been influenced by this market, but, while the influence is obvious, it may seem negligible to the specialist collector, who knows that the values listed herein are well below the current established norms within the circles he or she moves.. (The interested reader should note that captions to many of the photos throughout this edition make reference to the effects that the audiophile community has had on the collectibility of certain albums.)

There is also the issue of still-sealed copies of audiophile recordings, which often sell for many times the value of a mint copy. The demand here, which may be far in excess of that of the mainstream collector, is best placed in context by considering that many audiophiles have cartridges on their tone arms worth more than the average collector's entire sound system. The idea of subjecting said cartridge to the trauma of a worn record makes little sense. This does not apply across the board: Charlie Essmeier of Retro Records is one of several dealers specializing in audiophiles' needs; he was primarily responsible for the list below. Regarding the current state of the market, Charlie noted "It's hard to get a premium for sealed copies of the CBS titles, largely because they have a bad reputation sound-wise. Oddly enough, these are the hardest half-speed mastered LPs to find in sealed condition!"

The average consumer continues to spend their hard earned money on CDs, often liquidating their vinyl at a fraction of their value. (Anyone out there taking a quarter an album for their collection?) "Don't be fooled by the digital revolution," continues Essmeier. "The prices of these LPs are continuing to increase. Titles that were common just two years ago are commanding high prices today. The Ry Cooder *Jazz* has turned out to be the most highly sought-after Mobile Fidelity album and perhaps the rarest, as well. I'm also pleased to hear that they plan to release some new vinyl titles in 1993; they obviously feel that the demand is still there. Not that it's news to me: I sell lots of import titles that aren't pressed on vinyl here. And some that are. . . Who can find them?"

Promotional collectibles associated with these labels include test pressings made for each of Mobile Fidelity's "Original Master Recordings." These have plain white labels and were issued in plain cardboard jackets.; early titles have "JVC Sample Record-Not For Sale" printed on them (and possible hand-written information) while later pressings read "MFSL Inc." These generally sell for approximately twice the title's listed Near Mint value. They also manufactured test pressings for each of The Beatles' titles for their "Ultra High Quality Recording" (UHQR) series (the next step up from the "OMR"). These are very collectible and can be found under The Beatles section in the main listings. Similarly, Nautilus pressed promo copies of their titles on white labels and issued them in plain cardboard covers with a sticker of a nautilus shell. While these follow the general guidelines for promos elsewhere in the introduction to this book, it needs to be pointed out that the promo for John & Yoko's *Double Fantasy* is the rarest and most valuable ($400) of the Nautilus promos and can be found under Lennon & Ono in the listings.

The concerns of the audiophile has spawned several nationally distributed publications, the best known being *Stereo Review* and *Audio*. The more arcane aspects of the hobby has also spawned at least two publications that deal at least peripherally with the concerns of the software (i.e., the recorded medium, either vinyl or CD). Both *The Absolute Sound* and *Stereophile* devote space to reviewing exceptionally well recorded and manufactured music and, while the emphasis is often on the more spectacular classical realms, they do pay attention to the type of music covered in this book. (All four of the afore-mentioned periodicals are available at any well-stocked magazine stand.)

Finally, it should be interesting to observe where current standards are heading. CBS has just introduced their new series of [higher priced] CDs with superior mixes and sound due to the improved ability of the "bits" per sound that can be sampled. This from an industry that has told us that compact discs were already perfect. . .

Beatles Originals Vs. Counterfeits

In May 1970, as millions of expectant fans rushed to stores to purchase what would be the Beatles' ultimate album, *Let It Be* (Apple AR-34001), dirty deeds were done. Someone with enormous financial reserves and enviable contacts in the music business apparently acquired legitimate stampers for the album sides and proceeded to mass produce their own [counterfeit] copies of the album. Good quality copies of the labels and jacket art were acquired in the usual manner; i.e., photo-copying the originals. While the exact figure of how many counterfeits were pressed is, needless to say, unavailable, all reasonable sources estimate it at approximately 2,000,000 copies.

United Artists, who acted as distributors for this Apple release, remarked that *it was the only time in history that more returns were accepted than original copies shipped!* (Of course, we will not even begin to speculate how millions of copies of an illegal record found their way into the hands of hundreds of distributors and thousands of retail outlets throughout America without *someone* raising an eyebrow in the direction of justice. That's show biz, right?)

Sales of *Let It Be* are supposed to now exceed 4,000,000 copies. Thus the counterfeit's press run makes up half of the copies that were available for sale in the United States. As the counterfeits were returned to the manufacturer along with the legitimate copies, the two occupied the same cut-out bins throughout the '70s. So, depending on the figures above, any reader who purchased a copy of this album under the belief they were acquiring an "original"— and that includes collectors who have purchased copies from used records shops or mail-order dealers— have a 50% chance of owning a counterfeit just as many a seller at a record show stands a 50/50 chance of offering a fake for sale!

And, as Retro Records Charlie Essmeier explains, "There is no polite way to tell someone that the record they have for sale is a fake. They *always* get defensive... Still, as many collectors don't know what to look for, it's only fair to try to warn them, so that they don't get taken in by a dealer who doesn't know better. At times it seems like every interesting album has been counterfeited and now we have to deal with these records being offered for sale as originals!"

The reader needs to understand that there is a difference between a "second pressing," which must be an authorized reissue on the same label as the original, and a counterfeit or reproduction, which are unauthorized (and, in this country, always illegal). A counterfeit is an attempt at an exact copy of a legitimate record. Many are fairly obvious: The covers are blurred photocopies of the originals, the labels tend to be uneven, and the sound quality is obviously "mastered" from another record. At the time of their "release" they were almost always sold on the collectors market as second pressings or bootlegs. On the opposite end of the scale, many are of such professional duplication that it is damn near impossible to tell the real from the unreal without being made aware of the differences and having one of each to compare with one another.

So, getting back to *Let It Be*, just how does one ascertain which is which? While one can go through a variety of comparisons— the original covers are sharply defined while the counterfeits are a tad off with a bit too much red— the easiest way is to simply slide the disc out of the jacket and check the trail-off vinyl (the inch or so of vinyl between the last track and the label, also referred to as "dead wax"). No matter how good your copy looks and plays, legitimate copies *must* have "Bell Sound" machine-stamped in the dead wax. Period.

Unfortunately, the other fakes in the Fab's catalog are not so readily discerned. There were several variations in the legitimate pressing of the group's previous release, *Abbey Road* (Apple SO-383, 1969, and their last *recorded* album), and one was copied. Should your copy have an Apple label that reads "Mfd. by Apple" along the perimeter at the bottom (first pressings were manufactured by Capitol and bear the parent company's logo along the bottom), check your album against other copies. Should yours prove to have an inferior cover and label with somewhat diluted colors and less than sharp print, chances are you've got a fake.

Now for the reader who thinks that this heinous practice only bore its illegal head toward the end of the Fab Four's seven year hiatus as the world's most popular foursome, I bear more bad news: In 1963, when EMI/Parlophone offered the group's masters to Capitol, their American representative, the decision makers in Hollywood knew better than to think that a British "beat group" could score in the States and politely declined. The British company offered the group around, finding a reception in the more humble offices of Vee Jay Records, a Chicago based indie specializing in rhythm 'n blues.

America's most successful black owned and operated label prior to Berry Gordy's Tamla/Motown empire, Vee Jay had scored nationally with several quality r&b artists, notably Jerry Butler. At the time, it was another white group, the Four Seasons, which kept their cash flowing and their logo afloat. Taking a chance, the label issued a couple of Beatles singles and an album, *Introducing The Beatles*, Vee Jay 1062, in the summer of '63. . . to an unresponsive public.

When Capitol, no longer able to ignore the unprecedented cross-Atlantic success of John, Paul, George and Ringo, opted to pick up the rights to the group's new releases in January 1964, Beatlemania unfolded and a new definition of "youth culture" was born. By the second quarter of 1964 the Beatles were in the enviable position of having six companies pushing their product in the States: along with Capitol and Vee Jay, Swan, MGM and Atco each had some older material while United Artists had the rights to the enormously profitable soundtrack to *A Hard Day's Night.*

Vee Jay, on their last corporate legs, issued a slightly revamped version of the album, substituting the hit "Please Please Me" and "Ask Me Why" for the original version's "Love Me Do" and "P.S. I Love You." From January 1964 through the rest of the year, millions of copies of Vee Jay albums flooded the market as the label repackaged the same sixteen tracks into four different (sic) albums. But all of the copies were not real. . . As cash came in from the album's staggering sales, Vee Jay hired several pressing plants to make the record, resulting in a plethora of variations on the pressings. Perry Cox and Joe Lindsay's *The Beatles Price Guide For American Records* lists four different versions of the first [1963] pressings with "Love Me Do," while there are at least five mono and three stereo variations on the second [1964] pressing with "Please Please Me."

Exactly when the counterfeiting of the Beatles first American long-player began is still debated. The steady demand for the album left the door open for any entrepreneur with the willingness to circumvent the more traditional avenues of business in the record business. There are many, many counterfeits of *Introducing The Beatles*, but fortunately most are so obvious that it is often amazing to realize that anyone who collects records could be fooled. But there are also Vee Jay counterfeits of surpassing excellence.

Legitimate covers *always* have a glossy sheen on both the front and back cover (although the amount of sheen varies). The photo of the group is crisp and clear with an obvious shadow cast by the lads against the photographer's backdrop. The covers were made from gray or tan posterboard with the flaps over the top and bottom an even 1/4 inch each. Many— but not all— covers have "Printed in U.S.A." in the lower left corner. Legitimate labels are always a glossy black with sharp print. On those labels using the rainbow border, the shift in the color-band is smooth and lovely.

Both the albums title, *Introducing The Beatles*, and artist's credit, *The Beatles*, are printed above the spindle hole. The trail-off vinyl on all legitimate copies is between 7/8 inch and 1 inch long. Finally, should your copy have the "Stereo" printed on the label or "Audio Matrix," "MR" or "ARP" machine stamped in the trail-off vinyl, you have an original although not *all* originals have these identifying scores.

Counterfeits have a more normal, flat finish with the clarity of the photo's details compromised (on bad copies the shadow is more an indecipherable blur) and are made from white cardboard instead of the brown board of the original. Phonies may have the title above the hole and the group's name below; the label may be flat or *slightly* finished; the color gradation in the rainbow may be abrupt; or the trail-off varies, often visibly exceeding the one-inch mark.

The Beatles & Frank Ifields On Stage! (Vee Jay 1085, 1964) was issued with two separate covers: The first had a cartoon of an eccentric looking British chap (with a "Jolly What!" exclamation above the title). The second version, known as the "portrait cover," features a beautiful full-color painting of the group. Both legitimate versions have the normal printing along the jacket spine (title, catalog number, etc.) While both versions of the cover have been copied they are are easily identified: neither have printing on the spine!

Songs Picture And Stories Of The Fabulous Beatles (Vee Jay 1092, 1964, actually a new cover and catalogue number holding copies of 1062) was issued with a gatefold semi-cover, a book-like flap covering 2/3 of the jacket; counterfeits dispensed with this obvious luxury and issued the LP in a regular jacket. *Hear The Beatles Tell All* (Vee Jay PRO-202) was issued on the label's attractive black label with a rainbow perimeter. Fakes have solid black labels (and no printing on the spine of the cover).

The only Capitol album to be reproduced was the rare mono version of *Magical Mystery Tour* (MAL-2835), originally issued in November 1967. But anyone familiar with this album, with its gatefold cover and glued-in booklet from the film, should not be fooled by the single-pocket jacket lacking a booklet the counterfeiters opted for. Earlier in '67 Paul had contributed the score for *The Family Way*, technically the first "solo" album from the group. Issued in America on London, counterfeits are rather easily identified: While the originals covers were printed on heavy stock with cover slicks pasted on, the fakes were done on thinner stock with the graphics printed directly on to the board.

A pair of the many albums from the fabulous Beatles that have been counterfeited over the years: Paul McCartney's soundtrack for The Family Way *and* The Beatles Christmas Album, *a special compilation of their fan club messages from 1963 through 1969 that was issued to members as a farewell in 1970.*

Throughout their career, The Beatles had the delightful practice of recording a "message" of seasonal cheer and mailing them out for Christmas to the members of their fan club. While the first few were typically, er, cheeky, the messages from 1967 and 1968 in particular are memorable for the psychedelicism of the aural montages and the Lennon-in-Wonderland asides. These recordings are rarely covered by the group's chroniclers but belong in every collection, especially if you hope to assemble the definitive psychedelic Beatles!

While there were no Beatles for 1970's Christmas season, there was still an active fan club in need of Yuletide cheer. Apple collected the seven prior messages and assembled them as an album modestly titled *The Beatles Christmas Album* (Apple SBC-100), sending it out as a final gift. Since the demand for such an album was—and *is*—far greater than the miniscule print run, the album was counterfeited and easily found on the collectors market throughout the '70s and '80s. Again, the dupes vary with some quite close to the originals. The easiest way is to check out the print on the sundry photos on the cover: Each must be crisp and clear; any blurring of background detail indicates a forgery.

Original copies of Ed Rudy's *American Tour #2* (part of the initial exploitation of the group in 1964) are on the thick, non-flexible vinyl of the times and the covers have obviously red print on the front. Reproductions are on the more contemporary flimsy flexible vinyl with orange print on the cover. *American Tour #3*, also on non-flexible vinyl, features "The Beatles" in black print under the photo on the cover. Fakes are on flexible vinyl with "The Beatles" in red print *on top of the photo* on the cover.

The counterfeiting of the Fabs did not end with the break up of the group: *McCartney* was counterfeited in a manner similar to *Let It Be*. The easiest way to spot the fake is through their noticeably inferior quality of the graphics on both the cover and the label. The interview disc, *Brung To Ewe By*, that accompanied promo copies of *Ram*, has also been duplicated without permission but, while the spacing between the bands of the originals are even the spaces on the counterfeit are visibly uneven. The promotional *Band On The Run Interview Special* was issued with white labels; the phony has yellow labels. The promotional double-album *The McCartney Interview* are easy, as the labels on the originals have black print while the counterfeits are blank.

John & Yoko's *Two Virgins: Unfinished Music #1* was counterfeited, although originals are easily identified: All real records have an "MR" stamped—not etched—in the trail-off vinyl. They were also issued in a brown paper outer sleeve that is the same size as the album jacket and opens on the right. Originals have glossy labels. Legitimate later pressings have non-glossy labels and the brown outer sleeve is 3/4" shorter than the album jacket.) (Note that colored vinyl boots also surfaced.)

Roots: John Lennon Sings The Great Rock & Roll Hits on Adam V!!! was offered for sale through mail-order ads briefly before a court order on behalf of Lennon ended the project. Counterfeits immediately flooded the market, many difficult to discern from the originals on cursory inspection but originals have "A-8018" hand-etched in the label area. Covers have the art printed on the cardboard; fakes have slicks pasted on the jacket. On originals the song titles on the ad on the back cover for "20 Solid Gold Hits" are readable while on counterfeits they are illegible. Also, copies that read "John Lennon Sings The Greatest Rock & Roll Hits" along the spine are fake.

Apparently an employee of Polydor surreptitiously manufactured a few collectibles after the lights went out. That is, using legitimate pressers and labels at the company pressing plant, someone squeezed some colored vinyl into the machine and created green and gold versions of the album. These LPs occupy a no-man's land as some collectors insist they are merely bootlegs while others assign a higher, *almost* legitimate status to them (I subscribe to the latter and the reader will find these listed with Lennon's other releases).

While I centered on The Beatles for this article, there are many, *many* other counterfeits to deal with in this hobby including most, if not all, of the rare R&B albums of the '50s and early '60s, especially King and Aladdin; many rock'n rollers, including *Johnny Burnette & The Rock 'n' Roll Trio* and the first four volumes of *Elvis' Golden Records;* and such '60s stalwarts as the Epic Yardbirds stereo albums, the stereo Mothers Of Inventions on Verve, the stereo Left Banke on Smash, and The International Submarine Band's *Safe At Home.*

Most of the small pressing garage/punk/psych/hard rock albums have been reproduced, sometimes more than once. Other examples include collectible promos of the '70s and '80s, including the "Warner Brothers Radio Show" series of live albums by Van Morrison, The Pretenders, The Who and Talking Heads; Todd Rundgren's two Runt albums on Ampex; *Elvis Costello Live At The El Mocambo;* Nils Lofgren's *Authorized Bootleg* and Tom Petty's *Live 'leg;* David Bowie's *The Man Who Sold The World;* and such unexpected rarities (sic) as *It's A Beautiful Day, The City, Saturday Night Fever;* and the pre-Cheap Trick *Fuse.* There are even counterfeits of test pressings, acetates and RIAA Gold and Platinum Record Awards!

One last word on counterfeits: In 1992 a group vocal collector seeking a rare album worth four figures broke down and purchased the counterfeit (itself now twenty plus years old and hard to find) for $150 just to have the music. . .

The World's Most Valuable Album

On May 12, 1963, Bob Dylan was scheduled to appear on Ed Sullivan's Show, guaranteeing him his largest audience outside of the circumscribed world of folk music. Dylan was planning to perform "Talkin' John Birch Blues," a farcical romp from his upcoming album, *The Freewheelin' Bob Dylan*. He had auditioned the song for Sullivan and the show's producer, and both were enthusiastic. Needless to say, Dylan's manager, Albert Grossman, was ebullient at the possibilities such exposure meant. On the eve of the show during a dress rehearsal the editor in charge of CBS-TV programming decided there were some problems with the lyrics, which lampooned the absurdities of racism in general and Birchers in particular. CBS decided that the risk of offending viewers below the Mason-Dixon was too great and Dylan was informed that he would not be singing that particular song. It was suggested he opt for something less topical, perhaps something the audience might already be familiar with, "like a Clancy Brothers tune." Dylan walked out. The stories that circulated in the folk world riled up everybody, all of whom were righteously on the singer's side.

The song had already been recorded and the album, widely anticipated by retailers as a big seller, was ready for shipping. Suddenly, the album was pulled and taken back into the studio. There are two versions of this story: One has Columbia, the recording branch of CBS, taking the logical conclusion (at least, based on the Sullivan decision) that the song was potentially libelous and should not be on the album, thus dictating the change. Another has the vindictive singer claiming that what wasn't good enough for TV couldn't be fit for disc and, at Columbia's expense, he had the record remastered.

Along with the Birch track, also pulled were "Gamblin' Willie's Dead Man's Hand," "Rocks And Gravel," and "Let Me Die In My Footsteps," a powerful condemnation of the bunker mentality then permeating much of America when citizens were being scared into spending a fortune constructing [ultimately useless] underground shelters in case of nuclear war. The three additional tracks, requiring both sides to be remastered, stand as some proof that the album's callback was at least partially instigated by Dylan.

During the pressing of the new version of the album, at least one run using the original stampers was made, although the new labels listing the replacement songs were pressed onto the vinyl, and they were slipped into the second version cover. There is no way to know how many of these "mispressings" made it out on the market but there are few known in the hands of collectors. Each of these copies were mono pressings repeatedly played and nowhere near the type of condition that makes collectors drool. In 1990, Los Angeles' Rockaway Records sold a copy graded "VG-" (slightly better than abused) for $8,000 to a collector who wasn't about to miss out on a copy in the hopes of eventually finding one in collectable condition.

In 1991 a nearly mint mono copy was put up for auction through Yesterday Records of Portland, Oregon, in an open auction in *Goldmine* magazine. While the exact terms of the deal are private, the fact that the purchaser paid for a round trip ticket so the record could be delivered to him in New York put the final price in excess of $10,000.

It was assumed that only mono pressings would exist. In fact, in the entry for this album in the previous edition of this book, I noted that "all known copies are mono" and did not even list the possibility of a stereo version. The sale of the near mint copy for five figures and the notation in the book earned the mono version the unofficial title as the "world's most valuable album."

Then, in April 1992 a collector in New York found a stereo copy at a church thrift shop! While the record was well-played, the labels correctly listed the deleted tracks, something none of the monos had done. The record was offered for sale through Greenwich Village's Strider Records, again in the pages of *Goldmine*, and after some furious bidding, the album was eventually sold for more than $10,000 (although it is a given in the field that had the record been in better condition it might have fetched twice that). Thus the reader will find this title with an estimated near mint value of $12,000-20,000 in the listings.

Finally, while the John Birch song has been a staple of bootlegs since the early '70s where it is generally listed as "Talkin' John Birch Society Blues," on Columbia's recently released three CD boxed set of rare Dylan material, *the bootleg series, volumes 1-3*, it is listed as "Talkin' John Birch Paranoid Blues." It should be noted that the label on the 1963 stereo album lists the song as "Talkin' John Birch Blues."

While all known original mono copies of The Freewheelin' Bob Dylan *with the deleted tracks have later labels listing the replacement songs, the sole stereo copy—found in 1992 in a thrift shop in New York's Greenwich Village—does list the original line-up on the label. Side 1 (shown here) lists "Rocks And Gravel" and "Let Me Die In My Footsteps" as the second and third songs, respectively. Side 2 (not shown) lists "Gamblin' Willie's Dead Man's Hand" and "Talkin' John Birch Blues" as the second and fifth songs. Note that a U.S. copy of the cover with the deleted tracks listed has not been found. CBS of Canada did print such covers, although all copies of the records list and play the replacement tracks. Collectible copies of this Canadian cover are currently worth approximately $100-200.*

The 100 Most Valuable U.S. Albums

Below are the albums with the highest assigned current market values as of 1993. The criterion for this list is that the item must be a domestically manufactured vinyl album, either commercial or promotional. Acetates, incomplete cover slicks and Compact Discs are ineligible. The listings are rather fluid; not only are prices changing constantly, new collectibles are being discovered—or called to my attention—with each new edition. Titles are listed in descending order of value (naturally). Those with the same value are listed alphabetically by artist; two or more titles by the same artist with the same value are listed chronologically. Copies with an asterisk (*) after the price indicates that the value assigned *for this list* is an average taken from the suggested range of Near Mint values in the main listings of the book. That is, a near mint copy of that record could sell for quite a bit less or considerably more than the value listed below.

To spice up this list, I have solicited the opinions of several contributors to say what they want about individual titles, hopefully to educate and elucidate the record's value. These opinions remain the exclusive property of the individuals; don't hold me responsible for a statement that is either grossly inaccurate or is the polar opposite of yours, unless, of course, it's mine expressed. These remarks are in quotes and are followed by the initials of the remarker: Norman Feinberg (NF), Joe Goldmark (JG), Gary Johnson (GJ), Ashley Johnson (AJ), Neal Skok (NS) and myself (NU).

---

1.   BOB DYLAN
Columbia CS-8786   (S)   **The Freewheelin' Bob Dylan**   1963   **20,000.00** *
        (Original pressings contain four songs— "Talking John Birch Blues," "Let Me Die In My Footsteps," "Rocks And Gravel" and "Gamblin' Willie's Dead Man's Hand"— deleted from all subsequent pressings and replaced by four new tracks, "Masters Of War," "Talkin' World War III Blues," "Girl From North Country" and "Bob Dylan's Dream." This second version remained in print as a stereo album through the '80s. For more information on the this album refer to the article "The World's Most Valuable Album" in this book.)

2.   BOB DYLAN
Columbia CL-1986   (M)   **The Freewheelin' Bob Dylan**   1963   **10,000.00** *
        (This is the mono version of the album above. It is important to note that while the stereo album above lists the deleted tracks on the label, no mono copy containing the deleted tracks have been found with the labels listing those tracks. That is, mono copies of this album have first pressing records with second pressing labels. Therefore, to determine whether or not you have a copy of this album, you must listen to it. . . The second version remained in print as a mono album through 1968, undergoing several label changes, which currently command $25-40. "While Freewheelin' is a better album over all with the replacement tracks, it's a shame that 'Footstep' and 'Birch' couldn't have stayed. They would have added to the album's pre-WWIII paranoia. Also, the topicality of this album could just as easily have fit in the Reagan-Bush years as it did the early '60s. . ." — NU)

3.   THE BEATLES
Vee Jay LPS-1085   (S)   **The Beatles And Frank Ifield On Stage** (Portrait cover) 1964   **9,000.00** *
        (The front cover is a full-color painting of the Fab Four. Original pressings were titled "Jolly What! The Beatles And Frank Ifield On Stage" on the front cover and featured a cartoon of an eccentric British chap. These are worth less than 1/10 of the portrait cover version. The mono version of this album is worth $3,000 and is listed below.)

4a. THE BEATLES
Vee Jay SR-1062   (S)   **Introducing The Beatles** (Ad back)   1963   **8,000.00** *
        (First pressing with "Love Me Do" and "P.S. I Love You." The back cover features ads for 25 other Vee Jay albums. The mono version of this album is worth $3,000 and is listed below.)

4b. THE BEATLES
Vee Jay PRO-202   *(DJ)*   **Hear The Beatles Tell All** *(White label promo)*   1964   **8,000.00**   •
    (Interviews with the Mop Tops from 1964. The stock mono copies are worth $150 while "stereo" copies were issued by Vee Jay International in 1979 and are worth $15.)

5a. THE BEATLES
Capitol ST-2553   *(S)*   **Yesterday And Today** *(Butcher cover)*   1966   **7,500.00**   •
    (Throughout the first few years of the Beatles' American career, Capitol was paring the original EMI/Parlophone albums down from 14 tracks to eleven for U.S. consumption, butchering the group's work and its intent. The left-overs were used to compile "new" albums, none of which, for the most part, have counterparts anywhere else in the world. As a means of protest, this album sported a cover photo of the four Fabs in doctor smocks cheekily handling dismembered baby-doll parts and slabs of raw meat. . . After initial copies were distributed the album was withdrawn and a new cover with a shot off four nattily attired but docile lads posing with a steamer trunk was adapted. Hirelings were paid to remove the original cover and affix the new one but, as they were paid by the piece, many took to merely pasting the second, "trunk" cover over the "butcher cover." Copies of the album with the original cover never having had a second cover pasted on to it are referred to as "first state butchers." Copies with both covers—i.e., the original cover and the second cover pasted on it—are referred to as "second state butchers." The mono version of this album is worth $3,000 and is listed below.)

5b. THE ROLLING STONES
London LL-3402   *(M)*   **12 X 5** *(Blue vinyl)*   1966   **7,500.00**   •
    (One copy of The Stones' second American long-player was found in 1989 on blue vinyl. Its official original remains a mystery although the record, graded "Poor" by the seller, immediately sold for $2,000.)

5c. IKE & TINA TURNER
Philles PHLPS-4011   *(S)*   **River Deep-Mountain High**   1966   **7,500.00**   •
    ("River Deep-Mountain High" the single, often cited by both fans and critics as one of the genre's greatest achievements, was viewed as an event at the time of its release by both producer Phil Spector, his admirers and his detractors. After it failed to even dent the top 40, Uncle Phil blamed his "enemies" for the failure. And he could be right; it's almost impossible to hear this amazing single and not think "Hit Record!" After AM stations torpedoed the next single, the album was pressed in minute quantities, apparently without Spector's knowledge, to gain access to the stereo-only FM radio stations. No covers are known to have been completed. This was eventually issued by A&M in 1969. "Rockaway Records sold a copy I graded "Poor" for $2,000 in 1991." — GJ)

5d. BILLY WARD & THE DOMINOES
Federal 295-94 (10")   *(M)*   **Billy Ward & His Dominoes**   1955   **7,500.00**   •
    (The Dominoes were one of the most important of the early groups, marked by strong leads with great harmonies on highly influential material. Out of their ranks rose both Clyde McPhatter (and thus, The Drifters) and Jackie Wilson.. "The first R&B group LP. . . Mint copies are all but non-existent and could conceivably command $15,000 or more." — NF)

6. THE BEATLES
Apple SO-385   *(S)*   **Hey Jude/The Beatles Again** *(Alternate cover)*   1970   **6,000.00**   •
    (Alternate cover prototypes were designed for this album when it bore the working title "The Beatles Again." Several graphic variations—including one cover with the front and back cover photos switched—are known to exist and the suggested value refers to any of the variations. The value is entirely for the cover, with or without the record inside.)

7a. BOB DYLAN
Columbia PC-33235   *(DJ)*   **Blood On The Tracks** *(Original test pressing)*   1975   **5,000.00**   •
    (Original test pressings—issued in plain cardboard jackets—feature alternate takes of five songs of "Tangled Up In Blue," "If You See Her Say Hello," "You're A Big Girl Now," "Idiot Wind" and "Lily, Rosemary And The Jack Of Hearts." A copy graded VG+ fetched $5,000 in 1991. "Another case where Dylan's instincts are spot on. While the original versions all have something to offer, this is a better album for the often sloppy but genuinely inspired replacement versions." — NU)

7b. PRINCE
Warner Bros. 25677DJ   *(DJ)*   **The Black Album** *(2 LP promo)*   1987   **5,000.00**   •
    (This promotional version of Prince's withdrawn [by the artist] album is actually two 12" records that play at 45 RPM. There are two known copies in the hands of collectors, one of which, graded VG+, sold for $6,000 during the first weeks of 1993. This set contains the entire contents of the regular album, which is valued as $4,000 and listed below.)

8a. FRANK BALLARD
Phillips Inter.1985 *(M)* **Rhythm-Blues Party** *1962* **4,500.00** •
(*"Copies of this album in collectible condition are so rare that delineating a price for condition is ludicrous. There are probably fewer than ten copies known to exist." — NF*)

8b. THE MIDNIGHTERS
Federal 295-90 (10") *(M)* **The Midnighters: Their Greatest Hits** *1955* **4,500.00** •
(*The first long-player by this classic R&B ensemble. "Near Mint copies of this album are almost non-existent and are seldom for sale. A truly mint copy of this LP has not been available in years." — NF*)

9a. BOYD BENNETT
King 395-594 *(M)* **Boyd Bennett** *1956* **4,000.00** •
(*King is noted for having released hundreds of LPs of rhythm & blues and country music in the '50s and '60s, many of which received print runs of less than 5,000. If the album sold, more were run off. If not, it was forgotten. This is one of the rarest— and most desirable— of all the Kings.*)

9b. DAVID BOWIE
RCA Victor CPL1-0576 *(S)* **Diamond Dogs** *(Genitals cover)* *1974* **4,000.00** •
(*The cover, a painting of a dog with Bowie's head, clearly shows the canine's genitals. . . at rest. Prior to release the Bowiedog was effectively neutered by an airbrush. These "dickless" covers are as common as hen's beaks. The value here is entirely for the cover, with or without the record inside.. "Once only rumored to exist and then only as a slick not affixed to the cardboard, there are now four known copies, the two most recent sold for $4,000 and $6,000." — NF*)

9c. CHARLES BROWN
Aladdin 702 (10") *(M)* **Mood Music** *(Red vinyl)* *1952* **4,000.00** •
(*This classic by the legendary Brown— who is still doing personal appearances— is arguably the rarest of the rare Aladdin 10" albums. The black vinyl version is listed at $2,500 below.*)

9d. AMOS MILBURN
Aladdin 704 (10") *(M)* **Rockin' The Boogie** *(Red vinyl)* *1954* **4,000.00** •
(*This was Amos' first LP; his last was recorded for Motown when he was past his prime and released in 1963. The black vinyl version of this album is listed at $2,500 below.*)

9e. PRINCE
Warner Bros. 25677 *(S)* **The Black Album** *1987* **4,000.00** •
(*This is the version prepared for commercial release in 1987 but pulled by Prince. A sealed copy sold in 1990 for $5,000. The two-LP promo version of this album is valued at $5,000 and listed above.*)

10a. THE FENDERMEN
Soma MG-1240 *(M)* **Mule Skinner Blues** *(Blue vinyl)* *1960* **3,500.00** •
(*Long rumored to exist— as have other colors— a copy of this album on blue vinyl turned up in 1992 and was promptly sold for $4,000. . . Copies on both non-opaque black vinyl-valued at $2,000— and normal opaque black vinyl— $1,250— are listed below.*)

10b. JACK KEROUAC
Dot DLP-3154 *(M)* **Poetry For The Beat Generation** *1959* **3,500.00** •
(*Preposterously rare collection withdrawn by Dot and issued on their Hanover subsidiary, which is also rare and currently commands $300. The value assigned is based on the assumption that this album would attract the attention of literary aficionados as well as record collectors.*)

11a. THE BACHS
Raio *(No number)* *(S)* **Out Of The Bachs** *1967* **3,000.00** •
(*Recently unearthed punk/psych gem. A VG copy sold for $2,000 prior to the discovery of a small cache of sealed copies, three of which have reportedly sold for $5,000 each. "Minor key, haunting and melodic... like an American Zombies if they were in a garage/psych mood." — NS*)

11b. THE BEATLES
Vee Jay LP-1062 *(M)* **Introducing The Beatles** *(Ad back)* *1963* **3,000.00**
(*First pressing with "Love Me Do" and "P.S. I Love You." The back cover features ads for 25 other Vee Jay albums. The stereo version of this album is worth $8,000 and is listed above.*)

11c. THE BEATLES
Vee Jay SR-1062 *(S)* **Introducing The Beatles** *(Blank back)* *1963* **3,000.00**
(*First pressing with "Love Me Do" and "P.S. I Love You." The back cover is completely blank, devoid of any printing. Long rumored to be a promo it is now assumed to be a mis-pressing. The mono version is worth $1,200 and is listed below.*)

58

11d. THE BEATLES
Vee Jay LP-1085   (M)   **The Beatles And Frank Ifield On Stage** *(Portrait cover)*   1964   **3,000.00**
*(The front cover is a full-color painting of the Fab Four. Original pressings were titled "Jolly What!
The Beatles And Frank Ifield On Stage" on the front cover and featured a cartoon of an eccentric British
chap. These are worth less than 1/10 of the portrait cover version. The stereo version of this album is
worth $9,000 and is listed above.)*

11e. THE BEATLES
Capitol T-2553   (M)   **Yesterday And Today** *(Butcher cover)*   1966   **3,000.00**
*(First-state mono "butcher cover." Refer to the first-state stereo butcher "Yesterday And Today,"
listed above at $8,000, for the full story on this rarity.)*

11f. JOHNNY BURNETTE & THE ROCK 'N' ROLL TRIO
Coral CRL-57080   (M)   **Johnny Burnette & The Rock 'N' Roll Trio**   1956   **3,000.00** •
*(The "trio" in the title is deceptive: This is really Johnny Burnette with brother Dorsey and Paul
Burlison. Along with RCA Victor LPM-1254, Elvis Presley, this is one of the first—and definitive—
rockabilly albums. "Most copies fall into the VG or less grading, selling for $200-500. Mint copies are
virtually unknown and would command prices in the $5,000-10,000 range." — NF)*

11g. DAMON
Ankh 968   (S)   **Song Of A Gypsy** *(Gatefold cover)*   1970   **3,000.00**
*(Original versions of this privately pressed psych album have gatefold covers with both an
Egyptian ankh and the title embossed on the front. Reissues with a standard single-pocket cover are
listed below at $1,500.)*

11h. AMOS MILBURN / WYNONIE HARRIS / CROWN PRINCE WATERFORD
Aladdin 703 (10")   (M)   **Party After Hours** *(Red vinyl)*   1954   **3,000.00** •
*(This r&b collection features three of Aladdin's favorite artists; while Milburn rated an album of his
own, Aladdin 704, Rockin' The Boogie (also on this list), neither Harris nor Waterford saw their work on
LP other than collections such as this. The black vinyl version of this album is listed below at $2,000.)*

11i. THE ROLLING STONES
London NPS-3   (DJ)   **Through The Past, Darkly** *(Picture disc)*   1969   **3,000.00** •
*(Prototypes for a rejected picture disc back in '69. Two variations are known: one has the cover
from "High Tide & Green Grass" on both sides the other has "High Tide" backed with Ten Years After's
"Sssh." The value is entirely for the record whether or not it includes a cover.)*

11j. FRANK SINATRA
Reprise FS-1028   (S)   **Sinatra-Jobim** *(Test pressing)*   1969   **3,000.00** •
*(This album, a follow-up to 1967's successful "Francis Albert Sinatra And Antonio Carlos Jobim,"
[Reprise 1021] was cancelled after test pressings were made. I assigned this record the the widest
suggested range in the book, $1,000-5,000, due to both the lack of knowledge concerning its rarity and
the utter unpredictability of Sinatra collectors. Company notes show that 3,500 copies were manufactured as 8-track tapes and all but three ordered destroyed. . . Issued in a plain cardboard jacket.)*

12a. THE BEATLES
United Artists UAL-3366(DJ)   **A Hard Day's Night** *(White label promo)*   1964   **2,500.00** •
*(This is the white label promo edition of the commercially released album to the Fab Four's first
feature film. Exactly why this promo is so rare is unknown; this movie was heavily promoted by U.A. as
producers of both the film and the soundtrack. . .)*

12b. THE BEATLES
Apple KAL-1004   (DJ)   **Yellow Submarine** *(Radio spots)*   1968   **2,500.00** •
*(While this film is, of course, forever linked with John, Paul, George & Ringo, the group had
nothing to do with the film in any way, 'cepting the contribution of a few unreleased songs. This album
contains a series of brief "spots," or plugs, intended for radio broadcast to promote the animated film.
Issued in a plain cardboard jacket.)*

12c. CHARLES BROWN
Aladdin 702 (10")   (M)   **Mood Music** *(Black vinyl)*   1952   **2,500.00** •
(The red vinyl version of this album is listed at $4,000 above.)

12d. FRANK FROST & THE NIGHTHAWKS
Phillips Inter.1975   (M)   **Hey Boss Man!**   1961   **2,500.00** •
*(Supposedly there were only 500 copies of this LP pressed. In 1975 a noted West Coast collector
found 490 odd covers without records. "There are probably less than 10 complete copies in the hands of
collectors today." — NF)*

The picture disc above was an experimental prototype for Through The Past, Darkly. *One version features the cover of* High Tide And Green Grass *on both sides while the other features* Tide *backed by Ten Years After's* Sssh. *Pressed in minute quantities (reportedly only eighteen of each were pressed) for distribution among the company execs, this record has an estimated value that places it squarely in the 100 most valuable American albums.*

12e. JEFFERSON AIRPLANE
RCA Victor LPM-3584   *(M)*   **Jefferson Airplane Takes Off!**   *1966*   **2,500.00**   •
     (Original mono pressings contain "Runnin' 'Round This World" and alternate takes of both "Go To Her" and "Let Me In," whose lyrics make allusions to sex or LSD. These three were deleted from all subsequent pressings. The latter two were replaced by cleaned up versions while "Runnin'" sat on the shelf until it was gathered onto the "Early Flight" album five years later. Stereo copies with these tracks are not known to exist.)

12f. PAUL & LINDA McCARTNEY
Apple MAS-3375   *(DJ)*   **Ram** *(Mono promo)*   *1971*   **2,500.00**   •
     (The label does not identify this as a promotional release but it clearly states that the album in "Monaural." In most cases it was was shipped to radio stations in the same cover as the regular stereo version, sometimes the two LPs were side by side in the same jacket.)

12g. AMOS MILBURN
Aladdin 704 (10")   *(M)*   **Rockin' The Boogie** *(Black vinyl)*   *1954*   **2,500.00**   •
     (The red vinyl version of this album is listed at $$4,000 above.)

12h. GATEMOUTH MOORE
King 684   *(M)*   **Gatemouth Moore Sings The Blues**   *1960*   **2,500.00**   •
     (This album, Moore's sole release of the '50s and '60s, has been erroneously titled in previous editions of this book as I'm A Fool To Care. "One of the legendary King albums; only a few have survived the past four decades. A Near Mint copy recently sold for $3,000." — NF)

13a. LLOYD GLENN
Swing Time 1901 (10")   *(M)*   **Lloyd Glenn**   *1952*   **2,250.00**   •
     ("There are probably less than 10 copies in the hands of collectors. One sold for $2,750 in 1991." — NF.)

13b. THE INDEX
D. C. *(No number)*   *(M)*   **The Index**   *1968*   **2,250.00**   •
     (The price is for original record in an original cover, both featuring "New York Mining Disaster." Most copies have the original record in a second pressing cover which lists "Fire Eyes." These are worth $1,500 in Near Mint condition. Second pressings with "Fire Eyes" are worth $1,200. "Along with Tom Rapp's Yetti-Men, this is one of the missing links between surf and psych." — NS)

14a. THE BEATLES
Vee Jay SR-1062   *(S)*   **Introducing The Beatles**   *1964*   **2,000.00**
     (Second pressings with "Please Please Me" and "Ask Me Why." There are three known label variations for this title, each with the same approximate value. The mono versions are worth $200-400 depending on the label.)

14b. THE BEATLES
Vee Jay VJS-1092   *(S)*   **Songs, Pictures And Stories Of The Fabulous Beatles**   *1964*   **2,000.00**
     (Issued in a nifty gatefold cover where the front flap is only 8" across. This album contains second pressings of Vee Jay 1062, Introducing The Beatles with "Please Please Me" and "Ask Me Why." There are three known label variations for this title, each currently carrying the same approximate value. The mono version of this album, which has been heavily counterfeited, is worth only $300.)

14c. THE BEATLES
Vee Jay DXS-30   *(S)*   **The Beatles Vs. The Four Seasons**   *1964*   **2,000.00**
     (This double-album collects Vee Jay 1062, "Introducing The Beatles," with 1065, "The Golden Hits Of The Four Seasons." It was issued with a fold-open, full-color poster of the Liverpudlians, worth an additional $300 in Near Mint condition. The mono version of this album is worth $500. Beatles collectors seeking to piece together the most perfect set of this album— cover plus the two discs— have driven the value of The Four Seasons album up beyond what a Seasons' collector would normally value the album at!)

14d. THE BEATLES
United Artists Help-Show *(DJ)*   **Help!** *(One-sided, open-end interview)*   *1965*   **2,000.00**
     (This one-sided disc should not be confused with the more common [sic] two-sided interview album, valued at $1,500 and listed below. Issued in a plain cardboard jacket.)

14e. THE BEATLES
Capitol ST-2553   *(S)*   **Yesterday And Today** *(2nd state butcher cover)*   *1966*   **2,000.00**
     (For the story on this title, refer to the listing for the "first-state stereo" listed above at $7,500. This is the second-state "butcher cover" with the "trunk" cover pasted over the original "butcher" cover. Second-state monos are worth $600.)

14f. BRIGADE
Band'n Vocal BVRS-1066 *(S)*   **Last Laugh**   1970   **2,000.00** •
    (Privately pressed album from a NW group. "Highly over-rated album with a couple of high points, including a psychedelic Doorsish number." — NS)

14g. JACKSON BROWNE
(No label)   *(S)*   **"Jackson Browne's First Album"**   1967   **2,000.00** •
    (This double-album is the Holy Grail for Jackson's fan. Actually, this is an untitled publishers demo intended to get other, established artists to record the his songs. None of these recordings have been released to the public. Issued in a plain cardboard jacket.)

14h. THE FENDERMEN
Soma MG-1240   *(M)*   **Mule Skinner Blues** *(Non-opaque black vinyl)*   1960   **2,000.00** •
    (Copies exist on a non-opaque black vinyl that allows light to shine through with a reddish tinge when held up to a light source. Normal opaque black vinyl copies are worth $1,250 and are listed below while a few copies are known on colored vinyl and, valued at $3,500, are listed above.)

14i. THE FIVE ROYALES
Apollo LP-488   *(M)*   **The Rockin' Five Royales** *(Green label)*   1956   **2,000.00** •
    ("Later pressings with yellow labels are either second pressings issued in the '60s or repros from the early '70s. Copies with a purple label are known to exist but would seem to be later pressings done to confuse the collector." — NF)

14j. FRACTION
Angelus WR-5005   *(S)*   **Moon Blood**   197?   **2,000.00**
    (This privately pressed psychedelic collectible was issued in a cover with a die-cut "window" to allow the moon on the inner sleeve to show through.)

14k. JOHN LENNON & YOKO ONO
Nautilus NR-47   *(S)*   **Double Fantasy** *(Alternate cover)*   1980   **2,000.00** •
    (Alternate cover prototype has bright yellow strokes added to the background and a red heart drawn on Yoko's bosom. There is one known copy and it is not for sale. The estimate is for the cover alone and based wholly on assumption. . .)

14l. LITTLE ESTHER [PHILLIPS]
King 622   *(M)*   **Down Memory Lane With Little Esther**   1959   **2,000.00** •
    ("Among the best R&B albums ever made, this masterpiece is high on everyone's want-list. A Mint copy would command a price in the $3,000-4,000 range." — NF)

14m. MARIANI
Sonobeat 1001   *(M)*   **Perpetuum Mobile**   196?   **2,000.00** •

14n. AMOS MILBURN / WYNONIE HARRIS / CROWN PRINCE WATERFORD
Aladdin 703 (10")   *(M)*   **Party After Hours** *(Black vinyl)*   1954   **2,000.00**
    (The red vinyl version of this album is listed above at $3,000.)

14o. PHAPHNER
Dragon LP-101   *(S)*   **Overdrive**   197?   **2,000.00**
    ("People are finally deciding this privately pressed psych album is a really good record as well as a really rare record. . . after they have all disappeared." — AJ.)

14p. ELVIS PRESLEY
RCA Victor *(No number)*   *(S)*   **International Hotel Presents Elvis, 1969**   1969   **2,000.00** •
    (Complimentary boxed set supposedly limited to 2,000 copies presented to the hotel's dinner guests for Elvis' first show of the year. The box contains a copy of LPM-4088, "Elvis," a copy of LSP-4155, "From Elvis In Memphis;" a 1969 Elvis Record & Tape Catalog; a 1969 Elvis wallet calendar; an 8 x 10 full color photo; two 8 x 10 black & white photos; and a letter of introduction and thanks from Elvis, Colonel Parker and RCA. Note that approximately 80% of the value is for the box alone.)

14q. ELVIS PRESLEY
RCA Victor *(No number)*   *(S)*   **International Hotel Presents Elvis, 1970**   1970   **2,000.00** •
    (Complimentary boxed set supposedly limited to 2,000 copies presented to the hotel's dinner guests for Elvis' first show of the year. The box contains a copy of LSP-6020, "From Memphis To Vegas / From Vegas To Memphis;" a copy of 47-9791, "Kentucky rain" / "My Little Friend" with picture sleeve; a 1970 Elvis Record & Tape Catalog; a 1970 Elvis wallet calendar; a photo booklet; an 8 x 10 black & white photo; a hotel menu with Elvis on the front; and a letter of introduction and thanks from Elvis, Colonel Parker and RCA. Note that approximately 80% of the value is for the box alone.)

14r. ELVIS PRESLEY
RCA Victor VPSX-6089   *(Q)*   **Aloha From Hawaii Via Satellite**   1973   **2,000.00**
(Van Camp, the sponsors of Elvis' 1973 CBS TV Special, acquired stock copies of the album and affixed stickers to the cover with their Chicken Of The Sea tuna maid noting the TV special. A single sheet with a picture of Elvis and a description of the show was included and these LPs were distributed to members of the corporate office.)

14s. THE ROLLING STONES
London NP-1   *(DJ)*   **High Tide & Green Grass** *(Alternate cover)*   1966   **2,000.00** •
(This rejected cover prototype has the same graphics as the released version except title on the front is on two lines [the released version has the title on three lines] and in radically different type. One copy is known to exist. The value is for the cover alone.)

14t. VARIOUS ARTISTS
Tamla TM-222   *(M)*   **The Great Gospel Stars**   1961   **2,000.00** •
("This is by far the rarest LP on any Motown related label; there are only a few copies known to exist. A Mint copy sold for $3,000 in 1991." — NF)

14u. VARIOUS ARTISTS
Warner Bros. *(No #)*   *(DJ)*   **Jamboree** *(Soundtrack)*   1955   **2,000.00** •
(This soundtrack contains snippets of songs by a potpourri of artists of the time and was shipped out to radio stations. It is one of the rarest albums of the rock 'n roll era and sells for $300-500 in VG or less condition.)

14v. WEST COAST POP ART EXPERIMENTAL BAND, THE
Fifo M101   *(M)*   **West Coast Pop Art Experimental Band**   1966   **2,000.00** •
(A privately pressed psych album from a group that later recorded several fine albums for Reprise. Copies of this album recently turned up without covers and quickly sold out. . .)

15a. THE MUSIC EMPORIUM
Sentinal 69001   *(S)*   **The Music Emporium**   1969   **1,750.00**
(Privately pressed psych album is one of the classics of its genre. "Typifies West Coast acid/psych with some nice raga type songs." — NS)

15b. VARIOUS ARTISTS
(No label)   *(DJ)*   **Carnival Rock** *(Soundtrack)*   1956   **1,750.00** •
(This sampler from the movie of the same name was pressed on red vinyl and shipped to radio stations in a plain cardboard or paper sleeve.)

15c. VARIOUS ARTISTS
DCA Prod. (No number)   *(DJ)*   **Rock, Rock, Rock**   1956   **1,750.00** •
(Publisher's demo disc intended for inclusion in the soundtrack for the movie of the same name.)

16a. LONNIE JOHNSON
King 395-520   *(M)*   **Lonesome Road**   1958   **1,600.00** •
("One of the most sought-after LPs on King. Mint copies are impossible to find and would fetch prices in excess of $2,500." — NF)

16b. BIG JAY McNEELY
Federal 295-96 (10")   *(M)*   **Big Jay McNeely**   1954   **1,600.00** •
(Primarily a major R&B session man given a shot at solo success by Federal and King.)

16c. THE MIDNIGHTERS
Federal 395-541   *(M)*   **The Midnighters: Their Greatest Hits**   1955   **1,600.00** •
(This is the 12" repackage of the 10" version, 295-90, valued at $4,000 and listed above. "Very rare in collectible condition and generally sold in VG or less for $100-200." — NF)

16d. THE PENGUINS
Dootone DTL-204   *(M)*   **Best In Rhythm 'N Blues** *(Red vinyl)*   1957   **1,600.00** •
(Although this is a various artists album with the second side containing tracks by The Dootones, Meadowlarks and Medallions, as all of side one is by The Penguins this is generally considered their first album by collectors. Black vinyl reissues are worth $150.)

17a. THE BEATLES
United Artists Help-Int.   *(DJ)*   **Help!** *(Open-end interview)*   1965   **1,500.00**
(This two-sided disc should not be confused with the rarer one-sided interview album, valued at $2,000 and listed above. Issued in a plain cardboard jacket.)

17b. ROY BROWN / WYNONIE HARRIS / EDDIE VINSON
King 668   (M)   **Battle Of The Blues, Volume 4**   *1960*   **1,500.00**
(This various artists compilation features tracks by each of the three R&B giants. "One of the rarest and most sought-after numbers on King. A recent auction of a NM copy had several bids in excess of $1,500." — NF)

17c. C. A. QUINTET
Candy Floss 7764   (M)   **A Trip Through Hell**   *1969*   **1,500.00**
(A legendary private pressing psychedelic album. "While this psych classic is not a mega-rarity— copies do turn up for sale— it virtually never shows up in truly Near Mint condition." — AJ)

17d. THE CHAMPS
Challenge CHL-601   (M)   **Go Champs Go** *(Blue vinyl)*   *1958*   **1,500.00** •
(Regular black vinyl copies of this album are worth $250.)

17e. THE CRYSTALS
Philles DT-90722   (E)   **Twist Uptown**   *1963*   **1,500.00**
(This is the electronically rechanneled— using Capitol's patented "Duophonic" system— version from the Capitol Record Club.)

17f. DAMON
Ankh 968   (S)   **Song Of A Gypsy** *(Standard cover)*   *1970*   **1,500.00**
(A private pressing from the garage/psych '60s/'70s. Original versions with gatefold covers are listed above at $3,000.)

17g. DION & THE BELMONTS
Laurie LLPS-2002   (S)   **Presenting Dion & The Belmonts**   *1959*   **1,500.00** •
("A few copies of this album exist in stereo although they have been grossly overlooked by collectors." — NF. Mono versions of this album are worth $100.)

17h. BOB DYLAN
Columbia CL-1986   (DJ)   **The Freewheelin' Bob Dylan** *(White label promo)*   *1963*   **1,500.00** •
(For the story on this title, refer to the first listing of this list. This white label promo plays the second version with "Masters Of War," etc., but the front cover has a DJ title & timing strip listing the deleted tracks, including "Talkin' John Birch Blues.")

17i. THE EBON-KNIGHTS
Stepheny MF-401   (M)   **First Date With The Ebon-Knights**   *1963*   **1,500.00**
(Early soul group from the Chicago-based Stepheny label.)

17j. THE FIVE KEYS
Aladdin 806   (M)   **The Best Of The Five Keys** *(Maroon label)*   *1956*   **1,500.00**
(Contrary to previously published listings, legitimate blue label pressings of this album do not exist. "Truly Mint copies of this marvelous group LP are virtually impossible to find and would command prices in the $2,000-3,000 range." — NF)

17k. THE FUGITIVES
Hideout 1001   (M)   **The Fugitives At Dave's Hideout**   *1968*   **1,500.00**
(Privately pressed album contains punkish covers of current hits. "There are less than five copies known to exist." — NF)

17l. GRANMA'S ROCKERS
Fredlo 6727   (M)   **Homemade Apple Pie**   *1967*   **1,500.00**
(A private pressing from the garage/psych '60s/'70s.)

17m. HAYMARKET SQUARE
Chaparral 201   (S)   **Magic Lantern**   *1969*   **1,500.00**
(After the first batch of this [privately pressed psych] album disappeared there have been no copies for sale in years." — AJ)

17n. THE JACKS
RPM LRP-3006   (M)   **Jumpin' With The Jacks**   *1956*   **1,500.00**
("Mint copies of this extremely rare LP are unheard of. . . Prices in the $2,000-3,000 range would be readily forthcoming if one were found." — NF)

17o. AMOS MILBURN
Motown 608   (M)   **Return Of The Blues Boss**   *1963*   **1,500.00** •
(Subtitled "The Return Of Amos Milburn," this is one of the rarest of all Motown collectibles.)

17p. ELVIS PRESLEY
RCA Victor AFL1-2428   *(S)*   **Moody Blue** *(Multi-colored vinyl)*   *1977*   **1,500.00**
    (Three variations are known of this colored vinyl prototype: purple-on-white, red-on-white and yellow-on-white. The price is for the record alone. "This album— Elvis' last release prior to his death— was mediocre even by the less than inspiring standards he had been setting for himself the previous half-dozen years." — NU)

17q. LULA REED
King 604   *(M)*   **Blue And Moody**   *1959*   **1,500.00**
    ("Mint copies of this album are extremely rare commanding prices in excess of $2,000." — NF)

17r. THE SHAGS
Third World 3001   *(S)*   **Philosophy Of The World**   *1970*   **1,500.00** •
    (This legendary piece of ultimate anti-commercialism, recorded by a trio of sisters under the guidance of their father, moved noted avant garde composer Carla Bley to remark "They bring my mind to a complete halt." This was eventually issued on Rounder and is worth $10.)

17s. VARIOUS ARTISTS
Celebrity 1000   *(M)*   **World Famous Rhythm And Blues**   *1959*   **1,500.00**
    (Perhaps the most valuable generally distributed commercial compilation of great group records from the '50s.)

17t. VARIOUS ARTISTS
RCA Victor SP-33-66   *(DJ)*   **Christmas Programming From RCA Victor**   *1959*   **1,500.00**
    (This special seasonal sampler features one Elvis track and was issued in a full-color paper jacket with photos of the artists, including EP. Counterfeits of the sleeve exist but are black & white reproductions.)

18a. THE ROLLING STONES
London LL-3375   *(DJ)*   **The Rolling Stones** *(White label promo)*   *1964*   **1,400.00** •
    (This is the only white label promo Stones album until 1971's "Sticky Fingers.")

18b. VARIOUS ARTISTS
(No label)   *(DJ)*   **Go, Johnny, Go** *(Soundtrack)*   *1959*   **1,400.00** •
    (Sent out to radio stations in a plain cardboard jacket. Copies were handed out at the movie's premiere in a deluxe box that also included a a lobby card and a "press pass" to the showing. The box is preposterously rare with no reasonable way to suggest a value.)

19a. THE FIVE SATINS
Ember ELP-100   *(M)*   **The Five Satins Sing** *(Blue vinyl)*   *1957*   **1,300.00** •
    ("The blue vinyl pressing of this album is a second pressing with the multi-color Ember label in the second jacket. It was probably pressed in a semi-authorized manner. However, it is extremely rare." — NF)

19b. JIM REEVES
Abbott LP-5001   *(M)*   **Jim Reeves Sings**   *1956*   **1,300.00** •
    ("Probably the rarest C&W album. . . I've never seen a copy." — JG)

20a. THE BEATLES
Savage BM-69   *(M)*   **The Savage Young Beatles** *(Yellow label)*   *1964*   **1,250.00** •
    (This album collects material recorded by Tony Sheridan in Hamburg in 1961 and features John, Paul, George and Pete Best as The Beat Brothers on four tracks. This pressing has a yellow label and was issued in a jacket with a glossy orange cover. This album exists with an orange label and yellow jacket, valued at $100, that has been reproduced.)

20b. THE FENDERMEN
Soma MG-1240   *(M)*   **Mule Skinner Blues** *(Opaque black vinyl)*   *1960*   **1,250.00** •
    (This is the regular black vinyl pressing; copies exist pressed on non-opaque black vinyl. Valued at $2,000 it is listed above, as is a colored vinyl version, listed at $3,500.)

20c. THE NEW TWEEDY BROTHERS
Ridon 234   *(S)*   **The New Tweedy Brothers**   *196?*   **1,250.00** •
    (Classic private pressing from a Portland psych group originally issued in an oversized, hexagonal cover. "Although they're from Portland they sound more like a Bay Area group with a tremeloed guitar sound ala John Cipollina." — NS)

20d. THE ROLLING STONES
Abkco MPD-1   (DJ)   **Songs Of The Rolling Stones** (Orange cover)   1975   **1,250.00** •
    (This collection of song snippets has an orange-tinted photo taken from the group's aborted TV Special, "The Rolling Stones' Rock & Roll Circus." Another version of this album has an inset shot of the group in a country field setting and is worth $300.)

21a. THE BEATLES
Vee Jay LP-1062   (M)   **Introducing The Beatles** (Blank back)   1963   **1,200.00**
    (First pressing with "Love Me Do" and "P.S. I Love You." The back cover is completely blank, devoid of any printing. Long rumored to be a promo pressing it is now assumed to be a mis-pressing. The stereo version is worth $3,000 and is listed above.)

21b. THE BEATLES
United Artists SP-2359 (DJ)   **A Hard Day's Night** (Open-end interview)   1964   **1,200.00**
                     (Issued in a plain cardboard jacket.)

21c. BOLDER DAMN
Hit HRI-5061   (S)   **Mourning**   1971   **1,200.00**
                    (Another privately pressed collectible from the early '70s.)

21d. BUDDY HOLLY & THE CRICKETS
Decca DL-8707   (M)   **That'll Be The Day** (Black & silver label)   1958   **1,200.00**
    (This album was reissued with a black label and a rainbow color spectrum through the center that is worth $250.)

21e. INDEX
D. C. (No number)   (M)   **The Index**   1968   **1,200.00**
    (Later copies of this privately pressed album feature "Fire Eyes." Original pressings with "New York Mining Disaster" are worth $2,000 and are listed above.)

21f. THE MARVELETTES
Tamla 229   (M)   **The Marvelettes Sing The Hits Of '62**   1962   **1,200.00**
    (Original covers have a large "M" with a '62' inside a circle. Later pressing covers are basically black with each of the song titles inside white circles and are worth $500.)

21g. THE PATRON SAINTS
(No label)   (M)   **Fohhoh Bohob**   1969   **1,200.00**
    (A legendary psych album pressed up by the band for local distribution.)

21h. ELVIS PRESLEY
RCA Victor LPM-1382 (M)   **Elvis**   1956   **1,200.00**
    (Black label with "Long Play" on the bottom. Some later pressings contain an alternate take of "Old Shep." The matrix number in the trail-off vinyl ends with either "17S" or "19S.")

21i. SHANNON, DEL
Big Top 12-3003   (S)   **Runaway**   1961   **1,200.00**
    ("This legendary stereo album was never even listed in the Schwann catalog! Apparently the stereo masters were cut without Del's knowledge [as sales of stereo albums meant a higher royalty to the artist]. When Del was shown a copy at the Bottom Line in 1980, he was totally surprised." — NF)

21j. BILLY WARD & THE DOMINOES
Federal 395-548   (M)   **Billy Ward & His Dominoes**   1956   **1,200.00**
    (This is a 12" reissue of the 10" album valued at $7,500 and listed above.)

21k. BILLY WARD & THE DOMINOES
Federal 395-559   (M)   **Clyde McPhatter With Billy Ward & His Dominoes**   1957   **1,200.00**
    (This album collects sides featuring Clyde McPhatter prior to his formation of The Drifters.)

The Godfather Of Soul At 33 1/3 RPM

The man we know as the "Godfather of Soul" was born James Joe Brown, Jr. and, before ascending to that more than justified title, was called, among others, "Crip," "Music Box," and, later, as a professional, the "Hardest Working Man in Showbiz" and "Mr. Dynamite." When the fledgling soul singer named his band the Famous Flames, no less an authority than Richard Penniman ("Little Richard" to the masses) exclaimed "You are the *onliest* people who ever made yourselves famous before you *were* famous," not only accurately gauging James' ambition (and ego), but aptly summing up what the Warholian decades ahead were to make commonplace.

Signing with King/Federal, Brown proceeded to define soul music over the course of a fifteen year stay with the label. From 1958 through 1971 the company issued 38 albums of studio and now legendary live recordings. From these sessions, he placed 61 sides on *Billboard's* Hot 100 and another 23 albums on the LP charts. Like many smaller labels, especially those marketing their products to a primarily black audience, pressings of LPs were minimal; King is reputed to have pressed dozens of titles in runs of less than 5,000, shipped them to a reliable market and, if the response was slow, discontinued the title and moved on to the next release. Even a big seller like JB had a difficult time moving the expensive LP in the basically black markets that R 'n B reached in the '50s and early '60s.

In the second half of the '60s, working around a contract that forbade him to record as a singing artist for any other label, JB managed a quick one by signing with Mercury's Smash Records as an instrumentalist, releasing eight albums in a four year period. He spent the '70s with Polydor, with whom he experienced a renaissance as the "Sex Machine," placing bottom heavy dance music on both the singles and album charts. This paved the way for the latter half of the decade's obsession with repetitive dance music in the form of the ubiquitous and, unlike Brown's often delirious attacks on rhythm and beat, utterly predictable disco music.

The Smash albums have slowly escalated in value (they were virtual giveaways a few years ago), while the Polydor albums have long commanded relatively big bucks *for '70s albums.* But it is the King recordings which serve as the foundation for most of the soul music that followed, inspiring not only countless young black singers and bands since, but also putting a burr in the sides of many of the original British Invasion bands, notably The Rolling Stones.

Original King LPs can be identified by both the label and the style of the logo used on the cover. King albums were initially issued on a black label with silver print and "KING" in an arc across the top; collectors refer to these as the "crownless black label." In 1966, the company switched to a blue label with "KING" in straight letters with a crown above it. The crownless black label releases are rare in anything resembling collectable (i.e., very-good-plus, or VG+, or better) condition. For a more detailed account refer to the listing for King Records in the "Record Label Directory" in this book.

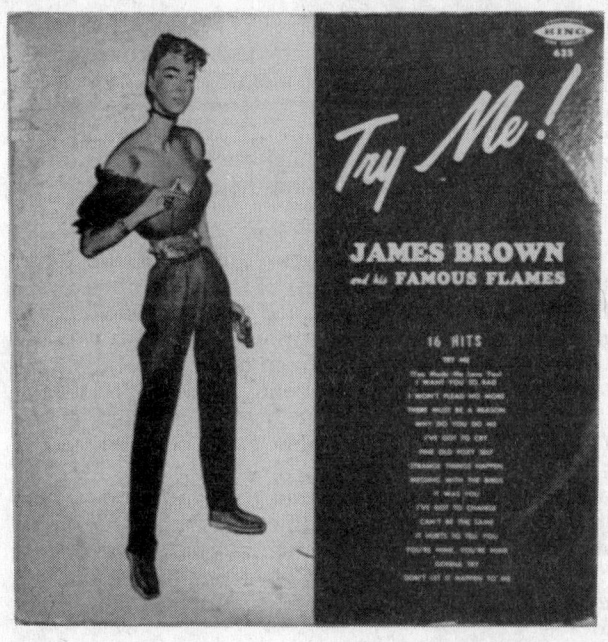

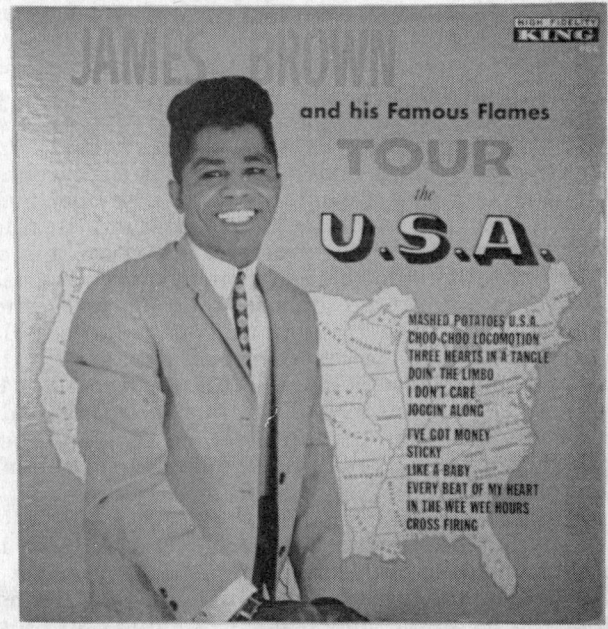

James Brown's second album, Try Me!, *featured this arresting cover art, alternately referred to as the "smoking gun" cover or the "smoking lady" cover. The* Tour The U.S.A. *album was originally issued on the crownless black label in mono in 1962; an electronically rechanneled stereo version on the blue crown label followed years later.*

The later original titles on the blue crown label are also escalating, albeit at a more moderate pace. While most collectors prefer mono, which were a far more accurate representation of the band's sound, the few stereo releases on this label are very rare and highly sought after by collectors of early stereo. (Many titles originally issued only in mono on the crownless label were reissued on the later label with a crown, many were electronically rechanneled for stereo and sound abysmal.)

While *Please Please Please* (King 610, 1959) is considered the most desirable, it's possible that *Think* (683, 1960) is the rarest of the early titles. *Pure Dynamite! Live At The Royal* (883, 1964) was initially issued with a gatefold cover and then replaced by a regular, single sleeve jacket. A curious collectable version of *I Got You, I Feel Good* (946, 1966) exists with a light green cover. Several of the early albums have notable art covers, the most popular being *Try Me* (635, 1959), which has a neat drawing of an attractive [white] woman holding a smoking gun years before the James Bond fad would make such a femme fatale common.

King also had no qualms about recycling JB and in a variety of ways: *Please Please Me* was reissued as King 909 with the same title while *Think* was reissued as 919 as *The Unbeatable James Brown*. Some albums were issued with different covers and titles; King 780 saw the light of day as *Good, Good Twistin', Shout And Shimmy* and *Excitement* while King 771 can be found as *Night Train, Twist Around* and *Jump Around*.

Traditionally, the Smash albums have been all but ignored by collectors but in the past few years completists have been searching them out and the prices are escalating. Note that Smash 2/67058, *Out Of Sight*, was withdrawn immediately after release and is among the rarest of all JB's albums. It was eventually issued in 1968 as 67109. Mercury also issued a compilation, *Soulful* (7083), in the early '70s that is currently impossible to find.

Beginning with 1971's *Hot Pants*, Brown found himself releasing a series of monstrously influential dance albums on Polydor. Over the next ten years he would issue twenty-five albums for his new label, including seven doubles (and a couple of collections of *Soul Classics* from his earlier heyday). The rhythms of these albums have influenced virtually every form of black dance music since, from the early disco through contemporary rap-based music. As these albums have been out of print for more than ten years, they are currently among the hottest of all collectible albums from the '70s, although many collectors and dealers believe the prices will drop [dramatically] when the music finally shows up on compact disc. While this does tend to affect the values of fairly common albums (i.e., the LP's release on CD), my own observations tend to confirm that JB collectors will damn the torpedoes, er, CDs, and continue to actively and avariciously pursue the vinyl with the albums continuing to escalate in collectibility and value.

Finally, while JB sold millions of records, he has received a mere two R.I.A.A. Gold Record Awards for singles and one for albums, and these were on Polydor. Like many independent labels, King did not make a habit of opening their books to any independent auditors, so those artists who comfortably passed the million mark (and it must be assumed that Brown did so with regularity) were destined not to see their walls hung with the industry's official recognition of sales achievement. . .

The Big Sound Of The Cars

While the collecting of records relating to cars and hot rods has been a part of the hobby for decades, for the most part the records collected were vocal songs about the four wheel passion, generally sung by a group. Most of these were another manifestation of the "West Coast Sound" of the '60s originated by Brian Wilson's Beach Boys with a nod to the early Jan & Dean recordings. Yet there is *another* aspect of collecting car records and that is the collecting of albums that deal directly with the world of racing, primarily sound effects and documentaries. These albums are usually collected outside of the mainstream record collecting hobby by men and women who are motor enthusiasts. While some of these collectors seek out only those records that deal with a specific car (say, a '64 Mustang), others collect those records that deal with a type of car, such as the ever popular Pontiac GTO. And, of even more interest, is the fact that the record itself (both its contents and its condition) may be of secondary import; what many of these collectors are looking for is the photo of the car on the cover and corresponding information in the liner notes!

The most common car collectible is any album that pictures a car on the cover and a collector of a specific type of car might find a need for each and every album with that car pictured. . . The list below is for non-musical automotive albums; the vocal and instrumental albums can be found in the main section under the artist. Rather than list two specific values as per the rest of the book, I have opted for a suggested price spread for albums in collectible condition (VG+ to NM) for automotive enthusiasts, as overall condition of the LP is often of secondary importance as long as the cover is clean.

Each listing is preceded by a parenthetical code that identifies the type of recording the album contains. The key to the abbreviations is:

E.	*Sound Effects*
G.	*Grand Prix / Formula One*
H.	*Hot Rods, Dragsters & Super Stocks*
I.	*Indianapolis 500*
L.	*Land Speed Trials*
M.	*Miscellaneous Cycles, karts, drag boats, etc*
N.	*NASCAR Stock cars*
P.	*Personality Interview or profile*
S.	*Sports Car Racing*

The data below was provided primarily by Jon Hardgrove, proprietor of the Carburetor Shop in Eldon, MO, and a collector of Pontiac GTO memorabilia. Much of the information for this aspect of record collecting is owed to the efforts of Tim Goebel of Tempe, AZ. For the interested reader/listener of this genre, John Blair's *Illustrated Discography Of Hot Rod Music 1961-1965* from Popular Culture, Ann Arbor, MI, is recommended.

P.	Allendor USR-8684	(S)	**I've Never Been Scared In A Race Car** *(Interview with Richard Petty)*	197?	40.00-75.00
P.	Amherst AMH-1003	(M)	**Evel Knievel**	1974	20.00-35.00
S.	Arkay AR-1009	(M)	**Sounds Of Laguna Seca 1957**	1958	20.00-35.00

M.	Associated Four A4-102	(M)	Race-A-Rama	196?	30.00-50.00
S.	Audio Fid. DFM-3031	(M)	Sound Effects: Daytona Speedway	1964	8.00-12.00
S.	Audio Fid. DFS-7031	(S)	Sound Effects: Daytona Speedway	1964	10.00-15.00
H.	Audio Fid. DFM-3032	(M)	The 1964 Winternationals	1964	10.00-20.00
H.	Audio Fid. DFS-7032	(S)	The 1964 Winternationals	1964	15.00-25.00
H.	Audio Fid. DFM-3033	(M)	Drag Race Sound Effects	1964	10.00-20.00
H.	Audio Fid. DFS-7033	(S)	Drag Race Sound Effects	1964	15.00-25.00
E.	Audio Fid. DFM-3034	(M)	Demolition Derby Sound Effects	1964	8.00-12.00
E.	Audio Fid. DFMS-7034	(S)	Demolition Derby Sound Effects	1964	10.00-15.00
H.	Audio Fid. DFM-3035	(M)	Motorcycle Scramble Sound Effects	1964	8.00-12.00
H.	Audio Fid. DFS-7035	(S)	Motorcycle Scramble Sound Effects	1964	10.00-15.00
E.	Audio Fid. DFS-5890	(S)	Sound Effects	197?	10.00-15.00
E.	Audio Fid. DFS-7777	(S)	Sound Effects	197?	10.00-15.00
H.	Battle 6130	(M)	Hot Rod Caravan	196?	10.00-20.00
H.	Battle 96130	(S)	Hot Rod Caravan	196?	15.00-25.00
H.	Battle 6131	(M)	Hot Rods-U.S.A.	196?	10.00-20.00
H.	Battle 96131	(S)	Hot Rods-U.S.A.	196?	15.00-25.00
H.	Battle 6132	(M)	Cement Roasters	196?	10.00-20.00
H.	Battle 96132	(S)	Cement Roasters	196?	15.00-25.00
H.	Battle 6133	(M)	Hot Stuff On The Asphalt	196?	10.00-20.00
H.	Battle 96133	(S)	Hot Stuff On The Asphalt	196?	15.00-25.00
H.	Battle 6134	(M)	Rods And Drags Forever	196?	10.00-20.00
H.	Battle 96134	(S)	Rods And Drags Forever	196?	15.00-25.00
H.	Battle 6135	(M)	Chrome On The Range	196?	10.00-20.00
H.	Battle 96135	(S)	Chrome On The Range	196?	15.00-25.00
H.	Battle 6136	(M)	Dig Out!	196?	10.00-20.00
H.	Battle 96136	(S)	Dig Out!	196?	15.00-25.00
G.	Battle 6137	(M)	Sports Car Caravan	196?	8.00-12.00
G.	Battle 96137	(S)	Sports Car Caravan	196?	10.00-15.00
G.	Battle 6138	(M)	Grand Prix USA	196?	10.00-20.00
G.	Battle 96138	(S)	Grand Prix USA	196?	15.00-25.00
S.	Battle 6139	(M)	Road Racing America	196?	10.00-20.00
S.	Battle 96139	(S)	Road Racing America	196?	15.00-25.00
S.	Battle 6140	(M)	'Sickels Galore!	196?	10.00-20.00
S.	Battle 96140	(S)	'Sickels Galore!	196?	15.00-25.00
H.	Bowmar B-573	(M)	Drag Racing Pix Dix	196?	20.00-35.00
H.	Capitol T-2001	(M)	The Big Sounds Of The Drags	1963	8.00-12.00
H.	Capitol ST-2001	(S)	The Big Sounds Of The Drags	1963	10.00-15.00
S.	Capitol T-2004	(M)	The Big Sounds Of The Sports Cars	1963	8.00-12.00
S.	Capitol ST-2004	(S)	The Big Sounds Of The Sports Cars	1963	10.00-15.00
M.	Capitol T-2049	(M)	The Big Sounds Of The Drag Boats	1963	10.00-20.00
M.	Capitol ST-2049	(S)	The Big Sounds Of The Drag Boats	1963	15.00-25.00
H.	Capitol TAO-2145	(M)	The History Of Drag Racing	1964	25.00-40.00
H.	Capitol STAO-2145	(S)	The History Of Drag Racing	1964	30.00-50.00
H.	Capitol T-2146	(M)	The Big Sounds Of The Drags, Volume 2	1964	8.00-12.00
H.	Capitol ST-2146	(S)	The Big Sounds Of The Drags, Volume 2	1964	10.00-15.00
H.	Capitol T-2147	(M)	The Big Sounds Of The Go-Karts	1964	10.00-20.00
H.	Capitol ST-2147	(S)	The Big Sounds Of The Go-Karts	1964	15.00-25.00
L.	Capitol KAO-2175	(M)	Breedlove 500+	1964	25.00-40.00
L.	Capitol SKAO-2175	(S)	Breedlove 500+	1964	30.00-50.00
H.	Dot DLP-3566	(M)	Drag Strip Sounds	1963	20.00-30.00
H.	Dot DLP-25566	(S)	Drag Strip Sounds	1963	20.00-35.00
H.	E.G. Kaiser LP-602	(M)	AHRA Summer Nationals Drag Sounds	196?	10.00-15.00
H.	E.T. LPM-7001	(M)	Soundsville, Vol. 1	196?	30.00-50.00
H.	Fleetwood FLD-1	(M)	The Sounds Of Auto Racing	1963	10.00-20.00
H.	Fleetwood FLD-1S	(S)	The Sounds Of Auto Racing	1963	15.00-25.00
H.	Fleetwood FLP-4001	(M)	Sounds Of Sanford	1963	10.00-20.00
H.	Fleetwood FLP-4001S	(S)	Sounds Of Sanford	1963	15.00-25.00
H.	Fleetwood FLP-4002	(M)	The 1963 Winternationals	1963	10.00-20.00
H.	Fleetwood FLP-4002S	(S)	The 1963 Winternationals	1963	15.00-25.00

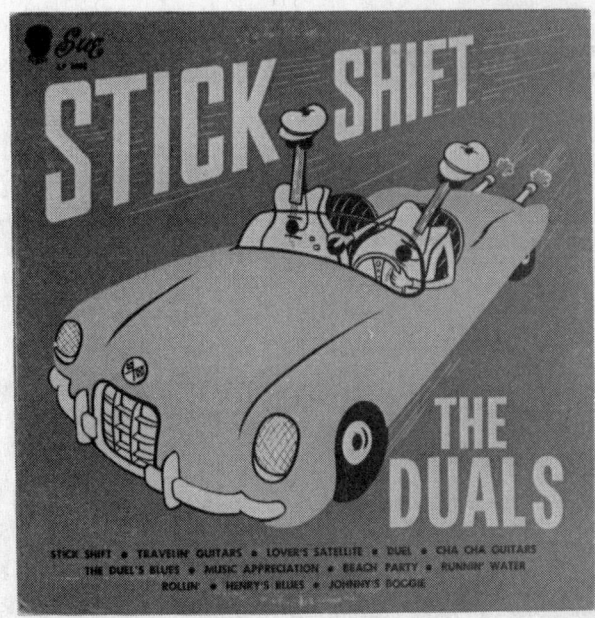

There are more than 200 vocal albums that feature music or covers devoted to cars. These include The Astronauts' Competition Coupe; The Beach Boys' Little Deuce Coupe; Jerry Cole's Hot Rod Dance Party (pictured above); Jan & Dean's Drag City; The Custom Kings' Kustom City; The Rip Chords' Three Window Coupe; Ronny & The Daytonas' G.T.O.; The Tokens' Wheels; and The Zip Codes' Mustang. A major player in this field was Gary Usher, who worked as Brian Wilson's lyricist on his early car songs and ended up recording as or producing The Competitors' Hits Of The Street and Strip; The Hondells' Go, Little Honda; The Knights' Hot Rod High; The Super Stocks' Thunder Road; and The Surfaris' Hit City '65. Instrumental albums in this field include Hal Blaine's Deuces "T's," Roadsters & Drums; Dick Dale's Checkered Flag; The Duals' Stick Shift (above) and The T-Bones' Boss Drag.

H.	Fleetwood FLP-4003	(M)	**AHRA 1963 Winter Championships**	1963	10.00-20.00
H.	Fleetwood FLP-4003S	(S)	**AHRA 1963 Winter Championships**	1963	15.00-25.00
H.	Fleetwood FLP-4004	(M)	**Bakersfield '63**	1963	10.00-20.00
H.	Fleetwood FLP-4004S	(S)	**Bakersfield '63**	1963	15.00-25.00
H.	Fleetwood FLP-4005	(M)	**1320 Special**	1963	75.00-125.00
H.	Fleetwood FLP-4005S	(S)	**1320 Special**	1963	100.00-150.00
N.	Fleetwood FLP-4006	(M)	**Rebel 300**	1963	20.00-30.00
N.	Fleetwood FLP-4006S	(S)	**Rebel 300**	1963	20.00-35.00
N.	Fleetwood FLP-4007	(M)	**Indianapolis 500**	1963	10.00-20.00
N.	Fleetwood FLP-4007S	(S)	**Indianapolis 500**	1963	15.00-25.00
N.	Fleetwood FLP-4008	(M)	**The World 600**	1963	20.00-30.00
N.	Fleetwood FLP-4008S	(S)	**The World 600**	1963	20.00-35.00
N.	Fleetwood FLP-4009	(M)	**Daytona "Firecracker" 400**	1963	20.00-30.00
N.	Fleetwood FLP-4009S	(S)	**Daytona "Firecracker" 400**	1963	20.00-35.00
L.	Fleetwood FLP-4010	(M)	**407.45**	1963	25.00-40.00
L.	Fleetwood FLP-4010S	(S)	**407.45**	1963	30.00-50.00
H.	Fleetwood FLP-4011	(M)	**The 1963 Nationals**	1964	10.00-20.00
H.	Fleetwood FLP-4011S	(S)	**The 1963 Nationals**	1964	15.00-25.00
S.	Fleetwood FLP-4012	(M)	**Road America 500 (SCCA) Elkhart Lake**	1964	10.00-20.00
S.	Fleetwood FLP-4012S	(S)	**Road America 500 (SCCA) Elkhart Lake**	1964	15.00-25.00
G.	Fleetwood FLP-4013	(M)	**Grand Prix Of The United States**	1964	20.00-30.00
G.	Fleetwood FLP-4013S	(S)	**Grand Prix Of The United States**	1964	20.00-35.00
M.	Fleetwood FLP-4014	(M)	**Drag Boats**	1964	20.00-30.00
M.	Fleetwood FLP-4014S	(S)	**Drag Boats**	1964	20.00-35.00
H.	Fleetwood FLP-4016	(M)	**The 1964 Winternationals**	1964	10.00-20.00
H.	Fleetwood FLP-4016S	(S)	**The 1964 Winternationals**	1964	15.00-25.00
H.	Fleetwood FLP-4017	(M)	**Bakersfield '64**	1964	20.00-30.00
H.	Fleetwood FLP-4017S	(S)	**Bakersfield '64**	1964	20.00-35.00
N.	Fleetwood FLP-4018	(M)	**Daytona 500**	1964	20.00-30.00
N.	Fleetwood FLP-4018S	(S)	**Daytona 500**	1964	20.00-35.00
S.	Fleetwood FLP-4019	(M)	**Sebring 1964**	1964	20.00-30.00
S.	Fleetwood FLP-4019S	(S)	**Sebring 1964**	1964	20.00-35.00
L.	Fleetwood FMS-1006	(S)	**Great Moments From The Indy 500**	1974	20.00-35.00
S.	Folkways FX-6140	(M)	**Sports Car Grand Prix Of Watkins Glen**	1956	30.00-50.00
S.	Fortissimo XK-8003	(S)	**Racing Cars**	1959	40.00-75.00
			(This unique stereo album plays the grooves from the inside out; i.e., from the label out to the edge!)		
H.	High Perform. HP-8000	(M)	**Hurst Takes You The The '64 Nationals**	1964	20.00-30.00
H.	High Perform. HPS-8000	(S)	**Hurst Takes You The The '64 Nationals**	1964	20.00-35.00
G.	High Perform. HP-8001	(M)	**Hurst '64-United States Grand Prix**	1964	20.00-30.00
G.	High Perform. HPS-8001	(S)	**Hurst '64-United States Grand Prix**	1964	20.00-35.00
G.	International 56007	(M)	**The Exciting Sounds Of Le Mans**	1966	40.00-60.00
G.	International 56007S	(S)	**The Exciting Sounds Of Le Mans**	1966	40.00-75.00
H.	Keystone	(M)	**Sox & Martin's "The Drags"**	196?	40.00-75.00
H.	Kiderian KPR-3333	(M)	**Sounds Of Drag Racing**	1974	10.00-15.00
H.	Lesco LE-200	(M)	**Sounds Of The Indy Nationals**	1967	20.00-35.00
E.	Major LP-1024	(M)	**Sound Effects, Volume 9**	196?	10.00-15.00
P.	MCA MCKS-506	(S)	**Championship Year**	1970	40.00-75.00
			(Interview with Jackie Stewart)		
L.	Mercury MG-20315	(M)	**500 Miles To Glory**	1959	25.00-40.00
L.	Mercury SR-60024	(S)	**500 Miles To Glory**	1959	30.00-50.00
G.	MGM E-4457	(M)	**The Grand Prix Challenge Of Champions**	1967	10.00-20.00
G.	MGM SE-4457	(S)	**The Grand Prix Challenge Of Champions**	1967	15.00-25.00
P.	Mobile Fidelity MF-101	(M)	**Dan Gurney: His World Of Racing**	1965	75.00-125.00
P.	Mobile Fidelity MFS-101	(S)	**Dan Gurney: His World Of Racing**	196?	100.00-150.00

M.	Newhall NN-101	(M)	Motorcycle Man	196?	10.00-15.00
H.	Performance PPPS-1001	(M)	13th Annual Winternationals	1973	15.00-25.00
H.	Performance PPPS-1002	(S)	4th Annual Gatornationals	1973	15.00-25.00
H.	Performance PPPS-1003	(M)	9th Annual Springnationals	1973	15.00-25.00
H.	Performance PPPS-1004	(S)	4th Annual Summernationals	1973	15.00-25.00
S.	Pirelli PLP-9	(M)	The Grand Prix Of Gibraltar	196?	10.00-15.00
S.	Riverside RLP-6	(M)	Sounds Of Speed	1960	10.00-20.00
S.	Riverside RS-96	(S)	Sounds Of Speed	1960	15.00-25.00
S.	Riverside RLP-12-833	(M)	The Grand Prix Of Gibraltar	1958	20.00-35.00
S.	Riverside RLP-5001	(M)	Sounds Of Sebring	1957	30.00-50.00
S.	Riverside RLP-5002	(M)	Sports Cars In Hi-Fi	1957	15.00-25.00
S.	Riverside RLP-1101	(S)	Sports Cars In Stereo	1957	15.00-25.00
S.	Riverside RLP-5003	(M)	Pit Stop	1957	15.00-25.00
P.	Riverside RLP-5004	(M)	Britain's Greatest Racing Driver (Interview with Stirling Moss)	1957	75.00-100.00
P.	Riverside RLP-5005	(M)	Around The Racing Circuit With Phil Hill	1957	75.00-100.00
P.	Riverside RLP-5006	(M)	The Career Of A Great Racing Driver (Interview with Carroll Shelby)	1957	150.00-250.00
P.	Riverside RLP-5007	(M)	A Memorial Tribute (For Marquis d'Portago)	1957	75.00-100.00
S.	Riverside RLP-5008	(M)	Sounds Of Sebring 1957	1957	30.00-50.00
S.	Riverside RLP-5010	(M)	Cuban Corners	1958	15.00-25.00
S.	Riverside RLP-5011	(M)	Sounds Of Sebring 1958	1958	15.00-25.00
S.	Riverside RLP-5012	(M)	Mercedes-Benz, The W125 And W163	1959	15.00-25.00
S.	Riverside RLP-5013	(M)	Vintage Sports Cars In Hi-Fi	1959	10.00-20.00
S.	Riverside RLP-1115	(S)	Vintage Sports Cars In Stereo	1959	15.00-25.00
S.	Riverside RLP-5014	(M)	Sounds Of Sebring 1959	1959	15.00-25.00
S.	Riverside RLP-1146	(S)	Sounds Of Sebring 1959	1959	10.00-20.00
S.	Riverside RLP-5015	(M)	Sports Cars At Sebring In Hi-Fi	1960	10.00-20.00
S.	Riverside RLP-1144	(S)	Sports Cars At Sebring In Stereo	1960	15.00-25.00
G.	Riverside RLP-5016	(M)	United States Grand Prix-Sebring 1959	1960	10.00-20.00
G.	Riverside RLP-1165	(S)	United States Grand Prix-Sebring 1959	1960	15.00-25.00
G.	Riverside RLP-5017	(M)	Grand Prix Cars In Action At Sebring	1960	10.00-20.00
G.	Riverside RLP-1166	(S)	Grand Prix Cars In Action At Sebring	1960	15.00-25.00
S.	Riverside RLP-5018	(M)	Sounds Of Sebring 1960	1960	10.00-20.00
S.	Riverside RLP-1173	(S)	Sounds Of Sebring 1960	1960	15.00-25.00
S.	Riverside RLP-5019	(M)	Sing A Song Of Sports Cars	1961	10.00-20.00
S.	Riverside RLP-1181	(S)	Sing A Song Of Sports Cars	1961	15.00-25.00
S.	Riverside RLP-5020	(M)	The Race/Mercedes-Benz 1937-1955	1961	15.00-25.00
G.	Riverside RLP-5021	(M)	The Grand Prix Of The United States	1961	10.00-20.00
G.	Riverside RS-95021	(S)	The Grand Prix Of The United States	1961	15.00-25.00
G.	Riverside RLP-5022	(M)	Farewell To A Formula	1961	10.00-20.00
G.	Riverside RS-95022	(S)	Farewell To A Formula	1961	15.00-25.00
S.	Riverside RLP-5023	(M)	Sounds Of Sebring 1961	1961	10.00-20.00
S.	Riverside RS-95023	(S)	Sounds Of Sebring 1961	1961	15.00-25.00
S.	Riverside RLP-5024	(M)	Sebring Corners	1962	10.00-20.00
S.	Riverside RS-95024	(S)	Sebring Corners	1962	15.00-25.00
S.	Riverside RLP-5025	(M)	Mercedes-Benz 75th Anniversary	1962	65.00-90.00
S.	Riverside RS-95025	(S)	Mercedes-Benz 75th Anniversary	1962	75.00-100.00
S.	Riverside RLP-5027	(M)	Sounds Of Sebring 1962	1962	10.00-20.00
S.	Riverside RS-95027	(S)	Sounds Of Sebring 1962	1962	15.00-25.00
G.	Riverside RLP-5028	(M)	Grand Prix Cars At Watkins Glen 1962	1962	10.00-20.00
G.	Riverside RS-95028	(S)	Grand Prix Cars At Watkins Glen 1962	1962	15.00-25.00
H.	Riverside RLP-5502	(M)	Hot Rods And Dragsters In Hi-Fi	1960	20.00-30.00
H.	Riverside RLP-1154	(S)	Hot Rods And Dragsters In Stereo	1960	20.00-35.00
H.	Riverside RLP-5503	(M)	Hot Rods In Action	1960	20.00-30.00
H.	Riverside RLP-1161	(S)	Hot Rods In Action	1960	20.00-35.00
L.	Riverside RLP-5504	(M)	On The Drag Strip	1960	25.00-40.00
L.	Riverside RLP-1184	(S)	On The Drag Strip	1960	30.00-50.00
L.	Riverside RLP-5506	(M)	Bonneville 1960	1960	65.00-90.00
L.	Riverside RS-95506	(S)	Bonneville 1960	1960	75.00-100.00
M.	Riverside RLP-5507	(M)	Karts In Action	1960	20.00-30.00
M.	Riverside RS-95507	(S)	Karts In Action	1960	20.00-35.00
H.	Riverside RLP-5509	(M)	Hot Rod Heaven/Bakersfield Smoker	1961	10.00-20.00
H.	Riverside RS-95509	(S)	Hot Rod Heaven/Bakersfield Smoker	1961	15.00-25.00
M.	Riverside RLP-5511	(M)	Scramble	1961	10.00-20.00
M.	Riverside RS-59511	(S)	Scramble	1961	15.00-25.00

L	Riverside RLP-5513	(M)	The Fastest 500	1961	20.00-30.00
L	Riverside RS-95513	(S)	The Fastest 500	1961	20.00-35.00
H	Riverside RLP-5515	(M)	Hot Cars At The Winternationals	1961	10.00-20.00
H	Riverside RS-95515	(S)	Hot Cars At The Winternationals	1961	15.00-25.00
H	Riverside RLP-5516	(M)	Super Stocks	1962	20.00-30.00
H	Riverside RS-95516	(S)	Super Stocks	1962	20.00-35.00
H	Riverside RLP-5517	(M)	Rods 'N' Rails	1962	10.00-20.00
H	Riverside RS-95517	(S)	Rods 'N' Rails	1962	15.00-25.00
H	Riverside RLP-5518	(M)	Hot Rods, Dragsters And Super Stocks	1962	20.00-30.00
H	Riverside RS-95518	(S)	Hot Rods, Dragsters And Super Stocks	1962	20.00-35.00
H	Riverside RLP-5519	(M)	Burning Slicks	1962	10.00-20.00
H	Riverside RS-95519	(S)	Burning Slicks	1962	15.00-25.00
H	Riverside RLP-5544	(M)	On The Drag Strip	1959	10.00-20.00
H	Riverside RLP-1184	(S)	On The Drag Strip	1959	15.00-25.00
S	Riverside RLP-12833	(M)	The Grand Prix Of Gibraltar	1959	65.00-90.00
S	Riverside SDP-33	(M)	The Golden Age Of Sebring	1959	75.00-100.00
S	Riverside SDP-44	(M)	The Wonderful World Of Sports Cars	1959	75.00-100.00
S	Rosemont RPLP-1160	(M)	The Pure Sound Of Speed	1960	40.00-75.00
H	Schofield	(M)	Dragsters And Hot Rods In Action	1960	30.00-50.00
H	Schofield LP-400	(M)	Dragsters And Competition Cars In Action	1960	25.00-40.00
H	Schofield LP-401	(S)	Dragsters And Competition Cars In Action	1960	30.00-50.00
S	Schofield LP-550	(M)	Senior TT: Isle Of Man 1959	1959	15.00-25.00
G	Schofield LP-551	(M)	The Formula One Grand Prix Car	1959	30.00-50.00
S	Schofield LP-552	(M)	1959 Isle Of Man TT	1959	15.00-25.00
G	Schofield LP-553	(M)	The Monaco Grand Prix 1959	1960	30.00-50.00
S	Schofield LP-559	(M)	1960 Isle Of Man TT	1960	15.00-25.00
S	Schofield LP-560	(M)	1961 Isle Of Man TT (Part 1)	1961	15.00-25.00
S	Schofield LP-561	(M)	1961 Isle Of Man TT (Part 2)	1961	15.00-25.00
S	Schofield LP-562	(M)	1962 Isle Of Man TT (Part 1)	1962	15.00-25.00
S	Schofield LP-563	(M)	1962 Isle Of Man TT (Part 2)	1962	15.00-25.00
S	Schofield LP-564	(M)	1963 Isle Of Man TT (Part 1)	1963	15.00-25.00
S	Schofield LP-565	(M)	1963 Isle Of Man TT (Part 2)	1963	15.00-25.00
S	Schofield LP-566	(M)	1964 Isle Of Man TT (Part 1)	1964	15.00-25.00
S	Schofield LP-567	(M)	1964 Isle Of Man TT (Part 2)	1964	15.00-25.00
H	Schofield LP-570	(M)	Dragfest	1965	25.00-40.00
H	Schofield LPS-570	(S)	Dragfest	1965	30.00-50.00
S	Schofield LP-574	(M)	1965 Isle Of Man TT (Part 1)	1965	15.00-25.00
S	Schofield LP-575	(M)	1965 Isle Of Man TT (Part 2)	1965	15.00-25.00
S	Schofield LP-577	(M)	1967 Isle Of Man TT (Part 1)	1967	15.00-25.00
S	Schofield LP-578	(M)	1967 Isle Of Man TT (Part 2)	1967	15.00-25.00
P.	Souvenir S-2692	(M)	George Hurst And Don Garlits Interview	196?	20.00-35.00
P.	SSN NI-676	(S)	One Who Dared (Interview with Gary Irvin)	197?	20.00-35.00
P.	TGR 720	(S)	Meet Richard Petty	197?	10.00-15.00

Record Company Label Directory

This section outlines the many graphic changes record companies' labels have undergone through the years and will assist the reader in identifying original albums from later pressings. I have kept the explanations as brief and to the point as possible. The dates and catalog numbers during the label transitions are approximate; you may find that you have pressings of an album on an earlier label than I have listed. I would certainly appreciate having any such errors of this type called to my attention so that future editions can be corrected.

One area that needs a little exposition is that of promotional releases. The most common method of printing promotional records has been to press them with white labels with plain black print, hence the term "white label promo." As these white labels are obvious manifestations of the labels special attention, they are the most popular with collectors. Some labels used their regular label, or a slightly modified version, and had such mottos as "Audition Copy" or "Promotional Copy" incorporated into the label's typesetting; these are also promos. *In this book records with such notices stamped on the label in ink after the fact are not the same!*

Promotional records are usually pressed in small runs on quality vinyl—often at plants that specialize in small print runs—making it a better pressing than the stock copies. Needless to say, they are quite collectible and generally command a premium above the normal value of the record, although the premium may be minimal.

To list each and every promo version of the albums in this book would practically double the size of the book. Instead, the reader should assume that a promo of most records exist and, in pricing, that such a promo is worth no less than the value listed for the stock copy and, generally, no more than twice the listed value. Listed exceptions are those albums that are more common than the stock version or those promos that are worth considerably more than the stock or, in a very few cases, where the promo is different or noteworthy.

In a money saving move, many companies dropped the practice of printing special promo records and simply took to designating stock copies as intended for promotional purposes by affixing a disclaimer to the cover usually reading "For Promotional Use Only-Not Intended For Sale." This took the most common form of stamping the disclaimer in [black] ink or embossing it with gold print. For a while in the mid-'60s Columbia affixed a gold "promo" sticker to the cover. Generally, these do not command a great deal of attention from collectors. Certainly a slight premium may be attached to a record so designated, but these disclaimers do not, for the most part, set the hearts of collectors afire.

One exception is Capitol Records, who, during the '60s, often added the word "PROMO" or "FREE" in perforated lettering in the upper right corner. While this is a blatant damage to the artwork, albums so marked do draw collectors' attention and regularly fetch a reasonable premium. Capitol also took to the practice of punching a hole in the corner of the cover and handing these out as promos. *These so-called "promo-holes" are not recognized by this book as worth attention.* Anyone with a hole-punch can construct all of such promos he or she might need to soak gullible collectors. The reader is advised that this position is not generally shared and many collectors seek out these albums, even though they should really be classified as cut-outs.

When large amounts of records were deleted in the mid-'60s, many of which were monos, most companies simply "cut out" the number from their catalogs and sold the remaining copies to wholesalers, where they ended up in "5 & 10s" around the country for 99¢. By the '80s, companies began clipping the corners of deleted titles; this was originally a small clip but grew to the point where huge portions of covers were left lying on the floor after the record was sent out to the distributors. Almost without exception cut-out marks on albums reduce any record's value. The sole exception being Warner Bros. and Reprise, who had the novel idea of placing a small brass rivet in the upper left corner of their cut-outs during the waning '60s. These tend to attract some collectors, who will pay a regular price for such a cut-out.

A&M From 1963 through mid-'73, A&M used a brown label. From then until 1985 the label was a silver gray with a large brown "AM" fading into the background.

ABC-Paramount From 1956 through 1961 (#101-400) a black label was issued with ABC-Paramount on top and "A Product of Am-Par Record Corp" on the bottom. From 1962 through 1966 (#400-560s) the black label reads "A Product of ABC-Paramount Records Inc." During 1966 and 1967, the logo was changed to "abc records" in a box at the top. Throughout these years, mono albums bore an "ABC" prefix; stereo had an "ABCS" prefix. White label promos were issued.

From 1968 to 1974, the label was black with "abc" on top and "New York, NY" on the bottom. Other labels include black with the logo in children's blocks in and purple on gold from 1973 to 1978. In 1979 ABC came under MCA's control.

Ace From inception through the early '60s a black label was issued with "Ace" in silver print on top. This was replaced by a black label with "ACE" in an oval.

Apple From November 1968 through early 1970 the Apple label read "A subsidiary of Capitol Industries, Inc" on the bottom. This was replaced with "Mfd. by Apple Records, Inc" from 1970 until 1974. The final run of albums from 1974 and 1975 included an "All Rights Reserved" disclaimer.

Argo From inception through 1964 Argo, primarlily a jazz label, used a black label with silver print. During 1965 the company also issued a silver label with black print and a brown label with pink print along with the original label. Throughout these years, mono albums bore an "LP" prefix; stereo albums had an "LPS" prefix. By 1966 Argo albums were released on Cadet.

Arista From 1972 through 1976 (#4000-4105) the label was light blue with "Arista Records" beneath the logo on top. For a few months in late 1976 and early 1977 the blue label read "Arista" beneath the logo on top. This was replaced with a black label (#4110-4205). From 1978 until 1984 the company returned to a blue label with "Arista" on the left side of the logo on top. Beginning in 1985 a black and blue label was used with "Arista" floating above a mountain skyline.

Asylum   For the first few releases (#5051-5066) the label was white with the company's logo in a circle on top. In 1973 the label used a sky with clouds motif (#5067-5099, 1000-1040s). This label was modified slightly in 1975 to include the Warner Bros. logo in the lower right; this label ran through 1984. Note: A solid blue label was used briefly in 1976. In 1985 the label turned black and orange.

Atco   A subsidiary of Atlantic, initial pressings from 1958 through the latter part of 1961 (#101-134) were on a solid yellow label with a harp in the upper left. From 1961 through 1968, mono albums had a gold and gray label with a white stripe through the center with "ATCO" in large print (#138-226). Stereo albums were purple and brown with the white stripe (#138-256).

In 1969, after the demise of mono, all albums returned to a solid yellow with an 1841 Broadway, NYC address printed on the bottom. When Atlantic was sold to the Warner conglomerate, the address was changed to 75 Rockefeller Plaza, NYC. From 1978 through 1984 the company used a solid gray label; since then Atlantic has used a gray label made up of countless tiny "Atco" logos.

Atlantic   From 1950 through mid 1960, mono albums were issued on a black label with silver print (#8000-8036 and 1200-1328). In 1958 select titles were mixed into stereo and issued on a green label, all of which are difficult to find. From 1960 through 1962 (#8032-8059 and 1330-1378) Atlantic mono albums were orange and purple while stereo albums were green and blue. Each label had a white band through the center with a white pinwheel logo— known as the "fan"— in a black box on the right side.

From 1962 through 1966 (#8060-8125 and 1379-1463) the fan switched to black on white with "Atlantic" running vertically alongside it. From 1966 through 1968 (#8126-8178 and 1464-1499) "Atlantic" ran horizontally beneath the fan. After 1968 the label, now stereo only, switched to a green and orange with the company's 1841 Broadway, NYC address on the bottom.

From 1973 through 1975 a Rockefeller Plaza address appeared at the bottom, and from 1975 through the late '80s "A Warner Communications Company" appeared on the bottom. White label promos were issued from the mid-'60s on.

Bang   From inception through the mid-'70s Bang used a red and white label with a derringer on top. From 1973 through 1977 a sky with clouds design was employed. This was followed by a light brown label with a red logo on top.

Bearsville   Initial releases had a light brown label with "Distributed by Ampex" on the bottom. From 1971 through the mid-'70s the label read "Distributed by Warner Bros." on the bottom. 1977 until 1981 saw no distribution motto; however, in 1981 a "3300 Warner Blvd" address was added.

Bell   From inception through 1969 a blue label was issued with silver print. The label was silver from 1970 through 1975.

Bethlehem   Throughout the '50s Bethlehem, primarlily a jazz label, featured a maroon label with silver print and"Bethlehem" in an arc across the top. In the late '50s, the "Bethlehem" logo changed to black letters in a silver border across the top. Finally, in the '60s, "King Records" was added to the bottom.

Big Tree   In 1970 the label was red with "Product of Big Tree Enterprises Limited" on the bottom. This was replaced by "Distributed by Ampex" in 1971 and 1972; "Distributed by Bell" in 1972 and 1973; and "Distributed by Atlantic" from 1974 until 1976.

Blue Thumb   The first four LPs had a black label. From the fifth release through approximately the mid-60s the off-white label had a thumb print on top. This was finally replaced with a purple label with the "abc" logo on top in 1974.

BluesWay   During the first year, 1967 and 1968, the label was blue. This was replaced by a black label with a blue perimeter.

Brother   The Beach Boys' label saw one LP issued in 1967, *Smiley Smile,* on a drab brown label manufactured by Capitol. The label was resurrected in 1970 under the Warner/Reprise corporate umbrella. From 1970 through 1976 the pale yellow label read "A Subsidiary and Licensee of Warner Bros., Inc" on the bottom. From mid-'76 through 1979 the label read "A Division of Warner Bros. Records, Inc" on the bottom.

Brunswick   From 1950 through the early '60s, Brunswick used a black label with silver print. Yellow label promos were issued. In late 1962 through 1972, the company switched to a black label with a rainbow through the center and "A Division of Decca Records" along the perimeter. Throughout these years mono albums bore a "BL" prefix, while stereo LPs carried a "BL-7" prefix. Since 1972 a black label was used with the rainbow and "Manufactured by Brunswick Record Corp" along the perimeter.

Buddah   From 1968 until 1973 the multi-color label had a silhouette of a Buddah on the bottom. From 1973 through 1978 an orange label was used with a smiling Buddah on the bottom. This was replaced by a black label with the Arista logo on the bottom.

Cadence   From inception through 1962 a maroon label was used with a silver top. During the company's final year the label was red with a black border.

Cadet   From 1965, when Cadet took over Argo, through 1968, the company used a blue label. In 1969 a blue label fading into white was issued. A pink and yellow label was in effect in the early '70s, replaced briefly by a pink and orange label.

Calendar   During 1967 and 1968 the label was orange with Zodiac figures around the perimeter. During late 1968 and 1969 it was orange with a "K" on top. The label then became Kirshner Records.

Camden   This budget subsidiary of RCA Victor repackaged material from the parent label's catalog, sometimes using obscure 45 and EP tracks. Camden's original label was a pink/purple. From 1958 through 1964, a blue label was used with a purple perimeter. From 1964 until 1968, a blue label was used with a dark blue perimeter fading into light blue. Throughout this time mono albums bore a "CAL" prefix; stereo titles had a "CAS" prefix. Stereo numbers ending with an "e" denoted reprocessed stereo. From 1969 until 1975 a dark blue label was in effect. In 1976 the entire line was turned over to Pickwick.

Cameo From 1959 until 1961 the label was orange with a cameo logo on top. From 1961 through the rest of the decade it was a red and black label with the cameo on the right. In the late '60s a purple label was used with the cameo on

Capitol From 1949 through 1953 (#100-344), they basically issued a green label with "Long Playing Microgroove" on the bottom. Ten-inch albums bore an "H" prefix. From 1953 through 1958 (#345-1008) a turquoise label with "Long Playing" on the bottom was in effect, with a gray or black label also used during this time. The twelve-inch albums generally carried a "T" prefix although certain titles carried a "W." Yellow label promos were issued.

In 1958 and 1959 (#1021-1225) Capitol switched to a black label with a rainbow perimeter and both the Capitol dome logo and "Long Playing High-Fidelity" printed on the left side. From 1959 until 1962 (#1225-1660s), the black/rainbow label had the logo and a silver line on the left. Black label promos were issued with "Not For Sale" on the bottom. The "T" and "W" prefixes were used for monos while an "ST" or "SW" was saved for stereos. A "DT" or "DW" indicates that the album was electronically rechanneled stereo using Capitol's patented "duophonic stereo" process ethod of altering the mono signal beyond recognition. Special releases with gatefold covers received "KAO" or "MAS" prefixes with either an "S" or "D" added for stereo.

From 1962 through 1969 (#1658-2999 and the new series beginning with 100 through the early 200s), Capitol issued a black label with the logo on top, using the "T"/"ST" prefix. Note: On each of these black rainbow labels the copyright data is along the lower perimeter in white print on the black label

After 1969 the situation is rather confusing: A [lime] green label was used from mid-'69 through mid-'72 (#208-11105). A red label with a purple target-like logo on top was used from mid-'72 through mid-'75. Simultaneously, an orange label was used with "Capitol" on the bottom from late 1972 through late 1975. In late 1975 an "Unauthorized duplication" disclaimer was added to the perimeter print on top of the orange label from late 1975 through early 1978. From mid-'78 through 1983 the label was purple. During this time a variety of prefixes were used, although "ST" remained the primary designation. In 1984 Capitol returned to the classic black rainbow label of the '60s except this time the copyright data was on top in black print in the rainbow. And, the company began manufacturing white label promos.

Capricorn In 1970 the label was a yellow Atco label with "Capricorn Records Series" on the bottom. In 1971 it was pink. From 1972 through 1974 the label was a plain tan. From 1975 until 1978 it was light brown with a large goat facing right. This was replaced by a light brown label with a [different] goat facing left.

Casablanca In 1974 the label was blue with "Manufactured and Distributed by Warner Bros. Records, Inc." on the bottom. In 1975 and early 1976 the blue label read "Manufactured and Distributed by Casablanca Records" on the bottom. From 1976 through 1977 (#7026-7050) the label featured a desert scene with three camels in the foreground. 1976 until 1981 (#7050s-7250s) saw the camels replaced with a film crew and "Manufactured and Distributed by Casablanca Records" on the bottom. Since 1981 the label has read "Manufactured and Distributed by Polygram Records" on the bottom.

Challenge From inception through the mid-'60s the label was blue with "Challenge" in an oval on top. During the '60s the label carried a plain "CHALLENGE" logo.

Chancellor   Initial releases in 1958 and 1959 had pink labels; after that they were black.

Checker From inception through 1966 (the 1400 series and 2900-2996) the label was black and occasionally maroon. In 1966 (#2997-3001) a light blue label was used with checkers on top. From 1967 through the early '70s a blue label that fades into white at the bottom was in effect. Finally, a blue label was used with a purple band through the center.

Chess Through 1966 (#1400-1490s), Chess used a black label with silver print. During 1966 they used a black label with a chess piece on top. From 1967 through the early '70s a blue label that fades into white at the bottom was used. From 1972 until 1977 the label was orange with a blue band through the center. The 50000 and 60000 series used then was under the direction of the GRT Corporation. Later issues were owned by the All Platinum Record Group. The '80s had a blue label with a checker-like effect along the lower perimeter.

Chrysalis From 1972 until 1976 (#1000-1130s) the label was green. In 1977 a blue label fading up into white was used with an "All Rights Reserved" disclaimer added in 1982.

Clarion This budget subsidiary of Atlantic/Atco repackaged material from the parent label's catalog.

Colgems The red and white label in 1966 and 1967 read "TM of Colgems Records" beneath the logo on top. This motto was dropped in 1968.

Colpix From inception through the early '60s the company used a gold label with "Colpix" in large red letters on top. In 1963 a strip of movie film was added. Later pressings were on a blue label. Stereo numbers are decidedly rarer than their mono counterparts.

Columbia   From 1949 through 1955 Columbia used a red label with gold print and "Long Playing" on the bottom (#500-650). A variety of prefixes, "CL," "GL" and "ML," were used before the company settled on "CL." From 1955 through 1962 (#650 through the early 1800s) mono albums had red labels with six white-on-black, highly stylized camera "eye"-on-a-tripod logos on each side of the label.

From 1962 through 1965 (#1780-2379) the white-on-black eye logos were replaced with two white eye logos, one on each side of the spindle hole, and read "Guaranteed High Fidelity" on the bottom. From 1965 through 1968 (#2380-2811) the red mono label read "360 Sound Mono" in white on the bottom. Note: Some later pressings from 1967 and 1968 read "Mono" only.

Columbia apparently began manufacturing stereo albums (the 8000 series) in early 1959; the initial 8000 numbers were assigned randomly as mono albums were mixed into stereo and released. By 1960 designating stereo was simple: CS-6800 was added to the mono catalog number to denote stereo. Thus, Columbia CL-2372, The Byrds' *Mr. Tambourine Man*, would be CS-9172!

The illustrations above may help to clarify certain differences in Columbia labels: The design used throughout the '50s and into 1962 (illustrated above by Adventures Of The Heart) is often referred to as the "eyes logo" label as it carried three highly stylized, white-on-black camera logos on each side of the spindle hole (a total of six per label). This should not be confused with the last label introduced in 1970 and shown above on Johnny's Newest Hits: Here the eye logo also appears a half-dozen times on each side but in gold print equally spaced around the perimeter between six "Columbias."

The stereo label with "360 Sound" in black print was issued in 1962 without arrows (Bob Dylan). By 1963 the arrows were added (Another Side Of Bob Dylan). In 1965 the color of the print was changed to white.

8000-8579 featured the red label with the six eye logos. From 1962 through 1965 (#8630-9128) stereo labels featured the two white eye logos with "360 Sound Stereo" in black on the bottom. Two arrows, one on each side pointing up, were added to the "360 Sound Stereo" in the last 1/3 of 1963. From 1965 through 1970 (#9130-9999, 1-30, and 30000-30050), stereo labels read "360 Sound Stereo" with the arrows in white at the bottom.

After 1970 the red label reads "Columbia" in gold letters a half-dozen times around the perimeter. The only way to note a first pressings is by the prefix in the catalog number, which have included, but are not limited to, "CS," "C," "G," "KC," and "PC," although some of these prefixes have been used on reissues of earlier titles. Columbia subsidiaries include Epic and Harmony.

Coral   From inception through 1963 Coral albums were issued on a maroon label; blue label promos were issued. From 1963 through 1968 a black label was used with a rainbow center and read "A Subsidiary of Decca Records." From 1968 through 1970 "A Subsidiary of MCA" replaced the Decca motto. Throughout these years, mono albums bore a "CRL" prefix; stereo albums, a "CRL-7." Refer to MCA.

Cotillion   From 1969 till late 1972 this Atlantic subsidiary used a grey label with an "1841 Broadway" address on the bottom. The address was changed to "75 Rockefeller Plaza" in the mid-'70s. Finally, Cotillion switched to a purple label.

Crown   Arising from the ashes of Modern Records, Crown used a black label with silver print through 1960, often reissuing the earlier label's titles. By 1960, Crown specialized in low budget reissues, pressed on the cheapest vinyl available and often with completely misleading credits. Note: When Crown began issuing albums in rechanneled stereo, the sound was among the worse ever developed. Consequently, the fake stereo titles are avoided by all but completists.

Curtom   From 1968 until 1972 the plain yellow label had a Broadway address on the bottom; 1973 until 1975 saw the address changed to 7th Ave. After the mid-'70s the yellow label sported a psychedelic multi-color top.

Decca   From 1949 through 1954 Decca used a black label with gold print (the early 8000 series). From 1954 through 1960 (through #8981) they used a black label with silver print. Pink label promos were issued. From 1960 through 1966 (#4000-4830s), the label was black with a rainbow stripe and reads "Mfrd. by Decca Records." From 1967 through 1971 "A Division of MCA" was printed beneath the rainbow. White label promos were issued. For approximately one year, 1971 and 1972, "Mfd. by MCA" was added. After that, reissues appeared on the MCA label. Mono albums bore a "DL" prefix; stereo albums with a "DL-7."

Del-Fi   Original labels had a blue logo; reissues from the '80s have a gold label.

Deram   From inception through the early '70s the label was basically white with "London" beneath the Deram logo on top. During the '70s the white label had a brown top. The '80s versions read "Manufactured by Phonogram, Inc" on top.

Dolton   From 1959 until 1962 the mono 2000 series and the stereo 8000s had a light blue label with a Sunset Blvd. address on the bottom. From late 1962 through late 1965 Dolton used a dark blue label with a fish logo on the left. This was replaced in 1966 by a black label with a "D" logo on the left. By 1967 Dolton was owned by Liberty.

Dore   Initial releases in the early '60s were on a light blue label with a feather on top. The '70s version was a dark blue with a larger feather on top. The late '70s saw a black label with a still larger feather.

Dot   During 1955 and 1956 (the 3000 series), Dot issued a maroon label with "Gallatin, Tennessee" on the bottom. During late 1956 and 1957 the address was "Hollywood, California." From 1957 through 1967 (#3030-3050), a black label was used with "Long Play" and "Dot" in script on the top. In 1968 "A Division of Paramount" appeared on the bottom. Throughout these years, mono albums bore a "DLP" prefix with a 3000 number; stereo albums bore the same "DLP" but were a 25000 series; i.e., the last three digits of the mono and stereos were identical.

From 1968 through 1970 the Paramount mountain logo appeared in a box with the Dot logo at the top of the label. From 1970 through 1974, the Dot logo appeared in a box on top with "A Division of Famous Music Corp" on the bottom. During 1974 until 1978, a purple and yellow label was in effect. After 1978 select Dot titles were reissued on ABC.

Duke   From inception through 1961 the label was purple and yellow. During the remainder of the decade the label was orange.

Dunhill   From 1965 through 1968 (#50000-50020s) the label was black with "Dunhill" on top with "Distributed by ABC Records" on the bottom. From 50020s - 50031 the label read "A Subsidiary of ABC Records." From 1968 through 1974 (#50032-50170s) both "Dunhill" and the "abc" logo were in a box on top. In 1973 a black label was used that featured children's blocks on top. During its final year, 1974 and 1975, the label was purple. By 1975 Dunhill was a part of ABC.

Elektra   During the '50s a white label was used with an electron logo on top. This was replaced with a grey label a small guitar player on top. From 1961 until 1966 a gold label was used with a large guitar player on top. The gold label was replaced from 1966 until 1969 (#4007-4040s) with a flat brownish label. During 1969 and 1970 the label was red (#4040s-5007). Throughout the rest of the decade the label was multi-colored with a butterfly in the upper right. This was replaced by a red label with a Warner Bros. logo on the bottom. After 1983 the label was black.

EmArcy   From 1954 through 1958 EmArcy, primarily a jazz label, used a blue label with silver print and a drummer at the top. Like other Mercury subsidiaries, an "MG" prefix was used on the mono 36000 series. When titles were released in stereo, an "SR" prefix was used with an 80000 number. In the '60s a gray label was issued. Reissues in the '80s featured a brown and gold label with the drummer. Note: Some titles were reissued on special blue Mercury/EmArcy Jazz labels, often appearing here in stereo for the first time.

End   The label was originally gray with a dog on top. This was replaced in the early '60s with a label that had "End" on end on either side.

Epic   As Columbia's primary subsidiary, from inception through 1962 Epic carried a yellow label with black lines radiating out along the perimeter; stereo issues read "Stereorama" across the top. During 1962 and 1963, a yellow label was used with "Epic" appearing eight times around the perimeter for mono albums; stereos read "Stereo" and "Epic" three times each around the perimeter.

From 1963 through 1965 (#24/26040s-24/26150s) a yellow label was used with "A Product of CBS" on the bottom. From 1965 through 1972 (#24/26150s-31992) the same yellow label deleted the CBS motto was in print. From 1973 until 1978 Epic issued an orange label and replaced that with a black label in 1978.

Initially, mono albums bore an "LG" or "LN" prefix. When titles from the 3000 series were issued in stereo they carried a "BN" prefix and were part of the 500 series. By the '60s, the bulk of the releases were either in the LN-24000 mono series or the BN-26000 stereo series.

Etiquette   Original labels were red with a Tacoma, WA address on the bottom. Reissues have a red label but bear a Seattle, WA address and the copyright date along with a 1984 on the bottom.

Excello   The company's original orange label was replaced in the latter '60s with a white label with a colored arrow on top.

Fantasy   From inception through the '60s, mono albums had a red/maroon label. When the label added stereo in the early '60s, they used an 8000 series number; these originals had a blue label with silver print and were pressed on stiff, non-flexible vinyl. White label promos were issued. Fantasy began pressing its albums on colored vinyl with their 10" series; copies of these albums have been seen on red, blue, green and purple vinyl. Some were on rainbow-like pressings of different colors; these are rare. With the inception of their 12" line in 1955, all new albums were pressed on thick, dark red vinyl, often with a mottling effect of the red dye in the vinyl.

For a brief period during 1957 and 1958, new releases were pressed on black vinyl. By 1958 red wax was back. . . Pressings from this point on were still made with the thick vinyl but were a lovely, translucent red. In-print titles were pressed on this wax before reverting the black in the early '60s. When Fantasy began issuing stereo in 1962, these albums were pressed on the same thick vinyl as the mono only using a translucent blue. These would then revert to modern black vinyl for the duration of the decade.

Hypothetically, an early Fantasy title could have seen four distinct mono pressings and two stereo! For example, a popular title such as Dave Brubeck's *Jazz At The College Of Pacific* could have been pressed first on thick, dark red vinyl in 1956. Second pressings in 1957 would have been on the thick black vinyl of the '50s with little or no "grooveguard" around the disc's perimeter to keep the stylus from sliding off. Third pressings in 1958/59 would be on the thick translucent red vinyl; final mono pressings from the early '60s would have been on thinner, more modern black vinyl with the now familiar grooveguard. Then a blue stereo pressing in 1962 followed by a black vinyl stereo reissue through the rest of the decade.

Gee   In the '50s the label was red label; they switched to a gray label in the '60s.

Geffen   In the early '80s the cream label had technical information printed around the perimeter. In 1984 the print was not used and in 1985 the label was changed to black.

Gordy A purple label with "Gordy" in yellow script on top was used from 1962 through 1967. After 1967 the purple label had a yellow slash through the middle with the logo on the left side.

Harmony This budget subsidiary of Columbia repackaged material from the parent label's catalog. Harmony used a maroon label from 1957 through 1959 (#7000-7150). For the next twelve years they issued a black label.

Harvest A yellow and green label was used from 1969 until 1976. From 1977 until 1985 the label had an EMI Records Ltd. copyright notice on the bottom.

Hi A plain gray/silver label with "Hi" on the left was used from inception through 1976. A few titles in 1972 and 1973 were issued with a white label with the "Hi" logo on top with the "London" logo beneath it. After 1976 the label was black.

Hickory Through the early '60s a black label was used with "Hickory" in silver print on top. From 1964 until 1972 a black label with colored stripes on top was in effect, and from 1973 until 1975 the label was brown with the MGM logo on the right. The rest of the '70s saw a purple and yellow label with the "abc" logo on top.

I.R.S. From the late '70s through the first years of the '80s the label was white. It was replaced in 1981 by a silver label and, again in 1985 by a goldish label.

Imperial From 1950 through 1958 (#9000-9040s) Imperial featured a maroon label. From 1958 through 1964 (#9045-9267) they used a black label with stars and colored rays on top. White label promos were issued. A black and pink label was in effect from 1964 through 1966 (#9268-9320s). From 1966 through 1969, a black and green label was used with "Product Of Liberty Records" on the bottom.

Mono albums bore an "LP" prefix and were part of the 9000 series. When stereo was added in the late '50s, these albums carried the same "LP" prefix but were part of the 12000 series. Original stereo albums featured a black label with silver print; later pressings had the black label with the stars. After Liberty was purchased by United Artists in 1970, "Liberty/UA, Inc" was added to the label.

International Artists Each of this company's original '60s albums were reissued in 1979 with identical covers and labels. The originals are on thick vinyl; reissues are on the thinner vinyl and have "Masterfonics" stamped in the trail-off vinyl.

Island In 1972 and 1973 the label had a sunray motif with the logo. In 1974 the label featured a stylized figure on water skies. From 1975 until 1978 the label was black. From 1978 until 1981 it was orange and blue. In 1982 and 1983 the label had a purple top with a skyscraper on the left. After 1983 the blue or black label noted the Warner Communication Corporation along the bottom.

Jamie In 1958 the label was yellow. From 1959 until 1967 it was white and gold and from 1967 through 1970, brown and orange.

Janus From 1970 until 1976 (the 3000 series and the early 7000s) the label was light brownish gold. In 1977 and 1978 the label was a reddish orange.

Josie From inception through the early '60s the label was a cream color with blue print. Through the latter '60s and into the '70s the label was light brown.

Jubilee   From inception through 1958 Jubilee used a blue label. From 1958 through 1960, a black label was used with "jubilee" in a silver "sunburst" oval on top. Throughout the '60s, a black label was used with "jubilee" in a multi-colored "sunburst." Mono albums carried a "JGL" prefix; stereos had a "JGS."

Kama Sutra   From 1965 until 1969 (#8000-8070s) the label was yellow. From 1969 until 1972 (#2000-2050s) the label was pink. After 1972 the label had a forest scene on top.

Kapp   From 1956 through 1959 Kapp used a maroon or blue label. A black and blue label with a "K" logo was in effect from 1959 through 1962. A black and blue label with a red major's hat was used from 1962 through 1964. From 1964 through 1971 black label was black with the major's hat on top. Throughout these years, mono albums bore a "KL" prefix and were part of the 1000 series; white label promos were issued. Stereo albums were designated with a "KS" and a 5000 number. An orange and purple label was used from 1971 until 1973.

King   From inception through 1966 original King albums had a black label with silver print. From 1966 through the mid-'70s a blue or black label was used with a crown on top. Throughout the rest of the label's run a brownish gold or black label with a "K" logo on top was in service. King 10" albums bore a "295" prefix for the suggested retail price of $2.95. The first 12" albums carried a "395" prefix through 1960; afterwards the monos were simply designated "LP." Stereo albums on this label were virtually non-existent until 1966; those in true stereo from 1960 until 1966 are rare and highly sought after by non-jazz collectors running the label.

From the first 12" album in 1956 through early 1958 (#500 through approximately 610), the logo on the cover was a box in the upper right with "King" in script and "HiFi" in block print. From 1958 through 1960 (#610-690), the logo was an ellipse with "KING" in block letters. From 1960 through 1962 (#690-810), the logo read "High Fidelity" with "KING" in open block letters. A crown atop "KING" in open block letters was used from 1963 through 1968 (#810-1040s). After 1969, the logo was a stylized "K" with "KING" in capital letters as the K's leg.

Kirshner   From 1969 until 1973 the label was the same as the latter Calendar label: Orange with a "K" logo on top. After 1974 it was white with a multi-color top.

Laurie   This one is confusing: The labels of originals and reissues are essentially the same except on the original pressings the dots in the five points of the star are large with plenty of white space. On later pressings the dots are noticeably smaller with considerably less white space.

LeGrand   The original '60s releases have a red and gold label without a crown on top. Reissues from the '80s have a crown on top and a white band in the middle.

Liberty   From inception through 1960 (#3000-3130s) Liberty boasted an aqua blue, or turquoise, label with silver print. When stereo albums, many of which were reprocessed, were issued on the 7000 series in the late '50s, a black label was used with silver print. Throughout these years, mono albums bore an "LRS" prefix; white label promos were issued. Some titles were issued as part of the 6000 series with an "LRS" prefix. Stereo albums were designated with "LST."

A black label with a rainbow and a gold logo was used from 1960 through 1966 (#3150-3440 and 13/14000s). From 1966 through 1969 (#3440-7620s and 13/14000s) "Liberty Records, Inc" was added beneath a blue logo. Off-white or cream label promos were issued. After Liberty was sold in 1970, "Liberty/UA, Inc" was added beneath the blue logo. In the '80s a gray label was in use.

London   From inception through 1964, mono albums had a red or maroon label with silver print and featured an "ffrr"/ear logo on top. White label promos were issued. When stereo was added, a blue label was issued with "ffss" in a circle on top; all are true stereo. From 1963 through 1965 mono albums had a red/maroon label, and stereo LPs had a blue label with a plain "London" in silver print on top. From 1965 until 1969 "London" appeared in a box on top. After 1969 "London" appeared in blue print in a silver box at the top. Throughout these years, mono albums bore an "LL" prefix and carried a four digit number. Stereo releases had a "PS" prefix and a three digit number, usually dropping the first number from the mono designation.

Mainstream   Original albums from 1965 and 1966 bore a light, silvery-blue label. White label promos were issued. Later pressings had a "Red Lion Production" in the upper right.

MCA   From 1973 through 1978 (#2000-2300s) a black label was used with a rainbow. A light brown label with a darker perimeter was in used from 1977 until 1979 (the 3000 series and the early 5000s). After 1980 the label showed a blue sky and clouds motif. Note: A blue label with rainbow was used on the MCA reissues.

Mercury   Original albums in 1949 on the 1000 series had a black label with gold print. From the mid-'50s through 1963 (#20000-20700) mono albums had a black label with silver print and a plain logo on top. Mono albums carried an "MG" prefix; yellow label promos were issued. The first stereo albums (the SR-60000 series) appeared in 1957 with a black label with silver print. From 1961 through 1964 (#20600-20900) the label for mono and stereo was black with an oval logo on top.

From 1964 through 1968 (#20900-61190) a red label was used with Mercury's head on top. White label promos were issued. A red label with twelve oval logos around perimeter was used from 1969 through 1973 (#61200-61300s and 600-670s). During 1973 and 1974 (#680-on) Mercury issued a red label with seven oval logos around perimeter. A colored label with a skyscraper was in print from 1974 through 1982 (the 1000 series). After 1982 the label was black with "Marketed by Polygram" on the bottom.

Mercury's budget label was Wing and they distributed several others, primarily the Norman Granz labels, Clef, Down Home, Norgran and Verve through 1960, along with Savoy and Regent.

MGM   Original MGM albums of the '50s (#3000-3770s) have a yellow and black label. From 1960 through 1968 (#3770s-4515) MGM used a black label with a multi-color logo. Yellow and white label promos were issued. Throughout these years, mono albums bore an "E" prefix; stereo albums carried an "SE."

From 1968 through 1976 the label was a blue and gold swirl label with "A Division of Metro-Goldwyn-Mayer" on the bottom. From 1976 on the blue and gold swirl label had a street address on the bottom. Yellow label promos were issued.

MGM's subsidiaries include Metrojazz and later the budget label, Metro. In 1961 they purchased Verve from Norman Granz, altering that label's cataloging system. For more information refer to Verve below.

Minit   Through most of the '60s the label was orange. This was replaced by a black label in the late '60s and early '70s.

Monument   1961 and 1962 releases had a copper and white swirl label. This was replaced in 1962 and 1963 with a white and rainbow swirl label. From 1963 until 1976 a light green label was used with a gold perimeter and a Henderson, Tenn, address on the bottom. From 1966 until 1971 the Tenn. location was dropped. A brownish orange label was used from 1971 until 1976. This was replaced in 1976 with a black label. Finally, a silver label was used in the early '80s.

Motown   From 1962 on Motown used a blue label with a map pinpointing Detroit at the top of the label. On original pressings from 1962 and 1963 the map extended from the East Coast to Kansas; there was a W. Grand Blvd. address beneath the map. From 1963 until 1969 the map was scaled down to extend from Pennsylvania to Indiana, and the W. Grand Blvd. address was printed at the bottom. From 1969 until 1983 "A Product of Motown" appeared on the bottom in lieu of the Detroit address. After 1983 the label notes MCA as the distributor.

Musicor   Initial pressings in 1962 were on a brown label. A black label with "Distributed by United Artists" on the bottom was used from 1962 into 1964. The United Artists reference was dropped from 1962 until 1964. During the first half of the '70s the label was orange; later, the label was green and yellow.

Ode   From 1968 until 1970 the label was yellow. During 1970 and 1971 it was white and silver with "Ode 70" in the upper right. From 1971 until 1975 the white and silver label specified "Ode Records Inc." Finally, a light brown label with the Epic logo was in effect from 1975 until 1978.

Paramount   In 1969 the label was gray with "A Division of Paramount Pictures" on the bottom. In the early '70s the gray label read "A Division of Famous Music." A few titles in 1971 and 1972 featured a blue label. Note: This company is not affiliated with ABC-Paramount.

Parkway   In 1960 and 1961 the label was orange with a "harp, horns & score" logo on each side. From 1961 until 1966 the label was orange and yellow with two harps on top. During 1967 and 1968 the label was gold.

Parrot   From 1965 until 1971 the label was black with "Distributed by London Records, Inc" on the bottom. From 1972 until 1974 the black label read "A Product of London Records."

Philips   From inception through 1963 (#001-120s) Philips used a black label with "Chicago 1, Illinois" on the bottom. From 1964 until 1966, the black label had "Vendor: Mercury" on the bottom. From 1966 until 1970, the black label was used with no disclaimers on the bottom. Throughout this time, mono albums bore a "PHM" prefix and were part of the 200-000 series; stereo titles had a "PHS" prefix and were part of the 600-000 series. Gold or white label promos were issued. From 1970 until 1974 a black label was used with "Manufactured and Distributed by Mercury" on the bottom.

Polydor   From 1969 until 1978 the label was red with no street address. From 1978 until 1982 the red label carried a Seventh Ave. address on the bottom.

RCA Victor   From 1950 through 1954, RCA Victor albums had a green label. For one year, 1954 and 1955, the company switched to a glossy black label with Nipper the dog on top in outline only. The 10" albums bore an "LPT" or "LPM" prefix and were issued with a 3000 number.

From 1955 through 1963 (LPM 2000-2700s) the classic shiny black label with the full-bodied Nipper on top appeared with "Long Play" on the bottom. During 1963 and 1964, (LPM 2700-2999), "Mono" was printed on the bottom, which was ultimately replaced by "Monaural" from 1964 until 1968 (LPM 3000-3900s). Note: Some albums issued in 1966 and 1967 read "Mono Dynagroove."

Stereo albums from 1958 through 1964 (LSP 2000-2999) had a shiny black label with the full-bodied Nipper on top appeared with "Living Stereo" on the bottom. From 1964 through 1968 (LSP 3000-4000s) only "Stereo" appeared on the bottom. Note: Some albums issued in 1966 and 1967 read "Stereo Dynagroove."

From late 1968 through 1971 (LSP 4000-4460s) an orange label was issued on stiff, non-flexible vinyl. Many, if not most, of these were reissued with identical labels on RCA's ridiculously flimsy "dynaflex" vinyl. From 1971 through 1976 (LSP 4460s-1039) the same orange label was in effect but with "dynaflex" printed on the bottom. During 1975 and 1976 the label was a light brown label. In 1976, the label was again black except Nipper was now located in the upper right at approximately 1 or 2 o'clock.

Regent   A subsidiary of Savoy, Regent, primarily a jazz label, was distributed by Mercury and carried an "MG" prefix. Original Regent releases used a green label; red labels are reissues.

Reprise   Initially Frank Sinatra's pet project, Reprise was incorporated into Warner Bros. within a few years. From inception through 1968, Reprise used a pink, gold, and green label with a large steamboat in the upper left (#6000-6280s). Note: Reprise had a jazz series that was yellow, red, and green with an angel in the upper left in print during the early '60s. From 1968 through 1970, a brown and orange label was used with a smaller steamboat and the "W7" logo on top (#6280s-6400s and 2000-2025). White label promos were issued.

Throughout this time, mono albums on the 1000 series had an "F" prefix; stereo LPs had an "FS" for Frank Sinatra prefix. Mono titles on the 6000 series had an "R" prefix; stereo titles were originally issued with an "R6" and then an "RS" prefix. From 1970 through 1976 a brown label was used without the "W7" logo (the early 6400s on). White label promos were issued.

Riverside   From inception through 1956 (#100-240s) Riverside, primarlily a jazz label, used a blue on white label. From 1956 through 1963 (#240s-476) the label was blue with a mike and two reels of tape on top. Stereo titles beginning in late 1958 had a black label with the mike and reels logo. For a brief period in 1963 and 1964, mono and stereo labels were blue without the mike and reels logo; this was definitely used on 477 and may have turned up on a few others and some reissues. These labels read "Bill Grauer Productions" on the bottom.

Reprise Records, started by and almost solely supported by Frank Sinatra's sales, used a steamboat on their label through the early '70s. Originally a pink, gold and green label with a large steamboat and "reprise:" in a banner (illustrated here by Movin' With Nancy), in 1968 it switched to a brown and orange label with a noticeably smaller boat and both a "W7" and ":r" logo on top (Are You Experienced?). By 1970 the label was brown and the "W7" had been dropped from the top (The Great Lost Kinks Album).

Initially, the mono albums began with 100 and carried an "RLP-12" prefix. Initial stereo releases were on an 1100 series with the new numbers assigned as the remixes for mono titles were made available; i.e., the stereo numbers do not necessarily correspond with their original mono counterparts. When new titles were automatically released in both mono and stereo, the monos retained the three digit figure (the late 200s or early 300s) and the "RLP" prefix. Stereo titles had the same three digit number but bore an "RS-9" prefix.

From 1964 through 1967 (#478-499) the label was turquoise with "Orpheum Prod." on the bottom. After ABC took over distribution of the label in 1967 the earlier material was reissued with black on brown labels. In the mid-'80s select titles were reissued, often in stereo, by Fantasy with a facsimile of the original blue on white label but with an OJC prefix for "Original Jazz Classic."

Roulette   Original issues in 1957 and 1958 (#25000-25050) had black labels. From 1959 through 1962 (#25050-25180 and 52000-52050) a white label was issued with criss-crossed color bars. For a brief period in 1962 and 1963, an orange and pink label was used. After 1963 Roulette used an orange and yellow label with a roulette wheel design. Throughout this time, mono albums bore a "R" prefix; white label promos were issued. Stereo titles had a "SR" prefix. Since 1977, the orange and yellow label with a roulette wheel label shows "Made in USA by Roulette Inc" at the bottom.

RSO   From 1973 until 1981 a light brown label was used with a red cow logo on top. This was replaced by a silver label with a red cow in 1981.

Savoy   All original issues on Savoy, primarlily a jazz label, from 1950 through the '60s had maroon labels. Distributed by Mercury, this label also used an "MG" prefix. Their subsidiary was Regent. When titles were reissued in the '70s a red or brown label was used with "Distributed by Arista" on the bottom.

Scepter   From 1962 until 1971 the label was orange with an oval-like center. Although a few titles had solid white or red labels. In 1972 and 1973 a multi-color label was in use on general releases with the special "Citation Series" carrying a yellow label. From 1974 until 1976 the label was blue.

Shelter   The first dozen titles in 1971 and 1972 (#8900-8910) had a red label with a Superman-like logo on the left. From 1972 through the latter part of 1973 the red label had a blacked out Superman logo on top. In 1974 and 1975 a gold label was used with "Distributed by MCA Records, Inc" on the bottom. In 1976 a yellowish gold label had "Distributed by ABC Records" on the bottom. From 1977 until 1979 the label had a crescent moon along the left side.

Sire   From 1968 through 1970 a white label was used with both the Sire and London logos on top. Since then, a yellow label was used with a blue or purple stylized "S" on top. During 1970 and 1971 the label read "Distributed by Polydor Records" on the bottom. From 1972 until 1974 the label read "Distributed by Famous Music Corp." From 1974 until 1976 it read "Distributed by ABC Records." During the rest of the '70s the label read "Marketed by Warner Bros." In the '80s the Warner motto was joined by a "3300 Warner Blvd" address.

Smash   From 1961 through 1968 a flat red label was used with black print. From 1968 until 1971 the red label carried a Mercury logo in an oval on top.

Soul   This Motown subsidiary's first few releases had a white and red label. This was immediately changed to a purple label in late 1965.

Specialty   From 1957 through the early '70s the label was gold with a black top. The '80s reissues had a white label with a black top.

Stax   From 1962 until 1967 the label was blue. with a stack of records on top. In 1967 and 1968 it was yellow with the stack of records. From 1968 until 1971 the yellow label had a finger-snapping logo in a blue box on the left and then in a brown box. Since the mid-'70s the label was purple fading into white.

Sue   From 1961 through the mid-'60s the label was orange; later titles and reissues are black.

Sunset This budget subsidiary of Liberty repackaged material from the parent label's catalog. Original releases through 1969 had a black and blue label that read "A Division of Liberty Records" on the bottom. After 1970 the same label read "Liberty/U.A." on the bottom.

Tamla   From 1961 through 1963 the label was yellow with overlapping globes on top. From 1963 until 1968 the yellow label showed two discs on top, one a record and one with the company imprint. After 1968 the yellow label had a brown top.

Threshold   From 1970 until 1973 the label was white. This was replaced with a blue label in 1973.

Tower   This subsidiary of Capitol used a dull orange label from 1965 until 1968. Several titles were reissued in 1968 on a striped label. Mono albums carried a "T" prefix while stereo LPs were "ST" and rechanneled stereo, "DT."

Track   From 1967 until 1971 the label was black; during 1972, it was silver. After 1973 the label was a dark brown.

20th Century Fox   From inception through the early '60s, the label was a light blue with "20th Fox" on top. From the early '60s through the early '70s, a black label was issued. During the '70s the label changed to aquamarine. From 1977 though the '80s, a light brown label was used with spotlights on top.

United Artists   In 1958 and 1959, U.A. used a red and black label. In 1959 mono albums had red labels, while stereos were blue. A black label with a large "UA" logo on top was briefly issued in 1960. From 1960 through 1968 (#3120-6640) the label was black with "United Artists" in a box on top. From 1968 through 1970 (#6640-6710s) the label was purple and orange. White label promos were issued. Throughout this period, mono albums (the UAL 3000 and 4000 series) and stereos (UAS 6000s and 5000s) had a "UAS" prefix.

During 1970 and 1971 (#6710-6700s and early 5500s and 5200s) the label was black and orange. From 1971 through 1975 (#6780 on and 100-540) the label was a light brown. From 1975 through 1977 (#540-760) "Music & Record Group" was added to the bottom of the brown label. After 1977 a "sun burst" design was used on the label.

Valiant   During the first half of the '60s the label was blue; during the latter half it was red.

Vanguard   From inception through 1963 (the 9000 mono series) Vanguard used a maroon label with silver print and a horseman logo on top. Stereo albums (the 2000 and 79000 series) had a black label with silver print. From 1963 through 1970 the company issued a gold-brown or silvery-gray label with a white horseman logo on the bottom. White label promos were issued. Throughout these years, monos bore a "VRS" prefix while stereos had a "VSD." During the '70s a marble "swirl" effect label was issued.

Vee Jay   From inception through 1959 the first few albums had a maroon label with silver print (#1000-1008). From 1960 through 1963 a glossy black label was used with a rainbow perimeter and the Vee Jay logo in an oval at the top of the label (#1010s-1070s and the 3000 series). From 1963 through 1965 (#1060-1070s) the glossy black rainbow label featured the logo in brackets. During 1965 and 1966, a flat black label was used with silver print. Throughout these years Vee Jay's basic prefix was the common "LP." White label promos were issued.

When stereos were issued they bore either an "LPS," SR" or "VRS" prefix. Note: Stereo Vee Jay albums are very rare; while this book notes the staggering difference between some monos and stereos, the necessary data is not currently available to note all of these rarities. Thus, when happening across a stereo Vee Jay bear in mind that it may be rarer than the prices in this book indicate. . .

When Vee Jay went bankrupt in 1966, the demand for a lot of their product remained and was met illegally. Many Vee Jay titles remained available throughout the '70s with black labels on pressings that are dramatically inferior to the originals. In fact, they resemble barely professional counterfeits: the covers are photo-reproductions of the originals, and the pressings are abominable, with poor sound and noticeable noise from recycled vinyl. While the most common was *Introducing The Beatles*, poorly reproduced Jimmy Reed albums and several jazz titles proliferated.

During the '70s "VJ International" and a "Vintage Series" appeared. During the '70s and the '80s, a red label with the brackets logo was also used.

Verve . Verve was jazz impressario Norman Granz' flagship label. He began this by consolidating his previous Clef, Down Home, and Norgran labels, and reissuing the bulk of the earlier titles. From 1956 through 1960 Verve used a black label with silver print and "Long Playing Microgroove Verve Records, Inc" on the bottom. While several series were used (the 1000s was for traditional jazz; the 2000s for popular selections, although some jazz, especially vocals, found their way here; and the 4000s, apparently created for Ella Fitzgerald's protean output), the bulk of the label's product was on the 8000 jazz series. Verve titles carried an "MGV" prefix and were issued exclusively in mono. When select titles were remixed in stereo and issued on the 6000 series in late 1959 and 1960, they carried an "MGVS" prefix.

When the label was purchased by MGM in 1960, most of the catalog was reissued with the monos designated with a "V" and the stereos with a "V6." The original 8000 series number was kept for both. The new parent company retained the original black with silver print label but "MGM Records-A Division Of Metro-Goldwyn-Mayer, Inc." was included on the bottom. From 1966 through 1971 MGM's Sunset address is also on the bottom. From 1972 until 1975, a white label was used with blue MGM and Verve logos. White label promos were issued.

When Warner Bros. switched their albums over to a lime green label in 1967, they carried their "Warner Bros.-Seven Arts Records" motto along the perimeter at the top with a "W7" logo in a box beneath it, shown above on Live/Dead. By 1970 the same green labels read "Warner Bros. Records" with the "WB" shield logo, illustrated here by Tupelo Honey.

Vik   This RCA subsidiary had black labels with a multi-color logo on top.

Virgin   From 1972 until 1975 the label was a full color picture of two young women—one must suppose they are the artist's, ahem, ideal virgins—with "Dist. by Atlantic Recording Corp." on the bottom. From 1975 until 1978 it read "Distributed by CBS Records." After 1978 the label was white.

Volt   From 1967 until 1969 the label was yellow. From 1969 until 1973 it was blue. After 1973 the label was brown.

Wand   Through most of the '60s (#650-690s) the label was white with a black top. From 1970 until 1974 the label had a marble effect. After 1974 the label was a dark orange.

Warner Brothers   From 1958 through 1962 (#1200-1470) Warner Bros. used a gray label with a black and yellow logo on top for mono albums. From 1962 until 1965 (#1470-1620) a gray label was used with a black and white logo on top. During this period stero albums carried a gold label.

From 1966 through 1968 (#1920-1730) both the mono and the stereo releases had a gold label. From 1968 through 1970 a green label was used with the "W7" logo on top. Throughout these years, mono albums carried a "W" prefix; stereos had a "WS" prefix. White label promos were issued.

From 1970 through 1977, the "W7" on the green label was changed to a "WB" logo. From 1973 until 1975, the label featured a Burbank street scene. From 1978 through the '80s, a tan label was issued.

White Whale   From 1965 until 1970 (#7100-7120s) the label was solid blue; after 1970 it was blue with concentric white circles.

Wing This budget subsidiary of Mercury repackaged material from the parent label's catalog. From inception through the '50s Wing had a blue label with silver print and the "Wing" logo in an oval on top, often with "Jazz" above it. Several titles were issued simultaneously on Mercury and Wing. Throughout the '60s, when Wing was exclusively a budget label, a blue or black label was used with "Mercury" above the "Wing" logo. Mono albums were on the 12000 series with an "MGW" prefix, while stereo LPs carried an "SRW" prefix on the 16000 series. From 1970 through 1971, a blue label featured both the Wing logo and the oval Mercury logo alongside it on top.

World Pacific   In 1957 Pacific Jazz changed its name to World Pacific; both new titles and older catalog titles were issued on the new imprints. From 1960 until 1965, the Pacific Jazz label was back, starting all over with number "1." From 1965 until 1970, both Pacific Jazz and World Pacific ran, with the later issuing non-jazz material covering the gamut from rock to pop to international. Both companies used a black, orange, and yellow label. During the late '70s and early '80s, the company used a blue and green "waves" design for the label.

"X"   The RCA subsidiary had white labels with a huge red "X" on top.

A. B. SKHY

MGM SE-4628	(S)	A. B. Skhy	1969	6.00	15.00
MGM SE-4676	(S)	Ramblin'	1970	6.00	15.00

A. F. O. EXECUTIVES, THE

A. F. O. LP-0002	(M)	A Compendium	196?	80.00	200.00

AARONKOFF, BENJY

Prestige PRLP-7416	(M)	Folk Songs	1966	6.00	15.00
Prestige PRST-7416	(S)	Folk Songs	1966	8.00	20.00

ABBA

Atlantic PR-300	(DJ)	Abba	1978	12.00	30.00
Atlantic PR-432	(DJ)	A Collection Of Hits	1982	12.00	30.00
Atlantic PR-436	(DJ)	The Abba Special (2 LPs)	1983	20.00	50.00
Nautilus NR-20	(S)	Arrival	198?	5.00	15.00

ABICAIR, SHIRLEY

Columbia CL-1531	(M)	With The Gentle Air	1960	6.00	15.00
Columbia CS-8331	(S)	With The Gentle Air	1960	8.00	20.00

ABDNOR INVOLVEMENT, JOHN HOWARD

Abnak ABST-2072	(S)	Intro To Change	1968	6.00	15.00

ACE, JOHNNY

Duke DLP-70 (10")	(M)	Memorial Album For Johnny Ace	1955	400.00	1,000.00
Duke DLP-71	(M)	Memorial Album For Johnny Ace	1956	150.00	300.00
		(Purple & yellow label. No card on the cover.)			
Duke DLP-71	(M)	Memorial Album For Johnny Ace	1961	60.00	150.00
		(Purple & yellow label. The cover has a playing card.)			
Duke DLPX-71	(E)	Memorial Album	1974	8.00	20.00

ACUFF, ROY

Columbia HL-9004 (10")	(M)	Songs Of The Smokey Mountains	1949	40.00	100.00
Columbia HL-9010 (10")	(M)	Old Time Barn Music	1949	40.00	100.00
Columbia HL-9013 (10")	(M)	Songs Of The Saddle	1949	40.00	100.00
Capitol T-617	(M)	Songs Of The Smoky Mountains	1955	20.00	50.00
Harmony HL-7082	(M)	Great Speckled Bird	1958	10.00	25.00
MGM E-3707	(M)	Favorite Hymns	1958	20.00	50.00
MGM E-4044	(M)	Hymn Time	1962	8.00	20.00
MGM SE-4044	(S)	Hymn Time	1962	10.00	25.00
Capitol T-1870	(M)	Songs Of The Smoky Mountains	1963	8.00	20.00
Capitol ST-1870	(S)	Songs Of The Smoky Mountains	1963	10.00	25.00
Capitol T-2103	(M)	The Great Roy Acuff	1964	8.00	20.00
Capitol ST-2103	(S)	The Great Roy Acuff	1964	10.00	25.00
Capitol T-2276	(M)	The Voice Of Country Music	1965	8.00	20.00
Capitol ST-2276	(S)	The Voice Of Country Music	1965	10.00	25.00

ADAMS, DON

Signature SM-1010	(M)	Don Adams	1960	12.00	30.00
Crescendo GNP-91	(M)	Don Adams Meets The Roving Reporter	1963	5.00	12.00
Crescendo GNPS-91	(S)	Don Adams Meets The Roving Reporter	1963	6.00	15.00
Roulette R-25317	(M)	The Detective	1966	6.00	15.00
Roulette SR-25317	(S)	The Detective	1966	8.00	20.00
United Arts. UAL-3533	(M)	Get Smart (TV Soundtrack)	1966	10.00	25.00
United Arts. UAS-6533	(S)	Get Smart (TV Soundtrack)	1966	12.00	30.00
United Arts. UAL-3604	(M)	Don Adams Live	1967	6.00	15.00
United Arts. UAS-6604	(S)	Don Adams Live	1967	8.00	20.00

Label & Catalog #		Title	Year	VG+	NM

ADAMS, EDIE

MGM E-3751	(M)	Music To Listen To Records To	1959	16.00	40.00
MGM SE-3751	(S)	Music To Listen To Records To	1959	20.00	50.00

ADAMS, FAYE

Warwick W-2031	(M)	Shake A Hand	1961	150.00	350.00
Zion 2104	(M)	Faye Adams Sings The Lord's Prayer	196?	20.00	50.00

ADAMS, J. T.

Bluesville BVLP-1077	(M)	Indiana Ave. Blues	1964	16.00	40.00

ADAMS, JERRI: *Refer to* GOLDMINE'S PRICE GUIDE TO COLLECTIBLE JAZZ ALBUMS

ADAMS, MIKE, & THE RED JACKETS

Crown CLP-5312	(M)	Surfer's Beat	1963	6.00	15.00
Crown CST-312	(S)	Surfer's Beat	1963	8.00	20.00
Crown CST-312	(S)	Surfer's Beat (Colored vinyl)	1963	16.00	40.00

ADRIAN & THE SUNSETS

Sunset 63-601	(M)	Breakthrough	1963	40.00	100.00
Sunset 63-601	(M)	Breakthrough (Multi-colored vinyl)	1963	60.00	150.00
Sunset SE-63-601	(S)	Breakthrough	1963	60.00	150.00
Sunset SE-63-601	(S)	Breakthrough (Multi-colored vinyl)	1963	100.00	250.00

ADVANCE

Han-O-Disk	(DJ)	American Excello (Picture disc)	1981	6.00	15.00

ADVANCEMENT, THE

Philips PHS-600-328	(S)	The Advancement	1969	6.00	15.00

ADVENTURERS, THE

Columbia CL-2147	(M)	Can't Stop Twistin'	1961	20.00	50.00
Columbia CS-8547	(S)	Can't Stop Twistin'	1961	30.00	75.00

AEROSMITH

Columbia KC-32005	(S)	Aerosmith (Orange cover)	1973	10.00	25.00
Columbia KCQ-32847	(Q)	Get Your Wings	1974	10.00	25.00
Columbia JCQ-33479	(Q)	Toys In The Attic	1975	10.00	25.00
Columbia PCQ-34165	(Q)	Rocks	1976	10.00	25.00
Columbia A3S-187	(DJ)	Pure Gold (3 LPs)	1976	20.00	50.00
Columbia (No number)	(DJ)	The First Decade (8 LP box)	1980	50.00	125.00

AESOPS FABLE

Cadet Concept LPS-323	(S)	In Due Time	1969	8.00	20.00

AFFECTION COLLECTION, THE

Evolution 2007	(S)	The Affection Collection	196?	6.00	15.00

AFFINITY

Paramount PAS-5027	(S)	Affinity	1970	10.00	25.00

AFTERGLOW

M. T. A. 5010	(M)	Afterglow	1967	12.00	30.00

AGAPE

Mark MRS-2170	(M)	Agape	196?	60.00	150.00
Renrut 101	(S)	Victims Of Tradition	197?	80.00	200.00

AGE OF REASON, THE

Georgetown	(M)	The Age Of Reason	196?	60.00	150.00

AGGREGATION

L. H. I. 12008	(S)	Mind Odyssey	1967	60.00	150.00

AIR SUPPLY

Mobile Fidelity MFSL-113	(S)	The One That You Love	198?	4.00	12.00
Nautilus NR-31	(S)	Lost In Love	198?	4.00	12.00

Label & Catalog #		Title	Year	VG+	NM

AKENS, JEWEL

Era EL-110	(M)	The Birds And The Bees	1965	12.00	30.00
Era ES-110	(S)	The Birds And The Bees	1965	16.00	40.00

ALABAMA

Alabama originally recorded as Wild Country, under which the L. S. I. albums below were released. After signing with RCA the masters for these albums and the remaining copies were destroyed.

L. S. I. LP-1??	(S)	Wild Country	1977	500.00	Rare
		(Near Mint copies have a suggested value of $800-1,200.)			
L. S. I. LP-177	(S)	Deuces Wild	1978	500.00	Rare
		(Near Mint copies have a suggested value of $800-1,200.)			
Plantation PLP-44	(S)	Wild Country	1981	10.00	25.00
Plantation PLP-44	(S)	Wild Country *(Gold vinyl)*	1981	20.00	50.00
		(This is not a reissue of the LSI album; it is a compilation of 45 sides and other odds & ends.)			

ALAIMO, STEVE

Checker LP-2981	(M)	Twist With Steve Alaimo	1961	24.00	60.00
Checker LP-2983	(M)	Mashed Potatoes	1962	24.00	60.00
Checker LP-2986	(M)	Every Day I Have To Cry	1963	24.00	60.00
ABC-Paramount 501	(M)	Starring Steve Alaimo	1965	12.00	30.00
ABC-Paramount S-501	(S)	Starring Steve Alaimo	1965	16.00	40.00
ABC-Paramount 531	(M)	Where The Action Is	1965	12.00	30.00
ABC-Paramount S-531	(S)	Where The Action Is	1965	16.00	40.00
ABC-Paramount 551	(M)	Steve Alaimo Sings And Swings	1966	12.00	30.00
ABC-Paramount S-551	(S)	Steve Alaimo Sings And Swings	1966	16.00	40.00

ALBATROSS

Anvil 8100	(S)	Albatross	197?	150.00	300.00

ALBERGHETTI, ANNA MARIA

Mercury MG-20056	(M)	Songs By Anna Maria Alberghetti	1956	12.00	30.00
Capitol T-887	(M)	I Can't Resist You	1957	12.00	30.00
MGM E-3946	(M)	Carnival *(With Kaye Ballard)*	1961	6.00	15.00
MGM SE-3946	(S)	Carnival *(With Kaye Ballard)*	1961	8.00	20.00
MGM E-4001	(M)	Love Makes The World Go 'Round	1962	6.00	15.00
MGM SE-4001	(S)	Love Makes The World Go 'Round	1962	8.00	20.00

ALBERT, THE

Perception 9	(S)	The Albert	1971	8.00	20.00

ALBERT, EDDIE

Kapp KP-1000	(M)	One God	1954	12.00	30.00
Kapp KP-1017	(M)	Eddie Albert And Margo	1956	12.00	30.00
Kapp KP-1083	(M)	September Song	1957	12.00	30.00
Dot DLP-3109	(M)	High Upon A Mountain	1960	6.00	15.00
Dot DLP-25109	(S)	High Upon A Mountain	1960	8.00	20.00
Columbia CL-2599	(M)	The Eddie Albert Album	1966	6.00	15.00
Columbia CS-9399	(S)	The Eddie Albert Album	1966	8.00	20.00

ALBERTS, AL

Alberts was formerly the lead singer of The Four Aces.

Coral CRL-57259	(M)	Man Has Got To Sing	1959	12.00	30.00
Coral CRL-757259	(S)	Man Has Got To Sing	1959	16.00	40.00

ALBRIGHT, LOLA: *Refer to* GOLDMINE'S PRICE GUIDE TO COLLECTIBLE JAZZ ALBUMS

ALDA, ROBERT

Tops L-1589	(M)	Romance Of Rome	195?	10.00	25.00
Treasure TLP-804	(M)	For Continental Lovers	195?	10.00	25.00

ALEONG, ALI, & THE NOBLES

Reprise R-6020	(M)	C'mon Baby, Let's Dance	1962	8.00	20.00
Reprise R9-6020	(S)	C'mon Baby, Let's Dance	1962	10.00	25.00
Reprise R-6011	(M)	Twistin' The Hits	1962	8.00	20.00
Reprise R9-6011	(S)	Twistin' The Hits	1962	10.00	25.00
Vee Jay LP-1060	(M)	Come Surf With Me	1963	2.00	30.00
Vee Jay SR-1060	(S)	Come Surf With Me	1963	16.00	40.00

Label & Catalog #		Title	Year	VG+	NM

ALEXANDER, ARTHUR

Dot DLP-3434	(M)	You Better Move On	1962	60.00	150.00
Dot DLP-25434	(E)	You Better Move On	1962	40.00	100.00
Warner Bros. B-2592	(S)	Arthur Alexander	1972	8.00	20.00

ALEXANDER, GORDON

Columbia CS-9693	(S)	Gordon's Buster	1968	5.00	12.00

ALEXANDER RABBIT

Mercury SR-61291	(S)	Alexander Rabbit	1970	5.00	12.00

ALEXANDER'S TIMELESS BLOOZBAND

Smack 1001	(M)	Alexander's Timeless Bloozband	1967	50.00	125.00
Uni 73021	(S)	For Sale	1968	10.00	20.00

ALEXANDRIA, LOREZ: *Refer to GOLDMINE'S PRICE GUIDE TO COLLECTIBLE JAZZ ALBUMS*

ALEXYS

Dot DLP-3713	(M)	Alexys	1966	10.00	25.00
Dot DLP-25713	(E)	Alexys	1966	8.00	20.00

ALIOTTA-HAYNES [ALIOTTA-HAYNES-JEREMIAH]

Ampex 10108	(S)	Aliotta-Haynes Music	1970	6.00	15.00
Ampex 10119	(S)	Aliotta-Haynes-Jeremiah	1970	6.00	15.00
Little Foot 711	(S)	Slippin' Away	1977	6.00	15.00
Big Foot 714	(S)	Lakeshore Drive	1978	10.00	20.00

ALIVE 'N KICKIN'

Roulette SR-42052	(S)	Alive 'N Kickin'	1969	6.00	15.00

ALKIRE, EDDIE

Full-Tone FM-646	(M)	Exciting New Colors	196?	12.00	30.00
Full-Tone FM-647	(M)	Exotic Steel Guitar	196?	12.00	30.00
Full-Tone FM-648	(M)	Steel Guitar Style	196?	12.00	30.00
Full-Tone FM-649	(M)	Jazz Steel Guitar	196?	12.00	30.00

ALL STARS, THE

Gramophone 20192	(M)	Boogie Woogie	196?	20.00	50.00

ALLAN, CHAD, & THE EXPRESSIONS
Chad Allan was an original member of The Guess Who. Refer to Brave Belt.

Scepter 533	(M)	Shakin' All Over	1966	16.00	40.00
Scepter SPS-533	(E)	Shakin' All Over	1966	12.00	30.00

ALLAN, DAVIE (& THE ARROWS)

Tower T-5002	(M)	Apache '65	1965	20.00	50.00
Tower DT-5002	(E)	Apache '65	1965	16.00	40.00
Tower T-5043	(M)	The Wild Angels (Soundtrack)	1966	10.00	25.00
Tower DT-5043	(E)	The Wild Angels (Soundtrack)	1966	8.00	20.00
Tower T-5056	(M)	The Wild Angels, Volume 2 (Soundtrack)	1967	10.00	25.00
Tower DT-5056	(E)	The Wild Angels, Volume 2 (Soundtrack)	1967	8.00	20.00
Tower T-5074	(M)	Devil's Angels (Soundtrack)	1967	10.00	25.00
Tower DT-5074	(E)	Devil's Angels (Soundtrack)	1967	8.00	20.00
Tower T-5078	(M)	Blues Theme	1967	20.00	50.00
Tower DT-5078	(E)	Blues Theme	1967	16.00	40.00
Tower T-5083	(M)	Mondo Hollywood (Soundtrack)	1968	12.00	30.00
Tower DT-5083	(E)	Mondo Hollywood (Soundtrack)	1968	8.00	20.00
Tower DT-5094	(E)	Cycledelic Sounds	1968	20.00	50.00
Tower SKAO-5099	(S)	Wild In The Streets (Soundtrack)	1968	12.00	30.00
Tower ST-5124	(E)	The Hellcats (Soundtrack)	1968	10.00	25.00
Tower ST-5141	(S)	Killers Three (Soundtrack)	1968	10.00	25.00
Sidewalk T-5902	(M)	Thunder Alley (Soundtrack)	1967	8.00	20.00
Sidewalk ST-5902	(S)	Thunder Alley (Soundtrack)	1967	10.00	25.00
Sidewalk T-5903	(M)	Teenage Rebellion (Soundtrack)	1967	10.00	25.00
Sidewalk DT-5903	(E)	Teenage Rebellion (Soundtrack)	1967	8.00	20.00
Sidewalk T-5910	(M)	Glory Stompers (Soundtrack)	1967	12.00	30.00
Sidewalk DT-5910	(E)	Glory Stompers (Soundtrack)	1967	8.00	20.00
Sidewalk DT-5911	(P)	Mary Jane (Soundtrack)	1968	8.00	20.00
Sidewalk ST-5914	(S)	Wild Racers (Soundtrack)	1968	12.00	30.00

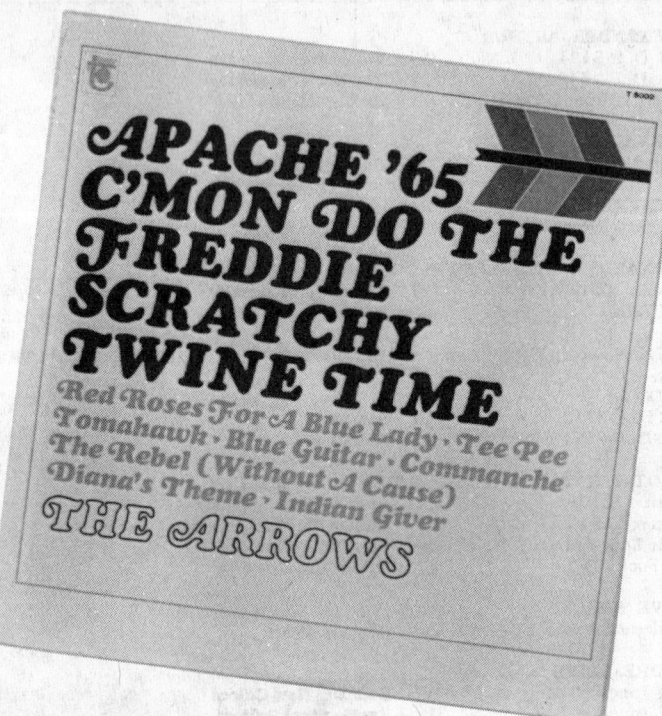

Originally scoring for Tower with the proto-psych "Apache '65," as The Arrows, Davie Allan and band quickly developed into the most sought-after musicians in Hollywood when it came to filling soundtracks for grade-B youth exploitation films, especially if there was a biker theme . . .

Label & Catalog #		Title	Year	VG+	NM

ALLEN, DAVE

International Art. 11	(S)	Color Blind	1969	20.00	50.00
International Art. 11	(S)	Color Blind	1979	6.00	15.00
		(Reissues have "Masterfonics" in the trail-off vinyl.)			

ALLEN, LEE

Ember ELP-200	(M)	Walkin' With Mr. Lee *(Red label)*	1958	150.00	400.00
Ember ELP-200	(M)	Walkin' With Mr. Lee *(Black label)*	196?	60.00	150.00

ALLEN, RAY, & THE UPBEATS

Blast BLP-6804	(M)	A Tribute To Six	196?	50.00	150.00

ALLEN, REX

Decca DL-8402	(M)	Under Western Skies	1956	20.00	50.00
Decca DL-8776	(M)	Mister Cowboy	1959	14.00	35.00
Decca DL-78776	(S)	Mister Cowboy	1959	20.00	50.00
Hacienda LP-101	(M)	Rex Allen Sings	1960	60.00	150.00
Buena Vista BV-3307	(M)	Rex Allen Sings 16 Favorites	1961	20.00	50.00
Mercury MG-20719	(M)	Faith Of A Man	1962	10.00	25.00
Mercury SR-60719	(S)	Faith Of A Man	1962	14.00	35.00
Mercury MG-20752	(M)	Rex Allen Sings And Tells Tales	1962	10.00	25.00
Mercury SR-60752	(S)	Rex Allen Sings And Tells Tales	1962	14.00	35.00

ALLEN, RICHIE (& THE PACIFIC SURFERS)

Imperial LP-9212	(M)	Stranger From Durango	1963	12.00	30.00
Imperial LP-12212	(S)	Stranger From Durango	1963	16.00	40.00
Imperial LP-9229	(M)	The Rising Surf	1963	20.00	50.00
Imperial LP-12229	(S)	The Rising Surf	1963	30.00	75.00
Imperial LP-9243	(M)	Surfer's Slide	1963	20.00	50.00
Imperial LP-12243	(S)	Surfer's Slide	1963	30.00	75.00

ALLEN, ROSALIE

Waldorf Music 33-150 (10")	(M)	Rosalie Allen Sings Country & Western	1955	30.00	75.00
Grand Award 330	(M)	Songs Of The Golden West	1957	14.00	35.00

ALLEN, TONY, & THE NIGHT OWLS

Crown CLP-5231	(M)	Rock & Roll With Tony Allen	1960	40.00	100.00
Crown CST-249	(S)	Rock & Roll With Tony Allen	1960	60.00	150.00

ALLEN, WOODY

Colpix CP-488	(M)	Woody Allen	1964	10.00	25.00
Colpix SCP-488	(S)	Woody Allen	1964	16.00	40.00
Colpix CP-518	(M)	Woody Allen 2	1965	10.00	25.00
Colpix SCP-518	(S)	Woody Allen 2	1965	16.00	40.00
Capitol T-2986	(M)	The Third Woody Allen Album	1968	10.00	25.00
Bell 6008	(S)	Wonderful Wacky World Of Woody Allen	1968	8.00	20.00
United Arts. UAS-9968	(S)	The Night Club Years 1964-1968	1972	6.00	15.00
Paramount PAS-1004	(S)	Play It Again, Sam *(Soundtrack)*	1972	8.00	20.00

ALLISON, GENE

Vee Jay LP-1009	(M)	Gene Allison *(Maroon label)*	1959	60.00	150.00
Vee Jay LP-1009	(M)	Gene Allison *(Black label)*	196?	20.00	50.00

ALLISON, KEITH
Produced by Gary Usher. Refer to The Falconaires; Paul Revere & The Raiders.

Columbia CL-2641	(M)	Keith Allison In Action	1967	10.00	25.00
Columbia CS-9441	(S)	Keith Allison In Action	1967	12.00	30.00

ALLISON, MOSE: *Refer to* GOLDMINE'S PRICE GUIDE TO COLLECTIBLE JAZZ ALBUMS

ALLMAN, DUANE & GREGG

Bold 33-301	(S)	Duane And Gregg Allman	1972	8.00	20.00
Bold 33-302	(S)	Duane And Gregg Allman	1973	4.00	10.00

ALLMAN, SHELDON

HiFi R-415	(M)	Folk Songs For The 21st Century	1960	12.00	30.00
Del Fi DFLP-1213	(M)	Sing Along With Drac	1961	12.00	30.00
Del Fi DFST-1213	(S)	Sing Along With Drac	1961	16.00	40.00

Lee Allen's saxophone can be heard on his sole pop hit, 1958's "Walkin' With Mr. Lee," and as a session player on hits by many rhythm 'n blues artists of the '50s, including Fats Domino and Little Richard. Tony Allen's rhythm 'n blues career saw him record with at least nine different labels with vocal backing from such notable groups as The Chimes and The Twilighters. This, his sole LP, is one of the most collectible titles from Crown Records.

Label & Catalog #		Title	Year	VG+	NM

ALLMAN BROTHERS BAND, THE
The Allman Brothers feature Duane and Gregg.

Atco SD-33-308	(S)	The Allman Brothers Band	1969	6.00	15.00
Atco SD-33-342	(S)	Idlewild South	1970	6.00	15.00
Atco SD-33-805	(S)	Beginnings	1973	6.00	15.00
Capricorn SD2-802	(S)	At Fillmore East *(2 LPs)*	1971	8.00	20.00
Capricorn SD-805	(S)	At Fillmore East *(2 LPs)*	1972	3.00	15.00
Capricorn 2CP-0102	(S)	Eat A Peach *(2 LPs)*	1972	3.00	15.00
Capricorn CX4-0102	(Q)	Eat A Peach *(2 LPs)*	1974	10.00	25.00
Capricorn PRO-545	(DJ)	Duane Allman Dialogs	1972	40.00	100.00
Capricorn 2CP-0108	(S)	Duane Allman Anthology *(2 LPs)*	1972	3.00	15.00
Capricorn CX4-0131	(Q)	At Fillmore East *(2 LPs)*	1974	10.00	25.00
Capricorn 2CP-0139	(S)	Duane Allman Anthology, Volume II *(2 LPs)*	1974	3.00	15.00
Springboard SPB-4046	(S)	Duane & Gregg	1973	6.00	15.00
Nautilus NR-30	(S)	At Fillmore East *(2 LPs)*	1980	30.00	90.00
Mobile Fidelity MFSL-157	(S)	Eat A Peach *(2 LPs)*	1984	50.00	150.00

ALLSUP, TOMMY
Allsup was a member of The Crickets.

| Reprise R-6182 | (M) | The Buddy Holly Songbook | 1965 | 20.00 | 50.00 |
| Reprise RS-6182 | (S) | The Buddy Holly Songbook | 1965 | 30.00 | 75.00 |

ALPAKA, ALFRED

| Decca DL-5423 (10") | (M) | My Isle Of Golden Dreams | 195? | 14.00 | 35.00 |

ALPERT, HERB (& THE TIJUANA BRASS)

A&M LP-101	(M)	The Lonely Bull	1962	6.00	15.00
A&M SP-101	(S)	The Lonely Bull	1962	8.00	20.00
		— Original A&M albums above have off-white labels.—			
Mobile Fidelity MFSL-053	(S)	Rise	1981	6.00	18.00

ALPHA CENTAURI

| Salt SAD-003 | (S) | Alpha Centauri | 1977 | 30.00 | 75.00 |

AMBOY DUKES, THE
The Amboy Dukes feature Ted Nugent.

Mainstream 56104	(M)	The Amboy Dukes	1968	16.00	40.00
Mainstream 6104	(S)	The Amboy Dukes	1968	12.00	30.00
Mainstream 6112	(S)	Journey To The Center Of The Mind	1968	12.00	30.00
Mainstream 6118	(S)	Migration	1968	12.00	30.00
Mainstream 6125	(S)	The Best Of The Original Amboy Dukes	1969	8.00	20.00
Mainstream 421	(S)	Ted Nugent & The Amboy Dukes	197?	8.00	20.00
Mainstream S-801	(S)	Journeys And Migrations *(2 LPs)*	1974	6.00	15.00
Polydor 24-4012	(S)	Marriage On The Rocks	1970	8.00	20.00
Polydor 24-4035	(S)	Survival Of The Fittest	1970	8.00	20.00
DiscReet 2181	(S)	Call Of The Wild	1974	6.00	15.00
DiscReet 2203	(S)	Tooth, Fang And Claw	1974	6.00	15.00

AMBROSE, AMANDA

| Dunwich 668 | (M) | Amanda | 1966 | 6.00 | 15.00 |
| Dunwich S-668 | (S) | Amanda | 1966 | 8.00 | 20.00 |

AMBROSE SLADE : Refer to SLADE

AMBROSIA

| Nautilus NR-23 | (S) | Life Beyond L.A. | 198? | 5.00 | 15.00 |

AMERICA

| Warner Bros. BS4-2808 | (Q) | Holiday | 1974 | 6.00 | 15.00 |
| Warner Bros. BS4-2852 | (Q) | Hearts | 1975 | 6.00 | 15.00 |

AMERICAN BLUES, THE

| Karma KLP-1001 | (M) | The American Blues Is Here | 1967 | 70.00 | 175.00 |
| Uni 73044 | (S) | The American Blues Do Their Thing | 1969 | 20.00 | 50.00 |

AMERICAN BLUES EXCHANGE, THE

| Tayl TLS-1 | (M) | Blueprint | 1969 | 50.00 | 125.00 |

Label & Catalog #		Title	Year	VG+	NM
AMERICAN BREED, THE					
Acta 8002	(M)	The American Breed	1967	6.00	15.00
Acta 38002	(S)	The American Breed	1967	8.00	20.00
Acta 8003	(M)	Bend Me, Shape Me	1968	6.00	15.00
Acta 38003	(S)	Bend Me, Shape Me	1968	8.00	20.00
Dot DLP-25846	(S)	No Way To Treat A Lady (Soundtrack)	1968	8.00	20.00
Acta 8006	(M)	Pumpkin, Powder, Scarlet & Green	1968	5.00	12.00
Acta 38006	(S)	Pumpkin, Powder, Scarlet & Green	1968	6.00	15.00
Acta 8008	(M)	Lonely Side Of The City	1968	5.00	12.00
Acta 38008	(S)	Lonely Side Of The City	1968	6.00	15.00
AMERICAN DREAM, THE					
Ampex 10101	(S)	The American Dream	1970	10.00	25.00
AMERICAN EAGLE					
Decca DL-75258	(S)	American Eagle	1971	8.00	20.00
AMERICAN REVOULTION					
Flick Disc FLS-54002	(S)	American Revolution	1968	10.00	25.00
AMES, NANCY					
Liberty LRP-3299	(M)	A Portrait Of Nancy	1963	6.00	15.00
Liberty LST-7299	(S)	A Portrait Of Nancy	1963	8.00	20.00
AMES BROTHERS, THE					
Coral CRL-56014 (10")	(M)	Sing A Song Of Christmas	1950	20.00	50.00
Coral CRL-56017 (10")	(M)	In The Evening By The Moonlight	1951	20.00	50.00
Coral CRL-56024 (10")	(M)	Sentimental Me	1951	20.00	50.00
Coral CRL-56025 (10")	(M)	Hoop-De-Hoo	1951	20.00	50.00
Coral CRL-56042 (10")	(M)	Sweet Leilani	1951	20.00	50.00
Coral CRL-56050 (10")	(M)	Favorite Spirituals	1952	20.00	50.00
Coral CRL-56079 (10")	(M)	Home On The Range	1952	20.00	50.00
Coral CRL-56080 (10")	(M)	Merry Christmas 1952	1952	20.00	50.00
Coral CRL-56097 (10")	(M)	Favorite Songs	1954	20.00	50.00
RCA Victor LPM-3186 (10")	(M)	It Must Be True	1954	20.00	50.00
Coral CRL-57031	(M)	Ames Brothers Concert	1956	12.00	30.00
Coral CRL-57054	(M)	Love's Old Sweet Song	1956	12.00	30.00
Coral CRL-57166	(M)	Sounds Of Christmas Harmony	1957	12.00	30.00
Coral CRL-57176	(M)	Love Serenade	1957	12.00	30.00
Coral CRL-57338	(M)	Our Golden Favorites	1960	10.00	25.00
Coral CRL-757338	(S)	Our Golden Favorites	1960	12.00	30.00
RCA Victor LPM-1142	(M)	Exactly Like You	1956	12.00	30.00
RCA Victor LPM-1157	(M)	Four Brothers	1956	12.00	30.00
RCA Victor LPM-1228	(M)	The Ames Brothers With Hugo Winterhalter	1956	12.00	30.00
RCA Victor LPM-1487	(M)	Sweet Seventeen	1957	12.00	30.00
RCA Victor LPM-1541	(M)	There'll Always Be A Christmas	1957	12.00	30.00
RCA Victor LPM-1680	(M)	Destination Moon	1958	12.00	30.00
RCA Victor LPM-1855	(M)	Smoochin' Time	1958	12.00	30.00
RCA Victor LPM-1859	(M)	The Best Of The Ames Brothers	1958	8.00	20.00
RCA Victor LPM-1954	(M)	Famous Hits Of Famous Quartets	1959	8.00	20.00
RCA Victor LSP-1954	(S)	Famous Hits Of Famous Quartets	1959	10.00	25.00
RCA Victor LPM-1998	(M)	The Best In The Country	1959	8.00	20.00
RCA Victor LSP-1998	(S)	The Best In The Country	1959	10.00	25.00
RCA Victor LPM-2009	(M)	Words And Music	1959	8.00	20.00
RCA Victor LSP-2009	(S)	Words And Music	1959	10.00	25.00
RCA Victor LPM-2100	(M)	Hello, Amigos	1960	6.00	15.00
RCA Victor LSP-2100	(S)	Hello, Amigos	1960	8.00	20.00
RCA Victor LPM-2182	(M)	The Blend And The Beat	1960	6.00	15.00
RCA Victor LSP-2182	(S)	The Blend And The Beat	1960	6.00	20.00
RCA Victor LPM-2273	(M)	The Best Of The Bands	1960	6.00	15.00
RCA Victor LSP-2273	(S)	The Best Of The Bands	1960	6.00	20.00
— Original RCA mono albums above have "Long Play" on the bottom of the label;					
stereo albums have "Living Stereo" on the bottom.—					
Epic LN-24036	(M)	Hello Italy	1963	5.00	12.00
Epic BN-26036	(S)	Hello Italy	1963	6.00	15.00
Epic LN-24069	(M)	Knees Up, Mother Brown	1963	5.00	12.00
Epic BN-26069	(S)	Knees Up, Mother Brown	1963	6.00	15.00
RCA Victor LPM-2876	(M)	For Sentimental Reasons	1964	5.00	12.00
RCA Victor LSP-2876	(S)	For Sentimental Reasons	1964	6.00	15.00

Label & Catalog #		Title	Year	VG+	NM
RCA Victor LPM-2981	(M)	**Down Memory Lane**	1964	5.00	12.00
RCA Victor LSP-2981	(S)	**Down Memory Lane**	1964	6.00	15.00
		— Original RCA albums above have black labels.—			
AMON DUUL [AMON DUUL II]					
Prophesy PRS-1003	(S)	**Amon Duul**	1970	10.00	25.00
United Arts. UAS-9954	(S)	**Dance Of The Lemmings** *(2 LPs)*	1971	6.00	15.00
United Arts. UAS-5586	(S)	**Carnival In Babylon**	1972	4.00	10.00
United Arts. LA017	(S)	**Wolf City**	1973	4.00	10.00
United Arts. LA198	(S)	**Vive La Trance**	1973	4.00	10.00
AMULET					
Shadow AC-00084	(S)	**Amulet**	1980	40.00	100.00
ANCIENT GREASE					
Mercury SR-61305	(S)	**Women And Children First**	1970	10.00	25.00
ANDERS & PONCIA					
Anders & Poncia also recorded as The Innocence; The Tradewinds.					
Warner Bros. WS-1778	(S)	**The Anders & Poncia Album**	1969	10.00	25.00
ANDERSON, AL					
Anderson originally recorded with Wildweeds and later with NRBQ.					
Vanguard VSD-79324	(S)	**Al Anderson**	1972	8.00	20.00
Vanguard VSQ-79324	(Q)	**Al Anderson**	1973	10.00	25.00
ANDERSON, BILL					
Decca DL-4192	(M)	**Bill Anderson Sings Country Songs**	1962	8.00	20.00
Decca DL-74192	(S)	**Bill Anderson Sings Country Songs**	1962	10.00	25.00
Decca DL-4427	(M)	**Still**	1963	8.00	20.00
Decca DL-74427	(S)	**Still**	1963	10.00	25.00
Decca DL-4499	(M)	**Bill Anderson Sings**	1964	8.00	20.00
Decca DL-74499	(S)	**Bill Anderson Sings**	1964	10.00	25.00
Decca DL-4600	(M)	**Bill Anderson Showcase**	1964	8.00	20.00
Decca DL-74600	(S)	**Bill Anderson Showcase**	1964	10.00	25.00
Decca DL-4646	(M)	**From This Pen**	1965	8.00	20.00
Decca DL-74646	(S)	**From This Pen**	1965	10.00	25.00
Decca DL-4686	(M)	**Bright Lights And Country Music**	1965	8.00	20.00
Decca DL-74686	(S)	**Bright Lights And Country Music**	1965	10.00	25.00
Decca DL-4771	(M)	**I Love You Drops**	1966	6.00	15.00
Decca DL-74771	(S)	**I Love You Drops**	1966	8.00	20.00
Decca DL-4855	(M)	**Get While The Gettin's Good**	1967	8.00	20.00
Decca DL-74855	(S)	**Get While The Gettin's Good**	1967	8.00	20.00
Decca DL-4859	(M)	**Bill Anderson's Greatest Hits**	1967	8.00	20.00
Decca DL-74859	(S)	**Bill Anderson's Greatest Hits**	1967	8.00	20.00
Decca DL-4886	(M)	**I Can Do Nothing Alone**	1967	8.00	20.00
Decca DL-74886	(S)	**I Can Do Nothing Alone**	1967	8.00	20.00
Decca DL-4998	(M)	**Wild Weekend**	1968	10.00	25.00
Decca DL-74998	(S)	**Wild Weekend**	1968	6.00	15.00
ANDERSON, BILL, & JAN HOWARD					
Decca DL-4959	(M)	**For Loving You**	1968	10.00	25.00
Decca DL-74959	(S)	**For Loving You**	1968	6.00	15.00
ANDERSON, CASEY					
Elektra EKL-192	(M)	**Goin' Places**	1960	8.00	20.00
Elektra EKS-7192	(S)	**Goin' Places**	1960	10.00	25.00
Atco 33-149	(M)	**The Bag I'm In**	1962	8.00	20.00
Atco SD-33-149	(S)	**The Bag I'm In**	1962	10.00	25.00
Atco 33-166	(M)	**More Pretty Girls Than One**	1964	8.00	20.00
Atco SD-33-166	(S)	**More Pretty Girls Than One**	1964	10.00	25.00
Atco 33-172	(M)	**Live At The Ice House**	1965	6.00	15.00
Atco SD-33-172	(S)	**Live At The Ice House**	1965	8.00	20.00
Atco 33-176	(M)	**Blues Is A Woman Gone**	1965	6.00	15.00
Atco SD-33-176	(S)	**Blues Is A Woman Gone**	1965	8.00	20.00

ANDERSON, ERNESTINE : *Refer to* GOLDMINE'S PRICE GUIDE TO COLLECTIBLE JAZZ ALBUMS

Label & Catalog #		Title	Year	VG+	NM

ANDERSON, PINK

Label & Catalog #		Title	Year	VG+	NM
Bluesville BVLP-1038	(M)	Carolina Blues Man	1961	16.00	40.00
Bluesville BVLP-1051	(M)	Medicine Show Man	1962	16.00	40.00
Bluesville BVLP-1071	(M)	Ballad And Folksinger	1963	16.00	40.00

ANDREWS, JULIE

Label & Catalog #		Title	Year	VG+	NM
RCA Victor LOC-1018	(M)	The Boy Friend (Original Cast)	1954	20.00	50.00
Columbia OL-5090	(M)	My Fair Lady (Original Cast)	1956	12.00	30.00
Columbia OL-5190	(M)	Cinderella (Soundtrack)	1957	12.00	30.00
RCA Victor LPM-1403	(M)	The Lass With The Delicate Air	1957	12.00	30.00
RCA Victor LPM-1681	(M)	Julie Andrews Sings	1958	12.00	30.00
RCA Victor LSP-1681	(S)	Julie Andrews Sings	1958	16.00	40.00
RCA Victor LOP-1001	(M)	Rose Marie (Soundtrack)	1958	8.00	20.00
RCA Victor LSO-1001	(S)	Rose Marie (Soundtrack)	1958	12.00	30.00

— Original RCA mono albums above have black labels with "Long Play" on the bottom;
stereo albums have "Living Stereo" on the bottom. —

Label & Catalog #		Title	Year	VG+	NM
Columbia OL-5615	(M)	My Fair Lady (Original Cast)	1959	8.00	20.00
Columbia OS-2015	(S)	My Fair Lady (Original Cast)	1959	10.00	25.00
Columbia OL-5620	(M)	Camelot (Original Cast)	1960	6.00	15.00
Columbia OS-2031	(S)	Camelot (Original Cast)	1960	8.00	20.00
Columbia OL-5840	(M)	Julie And Carol At Carnegie Hall	1962	6.00	15.00
Columbia OS-2240	(S)	Julie And Carol At Carnegie Hall	1962	8.00	20.00
Columbia CL-1712	(M)	Broadway's Fair Julie	1962	6.00	15.00
Columbia CS-8512	(S)	Broadway's Fair Julie	1962	8.00	20.00
Columbia CL-1886	(M)	Don't Go In The Lion's Cage Tonight	1962	6.00	15.00
Columbia CS-8686	(S)	Don't Go In The Lion's Cage Tonight	1962	8.00	20.00

— Original Columbia albums above have three white "eye" logos on each side of the spindle hole. —

Label & Catalog #		Title	Year	VG+	NM
Buena Vista BV-4026	(M)	Mary Poppins (Soundtrack)	1964	5.00	12.00
Buena Vista STER-4026	(S)	Mary Poppins (Soundtrack)	1964	6.00	15.00
RCA Victor LOCD-2005	(M)	The Sound Of Music (Soundtrack)	1965	4.00	10.00
RCA Victor LSOD-2005	(S)	The Sound Of Music (Soundtrack)	1965	5.00	12.00
Decca DL-1500	(M)	Thoroughly Modern Millie (Soundtrack)	1967	5.00	12.00
Decca DL-71500	(S)	Thoroughly Modern Millie (Soundtrack)	1967	6.00	15.00
RCA Victor LPM-3829	(M)	Christmas Treasure	1967	4.00	10.00
RCA Victor LSP-3829	(S)	Christmas Treasure	1967	5.00	12.00

— Original RCA albums above have black labels. —

ANDREWS, LEE, & THE HEARTS

Label & Catalog #		Title	Year	VG+	NM
Lost-Nite LP-101	(M)	Lee Andrews & The Hearts' Biggest Hits	1964	20.00	50.00
Lost-Nite LP-113	(M)	Dean Tyler Presents Lee Andrews			
		& The Hearts Live	1965	20.00	50.00

ANDREWS SISTERS, THE

The Sisters recorded with Bing Crosby.

Label & Catalog #		Title	Year	VG+	NM
Decca DL-5019 (10")	(M)	Merry Christmas	1950	16.00	40.00
Decca DL-5020 (10")	(M)	Christmas Greetings	1950	16.00	40.00
Decca DL-5065 (10")	(M)	Tropical Songs	1950	16.00	40.00
Decca DL-5120 (10")	(M)	The Andrews Sisters	1950	16.00	40.00
Decca DL-5155 (10")	(M)	Club 15	1950	16.00	40.00
Decca DL-5264 (10")	(M)	Berlin Songs	1950	16.00	40.00
Decca DL-5282 (10")	(M)	Christmas Cheer	1950	16.00	40.00
Decca DL-5284 (10")	(M)	Mr. Music (Soundtrack)	1951	40.00	100.00
Decca DL-5306 (10")	(M)	I Love To Tell The Story	1951	16.00	40.00
Decca DL-5331 (10")	(M)	Country Style	1952	16.00	40.00
Decca DL-5423 (10")	(M)	My Isle Of Golden Dreams	1952	16.00	40.00
Decca DL-5438 (10")	(M)	Sing, Sing, Sing	1953	16.00	40.00
Decca DL-8354	(M)	Jingle Bells	1956	12.00	30.00
Decca DL-8360	(M)	By Popular Demand	1957	12.00	30.00
Capitol T-790	(M)	The Andrews Sisters In Hi-Fi	1957	12.00	30.00
Capitol T-860	(M)	Fresh And Fancy Free	1957	12.00	30.00
Capitol T-973	(M)	Dancing Twenties	1958	12.00	30.00
Dot DLP-3406	(M)	The Andrews Sisters' Greatest Hits	1961	6.00	15.00
Dot DLP-25406	(S)	The Andrews Sisters' Greatest Hits	1961	10.00	25.00
Dot DLP-3452	(M)	Great Golden Hits	1962	6.00	15.00
Dot DLP-25452	(S)	Great Golden Hits	1962	10.00	25.00
Dot DLP-3529	(M)	The Andrews Sisters Present	1963	6.00	15.00
Dot DLP-25529	(S)	The Andrews Sisters Present	1963	8.00	20.00
Dot DLP-3543	(M)	The Andrews Sisters' Greatest Hits	1963	6.00	15.00
Dot DLP-25543	(S)	The Andrews Sisters' Greatest Hits	1963	8.00	20.00

Label & Catalog #		Title	Year	VG+	NM
Capitol T-1924	(M)	The Hits Of The Andrews Sisters	1964	6.00	15.00
Capitol ST-1924	(S)	The Hits Of The Andrews Sisters	1964	8.00	20.00
Dot DLP-3567	(M)	Great Country Hits	1964	6.00	15.00
Dot DLP-25567	(S)	Great Country Hits	1964	8.00	20.00
Dot DLP-3632	(M)	The Andrews Sisters Go Hawaiian	1965	6.00	15.00
Dot DLP-25632	(S)	The Andrews Sisters Go Hawaiian	1965	8.00	20.00

ANGELS, THE

Label & Catalog #		Title	Year	VG+	NM
Caprice LP-1001	(M)	And The Angels Sing	1962	24.00	60.00
Caprice SLP-1001	(S)	And The Angels Sing	1962	30.00	75.00
Smash MGS-27039	(M)	My Boyfriend's Back	1963	14.00	35.00
Smash SRS-67039	(S)	My Boyfriend's Back	1963	20.00	50.00
		("Til" is rechanneled on this album.)			
Smash MGS-27048	(M)	A Halo To You	1964	12.00	30.00
Smash SRS-67048	(S)	A Halo To You	1964	16.00	40.00
Ascot AM-13009	(M)	Twelve Of Their Greatest Hits	1964	10.00	25.00
Ascot ALS-6009	(S)	Twelve Of Their Greatest Hits	1964	12.00	30.00
		(The Ascot album is a repackage of Caprice 1001.)			

ANIMALS, THE [ERIC BURDON & THE ANIMALS]

The original Animals were Eric Burdon, Chas Chandler, Alan Price, John Steel and Hilton Valentine. By early 1966 Price and Steel left, replaced by Dave Rowberry and Barry Jenkins. By the end of 1966 the group split with Burdon and Jenkins forming Eric Burdon & The Animals (MGM 4433 on).

Label & Catalog #		Title	Year	VG+	NM
MGM E-4264	(DJ)	The Animals (Yellow label)	1964	60.00	150.00
MGM E-4264	(M)	The Animals	1964	16.00	40.00
MGM SE-4264	(E)	The Animals	1964	12.00	30.00
MGM T-90687	(M)	The Animals (Capitol Record Club)	1965	40.00	100.00
		(With photos of the five Animals on the back cover.)			
MGM E-4281	(DJ)	The Animals On Tour (Yellow label)	1965	60.00	150.00
MGM E-4281	(M)	The Animals On Tour	1965	16.00	40.00
MGM SE-4281	(E)	The Animals On Tour	1965	12.00	30.00
MGM E-4305	(DJ)	Animal Tracks (Yellow label)	1965	60.00	150.00
MGM E-4305	(M)	Animal Tracks	1965	20.00	50.00
MGM SE-4305	(E)	Animal Tracks	1965	16.00	40.00
MGM E-4324	(DJ)	The Best Of The Animals (Yellow label)	1966	40.00	100.00
MGM E-4324	(M)	The Best Of The Animals	1966	8.00	20.00
MGM SE-4324	(P)	The Best Of The Animals	1966	10.00	25.00
ABC-Paramount 536	(M)	The Dangerous Christmas Of Red Riding Hood (Soundtrack)	1965	12.00	30.00
ABC-Paramount S-536	(M)	The Dangerous Christmas Of Red Riding Hood (Soundtrack)	1965	16.00	40.00
MGM E-4384	(DJ)	Animalization (Yellow label)	1966	60.00	150.00
MGM E-4384	(M)	Animalization	1966	10.00	25.00
MGM SE-4384	(S)	Animalization	1966	12.00	30.00
		("Inside Looking Out" is rechanneled on this album.)			
MGM E-4414	(DJ)	Animalism (Yellow label)	1966	60.00	150.00
MGM E-4414	(M)	Animalism	1966	10.00	25.00
MGM SE-4414	(S)	Animalism	1966	12.00	30.00
		("All Night Long" and "The Other Side Of This Life" were arranged by Frank Zappa.)			
MGM E-4433	(M)	Eric Is Here	1967	6.00	15.00
MGM SE-4433	(S)	Eric Is Here	1967	8.00	20.00
MGM E-4454	(M)	Best Of Eric Burdon & The Animals, Vol. 2	1967	8.00	20.00
MGM SE-4454	(P)	Best Of Eric Burdon & The Animals, Vol. 2	1967	8.00	20.00
MGM E-4484	(M)	Winds Of Change	1967	8.00	20.00
MGM SE-4484	(S)	Winds Of Change	1967	10.00	25.00
MGM E-4537	(M)	The Twain Shall Meet	1968	12.00	30.00
MGM SE-4537	(S)	The Twain Shall Meet	1968	10.00	25.00
MGM E-4553	(M)	Every One Of Us	1968	12.00	30.00
MGM SE-4553	(S)	Every One Of Us	1968	10.00	25.00
MGM SE-4591	(S)	Love Is (2 LPs)	1969	20.00	50.00
MGM SE-4602	(S)	Greatest Hits Of Eric Burdon & The Animals	1969	6.00	15.00
Wand WDS-690	(S)	In The Beginning	1970	5.00	12.00
Pickwick SPC-3330	(E)	The Early Animals With Eric Burdon	1971	4.00	10.00
Springboard SPB-4025	(E)	The Best Of The Animals	1972	5.00	12.00
Springboard SPB-4065	(E)	The Night Time Is The Right Time	1973	5.00	12.00
Abkco AB-4226	(S)	The Best Of The Animals (2 LPs)	1973	6.00	15.00
Scepter/Citation 18026	(S)	The Best Of The Animals	1976	4.00	10.00
United Arts. LA790-H	(S)	Before We Were So Rudely Interrupted	1977	4.00	10.00

Label & Catalog #		Title	Year	VG+	NM
ANIMATED EGG					
Alshire SF-5104	(S)	**Animated Egg**	1967	6.00	15.00
ANKA, PAUL					
Riviera 0047	(M)	**Paul Anka & Others**	1959	50.00	100.00
		(This is actually a various artists album containing			
		Anka's early, pre-ABC Paramount sides.)			
ABC-Paramount 240	(M)	**Paul Anka**	1958	20.00	50.00
ABC-Paramount 296	(M)	**My Heart Sings**	1959	14.00	35.00
ABC-Paramount S-296	(S)	**My Heart Sings**	1959	20.00	50.00
ABC-Paramount 323	(M)	**Paul Anka Sings His Big 15**	1960	20.00	50.00
ABC-Paramount S-323	(E)	**Paul Anka Sings His Big 15**	1960	16.00	40.00
ABC-Paramount 347	(M)	**Paul Anka Swings For Young Lovers**	1960	12.00	30.00
ABC-Paramount S-347	(S)	**Paul Anka Swings For Young Lovers**	1960	16.00	40.00
ABC-Paramount 353	(M)	**Anka At The Copa**	1960	12.00	30.00
ABC-Paramount S-353	(S)	**Anka At The Copa**	1960	16.00	40.00
ABC-Paramount 360	(M)	**It's Christmas Everywhere**	1960	12.00	30.00
ABC-Paramount S-360	(S)	**It's Christmas Everywhere**	1960	16.00	40.00
ABC-Paramount 371	(M)	**Strictly Instrumental**	1961	12.00	30.00
ABC-Paramount S-371	(S)	**Strictly Instrumental**	1961	16.00	40.00
ABC-Paramount 390	(M)	**Paul Anka Sings His Big 15, Volume 2**	1961	12.00	30.00
ABC-Paramount S-390	(S)	**Paul Anka Sings His Big 15, Volume 2**	1961	16.00	40.00
ABC-Paramount 409	(M)	**Paul Anka Sings His Big 15, Volume 3**	1962	12.00	30.00
ABC-Paramount S-409	(S)	**Paul Anka Sings His Big 15, Volume 3**	1962	16.00	40.00
ABC-Paramount 420	(M)	**Diana**	1962	12.00	30.00
ABC-Paramount S-420	(S)	**Diana**	1962	16.00	40.00
RCA Victor LPM-2502	(M)	**Young, Alive And In Love!**	1962	8.00	20.00
RCA Victor LSP-2502	(S)	**Young, Alive And In Love!**	1962	12.00	30.00
RCA Victor LPM-2575	(M)	**Let's Sit This One Out!**	1962	8.00	20.00
RCA Victor LSP-2575	(S)	**Let's Sit This One Out!**	1962	12.00	30.00
RCA Victor LPM-2614	(M)	**Our Man Around The World**	1963	8.00	20.00
RCA Victor LSP-2614	(S)	**Our Man Around The World**	1963	12.00	30.00
RCA Victor LPM-2691	(M)	**Paul Anka's 21 Golden Hits**	1963	8.00	20.00
RCA Victor LSP-2691	(S)	**Paul Anka's 21 Golden Hits**	1963	12.00	30.00
		— Original RCA mono albums above have "Long Play" on the bottom of the label;			
		stereo albums have "Living Stereo" on the bottom.—			
RCA Victor LPM-2744	(M)	**Songs I Wish I'd Written**	1963	6.00	15.00
RCA Victor LSP-2744	(S)	**Songs I Wish I'd Written**	1963	8.00	20.00
RCA Victor LPM-2996	(M)	**Excitement On Park Avenue**	1964	6.00	15.00
RCA Victor LSP-2996	(S)	**Excitement On Park Avenue**	1964	8.00	20.00
RCA Victor LPM-3580	(M)	**Strictly Nashville**	1966	6.00	15.00
RCA Victor LSP-3580	(S)	**Strictly Nashville**	1966	8.00	20.00
RCA Victor LPM-3875	(M)	**Paul Anka Alive**	1967	6.00	15.00
RCA Victor LSP-3875	(S)	**Paul Anka Alive**	1967	8.00	20.00
		— Original RCA albums above have black labels.—			
RCA Victor LSP-4142	(S)	**Goodnight My Love**	1969	4.00	10.00
RCA Victor LSP-4203	(S)	**Sincerely/Recorded Live At The Copa**	1969	4.00	10.00
RCA Victor LSP-4250	(S)	**Life Goes On**	1969	4.00	10.00
RCA Victor LSP-4300	(S)	**Paul Anka 70's**	1970	4.00	10.00
		— Original RCA albums above have orange labels.—			
Sire K-6043	(P)	**Vintage Years 1957-1961 (2 LPs)**	1978	6.00	15.00
ANN-MARGRET					
RCA Victor LPM-2399	(M)	**And Here She Is**	1961	12.00	30.00
RCA Victor LSP-2399	(S)	**And Here She Is**	1961	16.00	40.00
RCA Victor LPM-2453	(M)	**On The Way Up**	1961	12.00	30.00
RCA Victor LSP-2453	(S)	**On The Way Up**	1961	16.00	40.00
Dot DLP-9011	(M)	**State Fair** *(Soundtrack)*	1962	12.00	30.00
Dot DLP-25011	(S)	**State Fair** *(Soundtrack)*	1962	16.00	40.00
RCA Victor LPM-2551	(M)	**The Vivacious One**	1962	10.00	25.00
RCA Victor LSP-2551	(S)	**The Vivacious One**	1962	14.00	35.00
RCA Victor LPM-2659	(M)	**Bachelor's Paradise**	1963	10.00	25.00
RCA Victor LSP-2659	(S)	**Bachelor's Paradise**	1963	14.00	35.00
RCA Victor LOC-1081	(M)	**Bye Bye Birdie** *(Soundtrack)*	1963	8.00	20.00
RCA Victor LSO-1081	(S)	**Bye Bye Birdie** *(Soundtrack)*	1963	12.00	30.00
		(First pressings: Ann-Margret is not pictured on the cover.)			
RCA Victor LOC-1081	(M)	**Bye Bye Birdie** *(Soundtrack)*	1963	5.00	12.00
RCA Victor LSO-1081	(S)	**Bye Bye Birdie** *(Soundtrack)*	1963	6.00	15.00
		(Second pressings: Ann-Margret is pictured on the cover.)			

Label & Catalog #		Title	Year	VG+	NM
RCA Victor LOC-1101	(M)	The Pleasure Seekers *(Soundtrack)*	1965	16.00	40.00
RCA Victor LSO-1101	(S)	The Pleasure Seekers *(Soundtrack)*	1965	20.00	50.00
RCA Victor LPM-3710	(M)	The Swinger *(Soundtrack)*	1966	24.00	60.00
RCA Victor LSP-3710	(S)	The Swinger *(Soundtrack)*	1966	30.00	75.00

ANN-MARGRET, & JOHN GARY

RCA Victor LPM-2947	(M)	Hits From Broadway Shows	1964	6.00	15.00
RCA Victor LSP-2947	(S)	Hits From Broadway Shows	1964	8.00	20.00

ANN-MARGRET, & LEE HAZLEWOOD

L. H. I. 12007	(S)	The Cowboy And The Lady	1969	6.00	15.00

ANN-MARGRET, & AL HIRT

RCA Victor LPM-2690	(M)	Beauty And The Beard	1963	6.00	15.00
RCA Victor LSP-2690	(S)	Beauty And The Beard	1963	8.00	20.00

ANN-MARGRET / KITTY KALLEN / DELLA REESE

RCA Victor LPM-2724	(M)	Three Great Girls	1963	5.00	12.00
RCA Victor LSP-2724	(S)	Three Great Girls	1963	6.00	15.00

ANNETTE [ANNETTE FUNICELLO]

Mickey Mouse MM-24	(M)	Songs From Annette	1959	40.00	100.00
Buena Vista BV-3301	(M)	Annette	1959	40.00	100.00
Buena Vista BV-3302	(M)	Annette Sings Anka	1960	40.00	100.00
Buena Vista BV-3303	(M)	Hawaiiannette	1960	30.00	75.00
Buena Vista BV-3304	(M)	Italiannette	1960	30.00	75.00
Buena Vista BV-3305	(M)	Dance Annette	1961	30.00	75.00
Buena Vista BV-3312	(M)	The Story Of My Teens	1962	30.00	75.00
Buena Vista BV-3313	(M)	Teen Street	1962	30.00	75.00
Buena Vista BV-3314	(M)	Muscle Beach Party	1963	30.00	75.00
Buena Vista STER-3314	(S)	Muscle Beach Party	1963	60.00	150.00
		(Features Annette's songs from the movie "Muscle Beach Party.")			
Buena Vista BV-3316	(M)	Beach Party	1963	30.00	75.00
Buena Vista STER-3316	(S)	Beach Party	1963	50.00	125.00
		(Features Annette's songs from the movie "Beach Party.")			
Buena Vista CR2567-70	(DJ)	Merlin Jones *(Radio spots & interview)*	1963	100.00	250.00
Buena Vista BV-3320	(M)	Annette On Campus	1964	20.00	50.00
Buena Vista STER-3320	(S)	Annette On Campus	1964	40.00	100.00
Buena Vista BV-3324	(M)	Annette At Bikini Beach	1964	20.00	50.00
Buena Vista STER-3324	(S)	Annette At Bikini Beach	1964	40.00	100.00
		("The Monkey's Uncle" also features The Beach Boys.)			
Buena Vista BV-3325	(M)	Annette's Pajama Party	1964	16.00	40.00
Buena Vista STER-3325	(S)	Annette's Pajama Party	1964	40.00	100.00
Buena Vista BV-3327	(M)	Annette Sings Golden Surfin' Hits	1964	40.00	100.00
Buena Vista STER-3327	(S)	Annette Sings Golden Surfin' Hits	1964	60.00	150.00
		("The Monkey's Uncle" also features The Beach Boys.)			
Buena Vista BV-3328	(M)	Something Borrowed, Something Blue	1964	30.00	75.00
Buena Vista STER-3328	(S)	Something Borrowed, Something Blue	1964	60.00	150.00
		("Ma, He's Makin' Eyes At Me," "Mr. Piano Man," "Crystal Ball," and "Canzoni D'Amore" are rechanneled on this album.)			
Disneyland DQ-1245	(M)	Walt Disney's Wonderful World Of Color	1964	10.00	25.00
Disneyland DQS-1245	(S)	Walt Disney's Wonderful World Of Color	1964	16.00	40.00
Disneyland DQ-1267	(M)	The Best Of Broadway	1965	12.00	30.00
Disneyland DQ-1287	(M)	Tubby The Tuba	1966	10.00	25.00
Disneyland DQS-1287	(S)	Tubby The Tuba	1966	16.00	40.00
Disneyland DQ-1293	(M)	State And College Songs	1967	10.00	25.00
Disneyland DQS-1293	(S)	State And College Songs	1967	16.00	40.00
Sidewalk T-5902	(M)	Thunder Alley *(Soundtrack)*	1967	8.00	20.00
Sidewalk ST-5902	(S)	Thunder Alley *(Soundtrack)*	1967	10.00	25.00
Buena Vista BV-4037	(M)	Annette Funicello	1972	20.00	50.00
Disneyland DQS-1362	(S)	Walt Disney's MM Club Mousekedances And Other Mousketeer Favorites	1974	6.00	15.00

ANNETTE & HAYLEY MILLS

Buena Vista BV-3508	(M)	Annette And Hayley *(Paper sleeve)*	1964	300.00	600.00

ANNETTE & TOMMY SANDS

Buena Vista BV-3309	(M)	The Parent Trap *(Soundtrack)*	1961	20.00	50.00
Buena Vista STER-3309	(S)	The Parent Trap *(Soundtrack)*	1961	30.00	75.00

Label & Catalog #		Title	Year	VG+	NM
Buena Vista BV-4022	(M)	**Babes In Toyland** (Soundtrack)	1961	20.00	50.00
Buena Vista STER-4022	(S)	**Babes In Toyland** (Soundtrack)	1961	30.00	75.00
ANONYMOUS					
A-Major AMLS-1002	(S)	**Inside The Shadow** (Blue cover with booklet)	1976	100.00	250.00
A-Major AMLS-1002	(S)	**Inside The Shadow** (Black on white cover)	1981	20.00	50.00
ANT TRIP CEREMONY					
C. R. C. 2129	(M)	**Twenty-Four Hours**	1967	360.00	600.00
AORTA					
Columbia CS-9785	(S)	**Aorta**	1968	8.00	20.00
Happy Tiger HT-1010	(S)	**Aorta 2**	1970	8.00	20.00
APHRODITE'S CHILD					
Vertigo 2-500	(S)	**666** (2 LPs)	196?	8.00	20.00
APPEL, DAVE					
Cameo C-1004	(M)	**Alone Together**	1959	12.00	30.00
APPLE CORE					
SSS Inter.	(S)	**Apple Core** (Blue vinyl)	197?	10.00	25.00
J. S. R.	(S)	**Behind The Rear**	1979	10.00	25.00
APPLETREE THEATRE					
Verve/Forecast FT-3042	(M)	**Playback**	1968	10.00	25.00
Verve/Forecast FTS-3042	(S)	**Playback**	1968	12.00	30.00
APOSTLES, THE					
M. G. 79909	(M)	**On Crusade**	196?	60.00	150.00
APOSTLES, THE					
Sound Recording CO-1245	(M)	**An Hour Of Prayer**	196?	60.00	150.00
AQUATONES, THE					
Fargo 3001	(M)	**The Aquatones Sing**	1964	150.00	300.00
ARBORS, THE					
Date DE-1003	(M)	**A Symphony For Susan**	1967	6.00	15.00
Date DES-3003	(S)	**A Symphony For Susan**	1967	8.00	20.00
Date TES-4017	(S)	**I Can't Quit Her / The Letter**	1968	8.00	20.00
ARCESIA					
Alpha 103	(S)	**Arcesia (Reachin')**	197?	300.00	600.00
ARCHIES, THE					
The sound of The Archies is a creation of Ron Dante.					
Calendar KES-101	(S)	**The Archies**	1968	10.00	25.00
Calendar (No number)	(DJ)	**Everything's Archie Box**	1969	40.00	100.00
		(Promotional boxed set includes a sealed copy of "The Archies," buttons, photos and press kit.)			
Calendar KES-103	(S)	**Everything's Archie**	1969	8.00	20.00
Kirshner KES-103	(S)	**Sugar Sugar**	1969	8.00	20.00
		("Sugar Sugar" is a repackage of "Everything's Archie.")			
Calendar KES-105	(S)	**Jingle Jangle**	1969	8.00	20.00
Kirshner KES-107	(S)	**Sunshine**	1969	8.00	20.00
Kirshner KES-109	(S)	**The Archies' Greatest Hits**	1970	6.00	15.00
Kirshner KES-110	(S)	**This Is Love**	1971	10.00	25.00
Morgan Music A6-2345	(S)	**Drive The Boulevard**	1980	6.00	15.00
51 West Q-16002	(S)	**The Archies**	1979	5.00	12.00
ARCHITECT					
Architect AR-101	(S)	**Architect**	197?	40.00	100.00
ARDEN, TONI					
Decca DL-8651	(M)	**Miss Toni Arden**	1957	12.00	30.00
Decca DL-8875	(M)	**Besame**	1959	10.00	25.00
Decca DL-78875	(S)	**Besame**	1959	12.00	30.00

Label & Catalog #		Title	Year	VG+	NM
AREA CODE 615					
Polydor 24-4002	(S)	Area Code 615	1969	6.00	15.00
Polydor 24-4025	(S)	A Trip in the Country	1970	6.00	15.00
ARGENT					
Argent features Rod Argent; Russ Ballard.					
Epic BN-26525	(S)	Argent (Yellow label)	1969	6.00	15.00
Epic KE-30128	(S)	Ring of Hands (Yellow label)	1971	6.00	15.00
Epic EQ-32195	(Q)	In Deep	1974	8.00	20.00
ARISTOCATS, THE					
High Fidelity R-610	(M)	Boogie And Blues	1959	12.00	30.00
High Fidelity SR-610	(S)	Boogie And Blues	1959	16.00	40.00
ARK					
Ark 810-71	(S)	Voyages	1978	360.00	600.00
ARKANGEL					
Joyeuse Garde JGR-001	(S)	Wind Face	1980	12.00	30.00
ARKANSAS BLUEGRASS BOYS, THE					
Smigar 6275	(M)	Bluegrass Special	1962	16.00	40.00
ARMAGEDDON					
Amos 73075	(S)	Armageddon	1969	10.00	25.00
ARMAGEDDON					
Armageddon features Keith Relf, formerly of The Yardbirds.					
A&M SP-4513	(S)	Armageddon	1975	8.00	20.00
ARMATRADING, JOAN					
A&M SP-8414	(DJ)	Superstar Radio Network	1977	6.00	15.00
ARNAZ, DESI					
RCA Victor LPM-3096 (10")	(M)	Babalu!	1954	50.00	125.00
ARNOLD, BILLY BOY					
Prestige PRLP-7389	(M)	Blues On The South Side	1965	8.00	20.00
Prestige PRST-7389	(S)	Blues On The South Side	1965	8.00	20.00
ARNOLD, EDDY					
RCA Victor LPM-3027 (10")	(M)	Anytime	1952	40.00	100.00
RCA Victor LPM-3031 (10")	(M)	All-Time Hits From The Hills	1952	30.00	75.00
RCA Victor LPM-3117 (10")	(M)	All-Time Favorites	1953	30.00	75.00
RCA Victor LPM-3219 (10")	(M)	The Chapel On The Hill	1954	30.00	75.00
RCA Victor LPM-3230 (10")	(M)	An American Institution (With booklet)	1954	40.00	100.00
RCA Victor LPM-3230 (10")	(M)	An American Institution (Without booklet)	1954	30.00	75.00
RCA Victor LPM-1111	(M)	Wanderin'	1955	20.00	50.00
RCA Victor LPM-1223	(M)	All-Time Favorites	1955	20.00	50.00
RCA Victor LPM-1224	(M)	Anytime	1955	20.00	50.00
RCA Victor LPM-1225	(M)	The Chapel On The Hill	1955	20.00	50.00
RCA Victor LPM-1293	(M)	A Dozen Hits	1956	20.00	50.00
RCA Victor LPM-1377	(M)	A Little On The Lonely Side	1956	20.00	50.00
RCA Victor LPM-1484	(M)	When They Were Young	1957	16.00	40.00
RCA Victor LPM-1575	(M)	My Darling, My Darling	1957	16.00	40.00
RCA Victor LPM-1733	(M)	Praise Him, Praise Him	1958	16.00	40.00
RCA Victor LPM-1928	(M)	Have Guitar, Will Travel	1959	12.00	30.00
RCA Victor LSP-1928	(S)	Have Guitar, Will Travel	1959	16.00	40.00
RCA Victor LPM-2036	(M)	Thereby Hangs A Tale	1959	12.00	30.00
RCA Victor LSP-2036	(S)	Thereby Hangs A Tale	1959	16.00	40.00
RCA Victor LPM-2185	(M)	Eddy Arnold Sings Them Again	1960	10.00	25.00
RCA Victor LSP-2185	(S)	Eddy Arnold Sings Them Again	1960	12.00	30.00
RCA Victor LPM-2268	(M)	You Gotta Have Love	1960	10.00	25.00
RCA Victor LSP-2268	(S)	You Gotta Have Love	1960	12.00	30.00
RCA Victor LPM-2337	(M)	Let's Make Memories Tonight	1961	10.00	25.00
RCA Victor LSP-2337	(S)	Let's Make Memories Tonight	1961	12.00	30.00
RCA Victor LPM-2471	(M)	One More Time	1961	10.00	25.00
RCA Victor LSP-2471	(S)	One More Time	1961	12.00	30.00

Label & Catalog #		Title	Year	VG+	NM
RCA Victor PRS-346	(DJ)	Christmas With Eddy Arnold	1961	20.00	50.00
RCA Victor LPM-2554	(M)	Christmas With Eddy Arnold	1961	10.00	25.00
RCA Victor LSP-2554	(S)	Christmas With Eddy Arnold	1961	12.00	30.00
RCA Victor LPM-2578	(M)	Cattle Call	1962	10.00	25.00
RCA Victor LSP-2578	(S)	Cattle Call	1962	12.00	30.00
RCA Victor LPM-2596	(M)	Our Man Down South	1962	10.00	25.00
RCA Victor LSP-2596	(S)	Our Man Down South	1962	12.00	30.00
RCA Victor LPM-2629	(M)	Faithfully Yours	1963	10.00	25.00
RCA Victor LSP-2629	(S)	Faithfully Yours	1963	12.00	30.00

— Original RCA mono albums above have "Long Play" on the bottom of the label; stereo albums have "Living Stereo" on the bottom.—

RCA Victor LPM-2811	(M)	Folk Song Book	1964	6.00	15.00
RCA Victor LSP-2811	(S)	Folk Song Book	1964	8.00	20.00
RCA Victor LPM-2909	(M)	Sometimes I'm Happy, Sometimes I'm Blue	1964	5.00	12.00
RCA Victor LSP-2909	(S)	Sometimes I'm Happy, Sometimes I'm Blue	1964	6.00	15.00
RCA Victor LPM-2951	(M)	Pop Hits From The Country Side	1964	5.00	12.00
RCA Victor LSP-2951	(S)	Pop Hits From The Country Side	1964	6.00	15.00
RCA Victor LPM-3361	(M)	The Easy Way	1965	5.00	12.00
RCA Victor LSP-3361	(S)	The Easy Way	1965	6.00	15.00
RCA Victor LPM-3466	(M)	My World	1965	5.00	12.00
RCA Victor LSP-3466	(S)	My World	1965	6.00	15.00
RCA Victor LPM-3507	(M)	I Want To Go With You	1966	5.00	12.00
RCA Victor LSP-3507	(S)	I Want To Go With You	1966	6.00	15.00
RCA Victor LPM-3565	(M)	The Best Of Eddy Arnold	1966	5.00	12.00
RCA Victor LSP-3565	(S)	The Best Of Eddy Arnold	1966	6.00	15.00
RCA Victor LPM-3622	(M)	The Last Word In Lonesome	1966	5.00	12.00
RCA Victor LSP-3622	(S)	The Last Word In Lonesome	1966	6.00	15.00
RCA Victor LPM-3715	(M)	Somebody Like Me	1966	5.00	12.00
RCA Victor LSP-3715	(S)	Somebody Like Me	1966	6.00	15.00
RCA Victor LPM-3753	(M)	Lonely Again	1967	8.00	20.00
RCA Victor LSP-3753	(S)	Lonely Again	1967	6.00	15.00
RCA Victor LPM-3869	(M)	Turn The World Around	1967	8.00	20.00
RCA Victor LSP-3869	(S)	Turn The World Around	1967	6.00	15.00
RCA Victor LPM-3931	(M)	The Everlovin' World Of Eddy Arnold	1968	20.00	50.00
RCA Victor LSP-3931	(S)	The Everlovin' World Of Eddy Arnold	1968	6.00	15.00

— Original RCA albums above have black labels.—

ARROWS, THE: *Refer to* DAVIE ALLAN

ARS NOVA

Elektra EKS-74020	(S)	Ars Nova	1968	6.00	15.00
Atlantic SD-8221	(S)	Sunshine And Shadows	1969	6.00	15.00

ART OF LOVIN'

Mainstream S-6113	(S)	Art Of Lovin'	1968	10.00	25.00

ARTHUR [ARTHUR LEE HARPER]

L. H. I. 12000	(S)	Dreams And Images	1968	10.00	25.00

ARTISTICS, THE

OKeh OKL-4119	(M)	Get My Hands On Some Lovin'	1967	12.00	30.00
OKeh OKS-14119	(S)	Get My Hands On Some Lovin'	1967	16.00	40.00
Brunswick BL-54123	(M)	I'm Gonna Miss You	1967	6.00	15.00
Brunswick BL-754123	(S)	I'm Gonna Miss You	1967	8.00	20.00
Brunswick BL-754139	(S)	The Articulate Artistics	1968	6.00	15.00
Brunswick BL-754153	(S)	What Happened	1969	6.00	15.00

ARZACHEL

Roulette SR-42036	(S)	Arzachel	1969	50.00	125.00

ASGAERD

Threshold THS-6	(S)	In The Realm Of Asgaerd	1972	6.00	15.00

ASHER, JANE

London OSA-1206	(M)	Alice In Wonderland	1965	20.00	50.00

ASHER & LITTLE JIMMY

Decca DL-4785	(M)	Mountain Ballads And Old Hymns	1966	10.00	25.00
Decca DL-74785	(S)	Mountain Ballads And Old Hymns	1966	12.00	30.00

Label & Catalog #		Title	Year	VG+	NM

ASHES

Vault 125	(S)	Ashes	1968	10.00	25.00

ASHKAN

Sire SES-97017	(S)	In From The Cold	1970	16.00	40.00

ASSOCIATION, THE

Valiant VLM-5002	(M)	And Then Along Comes The Association	1966	8.00	20.00
Valiant VLS-25002	(S)	And Then Along Comes The Association	1966	10.00	25.00
Valiant VLM-5004	(M)	Renaissance	1966	8.00	20.00
Valiant VLS-25004	(S)	Renaissance	1966	10.00	25.00
		(First pressing covers do not mention "No Fair At All.")			
Valiant VLM-5004	(M)	Renaissance	1966	6.00	15.00
Valiant VLS-25004	(S)	Renaissance	1966	8.00	20.00
		(Second pressing covers have a blurb for "No Fair At All.")			
Warner Bros. W-1696	(M)	Insight Out	1967	6.00	15.00
Warner Bros. WS-1696	(S)	Insight Out	1967	8.00	20.00
		— Original Warner Bros. albums above have gold labels.—			

ASTAIRE, FRED

Clef *(No number)*	(M)	The Fred Astaire Story	1954	150.00	250.00
		(Limited edition boxed set of four albums with a booklet.)			
Clef MGC-1001	(M)	The Fred Astaire Story, Volume 1	1954	20.00	50.00
Clef MGC-1002	(M)	The Fred Astaire Story, Volume 2	1954	20.00	50.00
Clef MGC-1003	(M)	The Fred Astaire Story, Volume 3	1954	20.00	50.00
Clef MGC-1004	(M)	The Fred Astaire Story, Volume 4	1954	20.00	50.00
		(Clef 1001-1004 are reissues of the four albums in the box set.)			
Clef MGC-662	(M)	The Fred Astaire Story, Volume 1	1955	16.00	40.00
Clef MGC-663	(M)	The Fred Astaire Story, Volume 2	1955	16.00	40.00
Clef MGC-664	(M)	The Fred Astaire Story, Volume 3	1955	16.00	40.00
Clef MGC-665	(M)	The Fred Astaire Story, Volume 4	1955	16.00	40.00
		(Clef 662-665 are reissues of 1001-1004.)			
"X" LVA-1001	(M)	Fred Astaire With Leo Reisman	1955	20.00	50.00
Coral CRL-57008	M)	Cavalcade Of Dance	1955	20.00	50.00
Epic LN-3103	(M)	Nothing Thrilled Us Half As Much	1955	20.00	50.00
Epic LN-3137	(M)	The Best Of Fred Astaire	1955	20.00	50.00
MGM E-3413	(M)	Shoes With Wings	1956	20.00	50.00
Verve V-2010	(M)	Mr. Top Hat	1956	20.00	50.00
Verve V-2114	(M)	Easy To Dance With	1958	20.00	50.00
		(Verve 2010 and 2114 are repackages Clef material.)			
Kapp KL-1165	(M)	Now	1959	10.00	25.00
Kapp KS-3165	(S)	Now	1959	14.00	35.00
MGM CC-2	(M)	Chrysler Presents Fred Astaire	196?	6.00	15.00

ASTRONAUTS, THE

The Astronauts later recorded as Hardwater.

RCA Victor LPM-2760	(M)	Surfin' With The Astronauts	1963	16.00	40.00
RCA Victor LSP-2760	(S)	Surfin' With The Astronauts	1963	20.00	50.00
RCA Victor LPM-2782	(M)	Everything Is A-OK	1964	12.00	30.00
RCA Victor LSP-2782	(S)	Everything Is A-OK	1964	16.00	40.00
RCA Victor LPM-2858	(M)	Competition Coupe	1964	20.00	50.00
RCA Victor LSP-2858	(S)	Competition Coupe	1964	30.00	75.00
RCA Victor LPM-2903	(M)	The Astronauts Orbit Campus	1964	12.00	30.00
RCA Victor LSP-2903	(S)	The Astronauts Orbit Campus	1964	16.00	40.00
RCA Victor PRM-183	(DJ)	Rockin' With The Astronauts	1964	12.00	30.00
RCA Victor LPM-3441	(M)	Wild On The Beach *(Soundtrack)*	1965	12.00	30.00
RCA Victor LSP-3441	(S)	Wild On The Beach *(Soundtrack)*	1965	16.00	40.00
RCA Victor LPM-3307	(M)	The Astronauts Go Go Go	1965	12.00	30.00
RCA Victor LSP-3307	(S)	The Astronauts Go Go Go	1965	16.00	40.00
RCA Victor LPM-3359	(M)	Favorites For You From Us	1965	12.00	30.00
RCA Victor LSP-3359	(S)	Favorites For You From Us	1965	16.00	40.00
RCA Victor LPM-3454	(M)	Down The Line	1966	12.00	30.00
RCA Victor LSP-3454	(S)	Down The Line	1966	16.00	40.00
RCA Victor LPM-3733	(M)	Travelin' Men	1967	20.00	50.00
RCA Victor LSP-3733	(S)	Travelin' Men	1967	16.00	40.00

ASTRONAUTS, THE / THE LIVERPOOL FIVE

RCA Victor PRS-251	(S)	Stereo Festival *(Sampler)*	1967	60.00	150.00

Label & Catalog #		Title	Year	VG+	NM

ASYLUM CHOIR
The Asylum Choir is Leon Russell and Mark Benno.

Smash SRS-67107	(S)	**Look Inside The Asylum Choir**	1970	6.00	15.00
		(The cover features a roll of toilet paper.)			
Smash SRS-67107	(S)	**Look Inside The Asylum Choir**	1970	4.00	10.00
		(The cover features a group photo.)			

ATCHER, BOBBY, & THE COUNTRYMEN

Columbia HL-9006 (10")	(M)	**Early American Folk Songs**	1949	30.00	75.00
Columbia HL-9013 (10")	(M)	**Songs Of The Saddle**	1949	30.00	75.00
Columbia CL-2232	(M)	**The Dean Of Cowboy Singers**	1964	10.00	25.00
Columbia CS-9032	(E)	**The Dean Of Cowboy Singers**	1964	6.00	15.00

ATKINS, CHET
Refer to The Country All-Stars; The Nashville All-Stars.

RCA Victor LPM-3079 (10")	(M)	**Chet Atkins' Gallopin' Guitar**	1952	60.00	150.00
RCA Victor LPM-3169 (10")	(M)	**Stringin' Along With Chet Atkins**	1953	50.00	125.00
RCA Victor LPM-1090	(M)	**A Session With Chet Atkins**	1954	24.00	60.00
RCA Victor LPM-1197	(M)	**Chet Atkins In Three Dimensions**	1956	20.00	50.00
RCA Victor LPM-1236	(M)	**Stringin' Along With Chet Atkins**	1956	20.00	50.00
RCA Victor LPM-1383	(M)	**Finger Style Guitar**	1956	16.00	40.00
RCA Victor LPM-1544	(M)	**Chet Atkins At Home**	1957	16.00	40.00
RCA Victor LPM-1577	(M)	**Hi Fi In Focus**	1957	16.00	40.00
RCA Victor LPM-1993	(M)	**Chet Atkins In Hollywood**	1959	12.00	30.00
RCA Victor LSP-1993	(S)	**Chet Atkins In Hollywood**	1959	20.00	50.00
		(First pressing covers feature a shapely guitar			
		against the night skyline of Hollywood.)			
RCA Victor LPM-1993	(M)	**Chet Atkins In Hollywood**	1961	12.00	30.00
RCA Victor LSP-1993	(S)	**Chet Atkins In Hollywood**	1961	20.00	50.00
		(Later pressing covers feature an even more shapely model			
		on the corner of Hollywood and Vine.)			
RCA Victor LPM-2025	(M)	**Hum And Strung Along** *(With booklet)*	1959	12.00	30.00
RCA Victor LSP-2025	(S)	**Hum And Strung Along** *(With booklet)*	1959	16.00	40.00
RCA Victor LPM-2025	(M)	**Hum And Strung Along** *(Without booklet)*	1959	8.00	20.00
RCA Victor LSP-2025	(S)	**Hum And Strung Along** *(Without booklet)*	1959	12.00	30.00
RCA Victor LPM-2103	(M)	**Mister Guitar**	1959	8.00	20.00
RCA Victor LSP-2103	(S)	**Mister Guitar**	1959	12.00	30.00
RCA Victor LPM-2161	(M)	**Teensville**	1960	8.00	20.00
RCA Victor LSP-2161	(S)	**Teensville**	1960	12.00	30.00
RCA Victor LPM-2175	(M)	**The Other Chet Atkins**	1960	8.00	20.00
RCA Victor LSP-2175	(S)	**The Other Chet Atkins**	1960	12.00	30.00
RCA Victor LPM-2232	(M)	**Chet Atkins' Workshop**	1961	6.00	15.00
RCA Victor LSP-2232	(S)	**Chet Atkins' Workshop**	1961	10.00	25.00
RCA Victor LPM-2346	(M)	**The Most Popular Guitar**	1961	6.00	15.00
RCA Victor LSP-2346	(S)	**The Most Popular Guitar**	1961	10.00	25.00
RCA Victor LPM-2424	(M)	**Christmas With Chet Atkins**	1961	6.00	15.00
RCA Victor LSP-2424	(S)	**Christmas With Chet Atkins**	1961	10.00	25.00
RCA Victor LPM-2450	(M)	**Down Home**	1962	6.00	15.00
RCA Victor LSP-2450	(S)	**Down Home**	1962	10.00	25.00
RCA Victor LPM-2549	(M)	**Caribbean Guitar**	1962	6.00	15.00
RCA Victor LSP-2549	(S)	**Caribbean Guitar**	1962	10.00	25.00
RCA Victor LPM-2601	(M)	**Back Home Hymns**	1962	6.00	15.00
RCA Victor LSP-2601	(S)	**Back Home Hymns**	1962	10.00	25.00
RCA Victor LPM-2616	(M)	**Our Man In Nashville**	1963	6.00	15.00
RCA Victor LSP-2616	(S)	**Our Man In Nashville**	1963	10.00	25.00
RCA Victor LPM-2678	(M)	**Travelin'**	1963	6.00	15.00
RCA Victor LSP-2678	(S)	**Travelin'**	1963	10.00	25.00
RCA Victor LPM-2719	(M)	**Teen Scene**	1963	6.00	15.00
RCA Victor LSP-2719	(S)	**Teen Scene**	1963	10.00	25.00
		—Original RCA mono albums above have "Long Play" on the bottom of the label;			
		stereo albums have "Living Stereo" on the bottom.—			
RCA Victor LPM-2783	(M)	**Guitar Country**	1964	5.00	12.00
RCA Victor LSP-2783	(S)	**Guitar Country**	1964	6.00	15.00
RCA Victor LPM-2887	(M)	**The Best Of Chet Atkins**	1964	5.00	12.00
RCA Victor LSP-2887	(S)	**The Best Of Chet Atkins**	1964	4.00	12.00
RCA Victor LPM-2908	(M)	**Progressive Pickin'**	1964	5.00	12.00
RCA Victor LSP-2908	(S)	**Progressive Pickin'**	1964	6.00	15.00
RCA Victor LPM-2952	(M)	**Reminiscing**	1964	5.00	12.00
RCA Victor LSP-2952	(S)	**Reminiscing**	1964	6.00	15.00

Unquestionably the most collectible single country 'n western guitarist— if not the most prolific and influential— Chet Atkins placed nineteen albums on the pop charts through 1976, although he has yet to receive an RIAA Gold Record. He literally defines a period of Nashville's famed sound as both instrumentalist and producer. Please note that first pressings of the popular Chet Atkins In Hollywood(above) bare the eye-catching "Living Stereo" banner across the top of the cover. This album also enjoys a solid reputation in the audiophile community.

Label & Catalog #		Title	Year	VG+	NM
RCA Victor LPM-3316	(M)	My Favorite Guitars	1964	5.00	12.00
RCA Victor LSP-3316	(S)	My Favorite Guitars	1964	6.00	15.00
RCA Victor LPM-3429	(M)	More Of That Guitar Country	1965	5.00	12.00
RCA Victor LSP-3429	(S)	More Of That Guitar Country	1965	6.00	15.00
RCA Victor LPM-3531	(M)	Chet Atkins Picks On The Beatles	1965	10.00	25.00
RCA Victor LSP-3531	(S)	Chet Atkins Picks On The Beatles	1965	12.00	30.00

—RCA Victor albums above have black labels with Nipper on top.—

ATLANTA RHYTHM SECTION, THE

Mobile Fidelity MFSL-038	(S)	Champagne Jam	1980	10.00	30.00

ATLEE: *Refer to* **ATLEE YEAGER**

ATOMIC ROOSTER

Elektra EKS-74094	(S)	Death Walks Behind You	1971	6.00	15.00
Elektra EKS-74109	(S)	In Hearing Of	1971	6.00	15.00
Elektra EKS-75039	(S)	Made In England	1972	5.00	12.00
Elektra EKS-75074	(S)	Atomic Rooster IV	1973	5.00	12.00

ATTILA
Attila features Billy Joel.

Epic E-30030	(S)	Attila	1970	10.00	25.00

AU-GO-GO SINGERS, THE
The Au-Go-Gos feature Steve Stills and Rich Furay, later of The Buffalo Springfield.

Roulette R-25280	(M)	They Call Us The Au Go-Go Singers	1964	20.00	50.00
Roulette SR-25280	(S)	They Call Us The Au Go-Go Singers	1964	30.00	75.00

AUGER, BRIAN

Atco SD-33-258	(S)	Open (With Jools Driscoll)	1968	6.00	15.00
Atco SD-33-273	(S)	Definitely What!...	1969	6.00	15.00
Atco SD-2-701	(S)	Streetnoise (2 LPs)	1969	8.00	20.00
Capitol ST-136	(S)	Jools & Brian (With Jools Driscoll)	1969	6.00	15.00
RCA Victor LSP-4372	(S)	Befour	1970	4.00	10.00
RCA Victor LSP-4462	(S)	Brian Auger's Oblivion Express	1971	4.00	10.00
RCA Victor LSP-4540	(S)	Better Land	1971	4.00	10.00
RCA Victor LSP-4703	(S)	Second Wind	1972	4.00	10.00
Headfirst	(S)	Search Party	198?	6.00	15.00

AUM

Sire SES-97007	(S)	Bluesvibes	1969	8.00	20.00
Fillmore F-30002	(S)	Resurrection	1969	10.00	25.00

AUSTIN, CLAIRE: *Refer to* **GOLDMINE'S PRICE GUIDE TO COLLECTIBLE JAZZ ALBUMS**

AUSTIN, GENE

RCA Victor LPM-3200 (10")	(M)	My Blue Heaven	195?	20.00	50.00
"X" LVA-1007	(M)	Gene Austin Sings All-Time Favorites	195?	16.00	40.00
Decca DL-8433	(M)	My Blue Heaven	1957	16.00	40.00
Dot DLP-3300	(M)	Great Hits	1960	8.00	20.00
Dot DLP-25300	(S)	Great Hits	1960	12.00	30.00

AUTOSALVAGE

RCA Victor LPM-3940	(M)	Autosalvage	1968	20.00	50.00
RCA Victor LSP-3940	(S)	Autosalvage	1968	10.00	25.00

AUTRY, GENE

Columbia JL-8001 (10")	(M)	Gene Autry At The Rodeo	1949	50.00	125.00
Columbia JL-8009 (10")	(M)	Stampede	1949	50.00	125.00
Columbia JL-8012 (10")	(M)	Champion	1950	50.00	125.00
Columbia HL-9001 (10")	(M)	Western Classic, Volume 1	1949	50.00	125.00
Columbia HL-9002 (10")	(M)	Western Classic, Volume 2	1949	50.00	125.00
Columbia CL-6020 (10")	(M)	Easter Favorites	1949	40.00	100.00
Columbia CL-6137 (10")	(M)	Merry Christmas	1950	40.00	100.00
Columbia MJV-82 (10")	(M)	The Story Of The Nativity	1955	30.00	75.00
Columbia MJV-83 (10")	(M)	Little Johnny Pilgrim And Guffy	1955	30.00	75.00
Columbia MJV-94 (10")	(M)	Rusty, The Rocking Horse	1955	30.00	75.00

Label & Catalog #		Title	Year	VG+	NM
Columbia CL-2547 (10")	(M)	Merry Christmas	1955	30.00	75.00
Columbia CL-2568 (10")	(M)	Gene Autry Sings Peter Cottontail	1955	30.00	75.00
Columbia CL-677	(M)	Champion Western Adventures	1955	30.00	75.00
Challenge CHL-600	(M)	Christmas With Gene Autry	1958	20.00	50.00
Columbia CL-1575	(M)	Gene Autry's Greatest Hits	1961	14.00	35.00
Harmony HL-9505	(M)	Champion Western Adventures	1959	16.00	40.00
Harmony HL-9550	(M)	Christmas Favorites	1960	12.00	30.00
Harmony HL-7332	(M)	Gene Autry's Great Western Hits	1965	10.00	25.00
RCA Victor LPM-2623	(M)	Gene Autry's Golden Hits	1962	10.00	25.00
RCA Victor LSP-2623	(S)	Gene Autry's Golden Hits	1962	10.00	25.00
Melody Ranch 101	(M)	Melody Ranch	1965	16.00	40.00
Republic 1970	(S)	South Of The Border	1970	12.00	30.00

AVALANCHES, THE

Warner Bros. W-1525	(M)	Ski Surfin'	1963	12.00	30.00
Warner Bros. WS-1525	(S)	Ski Surfin'	1963	16.00	40.00

AVALON, FRANKIE
Refer to Fabian / Frankie Avalon.

Chancellor CHL-5001	(M)	Frankie Avalon	1958	30.00	75.00
Chancellor CHL-5002	(M)	The Young Frankie Avalon	1959	30.00	75.00
		— Chancellor albums above have pink labels.—			
Chancellor CHL-5001	(M)	Frankie Avalon	1960	20.00	50.00
Chancellor CHL-5002	(M)	The Young Frankie Avalon	1960	20.00	50.00
Chancellor CHLS-5002	(S)	The Young Frankie Avalon	1960	30.00	75.00
Chancellor CHLX-5004	(M)	Swingin' On A Rainbow	1960	24.00	60.00
Chancellor CHLS-5004	(S)	Swingin' On A Rainbow	1960	30.00	75.00
Chancellor CHL-69801	(M)	Young And In Love	1960	30.00	75.00
		(Boxed set with photos and a 3-D portrait.)			
Chancellor CHL-5011	(M)	Summer Scene	1960	16.00	40.00
Chancellor CHLS-5011	(S)	Summer Scene	1960	24.00	60.00
Chancellor CHL-5018	(M)	A Whole Lot Of Frankie	1961	16.00	40.00
Chancellor CHL-5022	(M)	And Now About Mr. Avalon	1961	16.00	40.00
Chancellor CHLS-5022	(S)	And Now About Mr. Avalon	1961	20.00	50.00
Chancellor CHL-5025	(M)	Italiano	1962	10.00	25.00
Chancellor CHLS-5025	(S)	Italiano	1962	16.00	40.00
Chancellor CHL-5027	(M)	You Are Mine	1962	10.00	25.00
Chancellor CHLS-5027	(S)	You Are Mine	1962	16.00	40.00
Chancellor CHL-5031	(M)	Frankie Avalon's Christmas Album	1962	10.00	25.00
Chancellor CHLS-5031	(S)	Frankie Avalon's Christmas Album	1962	16.00	40.00
Chancellor CHL-5032	(M)	Cleopatra Plus 13 Other Great Hits	1963	10.00	25.00
Chancellor CHLS-5032	(S)	Cleopatra Plus 13 Other Great Hits	1963	16.00	40.00
		— Chancellor albums above have pink labels.—			
United Arts. UAL-3371	(M)	Songs From Muscle Beach Party	1964	8.00	20.00
United Arts. UAS-6371	(S)	Songs From Muscle Beach Party	1964	12.00	30.00
United Arts. UAL-3382	(M)	Frankie Avalon's 15 Greatest Hits	1964	8.00	20.00
United Arts. UAS-6382	(P)	Frankie Avalon's 15 Greatest Hits	1964	10.00	25.00
		(A collection of hits originally issued on Chancellor.)			
United Arts. UAL-4121	(M)	I'll Take Sweden *(Soundtrack)*	1965	8.00	20.00
United Arts. UAS-5121	(S)	I'll Take Sweden *(Soundtrack)*	1965	10.00	25.00
Sunset SUS-5244	(S)	Frankie Avalon	1969	6.00	15.00
Metromedia 1034	(S)	I Want You Near Me	1970	6.00	15.00
ABC X-805	(S)	16 Greatest Hits	1973	5.00	12.00

AVENGERS VI, THE

Mark-56 Records	(M)	Real Cool Hits	1965	100.00	250.00

AVERAGE WHITE BAND, THE [AWB]

Atlantic QD-7308	(Q)	AWB	1975	6.00	15.00

AVERNE, HARVEY

Atlantic SD-8168	(S)	Viva Soul	1968	8.00	20.00

AVONS, THE

Hull HLP-1000	(M)	The Avons *(Red label)*	1960	400.00	1,000.00

AXELROD, DAVID

Capitol ST-2982	(S)	Songs Of Experience	1969	6.00	15.00

Label & Catalog #		Title	Year	VG+	NM

AYCOCK, EARL
| Mercury MG-20282 | (M) | Earl Aycock | 1958 | 10.00 | 25.00 |

AZTECA
| Columbia CQ-31776 | (Q) | Azteca | 1973 | 6.00 | 15.00 |

AZTECS, THE
| World Artists WAM-2001 | (M) | Live At The Ad-Lib Club Of London | 1964 | 16.00 | 40.00 |

AZITIS
| Elco SC-EC-5555 | (S) | Help! | 1974 | 100.00 | 250.00 |

B. F. TRIKE
| Rockadellic | (S) | B. F. Trike | 1989 | 24.00 | 60.00 |

BABY
| Lone Starr 9782 | (S) | Baby | 1974 | 8.00 | 20.00 |

BABY HUEY
| Curtom CRS-8007 | (S) | The Living Legend | 1970 | 16.00 | 40.00 |

BABY RAY [RAY STEVENS]
| Imperial LP-9335 | (M) | Where Soul Lives | 1967 | 6.00 | 15.00 |
| Imperial LP-12335 | (S) | Where Soul Lives | 1967 | 8.00 | 20.00 |

BABYSITTERS, THE
The Babysitters were Alan Arkin, Lee Hays and Doris Kaplan.
| Vanguard VRS-9042 | (M) | The Babysitters | 195? | 8.00 | 20.00 |

BACHS, THE
| Raio (No number) | (S) | Out Of The Bachs | 1967 | 1,500.00 | 3,000.00 |

BACK PORCH MAJORITY, THE
The Back Porch Majority features Randy Sparks.
Epic LN-24134	(M)	Live From Ledbetter's	1965	6.00	15.00
Epic BN-26134	(S)	Live From Ledbetter's	1965	8.00	20.00
Epic LN-24149	(M)	Riverboat Days	1965	6.00	15.00
Epic BN-26149	(S)	Riverboat Days	1965	8.00	20.00
Epic LN-24184	(M)	That's The Way It's Gonna Be	1966	6.00	15.00
Epic BN-26184	(S)	That's The Way It's Gonna Be	1966	8.00	20.00
Epic LN-24319	(M)	Willy Nilly Wonder Of Illusion	1967	6.00	15.00
Epic BN-26319	(S)	Willy Nilly Wonder Of Illusion	1967	8.00	20.00

BADFINGER
Badfinger originally recorded as The Iveys. Refer to George Harrison & Friends.
Commonwealth UN. 6004	(S)	The Magic Christian (Sdtk with Ringo)	1970	10.00	25.00
Apple ST-3364	(S)	Magic Christian Music	1970	10.00	25.00
		(Apple label with "A Subsidiary of Capitol" on the bottom.)			
Apple ST-3364	(S)	Magic Christian Music	1970	6.00	15.00
		(Apple label with "Manufactured by Apple" on the bottom.)			
Apple SKAO-3367	(S)	No Dice	1970	16.00	40.00
Apple SW-3387	(S)	Straight Up	1971	30.00	75.00
Apple SW-3411	(S)	Ass	1973	8.00	20.00

Label & Catalog #		Title	Year	VG+	NM
Warner Bros. BS-2762	(S)	Badfinger	1974	6.00	15.00
Warner Bros. BS-2827	(S)	Wish You Were Here	1974	8.00	20.00
Elektra 6E-175	(S)	Airwaves	1979	4.00	10.00

BADGE

Label & Catalog #		Title	Year	VG+	NM
LPS-1	(S)	Badge & Co.	1977	150.00	300.00

BAEZ, JOAN

Label & Catalog #		Title	Year	VG+	NM
Veritas XTV-62202	(M)	Folksingers 'Round Harvard Square	1959	80.00	200.00
Vanguard VRS-9077	(M)	Joan Baez	1960	10.00	25.00
Vanguard VSD-2077	(S)	Joan Baez	1960	12.00	30.00
Vanguard VRS-9097	(M)	Joan Baez, Volume 2	1961	10.00	25.00
Vanguard VSD-2097	(S)	Joan Baez, Volume 2	1961	12.00	30.00
Vanguard VRS-9122	(M)	Joan Baez In Concert, Volume 1	1962	10.00	25.00
Vanguard VSD-2122	(S)	Joan Baez In Concert, Volume 1	1962	12.00	30.00
Vanguard VRS-9123	(M)	Joan Baez In Concert, Volume 2	1963	10.00	25.00
Vanguard VSD-2123	(S)	Joan Baez In Concert, Volume 2	1963	12.00	30.00
— Original Vanguard mono albums above have maroon labels; stereo albums have black labels.—					
Vanguard VRS-9160	(M)	Joan Baez/5	1964	6.00	15.00
Vanguard VSD-79160	(M)	Joan Baez/5	1964	8.00	20.00
Vanguard VRS-9200	(M)	Farewell Angelina	1965	6.00	15.00
Vanguard VSD-79200	(S)	Farewell Angelina	1965	8.00	20.00
Vanguard VRS-9230	(M)	Noel	1966	6.00	15.00
Vanguard VSD-79230	(S)	Noel	1966	8.00	20.00
Vanguard VRS-9240	(M)	Joan	1967	6.00	15.00
Vanguard VSD-79240	(S)	Joan	1967	8.00	20.00
Fantasy	(M)	Joan Baez In San Francisco	196?	12.00	30.00
Fantasy	(S)	Joan Baez In San Francisco	196?	16.00	40.00
Vanguard Q-40001	(Q)	Blessed Are (2 LPs)	1974	6.00	15.00
Vanguard Q-40332	(Q)	Hits/Greatest And Others	1974	6.00	15.00
A&M QU-54339	(Q)	Come From The Shadows	1974	6.00	15.00
A&M QU-54527	(Q)	Diamonds And Rust	1975	6.00	15.00
A&M SP-8375	(DJ)	For Every Stage (White label promo)	1976	60.00	150.00
Portrait PRQ-34697	(Q)	Blowin' Away	1977	6.00	15.00
Nautilus NR-12	(S)	Diamonds And Rust	198?	12.00	36.00

BAG, THE

Label & Catalog #		Title	Year	VG+	NM
Decca DL-75057	(S)	Real	1968	6.00	15.00

BAGDASARIAN, ROSS

Bagdasarian as David Seville was the mastermind behind The Chipmunks.

Label & Catalog #		Title	Year	VG+	NM
Liberty LRP-3451	(M)	The Crazy, Mixed-Up World Of Ross Bagdasarian	1966	16.00	40.00
Liberty LST-7451	(S)	The Crazy, Mixed-Up World Of Ross Bagdasarian	1966	20.00	50.00

BAILEY, MILDRED: Refer to GOLDMINE'S PRICE GUIDE TO COLLECTIBLE JAZZ ALBUMS

BAILEY, PEARL

Label & Catalog #		Title	Year	VG+	NM
Columbia CL-6099 (10")	(M)	Pearl Bailey Entertains	1950	20.00	50.00
Coral CRL-56068 (10")	(M)	Say Si Si	1953	20.00	50.00
Coral CRL-56078 (10")	(M)	I'm With You	1953	20.00	50.00
Columbia ML-4969	(M)	House Of Flowers (Soundtrack)	1954	20.00	50.00
Capitol L-355	(M)	St. Louis Woman (Soundtrack)	1955	40.00	100.00
Mercury MG-20187	(M)	The One And Only Pearl Bailey Sings	1956	16.00	40.00
Mercury MG-20277	(M)	The Intoxicating Pearl Bailey	1957	16.00	40.00
Coral CRL-57037	(M)	Birth Of The Blues	1956	16.00	40.00
Coral CRL-57162	(M)	Cultured Pearl	1957	16.00	40.00
Vocalion VL-3621	(M)	Gems By Pearl Bailey	1958	10.00	25.00
Columbia OL-5410	(M)	Porgy And Bess (Soundtrack)	1959	8.00	20.00
Columbia OS-2016	(S)	Porgy And Bess (Soundtrack)	1959	12.00	30.00
Roulette R-25012	(M)	Pearl Bailey A-Broad	1959	8.00	20.00
Roulette R-25016	(M)	Pearl Bailey Sings For Adults Only	1959	6.00	15.00
Roulette SR-25016	(S)	Pearl Bailey Sings For Adults Only	1959	8.00	20.00
Roulette R-25037	(M)	St. Louis Blues	1959	6.00	15.00
Roulette SR-25037	(S)	St. Louis Blues	1959	8.00	20.00
— Original Roulette albums above have black labels.—					
Roulette R-25063	(M)	Porgy And Bess	1959	6.00	15.00
Roulette SR-25063	(S)	Porgy And Bess	1959	8.00	20.00

Label & Catalog #		Title	Year	VG+	NM
Roulette R-25101	(M)	More Songs For Adults Only	1960	6.00	15.00
Roulette SR-25101	(S)	More Songs For Adults Only	1960	8.00	20.00
Roulette R-25116	(M)	Songs Of The Bad Old Days	1960	6.00	15.00
Roulette SR-25116	(S)	Songs Of The Bad Old Days	1960	8.00	20.00
Roulette R-25125	(M)	Naughty But Nice	1960	6.00	15.00
Roulette SR-25125	(S)	Naughty But Nice	1960	8.00	20.00
Roulette R-25144	(M)	The Best Of Pearl Bailey	1961	5.00	12.00
Roulette SR-25144	(S)	The Best Of Pearl Bailey	1961	6.00	15.00
Roulette R-25155	(M)	Songs Of Harold Arlen	1961	5.00	12.00
Roulette SR-25155	(S)	Songs Of Harold Arlen	1961	6.00	15.00
Roulette R-25167	(M)	Happy Sounds	1962	5.00	12.00
Roulette SR-25167	(S)	Happy Sounds	1962	6.00	15.00
Roulette R-25181	(M)	Come On, Let's Play With Pearlie Mae	1962	5.00	12.00
Roulette SR-25181	(S)	Come On, Let's Play With Pearlie Mae	1962	6.00	15.00
		— Original Roulette albums above have white labels.—			
Roulette R-25195	(M)	All About Good Little Girls & Bad Little Boys	1963	5.00	12.00
Roulette SR-25195	(S)	All About Good Little Girls & Bad Little Boys	1963	6.00	15.00
Roulette R-25222	(M)	C'est La Vie	1963	5.00	12.00
Roulette SR-25222	(S)	C'est La Vie	1963	6.00	15.00
Roulette R-25259	(M)	The Risque World Of Pearl Bailey	1964	5.00	12.00
Roulette SR-25259	(S)	The Risque World Of Pearl Bailey	1964	6.00	15.00
RCA Victor LOC-1090	(M)	Les Poupees De Paris (Soundtrack)	1964	14.00	35.00
RCA Victor LSO-1090	(S)	Les Poupees De Paris (Soundtrack)	1964	20.00	50.00
RCA Victor LOC-1147	(M)	Hello, Dolly (Soundtrack)	1964	8.00	20.00
RCA Victor LSO-1147	(S)	Hello, Dolly (Soundtrack)	1964	10.00	25.00
Roulette R-25271	(M)	Songs By James Van Heusen	1964	5.00	12.00
Roulette SR-25271	(S)	Songs By James Van Heusen	1964	5.00	12.00
Roulette R-25300	(M)	For Women Only	1965	6.00	15.00
Roulette SR-25300	(S)	For Women Only	1965	5.00	12.00
Regent MG-6022	(M)	The Jazz Singer	1965	8.00	20.00
Regent MG-6032	(M)	Me And The Blues	1965	8.00	20.00

BAIN, BOB

Capitol T-965	(M)	Rockin,' Rollin' And Strollin'	1958	40.00	100.00
Capitol T-1201	(M)	Latin Love	1959	16.00	40.00
Capitol ST-1201	(S)	Latin Love	1959	20.00	50.00
Capitol T-1500	(M)	Guitar De Amor	1961	12.00	30.00
Capitol ST-1500	(S)	Guitar De Amor	1961	16.00	40.00

BAKER, GEORGE

Colossus CS-1002	(S)	Little Green Bag	1970	6.00	15.00
		("Little Green Bag" is rechanneled on this album.)			

BAKER, GINGER [GINGER BAKER'S AIRFORCE]
Refer to Baker-Gurvitz Army; Blind Faith; Cream.

Atco SD-2-703	(S)	Ginger Baker's Air Force (2 LPs)	1970	8.00	20.00
Atco SD-33-343	(S)	Ginger Baker's Air Force 2	1970	6.00	15.00
Atco SD-7012	(S)	Stratavarious	1972	6.00	15.00

BAKER, JOSEPHINE

Columbia FL-9532 (10")	(M)	Josephine Baker	1951	30.00	75.00
Columbia FL-9533 (10")	(M)	Chansons Americaines	1951	30.00	75.00
Columbia ML-2608 (10")	(M)	Josephine Baker Sings	1952	30.00	75.00
Columbia ML-2609 (10")	(M)	Chansons Americaines	1952	30.00	75.00
Columbia ML-2613 (10")	(M)	Encores Americaines	1952	30.00	75.00
Jolly Roger 5015 (10")	(M)	Josephine Baker	1951	20.00	50.00
Mercury MG-25105 (10")	(M)	The Inimitable Josephine Baker	1952	20.00	50.00
Mercury MG-25151 (10")	(M)	Avec Josephine Baker	1952	20.00	50.00
RCA Victor LPM-2475	(M)	The Fabulous Josephine Baker	1962	12.00	30.00
RCA Victor LSP-2475	(S)	The Fabulous Josephine Baker	1962	16.00	40.00

BAKER, LAVERN

Atlantic 8002	(M)	LaVern	1956	60.00	150.00
Atlantic 8007	(M)	LaVern Baker	1957	60.00	150.00
Atlantic 1281	(M)	LaVern Baker Sings Bessie Smith	1958	50.00	125.00
Atlantic 8030	(M)	Blues Ballads	1959	50.00	125.00
Atlantic 8036	(M)	Precious Memories	1959	50.00	125.00
		— Original Atlantic albums above have black labels.—			

Label & Catalog #		Title	Year	VG+	NM
Atlantic 8002	(M)	LaVern	1961	30.00	75.00
Atlantic 1281	(M)	LaVern Baker Sings Bessie Smith	1961	30.00	75.00
Atlantic SD-1281	(S)	LaVern Baker Sings Bessie Smith	1961	40.00	100.00
Atlantic 8030	(M)	Blues Ballads	1961	24.00	60.00
Atlantic 8050	(M)	Saved	1961	20.00	50.00
Atlantic SD-8050	(S)	Saved	1961	30.00	75.00
Atlantic 8071	(M)	See See Rider	1963	20.00	50.00
Atlantic SD-8071	(S)	See See Rider	1963	30.00	75.00
Atlantic 8078	(M)	The Best Of LaVern Baker	1963	20.00	50.00
Atlantic SD-8078	(P)	The Best Of LaVern Baker	1963	30.00	75.00

—Mono Atlantic albums above have orange & purple labels with a white fan;
stereo albums have green & blue labels with a white fan.—

Brunswick BL-754160	(S)	Let Me Belong To You	1970	8.00	20.00

BAKER, MICKEY
Formerly one half of Mickey & Sylvia. Refer to Champion Jack Dupree; Brother John Sellers.

Atlantic 8035	(M)	Wildest Guitar (Black label)	1959	60.00	150.00
Atlantic SD-8035	(S)	Wildest Guitar (Green label)	1959	80.00	200.00
King 839	(M)	But Wild (Black crownless label)	1963	100.00	250.00
King KS-839	(E)	But Wild (Blue label with a crown)	196?	10.00	25.00

BALDRY, LONG JOHN

Ascot ALM-13022	(M)	Long John's Blues	1965	10.00	25.00
Ascot ALS-16022	(S)	Long John's Blues	1965	12.00	30.00
United Arts. UAS-5543	(S)	Long John's Blues	1971	6.00	15.00

(United Arts. 5543 is a reissue of Ascot 16002.)

Warner Bros. WS-1921	(S)	It Ain't Easy	1971	6.00	15.00
Warner Bros. BS-2614	(S)	Everything Stops For Tea	1972	6.00	15.00

BALIN, MARTY
Marty Balin was a founding member of Jefferson Airplane. Refer to Grootna.

EMI SPRO-9673	(DJ)	Balin (Red vinyl)	1981	5.00	12.00

BALLADEERS, THE

Del-Fi DFLP-1204	(M)	Alive-O	1959	16.00	40.00

BALLARD, FRANK

Phillips Int. 1985	(M)	Rhythm-Blues Party	1962	1,500.00	Rare

(Near Mint copies have a suggested value of $3,000-6,000.)

BALLARD, HANK (& THE MIDNIGHTERS)

Federal 295-90 (10")	(M)	The Midnighters: Their Greatest Hits	1952	1,500.00	Rare

(Near Mint copies have a suggested value of $3,000-6,000.)

Federal 395-541	(M)	The Midnighters: Their Greatest Hits	1955	600.00	Rare

(Near Mint copies have a suggested value of $1,200-2,000.)

Federal 395-581	(M)	The Midnighters, Volume 2	1955	500.00	1,000.00
King 541	(M)	Their Greatest Jukebox Hits	1958	150.00	300.00

(King 541 is a reissue of Federal 541.)

King 581	(M)	The Midnighters, Volume 2	1958	150.00	300.00

(King 541 and 581 are reissues of Federal 541 and 581.)

King 618	(M)	Singin And Swingin'	1959	70.00	175.00
King 674	(M)	The One And Only Hank Ballard	1960	70.00	175.00
King 700	(M)	Mr. Rhythm And Blues	1960	70.00	175.00
King 740	(M)	Spotlight On Hank Ballard	1961	70.00	175.00
King KS-740	(S)	Spotlight On Hank Ballard	1961	100.00	250.00
King 748	(M)	Let's Go Again	1961	40.00	100.00
King 759	(M)	Sing Along	1961	40.00	100.00
King 781	(M)	The Twistin' Fools	1962	40.00	100.00
King 793	(M)	Jumpin' Hank Ballard	1962	40.00	100.00
King 815	(M)	The 1963 Sound Of Hank Ballard	1963	40.00	100.00
King 867	(M)	Biggest Hits	1963	40.00	100.00
King 896	(M)	A Star In Your Eyes	1964	40.00	100.00

—Original King albums above have crownless black labels.—

King 913	(M)	Those Lazy, Lazy Days	1965	30.00	75.00
King 927	(M)	Glad Songs, Sad Songs	1966	30.00	75.00
King 950	(M)	24 Hit Tunes	1966	24.00	60.00
King 981	(M)	24 Great Songs	1968	16.00	40.00
King KSD-1052	(S)	You Keep A Good Man Down	1969	16.00	40.00

(Produced by James Brown.)

Label & Catalog #		Title	Year	VG+	NM

BALLARD, RUSS
Russ Ballard recorded with Argent.

EMI SPRO-9404/5	(DJ)	The Fire Still Burns (2 LPs)	1985	8.00	20.00

BANANA & THE BUNCH
Banana is Lowell Levinger of The Youngbloods.

Raccoon/Warners BS-2626	(S)	Mid Mountain Ranch	1972	4.00	10.00

BANANA SPLITS, THE

Decca DL-75075	(S)	We're The Banana Splits	1969	70.00	175.00
Rhodes Prod.	(S)	We're The Banana Splits (Picture disc)	1985	40.00	100.00

BAND, THE
The Band is Rick Danko, Levon Helm, Garth Hudson, Richard Manuel and Robbie Robertson. Refer to Bob Dylan; John Hammond; Ronnie Hawkins; Steve Miller / Quicksilver / The Band.

Capitol SKAO-2955	(S)	Music From Big Pink	1968	8.00	20.00
Capitol ST-132	(S)	The Band	1969	10.00	25.00
— Original Capitol albums above have black rainbow labels.—					
Capitol SKAO-2955	(S)	Music From Big Pink	1970	5.00	12.00
Capitol ST-132	(S)	The Band	1970	5.00	12.00
Capitol SW-425	(S)	Stage Fright	1970	5.00	12.00
Capitol ST-651	(S)	Cahoots	1971	5.00	12.00
— Capitol albums above have green labels.—					
Capitol SABB-11045	(S)	Rock Of Ages (2 LPs. Red label)	1972	10.00	25.00
Capitol SABB-11045	(S)	Rock Of Ages (2 LPs. Orange label)	1972	6.00	15.00
Capitol SW-11214	(S)	Moondog Matinee	1973	8.00	20.00
		(Orange label. Originally issued with a fold-open "false" cover insert with a painting portraying the group in a bar scene.)			
Warner Bros. PRO-737	(DJ)	The Last Waltz (Sampler)	1978	6.00	15.00
Warner Bros. 3WS-3146	(S)	The Last Waltz (3 LPs)	1978	5.00	12.00
Mobile Fidelity MFSL-039	(S)	Music From Big Pink	198?	15.00	46.00

BANDITS, THE
The Bandits feature Glen Campbell.

World Pacific T-1833	(M)	The Electric 12 String	1964	6.00	15.00
World Pacific ST-1833	(S)	The Electric 12 String	1964	8.00	20.00

BANGLES, THE

Faulty 1302	(S)	The Bangles (5 tracks)	1982	8.00	20.00
Columbia CAS-2270	(DJ)	Interchords (Interview)	1986	10.00	25.00

BANGOR FLYING CIRCUS, THE

Dunhill DS-50069	(S)	The Bangor Flying Circus	1969	6.00	15.00

BANKS, DARRELL

Atco 33-216	(M)	Darrell Banks Is Here	1967	8.00	20.00
Atco SD-33-216	(S)	Darrell Banks Is Here	1967	10.00	25.00
		("Open The Door To Your Heart" is rechanneled for this album.)			
Volt VOS-6002	(S)	Here To Stay	1969	8.00	20.00

BANTAMS, THE

Warner Bros. W-1625	(M)	Beware The Bantams	1966	8.00	20.00
Warner Bros. WS-1625	(S)	Beware The Bantams	1966	10.00	25.00

BAR-KAYS, THE

Volt 417	(M)	Soul Finger	1967	10.00	25.00
Volt S-417	(S)	Soul Finger	1967	8.00	20.00
Volt S-6004	(S)	Gotta Groove	1969	8.00	20.00
Volt S-6011	(S)	Black Rock	1971	6.00	15.00
Volt S-8001	(S)	Do You See What I See?	1972	6.00	15.00
Volt S-6023	(S)	Cold Blooded	1974	6.00	15.00

BARBARIANS, THE

Laurie LLP-2033	(M)	Are You A Boy Or Are You A Girl?	1966	30.00	75.00
Laurie SLP-2033	(S)	Are You A Boy Or Are You A Girl?	1966	60.00	150.00

BARDOT, BRIGITTE

Poplar 33-1002	(M)	The Girl In The Bikini (Soundtrack)	1952	200.00	400.00
Decca DL-8685	(M)	And God Created Woman (Soundtrack)	1957	40.00	100.00

Label & Catalog #		Title	Year	VG+	NM
Warner Bros. W-1371	(M)	**Behind Brigitte Bardot**	*1960*	**12.00**	**30.00**
Warner Bros. WS-1371	(S)	**Behind Brigitte Bardot**	*1960*	**16.00**	**40.00**
Philips PC-204	(M)	**Brigitte Bardot Sings**	*1963*	**12.00**	**30.00**
Philips PCC-604	(S)	**Brigitte Bardot Sings**	*1963*	**16.00**	**40.00**
Burlington-Cameo 1000	(DJ)	**Special Bardot** (TV Soundtrack)	*1968*	**60.00**	**150.00**
BARDS, THE					
Piccadilly PIC-3419	(S)	**The Bards**	*1980*	**8.00**	**20.00**
BARE, BOBBY					
RCA Victor LPM-2776	(M)	**Detroit City And Other Hits**	*1963*	**8.00**	**20.00**
RCA Victor LSP-2776	(S)	**Detroit City And Other Hits**	*1963*	**10.00**	**25.00**
RCA Victor LPM-2835	(M)	**500 Miles Away From Home**	*1963*	**8.00**	**20.00**
RCA Victor LSP-2835	(S)	**500 Miles Away From Home**	*1963*	**10.00**	**25.00**
RCA Victor LPM-2955	(M)	**The Travelin' Bare**	*1964*	**8.00**	**20.00**
RCA Victor LSP-2955	(S)	**The Travelin' Bare**	*1964*	**10.00**	**25.00**
RCA Victor LPM-3336	(M)	**Tunes For Two**	*1965*	**6.00**	**15.00**
RCA Victor LSP-3336	(S)	**Tunes For Two**	*1965*	**8.00**	**20.00**
RCA Victor LPM-3395	(M)	**Constant Sorrow**	*1965*	**6.00**	**15.00**
RCA Victor LSP-3395	(S)	**Constant Sorrow**	*1965*	**8.00**	**20.00**
RCA Victor LPM-3479	(M)	**The Best Of Bobby Bare**	*1965*	**6.00**	**15.00**
RCA Victor LSP-3479	(S)	**The Best Of Bobby Bare**	*1965*	**8.00**	**20.00**
RCA Victor LPM-3515	(M)	**Talk Me Some Sense**	*1966*	**6.00**	**15.00**
RCA Victor LSP-3515	(S)	**Talk Me Some Sense**	*1966*	**8.00**	**20.00**
RCA Victor LPM-3618	(M)	**The Streets Of Baltimore**	*1966*	**6.00**	**15.00**
RCA Victor LSP-3618	(S)	**The Streets Of Baltimore**	*1966*	**8.00**	**20.00**
RCA Victor LPM-3688	(M)	**This I Believe**	*1966*	**6.00**	**15.00**
RCA Victor LSP-3688	(S)	**This I Believe**	*1966*	**8.00**	**20.00**
RCA Victor LPM-3764	(M)	**The Game Of Triangles**	*1967*	**8.00**	**20.00**
RCA Victor LSP-3764	(S)	**The Game Of Triangles**	*1967*	**6.00**	**15.00**
RCA Victor LPM-3831	(M)	**A Bird Named Yesterday**	*1967*	**8.00**	**20.00**
RCA Victor LSP-3831	(S)	**A Bird Named Yesterday**	*1967*	**6.00**	**15.00**
RCA Victor LPM-3896	(M)	**The English Country Side**	*1967*	**8.00**	**20.00**
RCA Victor LSP-3896	(S)	**The English Country Side**	*1967*	**6.00**	**15.00**
RCA Victor LSP-3994	(S)	**The Best Of Bobby Bare, Volume II**	*1968*	**6.00**	**15.00**
		— Original RCA albums above have black labels.—			
BARGE, GENE					
Checker LP-2994	(M)	**Dance With Daddy G**	*1965*	**20.00**	**50.00**
BARKER, WARREN					
Warner Bros. W-1289	(M)	**77 Sunset Strip** (TV Soundtrack)	*1959*	**12.00**	**30.00**
Warner Bros. WS-1289	(S)	**77 Sunset Strip** (TV Soundtrack)	*1959*	**16.00**	**40.00**
Warner Bros. W-1290	(M)	**TV Guide/Top TV Themes**	*1959*	**10.00**	**25.00**
Warner Bros. WS-1290	(S)	**TV Guide/Top TV Themes**	*1959*	**12.00**	**30.00**
BARNES, GEORGE					
Decca DL-8658	(M)	**Guitars By George**	*1957*	**16.00**	**40.00**
BARNES, J. J., & STEVE MANCHA					
Volt VOS-6001	(S)	**Rare Stamps**	*1969*	**6.00**	**15.00**
BARNES, MAE					
Atlantic ALS-404 (10")	(M)	**Fun With Mae Barnes**	*1953*	**200.00**	**400.00**
BARNETT, BOBBY					
Sims 198	(M)	**At The World Famous Crystal Palace**	*1964*	**12.00**	**30.00**
BAROQUE INEVITABLE, THE					
Columbia CL-2587	(M)	**The Baroque Inevitable Album**	*1966*	**5.00**	**12.00**
Columbia CS-9387	(S)	**The Baroque Inevitable Album**	*1966*	**6.00**	**15.00**
BAROQUES, THE					
Chess LP-1516	(M)	**The Baroques**	*1967*	**16.00**	**40.00**
Chess LPS-1516	(S)	**The Baroques**	*1967*	**20.00**	**50.00**
BARRACUDAS, THE					
Justice 143	(M)	**A Plane View**	*1968*	**150.00**	**300.00**

Label & Catalog #		Title	Year	VG+	NM
BARRIER BROTHERS, THE					
Philips PHM-200-003	(M)	**Golden Bluegrass Hits**	1962	10.00	25.00
Philips PHS-600-003	(S)	**Golden Bluegrass Hits**	1962	12.00	30.00
Philips PHM-200-049	(M)	**More Golden Bluegrass Hits**	1962	10.00	25.00
Philips PHS-600-049	(S)	**More Golden Bluegrass Hits**	1962	12.00	30.00
Philips PHM-200-083	(M)	**Gospel Songs, Bluegrass Style**	1962	10.00	25.00
Philips PHS-600-083	(S)	**Gospel Songs, Bluegrass Style**	1962	12.00	30.00
BARRY & THE TAMERLANES					
Valiant LP-406	(M)	**I Wonder What She's Doing Tonight**	1963	60.00	150.00
Valiant LPS-406	(S)	**I Wonder What She's Doing Tonight**	1963	300.00	500.00
BARRY, GENE					
RCA Victor LPM-2975	(M)	**The Star Of "Burke's Law" Sings**	1964	6.00	15.00
RCA Victor LSP-2975	(S)	**The Star Of "Burke's Law" Sings**	1964	8.00	20.00
BARRY, JEFF					
Jeff Barry was formerly a member of The Raindrops.					
A&M SP-4393	(S)	**Walkin' In The Sun**	1973	5.00	12.00
BARRY, LEN					
Len Barry was formerly a member of The Dovells.					
Decca DL-4720	(M)	**1-2-3**	1965	10.00	25.00
Decca DL-74720	(S)	**1-2-3**	1965	12.00	30.00
		("Lip Sync" is rechanneled for this album.)			
RCA Victor LPM-3823	(M)	**My Kind Of Soul**	1967	6.00	15.00
RCA Victor LSP-3823	(S)	**My Kind Of Soul**	1967	8.00	20.00
Buddah BDS-5105	(S)	**Ups & Downs**	1972	6.00	15.00
BARTHOLOMEW, DAVE					
Imperial LP-9162	(M)	**Fats Domino Presents David Bartholomew**	1961	30.00	75.00
Imperial LP-12076	(S)	**Fats Domino Presents David Bartholomew**	1961	40.00	100.00
Imperial LP-9217	(M)	**New Orleans House Party**	1963	30.00	75.00
Imperial LP-12217	(S)	**New Orleans House Party**	1963	40.00	100.00
BARTLEY, CHARLENE					
RCA Victor LPM-1478	(M)	**Weekend Of A Private Secretary**	1957	10.00	25.00
BASKERVILLE HOUNDS, THE					
Dot DLP-3823	(M)	**The Baskerville Hounds**	1967	16.00	40.00
Dot DLP-25823	(S)	**The Baskerville Hounds**	1967	20.00	50.00
BASS, FONTELLA					
Checker LP-2997	(M)	**The New Look**	1966	10.00	25.00
Checker LPS-2997	(S)	**The New Look**	1966	14.00	35.00
Paula LPS-2203	(S)	**Free**	1972	4.00	10.00
BATTERED ORNAMENTS					
Harvest SKAO-422	(S)	**Mantle-Piece**	1970	14.00	35.00
BAUGH, PHIL					
Longhorn LP-002	(M)	**Country Guitar**	1965	24.00	60.00
Toro T-502	(M)	**Country Guitar II**	1965	16.00	40.00
Era ES-801	(S)	**California Guitar**	196?	12.00	30.00
BAYSIDERS, THE					
Everest LPBR-5124	(M)	**Over The Rainbow**	1961	60.00	150.00
Everest BRST-5124	(S)	**Over The Rainbow**	1961	100.00	250.00
BE-BOP DELUXE					
Harvest ST-11432	(S)	**Futurama**	1976	4.00	10.00
Harvest ST-11478	(S)	**Sunburst Finish**	1976	4.00	10.00
Harvest SPRO-8531	(DJ)	**Be-Bop's Biggest**	1976	12.00	30.00
Harvest SKBB-11666	(DJ)	**Live! In The Air Age** (2 LPs)	1977	10.00	25.00
Harvest ST-11575	(S)	**Modern Music**	1977	4.00	10.00
Harvest ST-11689	(S)	**Axe Victim**	1977	4.00	10.00
Harvest SW-11750	(DJ)	**Drastic Plastic** (White vinyl)	1978	8.00	20.00
Harvest SW-11750	(S)	**Drastic Plastic**	1978	4.00	10.00
Harvest SKBO-11870	(S)	**The Best Of & The Rest Of** (2 LPs)	1978	4.00	10.00

Label & Catalog #		Title	Year	VG+	NM

BEACH BOYS, THE

Original members were Brian Wilson with brothers Carl and Dennis, cousin Mike Love, and neighbor Al Jardine. Jardine left in 1963 and returned in 1964, replaced during that time by David Marks. With Brian's increasing involvement in producing the group's albums, his role in the touring band was filled by Bruce Johnston. Johnston left in 1971 over difficulties with management; he returned in 1978. From 1971 through 1973, Rickie Fataar and Blondie Chaplin, formerly of The Flame, were Beach Boys.

The group initially laid down a set of tracks in the tiny studios of Hite Morgan; their first single, "Surfin'" / "Luau," was issued on Morgan's "X" and Candix labels in November 1961. They also released a second Morgan single on Randy as Kenny & The Cadets. After signing with Capitol in '62, their early recordings languished until the end of the decades, when they were issued on the budget label, Era. They have since appeared on sundry labels, several of which are hard to find. The first section below lists several of those albums; note that along with the Candix and Randy sides, there are several outtakes and filler from other Morgan groups.

The Beach Boys were produced by Brian Wilson through 1967, although Capitol staff producer is credited on the first two albums and the group is credited on "Smiley Smile" and "Wild Honey." Brian is virtually deaf in one ear so he works exclusively in mono; stereo mixes that exist during this time were done by engineer Chuck Britz. Capitol 1890, 1981, 2164 and 2198 were issued completely in stereo; 1998, 2027 and 2110 are partially stereo. The other albums— 1808, 2269, 2354, 2398, 2458, 2545, 2813, 2859 and Brother 9001— are "duophonically" (sic) rechanneled. On SKAO-133 "Do It Again" and "Time To Get Alone" are rechanneled while the original 1966 tracks for "Our Prayer" and "Cabinessence" are mono with additional stereo overdubs.

Section 1. includes the earliest albums tomcontain the Hite Morgan recordings. While these records often turn up for a cuppla bucks at shows, finding them in NM condition can be difficult. Section 2. covers the Capitol years, the main source of collector interest. The listings of the group's Capitol catalog below include every known variation of the original black rainbow label, record club versions and other important reissues. Several albums remained in print through the '70s and '80s; the prefix was changed to "SM" and at least five albums were reissued with a yellow label. In the early '80s several albums— including the long out of print post '66 tiles— were reinstated as part of the label's budget series (the 16000 series with green labels). At this time, most of these reissues are easily found. . .

The interested reader can peruse the Capitol listings in the Various Artists section and safely assume that any surf or hot rod compilation features The Beach Boys. Of particlular note are 1918 (the first Shut Down, an automotive sampler compiled without the group's knowledge and from whence Shut Down, Volume 2 derived its name) and both 1995 and 2024 along with PRO 2396 and 2480. These albums could easily function as Beach Boys titles. . .

Section 3. gathers together tose items of collectible interest fromthe group's rejuvenation of their Brother Records imprint under the wing of Warner/Reprise. and their stay with CBS' Caribou subsidiary. For more listtings refer to Annette; Jan & Dean; Brian, Carl, Dennis and Murray Wilson.

1. Hite Morgan Recordings 1961

Label & Catalog #		Title	Year	VG+	NM
Era HTE-805	(M)	The Beach Boys' Biggest Beach Hits	1969	8.00	20.00
Orbit OR-688	(M)	The Beach Boys' Greatest Hits (1961-63)	1972	5.00	12.00
Wand WDS-688	(M)	The Beach Boys' Greatest Hits (1961-63)	1972	5.00	12.00
Scepter CTN-18004	(M)	The Best Of Beach Boys	1972	5.00	12.00
Springboard SPB-4021	(M)	The Beach Boys 1961	1977	4.00	10.00
Gateway GSLP-10104	(M)	Surfing With The Beach Boys, The Marketts And Frogmen	1979	4.00	10.00
Everest 4108	(M)	Rare Early Recordings	1981	4.00	10.00

2. The Capitol Years, 1962-69

Label & Catalog #		Title	Year	VG+	NM
Capitol T-1808	(M)	Surfin' Safari	1962	20.00	50.00
Capitol DT-1808	(E)	Surfin' Safari	1962	30.00	75.00
		(Originally issued in a "Full Dimensional Stereo" cover.)			
Capitol DT-1808	(E)	Surfin' Safari	1963	16.00	40.00
		(Second pressings have the correct "Duophonic Stereo" cover.)			
Capitol T-1890	(M)	Surfin' U.S.A.	1963	14.00	35.00
Capitol ST-1890	(S)	Surfin' U.S.A.	1963	16.00	40.00
Capitol T-1981	(M)	Surfer Girl	1963	14.00	35.00
Capitol ST-1981	(S)	Surfer Girl	1963	16.00	40.00
		(Original covers mention the influence of The Four Freshmen style on "Your Summer Dreams" in the liner notes on the back.)			

Label & Catalog #		Title	Year	VG+	NM
Capitol T-1981	(M)	**Surfer Girl**	1963	16.00	40.00
Capitol ST-1981	(S)	**Surfer Girl**	1963	20.00	50.00
		(Later pressings make mention of "Their other new single-record hit Little Deuce Coupe" in the liner notes on the back.)			
Capitol T-1998	(M)	**Little Deuce Coupe**	1963	14.00	35.00
Capitol ST-1998	(S)	**Little Deuce Coupe**	1963	16.00	40.00
Capitol ST-1998	(S)	**Little Deuce Coupe** *(Red label)*	197?	6.00	15.00
Capitol T-2027	(M)	**Shut Down, Volume 2**	1964	14.00	35.00
Capitol ST-2027	(P)	**Shut Down, Volume 2**	1964	16.00	40.00
		("Fun, Fun, Fun" is a shorter, different mix on the stereo album.)			
Capitol T-2110	(M)	**All Summer Long**	1964	16.00	40.00
Capitol ST-2110	(S)	**All Summer Long**	1964	20.00	50.00
		(The front cover erroneously lists the last song on the album as "Don't Break Down.")			
Capitol T-2110	(M)	**All Summer Long**	1964	14.00	35.00
Capitol ST-2110	(P)	**All Summer Long**	1964	16.00	40.00
		(The front cover correctly lists the last song on the album as "Don't Back Down.")			
Capitol T-2164	(M)	**The Beach Boys' Christmas Album**	1964	14.00	35.00
Capitol ST-2164	(S)	**The Beach Boys' Christmas Album**	1964	16.00	40.00
		("Merry Christmas Baby" is 28 seconds longer on the stereo album than on the mono.)			
Capitol SM-502164	(S)	**The Beach Boys' Christmas Album**	197?	6.00	15.00
		(Columbia Record Club also known as 2P-6508.)			
Capitol R-133854	(S)	**The Beach Boys' Christmas Album**	197?	6.00	15.00
		(RCA Record Club)			
Capitol PRO-3133	(DJ)	**The Beach Boys Christmas Special**	1964	200.00	400.00
		(Promotional radio show built around the group's new LP.)			
Capitol TAO-2198	(M)	**Beach Boys Concert**	1964	14.00	35.00
Capitol STAO-2198	(S)	**Beach Boys Concert**	1964	16.00	40.00
Capitol STAO-8-2198	(S)	**Beach Boys Concert** *(Record Club)*	1964	30.00	75.00
Capitol T-2269	(M)	**The Beach Boys Today!**	1965	16.00	40.00
Capitol DT-2269	(E)	**The Beach Boys Today!**	1965	14.00	35.00
Capitol DT-8-2269	(E)	**The Beach Boys Today!** *(Record Club)*	1965	30.00	75.00
Capitol T-2354	(M)	**Summer Days (And Summer Nights!!)**	1965	16.00	40.00
Capitol DT-2354	(E)	**Summer Days (And Summer Nights!!)**	1965	20.00	50.00
		(DT-2354 was originally issued with an erroneous "Full Dimensional Stereo" banner across the top of the cover.)			
Capitol DT-2354	(E)	**Summer Days (And Summer Nights!!)**	1965	14.00	35.00
		(Later pressings have the correct "Duophonic Stereo" banner across the top of the cover.)			
Capitol MAS-2398	(M)	**Beach Boys Party!**	1965	16.00	40.00
Capitol DMAS-2398	(E)	**Beach Boys Party!**	1965	14.00	35.00
		(Issued with a sheet of perforated wallet photos.)			
Capitol MAS-2398	(M)	**Beach Boys Party!**	1965	12.00	30.00
Capitol DMAS-2398	(E)	**Beach Boys Party!**	1965	10.00	25.00
		(The prices above are for the albums without the photos.)			
Capitol T-2458	(M)	**Pet Sounds**	1966	12.00	30.00
Capitol DT-2458	(E)	**Pet Sounds**	1966	10.00	25.00
Capitol T-2545	(M)	**Best Of The Beach Boys, Volume 1**	1966	10.00	25.00
Capitol DT-2545	(E)	**Best Of The Beach Boys, Volume 1**	1966	8.00	20.00
		(Black rainbow label.)			
Capitol T-2545	(M)	**Best Of The Beach Boys, Volume 1**	1966	12.00	30.00
Capitol DT-2545	(E)	**Best Of The Beach Boys, Volume 1**	1966	10.00	25.00
		(Black Starline label.)			
Capitol T-2545	(M)	**Best Of The Beach Boys, Volume 1**	1967	16.00	40.00
Capitol DT-2545	(E)	**Best Of The Beach Boys, Volume 1**	1967	6.00	15.00
		(Red & white "bullseye" Starline label.)			
Capitol DT-2545	(E)	**Best Of The Beach Boys, Volume 1**	1969	10.00	25.00
		(Red & white "star" Starline label.)			
Capitol DT-2545	(E)	**Best Of The Beach Boys, Volume 1**	1970	6.00	15.00
		(Green Starline label)			
Capitol DT-502545	(E)	**Best Of The Beach Boys, Volume 1**	197?	6.00	15.00
		(Columbia Record Club)			
Capitol R-123946	(E)	**Best Of The Beach Boys, Volume 1**	197?	6.00	15.00
		(RCA Record Club)			
Capitol DT-602524	(E)	**Best Of The Beach Boys, Volume 1**	197?	6.00	15.00
		(Record Club of America)			

Label & Catalog #		Title	Year	VG+	NM
Capitol T-2580	(M)	Smile	1966		See note below
Capitol DT-2580	(E)	Smile	1966		See note below
		("Smile" remains Brian Wilson's legendary unreleased masterpiece. For Christmas 1966 Capitol printed 400,000 front and back cover slicks and a similar number of booklets with graphics and lyrics. Both the cover slicks and the booklets are priced separately below.)			
Capitol T/DT-2580		Smile Cover Slick (Reproductions exist)	1966	300.00	Rare
		(Near Mint copies have a suggested value of $500-1,000.)			
Capitol T/DT-2580		Smile Bonus Book (Reproductions exist)	1966	100.00	300.00
Capitol T-2706	(M)	Best Of The Beach Boys, Volume 2	1967	10.00	25.00
Capitol DT-2706	(E)	Best Of The Beach Boys, Volume 2	1967	6.00	15.00
		(Red & white "bullseye" Starline label.)			
Capitol DT-2706	(E)	Best Of The Beach Boys, Volume 2	1969	6.00	15.00
		(Red & white "star" Starline label.)			
Capitol DT-502706	(E)	Best Of The Beach Boys, Volume 2	1970	6.00	15.00
		(Green Starline label)			
Capitol DT-502706	(E)	Best Of The Beach Boys, Volume 2	197?	10.00	25.00
		(Columbia Record Club)			
Brother T-9001	(M)	Smiley Smile	1967	12.00	30.00
Brother ST-9001	(E)	Smiley Smile	1967	8.00	20.00
		(First pressing covers do not credit Barry Turnbull.)			
Brother T-9001	(M)	Smiley Smile	1967	10.00	25.00
Brother ST-9001	(E)	Smiley Smile	1967	6.00	15.00
		(Later pressings read "Title for this album by Barry Turnbull" on the back cover)			
Capitol TCL-2813	(M)	The Beach Boys Deluxe Set (3 LP box)	1967	80.00	200.00
		(The mono box has a black border and contains standard copies of the albums with a "T" prefix.)			
Capitol DTCL-2813	(E)	The Beach Boys Deluxe Set (3 LP box)	1967	30.00	75.00
		(The stereo box has a maroon border and contains custom copies of the albums with a "DTCL" prefix.)			
Capitol DTCL-8-2813	(E)	The Beach Boys Deluxe Set (Record Club)	1967	100.00	250.00
		(The stereo box has a blue border and contains custom copies of the albums with a "DTCL" prefix.)			
Capitol T-2859	(M)	Wild Honey	1967	12.00	30.00
Capitol ST-2859	(E)	Wild Honey	1967	8.00	20.00
Capitol ST-8-2891	(E)	Smiley Smile (Record Club)	1968	150.00	300.00
Capitol DKAO-2893	(E)	Stack O' Tracks (With booklet)	1968	30.00	75.00
Capitol DKAO-2893	(E)	Stack O' Tracks (Without booklet)	1968	16.00	40.00
Capitol DKAO-8-2893	(E)	Stack O' Tracks (Record Club with booklet)	1968	60.00	150.00
Capitol ST-2895	(S)	Friends	1968	10.00	25.00
Capitol DKAO-2945	(P)	Best Of The Beach Boys, Volume 3	1969	6.00	15.00
		(Black rainbow label.)			
Capitol DKAO-2945	(P)	Best Of The Beach Boys, Volume 3	1969	8.00	20.00
		(Red & white "star" Starline label.)			
Capitol SKAO-133	(P)	20/20 (Black rainbow label)	1969	10.00	25.00
Capitol SKAO-133	(P)	20/20 (Red & white "star" Starline label)	1969	12.00	30.00
Capitol SKAO-8-0133	(P)	20/20 (Record Club. Black label)	1969	16.00	40.00
Capitol SKAO-8-0133	(P)	20/20 (Record Club. Green label)	197?	20.00	50.00
Capitol SWBB-253	(E)	Close-Up (2 LPs. Black rainbow label)	1969	8.00	20.00
Capitol SWBB-253	(E)	Close-Up (2 LPs. Green label)	197?	16.00	40.00
Sears SPS-609	(E)	Summertime Blues	1970	20.00	50.00
		(Sears 608 reissues material from the first two Capitol albums.)			
Capitol ST-442	(P)	Good Vibrations (Green label)	1970	6.00	15.00
Capitol DT-8-442	(P)	Good Vibrations (Record Club)	1970	10.00	25.00
Capitol ST-442	(P)	Good Vibrations (Orange label)	1972	8.00	20.00
Capitol STBB-500	(E)	All Summer Long / California Girls	1970	8.00	20.00
		(Lime label. Two single albums, edited versions of 2110 and 2354, bound together with a Special Double Play sticker.			
Capitol STBB-500	(E)	All Summer Long / California Girls (2 LPs)	1971	12.00	30.00
		(Orange label with a purple "C" on top. This is two single albums bound together with a Special Double Play sticker.)			
Capitol SF-8-0501	(E)	All Summer Long (Capitol Record Club)	1971	4.00	10.00
Capitol SF-500501	(E)	All Summer Long (Columbia Record Club)	1971	4.00	10.00
Capitol DF-8-0502	(E)	California Girls (Capitol Record Club)	1971	4.00	10.00
Capitol SF-500502	(E)	California Girls (Columbia Record Club)	1971	4.00	10.00
Capitol STBB-701	(P)	Fun, Fun, Fun / Dance, Dance, Dance	1970	8.00	20.00
		(Lime label. Two single albums, edited versions of 2027 and 2269, bound together with a Special Double Play sticker.)			

This little printing defect identifies The Beach Boys' first album as being in both "Duophonic For Stereo Phonogrpahs" (i.e., electronically created from a mono signal) and "Full Dimensional Stereo." This occurred when the cover slicks were improperly trimmed and pasted on the cover. Normally, the [incorrect] "Full Dimensional Stereo" banner would have been covered over by the [correct] Duophonic banner. While such errors are probably inevitable, thier occurrence in the face of hundreds of thousands of copies printed are miniscule. While such an error will doubtfully attract the interest of a few Beach Boy completists, had this been a Beatles title it would instantly command big bucks.

Label & Catalog #		Title	Year	VG+	NM
Capitol SF-702/DF-703	(P)	**Fun, Fun, Fun / Dance, Dance, Dance** *(2 LPs.)*	1971	12.00	30.00
		(Orange label with a purple "C" on top. This is two single albums bound together with a Special Double Play sticker.)			
Capitol ST-8-0702	(P)	**Fun, Fun, Fun** *(Record Club)*	1971	4.00	10.00
Capitol DF-8-0703	(E)	**Dance, Dance, Dance** *(Record Club)*	1971	4.00	10.00
Capitol R-233593	(P)	**American Summer** *(RCA Record Club)*	1975	4.00	10.00
Capitol SVBB-511307	(P)	**Endless Summer** *(Columbia RecordClub)*	1974	6.00	15.00
Capitol R-223559	(P)	**Endless Summer** *(RCA RecordClub)*	1974	6.00	15.00
Capitol SVBB-511384	(P)	**Spirit Of America** *(Columbia RecordClub)*	1975	6.00	15.00
Capitol SLB-6994	(P)	**Golden Years Of The Beach Boys** *(2 LPs)*	1975	6.00	15.00
Capitol ST-11584	(S)	**Beach Boys '69 (Live In London)**	1976	4.00	10.00
Candlelite SLB-6994	(P)	**The Golden Years Of The Beach Boys** *(2 LPs)*	1975	6.00	15.00
Ronco R-2230	(P)	**Beach Boys Super Hits**	1978	4.00	10.00
Sessions SLB-8134	(P)	**The Beach Boys** *(2 LPs)*	1980	6.00	15.00
Mobile Fidelity MFSL-116	(S)	**Surfer Girl**	198?	6.00	18.00

3. Brother/Reprise And Caribou

Label & Catalog #		Title	Year	VG+	NM
Reprise RS-6382	(DJ)	**Sunflower** *(White label)*	1970	12.00	30.00
Reprise RS-6382	(S)	**Sunflower** *(Orange label)*	1970	30.00	75.00
Capitol SKAO-93352	(S)	**Sunflower** *(Capitol Record Club)*	1970	60.00	150.00
Reprise RS-6453	(DJ)	**Surf's Up** *(White label)*	1971	16.00	40.00
Reprise RS-6453	(S)	**Surf's Up** *(With lyric sheet)*	1971	4.00	10.00
Reprise R-113793	(S)	**Surf's Up** *(RCA Record Club)*	1971	8.00	20.00
Asylum R-113793	(S)	**Surf's Up** *(RCA Record Club)*	1971	60.00	150.00
Reprise 2MS-2083	(DJ)	**Carl And The Passion-So Tough / Pet Sounds** *(2 LPs. White label)*	1972	12.00	30.00
Reprise 2MS-2083	(S)	**Carl And The Passion-So Tough / Pet Sounds** *(2 LPs)*	1972	8.00	20.00
Reprise MS-2118	(DJ)	**Holland** *(Test pressing with "We Got Love")*	1973	300.00	500.00
Reprise MS-2118	(DJ)	**Holland** *(White label)*	1973	16.00	40.00
		(Issued with a white label EP, "Mt. Vernon & Fairway," with a PS.)			
Reprise MS-2118	(S)	**Holland**	1973	6.00	15.00
		(Issued with an EP, "Mt. Vernon & Fairway," in a PS, taped to the back cover; small tape tears in the EP sleeve are common)			
Reprise 2MS-6484	(DJ)	**Beach Boys In Concert** *(2 LPs. White label)*	1973	12.00	30.00
Reprise 2MS-6484	(S)	**The Beach Boys In Concert** *(2 LPs)*	1973	5.00	12.00
Reprise R-223569	(S)	**The Beach Boys In Concert** *(2 LPs)*	1973	6.00	15.00
		(RCA Record Club.)			
Reprise 2MS-2166	(DJ)	**Wild Honey / 20/20** *(2 LPs)*	1974	10.00	25.00
Reprise 2MS-2166	(S)	**Wild Honey / 20/20** *(2 LPs)*	1974	6.00	15.00
Reprise 2MS-2167	(DJ)	**Friends / Smiley Smile** *(2 LPs)*	1974	10.00	25.00
Reprise 2MS-2167	(S)	**Friends / Smiley Smile** *(2 LPs)*	1974	6.00	15.00
Reprise MS-2197	(M)	**Pet Sounds**	1974	6.00	15.00
Reprise MS-2223	(S)	**Good Vibrations-Best Of The Beach Boys**	1975	6.00	15.00
Reprise *(No number)*	(DJ)	**The Beach Boys Radio Special Promo Spot**	1976	12.00	30.00
— *Original Reprise albums above have yellow labels without the Warner Communication logo.*—					
Reprise MS-2251	(S)	**15 Big Ones**	1976	3.50	8.00
Reprise MS-2258	(S)	**The Beach Boys Love You**	1977	3.50	8.00
Reprise MS-2269	(S)	**M.I.U. Album**	1978	3.50	8.00
Caribou JZ-35752	(DJ)	**L.A. (Light Album)** *(White label)*	1979	6.00	15.00
Caribou JZ-35752	(S)	**L.A. (Light Album)**	1979	3.50	8.00
Caribou JZ-36293	(DJ)	**Keepin' The Summer Alive** *(White label)*	1980	6.00	15.00
Caribou JZ-36293	(S)	**Keepin' The Summer Alive**	1980	3.50	8.00

BEACON STREET UNION
The Beacon Street Union later recorded as Eagle.

MGM E-4517	(M)	**The Eyes Of The Beacon Street Union**	1968	8.00	20.00
MGM SE-4517	(S)	**The Eyes Of The Beacon Street Union**	1968	12.00	25.00
MGM SE-4568	(S)	**The Clown Died In Marvin Gardens**	1968	12.00	25.00

BEAGLES, THE, & THE FOUR LIVERPOOL WHIGS

Sutton SU-329	(M)	**I Want To Hold Your Hand & Other Favorites**	1964	12.00	25.00
Sutton SSU-329	(S)	**I Want To Hold Your Hand & Other Favorites**	1964	12.00	30.00

BEAGLES, THE

Harmony HL-14561	(M)	**Here Come The Beagles**	1967	5.00	12.00
Harmony HS-14561	(S)	**Here Come The Beagles**	1967	6.00	15.00

Label & Catalog #		Title	Year	VG+	NM
BEANS					
Avalanche 9200	(S)	**Beans**	1971	8.00	20.00
BEAR					
Verve/Forecast FTS-3059	(S)	**Greetings**	1969	6.00	15.00
BEAR, YOGI, & THE THREE STOOGES					
HBR HLP-2050	(M)	**The Mad, Mad Dr. No No**	1962	20.00	50.00
BEAR, YOGI					
Colpix CP-472	(M)	**Hey There, It's Yogi Bear** *(TV Soundtrack)*	1964	20.00	50.00
Colpix SCP-472	(S)	**Hey There, It's Yogi Bear** *(TV Soundtrack)*	1964	30.00	75.00
BEARCUTS, THE					
Somerset P-20800	(M)	**Beatlemania**	1964	10.00	25.00
Somerset SP-20800	(S)	**Beatlemania**	1964	12.00	30.00
BEASLEY, JIMMY					
Modern LMP-1214	(M)	**The Fabulous Jimmy Beasley**	1956	100.00	250.00
Crown CLP-5014	(M)	**The Fabulous Jimmy Beasley**	1957	40.00	100.00
Crown CLP-5247	(M)	**Twist With Jimmy Beasley**	1961	20.00	50.00
Crown CST-247	(E)	**Twist With Jimmy Beasley**	1961	8.00	20.00
BEAT-A-MANIA					
Spectrum 172	(M)	**Beat-A-Mania**	1964	10.00	25.00
BEAT OF THE EARTH					
Ardish AS-001	(S)	**Beat Of The Earth**	196?	150.00	300.00
BEATLE BUDDIES, THE					
Diplomat D-2313	(M)	**The Beatle Buddies**	1964	8.00	20.00
Diplomat DS-2313	(S)	**The Beatle Buddies**	1964	10.00	25.00

BEATLES, THE

The Beatles are the single most collectible group in the hobby; every variation in sound, label or cover is pursued, documented and valued among aficionados. While the listings here are more than adequate for most dealers and collectors to assess their acquisitions, they may be less so for the completist. I recommend The Beatles Price Guide For American Records by Perry Cox and Joe Lindsay. For more information on this book, contact Perry Cox Ent., P.O. Box 82278, Phoenix, AZ 85071.

Prior to international stardom, John Lennon, Paul McCartney and George Harrison with drummer Pete Best backed up Tony Sheridan on a number of studio sessions recorded in Hamburg, Germany, in 1961 (they were billed as "The Beat Brothers"). After the group's initial U.S. success in 1964, a number of companies recycled thesesides on various 45s and LPs. By 1962 Mr. Best was history and Richard Starkey, a.k.a. Ringo Starr, was about to make history as The Beatles' irrepressible drummer. Their now legendary audition for Decca Records (who, ahem, saw no commercial potential in a British beat group) made the rounds of various labels after a copyright lapse in 1982. For chronological purposes, the Decca and Hamburg material (including live recordings) are listed below in Section 1, "Early Recordings 1962."

The group finally signed with Parlophone, an EMI subsidiary, which was both a last ditch effort (Parlophone was a budget label with no major stars to claim) and arguably their greatest stroke of luck, as it placed them under the talented and sympathetic wing of staff producer George Martin. After taking most of the civilized world by storm in 1963, EMI offered them to their American licensee, Capitol, who, like Decca U.K., saw no reason to bite. Consequently, their first recordings ended up on a variety of smaller, independent U.S. labels, the most significant being Vee Jay (aside from being the only label to have enough material to issue an LP).

Section 2, "Vee Jay 1963-1964," lists the many attempts of that company to successfully package the fourteen tracks to which they possessed the rights. As Vee Jay issued mono albums with stereo labels, check for an "S" suffix on the master number in the trail-off vinyl. Also, many counterfeits of the Vee Jay albums exist.

Section 3, "Capitol Originals 1964-1967," covers the main period of the group's history in this country. During this time all of the group's new recordings were issued on Capitol, who had finally picked up their option on the group's American releases in late 1963, except the new songs prepared for the film "A Hard Day's Night," to which United Artists had the rights in this country. So the third section collects the Capitol releases, including later pressings, and Capitol Record Club issues (designated with an "8" added to their catalogue number), along with the United Artists material. This section also includes what must surely be the most collectible album in the world, the now-legendary Beatles butcher cover...

The "butcher" cover. *Capitol 2553, "Yesterday" ...And Today was a U.S. only compilation of tracks cribbed from the group's previous EMI album releases. The original cover photo for this album depicted the smiling Fabs dressed in butcher's smocks, covered with pieces of raw meat and baby doll parts. Capitol, after pressing up hundreds of thousands of covers and sending out advance copies, did a turnabout and pulled the album from distribution almost immediately. A new cover with an innocuous photo of an unsmiling, some might say dour, group posing around a steamer trunk, was designed. Rather than destroy the original covers, Capitol simply pasted this new "trunk" cover over the "butcher cover" and sent them back out to their distributors. This has created a situation for collectors where this album has a variety of terms applied to it according to the state the cover is in:*

"First state" refers to the original cover as it was manufactured. That is, the butcher cover has never had the trunk cover pasted over it. First-state stereo butcher covers are the most talked-about and widely sought-after LPs in and outside of the hobby. The Beatles Price Guide For American Records recommends "to lightly moisten a small piece of tissue paper. Gently press the moistened tissue on any area of the front cover and allow to dry. If the cover is a true first-state the tissue will brush or blow off easily. If the [tissue] paper sticks to the cover, it is most likely not a first-state." (That is, it is a third state, discussed below.)

"Second state" refers to the album as it was sent out for sale with the trunk cover pasted over the original butcher cover. Whether or not a copy of the album is a second-state is readily apparent: The black "V" of Ringo's sweater on the original cover can be seen through the paste-over midway up the right side of the cover, beneath the album title. Second states are also referred to as "paste-overs."

"Third state" refers to the various attempts to make a second state a first state. That is, to remove the trunk cover from the butcher cover. These are also referred to as "peel jobs." Of course the success of the peel would dictate the value of the third-state; the closer to Near Mint the finished peel looks the more it would be worth to a collector seeking a first-state but unable or unwilling to pay for a first-state. Poorly peeled copies are a staple of the hobby and yet, even covers that have been decimated by hasty fingers are in demand and fetch hundreds of dollars from some would-be owner. If a lightly moistened piece of tissue paper drys and adheres to what appears to be a first-state cover, it indicates that is more than likely a first-rate peel.

Due to the fact that so many collectors are interested in owning an original butcher cover, the stock of second states are being depleted (especially in light of the contemporary means of removing the extraneous cover using chemicals that dissolve the adhesive without marring the paper). Collectors— and historians— should consider the fact that it is the existence of the second state covers that are the centerpiece for this bit of cultural history and that without them, the story is incomplete. Should every collector remove their trunk cover to reveal the butcher cover below, eventually the second state covers would become rarer than the first states.

Of particular note are still-sealed "butcher cover." Sealed first and second-state butchers command a hefty premium, but it is the first state that deserves some attention here. A still-sealed first-state stereo butcher cover currently ranks as the most sought-after album in the hobby. In the past few years, at least four copies have sold in excess of $10,000 with two of them topping $15,000. The next few years will probably see this particular item reach undreamt of heights. . .

Collecting still-sealed Beatles albums represents a real test for the diehard: Factory sealed Capitol albums are easily worth three times the listed Near Mint value. While any sealed mono album is an original (mono was discontinued by Capitol in 1968 and thus saw none of the later label changes) stereo albums are a different matter. The easiest way to identify an original stereo album in a sealed jacket is to tap the album till the inner sleeve is flush against the plastic wrap along the edge. As Capitol invariably issued all their albums in different colored paper sleeves (advertising other LPs), the appearance of such a colored sleeve would almost certainly assure an original stereo album within.

These parameters apply to most of the other companies who manufactured Beatles albums during the '60s with the sole exception of Vee Jay. Unfortunately, due to complications brought about by the company's financial problems in 1963 and 1964, one can never be sure that the record in a cover matches that cover. So, in the case of Vee Jay albums, it is in the interest of both the buyer and the seller to know exactly what any given Vee Jay cover holds.

These albums along with all of the others in Section 3 were all issued on Capitol's classic black label with the rainbow perimeter. This particular label is not to be confused with two later permutations: The original '60s version has the perimeter data along the bottom in white print on the black label and reads "Mfd. by Capitol Records, Inc., U.S.A." A second version of this label, used briefly in 1969, is identical to the above except the perimeter data reads "Mfd. by Capitol Records, Inc. A Subsidiary of Capitol Industries, Inc. U.S.A." After undergoing several major color changes through the next fourteen years, Capitol returned to the black label in 1983 except this time the perimeter data was in black print in the rainbow.

Label & Catalog #		Title	Year	VG+	NM

With the formation of their own Apple Records in 1968, things become complicated: Aside from new titles being issued exclusively on Apple (listed in Section 5, "Apple Originals, 1968-1973"), the earlier catalog titles were kept in print on Capitol and reissued on Apple with the same covers and catalog numbers. Further complicating matters is the fact that early pressings of the Apple reissues can be found inside Capitol covers. (And, for the O/C, later copies of Meet The Beatles, The Beatles' Second Album, Beatles '65, Beatles VI and "Yesterday" ...And Today can be found with and without the RIAA Gold Record seal on the cover.) The reissues can be found in Section 4, "Capitol & Apple Reissues 1968-1974."

After the collapse of Apple, the material reverted to Capitol and has remained in print since. From 1976-78 the entire catalog of albums were reissued with an orange label followed by a purple label during 1978-83. From 1983-88 the company brought back the black rainbow label (noted above). It was during this time that Capitol issued the Parlophone versions for the first time. Finally, in 1988, a second purple label was used and all of the albums were reissued, this time with new catalog numbers (the Parlophone versions were also in print on this label). While these variations are nor listed below, most are readily found in shops and shows fetching $6-12 each. Note: The orange label pressings and the latter purple label issues are quickly escalating in value and may bring $15 or more from completists.

Section 6, "Capitol Repackagings 1976-1984," lists the new titles composed of previously released material including Capitol's finally releasing the original Parlophone versions of the first seven albums. Section 7, "Miscellaneous Releases," collects a few odds 'n' ends while while Section 8 collect the Original Master Recording and Ultra High Quality Recording audiophile releases from Mobile Fidelity Sound Labs.

A number of Beatles recordings are rather difficult;t to track down in stereo, especially if the reader has a basic collection made up of the American albums. For more information on how to assemble a more or less complete stereo catalog, refer to the appendix "The Beatles Uncommon Stereo."

In the wake of 1964's Beatlemania in the U.S., the inevitable exploitation of the group, their sound and their image, commenced with a vengeance. While countless artists recorded Lennon-McCartney songs and several entire albums of the Fabs' music, it is the "exploitation records" that attract some collectors interest. For those with a taste for the obscure, the hilarious, the offensive and, occasionally, the creative, refer to The Beagle & The Four Liverpool Whigs; The Bearcuts; Beat-A-Mania; The Beatle Buddies; The Beats; Pete Best (yes, he was a Beatle briefly but this is exploitational nonetheless); The Blue Beats; B. Brock & The Sultans; The Buggs; Louise Harrison Caldwell (George's sister tells all); The Liverpool Lads; The Liverpools; The Merseybeats; The Merseyboys; Sing Along With The Beatles; The Sparrows; and The Weasels. Also refer to Elvis Presley / The Silver Beatles.

1. Early Recordings 1962

— Tony Sheridan Sessions —

Label & Catalog #		Title	Year	VG+	NM
Savage BM-69	(M)	The Savage Young Beatles	1964	60.00	150.00
		(This album of dubious legality collects Tony Sheridan material with and without The Beat Brothers. Orange label and a yellow cover. Counterfeits have "Stereo" in the upper right corner of the cover.)			
Savage BM-69	(M)	The Savage Young Beatles	1964	660.00	Rare
		(Some copies have a yellow label and a glossy orange cover. Near Mint copies have a suggested value of $1,000-1,500.)			
Atco 33-169	(DJ)	Ain't She Sweet	1964	500.00	1,000.00
Atco 33-169	(M)	Ain't She Sweet	1964	80.00	200.00
Atco SD-33-169	(S)	Ain't She Sweet	1964	150.00	300.00
		(Original stereo pressings have purple & brown labels.)			
Atco SD-33-169	(S)	Ain't She Sweet	1969	200.00	400.00
		(Later pressings have yellow labels with a white border on the cover.)			
MGM E-4215	(M)	The Beatles With Tony Sheridan & Their Guests & Others	1964	80.00	200.00
MGM SE-4215	(S)	The Beatles With Tony Sheridan & Their Guests & Others	1964	300.00	500.00
MGM E-4215	(M)	The Beatles With Tony Sheridan & Their Guests	1964	60.00	150.00
MGM SE-4215	(S)	The Beatles With Tony Sheridan & Their Guests	1964	200.00	400.00
		(Later pressings drop "& Others" from the cover title.)			
Metro M-563	(M)	This Is Where It Started	1966	30.00	75.00
Metro MS-563	(S)	This Is Where It Started	1966	60.00	150.00
		(Metro 563 is a reissue of MGM 4215.)			
Clarion 601	(M)	The Amazing Beatles & Other Great English Group Sounds	1966	50.00	125.00
Clarion SD-601	(S)	The Amazing Beatles & Other Great English Group Sounds	1966	100.00	250.00
		(Clarion 601 is a reissue of Atco 169.)			

Label & Catalog #		Title	Year	VG+	NM
Polydor 24-4504	(S)	The Beatles Circa 1960: In The Beginning Featuring Tony Sheridan (Red label)	1970	8.00	20.00
Polydor SKAO-93199	(S)	The Beatles Circa 1960: In The Beginning Featuring Tony Sheridan (Record Club)	1970	16.00	40.00
Polydor PD-4504	(S)	In The Beginning: The Beatles	197?	16.00	40.00
		(This rare reissue alters the LP's title.)			

— Live In Germany—

Lingasong LS-2-7001	(DJ)	Live! At The Star-Club In Hamburg, Germany; 1962 (2 LPs. Blue vinyl)	1977	180.00	300.00
Lingasong LS-2-7001	(DJ)	Live! At The Star-Club In Hamburg, Germany; 1962 (2 LPs. Red vinyl)	1977	50.00	125.00
Lingasong LS-2-7001	(DJ)	Live! At The Star-Club In Hamburg, Germany; 1962 (2 LPs. Black vinyl)	1977	12.00	30.00
Lingasong LS-2-7001	(E)	Live! At The Star-Club In Hamburg, Germany; 1962 (2 LPs)	1977	6.00	15.00

—Decca Audition Sessions—

Backstage BSR-1111	(M)	Like Dreamers Do (Gray vinyl promo)	1982	12.00	30.00
Backstage BSR-1111	(M)	Like Dreamers Do (White vinyl promo)	1982	10.00	25.00
Backstage BSR-1111	(M)	Like Dreamers Do (3 LPs)	1982	12.00	30.00
		(Two picture discs, one an interview and one from the Decca sessions with a white vinyl LP that duplicates the Decca disc. Contains ten of the fifteen Decca audition tracks.)			
Backstage 2-201	(M)	Like Dreamers Do (2 LPs)	1982	10.00	25.00
		(Double album of the above with one picture disc and the white LP. Contains ten of the fifteen Decca audition tracks.)			
Pac UDL-2333	(M)	Dawn Of The Silver Beatles	1981	30.00	75.00
		(First pressings were hand numbered on the label and back cover. Contains ten of the fifteen Decca audition tracks.)			
Pac UDL-2333	(M)	Dawn Of The Silver Beatles	1981	20.00	50.00
		(Second pressings included numbered registration cards. Contains ten of the fifteen Decca audition tracks.)			
Audio Rarities AR-2452	(M)	The Complete Silver Beatles	1982	6.00	15.00
		(Contains twelve of the fifteen Decca audition tracks.)			
Orange ORC-12280	(M)	The Silver Beatles (Half-speed master)	1985	80.00	200.00
		(Test pressing in a plain jacket with a full-color cover-slick insert. Contains all fifteen of the Decca audition tracks.)			
Orange ORC-12280	(M)	The Silver Beatles (Half-speed master)	1985	60.00	150.00
		(Test pressing in a plain cardboard jacket with a title sticker. Contains all fifteen of the Decca audition tracks.)			

2. Vee Jay, 1963-1964

Vee Jay LP-1062	(M)	Introducing The Beatles ("Ad back")	1963	2,000.00	3,000.00
Vee Jay SR-1062	(P)	Introducing The Beatles ("Ad back")	1963	3,000.00	Rare
		(Includes "Love Me Do" and "P.S. I Love You." The back cover has ads for 25 other Vee Jay albums. Near Mint stereo copies have a suggested value of $6,000-10,000.)			
Vee Jay LP-1062	(M)	Introducing The Beatles ("Blank back")	1963	800.00	1,200.00
Vee Jay SR-1062	(P)	Introducing The Beatles ("Blank back")	1963	1,800.00	3,000.00
		(Includes "Love Me Do" and "P.S. I Love You." The back cover is completely blank.)			
Vee Jay LP-1062	(M)	Introducing The Beatles	1963	200.00	400.00
		(Includes "Love Me Do" and "P.S. I Love You." Black rainbow label with an oval logo. The back cover lists the song titles.)			
Vee Jay LP-1062	(M)	Introducing The Beatles	1963	300.00	500.00
		(Includes "Love Me Do" and "P.S. I Love You." Black rainbow label with a brackets logo. The back cover lists the song titles.)			
Vee Jay LP-1062	(M)	Introducing The Beatles	1964	200.00	400.00
Vee Jay SR-1062	(S)	Introducing The Beatles	1964	1,000.00	2,000.00
		(Includes "Please Please Me" and "Ask Me Why." Black rainbow label with a "Vee Jay" logo in an oval.)			
Vee Jay LP-1062	(M)	Introducing The Beatles	1964	100.00	250.00
Vee Jay SR-1062	(S)	Introducing The Beatles	1964	1,000.00	2,000.00
		(Includes "Please Please Me" and "Ask Me Why." Black rainbow label a "Vee Jay' logo in brackets.)			

Label & Catalog #		Title	Year	VG+	NM
Vee Jay LP-1062	(M)	**Introducing The Beatles**	1964	150.00	300.00
Vee Jay SR-1062	(S)	**Introducing The Beatles**	1964	1,000.00	2,000.00
		(Includes "Please Please Me" and "Ask Me Why." Solid black label with plain "VJ" logo.)			
Vee Jay LP-1062	(M)	**Introducing The Beatles**	1964	150.00	300.00
		(Includes "Please Please Me" and "Ask Me Why." Solid black label with the "VJ" logo in an oval.)			
Vee Jay LP-1062	(M)	**Introducing The Beatles**	1964	200.00	400.00
		(Includes "Please Please Me" and "Ask Me Why." Solid black label with "VJ" logo in brackets.)			
Vee Jay LP-1085	(M)	**The Beatles And Frank Ifield On Stage**	1964	100.00	250.00
Vee Jay LPS-1085	(P)	**The Beatles And Frank Ifield On Stage**	1964	300.00	500.00
		(The cover has a drawing of a Victorian gentleman with a Beatles haircut. Original covers have printing along the spine.)			
Vee Jay LP-1085	(M)	**The Beatles And Frank Ifield On Stage**	1964	2,000.00	3,000.00
Vee Jay LPS-1085	(P)	**The Beatles And Frank Ifield On Stage**	1964	4,000.00	Rare
		(The cover has a full-color, painted portrait of John, Paul, George and Ringo. Counterfeits have slightly blurred covers, no printing on the spine, and the markings in the disc's trail-off area are almost illegible. This was issued with three labels— black rainbow with oval or brackets logo and plain black— with most of the value in the cover. Near Mint stereo copies have a suggested value of $6,000-12,000.)			
Vee Jay DX-30	(M)	**The Beatles Vs. The Four Seasons** (2 LPs)	1964	300.00	500.00
Vee Jay DXS-30	(S)	**The Beatles Vs. The Four Seasons** (2 LPs)	1964	1,200.00	2,000.00
		(Vee Jay 30 repackages 1065, "Golden Hits Of The Four Seasons," with the second version of Vee Jay 1062, "Introducing The Beatles." Original front covers must read "Free Bonus 8" x 15" Full Color Beatle Picture Suitable For Framing," priced separately below.)			
Vee Jay DXS-30		**The Beatles Vs. The Four Seasons Bonus**	1964	180.00	300.00
Vee Jay VJ-1092	(M)	**Songs, Pictures And Stories Of The Fabulous Beatles** (Gatefold cover)	1964	200.00	400.00
Vee Jay VJS-1092	(S)	**Songs, Pictures And Stories Of The Fabulous Beatles** (Gatefold cover)	1964	1,000.00	2,000.00
		(Vee Jay 1092 repackages the second version of Vee Jay 1062, with the black rainbow label with the oval logo.)			
Vee Jay VJ-1092	(M)	**Songs, Pictures And Stories Of The Fabulous Beatles** (Gatefold cover)	1964	180.00	300.00
Vee Jay VJS-1092	(S)	**Songs, Pictures And Stories Of The Fabulous Beatles** (Gatefold cover)	1964	1,000.00	2,000.00
		(Vee Jay 1092 repackages the second version of Vee Jay 1062, with the black rainbow label with the brackets logo.)			
Vee Jay VJ-1092	(M)	**Songs, Pictures And Stories Of The Fabulous Beatles** (Gatefold cover)	1964	180.00	300.00
Vee Jay VJS-1092	(S)	**Songs, Pictures And Stories Of The Fabulous Beatles** (Gatefold cover)	1964	1,000.00	2,000.00
		(Vee Jay 1092 repackages the second version of Vee Jay 1062, with the solid black label with silver print.)			
Vee Jay PRO-202	(DJ)	**Hear The Beatles Tell All** (White label)	1964	3,000.00	Rare
		(Near Mint copies have a suggested value of $6,000-10,000.)			
Vee Jay PRO-202	(M)	**Hear The Beatles Tell All**	1964	60.00	150.00
		(Original pressings have black rainbow labels. Counterfeits have plain black labels and no print on the spine of the cover.)			
Vee Jay 202	(M)	**Hear The Beatles Tell All**	1964	100.00	250.00
		(Later pressings have black rainbow labels but drop the "PRO" prefix from the catalog number.)			

3. Capitol Originals 1964-1967

Label & Catalog #		Title	Year	VG+	NM
Capitol T-2047	(M)	**Meet The Beatles**	1964	35.00	85.00
Capitol ST-2047	(P)	**Meet The Beatles**	1964	24.00	60.00
		(Original front covers have "Beatles!" in a brown print.)			
Capitol T-2047	(M)	**Meet The Beatles**	1964	30.00	75.00
Capitol ST-2047	(P)	**Meet The Beatles**	1964	20.00	50.00
		(Later front covers have "Beatles!" in an olive green print.)			
Capitol ST-8-2047	(P)	**Meet The Beatles** (Record Club)	1964	150.00	300.00
Capitol T-2080	(M)	**The Beatles' Second Album**	1964	30.00	75.00
Capitol ST-2080	(P)	**The Beatles' Second Album**	1964	20.00	50.00
Capitol ST-8-2080	(P)	**The Beatles' Second Album** (Record Club)	1964	200.00	400.00

Label & Catalog #		Title	Year	VG+	NM
United Artists SP-2359	(DJ)	**A Hard Day's Night** *(Open-end interview)*	1964	800.00	1,200.00
		(Issued with a script in a plain cardboard jacket.)			
United Artists SP-2362	(DJ)	**A Hard Day's Night** *(Radio Spots)*	1964	660.00	1,000.00
		(Issued in a plain cardboard jacket.)			
United Artists UAL-3366	(DJ)	**A Hard Day's Night** *(White label)*	1964	*See note below*	
		(Rare with suggested values in collectible condition of 2,000-3,000.)			
United Artists UAL-3366	(M)	**A Hard Day's Night** *(Soundtrack)*	1964	60.00	150.00
United Artists UAS-6366	(P)	**A Hard Day's Night** *(Soundtrack)*	1964	80.00	200.00
		(Black label. The back cover correctly lists "I'll Cry Instead."			
		Note that four tracks are by George Martin & Orchestra			
		on this and all subsequent pressings.)			
United Artists UAL-3366	(M)	**A Hard Day's Night** *(Soundtrack)*	1964	40.00	100.00
United Artists UAS-6366	(P)	**A Hard Day's Night** *(Soundtrack)*	1964	60.00	150.00
		(Black label. The back cover incorrectly lists "I Cry Instead.")			
United Artists T-90828	(M)	**A Hard Day's Night** *(Sdtk. Record Club)*	1964	500.00	750.00
United Artists ST-90828	(P)	**A Hard Day's Night** *(Sdtk. Record Club)*	1964	300.00	500.00
United Artists UAS-6366	(P)	**A Hard Day's Night** *(Soundtrack)*	1968	16.00	40.00
		(Pink & orange label)			
United Artists UAS-6366	(P)	**A Hard Day's Night** *(Soundtrack)*	1970	12.00	30.00
		(Pink & black label)			
United Artists UAS-6366	(P)	**A Hard Day's Night** *(Soundtrack)*	1971	60.00	150.00
		(Tan label. The back cover is completely blank.)			
Capitol T-2108	(M)	**Something New**	1964	30.00	75.00
Capitol ST-2108	(S)	**Something New**	1964	20.00	50.00
Capitol ST-8-2108	(S)	**Something New** *(Record Club)*	1964	150.00	300.00
Capitol TBO-2222	(M)	**The Beatles' Story** *(2 LPs)*	1964	40.00	100.00
Capitol STBO-2222	(P)	**The Beatles' Story** *(2 LPs)*	1969	30.00	75.00
		(Assembled and produced by Gary Usher and Roger Christian.)			
Capitol T-2228	(M)	**Beatles '65**	1964	30.00	75.00
Capitol T-2228	(P)	**Beatles '65**	1964	20.00	50.00
Capitol T-2309	(M)	**The Early Beatles**	1965	30.00	75.00
Capitol ST-2309	(P)	**The Early Beatles**	1965	20.00	50.00
Capitol T-2358	(M)	**Beatles VI**	1965	35.00	85.00
Capitol ST-2358	(P)	**Beatles VI**	1965	24.00	60.00
		(The back cover reads "See label for correct playing order.")			
Capitol ST-8-2358	(P)	**Beatles VI** *(Record Club)*	1965	200.00	400.00
Capitol T-2358	(M)	**Beatles VI**	1965	30.00	75.00
Capitol ST-2358	(P)	**Beatles VI**	1965	20.00	50.00
		(Second pressings list the tracks in correct order.)			
United Artists Help-A/B	(DJ)	**Help!** *(Radio spots)*	1965	660.00	1,000.00
		(Issued in a plain cardboard jacket.)			
United Artists Help-INT	(DJ)	**Help!** *(Open-end Interview)*	1965	900.00	1,500.00
		(Issued with a script in a plain cardboard jacket.)			
United Artists Help-Show	(DJ)	**Help!** *(One-sided open-end interview)*	1965	1,300.00	2,000.00
		(Issued with a script in a plain cardboard jacket.)			
Capitol MAS-2386	(M)	**Help!** *(Soundtrack)*	1965	30.00	75.00
Capitol SMAS-2386	(P)	**Help!** *(Soundtrack)*	1965	20.00	50.00
		(Note that six tracks are by George Martin & Orchestra			
		on this and all subsequent pressings.)			
Capitol SMAS-8-2386	(P)	**Help!** *(Soundtrack. Record Club)*	1965	150.00	300.00
		(The cover catalogue number is SMAS-2386.)			
Capitol SMAS-8-2386	(P)	**Help!** *(Soundtrack. Record Club)*	1965	300.00	500.00
		(The cover catalogue number is SMAS-8-2386.)			
Capitol T-2442	(M)	**Rubber Soul**	1965	30.00	75.00
Capitol ST-2442	(S)	**Rubber Soul**	1965	20.00	50.00
Capitol ST-8-2442	(S)	**Rubber Soul** *(Record Club)*	1965	150.00	300.00
Capitol T-2553	(M)	**"Yesterday" ...And Today** *("Butcher cover")*	1966	2,000.00	3,000.00
Capitol ST-2553	(P)	**"Yesterday" ...And Today** *("Butcher cover")*	1966	3,000.00	Rare
		(First state butcher cover. Refer to the notes in the text at the be-			
		ginning of THE BEATLES listing above. Near Mint stereo copies have			
		a suggested value of $5,000-10,000, all which is for the cover alone.			
		Copies of the black rainbow label LP can be found for $10-30.)			
Capitol T-2553	(M)	**"Yesterday" ...And Today** *("Butcher cover")*	1966	500.00	800.00
Capitol ST-2553	(P)	**"Yesterday" ...And Today** *("Butcher cover")*	1966	1,300.00	2,000.00
		(Second state butcher cover. Refer to the notes in the text at the			
		beginning of THE BEATLES listing above. The price is for the cover;			
		copies of the black rainbow label can be found for $10-30.)			

Label & Catalog #		Title	Year	VG+	NM
Capitol T-2553	(M)	"Yesterday" ...And Today ("Butcher cover")	1966	See note below	
Capitol ST-2553	(P)	"Yesterday" ...And Today ("Butcher cover")	1966	See note below	
		(Third state butcher cover. Refer to the notes in the text at the beginning of THE BEATLES listing above for complete details on this title. Suggested values for mono copies in collectible condition would be $250-750. Suggested values for stereo copies in collectible condition would be $500-1,500.)			
Capitol T-2553	(M)	"Yesterday" ...And Today ("Trunk cover")	1966	30.00	75.00
Capitol ST-2553	(P)	"Yesterday" ...And Today ("Trunk cover")	1966	20.00	50.00
		(Trunk cover. Black rainbow label without "A Subsidiary of Capitol." All subsequent pressings of this album feature this "trunk cover." Refer to the notes in the text at the beginning of THE BEATLES listing above for complete details on this title.)			
Capitol ST-8-2553	(P)	"Yesterday" ...And Today (Record Club)	1966	150.00	300.00
Capitol T-2576	(M)	Revolver	1966	30.00	75.00
Capitol ST-2576	(S)	Revolver	1964	20.00	50.00
Capitol ST-8-2576	(S)	Revolver (Record Club)	1966	150.00	300.00
Capitol MAS-2653	(M)	Sgt. Pepper's Lonely Heart's Club Band	1967	60.00	150.00
Capitol SMAS-2653	(S)	Sgt. Pepper's Lonely Heart's Club Band	1967	20.00	50.00
		(Issued in a gatefold cover with a sheet of cutouts and a psychedelic inner sleeve. Counterfeits were issued in a standard, single-pocket jacket, a plain white inner sleeve and without the cut-outs.)			
Capitol MAL-2835	(M)	Magical Mystery Tour	1967	80.00	200.00
		(Gatefold covers; counterfeits have single-pocket covers.)			
Capitol SMAL-2835	(P)	Magical Mystery Tour	1967	20.00	50.00

— Original Capitol albums above have black labels without "A Subsidiary of Capitol" on the bottom.—

4. Capitol & Apple Reissues 1968-1974

Label & Catalog #		Title	Year	VG+	NM
Capitol ST-2047	(P)	Meet The Beatles	1969	16.00	40.00
Capitol ST-2080	(P)	The Beatles' Second Album	1969	16.00	40.00
Capitol ST-2108	(S)	Something New	1969	16.00	40.00
Capitol STBO-2222	(P)	The Beatles' Story	1969	20.00	50.00
Capitol ST-2228	(P)	Beatles '65	1969	16.00	40.00
Capitol ST-2309	(P)	The Early Beatles	1969	16.00	40.00
Capitol ST-2358	(P)	Beatles VI	1969	16.00	40.00
Capitol SMAS-8-2386	(P)	Help! (Soundtrack)	1969	16.00	40.00
Capitol ST-2442	(S)	Rubber Soul	1969	16.00	40.00
Capitol ST-2553	(P)	"Yesterday" ...And Today	1969	16.00	40.00
Capitol ST-2576	(S)	Revolver	1969	16.00	40.00
Capitol SMAS-2653	(S)	Sgt. Pepper's Lonely Heart's Club Band	1969	16.00	40.00
Capitol SMAL-2835	(P)	Magical Mystery Tour	1969	16.00	40.00

— Capitol albums above have black rainbow labels with "A Subsidiary of Capitol" on the bottom.—

Label & Catalog #		Title	Year	VG+	NM
Capitol ST-2047	(P)	Meet The Beatles	1969	16.00	40.00
Capitol ST-8-2047	(P)	Meet The Beatles (Record Club)	1969	60.00	150.00
Capitol ST-2080	(P)	The Beatles' Second Album	1969	16.00	40.00
Capitol ST-8-2080	(P)	The Beatles' Second Album (Record Club)	1969	80.00	200.00
Capitol ST-2108	(S)	Something New	1969	16.00	40.00
Capitol ST-8-2108	(S)	Something New (Record Club)	1969	60.00	150.00
Capitol ST-8-2108	(S)	Something New (Longines Sym. issue)	1969	80.00	200.00
Capitol STBO-2222	(P)	The Beatles' Story (2 LPs)	1969	20.00	50.00
Capitol ST-2228	(P)	Beatles '65	1969	16.00	40.00
Capitol ST-2309	(P)	The Early Beatles	1969	16.00	40.00
Capitol ST-2358	(P)	Beatles VI	1969	16.00	40.00
Capitol ST-8-2358	(P)	Beatles VI (Record Club)	1969	80.00	200.00
Capitol SMAS-2386	(P)	Help! (Soundtrack)	1969	16.00	40.00
Capitol SMAS-8-2386	(P)	Help! (Soundtrack. Record Club)	1969	80.00	200.00
		(The cover catalogue number is SMAS-2386.)			
Capitol SMAS-8-2386	(P)	Help! (Soundtrack. Record Club)	1969	150.00	300.00
		(The cover catalogue number is SMAS-8-2386.)			
Capitol ST-2442	(S)	Rubber Soul	1969	16.00	40.00
Capitol ST-8-2442	(S)	Rubber Soul (Record Club)	1969	60.00	150.00
Capitol ST-2553	(P)	"Yesterday" ...And Today	1969	16.00	40.00
Capitol ST-8-2553	(P)	"Yesterday" ...And Today (Record Club)	1969	60.00	150.00
Capitol ST-2576	(S)	Revolver	1969	12.00	30.00
Capitol ST-2576	(S)	Revolver (Red label)	197?	60.00	150.00
Capitol ST-8-2576	(S)	Revolver (Record Club)	1969	60.00	150.00

Label & Catalog #		Title	Year	VG+	NM
Capitol ST-2576	(S)	**Revolver** *(Orange label)*	*1976*	**40.00**	**100.00**
Capitol SMAS-2653	(S)	**Sgt. Pepper's Lonely Heart's Club Band**	*1969*	**16.00**	**40.00**
Capitol SMAL-2835	(P)	**Magical Mystery Tour**	*1969*	**16.00**	**40.00**

— Capitol albums above have lime-green labels except where noted,.—

Apple ST-2047	(P)	**Meet The Beatles**	*1969*	**16.00**	**40.00**
Apple ST-2080	(P)	**The Beatles' Second Album**	*1969*	**16.00**	**40.00**
Apple ST-2108	(S)	**Something New**	*1969*	**16.00**	**40.00**
Apple ST-2222	(P)	**The Beatles' Story** *(2 LPs)*	*1969*	**20.00**	**50.00**
Apple ST-2228	(P)	**Beatles '65**	*1969*	**16.00**	**40.00**
Apple ST-2309	(P)	**The Early Beatles**	*1969*	**16.00**	**40.00**
Apple ST-2358	(P)	**Beatles VI**	*1969*	**16.00**	**40.00**
Apple ST-2386	(P)	**Help!** *(Soundtrack)*	*1969*	**16.00**	**40.00**
Apple ST-2442	(S)	**Rubber Soul**	*1969*	**16.00**	**40.00**
Apple ST-2553	(P)	**"Yesterday" ...And Today**	*1969*	**16.00**	**40.00**
Apple ST-2576	(S)	**Revolver**	*1969*	**16.00**	**40.00**
Apple SMAS-2653	(S)	**Sgt. Pepper's Lonely Heart's Club Band**	*1969*	**16.00**	**40.00**
Apple SMAL-2835	(P)	**Magical Mystery Tour**	*1969*	**16.00**	**40.00**

— Apple albums above have green Apple labels with "A Subsidiary of Capitol" on the bottom.—

Apple ST-2047	(P)	**Meet The Beatles**	*1971*	**6.00**	**15.00**
Apple ST-2080	(P)	**The Beatles' Second Album**	*1971*	**6.00**	**15.00**
Apple ST-2108	(S)	**Something New**	*1971*	**6.00**	**15.00**
Apple ST-2222	(P)	**The Beatles' Story** *(2 LPs)*	*1971*	**8.00**	**20.00**
Apple ST-2228	(P)	**Beatles '65**	*1971*	**6.00**	**15.00**
Apple ST-2309	(P)	**The Early Beatles**	*1971*	**6.00**	**15.00**
Apple ST-2358	(P)	**Beatles VI**	*1971*	**6.00**	**15.00**
Apple ST-2386	(P)	**Help!** *(Soundtrack)*	*1971*	**6.00**	**15.00**
Apple ST-2442	(S)	**Rubber Soul**	*1971*	**6.00**	**15.00**
Apple ST-2553	(P)	**"Yesterday" ...And Today**	*1971*	**6.00**	**15.00**
Apple ST-2576	(S)	**Revolver**	*1971*	**6.00**	**15.00**
Apple SMAS-2653	(S)	**Sgt. Pepper's Lonely Heart's Club Band**	*1971*	**6.00**	**15.00**
Apple SMAL-2835	(P)	**Magical Mystery Tour**	*1971*	**6.00**	**15.00**

— Apple albums above have green Apple labels with "Mfd. by Apple Records" on the bottom.—

Apple ST-2047	(P)	**Meet The Beatles**	*1975*	**8.00**	**20.00**
Apple ST-2080	(P)	**The Beatles' Second Album**	*1975*	**8.00**	**20.00**
Apple ST-2108	(S)	**Something New**	*1975*	**8.00**	**20.00**
Apple ST-2222	(P)	**The Beatles' Story** *(2 LPs)*	*1975*	**10.00**	**25.00**
Apple ST-2228	(P)	**Beatles '65**	*1975*	**8.00**	**20.00**
Apple ST-2309	(P)	**The Early Beatles**	*1975*	**8.00**	**20.00**
Apple ST-2358	(P)	**Beatles VI**	*1975*	**8.00**	**20.00**
Apple ST-2386	(S)	**Help!** *(Soundtrack)*	*1975*	**8.00**	**20.00**
Apple ST-2442	(S)	**Rubber Soul**	*1975*	**8.00**	**20.00**
Apple ST-2553	(P)	**"Yesterday" ...And Today**	*1975*	**8.00**	**20.00**
Apple ST-2576	(S)	**Revolver**	*1975*	**8.00**	**20.00**
Apple SMAS-2653	(S)	**Sgt. Pepper's Lonely Heart's Club Band**	*1975*	**8.00**	**20.00**
Apple SMAL-2835	(P)	**Magical Mystery Tour**	*1975*	**8.00**	**20.00**

— Apple albums above have green Apple labels with an "All rights reserved" disclaimer.—

5. Apple Originals 1968-1974

Apple SWBO-101	(S)	**The Beatles** *(2 LPs)*	*1968*	**40.00**	**100.00**

(First pressing labels read "A subsidiary of Capitol" on the bottom. First pressing covers have "The Beatles" in raised white letters and are sequentially numbered 1-3,000,000 in black. Copies with numbers under #10,000 affect the value— under #1,000, the value is raised substantially. Issued with a fold-open poster/lyric sheet and four glossy, full-color portraits of the group, included in the price. Note: Because of the lack of graphics on the front and back cover, this album is also known as "The White Album.")

Apple SWBO-101	(S)	**The Beatles** *(2 LPs)*	*1968*	**200.00**	**400.00**

(First pressing same as above with a large, fluorescent red sticker on the front cover with song titles, etc.)

Apple SWBO-101	(S)	**The Beatles** *(2 LPs)*	*1968*	**100.00**	**250.00**

(First pressing same as above with a small sticker on the back cover with song titles, etc.)

Label & Catalog #		Title	Year	VG+	NM
Apple SWBO-101	(S)	**The Beatles** *(2 LPs)*	1968	**28.00**	70.00
		(First pressing without the poster and photos.)			
Apple SWBO-101	(S)	**The Beatles** *(2 LPs)*	1969	**24.00**	60.00
		(Second pressing label read "Manufactured by Apple" on the bottom. Covers are similar to the first except there is no number stamped on the cover. Issued with the poster and the four glossy photos.)			
Apple SWBO-101	(S)	**The Beatles** *(2 LPs)*	1969	**12.00**	30.00
		(Second pressing without the poster and photos.)			
Apple SWBO-101	(S)	**The Beatles** *(2 LPs)*	1975	**24.00**	60.00
		(Third pressing labels have an "All rights reserved" disclaimer. This and all subsequent pressings have the title printed in black on the cover and the photos are on thin stock with less gloss.)			
Apple KAL-1004	(DJ)	**Yellow Submarine** *(Radio spots)*	1968	**1,000.00**	Rare
		(Near Mint copies have a suggested value of $2,000-3,000.)			
Apple SW-153	(P)	**Yellow Submarine**	1969	**10.00**	25.00
		(First pressing labels read "A subsidiary of Capitol" on the bottom. Note that side two is by George Martin & Orchestra on this and all subsequent pressings.)			
Apple SW-153	(P)	**Yellow Submarine**	1969	**6.00**	15.00
		(Second pressing label read "Mfd. by Apple" on the bottom.)			
Apple SW-153	(P)	**Yellow Submarine**	1975	**8.00**	20.00
		(Third pressing labels have an "All rights reserved" disclaimer.)			
Apple SO-383	(S)	**Abbey Road**	1969	**12.00**	30.00
		(First pressing labels read "A subsidiary of Capitol" on the bottom. "Her Majesty" is listed on the cover and the label.)			
Apple SO-383	(S)	**Abbey Road**	1969	**10.00**	25.00
		(First pressing labels read "A subsidiary of Capitol" on the bottom. "Her Majesty" is not listed on either the cover or the label.)			
Apple SO-383	(S)	**Abbey Road**	1969	**6.00**	15.00
		(Second pressing label read "Mfd. by Apple" on the bottom. and may or may not list "Her Majesty" on the cover or label. Counterfeits exist; the print and colors tend to be fuzzy.)			
Apple SO-383	(S)	**Abbey Road**	1975	**8.00**	20.00
		(Third pressing labels have an "All rights reserved" disclaimer. This and all subsequent Capitol pressings list "Her Majesty.")			
Apple SO-385	(S)	**Beatles Again** *(Alternate covers)*	1970		See note below
		(At least two variations were made for this album when its title was "Beatles Again." One has the same photos but the back cover is purple while the other has the front and back photos reversed. Suggested values in collectible condition are $4,000-8,000 each.)			
Apple SO-385	(S)	**Hey Jude/The Beatles Again**	1970	**8.00**	20.00
		(First pressings read "Manufactured by Apple" on the label and have an "SO" prefix. While the title on the cover is "Hey Jude," on the label it is "The Beatles Again.")			
Apple SW-385	(S)	**Hey Jude/The Beatles Again**	1970	**10.00**	25.00
		(Second pressings read "Manufactured by Apple" on the label. and have an "SW" prefix. While the title on the cover is "Hey Jude," on the label it is "The Beatles Again.")			
Apple SW-385	(S)	**Hey Jude**	1970	**20.00**	50.00
		(Third pressings read "Manufactured by Capitol" on the label. Both the cover and the label on this and all subsequent Apple and Capitol pressings list the title as "Hey Jude.")			
Apple SW-385	(S)	**Hey Jude**	1970	**6.00**	15.00
		(Fourth pressing label read "Mfd. by Apple" on the bottom.)			
Apple SW-385	(S)	**Hey Jude**	1975	**8.00**	20.00
		(Fifth pressing labels have an "All rights reserved" disclaimer.)			
Apple AR-34001	(S)	**Let It Be**	1970	**10.00**	25.00
		(Red Apple label. Originals have "Bell Sound" stamped in the trail-off vinyl; counterfeits do not.)			
Apple SBC-100	(M)	**The Beatles Christmas Album** *(Fan club)*	1970	**100.00**	250.00
		(Convincing counterfeits exist: Both the photos on the cover— especially the background details— and the print in the trail-off vinyl are slightly blurred.)			
Apple SKBO-3403	(P)	**The Beatles 1962-1966** *(2 LPs)*	1973	**8.00**	20.00
		(First pressings have custom Apple labels.)			
Apple SKBO-3403	(P)	**The Beatles 1962-1966** *(2 LPs)*	1975	**10.00**	25.00
		(Second pressing labels have an "All rights reserved" disclaimer.)			
Apple SKBO-3404	(P)	**The Beatles 1967-1970** *(2 LPs)*	1973	**8.00**	20.00
		(First pressings have custom Apple labels.)			

Label & Catalog #		Title	Year	VG+	NM
Apple SKBO-3404	(P)	The Beatles 1967-1970 (2 LPs)	1975	10.00	25.00
		(Second pressing labels have an "All rights reserved" disclaimer.)			
Apple (No number)	(P)	The Beatles Special Limited Edition	1974	660.00	1,000.00
		(Boxed set of nine Apple label albums.)			

6. Capitol Repackagings 1976-1983

Label & Catalog #		Title	Year	VG+	NM
Capitol (No number)	(DJ)	The Beatles 10th Anniversary Box Set	1974	900.00	1,500.00
		(Boxed set of seventeen Apple label albums.)			
Capitol SKBO-11537	(S)	Rock 'n' Roll Music (2 LPs)	1977	8.00	20.00
Capitol SMAS-11638	(DJ)	The Beatles At The Hollywood Bowl	1977	150.00	300.00
		(White label issued in a plain white jacket.)			
Capitol SMAS-11638	(S)	The Beatles At The Hollywood Bowl	1977	6.00	15.00
		(Both the title and the graphics on the front cover are raised.)			
Capitol SKBL-11711	(P)	Love Songs (2 LPs with lyric booklet)	1977	6.00	15.00
		(Original pressings have an embossed front cover.)			
Capitol SEAX-11840	(S)	Sgt. Pepper's Lonely Heart's Club Band	1978	6.00	15.00
		(Picture disc in die cut cover.)			
Capitol SEBX-11841	(S)	The Beatles (2 LPs. White vinyl)	1978	16.00	40.00
Capitol SEBX-11842	(P)	The Beatles 1962-1966 (2 LPs. Red vinyl)	1978	12.00	30.00
Capitol SEBX-11843	(P)	The Beatles 1967-1970 (2 LPs. Blue vinyl)	1978	12.00	30.00
Capitol SEBX-11844	(P)	Love Songs (2 LPs. Canadian gold vinyl)	1978	40.00	100.00
		(Issued with a lyric booklet.)			
Capitol SEAX-11900	(S)	Abbey Road (Picture disc)	1978	16.00	40.00
Capitol SN-12009	(P)	The Beatles Rarities (Green label)	1978	80.00	200.00
		(Capitol 12009 is a reissue of the British EMI/Parlophone release with 17 tracks and was issued without a cover.)			
Capitol/EMI BC-13	(P)	The Beatles Collection (14 LP box)	1978	100.00	250.00
Capitol SPRO-8969	(DJ)	The Beatles Rarities (Purple label)	1980	16.00	40.00
Capitol SN-16020	(S)	Rock 'n' Roll Music, Volume 1	1980	5.00	12.00
Capitol SN-16021	(S)	Rock 'n' Roll Music, Volume 2	1980	5.00	12.00
		(Capitol 16020 and 16021 are reissues of 11537.)			
Capitol SHAL-12080	(P)	Rarities (Rainbow label)	1980	6.00	15.00
		("Rarities" contains 15 tracks and is a different album than 12009 above. Original covers do not credit George Martin as producer.)			
Capitol SV-12199	(DJ)	Reel Music (Gold vinyl)	1982	16.00	40.00
		(Back cover stamped with a "Limited Edition" number and included a souvenir program.)			
Capitol SV-12199	(S)	Reel Music (Gold vinyl)	1982	12.00	30.00
		(Without the "Limited Edition" number with program.)			
Capitol SV-12199	(S)	Reel Music (Black vinyl)	1982	4.00	10.00
Capitol SV-12245	(P)	20 Greatest Hits	1982	4.00	10.00
Capitol (No number)	(DJ)	The Platinum Collection (18 LP box)	1984	30.00	500.00
Capitol BBX1-91302	(DJ)	The Deluxe Box Set (14 LP box)	1984	80.00	200.00

7. Miscellaneous Releases

Label & Catalog #		Title	Year	VG+	NM
INS Radio News DOC-1	(DJ)	Beatlemania Tour Coverage	1964	600.00	1,000.00
		(Open-end interview issued with a script in a plain cardboard jacket.)			
Radio Pulsebeat #2	(M)	American Tour With Ed Rudy (Yellow label)	1964	40.00	100.00
		(Counterfeits are on flexible vinyl with no writing in the trail-off area and the covers have bo print on the spine.)			
Radio Pulsebeat	(M)	1965 Talk Album, Ed Rudy With New U.S. Tour	1965	60.00	150.00
		(Original covers have "The Beatles" in black print under the photo; counterfeit covers have "The Beatles" in red print above the photo.)			
Sterling Prod. 8895-6481	(M)	I Apologize (With bonus photo)	1966	150.00	300.00
Sterling Prod. 8895-6481	(M)	I Apologize (Without photo)	1966	100.00	250.00

8. Original Master Recordings & UHQRs

Label & Catalog #		Title	Year	VG+	NM
Mobile Fidelity MFSL-023	(S)	Abbey Road	1979	13.00	40.00
Mobile Fidelity MFSL-047	(P)	Magical Mystery Tour	1980	20.00	50.00
Mobile Fidelity MFSL-072	(S)	The Beatles (2 LPs)	1982	13.00	40.00
Mobile Fidelity MFSL-100	(S)	Sgt. Pepper's Lonely Heart's Club Band	1982	10.00	30.00
Mobile Fidelity MFSL-101	(P)	Please Please Me	1986	10.00	30.00

Beginning as a five man group, The Beau Brummels emulated the sound of the British Invasion, achieving big chart success in 1964-65 with "Laugh Laugh," "Just A Little" and "Tell Me Why." By 1967 the group was a studio trio. Both of these albums are astonishing; Ron Elliot's guitar(s) and Sal Valentino's vocals are breath-taking. 1967's Triangle is a minor masterpiece of late '60s mood music while 1968's Bradley's Barn was one of the earliest forays into country rock, recorded in Owen Bradley's famed Nashville studios with local pickers.

Label & Catalog #		Title	Year	VG+	NM
Mobile Fidelity MFSL-102	(S)	With The Beatles	1986	50.00	150.00
Mobile Fidelity MFSL-103	(S)	A Hard Day's Night	1986	10.00	30.00
Mobile Fidelity MFSL-104	(S)	Beatles For Sale	1986	10.00	30.00
Mobile Fidelity MFSL-105	(S)	Help!	1986	10.00	30.00
Mobile Fidelity MFSL-106	(S)	Rubber Soul	1986	12.00	35.00
Mobile Fidelity MFSL-107	(S)	Revolver	1987	10.00	30.00
Mobile Fidelity MFSL-108	(P)	Yellow Submarine	1987	12.00	35.00
Mobile Fidelity MFSL-109	(S)	Let It Be	1987	10.00	30.00
Mobile Fidelity MFSL-110	(DJ)	Rarities (One-sided test pressing)	1987	50.00	150.00
Mobile Fidelity BC-1	(P)	The Beatles: The Collection (14 LP box)	1982	150.00	450.00

— The Mobile Fidelity albums above are Original Master Recordings.—

Mobile Fidelity MFQR-023	(S)	Abbey Road (Test pressing)	1979	300.00	900.00
Mobile Fidelity MFQR-047	(P)	Magical Mystery Tour (Test pressing)	1980	300.00	900.00
Mobile Fidelity MFQR-072	(S)	The Beatles (2 LPs. Test pressing)	1982	300.00	900.00
Mobile Fidelity MFQR-100	(S)	Sgt. Pepper's Lonely Heart's Club Band	1982	100.00	300.00

(Issued in a box with a Geodisc cartridge alignment tool.)

Mobile Fidelity MFQR-101	(P)	Please Please Me (Test pressing)	1986	300.00	900.00
Mobile Fidelity MFQR-102	(S)	With The Beatles (Test pressing)	1986	300.00	900.00
Mobile Fidelity MFQR-103	(S)	A Hard Day's Night (Test pressing)	1986	300.00	900.00
Mobile Fidelity MFQR-104	(S)	Beatles For Sale (Test pressing)	1986	300.00	900.00
Mobile Fidelity MFQR-105	(S)	Help! (Test pressing)	1986	300.00	900.00
Mobile Fidelity MFQR-106	(S)	Rubber Soul (Test pressing)	1986	300.00	900.00
Mobile Fidelity MFQR-107	(S)	Revolver (Test pressing)	1987	300.00	900.00
Mobile Fidelity MFQR-108	(P)	Yellow Submarine (Test pressing)	1987	300.00	900.00
Mobile Fidelity MFQR-109	(S)	Let It Be (Test pressing)	1987	300.00	900.00

— The Mobile Fidelity albums above are Ultra High Quality Recordings.
The test pressings were issued in plain cardboard jackets.—

BEATS, THE

Design 170	(M)	The New Merseyside Sound	1964	20.00	50.00

(This was also released on Rondo credited to The Liverpool Beats.)

BEAU BRUMMELS, THE
Originally Ron Elliot, Declan Mulligan, Ron Meagher, John Petersen and Sal Valentino, by 1967 The Beau Brummels were a duo, Valentino and Elliot.

Autumn LP-103	(M)	Introducing The Beau Brummels	1965	16.00	40.00
Autumn SLP-103	(S)	Introducing The Beau Brummels	1965	20.00	50.00

("I Would Be Happy" is in mono on this album.)

Autumn LP-104	(M)	The Beau Brummels, Volume 2	1965	16.00	40.00
Autumn SLP-104	(S)	The Beau Brummels, Volume 2	1965	20.00	50.00
Warner Bros. WS-1644	(M)	Beau Brummels '66	1966	10.00	25.00
Warner Bros. WS-1644	(S)	Beau Brummels '66	1966	12.00	30.00
Warner Bros. W-1692	(M)	Triangle	1967	8.00	20.00
Warner Bros. WS-1692	(S)	Triangle	1967	10.00	25.00
Warner Bros. WS-1760	(S)	Bradley's Barn	1968	8.00	20.00
Vault LP-114	(M)	The Best Of The Beau Brummels	1967	10.00	25.00
Vault SLP-114	(S)	The Best Of The Beau Brummels	1967	8.00	20.00
Vault SLP-121	(P)	The Beau Brummels, Volume 44	1968	8.00	20.00
Post 6000	(P)	The Beau Brummels Sing	196?	8.00	20.00
JAS 5000	(S)	Original Hits Of The Beau Brummels	1976	8.00	20.00

BEAUREGARDE

F-Empire	(S)	Beauregarde	196?	24.00	60.00

BEAVER, PAUL

Rapture 11111	(S)	Perchance To Dream	196?	20.00	50.00

BEAVER, PAUL, & BERNIE KRAUSE

Limelight 86069	(S)	Ragnarok	1969	12.00	30.00
Warner Bros. WS-1850	(S)	In A Wild Sanctuary	1969	8.00	20.00
Warner Bros. WS-1909	(S)	Gandharva	1971	6.00	15.00
Warner Bros. BS-2624	(S)	All Good Men	1972	6.00	15.00

BECK, JEFF
Beck was formerly a member of The Yardbirds. Epic 26413-26478 feature Rod Stewart and Ron Wood.

Epic BN-26413	(S)	Truth	1968	6.00	15.00
Epic BN-26478	(S)	Beck-Ola	1969	6.00	15.00

— Original Epic albums above have yellow labels.—

Label & Catalog #		Title	Year	VG+	NM
Epic EQ-30973	(Q)	Rough And Ready	1973	8.00	20.00
Epic EQ-31331	(Q)	The Jeff Beck Group	1973	8.00	20.00
Epic PEQ-33409	(Q)	Blow By Blow	1975	8.00	20.00
Epic PEQ-33849	(Q)	Wired	1976	8.00	20.00
Epic PEQ-34433	(Q)	Live	1977	8.00	20.00
Epic AS-151	(DJ)	Everything You Always Wanted To Hear	1977	8.00	20.00
Epic AS-796	(DJ)	Musical Montage	1979	8.00	20.00
Epic HE-43409	(S)	Blow By Blow (Half-speed master)	1982	15.00	45.00
Epic HE-43849	(S)	Wired (Half-speed master)	1982	15.00	45.00

BECK, BOGERT & APPICE
Jeff Beck with Tim Bogert and Carmine Appice of The Vanilla Fudge.

Epic EQ-32140	(Q)	Beck, Bogert, & Appice	1973	6.00	15.00

BECK, PIA

Epic LN-3269	(M)	Dutch Treat	1957	16.00	40.00

BEDIENT, JACK, & THE CHESSMEN

Executive Prods.	(M)	Jack Bedient	196?	20.00	50.00
Trophy 101	(M)	Two Sides Of Jack Bedient	1964	20.00	50.00
Fantasy 3365	(M)	Live At Harvey's	1965	20.00	50.00
Satori LP-1001	(M)	Where Did She Go?	1966	30.00	75.00

BEE, MOLLY

Capitol T-1097	(M)	Young Romance	1958	16.00	40.00
MGM E-4303	(M)	It's Great, It's Molly Bee	1965	6.00	15.00
MGM SE-4303	(S)	It's Great, It's Molly Bee	1965	8.00	20.00
MGM E-4423	(M)	Swingin' Country	1967	6.00	15.00
MGM SE-4423	(S)	Swingin' Country	1967	8.00	20.00

BEE GEES, THE
The Bee Gees are the brothers Gibb: Barry, Maurice and Robin.

Atco 33-223	(M)	The Bee Gees First	1967	10.00	25.00
Atco SD-33-223	(S)	The Bee Gees First	1967	8.00	20.00
Atco 33-233	(M)	Horizontal	1968	12.00	30.00
Atco SD-33-233	(S)	Horizontal	1968	8.00	20.00
Atco SD-33-253	(S)	Idea	1968	8.00	20.00
Atco SD-33-264	(E)	Rare, Precious And Beautiful	1968	8.00	20.00
— Original Atco stereo albums above have brown & purple labels.—					
Atco SD-33-292	(S)	The Best Of The Bee Gees	1969	5.00	12.00
Atco ST-142	(DJ)	Odessa (In-store sampler)	1969	30.00	75.00
Atco SD-2-702	(S)	Odessa (Red felt cover)	1969	12.00	30.00
Atco SD-2-702	(S)	Odessa (Record Club. Plain red cover)	1969	20.00	50.00
Atco SD-33-321	(E)	Rare, Precious And Beautiful, Volume 2	1970	5.00	12.00
Atco SD-33-327	(S)	Cucumber Castle	1970	5.00	12.00
Atco SD-33-353	(S)	Two Years On	1971	5.00	12.00
Atco SD-33-363	(S)	Melody (Soundtrack)	1971	6.00	15.00
Atco SD-7003	(S)	Trafalgar	1971	5.00	12.00
Atco SD-7012	(S)	To Whom It May Concern	1972	5.00	12.00
— Original Atco albums above have yellow labels with an 1841 Broadway address on the bottom.—					
RSO SMP-1	(DJ)	The Words And Music Of Maurice, Barry And Robin Gibb (Sampler)	197?	12.00	30.00
RSO 3042	(S)	Spirits Having Flown (Picture disc)	1979	4.00	10.00
Nautilus NR-17	(S)	Spirits Having Flown	1981	5.00	15.00
Nautilus NR-42	(DJ)	Living Eyes (Test pressing)	1981	30.00	90.00

BEEFHEART, CAPTAIN: *Refer to* CAPTAIN BEEFHEART & THE MAGIC BAND

BEETHOVEN SOUL, THE

Dot DLP-3821	(M)	The Beethoven Soul	1967	8.00	20.00
Dot DLP-25821	(S)	The Beethoven Soul	1967	10.00	25.00

BEHRKE TRIO, RICHARD

Atco 33-141	(M)	The Richard Behrke Trio	1962	6.00	15.00
Atco SD-33-141	(S)	The Richard Behrke Trio	1962	8.00	20.00

BELAFONTE, HARRY

RCA Victor LPM-1022	(M)	Mark Twain & Other Folk Favorites	1954	20.00	50.00
RCA Victor LPM-1150	(M)	Belafonte	1955	20.00	50.00

Label & Catalog #		Title	Year	VG+	NM
RCA Victor LPM-1248	(M)	Calypso	1956	12.00	30.00
RCA Victor LPM-1402	(M)	An Evening With Belafonte	1957	12.00	30.00
RCA Victor LPM-1505	(M)	Belafonte Sings Of The Caribbean	1957	12.00	30.00
RCA Victor LOP-1006	(M)	Belafonte Sings The Blues	1958	10.00	25.00
RCA Victor LPM-1887	(M)	To Wish You A Merry Christmas	1958	10.00	25.00
RCA Victor LPM-1927	(M)	Love Is A Gentle Thing	1959	8.00	20.00
RCA Victor LSP-1927	(S)	Love Is A Gentle Thing	1959	10.00	25.00
RCA Victor LOC-1507	(M)	Porgy And Bess	1959	8.00	20.00
RCA Victor LSO-1507	(S)	Porgy And Bess	1959	10.00	25.00
RCA Victor LOC-6006	(M)	Belafonte At Carnegie Hall	1959	8.00	20.00
RCA Victor LSO-6006	(S)	Belafonte At Carnegie Hall	1959	10.00	25.00
RCA Victor LPM-2022	(M)	My Lord What A Mornin'	1960	8.00	20.00
RCA Victor LSP-2022	(S)	My Lord What A Mornin'	1960	10.00	25.00
RCA Victor LOC-6007	(M)	Belafonte Returns To Carnegie Hall	1960	8.00	20.00
RCA Victor LSO-6007	(S)	Belafonte Returns To Carnegie Hall	1960	10.00	25.00
RCA Victor LPM-2194	(M)	Swing Dat Hammer	1960	8.00	20.00
RCA Victor LSP-2194	(S)	Swing Dat Hammer	1960	10.00	25.00
RCA Victor LPM-2388	(M)	Jump Up Calypso	1961	8.00	20.00
RCA Victor LSP-2388	(S)	Jump Up Calypso	1961	10.00	25.00
RCA Victor LPM-2499	(M)	The Midnight Special	1962	10.00	25.00
RCA Victor LSP-2499	(S)	The Midnight Special	1962	14.00	35.00
		(RCA 2499 features Bob Dylan's first appearance on record, playing harmonica on one track.)			
RCA Victor LPM-2574	(M)	The Many Moods Of Belafonte	1962	6.00	15.00
RCA Victor LSP-2574	(S)	The Many Moods Of Belafonte	1962	8.00	20.00
RCA Victor LPM-2626	(M)	To Wish You A Merry Christmas	1962	6.00	15.00
RCA Victor LSP-2626	(S)	To Wish You A Merry Christmas	1962	8.00	20.00
RCA Victor LPM-2695	(M)	Streets I Have Walked	1963	6.00	15.00
RCA Victor LSP-2695	(S)	Streets I Have Walked	1963	8.00	20.00
— Original RCA mono albums above have "Long Play" on the bottom of the label; stereo albums have "Living Stereo" on the bottom.—					
RCA Victor LOC-6009	(M)	Belafonte At The Greek Theatre (2 LPs)	1964	5.00	12.00
RCA Victor LSO-6009	(S)	Belafonte At The Greek Theatre (2 LPs)	1964	6.00	15.00
RCA Victor LPM-2953	(M)	Ballads, Blues And Boasters	1964	5.00	12.00
RCA Victor LSP-2953	(S)	Ballads, Blues And Boasters	1964	6.00	15.00
RCA Victor LPM-3571	(M)	In My Quiet Room	1966	5.00	12.00
RCA Victor LSP-3571	(S)	In My Quiet Room	1966	6.00	15.00
RCA Victor LPM-3658	(M)	Calypso In Brass	1966	5.00	12.00
RCA Victor LSP-3658	(S)	Calypso In Brass	1966	6.00	15.00
RCA Victor LPM-3779	(M)	Belafonte On Campus	1967	6.00	15.00
RCA Victor LSP-3779	(S)	Belafonte On Campus	1967	6.00	15.00

BELAFONTE, HARRY, & MOUSKOURI

RCA Victor LPM-3415	(M)	An Evening with Belafonte/Mouskouri	1965	5.00	12.00
RCA Victor LSP-3415	(S)	An Evening with Belafonte/Mouskouri	1965	6.00	15.00

BELAFONTE, HARRY, & MIRIAM MAKEBA

RCA Victor LPM-3420	(M)	An Evening With Belafonte/Makeba	1965	5.00	12.00
RCA Victor LSP-3420	(S)	An Evening With Belafonte/Makeba	1965	6.00	15.00

BELAFONTE FOLK SINGERS, THE

RCA Victor LMP-2309	(M)	At Home And Abroad	1961	5.00	12.00
RCA Victor LSP-2309	(S)	At Home And Abroad	1961	6.00	15.00

BELEW, CARL

Decca DL-4074	(M)	Carl Belew	1960	12.00	30.00
Decca DL-74074	(S)	Carl Belew	1960	16.00	40.00
Wrangler 31007	(M)	Carl Belew	1962	16.00	40.00
RCA Victor LPM-2848	(M)	Hello Out There	1964	8.00	20.00
RCA Victor LSP-2848	(S)	Hello Out There	1964	10.00	25.00
RCA Victor LPM-3381	(M)	Am I That Easy To Forget?	1965	8.00	20.00
Victor LSP-3381	(S)	Am I That Easy To Forget?	1965	10.00	25.00
Hilltop JM-6013	M	Another Lonely Night	1965	10.00	25.00
Vocalion VL-3774	(M)	Country Songs	1966	6.00	15.00
Vocalion VL-73774	(S)	Country Songs	1966	6.00	15.00
Vocalion VL-3797	(M)	Lonely Street	1967	6.00	15.00
Vocalion VL-73797	(S)	Lonely Street	1967	6.00	15.00
RCA Victor LPM-3919	(M)	Twelve Shades Of Belew	1968	20.00	50.00
RCA Victor LSP-3919	(S)	Twelve Shades Of Belew	1968	8.00	20.00

Jesse Lorenzo Belvin is another virtually unsung mover of the '50s rhythm 'n blues scene. Aside from recording with several groups (including The Three Dots & A Dash for Jig Jay McNeely, The Capris, The Chargers and The Cliques), he had a hand in the writing of "Earth Angel" and "Goodnight My Love." He was beginning to enjoy success outside of rhythm 'n blues as a pop singer (ala Sam Cooke) for RCA Victor when he was tragically killed in an automobile accident in 1960.

Label & Catalog #		Title	Year	VG+	NM

BELL, ARCHIE, & THE DRELLS

Atlantic 8181	(M)	Tighten Up	1968	12.00	30.00
Atlantic SD-8181	(S)	Tighten Up	1968	16.00	40.00
Atlantic SD-8204	(S)	I Can't Stop Dancing	1968	12.00	30.00
Atlantic SD-8226	(S)	There's Gonna Be A Showdown	1969	12.00	30.00

BELL, FREDDIE, & THE BELL BOYS

Mercury MG-20289	(M)	Rock And Roll—All Flavors	1958	40.00	100.00
20th Century TF-4146	(M)	Bells Are Swinging	1964	8.00	20.00
20th Century TFS-4146	(S)	Bells Are Swinging	1964	10.00	25.00

BELL, WILLIAM

Stax 719	(M)	Soul Of A Bell	1967	6.00	15.00
Stax S-719	(S)	Soul Of A Bell	1967	8.00	20.00
Stax STS-2014	(S)	Bound To Happen	1969	6.00	15.00
Stax STS-2037	(S)	Wow...	1971	5.00	12.00
Stax STS-3005	(S)	Phases To Reality	1973	5.00	12.00
Stax STS-5502	(S)	Relating	1974	5.00	12.00

BELL SHANNY MEN, THE

Orco 1002	(S)	The Bell Shanny Men	1967	6.00	15.00

BELLINE, DENNY, & THE RICH KIDS

RCA Victor LPM-3655	(M)	Denny Belline And The Rich Kids	1966	6.00	15.00
RCA Victor LSP-3655	(S)	Denny Belline And The Rich Kids	1966	8.00	20.00

BELLUS, TONY

N.R.C. LPA-8	(M)	Robbin' The Cradle	1960	50.00	125.00

BELMONTS, THE
Refer to Dion & The Belmonts.

Sabina SALP-5001	(M)	The Belmonts' Carnival Of Hits	1962	50.00	125.00
Dot DLP-25949	(S)	Summer Love	1969	12.00	30.00
Buddah BDS-5123	(S)	Cigars, Acappella, Candy	1972	20.00	50.00
Strawberry 6001	(S)	Cheek To Cheek	1978	6.00	15.00

BELVIN, JESSE
Refer to Brook Benton / Jesse Belvin.

Crown CLP-5145	(M)	The Casual Jessie Belvin	1959	16.00	40.00
Crown CLP-5187	(M)	The Unforgettable Jessie Belvin	1959	16.00	40.00
RCA Victor LPM-2089	(M)	Just Jesse Belvin	1959	14.00	35.00
RCA Victor LSP-2089	(S)	Just Jesse Belvin	1959	20.00	50.00
RCA Victor LPM-2105	(M)	Mr. Easy	1960	12.00	30.00
RCA Victor LSP-2105	(S)	Mr. Easy	1960	16.00	40.00

— Original RCA mono albums above have black labels with "Long Play" on the bottom; stereo albums have "Living Stereo" on the bottom.—

Camden CAL-960	(M)	Jesse Belvin's Best	1966	5.00	12.00
Camden CAS-960	(S)	Jesse Belvin's Best	1966	6.00	15.00

BENATAR, PAT
Pat was formerly a member of Coxan's Army.

Mobile Fidelity MFSL-057	(S)	In The Heat Of The Night	197?	6.00	18.00

BENDIX, WILLIAM

Cricket CR-30	(M)	Famous Pirate Stories	1959	16.00	40.00

BENET, VICKI

Decca DL-8233	(M)	Woman Of Paris	1956	16.00	40.00
Decca DL-8381	(M)	The French Touch	1957	16.00	40.00
Decca DL-8987	(M)	a' Paris	1959	12.00	30.00
Liberty LRP-3103	(M)	Sing To Me Of Love	1960	10.00	25.00
Liberty LST-7103	(S)	Sing To Me Of Love	1960	14.00	35.00

BENNETT, BETTY : Refer to GOLDMINE'S PRICE GUIDE TO COLLECTIBLE JAZZ ALBUMS

BENNETT, BOYD

King 395-594	(M)	Boyd Bennett	1955	1,500.00	Rare

(Near Mint copies have a suggested value of $3,000-5,000.)

Label & Catalog #		Title	Year	VG+	NM
BENNETT, CONNIE; BILL SMYTH & THE HARLEM-AIRES					
Hollywood LPH-30	*(M)*	**Rhythm 'N Blues In The Night**	1957	**300.00**	**500.00**
		(The cover, a generic pretty white girl common on R&B albums of the time, features a very young— and scantily clad—Julie Newmar.)			
BENNETT, TONY					
Columbia CL-6221 (10")	*(M)*	**Because Of You**	1952	**30.00**	**75.00**
Columbia CL-2507 (10")	*(M)*	**Alone At Last With Tony Bennett**	1955	**20.00**	**50.00**
Columbia CL-2550 (10")	*(M)*	**Because Of You** *(Reissue of 6221)*	1956	**20.00**	**50.00**
Columbia CL-621	*(M)*	**Cloud Seven**	1955	**16.00**	**40.00**
		— Original Columbia albums above have "Long Playing" on the bottom.—			
Columbia CL-938	*(M)*	**Tony**	1957	**14.00**	**35.00**
Columbia CL-1079	*(M)*	**The Beat Of My Heart**	1957	**14.00**	**35.00**
Columbia CL-1186	*(M)*	**Long Ago And Far Away**	1958	**14.00**	**35.00**
Columbia CL-1229	*(M)*	**Tony's Greatest Hits**	1958	**14.00**	**35.00**
Columbia CL-1292	*(M)*	**Blue Velvet**	1959	**14.00**	**35.00**
Columbia CL-2343	*(M)*	**If I Ruled The World**	1959	**14.00**	**35.00**
Columbia CL-1294	*(M)*	**Tony Bennett In Person**	1959	**10.00**	**25.00**
Columbia CS-8104	*(S)*	**Tony Bennett In Person**	1959	**14.00**	**35.00**
Columbia CL-1301	*(M)*	**Hometown, My Hometown**	1959	**10.00**	**25.00**
Columbia CS-8107	*(S)*	**Hometown, My Hometown**	1959	**14.00**	**35.00**
Columbia CL-1429	*(M)*	**To My Wonderful One**	1960	**10.00**	**25.00**
Columbia CS-8226	*(S)*	**To My Wonderful One**	1960	**14.00**	**35.00**
Columbia CL-1446	*(M)*	**Tony Sings For Two**	1960	**10.00**	**25.00**
Columbia CS-8242	*(S)*	**Tony Sings For Two**	1960	**14.00**	**35.00**
Columbia CL-1471	*(M)*	**Alone Together**	1960	**10.00**	**25.00**
Columbia CS-8262	*(S)*	**Alone Together**	1960	**14.00**	**35.00**
Columbia CL-1535	*(M)*	**More Tony's Greatest Hits**	1960	**10.00**	**25.00**
Columbia CS-8335	*(S)*	**More Tony's Greatest Hits**	1960	**10.00**	**25.00**
Columbia CL-1559	*(M)*	**A String Of Harold Arlen**	1960	**10.00**	**25.00**
Columbia CS-8359	*(S)*	**A String Of Harold Arlen**	1960	**12.00**	**30.00**
Roulette R-25072	*(M)*	**Count Basie Swings/Tony Sings**	1961	**10.00**	**25.00**
Roulette SR-25072	*(S)*	**Count Basie Swings/Tony Sings**	1961	**12.00**	**30.00**
Roulette R-25231	*(M)*	**Bennett And Basie Strike Up The Band**	1961	**10.00**	**25.00**
Roulette SR-25231	*(S)*	**Bennett And Basie Strike Up The Band**	1961	**12.00**	**30.00**
Columbia CL-1658	*(M)*	**My Heart Sings**	1961	**10.00**	**25.00**
Columbia CS-8458	*(S)*	**My Heart Sings**	1961	**12.00**	**30.00**
Columbia CL-1763	*(M)*	**Mr. Broadway**	1962	**10.00**	**25.00**
Columbia CS-8563	*(S)*	**Mr. Broadway**	1962	**12.00**	**30.00**
Columbia CL-1852	*(M)*	**Tony's Greatest Hits**	1962	**10.00**	**25.00**
Columbia CS-8652	*(E)*	**Tony's Greatest Hits**	1962	**6.00**	**15.00**
Columbia CL-1869	*(M)*	**I Left My Heart In San Francisco**	1962	**10.00**	**25.00**
Columbia CS-8669	*(S)*	**I Left My Heart In San Francisco**	1962	**12.00**	**30.00**
Columbia C2L-23	*(M)*	**Tony Bennett At Carnegie Hall**	1962	**10.00**	**25.00**
Columbia C2S-23	*(S)*	**Tony Bennett At Carnegie Hall**	1962	**12.00**	**30.00**
		— Original Columbia albums above have three white "eye" logos on each side of the spindle hole.—			
Columbia CL-2000	*(M)*	**I Wanna Be Around**	1963	**6.00**	**15.00**
Columbia CS-8800	*(S)*	**I Wanna Be Around**	1963	**8.00**	**20.00**
Columbia CL-2056	*(M)*	**This Is All I Ask**	1963	**6.00**	**15.00**
Columbia CS-8856	*(S)*	**This Is All I Ask**	1963	**8.00**	**20.00**
Columbia CL-2141	*(M)*	**The Many Moods Of Tony**	1964	**6.00**	**15.00**
Columbia CS-8941	*(S)*	**The Many Moods Of Tony**	1964	**8.00**	**20.00**
Columbia CL-2175	*(M)*	**When Lights Are Low**	1964	**6.00**	**15.00**
Columbia CS-8975	*(S)*	**When Lights Are Low**	1964	**8.00**	**20.00**
Columbia CL-2285	*(M)*	**Who Can I Turn To?**	1964	**6.00**	**15.00**
Columbia CS-9085	*(S)*	**Who Can I Turn To?**	1964	**8.00**	**20.00**
Columbia CL-2343	*(M)*	**Songs For The Jet Set**	1965	**6.00**	**15.00**
Columbia CS-9143	*(S)*	**Songs For The Jet Set**	1965	**8.00**	**20.00**
Columbia CL-2373	*(M)*	**Tony's Greatest Hits, Volume 3**	1965	**6.00**	**15.00**
Columbia CS-9173	*(S)*	**Tony's Greatest Hits, Volume 3**	1965	**8.00**	**20.00**
Columbia CL-2472	*(M)*	**The Movie Song Album**	1966	**6.00**	**15.00**
Columbia CS-9272	*(S)*	**The Movie Song Album**	1966	**8.00**	**20.00**
Columbia CL-2560	*(M)*	**A Time For Love**	1966	**6.00**	**15.00**
Columbia CS-9360	*(S)*	**A Time For Love**	1966	**8.00**	**20.00**
Columbia OL-6550	*(M)*	**The Oscar** *(Soundtrack)*	1966	**20.00**	**50.00**
Columbia OS-2950	*(S)*	**The Oscar** *(Soundtrack)*	1966	**24.00**	**60.00**
Columbia CSL-552	*(M)*	**Singer Presents Tony Bennett**	1966	**6.00**	**15.00**
Columbia CSS-552	*(S)*	**Singer Presents Tony Bennett**	1966	**8.00**	**20.00**

Label & Catalog #		Title	Year	VG+	NM
Columbia CL-2653	(M)	Tony Makes It Happen!	1967	6.00	15.00
Columbia CS-9453	(S)	Tony Makes It Happen!	1967	6.00	15.00
Columbia CS-9573	(S)	For Once In My Life	1968	6.00	15.00
Columbia CS-9678	(S)	Yesterday I Heard The Rain	1968	6.00	15.00
Columbia CS-9814	(S)	Tony Bennett's Greatest Hits, Volume 4	1969	6.00	15.00
Columbia CS-9882	(S)	I've Gotta Be Me	1969	6.00	15.00
Columbia CS-9980	(S)	Tony Sings The Great Hits Of Today	1970	6.00	15.00
—Original Columbia albums above have "360 Sound" on the bottom of the label.—					
Mobile Fidelity MFSL-117	(S)	The Bennett/Evans Album	1981	12.00	36.00

BENSON, GEORGE

Mobile Fidelity MFSL-011	(S)	Breezin'	1979	10.00	30.00

BENT WIND

Trend T-1015	(S)	Sussex (Canadian)	196?	2,000.00	Rare
(Near Mint copies have a suggested value of $3,000-5,000.)					

BENTON, BARBI

Playboy 404	(S)	Barbi Doll (Includes poster)	1974	10.00	25.00
Playboy 404	(S)	Barbi Doll (Without poster)	1974	6.00	15.00
Playboy 406	(S)	Barbi Benton	1975	6.00	15.00
Playboy 411	(S)	Something New	1976	6.00	15.00

BENTON, BROOK

Epic LG-3573	(M)	Brook Benton At His Best	195?	16.00	40.00
Mercury MG-20421	(M)	It's Just A Matter Of Time	1959	16.00	40.00
Mercury SR-60421	(S)	It's Just A Matter Of Time	1959	20.00	50.00
Mercury MG-20464	(M)	Brook Benton	1959	12.00	30.00
Mercury SR-60146	(S)	Brook Benton	1959	16.00	40.00
Mercury MG-20565	(M)	So Many Ways I Love You	1959	12.00	30.00
Mercury SR-60225	(S)	So Many Ways I Love You	1959	16.00	40.00
Mercury MG-20602	(M)	Songs I Love To Sing	1960	8.00	20.00
Mercury SR-60602	(S)	Songs I Love To Sing	1960	12.00	30.00
Mercury MG-20607	(M)	Brook Benton's Golden Hits	1961	8.00	20.00
Mercury SR-60607	(S)	Brook Benton's Golden Hits	1961	12.00	30.00
Mercury MG-20619	(M)	If You Believe	1961	8.00	20.00
Mercury SR-60619	(S)	If You Believe	1961	10.00	25.00
Mercury MG-20641	(M)	The Boll Weevil Song	1961	8.00	20.00
Mercury SR-60641	(S)	The Boll Weevil Song	1961	10.00	25.00
Mercury MG-20673	(M)	There Goes That Song Again	1962	8.00	20.00
Mercury SR-60673	(S)	There Goes That Song Again	1962	10.00	25.00
Mercury MG-20740	(M)	Singing The Blues	1962	8.00	20.00
Mercury SR-60740	(S)	Singing The Blues	1962	10.00	25.00
Mercury MG-20774	(M)	Brook Benton's Golden Hits, Volume 2	1963	8.00	20.00
Mercury SR-60774	(S)	Brook Benton's Golden Hits, Volume 2	1963	10.00	25.00
Mercury MG-20830	(M)	Best Ballads Of Broadway	1963	8.00	20.00
Mercury SR-60830	(S)	Best Ballads Of Broadway	1963	10.00	25.00
Mercury MG-20886	(M)	Born To Sing The Blues	1964	8.00	20.00
Mercury SR-60886	(S)	Born To Sing The Blues	1964	10.00	25.00
—Original Mercury albums above have black labels with silver print.—					
Mercury MG-20918	(M)	On The Country Side	1964	6.00	15.00
Mercury SR-60918	(S)	On The Country Side	1964	8.00	20.00
Mercury MG-20934	(M)	This Bitter Earth	1964	6.00	15.00
Mercury SR-60934	(S)	This Bitter Earth	1964	8.00	20.00
RCA Victor LPM-3514	(M)	That Old Feeling	1966	6.00	15.00
RCA Victor LSP-3514	(S)	That Old Feeling	1966	8.00	20.00
RCA Victor LPM-3526	(M)	Mother Nature, Father Time	1966	6.00	15.00
RCA Victor LSP-3526	(S)	Mother Nature, Father Time	1966	8.00	20.00
RCA Victor LPM-3590	(M)	My Country	1966	6.00	15.00
RCA Victor LSP-3590	(S)	My Country	1966	8.00	20.00
Reprise R-6268	(M)	Laura, What's He Got That I Ain't Got?	1967	6.00	15.00
Reprise RS-6268	(S)	Laura, What's He Got That I Ain't Got?	1967	8.00	20.00

BENTON, BROOK / JESSE BELVIN

Crown CLP-5350	(M)	Brook Benton & Jesse Belvin	1963	8.00	20.00
Crown CST-350	(E)	Brook Benton & Jesse Belvin	1963	4.00	10.00

Label & Catalog #		Title	Year	VG+	NM
BENTON, BROOK, & DINAH WASHINGTON					
Mercury MG-20588	(M)	The Two Of Us	1960	8.00	20.00
Mercury SR-60244	(S)	The Two Of Us	1960	10.00	25.00
BERGEN, POLLY					
Jubilee JGL-14 (10")	(M)	Polly Bergen	1955	20.00	50.00
Columbia CL-994	(M)	Bergen Sings Morgan	1957	12.00	30.00
Columbia CL-1031	(M)	The Party's Over	1957	12.00	30.00
Columbia CL-1138	(M)	Polly And Her Pop	1958	10.00	25.00
Columbia OL-2014	(M)	First Impressions	1959	10.00	25.00
Columbia CL-1218	(M)	My Heart Sings	1959	8.00	20.00
Columbia CS-8018	(S)	My Heart Sings	1959	10.00	25.00
Columbia CL-1300	(M)	All Alone By The Telephone	1959	8.00	20.00
Columbia CS-8100	(S)	All Alone By The Telephone	1959	10.00	25.00
Columbia CL-1481	(M)	Four Seasons Of Love	1960	6.00	15.00
Columbia CS-8246	(S)	Four Seasons Of Love	1960	8.00	20.00
Columbia CL-1632	(M)	"Do Re Mi" And "Annie Get Your Gun"	1961	6.00	15.00
Columbia CS-8432	(S)	"Do Re Mi" And "Annie Get Your Gun"	1961	8.00	20.00
— Original Columbia albums above have three white "eye" logos on each side of the spindle hole.—					
Columbia CL-2171	(M)	My Heart Sings	1964	5.00	12.00
Columbia CS-8971	(S)	My Heart Sings	1964	6.00	15.00
Philips PHM-200-084	(M)	Act One-Sing, Too	1963	5.00	12.00
Philips PHS-600-084	(S)	Act One-Sing, Too	1963	6.00	15.00
BERGEN, FRANCES					
Columbia CL-873	(M)	Beguiling Miss	1956	12.00	30.00
BERLE, MILTON					
Forum F-9005	(M)	Songs My Mother Loved	195?	12.00	30.00
BERMAN, SHELLY					
Refer to Jonathan Winters / Shelly Berman / Mort Sahl.					
MGV-15003	(M)	Inside Shelly Berman	1959	6.00	15.00
MGV-15007	(M)	Outside Shelly Berman	1959	6.00	15.00
MGV-15008	(M)	Inside And Outside Shelly Berman (2 LPs)	1959	6.00	15.00
		(Verve 15008 is a reissue of 15003 and 15007.)			
MGV-15013	(M)	The Edge Of Shelly Berman	1960	6.00	15.00
MGV-15027	(M)	A Personal Appearance	1961	6.00	15.00
— Original Verve albums above have black labels with "Verve Records, Inc." on the bottom.—					
V6-15027	(S)	A Personal Appearance	1962	5.00	12.00
V-15036	(M)	The New Sides Of Shelly Berman	1962	4.00	10.00
V6-15036	(S)	The New Sides Of Shelly Berman	1962	5.00	12.00
V-15043	(M)	Sex Life Of The Primate	1964	4.00	10.00
V6-15043	(S)	Sex Life Of The Primate	1964	5.00	12.00
V-15048	(M)	Great Moments	1964	4.00	10.00
BERMUDA JAM					
Dynovoice 31907	(S)	Bermuda Jam	1969	6.00	15.00
BERNARD, ROD					
Jin LP-4007	(M)	Rod Bernard	196?	20.00	50.00
BERRY, BROOKS, & SCRAPPER BLACKWELL					
Bluesville BVLP-1074	(M)	My Heart Struck Sorrow	1963	16.00	40.00
BERRY, CHUCK					
Mr. Berry also recorded with Bo Diddley.					
Chess LP-1426	(DJ)	After School Session	1958	200.00	400.00
Chess LP-1426	(M)	After School Session	1958	60.00	150.00
Chess LP-1432	(DJ)	One Dozen Berrys	1958	200.00	400.00
Chess LP-1432	(M)	One Dozen Berrys	1958	60.00	150.00
Chess LP-1435	(DJ)	Berry Is On Top	1959	20.00	400.00
Chess LP-1435	(M)	Berry Is On Top	1959	60.00	150.00
Chess LP-1448	(DJ)	Rockin' At The Hops	1960	150.00	300.00
Chess LP-1448	(M)	Rockin' At The Hops	1960	60.00	150.00
Chess LP-1456	(DJ)	New Juke Box Hits	1961	150.00	300.00
Chess LP-1456	(M)	New Juke Box Hits	1961	60.00	150.00
Chess LP-1465	(DJ)	Chuck Berry Twist	1962	100.00	250.00
Chess LP-1465	(M)	Chuck Berry Twist	1962	30.00	75.00

Label & Catalog #		Title	Year	VG+	NM
Chess LP-1465	(DJ)	More Chuck Berry	1963	100.00	250.00
Chess LP-1465	(M)	More Chuck Berry	1963	30.00	75.00
Chess LP-1480	(DJ)	Chuck Berry On Stage	1963	100.00	250.00
Chess LP-1480	(M)	Chuck Berry On Stage	1963	30.00	75.00
Chess LP-1485	(DJ)	Chuck Berry's Greatest Hits	1964	80.00	200.00
Chess LP-1485	(M)	Chuck Berry's Greatest Hits	1964	20.00	50.00
Chess LP-1488	(DJ)	St. Louis To Liverpool	1964	80.00	200.00
Chess LP-1488	(M)	St. Louis To Liverpool	1964	20.00	50.00
Chess LPS-1488	(S)	St. Louis To Liverpool	1964	30.00	75.00
		— Original Chess albums above have black & silver labels.—			
Chess LP-1495	(DJ)	Chuck Berry In London (White label)	1965	80.00	200.00
Chess LP-1495	(M)	Chuck Berry In London	1965	14.00	35.00
Chess LPS-1495	(S)	Chuck Berry In London	1965	16.00	40.00
Chess LP-1498	(DJ)	Fresh Berry's (White label)	1965	80.00	200.00
Chess LP-1498	(M)	Fresh Berry's	1965	14.00	35.00
Chess LPS-1498	(S)	Fresh Berry's	1965	16.00	40.00
		—Original Chess albums above have blue labels with a gold logo on top.—			
Chess LPS-1426	(E)	After School Session	1966	8.00	20.00
Chess LPS-1432	(E)	One Dozen Berrys	1966	8.00	20.00
Chess LPS-1435	(E)	Berry Is On Top	1966	8.00	20.00
Chess LPS-1448	(E)	Rockin' At The Hops	1966	8.00	20.00
Chess LPS-1456	(E)	New Juke Box Hits	1966	8.00	20.00
Chess LPS-1465	(E)	More Chuck Berry	1966	8.00	20.00
Chess LPS-1480	(E)	Chuck Berry On Stage	1966	8.00	20.00
Chess LPS-1485	(E)	Chuck Berry's Greatest Hits	1966	8.00	20.00
Chess LPS-1488	(P)	St. Louis To Liverpool	1966	8.00	20.00
Chess LPS-1495	(S)	Chuck Berry In London	1966	8.00	20.00
Chess LPS-1498	(S)	Fresh Berry's	1966	8.00	20.00
Chess LP-1514	(M)	Chuck Berry's Golden Decade	1967	10.00	25.00
Chess LPS-1514	(E)	Chuck Berry's Golden Decade	1967	6.00	15.00
		—Chess albums above have blue & white labels.—			
Mercury MG-21103	(M)	Chuck Berry's Golden Hits	1967	6.00	15.00
Mercury SR-61103	(S)	Chuck Berry's Golden Hits	1967	6.00	15.00
Mercury MG-21123	(M)	Chuck Berry In Memphis	1967	8.00	20.00
Mercury SR-61123	(S)	Chuck Berry In Memphis	1967	10.00	25.00
Mercury MG-21138	(M)	Live At The Fillmore Auditorium	1967	8.00	20.00
Mercury SR-61138	(S)	Live At The Fillmore Auditorium	1967	10.00	25.00
		(Berry is backed by The Steve Miller Blues Band.)			
Mercury SR-61176	(S)	From St. Louis To Frisco	1968	8.00	20.00
Mercury SR-61223	(S)	Concerto In B. Goode	1969	8.00	20.00
Mercury SRM-2-6501	(S)	St. Louie To Frisco To Memphis (2 LPs)	1972	6.00	15.00
		(Repackage of previous Mercury material.)			
Chess LPS-1550	(S)	Back Home	1970	8.00	20.00
Chess CH-50008	(S)	San Francisco Dues	1971	8.00	20.00
Chess CH-60020	(S)	The Chuck Berry London Sessions	1972	6.00	15.00
		(Gatefold cover. "My Ding-A-Ling" is rechanneled on this album.)			
Chess 2CH-60023	(P)	Golden Decade, Volume 2 (2 LPs)	1973	6.00	15.00
Chess CH-50043	(S)	Bio (Gatefold cover)	1973	5.00	12.00
Chess 2CH-60028	(P)	Golden Decade, Volume 3 (2 LPs)	1974	6.00	15.00

BERRY, RICHARD (& THE SOUL SEARCHERS)

Crown CLP-5371	(M)	Richard Berry And The Dreamers	1963	20.00	50.00
Crown CST-371	(E)	Richard Berry And The Dreamers	1963	10.00	25.00
Pam 1001	(M)	Live At The Century Club	196?	20.00	50.00
Pam 1002	(M)	Wild Berry	196?	20.00	50.00

BEST, PETE
Best was a member of the Beatles before they recorded for EMI/Parlophone.

Savage BM-71	(M)	Best Of The Beatles	1965	80.00	200.00
		(Originals have orange labels and a white oval logo on the cover.			
		Counterfeits have red labels and a yellow oval logo on the cover.)			

BETHLEHEM ASYLUM

Ampex 10106	(S)	Commit Yourself	1970	6.00	15.00
Ampex 10124	(S)	Bethlehem Asylum	1971	6.00	15.00

BEVERLY HILL BILLIES, THE
The Hill Billies are a studio concoction featuring Elton Britt.

Rar-Arts 1000	(M)	Those Fabulous Beverly Hill Billies	196?	30.00	75.00

Label & Catalog #		Title	Year	VG+	NM

BIBB, LEON

Label & Catalog #		Title	Year	VG+	NM
Vanguard VRS-9067	(M)	Love Songs	1960	8.00	20.00
Vanguard VSD-2067	(S)	Love Songs	1960	10.00	25.00
Vanguard VRS-9041	(M)	Folksongs	1961	8.00	20.00
Vanguard VSD-2041	(S)	Folksongs	1961	10.00	25.00
Vanguard VRS-9058	(M)	Tol' My Captain	1961	8.00	20.00
Vanguard VSD-2058	(S)	Tol' My Captain	1961	10.00	25.00

BIG BEATS, THE

Liberty LRP-3407	(M)	The Big Beats Live	1965	8.00	20.00
Liberty LST-7407	(S)	The Big Beats Live	1965	10.00	25.00

BIG BLACK

Uni 73018	(S)	Elements Of Now	1968	6.00	15.00
Uni 73033	(S)	Lion Walk	1969	6.00	15.00
Uni 73134	(S)	Big Black And The Blues	1972	6.00	15.00

BIG BOPPER, THE
The Big Bopper is a pseudonym for J. P. "Jape" Richardson.

Mercury MG-20402	(M)	Chantilly Lace (Black label)	1959	200.00	400.00
Mercury MG-20402	(M)	Chantilly Lace	1964	60.00	150.00
		(Red label with black & white logo on top.)			
Mercury MG-20402	(M)	Chantilly Lace	1971	10.00	25.00
		(Red label with twelve oval logos around the perimeter.)			
Pickwick SPC-3365	(E)	Chantilly Lace	1973	6.00	15.00

BIG BROTHER

All American 5770	(M)	Big Brother Featuring Ernie Joseph	1970	60.00	150.00

BIG BROTHER & THE HOLDING COMPANY
BB&THC were Peter Albin, Sam Andrews, David Getz and James Gurley. The first two albums feature Janis Joplin; the final two feature Nick Gravenites.

Mainstream 56099	(M)	Big Brother & The Holding Company	1967	12.00	30.00
Mainstream S-6099	(S)	Big Brother & The Holding Company	1967	10.00	25.00
Columbia KCL-2900	(M)	Cheap Thrills	1968	20.00	50.00
Columbia KCS-9700	(S)	Cheap Thrills ("360 Sound" label)	1968	10.00	25.00
Columbia C-30222	(S)	Be A Brother	1970	10.00	25.00
Columbia C-30631	(S)	Big Brother & The Holding Company	1971	6.00	15.00
		(Columbia 30631 is a reissue of Mainstream 6099 plus both sides of their final Mainstream single in stereo			
Columbia C-30738	(S)	How Hard It Is	1971	10.00	25.00

BIG DADDY

Gee G-704	(M)	Big Daddy's Blues (Red label)	1960	20.00	50.00
Gee SG-704	(S)	Big Daddy's Blues (Red label)	1960	40.00	100.00
Regent MG-6106	(M)	Twist Party	1962	10.00	25.00

BIG FOOT

Winro 1004	(S)	Big Foot	1968	8.00	20.00

BIG MAYBELLE

Savoy MG-14005	(M)	Big Maybelle Sings	1957	50.00	150.00
Savoy MG-14011	(M)	Blues, Candy And Big Maybelle	1958	50.00	150.00
Brunswick BL-54107	(M)	What More Can A Woman Do	1962	10.00	25.00
Brunswick BL-754107	(S)	What More Can A Woman Do	1962	12.00	30.00
Brunswick BL-541??	(M)	The Gospel Sound Of Big Maybelle	1962	8.00	20.00
Brunswick BL-7541??	(S)	The Gospel Sound Of Big Maybelle	1962	10.00	25.00
Scepter S-522	(M)	The Soul Of Big Maybelle	1964	8.00	20.00
Scepter SS-522	(S)	The Soul Of Big Maybelle	1964	12.00	30.00
Rojac R-522	(M)	Got A Brand New Bag	1967	12.00	30.00
Rojac RS-522	(S)	Got A Brand New Bag	1967	20.00	50.00
Rojac RS-123	(S)	Saga Of The Good Life And Hard Times	196?	12.00	30.00
Paramount PAS-1011	(S)	The Last Of Big Maybelle (2 LPs)	1970	6.00	15.00

BIG STAR
Big Star features Alex Chilton, formerly of The Box Tops.

Ardent ADS-2803	(S)	#1 Record	1972	10.00	25.00
Ardent ADS-1501	(S)	Radio City ("O My Soul" is in mono)	1974	10.00	25.00
PVC 7903	(S)	Big Star's Third	1978	10.00	25.00

Label & Catalog #		Title	Year	VG+	NM

BIG THREE, THE
The Big Three are Cass Elliot, James Hendricks and Tim Rose.

FM 307	(M)	The Big Three	1963	12.00	30.00
FM FS-307	(S)	The Big Three	1963	16.00	40.00
FM 311	(M)	Live At The Recording Studio	1964	12.00	30.00
FM FS-311	(S)	Live At The Recording Studio	1964	16.00	40.00
Roulette R-42000	(M)	The Big Three Featuring Cass Elliot	1967	6.00	15.00
Roulette SR-42000	(S)	The Big Three Featuring Cass Elliot	1967	8.00	20.00

BIKEL, THEODORE

Elektra EKL-32	(M)	Songs Of Israel	195?	8.00	20.00
Elektra EKL-105	(M)	Actor's Holiday	195?	8.00	20.00
Elektra EKL-175	(M)	Bravo Bikel	195?	8.00	20.00

BIKEL, THEODORE, & GEULA GILL

Elektra EKL-150	(M)	Russian Gypsy	195?	8.00	20.00
Elektra EKL-161	(M)	Songs From Just About Everywhere	195?	8.00	20.00
Elektra EKL-185	(M)	Songs Old And New	195?	8.00	20.00

BIKEL, THEODORE, & CYNTHIA GOODING

Elektra EKL-109	(M)	A Young Man And A Maid	195?	8.00	20.00

BILLION DOLLAR BABIES, THE
The Babies were former members of Alice Cooper's band.

Polydor PRO-022	(DJ)	Battle Axe (Sampler)	1977	8.00	20.00
Polydor PD1-6100	(S)	Battle Axe	1977	5.00	12.00

BIRMINGHAM SUNDAY

All-American	(S)	Birmingham Sunday	197?	200.00	400.00

BIRTH CONTROL

Prophesy PRS-1002	(S)	A New German Rock Group	1970	10.00	25.00

BISHOP, ELVIN [THE ELVIN BISHOP GROUP]
Bishop was formerly a member of Paul Butterfield's Blues Band.

Fillmore F-30001	(S)	The Elvin Bishop Group	1969	6.00	15.00
Fillmore Z-30239	(S)	Feel It	1970	6.00	15.00

BISHOP, JOEY

ABC-Paramount 408	(M)	Joey Bishop Sings Country & Western	1962	8.00	20.00
ABC-Paramount S-408	(S)	Joey Bishop Sings Country & Western	1962	10.00	25.00

BIT-A-SWEET

ABC S-640	(S)	Hypnotic 1	1968	6.00	15.00

BITTER END SINGERS, THE

Mercury MG-20986	(M)	Discover The Bitter End Singers	1965	6.00	15.00
Mercury SR-60986	(S)	Discover The Bitter End Singers	1965	8.00	20.00
Mercury MG-21018	(M)	Through Our Eyes	1965	6.00	15.00
Mercury SR-61018	(S)	Through Our Eyes	1965	8.00	20.00

BLACK , BILL
Bill Black was Elvis Presley's bass player from 1954 through his first golden era with RCA, 1956-1959.

Hi HL-12001	(M)	Smokie	1960	12.00	40.00
Hi SHL-32001	(E)	Smokie	196?	8.00	20.00
Hi HL-12002	(M)	Saxy Jazz	1960	12.00	40.00
Hi SHL-32002	(E)	Saxy Jazz	196?	8.00	20.00
Hi HL-12003	(M)	Solid And Raunchy	1960	12.00	40.00
Hi SHL-32003	(E)	Solid And Raunchy	1960	8.00	20.00
Hi HL-12004	(M)	That Wonderful Feeling	1961	8.00	20.00
Hi SHL-32004	(S)	That Wonderful Feeling	1961	10.00	30.00
Hi HL-12005	(M)	Movin'	1961	8.00	20.00
Hi SHL-32005	(S)	Movin'	1961	10.00	30.00
Hi HL-12006	(M)	Bill Black's Record Hop	1961	8.00	20.00
Hi SHL-32006	(S)	Bill Black's Record Hop	1961	10.00	30.00
Hi HL-12006	(M)	Let's Twist Her	1962	6.00	15.00
Hi SHL-32006	(S)	Let's Twist Her	1962	8.00	20.00

("Let's Twist Her" is a repackage of "Bill Black's Record Hop.")

Label & Catalog #		Title	Year	VG+	NM
Hi HL-12009	(M)	The Untouchable Sound	1963	6.00	15.00
Hi SHL-32009	(S)	The Untouchable Sound	1963	8.00	20.00
Hi SR-8689	(DJ)	Sears Silvertone Presents (Stereo demo LP)	1963	12.00	30.00
Hi HL-12012	(M)	Bill Black's Greatest Hits	1963	5.00	12.00
Hi SHL-32012	(P)	Bill Black's Greatest Hits	1963	6.00	15.00
Hi HL-12013	(M)	Bill Black's Combo Goes West	1963	5.00	12.00
Hi SHL-32013	(S)	Bill Black's Combo Goes West	1963	6.00	15.00
Hi HL-12015	(M)	Bill Black Plays The Blues	1964	6.00	15.00
Hi SHL-32015	(S)	Bill Black Plays The Blues	1964	8.00	20.00
Hi HL-12017	(M)	Bill Black Plays Tunes By Chuck Berry	1964	6.00	15.00
Hi SHL-32017	(S)	Bill Black Plays Tunes By Chuck Berry	1964	8.00	20.00
Hi HL-12020	(M)	Bill Black's Combo Goes Big Band	1964	5.00	12.00
Hi SHL-32020	(S)	Bill Black's Combo Goes Big Band	1964	6.00	15.00
Hi HL-12023	(M)	More Solid And Raunchy	1965	5.00	12.00
Hi SHL-32023	(S)	More Solid And Raunchy	1965	6.00	15.00
Hi HL-12027	(M)	Mr. Beat	1965	5.00	12.00
Hi SHL-32027	(S)	Mr. Beat	1965	6.00	15.00
Hi HL-12032	(M)	All Timers	1966	5.00	12.00
Hi SHL-32032	(S)	All Timers	1966	6.00	15.00
Hi HL-12033	(M)	Black Lace	1967	5.00	12.00
Hi SHL-32033	(S)	Black Lace	1967	6.00	15.00
Hi HL-12041	(M)	Beat Goes On	1968	6.00	15.00
Hi SHL-32041	(S)	Beat Goes On	1968	6.00	15.00

— Original Hi albums above have gray labels.—

BLACK, CILLA

Capitol T-2308	(M)	Is It Love?	1965	12.00	30.00
Capitol ST-2308	(S)	Is It Love?	1965	16.00	40.00

BLACK, JEANNE

Capitol T-1513	(M)	A Little Bit Lonely	1961	6.00	15.00
Capitol ST-1513	(S)	A Little Bit Lonely	1961	8.00	20.00

BLACK DIAMONDS, THE

Alshire 5220	(S)	Tribute To Jimi Hendrix	1971	6.00	15.00

BLACK LIGHTNING

Tower ST-5129	(S)	Shades Of Black Lightning	1968	6.00	15.00

BLACK MERDA

Chess LP-1551	(S)	Black Merda	1970	20.00	50.00

BLACK OAK ARKANSAS

Atco QD-7019	(Q)	Raunch And Roll/Live	1973	8.00	20.00
Capricorn CEP-0005	(DJ)	I'd Rather Be Sailing	1978	8.00	20.00

BLACK ORCHIDS, THE

"NR" 4680	(S)	The Black Orchids (No cover)	1972	30.00	75.00

BLACK PEARL

Atlantic SD-8220	(S)	Black Pearl	1969	8.00	20.00
Prophesy PRS-1001	(S)	Black Pearl Live	1970	10.00	25.00

BLACK SABBATH

The original Sabbath featured Ozzie Osbourne, later replaced by Ronnie James Dio and Ian Gillan.

Warner Bros. WS-1871	(S)	Black Sabbath	1969	6.00	15.00
Warner Bros. WS-1887	(S)	Paranoid	1971	6.00	15.00
Warner Bros. BS-2562	(S)	Master Of Reality (With poster)	1971	16.00	40.00
Warner Bros. BS-2562	(S)	Master Of Reality (Without poster)	1971	6.00	15.00
Warner Bros. BS-2602	(S)	Black Sabbath, Volume 4	1972	6.00	15.00
— Original Warner Bros. albums above have green labels.—					
Warner Bros. WS4-1887	(Q)	Paranoid	1974	10.00	25.00

BLACK SATIN

Black Satin features Fred Parris of The Five Satins.

Buddah BDS-5654	(S)	Black Satin	1976	6.00	15.00

BLACK VELVET

OKeh OKS-14130	(S)	Love City	1969	6.00	15.00

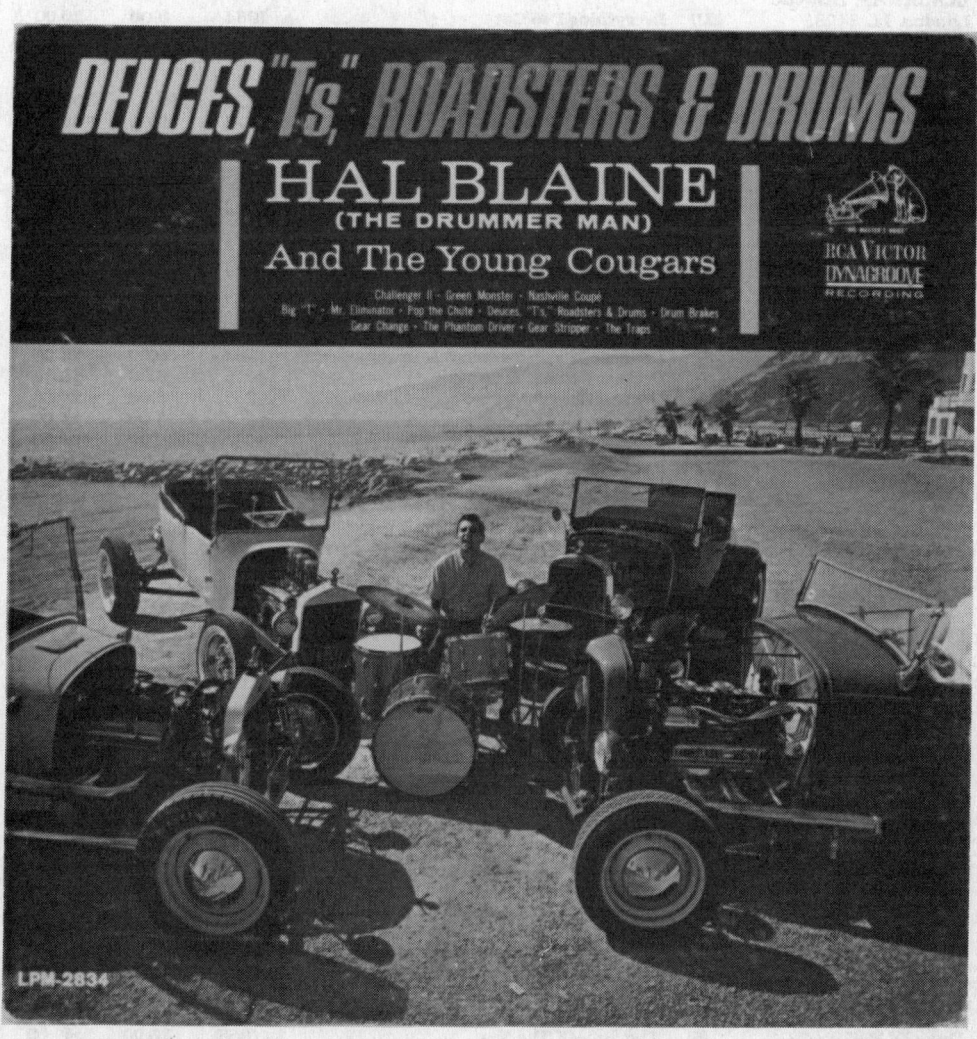

Hal Blaine is the drummer's drummer, a session musician who claims more hit records than any percussionist in the history of recorded music; the RIAA Gold Records lining his walls are testimony to his claim. Of his solo albums, Deuces, "Ts", Roadsters & Drums with The Young Cougars is easily his most sought-after, not only for the music but for the great cover shot of the classic rods against the Southern California background, which piques the automotive collector's intrest.

Label & Catalog #		Title	Year	VG+	NM

BLACKFOOT, J. D.

| Mercury SRM-1-61288 | (S) | The Ultimate Prophecy | 1970 | 20.00 | 50.00 |

BLACKHORSE

| DSDA 001 | (S) | Blackhorse | 197? | 30.00 | 75.00 |

BLACKMAN, HONOR

| London LL-3408 | (M) | Everything I've Got | 1964 | 8.00 | 20.00 |
| London PS-408 | (S) | Everything I've Got | 1964 | 12.00 | 30.00 |

BLACKWELL, OTIS

| Davis 109 | (M) | Singin' The Blues | 1956 | 150.00 | 300.00 |
| Inner City 1032 | (S) | These Are My Songs | 1977 | 6.00 | 15.00 |

BLACKWELL, SCRAPPER

Scrapper also recorded with Brooks Berry.

| Bluesville BVLP-1047 | (M) | Mr. Scrapper's Blues | 1962 | 16.00 | 40.00 |

BLACKWOOD APOLOGY

| Fontana SRF-67591 | (S) | House Of Leather | 1969 | 6.00 | 15.00 |

BLAINE, HAL (& THE YOUNG COUGARS)

RCA Victor LPM-2834	(M)	Deuces, "T's," Roadsters & Drums	1963	24.00	60.00
RCA Victor LSP-2834	(S)	Deuces, "T's," Roadsters & Drums	1963	30.00	75.00
Dunhill D-50002	(M)	Drums! Drums! A Go Go	1966	6.00	15.00
Dunhill DS-50002	(S)	Drums! Drums! A Go Go	1966	8.00	20.00
Dunhill D-50019	(M)	Psychedelic Percussion	1967	6.00	15.00
Dunhill DS-50019	(S)	Psychedelic Percussion	1967	8.00	20.00

BLAINE, VIVIAN

Mercury MG-20233	(M)	Songs From The Ziegfeld Follies	1957	12.00	30.00
Mercury MG-20234	(M)	Songs From "The Great White Way"	1957	12.00	30.00
Mercury MG-20321	(M)	Pal Joey	1958	12.00	30.00

BLAIR, SALLIE : *Refer to* GOLDMINE'S PRICE GUIDE TO COLLECTIBLE JAZZ ALBUMS

BLAKE, BETTY : *Refer to* GOLDMINE'S PRICE GUIDE TO COLLECTIBLE JAZZ ALBUMS

BLANC, MEL

Refer to Bugs Bunny; The Flintstones; Woody Woodpecker; and Tweety Pie.

| Capitol H-436 (10") | (M) | Party Panic | 1953 | 40.00 | 100.00 |

BLAND, BOBBY "BLUE"

Duke DLP-74	(M)	Two Steps From The Blues	1961	50.00	150.00
		(Originally issued on a purple & yellow label.)			
Duke DLP-74	(M)	Two Steps From The Blues	1961	20.00	50.00
Duke DLPS-74	(E)	Two Steps From The Blues	1961	16.00	40.00
Duke DLP-75	(M)	Here's The Man	1962	20.00	50.00
Duke DLPS-75	(S)	Here's The Man	1962	40.00	100.00
		(Original pressings include a spoken into to "36-22-36.")			
Duke DLPS-75	(S)	Here's The Man	196?	16.00	40.00
		(Later pressings delete the spoken intro.)			
Duke DLP-77	(M)	Call On Me	1963	20.00	50.00
Duke DLP-78	(M)	Ain't Nothing You Can Do	1964	20.00	50.00
Duke DLP-79	(M)	The Soul Of The Man	1966	12.00	30.00
Duke DLPS-79	(S)	The Soul Of The Man	1966	16.00	40.00
Duke DLP-84	(M)	The Best Of Bobby Bland	1967	6.00	20.00
Duke DLPS-84	(P)	The Best Of Bobby Bland	1967	6.00	25.00
Duke DLP-88	(M)	Touch Of The Blues	1967	8.00	20.00
Duke DLPS-88	(S)	Touch Of The Blues	1967	6.00	25.00
Duke DLP-86	(M)	The Best Of Bobby Bland, Volume 2	1968	10.00	25.00
Duke DLPS-86	(P)	The Best Of Bobby Bland, Volume 2	1968	8.00	20.00
Duke DLPS-89	(S)	Spotlighting The Man	1969	8.00	20.00
Duke X-90	(S)	If Loving You Is Wrong	1970	8.00	20.00
		— Original Duke albums above have orange labels.—			
BluesWay BLS-6065	(S)	Call On Me	1973	6.00	15.00
Dunhill DSX-50163	(S)	His California Album	1973	6.00	15.00
Dunhill DSX-50169	(S)	Dreamer	1974	6.00	15.00

Label & Catalog #		Title	Year	VG+	NM

BLAND, BOBBY "BLUE," & B.B. KING

Dunhill DS-50190	(S)	Together For The First Time (2 LPs)	1974	6.00	15.00
Impulse AS-9317	(S)	Together Again	1975	4.00	10.00

BLAND, BOBBY "BLUE" / JIMMY SOUL / JOHNNY "GUITAR" WATSON

Crown CLP-5358	(M)	Bobby Bland-Jimmy Soul-Johnny Watson	196?	10.00	25.00
Crown CST-358	(E)	Bobby Bland-Jimmy Soul-Johnny Watson	196?	4.00	10.00

BLASTERS, THE

Crown CLP-5392	(M)	Sounds Of The Drags	1963	8.00	20.00
Crown CST-392	(S)	Sounds Of The Drags	1963	10.00	25.00

BLASTERS, THE

Rollin' Rock 021	(S)	American Music	1980	30.00	75.00

BLENDELLS, THE: *Refer to* **SONNY & CHER**

BLESSED END

T. N. S.	(M)	Movin' On	1971	70.00	175.00

BLIND FAITH
Blind Faith is Ginger Baker, Eric Clapton, Rick Grech and Steve Winwood.

Atco SD-33-304A	(S)	Blind Faith (Naked girl on cover)	1969	10.00	25.00
Atco SD-33-304B	(S)	Blind Faith (Attired group on cover)	1969	6.00	15.00
Mobile Fidelity MFSL-086	(S)	Blind Faith	198?	6.00	18.00

BLOCKER, DAN

Trey TLP-903	(M)	Tales For Young 'Uns	196?	20.00	50.00
RCA Victor LPM-2896	(M)	Our Land, Our Heritage	1964	8.00	20.00
RCA Victor LSP-2896	(S)	Our Land, Our Heritage	1964	10.00	25.00

BLODWYN PIG

A&M SP-4210	(S)	Ahead Rings Out	1969	8.00	20.00
A&M SP-4243	(S)	Getting To This	1970	8.00	20.00

BLOND

Fontana SRF-67607	(S)	Blond	1969	8.00	20.00

BLONDE ON BLONDE

Janus JLS-3003	(S)	Contrasts	1969	10.00	25.00

BLONDIE
Blondie features Debbie Harry, formerly of Wind In The Willows.

Private Stock PS-2035	(S)	Blondie	1975	8.00	20.00
Chrysalis CHP-5001	(S)	Parallel Lines (Picture disc)	1978	8.00	20.00
Chrysalis CHS-24	(DJ)	At Home With Debbie Harry & Chris Stein	1981	10.00	25.00
		(Open-end interview with script.)			
Mobile Fidelity MFSL-50	(S)	Parallel Lines	1981	10.00	30.00

BLOOD ROCK

Capitol ST-435	(S)	Bloodrock	1969	3.00	15.00
Capitol ST-491	(S)	Bloodrock 2	1970	5.00	12.00
Capitol SMAS-645	(S)	U.S.A.	1971	5.00	12.00
Capitol ST-765	(S)	Bloodrock 3	1971	5.00	12.00
Capitol SVBB-11038	(S)	Bloodrock Live (2 LPs)	1972	3.00	15.00

BLOOD, SWEAT & TEARS
Originally the brainchild of Blues Project members Al Kooper and Steve Katz, by the second album BS&T was later fronted by David Clayton-Thomas.

Columbia CS-9616	(S)	Child Is Father To The Man	1968	8.00	20.00
Columbia CS-9720	(S)	Blood, Sweat And Tears	1969	6.00	15.00
— Original Columbia albums above have "360 Sound" on the bottom of the label. —					
Columbia CQ-30994	(Q)	Blood, Sweat And Tears	1973	8.00	20.00
Columbia CQ-31170	(Q)	Blood, Sweat And Tears' Greatest Hits	1973	6.00	15.00
Columbia PCQ-32929	(Q)	Mirror Image	1974	6.00	15.00
Columbia HC-49619	(S)	Child Is Father To The Man (Half-speed)	1981	25.00	75.00
LAX L33-1865	(DJ)	Nuclear Blues (Gold vinyl)	1980	6.00	15.00
Direct Disk SD-16605	(S)	Blood, Sweat And Tears	198?	20.00	60.00

Label & Catalog #		Title	Year	VG+	NM
BLOODY MARY					
Family 2707	(S)	**Bloody Mary**	*1972*	**6.00**	**15.00**
BLOOMFIELD, MIKE; AL KOOPER & STEVE STILL					
Columbia CS-9701	(S)	**Super Session** (*"360 Sound" label*)	*1968*	**6.00**	**15.00**
Columbia PCQ-9701	(Q)	**Super Session** (*Gold label*)	*1974*	**8.00**	**20.00**
BLOOMFIELD, MIKE, & AL KOOPER					
Columbia KGP-6	(S)	**The Live Adventures Of Mike Bloomfield & Al Kooper** (*2 LPs. "360 Sound" label*)	*1969*	**8.00**	**20.00**
BLOOMFIELD, MIKE					
Refer to Paul Butterfield's Blues Band; The Electric Flag.					
Columbia CS-9883	(S)	**It's Not Killing Me** (*"360 Sound" label*)	*1969*	**5.00**	**12.00**
BLOOMFIELD, MIKE, & NICK GRAVENITES					
Columbia KC-9893	(S)	**Live At Fillmore West** (*"360 Sound" label*)	*1969*	**5.00**	**12.00**
BLOSSOM DEARIE					
Verve MGV-2037	(M)	**Blossom Dearie**	*1956*	**20.00**	**50.00**
Verve MGV-2081	(M)	**Give Him The Ooh-La-La**	*1958*	**16.00**	**40.00**
Verve MGV-2109	(M)	**Comden And Green**	*1959*	**12.00**	**30.00**
Verve MGVS-6050	(S)	**Comden And Green**	*1959*	**16.00**	**40.00**
Verve MGV-2111	(M)	**Once Upon A Summertime**	*1959*	**12.00**	**30.00**
Verve MGVS-6020	(S)	**Once Upon A Summertime**	*1959*	**16.00**	**40.00**
Verve MGV-2125	(M)	**My Gentleman Friend**	*1959*	**12.00**	**30.00**
Verve MGVS-6112	(S)	**My Gentleman Friend**	*1959*	**16.00**	**40.00**
Verve MGV-2133	(M)	**Broadway Hit Songs**	*1960*	**10.00**	**25.00**
Verve MGV6-2133	(S)	**Broadway Hit Songs**	*1960*	**14.00**	**35.00**
BLOSSOMS, THE					
Lion 1007	(S)	**Shockwave**	*1972*	**6.00**	**15.00**
BLUE BARONS, THE					
Philips PHM-200-017	(M)	**Twist To The Great Blues Hits**	*1962*	**8.00**	**20.00**
Philips PHS-600-017	(S)	**Twist To The Great Blues Hits**	*1962*	**10.00**	**25.00**
BLUE BEATS, THE					
A.A. 133	(M)	**The Beatle Beat**	*1964*	**20.00**	**50.00**
BLUE CHEER					
The original Blue Cheer was Dickie Peterson, Leigh Stevens and Paul Whaley.					
Philips PHM-200-264	(M)	**Vincebus Eruptum**	*1968*	**16.00**	**40.00**
Philips PHS-600-264	(S)	**Vincebus Eruptum**	*1968*	**12.00**	**30.00**
Philips PHS-600-278	(S)	**Outsideinside**	*1968*	**12.00**	**30.00**
Philips PHS-600-305	(S)	**New! Improved! Blue Cheer**	*1969*	**12.00**	**30.00**
Philips PHS-600-333	(S)	**Blue Cheer**	*1970*	**12.00**	**30.00**
— Original Philips albums above have black labels with no print on the bottom perimeter.—					
Philips PHS-600-264	(S)	**Vincebus Eruptum**	*1970*	**6.00**	**15.00**
Philips PHS-600-278	(S)	**Outsideinside**	*1970*	**6.00**	**15.00**
Philips PHS-600-305	(S)	**New! Improved! Blue Cheer**	*1970*	**6.00**	**15.00**
Philips PHS-600-333	(S)	**Blue Cheer**	*1970*	**6.00**	**15.00**
Philips PHS-600-347	(S)	**The Original Human Being**	*1970*	**8.00**	**20.00**
Philips PHS-600-350	(S)	**Oh! Pleasant Hope**	*1971*	**8.00**	**20.00**
— Philips albums above have black labels with "Distributed by Mercury" on the bottom.—					
BLUE DIAMONDS, THE					
London LL-3235	(M)	**Ramona**	*1963*	**10.00**	**25.00**
BLUE EMOTIONS, THE					
Ambient Sound 38346	(S)	**Doo-Wop Doo-Wop**	*1982*	**5.00**	**12.00**
BLUE JAYS, THE					
Milestone 1001	(M)	**The Blue Jays Meet Little Caesar**	*196?*	**20.00**	**50.00**
BLUE MOUNTAIN EAGLE					
Atco SD-33-324	(S)	**Blue Mountain Eagle**	*1970*	**8.00**	**20.00**
Atco *(No number)*	(DJ)	**Blue Mountain Eagle 2**	*1970*	*See note below*	
		(There is cause to doubt the existence of this album.)			

Label & Catalog #		Title	Year	VG+	NM

BLUE OYSTER CULT

Columbia XSM-157265	(DJ)	Live 'Leg (No cover)	1972	30.00	75.00
Columbia PCQ-32017	(Q)	Tyranny And Mutation	1973	8.00	20.00
Columbia PCQ-32858	(Q)	Secret Treaties	1974	8.00	20.00
Columbia AS-986	(DJ)	Blue Oyster Cult (Sampler)	1981	8.00	20.00
Columbia AS-1441	(DJ)	Blue Oyster Cult Live (Sampler)	1982	8.00	20.00

BLUE RIDGE RANGERS , THE
The Blue Ridge Rangers are John Fogerty of Creedence Clearwater.

| Fantasy F-9415 | (S) | The Blue Ridge Rangers | 1973 | 8.00 | 20.00 |

BLUE SKY BOYS, THE

Starday SLP-205	(M)	Rare Treasury Of Old Song Gems	1963	20.00	50.00
Starday SLP-257	(M)	Together Again	1964	16.00	40.00
Starday SLP-269	(M)	The Blue Sky Boys	1964	16.00	40.00
Capitol T-2483	(M)	Presenting The Blue Sky Boys	1966	6.00	15.00
Capitol ST-2483	(S)	Presenting The Blue Sky Boys	1966	8.00	20.00

BLUE THINGS, THE

| RCA Victor LPM-3603 | (M) | The Blue Things | 1966 | 30.00 | 75.00 |
| RCA Victor LSP-3603 | (S) | The Blue Things | 1966 | 40.00 | 100.00 |

BLUE VELVET BAND, THE

| Warner Bros. WS-1802 | (S) | Sweet Moments | 1969 | 12.00 | 30.00 |

BLUEBIRD

| Piccadilly PIC- | (S) | Bluebird | 1980 | 16.00 | 40.00 |

BLUES CLIMAX

| Horne JC-333 | (S) | Blues Climax | 196? | 20.00 | 50.00 |

BLUES IMAGE

| Atco SD-33-300 | (S) | Blues Image | 1969 | 8.00 | 20.00 |

BLUES MAGOOS, THE

Mercury MG-21096	(M)	Psychedelic Lollipop	1966	12.00	30.00
Mercury SR-61096	(S)	Psychedelic Lollipop	1966	16.00	40.00
Mercury MG-21104	(M)	Electric Comic Book	1967	16.00	40.00
Mercury SR-61104	(S)	Electric Comic Book	1967	20.00	50.00
		(The price includes a small black & white comic book.)			
Mercury MG-21104	(M)	Electric Comic Book	1967	12.00	30.00
Mercury SR-61104	(S)	Electric Comic Book	1967	16.00	40.00
		(The price here is for the album without the comic book.)			
Mercury SR-61167	(M)	Basic Blues Magoos	1968	10.00	25.00
Mercury SR-61167	(S)	Basic Blues Magoos	1968	10.00	25.00
		— Original Mercury albums above have red labels with a black & white logo on top.—			
ABC S-697	(S)	Never Goin' Back To Georgia	1969	8.00	20.00
ABC S-710	(S)	Gulf Coast Bound	1970	8.00	20.00

BLUES PROJECT, THE
The Blues Project consisted of Roy Blumenfeld, Tommy Flanders, Danny Kalb, Steve Katz, Al Kooper and Andy Kulberg. Refer to Blood, Sweat & Tears; Seatrain.

Verve/Folkways FV-9024	(M)	Live At The Cafe Au-Go-Go	1966	10.00	25.00
Verve/Folkways FVS-9024	(S)	Live At The Cafe Au-Go-Go	1966	12.00	30.00
Verve/Folkways FT-3000	(M)	Live At The Cafe Au-Go-Go	1966	8.00	20.00
Verve/Folkways FTS-3000	(S)	Live At The Cafe Au-Go-Go	1966	10.00	25.00
		(Folkways 3000 is a reissue of 9024.)			
Verve/Forecast FT-3008	(M)	Projections	1966	8.00	20.00
Verve/Forecast FTS-3008	(S)	Projections	1966	10.00	25.00
Verve/Forecast FTS-3025	(S)	Live At Town Hall	1967	10.00	25.00
Verve/Forecast FTS-3046	(S)	Planned Obsolescence	1968	8.00	20.00
Verve/Forecast FTS-3069	(S)	Flanders/Kalb/Katz, Etc.	1969	8.00	20.00
Verve/Forecast FTS-3077	(S)	The Best Of The Blues Project	1969	6.00	15.00
Capitol ST-782	(S)	Lazarus	1971	5.00	12.00
Capitol SMAS-11017	(S)	The Blues Project	1972	5.00	12.00
MGM GAS-118	(S)	The Blues Project	1972	5.00	12.00
MGM SE-2-8003	(S)	Reunion In Central Park	1973	5.00	12.00
MGM SE-4953	(S)	Archetypes	1974	5.00	12.00

One of only a handful of LPs issued on Phil Spector's Philles label, Bobb-B-Soxx features Bobby Sheen with Darlene Love & The Blossoms. As Uncle Phil cut as many financial corners as possible—including using the lowest quality vinyl available—finding copies that both look and play nearly mint is an adventure. And, like other Philles albums, white label promos of this were another luxury Spector barely tolerated. . . or manufactured.

Label & Catalog #		Title	Year	VG+	NM
BLUES SPECTRUM, THE					
DB 8970	(S)	We Were The Blues Spectrum	1970	60.00	150.00
BLYTHE, STERLING					
Sage C-14	(M)	Night At The Showboat (Red vinyl)	1962	16.00	40.00
BO GRUMPUS					
Atco 33-246	(S)	Before The War	1968	8.00	20.00
BO STREET RUNNERS, THE					
B.T. Puppy BTPS-1026	(S)	The Bo Street Runners	1969	500.00	800.00
BOA					
Snakefield SN-001	(S)	Wrong Road	1969	60.00	150.00
BOAZ					
Blue Moon	(S)	Three Of A Kind	1978	40.00	100.00
BOB & EARL					
Bob Garrett and Earl Cosby.					
Tip TLP-1011	(M)	Harlem Shuffle	1964	14.00	35.00
Tip TLS-9011	(P)	Harlem Shuffle	1964	20.00	50.00
BOB & RAY					
Unicorn 1001 (10")	(M)	Bob & Ray	1954	30.00	75.00
RCA Victor LPM-2131	(M)	On A Platter	1960	8.00	20.00
RCA Victor LSP-2131	(S)	On A Platter	1960	10.00	25.00
BOBB B. SOXX & THE BLUE JEANS					
The Blue Jeans feature Darlene Love. Produced by Phil Spector.					
Philles PHLP-4002	(DJ)	Zip-A-Dee-Doo-Dah (White label)	1963	300.00	750.00
Philles PHLP-4002	(M)	Zip-A-Dee-Doo-Dah	1963	150.00	300.00
BODACIOUS D. F.					
Bodacious D. F. features Marty Balin, formerly of Jefferson Airplane.					
RCA Victor APL1-0206	(S)	Bodacious D. F.	1973	6.00	15.00
BOETCHER, CURT					
Produced by Gary Usher. Boetcher was formerly a member of Milenntum.					
Elektra EKS-75037	(DJ)	There's An Innocent Face	1972	4.00	10.00
Elektra EKS-75037	(S)	There's An Innocent Face	1972	6.00	15.00
BOGARDE, DIRK					
London LL-3147	(M)	Lyrics For Lovers	1960	10.00	25.00
BOGGS, DOCK					
Verve/Folkways FV-9025	(M)	The Legendary Dock Boggs	1965	8.00	20.00
Verve/Folkways FVS-9025	(S)	The Legendary Dock Boggs	1965	10.00	25.00
BOGGS, NOEL					
Repeat 100-10	(M)	Anytime	196?	20.00	50.00
Repeat 310-8	(M)	Western Swing	196?	20.00	50.00
Shasta 503	(M)	Magic Steel Guitar (Red cover)	196?	20.00	50.00
BOHEMIAN VENDETTA					
Mainstream 56106	(M)	Bohemian Vendetta	1968	14.00	35.00
Mainstream S-6106	(S)	Bohemian Vendetta	1968	20.00	50.00
BOLDER DAMN					
Hit HRI-5061	(S)	Mourning	1971	800.00	1,200.00
BOK, GORGON					
Verve/Forecast FT-3016	(M)	Gordon Bok	1966	6.00	15.00
Verve/Forecast FTS-3016	(S)	Gordon Bok	1966	8.00	20.00
BOMBERS, THE					
West End 104	(S)	The Bombers	1979	6.00	15.00
West End 106	(S)	The Bombers 2	1979	6.00	15.00

Label & Catalog #		Title	Year	VG+	NM

BONADUCE, DANNY

Lion LN-1015	(S)	Danny Bonaduce	1973	10.00	25.00

BOND, EDDIE

Philips Int. 1980	(M)	The Greatest Country Gospel Hits	1961	150.00	300.00

BOND, GRAHAM [GRAHAM BOND ORGANIZATION]

Pulsar 10604	(S)	Love Is The Law	1969	8.00	20.00
Pulsar 10606	(S)	Mighty Graham Bond	1969	8.00	20.00
Mercury SR-61327	(S)	Holy Magick	1970	6.00	15.00
Mercury SRM-1-612	(S)	We Put Our Magick On You	1971	6.00	15.00
Warner Bros. 2BS-2555	(S)	Solid Bond (2 LPs)	1971	6.00	15.00

BOND, JOHNNY
Johnny also recorded with Merle Travis.

Starday SLP-147	(M)	That Wild, Wicked, But Wonderful West	1961	20.00	50.00
Starday SLP-227	(M)	Songs That Made Him Famous	1963	16.00	40.00
Starday SLP-298	(M)	Hot Rod Lincoln	1964	24.00	60.00
Starday SLP-333	(M)	Ten Little Bottles	1965	16.00	40.00
Starday SLP-354	(M)	Famous Hot Rodders I Have Known	1965	30.00	75.00
Harmony HL-7308	(M)	Johnny Bond's Best	1964	8.00	20.00
Harmony HL-7353	(M)	Bottled In Bond	1965	8.00	20.00

BONDS, GARY "U.S."

Legrand LLP-3001	(M)	Dance 'Til Quarter To Three	1961	30.00	75.00
Legrand LLP-3002	(M)	Twist Up Calypso	1962	24.00	60.00
Legrand LLP-3003	(M)	Greatest Hits Of Gary U.S. Bonds	1962	24.00	60.00

BONFIRE, MARS

Uni 73027	(S)	Mars Bonfire	1968	8.00	20.00
Columbia CS-9834	(S)	Faster Than The Speed Of Life	1969	6.00	15.00

BONNEVILLES, THE

Drum Boy DLM-1001	(M)	Meet The Bonnevilles	1963	30.00	75.00
Drum Boy DLS-1001	(S)	Meet The Bonnevilles	1963	50.00	125.00

BONNIE LOU

King 335	(M)	Bonnie Lou Sings	1958	30.00	75.00
King 389	(M)	Daddy-O	1958	30.00	75.00
King 595	(M)	Bonnie Lou Sings	1958	30.00	75.00

BONNIWELL, T. S.

Capitol ST-277	(S)	Close	1969	8.00	20.00

BONNIWELL'S MUSIC MACHINE
Sean Bonniwell was formerly a member of The Music Machine.

Warner Bros. W-1732	(M)	Bonniwell's Music Machine	1967	10.00	25.00
Warner Bros. WS-1732	(S)	Bonniwell's Music Machine	1967	16.00	40.00

BONZO DOG (DOO DAH) BAND, THE
Refer to Roger Ruskin-Spear; The Rutles.

Imperial LP-9370	(M)	Gorilla (Includes booklet)	1968	12.00	30.00
Imperial LP-12370	(S)	Gorilla (Includes booklet)	1968	12.00	30.00
Imperial LP-9370	(M)	Gorilla (Without booklet)	1968	10.00	25.00
Imperial LP-12370	(S)	Gorilla (Without booklet)	1968	10.00	25.00
Imperial LP-12432	(S)	Urban Spaceman (Includes booklet)	1969	12.00	30.00
Imperial LP-12432	(S)	Urban Spaceman (Without booklet)	1969	10.00	25.00
Imperial LP-12445	(S)	Tadpoles	1969	10.00	25.00
Imperial LP-12457	(S)	Keynsham	1970	10.00	25.00
United Arts. UAS-5517	(S)	Beast Of The Bonzos	1972	6.00	15.00
United Arts. UAS-5584	(S)	Let's Make Up And Be Friendly	1972	8.00	20.00
		(With postcard still attached to the cover.)			
United Arts. LA321H2	(S)	The History Of The Bonzos (2 LPs)	1974	8.00	20.00

BOOGIE KINGS, THE

Montel LP-104	(M)	The Boogie Kings	1966	10.00	25.00
Montel LP-109	(M)	Blue Eyed Soul	1967	10.00	25.00

Label & Catalog #		Title	Year	VG+	NM

BOOKER T. & THE M.G.'S
Refer to The Mar-Keys & Booket T. & The M.G.'s

Label & Catalog #		Title	Year	VG+	NM
Stax 701	(M)	Green Onions	1962	20.00	40.00
Stax STS-701	(E)	Green Onions	1965	10.00	25.00
Stax 705	(M)	Soul Dressing	1965	12.00	30.00
Stax STS-705	(E)	Soul Dressing	1965	8.00	20.00
Stax 711	(M)	And Now	1966	8.00	20.00
Stax STS-711	(S)	And Now	1966	12.00	30.00
Stax 713	(M)	In The Christmas Spirit	1966	10.00	25.00
Stax STS-713	(S)	In The Christmas Spirit	1966	12.00	30.00
Stax 717	(M)	Hip Hug-Her	1967	10.00	25.00
Stax STS-717	(S)	Hip Hug-Her	1967	8.00	20.00
Stax 724	(M)	Doin' Our Thing	1968	12.00	30.00
Stax STS-724	(S)	Doin' Our Thing	1968	10.00	25.00
Atlantic 8202	(S)	The Best Of Booker T. & The M.G.'s	1968	6.00	15.00
Stax STS-2033	(S)	Booker T. & The M.G.'s' Greatest Hits	1970	5.00	12.00
Stax	(DJ)	Funktion *(In-store sampler)*	1972	8.00	20.00

BOONE, PAT

Label & Catalog #		Title	Year	VG+	NM
Dot DLP-3012	(M)	Pat Boone	1956	16.00	40.00
Dot DLP-3030	(M)	Howdy!	1956	16.00	40.00
		— Original Dot albums above have maroon labels.—			
Dot DLP-3012	(M)	Pat Boone	1957	10.00	25.00
Dot DLP-25012	(E)	Pat Boone	196?	4.00	10.00
Dot DLP-3030	(M)	Howdy!	1957	10.00	25.00
Dot DLP-25030	(E)	Howdy!	196?	4.00	10.00
Dot DLP-3050	(M)	Pat	1957	10.00	25.00
Dot DLP-25050	(E)	Pat	196?	4.00	10.00
Dot DLP-3068	(M)	Hymns We Love	1957	10.00	25.00
Dot DLP-25068	(S)	Hymns We Love	1957	12.00	30.00
Dot DLP-3071	(M)	Pat's Great Hits	1957	10.00	25.00
Dot DLP-25071	(P)	Pat's Great Hits	1957	12.00	30.00
Dot DLP-9000	(M)	April Love	1957	10.00	25.00
Dot DLP-3077	(M)	Pat Boone Sings Irving Berlin	1958	8.00	20.00
Dot DLP-25077	(S)	Pat Boone Sings Irving Berlin	1958	10.00	25.00
Dot DLP-3118	(M)	Star Dust	1958	8.00	20.00
Dot DLP-25118	(S)	Star Dust	1958	10.00	25.00
Dot DLP-3121	(M)	Yes Indeed!	1958	8.00	20.00
Dot DLP-3158	(M)	Pat Boone Sings	1959	8.00	20.00
Dot DLP-25158	(S)	Pat Boone Sings	1959	10.00	25.00
Dot DLP-3180	(M)	Tenderly	1959	8.00	20.00
Dot DLP-25180	(S)	Tenderly	1959	10.00	25.00
Dot DLP-3181	(M)	Great Millions	1959	8.00	20.00
Dot DLP-25181	(S)	Great Millions	1959	10.00	25.00
Dot DLP-3199	(M)	Side By Side	1959	8.00	20.00
Dot DLP-25199	(S)	Side By Side	1959	10.00	25.00
Dot DLP-3222	(M)	White Christmas	1959	8.00	20.00
Dot DLP-25222	(S)	White Christmas	1959	10.00	25.00
Dot DLP-3234	(M)	He Leadeth Me	1960	8.00	20.00
Dot DLP-25234	(S)	He Leadeth Me	1960	10.00	25.00
Dot DLP-3261	(M)	Pat's Great Hits, Volume 2	1960	8.00	20.00
Dot DLP-25261	(S)	Pat's Great Hits, Volume 2	1960	10.00	25.00
Dot DLP-3270	(M)	Moonglow	1960	8.00	20.00
Dot DLP-25270	(S)	Moonglow	1960	10.00	25.00
Dot DLP-25270	(S)	Moonglow *(Blue vinyl)*	1960	20.00	50.00
Dot DLP-3285	(M)	This And That	1960	6.00	15.00
Dot DLP-25285	(S)	This And That	1960	8.00	20.00
Dot DLP-3346	(M)	Great! Great! Great!	1961	5.00	12.00
Dot DLP-25346	(S)	Great! Great! Great!	1961	6.00	15.00
Dot DLP-3384	(M)	Moody River	1961	6.00	15.00
Dot DLP-25384	(S)	Moody River	1961	8.00	20.00
Dot DLP-3386	(M)	My God And I	1961	5.00	12.00
Dot DLP-25386	(S)	My God And I	1961	6.00	15.00
Dot DLP-3399	(M)	I'll See You In My Dreams	1962	5.00	12.00
Dot DLP-25399	(S)	I'll See You In My Dreams	1962	6.00	15.00
Dot DLP-3402	(M)	Pat Boone Reads From The Holy Bible	1962	6.00	15.00
Dot DLP-3455	(M)	Pat Boone's Golden Hits	1962	5.00	12.00
Dot DLP-25455	(S)	Pat Boone's Golden Hits	1962	6.00	15.00

Label & Catalog #		Title	Year	VG+	NM
Dot DLP-9011	(M)	State Fair *(Soundtrack)*	1962	6.00	15.00
Dot DLP-29011	(S)	State Fair *(Soundtrack)*	1962	8.00	20.00
Dot DLP-3475	(M)	I Love You Truly	1962	5.00	12.00
Dot DLP-25475	(S)	I Love You Truly	1962	6.00	15.00
Dot DLP-3501	(M)	Pat Boone Sings Guess Who?	1963	20.00	50.00
Dot DLP-25501	(S)	Pat Boone Sings Guess Who?	1963	30.00	75.00
		("White Bucks" Boone sings "Blue Suede" Presley.)			
Dot DLP-3504	(M)	Days Of Wine And Roses			
		(And Other Movie Themes)	1963	5.00	12.00
Dot DLP-25504	(S)	Days Of Wine And Roses			
		(And Other Movie Themes)	1963	6.00	15.00
Dot DLP-3513	(M)	Sing Along Without Pat Boone	1963	5.00	12.00
Dot DLP-3513	(M)	Sing Along Without Pat Boone	1963	6.00	15.00
Dot DLP-3520	(M)	The Star Spangled Banner	1963	5.00	12.00
Dot DLP-25520	(S)	The Star Spangled Banner	1963	6.00	15.00
Dot DLP-3534	(M)	Tie Me Kangaroo Down, Sport	1963	5.00	12.00
Dot DLP-25534	(S)	Tie Me Kangaroo Down, Sport	1963	6.00	15.00
Dot DLP-3546	(M)	The Touch Of Your Lips	1963	5.00	12.00
Dot DLP-25546	(S)	The Touch Of Your Lips	1963	6.00	15.00
Dot DLP-3573	(M)	Ain't That A Shame	1964	5.00	12.00
Dot DLP-25573	(S)	Ain't That A Shame	1964	6.00	15.00
Dot DLP-3582	(M)	The Lord's Prayer (& Other Great Hymns)	1964	5.00	12.00
Dot DLP-25582	(S)	The Lord's Prayer (& Other Great Hymns)	1964	6.00	15.00
Dot DLP-3594	(M)	Boss Beat	1964	5.00	12.00
Dot DLP-25594	(S)	Boss Beat	1964	6.00	15.00
Hamilton HL-60010	(M)	12 Great Hits	1964	4.00	10.00
Hamilton HLS-60010	(S)	12 Great Hits	1964	5.00	12.00
Hamilton HL-60081	(M)	Pat Boone 1965	1965	4.00	10.00
Hamilton HLS-60081	(S)	Pat Boone 1965	1965	5.00	12.00
Dot DLP-3601	(M)	Blest Be The Tie That Binds	1965	5.00	12.00
Dot DLP-25601	(S)	Blest Be The Tie That Binds	1965	6.00	15.00
Dot DLP-3606	(M)	Near You	1965	5.00	12.00
Dot DLP-25606	(S)	Near You	1965	6.00	15.00
Dot DLP-3626	(M)	The Golden Era Of Country Hits	1965	5.00	12.00
Dot DLP-25626	(S)	The Golden Era Of Country Hits	1965	6.00	15.00
Dot DLP-3650	(M)	My Tenth Anniversary With Dot Records	1964	4.50	12.00
Dot DLP-25560	(S)	My Tenth Anniversary With Dot Records	1964	6.00	15.00
Dot DLP-3667	(M)	Winners Of The Reader's Digest Poll	1965	5.00	12.00
Dot DLP-25667	(S)	Winners Of The Reader's Digest Poll	1965	6.00	15.00
Dot DLP-3685	(M)	Great Hits Of 1965	1965	5.00	12.00
Dot DLP-25685	(S)	Great Hits Of 1965	1965	6.00	15.00
Dot DLP-3748	(M)	Memories	1966	5.00	12.00
Dot DLP-25748	(S)	Memories	1966	6.00	15.00
Dot DLP-3764	(M)	Wish You Were Here, Buddy	1966	5.00	12.00
Dot DLP-25764	(S)	Wish You Were Here, Buddy	1966	6.00	15.00
Dot DLP-3770	(M)	Christmas Is A Comin'	1966	5.00	12.00
Dot DLP-25770	(S)	Christmas Is A Comin'	1966	6.00	15.00
Dot DLP-3798	(M)	How Great Thou Art	1967	5.00	12.00
Dot DLP-25798	(S)	How Great Thou Art	1967	6.00	15.00
Dot DLP-3805	(M)	I Was Kaiser Bill's Batman	1967	5.00	12.00
Dot DLP-25805	(S)	I Was Kaiser Bill's Batman	1967	6.00	15.00
Dot DLP-3814	(M)	Golden Hits/15 Hits Of Pat Boone	1967	5.00	12.00
Dot DLP-25814	(S)	Golden Hits/15 Hits Of Pat Boone	1967	6.00	15.00
Dot DLP-3876	(M)	Look Ahead	1968	6.00	15.00
Dot DLP-25876	(S)	Look Ahead	1968	4.00	10.00
Tetragrammaton 118	(S)	Departure	1969	4.00	10.00

BOONE, RANDY

Decca DL-4619	(M)	The Singing Star Of The Virginian	1965	12.00	30.00
Decca DL-74619	(S)	The Singing Star Of The Virginian	1965	14.00	35.00
Decca DL-4663	(M)	Ramblin' Randy	1965	8.00	20.00
Decca DL-74663	(S)	Ramblin' Randy	1965	10.00	25.00
Gre-Gar 22170006	(S)	Randy Boone	196?	8.00	20.00

BOOT

Agape 2601	(S)	Boot	197?	10.00	25.00
Guinness 36002	(S)	Turn The Other Cheek	197?	6.00	15.00

BOOTSY / BOOTSY'S RUBBER BAND: *Refer to* **WILLIAM COLLINS**

Label & Catalog #		Title	Year	VG+	NM

BORDERSONG
Ann and Nancy Wilson of Heart provide backing vocals on "It's Time Again."

Label & Catalog #		Title	Year	VG+	NM
Real Good 1001	(S)	Morning *(Canadian)*	1975	24.00	60.00

BOSTIC, EARL

King 295-72 (10")	(M)	Earl Bostic And His Alto Sax	195?	16.00	40.00
King 295-76 (10")	(M)	Earl Bostic And His Alto Sax	195?	16.00	40.00
King 295-77 (10")	(M)	Earl Bostic And His Alto Sax	195?	16.00	40.00
King 295-78 (10")	(M)	Earl Bostic And His Alto Sax	195?	16.00	40.00
King 295-79 (10")	(M)	Earl Bostic And His Alto Sax	195?	16.00	40.00
King 295-95 (10")	(M)	Earl Bostic Plays Old Standards	195?	16.00	40.00
King 295-103 (10")	(M)	Earl Bostic And His Alto Sax	195?	16.00	40.00
King 295-119 (10")	(M)	Earl Bostic And His Alto Sax	195?	16.00	40.00
King 395-500	(M)	The Best Of Earl Bostic	1956	10.00	25.00
King 395-503	(M)	Bostic For You	1956	10.00	25.00
King 395-515	(M)	Alto-Tude	1956	10.00	25.00
King 395-525	(M)	Dance Time	1956	10.00	25.00
King 395-529	(M)	Let's Dance With Earl Bostic	1958	8.00	20.00
King 395-547	(M)	Invitation To Dance	1958	8.00	20.00
King 395-558	(M)	C'mon And Dance With Earl Bostic	1958	8.00	20.00
King 395-571	(M)	Bostic Rocks	1958	8.00	20.00
King 395-583	(M)	Showcase Of Swinging Dance Hits	1958	8.00	20.00
King 395-597	(M)	Alto Magic In Hi-Fi	1958	8.00	20.00
King 395-602	(M)	Sweet Tunes Of The Fantastic Fifties	1959	8.00	20.00
King 395-613	(M)	Workshop	1959	8.00	20.00
King 395-620	(M)	Sweet Tunes Of The Roaring Twenties	1959	6.00	15.00
King 640	(M)	Sweet Tunes Of The Sentimental Forties	1959	6.00	15.00
King KS-640	(S)	Sweet Tunes Of The Sentimental Forties	1959	10.00	25.00
King 500	(M)	The Best Of Earl Bostic	1959	6.00	15.00
King 525	(M)	Ain't Misbehavin'	1959	6.00	15.00
King 705	(M)	Hit Tunes Of Big Broadway Shows	1960	6.00	15.00
King 725	(M)	25 Years Of Rhythm And Blues Hits	1960	6.00	15.00
King 786	(M)	By Popular Demand	1962	6.00	15.00
King KS-786	(S)	By Popular Demand	1962	10.00	25.00
King 827	(M)	Earl Bostic Plays Bossa Nova	1963	6.00	15.00
King KS-827	(S)	Earl Bostic Plays Bossa Nova	1963	10.00	25.00
King 838	(M)	Fantastic Fifties	1963	6.00	15.00
King 846	(M)	Jazz As I Feel It	1963	6.00	15.00
King KS-846	(S)	Jazz As I Feel It	1963	10.00	25.00
King 881	(M)	The Best Of Earl Bostic	1964	6.00	15.00
King 900	(M)	New Sound	1964	6.00	15.00
King KS-900	(S)	New Sound	1964	10.00	25.00
King 921	(M)	The Great Hits Of 1964	1964	6.00	15.00
King KS-921	(S)	The Great Hits Of 1964	1964	10.00	25.00
King KS-1048	(S)	Harlem Nocturne	1969	6.00	15.00

BOSTON

Epic E99-44188	(S)	Boston *(Picture disc)*	1978	6.00	15.00
Epic HE-34188	(S)	Boston *(Half-speed master)*	1981	15.00	45.00
Epic HE-44188	(S)	Boston *(Half-speed master)*	1982	12.00	35.00
Epic E99-45050	(DJ)	Don't Look Back *(Picture disc)*	1982	12.00	30.00
Epic HE-45050	(S)	Don't Look Back *(Half-speed master)*	1982	25.00	75.00

BOSTON TEA PARTY, THE

Flick Disc 45000	(S)	The Boston Tea Party	1968	6.00	15.00
American Inter. ST-A-1033	(S)	The Cycle Savages *(Soundtrack)*	1970	10.00	25.00

BOSWELL, CONNEE
Ms. Boswell also recorded with Bing Crosby.

Decca DL-6013 (10")	(M)	The Star Maker	1951	20.00	50.00
Decca DL-5390 (10")	(M)	Connee Boswell	1952	20.00	50.00
Decca DL-5445 (10")	(M)	Singing The Blues	1953	20.00	50.00
RCA Victor LPM-1426	(M)	Connee Boswell & The Original Memphis 5	1957	12.00	30.00
Decca DL-8356	(M)	Connee	1956	12.00	30.00
Design 68	(M)	Connee Boswell Sings Irving Berlin	195?	10.00	25.00
Design 101	(M)	The New Sound Of Connee Boswell	195?	10.00	25.00
Decca DL-4254	(M)	The Star Maker	1962	8.00	20.00
Decca DL-74254	(S)	The Star Maker	1962	10.00	25.00

Label & Catalog #		Title	Year	VG+	NM

BOWEN, JIMMY
Jimmy also recorded with Buddy Knox.

Roulette R-25004	(M)	Jimmy Bowen (Black label)	1957	60.00	150.00
Reprise R-6210	(M)	Sunday Morning With The Comics	1966	12.00	30.00
Reprise RS-6210	(S)	Sunday Morning With The Comics	1966	16.00	40.00

BOWIE, DAVID

Deram DE-16003	(M)	David Bowie	1967	50.00	125.00
Deram DES-18003	(S)	David Bowie	1967	80.00	200.00
Mercury SR-61246	(S)	Man Of Words, Man Of Music	1969	70.00	175.00
Mercury SR-61325	(S)	The Man Who Sold The World	1971	30.00	75.00
		(The matrix number is stamped in the trail-off vinyl of originals;			
		counterfeits have those numbers hand-etched.)			
London 628/9	(P)	Images 1966-1967 (2 LPs)	1973	12.00	30.00
London 50007	(S)	Starting Point	1977	4.00	10.00
		(The London albums recycle material from Deram and Mercury)			
RCA Victor LSP-4623	(S)	Hunky Dory	1972	8.00	20.00
RCA Victor LSP-4702	(S)	The Rise And Fall Of Ziggy Stardust			
		& The Spiders From Mars	1972	8.00	20.00
RCA Victor LSP-4813	(S)	Space Oddity (With poster)	1972	12.00	30.00
RCA Victor LSP-4813	(S)	Space Oddity (Without poster)	1972	8.00	20.00
RCA Victor LSP-4816	(S)	Man Who Sold The World (With poster)	1972	12.00	30.00
RCA Victor LSP-4816	(S)	Man Who Sold The World (Without poster)	1972	8.00	20.00
RCA Victor LSP-4852	(S)	Aladdin Sane	1973	8.00	20.00
RCA Victor APL1-0291	(S)	Pin Ups	1974	8.00	20.00
RCA Victor CPL1-0576	(S)	Diamond Dogs	1974	2,000.00	Rare
		(Original covers show the Bowie-dog's genitals clearly. This was			
		withdrawn and the offending member airbrushed out for release.			
		Near Mint copies have a suggested value of $3,000-5,000.)			
RCA Victor APL1-0576	(S)	Diamond Dogs	1974	6.00	15.00
RCA Victor CPL2-0771	(S)	David Live (2 LPs)	1974	8.00	20.00
RCA Victor APL1-0998	(S)	Young Americans	1975	6.00	15.00
		— Original RCA albums above have orange labels.—			
RCA Victor APL1-1327	(S)	Station To Station (Brown label)	1975	4.00	10.00
RCA Victor APL1-1732	(S)	Changesonebowie	1976	50.00	125.00
		(Contains an alternate take of "John, I'm Only Dancing.")			
RCA Victor APL1-1732	(S)	Changesonebowie	1976	4.00	10.00
RCA Victor DJL1-2697	(DJ)	Bowie Now	1978	14.00	35.00
RCA Victor JD-11306	(DJ	Peter And The Wolf (Black vinyl)	1978	16.00	40.00
RCA Victor ARL1-2743	(S)	Peter And The Wolf (Black vinyl)	1978	6.00	15.00
RCA Victor ARL1-2743	(S)	Peter And The Wolf (Green vinyl)	1978	6.00	15.00
RCA Victor CPL2-2913	(S)	Stage (2 LPs)	1978	4.00	10.00
RCA Victor DJL1-3016	(DJ)	An Evening With David Bowie	1978	30.00	75.00
		(Originals have a black border along the bottom of the cover.)			
RCA Victor DJL1-3545	(DJ)	1980 All Clear	1979	10.00	25.00
RCA Victor DJL1-3829	(DJ)	Special Radio Series, Volume 1:			
		Scary Monsters Interview Album	1980	10.00	25.00
RCA Victor DJL1-3829	(DJ)	College Radio Series, Volume 1:			
		Scary Monsters Interview Album	1980	12.00	30.00
RCA Victor DJL1-3840	(DJ)	Scary Monsters Interview Album	1980	12.00	30.00
RCA Victor CPL2-4862	(DJ)	Ziggy Stardust, The Motion Picture (2 LPs)	1983	40.00	100.00
		(Promo issued on clear vinyl.)			
EMI SPRO-9960/1	(DJ)	Let's Talk	1983	12.00	30.00
EMI SPRO-79112/3	(DJ)	Never Let Me Down: The Interview	1987	30.00	75.00
Mobile Fidelity MFSL-064	(S)	The Rise And Fall Of Ziggy Stardust			
		& The Spiders From Mars	1983	15.00	45.00
Mobile Fidelity MFSL-083	(S)	Let's Dance	1983	6.00	18.00
Rykodisc LSD-4702	(DJ)	The Rise And Fall Of Ziggy Stardust			
		& The Spiders From Mars	1990	40.00	100.00
		(Rykodisc 4702 contains an album and a CD.)			

BOWN, ALAN

| Verve/Forecast FTS-3062 | (S) | The Alan Bown Group | 1969 | 6.00 | 15.00 |

BOX TOPS, THE
The Box Tops feature Alex Chilton. Refer to Big Star.

Bell 6011	(M)	The Letter/Neon Rainbow	1967	10.00	25.00
Bell S-6011	(S)	The Letter/Neon Rainbow	1967	12.00	30.00
Bell S-6017	(S)	Cry Like A Baby	1968	10.00	25.00

Label & Catalog #		Title	Year	VG+	NM
Bell S-6023	(S)	Non-Stop	1968	10.00	25.00
Bell S-6025	(S)	Super Hits	1968	8.00	20.00
Bell S-6032	(S)	Dimensions	1969	8.00	20.00
Cotillion SD-057	(S)	A Lifetime Believing	1971	8.00	20.00
BOYCE, TOMMY					
Camden CAL-2202	(M)	A Twofold Talent	1967	6.00	15.00
Camden CAS-2202	(S)	A Twofold Talent	1967	8.00	20.00
BOYCE, TOMMY, & BOBBY HART					
Refer to Dolenz, Jones, Boyce & Hart.					
A&M LP-126	(M)	Test Patterns	1967	8.00	20.00
A&M SP-4126	(S)	Test Patterns	1967	10.00	25.00
A&M LP-143	(M)	I Wonder What She's Doing Tonight	1968	12.00	30.00
A&M SP-4143	(S)	I Wonder What She's Doing Tonight	1968	10.00	25.00
A&M SP-4162	(S)	It's All Happening On The Inside	1968	8.00	20.00
BOYD, BILLY					
Crown CLP-5196	(M)	Twangy Guitars	1960	10.00	25.00
Crown CST-196	(E)	Twangy Guitars	1960	4.00	10.00
Crown CST-196	(E)	Twangy Guitars (Red vinyl)	1960	16.00	40.00
BOYD, EDDIE					
Epic BN-26409	(S)	7936 South Rhodes	1968	16.00	40.00
London PS-554	(S)	I'll Dust My Broom	1969	16.00	40.00
BRACKEN, EDDIE					
Sea Horse CSH-7002	(M)	Bat Masterson	1960	20.00	50.00
BRADBURY, RAY					
Tower ST-5172	(S)	Dark Carnival	1968	12.00	30.00
BRADLEY, OWEN					
Decca DL-8868	(M)	Big Guitar	1958	12.00	30.00
Decca DL-78868	(S)	Big Guitar	1958	16.00	40.00
BRADLEY, WILL					
Epic LG-1005 (10")	(M)	Boogie Woogie	1954	60.00	150.00
Epic LG-1127 (10")	(M)	Will Bradley	1955	60.00	150.00
Epic LN-3115	(M)	Boogie Woogie	1955	30.00	75.00
Epic LN-3119	(M)	The House Of Bradley	1956	30.00	75.00
BRADSHAW, TINY					
King 295-74 (10")	(M)	Off And On	1955	150.00	350.00
King 395-501	(M)	Selections	1958	150.00	400.00
King 653	(M)	Great Composer	1959	40.00	100.00
King 953	(M)	24 Great Songs	1966	10.00	25.00
BRADY BUNCH, THE					
Paramount PAS-6032	(S)	Meet The Brady Bunch	1972	8.00	20.00
Paramount PAS-6037	(S)	The Kids From The Brady Bunch	1972	8.00	20.00
Paramount PAS-5026	(S)	Merry Christmas From The Brady Bunch	1972	10.00	25.00
Paramount PAS-6058	(S)	The Brady Bunch Phonograph Record	1973	12.00	30.00
BRAHMAN					
Mercury SR-61348	(S)	Brahman	1971	6.00	15.00
BRAINBOX					
Capitol ST-596	(S)	Brainbox	1970	6.00	15.00
BRAND, OSCAR					
Oscar Brand also recorded with Jean Ritchie.					
Riverside RLP-12-630	(M)	Absolute Nonsense	195?	12.00	30.00
Riverside RLP-12-639	(M)	American Drinking Songs	195?	12.00	30.00
Riverside RLP-12-825	(M)	G.I. American Army Songs	195?	12.00	30.00
Chesterfield 101	(M)	Back Room Ballads	195?	10.00	25.00
Elektra EKL-188	(M)	Sports Car Songs For Big Wheels	195?	10.00	25.00
Audio Fidelity LP-1800	(M)	Bawdy Songs & Back Room Ballads, Vol. 1	1957	8.00	20.00
Audio Fidelity LP-1806	(M)	Bawdy Songs & Back Room Ballads, Vol. 2	1957	8.00	20.00

Label & Catalog #		Title	Year	VG+	NM
Audio Fidelity LP-1824	(M)	Bawdy Songs & Back Room Ballads, Vol. 3	957	8.00	20.00
Audio Fidelity LP-1847	(M)	Bawdy Songs & Back Room Ballads, Vol. 4	1958	8.00	20.00
Audio Fidelity SD-5847	(S)	Bawdy Songs & Back Room Ballads, Vol. 4	1958	10.00	25.00
Audio Fidelity LP-1884	(M)	Bawdy Sea Shanties	1959	8.00	20.00
Audio Fidelity SD-5884	(S)	Bawdy Sea Shanties	1959	10.00	25.00
Audio Fidelity LP-1920	(M)	Bawdy Western Songs	1960	8.00	20.00
Audio Fidelity SD-5920	(S)	Bawdy Western Songs	1960	10.00	25.00
Audio Fidelity LP-1952	(M)	Bawdy Songs Goes To College	1961	8.00	20.00
Audio Fidelity SD-5952	(S)	Bawdy Songs Goes To College	1961	10.00	25.00
ABC-Paramount 388	(M)	Oscar Brand Sings For Adults	1961	8.00	20.00
ABC-Paramount S-388	(S)	Oscar Brand Sings For Adults	1961	10.00	25.00
Decca DL-4275	(M)	Folk Songs For Fun	1962	6.00	15.00
Decca DL-74275	(S)	Folk Songs For Fun	1962	8.00	20.00
Tradition TLP-1014	(M)	Laughing America	196?	6.00	15.00
Tradition TLP-1022	(M)	Pie In The Sky	196?	6.00	15.00

BRAND X

Mirror Image	(S)	Brand X Squared	198?	8.00	20.00

BRASSELLE, KEEFE

Coral CRL-57295	(M)	Minstrel Man	1959	8.00	20.00
Coral CRL-757295	(S)	Minstrel Man	1959	10.00	25.00

BRAUTIGAN, RICHARD

Harvest ST-424	(S)	Listening To Richard Brautigan	1969	8.00	20.00

BRAVE BELT
Brave Belt is former Guess Who members Chad Allan and Randy Bachman.

Reprise RS-9447	(S)	Brave Belt	1971	5.00	12.00
Reprise MS-2057	(S)	Brave Belt II	1972	5.00	12.00

BREAD
Bread was David Gates and James Griffin.

Elektra BRD-1	(DJ)	Bread (In-store sampler)	1969	10.00	25.00
Elektra EQ-5015	(Q)	Baby, I'm A-Want You	1973	6.00	15.00
Elektra EQ-5056	(Q)	The Best Of Bread	1973	6.00	15.00

BRENDA & THE TABULATIONS

Dionn LPM-2000	(M)	Dry Your Eyes	1967	12.00	30.00
Dionn LPS-2000	(S)	Dry Your Eyes	1967	16.00	40.00
		("Dry Your Eyes" is rechanneled for this album.)			

BRENNAN, WALTER

Dot DLP-3309	(M)	Dutchman's Gold	1960	6.00	15.00
Dot DLP-25309	(M)	Dutchman's Gold	1960	8.00	20.00
Everest DBR-5103	(M)	World Of Miracles	1960	6.00	15.00
Everest SDBR-1103	(S)	World Of Miracles	1960	8.00	20.00
Everest DBR-5123	(M)	The President	1960	6.00	15.00
Everest SDBR-1123	(S)	The President	1960	8.00	20.00
Liberty LRP-3233	(M)	Old Rivers	1962	6.00	15.00
Liberty LST-7233	(S)	Old Rivers	1962	8.00	20.00
Liberty LRP-3241	(M)	The President	1962	6.00	15.00
Liberty LST-7241	(S)	The President	1962	8.00	20.00
Liberty LRP-3244	(M)	World Of Miracles	1962	6.00	15.00
Liberty LST-7244	(S)	World Of Miracles	1962	8.00	20.00
Liberty LRP-3257	(M)	'Twas The Night Before Christmas Back Home	1962		15.00
Liberty LST-7257	(S)	'Twas The Night Before Christmas Back Home	1962	8.00	20.00
Liberty LRP-3266	(M)	Mama Sang A Song	1963	6.00	15.00
Liberty LST-7266	(S)	Mama Sang A Song	1963	8.00	20.00
Liberty LRP-3317	(M)	Talkin' From The Heart	1964	6.00	15.00
Liberty LST-7317	(S)	Talkin' From The Heart	1964	8.00	20.00
Liberty LRP-3372	(M)	Gunfight At The O.K. Corral	1964	6.00	15.00
Liberty LST-7372	(S)	Gunfight At The O.K. Corral	1964	8.00	20.00

BRETT, PAUL

Janus 3026	(S)	Paul Brett Sage	1971	6.00	15.00

Label & Catalog #		Title	Year	VG+	NM

BREWER, TERESA

London APB-1006 (10")	(M)	Teresa Brewer	1952	16.00	40.00
Coral CRL-56072 (10")	(M)	A Bouquet Of Hits	1952	16.00	40.00
Coral CRL-56093 (10")	(M)	Till I Waltz Again With You	1954	16.00	40.00
Coral CRL-57027	(M)	Music, Music, Music	1956	12.00	30.00
Coral CRL-57053	(M)	Teresa	1956	12.00	30.00
Coral CRL-57135	(M)	For Teenagers In Love	1957	12.00	30.00
Coral CRL-57144	(M)	Teresa Brewer At Christmas Time	1957	12.00	30.00
Coral CRL-57179	(M)	Miss Music	1958	12.00	30.00
Coral CRL-57232	(M)	Time For Teresa	1958	12.00	30.00
Coral CRL-57245	(M)	Teresa Brewer And The Dixieland Band	1959	8.00	20.00
Coral CRL-757245	(S)	Teresa Brewer And The Dixieland Band	1959	10.00	25.00
Coral CRL-57257	(M)	When Your Love Has Gone	1959	8.00	20.00
Coral CRL-757257	(S)	When Your Love Has Gone	1959	10.00	25.00
Coral CRL-57297	(M)	Heavenly Lover	1959	8.00	20.00
Coral CRL-757297	(S)	Heavenly Lover	1959	10.00	25.00
Coral CRL-57315	(M)	Ridin' High	1960	6.00	15.00
Coral CRL-757315	(S)	Ridin' High	1960	8.00	20.00
Coral CRL-57329	(M)	Naughty, Naughty, Naughty	1960	6.00	15.00
Coral CRL-757329	(S)	Naughty, Naughty, Naughty	1960	8.00	20.00
Coral CRL-57351	(M)	My Golden Favorites	1960	6.00	15.00
Coral CRL-757351	(S)	My Golden Favorites	1960	8.00	20.00
Coral CRL-57361	(M)	Songs Everybody Knows	1961	6.00	15.00
Coral CRL-757361	(S)	Songs Everybody Knows	1961	8.00	20.00
Coral CRL-57374	(M)	Aloha From Teresa	1961	6.00	15.00
Coral CRL-757374	(S)	Aloha From Teresa	1961	8.00	20.00
Coral CRL-57414	(M)	Don't Mess With Tess	1962	6.00	15.00
Coral CRL-757414	(S)	Don't Mess With Tess	1962	8.00	20.00
Philips PHM-200-062	(M)	Teresa Brewer's Greatest Hits	1962	6.00	15.00
Philips PHS-600-062	(S)	Teresa Brewer's Greatest Hits	1962	8.00	20.00
Philips PHM-200-099	(M)	Terrific Teresa	1963	5.00	12.00
Philips PHS-600-099	(S)	Terrific Teresa	1963	6.00	15.00
Philips PHM-200-119	(M)	Moments To Remember	1964	5.00	12.00
Philips PHS-600-119	(S)	Moments To Remember	1964	6.00	15.00
Philips PHM-200-147	(M)	Golden Hits Of 1964	1964	5.00	12.00
Philips PHS-600-147	(S)	Golden Hits Of 1964	1964	6.00	15.00
Philips PHM-200-163	(M)	Goldfinger/Other Great Movie Songs	1965	5.00	12.00
Philips PHS-600-163	(S)	Goldfinger/Other Great Movie Songs	1965	6.00	15.00
Philips PHM-200-200	(M)	Songs For Our Fighting Men	1966	5.00	12.00
Philips PHS-600-200	(S)	Songs For Our Fighting Men	1966	6.00	15.00
Philips PHM-200-216	(M)	Gold Country	1966	5.00	12.00
Philips PHS-600-216	(S)	Gold Country	1966	6.00	15.00
Philips PHM-200-230	(M)	Texas Leather And Mexican Lace	1967	5.00	12.00
Philips PHS-600-230	(S)	Texas Leather And Mexican Lace	1967	6.00	15.00

BRICE, FANNY, & HELEN MORGAN

Vik 997	(M)	Torch Songs	195?	20.00	50.00

BRIDES OF FUNKENSTEIN, THE
The Brides are members of the Parliament/Funkadelic community.

Atlantic 19201	(S)	Funk Or Walk	1978	6.00	15.00
Atlantic 19261	(S)	Never Buy Texas From A Cowboy	1979	6.00	15.00

BRIDGES, LLOYD

Carlton CHH-17	(M)	Hear How To Skin Dive	195?	16.00	40.00

BRIGADE

Band'n Vocal BVRS-1066	(S)	Last Laugh	1970	1,000.00	Rare
		(Near Mint copies have a suggested value of $1,500-2,500)			

BRIGG

Susquehanna LP-301	(S)	Brigg	1973	60.00	150.00

BRIGMAN, GEORGE

Solid SR-001	(S)	Jungle Rot	1975	40.00	100.00

BRILL, MARTY

Mercury MG-20178	(M)	A Roving Balladeer	1956	12.00	30.00

Label & Catalog #		Title	Year	VG+	NM
BRILLIANT, ASHLEIGH					
Dorash 1001	(M)	In The Haight-Ashbury (Documentary)	1967	40.00	100.00
BRIMSTONE					
"S" 30534	(M)	Paper Winged Dreams	1968	70.00	175.00
BRINSLEY SCHWARZ					
Brinsley Schwarz features Nick Lowe.					
Capitol ST-589	(S)	Brinsley Schwarz	1970	8.00	20.00
Capitol ST-744	(S)	Despite It All	1971	8.00	20.00
United Arts. UAS-5566	(S)	Silver Pistol	1972	6.00	15.00
United Arts. UAS-5647	(S)	Nervous On The Road	1972	6.00	15.00
BRITT, ELTON					
Elton Britt also recorded as a member of The Beverly Hill Billies.					
RCA Victor LPM-3222 (10")	(M)	Yodel Songs	1954	40.00	100.00
RCA Victor LPM-1288	(M)	Yodel Songs	1956	20.00	50.00
ABC-Paramount 293	(M)	The Wandering Cowboy	1959	14.00	35.00
ABC-Paramount S-293	(S)	The Wandering Cowboy	1959	20.00	50.00
ABC-Paramount 322	(M)	Beyond The Sunset	1960	10.00	25.00
ABC-Paramount S-322	(S)	Beyond The Sunset	1960	14.00	35.00
ABC-Paramount 331	(M)	I Heard A Forest Praying	1960	10.00	25.00
ABC-Paramount S-331	(S)	I Heard A Forest Praying	1960	14.00	35.00
ABC-Paramount 521	(M)	The Singing Hills	1965	8.00	20.00
ABC-Paramount S-521	(S)	The Singing Hills	1965	10.00	25.00
ABC-Paramount 566	(M)	Somethin' For Everybody	1966	8.00	20.00
ABC-Paramount S-566	(S)	Somethin' For Everybody	1966	10.00	25.00
RCA Victor LPM-2669	(M)	The Best Of Elton Britt (Black label)	1963	10.00	25.00
RCA Victor LSP-2669	(E)	The Best Of Elton Britt (Black label)	1963	6.00	15.00
RCA Victor LSP-4073	(S)	When Evening Shadows Fall	1968	6.00	15.00
BROCK, B., & THE SULTANS					
Crown CLP-5399	(M)	Do The Beetle	1964	16.00	40.00
Crown CST-399	(S)	Do The Beetle	1964	20.00	50.00
BROOKLYN BRIDGE, THE					
Brooklyn Bridge features Johnny Maestro of The Crests.					
Buddah BDS-5034	(S)	The Brooklyn Bridge	1969	6.00	15.00
Buddah BDS-5042	(S)	The Second Brooklyn Bridge	1969	6.00	15.00
National General 1001	(S)	Grasshopper (Soundtrack)	1970	6.00	15.00
Buddah BDS-5065	(S)	The Brooklyn Bridge	1970	6.00	15.00
Buddah BDS-5107	(S)	Bridge In Blue	1972	6.00	15.00
BROOKS, DONNA					
Dawn DLP-1105	(M)	I'll Take Romance	1956	16.00	40.00
BROOKS, DONNIE					
Era EL-105	(M)	The Happiest	1961	50.00	125.00
BROOKS, HADDA					
Modern LMP-1210	(M)	Femme Fatale	1956	80.00	200.00
Crown CLP-5010	(M)	Femme Fatale	1957	20.00	50.00
Crown CLP-5374	(M)	Hadda Brooks Sings And Swings	1963	10.00	25.00
Crown CST-374	(E)	Hadda Brooks Sings And Swings	1963	4.00	10.00
BROOKS, HADDA / PETE JOHNSON					
Crown CLP-5058	(M)	Boogie	1958	20.00	50.00
BROONZY, BIG BILL					
Big Bill also recorded with Pete Seeger; Josh White.					
Dial 306 (10")	(M)	Blues Concert	1952	80.00	200.00
Period 1114 (10")	(M)	Big Bill Broonzy Sings	1955	150.00	300.00
EmArcy MG-20634 (10")	(M)	Folk Blues	1954	50.00	125.00
Folkways FA-2315	(M)	Big Bill Broonzy	1957	20.00	50.00
Folkways FA-2326	(M)	Country Blues	1957	20.00	50.00
Folkways FA-3586	(M)	His Songs And Story	1957	20.00	50.00
EmArcy MG-36137	(M)	Blues By Broonzy	1958	30.00	75.00
Columbia WL-111	(M)	Big Bill's Blues	1958	30.00	75.00
Verve MGV-3000	(M)	The Big Bill Broonzy Story (5 LP box)	1959	80.00	200.00

Label & Catalog #		Title	Year	VG+	NM
Verve MGV-3001	(M)	Last Session, Part 1	1959	16.00	40.00
Verve MGV-3002	(M)	Last Session, Part 2	1959	16.00	40.00
Verve MGV-3003	(M)	Last Session, Part 3	1959	16.00	40.00
		(The "Last Sessions" are taken from the boxed set above.)			
Mercury MG-20822	(M)	Memorial	1963	8.00	20.00
Mercury SR-60822	(S)	Memorial	1963	10.00	25.00
Mercury MG-20905	(M)	Remembering Big Bill Broonzy	1964	8.00	20.00
Mercury SR-60905	(S)	Remembering Big Bill Broonzy	1964	10.00	25.00
Epic EE-22017	(M)	Big Bill's Blues	1969	12.00	30.00

BROONZY, BIG BILL; SONNY TERRY & BROWNIE McGHEE

Folkways FA-3817	(M)	Big Bill Broonzy, Sonny Terry And Brownie McGhee	1959	14.00	35.00

BROONZY, BIG BILL, & WASHBOARD SAM

Chess LP-1468	(M)	Big Bill Broonzy And Washboard Sam	1962	70.00	175.00

BROTHER FOX & TAR BABY

Oracle 1001	(S)	Brother Fox & Tar Baby	1969	12.00	30.00
Capitol ST-544	(S)	Brother Fox & Tar Baby	1969	8.00	20.00

BROTHERHOOD

Smitty, Drake and Fang of Paul Revere's Raiders, who also recorded as Friendsound.

RCA Victor LSP-4092	(S)	Brotherhood	1968	6.00	15.00
RCA Victor LSP-4228	(S)	Brotherhood, Brotherhood	1969	6.00	15.00

BROTHERHOOD

BH 501	(S)	Stavia	1972	50.00	125.00

BROTHERHOOD OF MAN, THE

Deram DES-18046	(S)	United We Stand	1970	6.00	15.00

BROTHERS FOUR, THE

Columbia CL-1402	(M)	The Brothers Four	1960	6.00	15.00
Columbia CS-8197	(S)	The Brothers Four	1960	8.00	20.00
Columbia CL-1479	(M)	Rally 'Round The Brothers Four	1960	6.00	15.00
Columbia CS-8270	(S)	Rally 'Round The Brothers Four	1960	8.00	20.00
Columbia CL-1558	(M)	The Alamo (Soundtrack)	1960	12.00	30.00
Columbia CS-8358	(S)	The Alamo (Soundtrack)	1960	16.00	40.00
Columbia CL-1578	(M)	BMOC-Best Music On/Off Campus	1961	6.00	15.00
Columbia CS-8378	(S)	BMOC-Best Music On/Off Campus	1961	8.00	20.00
Columbia CL-1625	(M)	Roamin' With The Brothers Four	1961	6.00	15.00
Columbia CS-8425	(S)	Roamin' With The Brothers Four	1961	8.00	20.00
Columbia CL-1697	(M)	The Brothers Four Songbook	1961	6.00	15.00
Columbia CS-8497	(S)	The Brothers Four Songbook	1961	8.00	20.00
Columbia CL-1803	(M)	The Brothers Four's Greatest Hits	1962	6.00	15.00
Columbia CS-8603	(S)	The Brothers Four's Greatest Hits	1962	8.00	20.00
— Original Columbia albums above have six white-on-black eye logos around the perimeter of the label.—					
Columbia CL-1828	(M)	The Brothers Four In Person	1962	5.00	12.00
Columbia CS-8628	(S)	The Brothers Four In Person	1962	6.00	15.00
Columbia CL-1946	(M)	Cross-Country Concert	1963	5.00	12.00
Columbia CS-8746	(S)	Cross-Country Concert	1963	6.00	15.00
Columbia CL-2033	(M)	The Big Folk Hits	1963	5.00	12.00
Columbia CS-8833	(S)	The Big Folk Hits	1963	6.00	15.00
Columbia CL-2128	(M)	The Brothers Four Sing Of Our Times	1964	5.00	12.00
Columbia CS-8928	(S)	The Brothers Four Sing Of Our Times	1964	6.00	15.00
Columbia CL-2213	(M)	More Big Folk Hits	1964	5.00	12.00
Columbia CS-9013	(S)	More Big Folk Hits	1964	6.00	15.00
Columbia CL-2305	(M)	The Honey Wind Blows	1965	5.00	12.00
Columbia CS-9105	(S)	The Honey Wind Blows	1965	6.00	15.00
Columbia CL-2379	(M)	Try To Remember	1965	5.00	12.00
Columbia CS-9179	(S)	Try To Remember	1965	6.00	15.00
Columbia CL-2502	(M)	The Beatles' Songbook	1966	8.00	20.00
Columbia CS-9302	(S)	The Beatles' Songbook	1966	10.00	25.00
Columbia CL-2568	(M)	Merry Christmas	1966	5.00	12.00
Columbia CS-9368	(S)	Merry Christmas	1966	6.00	15.00
Columbia CL-2702	(M)	A New World's Record	1967	5.00	12.00
Columbia CS-9502	(S)	A New World's Record	1967	6.00	15.00
Columbia CS-9818	(S)	Let's Get Together	1969	5.00	12.00

Label & Catalog #		Title	Year	VG+	NM
BROTHERS JOHNSON					
A&M PR-4714	(DJ)	Blam! *(Picture disc)*	1978	8.00	20.00
		(B-side promotes the group's Japanese tour.)			
A&M PR-4714	(S)	Blam! *(Picture disc)*	1978	4.00	10.00
A&M PR-4714	(S)	Blam! *(Picture disc)*	1978	8.00	20.00
		(Mispressing with same graphics on both sides.)			
Sweet Thunder 10	(S)	Light Up The Night	198?	8.00	25.00
BROWN, AL, & HIS TUNE TOPPERS					
Amy A-1	(M)	The Madison Dance Party	1960	14.00	35.00
Amy AS-1	(S)	The Madison Dance Party	1960	16.00	40.00
		("The Madison" is rechanneled for this album.)			
BROWN, ARTHUR					
Atlantic/Track SD-8198	(S)	The Crazy World Of Arthur Brown	1968	10.00	25.00
BROWN, BOBBY					
Destiny 4001	(S)	Bobby Brown Live	1972	6.00	15.00
Destiny 4002	(S)	The Enlightening Beam Of Axonda	1972	10.00	25.00
BROWN, BOOTS, & HIS BLOCKBUSTERS / DAN DREW & HIS DAREDEVILS					
Both the "artists" on this album are pseudonyms for two groups of jazz luminaries including Shelly Manne, Gerry Mulligan and Shorty Rogers (as the West Coast's Blockbusters) and Al Cohn, Elliott Lawrence and Nick Travis (the East Coast's Daredevils).					
Groove LG-1000	(M)	Rock That Beat	1958	100.00	250.00
BROWN, BUSTER					
Fire FLP-102	(M)	The New King Of The Blues	1960	300.00	600.00
		(Original covers are white with a photo of Brown filling the cover.)			
Fire FLP-102	(M)	The New King Of The Blues	1960	200.00	400.00
		(Later covers are blue with a photo of Brown in the lower left corner and a drawing of a crown above his head.)			
BROWN, CHARLES					
Aladdin 702 (10")	(M)	Mood Music *(Red vinyl)*	1952	1,500.00	Rare
		(Near Mint copies have a suggested value of $3,000-5,000.)			
Aladdin 702 (10")	(M)	Mood Music	1955	1,000.00	Rare
		(Near Mint copies have a suggested value of $2,000-3,000.)			
Aladdin 809	(M)	Mood Music	1956	300.00	500.00
Score SLP-4011	(M)	Driftin' Blues	1958	200.00	400.00
Imperial A-9178	(M)	Million Sellers	1961	50.00	125.00
King 775	(M)	Sings Christmas Songs	1961	50.00	125.00
King 878	(M)	Great Charles Brown	1963	50.00	125.00
Mainstream 56035	(M)	Ballads My Way	1965	8.00	20.00
Mainstream S-6035	(S)	Ballads My Way	1965	12.00	30.00
BluesWay BLS-6039	(S)	Legend	1970	6.00	15.00
BROWN, CHARLES / AMOS MILBURN					
Grand Prix K-421	(M)	Original Blues Sounds	196?	10.00	25.00
Grand Prix KS-421	(E)	Original Blues Sounds	196?	4.00	10.00
BROWN, GEORGIA					
London LL-3286	(M)	Georgia Brown	1962	8.00	20.00
London LL-3331	(M)	Georgia Brown Loves Gershwin	1963	6.00	15.00
London PS-331	(S)	Georgia Brown Loves Gershwin	1963	8.00	20.00
Coral CRL-57436	(M)	Georgia Brown	1964	6.00	15.00
Coral CRL-757436	(S)	Georgia Brown	1964	8.00	20.00
Capitol T-2329	(M)	The Many Shades Of Georgia Brown	1965	6.00	15.00
Capitol ST-2329	(S)	The Many Shades Of Georgia Brown	1965	8.00	20.00
BROWN, HYLO					
Capitol T-1168	(M)	Hylo Brown	1959	30.00	75.00
Starday SLP-185	(M)	Bluegrass Balladeer	196?	24.00	60.00
Starday SLP-204	(M)	Bluegrass Goes To College	196?	20.00	50.00
Starday SLP-220	(M)	Hylo Brown Meets The Lonesome Pine Fiddlers	196?	20.00	50.00
Starday SLP-249	(M)	Sing Me A Bluegrass Song	196?	16.00	40.00

Label & Catalog #		Title	Year	VG+	NM

BROWN, JAMES (& HIS FAMOUS FLAMES)

Many of JB's albums were in and out of print with different labels, covers, titles and catalogue numbers. The listing below covers first pressings and many, but not all, of the changes. Refer to Hank Ballard; Bobby Byrd; Lynn Collins; Bill Doggett; Dee Felice; Fred & The New JB's; Martha High; The JB's; Anna King; Maceo; Sweet Charles; Fred Wesley; Marva Whitney.

Label & Catalog #		Title	Year	VG+	NM
King 610	(M)	**Please Please Please**	1959	**500.00**	**1,000.00**
		(Original covers have a photo of a woman's legs ascending steps.)			
King 635	(M)	**Try Me**	1959	**300.00**	**600.00**
		(Original covers have a drawing of a woman holding a smoking gun.)			
King 683	(M)	**Think!**	1960	**300.00**	**600.00**
		(Original covers have a photo of a baby.)			
King 683	(M)	**Think!**	196?	**40.00**	**100.00**
		(Later covers have photos of JB.)			
King 743	(M)	**The Amazing James Brown**	1961	**80.00**	**200.00**
		(First pressings have the crownless black label.)			
King 743	(M)	**The Amazing James Brown**	196?	**80.00**	**200.00**
		(Second pressings have a black label with a crown.)			
King KS-743	(E)	**The Amazing James Brown**	196?	**20.00**	**50.00**
		(Later pressings have a black & orange label with JB's face.)			
King 771	(M)	**Night Train**	1961	**60.00**	**150.00**
King 771	(M)	**Twist Around**	1962	**50.00**	**125.00**
King 771	(M)	**Jump Around**	1963	**40.00**	**100.00**
King KS-771	(S)	**Jump Around**	1963	**60.00**	**150.00**
		(King 771 s actually a various artists album featuring JB. "Twist Around" and "Jump Around" are reissues of "Night Train.")			
King 780	(M)	**Shout And Shimmy**	1962	**60.00**	**150.00**
King 780	(M)	**Good, Good Twistin'**	1962	**40.00**	**100.00**
		("Good Good Twistin'" is a reissue of "Shout And Shimmy.")			
King 780	(M)	**Excitement**	1963	**40.00**	**100.00**
		("Excitement" is a reissue of "Shout And Shimmy.")			
King KS-780	(E)	**Excitement**	196?	**20.00**	**50.00**
		(The stereo reissue has a blue label with a crown.)			
King 804	(M)	**James Brown & His Famous Flames Tour The U.S.A.**	1962	**60.00**	**150.00**
King KS-804	(E)	**James Brown & His Famous Flames Tour The U.S.A.**	196?	**20.00**	**50.00**
		(The stereo reissue has a blue label with a crown.)			
King 826	(DJ)	**Live At The Apollo!** *(Banded for airplay)*	1963	**300.00**	**500.00**
zKing 826	(M)	**Live At The Apollo!**	1963	**40.00**	**100.00**
King KS-826	(S)	**Live At The Apollo!**	1963	**60.00**	**150.00**
King 851	(M)	**Prisoner Of Love**	1963	**40.00**	**100.00**
King KS-851	(E)	**Prisoner Of Love**	196?	**20.00**	**50.00**
		(The stereo reissue has a blue label with a crown.)			
King 883	(M)	**Pure Dynamite! Live At The Royal**	1964	**60.00**	**150.00**
		(Gatefold cover)			
King 909	(M)	**Please Please Please**	1964	**40.00**	**100.00**
King KS-909	(E)	**Please Please Please**	1964	**20.00**	**50.00**
		(King 909 is a reissue of 610.)			
King 919	(M)	**The Unbeatable James Brown/16 Hits**	1964	**40.00**	**100.00**
King KS-919	(E)	**The Unbeatable James Brown/16 Hits**	1964	**20.00**	**50.00**
		(King 919 is a reissue of 683.)			
King 938	(M)	**Papa's Got A Brand New Bag**	1965	**30.00**	**75.00**
King LPS-938	(P)	**Papa's Got A Brand New Bag**	1965	**30.00**	**75.00**
King 946	(M)	**I Got You (I Feel Good)**	1966	**40.00**	**100.00**
King KSD-946	(S)	**I Got You (I Feel Good)**	1966	**60.00**	**150.00**
King 961	(M)	**Mighty Instrumentals**	1966	**40.00**	**100.00**
King 985	(M)	**It's A Man's Man's Man's World**	1966	**40.00**	**100.00**
King KS-985	(S)	**It's A Man's Man's Man's World**	1966	**60.00**	**150.00**
King 1010	(M)	**Christmas Songs**	1966	**60.00**	**150.00**
		— Original King albums above have crownless black or blue labels. The logo on the covers have a crown with "King" in open capital block letters below.—			
King 1016	(M)	**Raw Soul**	1967	**20.00**	**50.00**
King KS-1016	(E)	**Raw Soul**	1967	**14.00**	**35.00**
King 1018	(M)	**Live At The Garden**	1967	**20.00**	**50.00**
King KS-1018	(S)	**Live At The Garden**	1967	**30.00**	**75.00**
King K-1020	(M)	**Cold Sweat**	1967	**20.00**	**50.00**
King KS-1020	(E)	**Cold Sweat**	1967	**14.00**	**35.00**
King KS-1022	(S)	**Live At The Apollo, Vol. 2** *(2 LPs)*	1968	**24.00**	**60.00**
King KS-1024	(S)	**JB Presents His Show Of Tomorrow**	1968	**20.00**	**50.00**

Label & Catalog #		Title	Year	VG+	NM
		(King 1024 is actually a various artists album.)			
King KS-1030	(S)	I Can't Stand Myself (When You Touch Me)	1968	20.00	50.00
King KS-1031	(S)	I Got The Feelin'	1968	20.00	50.00
King KS-1034	(S)	JB Plays Nothing But Soul	1968	20.00	50.00
King KS-1038	(S)	Thinking About Little Willie John			
		And A Few Nice Things	1968	20.00	50.00
		—The covers of original King album above have a crown with "King" in open capital block letters.—			
King KS-1040	(S)	A Soulful Christmas	1968	16.00	40.00
King KS-1047	(S)	Say It Loud—I'm Black And I'm Proud	1969	16.00	40.00
King KS-1051	(S)	Gettin' Down To It	1969	16.00	40.00
King KSD-1055	(S)	The Popcorn	1969	16.00	40.00
King KS-1063	(S)	It's A Mother	1969	16.00	40.00
King KSD-1092	(S)	Ain't It Funky	1970	16.00	40.00
King KS-1095	(S)	It's A New Day—Let A Man Come In	1970	20.00	50.00
King KS-1100	(S)	Soul On Top	1970	16.00	40.00
King KSD-1110	(S)	Sho Is Funky Down Here	1971	16.00	40.00
King KSD-1115	(S)	Sex Machine (2 LPs)	1970	20.00	50.00
King KSD-1124	(S)	Hey, America!	1970	20.00	50.00
King KS-1127	(S)	Super Bad	1971	16.00	40.00
Smash MGS-27054	(M)	Showtime	1964	12.00	30.00
Smash SRS-67054	(S)	Showtime	1964	16.00	40.00
Smash MGS-27057	(M)	Grits And Soul	1965	12.00	30.00
Smash SRS-67057	(S)	Grits And Soul	1965	16.00	40.00
Smash MGS-27058	(S)	Out Of Sight	1965	30.00	75.00
Smash SRS-67058	(S)	Out Of Sight	1965	40.00	100.00
		(Deleted shortly after release.)			
Smash MGS-27072	(M)	JB Plays JB Today And Yesterday	1965	12.00	30.00
Smash SRS-67072	(S)	JB Plays JB Today And Yesterday	1965	16.00	40.00
Smash MGS-27080	(M)	JB Plays New Breed (The Boo-Ga-Loo)	1966	12.00	30.00
Smash SRS-67080	(S)	JB Plays New Breed (The Boo-Ga-Loo)	1966	16.00	40.00
Smash MGS-27084	(M)	Handful Of Soul	1966	12.00	30.00
Smash SRS-67084	(S)	Handful Of Soul	1966	16.00	40.00
Smash MGS-27087	(M)	The James Brown Show	1967	12.00	30.00
Smash SRS-67087	(S)	The James Brown Show	1967	16.00	40.00
		("The JB Show" is a various artists album.)			
Smash MGS-27093	(M)	JB Plays The Real Thing	1967	12.00	30.00
Smash SRS-67093	(S)	JB Plays The Real Thing	1967	16.00	40.00
Smash SRS-67109	(S)	James Brown Sings Out Of Sight	1968	12.00	30.00
		(Smash 67109 is a reissue of 67058 minus one track.)			
Mercury SMX-7083	(S)	Soulful James Brown	197?	30.00	75.00
Polydor PD-4054	(S)	Hot Pants	1971	16.00	40.00
Polydor PD2-3003	(S)	Revolution Of The Mind			
		(Live At The Apollo, Volume III) (2 LPs)	1971	30.00	75.00
Polydor PD-5028	(S)	There It Is	1972	16.00	40.00
Polydor PD-5401	(S)	Soul Classics	1972	8.00	20.00
Polydor PD2-3004	(S)	Get On The Good Foot (2 LPs)	1972	30.00	75.00
Polydor PD1-6014	(S)	Black Caesar (Soundtrack)	1973	24.00	60.00
Polydor PD1-6015	(S)	Slaughter's Big Rip Off (Soundtrack)	1973	20.00	50.00
Polydor PD-5402	(S)	Soul Classics, Volume 2	1973	8.00	20.00
Polydor PD2-3007	(S)	The Payback (2 LPs)	1974	20.00	50.00
Polydor PD2-9001	(S)	Hell (2 LPs)	1974	30.00	75.00
Polydor PD1-6039	(S)	Reality	1975	16.00	40.00
Polydor PD1-6042	(S)	Sex Machine Today	1975	16.00	40.00
Polydor PD1-6054	(S)	Everybody's Doin' The Hustle			
		& Dead On The Double Bump	1975	16.00	40.00
Polydor PD2-6059	(S)	Hot	1976	16.00	40.00
Polydor PD2-9004	(S)	Sex Machine Live (2 LPs)	1976	20.00	50.00
Polydor PD1-6071	(S)	Get Up Offa That Thing	1976	16.00	40.00
Polydor PD1-6093	(S)	Bodyheat	1976	16.00	40.00
Polydor PD1-6111	(S)	Mutha's Nature	1977	16.00	40.00
Polydor PD1-6140	(S)	Jam 1980s	1973	16.00	40.00
HRB 1004	(S)	The Fabulous James Brown (2 LPs)	1978	10.00	25.00
Polydor PD1-6181	(S)	Take A Look At Those Cakes	1979	12.00	30.00
Polydor PD1-6212	(S)	The Original Disco Man	1979	8.00	20.00
Polydor PD1-6258	(S)	People	1980	12.00	30.00
Polydor PD2-6290	(S)	Live/Hot On The One (2 LPs)	1980	20.00	50.00
Polydor PD1-6318	(S)	Nonstop!	1981	12.00	30.00
Polydor PD-6340	(S)	The Best Of James Brown	1981	8.00	20.00

Label & Catalog #		Title	Year	VG+	NM

BROWN, MAXINE
Maxine Brown also recorded with Chuck Jackson.

Wand WD-656	(M)	The Fabulous Sound Of Maxine Brown	1963	14.00	35.00
Wand WDS-656	(S)	The Fabulous Sound Of Maxine Brown	1963	20.00	50.00
Wand WD-663	(M)	Spotlight On Maxine Brown	1965	8.00	20.00
Wand WDS-663	(S)	Spotlight On Maxine Brown	1965	10.00	25.00
Wand WD-684	(M)	Maxine Brown's Greatest Hits	1967	6.00	15.00
Wand WDS-684	(P)	Maxine Brown's Greatest Hits	1967	8.00	20.00

BROWN, MAXINE, & IRMA THOMAS

Grand Prix K-426	(M)	Maxine Brown And Irma Thomas	1964	8.00	20.00
Grand Prix KS-426	(E)	Maxine Brown And Irma Thomas	1964	4.00	10.00

BROWN, MILTON

Decca DL-5561 (10")	(M)	Dance-O-Rama #1	1955	100.00	250.00

BROWN, NAPPY

Savoy MG-14002	(M)	Nappy Brown Sings	1958	150.00	300.00
Savoy MG-14025	(M)	The Right Time	1960	80.00	200.00
Savoy 14427	(S)	Nappy Brown	1977	4.00	10.00

BROWN, ROY

King 956	(M)	Roy Brown Sings 24 Hits	1966	20.00	50.00
King KS-956	(E)	Roy Brown Sings 24 Hits	1966	20.00	50.00
BluesWay BLS-6019	(S)	The Blues Are Brown	1968	6.00	15.00
BluesWay BLS-6056	(S)	Hard Times	197?	6.00	15.00
King KS-1130	(M)	Hard Luck Blues	1971	6.00	15.00
Epic BG-30473	(S)	Live At Monterey	1971	6.00	15.00

BROWN, ROY / WYNONIE HARRIS

King 607	(M)	Battle Of The Blues, Volume 1	1958	200.00	400.00
King 627	(M)	Battle Of The Blues, Volume 2	1959	250.00	500.00

BROWN, ROY / WYNONIE HARRIS / EDDIE VINSON

King 668	(M)	Battle Of The Blues, Volume 4	1960	750.00	1,500.00

BROWN, RUTH

Atlantic 115 (10")	(M)	Ruth Brown Sings Favorites	1952	Unreleased	
Atlantic 8004	(M)	Ruth Brown (Black label)	1957	60.00	150.00
Atlantic 1308	(M)	Late Date With Ruth Brown (Black label)	1959	60.00	150.00
Atlantic SD-1308	(S)	Late Date With Ruth Brown (Green label)	1959	100.0	250.00
Atlantic 8026	(M)	Miss Rhythm (Black label)	1959	50.00	125.00
Atlantic 8026	(M)	Miss Rhythm (White label)	1959	80.00	200.00
Atlantic 8080	(M)	The Best Of Ruth Brown	1963	16.00	40.00
Atlantic SD-8080	(P)	The Best Of Ruth Brown	1963	20.00	50.00
Philips PHM-200-028	(M)	Along Comes Ruth	1962	16.00	40.00
Philips PHS-600-028	(S)	Along Comes Ruth	1962	20.00	50.00
Philips PH-200-055	(M)	Gospel Time	1962	12.00	30.00
Philips PHS-600-055	(S)	Gospel Time	1962	16.00	40.00
Mainstream 16044	(S)	Ruth Brown '65	1965	10.00	25.00
Mainstream S-6044	(S)	Ruth Brown '65	1965	12.00	30.00

BROWN, WALT

Warner Bros. W-1568	(M)	The Walt Brown Show With Bill Collins	1965	8.00	20.00
Warner Bros. WS-1568	(S)	The Walt Brown Show With Bill Collins	1965	10.00	25.00

BROWN'S FERRY FOUR, THE
Country "supergroup" features Granpa Jones, The Delmore Brothers and Merle Travis.

King 551	(M)	Sacred Songs	1957	30.00	75.00
King 590	(M)	Sacred Songs	1958	30.00	75.00
King 943	(M)	Sacred Songs	1964	12.00	30.00

BROWNE, JACKSON

(No label)	(DJ)	"Jackson Browne's First Album" (2 LPs)	1967	1,000.00	Rare

(This is a publishers demo issued in plain cardboard jackets. Near Mint copis have a suggested value of $1,500-2,500.)

Asylum SD-5051	(S)	Jackson Browne (With burlap cover)	1972	12.00	30.00
Asylum SD-5067	(S)	For Everyman	1973	10.00	25.00

(Asylum 5051-5067 have white labels with a door-in-a-circle logo.)

Label & Catalog #		Title	Year	VG+	NM
Reprise RS-	(S)	Late For The Sky	197?	12.00	30.00
Mobile Fidelity MFSL-055	(S)	The Pretender	1983	10.00	30.00

BROWNS, THE

RCA Victor LPM-1438	(M)	Jim Edward, Maxine And Bonnie Brown	1957	20.00	50.00
RCA Victor LPM-2144	(M)	Sweet Sounds By The Browns	1959	12.00	30.00
RCA Victor LSP-2144	(S)	Sweet Sounds By The Browns	1959	16.00	40.00
RCA Victor LPM-2174	(M)	Town And Country	1960	8.00	20.00
RCA Victor LSP-2174	(S)	Town And Country	1960	10.00	25.00
RCA Victor LPM-2260	(M)	The Browns Sing Their Hits	1960	8.00	20.00
RCA Victor LSP-2260	(S)	The Browns Sing Their Hits	1960	10.00	25.00
RCA Victor LPM-2333	(M)	Our Favorite Folk Songs	1961	8.00	20.00
RCA Victor LSP-2333	(S)	Our Favorite Folk Songs	1961	10.00	25.00
RCA Victor LPM-2345	(M)	The Little Brown Church Hymnal	1961	8.00	20.00
RCA Victor LSP-2345	(S)	The Little Brown Church Hymnal	1961	10.00	25.00

— Original RCA mono albums above have "Long Play" on the bottom of the label;
stereo albums have "Living Stereo" on the bottom.—

RCA Victor LPM-2860	(M)	This Young Land	1964	6.00	15.00
RCA Victor LSP-2860	(S)	This Young Land	1964	8.00	20.00
RCA Victor LPM-2784	(M)	Grand Ole Opry Favorites	1965	6.00	15.00
RCA Victor LSP-2784	(S)	Grand Ole Opry Favorites	1965	8.00	20.00
RCA Victor LPM-2987	(M)	Three Shades Of Brown	1965	6.00	15.00
RCA Victor LSP-2987	(S)	Three Shades Of Brown	1965	8.00	20.00
RCA Victor LPM-3423	(M)	When Love Is Gone	1965	6.00	15.00
RCA Victor LSP-3423	(S)	When Love Is Gone	1965	8.00	20.00
RCA Victor LPM-3561	(M)	The Best Of The Browns	1966	6.00	15.00
RCA Victor LSP-3561	(P)	The Best Of The Browns	1966	8.00	20.00
RCA Victor LPM-3668	(M)	Our Kind Of Country	1966	6.00	15.00
RCA Victor LSP-3668	(S)	Our Kind Of Country	1966	8.00	20.00
RCA Victor LPM-3798	(M)	The Old Country Church	1967	8.00	20.00
RCA Victor LSP-3798	(S)	The Old Country Church	1967	6.00	15.00

— Original RCA albums above have black labels.—

BROWNSVILLE STATION [BROWNSVILLE]

Palladium P-1004	(S)	Brownsville Station	1970	12.00	30.00
Epic JE-35606	(DJ)	Air Special (Orange vinyl)	1979	6.00	15.00

BRUCE, CAROL

Tops L-1574	(M)	Carol Bruce Sings	195?	10.00	25.00

BRUCE, JACK
Jack Bruce was formerly a member of Cream.

Atco SD-33-306	(S)	Songs For A Tailor	1969	8.00	20.00
Atco SD-33-349	(S)	Things We Like	1971	6.00	15.00
Atco SD-33-365	(S)	Harmony Row	1971	6.00	15.00

BRUCE, LENNY
Refer to Lawrence Schiller.

Fantasy 7001	(M)	Interviews Of Our Times (Thick red vinyl)	1959	30.00	75.00
Fantasy 7001	(M)	Interviews Of Our Times (Thin red vinyl)	196?	12.00	30.00
Fantasy 7001	(M)	Interviews Of Our Times	1959	10.00	25.00
Fantasy 7003	(M)	Sick Humor (Thick red vinyl)	1959	30.00	75.00
Fantasy 7003	(M)	Sick Humor (Thin red vinyl)	196?	12.00	30.00
Fantasy 7003	(M)	Sick Humor Of Lenny Bruce	1959	10.00	25.00
Fantasy 7007	(M)	I Am Not A Nut, Elect Me (Thick red vinyl)	1960	30.00	75.00
Fantasy 7007	(M)	I Am Not A Nut, Elect Me (Thin red vinyl)	196?	12.00	30.00
Fantasy 7007	(M)	I Am Not A Nut, Elect Me	1960	10.00	25.00
Fantasy 7011	(M)	Lenny Bruce, American (Thick red vinyl)	1962	30.00	75.00
Fantasy 7011	(M)	Lenny Bruce, American (Thin red vinyl)	196?	12.00	30.00
Fantasy 7011	(M)	Lenny Bruce, American	1962	10.00	25.00

—Fantasy 7001-7011 were originally pressed on thick, non-flexible red vinyl.
Later pressings were on a thinner, more flexible red and black vinyl.—

Fantasy 7012	(M)	The Best Of Lenny Bruce (Thin red vinyl)	1962	12.00	30.00
Fantasy 7012	(M)	The Best Of Lenny Bruce	1962	8.00	20.00
Philles PHLP-4010	(M)	Lenny Bruce Is Out Again	1966	30.00	75.00
United Arts. UAL-3580	(M)	Lenny Bruce	1967	10.00	25.00
United Arts. UAS-6580	(E)	Lenny Bruce	1967	6.00	15.00
Douglas SD-788	(M)	The Essential Lenny Bruce	1968	6.00	15.00
Verve/Forecast FTS-3035	(E)	Lenny Bruce	1968	Unreleased	

Label & Catalog #		Title	Year	VG+	NM
Bizarre 6329	(M)	The Berkeley Concert	1969	10.00	25.00
Douglas 2	(M)	To Is A Preposition, Come Is A Verb	196?	8.00	20.00
Douglas 30872	(M)	What I Was Arrested For	1971	6.00	15.00
		(Douglas 30872 is a reissue of 2.)			
Fantasy 7017	(M)	Thank You, Masked Man	1972	6.00	15.00
Fantasy 34201	(M)	Live At The Curran Theater	1972	6.00	15.00
United Arts. UAS-6794	(M)	The Midnight Concert	197?	6.00	15.00
United Arts. UAS-9800	(M)	Carnegie Hall (3 LPs)	1975	6.00	15.00
Fantasy 79003	(M)	The Real Lenny Bruce (2 LPs)	1975	6.00	15.00
Warner Bros. SP- 9101	(M)	The Law, The Language And Lenny Bruce	1975	4.00	10.00
Fantasy FP-1	(DJ)	Lenny Bruce Promo Album	197?	8.00	20.00

BRUTE FORCE

Columbia CL-2615	(M)	Confections Of Love	1967	6.00	15.00
Columbia CS-9415	(M)	Confections Of Love	1967	8.00	20.00

BRYAN, JOY: *Refer to* GOLDMINE'S PRICE GUIDE TO COLLECTIBLE JAZZ ALBUMS

BRYANT, JIMMY
Bryant also recorded with Speedy West.

Capitol T-1314	(M)	Country Cabin Jazz	1960	40.00	100.00
Capitol ST-1314	(S)	Country Cabin Jazz	1960	50.00	125.00
Dolton BLP-16505	(M)	Play Country Guitar With Jimmy Bryant	1965	6.00	15.00
Dolton BST-17505	(S)	Play Country Guitar With Jimmy Bryant	1965	8.00	20.00
Imperial LP-9310	(M)	Bryant's Back In Town	1966	6.00	15.00
Imperial LP-12310	(S)	Bryant's Back In Town	1966	8.00	20.00
Imperial LP-9315	(M)	Laughing Guitar, Crying Guitar	1966	6.00	15.00
Imperial LP-12315	(S)	Laughing Guitar, Crying Guitar	1966	8.00	20.00
Imperial LP-9338	(M)	We Are Young	1966	6.00	15.00
Imperial LP-12338	(S)	We Are Young	1966	8.00	20.00
Imperial LP-9349	(M)	Wingin' It With Norval & Ivy	1967	6.00	15.00
Imperial LP-12349	(S)	Wingin' It With Norval & Ivy	1967	8.00	20.00
Imperial LP-9360	(M)	The Fastest Guitar In The Country	1967	6.00	15.00
Imperial LP-12360	(S)	The Fastest Guitar In The Country	1967	8.00	20.00

BRYANT, RAY: *Refer to* GOLDMINE'S PRICE GUIDE TO COLLECTIBLE JAZZ ALBUMS

BUBBLE GUM MACHINE, THE

Senate 1002	(M)	The Bubble Gum Machine	1967	10.00	25.00
Senate 21002	(S)	The Bubble Gum Machine	1967	12.00	30.00

BUBBLE PUPPY
Bubble Puppy later recorded as Demian.

International Arts. 10	(S)	A Gathering Of Promises	1969	30.00	75.00
International Arts. 10	(S)	A Gathering Of Promises	1979	10.00	25.00
		(Reissues have "Masterfonics" stamped in the trail-off vinyl.)			

BUCCANEER
A recent warehouse find has halved the value of these records.

Blunderbuss	(S)	Buccaneer	1980	20.00	50.00
		(The title on the cover is gold; issued with two singles.)			
Blunderbuss	(S)	Buccaneer	198?	12.00	30.00
		(Second pressings: the title on the cover is red.)			

BUCHANAN, ROY

Bioya MM-519	(S)	Buch & The Snake Stretchers	1971	60.00	150.00
		(Issued in a burlap bag.)			
Polydor PD-5033	(S)	Buch & The Snake Stretchers	1972	8.00	20.00
Polydor PD-5046	(S)	Second Album	1973	8.00	20.00
Polydor PD-6020	(S)	That's What I Am Here For	1973	8.00	20.00
Polydor PD-6035	(S)	In The Beginning	1974	8.00	20.00
Polydor PD-6048	(S)	Live Stock	1975	8.00	20.00
Atlantic SD-18170	(S)	A Street Called Straight	1976	6.00	15.00
Atlantic SD-18219	(S)	Leading Zone	1977	6.00	15.00
Atlantic SD-19170	(S)	You're Not Alone	1977	6.00	15.00

BUCHANAN & GOODMAN

Rori 3301	(M)	The Many Heads Of Buchanan & Goodman	195?	40.00	100.00

Label & Catalog #		Title	Year	VG+	NM

BUCHANAN BROTHERS, THE
The Buchanan Brothers are Terry Cashman, Gene Pistilli and Tommy West.

Event 101	(S)	**Medicine Man**	1969	10.00	25.00

BUCKAROOS, THE [BUCK OWENS' BUCKAROOS]

Capitol T-2436	(M)	**The Buck Owens' Songbook**	1965	10.00	25.00
Capitol ST-2436	(S)	**The Buck Owens' Songbook**	1965	12.00	30.00
Capitol T-2722	(M)	**America's Most Wanted Band**	1967	8.00	20.00
Capitol ST-2722	(S)	**America's Most Wanted Band**	1967	10.00	25.00
Capitol T-2828	(M)	**Again**	1967	8.00	20.00
Capitol ST-2828	(S)	**Again**	1967	8.00	20.00
Capitol ST-2902	(S)	**A Night On The Town**	1968	8.00	20.00
Capitol ST-2973	(S)	**Meanwhile, Back At The Ranch**	1968	8.00	20.00
Capitol ST-194	(S)	**Anywhere, U.S.A.**	1969	6.00	15.00
Capitol ST-322	(S)	**Roll Your Own With Buck Owens' Buckaroos**	1969	6.00	15.00
Capitol ST-440	(S)	**Rompin' And Stompin'**	1970	6.00	15.00
Capitol ST-550	(S)	**Boot Hill**	1970	6.00	15.00
Capitol ST-767	(S)	**The Buckaroos Play The Hits**	1971	6.00	15.00

BUCKINGHAM/NICKS
Lindsay Buckingham and Stevie Nicks. Refer to Fleetwood Mac.

Polydor PD-5058	(S)	**Buckingham/Nicks** *(Gatefold cover)*	1973	20.00	50.00
Polydor PD-5058	(S)	**Buckingham/Nicks** *(Standard cover)*	1973	10.00	25.00

BUCKINGHAMS, THE

U.S.A. 107	(M)	**Kind Of A Drag**	1967	300.00	500.00
		(Original mono pressings contain "I'm A Man;"			
		stereo copies are not known to exist.)			
U.S.A. 107	(M)	**Kind Of A Drag**	1967	10.00	25.00
U.S.A. 107	(S)	**Kind Of A Drag**	1967	12.00	30.00
Columbia CL-2669	(M)	**Time And Charges**	1967	8.00	20.00
Columbia CS-9469	(S)	**Time And Charges**	1967	10.00	25.00
Columbia CL-2798	(M)	**Portraits**	1968	12.00	30.00
Columbia CS-9598	(S)	**Portraits**	1968	8.00	20.00
Columbia CS-9703	(S)	**In One Ear And Gone Tomorrow**	1968	8.00	20.00
Columbia CS-9812	(S)	**The Buckinghams' Greatest Hits**	1969	6.00	15.00
		— Original Columbia albums above have "360 Sound " on the bottom of the label —			

BUCKLEY, LORD

RCA Victor LPM-3246 (10")	(M)	**Hipsters, Flipsters And Finger Poppin' Daddies, Knock Me Your Lobes**	1955	80.00	200.00
Vaya 101 (10")	(M)	**Euphoria**	1955	70.00	175.00
Vaya 107/8	(M)	**Euphoria, Volume 2**	1957	40.00	100.00
World Pacific WP-1279	(M)	**The Way Out Humor Of Lord Buckley**	1959	30.00	75.00
Crestview CRV-801	(M)	**The Best Of Lord Buckley**	1963	14.00	35.00
Crestview CRV7-801	(S)	**The Best Of Lord Buckley**	1963	14.00	35.00
World Pacific WP-1815	(M)	**Lord Buckley In Concert**	1964	14.00	35.00
World Pacific WP-1849	(M)	**Blowing His Mind And Yours, Too**	1966	14.00	35.00
World Pacific WPS-21879	(S)	**Buckley's Best**	1968	14.00	35.00
World Pacific WPS-21889	(S)	**Bad Rapping The Marquis De Sade**	1969	14.00	35.00
Elektra EKS-74047	(S)	**The Best Of Lord Buckley**	1969	10.00	25.00
Straight STS-1054	(S)	**A Most Immaculately Hip Autocrat**	1970	14.00	35.00
Bizarre RS-6389	(S)	**Lord Buckley**	1970	10.00	25.00

BUCKLEY, TIM

Elektra EKL-4004	(M)	**Tim Buckley**	1966	6.00	15.00
Elektra EKS-4004	(S)	**Tim Buckley**	1966	8.00	20.00
Elektra EKL-4028	(M)	**Goodbye And Hello**	1967	6.00	15.00
Elektra EKS-74028	(S)	**Goodbye And Hello**	1967	8.00	20.00
Elektra EKS-74045	(S)	**Happy Sad**	1969	6.00	15.00
Elektra EKS-74074	(S)	**Lorca**	1970	6.00	15.00
Straight STS-1060	(S)	**Blue Afternoon**	1969	10.00	25.00
Warner Bros. WS-1842	(S)	**Blue Afternoon**	1970	6.00	15.00
Warner Bros. WS-1881	(S)	**Starsailor**	1970	6.00	15.00
Warner Bros. B-2631	(S)	**Greetings From L.A.** *(Gatefold cover)*	1972	8.00	20.00
DiscReet 2157	(S)	**Sefronia**	1973	8.00	20.00
DiscReet 2201	(S)	**Look At The Fool**	1974	6.00	15.00

Label & Catalog #		Title	Year	VG+	NM
BUD & TRAVIS					
Bud Dashiell and Travis Edmonson.					
Liberty LRP-3125	(M)	**Bud & Travis**	1959	10.00	25.00
Liberty LST-7125	(S)	**Bud & Travis**	1959	16.00	40.00
Liberty LDR-8001	(M)	**Bud & Travis In Concert**	1960	8.00	20.00
Liberty LDS-12001	(S)	**Bud & Travis In Concert**	1960	10.00	25.00
Liberty LRP-3138	(M)	**Spotlight On Bud & Travis**	1961	8.00	20.00
Liberty LST-7138	(S)	**Spotlight On Bud & Travis**	1961	10.00	25.00
Liberty LRP-3222	(M)	**Bud & Travis In Concert, Volume 2**	1962	8.00	20.00
Liberty LST-7222	(S)	**Bud & Travis In Concert, Volume 2**	1962	10.00	25.00
Liberty LRP-3295	(M)	**Naturally**	1963	6.00	15.00
Liberty LST-7295	(S)	**Naturally**	1963	8.00	20.00
Liberty LRP-3341	(M)	**Perspective On Bud & Travis**	1964	6.00	15.00
Liberty LST-7341	(S)	**Perspective On Bud & Travis**	1964	8.00	20.00
Liberty LRP-3386	(M)	**Bud & Travis In Person**	1964	6.00	15.00
Liberty LST-7386	(S)	**Bud & Travis In Person**	1964	8.00	20.00
Liberty LRP-3398	(M)	**Bud & Travis' Latin Album**	1965	6.00	15.00
Liberty LST-7398	(S)	**Bud & Travis' Latin Album**	1965	8.00	20.00
BUDDIES, THE					
Wing MGW-12293	(M)	**The Buddies And The Compacts**	1965	16.00	40.00
Wing SRW-16293	(S)	**The Buddies And The Compacts**	1965	20.00	50.00
Wing MGW-12306	(M)	**Go Go With The Buddies**	1965	16.00	40.00
Wing SRW-16306	(S)	**Go Go With The Buddies**	1965	20.00	50.00
BUDGIE					
Kapp KS-3656	(S)	**Budgie**	1971	16.00	40.00
Kapp KS-3669	(S)	**Squawk**	1972	12.00	30.00
MCA 429	(S)	**In For The Kill**	1973	8.00	20.00
A&M SP-4593	(S)	**If I Were Brittania, I'd Waive The Rules**	1976	6.00	15.00
A&M SP-4618	(S)	**Bandolier**	1977	6.00	15.00
A&M SP-4675	(S)	**IImpeckable**	1978	6.00	15.00
BUFFALO NICKEL JUGBAND, THE					
Happy Tiger 1018	(S)	**The Buffalo Nickel Jugband**	1971	10.00	25.00

BUFFALO SPRINGFIELD, THE
The Springfield consisted of Neil Young, Steve Stills, Richie Furay, Dewey Martin and Bruce Palmer,
replaced by Jim Messina in 1968. Refer to The Au Go-Go Singers.

Atco 33-200	(M)	**Buffalo Springfield**	1966	60.00	150.00
Atco SD-33-200	(S)	**Buffalo Springfield**	1966	80.00	200.00
		(First pressings contain the track "Baby Don't Scold Me."			
		Also, "Burned" is rechanneled on all pressings of this album.)			
Atco 33-200-A	(M)	**Buffalo Springfield**	1967	12.00	30.00
Atco SD-33-200-A	(S)	**Buffalo Springfield**	1967	10.00	25.00
		(Later pressings feature "For What It's Worth.")			
Atco 33-226	(M)	**Buffalo Springfield Again**	1967	12.00	30.00
Atco SD-33-226	(S)	**Buffalo Springfield Again**	1967	10.00	25.00
Atco SD-33-256	(S)	**Last Time Around**	1968	16.00	40.00
		— Original Atco stereo albums above purple & brown labels.—			
Atco SD-33-200A	(S)	**Buffalo Springfield**	1968	4.00	10.00
Atco SD-33-226	(S)	**Buffalo Springfield Again**	1968	4.00	10.00
Atco SD-33-256	(S)	**Last Time Around**	1968	6.00	15.00
		— Atco albums above yellow labels with "Atlantic Recording Co." on the bottom.—			
Atco SD-33-283	(S)	**Retrospective**	1969	20.00	50.00
		(Gold & gray label with laminated cover manufactured for export.)			

BUFFETT, JIMMY					
ABC SPDJ-43	(DJ)	**Special Jimmy Buffett Sampler**	1978	6.00	15.00
BUGALOOS, THE					
Capitol SW-621	(S)	**Bugaloos**	1970	8.00	20.00
BUGGS, THE					
Coronet CX-212	(M)	**The Beetle Beat**	1964	6.00	15.00
Coronet CXS-212	(S)	**The Beetle Beat**	1964	8.00	20.00
BUMP					
Pioneer	(S)	**Bump** *(Canadian)*	1970	60.00	250.00

Label & Catalog #		Title	Year	VG+	NM
BUNNY, BUGS					
Bugs and most of the other WB characters were done by Mel Blanc.					
Capitol J-3257	(M)	**Bugs Bunny And His Friends**	1961	20.00	50.00
Capitol J-3266	(M)	**Bugs Bunny In Storyland**	1963	20.00	50.00
BUOYS, THE					
Scepter SPS-593	(S)	**Timothy**	1971	6.00	15.00
BURDON, ERIC, & THE ANIMALS: *Refer to* THE ANIMALS					
BURDON, ERIC, & WAR					
For additional listings refer to War.					
MGM SE-4663	(S)	**Eric Burdon Declares War**	1970	6.00	15.00
MGM SAMP-4710	(DJ)	**Black Man's Burdon** *(Radio sampler)*	1970	12.00	30.00
MGM SE-4710	(S)	**Black Man's Burdon** *(2 LPs)*	1970	8.00	20.00
BURDON, ERIC, & JIMMY WITHERSPOON					
MGM SE-4791	(S)	**Guilty**	1971	8.00	20.00
BURDON, ERIC					
Capitol ST-11359	(S)	**Sun Secrets**	1974	6.00	15.00
Capitol ST-11426	(S)	**Stop** *(Hexagonal cover)*	1974	6.00	15.00
Capitol ST-11426	(S)	**Stop** *(Square cover)*	1975	5.00	12.00
BURKE, SOLOMON					
Apollo ALP-498	(M)	**Solomon Burke**	1962	250.00	500.00
Atlantic 8067	(M)	**Solomon Burke's Greatest Hits**	1962	20.00	50.00
Atlantic SD-8067	(S)	**Solomon Burke's Greatest Hits**	1962	30.00	75.00
Atlantic 8085	(M)	**If You Need Me**	1963	20.00	50.00
Atlantic SD-8085	(S)	**If You Need Me**	1963	30.00	75.00
Atlantic 8096	(M)	**Rock 'N' Roll Soul**	1964	20.00	50.00
Atlantic SD-8096	(S)	**Rock 'N' Roll Soul**	1964	30.00	75.00
Clarion 607	(M)	**I Almost Lost My Mind**	1965	8.00	20.00
Clarion SD-607	(S)	**I Almost Lost My Mind**	1965	10.00	25.00
Atlantic 8109	(M)	**The Best Of Solomon Burke**	1965	12.00	30.00
Atlantic SD-8109	(S)	**The Best Of Solomon Burke**	1965	16.00	40.00
Atlantic SD-8185	(S)	**I Wish I Knew**	1968	10.00	25.00
Atlantic SD-8158	(S)	**King Solomon**	1968	10.00	25.00
Bell 6033	(S)	**Proud Mary**	1969	6.00	15.00
Pride 0011	(S)	**The History Of Solomon Burke**	1971	6.00	15.00
MGM SE-4767	(S)	**Electronic Magnetism**	1971	6.00	15.00
MGM SE-4830	(S)	**We're Almost Home**	1972	6.00	15.00
MGM SE-35	(S)	**Cool Breeze** *(Soundtrack)*	1972	6.00	15.00
Dunhill DSX-50161	(S)	**I Have A Dream**	1974	5.00	12.00
Chess CH-19002	(S)	**Back To My Roots**	1976	5.00	12.00
BURNETTE, J. HENRY : *Refer to* T-BONE BURNETTE					
BURNETTE, DORSEY					
Era EL-102	(M)	**Tall Oak Tree**	1960	60.00	150.00
Era ES-102	(S)	**Tall Oak Tree**	1960	150.00	300.00
Dot DLP-3456	(M)	**Dorsey Burnette Sings**	1963	16.00	40.00
Dot DLP-25456	(S)	**Dorsey Burnette Sings**	1963	20.00	50.00
Era ES-800	(S)	**Dorsey Burnette's Greatest Hits**	1969	10.00	25.00
Capitol ST-11094	(S)	**Here And Now**	1972	6.00	15.00
Capitol ST-11219	(S)	**Dorsey Burnette**	1973	6.00	15.00
BURNETTE, JOHNNY, & THE ROCK 'N' ROLL TRIO					
Coral CRL-57080	(M)	**Johnny Burnette & The Rock 'N' Roll Trio**	1956	1,000.00	*Rare*
		(Near Mint copies have a suggested value of $2,000-4,000. Originals have printing on the spine and "Made in USA" on the lower right back cover; counterfeits do not. Finally, contrary to rumors, there are no blue label promos for this album.)			
Solid Smoke SS-8001	(M)	**Tear It Up!**	1978	6.00	15.00
Solid Smoke SS-8001	(M)	**Tear It Up!** *(Blue vinyl)*	1978	10.00	25.00
		("Tear It Up" repackages the Coral album with bonus tracks.)			
Solid Smoke SS-8005	(M)	**Together Again**	1978	6.00	15.00

Ms. Bush is one of the most idiosyncratic and striking talents of the post Beatles era. She has produced a lengthy string of hits in her native U.K. although her success here in the States has been negligible. Her first album, The Kick Inside, was originally issued on Capitol's Harvest label (above) and then reissued on EMI-America (below), with neither having any substantial chart success.

Label & Catalog #		Title	Year	VG+	NM

BURNETTE, JOHNNY

Liberty LRP-3179	(M)	Dreamin'	1960	16.00	40.00
Liberty LST-7179	(S)	Dreamin'	1960	20.00	50.00
Liberty LRP-3183	(M)	Johnny Burnette	1961	16.00	40.00
Liberty LST-7183	(S)	Johnny Burnette	1961	20.00	50.00
Liberty LRP-3190	(M)	Johnny Burnette Sings	1961	16.00	40.00
Liberty LST-7190	(S)	Johnny Burnette Sings	1961	20.00	50.00
Liberty LRP-3206	(M)	Hits And Other Favorites	1962	16.00	40.00
Liberty LST-7206	(S)	Hits And Other Favorites	1962	20.00	50.00
Liberty LRP-3255	(M)	Roses Are Red	1962	16.00	40.00
Liberty LST-7255	(S)	Roses Are Red	1962	20.00	50.00
Liberty LRP-3389	(M)	The Johnny Burnette Story	1964	16.00	40.00
Liberty LST-7389	(S)	The Johnny Burnette Story	1964	20.00	50.00
Sunset SUM-1179	(M)	Dreamin'	1967	6.00	15.00
Sunset SUS-5179	(S)	Dreamin'	1967	8.00	20.00

BURNETTE, T-BONE
T-Bone is a pseudonym for J. Henry Burnette.

Uni 73125	(S)	The B-52 Band & The Fabulous Skyhawks	1972	12.00	30.00
Warner Bros. 23921	(DJ)	Proof Through The Night (Quiex II vinyl)	1983	6.00	15.00

BURNS, RANDY, & THE SKY DOG BAND

ESP-Disk' 1039S	(S)	Sons Of Love And War	1966	10.00	25.00
ESP-Disk' 1089S	(S)	Evening Of The Magician	1968	8.00	20.00
ESP-Disk' 2007	(S)	Song For An Uncertain Lady	1971	6.00	15.00

BURNT SUITE

B. J. W. 9	(M)	Burnt Suite	1967	60.00	150.00

BURRITO BROTHERS: *Refer to* FLYING BURRITO BROTHERS

BURROUGHS, WILLIAM

ESP-Disk' 1050	(M)	Call Me Burroughs	196?	40.00	100.00

BURROWS, ABE

Columbia CL-6128 (10")	(M)	Abe Burrows Sings	195?	16.00	40.00
Decca DL-5288 (10")	(M)	The Girl With The Three Blue Eyes	1950	16.00	40.00

BURTON, JAMES
Refer to Longbranch Pennywhistle; Ralph Mooney.

A&M SP-4293	(S)	James Burton	1971	10.00	25.00

BUSH, JOHNNY

Million 1001	(M)	The Best Of Johnny Bush	1972	16.00	40.00

BUSH, KATE

Harvest SW-11761	(S)	The Kick Inside	1978	16.00	40.00
EMI SW-17003	(DJ)	Kate Bush Interview Album	1982	60.00	150.00
		(EMI issued this promo interview with copies of "The Kick Inside.")			
EMI SW-17003	(S)	The Kick Inside	1982	4.00	10.00
EMI SW-17084	(S)	The Dreaming	1982	4.00	10.00
EMI ST-19004	(S)	Kate Bush	1983	4.00	10.00
EMI ST-17171	(DJ)	Hounds Of Love (Marble vinyl)	1986	16.00	40.00
EMI ST-17171	(S)	Hounds Of Love	1986	4.00	10.00

BUSHES, THE

Growth LPS-200-08	(S)	Assorted Shrubbery	197?	40.00	100.00

BUSKERS, THE

RCA Victor LPM-104	(M)	Ave A Go With The Buskers	1961	6.00	15.00
RCA Victor LSP-104	(S)	Ave A Go With The Buskers	1961	8.00	20.00

BUTCH

Sunndial	(S)	The Bitch Of Rock & Roll	1977	30.00	75.00

BUTERA, SAM, & THE WITNESSES

Dot DLP-3272	(M)	The Wildest Clan	1960	8.00	20.00
Dot DLP-25272	(S)	The Wildest Clan	1960	10.00	25.00

Label & Catalog #		Title	Year	VG+	NM

BUTLER, BILLY

OKeh OKM-12115	(M)	Right Track	1966	8.00	20.00
OKeh OKS-12115	(S)	Right Track	1966	10.00	25.00
Prestige PRST-7734	(S)	Guitar Soul	1969	6.00	15.00

BUTLER, CARL

Columbia CL-2002	(M)	Don't Let Me Cross Over	1963	6.00	15.00
Columbia CS-8802	(S)	Don't Let Me Cross Over	1963	8.00	20.00

BUTLER, CARL & PEARL

Columbia CL-2125	(M)	Loving Arms	1964	5.00	12.00
Columbia CS-8925	(S)	Loving Arms	1964	6.00	15.00
Columbia CL-2308	(M)	The Old And The New	1965	5.00	12.00
Columbia CS-9108	(S)	The Old And The New	1965	6.00	15.00
Columbia CL-2640	(M)	Avenue Of Prayer	1967	5.00	12.00
Columbia CS-9440	(S)	Avenue Of Prayer	1967	6.00	15.00

BUTLER, FREDDY

Kapp KL-1519	(M)	With A Dab Of Soul	1968	5.00	12.00
Kapp KS-3519	(S)	With A Dab Of Soul	1968	6.00	15.00

BUTLER, JERRY
Refer to The Ice Man's Band.

Abner R-2001	(M)	Jerry Butler Esquire	1959	150.00	300.00
Vee Jay LP-1027	(M)	Jerry Butler Esquire	1960	30.00	75.00
		(Vee Jay 1027 is a reissue of the Abner album.)			
Vee Jay LP-1029	(M)	He Will Break Your Heart	1960	30.00	75.00
Vee Jay LP-1034	(M)	Love Me	1961	14.00	35.00
		(Vee Jay 1034 is a reissue of 1027.)			
Vee Jay LP-1038	(M)	Aware Of Love	1961	10.00	25.00
Vee Jay SR-1038	(S)	Aware Of Love	1961	12.00	30.00
Vee Jay LP-1046	(M)	Moon River	1962	10.00	25.00
Vee Jay SR-1046	(S)	Moon River	1962	12.00	30.00
Vee Jay LP-1048	(M)	The Best Of Jerry Butler	1962	10.00	25.00
Vee Jay SR-1048	(P)	The Best Of Jerry Butler	1962	12.00	30.00
Vee Jay LP-1057	(M)	Folk Songs	1963	10.00	25.00
Vee Jay SR-1057	(S)	Folk Songs	1963	12.00	30.00
Vee Jay LP-1075	(M)	For Your Precious Love	1963	10.00	25.00
Vee Jay VJS-1075	(S)	For Your Precious Love	1963	12.00	30.00
Vee Jay LP-1076	(M)	Giving Up On Love/Need To Belong	1963	10.00	25.00
Vee Jay VJS-1076	(S)	Giving Up On Love/Need To Belong	1963	12.00	30.00
Vee Jay LP-1119	(M)	More Of The Best Of Jerry Butler	1965	10.00	25.00
Vee Jay VJS-1119	(S)	More Of The Best Of Jerry Butler	1965	12.00	30.00
Vee Jay VJS-2-1003	(M)	Jerry Butler's Gold *(2 LPs)*	196?	6.00	15.00
Mercury MG-21005	(M)	The Soul Artistry Of Jerry Butler	1967	8.00	20.00
Mercury SR-61005	(S)	The Soul Artistry Of Jerry Butler	1967	6.00	15.00
Mercury MG-21146	(M)	Mr. Dream Merchant	1967	8.00	20.00
Mercury SR-61146	(S)	Mr. Dream Merchant	1967	6.00	15.00
Mercury SR-61151	(S)	Golden Hits Live	1968	6.00	15.00
Mercury SR-61171	(S)	The Soul Goes On	1968	6.00	15.00
Mercury SR-61198	(S)	The Ice Man Cometh	1969	6.00	15.00
Mercury SR-61234	(S)	Ice On Ice	1969	6.00	15.00
Buddah BDS-4001	(S)	The Very Best Of Jerry Butler	1969	6.00	15.00
		(Buddah 4001 repackages Vee Jay material.)			
Mercury SR-61269	(S)	You And Me	1970	5.00	12.00
Mercury SR-61281	(S)	The Best Of Jerry Butler	1970	5.00	12.00
Mercury SR-61320	(S)	Assorted Sounds	1971	4.00	10.00
Mercury SR-61347	(S)	The Sagittarius Movement	1971	4.00	10.00
Mercury SRM-7502	(S)	The Spice Of Life *(2 LPs)*	1972	4.00	10.00
Mercury SRM-660	(S)	Love We Have, Love We Had	1973	4.00	10.00
Mercury SRM-689	(S)	The Power Of Love	1973	4.00	10.00
Mercury SRM-006	(S)	Sweet Sixteen	1974	4.00	10.00
Sire SASH-3717	(P)	The Vintage Years *(2 LPs)*	1977	8.00	20.00

BUTLER, JERRY, & BETTY EVERETT

Vee Jay LP-1099	(M)	Delicious Together	1964	8.00	20.00
Vee Jay VJS-1099	(S)	Delicious Together	1964	10.00	25.00
Buddah BDS-7505	(S)	Together	1969	6.00	15.00
		(Buddah 7505 is a reissue of Vee Jay 1099.)			

Label & Catalog #		Title	Year	VG+	NM

BUTLER, JERRY, & GENE CHANDLER

Mercury SR-61330	(S)	One & One	1971	4.00	10.00

BUTTERFIELD, PAUL [THE BUTTERFIELD BLUES BAND]
Butterfield's original band included Jerome Arnold, Elvin Bishop, Mike Bloomfield and Mark Naftalin.

Elektra EKL-294	(M)	Paul Butterfield Blues Band	1965	6.00	15.00
Elektra EKS-7294	(S)	Paul Butterfield Blues Band	1965	8.00	20.00
Elektra EKL-315	(M)	East-West	1966	6.00	15.00
Elektra EKS-7315	(S)	East-West	1966	8.00	20.00
Elektra EKL-4015	(M)	Resurrection Of Pigboy Crabshaw	1967	6.00	15.00
Elektra EKS-74015	(S)	Resurrection Of Pigboy Crabshaw	1967	8.00	20.00
Elektra EKS-74025	(S)	In My Own Dream	1968	6.00	15.00
Elektra EKS-75031	(S)	Sometimes I Just Feel Like Smilin'	1971	5.00	12.00
Elektra EKS-75053	(S)	Keep On Moving	1971	5.00	12.00
Elektra 7E-2001	(S)	Paul Butterfield Blues Band Live (2 LPs)	1971	6.00	15.00
Elektra 7E-2005	(S)	Golden Butter (2 LPs)	1972	5.00	12.00
Red Lightnin'	(M)	Offer You Can't Refuse	1972	12.00	30.00
Bearsville BS-2119	(S)	Paul Butterfield's Better Days	1973	5.00	12.00
Bearsville BRK-6960	(S)	Put It In Your Ear	1975	5.00	12.00
Bearsville BRK-6995	(S)	North-South	1976	5.00	12.00

BUTTERFINGERS

Pot SLP-457	(S)	Butterfingers	1972	500.00	1,000.00

BUTTERSWORTH, MARY: *Refer to* MARY BUTTERSWORTH

BYRD, BOBBY
Bobby Byrd originally recorded as Bobby Day.

King KS-1118	(S)	I Need Help (Produced by James Brown)	1970	16.00	40.00

BYRD, JERRY
Jerry also recorded as a member of The Country All-Stars.

Mercury MG-25077 (10")	(M)	Nani Hawaii	1954	30.00	75.00
Mercury MG-25134 (10")	(M)	Pagan Love Song	1954	30.00	75.00
Mercury MG-25169 (10")	(M)	Byrd's Expedition	1954	30.00	75.00
Mercury MG-20230	(M)	On The Shores Of Waikiki	1960	12.00	30.00
Mercury SR-60230	(S)	On The Shores Of Waikiki	1960	16.00	40.00
Mercury MG-20345	(M)	Steel Guitar Favorites	1961	12.00	30.00
Mercury SR-60345	(S)	Steel Guitar Favorites	1961	16.00	40.00
Mercury MG-20693	(M)	Hawaiian Golden Hits	1962	12.00	30.00
Mercury SR-60693	(S)	Hawaiian Golden Hits	1962	16.00	40.00
Mercury MG-20856	(M)	Blue Hawaiian Steel Guitar	1963	12.00	30.00
Mercury SR-60856	(S)	Blue Hawaiian Steel Guitar	1963	16.00	40.00
Mercury MG-20932	(M)	The Man Of Steel	1964	12.00	30.00
Mercury SR-60932	(S)	The Man Of Steel	1964	16.00	40.00
Decca DL-8643	(M)	Hi Fi Guitar	1958	16.00	40.00
Decca DL-4078	(M)	Paradise Island	1961	8.00	20.00
Decca DL-74078	(S)	Paradise Island	1961	12.00	30.00
Wing MGW-12315	(M)	Country Steel Guitar Hits	196?	8.00	20.00
Wing SRW-16315	(S)	Country Steel Guitar Hits	196?	12.00	30.00
Monument M-4003	(M)	Byrd Of Paradise	1961	6.00	15.00
Monument SM-14008	(S)	Memories Of Maria	1962	8.00	20.00
Monument LP-8018	(M)	Admirable Byrd	1963	6.00	15.00
Monument SLP-18018	(S)	Admirable Byrd	1963	8.00	20.00
Monument LP-8033	(M)	Satin Strings Of Steel	1965	8.00	20.00
Monument SLP-18033	(S)	Satin Strings Of Steel	1965	12.00	30.00
Monument LP-8040	(M)	Potpourri	1965	6.00	15.00
Monument SLP-18040	(S)	Potpourri	1965	8.00	20.00
Monument LP-8081	(M)	Burning Sands/Pearly Shells	1966	6.00	15.00
Monument SLP-18081	(S)	Burning Sands/Pearly Shells	1966	8.00	20.00
Monument LP-8107	(M)	Polynesian Suite	1967	6.00	15.00
Monument SLP-18107	(S)	Polynesian Suite	1967	8.00	20.00

BYRD, JERRY / SHOT JACKSON

Sesac PA-228	(M)	Just A Minute	195?	40.00	100.00

Label & Catalog #		Title	Year	VG+	NM

BYRDS, THE

Gene Clark, David Crosby and Jim McGuinn originally recorded as The Jet Set (refer to Early L.A. on Together Records in the various artists section) and then a lone single for Elektra as The Beefeaters with no success. With Chris Hillman and Michael Clarke they form The Byrds, recording a series of demos in 1964 that are eventually released in 1969 on Together as Preflyte.

After signing with Columbia the original five man band last through two album as Clark leaves at the beginning of the Fifth Dimension sessions. While Notorious Byrd Brothers features all of the members in some capacity— Clark plays tambourine and possibly contributes backing vocals on a track or two— it is basically McGuinn and Hillman backed by studio musicians.

By Sweetheart of The Rodeo the members are McGuinn (now Roger) and Hillman with Gram Parsons and Kevin Kelly. For Dr. Byrds it is McGuinn with Gene Parsons, Clarence White and John York, who is replaced by Skip Battin in late 1969. Finally, the five original members reunited for the eponymous album on Asylum. Refer to The International Submarine Band; The Kentucky Colonels; The Flying Buritto Brothers; The Scottsville Squirrel Barkers.

Label & Catalog #		Title	Year	VG+	NM
Columbia CL-2372	(DJ)	Mr. Tambourine Man *(White label)*	1965	40.00	100.00
Columbia CL-2372	(M)	Mr. Tambourine Man	1965	20.00	50.00
		(Original mono pressing labels read "Guaranteed High Fidelity.")			
Columbia CL-2372	(M)	Mr. Tambourine Man	1965	12.00	30.00
Columbia CS-9172	(S)	Mr. Tambourine Man	1965	10.00	25.00
		("Mr. Tambourine Man" and "I Knew I'd Want You" are rechanneled on this album.)			
Columbia CL-2454	(DJ)	Turn, Turn, Turn *(White label)*	1965	40.00	100.00
Columbia CL-2454	(M)	Turn, Turn, Turn	1965	12.00	30.00
Columbia CS-9254	(S)	Turn, Turn, Turn	1965	10.00	25.00
		("Turn, Turn, Turn" is rechanneled on this album.)			
Columbia CL-2549	(DJ)	5D (Fifth Dimension) *(White label)*	1966	40.00	100.00
Columbia CL-2549	(M)	5D (Fifth Dimension)	1966	12.00	30.00
Columbia CS-9349	(S)	5D (Fifth Dimension)	1966	10.00	25.00
Columbia CL-2642	(DJ)	Younger Than Yesterday *(White label)*	1967	40.00	100.00
Columbia CL-2642	(M)	Younger Than Yesterday	1967	16.00	40.00
Columbia CS-9442	(S)	Younger Than Yesterday	1967	10.00	25.00
		(Produced by Gary Usher.)			
MGM E-4484	(M)	Don't Make Waves *(Soundtrack)*	1967	8.00	20.00
MGM SE-4484	(S)	Don't Make Waves *(Soundtrack)*	1967	10.00	25.00
Columbia CL-2716	(DJ)	The Byrds' Greatest Hits *(White label)*	1967	30.00	75.00
Columbia CL-2716	(M)	The Byrds' Greatest Hits	1967	12.00	30.00
Columbia CS-9516	(S)	The Byrds' Greatest Hits	1967	8.00	20.00
Columbia CL-2775	(DJ)	The Notorious Byrd Brothers *(White label)*	1968	30.00	75.00
Columbia CL-2775	(M)	The Notorious Byrd Brothers	1968	20.00	50.00
Columbia CS-9575	(S)	The Notorious Byrd Brothers	1968	8.00	20.00
		(Produced by Gary Usher.)			
Columbia CS-9670	(DJ)	Sweetheart Of The Rodeo *(White label)*	1968	20.00	50.00
Columbia CS-9670	(S)	Sweetheart Of The Rodeo	1968	8.00	20.00
		(Produced by Gary Usher.)			
ABC S-OC-9	(S)	Candy *(Soundtrack)*	1968	6.00	15.00
Columbia CS-9755	(DJ)	Dr. Byrds And Mr. Hyde *(White label)*	1969	20.00	50.00
Columbia CS-9755	(S)	Dr. Byrds And Mr. Hyde	1969	6.00	15.00
Columbia CS-9942	(DJ)	The Ballad Of Easy Rider *(White label)*	1969	20.00	50.00
Columbia CS-9942	(S)	The Ballad Of Easy Rider	1969	6.00	15.00
		—Original Columbia albums above have "360 Sound" on the bottom of the label.—			
Together ST-1-1001	(S)	Preflyte	1969	8.00	20.00
Columbia G-30127	(S)	Untitled *(2 LPs)*	1970	8.00	20.00
		(Originals list "Kathleen" as a song on the back cover.)			
Columbia G-30127	(S)	Untitled *(2 LPs)*	1970	5.00	12.00
		(Later pressings correctly delete "Kathleen" from the back cover.)			
Columbia KC-30640	(S)	Byrdmaniax	1971	4.00	10.00
Columbia KC-31050	(S)	Farther Along	1971	4.00	10.00
Columbia KC-31795	(S)	The Best Of The Byrds, Volume 2	1972	4.00	10.00
Columbia KC-32183	(S)	Preflyte *(Reissue of Together 1001)*	1973	4.00	10.00

BYRNES, ED "KOOKIE"

Label & Catalog #		Title	Year	VG+	NM
Warner Bros. W-1309	(M)	Kookie	1959	14.00	35.00
Warner Bros. WS-1309	(S)	Kookie	1959	20.00	50.00

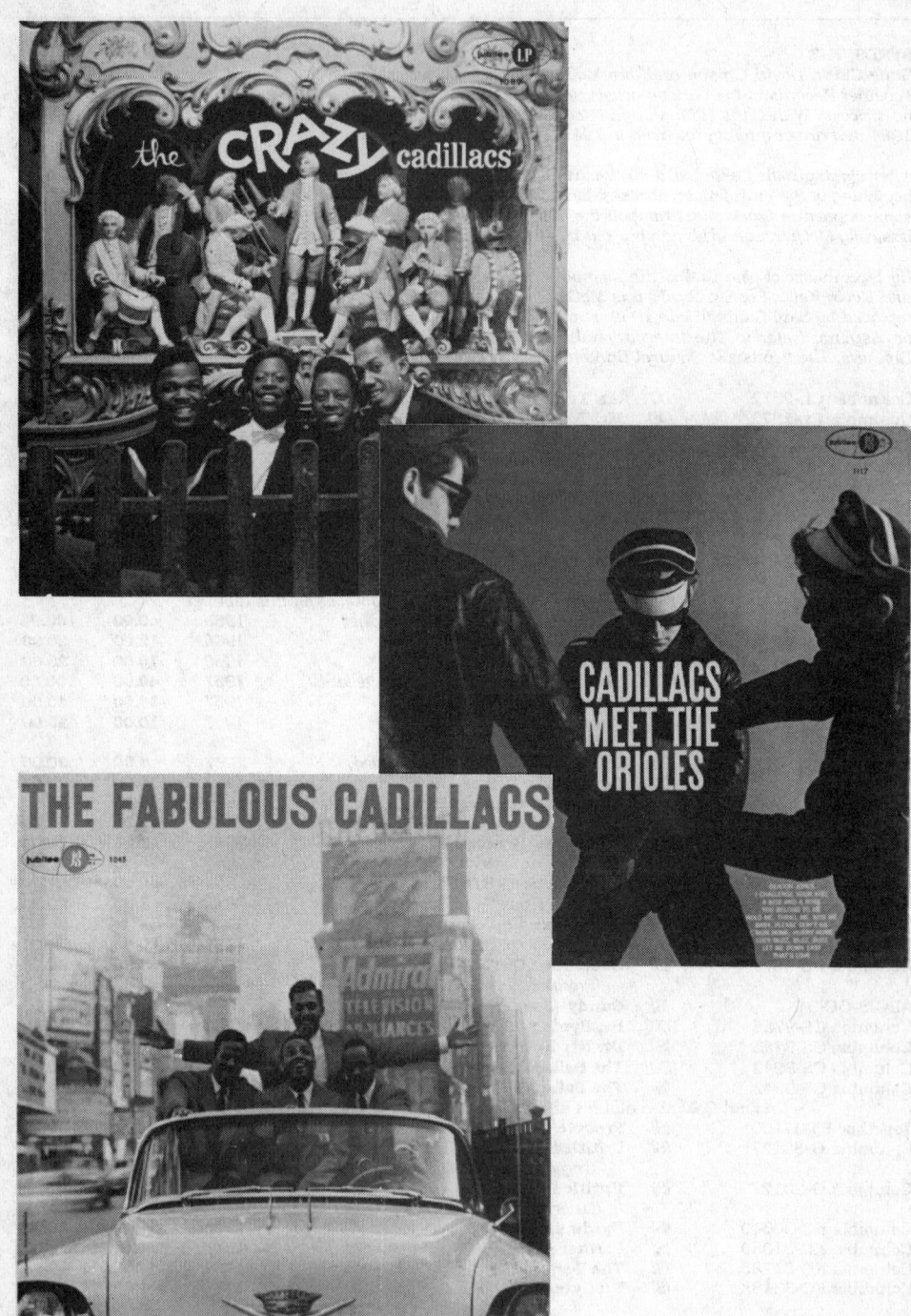

The Cadillacs were one of the few rhythm 'n blues vocal groups to be graced by the powers-that-be with an album. While they eventually recorded for Mercury/Smash and Capitol, it was well past the heyday of doo wop and these companies never released any albums, leaving the group's entire LP catalog to Jubilee.

C. A. QUINTET, THE

Candy Floss 7764	(M)	A Trip Through Hell	1969	750.00	1,500.00

("A Trip Through Hell" is in stereo on this album.)

C. C. S.

Rak KZ-30559	(S)	Whole Lotta Love	1971	12.00	30.00
Rak KZ-31569	(S)	C. C. S.	1972	12.00	30.00

CABOT, SEBASTIAN

MGM E-4431	(M)	Sebastian Cabot, Actor/Bob Dylan, Poet	1967	6.00	15.00
MGM SE-4431	(S)	Sebastian Cabot, Actor/Bob Dylan, Poet	1967	8.00	20.00

CACTUS

Atco SD-33-340	(S)	Cactus	1970	6.00	15.00
Atco SD-33-356	(S)	One Way... Or Another	1970	6.00	15.00
Atco SD-33-337	(S)	Restrictions	1971	6.00	15.00
Atco SD-36-7011	(S)	'Ot 'N' Sweaty	1972	6.00	15.00

CADETS, THE

The Cadets also recorded as The Jacks. Refer to Aaron Collins.

Crown CLP-5015	(M)	Rockin' 'N' Reelin	1957	100.00	250.00
Crown CLP-5370	(M)	The Cadets	1963	60.00	150.00
Crown CST-370	(E)	The Cadets	1963	50.00	100.00

CADILLACS, THE

Jubilee JGM-1045	(M)	The Fabulous Cadillacs (Blue label)	1957	150.00	350.00
Jubilee JGM-1045	(M)	The Fabulous Cadillacs (Flat black label)	1959	100.00	250.00
Jubilee JGM-1045	(M)	The Fabulous Cadillacs (Glossy black label)	1960	40.00	100.00
Jubilee JGM-1089	(M)	The Crazy Cadillacs (Flat black label)	1959	100.00	250.00
Jubilee JGM-1089	(M)	The Crazy Cadillacs (Glossy black label)	1960	40.00	100.00
Jubilee JGM-5009	(M)	Twisting With The Cadillacs	1962	80.00	200.00

CADILLACS, THE / THE ORIOLES

Jubilee JGM-1117	(M)	The Cadillacs Meet The Orioles	1961	60.00	150.00

CAESAR & CLEO: Refer to SONNY & CHER

CAIN

A.S.I. 204	(S)	A Pound Of Flesh	1974	24.00	60.00
A.S.I. 214	(S)	Stinger	1975	12.00	30.00

CAIN, JACKIE, & ROY KRAL: Refer to GOLDMINE'S PRICE GUIDE TO COLLECTIBLE JAZZ ALBUMS

CAKE, THE

Decca DL-4927	(M)	The Cake	1967	6.00	15.00
Decca DL-74927	(S)	The Cake	1967	8.00	20.00
Decca DL-75039	(S)	A Slice Of The Cake	1968	8.00	20.00

CALDWELL, LOUISE HARRISON

Mrs. Caldwell is the sister of George Beatle and this is a wonderful exploitation of her sibling's fame.

Recar 2012	(M)	Questions All About The Beatles Answered By Louise Harrison Caldwell	1965	40.00	100.00

CALE, JOHN

Cale was formerly a member of the Velvet Underground.

Columbia CS-1037	(P)	Vintage Violence ("360 Sound" label)	1970	8.00	20.00
Reprise MS-2079	(S)	The Academy In Peril	1972	6.00	15.00
Reprise MS-2131	(S)	Paris, 1919	1973	5.00	12.00

Label & Catalog #		Title	Year	VG+	NM
CALE, JOHN, & TERRY RILEY					
Columbia CS-30131	(S)	**Church Of Anthrax**	1971	6.00	15.00
CALIFORNIA, RANDY					
California was formerly a member of Spirit.					
Epic KE-31755	(S)	**Kapt. Kopter & The Fabulous Twirly Birds** *(Yellow label)*	1972	8.00	20.00
Epic KE-31755	(S)	**Kapt. Kopter & The Fabulous Twirly Birds** *(Orange label)*	1973	4.00	10.00
CALIFORNIA POPPY PICKERS, THE					
The C.P.P.'s was a house name for various artists who recorded without credit. While rumors that Gene Clark was involved remain unconfirmed, Wilson McKinley can he found on "Honkey Tonk Women."					
Alshire	(S)	**Sounds Of '69**	1969	10.00	25.00
Alshire	(S)	**Let The Sunshine In**	1969	10.00	25.00
Alshire	(S)	**Today's Chart Busters**	1969	10.00	25.00
Alshire	(S)	**Honkey Tonk Women**	1969	20.00	50.00
CALLIER, TERRY					
Prestige PRLP-7383	(M)	**The New Folk Sound**	1966	6.00	15.00
Prestige PRST-7383	(S)	**The New Folk Sound**	1966	8.00	20.00
CALLIOPE					
Calliope features Danny O'Keefe.					
Buddah BDS-5023	(S)	**Steamed**	1968	10.00	25.00
CALLOWAY, CAB: *Refer to* **GOLDMINE'S PRICE GUIDE TO COLLECTIBLE JAZZ ALBUMS**					
CAMPBELL, CECIL					
Starday SLP-254	(M)	**Steel Guitar Jamboree**	1963	16.00	40.00
Winston 1001	(M)	**Greatest Hawaiian Instrumentals**	196?	8.00	20.00
CAMPBELL, CHOKER					
Motown 620	(M)	**Hits Of The Sixties**	1965	8.00	20.00
Motown MS-620	(S)	**Hits Of The Sixties**	1965	12.00	30.00
CAMPBELL, DICK					
Mercury MG-21060	(M)	**Dick Campbell Sings Where It's At**	1966	12.00	30.00
Mercury SR-61060	(S)	**Dick Campbell Sings Where It's At**	1966	16.00	40.00
CAMPBELL, GLEN					
Campbell also recorded with The Bandits; The Folkswingers.					
Capitol T-1810	(M)	**Big Bluegrass Special**	1962	30.00	75.00
Capitol T-1810	(S)	**Big Bluegrass Special** *(With The Green River Boys.)*	1962	40.00	100.00
Capitol T-1881	(M)	**Too Late To Worry, Too Blue To Cry**	1963	8.00	20.00
Capitol ST-1881	(S)	**Too Late To Worry, Too Blue To Cry**	1963	10.00	25.00
Capitol T-2023	(M)	**Astounding 12-String Guitar**	1964	6.00	15.00
Capitol ST-2023	(S)	**Astounding 12-String Guitar**	1964	8.00	20.00
Capitol T-2392	(M)	**The Big Bad Rock Guitar Of Glen Campbell**	1965	6.00	15.00
Capitol ST-2392	(S)	**The Big Bad Rock Guitar Of Glen Campbell**	1965	8.00	20.00
Capitol SW-11722	(DJ)	**Basic** *(Picture disc)*	1978	20.00	50.00
CAMPBELL, IAN					
Elektra EKL-268	(M)	**The Ian Campbell Folk Group**	1964	6.00	15.00
Elektra EKS-7268	(S)	**The Ian Campbell Folk Group**	1964	8.00	20.00
Elektra EKL-309	(M)	**Rights Of Man**	1966	6.00	15.00
Elektra EKS-7309	(S)	**Rights Of Man**	1966	8.00	20.00
CAMPBELL, JO ANN					
End LP-306	(M)	**I'm Nobody's Baby**	1959	40.00	100.00
ABC-Paramount 393	(M)	**Twistin' And Listenin'**	1962	40.00	100.00
ABC-Paramount S-393	(S)	**Twistin' And Listenin'**	1962	60.00	150.00
Cameo C-1026	(M)	**All The Hits Of Jo Ann Campbell**	1962	20.00	50.00
Cameo SC-1026	(S)	**All The Hits Of Jo Ann Campbell**	1962	30.00	75.00
Roulette R-25168	(M)	**Hey, Let's Twist** *(Soundtrack)*	1962	16.00	40.00
Roulette SR-25168	(S)	**Hey, Let's Twist** *(Soundtrack)*	1962	20.00	50.00
Coronet CX-199	(M)	**Starring Jo Ann Campbell**	196?	8.00	20.00
Coronet CXS-199	(E)	**Starring Jo Ann Campbell**	196?	5.00	12.00

Label & Catalog #		Title	Year	VG+	NM
CAMPUS SINGERS, THE					
Argo 4023	(M)	The Campus Singers At The Fickle Pickle	1963	10.00	25.00
CANADIAN BEADLES, THE					
Tide 2005	(M)	Three Faces North	1964	20.00	50.00
CANADIAN SWEETHEARTS, THE					
A&M LP-106	(M)	Introducing The Canadian Sweethearts	1964	8.00	20.00
A&M SP-106	(S)	Introducing The Canadian Sweethearts	1964	12.00	30.00
CANARIES, THE					
B.T. Puppy BTS-1007	(S)	Flying High With The Canaries	1970	30.00	75.00
CANDY STORE, THE					
Decca DL-75147	(S)	Turned On Christmas	1969	10.00	25.00
CANDYMEN, THE					
ABC 616	(M)	The Candymen	1967	6.00	15.00
ABC S-616	(S)	The Candymen	1967	8.00	20.00
ABC S-633	(S)	The Candymen Bring You Candypower	1968	8.00	20.00
CANNED HEAT					
Liberty LRP-3526	(M)	Canned Heat	1967	10.00	25.00
Liberty LST-7526	(S)	Canned Heat	1967	10.00	25.00
Liberty LST-7541	(S)	Boogie With Canned Heat	1968	10.00	25.00
Liberty LST-7618	(S)	Hallelujah	1968	10.00	25.00
Liberty LST-27200	(S)	Living The Blues	1968	10.00	25.00
Liberty LST-11000	(S)	Canned Heat Cookbook	1969	8.00	20.00
Liberty LST-11002	(S)	Future Blues	1970	8.00	20.00
		("Let's Work Together" is in mono on this album.)			
Liberty LST-35002	(S)	Hooker 'N' Heat (2 LPs)	1971	10.00	25.00
		(John Lee Hooker boogies with Canned Heat.)			
Wand WDS-693	(S)	Live At Topanga Canyon	1970	10.00	25.00
Sunset SUS-5298	(S)	Collage	1971	4.00	10.00
Scepter CTN-18017	(S)	The Best Of Canned Heat	1971	4.00	10.00
United Arts. UAS-9955	(S)	Living The Blues (2 LPs)	1971	6.00	15.00
United Arts. UAS-5509	(S)	Live In Europe	1971	5.00	12.00
United Arts. UAS-5557	(S)	Historical Figures & Ancient Heads	1972	6.00	15.00
		(Little Richard rocks with Canned Heat. Issued with a comic book)			
United Arts. LA049	(S)	New Age	1973	6.00	15.00
United Arts. LA431	(S)	The Very Best Of Canned Heat	1975	4.00	10.00
Atlantic SD-7239	(S)	One More River To Cross	1973	4.00	10.00
CANNIBAL & THE HEADHUNTERS					
Rampart RM-3302	(M)	Land Of 1,000 Dances	1966	20.00	50.00
Rampart RS-3302	(S)	Land Of 1,000 Dances	1966	24.00	60.00
Date TEM-3001	(M)	Land Of 1,000 Dances	1966	16.00	40.00
Date TES-3001	(S)	Land Of 1,000 Dances	1966	20.00	50.00
CANNON, ACE					
Hi HL-12007	(M)	Tuff Sax	1962	8.00	20.00
Hi SHL-32007	(S)	Tuff Sax	1962	10.00	25.00
Hi HL-12008	(M)	Looking Back	1962	8.00	20.00
Hi SHL-32008	(S)	Looking Back	1962	10.00	25.00
Hi HL-12014	(M)	The Moanin' Sax Of Ace Cannon	1963	8.00	20.00
Hi SHL-32014	(S)	The Moanin' Sax Of Ace Cannon	1963	10.00	25.00
Hi HL-12016	(M)	Aces Hi	1964	6.00	15.00
Hi SHL-32016	(S)	Aces Hi	1964	8.00	20.00
Hi HL-12019	(M)	Great Show Tunes	1964	6.00	15.00
Hi SHL-32019	(S)	Great Show Tunes	1964	8.00	20.00
Hi HL-12022	(M)	Christmas Cheers	1964	6.00	15.00
Hi SHL-32022	(S)	Christmas Cheers	1964	8.00	20.00
Hi HL-12025	(M)	Ace Cannon Live	1965	5.00	12.00
Hi SHL-32025	(S)	Ace Cannon Live	1965	6.00	15.00
Hi HL-12028	(M)	Nashville Hits	1965	5.00	12.00
Hi SHL-32028	(S)	Nashville Hits	1965	6.00	15.00
Hi HL-12030	(M)	Sweet And Tuff	1966	5.00	12.00
Hi SHL-32030	(S)	Sweet And Tuff	1966	6.00	15.00

Label & Catalog #		Title	Year	VG+	NM
Hi HL-12035	(M)	The Misty Sax Of Ace Cannon	1967	5.00	12.00
Hi SHL-32035	(S)	The Misty Sax Of Ace Cannon	1967	6.00	15.00
Hi HL-12040	(M)	Memphis' Golden Hits	1967	5.00	12.00
Hi SHL-32040	(S)	Memphis' Golden Hits	1967	6.00	15.00

CANNON, FREDDY

Swan LP-502	(M)	The Explosive! Freddie Cannon	1960	50.00	125.00
Swan LPS-502	(S)	The Explosive! Freddie Cannon	1960	80.00	200.00

("Way Down Yonder In New Orleans" and "Okefenokee" are rechanneled while "Tallahassee Lassie" was rerecorded.)

Swan LP-504	(M)	Happy Shades Of Blue	1960	50.00	125.00
Swan LP-505	(M)	Solid Gold Hits	1961	50.00	125.00
Swan LP-506	(M)	Twistin' All Night Long	1961	50.00	125.00

(Freddy is backed by Danny & The Juniors.)

Swan LP-507	(M)	Freddie Cannon At Palisades Park	1962	50.00	125.00
Swan LP-511	(M)	Freddie Cannon Steps Out	1963	50.00	125.00
Warner Bros. W-1544	(M)	Freddie Cannon	1964	10.00	25.00
Warner Bros. WS-1544	(S)	Freddie Cannon	1964	12.00	30.00
Warner Bros. W-1612	(M)	Action!	1965	10.00	25.00
Warner Bros. WS-1612	(S)	Action!	1965	12.00	30.00
Warner Bros. W-1628	(M)	Freddie Cannon's Greatest Hits	1966	8.00	20.00
Warner Bros. WS-1628	(S)	Freddie Cannon's Greatest Hits	1966	10.00	25.00

CANNON, GUS

Stax 702	(M)	Walk Right In	1962	300.00	500.00

CANOVA, JUDY

Tops L-1613	(M)	Judy Canova In Hi-Fi	1958	8.00	20.00

CANTELON, WILLARD

Supreme M-113	(M)	L.S.D. Battle For The Mind	1966	10.00	25.00
Supreme S-113	(S)	L.S.D. Battle For The Mind	1966	12.00	30.00

CAPES & MASKS, THE

Mainstream 16069	(M)	Comic Book Heroes	1966	5.00	12.00
Mainstream S-6069	(S)	Comic Book Heroes	1966	6.00	15.00

CAPITAL CITY ROCKETS, THE

Elektra EKS-75059	(S)	Capital City Rockets	1973	6.00	15.00

CAPITOLS, THE

Atco 33-190	(M)	Dance The Cool Jerk	1966	12.00	30.00
Atco SD-33-190	(S)	Dance The Cool Jerk	1966	16.00	40.00
Atco 33-201	(M)	We Got A Thing That's In The Groove	1966	12.00	30.00
Atco SD-33-201	(S)	We Got A Thing That's In The Groove	1966	14.00	40.00

CAPOTE, TRUMAN

United Arts. UAS-6621	(S)	Christmas Memory	1968	8.00	20.00
United Arts. UAS-6682	(S)	Thanksgiving Visitor	1968	8.00	20.00

CAPRIS, THE

Ambient Sound 37714	(S)	There's A Moon Out Again	1982	5.00	12.00

CAPTAIN & TENNILLE, THE
Daryl Dragon and Toni Tenille.

A&M QU-54552	(Q)	Love Will Keep Us Together	1975	6.00	15.00

CAPTAIN BEEFHEART & THE MAGIC BAND
The Captain also recorded with Frank Zappa.

Buddah BDM-1001	(DJ)	Safe As Milk (White label promo. Mono)	1967	30.00	75.00
Buddah BDS-5001	(DJ)	Safe As Milk (White label promo. Stereo)	1967	40.00	100.00
Buddah BDM-1001	(M)	Safe As Milk	1967	12.00	30.00
Buddah BDS-5001	(S)	Safe As Milk (Red label)	1967	16.00	40.00

(With custom inner sleeve and bumper sticker.)

Buddah BDS-5063	(S)	Safe As Milk (Multi-color label)	1969	8.00	20.00
Verve/Forecast FTS-3054	(S)	Captain Beefheart & The Magic Band	1968	Unreleased	
Blue Thumb BTS-1	(S)	Strictly Personal (Black label)	1968	16.00	40.00

(Black label with un-banded tracks.)

Label & Catalog #		Title	Year	VG+	NM
Blue Thumb BTS-1	(S)	**Strictly Personal** (White label with un-banded tracks.)	1969	8.00	20.00
Blue Thumb BTS-1	(S)	**Strictly Personal** (White label with banded tracks.)	1969	6.00	15.00
Straight STS-1053	(S)	**Trout Mask Replica** (2 LPs prod. by Zappa)	1969	16.00	40.00
Straight RS-6420	(S)	**Lick My Decals Off, Baby**	1970	12.00	30.00
Reprise RS-6420	(S)	**Lick My Decals Off, Baby** (Brown label with the lyric sheet.)	197?	6.00	15.00
Buddah BDS-5077	(S)	**Mirror Man** (Fold open, die-cut cover)	1971	10.00	25.00
Reprise M2S-2027	(S)	**Trout Mask Replica** (2 LPs)	1972	6.00	15.00
Reprise MS-2050	(S)	**Spotlight Kid** (Orange label)	1972	10.00	25.00
Reprise MS-2050	(S)	**Spotlight Kid** (Brown label)	197?	6.00	15.00
Reprise MS-2115	(S)	**Clear Spot** (Clear jacket)	1972	10.00	25.00
Mercury SRM-1-709	(S)	**Unconditionally Guaranteed**	1974	4.00	10.00
Mercury SRM-1-1018	(S)	**Bluejeans And Moonbeams**	1974	6.00	15.00
Warner Bros. BSK-3256	(S)	**Shiny Beast (Bat Chain Puller)**	1978	4.00	10.00

CAPTAIN BEEFHEART / RY COODER

Reprise PRO-447	(DJ)	**Capt. Beefheart / Ry Cooder Interview**	1972	150.00	300.00

CAPTAIN BEYOND

Capricorn CP-0105	(S)	**Captain Beyond** (3-D cover)	1972	10.00	25.00
Capricorn CP-0105	(S)	**Captain Beyond** (2-D cover)	1972	6.00	15.00
Capricorn CP-0115	(S)	**Sufficiently Breathless**	1973	6.00	15.00

CARAVAN

Verve/Forecast FTS-3066	(S)	**Caravan**	1969	6.00	15.00

CARAVAN, JIMMY

Tower ST-5103	(S)	**Look Into the Flower**	1968	8.00	20.00
Vault 9007	(S)	**Hey Jude**	1969	6.00	15.00

CARAVELLES, THE

Smash MGS-27044	(M)	**You Don't Have To Be A Baby To Cry**	1963	20.00	50.00
Smash SRS-67044	(E)	**You Don't Have To Be A Baby To Cry**	1963	16.00	40.00

CARAWAN, GUY

Folkways FA-3544	(M)	**Guy Carawan**	195?	8.00	20.00

CAREFREES, THE

London LL-3379	(M)	**From England! The Carefrees**	1964	16.00	40.00
London PS-379	(S)	**From England! The Carefree**	1964	20.00	50.00

CARLISLE, BILL

Hickory HL-129	(M)	**The Best Of Bill Carlisle**	1966	6.00	15.00
Hickory HLS-129	(S)	**The Best Of Bill Carlisle**	1966	8.00	20.00

CARLISLE BROTHERS, THE

Mercury MG-20359	(M)	**On Stage With The Carlisles**	1958	20.00	50.00
King 643	(M)	**Fresh From The Country**	1959	20.00	50.00

CARLTON, LARRY

Uni 73036	(S)	**With A Little Help From My Friends**	1968	6.00	15.00

CARMEN, ERIC
Carmen was formerly a member of The Raspberries.

Arista AQ-4057	(Q)	**Eric Carmen**	1975	6.00	15.00

CARMEN, JENKS "TEX"

Modern 7037	(M)	**Country Caravan**	1959	12.00	30.00
Sage 9	(M)	**Jenks "Tex" Carmen**	1962	12.00	30.00
Sage 26	(M)	**The Ole Indian** (Red vinyl)	1962	16.00	40.00
Sage 40	(M)	**Tex Carmen Plays And Sings**	1962	12.00	30.00

CARMICHAEL, HOAGY: Refer to GOLDMINE'S PRICE GUIDE TO COLLECTIBLE JAZZ ALBUMS

CARNES, KIM
Refer to The Sugar Bears.

Amos 7016	(S)	**Rest On Me**	1971	6.00	15.00

Label & Catalog #		Title	Year	VG+	NM
EMI SPRO-9626/7	(DJ)	Kim Carnes & The Hate Boys (Sampler)	1981	6.00	15.00
Mobile Fidelity MFSL-073	(S)	Mistaken Identity	1982	5.00	15.00

CARNEY, ART

| Columbia CL-2595 (10") | (M) | Doodle-Li-Boops And Rhinocelopes | 195? | 16.00 | 40.00 |

CAROLINA SLIM

| Sharp 2002 | (M) | Blues From The Cotton Fields | 195? | 100.00 | 250.00 |

CARPENTER, IKE

Discovery DL-3003 (10")	(M)	Dancers In Love	1949	150.00	300.00
Intro 950 (10")	(M)	Lights Out	1952	150.00	300.00
Aladdin LP-811	(M)	Lights Out	1956	150.00	300.00
Score SLP-4010	(M)	Lights Out	1957	70.00	175.00

CARPENTERS, THE
The Carpenters are siblings Karen and Richard.

A&M SP-4205	(S)	Offering	1969	16.00	40.00
A&M SP-4205	(S)	Ticket To Ride	1970	8.00	20.00
		("Ticket To Ride" is a repackage of "Offering.")			
A&M SP-4271	(S)	Close To You	1970	6.00	15.00
A&M QU-54271	(Q)	Close To You	1970	10.00	25.00
A&M SP-4322	(S)	Bless The Beasts And The Children	1971	6.00	15.00
A&M SP-3502	(S)	Carpenters	1971	6.00	15.00
A&M QU-53502	(Q)	Carpenters	1971	10.00	25.00
A&M SP-3511	(S)	A Song For You	1972	6.00	15.00
A&M QU-53511	(Q)	A Song For You	1972	10.00	25.00
A&M SP-3519	(S)	Now & Then	1973	6.00	15.00
A&M QU-53519	(Q)	Now & Then	1973	10.00	25.00
A&M QU-53601	(Q)	The Singles 1969-1973	1973	10.00	25.00
A&M QU-54530	(Q)	Horizon	1975	10.00	25.00
		— Original A&M albums above have brown labels.—			

CARR, CATHY

Fraternity 1005	(M)	Ivory Tower	1957	20.00	50.00
Dot DLP-3674	(M)	Ivory Tower	1964	8.00	20.00
Dot DLP-25674	(S)	Ivory Tower	1964	12.00	30.00

CARR, GEORGIA: *Refer to* GOLDMINE'S PRICE GUIDE TO COLLECTIBLE JAZZ ALBUMS

CARR, HELEN: *Refer to* GOLDMINE'S PRICE GUIDE TO COLLECTIBLE JAZZ ALBUMS

CARR, JAMES

| Goldwax 3001S | (S) | You've Got My Mind Messed Up | 1968 | 50.00 | 100.00 |
| Goldwax 3002S | (S) | A Man Needs A Woman | 1968 | 50.00 | 100.00 |

CARR, LEROY

| Columbia CL-1911 | (M) | Blues Before Sunrise | 1962 | 10.00 | 25.00 |
| Columbia CS-8511 | (E) | Blues Before Sunrise | 1962 | 8.00 | 20.00 |

CARROLL, DIAHANN

RCA Victor LPM-1467	(M)	Diahann Carroll Sings Harold Arlen	1957	14.00	35.00
United Arts. UAL-4021	(M)	Porgy And Bess	1960	6.00	15.00
United Arts. UAS-5021	(S)	Porgy And Bess	1960	8.00	20.00
United Arts. UAL-3069	(M)	Diahann Carroll And Andre Previn	1960	6.00	15.00
United Arts. UAS-6069	(S)	Diahann Carroll And Andre Previn	1960	8.00	20.00
United Arts. UAL-3080	(M)	Diahann Carroll At The Persian Room	1960	6.00	15.00
United Arts. UAS-6080	(S)	Diahann Carroll At The Persian Room	1960	8.00	20.00
Atlantic 8048	(M)	Fun Life	1961	6.00	15.00
Atlantic SD-8048	(S)	Fun Life	1961	10.00	25.00
United Arts. UAL-4091	(M)	Goodbye Again (Soundtrack)	1961	14.00	35.00
United Arts. UAS-5091	(S)	Goodbye Again (Soundtrack)	1961	20.00	50.00
United Arts. UAL-3229	(M)	The Fabulous Diahann Carroll	1962	5.00	12.00
United Arts. UAS-6229	(S)	The Fabulous Diahann Carroll	1962	6.00	15.00
Columbia CL-2571	(M)	Nobody Sees Me Cry	1967	6.00	15.00
Columbia CS-9371	(S)	Nobody Sees Me Cry	1967	5.00	12.00

Label & Catalog #		Title	Year	VG+	NM

CARROLL BROTHERS

Cameo C-1015	(M)	College Twist Party	1962	8.00	20.00
Cameo CS-1015	(S)	College Twist Party	1962	12.00	30.00

CARS, THE

Elektra 5E-567	(DJ)	Shake It Up (Picture disc) (The back advertises KMET FM Radio.)	1981	20.00	50.00
Elektra 5E-567	(DJ)	Shake It Up (Picture disc. Blank back)	1981	16.00	40.00
Elektra 60296	(DJ)	Heartbeat City (Quiex II vinyl)	198?	6.00	15.00
Nautilus NR-14	(S)	The Cars	198?	7.00	20.00
Nautilus NR-49	(S)	Candy-O	198?	8.00	25.00

CARSON, MARTHA (LOU)

RCA Victor LPM-1145	(M)	Journey To The Sky	1955	14.00	35.00
RCA Victor LPM-1490	(M)	Rock-A My Soul	1957	14.00	35.00
Sims LP-100	(M)	Martha Carson	195?	12.00	30.00
Sims LP-109	(M)	Martha Carson	195?	10.00	25.00
Capitol T-1507	(M)	Satisfied	1960	8.00	20.00
Capitol T-1607	(M)	A Talk With The Lord	1962	6.00	15.00
Capitol ST-1607	(S)	A Talk With The Lord	1962	8.00	20.00

CARTER, ANITA

Mercury MG-20770	(M)	Folk Songs Old And New	1963	8.00	20.00
Mercury SR-60770	(S)	Folk Songs Old And New	1963	10.00	25.00

CARTER, BETTY: Refer to GOLDMINE'S PRICE GUIDE TO COLLECTIBLE JAZZ ALBUMS

CARTER, CALVIN

Vee Jay LP-1041	(M)	Twist Along With Calvin Carter	1962	12.00	30.00

CARTER, CLARENCE

Atlantic SD-8192	(S)	This Is Clarence Carter	1968	12.00	30.00
Atlantic SD-8199	(S)	The Dynamic Clarence Carter	1969	10.00	25.00
Atlantic SD-8238	(S)	Testifyin'	1969	10.00	25.00
Atlantic SD-8267	(S)	Patches	1970	10.00	25.00
Atlantic SD-8282	(S)	The Best Of Clarence Carter	1971	8.00	20.00
ABC X-633	(S)	Real	1974	6.00	15.00
ABC X-943	(S)	A Heart Full Of Song	1976	6.00	15.00

CARTER, LYNDA

Epic JE-35308	(S)	Portrait (Picture disc)	1978	12.00	30.00

CARTER, "MOTHER" MAYBELLE
Refer to The Carter Family.

Ambassador 98069	(M)	Mother Maybelle Carter	195?	80.00	200.00
Kapp KL-1413	(M)	Queen Of The Autoharp	1964	8.00	20.00
Kapp KS-3413	(S)	Queen Of The Autoharp	1964	10.00	25.00
Columbia CL-2475	(M)	A Living Legend	1965	6.00	15.00
Columbia CS-9275	(S)	A Living Legend	1965	8.00	20.00

CARTER, MEL

Derby LPM-702	(M)	When A Boy Falls In Love	1963	150.00	300.00
Imperial LP-9289	(M)	Hold Me, Thrill Me, Kiss Me	1965	8.00	20.00
Imperial LP-12289	(S)	Hold Me, Thrill Me, Kiss Me	1965	10.00	25.00
Imperial LP-9300	(M)	My Heart Sings	1965	6.00	15.00
Imperial LP-12300	(S)	My Heart Sings	1965	8.00	20.00
Imperial LP-9319	(M)	Easy Listening	1966	5.00	12.00
Imperial LP-12319	(S)	Easy Listening	1966	6.00	15.00
Liberty LRP-3530	(M)	Be My Love	1967	5.00	12.00
Liberty LSP-7530	(S)	Be My Love	1967	6.00	15.00

CARTER FAMILY, THE
The Carters feature Mother Maybelle.

Acme LP-1	(M)	All Time Favorites	195?	70.00	175.00
Acme LP-2	(M)	In Memory Of A.P. Carter	195?	18.00	200.00
Camden CAL-586	(M)	The Original And Great Carter Family	195?	6.00	15.00
Decca DL-4404	(M)	The Carter Family	1960	16.00	40.00
Decca DL-4404	(M)	A Collection Of Favorites	1963	12.00	30.00

Label & Catalog #		Title	Year	VG+	NM
Decca DL-4557	(M)	More Favorites By The Carter Family	1964	16.00	40.00
Columbia CL-2152	(M)	Keep On The Sunny Side	1964	6.00	15.00
Columbia CS-8952	(S)	Keep On The Sunny Side	1964	8.00	20.00
Columbia CL-2617	(M)	The Country Album	1966	6.00	15.00
Columbia CS-9417	(S)	The Country Album	1966	8.00	20.00

CARTOONE

Atlantic SD-8219	(S)	Cartoone (With Jimmy Page)	1969	8.00	20.00

CARTWRIGHT, ANGELA

Star-Bright HLP-102	(M)	Angela Cartwright Sings	195?	16.00	40.00

CASCADES

Valiant W-405	(M)	Rhythm Of The Rain	1963	40.00	100.00
Valiant WS-405	(S)	Rhythm Of The Rain	1963	100.00	250.00
		("Rhythm Of The Rain" is rechanneled for this album.)			
Cascade 681001	(S)	What Goes On	1968	20.00	50.00
Uni 73069	(S)	Maybe The Rain Will Fall	1969	8.00	20.00

CASE, ALAN

Columbia CL-1402	(M)	The "Deputy" Sings	1960	8.00	20.00
Columbia CS-8202	(S)	The "Deputy" Sings	1960	12.00	30.00

CASEY, AL

Prestige W-2007	(M)	Buck Jumpin'	1960	20.00	50.00
Prestige MV-12	(M)	The Al Casey Quartet	1961	16.00	40.00
Stacy STM-100	(M)	Surfin' Hootenanny (Surf-colored vinyl)	1963	40.00	100.00
Stacy STMS-100	(S)	Surfin' Hootenanny (Surf-colored vinyl)	1963	60.00	150.00

CASH, JOHNNY

Sun SLP-1220	(M)	Johnny Cash With His Hot & Blue Guitar	1956	30.00	75.00
Sun SLP-1235	(M)	The Songs That Made Him Famous	1958	30.00	75.00
Sun SLP-1240	(M)	Johnny Cash's Greatest!	1959	20.00	50.00
Sun SLP-1245	(M)	Johnny Cash Sings Hank Williams	1960	20.00	50.00
Sun SLP-1255	(M)	Now Here's Johnny Cash	1961	16.00	40.00
Sun SLP-1270	(M)	All Aboard The Blue Train	1963	14.00	35.00
Sun SLP-1275	(M)	The Original Sun Sound Of Johnny Cash	1965	14.00	35.00
Columbia CL-1253	(M)	The Fabulous Johnny Cash	1958	10.00	25.00
Columbia CS-8122	(S)	The Fabulous Johnny Cash	1958	14.00	35.00
Columbia CL-1284	(M)	Hymns By Johnny Cash	1959	8.00	20.00
Columbia CS-8125	(S)	Hymns By Johnny Cash	1959	12.00	30.00
Columbia CL-1339	(M)	Songs Of Our Soil	1959	8.00	20.00
Columbia CS-8148	(S)	Songs Of Our Soil	1959	12.00	30.00
Columbia CL-1463	(M)	Now, There Was A Song!	1960	8.00	20.00
Columbia CS-8254	(S)	Now, There Was A Song!	1960	12.00	30.00
Columbia CL-1464	(M)	Ride This Train	1960	8.00	20.00
Columbia CS-8255	(S)	Ride This Train	1960	12.00	30.00
Columbia CL-1622	(M)	The Lure Of The Grand Canyon	1961	12.00	30.00
Columbia CS-8422	(S)	The Lure Of The Grand Canyon	1961	16.00	40.00
Columbia CL-1722	(M)	Hymns From The Heart	1962	8.00	20.00
Columbia CS-8522	(S)	Hymns From The Heart	1962	10.00	25.00
Columbia CL-1802	(M)	The Sound Of Johnny Cash	1962	8.00	20.00
Columbia CS-8602	(S)	The Sound Of Johnny Cash	1962	10.00	25.00
		— Original Columbia albums above have three white "eye" logos on each side of the spindle hole.—			
Columbia CL-1930	(M)	Blood, Sweat And Tears	1963	6.00	15.00
Columbia CS-8730	(S)	Blood, Sweat And Tears	1963	8.00	20.00
Columbia CL-2053	(M)	Ring Of Fire/The Best Of Johnny Cash	1963	6.00	15.00
Columbia CS-8853	(S)	Ring Of Fire/The Best Of Johnny Cash	1963	8.00	20.00
Columbia CL-2117	(M)	Christmas Spirit	1963	6.00	15.00
Columbia CS-8917	(S)	Christmas Spirit	1963	8.00	20.00
Columbia CL-2190	(M)	I Walk The Line	1964	6.00	15.00
Columbia CS-8990	(S)	I Walk The Line	1964	8.00	20.00
Columbia CL-2248	(M)	Bitter Tears	1964	6.00	15.00
Columbia CS-9048	(S)	Bitter Tears	1964	8.00	20.00
Columbia C2L-838	(M)	Ballads Of The True West (2 LPs)	1965	8.00	20.00
Columbia C2S-838	(S)	Ballads Of The True West (2 LPs)	1965	10.00	25.00
Columbia CL-2309	(M)	Orange Blossom Special	1965	6.00	15.00
Columbia CS-9109	(S)	Orange Blossom Special	1965	8.00	20.00

Label & Catalog #		Title	Year	VG+	NM
Columbia CL-2446	(M)	Mean As Hell	1965	6.00	15.00
Columbia CS-9246	(S)	Mean As Hell	1965	8.00	20.00
Columbia OL-6420	(M)	The Sons Of Katie Elder (Soundtrack)	1965	75.00	150.00
Columbia OS-2820	(S)	The Sons Of Katie Elder (Soundtrack)	1965	100.00	200.00
Columbia CL-2492	(M)	Everybody Loves A Nut	1966	5.00	12.00
Columbia CS-9292	(S)	Everybody Loves A Nut	1966	6.00	15.00
Columbia CL-2537	(M)	Happiness Is You	1966	5.00	12.00
Columbia CS-9337	(S)	Happiness Is You	1966	6.00	15.00
Columbia CL-2537	(M)	That's What You Get For Loving Me	1966	5.00	12.00
Columbia CS-9337	(S)	That's What You Get For Loving Me	1966	6.00	15.00
Columbia CL-2647	(M)	From Sea To Shining Sea	1967	5.00	12.00
Columbia CS-9447	(S)	From Sea To Shining Sea	1967	6.00	15.00
Columbia CL-2678	(M)	Johnny Cash's Greatest Hits, Volume 1	1967	6.00	15.00
Columbia CS-9478	(S)	Johnny Cash's Greatest Hits, Volume 1	1967	6.00	15.00
Columbia CL-2728	(M)	Carryin' On	1967	6.00	15.00
Columbia CS-9528	(S)	Carryin' On	1967	6.00	15.00
Columbia CS-9639	(S)	Johnny Cash At Folsom Prison	1968	4.00	10.00
Columbia CS-9726	(S)	The Holy Land (3D cover)	1969	6.00	15.00
Columbia CS-9726	(S)	The Holy Land (2D cover)	1969	4.00	10.00
Columbia CS-9827	(S)	Johnny Cash At San Quentin	1969	4.00	10.00
Columbia CS-9943	(S)	Hello, I'm Johnny Cash	1970	4.00	10.00
— Original Columbia albums above have "360 Sound" labels. —					
Columbia 7425	(S)	Grand Canyon Suite	1969	8.00	20.00
		(Grey label with white "Masterworks" logo)			
Columbia 32253	(S)	The Gospel Road	1973	8.00	20.00
Sun LP-100	(E)	Original Golden Hits, Volume 1	1969	4.00	10.00
Sun LP-101	(E)	Original Golden Hits, Volume 2	1969	4.00	10.00
Sun LP-104	(E)	Story Songs Of The Trains And Rivers	1969	4.00	10.00
Sun LP-105	(E)	Get Rhythm	1969	4.00	10.00
Sun LP-115	(E)	Johnny Cash	1970	4.00	10.00
Sun LP-118	(E)	The Legend (2 LPs)	1970	4.00	10.00
Sun LP-122	(E)	The Rough Cut King Of Country Music	1970	4.00	10.00
Sun LP-126	(E)	The Man, The World, His Music (2 LPs)	1971	4.00	10.00
Sun LP-127	(E)	Original Golden Hits, Volume 3	1971	4.00	10.00
Sun LP-147	(E)	Original Rockabilly	1972	4.00	10.00
		(The Sun 100 series collects material recorded 1956-60.)			
Doral	(E)	Doral Presents Johnny Cash	1971	8.00	20.00
		(Promotional compilation of previously released material.)			

CASH, JOHNNY / JERRY LEE LEWIS

Sun LP-119	(E)	Sunday Down South	1970	4.00	10.00
Sun LP-125	(E)	Sing Hank Williams	1971	4.00	10.00

CASHMAN & WEST
Terry Cashman and Tommy West. Refer to The Chevrons.

Dunhill SPDJ-17	(DJ)	Tale Of Two Cities (American City Suite)	1972	6.00	15.00

CASINOS, THE

Fraternity 1019	(M)	Then You Can Tell Me Goodbye	1967	14.00	35.00
Fraternity LPS-1019	(S)	Then You Can Tell Me Goodbye	1967	20.00	50.00

CASSIDY, DAVID
David was formerly a member of The Partridge Family.

Bell 6070	(S)	Cherish	1972	8.00	20.00
Bell 1109	(S)	Rock Me, Baby	1972	8.00	20.00
Bell 1132	(S)	Dreams Are Nothin' More Than Wishes	1973	8.00	20.00
Bell 1321	(S)	David Cassidy's Greatest Hits	1974	6.00	15.00
Bell 1312	(S)	Cassidy Live	1974	10.00	25.00
RCA Victor APL1-1066	(DJ)	The Higher They Climb... (Blue vinyl)	1975	20.00	50.00
RCA Victor APL1-1066	(S)	The Higher They Climb...	1975	5.00	12.00
RCA Victor APL1-1309	(S)	Home Is Where The Heart Is	1976	5.00	12.00
RCA Victor APL1-1852	(S)	Gettin' It In The Street	1976	5.00	12.00

CASTELLS, THE

Era EL-109	(M)	So This Is Love	1962	40.00	100.00
Era ES-109	(S)	So This Is Love	1962	150.00	300.00

CASTLE, PAULA

Bethlehem BCP-1036 (10")	(M)	Lost Love	1955	35.00	70.00

Label & Catalog #		Title	Year	VG+	NM

CASTOR BUNCH, JIMMY
| Smash MGS-27091 | (M) | Hey Leroy! | 1967 | 8.00 | 20.00 |
| Smash SRW-67091 | (S) | Hey Leroy! | 1967 | 10.00 | 25.00 |

CATALINAS, THE
The Catalinas feature Bruce Johnston and Terry Melcher.
| Ric M-1006 | (M) | Fun, Fun, Fun | 1964 | 30.00 | 75.00 |
| Ric S-1006 | (S) | Fun, Fun, Fun | 1964 | 50.00 | 125.00 |

CATHEDRAL
| Delta DRC-1002 | (S) | Stained Glass Stories | 197? | 150.00 | 300.00 |
| Symphonic | (S) | Stained Glass Stories | 198? | 8.00 | 20.00 |

CATHY JEAN & THE ROOMATES
| Valmor 78 | (M) | Great Oldies | 1961 | 300.00 | 750.00 |
| Valmor 789 | (M) | At The Hop! *(Reissue of "Great Oldies")* | 1961 | 100.00 | 250.00 |

CAVALIERE, FELIX
Felix was formerly a member of The Young Rascals/Rascals.
| Epic AS-705 | (DJ) | Castles In The Air Sampler/Interview | 197? | 8.00 | 20.00 |

CENTRAL NERVOUS SYSTEM
| Music Factory MFS-12003 | (S) | I Could Have Danced All Night | 1968 | 6.00 | 15.00 |

CENTURIONS, THE
| Del-Fi DFLP-1228 | (M) | Surfer's Pajama Party | 1963 | 12.00 | 30.00 |
| Del-Fi DFST-1228 | (S) | Surfer's Pajama Party | 1963 | 16.00 | 40.00 |

(This album has the same title, catalog number and cover as The Bruce Johnston Surfing Band, but plays The Centurions.)

CESANA
| Modern M-100 | (M) | Tender Emotions | 1964 | 8.00 | 20.00 |

CEYLIB PEOPLE, THE
The Cetlib People feature Ry Cooder.
| Vault LP-117 | (S) | Tanyet | 1968 | 16.00 | 40.00 |

CHAD & JEREMY
Chad Stuart and Jeremy Clyde.
| World Artists WAM-2002 | (M) | Yesterday's Gone | 1964 | 5.00 | 12.00 |
| World Artists WAS-3002 | (S) | Yesterday's Gone | 1964 | 6.00 | 15.00 |

("Yesterday's Gone" is rechanneled on this album.)

World Artists WAM-2005	(M)	Chad & Jeremy Sing For You	1965	5.00	12.00
World Artists WAS-3005	(S)	Chad & Jeremy Sing For You	1965	6.00	15.00
Fidu FM-101	(M)	5 + 10 = 15 Fabulous Hits	1965	5.00	12.00
Fidu FS-101	(P)	5 + 10 = 15 Fabulous Hits	1965	6.00	15.00
Capitol T-2470	(M)	The Best Of Chad & Jeremy	1966	6.00	15.00
Capitol ST-2470	(P)	The Best Of Chad & Jeremy	1966	8.00	20.00

(Black "Starline" label.)

| Capitol ST-2470 | (P) | The Best Of Chad & Jeremy | 196? | 6.00 | 15.00 |

(Red & white "Starline" label.)

| Capitol TT-2546 | (M) | More Chad & Jeremy | 1966 | 6.00 | 15.00 |
| Capitol ST-2546 | (P) | More Chad & Jeremy | 1966 | 8.00 | 20.00 |

(Black "Starline" label.)

—The Fido and Capitol albums above repackage World Artists material.—

Columbia CL-2374	(M)	Before And After	1965	8.00	20.00
Columbia CS-9174	(S)	Before And After	1965	10.00	25.00
Columbia CL-2398	(M)	I Don't Want To Lose You Baby	1965	8.00	20.00
Columbia CS-9198	(S)	I Don't Want To Lose You Baby	1965	10.00	25.00
Columbia CL-2564	(M)	Distant Shores	1966	6.00	15.00
Columbia CS-9364	(S)	Distant Shores	1966	8.00	20.00

("Distant Shores" is rechanneled on this album.)

Columbia CL-2657	(M)	Of Cabbages And Kings	1967	6.00	15.00
Columbia CS-9457	(S)	Of Cabbages And Kings	1967	8.00	20.00
Columbia CL-2899	(M)	The Ark	1968	12.00	30.00
Columbia CS-9699	(S)	The Ark	1968	8.00	20.00

(Columbia 9457 and 9699 produced by Gary Usher.)

| Sidewalk ST-5918 | (S) | Three In The Attic *(Soundtrack)* | 1969 | 8.00 | 20.00 |
| Harmony HS-11357 | (S) | Chad & Jeremy | 196? | 6.00 | 15.00 |

Label & Catalog #		Title	Year	VG+	NM

CHAIRMEN OF THE BOARD

Invictus SKAO-7300	(S)	Chairmen Of The Board	1970	12.00	30.00
Invictus SKAO-7304	(S)	In Session	1971	12.00	30.00
Invictus ST-9801	(S)	Bittersweet	1972	12.00	30.00
Invictus KZ-32526	(S)	The Skin I'm In	1974	12.00	30.00

CHALKER, CURLY

Columbia CL-2496	(M)	Big Hits On Big Steel	1965	12.00	30.00
Columbia CS-9296	(S)	Big Hits On Big Steel	1965	16.00	40.00

CHALLENGERS, THE
The Challengers also recorded as The Good Guys. Refer to The Surfaris.

Vault LP-100	(M)	Surfbeat	1963	20.00	50.00
Vault VS-100	(S)	Surfbeat	1963	30.00	75.00
Vault VS-100	(S)	Surfbeat (Orange vinyl)	1963	60.00	150.00
Vault VS-100	(S)	Surfbeat (Red vinyl)	1963	60.00	150.00
Vault VS-100	(S)	Surfbeat (Yellow vinyl)	1963	60.00	150.00
Vault LP-101	(M)	Surfing	1963	20.00	50.00
Vault VS-101	(S)	Surfing	1963	30.00	75.00
Vault VS-101	(S)	Surfing (Orange vinyl)	1963	60.00	150.00
Vault VS-101	(S)	Surfing (Red vinyl)	1963	60.00	150.00
Vault VS-101	(S)	Surfing (Yellow vinyl)	1963	60.00	150.00
Vault VS-101	(S)	Surfing (Blue vinyl)	1963	60.00	150.00
Vault LP-102	(M)	The Challengers On The Move	1963	14.00	35.00
Vault VS-102	(S)	The Challengers On The Move	1963	20.00	50.00
Vault LP-107	(M)	K-39	1964	30.00	75.00
Vault LP-109	(M)	The Surf's Up	1965	20.00	50.00
Vault VS-109	(S)	The Surf's Up	1965	14.00	35.00
Vault LP-110	(M)	The Challengers A Go Go	1966	14.00	35.00
Vault VS-110	(S)	The Challengers A Go Go	1966	20.00	50.00
Vault LP-111	(M)	The Challengers' Greatest Hits	1967	10.00	25.00
Vault VS-111	(S)	The Challengers' Greatest Hits	1967	8.00	20.00
Triumph 100	(M)	Sidewalk Surfing	1965	8.00	20.00
Triumph TR-100	(S)	Sidewalk Surfing	1965	10.00	25.00
Crescendo GNP-2010	(M)	The Challengers At The Teenage Fair	1965	6.00	15.00
Crescendo GNPS-2010	(S)	The Challengers At The Teenage Fair	1965	8.00	20.00
Crescendo GNP-2018	(M)	The Man From U.N.C.L.E.	1965	6.00	15.00
Crescendo GNPS-2018	(S)	The Man From U.N.C.L.E.	1965	8.00	20.00
Crescendo GNP-2025	(M)	California Kicks	1966	6.00	15.00
Crescendo GNPS-2025	(S)	California Kicks	1966	8.00	20.00
Crescendo GNP-2030	(M)	Billy Strange And The Challengers	1966	6.00	15.00
Crescendo GNPS-2030	(S)	Billy Strange And The Challengers	1966	8.00	20.00
Crescendo GNP-2031	(M)	Wipe Out	1966	6.00	15.00
Crescendo GNPS-2031	(S)	Wipe Out	1966	8.00	20.00
Crescendo GNP-609	(M)	25 Great Instrumental Hits (2 LPs)	1967	6.00	15.00
Crescendo GNPS-609	(S)	25 Great Instrumental Hits (2 LPs)	1967	8.00	20.00
Crescendo GNPS-2045	(S)	Light My Fire With Classical Gas	1968	6.00	15.00
Crescendo GNPS-2056	(S)	Vanilla Funk	1970	6.00	15.00

— Original GNP Crescendo albums above have red labels. —

Fantasy F-9443	(S)	Where Were You In The Summer Of '62	1970	4.00	10.00

CHALLENGERS, THE

Nariel LPMS-104	(S)	The Challengers	196?	60.00	150.00

CHAMBERLAIN, RICHARD

MGM E-4088	(M)	Richard Chamberlain Sings	1963	6.00	15.00
MGM SE-4088	(S)	Richard Chamberlain Sings	1963	8.00	20.00
MGM E-4185	(M)	Twilight Of Honor (Soundtrack)	1963	6.00	15.00
MGM SE-4185	(S)	Twilight Of Honor (Soundtrack)	1963	8.00	20.00
MGM E-4287	(M)	Joy In The Morning	1964	6.00	15.00
MGM SE-4287	(S)	Joy In The Morning	1964	8.00	20.00
Metro M-564	(M)	Theme From "Dr. Kildare"	1966	6.00	15.00
Metro MS-564	(S)	Theme From "Dr. Kildare"	1966	8.00	20.00

CHAMBERS BROTHERS, THE

Vault 9003	(M)	People Get Ready	1966	6.00	15.00
Vault 9003	(S)	People Get Ready	1966	8.00	20.00
Vault LP-115	(M)	The Chambers Brothers Now	1967	6.00	15.00
Vault VS-115	(S)	The Chambers Brothers Now	1967	8.00	20.00

Like many Vee Jay albums, the stereo release of Gene Chandler's Duke Of Earl *is damn near impossible to find. Complicating the matter was the dumping of counterfeits on the market years ago. While collectors have tended to use the existence of the "Stereophonic" across the top of the front cover or the stereo notice on top of the back cover that begins "Important Notice" in identifying originals from fakes, both of these can be found on the counterfeit covers! But. . . thus far there are no known counterfeits of the stereo disc. So, when purchasing this or any other stereo Vee Jay album, check the record.*

Label & Catalog #		Title	Year	VG+	NM
Vault VS-120	(S)	The Chambers Brothers Shout	1968	6.00	15.00
Vault VS-128	(S)	Feelin' The Blues	1969	6.00	15.00
Vault VS-135	(S)	Chambers Brothers' Greatest Hits (2 LPs)	1970	6.00	15.00
Columbia CL-2722	(M)	The Time Has Come	1967	6.00	15.00
Columbia CS-9522	(S)	The Time Has Come	1967	6.00	15.00
Columbia CS-9671	(S)	A New Time/A New Day	1968	6.00	15.00
Columbia KGP-20	(S)	Love, Peace & Happiness (2 LPs)	1969	8.00	20.00

— Original Columbia albums above have "360 Sound " on the bottom of the label.—

CHAMPS, THE

Challenge CHL-601	(M)	Go Champs Go	1958	100.00	250.00
Challenge CHL-601	(M)	Go Champs Go (Blue vinyl)	1958	660.00	Rare

(Near Mint copies have a suggested value of $1,000-2,000.)

Challenge CHL-605	(M)	Everybody's Rockin' With The Champs	1959	50.00	125.00
Challenge CHS-605	(S)	Everybody's Rockin' With The Champs	1959	70.00	175.00
Challenge CHL-613	(M)	Great Dance Hits	1962	20.00	50.00
Challenge CHS-613	(S)	Great Dance Hits	1962	30.00	75.00
Challenge CHL-614	(M)	All American Music From The Champs	1962	20.00	50.00
Challenge CHS-614	(S)	All American Music From The Champs	1962	30.00	75.00

CHAMPS, THE / THE CYCLONES

Design DLP-159	(M)	Spotlight On The Champs & The Cyclones	196?	6.00	15.00
Design DLS-159	(E)	Spotlight On The Champs & The Cyclones	196?	4.00	10.00
Inter. Award AK-223	(M)	The Champs & The Fabulous Cyclones	196?	6.00	15.00
Inter. Award AKS-223	(E)	The Champs & The Fabulous Cyclones	196?	4.00	10.00

CHANDLER, GENE
Gene Chandler also recorded with Jerry Butler.

Vee Jay MR-1040	(M)	The Duke Of Earl	1962	40.00	100.00
Vee Jay SR-1040	(S)	The Duke Of Earl	1962	300.00	500.00

(Original stereo albums exist with "Stereophonic" across the top of the front cover and/or the stereo indica strip across the back. Counterfeits of both of these cover variations also exists, but there are no known counterfeits of the stereo record.)

Constellation LP-1421	(M)	Greatest Hits By Gene Chandler	1964	12.00	30.00
Constellation LP-1423	(M)	Just Be True	1964	12.00	30.00
Constellation LP-1425	(M)	Gene Chandler/Live On Stage In '65	1965	12.00	30.00
Checker LP-3003	(M)	The Duke Of Soul	1967	12.00	30.00
Checker LPS-3003	(E)	The Duke Of Soul	1967	8.00	20.00
Brunswick BL-54124	(M)	The Girl Don't Care	1967	8.00	20.00
Brunswick BL-754124	(S)	The Girl Don't Care	1967	6.00	15.00
Brunswick BL-754131	(S)	There Was A Time	1968	6.00	15.00
Brunswick BL-75149	(S)	The Two Sides Of Gene Chandler	1969	6.00	15.00
Mercury SR-61304	(S)	The Gene Chandler Situation	1970	4.00	10.00

CHANDLER, JEFF

Liberty LRP-3067	(M)	Jeff Chandler Sings To You	1957	16.00	40.00
Liberty LRP-3074	(M)	Warm And Easy	1957	16.00	40.00
Sunset SUM-1127	(M)	Sincerely Yours	196?	6.00	15.00
Sunset SUS-5127	(E)	Sincerely Yours	196?	5.00	12.00

CHANNEL, BRUCE

Smash MGS-27008	(M)	Hey! Baby	1962	30.00	75.00
Smash SRS-67008	(E)	Hey! Baby	1962	20.00	50.00

CHANTAYS, THE

Downey DLP-1002	(M)	Pipeline	1963	60.00	150.00
Downey DLPS-1002	(S)	Pipeline	1963	80.00	200.00
Dot DLP-3516	(M)	Pipeline	1963	16.00	40.00
Dot DLP-25516	(S)	Pipeline	1963	20.00	50.00
Dot DLP-3771	(M)	Two Sides Of The Chantays	1966	16.00	40.00
Dot DLP-25771	(S)	Two Sides Of The Chantays	1966	20.00	50.00

CHANTELS, THE

End LP-301	(M)	We're The Chantels	1958	500.00	800.00

(Original pressings have gray labels and a cover photo of the girls dressed in Southern plantation finery that apparently brought accusations of racial stereotyping and was quickly withrawn.)

Label & Catalog #		Title	Year	VG+	NM
End LP-301	(M)	We're The Chantels	1959	100.00	200.00
		(Gray label. Second pressings have gray labels but the covers replace the group with a photo of a jukebox.)			
End LP-301	(M)	We're The Chantels	1962	40.00	100.00
		(Third pressings have gray labels with 1962 in the trail-off vinyl and were issued in the jukebox cover.)			
End LP-301	(M)	We're The Chantels	1965	12.00	30.00
		(Later pressings have a color label with 1965 in the trail-off vinyl and were issued in the jukebox cover.)			
Carlton LP-144	(M)	The Chantels On Tour	1961	50.00	125.00
Carlton STLP-144	(S)	The Chantels On Tour	1961	100.00	250.00
		(Carlton 144 contains tracks by Chris Montez, The Imeprials without Little Anthony and Gus Backus of The Dell Vikings in mono and the Chantels' tracks in stereo.)			
End LP-312	(M)	There's Our Song Again	1962	30.00	75.00
Forum 9104	(M)	The Chantels Sing Their Favorites	196?	10.00	25.00

CHAPIN BROTHERS, THE [HARRY & TOM CHAPIN]

Rockland 66	(M)	Chapin Music	1966	12.00	30.00

CHARIOTEERS, THE

Columbia CL-6014 (10")	(M)	Sweet And Low	1950	100.00	250.00

CHARISMA

Roulette SR-42037	(S)	Charisma	1969	6.00	15.00

CHARITY

Uni 73061	(S)	Charity Now	1969	10.00	25.00

CHARLATANS, THE

Philips PHS-600-309	(S)	The Charlatans	1969	24.00	60.00

CHARLES, RAY

Atlantic 8006	(M)	Ray Charles	1957	30.00	75.00
Atlantic 1259	(M)	The Great Ray Charles	1957	30.00	75.00
Atlantic 1279	(M)	Soul Brothers	1958	20.00	50.00
Atlantic 1289	(M)	Ray Charles At Newport	1958	20.00	50.00
Atlantic 8025	(M)	Yes, Indeed! *(Screaming girls on cover)*	1959	20.00	50.00
Atlantic 8029	(M)	What'd I Say	1959	20.00	50.00
Atlantic 8039	(M)	Ray Charles In Person	1960	20.00	50.00
Atlantic 1312	(M)	The Genius Of Ray Charles	1960	20.00	50.00
Atlantic SD-1312	(S)	The Genius Of Ray Charles	1960	40.00	100.00
		— Original Atlantic albums above have black labels; stereo albums have green labels.—			
Hollywood 504	(M)	Ray Charles	1959	30.00	75.00
Hollywood 505	(M)	The Fabulous Ray Charles	1959	30.00	75.00
Atlantic 8006	(M)	Ray Charles	1960	8.00	20.00
Atlantic 1259	(M)	The Great Ray Charles	1960	8.00	20.00
Atlantic 1279	(M)	Soul Brothers	1960	8.00	20.00
Atlantic 1289	(M)	Ray Charles At Newport	1960	8.00	20.00
Atlantic 8025	(M)	Yes, Indeed!	1960	8.00	20.00
Atlantic 8029	(M)	What'd I Say	1960	8.00	20.00
Atlantic 8039	(M)	Ray Charles In Person	1960	8.00	20.00
Atlantic 1312	(M)	The Genius Of Ray Charles	1960	10.00	25.00
Atlantic SD-1312	(S)	The Genius Of Ray Charles	1960	14.00	35.00
Atlantic 8052	(M)	The Genius Sings The Blues	1961	10.00	25.00
Atlantic SD-8052	(E)	The Genius Sings The Blues	1961	8.00	20.00
Atlantic 8054	(M)	Do The Twist With Ray Charles!	1961	10.00	25.00
Atlantic 1360	(M)	Soul Meeting	1961	10.00	25.00
Atlantic SD-1360	(S)	Soul Meeting	1961	14.00	35.00
		—Atlantic mono albums above have orange & purple labels with a white fan; stereo albums have green and blue labels with a white fan.—			
Atlantic 8006	(M)	Hallelujah I Love Her So	1962	8.00	20.00
		("Hallelujah I Love Her So" is a reissue of "Rock And Roll.")			
Atlantic 8025	(M)	Yes, Indeed! *(Ray Charles on cover)*	1962	8.00	20.00
Atlantic 1369	(M)	The Genius After Hours	1961	10.00	25.00
Atlantic SD-1369	(S)	The Genius After Hours	1961	14.00	35.00
Atlantic 8063	(M)	The Ray Charles Story, Volume 1	1962	8.00	20.00
Atlantic SD-8063	(E)	The Ray Charles Story, Volume 1	1962	6.00	15.00

Label & Catalog #		Title	Year	VG+	NM
Atlantic 8064	(M)	The Ray Charles Story, Volume 2	1962	8.00	20.00
Atlantic SD-8064	(E)	The Ray Charles Story, Volume 2	1962	6.00	15.00
Atlantic 8083	(M)	The Ray Charles Story, Volume 3	1963	8.00	20.00
Atlantic SD-8083	(P)	The Ray Charles Story, Volume 3	1963	10.00	25.00
Atlantic 8094	(M)	The Ray Charles Story, Volume 4	1964	8.00	20.00
Atlantic SD-8094	(P)	The Ray Charles Story, Volume 4	1964	10.00	25.00
Atlantic SD-7101	(S)	Great Hits Recorded On 8-Track Stereo	1964	10.00	25.00
ABC-Paramount 335	(M)	The Genius Hits The Road	1960	8.00	20.00
ABC-Paramount S-335	(S)	The Genius Hits The Road	1960	12.00	30.00
ABC-Paramount 355	(M)	Dedicated To You	1961	8.00	20.00
ABC-Paramount S-355	(S)	Dedicated To You	1961	12.00	30.00

*— Original ABC albums above have black labels with "ABC-PARAMOUNT" on the top
and "Am-Par Record Corp." on the bottom.—*

Impulse A-2	(M)	Genius + Soul = Jazz	1961	12.00	30.00
Impulse AS-2	(S)	Genius + Soul = Jazz	1961	16.00	40.00
Baronet BM-111	(M)	The Artistry Of Ray Charles	1962	6.00	15.00
Baronet BS-111	(E)	The Artistry Of Ray Charles	1962	4.00	10.00
ABC-Paramount 410	(M)	Modern Sounds In Country And Western	1962	10.00	25.00
ABC-Paramount S-410	(S)	Modern Sounds In Country And Western	1962	12.00	30.00
		(Original pressings do not have the RIAA Gold Record Award seal on the cover.)			
ABC-Paramount S-410	(S)	Modern Sounds In Country And Western	196?	6.00	15.00
		(Later pressing covers have an RIAA Gold Record Award seal on the cover.)			
ABC-Paramount 415	(M)	Ray Charles' Greatest Hits	1962	6.00	15.00
ABC-Paramount S-415	(S)	Ray Charles' Greatest Hits	1962	8.00	20.00
ABC-Paramount 435	(M)	Modern Sounds In Country & Western, Volume 2	1962	6.00	15.00
ABC-Paramount S-435	(S)	Modern Sounds In Country & Western, Volume 2	1962	8.00	20.00
ABC-Paramount 465	(M)	Ingredients In A Recipe For Soul	1963	6.00	15.00
ABC-Paramount S-465	(S)	Ingredients In A Recipe For Soul	1963	8.00	20.00
ABC-Paramount 480	(M)	Sweet And Sour Tears	1964	6.00	15.00
ABC-Paramount S-480	(S)	Sweet And Sour Tears	1964	8.00	20.00
ABC-Paramount 495	(M)	Have A Smile With Me	1964	6.00	15.00
ABC-Paramount S-495	(S)	Have A Smile With Me	1964	8.00	20.00
MGM E-4313	(M)	The Cincinnati Kid *(Soundtrack)*	1965	6.00	15.00
MGM SE-4313	(S)	The Cincinnati Kid *(Soundtrack)*	1965	8.00	20.00
ABC-Paramount 500	(M)	Live In Concert	1965	4.00	10.00
ABC-Paramount S-500	(S)	Live In Concert	1965	5.00	12.00
ABC-Paramount 520	(M)	Country & Western Meets Rhythm & Blues	1965	6.00	15.00
ABC-Paramount S-520	(S)	Country & Western Meets Rhythm & Blues	1965	8.00	20.00
ABC-Paramount 520	(M)	Together Again	1966	5.00	12.00
ABC-Paramount S-520	(S)	Together Again	1966	6.00	15.00
		(Repackage of "Country & Western Meets Rhythm & Blues.")			
ABC-Paramount 544	(M)	Crying Time	1966	5.00	12.00
ABC-Paramount S-544	(S)	Crying Time	1966	6.00	15.00

— Original ABC albums above have black labels with "ABC-Paramount" on top.—

ABC 550	(M)	Ray's Moods	1966	5.00	12.00
ABC X-550	(S)	Ray's Moods	1966	6.00	15.00
ABC 2-590	(M)	A Man And His Soul *(2 LPs)*	1967	8.00	20.00
ABC Y-2-590	(S)	A Man And His Soul *(2 LPs)*	1967	10.00	25.00
ABC 595	(M)	Ray Charles Invites You To Listen	1967	5.00	12.00
ABC X-595	(S)	Ray Charles Invites You To Listen	1967	6.00	15.00
ABC X-625	(S)	A Portrait Of Ray	1968	4.00	10.00
ABC X-675	(S)	I'm All Yours, Baby	1969	4.00	10.00
ABC X-695	(S)	Doing His Thing	1969	4.00	10.00
ABC X-707	(S)	Love Country Style	1970	4.00	10.00
ABC X-726	(S)	Volcanic Action Of My Soul	1971	4.00	10.00
ABC H-731	(S)	25th Anniversary In Show Business *(2 LPs)*	1971	6.00	15.00
ABC X-755	(S)	A Message From The People	1972	4.00	10.00
ABC X-765	(S)	Through The Eyes Of Love	1972	4.00	10.00
United Artists UAL-4160	(M)	In The Heat Of The Night *(Soundtrack)*	1967	6.00	15.00
United Artists UAS-5160	(S)	In The Heat Of The Night *(Soundtrack)*	1967	8.00	20.00
Coronet CX-173	(M)	Ray Charles	196?	6.00	15.00
Coronet CXS-173	(E)	Ray Charles	196?	4.00	10.00
United Dist. 2-2318	(E)	Heart Breakers *(2 LPs)*	1983	5.00	12.00

Label & Catalog #		Title	Year	VG+	NM

CHARLES, RAY / HARRY BELAFONTE

Label & Catalog #		Title	Year	VG+	NM
Coronet CX-203	(M)	The Greatest Ever	196?	8.00	20.00
Coronet CXS-203	(E)	The Greatest Ever	196?	4.00	10.00

CHARLES, RAY, & BETTY CARTER

ABC-Paramount 385	(M)	Ray Charles And Betty Carter	1961	20.00	50.00
ABC-Paramount S-385	(S)	Ray Charles And Betty Carter	1961	30.00	75.00

CHARLES, RAY / IVORY JOE HUNTER / JIMMY RUSHING

Design DLP-909	(M)	Three Of A Kind	196?	6.00	15.00
Design DLS-909	(E)	Three Of A Kind	196?	4.00	10.00

CHARLES VALLEY RIVER BOYS, THE

Folklore FRLP-14017	(M)	Bluegrass And Old Timey Music	1964	8.00	20.00
Folklore FRST-14017	(S)	Bluegrass And Old Timey Music	1964	10.00	25.00
Folklore FRLP-14024	(M)	Bluegrass Get Together (With Tex Logan)	1964	8.00	20.00
Folklore FRST-14024	(S)	Bluegrass Get Together (With Tex Logan)	1964	10.00	25.00
Elektra EKL-4006	(M)	Beatles Country	1967	8.00	20.00
Elektra ES-74006	(S)	Beatles Country	1967	10.00	25.00

CHARLIE

Janus/GRT JXS-7036	(DJ)	Lines (Picture disc)	1978	20.00	50.00

CHARMER

Illusion CM-1070	(S)	Your Presence Requested	1976	40.00	100.00
Illusion CM-1071	(S)	Do It To It	1976	40.00	100.00

CHARTBUSTERS, THE: *Refer to* THE MANCHESTERS

CHASE

Epic EQ-30472	(Q)	Chase	1974	6.00	15.00
Epic EQ-32572	(Q)	Pure Music	1974	6.00	15.00

CHASE, LINCOLN

Liberty LRP-3076	(M)	The Explosive Lincoln Chase	1958	16.00	40.00

CHATANOOGA CATS, THE

Forward ST-F-1018	(S)	The Chatanooga Cats	1969	12.00	30.00

CHEAP TRICK

Epic 35773	(DJ)	Dream Police (Picture disc)	1980	12.00	30.00

CHECKER, CHUBBY

Chubby Checker is a pseudonym for Ernest Evans. Refer to Bobby Rydell; Dee Dee Sharp.

Parkway 5001	(M)	Chubby Checker	1960	30.00	75.00
Parkway P-7001	(M)	Twist With Chubby Checker	1960	20.00	50.00
Parkway P-7002	(M)	For Twisters Only	1960	20.00	50.00
Parkway P-7003	(M)	It's Pony Time	1961	20.00	50.00
Parkway P-7004	(M)	Let's Twist Again	1961	20.00	50.00
Parkway P-7007	(M)	Your Twist Party	1961	20.00	50.00
Parkway P-7008	(M)	Twistin' Round The World	1962	20.00	50.00
Parkway P-7009	(M)	For Teen Twisters Only	1962	20.00	50.00
Parkway SP-7009	(S)	For Teen Twisters Only	1962	30.00	75.00
Parkway P-7011	(M)	Don't Knock The Twist (Soundtrack)	1962	30.00	75.00
Parkway P-7014	(M)	All The Hits For Your Dancin' Party	1962	20.00	50.00
Parkway P-7020	(M)	Limbo Party	1962	20.00	50.00
Parkway SP-7020	(S)	Limbo Party	1962	30.00	75.00
Parkway P-7022	(M)	Chubby Checker's Biggest Hits	1962	20.00	50.00
Parkway SP-7022	(E)	Chubby Checker's Biggest Hits	1962	20.00	50.00
Parkway P-7026	(M)	Chubby Checker In Person	1963	20.00	50.00
Parkway SP-7026	(S)	Chubby Checker In Person	1963	30.00	75.00
Parkway P-7027	(M)	Let's Limbo Some More	1963	20.00	50.00
Parkway SP-7027	(S)	Let's Limbo Some More	1963	30.00	75.00
Parkway P-7030	(M)	Beach Party	1963	20.00	50.00
Parkway SP-7030	(S)	Beach Party	1963	30.00	75.00
Parkway P-7036	(M)	Chubby Checker With Sy Oliver	1964	20.00	50.00
Parkway SP-7036	(S)	Chubby Checker With Sy Oliver	1964	30.00	75.00
Parkway P-7040	(M)	Folk Album	1964	20.00	50.00
Parkway SP-7040	(S)	Folk Album	1964	30.00	75.00

Label & Catalog #		Title	Year	VG+	NM
Parkway P-7045	(M)	Discotheque	1965	20.00	50.00
Parkway SP-7045	(S)	Discotheque	1965	30.00	75.00
Parkway P-7048	(M)	Chubby Checker's Eighteen Golden Hits	1966	20.00	50.00
Parkway SP-7048	(P)	Chubby Checker's Eighteen Golden Hits	1966	30.00	75.00

CHECKMATES, THE

Justice JLP-149	(S)	The Checkmates	1966	100.00	250.00

CHECKMATES, LTD., THE

Ikon 122	(M)	Live At Harvey's	1965	10.00	25.00
Capitol T-2840	(M)	Live At Caesar's Palace	1966	6.00	15.00
Capitol ST-2840	(S)	Live At Caesar's Palace	1966	8.00	20.00
A&M SP-4183	(S)	Love Is All We Have To Give	1969	8.00	20.00
		(Produced by Phil Spector.)			
Rustic 2001	(S)	Bobby Stevens & The Checkmates, Ltd.	1971	8.00	20.00
Fantasy 9541	(S)	We Got The Moves	1978	6.00	15.00

CHELSEA

Chelsea features Peter Criss, later of Kiss.

Decca DL-75262	(S)	The Chelsea Album	1972	30.00	75.00

CHER

Refer to Sonny & Cher.

Imperial LP-9292	(M)	All I Really Want To Do	1965	8.00	20.00
Imperial LP-12292	(S)	All I Really Want To Do	1965	10.00	25.00
Imperial LP-9301	(M)	The Sonny Side Of Cher	1966	8.00	20.00
Imperial LP-12301	(S)	The Sonny Side Of Cher	1966	10.00	25.00
		— Original Imperial albums above have green & black labels. —			
Imperial LP-9320	(M)	Cher	1966	6.00	15.00
Imperial LP-12320	(S)	Cher	1966	8.00	20.00
Imperial LP-9358	(M)	With Love	1967	6.00	15.00
Imperial LP-12358	(S)	With Love	1967	8.00	20.00
Imperial LP-12373	(S)	Backstage	1968	6.00	15.00
Imperial LP-12406	(S)	Cher's Golden Greats	1968	8.00	20.00
Atco SD-33-2098	(S)	3614 Jackson Highway	1969	6.00	15.00
Casablanca NBPIX-7133	(S)	Take Me Home (Picture disc)	1979	5.00	12.00

CHEROKEE

ABC S-719	(S)	Cherokee	1970	6.00	15.00

CHESTER, GARY

DCP DCL-3803	(M)	Yeah, Yeah, Yeah	1964	6.00	15.00
DCP DCS-6803	(S)	Yeah, Yeah, Yeah	1964	8.00	20.00

CHEVRONS, THE

The Chevrons feature Terry Cashman.

Time 10008	(M)	Sing A Long Rock & Roll	1961	30.00	75.00

CHI-LITES, THE

Brunswick BL-754142	(S)	Give It Away	1969	8.00	20.00
Brunswick BL-754165	(S)	I Like Your Lovin', Do You Like Mine?	1971	8.00	20.00
Brunswick BL-754170	(S)	Give More Power To The People	1971	8.00	20.00
Brunswick BL-754179	(S)	Lonely Man	1972	8.00	20.00
Brunswick BL-754184	(S)	The Chi-Lites Greatest Hits	1972	6.00	15.00
Brunswick BL-754188	(S)	A Letter To Myself	1973	6.00	15.00
Brunswick BL-754197	(S)	The Chi-Lites	1973	6.00	15.00
Brunswick BL-754200	(S)	Toby	1974	6.00	15.00
Brunswick BL-754204	(S)	Half A Love	1974	6.00	15.00

CHICAGO [CHICAGO TRANSIT AUTHORITY]

Columbia GP-8	(S)	Chicago Transit Authority (2 LPs)	1969	16.00	40.00
Columbia KGP-24	(S)	Chicago (2 LPs)	1970	20.00	50.00
		— Original Columbia albums above have "360 Sound " on the bottom of the label. —			
Columbia GP-8	(S)	Chicago Transit Authority (2 LPs)	1970	4.00	10.00
Columbia KGP-24	(S)	Chicago (2 LPs)	1970	4.00	10.00
Columbia C2-30110	(S)	Chicago III (2 LPs)	1970	4.00	10.00
Columbia C2Q-30110	(Q)	Chicago III (2 LPs)	1974	12.00	30.00
Columbia C4X-30863	(S)	Chicago At Carnegie Hall, Vol. 1 & 2 (2 LPs)	1971	4.00	10.00
Columbia C4X-30864	(S)	Chicago At Carnegie Hall, Vol. 3 & 4 (2 LPs)	1971	4.00	10.00

Patricia Bennett, Judy Craig, Barbara Lee and Sylvia Patterson, four young women from the Bronx, virtually define "girl group" for many collectors. And, unlike so many others of the genre, they made several albums to go along with their classic singles. Both of their first two LPs on Laurie are far more difficult to find in collectible condition than their current market value indicates.

Label & Catalog #		Title	Year	VG+	NM
Columbia C4X-30865	(S)	**Chicago At Carnegie Hall** *(4 LP box)*	1971	20.00	50.00
Columbia C4Q-30865	(Q)	**Chicago At Carnegie Hall** *(4 LP box)*	1974	30.00	75.00
		(Columbia 30865 collects 30863 and 30864.)			
Columbia KC-31102	(S)	**Chicago V**	1972	3.60	8.00
Columbia CQ-31102	(Q)	**Chicago V**	1974	10.00	25.00
Columbia KC-32400	(S)	**Chicago VI**	1973	3.60	8.00
Columbia CQ-32400	(Q)	**Chicago VI**	1974	10.00	25.00
Columbia C2-32810	(S)	**Chicago VII** *(2 LPs)*	1974	4.00	10.00
Columbia C2Q-32810	(Q)	**Chicago VII** *(2 LPs)*	1974	12.00	30.00
Columbia PC-33100	(S)	**Chicago VIII**	1975	3.60	8.00
Columbia PCQ-33100	(Q)	**Chicago VIII**	1975	10.00	25.00
Columbia GQ-33255	(Q)	**Chicago Transit Authority** *(2 LPs)*	1975	10.00	25.00
Columbia GQ-33258	(Q)	**Chicago** *(2 LPs)*	1975	10.00	25.00
		(Columbia 33255 and 33258 are quad reissues of the first albums.)			
Columbia PC-33900	(S)	**Chicago IX/Greatest Hits**	1975	3.60	8.00
Columbia PCQ-33900	(Q)	**Chicago IX/Greatest Hits**	1975	10.00	25.00
Columbia HC-43900	(S)	**Chicago IX/Greatest Hits** *(Half-speed)*	1982	12.00	30.00
Columbia PC-34200	(S)	**Chicago X**	1976	10.00	25.00
Columbia PCQ-34200	(Q)	**Chicago X**	1976	3.60	8.00
Columbia HC-44200	(S)	**Chicago X** *(Half-speed master)*	1982	10.00	25.00
Columbia *(No number)*	(DJ)	**Chicago** *(17 LP box)*	1976	80.00	200.00
Mobile Fidelity MFSL-128	(S)	**Chicago Transit Authority** *(2 LPs)*	1983	15.00	45.00
		(Original Master Recording)			
Full Moon 25060	(DJ)	**Chicago 17** *(Quiex II vinyl)*	1984	6.00	15.00

CHICAGO SLIM

Capitol ST-344	(S)	**Scufflin'**	1969	6.00	15.00

CHICKEN SHACK
Chicken Shack features Christine Perfect a.k.a. Christine McVie, later of Fleetwood Mac.

Epic LN-24414	(M)	**Forty Blue Fingers, Freshly Packed And Ready To Serve** *(White label promo)*	1968	40.00	100.00
Epic BN-26414	(S)	**Forty Blue Fingers, Freshly Packed And Ready To Serve**	1968	10.00	25.00
Blue Horizon BH-7705	(S)	**O.K. Ken?**	1969	10.00	25.00
Blue Horizon BH-7706	(S)	**100 Ton Chicken**	1969	8.00	20.00
Blue Horizon BH-4809	(S)	**Accept Chicken Shack**	1970	8.00	20.00
Deram DES-18063	(S)	**Imagination Lady**	1972	8.00	20.00

CHIFFONS, THE

Laurie LLP-2018	(M)	**He's So Fine**	1963	40.00	100.00
Laurie DT-9075	(E)	**He's So Fine** *(Capitol Record Club)*	1963	80.00	200.00
Laurie LLP-2020	(M)	**One Fine Day**	1963	40.00	100.00
Laurie LLP-2036	(M)	**Sweet Talkin' Guy**	1966	20.00	50.00
Laurie SLP-2036	(S)	**Sweet Talkin' Guy**	1966	30.00	75.00
		("Nobody Knows What's Goin' On" is rechanneled on this album.)			
B.T. Puppy S-1011	(S)	**My Secret Love**	1970	30.00	75.00

CHILD'S ART

Gold 3000	(S)	**Uncut**	1982	24.00	60.00

CHILDREN, THE

Cinema CLP-1	(S)	**Rebirth**	1968	30.00	75.00
Atco SD-33-271	(S)	**Rebirth**	1968	6.00	15.00

CHIPMUNKS, THE
The Chipmunks are the creation of Ross Bagdasarian, a.k.a. David Seville.

Liberty LRP-3132	(M)	**Sing With The Chipmunks** *(Red vinyl)*	1959	30.00	75.00
Liberty LST-7132	(S)	**Sing With The Chipmunks** *(Red vinyl)*	1959	40.00	100.00
Liberty LRP-3132	(M)	**Sing With The Chipmunks**	1959	14.00	35.00
Liberty LST-7132	(S)	**Sing With The Chipmunks**	1959	20.00	50.00
Liberty LRP-3159	(M)	**Sing Again With The Chipmunks**	1960	14.00	35.00
Liberty LST-7159	(S)	**Sing Again With The Chipmunks**	1960	20.00	50.00
Liberty LRP-3170	(M)	**Around The World With The Chipmunks**	1960	14.00	35.00
Liberty LST-7170	(S)	**Around The World With The Chipmunks**	1960	20.00	50.00
		— Original pressings above have "realistic" drawings of the Chipmunks on the covers.—			
Liberty LRP-3132	(M)	**Sing With The Chipmunks**	1961	10.00	25.00
Liberty LST-7132	(S)	**Sing With The Chipmunks**	1961	12.00	30.00

Label & Catalog #		Title	Year	VG+	NM
Liberty LRP-3159	(M)	Sing Again With The Chipmunks	1961	10.00	25.00
Liberty LST-7159	(S)	Sing Again With The Chipmunks	1961	12.00	30.00
Liberty LRP-3170	(M)	Around The World With The Chipmunks	1961	10.00	25.00
Liberty LST-7170	(S)	Around The World With The Chipmunks	1961	12.00	30.00
—Later pressings have drawings of the Chipmunks on the covers as the familiar cartoons.—					
Liberty LRP-3209	(M)	The Alvin Show	1961	10.00	25.00
Liberty LST-7209	(S)	The Alvin Show	1961	12.00	30.00
Liberty LRP-3229	(M)	The Chipmunks Songbook	1962	10.00	25.00
Liberty LST-7229	(S)	The Chipmunks Songbook	1962	12.00	30.00
Liberty LRP-3256	(M)	Christmas With The Chipmunks	1962	10.00	25.00
Liberty LST-7256	(S)	Christmas With The Chipmunks	1962	12.00	30.00
Liberty LRP-3334	(M)	Christmas With The Chipmunks, Volume 2	1963	10.00	25.00
Liberty LST-7334	(S)	Christmas With The Chipmunks, Volume 2	1963	12.00	30.00
Liberty LRP-3388	(M)	The Chipmunks Sing The Beatles Hits	1964	12.00	30.00
Liberty LST-7388	(S)	The Chipmunks Sing The Beatles Hits	1964	16.00	40.00
Liberty LRP-3424	(M)	The Chipmunks A Go-Go	1965	8.00	20.00
Liberty LST-7424	(S)	The Chipmunks A Go-Go	1965	10.00	25.00
Liberty LRP-3405	(M)	The Chipmunks Sing With Children	1965	8.00	20.00
Liberty LST-7405	(S)	The Chipmunks Sing With Children	1965	10.00	25.00
CHOATE, BILL					
Sims LP-123	(M)	True Country & Western Songs	1964	40.00	100.00
CHOATES, HARRY					
"D" 7000	(M)	Jole Blon	195?	20.00	50.00
CHOCOLATE WATCH BAND, THE					
Tower T-5096	(M)	No Way Out	1967	80.00	200.00
Tower ST-5096	(S)	No Way Out	1967	80.00	200.00
Tower T-5016	(M)	The Inner Mystique	1968	80.00	200.00
Tower ST-5016	(S)	The Inner Mystique	1968	80.00	200.00
Tower ST-5153	(S)	One Step Beyond	1969	60.00	150.00
(Original copies have printing on the spine and "Printed in USA" on the cover; counterfeits do not.)					
CHORDETTES, THE					
Columbia CL-6111 (10")	(M)	Harmony Time	1950	20.00	50.00
Columbia CL-6170 (10")	(M)	Harmony Time, Volume 2	1951	20.00	50.00
Columbia CL-6218 (10")	(M)	Harmony Encores	1952	20.00	50.00
Columbia CL-6285 (10")	(M)	Your Requests	1953	16.00	40.00
Columbia CL-2519 (10")	(M)	The Chordettes	1955	16.00	40.00
Columbia CL-956	(M)	Listen	1957	12.00	30.00
Cadence CLP-1002 (10")	(M)	Close Harmony	1955	16.00	40.00
Cadence LP-3001	(M)	The Chordettes	1957	12.00	30.00
Cadence CLP-3002	(M)	Close Harmony	1957	12.00	30.00
Cadence CLP-3062	(M)	Never On Sunday	1962	8.00	20.00
Cadence CLP-25062	(S)	Never On Sunday	1962	12.00	30.00
CHOSEN FEW, THE					
RCA Victor LSP-4242	(S)	The Chosen Few	1969	8.00	20.00
CHRISTIE, LOU [LOU CHRISTIE SACCO]					
Lou Christie is a pseudonym for Lugee Sacco.					
Roulette R-25208	(M)	Lou Christie	1963	14.00	35.00
Roulette SR-25208	(P)	Lou Christie	1963	20.00	50.00
MGM E-4360	(M)	Lightnin' Strikes	1966	8.00	20.00
MGM SE-4360	(S)	Lightnin' Strikes	1966	10.00	25.00
Co&Ce LP-1231	(M)	Lou Christie Strikes Back	1966	16.00	40.00
Colpix CP-4001	(M)	Lou Christie Strikes Again	1966	10.00	25.00
Colpix SCP-4001	(S)	Lou Christie Strikes Again	1966	16.00	40.00
Roulette R-25332	(M)	Lou Christie Strikes Again	1966	8.00	20.00
Roulette SR-25332	(S)	Lou Christie Strikes Again	1966	10.00	25.00
(Roulette 25332 is a reissue of Colpix 4001.)					
MGM E-4394	(M)	Painter Of Hits	1966	8.00	20.00
MGM SE-4394	(S)	Painter Of Hits	1966	10.00	25.00
("Rhapsody In The Rain" is in mono on this album.)					
Spin-O-Rama M-173	(M)	Starring Lou Christie & The Classics	1966	8.00	20.00
Spin-O-Rama S-173	(E)	Starring Lou Christie & The Classics	1966	4.00	10.00

Label & Catalog #		Title	Year	VG+	NM
Buddah BDS-5052	(S)	I'm Gonna Make You Mine	1969	6.00	15.00
		("I'M Gonna Make You Mine" is rechanneled on this album.)			
Buddah BDS-5073	(S)	Paint America Love	1971	6.00	15.00
		(Buddah 5073 credits Lou Christie Sacco.)			
Three Brothers THB-2000	(S)	Lou Christie	1974	4.00	10.00

CHRISTOPHER

Chris Tee	(S)	What'cha Gonna Do? (Orange cover)	1969	500.00	Rare
		(Near Mint copies have a suggested value of $800-1,200.)			
Rockadelic	(S)	What'cha Gonna Do? (Reissue)	1990	16.00	40.00

CHRISTOPHER

| Metromedia 1024 | (DJ) | Christopher | 197? | 150.00 | 300.00 |

CHRISTY, JUNE

Capitol H-516 (10")	(M)	Something Cool	1954	30.00	75.00
Capitol T-516	(M)	Something Cool	1955	20.00	50.00
Capitol T-656	(M)	Duet	1955	20.00	50.00
Capitol T-725	(M)	The Misty Miss Christy	1955	20.00	50.00
Capitol T-833	(M)	June Fair And Warmer	1957	16.00	40.00
Capitol T-902	(M)	Gone For The Day	1957	16.00	40.00
Capitol T-1006	(M)	This Is June Christy!	1958	16.00	40.00
		— Original Capitol albums above have turquoise labels.—			
Capitol T-1076	(M)	June's Got Rhythm	1958	12.00	30.00
Capitol T-1114	(M)	The Song Is June!	1959	12.00	30.00
Capitol T-1202	(M)	June Christy Recalls Those Kenton Days	1959	12.00	30.00
Capitol T-1308	(M)	Ballads For Night People	1959	12.00	30.00
Capitol T-1327	(M)	Road Show	1959	12.00	30.00
Capitol ST-1327	(S)	Road Show	1959	16.00	40.00
Capitol T-1398	(M)	The Cool School	1960	12.00	30.00
Capitol ST-1398	(S)	The Cool School	1960	16.00	40.00
Capitol T-1498	(M)	Off Beat	1961	12.00	30.00
Capitol ST-1498	(S)	Off Beat	1961	16.00	40.00
Capitol T-1586	(M)	Do Re Mi	1961	12.00	30.00
Capitol ST-1586	(S)	Do Re Mi	1961	16.00	40.00
Capitol T-1605	(M)	That Time Of Year	1961	12.00	30.00
Capitol ST-1605	(S)	That Time Of Year	1961	16.00	40.00
		— Original Capitol albums above have black labels with the Capitol logo on the left side.—			
Capitol T-1693	(M)	The Best Of June Christy	1962	8.00	20.00
Capitol ST-1693	(S)	The Best Of June Christy	1962	10.00	25.00
Capitol T-1845	(M)	Big Band Specials	1962	8.00	20.00
Capitol ST-1845	(S)	Big Band Specials	1962	10.00	25.00
Capitol T-1953	(M)	The Intimate June Christy	1962	8.00	20.00
Capitol ST-1953	(S)	The Intimate June Christy	1962	10.00	25.00
Capitol T-2410	(M)	Something Broadway, Something Latin	1965	8.00	20.00
Capitol ST-2410	(S)	Something Broadway, Something Latin	1965	10.00	25.00
		— Original Capitol albums above have black label with the Capitol logo on the top.—			

CIRCUIT RIDER

| C.R. 666 | (S) | Circuit Rider | 1980 | 30.00 | 75.00 |

CIRCUS

| Metromedia LPS-7401 | (S) | Circus | 197? | 8.00 | 20.00 |

CIRCUS MAXIMUS
Circus Maximus features Jerry Jeff Walker.

Vanguard VRS-9260	(M)	Circus Maximus	1967	8.00	20.00
Vanguard VSD-79260	(S)	Circus Maximus	1967	10.00	25.00
Vanguard VSD-79274	(S)	Never Land Revisited	1968	12.00	30.00

CITY
City features Carole King.

| Ode Z-1244012 | (S) | Now That Everything's Been Said | 1969 | 20.00 | 50.00 |
| | | (Originals have color covers; counterfeits have black & white covers.) | | | |

CLANTON, JIMMY

Ace 1001	(M)	Just A Dream	1959	30.00	75.00
Ace 1007	(M)	Jimmy's Happy	1960	30.00	75.00
Ace 1007	(M)	Jimmy's Happy (Red vinyl)	1960	50.00	125.00

Label & Catalog #		Title	Year	VG+	NM
Ace 1008	(M)	Jimmy's Blue	1960	30.00	75.00
Ace 1008	(M)	Jimmy's Blue (Blue vinyl)	1960	50.00	125.00
		(The records for "Jimmy's Happy" and "Jimmy's Blue" on red and blue vinyl have both the single album catalog numbers, 1007-8 and the double album catalog number, 100, on their labels.)			
Ace DLP-100	(M)	Jimmy's Happy/Blue (2 LPs. Colored vinyl)	1960	100.00	200.00
		(Issued with a poster, priced separately below.)			
Ace DLP-100		Jimmy's Happy/Jimmy's Blue Poster	1960	20.00	50.00
Ace 1011	(M)	My Best To You	1961	30.00	75.00
Ace 1014	(M)	Teenage Millionaire	1961	30.00	75.00
Ace 1026	(M)	Venus In Bluejeans	1962	30.00	75.00
Philips PHM-200-154	(M)	The Best Of Jimmy Clanton	1964	8.00	20.00
Philips PHS-600-154	(S)	The Best Of Jimmy Clanton	1964	10.00	25.00
		(Contains rerecorded versions of the Ace material.)			

CLANTON, JIMMY / BRISTOW HOOPER

Design DLP-176	(M)	Jimmy Clanton / Brisow Hooper	196?	6.00	15.00
Design DLS-176	(E)	Jimmy Clanton / Brisow Hooper	196?	4.00	10.00

CLAP

Nova Sol 1001	(S)	Have You Reached Yet?	1970	300.00	Rare
		(Near Mint copies have a suggested value of $500-1,000.)			

CLAPTON, ERIC
Refer to Blind Faith; Cream; Delaney & Bonnie; Derek & The Dominos; John Mayall; The Yardbirds.

Atco SD-33-329	(S)	Eric Clapton	1970	6.00	15.00
Atco SD-2-803	(S)	The History Of Eric Clapton (2 LPs)	1972	6.00	15.00
Polydor PD-3503	(S)	Clapton At His Best (2 LPs)	1972	6.00	15.00
RSO QD-4801	(Q)	461 Ocean Boulevard	1974	10.00	25.00
RSO QD-4806	(Q)	There's One In Every Crowd	1975	10.00	25.00
RSO 035	(DJ)	Slowhand (White vinyl)	1978	12.00	30.00
RSO 1009	(DJ)	Backless (White vinyl)	1978	10.00	25.00
RSO PRO-22-015	(DJ)	Classic Cuts (2 LPs)	1980	12.00	30.00
Mobile Fidelity MFSL-030	(S)	Slowhand	1980	16.00	50.00
Nautilus NR-32	(S)	Just One Night	198?	16.00	50.00

CLARK, CHRIS

Motown 664	(M)	Soul Sounds	1967	12.00	30.00
Motown MS-664	(S)	Soul Sounds	1967	16.00	40.00
Weed 801	(S)	C.C. Rides Again	1969	12.00	30.00

CLARK, CLAUDINE

Chancellor CHL-5029	(M)	Party Lights	1962	50.00	200.00

CLARK, DAVE [THE DAVE CLARK FIVE]

Crown CLP-5400	(M)	The Dave Clark Five With The Playbacks	1964	12.00	30.00
Crown CST-400	(E)	The Dave Clark Five With The Playbacks	1964	8.00	20.00
Crown CLP-5473	(M)	Chaquita In Your Heart	1964	12.00	30.00
Crown CST-473	(E)	Chaquita In Your Heart	1964	8.00	20.00
Cortleigh C-1073	(M)	The Dave Clark Five With Ricky Astor	1964	12.00	30.00
Cortleigh CS-1073	(E)	The Dave Clark Five With Ricky Astor	1964	8.00	20.00
Epic LN-24093	(M)	Glad All Over	1964	40.00	100.00
Epic BN-26093	(E)	Glad All Over	1964	30.00	75.00
		(The band has no instruments on the cover.)			
Epic LN-24093	(M)	Glad All Over	1964	16.00	40.00
Epic BN-26093	(E)	Glad All Over	1964	12.00	30.00
		(The band has their instruments on the cover.)			
Epic LN-24104	(M)	The Dave Clark Five Return	1964	16.00	40.00
Epic BN-26104	(E)	The Dave Clark Five Return	1964	12.00	30.00
Epic LN-24117	(M)	American Tour, Volume 1	1964	16.00	40.00
Epic BN-26117	(E)	American Tour, Volume 1	1964	12.00	30.00
Epic XEM-77238	(DJ)	The Dave Clark 5 (Interview)	1964	150.00	300.00
Radio Pulsebeat	(M)	The Ed Rudy Interview	1964	50.00	125.00
Epic LN-24128	(M)	Coast To Coast	1965	16.00	40.00
Epic BN-26128	(E)	Coast To Coast	1965	12.00	30.00
Epic LN-24139	(M)	Weekend In London	1965	16.00	40.00
Epic BN-26139	(E)	Weekend In London	1965	12.00	30.00
Warner Bros. 3248	(DJ)	Having A Wild Weekend (Radio spots)	1965	150.00	300.00
Warner Bros. 3296	(DJ)	Having A Wild Weekend (Interview)	1965	300.00	500.00

Delecta "Dee" Clark originally recorded with The Kool Gents and The Delegates for Vee Jay. When Clark sought solo success, the other members recorded as The El Dorados, again for Vee Jay. The copy of You're Looking Good *(above) used here is a mono album with a stereo sticker affixed to the cover, a not uncommon practice in the latter half of the '60s when moving obsolete catalog items.*

Label & Catalog #		Title	Year	VG+	NM
Epic LN-24162	(M)	**Having A Wild Weekend** (Soundtrack)	1965	16.00	40.00
Epic BN-26162	(E)	**Having A Wild Weekend** (Soundtrack)	1965	12.00	30.00
Epic LN-24178	(M)	**I Like It Like That**	1965	16.00	40.00
Epic BN-26178	(E)	**I Like It Like That**	1965	12.00	30.00
Epic LN-24185	(M)	**Greatest Hits**	1966	12.00	30.00
Epic BN-26185	(E)	**Greatest Hits**	1966	10.00	25.00
Epic BN-26185	(E)	**Greatest Hits** (Orange label)	1973	16.00	40.00
Epic LN-24198	(M)	**Try Too Hard**	1966	12.00	30.00
Epic BN-26198	(E)	**Try Too Hard**	1966	10.00	25.00
Epic LN-24212	(M)	**Satisfied With You**	1966	12.00	30.00
Epic BN-26212	(E)	**Satisfied With You**	1966	10.00	25.00
Epic LN-24221	(M)	**More Greatest Hits**	1966	12.00	30.00
Epic BN-26221	(E)	**More Greatest Hits**	1966	10.00	25.00
Epic LN-24236	(M)	**Five By Five**	1967	10.00	25.00
Epic BN-26236	(S)	**Five By Five**	1967	12.00	30.00
Epic LN-24312	(M)	**You Got What It Takes**	1967	10.00	25.00
Epic BN-26312	(S)	**You Got What It Takes**	1967	12.00	30.00
Epic LN-24354	(M)	**Everybody Knows**	1968	10.00	25.00
Epic BN-26354	(S)	**Everybody Knows**	1968	12.00	30.00
— Original Epic albums above have yellow labels with a oval logo on top.—					
Epic EG-30434	(S)	**The Dave Clark Five** (2 LPs) COllection of hits and non-hits in honestogod stereo.)	1971	30.00	75.00
Epic KEG-33459	(M)	**Glad All Over Again**	1975	14.00	35.00

CLARK, DEE

Label & Catalog #		Title	Year	VG+	NM
Abner LP-2000	(M)	**Dee Clark**	1959	30.00	75.00
Abner SR-2000	(S)	**Dee Clark**	1959	60.00	150.00
		(Counterfeits of Abner SR-2000 exist.)			
Abner LP-2002	(M)	**How About That**	1960	24.00	60.00
Abner SR-2002	(S)	**How About That**	1960	40.00	100.00
Vee Jay LP-1019	(M)	**You're Looking Good**	1960	16.00	40.00
		(The existence of stereo copies of Vee jay 1019 is in doubt.)			
Vee Jay LP-1037	(M)	**Hold On, It's Dee Clark**	1961	16.00	40.00
Vee Jay SR-1037	(S)	**Hold On, It's Dee Clark**	1961	24.00	60.00
Vee Jay LP-1047	(M)	**The Best Of Dee Clark**	1964	16.00	40.00
Vee Jay SR-1047	(S)	**The Best Of Dee Clark**	1964	24.00	60.00

CLARK, DOTTIE

Label & Catalog #		Title	Year	VG+	NM
Mainstream 56006	(M)	**I'm Lost**	1966	6.00	15.00
Mainstream S-6006	(S)	**I'm Lost**	1966	8.00	20.00

CLARK, GENE

Clark was formerly a member of The Byrds. Refer to Dillard & Clark; McGuinn, Clark & Hillman

Label & Catalog #		Title	Year	VG+	NM
Columbia CL-2618	(M)	**Gene Clark With The Gosdin Brothers**	1967	12.00	30.00
Columbia CS-9418	(S)	**Gene Clark With The Gosdin Brothers**	1967	20.00	50.00
A&M SD-4292	(S)	**White Light**	1971	6.00	15.00
MediaArts 41-12	(S)	**American Flyer** (Soundtrack)	1971	6.00	15.00
Columbia KC-31123	(S)	**Early L.A. Sessions**	1972	5.00	12.00
		(Columbia 31123 is a remixed reissue of 9418 with new vocals.)			
Asylum 7E-1016	(S)	**No Other** (With bonus photo)	1974	5.00	12.00
RSO RS-1-3011	(S)	**Two Sides To Every Story**	1976	6.00	15.00

CLARK, PETULA

Label & Catalog #		Title	Year	VG+	NM
Imperial LP-9079	(M)	**Pet Clark**	1959	14.00	35.00
Imperial LP-12027	(S)	**Pet Clark**	1959	20.00	50.00
Imperial LP-9281	(M)	**Uptown With Petula Clark**	1965	8.00	20.00
Imperial LP-12281	(S)	**Uptown With Petula Clark**	1965	10.00	25.00
		(Imperial 9/12281 is a reissue of Imperial 9/12079.)			
Sunset SUM-1101	(M)	**This Is Petula Clark**	196?	5.00	12.00
Sunset SUS-5101	(S)	**This Is Petula Clark**	196?	6.00	15.00
		(Sunset1/5011 is a reissue of Imperial 9/12079.)			
Premier PM-9016	(M)	**The English Sound Starring Petula Clark**	1964	5.00	12.00
Premier PS-9016	(S)	**The English Sound Starring Petula Clark**	1964	6.00	15.00
Laurie LLP-2032	(M)	**In Love**	1966	8.00	20.00
Laurie LLPS-2032	(E)	**In Love**	1966	6.00	15.00
Laurie LLP-2043	(M)	**Petula Clark Sings For Everybody**	1967	6.00	15.00
Laurie LLPS-2043	(S)	**Petula Clark Sings For Everybody**	1967	8.00	20.00
Warner Bros. W-1590	(M)	**Downtown**	1964	6.00	15.00
Warner Bros. WS-1590	(S)	**Downtown**	1964	8.00	20.00

Label & Catalog #		Title	Year	VG+	NM
Warner Bros. W-1598	(M)	I Know A Place	1965	6.00	15.00
Warner Bros. WS-1598	(S)	I Know A Place	1965	8.00	20.00
Warner Bros. W-1608	(M)	The World's Greatest International Hits	1965	6.00	15.00
Warner Bros. WS-1608	(S)	The World's Greatest International Hits	1965	8.00	20.00
		— Original Warner mono albums above have grey labels; stereo albums ahve gold labels.—			
Warner Bros. W-1630	(M)	My Love	1966	5.00	12.00
Warner Bros. WS-1630	(S)	My Love	1966	6.00	15.00
Warner Bros. W-1645	(M)	I Couldn't Live Without Your Love	1966	5.00	12.00
Warner Bros. WS-1645	(S)	I Couldn't Live Without Your Love	1966	6.00	15.00
Warner Bros. W-1673	(M)	Color My World/Who Am I	1967	5.00	12.00
Warner Bros. WS-1673	(S)	Color My World/Who Am I	1967	6.00	15.00
Warner Bros. W-1698	(M)	These Are My Songs	1967	5.00	12.00
Warner Bros. WS-1698	(S)	These Are My Songs	1967	6.00	15.00
Warner Bros. W-1719	(M)	The Other Man's Grass Is Always Greener	1968	8.00	20.00
Warner Bros. WS-1719	(S)	The Other Man's Grass Is Always Greener	1968	6.00	15.00
		("The Other Man's Grass Is Always Greener" is rechanneled.)			
Warner Bros. W-1743	(M)	Petula	1968	8.00	20.00
Warner Bros. WS-1743	(S)	Petula	1968	6.00	15.00
		— Original Warner albums above have gold labels.—			
Warner Bros. 93215	(S)	Hits... My Way (2 LPs. Record Club)	196?	10.00	25.00
		("The Other Man's Grass Is Always Greener" is rechanneled.)			

CLARK, TODD
Todd originally recorded with Eyes.

World Theatre	(S)	We're Not Safe	197?	150.00	300.00
T.M.I. 020	(S)	Into Vision	198?	8.00	20.00

CLARK, "YODELING SLIM"

Playhouse 2017 (10")	(M)	Western Songs And Dances	1954	20.00	50.00
Continental 1505	(M)	Cowboy And Yodel Songs	1962	10.00	25.00
Masterseal 57	(M)	Cowboy Songs	1963	8.00	20.00
Masterseal 135	(M)	Cowboy Songs (Volume 2)	1964	8.00	20.00
Palomino 300	(M)	Yodeling Slim Clark Sings Jimmie Rodgers	1966	30.00	60.00
Palomino 301	(M)	Favorite Montana Slim Songs	1966	16.00	40.00
Palomino 303	(M)	Favorite Montana Slim Songs	1966	16.00	40.00
Palomino 306	(M)	I Feel A Trip Coming On	1966	12.00	30.00
Palomino 307	(M)	Old Chestnuts	1967	12.00	30.00
Palomino 314	(M)	50th Anniversary Album	1968	12.00	30.00

CLARK-HUTCHINSON

Sire SES-97027	(S)	A = MH^2	1969	6.00	15.00

CLARK SISTERS, THE

Coral CRL-57290	(M)	Beauty Shop Beat	1960	6.00	15.00
Coral CRL-757290	(S)	Beauty Shop Beat	1960	8.00	20.00

CLARY, ROBERT

Epic LN-3171	(M)	Meet Robert Clary	195?	10.00	25.00
Epic LN-3281	(M)	Hooray For Love	195?	10.00	25.00
Mercury MG-20367	(M)	Gigi	1958	8.00	20.00

CLASH, THE

Epic JE-35543	(S)	Give 'Em Enough Rope (Orange label)	1979	6.00	15.00
Epic 4E-36846 (10")	(S)	Black Market Clash	1980	6.00	15.00
Epic AS-952	(DJ)	Interchords	1981	12.00	30.00
Epic AS-1594	(DJ)	The World According To The Clash	1982	12.00	30.00
Epic AS-	(DJ)	Sandanista Now! (Sampler)	1981	10.00	25.00
Epic AS-99-1595	(DJ)	Combat Rock (Picture disc)	1983	6.00	30.00

CLASS-AIRES, THE

Honey Bee	(M)	Tears Start To Fall	195?	150.00	300.00

CLASSICS IV, THE
The Classics IV feature Dennis Yost.

Imperial LP-12371	(S)	Spooky	1968	8.00	20.00
Imperial LP-12407	(S)	Mamas & Papas/Soul Train	1969	6.00	15.00
Imperial LP-12429	(S)	Traces	1969	6.00	15.00
Imperial LP-16000	(S)	Greatest Hits	1969	5.00	12.00
MGM MSH-702	(S)	Dennis Yost & The Classics IV	1973	4.00	10.00

Label & Catalog #		Title	Year	VG+	NM
CLAY, CASSIUS					
Cassius Clay later performed as Muhammad Ali.					
Columbia CL-2093	(M)	I Am The Greatest!	1963	16.00	40.00
Columbia CS-8893	(S)	I Am The Greatest!	1963	20.00	50.00
CLAY, JUDY, & BILLY VERA					
Atlantic 8174	(M)	Storybook Children	1967	6.00	15.00
Atlantic 8174	(S)	Storybook Children	1967	8.00	20.00
CLAYTON, PAUL					
Folkways FA-2007	(M)	Cumberland Mountain Folksongs	195?	8.00	20.00
Folkways FA-2106	(M)	Bay State Ballads	195?	8.00	20.00
Folkways FA-2110	(M)	Folksongs And Ballads Of Virginia	195?	8.00	20.00
Folkways FA-2378	(M)	American Broadside			
		Ballads In Popular Tradition	195?	8.00	20.00
Folkways FA-2382	(M)	Dulcimer Songs And Solos	195?	8.00	20.00
Folkways FA-2429	(M)	Foc'sle Songs And Shanties	195?	8.00	20.00
Folkways FA-8708	(M)	British Broadside Ballads	195?	8.00	20.00
Riverside RLP-12-615	(M)	Bloody Ballads	195?	8.00	20.00
Riverside RLP-12-640	(M)	Wanted For Murder:			
		Songs Of Outlaws And Desperados	195?	8.00	20.00
Riverside RLP-12-648	(M)	Timber-r-r! Songs Of The Lumberjacks	195?	8.00	20.00
Elektra EKL-147	(M)	Unholy Matrimony	195?	8.00	20.00
Elektra EKL-155	(M)	Bobby Burns' Merry Muses Of Caledonia	195?	8.00	20.00
Tradition TLP-1005	(M)	Whaling And Sailing Songs			
		From The Days Of Moby Dick	196?	6.00	15.00
Stinson 69	(M)	Whaling Songs And Ballads	196?	6.00	15.00
Monument MLP-8017	(M)	Folk Singer	1965	6.00	15.00
Monument SLP-18017	(S)	Folk Singer	1965	8.00	20.00
CLAYTON-THOMAS, DAVID					
Refer to Blood, Sweat & Tears.					
Decca DL-75146	(S)	David Clayton-Thomas	1969	8.00	20.00
RCA Victor APD1-0173	(Q)	David Clayton-Thomas	1974	8.00	20.00
CLEANLINESS & GODLINESS SKIFFLE BAND, THE					
Vanguard VSD-79285	(S)	Greatest Hits	1968	12.00	30.00
CLEAR LIGHT					
Elektra EKL-4011	(M)	Clear Light	1967	8.00	20.00
Elektra EKS-74011	(S)	Clear Light	1967	10.00	25.00
CLEARY, DON					
Palomino 302	(M)	Traditional Cowboy Songs	1966	12.00	30.00
CLEFTONES, THE					
Gee GLP-705	(M)	Heart And Soul	1961	70.00	175.00
Gee SGLP-705	(P)	Heart And Soul	1961	150.00	350.00
Gee GLP-707	(M)	For Sentimental Reasons	1962	70.00	175.00
Gee SGLP-707	(P)	For Sentimental Reasons	1962	300.00	750.00
		— Original Gee albums above have red labels.—			
CLIFFORD, BUZZ					
Columbia CL-1616	(M)	Baby Sittin' With Buzz	1961	30.00	75.00
Columbia CS-8416	(S)	Baby Sittin' With Buzz	1961	40.00	100.00
Dot DLP-25965	(S)	See Your Way Clear	1969	8.00	20.00
CLIFFORD, MIKE					
United Arts. UAL-6409	(M)	For The Love Of Mike	1965	8.00	20.00
United Arts. UAS-6409	(P)	For The Love Of Mike	1965	10.00	25.00
CLINE, PATSY					
Decca DL-8611	(M)	Patsy Cline *(Black & silver label)*	1957	40.00	100.00
Decca DL-8611	(M)	Patsy Cline	1958	20.00	50.00
Decca DL-4202	(M)	Patsy Cline Showcase	1961	16.00	40.00
Decca DL-74202	(S)	Patsy Cline Showcase	1961	20.00	50.00
Decca DL-4282	(M)	Sentimentally Yours	1962	10.00	25.00
Decca DL-74282	(S)	Sentimentally Yours	1962	14.00	35.00

Label & Catalog #		Title	Year	VG+	NM
Decca DXB-176	(M)	The Patsy Cline Story (With booklet)	1963	12.00	30.00
Decca DXSB-7176	(S)	The Patsy Cline Story (With booklet)	1963	16.00	40.00
Decca DL-4508	(M)	A Portrait Of Patsy Cline	1964	10.00	25.00
Decca DL-74508	(S)	A Portrait Of Patsy Cline	1964	14.00	35.00
Decca DL-4586	(M)	That's How A Heartache Begins	1964	10.00	25.00
Decca DL-74586	(S)	That's How A Heartache Begins	1964	14.00	35.00
— Decca albums above have black labels with "Mfrd. by Decca" beneath the rainbow.—					
Decca DL-4854	(M)	Patsy Cline's Greatest Hits	1967	8.00	20.00
Decca DL-74854	(S)	Patsy Cline's Greatest Hits	1967	10.00	25.00
Everest LPBR-5200	(M)	Patsy Cline's Golden Hits	1962	8.00	20.00
Everest SDBR-1200	(S)	Patsy Cline's Golden Hits	1962	10.00	25.00
Everest LPBR-5204	(M)	Encores	1963	6.00	15.00
Everest SDBR-1204	(S)	Encores	1963	8.00	20.00
Everest LPBR-5217	(M)	In Memoriam	1963	6.00	15.00
Everest SDBR-1217	(S)	In Memoriam	1963	8.00	20.00
Everest LPBR-5223	(M)	Patsy Cline-A Legend	1963	6.00	15.00
Everest SDBR-1223	(S)	Patsy Cline-A Legend	1963	8.00	20.00
Everest LPBR-5229	(M)	Reflections	1964	6.00	15.00
Everest SDBR-1229	(S)	Reflections	1964	8.00	20.00
Vocalion VL-3753	(M)	Here's Patsy Cline	1965	6.00	15.00
Vocalion VL-73753	(S)	Here's Patsy Cline	1965	8.00	20.00
Columbia CSP-5280	(S)	A Portrait Of Patsy (Record Club)	1969	8.00	20.00

CLINTON, GEORGE
George Clinton is the mastermind behind the Parliament/Funkadelic community. Refer to The Brides Of Funkenstein; William "Bootsy" Collins; Funkadelic; Eddie Hazel; The Incorporated Thang Band; Jimmy G; The P Funk All-Stars; Parlet; Parliament; The Fred Wesley Horns; Philippe Wynne.

Capitol ST-12246	(S)	Computer Games	1982	4.00	10.00
Capitol ST-12308	(S)	You Shouldn't-Nuf Bit Fish	1984	4.00	10.00
Capitol ST-12417	(S)	Some Of My Best Jokes Are Friends	1985	4.00	10.00
Capitol ST-12481	(S)	R&B Skeletons In The Closet	1986	4.00	10.00
Capitol ST-12534	(S)	The Best Of George Clinton	1986	4.00	10.00
Capitol ST-15021	(S)	The Mothership Connection Live From Houston	1986	4.00	10.00

CLIQUE, THE
White Whale WWS-7126	(S)	The Clique	1969	6.00	15.00

CLOCKWORK
Green Bottle 1013	(S)	Clockwork	1973	6.00	15.00

CLOONEY, ROSEMARY
Refer to The Clooney Sisters; Bing Crosby; The Ferrers; The Hi-Lo's; The Reprise Repertory Theatre.

Columbia CL-6224 (10")	(M)	Hollywood's Best	1952	20.00	50.00
Columbia CL-6297 (10")	(M)	Rosemary Clooney	1954	20.00	50.00
Columbia CL-6338 (10")	(M)	White Christmas	1954	20.00	50.00
Columbia CL-6282 (10")	(M)	Red Garters (Soundtrack)	1954	50.00	100.00
Columbia CL-2525 (10")	(M)	Tenderly	1955	20.00	50.00
Columbia CL-2569 (10")	(M)	Children's Favorites	1956	16.00	40.00
Columbia CL-2572 (10")	(M)	A Date With The King	1956	16.00	40.00
Columbia CL-2597 (10")	(M)	My Fair Lady	1956	16.00	40.00
MGM E-3153	(M)	Deep In My Heart (Soundtrack. Boxed set)	1954	40.00	100.00
MGM E-3153	(M)	Deep In My Heart (Soundtrack)	1955	20.00	50.00
Columbia CL-585	(M)	Hollywood's Best	1955	12.00	30.00
Columbia CL-872	(M)	Blue Rose	1956	12.00	30.00
Columbia CL-969	(M)	Clooney Tunes	1957	12.00	30.00
Columbia CL-1230	(M)	Rosie's Greatest Hits	1958	12.00	30.00
— Columbia albums above have three white "eye" logos on each side of the spindle hole.—					
Coral CRL-57266	(M)	Swing Around Rosie	1958	12.00	30.00
MGM E-3687	(M)	Oh, Captain!	1958	12.00	30.00
MGM E-3782	(M)	Hymns From The Heart	1959	8.00	20.00
MGM SE-3782	(S)	Hymns From The Heart	1959	12.00	30.00
MGM E-3834	(M)	Rosemary Clooney Swings Softly	1960	8.00	20.00
MGM SE-3834	(S)	Rosemary Clooney Swings Softly	1960	12.00	30.00
RCA Victor LPM-1854	(M)	Fancy Meeting You Here	1958	8.00	20.00
RCA Victor LSP-1854	(S)	Fancy Meeting You Here	1958	12.00	30.00
RCA Victor LPM-2133	(M)	A Touch Of Tabasco	1960	8.00	20.00
RCA Victor LSP-2133	(S)	A Touch Of Tabasco	1960	12.00	30.00

Label & Catalog #		Title	Year	VG+	NM
RCA Victor LPM-2212	(M)	**Clap Hands, Here Comes Rosie**	1960	8.00	20.00
RCA Victor LSP-2212	(S)	**Clap Hands, Here Comes Rosie**	1960	12.00	30.00
RCA Victor LPM-2265	(M)	**Rosie Solves The Swingin' Riddle**	1961	8.00	20.00
RCA Victor LSP-2265	(S)	**Rosie Solves The Swingin' Riddle**	1961	12.00	30.00
RCA Victor LPM-2565	(M)	**Country Hits From The Heart**	1963	8.00	20.00
RCA Victor LSP-2565	(S)	**Country Hits From The Heart**	1963	12.00	30.00
		— Mono RCA albums above have "Long Play" on the bottom of the label;			
		stereo albums have "Living Stereo" on the bottom.—			
Reprise R-6088	(M)	**Love**	1963	5.00	12.00
Reprise R-96088	(S)	**Love**	1963	6.00	15.00
Reprise R-6108	(M)	**Thanks For Nothing**	1964	5.00	12.00
Reprise R-96108	(S)	**Thanks For Nothing**	1964	6.00	15.00

CLOONEY SISTERS, THE
The Sisters feature Rosemary Clooney.

Epic LN-3160	(M)	**The Clooney Sisters With Tony Pastor**	1955	16.00	40.00

CLOUDS, THE

Deram DES-18044	(S)	**Up Above Our Heads**	1970	6.00	15.00
Deram DES-18058	(S)	**Watercolour Days**	1971	6.00	15.00

CLOVER
Clover backed Elvis Costello on his first album.

Mercury SRM-1-1169	(S)	**Clover**	1977	6.00	15.00
Mercury SRM-1-3708	(S)	**Love On The Wire**	1977	6.00	15.00

CLOVER

Fantasy 8395	(S)	**Clover**	1969	8.00	20.00
Fantasy 8405	(S)	**Forty-Niner**	1969	8.00	20.00

CLOVERS, THE

Atlantic LP-1248	(M)	**The Clovers**	1956	250.00	600.00
Atlantic LP-8009	(M)	**The Clovers**	1957	150.00	350.00
		(Atlantic 8009 is a reissue of 1248.)			
Atlantic LP-8034	(M)	**Dance Party**	1959	100.00	250.00
		— Original Atlantic albums above have black labels.—			
Atlantic LP-8009	(M)	**The Clovers**	196?	50.00	125.00
Atlantic LP-8034	(M)	**Dance Party**	196?	50.00	125.00
		— Original Atlantic albums above have purple & orange labels.—			
Poplar 1001	(M)	**In Clover**	1958	150.00	400.00
United Arts. UAL-3033	(M)	**In Clover**	1959	60.00	150.00
United Arts. UAS-6033	(E)	**In Clover**	1959	50.00	125.00
United Arts. UAL-3099	(M)	**Love Potion Number Nine**	1959	60.00	150.00
United Arts. UAS-6099	(S)	**Love Potion Number Nine**	1959	80.00	200.00
		("Love Potion Number Nine" and "Lovey Dovey"			
		were rerecorded for this album.)			
Design DLP-	(M)	**Love Potion Number Nine**	196?	16.00	40.00
Design DSLP-	(E)	**Love Potion Number Nine**	196?	6.00	15.00
Grand Prix K-428	(M)	**The Original Love Potion Number Nine**	1964	12.00	30.00
Grand Prix KS-428	(E)	**The Original Love Potion Number Nine**	1964	6.00	15.00
Atco SD-33-374	(P)	**Their Greatest Recordings/The Early Years**	1971	4.00	10.00

COASTERS, THE

Atco 33-101	(M)	**The Coasters**	1958	200.00	400.00
Atco 33-111	(M)	**The Coasters' Greatest Hits**	1959	80.00	200.00
		— Original Atco albums above have yellow labels with a harp on top.—			
Atco 33-101	(M)	**The Coasters**	1960	20.00	50.00
Atco SD-33-101	(E)	**The Coasters**	196?	10.00	25.00
Atco 33-111	(M)	**The Coasters' Greatest Hits**	1960	20.00	50.00
Atco SD-33-111	(E)	**The Coasters' Greatest Hits**	196?	10.00	25.00
Atco 33-123	(M)	**One By One**	1960	30.00	75.00
Atco SD-33-123	(S)	**One By One**	1960	50.00	125.00
Atco 33-135	(M)	**Coast Along With The Coasters**	1962	20.00	50.00
Atco SD-33-135	(P)	**Coast Along With The Coasters**	1962	30.00	75.00
		— Atco mono albums above have gold & gray labels; stereo albums have purple & brown labels.—			
Clarion 605	(M)	**That's Rock And Roll**	1964	8.00	20.00
Clarion 605	(P)	**That's Rock And Roll**	1964	10.00	25.00

NEVER TO BE FORGOTTEN

WEEKEND
TWENTY FLIGHT ROCK
LONG TALL SALLY
LONELY
CHERISHED MEMORIES
NERVOUS BREAKDOWN
BOLL WEEVIL
MILK COW BLUES
BLUE SUEDE SHOES
LITTLE ANGEL
LOVE AGAIN
SWEETIE PIE

Edward Ray Cochrane began his career as half of a country 'n western duo with Hank Cochran (no relation, although they did bill themselves as the Cochran Brothers). By the time of his unfortunate demise in the same automobile accident that crippled Gene Vincent, he had established himself as one of the most influential white rockers and guitar players following in the wake of Elvis. Both of these albums were released after his death; Eddie Cochran (above) is often referred to as the "Memorial Album."

Label & Catalog #		Title	Year	VG+	NM
COCHRAN, EDDIE					
Liberty LRP-3061	(M)	**Singin' To My Baby** (Green label)	1957	200.00	400.00
Liberty LRP-3061	(M)	**Singin' To My Baby** (Black label)	1960	40.00	100.00
Liberty LRP-3172	(DJ)	**Eddie Cochran** (White label)	1960	150.00	300.00
Liberty LRP-3172	(M)	**Eddie Cochran**	1960	40.00	100.00
Liberty LRP-3220	(M)	**Never To Be Forgotten**	1962	30.00	75.00
Sunset SUM-1123	(M)	**Summertime Blues**	1966	14.00	35.00
Sunset SUS-5123	(E)	**Summertime Blues**	1966	10.00	25.00
United Arts. UAS-9959	(M)	**Legendary Master** (2 LPs)	1971	10.00	25.00
COCHRAN, STEVIE					
(No label)	(DJ)	**No Need To Worry** (Test pressing)	1984	60.00	150.00
COCHRAN, WAYNE (& THE C.C. RIDERS)					
Chess LP-1519	(M)	**Wayne Cochran**	1967	10.00	25.00
Chess LPS-1519	(S)	**Wayne Cochran**	1967	12.00	30.00
King KS-1116	(S)	**Alive & Well**	1970	8.00	20.00
Bethlehem 10002	(S)	**High And Ridin'**	1970	6.00	15.00
Epic KE-30989	(S)	**Cochran**	1972	5.00	12.00
COCKBURN, BRUCE					
True North APHT-5008	(S)	**Dancing In The Dragon's Jaw** (Half-speed)	1982	12.00	35.00
True North APHT-5009	(S)	**Humans** (Half-speed master)	1982	12.00	35.00
COCKER, JOE					
A&M SP-4182	(S)	**With A Little Help From My Friends** (Brown label)	1969	6.00	15.00
A&M QU-54182	(Q)	**With A Little Help From My Friends**	1974	6.00	15.00
A&M QU-54224	(Q)	**Joe Cocker!**	1974	6.00	15.00
Asylum 6E-145	(DJ)	**Luxury You Can Afford** (Picture disc)	1978	4.00	10.00
COE, DAVID ALLAN					
SSS Inter. 9	(S)	**Penitentiary Blues**	196?	120.00	50.00
COLD BLOOD					
San Francisco 200	(S)	**Cold Blood**	1969	8.00	20.00
San Francisco 205	(S)	**Sisyphus**	1970	8.00	20.00
Reprise BS-2074	(S)	**First Taste Of Sin**	1972	4.00	10.00
Reprise BS-2130	(S)	**Thriller**	1973	4.00	10.00
COLD SUN: *Refer to* DARK SHADOWS					
COLDER, BEN					
Ben Colder is a pseudonym for Sheb Wooley.					
MGM E-4117	(M)	**Spoofing The Big Ones**	1961	12.00	30.00
MGM SE-4117	(S)	**Spoofing The Big Ones**	1961	16.00	40.00
MGM E-4173	(M)	**Ben Colder**	1963	10.00	25.00
MGM SE-4173	(S)	**Ben Colder**	1963	12.00	30.00
MGM E-4421	(M)	**Big Ben Strikes Again**	1966	6.00	15.00
MGM SE-4421	(S)	**Big Ben Strikes Again**	1966	8.00	20.00
MGM E-4482	(M)	**Wine, Women And Song**	1967	5.00	12.00
MGM SE-4482	(S)	**Wine, Women And Song**	1967	6.00	15.00
COLE, COZY					
Love 5000	(M)	**Topsy**	195?	40.00	100.00
Love 5000S	(S)	**Topsy**	195?	80.00	200.00
		("Topsy" was rerecorded in stereo for this album.)			
COLE, DON & ALLEYNE					
Tollie T-56001	(M)	**Live At The Whiskey A-Go-Go**	1964	6.00	15.00
Tollie S-56001	(S)	**Live At The Whiskey A-Go-Go**	1964	8.00	20.00
COLE, JERRY, & HIS SPACEMEN					
Mr. Cole also recorded as Jerry Kole.					
Capitol T-2044	(M)	**Outer Limits**	1963	12.00	30.00
Capitol ST-2044	(S)	**Outer Limits**	1963	16.00	40.00
Capitol T-2061	(M)	**Hot Rod Dance Party**	1964	20.00	50.00
Capitol ST-2601	(S)	**Hot Rod Dance Party**	1964	24.00	60.00

Label & Catalog #		Title	Year	VG+	NM
Capitol T-2112	(M)	Surf Age	1964	16.00	40.00
Capitol ST-2112	(S)	Surf Age	1964	20.00	50.00
		(Includes the bonus single "Thunder Wave" / "Spanish Kiss" by Dick Dale in a pocket on the cover.)			
Capitol T-2112	(M)	Surf Age (Without the single)	1964	12.00	30.00
Capitol ST-2112	(S)	Surf Age (Without the single)	1964	16.00	40.00
Liberty LRP-3362	(M)	Sounds Of The Big Irons	1964	12.00	30.00
Liberty LST-7362	(S)	Sounds Of The Big Irons	1964	16.00	40.00

COLE, MARIA

Label & Catalog #		Title	Year	VG+	NM
Kapp 102 (10")	(M)	Maria Cole	1954	20.00	50.00
Capitol T-2612	(M)	Love Is A Special Feeling	1966	5.00	12.00
Capitol ST-2612	(S)	Love Is A Special Feeling	1966	6.00	15.00

COLE, NAT "KING"

Label & Catalog #		Title	Year	VG+	NM
Capitol H-8 (10")	(M)	The King Cole Trio	1950	16.00	40.00
Capitol H-29 (10")	(M)	The King Cole Trio, Volume 2	1950	16.00	40.00
Capitol H-59 (10")	(M)	The King Cole Trio, Volume 3	1950	16.00	40.00
Capitol L-156 (10")	(M)	Nat King Cole At The Piano	1950	16.00	40.00
Capitol H-177 (10")	(M)	The King Cole Trio, Volume 4	1950	16.00	40.00
Capitol L-213 (10")	(M)	Harvest Of Hits	1950	16.00	40.00
Capitol H-220 (10")	(M)	The Nat King Cole Trio, Volume 1	1950	16.00	40.00
Capitol H-332 (10")	(M)	Penthouse Serenade	1952	16.00	40.00
Capitol H-357 (10")	(M)	Unforgettable	1952	16.00	40.00
Capitol H-420 (10")	(M)	Two In Love	1954	16.00	40.00
Capitol H-514 (10")	(M)	Tenth Anniversary Album	1954	16.00	40.00
Capitol T-9110	(M)	Nat Kink Cole's Top Pops	1954	12.00	30.00
Capitol T-332	(M)	Penthouse Serenade	1954	12.00	30.00
Capitol T-357	(M)	Unforgettable	1954	12.00	30.00
Capitol T-420	(M)	Two In Love	1954	12.00	30.00
Capitol W-514	(M)	Tenth Anniversary Album	1954	12.00	30.00
Capitol T-591	(M)	Vocal Classics	1955	12.00	30.00
Capitol T-592	(M)	Instrumental Classics	1955	12.00	30.00
Capitol T-680	(M)	Ballads Of The Day	1956	12.00	30.00
Capitol W-689	(M)	The Piano Style Of Nat King Cole	1956	12.00	30.00
Capitol W-782	(M)	After Midnight	1956	12.00	30.00
— Original Capitol albums above have turquoise or grey labels with "Long Playing" on the bottom.—					
Decca DL-8260	(M)	In The Beginning	1956	16.00	40.00
Score SLP-4019	(M)	The King Cole Trio And Lester Young	1957	30.00	75.00
Capitol W-824	(M)	Love Is The Thing	1957	8.00	20.00
Capitol SW-824	(S)	Love Is The Thing	1958	12.00	30.00
Capitol T-870	(M)	This Is Nat King Cole	1957	10.00	25.00
Capitol W-903	(M)	Just One Of Those Things	1958	8.00	20.00
Capitol SW-903	(S)	Just One Of Those Things	1958	12.00	30.00
Capitol W-993	(M)	Saint Louis Blues (Soundtrack)	1958	16.00	40.00
— Original Capitol albums above have turquoise or grey labels with "Long Playing High Fidelity."—					
Capitol W-1031	(M)	Cole Espanol	1958	8.00	20.00
Capitol DW-1031	(E)	Cole Espanol	196?	5.00	12.00
Capitol W-1084	(M)	The Very Thought Of You	1958	6.00	15.00
Capitol SW-1084	(S)	The Very Thought Of You	1958	8.00	20.00
Capitol W-1120	(M)	Welcome To The Club	1959	6.00	15.00
Capitol SW-1120	(S)	Welcome To The Club	1959	8.00	20.00
Capitol W-1190	(M)	To Whom It May Concern	1959	6.00	15.00
Capitol SW-1190	(S)	To Whom It May Concern	1959	8.00	20.00
Capitol W-1220	(M)	A Mis Amigos	1959	6.00	15.00
Capitol SW-1220	(S)	A Mis Amigos	1959	8.00	20.00
Capitol T-1249	(M)	Every Time I Feel The Spirit	1960	6.00	15.00
Capitol ST-1249	(S)	Every Time I Feel The Spirit	1960	8.00	20.00
Capitol W-1331	(M)	Tell Me All About Yourself	1960	6.00	15.00
Capitol SW-1331	(S)	Tell Me All About Yourself	1960	8.00	20.00
Capitol WAK-1392	(M)	Wild Is Love	1960	6.00	15.00
Capitol SWAK-1392	(S)	Wild Is Love	1960	8.00	20.00
Capitol W-1444	(M)	The Magic Of Christmas	1960	6.00	15.00
Capitol SW-1444	(S)	The Magic Of Christmas	1960	8.00	20.00
Capitol W-1574	(M)	The Touch Of Your Lips	1961	6.00	15.00
Capitol ST-1574	(S)	The Touch Of Your Lips	1961	8.00	20.00
Capitol WCL-1613	(M)	The Nat King Cole Story (3 LPs)	1961	10.00	25.00
Capitol SWCL-1613	(P)	The Nat King Cole Story (3 LPs)	1961	12.00	30.00

Label & Catalog #		Title	Year	VG+	NM
Capitol W-1675	(M)	Nat King Cole Sings/George Shearing Plays	1962	8.00	20.00
Capitol ST-1675	(S)	Nat King Cole Sings/George Shearing Plays	1962	10.00	25.00
		(Issued with a bonus album, PRO-2003.)			
Capitol W-1675	(M)	Nat King Cole Sings/George Shearing Plays	1962	5.00	12.00
Capitol ST-1675	(S)	Nat King Cole Sings/George Shearing Plays	1962	6.00	15.00
		(Without the bonus album.)			
Capitol W-1713	(M)	Nat King Cole Sings The Blues	1962	4.00	10.00
Capitol SW-1713	(S)	Nat King Cole Sings The Blues	1962	5.00	12.00

— Original Capitol albums above have black labels with the Capitol logo on the left side.—

Capitol T-1793	(M)	Ramblin' Rose	1962	4.00	10.00
Capitol ST-1793	(S)	Ramblin' Rose	1962	5.00	12.00
Capitol T-1838	(M)	Dear Lonely Heart	1963	4.00	10.00
Capitol ST-1838	(S)	Dear Lonely Heart	1963	5.00	12.00
Capitol W-1929	(M)	Nat King Cole Sings The Blues, Volume 2	1963	4.00	10.00
Capitol SW-1929	(S)	Nat King Cole Sings The Blues, Volume 2	1963	5.00	12.00
Capitol T-2311	(M)	The Nat King Cole Trio	1965	6.00	15.00
Capitol T-2340	(M)	"Cat Ballou" And Other Motion Pictures	1965	5.00	12.00
Capitol ST-2340	(S)	"Cat Ballou" And Other Motion Pictures	1965	6.00	15.00
Capitol T-2529	(M)	The Vintage Years	1966	6.00	15.00
Capitol TCL-2873	(M)	Deluxe Set (3 LP box)	1967	8.00	20.00
Capitol STCL-2873	(P)	Deluxe Set (3 LP box)	1967	10.00	25.00

— Original Capitol albums above have black labels with the Capitol logo on top.—

Capitol ST-2994	(P)	The Best Of Nat King Cole	1968	4.00	10.00
Capitol ST-2943	(S)	Smile	1969	4.00	10.00
Capitol SDWBB-252	(E)	Close-Up (2 LPs)	1969	4.00	10.00
Capitol ST-310	(S)	There, I've Said It Again	1969	4.00	10.00
Capitol SKAO-373	(S)	Nat Cole's Greatest	1969	4.00	10.00
Mobile Fidelity MFSL-081	(S)	Nat King Cole Sings/George Shearing Plays	198?	16.00	50.00

COLE, NATALIE

Mobile Fidelity MFSL-032	(S)	Thankful	197?	5.00	15.00

COLLAGE

Smash SRS-67101	(S)	The Collage	1968	8.00	20.00
Cream 9008	(S)	Collage	1971	6.00	15.00

COLLECTORS, THE

The Collectors later recorded as Chilliwack.

Warner Bros. WS-1746	(S)	The Collectors	1968	8.00	20.00
Warner Bros. WS-1774	(S)	Grass And Wild Strawberries	1969	6.00	15.00

COLLEGIANS, THE

Winley LP-6004	(M)	Sing Along With The Collegians	195?	100.00	250.00

COLLIER, MITTY

Chess LP-1492	(M)	Shades Of Genius	1965	14.00	35.00
Chess LPS-1492	(S)	Shades Of Genius	1965	20.00	50.00

COLLINS, AARON

Aaron Collins was the lead singer for The Cadets and The Jacks.

Crown CLP-5028	(M)	Calypso USA	1958	300.00	600.00

COLLINS, ALBERT

T.C.F. Hall 8002	(M)	The Cool Sound Of Albert Collins	1965	30.00	75.00
Imperial LP-12428	(S)	Love Can Be Found Anywhere	1968	8.00	20.00
Imperial LP-12438	(S)	Trash Talkin'	1969	8.00	20.00
Imperial LP-12449	(S)	The Complete Albert Collins	1969	8.00	20.00
Blue Thumb BTS-8	(S)	Truckin' With Albert Collins	1969	6.00	15.00
Tumbleweed TWS-103	(S)	There's Gotta Be A Change	1971	5.00	12.00

COLLINS, BILL: Refer to WALT BROWN

COLLINS, DOROTHY

Coral CRL-57105	(M)	At Home	1957	10.00	25.00
Coral CRL-57106	(M)	Songs By Dorothy Collins	1957	10.00	25.00

COLLINS, JUDY

Elektra EKL-209	(M)	Maid Of Constant Sorrow	1961	6.00	15.00
Elektra EKS-7209	(S)	Maid Of Constant Sorrow	1961	8.00	20.00

Label & Catalog #		Title	Year	VG+	NM
Elektra EKL-222	(M)	Golden Apples Of The Sun	1962	6.00	15.00
Elektra EKS-7222	(S)	Golden Apples Of The Sun	1962	8.00	20.00
Elektra EKL-243	(M)	Judy Collins #3	1964	6.00	15.00
Elektra EKS-7243	(S)	Judy Collins #3	1964	8.00	20.00
Elektra EKL-280	(M)	Judy Collins' Concert	1964	6.00	15.00
Elektra EKS-7280	(S)	Judy Collins Concert	1964	8.00	20.00
Elektra EKL-300	(M)	Judy Collins' Fifth Album	1965	6.00	15.00
Elektra EKS-7300	(S)	Judy Collins' Fifth Album	1965	8.00	20.00
Elektra EKL-320	(M)	In My Life	1967	8.00	20.00
Elektra EKS-7320	(S)	In My Life	1967	6.00	15.00
Elektra EKL-4012	(M)	Wildflowers	1967	10.00	25.00
Elektra EKS-74012	(S)	Wildflowers	1967	6.00	15.00
Elektra EQ-5030	(Q)	Colors Of The Day/Best Of Judy Collins	1972	6.00	15.00
Direct Disk SD-16607	(S)	Judith	197?	8.00	25.00

COLLINS, LYN
Produced by James Brown.

People PE-5602	(S)	Think (About It)	1972	6.00	15.00
People PE-6605	(S)	Check Me Out	1975	6.00	15.00

COLLINS, TOMMY

Capitol T-776	(M)	Words And Music Country Style	1957	40.00	100.00
Capitol T-1125	(M)	Light Of The Lord	1959	60.00	150.00
Capitol T-1196	(M)	This Is Tommy Collins	1959	30.00	75.00
Capitol T-1436	(M)	Songs I Love To Sing	1961	24.00	60.00
Capitol ST-1436	(S)	Songs I Love To Sing	1961	30.00	75.00
Tower T-5021	(M)	Let's Live A Little	1966	16.00	40.00
Tower DT-5021	(E)	Let's Live A Little	1966	10.00	25.00
Tower T-5107	(M)	Shindig	1968	20.00	50.00
Tower DT-5107	(E)	Shindig	1968	16.00	40.00
Columbia CL-2510	(M)	The Dynamic Tommy Collins	1966	14.00	35.00
Columbia CS-9310	(S)	The Dynamic Tommy Collins	1966	20.00	50.00
Columbia CL-2778	(M)	Tommy Collins On Tour	1968	30.00	75.00
Columbia CS-9578	(S)	Tommy Collins On Tour	1968	20.00	50.00
Starday SLP-474	(M)	Callin'	196?	10.00	25.00

COLLINS, WILLIAM "BOOTSY" [BOOTSY'S RUBBER BAND]
Formerly of James Brown's JBs, Bootsy is a member of the Parliament/Funkadelic community. Refer to Godmoma; Mico Wave; The Sweat Band.

Warner Bros. BS-2920	(S)	Stretchin' Out	1976	8.00	20.00
Warner Bros. BS-2972	(S)	Aah... The Name Is Bootsy, Baby	1977	8.00	20.00
Warner Bros. K-3093	(S)	Bootsy? Player Of The Year	1978	8.00	20.00
Warner Bros. K-3295	(S)	This Boot Is Made For Fonk'N	1979	8.00	20.00
Warner Bros. K-3433	(S)	Ultrawave	1980	8.00	20.00
Warner Bros. K-3667	(S)	One Giveth, The Count Taketh Away	1982	8.00	20.00
Columbia 44107	(S)	What's Bootsy Doin'?	1988	4.00	10.00

COLMAN, RONALD

Decca DL-9059	(M)	A Tale Of Two Cities	1959	8.00	20.00

COLONEL BAGSHOT

Cadet Concept 50010	(S)	Oh! What A Lovely War	1971	6.00	15.00

COLOURS

Dot DLP-25854	(S)	Colours	1968	6.00	15.00
Dot DLP-25935	(S)	Atmosphere	1969	6.00	15.00

COLWELL-WINFIELD BLUES BAND, THE

Verve/Forecast FVS-3056	(S)	Cold Wind Blues	1968	8.00	20.00
Verve/Forecast FVS-3072	(S)	Colwell-Winfield Blues Band	1969	Unreleased	
ZaZoo 1	(S)	Live Bust	1971	12.00	30.00

COMFORTABLE CHAIR, THE

Ode Z12-44005	(S)	The Comfortable Chair	1968	6.00	15.00

COMMON PEOPLE, THE

Capitol ST-266	(S)	Of The People, By The People	1969	30.00	75.00

Label & Catalog #		Title	Year	VG+	NM

COMO, PERRY

Label & Catalog #		Title	Year	VG+	NM
RCA Victor LPM-51 (10")	(M)	Merry Christmas	1951	16.00	40.00
RCA Victor LPM-3013 (10")	(M)	TV Favorites	1952	16.00	40.00
RCA Victor LPM-3035 (10")	(M)	Sentimental Date	1952	16.00	40.00
RCA Victor LPM-3044 (10")	(M)	Supper Club Favorites	1952	16.00	40.00
RCA Victor LPM-3124 (10")	(M)	Hits From Broadway Shows	1953	16.00	40.00
RCA Victor LPM-3133 (10")	(M)	Around The Christmas Tree	1953	16.00	40.00
RCA Victor LPM-3188 (10")	(M)	I Believe	1954	16.00	40.00
RCA Victor LPM-3224 (10")	(M)	Como's Golden Records	1954	16.00	40.00
RCA Victor LPM-1085	(M)	So Smooth	1955	12.00	30.00
RCA Victor LPM-1172	(M)	I Believe	1955	12.00	30.00
RCA Victor LPM-1176	(M)	Relaxing With Perry Como	1955	12.00	30.00
RCA Victor LPC-1177	(M)	A Sentimental Date With Perry Como	1955	12.00	30.00
RCA Victor LPM-1191	(M)	Hits From Broadway Shows	1956	12.00	30.00
RCA Victor LPM-1243	(M)	Merry Christmas Music	1956	12.00	30.00
RCA Victor LPM-1463	(M)	We Get Letters	1957	12.00	30.00
RCA Victor LOP-1004	(M)	Saturday Night With Mr. C	1958	12.00	30.00
RCA Victor LOP-1007	(M)	Como's Golden Records	1958	12.00	30.00
RCA Victor LPM-1885	(M)	When You Come To The End Of The Day	1959	8.00	20.00
RCA Victor LPM-2010	(M)	Como Swings	1959	8.00	20.00
RCA Victor LSP-2010	(S)	Como Swings	1959	10.00	25.00
RCA Victor LPM-2066	(M)	Season's Greetings	1959	8.00	20.00
RCA Victor LSP-2066	(S)	Season's Greetings	1959	10.00	25.00
RCA Victor LPM-2343	(M)	For The Young At Heart	1961	6.00	15.00
RCA Victor LSP-2343	(S)	For The Young At Heart	1961	8.00	20.00
RCA Victor LPM-2390	(M)	Sing To Me, Mr. C	1961	6.00	15.00
RCA Victor LSP-2390	(S)	Sing To Me, Mr. C	1961	8.00	20.00
RCA Victor LPM-2567	(M)	By Request	1962	6.00	15.00
RCA Victor LSP-2567	(S)	By Request	1962	8.00	20.00
RCA Victor LPM-2630	(M)	Irving Berlin's Songs For "Mr. President"	1962	6.00	15.00
RCA Victor LSP-2630	(S)	Irving Berlin's Songs For "Mr. President"	1962	8.00	20.00

— Original RCA mono albums above have "Long Play" on the bottom of the label;
stereo albums have "Living Stereo" on the bottom.—

Label & Catalog #		Title	Year	VG+	NM
RCA Victor LPM-2708	(M)	The Songs I Love	1963	5.00	12.00
RCA Victor LSP-2708	(S)	The Songs I Love	1963	6.00	15.00
RCA Victor LPM-3013	(M)	TV Favorites	1964	5.00	12.00
RCA Victor LSP-3013	(S)	TV Favorites	1964	6.00	15.00
RCA Victor LPM-3035	(M)	Sentimental Date	1964	5.00	12.00
RCA Victor LSP-3035	(S)	Sentimental Date	1964	6.00	15.00
RCA Victor LPM-3396	(M)	The Scene Changes	1965	5.00	12.00
RCA Victor LSP-3396	(S)	The Scene Changes	1965	6.00	15.00
RCA Victor LPM-3552	(M)	Lightly Latin	1966	5.00	12.00
RCA Victor LSP-3552	(S)	Lightly Latin	1966	6.00	15.00
RCA Victor LPM-3608	(M)	Perry Como In Italy	1966	5.00	12.00
RCA Victor LSP-3608	(S)	Perry Como In Italy	1966	6.00	15.00

— Original RCA albums above have black labels.—

COMPETITORS, THE

The Competitors are a creation of Gary Usher & Co.

Label & Catalog #		Title	Year	VG+	NM
Dot DLP-3542	(M)	Hits Of The Street And Strip	1963	60.00	150.00
Dot DLP-25542	(S)	Hits Of The Street And Strip	1963	80.00	200.00

COMSTOCK, BOBBY, & THE COUNTS

Label & Catalog #		Title	Year	VG+	NM
Ascot ALM-13026	(M)	Out Of Sight	1966	10.00	25.00
Ascot ALS-16026	(S)	Out Of Sight	1966	14.00	35.00

CONDELLO

Condello is Michael Condello.

Label & Catalog #		Title	Year	VG+	NM
Scepter SP-542	(M)	Phase 1	1968	8.00	20.00
Scepter SPS-542	(S)	Phase 1	1968	10.00	25.00

CONLEY, ARTHUR

Label & Catalog #		Title	Year	VG+	NM
Atco 33-215	(M)	Sweet Soul Music	1967	16.00	40.00
Atco SD-33-215	(E)	Sweet Soul Music	1967	12.00	30.00
Atco 33-220	(M)	Shake, Rattle And Roll	1967	12.00	30.00
Atco SD-33-220	(E)	Shake, Rattle And Roll	1967	10.00	25.00
Atco SD-33-243	(S)	Soul Directions	1968	12.00	30.00
Atco SD-33-276	(S)	More Sweet Soul	1969	12.00	30.00

With the demise of horror comic books in the '50s in the wake of Seduction Of The Innocent (a book espousing a treatise that claimed that since almost every convicted felon admitted to reading comics as a child then comics must lead to crime), fans found other forms to savor the unsavory. From Forrest Ackermann's "Famous Monsters Of Filmland" magazine to Aurora's plastic model kits of the Frankenstein, Mummy, the Wolfman, etc., the fad for celluloid horrors found its way onto vinyl in a variety of forms. RCA Victor's Monster Rally attracts both record collectors and comic art enthusiasts as it features a beautiful cover from EC's legendary Jack Davis.

Label & Catalog #		Title	Year	VG+	NM
CONNELLY, CHRIS					
Philips PHM-200-173	(M)	The Boy From Peyton Place	1965	6.00	15.00
Philips PHS-600-173	(S)	The Boy From Peyton Place	1965	8.00	20.00
CONNELLY, PEGGY: *Refer to* GOLDMINE'S PRICE GUIDE TO COLLECTIBLE JAZZ ALBUMS					
CONNOR, CHRIS: *Refer to* GOLDMINE'S PRICE GUIDE TO COLLECTIBLE JAZZ ALBUMS					
CONRAD, RAY					
Prestige Int. PRLP-13039	(M)	A Cotton Pickin' Lift Tower	1962	10.00	25.00
CONRIED, HANS					
RCA Victor LPM-1923	(M)	Monster Rally	1959	12.00	30.00
RCA Victor LSP-1923	(S)	Monster Rally	1959	16.00	40.00
CONTOURS, THE					
Gordy 901	(M)	Do You Love Me	1962	100.00	250.00
COODER, RY					
Refer to Capt. Beefheart / Ry Cooder; The Ceylib People; Longbranch Pennywhistle					
Reprise RS-6402	(S)	Ry Cooder	1970	6.00	15.00
Reprise MS-2117	(S)	Boomer's Story	1972	5.00	12.00
Reprise MS-2052	(S)	Into The Purple Valley	1972	5.00	12.00
Warner Bros. 238101	(S)	Live In Europe	198?	8.00	20.00
Mobile Fidelity MFSL-085	(S)	Jazz	1984	70.00	200.00
COOKE, SAM					
Refer to The Soul Stirrers.					
Keen A-2001	(M)	Sam Cooke	1958	50.00	150.00
Keen A-2003	(M)	Encore	1958	50.00	150.00
Keen A-2004	(M)	Tribute To The Lady—Billie Holiday	1959	40.00	125.00
Keen AS-2004	(S)	Tribute To The Lady—Billie Holiday	1959	70.00	175.00
Keen 86101	(M)	Hit Kit	1959	75.00	200.00
Keen 86103	(M)	I Thank God	1960	150.00	400.00
Keen 86106	(M)	The Wonderful World Of Sam Cooke	1960	100.00	300.00
RCA Victor LPM-2221	(M)	Cooke's Tour	1960	12.00	30.00
RCA Victor LSP-2221	(S)	Cooke's Tour	1960	16.00	40.00
RCA Victor LPM-2236	(M)	Hits Of The 50's	1960	12.00	30.00
RCA Victor LSP-2236	(S)	Hits Of The 50's	1960	16.00	40.00
RCA Victor LPM-2293	(M)	Swing Low	1960	12.00	30.00
RCA Victor LSP-2293	(S)	Swing Low	1960	16.00	40.00
RCA Victor LPM-2392	(M)	My Kind Of Blues	1961	12.00	30.00
RCA Victor LSP-2392	(S)	My Kind Of Blues	1961	16.00	40.00
RCA Victor LPM-2555	(M)	Twistin' The Night Away	1962	12.00	30.00
RCA Victor LSP-2555	(S)	Twistin' The Night Away	1962	16.00	40.00
RCA Victor LPM-2625	(M)	The Best Of Sam Cooke	1962	10.00	25.00
RCA Victor LSP-2625	(E)	The Best Of Sam Cooke	1962	8.00	20.00
RCA Victor LPM-2673	(M)	Mr. Soul	1963	8.00	20.00
RCA Victor LSP-2673	(S)	Mr. Soul	1963	12.00	30.00
RCA Victor LPM-2709	(M)	Night Beat	1963	8.00	20.00
RCA Victor LSP-2709	(S)	Night Beat	1963	12.00	30.00
— Original RCA mono albums above have "Long Play" on the bottom of the label; stereo albums have "Living Stereo" on the bottom.—					
RCA Victor LPM-2899	(M)	Ain't That Good News	1964	8.00	20.00
RCA Victor LSP-2899	(S)	Ain't That Good News	1964	10.00	25.00
RCA Victor LPM-2970	(M)	Sam Cooke At The Copa	1964	8.00	20.00
RCA Victor LSP-2970	(S)	Sam Cooke At The Copa	1964	10.00	25.00
RCA Victor LPM-3367	(M)	Shake	1965	8.00	20.00
RCA Victor LSP-3367	(S)	Shake	1965	10.00	25.00
RCA Victor LPM-3373	(M)	The Best Of Sam Cooke, Volume 2	1965	6.00	15.00
RCA Victor LSP-3373	(P)	The Best Of Sam Cooke, Volume 2	1965	8.00	20.00
RCA Victor LPM-3435	(M)	Try A Little Love	1965	8.00	20.00
RCA Victor LSP-3435	(S)	Try A Little Love	1965	10.00	25.00
RCA Victor LPM-3517	(M)	The Unforgettable Sam Cooke	1966	6.00	15.00
RCA Victor LSP-3517	(S)	The Unforgettable Sam Cooke	1966	8.00	20.00
RCA Victor LSP-3991	(S)	The Man Who Invented Soul	1968	6.00	15.00
— Original RCA albums above have black labels.—					
RCA Victor AYL1-3863	(E)	The Best Of Sam Cooke	1977	6.00	15.00
("Chain Gang" and "Sad Mood" are in stereo on this reissue.)					

Label & Catalog #		Title	Year	VG+	NM
Famous F-502	(M)	Sam's Songs	1969	14.00	35.00
Famous F-505	(M)	Only Sixteen	1969	14.00	35.00
Famous F-508	(M)	So Wonderful	1969	14.00	35.00
Famous F-509	(M)	You Send Me	1969	14.00	35.00
Famous F-512	(M)	Cha-Cha-Cha	1969	14.00	35.00
		(The Famous albums above repackage the Keen material.)			

COOKIES, THE / LITTLE EVA / CAROLE KING

Dimension DLP-6001	(M)	The Dimension Dolls	1964	80.00	200.00

COOL, CALVIN, & THE SURF KNOBS

Charter CLP-103	(M)	The Surfer's Beat	1963	12.00	30.00
Charter CLS-103	(S)	The Surfer's Beat	1963	16.00	40.00

COOLEY, SPADE

Columbia HL-9007 (10")	(M)	Sagebrush Swing	1949	60.00	150.00
Decca DL-5563 (10")	(M)	Dance-O-Rama #3	1955	100.00	250.00
Raynote R-5007	(M)	Fidoolin'	1959	16.00	40.00
Raynote RS-5007	(S)	Fidoolin'	1959	20.00	50.00
Roulette R-25145	(M)	Fidoolin'	1961	8.00	20.00
Roulette SR-25145	(M)	Fidoolin'	1961	12.00	30.00

COOLIDGE, RITA

Nautilus NR-16	(S)	Anytime... Anywhere	198?	6.00	18.00

COOPER, ALICE

Originally the name of the group, Alice Cooper has become pseudonymous with leader Vince Furnier. Refer to The Billion Dollar Babies.

Straight STS-1051	(S)	Pretties For You	1969	20.00	50.00
Straight WS-1845	(S)	Easy Action	1970	20.00	50.00
		("Alice Cooper" is in black letters on the cover)			
Straight WS-1845	(S)	Easy Action	1970	12.00	30.00
		("Alice Cooper" is in white letters on the cover)			
Straight WS-1883	(S)	Love It to Death	1971	20.00	50.00
Warner Bros. WS-1883	(S)	Love It to Death	1971	12.00	30.00
		(Cooper is gripping his cape in such a manner that his right thumb has a phallic appearance.)			
Warner Bros. WS-1883	(S)	Love It to Death	1971	8.00	20.00
		(The thumb remains and a white box that reads "Including Their Hit I'm Eighteen" in the corner.)			
Warner Bros. WS-1883	(S)	Love It to Death	197?	8.00	20.00
		(The cover has a broad white border at the top and bottom.)			
Warner Bros. WS-1883	(S)	Love It to Death	197?	5.00	12.00
		(Restored cover with the offending member airbrushed off.)			
Warner Bros. BS-2567	(S)	Killer *(With calendar and poster)*	1971	12.00	30.00
Warner Bros. BS-2623	(S)	School's Out *(With panties)*	1972	12.00	30.00
Warner Bros. BS4-2685	(Q)	Billion Dollar Babies	1974	8.00	20.00
Warner Bros. BS4-2748	(Q)	Muscle Of Love	1973	8.00	20.00
Mobile Fidelity MFSL-063	(S)	Welcome To My Nightmare	1980	12.00	35.00

COOPER, JACKIE

Dot DLP-3146	(M)	The Movies Swing!	1958	16.00	40.00
Signature SM-1049	(M)	Hennesey *(Soundtrack)*	195?	30.00	75.00

COOPER, LES, & THE SOUL ROCKERS

Everlast ELP-202	(M)	Wiggle Wobble	1963	16.00	40.00

COPAS, COWBOY

King 553	(M)	His All-Time Hits	1957	30.00	75.00
King 556	(M)	Favorite Scared Songs	1957	20.00	50.00
King 619	(M)	Sacred Songs	1969	20.00	50.00
King 714	(M)	Tragic Tales Of Love And Life	1960	20.00	50.00
King 720	(M)	Broken Hearted Melodies	1960	20.00	50.00
King 817	(M)	Country Gentleman Of Song	1963	16.00	40.00
King 824	(M)	As You Remember Cowboy Copas	1963	16.00	40.00
Starday SLP-118	(M)	All Time Country Music Great	1960	16.00	40.00
Starday SLP-133	(M)	Inspirational Songs	1961	14.00	35.00
Starday SLP-144	(M)	Cowboy Copas	1961	14.00	35.00
Starday SLP-175	(M)	Mr. Country Music	1962	14.00	35.00

Dave "Baby" Cortez Clowney began his career as singer and organist for The Pearls. After "The Happy Organ" hit the national charts for Clock in 1959, RCA Victor leased the material and issued his first album. By 1963 he was on Chess, who recycled the photo of Dave for their album art . . .

Label & Catalog #		Title	Year	VG+	NM
Starday SLP-184	(M)	Songs That Made Him Famous	1962	14.00	35.00
Starday SLP-208	(M)	Country Music Entertainer #1	1963	14.00	35.00
Starday SLP-212	(M)	Beyond The Sunset	1963	14.00	35.00
Starday SLP-234	(M)	The Unforgettable Cowboy Copas	1963	14.00	35.00
Starday SLP-247	(M)	Star Of The Grand Ole Opry	1963	12.00	30.00
Starday SLP-268	(M)	Cowboy Copas And His Friends	1964	12.00	30.00
Starday SLP-347	(M)	The Cowboy Copas Story	1965	12.00	30.00

COPAS, COWBOY / HAWKSHAW HAWKINS

King 835	(M)	In Memory	1963	16.00	40.00
King 850	(M)	Legend Of Cowboy Copas And Hawkshaw Hawkins	1964	16.00	40.00

CORBIN, HAROLD

Roulette R-25079	(M)	Soul Brother	1961	8.00	20.00
Roulette SR-25079	(S)	Soul Brother	1961	10.00	25.00

CORNELLS, THE

Garex LPGA-100	(M)	Beach Bound	1963	150.00	300.00

CORPORATE BODY, THE

MGM SE-4624	(S)	Prospectus '69	1969	6.00	15.00

CORPORATION, THE

Age of Aquarius 4150	(S)	Get On Our Swing	1969	8.00	20.00
Age of Aquarius 4250	(S)	Hassles In My Mind	1969	8.00	20.00
		(A warehouse find of the Aquarius titles halved their value.)			
Capitol ST-175	(S)	The Corporation	1969	12.00	30.00

CORPUS

Acorn 1001	(S)	Creation: A Child	1972	150.00	300.00

CORTEZ, DAVE "BABY"

RCA Victor LPM-2099	(M)	The Happy Organ	1959	20.00	50.00
RCA Victor LSP-2099	(P)	The Happy Organ	1959	30.00	75.00
Clock C-331	(M)	Dave "Baby" Cortez	1960	14.00	35.00
Clock CS-331	(P)	Dave "Baby" Cortez	1960	20.00	50.00
Chess LP-1473	(M)	Rinky Dink	1962	20.00	50.00
Roulette R-25298	(M)	Organ Shindig	1965	8.00	20.00
Roulette SR-25298	(S)	Organ Shindig	1965	10.00	25.00
Roulette R-25315	(M)	Tweety Pie	1966	8.00	20.00
Roulette SR-25315	(S)	Tweety Pie	1966	10.00	25.00
Roulette R-25328	(M)	In Orbit With Dave "Baby" Cortez	1966	8.00	20.00
Roulette SR-25328	(S)	In Orbit With Dave "Baby" Cortez	1966	10.00	25.00
Metro M-550	(M)	The Fabulous Organ Of Dave "Baby" Cortez	1965	5.00	12.00
Metro MS-550	(S)	The Fabulous Organ Of Dave "Baby" Cortez	1965	6.00	15.00

COSTELLO, ELVIS (& THE ATTRACTIONS)

Columbia JC-35037	(S)	My Aim Is True	1977	8.00	20.00
		(Original covers are yellow on the back. Costello is backed by the American group Clover on this album.)			
Columbia JC-35331	(S)	This Year's Model	1978	8.00	20.00
		(Red label with "Costello" around the perimeter.)			
CBS CDN-10	(DJ)	Live At The El Mocambo *(Canadian)*	1978	60.00	150.00
		(Counterfeits have excessive tape hiss.)			
Columbia *(No number)*	(DJ)	My Aim Is True *(Picture disc)*	1979	40.00	100.00
Columbia JC-35709	(S)	Armed Forces	1979	6.00	15.00
		(Issued with a 7" EP, "Live At Hollywood High.")			
Costello AS-847	(DJ)	Taking Liberties *(Radio sampler)*	1980	16.00	40.00
Columbia AS-958	(DJ)	The Tom Snyder Interview	1981	12.00	30.00
Columbia AS-1318	(DJ)	Almost Blue *(Radio sampler)*	1981	16.00	40.00
Columbia HC-48157	(S)	Imperial Bedroom *(Half-speed master)*	1982	16.00	50.00

COSTELLO, ELVIS / NICK LOWE / MINK DeVILLE

Columbia/Capitol AS-443	(DJ)	Radio Radio *(Orange vinyl)*	1979	10.00	25.00

COTTON, JAMES [THE JAMES COTTON BLUES BAND]

Verve/Forecast FT-3023	(M)	James Cotton Blues Band	1967	6.00	15.00
Verve/Forecast FTS-3023	(S)	James Cotton Blues Band	1967	8.00	20.00

Label & Catalog #		Title	Year	VG+	NM
Verve/Forecast FTS-3038	(S)	**Pure Cotton**	1968	8.00	20.00
Vanguard VSD-79283	(S)	**Cut You Loose**	1968	8.00	20.00
Verve/Forecast FTS-3060	(S)	**Cotton In Your Ears**	1969	8.00	20.00
Capitol ST-814	(S)	**Taking Care Of Business**	1971	5.00	12.00

COUGAR, JOHN: *Refer to* JOHN COUGAR MELLENCAMP

COUNT FIVE, THE

Double Shot DSM-1001	(M)	**Psychotic Reaction**	1966	16.00	40.00
Double Shot DSS-5001	(E)	**Psychotic Reaction**	1966	12.00	30.00
		(Reproductions of Double Shot DSS-5001 exist.)			

COUNTRY ALL-STARS, THE
The All-Stars feature Chet Atkins, Jerry Byrd and Henry "Homer" Haynes.

RCA Victor LPM-3167 (10")	(M)	**String Dustin'**	1953	60.00	150.00

COUNTRY CUT-UPS, THE

Town House 1000	(M)	**The Country Cut-Ups Go To College**	195?	30.00	75.00

COUNTRY GENTLEMEN, THE

Folkways FA-2409	(M)	**The Country Gentlemen**	195?	10.00	25.00
Cimarron 2001	(M)	**Songs Of The Pioneers**	1962	12.00	30.00

COUNTRY GENTLEMEN, THE

Starday SLP-109	(M)	**Traveling Dobro Blues**	1959	16.00	40.00

COUNTRY JOE & THE FISH
Country Joe MacDonald with Fish Barry Melton, Chicken Hirsch, Bruce Barthol and David Cohen.

Vanguard VRS-9244	(M)	**Electric Music For The Mind And Body**	1967	8.00	20.00
Vanguard VSD-79244	(S)	**Electric Music For The Mind And Body**	1967	8.00	20.00
Vanguard VRS-9266	(M)	**I-Feel-Like-I'm-Fixin'-To-Die**	1967	8.00	20.00
Vanguard VSD-79266	(S)	**I-Feel-Like-I'm-Fixin'-To-Die**	1967	8.00	20.00
		(Originally issued with a fold-open, "Fish game" poster, priced separately below.)			
Vanguard		**I-Feel-Like-I'm-Fixin'-To-Die Poster**	1967	6.00	15.00
Vanguard VSD-79277	(S)	**Together**	1968	8.00	20.00
Vanguard VSD-6545	(S)	**Country Joe & The Fish's Greatest Hits**	1969	8.00	20.00
Vanguard VSD-79299	(S)	**Here We Are Again**	1969	8.00	20.00
Vanguard VSD-6555	(S)	**C.J. Fish**	1970	8.00	20.00

COUNTRY JOE (McDONALD)

Vanguard VSD-6546	(S)	**Thinking Of Woody**	1969	6.00	15.00
Vanguard VSD-6557	(S)	**Tonight I'm Singing Just For You**	1970	6.00	15.00
Vanguard VSD-79303	(S)	**Quiet Days In Clichy** *(Soundtrack)*	1970	6.00	15.00
Vanguard VSD-79304	(S)	**Hold On It's Coming**	1971	4.00	10.00
Vanguard VSD-79315	(S)	**War, War, War**	1971	4.00	10.00
Vanguard VSD-79316	(S)	**Incredible! Live!**	1972	4.00	10.00
Vanguard VSD-79328	(S)	**Paris Sessions**	1973	4.00	10.00
Vanguard VSD-79348	(S)	**Country Joe**	1975	4.00	10.00
Mobile Fidelity MFSL-056	(S)	**Paradise With An Ocean View**	1980	5.00	15.00
Sweet Thunder 16	(S)	**Into The Fray**	198?	7.00	20.00

COUNTRY WEATHER

(No label)	(S)	**Country Weather** *(One-sided demo)*	1968	60.00	150.00

COUSINS, THE

Parkway P-7005	(M)	**Music Of The Strip**	1961	6.00	15.00
Parkway SP-7005	(S)	**Music Of The Strip**	1961	8.00	20.00

COVAY, DON

Atlantic 8104	(M)	**Mercy**	1965	16.00	40.00
Atlantic SD-8104	(S)	**Mercy**	1965	20.00	50.00
Atlantic 8120	(M)	**See Saw**	1966	16.00	40.00
Atlantic SD-8120	(S)	**See Saw**	1966	20.00	50.00
Atlantic SD-8237	(S)	**The House Of Blue Lights**	1969	10.00	25.00
Janus 3038	(S)	**Different Strokes From Different Folks**	1972	6.00	15.00
Mercury SRM-1-1020	(S)	**Hot Blood**	1974	5.00	12.00

Label & Catalog #		Title	Year	VG+	NM
COVEN, THE					
Mercury SR-61239	(S)	Witchcraft Destroys Minds & Reaps Souls	1969	6.00	15.00
MGM SE-4801	(S)	Coven	1971	4.00	10.00
Buddah BDS-5614	(S)	Blood On The Snow	1974	4.00	10.00
COWSILL, BILL					
MGM SE-4706	(S)	Nervous Breakthrough	1971	8.00	20.00
COWSILLS, THE					
MGM E-4498	(M)	The Cowsills	1967	6.00	15.00
MGM SE-4498	(S)	The Cowsills	1967	8.00	20.00
MGM SE-4534	(S)	We Can Fly	1968	6.00	15.00
MGM SE-4554	(S)	Captain Sad And His Ship Of Fools	1968	6.00	15.00
MGM SE-4597	(S)	The Best Of The Cowsills	1969	5.00	12.00
MGM SE-4619	(S)	The Cowsills In Concert	1969	6.00	15.00
MGM SE-4639	(S)	II By II	1970	8.00	20.00
London 587	(S)	On My Side	1971	12.00	30.00
COWSILLS, THE / THE LINCOLN PARK ZOO					
Wing SRW-16354	(S)	The Cowsills Plus The Lincoln Park Zoo	1968	5.00	12.00
COX, DANNY					
Pioneer 2125	(S)	Sunny	1966	12.00	30.00
Together ZR-1011	(S)	Birth Announcement (2 LPs)	1970	12.00	30.00
		(Produced by Gary Usher.)			
Sunflower 5002	(S)	Live At The Family Dog	1970	6.00	15.00
Dunhill 50114	(S)	Danny Cox	1971	4.00	10.00
COXAN'S ARMY					
Coxan's Army features Pat Benatar.					
(Label unknown)	(S)	Coxan's Army	1972	150.00	300.00
CRADDOCK, BILLY "CRASH"					
King 912	(M)	I'm Tore Up	1964	40.00	100.00
CRAIN, JIMMY					
Ray-O LP-2005	(M)	Miles To Go	196?	50.00	125.00
CRAMER, FLOYD					
MGM E-3502	(M)	That Honky-Tonk Piano	1957	16.00	40.00
RCA Victor LPM-2151	(M)	Hello Blues	1960	6.00	15.00
RCA Victor LSP-2151	(S)	Hello Blues	1960	8.00	20.00
RCA Victor LPM-2350	(M)	Last Date	1961	8.00	20.00
RCA Victor LSP-2350	(S)	Last Date	1961	10.00	25.00
RCA Victor LPM-2359	(M)	On The Rebound	1961	5.00	12.00
RCA Victor LSP-2359	(S)	On The Rebound	1961	6.00	15.00
RCA Victor LPM-2428	(M)	Floyd Cramer Gets Organ-ized	1962	5.00	12.00
RCA Victor LSP-2428	(S)	Floyd Cramer Gets Organ-ized	1962	6.00	15.00
RCA Victor LPM-2466	(M)	America's Biggest Selling Pianist	1962	5.00	12.00
RCA Victor LSP-2466	(S)	America's Biggest Selling Pianist	1962	6.00	15.00
RCA Victor LPM-2544	(M)	I Remember Hank Williams	1962	6.00	15.00
RCA Victor LSP-2544	(S)	I Remember Hank Williams	1962	8.00	20.00
		— Original RCA mono albums above have black labels with "Long Play" on the bottom;			
		stereo albums have "Living Stereo" on the bottom.—			
CRANE, BOB					
Epic LN-246224	(M)	The Funny Side Of TV	1967	8.00	20.00
Epic BN-26224	(S)	The Funny Side Of TV	1967	10.00	25.00
CRAWFORD, DON					
Verve/Folkways FT-3002	(M)	Don Crawford	1966	5.00	12.00
Verve/Folkways FTS-3002	(S)	Don Crawford	1966	6.00	15.00
CRAWFORD, JOHNNY					
Del-Fi DFLP-1220	(M)	The Captivating Johnny Crawford	1962	16.00	40.00
Del-Fi DFLP-1223	(M)	A Young Man's Fancy	1963	12.00	30.00
Del-Fi DFST-1223	(S)	A Young Man's Fancy	1963	16.00	40.00
Del-Fi DFLP-1224	(M)	Rumors	1963	12.00	30.00
Del-Fi DFST-1224	(S)	Rumors	1963	16.00	40.00

Label & Catalog #		Title	Year	VG+	NM
Del-Fi DFLP-1229	(M)	**Johnny Crawford: His Greatest Hits**	1963	12.00	30.00
Del-Fi DFST-1229	(S)	**Johnny Crawford: His Greatest Hits**	1963	16.00	40.00
Del-Fi DFLP-1248	(M)	**Greatest Hits, Volume 2**	1964	8.00	20.00
Del-Fi DFST-1248	(S)	**Greatest Hits, Volume 2**	1964	12.00	30.00
Supreme S-210	(S)	**Songs From "The Restless Ones"**	196?	12.00	30.00

CRAYTON, PEE WEE

Crown CLP-5175	(M)	**Pee Wee Crayton**	1959	40.00	100.00
Vanguard VSD-6566	(S)	**The Things I Used To Do**	1971	6.00	15.00

CRAZY ELEPHANT

Bell 6034	(S)	**Crazy Elephant**	1969	6.00	15.00

CRAZY HORSE
Original members include Danny Whitten, Billy Talbot and Ralph Molina, who had previously recorded as The Rockets. The first album includes Nils Lofgren and Jack Nitzsche. Refer to Neil Young.

Reprise RS-6438	(S)	**Crazy Horse**	1971	6.00	15.00
Reprise MS-2059	(S)	**Loose**	1972	4.00	10.00
Epic KE-31710	(S)	**At Crooked Lake**	1972	4.00	10.00

CREAM
Cream was Ginger Baker, Jack Bruce, and Eric Clapton with Felix Pappalardi.

Atco 33-206	(M)	**Fresh Cream**	1967	16.00	40.00
Atco SD-33-206	(S)	**Fresh Cream**	1967	12.00	30.00
Atco 33-232	(M)	**Disraeli Gears**	1967	20.00	50.00
Atco SD-33-232	(S)	**Disraeli Gears**	1967	12.00	30.00
Atco PR-119/20	(DJ)	**Wheels Of Fire** *(Radio sampler)*	1968	30.00	75.00
Atco 2-700	(DJ)	**Wheels Of Fire** *(2 LPs. White label. Mono)*	1968	40.00	100.00
Atco SD-2-700	(S)	**Wheels Of Fire** *(2 LPs)*	1968	16.00	40.00
		(Original covers have a silver foil-like backing.			
		Later pressing cover are a dull grey.)			
Atco SD-7001	(S)	**Goodbye**	1969	12.00	30.00
		— Original Atco stereo albums above have purple & brown labels.—			
Atco SD-33-206	(S)	**Fresh Cream**	1969	4.00	10.00
Atco SD-33-232	(S)	**Disraeli Gears**	1969	4.00	10.00
Atco SD-2-700	(S)	**Wheels Of Fire** *(2 LPs)*	1969	6.00	15.00
Atco SD-7001	(S)	**Goodbye**	1969	4.00	10.00
Atco SD-33-328	(S)	**Live Cream**	1970	6.00	15.00
Atco SD-7005	(S)	**Live Cream (Volume 2)**	1972	6.00	15.00
		— Atco albums above yellow labels with "Atlantic Recording Co." on the bottom.—			
Springboard SPB-4037	(S)	**Early Cream**	1972	6.00	15.00
RSO-015	(DJ)	**Classic Cuts** *(2 LPs)*	1975	16.00	40.00
Mobile Fidelity MFSL-066	(S)	**Wheels Of Fire**	1980	15.00	45.00

CREAM / THE VANILLA FUDGE

Atco TL-ST-141	(DJ)	**Goodbye / Rock'n Roll**	1969	20.00	50.00
		(Radio sampler with one side by each artist.)			

CREATION OF SUNLIGHT

Windi 1001	(S)	**Creation Of Sunlight**	196?	200.00	400.00

CREEDENCE CLEARWATER REVIVAL
CCR was John and Tom Fogerty, Stu Cook and Doug Clifford, who originally recorded as The Golliwogs.
Note: CCR albums on Liberty— other titles may exist— were manufactured for either record club or foreign distribution and have suggested Near Mint values of $50-100 each.)

Fantasy F-8382	(S)	**Creedence Clearwater Revival**	1968	8.00	20.00
		(Without the blurb for "Suzie Q" on the cover.)			
Fantasy F-8382	(S)	**Creedence Clearwater Revival**	1968	6.00	15.00
		(Later pressings have a blurb for "Suzie Q" on the cover.			
		"Porterville" is in mono on both pressings of this album.)			
Fantasy F-8387	(S)	**Bayou Country**	1969	6.00	15.00
		("Proud Mary" is in mono on this album.)			
Fantasy F-8393	(S)	**Green River**	1969	6.00	15.00
Fantasy F-8397	(S)	**Willy And The Poor Boys**	1969	6.00	15.00
Fantasy F-8402	(S)	**Cosmo's Factory**	1970	6.00	15.00
Fantasy F-8410	(S)	**Pendulum**	1970	6.00	15.00
Fantasy F-9404	(S)	**Mardi Gras**	1972	6.00	15.00
		— Original copies of Fantasy albums above have blue labels.—			

When Jerry Allison, Charles Hardin Holley, Joel Mauldin and Nikki Sullivan signed with Brunswick, their contract allowed them to record as a group, The Crickets, for the parent label, and their singer, guitarist and songwriter, known professionally as Buddy Holly, to record as a solo for their Coral subsidiary. The Chirping Crickets was their sole album released during Buddy's life, cut short by the now legendary airplane crash in the winter of 1959 that also took the lives of Ritchie Valens and The Big Bopper ("the day the music died"). In Style With The Crickets was the first album the trio made following their leader's death; the rare stereo version is listed here for the first time.

Label & Catalog #		Title	Year	VG+	NM
Mobile Fidelity MFSL-037	(S)	**Cosmo's Factory**	1979	25.00	75.00
K-Tel NU-9360	(S)	**20 Super Hits: The Best Of CCR**	1978	4.00	10.00
Fantasy F-4501	(S)	**The Royal Albert Hall Concert**	1980	4.00	10.00
Sweet Thunder 13	(S)	**Green River**	198?	30.00	90.00
CREME SODA					
Trinity CST-11	(S)	**Tricky Zingers** (Group photo cover)	1975	40.00	100.00
Trinity CST-11	(S)	**Tricky Zingers** (Plain white cover)	1976	20.00	50.00
CRESCENDOS, THE					
Guest Star G-1453	(M)	**Oh Julie**	196?	20.00	50.00
Guest Star GS-1453	(E)	**Oh Julie**	196?	10.00	25.00

CRESTS, THE
The Crests feature Johnny Maestro. Refer to The Brooklyn Bridge.

Coed LPC-901	(DJ)	**The Crests Sing All The Biggies** (Red label)	1960	350.00	750.00
Coed LPC-901	(M)	**The Crests Sing All The Biggies**	1960	100.00	250.00
Coed LPC-904	(M)	**The Best Of The Crests**	1961	100.00	350.00
Coed LPS-904	(S)	**The Best Of The Crests**	1961	*See note below*	
		(While a stereo cover of Coed 904 has been found, it contained a mono LP. Should a stereo copy be found, it would fetch four figures.)			
Post 3000	(E)	**The Crests Sing**	196?	20.00	50.00
		(Post 3000 is a reissue of Coed 904.)			

CREW CUTS, THE

Mercury MG-25200 (10")	(M)	**The Crew Cuts On The Campus**	1956	30.00	75.00
Mercury MG-20067	(M)	**The Crew Cuts Go Longhair**	1956	20.00	50.00
Mercury MG-20140	(M)	**The Crew Cuts On The Campus**	1957	20.00	50.00
Mercury MG-20143	(M)	**Crew Cut Capers**	1957	20.00	50.00
Mercury MG-20144	(M)	**Rock And Roll Bash**	1957	30.00	75.00
Mercury MG-20199	(M)	**Music Ala Carte**	1957	20.00	50.00
RCA Victor LPM-1933	(M)	**Surprise Package**	1958	10.00	25.00
RCA Victor LSP-1933	(S)	**Surprise Package**	1958	16.00	40.00
RCA Victor LPM-2037	(M)	**The Crew Cuts Sing**	1959	10.00	25.00
RCA Victor LSP-2037	(S)	**The Crew Cuts Sing**	1959	16.00	40.00
RCA Victor LPM-2067	(M)	**You Must Have Been A Beautiful Baby**	1960	10.00	25.00
RCA Victor LSP-2067	(S)	**You Must Have Been A Beautiful Baby**	1960	16.00	40.00
RCA Victor PR-102	(DJ)	**The Crew Cuts Sing Out!**	1960	10.00	25.00
Wing MGW-12177	(M)	**The Crew Cuts**	1962	8.00	20.00
Wing MGW-12180	(M)	**High School Favorites**	1962	8.00	20.00
Camay CA-1002	(M)	**The Crew Cuts Sing Folk**	196?	8.00	20.00
Camay CA-3002	(S)	**The Crew Cuts Sing Folk**	196?	10.00	25.00

CREWE, BOB [BOB CREWE GENERATION]

Warwick W-2009	(M)	**Kicks**	1966	6.00	15.00
Warwick WST-2009	(S)	**Kicks**	1966	10.00	25.00
Warwick W-2034	(M)	**Crazy In The Heart**	1967	6.00	15.00
Warwick WST-2034	(M)	**Crazy In The Heart**	1967	8.00	20.00

CRICKETS, THE
The Crickets featured Buddy Holly; refer to Holly for more listings. Original members were Jerry Allison, Don Guess and Sonny Curtis; later members included Tommy Allsup, Glen Hardin, and Niki Sullivan. Refer to Bobby Vee; The Ventures.

Coral CRL-57320	(M)	**In Style With The Crickets**	1960	60.00	150.00
Coral CRL-757320	(S)	**In Style With The Crickets**	1960	150.00	300.00
		("Deborah," "When You Ask About Love," "Time Will Tell," "I Fought The Law," and "Love's Made A Fool Of You" are rechanneled.)			
Liberty LRP-3272	(M)	**Something Old, Something New**	1962	30.00	75.00
Liberty LST-7272	(S)	**Something Old, Something New**	1962	40.00	100.00
Liberty LRP-7351	(M)	**California Sun**	1964	20.00	50.00
Liberty LST-7351	(S)	**California Sun**	1964	30.00	75.00
Barnaby Z-30268	(S)	**Rockin' 50's Rock 'N' Roll**	1970	8.00	20.00
Vertigo VEL-1020	(S)	**Remnants**	1973	8.00	20.00
Epic FE-44446	(S)	**T-Shirt** (With Paul McCartney)	1988	5.00	12.00

CRISS, PETER
Refer to Chelsea; Kiss.

Casablanca NBLP-7240	(S)	**Out Of Control**	1980	10.00	25.00

Label & Catalog #		Title	Year	VG+	NM

CRITTERS, THE

Kapp KL-1485	(M)	Younger Girl	1966	14.00	35.00
Kapp KS-3485	(S)	Younger Girl	1966	16.00	40.00
Project-3 PR-4001	(S)	Touch'n Go With The Critters	1968	8.00	20.00
Project-3 PR-4002	(S)	The Critters	1969	8.00	20.00

CROCE, JIM

Croce (No number)	(S)	Faucets	1966	150.00	300.00
Capitol ST-315	(S)	Croce	1969	8.00	20.00
Command QD-40006	(Q)	You Don't Mess Around With Jim	1974	8.00	20.00
Command QD-40007	(Q)	Life And Times	1974	8.00	20.00
Command QD-40008	(Q)	I Got A Name	1974	8.00	20.00
Command QD-40020	(Q)	Photographs And Memories	1974	8.00	20.00
Mobile Fidelity MFSL-079	(S)	You Don't Mess Around With Jim	1980	12.00	35.00

CROME SYRCUS, THE

Command 925	(S)	Love Cycle	1968	8.00	20.00

CROSBY, BING

Due to Der Bingle's prolific career, his albums are listed chronologically by label with no interruptions. Refer to The Reprise Repertory Theatre; Frank Sinatra.

Decca DL-5000 (10")	(M)	Hits From Musical Comedies	1949	20.00	50.00
Decca DL-5001 (10")	(M)	Jerome Kern Songs	1949	20.00	50.00
Decca DL-5010 (10")	(M)	Stephen Foster Songs	1949	20.00	50.00
Decca DL-5011 (10")	(M)	El Bingo	1949	16.00	40.00
Decca DL-5020 (10")	(M)	Christmas Greetings	1949	16.00	40.00
Decca DL-5028 (10")	(M)	Auld Lang Syne	1950	16.00	40.00
Decca DL-5037 (10")	(M)	St. Patrick's Day	1950	16.00	40.00
Decca DL-5039 (10")	(M)	St. Valentine's Day	1950	16.00	40.00
Decca DL-5042 (10")	(M)	Blue Skies	1950	16.00	40.00
Decca DL-5052 (10")	(M)	Going My Way	1950	16.00	40.00
Decca DL-5052 (10")	(M)	The Bells Of St. Mary's (Soundtrack)	1950	40.00	100.00
Decca DL-5060 (10")	(M)	Showboat Selections (Soundtrack)	1950	30.00	75.00
Decca DL-5063 (10")	(M)	Don't Fence Me In	1950	16.00	40.00
Decca DL-5064 (10")	(M)	Cole Porter Songs	1950	16.00	40.00
Decca DL-5081 (10")	(M)	Songs By Gershwin	1950	16.00	40.00
Decca DL-5092 (10")	(M)	Holiday Inn (Soundtrack)	1950	30.00	75.00
Decca DL-5102 (10")	(M)	Blue Of The Night	1950	16.00	40.00
Decca DL-5105 (10")	(M)	Blue Of The Night	1950	16.00	40.00
Decca DL-5107 (10")	(M)	Cowboy Songs	1950	16.00	40.00
Decca DL-5119 (10")	(M)	Drifting And Dreaming	1950	16.00	40.00
Decca DL-5122 (10")	(M)	Hawaiian Songs	1950	16.00	40.00
Decca DL-5126 (10")	(M)	Stardust	1950	16.00	40.00
Decca DL-5129 (10")	(M)	Cowboy Songs, Volume 2	1950	16.00	40.00
Decca DL-5207 (10")	(M)	South Pacific	1950	16.00	40.00
Decca DL-5220 (10")	(M)	Bing Sings Hits	1950	16.00	40.00
Decca DL-5272 (10")	(M)	Top O' The Morning	1950	16.00	40.00
Decca DL-5284 (10")	(M)	Mr. Music	1950	16.00	40.00
Decca DL-5298 (10")	(M)	Hits From Broadway Shows	1951	16.00	40.00
Decca DL-5299 (10")	(M)	Favorite Hawaiian Songs	1951	16.00	40.00
Decca DL-5302 (10")	(M)	Go West, Young Man	1951	16.00	40.00
Decca DL-5310 (10")	(M)	Way Back Home	1951	16.00	40.00
Decca DL-5316 (10")	(M)	Bing Crosby	1951	16.00	40.00
Decca DL-5323 (10")	(M)	Bing And The Dixieland Bands	1951	16.00	40.00
Decca DL-5326 (10")	(M)	Yours Is My Heart Alone	1951	16.00	40.00
Decca DL-5331 (10")	(M)	Country Style	1951	16.00	40.00
Decca DL-5340 (10")	(M)	Down Memory Lane	1951	16.00	40.00
Decca DL-5343 (10")	(M)	Down Memory Lane, Volume 2	1951	16.00	40.00
Decca DL-5351 (10")	(M)	Beloved Hymns	1951	16.00	40.00
Decca DL-5355 (10")	(M)	Bing Sings Victor Herbert	1951	16.00	40.00
Decca DL-5403 (10")	(M)	When Irish Eyes Are Smiling	1952	16.00	40.00
Decca DL-5417 (10")	(M)	Just For You	1952	16.00	40.00
Decca DL-5444 (10")	(M)	The Road To Bali (Soundtrack)	1952	30.00	75.00
Decca DL-5499 (10")	(M)	Song Hits Of Paris/Le Bing	1953	16.00	40.00
Decca DL-5508 (10")	(M)	Some Fine Old Chestnuts	1954	16.00	40.00
Decca DL-5520 (10")	(M)	Bing Sings The Hits	1954	16.00	40.00
Decca DL-5556 (10")	(M)	Country Girl	1953	16.00	40.00
Decca DL-6000 (10")	(M)	The Small One / The Happy Prince (Sdtk)	1950	30.00	75.00
Decca DL-6001 (10")	(M)	Ichabod Crane	1951	16.00	40.00

Label & Catalog #		Title	Year	VG+	NM
Decca DL-6008 (10")	(M)	Collector's Classics	1951	16.00	40.00
Decca DL-6009 (10")	(M)	Two For Tonight	1951	16.00	40.00
Decca DL-6010 (10")	(M)	Rhythm On The Range (Soundtrack)	1951	40.00	100.00
Decca DL-6011 (10")	(M)	Waikiki Wedding (Soundtrack)	1951	30.00	75.00
Decca DL-6012 (10")	(M)	Collector's Classics	1951	16.00	40.00
Decca DL-6013 (10")	(M)	The Star Maker (Soundtrack)	1951	30.00	75.00
Decca DL-6014 (10")	(M)	Collector's Classics	1951	16.00	40.00
Decca DL-6015 (10")	(M)	The Road To Singapore (Soundtrack)	1951	30.00	75.00

— Decca 6008-6015 are a series of "Collector's Classics" from Bing's '30s recordings; soundtrack titles are listed where known.—

Label & Catalog #		Title	Year	VG+	NM
Decca DX-151	(M)	A Musical Autobiography (5 LP box)	1954	60.00	150.00

(The five albums were released separately as Decca 8702-8706.)

Label & Catalog #		Title	Year	VG+	NM
Decca DX-152	(M)	Old Masters (3 LPs)	1954	60.00	150.00
Decca DL-8020	(M)	A Man Without A Country	1954	12.00	30.00
Decca DL-8083	(M)	White Christmas (Soundtrack)	1954	20.00	50.00
Decca DL-8110	(M)	Lullabye Time	1955	12.00	30.00
Decca DL-8128	(M)	Merry Christmas	1955	12.00	30.00
Decca DL-8207	(M)	Shillelaghs And Shamrocks	1956	12.00	30.00
Decca DL-8210	(M)	Home On The Range	1956	12.00	30.00
Decca DL-8262	(M)	When Irish Eyes Are Smiling	1956	12.00	30.00
Decca DL-8268	(M)	Drifting And Dreaming	1956	12.00	30.00
Decca DL-8269	(M)	Blue Hawaii	1956	12.00	30.00
Decca DL-8272	(M)	High Tor (Soundtrack)	1956	200.00	400.00
Decca DL-8318	(M)	Anything Goes (Soundtrack)	1956	12.00	30.00
Decca DL-8352	(M)	Songs I Wish I Had Sung	1956	12.00	30.00
Decca DL-8365	(M)	Twilight On The Trail	1956	12.00	30.00
Decca DL-8374	(M)	Some Fine Old Chestnuts	1957	12.00	30.00
Decca DL-8419	(M)	A Christmas Sing Around The World	1957	12.00	30.00
Decca DL-8493	(M)	Bing And The Dixieland Bands	1957	12.00	30.00
Decca DL-8575	(M)	New Tricks	1957	12.00	30.00
Decca DL-8687	(M)	Around The World	1958	12.00	30.00
Decca DL-8702	(M)	A Musical Autobiography 1927-1934	1958	12.00	30.00
Decca DL-8703	(M)	A Musical Autobiography 1934-1941	1958	12.00	30.00
Decca DL-8704	(M)	A Musical Autobiography 1941-1944	1958	12.00	30.00
Decca DL-8705	(M)	A Musical Autobiography 1944-1947	1958	12.00	30.00
Decca DL-8706	(M)	A Musical Autobiography 1947-1953	1958	12.00	30.00
Decca DL-8780	(M)	Bing In Paris	1958	12.00	30.00
Decca DL-8781	(M)	That Christmas Feeling	1958	12.00	30.00

—Original Decca albums above have black labels with silver print.—

Label & Catalog #		Title	Year	VG+	NM
Decca DL-8846	(M)	In A Little Spanish Town	1959	10.00	25.00
Decca DL-4086	(M)	My Golden Favorites	1961	8.00	20.00
Decca DL-4250	(M)	Easy To Remember	1962	8.00	20.00
Decca DL-4251	(M)	Pennies From Heaven	1962	8.00	20.00
Decca DL-4252	(M)	Pocketful Of Dreams	1962	8.00	20.00
Decca DL-4253	(M)	East Side Of Heaven	1962	8.00	20.00
Decca DL-4254	(M)	The Road Begins	1962	8.00	20.00
Decca DL-4255	(M)	Only Forever	1962	8.00	20.00
Decca DL-4256	(M)	Holiday Inn	1962	8.00	20.00
Decca DL-4257	(M)	Swinging On A Star	1962	8.00	20.00
Decca DL-4258	(M)	Accentuate The Positive	1962	8.00	20.00
Decca DL-4259	(M)	Blue Skies	1962	8.00	20.00
Decca DL-4260	(M)	But Beautiful	1962	8.00	20.00
Decca DL-4261	(M)	Sunshine Cake	1962	8.00	20.00
Decca DL-4262	(M)	Cool Of The Evening	1962	8.00	20.00
Decca DL-4263	(M)	Zing A Little Zong	1962	8.00	20.00
Decca DL-4264	(M)	Anything Goes	1962	8.00	20.00

— Decca 4250-4264 above are known as "Bing's Hollywood Series" and collect a variety of his earlier soundtrack recordings onto LP.—

Label & Catalog #		Title	Year	VG+	NM
Decca DL-4281	(M)	Holiday In Europe	1962	6.00	15.00
Decca DL-74281	(S)	Holiday In Europe	1962	8.00	20.00
Decca DL-4283	(M)	The Small One	1962	6.00	15.00
Decca DL-74283	(S)	The Small One	1962	8.00	20.00
Decca DL-4415	(M)	Songs Everybody Knows	1964	6.00	15.00
Decca DL-74415	(S)	Songs Everybody Knows	1964	8.00	20.00
Decca DX-184	(M)	The Best Of Bing Crosby (2 LPs)	1965	6.00	15.00
Decca DXK-151	(S)	Bing-A Musical Autobiography (2 LPs)	1965	6.00	15.00

— Original Decca albums above have black labels with "Mfrd By Decca" beneath the rainbow.—

Label & Catalog #		Title	Year	VG+	NM
Columbia CL-6027 (10")	(M)	Crosby Classics, Volume 1	1949	20.00	50.00
Columbia CL-6105 (10")	(M)	Crosby Classics, Volume 2	1950	20.00	50.00

Label & Catalog #		Title	Year	VG+	NM
Columbia CL-2502 (10")	(M)	Der Bingle	1955	16.00	40.00
Brunswick BL-58000 (10")	(M)	Bing Crosby, Volume 1	1950	20.00	50.00
Brunswick BL-58001(10")	(M)	Bing Crosby, Volume 2	1950	20.00	50.00
Brunswick BL-54005	(M)	The Voice Of Bing In The 30s	1955	10.00	25.00
"X" XLVA-4250	(M)	Young Bing Crosby	1955	20.00	50.00
Verve V-2020	(M)	Bing Sings Whilst Bregman Swings	1956	10.00	25.00
Capitol W-750	(M)	High Society (Soundtrack)	1956	16.00	40.00
United Arts. UAL-4001	(M)	Paris Holiday (Soundtrack)	1958	14.00	35.00
Grand Award 298:20	(M)	Ali Baba And The Forty Thieves	1957	8.00	20.00
Grand Award 298:21	(M)	Christmas Story	1957	8.00	20.00
RCA Victor LPM-1473	(M)	Bing With A Beat	1957	10.00	25.00
RCA Victor LPM-1854	(M)	Fancy Meeting You Here	1958	8.00	20.00
RCA Victor LSP-1854	(S)	Fancy Meeting You Here	1958	12.00	30.00
RCA Victor LPM-2071	(M)	Young Bing Crosby	1959	10.00	25.00
RCA Victor LPM-2314	(M)	High Time (Soundtrack)	1960	20.00	50.00
RCA Victor LSP-2314	(S)	High Time (Soundtrack)	1960	30.00	75.00
Warner Bros. W-1363	(M)	Join With Bing And Sing Along	1960	6.00	15.00
Warner Bros. WS-1363	(S)	Join With Bing And Sing Along	1960	8.00	20.00
Warner Bros. 2W-1401	(M)	101 Gang Songs (2 LPs)	1961	8.00	20.00
Warner Bros. 2WS-1401	(S)	101 Gang Songs (2 LPs)	1961	10.00	25.00
Warner Bros. W-1422	(M)	Join Bing In A Gang Sing Along	1961	6.00	15.00
Warner Bros. WS-1422	(S)	Join Bing In A Gang Sing Along	1961	8.00	20.00
Warner Bros. W-1435	(M)	Join Bing And Sing Along	1962	6.00	15.00
Warner Bros. WS-1435	(S)	Join Bing And Sing Along	1962	8.00	20.00
Warner Bros. W-1482	(M)	On The Happy Side	1962	6.00	15.00
Warner Bros. WS-1482	(S)	On The Happy Side	1962	8.00	20.00
Warner Bros. W-1484	(M)	I Wish You A Merry Christmas	1962	6.00	15.00
Warner Bros. WS-1484	(S)	I Wish You A Merry Christmas	1962	8.00	20.00
		—Original Warner albums above have grey labels.—			
MGM E-3890	(M)	Senor Bing	1961	6.00	15.00
MGM SE-3890	(S)	Senor Bing	1961	8.00	20.00
Liberty LOM-16002	(M)	The Road To Hong Kong (Soundtrack)	1962	14.00	35.00
Liberty LOS-17002	(S)	The Road To Hong Kong (Soundtrack)	1962	20.00	50.00
MGM E-4129	(M)	The Great Standards	1963	6.00	15.00
MGM SE-4129	(S)	The Great Standards	1963	8.00	20.00
MGM E-4203	(M)	The Very Best Of Bing Crosby	1964	6.00	15.00
MGM SE-4203	(S)	The Very Best Of Bing Crosby	1964	8.00	20.00
Reprise R-6106	(M)	Return To Paradise Islands	1964	6.00	15.00
Reprise R9-6106	(S)	Return To Paradise Islands	1964	8.00	20.00
Metro M-523	(M)	Bing Crosby	1965	4.00	10.00
Metro MS-523	(S)	Bing Crosby	1965	5.00	12.00
Capitol T-2300	(M)	That Travelin' Two-Beat	1965	6.00	15.00
Capitol ST-2300	(S)	That Travelin' Two-Beat	1965	8.00	20.00
Capitol T-2346	(M)	Great Country Hits	1965	6.00	15.00
Capitol ST-2346	(S)	Great Country Hits	1965	8.00	20.00
Columbia C2L-43	(M)	Bing In Hollywood (2 LPs)	1967	6.00	15.00
Columbia C2S-43	(E)	Bing In Hollywood (2 LPs)	1967	6.00	15.00

CROSBY, BING, & THE ANDREWS SITERS

Decca DL-5019 (10")	(M)	Merry Christmas	1949	14.00	35.00

CROSBY, BING, & CONNEE BOSWELL

Decca DL-5390 (10")	(M)	Bing And Connee	1951	20.00	50.00

CROSBY, BING, & LOUIS ARMSTRONG

MGM E-3882	(M)	Bing And Satchmo	1960	6.00	15.00
MGM SE-3882	(S)	Bing And Satchmo	1960	8.00	20.00

CROSBY, BING / WALTER HUSTON

Decca DL-9109	(M)	Ichabod / Rip Van Winkle	1959	10.00	25.00

CROSBY, CHRIS

MGM E-4226	(M)	Meet Chris Crosby	1964	6.00	15.00
MGM SE-4226	(S)	Meet Chris Crosby	1964	8.00	20.00

CROSBY, STILLS & NASH
David Crosby of The Byrds, Stephen Stills of The Buffalo Springfield, and Graham Nash of The Hollies.

Atlantic SD-8229	(S)	Crosby, Stills And Nash	1969	6.00	15.00
		(Original pressings have green & orange labels.)			

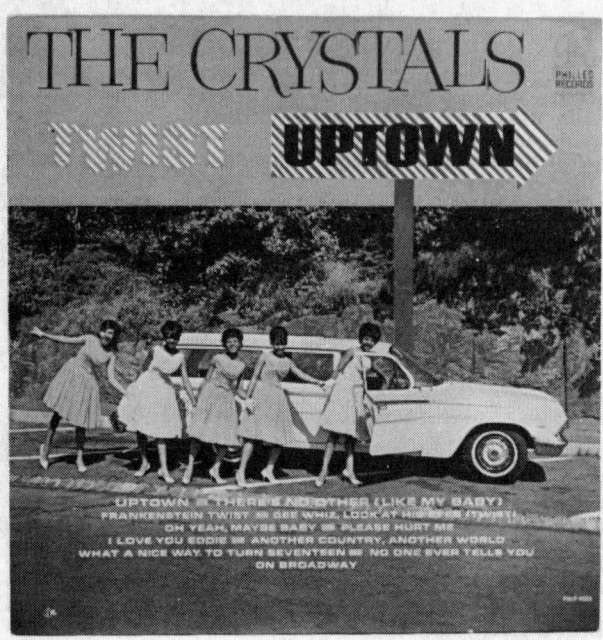

Barbara Alston, Lala Brooks, Dee Dee Kennibrew, Mary Thomas and Patricia Wright, better known as The Crystals, fared far better than the average protege of Phil Spector, realizing two full albums under Uncle Phil's magic production wand. As with all Philles albums, Spector cut post-production costs as much as possible, using low quality (read "cheap") vinyl and plating on all his product. Decades later, it is almost a miracle to find any of the Philles albums in a condition that plays without surface noise. (Note that two of the group's biggest hits, "He's A Rebel" and "He's Sure The Boy I Love," were sung not by them at all; they both feature Darlene Love's Blossoms, a typical Spectorian move. . .)

Label & Catalog #		Title	Year	VG+	NM
Atlantic PR-165	(DJ)	Celebration (Radio sampler)	197?	20.00	50.00
Nautilus NR-48	(S)	Crosby, Stills And Nash	1982	20.00	60.00

CROSBY, STILLS, NASH & YOUNG
The aforementioned trio plus ex-Buffalo Springfield Neil Young.

Atlantic SD-7200	(S)	Deja Vu	1970	6.00	15.00

(Original pressings have green & orange labels with the front photo is glued to the fake leatherette cover.)

Atlantic 18102	(DJ)	A Rap With C,S,N & Y (Interview)	197?	20.00	50.00
Mobile Fidelity MFSL-088	(S)	Deja Vu	1983	50.00	150.00

CROSSFIRES, THE

Strand SL-1083	(M)	Limbo Rock	1963	6.00	15.00
Strand SLS-1083	(S)	Limbo Rock	1963	8.00	20.00

CROSSRODE

Strawberry Jamm 801	(S)	Crossrode	1980	30.00	75.00

CROTHERS, SCATMAN

Tops 1511	(M)	Rock 'N Roll With Scatman	1956	40.00	100.00
Craftsman 8036	(M)	Gone With Scatman	1960	16.00	40.00
Motown M-777L	(S)	Big Ben Sings	1973	6.00	15.00

CROWS, THE / THE HARPTONES

Roulette RE-114	(M)	The Crows & The Harptones (2 LPs)	1972	8.00	20.00

CRUDUP, ARTHUR "BIG BOY"

Fire 103	(M)	Mean Ol' Frisco	1960	300.0	750.00
Delmark DS-614	(S)	Look On Yonders Wall	1969	10.00	25.00
Delmark DS-621	(S)	Crudup's Mood	1969	10.00	25.00
RCA Victor LVP-573	(M)	Father Of Rock And Roll	1971	8.00	20.00
Trip BSP-7501	(E)	Mean Ol' Frisco	1975	6.00	15.00

(Trip 7501 is a reissue of Fire 103.)

CRUM, SIMON
Simon Crum is a pseudonym for Ferlin Husky.

Capitol T-1880	(M)	The Unpredictable Simon Crum	1963	30.00	75.00
Capitol ST-1880	(S)	The Unpredictable Simon Crum	1963	50.00	100.00

CRYAN' SHAMES, THE
The Cryan' Shames feature Isaac Guillory.

Columbia CL-2589	(M)	Sugar And Spice	1966	16.00	40.00
Columbia CS-9389	(E)	Sugar And Spice	1966	10.00	25.00

("Sugar & Spice," "Ben Franklin's Almanac," "We Could Be Happy" and "I Wanna Meet You" are rechanneled on this album.)

Columbia CL-9586	(M)	A Scratch In The Sky	1967	8.00	20.00
Columbia CS-9586	(S)	A Scratch In The Sky	1967	10.00	25.00

— Original Columbia albums above have red labels with "360 Sound" on the bottom.—

Columbia CS-9719	(S)	Synthesis	1969	6.00	15.00

CRYSTAL HAZE

(No label)	(S)	Crystal Haze	1977	30.00	75.00

CRYSTAL CIRCUS
Crystal Circus features the former lead singer of The Strawberry Alarm Clock.

All-American	(S)	Crystal Circus (Issued without a cover)	197?	300.00	500.00

(The printed labels read "Strawberry SAC" with a label that reads "Crystal Circus" pasted over it.)

CRYSTALS, THE
The Crystals were produced by Phil Spector.

Philles PHLP-4000	(DJ)	Twist Uptown (White label)	1962	500.00	1,000.00
Philles PHLP-4000	(M)	Twist Uptown (Blue label)	1962	200.00	400.00
Philles T-90722	(M)	Twist Uptown (Capitol Record Club)	1963	500.00	1,000.00
Philles DT-90722	(E)	Twist Uptown (Capitol Record Club)	1963	900.00	1,500.00
Philles PHLP-4001	(DJ)	He's A Rebel (White label)	1963	500.00	1,000.00
Philles PHLP-4001	(M)	He's A Rebel (Blue label)	1963	150.00	300.00
Philles PHLP-4003	(M)	The Greatest Hits (Blue label)	1963	150.00	500.00

Label & Catalog #		Title	Year	VG+	NM
CUBY & THE BLIZZARDS					
Philips PHS-600-307	(S)	Cuby And The Blizzards/Live	1969	8.00	20.00
Philips PHS-600-331	(S)	King Of The World	1970	8.00	20.00
CUMBERLAND THREE, THE					
The Cumberland Three features John Stewart, later of The Kingston Trio.					
Roulette R-25121	(M)	Folk Scene, U.S.A.	1960	10.00	25.00
Roulette SR-25121	(S)	Folk Scene, U.S.A.	1960	12.00	30.00
Roulette R-25132	(M)	Civil War Almanac/The Yankees	1960	10.00	25.00
Roulette SR-25132	(S)	Civil War Almanac/The Yankees	1960	12.00	30.00
Roulette R-25133	(M)	Civil War Almanac/The Rebels	1960	10.00	25.00
Roulette SR-25133	(S)	Civil War Almanac/The Rebels	1960	12.00	30.00
CUMMINGS, BOB					
Renner RC-100	(M)	Sounds Of Aviation	195?	10.00	25.00
CUMMINGS, BURTON					
Cummings was formerly a member of The Guess Who.					
Portrait PRQ-34261	(Q)	Burton Cummings	1976	6.00	15.00
CURLESS, DICK					
Tiffany 1016	(M)	Songs Of The Open Country	1958	40.00	100.00
Tiffany 1028	(M)	Singing Just For Fun	1959	40.00	100.00
Tiffany 1033	(M)	I Love To Tell A Story	1960	40.00	100.00
CURTIS, KEN					
Capitol T-2418	(M)	Gunsmoke's Festus	1965	8.00	20.00
Capitol ST-2418	(S)	Gunsmoke's Festus	1965	10.00	25.00
Dot DLP-3859	(M)	Gunsmoke's Festus Calls Out Ken Curtis	1967	8.00	20.00
Dot DLP-25859	(S)	Gunsmoke's Festus Calls Out Ken Curtis	1967	10.00	25.00
CURTIS, SONNY					
Curtis was formerly a member of The Crickets.					
Imperial LP-9276	(M)	Beatle Hits Flamenco Style	1964	16.00	40.00
Imperial LP-12276	(S)	Beatle Hits Flamenco Style	1964	20.00	50.00
Viva V-36012	(S)	The First Of Sonny Curtis	1968	10.00	25.00
Viva V-36021	(S)	The Sonny Curtis Style	1969	10.00	25.00
CYCLONES, THE: Refer to THE CHAMPS / THE CYCLONES					
CYKLE, THE					
Label 9-261	(S)	The Cykle	1969	150.00	300.00
CYMBAL, JOHNNY					
Kapp KL-1324	(M)	Mr. Bass Man	1963	16.00	40.00
Kapp KS-3324	(S)	Mr. Bass Man	1963	20.00	50.00
CYRKLE, THE					
Columbia CL-2544	(M)	Red Rubber Ball	1966	10.00	25.00
Columbia CS-9344	(S)	Red Rubber Ball	1966	16.00	40.00
Columbia CL-2632	(M)	Neon	1967	5.00	12.00
Columbia CS-9432	(S)	Neon	1967	8.00	20.00
Amsterdam AMS-12007	(S)	The Minx (Soundtrack)	1970	8.00	20.00

The first album from the "King of the Surf Guitar" (above) was originally issued on his own Deltone label as LPM-1001. After signing with Capitol it was reissued on the Deltone label but with a Capitol catalog number, T-1886 (DT-1886 for the Duophonic stereo release), where it made the charts in the first quarter of 1963. Summer Surf (below) was one of a series of surf related albums that Capitol issued with a special bonus single tucked inside a "pocket" on the front cover.

DADA
Atco SD-33-352   (S)   **Dada**   1970   6.00   15.00

DADDY COOL
Reprise RS-6471   (S)   **Daddy Who? Daddy Cool**   1971   6.00   15.00
Reprise MS-2088   (S)   **Teenage Heaven**   1972   6.00   15.00

DADDY DEWDROP
Sunflower SNF-5006   (S)   **Daddy Dewdrop**   1971   6.00   15.00

DAILEY, DON
Crown CLP-5314   (M)   **Surf Stompin'**   1963   10.00   25.00
Crown CST-314   (E)   **Surf Stompin'**   1963   4.00   10.00

DAISEY CHAIN
United Int. LPM-13001   (M)   **Straight Or Lame**   1967   6.00   15.00
United Int. LPS-13001   (M)   **Straight Or Lame**   1967   8.00   20.00

DAKUS, WES, & THE REBELS
Kapp KL-1536   (M)   **Wes Dakus' Rebels**   1967   5.00   12.00
Kapp KS-3536   (S)   **Wes Dakus' Rebels**   1967   6.00   15.00

DALE, DICK (& HIS DEL-TONES)
Refer to Jerry Cole.
Deltone LPM-1001   (M)   **Surfer's Choice**   1962   40.00   100.00
Deltone T-1886   (M)   **Surfer's Choice**   1962   12.00   30.00
Deltone DT-1886   (E)   **Surfer's Choice**   1962   10.00   25.00
Capitol T-1930   (M)   **King Of The Surf Guitar**   1963   16.00   40.00
Capitol ST-1930   (S)   **King Of The Surf Guitar**   1963   20.00   50.00
Capitol T-2002   (M)   **Checkered Flag**   1963   20.00   50.00
Capitol ST-2002   (S)   **Checkered Flag**   1963   30.00   75.00
Capitol T-2053   (M)   **Mr. Eliminator**   1964   20.00   50.00
Capitol ST-2053   (S)   **Mr. Eliminator**   1964   30.00   75.00
Capitol T-2111   (M)   **Summer Surf**   1964   20.00   50.00
Capitol ST-2111   (S)   **Summer Surf**   1964   24.00   60.00
           (Includes the bonus single "Racing Waves" / "Movin' Surf"
           by Jerry Cole in a pocket on the cover.)
Capitol T-2111   (M)   **Summer Surf** *(Without the single)*   1964   16.00   40.00
Capitol ST-2111   (S)   **Summer Surf** *(Without the single)*   1964   20.00   50.00
Capitol T-2293   (M)   **Rock Out/Live At Ciro's**   1965   40.00   100.00
Capitol ST-2293   (S)   **Rock Out/Live At Ciro's**   1965   60.00   150.00

DALE, DICK / THE HOLLYWOOD SURFERS
Dub Tone LP-1246   (M)   **The Surf Family**   1964   14.00   35.00

DALE, DICK / THE STOMPERS
Cloister CLP-6301   (M)   **Silver Sounds Of The Surf** *(Felt cover)*   1963   80.00   200.00

DALE & GRACE
Dale Houston and Grace Broussard.
Montel LP-100   (M)   **I'm Leaving It Up To You**   1964   30.00   75.00

DALEY, JIMMY
Decca DL-8429   (M)   **Rock Pretty Baby** *(Soundtrack)*   1958   40.00   100.00

DALLAS
(No label)   (S)   **Casualty Of Love**   1979   8.00   20.00

Label & Catalog #		Title	Year	VG+	NM

DALLAS, DEAN
Dean Dallas is a pseudonym for Pete Drake.

Cumberland MGC-29516	(M)	**Golden Country Hits**	195?	10.00	25.00

DAMIN EIH [DAMIN EIH & BROTHER CLARK]

Demelot 7310	(S)	**Never Mind**	1974	80.00	200.00

DAMITA JO
Damita Jo was formerly a member of Steve Gibson's Red Caps.

ABC-Paramount 378	(M)	**The Big Fifteen**	1961	12.00	30.00
ABC-Paramount S-378	(S)	**The Big Fifteen**	1961	16.00	40.00
Mercury MG-20642	(M)	**I'll Save The Last Dance For You**	1961	10.00	25.00
Mercury SR-60642	(S)	**I'll Save The Last Dance For You**	1961	12.00	30.00
Mercury MG-20734	(M)	**Sing A Country Song**	1962	10.00	25.00
Mercury SR-60734	(S)	**Sing A Country Song**	1962	12.00	30.00
Mercury MG-20703	(M)	**Damita Jo At The Diplomat**	1962	10.00	25.00
Mercury SR-60703	(S)	**Damita Jo At The Diplomat**	1962	12.00	30.00
Vee Jay LP-1137	(M)	**Damita Jo Sings**	1965	10.00	25.00
Vee Jay SR-1137	(S)	**Damita Jo Sings**	1965	20.00	50.00
Epic LN-24131	(M)	**If You Go Away**	1965	6.00	15.00
Epic BN-26131	(S)	**If You Go Away**	1965	8.00	20.00
Epic LN-24244	(M)	**This Is Damita Jo**	1967	6.00	15.00
Epic BN-26244	(S)	**This Is Damita Jo**	1967	8.00	20.00
Ranwood 8037	(S)	**Miss Damita Jo**	1968	6.00	15.00

DAMNATION

United Arts. UAS-6738	(S)	**The Damnation Of Adam Blessing**	1969	6.00	15.00
United Arts. UAS-6773	(S)	**The Second Damnation**	1970	5.00	12.00
United Arts. UAS-5533	(S)	**Which Is The Justice, Which Is The Thief**	1971	5.00	12.00

DAMON
Damon features Atlee Yeager.

Ankh 968	(M)	**Song Of A Gypsy** *(Gatefold cover)*	1970	2,000.00	3,000.00
Ankh 968	(M)	**Song Of A Gypsy** *(Regular cover)*	1970	1,000.00	1,500.00

DAMONE, VIC

Mercury MG-25028 (10")	(M)	**Vic Damone**	1950	16.00	40.00
Mercury MG-25029 (10")	(M)	**Vic Damone**	1950	16.00	40.00
Mercury MG-25045 (10")	(M)	**Vic Damone**	1950	16.00	40.00
Mercury MG-25054 (10")	(M)	**Song Hits**	1950	16.00	40.00
Mercury MG-25092 (10")	(M)	**Christmas Favorites**	1951	16.00	40.00
Mercury MG-25100 (10")	(M)	**Vic Damone And Others**	1952	16.00	40.00
Mercury MG-25131 (10")	(M)	**The Night Has A Thousand Eyes**	1952	16.00	40.00
Mercury MG-25132 (10")	(M)	**Vocals By Vic**	1952	16.00	40.00
Mercury MG-25133 (10")	(M)	**April In Paris**	1952	16.00	40.00
Mercury MG-25156 (10")	(M)	**Vic Damone**	1952	16.00	40.00
Mercury MG-25202 (10")	(M)	**Athena** *(Soundtrack)*	1954	80.00	200.00
MGM E-86 (10")	(M)	**Rich, Young And Pretty** *(Soundtrack)*	1951	40.00	100.00
MGM E-3153	(M)	**Deep In My Heart** *(Soundtrack. Boxed set)*	1954	40.00	100.00
MGM E-3153	(M)	**Deep In My Heart** *(Soundtrack)*	1955	20.00	50.00
MGM E-3236	(M)	**Rich, Young And Pretty** *(Soundtrack)*	1955	20.00	50.00
Mercury MG-20163	(M)	**Yours For A Song**	1957	10.00	25.00
Mercury MG-20193	(M)	**The Voice Of Vic Damone**	1957	10.00	25.00
Mercury MG-25-0194	(M)	**My Favorites**	1957	10.00	25.00
Columbia CL-900	(M)	**That Towering Feeling!**	1956	10.00	25.00
Columbia CL-950	(M)	**The Stingiest Man In Town** *(Soundtrack)*	1956	20.00	50.00
Columbia CL-1113	(M)	**The Gift Of Love** *(Soundtrack)*	1958	40.00	100.00
Columbia CL-1219	(M)	**Closer Than A Kiss**	1959	6.00	15.00
Columbia CS-8019	(S)	**Closer Than A Kiss**	1959	8.00	20.00
Columbia CL-1246	(M)	**Angela Mia**	1959	6.00	15.00
Columbia CS-8046	(S)	**Angela Mia**	1959	8.00	20.00
Columbia CL-1369	(M)	**This Game Of Love**	1959	6.00	15.00
Columbia CS-8169	(S)	**This Game Of Love**	1959	8.00	20.00
Columbia CL-1573	(M)	**On The Swingin' Side**	1961	6.00	15.00
Columbia CS-8373	(S)	**On The Swingin' Side**	1961	8.00	20.00

— Original Columbia albums above have three white "eye" logos on each side of the spindle hole. —

Capitol T-1646	(M)	**Linger Awhile With Vic Damone**	1962	5.00	12.00
Capitol ST-1646	(S)	**Linger Awhile With Vic Damone**	1962	6.00	15.00

Label & Catalog #		Title	Year	VG+	NM
Capitol T-1691	(M)	Strange Enchantment	1962	5.00	12.00
Capitol ST-1691	(S)	Strange Enchantment	1962	6.00	15.00
Capitol T-1748	(M)	The Lively Ones	1962	5.00	12.00
Capitol ST-1748	(S)	The Lively Ones	1962	6.00	15.00
Capitol T-1811	(M)	My Baby Loves To Swing	1963	5.00	12.00
Capitol ST-1811	(S)	My Baby Loves To Swing	1963	6.00	15.00
Capitol T-1944	(M)	The Liveliest	1963	5.00	12.00
Capitol ST-1944	(S)	The Liveliest	1963	6.00	15.00
Capitol T-2123	(M)	On The Street Where You Live	1964	5.00	12.00
Capitol ST-2123	(S)	On The Street Where You Live	1964	6.00	15.00
RCA Victor LOC-1132	(M)	Arrivederci Baby (Soundtrack)	1966	8.00	20.00
RCA Victor LSO-1132	(S)	Arrivederci Baby (Soundtrack)	1966	10.00	25.00
RCA Victor LPM-3671	(M)	Stay With Me	1966	5.00	12.00
RCA Victor LSP-3671	(S)	Stay With Me	1966	6.00	15.00
RCA Victor LPM-3765	(M)	On The South Side Of Chicago	1967	6.00	15.00
RCA Victor LSP-3765	(S)	On The South Side Of Chicago	1967	6.00	15.00
RCA Victor LPM-3916	(M)	The Damone Type Of Thing	1968	6.00	15.00
RCA Victor LSP-3916	(S)	The Damone Type Of Thing	1968	6.00	15.00
RCA Victor LSP-3984	(S)	Why Can't I Walk Away	1968	6.00	15.00

DAN & DALE

| Tifton M-8002 | (M) | Batman And Robin | 1966 | 12.00 | 30.00 |
| Tifton S-78002 | (S) | Batman And Robin | 1966 | 16.00 | 40.00 |

DANE, BARBARA: Refer to GOLDMINE'S PRICE GUIDE TO COLLECTIBLE JAZZ ALBUMS

DANIELS, CHARLIE

Epic AS-273	(DJ)	Everything You Always Wanted To Hear	1976	8.00	20.00
Epic HE-44365	(S)	Fire On The Mountain (Half-speed master)	1982	8.00	25.00
Epic HE-45751	(S)	Million Mile Reflections (Half-speed master)	1982	8.00	25.00
Mobile Fidelity MFSL-176	(S)	Million Mile Reflections	1982	5.00	15.00

DANTE, RON
Dante was the mastermind behind The Detergents; The Archies; Mercy.

Kirshner KES-106	(S)	Ron Dante Brings You Up	1970	10.00	25.00
		(Includes bonus photo)			
Kirshner KES-106	(S)	Ron Dante Brings You Up (Without photo)	1970	6.00	15.00

DANTE & THE EVERGREENS

| Madison MA-1002 | (M) | Dante & The Evergreens | 1961 | 200.00 | 400.00 |

DARIN, BOBBY

Atco 22-102	(M)	Bobby Darin	1958	40.00	100.00
Atco 33-104	(M)	That's All	1959	20.00	50.00
Atco SD-33-104	(S)	That's All	1959	40.00	100.00
Atco 33-115	(M)	This Is Darin	1960	20.00	50.00
Atco SD-33-115	(S)	This Is Darin	1960	30.00	75.00
Atco 33-122	(M)	Darin At The Copa	1960	20.00	50.00
Atco SD-33-122	(S)	Darin At The Copa	1961	30.00	75.00
Atco SP-1001	(M)	For Teenagers Only (Gatefold cover)	1960	60.00	150.00
		(Includes a paper insert and a fold-open poster.)			
Atco 33-125	(M)	The 25th Of December	1960	20.00	50.00
Atco SD-33-125	(S)	The 25th Of December	1960	30.00	75.00
Colpix CP-507	(M)	Pepe (Soundtrack)	1960	16.00	40.00
Colpix SCP-507	(S)	Pepe (Soundtrack)	1960	20.00	50.00
Atco 33-126	(M)	Two Of A Kind	1961	16.00	40.00
Atco SD-33-126	(S)	Two Of A Kind	1961	20.00	50.00
Atco 33-131	(M)	The Bobby Darin Story	1961	16.00	40.00
Atco SD-33-131	(P)	The Bobby Darin Story	1961	20.00	50.00
Atco 33-134	(M)	Love Swings	1961	16.00	40.00
Atco SD-33-134	(S)	Love Swings	1961	20.00	50.00
		— Original Atco albums above have yellow labels with a harp on top. —			
Atco 22-102	(M)	Bobby Darin	1961	12.00	30.00
Atco 33-104	(M)	That's All	1961	8.00	20.00
Atco SD-33-104	(S)	That's All	1961	10.00	25.00
Atco 33-115	(M)	This Is Darin	1961	8.00	20.00
Atco SD-33-115	(S)	This Is Darin	1961	10.00	25.00
Atco 33-122	(M)	Darin At The Copa	1961	8.00	20.00
Atco 33-122	(S)	Darin At The Copa	1961	10.00	25.00

Label & Catalog #		Title	Year	VG+	NM
Atco 33-125	(M)	The 25th Of December	1961	8.00	20.00
Atco SD-33-125	(S)	The 25th Of December	1961	10.00	25.00
Atco 33-126	(M)	Two Of A Kind	1961	8.00	20.00
Atco SD-33-126	(S)	Two Of A Kind	1961	10.00	25.00
Atco 33-131	(M)	The Bobby Darin Story	1961	8.00	20.00
Atco SD-33-131	(S)	The Bobby Darin Story	1961	10.00	25.00
Atco 33-134	(M)	Love Swings	1961	8.00	20.00
Atco SD-33-134	(S)	Love Swings	1961	10.00	25.00

— Atco albums above have gold & gray labels; stereo albums have purple & brown labels.—

Label & Catalog #		Title	Year	VG+	NM
Atco 33-138	(M)	Twist With Bobby Darin	1961	10.00	25.00
Atco SD-33-138	(S)	Twist With Bobby Darin	1961	12.00	30.00
Atco 33-140	(M)	Bobby Darin Sings Ray Charles	1962	10.00	25.00
Atco SD-33-140	(S)	Bobby Darin Sings Ray Charles	1962	12.00	30.00
Dot DLP-9011	(M)	State Fair (Soundtrack)	1962	12.00	30.00
Dot DLP-25011	(S)	State Fair (Soundtrack)	1962	16.00	40.00
Atco 33-146	(M)	Things And Other Things	1962	10.00	25.00
Atco SD-33-146	(S)	Things And Other Things	1962	12.00	30.00
Atco 33-124	(M)	It's You Or No One	1963	10.00	25.00
Atco SD-33-124	(S)	It's You Or No One	1963	12.00	30.00
Atco 33-167	(M)	Winners	1964	10.00	25.00
Atco SD-33-167	(S)	Winners	1964	12.00	30.00
Capitol T-1791	(M)	Oh! Look At Me Now	1962	10.00	25.00
Capitol ST-1791	(S)	Oh! Look At Me Now	1962	12.00	30.00
Capitol T-1826	(M)	Earthy	1963	10.00	25.00
Capitol ST-1826	(S)	Earthy	1963	12.00	30.00
Capitol T-1866	(M)	You're The Reason I'm Living	1963	10.00	25.00
Capitol ST-1866	(S)	You're The Reason I'm Living	1963	12.00	30.00
Capitol T-1942	(M)	18 Yellow Roses	1963	10.00	25.00
Capitol ST-1942	(S)	18 Yellow Roses	1963	12.00	30.00
Capitol T-2007	(M)	Golden Folk Hits	1963	10.00	25.00
Capitol ST-2007	(S)	Golden Folk Hits	1963	12.00	30.00
Capitol T-2194	(M)	From "Hello Dolly" To "Goodbye Charlie"	1964	10.00	25.00
Capitol ST-2194	(S)	From "Hello Dolly" To "Goodbye Charlie"	1964	12.00	30.00
Decca DL-9119	(M)	The Lively Set (Soundtrack)	1964	14.00	35.00
Decca DL7-9119	(S)	The Lively Set (Soundtrack)	1964	20.00	50.00
Capitol T-2322	(M)	Venice Blue	1965	10.00	25.00
Capitol ST-2322	(S)	Venice Blue	1965	12.00	30.00
Capitol T-2571	(M)	The Best Of Bobby Darin	1966	8.00	20.00
Capitol ST-2571	(S)	The Best Of Bobby Darin	1966	10.00	25.00
Clarion 603	(M)	Clementine	1964	6.00	15.00
Clarion 603	(S)	Clementine	1964	8.00	20.00
Atlantic 8121	(M)	The Shadow Of Your Smile	1966	8.00	20.00
Atlantic SD-8121	(S)	The Shadow Of Your Smile	1966	10.00	25.00
Atlantic 8126	(M)	In A Broadway Bag	1966	8.00	20.00
Atlantic SD-8126	(S)	In A Broadway Bag	1966	10.00	25.00
Atlantic 8135	(M)	If I Were A Carpenter	1966	10.00	25.00
Atlantic SD-8135	(S)	If I Were A Carpenter	1966	20.00	50.00
Atlantic 8142	(M)	Inside Out	1967	10.00	25.00
Atlantic SD-8142	(S)	Inside Out	1967	12.00	30.00
Atlantic 8154	(M)	Bobby Darin Sings Doctor Doolittle	1967	8.00	20.00
Atlantic SD-8154	(S)	Bobby Darin Sings Doctor Doolittle	1967	10.00	25.00
Direction 1936	(S)	Born Walden Robert Cassotto	1968	10.00	25.00
Direction 1937	(S)	Commitment	1969	10.00	25.00
Motown M-753L	(S)	Bobby Darin	1972	8.00	20.00

DARIUS
| Chartmaker 1102 | (S) | Darius | 1969 | 100.00 | 250.00 |

DARK SHADOWS
| Rockadelic LP-2.5 | (S) | Dark Shadows | 198? | 40.00 | 100.00 |

(*"Dark Shadows" was recorded by the group Cold Sun. An acetate of that album exists. Due to technical reasons, Rockadelic had to release this credited to Dark Shadows.*)

DARLING, DENVER
| Audio Lab AL-107 | (M) | Denver Darling | 195? | 40.00 | 100.00 |

Label & Catalog #		Title	Year	VG+	NM
DARLING, ERIC					
Darling was a member of The Tarriers; The Rooftop Singers.					
Elektra EKL-154	(M)	**Folksongs**	*196?*	8.00	20.00
Vanguard VRS-9099	(M)	**True Religion**	*1961*	6.00	15.00
Vanguard VSD-2099	(S)	**True Religion**	*1961*	8.00	20.00
Vanguard VRS-9131	(M)	**Train Time**	*1962*	6.00	15.00
Vanguard VSD-2131	(S)	**Train Time**	*1962*	8.00	20.00
DARREN, JAMES					
Colpix CLP-406	(M)	**James Darren**	*1960*	20.00	50.00
Colpix CLP-406	(M)	**James Darren** (Green vinyl)	*1960*	60.00	150.00
Colpix CLP-418	(M)	**Gidget Goes Hawaiian**	*1961*	14.00	35.00
Colpix SCP-418	(S)	**Gidget Goes Hawaiian**	*1961*	20.00	50.00
Colpix CLP-424	(M)	**James Darren Sings For All Sizes**	*1962*	14.00	35.00
Colpix SCP-424	(S)	**James Darren Sings For All Sizes**	*1962*	20.00	50.00
Colpix CLP-428	(M)	**Love Among The Young**	*1962*	14.00	35.00
Colpix SCP-428	(S)	**Love Among The Young**	*1962*	20.00	50.00
Colpix CLP-454	(M)	**Bye Bye Birdie**	*1963*	14.00	35.00
Colpix SCP-454	(S)	**Bye Bye Birdie**	*1963*	20.00	50.00
Decca DL-9119	(M)	**The Lively Set** (Soundtrack)	*1964*	14.00	35.00
Decca DL7-9119	(S)	**The Lively Set** (Soundtrack)	*1964*	20.00	50.00
Warner Bros. W-1688	(M)	**All**	*1964*	5.00	12.00
Warner Bros. WS-1688	(S)	**All**	*1964*	6.00	15.00
Kirshner KES-115	(S)	**Mammy Blue**	*1971*	6.00	15.00
Kirshner KES-116	(S)	**Love Songs From The Movies**	*1972*	6.00	15.00
DARTELLS, THE					
Dot DLP-3522	(M)	**Hot Pastrami**	*1963*	10.00	25.00
Dot DLP-25522	(S)	**Hot Pastrami**	*1963*	14.00	35.00
DARTS, THE					
Del-Fi DF-1244	(M)	**Hollywood Drag**	*1963*	8.00	20.00
Del-Fi DFST-1244	(S)	**Hollywood Drag**	*1963*	12.00	30.00
DASHIEL, BUD, & THE KINSMEN					
Refer to Bud & Travis.					
Warner Bros. W-1429	(M)	**Folk Music In A Contemporary Manner**	*1961*	8.00	20.00
Warner Bros. WS-1429	(S)	**Folk Music In A Contemporary Manner**	*1961*	12.00	30.00
Warner Bros. W-1432	(M)	**Live Concert Extraordinary-Bud Dashiell & The Kinsmen Sing Everybody's Hits**	*1962*	8.00	20.00
Warner Bros. WS-1432	(S)	**Live Concert Extraordinary-Bud Dashiell & The Kinsmen Sing Everybody's Hits**	*1962*	12.00	30.00
Warner Bros. WS-1731	(S)	**I Think It's Gonna Rain Today**	*1968*	8.00	20.00
DAUGHTERS OF ALBION, THE					
Fontana SRF-68586	(S)	**The Daughters Of Albion** (With inserts)	*1968*	6.00	15.00
DAVE DEE, DOZY, BEAKY, MICK & TICH					
Fontana MGF-27567	(M)	**Greatest Hits**	*1967*	12.00	30.00
Fontana SRF-67567	(S)	**Greatest Hits**	*1967*	16.00	40.00
		("Bend It" and "Hold Tight" are rechanneled on this album.)			
Imperial LP-12402	(S)	**Time To Take Off**	*1968*	16.00	40.00
		("Zabadak" is rechanneled on this album.)			
DAVEY & THE BADMEN					
Gothic WA-63054	(M)	**Wanted**	*1963*	80.00	200.00
DAVID, THE					
V.M.C. 124	(S)	**Another Day, Another Lifetime**	*1968*	30.00	75.00
DAVID & JONATHAN					
David & Jonathan were Rogers Cook and Greenaway.					
Capitol T-2473	(M)	**Michelle**	*1966*	6.00	15.00
Capitol ST-2473	(S)	**Michelle**	*1966*	8.00	20.00
20th Century-Fox 3182	(M)	**Modesty Blaise** (Soundtrack)	*1966*	10.00	25.00
20th Century-Fox S-4182	(S)	**Modesty Blaise** (Soundtrack)	*1966*	12.00	30.00
DAVIS, BETTE					
Citadel CT-7030	(M)	**Miss Bette Davis Sings!**	*196?*	20.00	50.00

Label & Catalog #		Title	Year	VG+	NM
DAVIS, REV. GARY					
Bluesvile BVLP-1015	(M)	Harlem Street Singer	1961	16.00	40.00
Bluesvile BVLP-1032	(M)	Have A Little Faith	1961	16.00	40.00
Bluesvile BVLP-1049	(M)	Say No To The Devil	1961	16.00	40.00
Folklore FRLP-14028	(M)	Pure Religion	1964	8.00	20.00
Folklore FRST-14028	(S)	Pure Religion	1964	10.00	25.00
		(Folklore 14028 is a reissue of Bluesville 1015.)			
Folklore FRLP-14033	(M)	Guitar And Banjo	1964	8.00	20.00
Folklore FRST-14033	(S)	Guitar And Banjo	1964	10.00	25.00
Prestige PRST-7725	(S)	Blues Guitar And Banjo Of Rev. Gary Davis	1969	6.00	15.00
Prestige PRST-7805	(S)	Pure Religion	1969	6.00	15.00
		(Prestige 7805 is a reissue of Bluesville 1015.)			
DAVIS, JESSE ED					
Atco SD-33-346	(S)	Jesse Ed Davis	1970	6.00	15.00
Atco SD-33-382	(S)	Ululu	1972	6.00	15.00
Epic KE-32133	(S)	Keep On Comin'	1973	5.00	12.00
DAVIS, JIMMIE					
Decca DL-5500 (10")	(M)	Jimmie Davis	1954	20.00	50.00
Decca DL-8174	(M)	Jimmie Davis	1955	12.00	30.00
Decca DL-8572	(M)	Hymn Time With The Anita Kerr Singers	1957	12.00	30.00
Decca DL-8896	(M)	You Are My Sunshine	1959	12.00	30.00
Decca DL-8953	(M)	Suppertime	1960	12.00	30.00
DAVIS, JOHNNY					
King 626	(M)	Johnny "Scat" Davis	1959	20.00	50.00
DAVIS, LINK					
Mercury SR-61243	(S)	Cajun Crawdaddy	1969	10.00	25.00
DAVIS, SAMMY, Jr.					
Refer to The Reprise Repertory Theatre.					
Decca DL-8118	(M)	Starring Sammy Davis, Jr.	1955	12.00	30.00
Decca DL-8170	(M)	Just For Lovers	1955	12.00	30.00
Decca DL-9032	(M)	Mr. Wonderful *(Soundtrack)*	1956	16.00	40.00
Decca DL-8351	(M)	Here's Looking At You	1956	10.00	25.00
Decca DL-8486	(M)	Sammy Swings	1957	10.00	25.00
Decca DL-8641	(M)	It's All Over But The Swingin'	1957	10.00	25.00
Decca DL-8676	(M)	Mood To Be Wooed	1958	10.00	25.00
Decca DL-8779	(M)	All The Way And Then Some	1958	10.00	25.00
Decca DL-8841	(M)	Sammy Davis, Jr. At Town Hall	1959	8.00	20.00
Decca DL-78841	(S)	Sammy Davis, Jr. At Town Hall	1959	12.00	30.00
Decca DL-8854	(M)	Porgy And Bess	1959	8.00	20.00
Decca DL-78854	(S)	Porgy And Bess	1959	12.00	30.00
Decca DL-8921	(M)	Sammy Awards	1960	8.00	20.00
Decca DL-78921	(S)	Sammy Awards	1960	12.00	30.00
Decca DL-8981	(M)	I Got A Right To Swing	1960	8.00	20.00
Decca DL-78981	(S)	I Got A Right To Swing	1960	12.00	30.00
		—Original Decca albums above have black & silver labels.—			
Decca DL-4153	(M)	Mr. Entertainment	1961	6.00	15.00
Decca DL-74153	(S)	Mr. Entertainment	1961	8.00	20.00
Decca DL-4381	(M)	Forget-Me-Nots For First Nighters	1963	6.00	15.00
Decca DL-74381	(S)	Forget-Me-Nots For First Nighters	1963	8.00	20.00
Decca DL-4582	(M)	Try A Little Tenderness	1965	5.00	12.00
Decca DL-74582	(S)	Try A Little Tenderness	1965	6.00	15.00
Decca DXB-192	(M)	The Best Of Sammy Davis, Jr. *(2 LPs)*	1966	6.00	15.00
Decca DXSB-192	(S)	The Best Of Sammy Davis, Jr. *(2 LPs)*	1966	8.00	20.00
Decca DL-71502	(S)	Sweet Charity *(Soundtrack)*	1969	8.00	20.00
Reprise R-2003	(M)	The Wham Of Sam	1961	8.00	20.00
Reprise RS-2003	(S)	The Wham Of Sam	1961	6.00	15.00
Reprise R-2010	(M)	Belts The Best Of Broadway	1962	8.00	20.00
Reprise RS-2010	(S)	Belts The Best Of Broadway	1962	6.00	15.00
Reprise R-6033	(M)	All Star Spectacular	1962	8.00	20.00
Reprise R9-6033	(S)	All Star Spectacular	1962	6.00	15.00
Reprise R-6051	(M)	What Kind Of Fool Am I?	1962	8.00	20.00
Reprise R9-6051	(S)	What Kind Of Fool Am I?	1962	6.00	15.00
Reprise R-6063	(M)	At The Cocoanut Grove *(2 LPs)*	1963	10.00	25.00
Reprise R9-6063	(S)	At The Cocoanut Grove *(2 LPs)*	1963	8.00	20.00

Label & Catalog #		Title	Year	VG+	NM
Reprise R-6082	(M)	As Long As She Needs Me	1963	8.00	20.00
Reprise R9-6082	(S)	As Long As She Needs Me	1963	6.00	15.00
United Arts. UAL-4111	(M)	Johnny Cool (Soundtrack)	1963	10.00	25.00
United Arts. UAS-5111	(S)	Johnny Cool (Soundtrack)	1963	12.00	30.00
Capitol VAS-2124	(M)	Golden Boy (Soundtrack)	1964	10.00	25.00
Capitol SVAS-2124	(S)	Golden Boy (Soundtrack)	1964	12.00	30.00
Reprise R-6095	(M)	Salutes The Stars Of The London Palladium	1964	6.00	15.00
Reprise R9-6095	(S)	Salutes The Stars Of The London Palladium	1964	5.00	12.00
Reprise R-6096	(M)	A Treasury Of Golden Hits	1963	6.00	15.00
Reprise R9-6096	(S)	A Treasury Of Golden Hits	1963	5.00	12.00
Reprise R-6114	(M)	The Shelter Of Your Arms	1964	6.00	15.00
Reprise RS-6114	(S)	The Shelter Of Your Arms	1964	5.00	12.00
Reprise R-6126	(M)	California Suite	1964	6.00	15.00
Reprise RS-6126	(S)	California Suite	1964	5.00	12.00
Reprise R-6131	(M)	The Big Ones For Young Lovers	1964	6.00	15.00
Reprise RS-6131	(S)	The Big Ones For Young Lovers	1964	5.00	12.00
Reprise R-6144	(M)	When The Feeling Hits You	1965	6.00	15.00
Reprise RS-6144	(S)	When The Feeling Hits You	1965	5.00	12.00
Reprise R-6159	(M)	If I Ruled The World	1965	6.00	15.00
Reprise RS-6159	(S)	If I Ruled The World	1965	5.00	12.00
Reprise R-6164	(M)	The Nat King Cole Songbook	1965	6.00	15.00
Reprise RS-6164	(S)	The Nat King Cole Songbook	1965	5.00	12.00
Reprise R-6169	(M)	Sammy's Back On Broadway	1965	6.00	15.00
Reprise RS-6169	(S)	Sammy's Back On Broadway	1965	5.00	12.00
Reprise R-6180	(M)	A Man Called Adam (Soundtrack)	1966	10.00	25.00
Reprise RS-6180	(S)	A Man Called Adam (Soundtrack)	1966	12.00	30.00
— Original Reprise albums above have pink, gold & green labels.—					
Reprise RS-6291	(S)	Sammy Davis, Jr.'s Greatest Hits	1968	4.00	10.00
Reprise RS-6324	(S)	I've Gotta Be Me	1969	4.00	10.00
United Arts. UAS-5187	(S)	Salt And Pepper (Soundtrack)	1968	6.00	15.00

DAVIS, JR., SAMMY, & CARMEN McRAE

Label & Catalog #		Title	Year	VG+	NM
Decca DL-8490	(M)	Boy Meets Girl	1957	12.00	30.00

DAVIS, SKEETER

Ms. Davis also recorded with Porter Wagoner.

Label & Catalog #		Title	Year	VG+	NM
RCA Victor LPM-2197	(M)	I'll Sing You A Song And Harmonize, Too	1960	12.00	30.00
RCA Victor LSP-2197	(S)	I'll Sing You A Song And Harmonize, Too	1960	16.00	40.00
RCA Victor LPM-2327	(M)	Here's The Answer	1961	12.00	30.00
RCA Victor LSP-2327	(S)	Here's The Answer	1961	16.00	40.00
RCA Victor LPM-2699	(M)	The End Of The World	1962	12.00	30.00
RCA Victor LSP-2699	(S)	The End Of The World	1962	16.00	40.00
RCA Victor LPM-2736	(M)	Cloudy, With Occasional Tears	1963	12.00	30.00
RCA Victor LSP-2736	(S)	Cloudy, With Occasional Tears	1963	16.00	40.00
— Original RCA mono albums above have "Long Play" on the bottom of the label;					
stereo albums have "Living Stereo" on the bottom.—					
RCA Victor LPM-2980	(M)	Let Me Get Close To You	1964	10.00	25.00
RCA Victor LSP-2980	(S)	Let Me Get Close To You	1964	12.00	30.00
RCA Victor LPM-3374	(M)	The Best Of Skeeter Davis	1965	10.00	25.00
RCA Victor LSP-3374	(S)	The Best Of Skeeter Davis	1965	12.00	30.00
RCA Victor LPM-3382	(M)	Written By The Stars	1965	10.00	25.00
RCA Victor LSP-3382	(S)	Written By The Stars	1965	12.00	30.00
RCA Victor LPM-3463	(M)	Skeeter Sings Standards	1965	10.00	25.00
RCA Victor LSP-3463	(S)	Skeeter Sings Standards	1965	12.00	30.00
RCA Victor LPM-3567	(M)	Singin' In The Summer Sun	1966	10.00	25.00
RCA Victor LSP-3567	(S)	Singin' In The Summer Sun	1966	12.00	30.00
RCA Victor LPM-3667	(M)	My Heart's In The Country	1966	10.00	25.00
RCA Victor LSP-3667	(S)	My Heart's In The Country	1966	12.00	30.00
RCA Victor LPM-3763	(M)	Hand In Hand With Jesus	1967	14.00	35.00
RCA Victor LSP-3763	(S)	Hand In Hand With Jesus	1967	10.00	25.00
RCA Victor LPM-3790	(M)	Skeeter Davis Sings Buddy Holly	1967	20.00	50.00
RCA Victor LSP-3790	(S)	Skeeter Davis Sings Buddy Holly	1967	16.00	40.00
RCA Victor LPM-3876	(M)	What Does It Take	1967	14.00	35.00
RCA Victor LSP-3876	(S)	What Does It Take	1967	10.00	25.00
RCA Victor LPM-3960	(M)	Why So Lonely?	1968	20.00	50.00
RCA Victor LSP-3960	(S)	Why So Lonely?	1968	10.00	25.00
— Original RCA albums above have black labels.—					
Camden CAL-899	(M)	Blueberry Hill & Other Favorites	1965	5.00	12.00
Camden CAS-899	(S)	Blueberry Hill & Other Favorites	1965	6.00	15.00

Label & Catalog #		Title	Year	VG+	NM

DAVIS, SPENCER [THE SPENCER DAVIS GROUP]
Steve Winwood is featured on each album except 6652.

United Arts. UAL-3578	(M)	Gimme Some Lovin'	1967	20.00	50.00
United Arts. UAS-6578	(E)	Gimme Some Lovin'	1967	16.00	40.00
United Arts. UAL-3589	(M)	I'm A Man	1967	16.00	40.00
United Arts. UAS-6589	(P)	I'm A Man	1967	20.00	50.00
United Arts. UAS-6641	(P)	Spencer Davis' Greatest Hits	1968	8.00	20.00
United Arts. UAS-6652	(S)	With Their New Face On	1968	6.00	15.00
United Arts. UAS-6691	(S)	Heavies	1969	6.00	15.00

DAVIS, TYRONE

Daker DK-9005	(S)	Can I Change My Mind	1969	8.00	20.00
Daker DK-9027	(S)	Turn Back The Hands Of Time	1970	8.00	20.00
Daker DK-76901	(S)	I Had It All The Time	1972	8.00	20.00
Daker DK-76902	(S)	Greatest Hits	1972	6.00	15.00
Daker DK-76904	(S)	Without You In My Life	1973	6.00	15.00
Daker DK-76909	(S)	It's All In the Game	1974	6.00	15.00
Daker DK-76915	(S)	Homewrecker	1975	6.00	15.00
Daker DK-76918	(S)	Turning Point	1976	6.00	15.00

DAWE, TIM
Dawe was formerly a member of Iron Butterfly.

| Straight STS-1058 | (S) | Penrod | 1969 | 20.00 | 50.00 |
| Warner Bros. WS-1841 | (S) | Penrod | 1970 | 8.00 | 20.00 |

DAY, BOBBY
Bobby Day is a pseudonym for Bobby Byrd.

| Class LP-5002 | (M) | Rockin' With Robin | 1959 | 100.00 | 250.00 |
| Rendezvous M-1312 | (M) | Rockin' With Robin | 196? | 40.00 | 100.00 |

(Rendezvous 1312 is a reissue of Class 5002.)

DAY, DORIS
Ms. Day also recorded with Frank Sinatra.

Columbia CL-6071 (10")	(M)	You're My Thrill	1949	20.00	50.00
Columbia CL-6106 (10")	(M)	Young Man With A Horn (Soundtrack)	1950	40.00	100.00
Columbia CL-6149 (10")	(M)	Tea For Two (Soundtrack)	1950	40.00	100.00
Columbia CL-6168 (10")	(M)	Lullaby Of Broadway (Soundtrack)	1951	40.00	100.00
Columbia CL-6186 (10")	(M)	On Moonlight Bay (Soundtrack)	1951	40.00	100.00
Columbia CL-6198 (10")	(M)	I'll See You In My Dreams (Soundtrack)	1951	40.00	100.00
Columbia CL-6248 (10")	(M)	By The Light Of The Silvery Moon (Sdtk)	1953	40.00	100.00
Columbia CL-6273 (10")	(M)	Calamity Jane (Soundtrack)	1953	40.00	100.00
Columbia CL-2518 (10")	(M)	Lights, Cameras, Action	195?	12.00	30.00
Columbia CL-2530 (10")	(M)	Boys And Girls Together	195?	12.00	30.00
Columbia CL-2534 (10")	(M)	Hot Canaries (With Peggy Lee)	195?	12.00	30.00
Columbia CL-582	(M)	Young Man With A Horn	1954	10.00	25.00
Columbia CL-624	(M)	Day Dreams	1955	10.00	25.00
Columbia CL-710	(M)	Love Me Or Leave Me (Soundtrack)	1955	16.00	40.00
Columbia CL-749	(M)	Day In Hollywood	1955	10.00	25.00

— Original Columbia albums above have "Long Playing" on the bottom of the label. —

Columbia CL-942	(M)	Day By Day	1957	10.00	25.00
Columbia OL-5210	(M)	The Pajama Game (Soundtrack)	1957	10.00	25.00
Columbia CL-1210	(M)	Doris Day's Greatest Hits	1958	10.00	25.00
Columbia C2L-5	(M)	Hooray For Hollywood (2 LPs)	1959	12.00	30.00
Columbia C2S-5	(S)	Hooray For Hollywood (2 LPs)	1959	16.00	40.00
Columbia CL-1266	(M)	Hooray For Hollywood, Volume 1	1959	6.00	15.00
Columbia CS-8066	(S)	Hooray For Hollywood, Volume 1	1959	8.00	20.00
Columbia CL-1267	(M)	Hooray For Hollywood, Volume 2	1959	6.00	15.00
Columbia CS-8067	(S)	Hooray For Hollywood, Volume 2	1959	8.00	20.00
Columbia CL-1278	(M)	Cuttin' Capers	1959	6.00	15.00
Columbia CS-8078	(S)	Cuttin' Capers	1959	8.00	20.00
Columbia CL-1289	(M)	Day By Night	1959	6.00	15.00
Columbia CS-8089	(S)	Day By Night	1959	8.00	20.00
Columbia DD-1	(M)	Listen To Day	1960	6.00	15.00
Columbia DDS-1	(S)	Listen To Day	1960	8.00	20.00
Columbia CL-1434	(M)	What Every Girl Should Know	1960	6.00	15.00
Columbia CS-8234	(S)	What Every Girl Should Know	1960	8.00	20.00
Columbia CL-1461	(M)	Show Time	1960	6.00	15.00
Columbia CS-8261	(S)	Show Time	1960	8.00	20.00

For many, Ms. Day will always be the effervescently cute actress with the almost chipmunk like smile that made many mundane movies for the family in the '50s and '60s. But, as Day In Hollywood illustrates, she was originally discovered as a big band singer because she was a beautiful woman with a pleasing set of pipes.

Label & Catalog #		Title	Year	VG+	NM
Columbia CL-1660	(M)	I Have Dreamed	1961	6.00	15.00
Columbia CS-8460	(S)	I Have Dreamed	1961	8.00	20.00
Columbia OL-5860	(M)	Jumbo (Soundtrack)	1962	6.00	15.00
Columbia OS-2260	(S)	Jumbo (Soundtrack)	1962	8.00	20.00
Columbia CL-1752	(M)	Duet (With Andre Previn)	1962	6.00	15.00
Columbia CS-8552	(S)	Duet (With Andre Previn)	1962	8.00	20.00
— Original Columbia albums above have three white "eye" logos on each side of the spindle hole.—					
Columbia CL-1904	(M)	You'll Never Walk Alone	1962	5.00	12.00
Columbia CS-8704	(S)	You'll Never Walk Alone	1962	6.00	15.00
Columbia OL-5960	(M)	Annie Get Your Gun (Soundtrack)	1963	6.00	15.00
Columbia OS-2360	(S)	Annie Get Your Gun (Soundtrack)	1963	8.00	20.00
Columbia CL-1973	(M)	Love Me Or Leave Me (Soundtrack)	1963	6.00	15.00
Columbia CS-8773	(E)	Love Me Or Leave Me (Soundtrack)	1963	8.00	20.00
Columbia CL-2131	(M)	Love Him!	1964	5.00	12.00
Columbia CS-8931	(S)	Love Him!	1964	6.00	15.00
Columbia CL-2226	(M)	Christmas Album	1964	5.00	12.00
Columbia CS-9026	(S)	Christmas Album	1964	6.00	15.00
Columbia CL-2266	(M)	With A Smile And A Song	1964	5.00	12.00
Columbia CS-9066	(S)	With A Smile And A Song	1964	6.00	15.00
Columbia CL-2310	(M)	Latin For Lovers	1965	5.00	12.00
Columbia CS-9110	(S)	Latin For Lovers	1965	6.00	15.00
— Columbia albums above have "360 Sound Mono/Stereo" on the bottom of the label.—					

DAY, DORIS, & ROCK HUDSON

U.I. DCLA-1316	(DJ)	Selections From "Pillow Talk" (One sided)	195?	20.00	50.00

DAY, JIMMY

Philips PHM-200-016	(M)	Golden Steel Guitar Hits	196?	12.00	30.00
Philips PHS-600-016	(S)	Golden Steel Guitar Hits	196?	16.00	40.00
Philips PHM-200-075	(M)	Steel And Strings	196?	12.00	30.00
Philips PHS-600-075	(S)	Steel And Strings	196?	16.00	40.00

DAY BLINDNESS

Studio 10 DBX-101	(S)	Day Blindness	1969	16.00	40.00

DAYBREAK

R.P.C.	(S)	Daybreak	1971	300.00	600.00

DE-FENDERS, THE
The De-Fenders feature Bruce Johnston.

World Pacific WP-1810	(M)	The Big Ones	1963	16.00	40.00
World Pacific ST-1810	(S)	The Big Ones	1963	20.00	50.00
World Pacific ST-1810	(S)	The Big Ones (Green vinyl)	1963	50.00	125.00
World Pacific ST-1810	(S)	The Big Ones (Red vinyl)	1963	50.00	125.00
Del-Fi DFLP-1242	(M)	Drag Beat	1963	14.00	35.00
Del-Fi DFSP-1242	(S)	Drag Beat	1963	20.00	50.00

DEAD BOYS, THE

Sire SR-6038	(S)	Young, Loud And Snotty	1977	10.00	25.00
Sire SRK-6054	(S)	We Have Come For Your Children	1978	10.00	25.00

DEAD KENNEDYS, THE

I.R.S. SP-70014	(S)	Fresh Fruit For Rotting Vegetables	1981	8.00	20.00
		(Orange cover includes a poster/lyric sheet.)			
Alternate Tentacles	(S)	Fresh Fruit For Rotting Vegetables	1981	6.00	15.00

DEADLY ONES, THE

Vee Jay LP-1090	(M)	It's Monster Surfing Time	1964	16.00	40.00
Vee Jay VS-1090	(S)	It's Monster Surfing Time	1964	30.00	75.00

DEAL, BILL, & THE RHONDELLS

Heritage HTS-35003	(S)	Vintage Rock	1968	8.00	20.00
Heritage HTS-35006	(P)	The Best Of Bill Deal & The Rhondells	1969	8.00	20.00

DEAN, AL

Warrior 506	(M)	Fragile Heart	195?	50.00	125.00

DEAN, EDDIE

Sage & Sand C-1	(M)	Greatest Westerns	1956	20.00	50.00

Label & Catalog #		Title	Year	VG+	NM
Sage & Sand C-5	(M)	Hi-Country	1957	16.00	40.00
Sound 603	(M)	Greatest Westerns	1957	12.00	30.00
Sage & Sand C-16	(M)	Hillbilly Heaven	1961	12.00	30.00

DEAN, JIMMY

Mercury MG-20319	(M)	His Television Favorites	1957	16.00	40.00
Columbia CL-1025	(M)	Hour Of Prayer	1957	14.00	35.00
King 686	(M)	Favorites Of Jimmy Dean	1961	20.00	50.00
Starday SLP-325	(M)	Bummin' Around	1965	12.00	30.00

DEAUXVILLE TRIO, THE

Jubilee 1211	(M)	The Deauxville Trio On Campus	1961	6.00	15.00

DEBRIS

Static Disposal	(S)	Debris	1976	20.00	50.00

DeCARLO, YVONNE

Masterseal (No number)	(M)	Yvonne DeCarlo Sings	1957	20.00	50.00

DeCASTRO SISTERS, THE

Abbott 5002	(M)	The DeCastro Sisters	1960	20.00	50.00
Capitol T-1402	(M)	The DeCastros Sing	1960	8.00	20.00
Capitol ST-1402	(S)	The DeCastros Sing	1960	10.00	25.00
Capitol T-1501	(M)	The Rockin' Beat	1960	8.00	20.00
Capitol ST-1501	(S)	The Rockin' Beat	1960	10.00	25.00

DECEMBER'S CHILDREN

Mainstream S-6128	(S)	December's Children	1970	5.00	12.00

DEE, JOEY (& THE STARLIGHTERS)

Roulette R-25166	(M)	Doin' The Twist	1961	12.00	30.00
Roulette SR-25166	(S)	Doin' The Twist	1961	16.00	40.00
Roulette R-25168	(M)	Hey, Let's Twist (Soundtrack)	1961	16.00	40.00
Roulette SR-25168	(S)	Hey, Let's Twist (Soundtrack)	1961	20.00	50.00
Roulette R-25171	(M)	All The World Is Twistin'	1961	12.00	30.00
Roulette SR-25171	(S)	All The World Is Twistin'	1961	16.00	40.00
Roulette R-25173	(M)	Back To The Peppermint Lounge Twistin'	1961	12.00	30.00
Roulette SR-25173	(S)	Back To The Peppermint Lounge Twistin'	1961	16.00	40.00
Roulette R-25182	(M)	Two Tickets To Paris (Soundtrack)	1961	10.00	25.00
Roulette SR-25182	(S)	Two Tickets To Paris (Soundtrack)	1961	12.00	30.00
Roulette R-25197	(M)	Joey Dee	1961	10.00	25.00
Roulette SR-25197	(S)	Joey Dee	1961	12.00	30.00
Roulette R-25221	(M)	Dance, Dance, Dance	1961	10.00	25.00
Roulette SR-25221	(S)	Dance, Dance, Dance	1961	12.00	30.00

DEE, KIKI

Liberty LST-7613	(S)	Patterns	1969	6.00	15.00
Tamla TS-303	(S)	Great Expectations	1970	4.00	10.00

DEEP, THE

Parkway P-7051	(M)	Psychedelic Moods	1966	40.00	100.00
Parkway SP-7051	(S)	Psychedelic Moods	1966	60.00	150.00

DEEP PURPLE

Deep Purple features Ritchie Blackmore, Ian Paice and Jon Lord. Refer to Green Bullfrog.

Tetragrammaton T-102	(S)	Shades Of Deep Purple	1968	8.00	20.00
Tetragrammaton T-107	(S)	Book Of Taliesyn	1968	8.00	20.00
Tetragrammaton T-119	(S)	Deep Purple	1968	8.00	20.00
Tetragrammaton T-131	(S)	Deep Purple & The Royal Philharmonic	1968	8.00	20.00
Warner Bros. WS-1860	(S)	Deep Purple & The Royal Philharmonic	1970	4.00	10.00
Warner Bros. WS-1877	(S)	Deep Purple In Rock	1970	6.00	15.00
Warner Bros. BS-2607	(S)	Machine Head	1974	4.00	10.00
Warner Bros. BS4-2607	(Q)	Machine Head	1974	8.00	20.00
Warner Bros. BS4-2832	(Q)	Stormbringer	1974	8.00	20.00
Harvest SHVL-751	(S)	Book Of Taliesyn	197?	60.00	150.00
Harvest SHVL-777	(S)	Deep Purple In Rock	197?	60.00	150.00

(Harvest 751 and 777 are US discs inside UK jackets manu-factured for export during the early '70s. While the label and catalog number are British, the label reads "Made in USA.")

Label & Catalog #		Title	Year	VG+	NM

DEEP RIVER BOYS, THE

Waldorf 108 (10")	(M)	Spirituals And Jubilees	1956	60.00	150.00
Waldorf 120 (10")	(M)	Spirituals	1956	60.00	150.00
"X" LXA-1019	(M)	The Deep River Boys	1956	40.00	100.00
Camden CAL-303	(M)	Presenting The Deep River Boys	1957	20.00	50.00
Que FLS-104	(M)	Midnight Magic	1957	20.00	50.00

DEEP SIX, THE

| Liberty LRP-3475 | (M) | The Deep Six | 1966 | 5.00 | 12.00 |
| Liberty LST-7475 | (S) | The Deep Six | 1966 | 6.00 | 15.00 |

DEERFIELD

| Flat Rock FRS-1 | (S) | Nil Desperandum | 196? | 40.00 | 100.00 |

DEFIANT ONES, THE

| Essar SRLP-2000 | (M) | The Defiant Ones | 196? | Unreleased | |

DEKKER, DESMOND

| Uni 73059 | (S) | Israelites | 1969 | 12.00 | 30.00 |

("Tip Of My Finger," "Too Much Too Soon" and
"Nincompoop" are rechanneled.)

DEL SATINS, THE

| B.T. Puppy BTS-1019 | (S) | Out To Lunch | 1972 | 100.00 | 250.00 |

DEL VIKINGS, THE

The original all-black Del Vikings were Corinthian "Kripp" Johnson and Samuel Patterson, both lead, with Don Jackson, Clarence Quick and Bernard Robertson. Jackson, Patterson and Robertson were replaced by Norman Wright and white members Dave Lerchey and Donald "Gus" Backus. The all-black group recorded the acapella material that showed up on the Luniverse album (with strings over-dubbed), even though the cover depicts the later, racially integrated group. When their manager signed the group to Mercury, Johnson formed a second group, sometimes called The Dell Vikings, for Fee Bee. The group on the Mercury albums consisted of Backus, Lerchey, Quick, Wright and William Blakely; the group on the Dot album was original members Kripp Johnson and Don Jackson with Arthur Budd, Eddie Everette and Chuck Jackson*. Refer to The Chantels.

Luniverse LP-1000	(M)	Come Go With The Del Vikings	1957	200.00	400.00
		(Original copies have ten tracks; counterfeits have twelve.)			
Mercury MG-20314	(M)	They Sing-They Swing	1957	100.00	250.00
Mercury MG-20353	(M)	A Swinging, Singing Record Session	1958	60.00	150.00
Dot DLP-3695	(M)	Come Go With Me	1966	150.00	300.00
Dot DLP-25695	(E)	Come Go With Me	1966	200.00	400.00

DEL VIKINGS, THE / THE SONNETS

| Crown CLP-5368 | (M) | The Del Vikings And The Sonnets | 1963 | 12.00 | 30.00 |
| Crown CST-368 | (E) | The Del Vikings And The Sonnets | 1963 | 6.00 | 15.00 |

DELANEY & BONNIE

Delaney and Bonnie Bramlett.

Elektra EKS-74039	(S)	Accept No Substitutes	1969	6.00	15.00
Stax STS-2026	(S)	Home	1969	8.00	20.00
Atco SD-33-326	(S)	On Tour With Eric Clapton & Friends	1970	6.00	15.00
Atco SD-33-341	(S)	To Bonnie From Delaney	1970	5.00	12.00
Atco SD-33-358	(S)	Motel Shot	1971	5.00	12.00
Atco SD-33-383	(S)	Country Life	1972	4.00	10.00
Atco SD-33-7014	(S)	The Best Of Delaney & Bonnie	1972	4.00	10.00

DELBERT & GLEN

Delbert is Delbert McClinton.

| Clean 601 | (S) | Delbert & Glen | 1972 | 12.00 | 30.00 |
| Clean 602 | (S) | Subject To Change | 1973 | 12.00 | 30.00 |

DELFONICS, THE

The Delfonics featrue Major Harris.

Philly Groove 1150	(S)	La La Means I Love You	1968	20.00	50.00
Philly Groove 1151	(S)	The Sexy Sound Of Soul	1969	16.00	40.00
Philly Groove 1152	(S)	The Delfonics' Super Hits	1969	12.00	30.00
Philly Groove 1153	(S)	The Delfonics	1970	12.00	30.00
Philly Groove 1154	(S)	Tell Me This Is A Dream	1972	12.00	30.00

Label & Catalog #		Title	Year	VG+	NM

DELLS, THE

Vee Jay LP-1010	(M)	Oh What A Nite (Maroon label)	1959	300.00	500.00
Vee Jay LP-1010	(M)	Oh What A Nite (Black label)	1959	100.00	250.00
Vee Jay LP-1141	(M)	It's Not Unusual	1965	20.00	50.00
Vee Jay LPS-1141	(S)	It's Not Unusual	1965	30.00	75.00
Cadet LPS-804	(S)	There Is	1968	6.00	15.00
Cadet LPS-822	(S)	Musical Menu / Always Together	1969	6.00	15.00
Cadet LPS-824	(S)	The Dells' Greatest Hits	1969	6.00	15.00
Cadet LPS-829	(S)	Love Is Blue	1969	6.00	15.00
Cadet LPS-837	(S)	Like It Is, Like It Was	1970	6.00	15.00
Upfront UPF-105	(S)	Stay In My Corner	1968	5.00	12.00

DELLWOODS, THE

Big Top 1305	(M)	Mad Twists Rock N' Roll	1963	20.00	50.00
Big Top 1306	(M)	Fink Along With Mad	1963	20.00	50.00

DELMORE BROTHERS, THE

The Delmores also recorded as members of The Brown's Ferry Four.

King 589	(M)	Songs By The Delmore Brothers	1958	75.00	200.00
King 589	(M)	16 All-Time Favorites	1958	30.00	75.00
		("Favorites" is a reissue of "Songs By.")			
King 785	(M)	30th Anniversary Album	1962	30.00	75.00
King 910	(M)	In Memory	1964	20.00	50.00
King 920	(M)	In Memory, Volume 2	1964	20.00	50.00
King 983	(M)	24 Great Country Songs	1966	16.00	40.00
King KS-983	(E)	24 Great Country Songs	1966	12.00	30.00

DELTA RHYTHM, BOYS, THE

Mercury MG-25153 (10")	(M)	The Delta Rhythm Boys	1952	70.00	175.00
RCA Victor LPM-3085 (10")	(M)	Dry Bones	1953	40.00	100.00
Camden CAL-313	(M)	The Delta Rhythm Boys	1957	30.00	75.00
Elektra EKL-138	(M)	The Delta Rhythm Boys	1957	30.00	75.00
Jubilee LP-1022	(M)	Delta Rhythm Boys In Sweden (Red vinyl)	1957	60.00	150.00
Jubilee LP-1022	(M)	Delta Rhythm Boys In Sweden	1957	50.00	125.00
Coral CRL-57358	(M)	Singin' Spirituals	1961	20.00	50.00
Coral CRL-757358	(S)	Singin' Spirituals	1961	30.00	75.00

DEMEMSIONS, THE

Coral CRL-57430	(M)	My Foolish Heart	1963	50.00	125.00
Coral CRL-757430	(S)	My Foolish Heart	1963	100.00	300.00

DEMIAN

Demian originally recorded as Bubble Puppy.

ABC ABCS-718	(S)	Demian	1970	16.00	40.00

DEREK & THE DOMINOS

Derek is Eric Clapton while the Dominos feature Duane Allman.

Atco SD-2-704	(S)	Layla (2 LPs)	1970	12.00	30.00
RSO 2-8800	(S)	Derek & The Dominos In Concert (2 LPs)	1973	8.00	20.00
Direct Disk SD-16629	(S)	Layla (2 LPs)	198?	25.00	75.00

DERRINGER, RICK

Blue Sky PRO-265	(DJ)	Live In Cleveland	1977	8.00	20.00

DeSANTO, SUGAR PIE

Checker LP-2979	(M)	Sugar Pie DeSanto	1961	50.00	100.00

DeSHANNON, JACKIE

Liberty LRP-3320	(M)	Jackie DeShannon	1963	12.00	30.00
Liberty LRP-7320	(S)	Jackie DeShannon	1963	16.00	40.00
Liberty LRP-3390	(M)	Breakin' It Up On The Beatles Tour	1964	20.00	50.00
Liberty LRP-7390	(S)	Breakin' It Up On The Beatles Tour	1964	30.00	75.00
Imperial LP-9286	(M)	This Is Jackie DeShannon	1965	8.00	20.00
Imperial LP-12286	(S)	This Is Jackie DeShannon	1965	10.00	25.00
Imperial LP-9294	(M)	You Won't Forget Me	1965	8.00	20.00
Imperial LP-12294	(S)	You Won't Forget Me	1965	10.00	25.00
Imperial LP-9296	(M)	In The Wind	1965	8.00	20.00
Imperial LP-12296	(S)	In The Wind	1965	10.00	25.00

— Original Imperial albums above have black & pink labels.—

When Ron Dante booked session time in 1964 to cut a send-up of the Shangri-La's big hit, "Leader Of The Pack," he named his new studio group The Detergents. The album that followed featured an even dozen tracks of silliness, poking fun at just a variety of then happening sounds, including the West Coast scene and the British Invasion.

Label & Catalog #		Title	Year	VG+	NM
Imperial LP-9328	(M)	Are You Ready For This?	1966	6.00	15.00
Imperial LP-12328	(S)	Are You Ready For This?	1966	8.00	20.00
Imperial LP-9344	(M)	New Image	1967	6.00	15.00
Imperial LP-12344	(S)	New Image	1967	8.00	20.00
Imperial LP-9352	(M)	For You	1967	6.00	15.00
Imperial LP-12352	(S)	For You	1967	8.00	20.00
Imperial LP-9386	(M)	Me About You	1967	6.00	15.00
Imperial LP-12386	(S)	Me About You	1967	8.00	20.00
Imperial LP-9404	(M)	What The World Needs Now Is Love	1967	6.00	15.00
Imperial LP-12404	(S)	What The World Needs Now Is Love	1967	8.00	20.00
		("What The World Needs Now Is Love" is rechanneled on this LP.)			
Imperial LP-12415	(S)	Laurel Canyon	1968	6.00	15.00
Imperial LP-12442	(S)	Put A Little Love In Your Heart	1969	6.00	15.00
Imperial LP-12453	(S)	To Be Free	1970	6.00	15.00
Capitol ST-772	(S)	Songs	1971	4.00	10.00
Atlantic SD-7231	(S)	Jackie	1972	4.00	10.00
Columbia PC-33500	(S)	New Arrangement	1975	4.00	10.00

DETERGENTS, THE
The Detergents feature Ron Dante.

Roulette R-25308	(M)	The Many Faces Of The Detergents	1965	30.00	75.00
Roulette SR-25308	(E)	The Many Faces Of The Detergents	1965	20.00	50.00

DEUCE COUPES, THE

Del Fi DFLP-1243	(M)	Hotrodder's Choice	1963	12.00	30.00
Del Fi DFS-1243	(S)	Hotrodder's Choice	1963	16.00	40.00

DEUCE COUPES, THE

Crown CLP-5393	(M)	The Shut Downs	1963	8.00	20.00
Crown CST-393	(S)	The Shut Downs	1963	10.00	25.00

DEVIANTS, THE

Sire SES-97001	(S)	Ptoof!	1968	24.00	60.00
Sire SES-97005	(S)	Disposable	1969	24.00	60.00
Sire SES-97016	(S)	No. 3	1969	24.00	60.00

DEVILED HAM

Super-K SKS-6003	(M)	I Had Too Much To Dream Last Night	1968	8.00	20.00

DEVIL'S ANVIL, THE

Columbia CL-2664	(M)	Hard Rock From The Middle East	1967	10.00	25.00
Columbia CS-9464	(S)	Hard Rock From The Middle East	1967	14.00	35.00

DEVROE, BILLY, & THE DEVILAIRES

Tampa 31	(M)	Billy Devroe & The Devilaires, Volume 1	195?	12.00	30.00
Tampa 39	(M)	Billy Devroe & The Devilaires, Volume 1	195?	12.00	30.00

DEXTER, AL

Columbia CL-9005 (10")	(M)	Songs Of The Southwest	1954	24.00	60.00
Harmony HL-7293	(M)	Pistol Packin' Mama	1961	10.00	25.00
Capitol T-1701	(M)	His Greatest Hits	1962	16.00	40.00
Capitol ST-1701	(S)	His Greatest Hits	1962	20.00	50.00

DIALOGUE

Cold Studio	(M)	Dialogue (White cover includes insert)	196?	60.00	150.00
Cold Studio	(M)	Dialogue (Orange cover includes insert)	196?	20.00	50.00

DIALS, THE

Time 52100	(M)	It's Monkey Time	1964	6.00	15.00
Time S-2100	(S)	It's Monkey Time	1964	8.00	20.00

DIAMOND, NEIL
Refer to Diana Ross / Neil Diamond.

Bang BLP-214	(M)	The Feel Of Neil	1966	16.00	40.00
Bang BLPS-214	(S)	The Feel Of Neil	1966	30.00	75.00
Bang BLP-217	(M)	Just For You	1967	10.00	25.00
Bang BLPS-217	(S)	Just For You	1967	12.00	30.00
		("The Long Way Home," "You'll Forget" and the single version of "Solitary Man" are rechanneled.)			

Label & Catalog #		Title	Year	VG+	NM
Bang BLPS-219	(S)	Neil Diamond's Greatest Hits	1968	12.00	30.00
		("Do It," "Kentucky Woman" and the single version			
		of "Solitary Man" are rechanneled on this LP.)			
Bang BLPS-219	(S)	Neil Diamond's Greatest Hits	1968	6.00	15.00
		("Solitary Man" is rerecorded in stereo on later pressings.)			
Bang BLPS-221	(S)	Shilo	1970	12.00	30.00
Bang BLPS-224	(S)	Do It!	1970	10.00	25.00
		("Some Day Baby" is mono while "Shot Down," "You'll Forget"			
		and "The Long Way Home" are rechanneled.)			
Bang BLPS-227	(S)	Double Gold (2 LPs)	1970	8.00	20.00
		— Original Bang albums above have red & white labels.—			
Uni ST-73030	(S)	Velvet Gloves And Spit	1968	8.00	20.00
		(Original pressings have Neil's face on the cover.)			
Uni ST-73047	(S)	Brother Love's Traveling Salvation Show	1969	8.00	20.00
Uni ST-73071	(S)	Touching You, Touching Me	1970	8.00	20.00
Uni ST-73084	(S)	Gold	1970	8.00	20.00
Uni ST-73092	(S)	Tap Root Manuscript	1970	8.00	20.00
Uni ND-11	(DJ)	Neil Diamond (Radio sampler)	1970	60.00	150.00
Uni ST-1913	(DJ)	Open-End Interview	1971	100.00	250.00
Uni ST-93030	(S)	Velvet Gloves And Spit	1971	4.00	10.00
Uni ST-93047	(S)	Brother Love's Traveling Salvation Show	1971	4.00	10.00
Uni ST-93071	(S)	Touching You Touching Me	1971	4.00	10.00
Uni ST-93084	(S)	Neil Diamond Gold	1971	4.00	10.00
Uni ST-93092	(S)	Tap Root Manuscript	1971	4.00	10.00
Uni ST-93106	(S)	Stones	1971	5.00	12.00
Uni ST-93136	(S)	Moods	1972	5.00	12.00
Frog King AAR-1	(S)	Early Classics (Includes songbook)	1972	20.00	50.00
Frog King AAR-1	(S)	Early Classics (Without songbook)	1972	12.00	30.00
		("Kentucky Woman" is in stereo on this while "Do It" is mono.)			
Columbia PCQ032919	(Q)	Serenade	1974	10.00	25.00
Columbia HC-42550	(S)	Jonathan Livingston Seagull (Half-speed)	1982	16.00	50.00
Columbia HC-42625	(S)	You Don't Bring Me Flowers (Half-speed)	1982	13.00	40.00
Columbia HC-42628	(S)	On The Way To The Sky (Half-speed)	1982	16.00	50.00
Columbia HC-48068	(S)	His 12 Greatest Hits, Volume 2 (Half-speed)	1982	13.00	40.00
Columbia HC-48359	(S)	Heartlight (Half-speed master)	1982	13.00	40.00
Columbia 9C9-39915	(S)	Primitive (Picture disc)	1983	6.00	15.00
Mobile Fidelity MFSL-024	(S)	Hot August Night	1979	10.00	30.00
Mobile Fidelity MFSL-071	(S)	Jazz Singer	1981	8.00	25.00
Direct Disk SD-16612	(S)	His 12 Greatest Hits	1982	16.00	50.00

DIAMONDS, THE

Mercury MG-20213	(M)	Collection Of Golden Hits	1956	50.00	125.00
Mercury MG-20309	(M)	The Diamonds	1957	50.00	125.00
Mercury MG-20368	(M)	The Diamonds Meet Pete Rugolo	1958	20.00	50.00
Mercury SR-60076	(S)	The Diamonds Meet Pete Rugolo	1958	30.00	75.00
Mercury MG-20480	(M)	Songs From The Old West	1959	20.00	50.00
Mercury SR-60159	(S)	Songs From The Old West	1959	30.00	75.00
Wing MGW-12112	(M)	The Diamonds	1962	12.00	30.00
Wing MGW-12178	(M)	Pop Hits By The Diamonds	1962	12.00	30.00
Sound Recorders SRS-4644	(S)	The Diamonds '70	1971	8.00	20.00

DICK & DEE DEE
Dick St. John and Dee Dee Sperling.

Liberty LRP-3236	(M)	Tell Me/The Mountain's High	1962	16.00	40.00
Liberty LST-7236	(E)	Tell Me/The Mountain's High	1962	12.00	30.00
Warner Bros. W-1500	(M)	Young And In Love	1963	8.00	20.00
Warner Bros. WS-1500	(S)	Young And In Love	1963	10.00	25.00
Warner Bros. W-1538	(M)	Turn Around	1963	8.00	20.00
Warner Bros. WS-1538	(S)	Turn Around	1963	10.00	25.00
Warner Bros. W-1586	(M)	Thou Shalt Not Steal	1963	8.00	20.00
Warner Bros. WS-1586	(S)	Thou Shalt Not Steal	1963	10.00	25.00
Warner Bros. W-1623	(M)	Songs We've Sung On "Shindig"	1963	8.00	20.00
Warner Bros. WS-1623	(S)	Songs We've Sung On "Shindig"	1963	10.00	25.00

DICKENS, HAZEL, & ALICE FOSTER

Verve/Folkways FV-9005	(M)	Who's That Knocking?	1965	6.00	15.00
Verve/Folkways FVS-9005	(S)	Who's That Knocking?	1965	8.00	20.00

Label & Catalog #		Title	Year	VG+	NM
DICKENS, LITTLE JIMMY					
Columbia CL-9053 (10")	(M)	Old Country Church	1954	30.00	75.00
Columbia CL-1047	(M)	Raisin' The Dickens	1957	30.00	75.00
Columbia CL-1545	(M)	Big Songs	1960	8.00	20.00
Columbia CL-1545	(S)	Big Songs	1960	12.00	30.00
Columbia CL-1887	(M)	Out Behind The Barn	1962	8.00	20.00
Columbia CL-1887	(S)	Out Behind The Barn	1962	12.00	30.00
— Original Columbia albums above have three white "eye" logos on each side of the spindle hole.—					
Harmony HL-7311	(M)	Little Jimmy Dickens' Best	1964	6.00	15.00
Harmony HS-7311	(S)	Little Jimmy Dickens' Best	1964	8.00	20.00
DICKY DOO & THE DON'TS					
United Arts. UAL-3094	(M)	Madison And Other Dances	1959	12.00	30.00
United Arts. UAS-6094	(S)	Madison And Other Dances	1959	16.00	40.00
United Arts. UAL-3097	(M)	Teen Scene	1959	12.00	30.00
United Arts. UAS-6097	(S)	Teen Scene	1959	16.00	40.00
(No label)	(DJ)	Dicky Doo & The Don'ts Live	1962	300.00	Rare
(Near Mint copies have a suggested value of $500-1,000.)					
DIDDLEY, BO					
Bo Diddley is a pseudonym for Ellas McDaniel.					
Checker LP-1431	(M)	Bo Diddley	1958	60.00	150.00
Checker LP-1436	(M)	Go Bo Diddley	1959	50.00	125.00
Checker LP-2974	(M)	Have Guitar, Will Travel	1960	30.00	75.00
Checker LP-2976	(M)	Bo Diddley In The Spotlight	1960	30.00	75.00
Checker LP-2977	(M)	Bo Diddley Is A Gunslinger	1960	40.00	100.00
Checker LP-2980	(M)	Bo Diddley Is A Lover	1961	40.00	100.00
Checker LP-2982	(M)	Bo Diddley's A Twister	1962	30.00	75.00
Checker LP-2984	(M)	Bo Diddley	1962	30.00	75.00
Checker LP-2985	(M)	Bo Diddley And Company	1963	40.00	100.00
Checker LP-2987	(M)	Surfin' With Bo Diddley	1964	30.00	75.00
Checker LP-2987	(E)	Surfin' With Bo Diddley	1964	16.00	40.00
Checker LP-2988	(M)	Bo Diddley's Beach Party	1963	30.00	75.00
Checker LP-2988	(E)	Bo Diddley's Beach Party	1963	20.00	50.00
Checker LP-2989	(M)	16 All Time Greatest Hits	1964	16.00	40.00
Checker LP-2989	(E)	16 All Time Greatest Hits	1964	12.00	30.00
Checker LP-2992	(M)	Hey! Good Lookin'	1965	20.00	50.00
Checker LP-2992	(E)	Hey! Good Lookin'	1965	12.00	30.00
Checker LP-2996	(M)	500% More Man	1965	20.00	50.00
Checker LP-2996	(E)	500% More Man	1965	12.00	30.00
— Original Checker albums above have black labels with silver print—					
Checker LP-2982	(M)	Road Runner	1967	30.00	75.00
Checker LP-2982	(E)	Road Runner	1967	20.00	50.00
("Road Runner" is a repackage of "Bo Diddley's A Twister.")					
Checker LP-3001	(M)	The Originator	1966	12.00	30.00
Checker LP-3001	(S)	The Originator	1966	16.00	40.00
Checker LP-3006	(M)	Go Bo Diddley	1967	20.00	50.00
Checker LP-3006	(E)	Go Bo Diddley	1967	16.00	40.00
(Checker 3006 is a reissue of 1436.)					
Checker LP-3007	(M)	Boss Man	1967	30.00	75.00
Checker LP-3007	(E)	Boss Man	1967	20.00	50.00
(Checker 3007 is a reissue of 1431.)					
— Checker albums above have blue labels with checkers on top.—					
Checker LPS-3013	(S)	The Black Gladiator	1968	12.00	30.00
Chess CH-50001	(S)	Another Dimension	1971	16.00	40.00
Chess 2CH-60005	(E)	Got My Own Bag Of Tricks (2 LPs)	1972	10.00	25.00
Chess CH-50016	(S)	Where It All Began	1972	16.00	40.00
Chess CH-50029	(S)	The London Bo Diddley Sessions	1973	10.00	25.00
Chess CH-50047	(S)	Big Bad Bo	1974	10.00	25.00
RCA Victor APL1-1229	(S)	The 20th Anniversary Of Rock N' Roll	1976	8.00	20.00
M.F. 2002	(S)	I'm A Man (2 LPs)	1977	40.00	100.00
Accord SN-7812	(S)	Toronto Rock And Roll Revival, Volume 5	1982	8.00	20.00
Check Mate 1960	(S)	Give Me A Break	1988	6.00	15.00
DIDDLEY, BO, & CHUCK BERRY					
Checker LP-2991	(M)	Two Great Guitars	1964	30.00	75.00
Checker LPS-2991	(E)	Two Great Guitars	1964	16.00	40.00

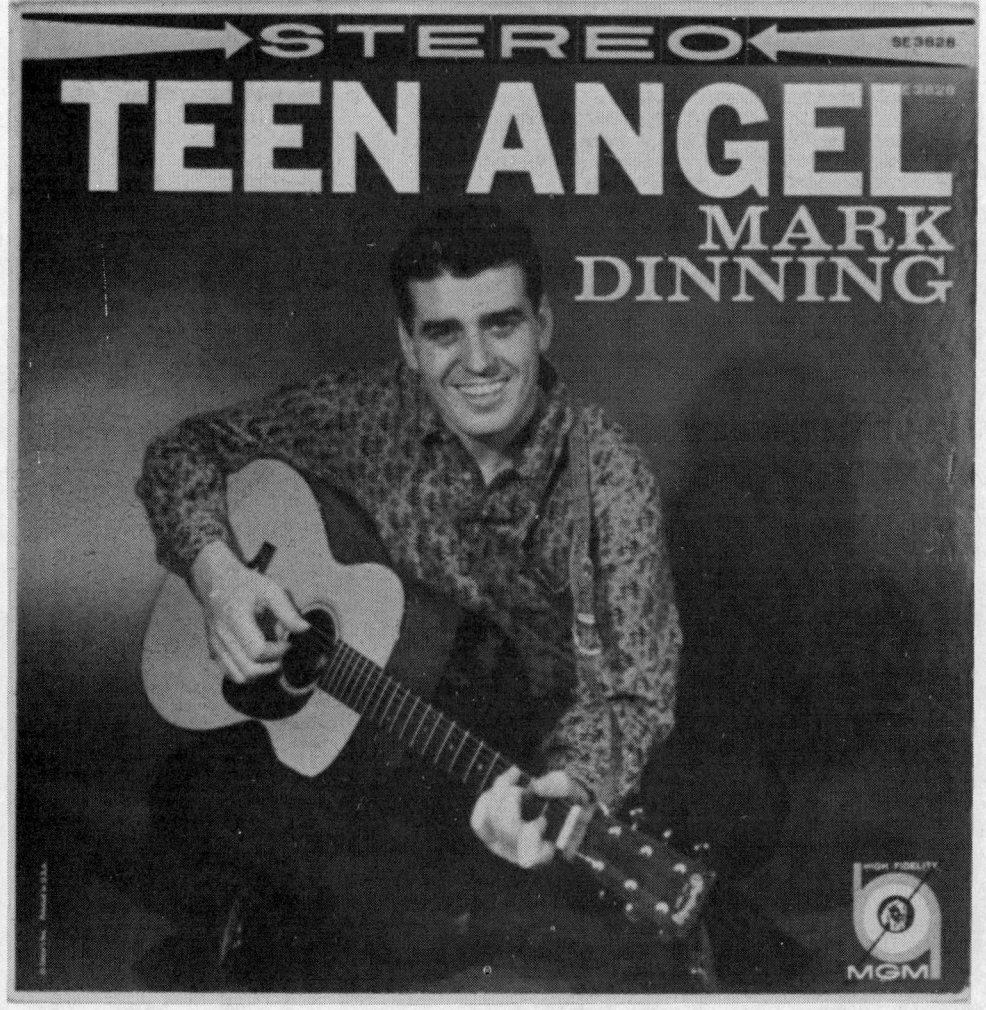

Mark Dinning's "Teen Angel," written by his sister in response to an actual accident, catapulted to the top of the charts in 1959. That the song was a virtual parody of itself from first hearing was noticed by few at the time. Dinning's album of the same name is another stereo rarity.

Label & Catalog #		Title	Year	VG+	NM
DIDDLEY, BO, & MUDDY WATERS & LITTLE WALTER					
Checker LP-3008	(M)	Super Blues Band	1968	20.00	50.00
Checker LPS-3008	(S)	Super Blues Band	1968	16.00	40.00
DIDDLEY, BO, & MUDDY WATERS & HOWLIN' WOLF					
Checker LP-3010	(M)	Super, Super Blues Band	1968	20.00	50.00
Checker LPS-3010	(S)	Super, Super Blues Band	1968	16.00	40.00
DIETRICH, MARLENE					
Decca DL-5100 (10")	(M)	Souvenir Album	1950	30.00	75.00
Vox PL-3040 (10")	(M)	Marlene Dietrich Sings	1951	30.00	75.00
Columbia GL-105	(M)	American Songs In German For The OSS	1952	30.00	75.00
Columbia GL-164	(M)	In Rio	1953	30.00	75.00
Columbia ML-4975	(M)	Cafe De Paris	1955	20.00	50.00
Decca DL-8465	(M)	Marlene Dietrich	1957	16.00	40.00
Columbia CL-1275	(M)	Lili Marlene	1959	12.00	30.00
Capitol Int. T-10397	(M)	Marlene	1965	10.00	25.00
Capitol Int. DT-10397	(E)	Marlene	1965	8.00	20.00
Capitol OTCR-300	(M)	The Magic Of Marlene	1969	10.00	25.00
DIGA RHYTHM BAND, THE					
The Digas are Mickey Hart and Bill Kreutzmann of the Grateful Dead.					
Round RX-110	(S)	The Diga Rhythm Band	1976	12.00	30.00
DILLARD, DOUG					
Together STT-1003	(S)	Banjo Album	1970	30.00	75.00
DILLARD & CLARK					
Doug Dillard & Gene Clark.					
A&M SP-4158	(S)	The Fantastic Expedition Of Dillard & Clark (Brown label)	1969	8.00	20.00
A&M SP-4158	(S)	The Fantastic Expedition Of Dillard & Clark (Silver label)	1970	4.00	10.00
A&M SP-4158	(S)	Through The Morning, Through The Night	1970	6.00	15.00
DILLARDS, THE					
Elektra EKL-232	(M)	Back Porch Bluegrass	1963	10.00	25.00
Elektra EKS-7232	(S)	Back Porch Bluegrass	1963	14.00	35.00
Elektra EKL-265	(M)	The Dillards Live! Almost!	1964	8.00	20.00
Elektra EKS-726	(S)	The Dillards Live! Almost!	1964	10.00	25.00
Elektra EKL-285	(M)	Pickin' And Fiddlin' With Byron Berline	1965	8.00	20.00
Elektra EKS-7285	(S)	Pickin' And Fiddlin' With Byron Berline	1965	10.00	25.00
Elektra EKS-74035	(S)	Wheatstraw Suite	1969	6.00	15.00
Elektra EKS-74054	(S)	Copperfields	1969	6.00	15.00
Crystal Clear CCS-5007	(S)	Mountain Rock	1979	8.00	20.00
DIMENSIONS, THE					
(No label)	(M)	From All Dimensions	1966	660.00	1,000.00
DING DONGS, THE					
Motown 716	(S)	Gimme Dat Ding	1970	6.00	15.00
DINNING, MARK					
MGM E-3828	(M)	Teen Angel	1960	30.00	75.00
MGM SE-3828	(S)	Teen Angel	1960	50.00	125.00
MGM E-3828	(M)	Wanderin'	1960	20.00	50.00
MGM SE-3828	(S)	Wanderin'	1960	30.00	75.00
DINO, DESI & BILLY					
Dino Martin, Desi Arnaz Jr, and Billy Hinsche.					
Reprise R-6176	(M)	I'm A Fool	1965	8.00	20.00
Reprise RS-6176	(S)	I'm A Fool	1965	10.00	25.00
Reprise R-6194	(M)	Our Times Are Coming	1966	6.00	15.00
Reprise RS-6194	(S)	Our Times Are Coming	1966	8.00	20.00
Reprise R-6198	(M)	Memories Are Made Of This	1966	6.00	15.00
Reprise RS-6198	(S)	Memories Are Made Of This	1966	8.00	20.00
Reprise R-6224	(M)	Souvenir	1966	8.00	20.00
Reprise RS-6224	(S)	Souvenir	1966	10.00	25.00
Uni ST-73056	(S)	Follow Me (Soundtrack)	1969	8.00	20.00

Label & Catalog #		Title	Year	VG+	NM

DION

Label & Catalog #		Title	Year	VG+	NM
Laurie LLP-2004	(M)	Alone With Dion	1960	40.00	100.00
Laurie LLP-2009	(M)	Runaround Sue (Green vinyl)	1961	80.00	200.00
Laurie LLP-2009	(M)	Runaround Sue	1961	30.00	75.00
Capitol DT-91027	(E)	Runaround Sue (Capitol Record Club)	1961	50.00	100.00
Laurie LLP-2012	(M)	Lovers Who Wander	1962	30.00	75.00
Laurie LLP-2015	(M)	Love Came To Me	1963	30.00	75.00
Laurie LLP-2017	(M)	Dion Sings To Sandy & All Other Girls	1963	30.00	75.00
Laurie LLP-2019	(M)	Dion Sings The 15 Million Sellers	1963	20.00	50.00
Laurie LLP-2022	(M)	More Of Dion's Greatest Hits	1963	20.00	50.00
Columbia CL-2010	(M)	Ruby Baby	1963	8.00	20.00
Columbia CS-8810	(S)	Ruby Baby	1963	12.00	30.00
Columbia CL-2107	(M)	Donna The Prima Donna	1963	8.00	20.00
Columbia CS-8907	(S)	Donna The Prima Donna	1963	12.00	30.00
Laurie SLP-2047	(S)	Dion	1968	8.00	20.00
Warner Bros. WS-1826	(S)	Sit Down, Old Friend ("360 Sound" label)	1969	8.00	20.00
Warner Bros. WS-1872	(S)	You're Not Alone	1971	6.00	15.00
Warner Bros. WS-1945	(S)	Sanctuary	1971	6.00	15.00
Warner Bros. BS-2642	(S)	Suite For Late Summer	1972	5.00	12.00
Warner Bros. BS-2954	(S)	Streetheart	1976	4.00	10.00

DION & THE BELMONTS
Refer to The Belmonts.

Label & Catalog #		Title	Year	VG+	NM
Laurie LLP-1002	(M)	Presenting Dion & The Belmonts	1959	150.00	300.00
		(First pressing have gold labels and the covers have "Master-works" under the Laurie label in the upper right corner.)			
Laurie LLP-2002	(M)	Presenting Dion & The Belmonts	1959	40.00	100.00
		(Second pressings have the gold & white label.)			
Laurie LLPS-2002	(S)	Presenting Dion & The Belmonts	1959	660.00	Rare
		(Near Mint copies have a suggested value of $1,000-2,000.)			
Laurie LLP-2006	(M)	Wish Upon A Star	1959	150.00	300.00
Laurie LLP-2013	(M)	Dion Sings His Greatest Hits	1959	40.00	100.00
Laurie LLPS-2013	(S)	Dion Sings His Greatest Hits	1959	80.00	200.00
Laurie LLP-2016	(M)	By Special Request	1959	20.00	50.00
ABC ABC-599	(M)	Together Again	1967	12.00	30.00
ABC ABCS-599	(S)	Together Again	1967	12.00	30.00
Reprise BS-2664	(S)	Dion & The Belmonts Live 1972	1973	12.00	30.00
Laurie SLP-6000	(P)	60 Greatest Hits (3 LP boxed set)	197?	8.00	20.00
Laurie SLP-6000	(P)	60 Greatest Hits (3 LPs)	197?	4.00	10.00
		(Tracks are in mono and stereo as recorded.)			
Laurie SLP-4002	(S)	Everything You Always Wanted To Hear	197?	4.00	10.00
Pickwick SPC-3521	(S)	Doo Wop	1975	4.00	10.00
		(Pickwick 3521 is a reissue of ABC 599.)			

DIRE STRAITS

Label & Catalog #		Title	Year	VG+	NM
Warner Bros. 23738	(S)	Love Over Gold (Quiex II vinyl)	1982	6.00	15.00
Warner Bros. 25264	(S)	Brothers In Arms (Quiex II vinyl)	1982	6.00	15.00
Warner Bros. 27085	(S)	Alchemy (2 LPs. Quiex II vinyl)	1982	8.00	20.00

DIRTY BLUES BAND, THE

Label & Catalog #		Title	Year	VG+	NM
BluesWay BLS-6010	(S)	The Dirty Blues Band	1968	10.00	25.00
BluesWay BLS-6020	(S)	Stone Dirt	1968	10.00	25.00

DIXIE CUPS, THE

Label & Catalog #		Title	Year	VG+	NM
Red Bird RB-20-100	(M)	Chapel Of Love	1964	20.00	50.00
Red Bird RBS-20-100	(S)	Chapel Of Love	1964	30.00	75.00
Red Bird RB-20-103	(M)	Iko Iko	1965	20.00	50.00
ABC-Paramount 525	(M)	Riding High	1965	14.00	35.00
ABC-Paramount S-525	(S)	Riding High	1965	20.00	50.00

DIXIE DREGS, THE

Label & Catalog #		Title	Year	VG+	NM
No label	(S)	The Great Spectacular	1975	60.00	150.00
Direct Disk SD-16620	(S)	Dregs Of The Earth	198?	13.00	40.00

DIXIE GENTLEMEN, THE

Label & Catalog #		Title	Year	VG+	NM
United Arts. UAL-3296	(M)	Country Style Of The Dixie Gentlemen	1963	5.00	12.00
United Arts. UAS-6296	(S)	Country Style Of The Dixie Gentlemen	1963	6.00	15.00

Label & Catalog #		Title	Year	VG+	NM

DIXIEBELLES, THE

Sound Stage-7 SSM-5000	(M)	Down At Papa Joe's	1963	16.00	40.00
Sound Stage-7 SSS-15000	(E)	Down At Papa Joe's	1963	12.00	30.00

DIXON, WILLIE

Bluesville BVLP-1003	(M)	Willie's Blues	1960	16.00	40.00
Columbia CS-9987	(S)	I Am The Blues ("360 Sound" label)	1970	8.00	20.00

DIXON, WILLIE, & MEMPHIS SLIM

Verve MGV-3007	(M)	Blues Every Which Way	1960	12.00	30.00
Verve MGV6-3007	(S)	Blues Every Which Way	1960	16.00	40.00
Battle BV-6122	(M)	In Paris	1963	8.00	20.00
Battle BVS-6122	(S)	In Paris	1963	10.00	25.00

DOBKINS, JR., CARL

Decca DL-8938	(M)	Carl Dobkins, Jr.	1959	30.00	75.00
Decca DL-78938	(S)	Carl Dobkins, Jr.	1959	40.00	100.00

DOBSON, BONNIE

Prestige Int. PRLP-13021	(M)	Like A Swallow	1962	10.00	25.00
Prestige Int. PRLP-13034	(M)	Dear Companion	1962	10.00	25.00
Prestige Int. PRLP-13064	(M)	Merry-Go-Round Of Children's Songs	1962	10.00	25.00
Folklore FRLP-14007	(M)	Dear Companion	1964	8.00	20.00
Folklore FRST-14007	(S)	Dear Companion	1964	10.00	25.00
		(Folklore 14007 is a reissue of Prestige 13034.)			
Folklore FRLP-14015	(M)	She's Like A Swallow	1964	8.00	20.00
Folklore FRST-14015	(S)	She's Like A Swallow	1964	10.00	25.00
		(Folklore 14015 is a reissue of Prestige 13021.)			
Folklore FRLP-14018	(M)	Hootenanny With Bonnie Gibson	1964	8.00	20.00
Folklore FRST-14018	(S)	Hootenanny With Bonnie Gibson	1964	10.00	25.00
Prestige PRST-7801	(S)	Dear Companion	1969	6.00	15.00
		(Prestige 7801 is a reissue of 13034.)			

DR. FEELGOOD & THE INTERNS
Dr. Feelgood also recorded as Piano Red.

OKeh OKM-12101	(M)	Doctor Feelgood & The Interns	1962	20.00	50.00
OKeh OKS-14101	(S)	Doctor Feelgood & The Interns	1962	30.00	75.00

DR. JOHN (THE NIGHT TRIPPER)
Dr. John is a pseudonym for Mac Rebennack.

Atco SD-33-234	(S)	Gris-Gris	1968	8.00	20.00
Atco SD-33-270	(S)	Babylon	1969	8.00	20.00
Atco SD-33-316	(S)	Remedies	1970	6.00	15.00
Atco SD-33-362	(S)	The Sun, Moon And Herbs	1971	6.00	15.00
Atco SD-36-7006	(S)	Gumbo	1972	5.00	12.00
Atco SD-7018	(S)	In The Right Place	1973	5.00	12.00

DR. MARIGOLD'S PRESCRIPTION

Alshire 5159	(S)	Doctor Marigold's Prescription	1969	5.00	12.00

DR. ROSS

Fortune F-3011	(M)	Doctor Ross, The Harmonica Boss	1962	14.00	35.00
Fortune FS-3011	(S)	Doctor Ross, The Harmonica Boss	1962	20.00	50.00
Testament 2206	(M)	Doctor Ross	196?	8.00	20.00

DR. WEST'S MEDICINE SHOW & JUG BAND
Dr. West's Band features Norman Greenbaum.

Go Go 22-17-002	(M)	The Eggplant That Ate Chicago	1967	8.00	20.00
Go Go 22-17-002	(E)	The Eggplant That Ate Chicago	1967	6.00	15.00

DOCTORS OF MADNESS, THE

United Arts. LA871	(S)	The Doctors Of Madness (2 LPs)	1976	6.00	15.00

DODD, DICK
Dodd was formerly a member of The Standells.

Tower ST-5142	(S)	First Evolution Of Dick Dodd	1968	20.00	50.00

Label & Catalog #		Title	Year	VG+	NM
DODD, JIMMIE					
Mercury MG-20315	(M)	**500 Miles To Glory**	1957	16.00	40.00
Imperial LP-9089	(M)	**Lonely Guitar**	1959	12.00	30.00
Imperial LP-9121	(M)	**Swing-A-Spell**	1960	12.00	30.00
Imperial LP-12121	(S)	**Swing-A-Spell**	1960	12.00	40.00
Disneyland DQ-1235	(M)	**Sing Along With Jimmie Dodd**	1962	12.00	30.00
Disneyland WDL-3014	(M)	**His Favorite Hymns**	1963	8.00	20.00

DODSON, MARGE: *Refer to* **GOLDMINE'S PRICE GUIDE TO COLLECTIBLE JAZZ ALBUMS**

Label & Catalog #		Title	Year	VG+	NM
DOGGETT, BILL					
King 295-82 (10")	(M)	**His Organ And Combo**	1955	12.00	30.00
King 295-83 (10")	(M)	**His Organ And Combo, Volume 2**	1955	12.00	30.00
King 295-85 (10")	(M)	**Christmas Songs**	1955	12.00	30.00
King 295-102 (10")	(M)	**Sentimentally Yours**	1956	12.00	30.00
King 395-502	(M)	**Moondust**	1957	8.00	20.00
King 395-514	(M)	**Hot Doggett**	1957	8.00	20.00
King 395-523	(M)	**As You Desire**	1958	8.00	20.00
King 395-531	(M)	**Everybody Dance To The Honky Tonk**	1958	8.00	20.00
King 395-532	(M)	**Dame Dreaming**	1958	8.00	20.00
King 395-533	(M)	**A Salute To Ellington**	1958	8.00	20.00
King 395-557	(M)	**The Doggett Beat For Dancing Feet**	1958	8.00	20.00
King 395-563	(M)	**Candle Glow**	1958	8.00	20.00
King 395-582	(M)	**Swingin' Easy**	1959	8.00	20.00
King 395-585	(M)	**Dance Awhile**	1959	8.00	20.00
King 395-600	(M)	**Bill Doggett Christmas**	1959	8.00	20.00
King 395-609	(M)	**Hold It**	1959	8.00	20.00
King 633	(M)	**High And Wide**	1959	8.00	20.00
King 641	(M)	**Big City Dance Party**	1959	8.00	20.00
King 667	(M)	**Bill Doggett On Tour**	1959	8.00	20.00
King 706	(M)	**For Reminiscent Lovers, Romantic Songs**	1960	8.00	20.00
King 723	(M)	**Back Again With More**	1960	8.00	20.00
King 759	(M)	**Bonanza Of 24 Songs**	1960	6.00	15.00
King 778	(M)	**The Many Moods Of Bill Doggett**	1963	6.00	15.00
King 830	(M)	**American Songs In The Bossa Nova Style**	1963	6.00	15.00
King 868	(S)	**Impressions**	1964	6.00	15.00
King 908	(S)	**The Best Of Bill Doggett**	1964	6.00	15.00
King 959	(S)	**Bonanza Of 24 Hit Songs**	1966	6.00	15.00

— Original King albums above have crownless black or blue labels. The logo on the covers have a crown with "King" in open capital block letters below.—

Label & Catalog #		Title	Year	VG+	NM
Warner Bros. W-1404	(M)	**3,046 People Danced 'Til 4 AM**	1960	4.00	10.00
Warner Bros. WS-1404	(S)	**3,046 People Danced 'Til 4 AM**	1960	5.00	12.00
Warner Bros. W-1421	(M)	**The Band With The Beat**	1961	4.00	10.00
Warner Bros. W-1421	(S)	**The Band With The Beat**	1961	5.00	12.00
Warner Bros. WS-1452	(M)	**Bill Doggett Swings**	1962	4.00	10.00
Warner Bros. WS-1452	(S)	**Bill Doggett Swings**	1962	5.00	12.00
Columbia CL-1814	(M)	**Oops!**	1962	4.00	10.00
Columbia CS-8614	(S)	**Oops!**	1962	5.00	12.00
Columbia CL-1942	(M)	**Prelude To The Blues**	1963	4.00	10.00
Columbia CS-8742	(S)	**Prelude To The Blues**	1963	5.00	12.00
Columbia CL-2082	(M)	**Fingertips**	1963	4.00	10.00
Columbia CS-8882	(S)	**Fingertips**	1963	5.00	12.00
Roulette R-25330	(M)	**Honky Tonk Ala Mod**	1966	4.00	10.00
Roulette SR-25330	(S)	**Honky Tonk Ala Mod**	1966	5.00	12.00
King 1078	(S)	**Honky Tonk Popcorn**	1969	20.00	50.00
		(Produced by James Brown.)			
King 1097	(S)	**The Nearness Of You**	1970	4.00	10.00
King 1101	(S)	**Ram Bunk Shush**	1970	4.00	10.00
King 1104	(S)	**Sentimental Journey**	1970	4.00	10.00
King 1108	(S)	**Soft**	1970	4.00	10.00

DOHERTY, DENNY
Mr. Doherty was formerly a member of The Mugwumps; The Mamas & The Papas.

Label & Catalog #		Title	Year	VG+	NM
Dunhill DS-50096	(S)	**Watcha' Gonna Do?**	1970	10.00	25.00
Ember EMS-1036	(S)	**Waiting For A Song**	1975	6.00	15.00

Label & Catalog #		Title	Year	VG+	NM
DOJO					
Eclipse ES-7309	(S)	**Down For The Last Time**	1971	10.00	25.00

Label & Catalog #		Title	Year	VG+	NM

DOLENZ, JONES, BOYCE & HART
Mickey Dolenz, Davey Jones, Tommy Boyce and Bobby Hart. Refer to The Monkees.

Label & Catalog #		Title	Year	VG+	NM
Capitol ST-11513	(S)	Dolenz, Jones, Boyce And Hart	1976	10.00	25.00

DOMINO, FATS

Label & Catalog #		Title	Year	VG+	NM
Imperial LP-9004	(M)	Rock And Rollin' With Fats Domino	1956	60.00	150.00
Imperial LP-9009	(M)	Rock And Rollin'	1956	60.00	150.00
Imperial LP-9028	(M)	This Is Fats Domino!	1957	60.00	150.00
Imperial LP-9038	(M)	Here Stands Fats Domino	1957	60.00	150.00
Imperial LP-9040	(M)	This Is Fats	1957	60.00	150.00
— Original Imperial albums above have maroon labels.—					
Imperial LP-9004	(M)	Rock And Rollin' With Fats Domino	1958	20.00	50.00
Imperial LP-9009	(M)	Rock And Rollin'	1958	20.00	50.00
Imperial LP-9028	(M)	This Is Fats Domino!	1958	20.00	50.00
Imperial LP-9038	(M)	Here Stands Fats Domino	1958	20.00	50.00
Imperial LP-9055	(M)	The Fabulous Mr. D	1958	20.00	50.00
Imperial LP-9062	(M)	Fats Domino Swings	1959	20.00	50.00
Imperial LP-9103	(M)	Million Record Hits	1960	20.00	50.00
Imperial LP-9127	(M)	A Lot Of Dominos	1961	16.00	40.00
Imperial LP-12066	(S)	A Lot Of Dominos	1961	40.00	100.00
Imperial LP-9138	(M)	I Miss You So	1961	16.00	40.00
Imperial LP-12398	(E)	I Miss You So	1961	16.00	40.00
Imperial LP-9153	(M)	Let The Four Winds Blow	1961	16.00	40.00
Imperial LP-12073	(S)	Let The Four Winds Blow	1961	40.00	100.00
Imperial LP-9164	(M)	What A Party	1962	16.00	40.00
Imperial LP-9170	(M)	Twistin' The Stomp	1962	16.00	40.00
Imperial LP-9195	(M)	Million Sellers By Fats	1962	12.00	30.00
Imperial LP-9208	(M)	Just Domino	1962	16.00	40.00
Imperial LP-9227	(M)	Walking To New Orleans	1963	12.00	30.00
Imperial LP-9239	(M)	Let's Dance With Domino	1963	12.00	30.00
Imperial LP-9248	(M)	Here He Comes Again	1963	12.00	30.00
— Imperial mono albums above have black labels with colored stars on top; stereo album have black labels with silver print.—					
Imperial LP-9004	(M)	Rock And Rollin' With Fats Domino	1964	10.00	25.00
Imperial LP-12387	(E)	Rock And Rollin' With Fats Domino	1964	8.00	20.00
Imperial LP-9009	(M)	Rock And Rollin'	1964	10.00	25.00
Imperial LP-12388	(E)	Rock And Rollin'	1964	8.00	20.00
Imperial LP-9028	(M)	This Is Fats Domino!	1964	10.00	25.00
Imperial LP-12389	(E)	This Is Fats Domino!	1964	8.00	20.00
Imperial LP-9038	(M)	Here Stands Fats Domino	1964	10.00	25.00
Imperial LP-12390	(E)	Here Stands Fats Domino	1964	8.00	20.00
Imperial LP-9040	(M)	This Is Fats	1964	10.00	25.00
Imperial LP-12391	(E)	This Is Fats	1964	8.00	20.00
Imperial LP-9055	(M)	The Fabulous Mr. D	1964	10.00	25.00
Imperial LP-12394	(E)	The Fabulous Mr. D	1964	8.00	20.00
Imperial LP-9062	(M)	Fats Domino Swings	1964	10.00	25.00
Imperial LP-12091	(E)	Fats Domino Swings	1964	8.00	20.00
Imperial LP-9065	(M)	Let's Play Fats Domino	1964	10.00	25.00
Imperial LP-12395	(E)	Let's Play Fats Domino	1964	8.00	20.00
Imperial LP-9103	(M)	Million Record Hits	1964	10.00	25.00
Imperial LP-12103	(E)	Million Record Hits	1964	8.00	20.00
Imperial LP-9127	(M)	A Lot Of Dominos	1964	10.00	25.00
Imperial LP-12066	(S)	A Lot Of Dominos	1964	14.00	35.00
Imperial LP-9138	(M)	I Miss You So	1964	10.00	25.00
Imperial LP-12398	(E)	I Miss You So	1964	8.00	20.00
Imperial LP-9153	(M)	Let The Four Winds Blow	1964	10.00	25.00
Imperial LP-12073	(S)	Let The Four Winds Blow	1964	14.00	35.00
Imperial LP-9195	(M)	Million Sellers By Fats	1964	10.00	25.00
Imperial LP-12195	(E)	Million Sellers By Fats	1964	8.00	20.00
Imperial LP-9227	(M)	Walking To New Orleans	1964	10.00	25.00
Imperial LP-12227	(E)	Walking To New Orleans	1964	8.00	20.00
Imperial LP-9239	(M)	Let's Dance With Domino	1964	10.00	25.00
Imperial LP-12239	(E)	Let's Dance With Domino	1964	8.00	20.00
Imperial LP-9248	(M)	Here He Comes Again	1964	10.00	25.00
Imperial LP-12248	(E)	Here He Comes Again	1964	8.00	20.00
— Imperial albums above have black & pink labels.—					
Imperial LP-9004	(M)	Rock And Rollin' With Fats Domino	1967	8.00	20.00
Imperial LP-12387	(E)	Rock And Rollin' With Fats Domino	1967	6.00	15.00

Antoine "Fats" Domino was already a rhythm 'n blues legend years before being "discovered" by young white record buyers and declared a rock 'n roll artist. Along with partner Dave Bartholomew (with whose orchestra and band he had began his career), Fats wrote most of his own hits; he also played piano on countless sessions for other New Orleans based artists. Fats has probably sold more records in the '50s than anyone but Presley. Of Fats' extensive Imperial LP catalog, only four of seventeen titles made the national charts, none receiving an RIAA Gold Record.

Label & Catalog #		Title	Year	VG+	NM
Imperial LP-9009	(M)	Rock And Rollin'	1967	8.00	20.00
Imperial LP-12388	(E)	Rock And Rollin'	1967	6.00	15.00
Imperial LP-9028	(M)	This Is Fats Domino!	1967	8.00	20.00
Imperial LP-12389	(E)	This Is Fats Domino!	1967	6.00	15.00
Imperial LP-9038	(M)	Here Stands Fats Domino	1967	8.00	20.00
Imperial LP-12390	(E)	Here Stands Fats Domino	1967	6.00	15.00
Imperial LP-9040	(M)	This Is Fats	1967	8.00	20.00
Imperial LP-12391	(E)	This Is Fats	1967	6.00	15.00
Imperial LP-9055	(M)	The Fabulous Mr. D	1967	8.00	20.00
Imperial LP-12394	(E)	The Fabulous Mr. D	1967	6.00	15.00
Imperial LP-9062	(M)	Fats Domino Swings	1967	8.00	20.00
Imperial LP-12091	(E)	Fats Domino Swings	1967	6.00	15.00
Imperial LP-9065	(M)	Let's Play Fats Domino	1967	8.00	20.00
Imperial LP-12395	(E)	Let's Play Fats Domino	1967	6.00	15.00
Imperial LP-9103	(M)	Fats Domino Sings Million Record Hits	1967	8.00	20.00
Imperial LP-12103	(E)	Fats Domino Sings Million Record Hits	1967	6.00	15.00
Imperial LP-9127	(M)	A Lot Of Dominos	1967	8.00	20.00
Imperial LP-12066	(S)	A Lot Of Dominos	1967	6.00	15.00
Imperial LP-9138	(M)	I Miss You So	1967	8.00	20.00
Imperial LP-12398	(E)	I Miss You So	1967	6.00	15.00
Imperial LP-9153	(M)	Let The Four Winds Blow	1967	8.00	20.00
Imperial LP-12073	(S)	Let The Four Winds Blow	1967	10.00	25.00
Imperial LP-9195	(M)	Million Sellers By Fats	1967	8.00	20.00
Imperial LP-12195	(S)	Million Sellers By Fats	1967	10.00	25.00
Imperial LP-9227	(M)	Walking To New Orleans	1967	8.00	20.00
Imperial LP-12227	(E)	Walking To New Orleans	1967	6.00	15.00
Imperial LP-9239	(M)	Let's Dance With Domino	1967	8.00	20.00
Imperial LP-12239	(E)	Let's Dance With Domino	1967	6.00	15.00
Imperial LP-9248	(M)	Here He Comes Again	1967	8.00	20.00
Imperial LP-12248	(E)	Here He Comes Again	1967	6.00	15.00
— Imperial albums above have black & green labels.—					
ABC Paramount 455	(M)	Here Comes Fats Domino	1963	8.00	20.00
ABC Paramount S-455	(S)	Here Comes Fats Domino	1963	10.00	25.00
ABC Paramount 479	(M)	Fats On Fire	1964	8.00	20.00
ABC Paramount S-479	(S)	Fats On Fire	1964	10.00	25.00
ABC Paramount 510	(M)	Getaway With Fats Domino	1965	8.00	20.00
ABC Paramount S-510	(S)	Getaway With Fats Domino	1965	10.00	25.00
Grand Award G-267	(M)	Fats Domino	196?	8.00	20.00
Grand Award GS-267	(E)	Fats Domino	196?	4.00	10.00
Mercury MG-21029	(M)	Fats Domino '65	1965	10.00	25.00
Mercury SR-61029	(S)	Fats Domino '65	1965	16.00	40.00
Mercury MG-21065	(M)	Southland U.S.A.	1966	Unreleased	
Mercury SR-61065	(S)	Southland U.S.A.	1966	Unreleased	
Sunset SUM-1103	(M)	Fats Domino	1966	5.00	12.00
Sunset SUS-5103	(E)	Fats Domino	1966	5.00	12.00
Sunset SUM-1158	(M)	Stompin' Fats Domino	1967	5.00	12.00
Sunset SUS-5158	(E)	Stompin' Fats Domino	1967	5.00	12.00
Sunset SUS-5200	(P)	Trouble In Mind	1968	8.00	20.00
Sunset SUS-5299	(E)	Ain't That A Shame	1970	5.00	12.00
Reprise RS-6304	(S)	Fats Is Back	1968	8.00	20.00
Reprise RS-6439	(S)	Fats (Test pressing)	1971	150.00	300.00
Reprise RS-6439	(S)	Fats	1971	Unreleased	
United Arts. UAS-9958	(M)	Legendary Masters (2 LPs)	1971	6.00	15.00
United Arts. UAMG-104	(DJ)	The Fats Domino Sound	1973	14.00	35.00
		(Promo only with edited versions of 30 tracks.)			
United Artists LA122	(DJ)	Cookin' With Fats (Multi-color vinyl)	1974	300.00	500.00
		(Single album promotional sampler.)			
United Artists LA122	(M)	Cookin' With Fats (2 LPs)	1974	12.00	30.00
United Arts. LA233G	(M)	The Very Best Of Fats Domino	1974	4.00	10.00
Candlelite Music P2-13197		The Legendary Music Man (2 LPs)	1976	6.00	15.00
"FD" Records WB-8000	(S)	Fats Domino 1980	1980	6.00	15.00

DON & DEWEY
Don "Sugarcane" Harris and Dewey Terry.

Specialty SPS-2131	(E)	They're Rockin' Til Midnight, Rollin' Til Dawn	1970	12.00	30.00
		("Pink Champagne" and "Mammer Jammer" are stereo on this LP.)			

While Lonnie Donegan is often dismissed by contemporary historians as a clever salesman (and his massive 1961 novelty hit, "Does Your Chewing Gum Lose Its Flavor On The Bed Post Over Night," certainly assists that observation), his most important recording, "Rock Island Line," started a small revolution in Great Britain in 1956, steering a generation of young musicians—including one John Winston Lennon—away from puerile pop into "honest" music.

Label & Catalog #		Title	Year	VG+	NM
DON & EDDIE					
Modern M-814	(M)	**Rock And Roll Party**	196?	12.00	30.00
Modern MST-814	(S)	**Rock And Roll Party**	196?	16.00	40.00
DON & THE GOOD TIMES					
Refer to Jim Valley.					
Burdette 300	(M)	**Don & The Goodtimes' Greatest Hits**	1966	20.00	50.00
Burdette 300-S	(S)	**Don & The Goodtimes' Greatest Hits**	1966	*See note below*	
		(Recently unearthed true stereo version with			
		no transactions from which to derive a value.)			
Epic LN-24311	(M)	**So Good**	1967	6.00	15.00
Epic BN-26311	(S)	**So Good**	1967	8.00	20.00
Wand WDS-679	(S)	**Where The Action Is**	1969	12.00	30.00
DON, DICK & JIMMY					
Modern LMP-1205	(M)	**Spring Fever**	195?	16.00	40.00
Verve MGV-2084	(M)	**Medium Rare**	195?	6.00	15.00
Verve MGV-2107	(M)	**Songs For The Hearth**	195?	6.00	15.00
DONEGAN, LONNIE					
Mercury MG-20229	(M)	**An Englishman Sings American Folk Songs**	1957	30.00	75.00
Dot DLP-3159	(M)	**Lonnie Donegan**	1959	14.00	35.00
Dot DLP-25159	(S)	**Lonnie Donegan**	1959	20.00	50.00
Dot DLP-3394	(M)	**Lonnie Donegan**	1961	10.00	25.00
Dot DLP-25394	(S)	**Lonnie Donegan**	1961	12.00	30.00
Atlantic 8038	(M)	**Skiffle Folk Music**	1960	10.00	25.00
Atlantic SD-8038	(S)	**Skiffle Folk Music**	1960	12.00	30.00
ABC-Paramount-433	(M)	**Sing Hallelujah**	1963	8.00	20.00
ABC-Paramount S-433	(S)	**Sing Hallelujah**	1963	10.00	25.00
DONNER, RAL					
Gone LP-5012	(M)	**Takin' Care Of Business**	1961	80.00	200.00
DONNER, RAL / RAY SMITH / BOBBY DALE					
Crown CLP-5335	(M)	**Ral Donner, Ray Smith And Bobby Dale**	1963	12.00	30.00
Crown CST-335	(E)	**Ral Donner, Ray Smith And Bobby Dale**	1963	6.00	15.00
DONNIE & THE DELCHORDS					
Taurus 1000	(S)	**Donnie & The Delchords With The Neons**	1967	100.00	250.00
DONOVAN (DONOVAN LEITCH)					
Hickory LPM-123	(M)	**Catch The Wind**	1965	10.00	25.00
Hickory LPS-123	(E)	**Catch The Wind**	1965	8.00	20.00
Hickory LPM-127	(M)	**Fairy Tale**	1965	8.00	20.00
Hickory LPS-127	(S)	**Fairy Tale**	1965	10.00	25.00
		("Colours" is rechanneled on this album.)			
Hickory LPM-135	(M)	**The Real Donovan**	1966	8.00	20.00
Hickory LPS-135	(P)	**The Real Donovan**	1966	10.00	25.00
		(While this compilation features rechanneled stereo tracks from			
		Hickory 128, the other tracks, including "Colours," are stereo.)			
Hickory LPS-143	(P)	**Like It Is, Was And Evermore Shall Be**	1968	8.00	20.00
Hickory LPS-149	(P)	**The Best Of Donovan**	1969	8.00	20.00
Epic LN-24217	(M)	**Sunshine Superman**	1966	10.00	25.00
Epic BN-26217	(E)	**Sunshine Superman**	1966	5.00	12.00
Epic LN-24239	(M)	**Mellow Yellow**	1967	10.00	25.00
Epic BN-26239	(E)	**Mellow Yellow**	1967	5.00	12.00
Epic LN-24349	(M)	**Wear Your Love Like Heaven**	1967	6.00	15.00
Epic BN-26349	(S)	**Wear Your Love Like Heaven**	1967	8.00	20.00
Epic LN-24350	(M)	**For Little Ones**	1967	6.00	15.00
Epic BN-26350	(S)	**For Little Ones**	1967	8.00	20.00
Epic L2N-171	(M)	**A Gift From A Flower To A Garden**	1968	16.00	40.00
Epic B2N-171	(S)	**A Gift From A Flower To A Garden**	1968	10.00	25.00
		(Boxed set of the two previous albums, "Wear Your Love Like			
		Heaven" and "For Little Ones." Issued with a portfolio of lyrics,			
		drawings, and poetry, which are included in the price.)			
Epic BN-26386	(S)	**Donovan In Concert**	1968	6.00	15.00
Epic BXN-26439	(S)	**Donovan's Greatest Hits**	1969	6.00	15.00
		("Catch The Wind" and "Colours" were rerecorded in stereo			
		for this album while "Mellow Yellow" is rechanneled.)			

Label & Catalog #		Title	Year	VG+	NM
Epic BN-26481	(S)	**Barabajagal**	1969	6.00	15.00
Epic E-30125	(S)	**Open Road**	1970	6.00	15.00
Epic KE-32156	(S)	**Cosmic Wheels** *(Includes poster)*	1970	5.00	12.00
		— Original Epic albums above have yellow labels.—			
DOOBIE BROTHERS, THE					
Warner Bros. BS4-2634	(Q)	**Toulouse Street**	1974	6.00	15.00
Warner Bros. BS4-2694	(Q)	**The Captain And Me**	1974	6.00	15.00
Warner Bros. WS4-2750	(Q)	**What Were Once Vices Are Now Habits**	1974	6.00	15.00
Warner Bros. BS4-2835	(Q)	**Stampede**	1975	6.00	15.00
Pickwick SPC-3721	(S)	**Introducing The Doobie Brothers**	1980	4.00	10.00
		(Collects pre-Warner Bros. recording.)			
Nautilus NR-5	(S)	**The Captain And Me**	1980	13.00	40.00
Nautilus NR-18	(S)	**Minute By Minute**	1981	5.00	15.00
Mobile Fidelity MFSL-122	(S)	**Takin' It To The Streets**	198?	6.00	18.00
DOONICAN, VAL					
Decca DL-4962	(M)	**If The Whole World Stopped Lovin'**	1966	6.00	15.00
Decca DL-74962	(S)	**If The Whole World Stopped Lovin'**	1966	8.00	20.00
London PL-3515	(M)	**The Many Shades Of Val Doonican**	1967	8.00	20.00
London PS-515	(S)	**The Many Shades Of Val Doonican**	1967	8.00	20.00
DOORS, THE					
The Doors are John Densmore, Robbie Krieger, Ray Manzarek and Jim Morrison.					
Elektra EKL-4007	(M)	**The Doors**	1967	20.00	50.00
Elektra EKS-74007	(S)	**The Doors**	1967	10.00	25.00
Elektra EKL-4014	(M)	**Strange Days**	1967	30.00	75.00
Elektra EKS-74014	(S)	**Strange Days**	1967	10.00	25.00
Elektra EKL-4024	(M)	**Waiting For The Sun**	1968	40.00	100.00
Elektra EKS-74024	(S)	**Waiting For The Sun**	1968	10.00	25.00
		— Original Elektra albums above have brown labels.—			
Elektra EKS-75005	(S)	**The Soft Parade**	1969	6.00	15.00
Elektra EKS-75007	(S)	**Morrison Hotel/Hard Rock Cafe**	1970	6.00	15.00
		— Original Elektra albums above have red labels.—			
Elektra EKS-2-9002	(S)	**Absolutely Live** *(2 LPs)*	1970	8.00	20.00
Elektra EKS-74079	(DJ)	**The Doors 13** *(White label)*	1970	16.00	40.00
Elektra EKS-74079	(S)	**The Doors 13**	1970	6.00	15.00
Elektra EKS-75011	(DJ)	**L.A. Woman** *(White label)*	1971	24.00	60.00
Elektra EKS-75011	(S)	**L.A. Woman**	1971	10.00	25.00
		(Originally issued in a cover with a die-cut window and a yellow inner sleeve with a photo of the group.)			
Elektra EKS-75017	(S)	**Other Voices**	1971	6.00	15.00
Elektra EKS-2-6001	(S)	**Weird Scenes Inside The Gold Mine** *(2 LPs)*	1972	6.00	15.00
Elektra EKS-75038	(S)	**Full Circle**	1972	6.00	15.00
Elektra EQ-5035	(Q)	**Best Of The Doors**	1973	10.00	25.00
		— Original Elektra albums above have "butterfly" labels.—			
Mobile Fidelity MSFL-051	(S)	**The Doors**	1980	20.00	60.00
DORS, DIANA					
Columbia CL-1436	(M)	**Swinging Dors**	1960	20.00	50.00
Columbia CS-8236	(S)	**Swinging Dors**	1960	30.00	75.00
DORSEY, LEE					
Fury 1002	(M)	**Ya Ya**	1962	100.00	250.00
Sphere Sound SR-7003	(M)	**Ya Ya**	1963	20.00	50.00
Sphere Sound SSR-7003	(E)	**Ya Ya**	1963	16.00	40.00
		(Sphere Sound 7003 is a reissue of Fury 1002.)			
Amy 8010	(M)	**Ride Your Pony**	1966	12.00	30.00
Amy S-8010	(S)	**Ride your Pony**	1966	16.00	40.00
Amy 8011	(M)	**The New Lee Dorsey**	1966	10.00	25.00
Amy S-8011	(S)	**The New Lee Dorsey**	1966	12.00	30.00
DOUGLAS, GLEN					
Decca DL-8748	(M)	**Heartbreak Alley**	1958	16.00	40.00
DOUGLAS, K. C.					
Cook LP-5002	(M)	**Road Recordings**	1954	100.00	250.00
Bluesville BVLP-1023	(M)	**K. C.'s Blues**	1961	20.00	50.00
Bluesville BVLP-1050	(M)	**Big Road Blues**	1962	20.00	50.00

Label & Catalog #		Title	Year	VG+	NM
DOVELLS, THE					
The Dovells feature Len Barry. Refer to the Orlons.					
Parkway P-7006	(M)	The Bristol Stomp	1961	40.00	100.00
Parkway P-7010	(M)	All The Hits Of The Teen Groups	1962	40.00	100.00
Parkway P-7011	(M)	Don't Knock The Twist *(Soundtrack)*	1962	40.00	100.00
Parkway P-7021	(M)	For Your Hully Gully Party	1963	30.00	75.00
Parkway P-7025	(M)	You Can't Sit Down	1963	30.00	75.00
Cameo C-1082	(M)	Len Barry Sings With The Dovells	1964	20.00	50.00
DOWELL, JOE					
Smash MGS-27000	(M)	Wooden Heart	1961	14.00	35.00
Smash SRS-67000	(S)	Wooden Heart	1961	20.00	50.00
Smash MGS-27011	(M)	German American Hits	1962	10.00	25.00
Smash SRS-67011	(S)	German American Hits	1962	12.00	30.00
DOWN FROM NOTHING					
No label	(S)	Down From Nothing	197?	100.00	250.00
DOWNS, HUGH					
Epic LN-3597	(M)	An Evening With Hugh Downs	195?	10.00	25.00
Epic BN-341	(S)	An Evening With Hugh Downs	195?	14.00	35.00
DOYLE, BOBBY					
Columbia CL-1858	(M)	In A Most Unusual Way	1962	8.00	20.00
Columbia CS-8658	(S)	In A Most Unusual Way	1962	10.00	25.00
DOYLE, MIKE					
Fleetwood FLP-3018	(M)	The Secrets Of Surfing	1963	10.00	25.00
DRAGONFLY					
Megaphone MS-1202	(S)	Dragonfly	1968	50.00	125.00
DRAGONWYCK					
(No label)	(S)	Dragonwyck *(Test pressing without a cover)*	197?	500.00	1,000.00
(No label)	(S)	Dragonwyck 2 *(Acetate without a cover)*	197?	500.00	Rare
		(Near Mint acetates have a suggested value of $1,000-2,000.)			
DRAGSTERS, THE					
Wing MGW-12269	(M)	Hot Rod Hits	1964	20.00	50.00
Wing SRW-16269	(S)	Hot Rod Hits	1964	30.00	75.00
DRAKE, NICK					
Island SMAS-9307	(S)	Nick Drake	1971	10.00	25.00
Island SMAS-9318	(S)	Pink Moon	1972	6.00	15.00
DRAKE, PETE					
Drake also recorded as Dean Dallas.					
Starday SLP-180	(M)	The Fabulous Steel Guitar Of Pete Drake	1962	16.00	40.00
Starday SLP-319	(M)	The Amazing And Incredible Pete Drake	1964	12.00	30.00
Smash MGS-27053	(M)	Forever	1964	6.00	15.00
Smash SRS-67053	(S)	Forever	1964	8.00	20.00
Smash MGS-27060	(M)	Talking Steel Guitar	1965	6.00	15.00
Smash SRS-67060	(S)	Talking Steel Guitar	1965	8.00	20.00
Smash MGS-27064	(M)	Talking Steel And Singing Strings	1965	6.00	15.00
Smash SRS-67064	(S)	Talking Steel And Singing Strings	1965	8.00	20.00
Cumberland MGC-29053	(M)	Country Steel Guitar	196?	8.00	20.00
Canaan LP-4640	(M)	Steel Away	196?	6.00	15.00
Canaan LP-9640	(S)	Steel Away	196?	8.00	20.00
DRAMATICS, THE					
Volt VOS-6018	(S)	Whatcha See Is Whatcha Get	197?	8.00	20.00
DRAPER, RUSTY					
Mercury MG-20068	(M)	Music For A Rainy Night	1956	12.00	30.00
Mercury MG-20117	(M)	Encores	1957	12.00	30.00
Mercury MG-20118	(M)	Rusty Draper Sings	1957	12.00	30.00
Mercury MG-20173	(M)	Rusty Meets Hoagy	1957	12.00	30.00

Label & Catalog #		Title	Year	VG+	NM
DREAMLOVERS, THE					
Columbia CL-2020	(M)	The Bird/Other Golden Dancing Grooves	1963	12.00	30.00
Columbia CS-8820	(S)	The Bird/Other Golden Dancing Grooves	1963	16.00	40.00
DREW, DORIS					
Mode MOD-126	(M)	Delightful Doris Drew	1957	30.00	75.00
DREW, PATTI					
Capitol T-2804	(M)	Tell Him	1967	6.00	15.00
Capitol ST-2804	(S)	Tell Him	1967	8.00	20.00
Capitol ST-156	(S)	I've Been Here All The Time	1969	5.00	12.00
Capitol ST-408	(S)	Wild Is Love	1970	5.00	12.00
Capitol ST-408	(DJ)	Wild Is Love (Picture disc)	1979	16.00	40.00

DRIFTERS, THE
Originally formed by Clyde McPhatter, lead singers over the years included Johnny Moore, Bobby Hendricks and Ben E. King.

Atlantic 8003	(M)	Clyde McPhatter & The Drifters	1956	200.00	400.00
Atlantic 8022	(M)	Rockin' And Driftin'	1958	200.00	400.00
		— Original Atlantic albums above have black labes.—			
Atlantic 8003	(M)	Clyde McPhatter & The Drifters	1960	60.00	150.00
Atlantic 8022	(M)	Rockin' And Driftin'	1960	60.00	150.00
Atlantic 8041	(M)	The Drifters' Greatest Hits	1960	30.00	75.00
Atlantic 8059	(M)	Save The Last Dance For Me	1962	30.00	75.00
Atlantic SD-8059	(S)	Save The Last Dance For Me	1962	50.00	125.00
Atlantic 8073	(M)	Up On The Roof	1963	20.00	50.00
Atlantic SD-8073	(S)	Up On The Roof	1963	30.00	75.00
Atlantic 8093	(M)	Our Biggest Hits	1964	20.00	50.00
Atlantic SD-8093	(S)	Our Biggest Hits	1964	30.00	75.00
Atlantic 8099	(M)	Under The Boardwalk	1964	20.00	50.00
Atlantic SD-8099	(S)	Under The Boardwalk	1964	30.00	75.00
Clarion 608	(M)	The Drifters	1964	8.00	20.00
Clarion SD-608	(P)	The Drifters	1964	12.00	30.00
Atlantic 8103	(M)	The Good Life With The Drifters	1965	12.00	30.00
Atlantic SD-8103	(S)	The Good Life With The Drifters	1965	20.00	50.00
Atlantic 8113	(M)	I'll Take You Where The Music's Playing	1965	12.00	30.00
Atlantic SD-8113	(S)	I'll Take You Where The Music's Playing	1965	20.00	50.00
Atlantic 8153	(M)	The Drifters' Golden Hits	1968	8.00	20.00
Atlantic SD-8153	(P)	The Drifters' Golden Hits	1968	8.00	20.00
		—Mono Atlantic albums above have orange & purple labels;			
		stereo albums have green & blue labels.—			
Atlantic SD-8153	(P)	The Drifters' Golden Hits (Green & blue label)	1968	8.00	20.00

DRIFTIN' SLIM
Driftin' Slim is a pseudonym for Elmon Mickle.

Milestone 93004	(M)	Driftin' Slim And His Blues Band (2 LPs)	1968	8.00	20.00

DRIFTWOOD, JIMMY

RCA Victor LPM-1635	(M)	Newly Discovered Early American Folk Songs	1958	20.00	50.00
RCA Victor LPM-1994	(M)	Wilderness Road	1959	12.00	30.00
RCA Victor LSP-1994	(S)	Wilderness Road	1959	20.00	50.00
RCA Victor LPM-2171	(M)	The Westward Movement	1959	12.00	30.00
RCA Victor LSP-2171	(S)	The Westward Movement	1959	20.00	50.00
RCA Victor LPM-2228	(M)	Tall Tales In Song	1960	8.00	20.00
RCA Victor LSP-2228	(S)	Tall Tales In Song	1960	16.00	40.00
RCA Victor LPM-2316	(M)	Songs Of Billy Yank And Johnny Reb	1961	8.00	20.00
RCA Victor LSP-2316	(S)	Songs Of Billy Yank And Johnny Reb	1961	12.00	30.00
RCA Victor LPM-2443	(M)	Driftwood At Sea	1962	8.00	20.00
RCA Victor LSP-2443	(S)	Driftwood At Sea	1962	12.00	30.00
		— Original RCA mono albums above have black labels with "Long Play" on the bottom;			
		stereo albums have "Living Stereo" on the bottom.—			
Monument MLP-8006	(M)	Voice Of The People	1963	6.00	15.00
Monument SLP-18006	(S)	Voice Of The People	1963	8.00	20.00
Monument MLP-8019	(M)	Down In The Arkansas	1965	6.00	15.00
Monument SLP-18019	(S)	Down In The Arkansas	1965	8.00	20.00
Monument MLP-8043	(M)	The Best Of Johnny Driftwood	1966	5.00	12.00
Monument SLP-18043	(S)	The Best Of Johnny Driftwood	1966	6.00	15.00

Label & Catalog #		Title	Year	VG+	NM

DRISCOOL, JOOLS: *Refer to* BRIAN AUGER

DRUIDS OF STONEHENGE, THE

Label & Catalog #		Title	Year	VG+	NM
Uni 3004	(M)	Creation	1967	16.00	40.00
Uni 73004	(S)	Creation	1967	20.00	50.00

DRUSKY, ROY

Decca DL-4160	(M)	Anymore With Roy Drusky	1961	8.00	20.00
Decca DL-74160	(S)	Anymore With Roy Drusky	1961	12.00	30.00
Decca DL-4340	(M)	It's My Way	1962	8.00	20.00
Decca DL-74340	(S)	It's My Way	1962	12.00	30.00
Mercury MG-20883	(M)	Songs Of The Cities	1964	6.00	15.00
Mercury SR-60883	(S)	Songs Of The Cities	1964	8.00	20.00
Mercury MG-20919	(M)	Yesterday's Gone	1964	6.00	15.00
Mercury SR-60919	(S)	Yesterday's Gone	1964	8.00	20.00
Mercury MG-20973	(M)	The Pick Of The Country	1964	6.00	15.00
Mercury SR-60973	(S)	The Pick Of The Country	1964	8.00	20.00
Mercury MG-21006	(M)	Country Music All Around The World	1965	6.00	15.00
Mercury SR-61006	(S)	Country Music All Around The World	1965	8.00	20.00
Mercury MG-21052	(M)	Roy Drusky's Greatest Hits	1965	6.00	15.00
Mercury SR-61052	(S)	Roy Drusky's Greatest Hits	1965	8.00	20.00
Mercury MG-21062	(M)	Country Song Express	1966	6.00	15.00
Mercury SR-61062	(S)	Country Song Express	1966	8.00	20.00
Mercury MG-21083	(M)	In A New Dimension	1966	6.00	15.00
Mercury SR-61083	(S)	In A New Dimension	1966	8.00	20.00
Mercury MG-21097	(M)	If The Whole World Stopped Lovin'	1966	6.00	15.00
Mercury SR-61097	(S)	If The Whole World Stopped Lovin'	1966	8.00	20.00
Mercury MG-21118	(M)	Now Is A Lonely Time	1967	8.00	20.00
Mercury SR-61118	(S)	Now Is A Lonely Time	1967	6.00	15.00
Mercury MG-21145	(M)	Roy Drusky's Greatest Hits, Volume 2	1968	10.00	25.00
Mercury SR-61145	(S)	Roy Drusky's Greatest Hits, Volume 2	1968	6.00	15.00

DRUSKY, ROY, & PRISCILLA MITCHELL

Mercury MG-21035	(M)	Love's Eternal Triangle	1965	5.00	12.00
Mercury SR-61035	(S)	Love's Eternal Triangle	1965	6.00	15.00
Mercury MG-21067	(M)	Together Again	1966	5.00	12.00
Mercury SR-61067	(S)	Together Again	1966	6.00	15.00

DRY CITY SCAT BAND, THE

Elektra EKL-292	(M)	Dry City Scat Band	1965	10.00	25.00
Elektra EKS-7292	(S)	Dry City Scat Band	1965	12.00	30.00

DRY DOCK COUNTY

Mercury SR-61286	(S)	Dry Dock County	1970	6.00	15.00

DRYEWATER

J. T. B. NRS-122	(S)	Dryewater	1974	30.00	75.00

DU SHON, JEAN

Argo LP-4039	(M)	Make Way For Jean Du Shon	1964	8.00	20.00
Argo LPS-4039	(S)	Make Way For Jean Du Shon	1964	10.00	25.00
Argo LP-750	(M)	You Better Believe It	1965	8.00	20.00
Argo LPS-750	(S)	You Better Believe It	1965	10.00	25.00

DUBS, THE

Josie JM-4001	(M)	The Dubs Meet The Shells	1962	60.00	150.00
Josie JSS-4001	(P)	The Dubs Meet The Shells	1962	150.00	350.00

DUDLEY, DAVE

Golden Ring 110	(M)	Six Days On The Road	1963	50.00	125.00

DUELS, THE

Sue LP-2002	(M)	Stick Shift (Cartoon cover)	1961	80.00	200.00
Sue LP-2002	(M)	Stick Shift (Photo cover)	1964	60.00	150.00

DUKE, PATTY, & NORMAN VINCENT PEALE

Guideposts GP-101	(M)	Guideposts For Christmas	1963	16.00	40.00

Label & Catalog #		Title	Year	VG+	NM
DUKE, PATTY					
United Arts. UAL-4131	(M)	**Billie** *(Soundtrack)*	1965	8.00	20.00
United Arts. UAS-5131	(S)	**Billie** *(Soundtrack)*	1965	10.00	25.00
United Arts. UAL-3452	(M)	**Don't Just Stand There**	1965	6.00	15.00
United Arts. UAS-6452	(S)	**Don't Just Stand There**	1965	8.00	20.00
United Arts. UAL-3492	(M)	**Patty**	1966	6.00	15.00
United Arts. UAS-6492	(S)	**Patty**	1966	8.00	20.00
United Arts. UAL-3535	(M)	**Patty Duke's Greatest Hits**	1966	6.00	15.00
United Arts. UAS-6535	(S)	**Patty Duke's Greatest Hits**	1966	8.00	20.00
Unart 20005	(M)	**TV's Teen Star**	1967	5.00	12.00
Unart 520005	(S)	**TV's Teen Star**	1967	6.00	15.00
United Arts. UAS-6632	(S)	**Songs From The Valley Of The Dolls**	1968	10.00	25.00
DUNBAR, AYNSLEY					
Aynsley Dunbar also recorded as a Mother with Frank Zappa.					
Blue Thumb BTS-4	(S)	**Retaliation**	1968	10.00	25.00
Blue Thumb BTS-6	(S)	**Doctor Dunbar's Prescription**	1969	10.00	25.00
Blue Thumb BTS-16	(S)	**To Mum, From Aynsley And The Boys**	1970	10.00	25.00
DUPREE, "CHAMPION" JACK					
Refer to Jimmy Rushing / Jack Dupree.					
Atlantic 8019	(M)	**Blues From The Gutter**	1959	70.00	175.00
Atlantic SD-8019	(S)	**Blues From The Gutter**	1959	100.00	250.00
—Atlantic mono albums above have black labels with a white fan; stereos have green labels.—					
Atlantic 8019	(S)	**Blues From The Gutter**	1961	20.00	50.00
Atlantic SD-8019	(S)	**Blues From The Gutter**	1961	30.00	75.00
Atlantic 8045	(S)	**Natural And Soulful Blues**	1961	20.00	50.00
Atlantic SD-8045	(S)	**Natural And Soulful Blues**	1961	30.00	75.00
Atlantic 8056	(M)	**Champion Of The Blues**	1961	16.00	40.00
Atlantic SD-8056	(S)	**Champion Of The Blues**	1961	20.00	50.00
—Atlantic mono albums above have orange & purple labels with a white fan;					
stereo albums have green & blue labels with a white fan.—					
King LP-735	(M)	**Champion Jack Dupree Sings The Blues**	1961	100.00	200.00
Folkways FS-3825	(M)	**Women Blues Of Champion Jack Dupree**	1961	10.00	25.00
OKeh OKM-12103	(M)	**Cabbage Greens**	1963	12.00	30.00
Blue Horizon 7702	(S)	**When You Feel The Feeling**	1969	10.00	25.00
London PS-553	(S)	**From New Orleans To Chicago**	1969	8.00	20.00
Atlantic SD-8255	(S)	**Blues From The Gutter**	1970	6.00	15.00
King KS-1084	(S)	**Walking The Blues**	1970	6.00	15.00
DUPREE, "CHAMPION" JACK, & MICKEY BAKER					
Sire SES-97010	(S)	**In Heavy Blues**	1969	10.00	25.00
DUPREE, SIMON, & THE BIG SOUND					
Tower ST-5097	(S)	**Without Reservations**	1968	10.00	25.00
DUPREES, THE					
Coed LPC-905	(M)	**You Belong To Me**	1962	50.00	125.00
Coed LPC-906	(M)	**Have You Heard**	1963	40.00	100.00
Heritage HTS-35002	(S)	**Total Recall**	1968	12.00	30.00
Post 1000	(E)	**The Duprees Sing**	196?	8.00	20.00
DURAN DURAN					
Mobile Fidelity MFSL-182	(S)	**Seven And The Ragged Tiger**	198?	6.00	18.00
Capitol SPRO-79097/8	(DJ)	**Duran Duran Goes Dutch**	1987	20.00	50.00
DURANTE, JIMMY					
Lion L-70053	(M)	**Jimmy Durante In Person**	1959	10.00	25.00
Decca DL-9040	(M)	**Club Durante**	1959	10.00	25.00
Decca DL-79040	(S)	**Club Durante**	1959	12.00	30.00
Roulette R-25123	(M)	**Jimmy Durante At The Copacabana**	1961	8.00	20.00
Roulette SR-25123	(S)	**Jimmy Durante At The Copacabana**	1961	10.00	25.00
Warner Bros. W-1506	(M)	**September Song**	1963	8.00	20.00
Warner Bros. WS-1506	(S)	**September Song**	1963	10.00	25.00
Warner Bros. W-1531	(M)	**Hello Young Lovers**	1964	8.00	20.00
Warner Bros. WS-1531	(S)	**Hello Young Lovers**	1964	10.00	25.00
MGM E-4207	(M)	**The Very Best Of Jimmy Durante**	1964	5.00	12.00
MGM SE-4207	(S)	**The Very Best Of Jimmy Durante**	1964	6.00	15.00

Label & Catalog #		Title	Year	VG+	NM
Warner Bros. W-1577	(M)	A Way Of Life	1965	6.00	15.00
Warner Bros. WS-1577	(S)	A Way Of Life	1965	8.00	20.00
Warner Bros. W-1655	(M)	One Of Those Songs	1966	6.00	15.00
Warner Bros. WS-1655	(S)	One Of Those Songs	1966	8.00	20.00
Warner Bros. W-1713	(M)	Songs For Sunday	1967	6.00	15.00
Warner Bros. WS-1713	(S)	Songs For Sunday	1967	8.00	20.00
Decca DL-78884	(S)	In Person At The Piano	1970	6.00	15.00

DURBIN, DEANNA

Decca DL-8785	(M)	Deanna Durbin	1958	20.00	50.00

DUROCS, THE

Capitol ST-11981	(S)	The Durocs	1979	6.00	15.00

DWARR

Brand-X	(S)	Starting Over	1985	14.00	35.00
Brand-X	(S)	Animals	1986	14.00	35.00

DYER-BENNET, RICHARD

Decca DLP-5046	(M)	Folksongs	195?	16.00	40.00
Stinson SLP-2	(M)	20th Century Minstrel	195?	16.00	40.00
StinsonSLP- 60	(M)	More Songs By The 20th Century Minstrel	195?	16.00	40.00
Dyer-Bennet 1	(M)	Richard Dyer-Bennet Songs, Volume 1	195?	8.00	20.00
Dyer-Bennet 2	(M)	Richard Dyer-Bennet Songs, Volume 2	195?	8.00	20.00
Dyer-Bennet 3	(M)	Richard Dyer-Bennet Songs, Volume 3	195?	8.00	20.00
Dyer-Bennet 4	(M)	Richard Dyer-Bennet Songs, Volume 4	195?	8.00	20.00
Dyer-Bennet 5	(M)	Richard Dyer-Bennet Songs, Volume 5	195?	8.00	20.00
Dyer-Bennet 6000	(M)	Songs With Young People In Mind	195?	8.00	20.00
Decca DL-9102	(M)	Twentieth Century Minstrel	195?	8.00	20.00
Decca DL-79102	(E)	Twentieth Century Minstrel	195?	8.00	20.00

DYKE & THE BLAZERS

Original Sound LP-8876	(M)	The Funky Broadway	1967	16.00	40.00
Original Sound LPS-8876	(S)	The Funky Broadway	1967	20.00	50.00
Original Sound LPS-8877	(S)	Dyke's Greatest Hits	1968	20.00	50.00

DYLAN, BOB

To avoid confusing label changes, the albums below are listed first in mono, then stereo. Refer to Harry Belafonte; Barry Goldberg; George Harrison & Friends; Carolyn Hester; Doug Sahm; Victoria Spivey.

Columbia CL-1779	(DJ)	Bob Dylan	1962	200.00	400.00

(The label has three white "eye" logo on each side of the spindle hole and is stamped for promotional use. The cover has a silver sticker that reads "A New Star On Columbia.")

Columbia CL-1779	(M)	Bob Dylan	1962	100.00	250.00

(The label has three white "eye" logo on each side of the spindle hole.)

Columbia CL-1779	(M)	Bob Dylan	1963	16.00	40.00

(The label reads "Guaranteed High Fidelity.")

Columbia CL-1779	(M)	Bob Dylan	1967	12.00	30.00

(The label reads "360 Sound Mono.")

Columbia CS-8579	(DJ)	Bob Dylan	1962	300.00	500.00

(The label has three white "eye" logo on each side of the spindle hole and is stamped for promotional use. The cover has a silver sticker that reads "A New Star On Columbia.")

Columbia CS-8579	(S)	Bob Dylan	1962	175.00	350.00

(The label has three white "eye" logo on each side of the spindle hole.)

Columbia CS-8579	(S)	Bob Dylan	1965	14.00	35.00

(The label reads "360 Sound Stereo" in black.)

Columbia CS-8579	(S)	Bob Dylan	1967	10.00	25.00

(The label reads "360 Sound Stereo" in white.)

Columbia CL-1986	(M)	The Freewheelin' Bob Dylan	1963	5,000.00	Rare

(Original pressings contain "Let Me Die In My Footsteps," "Talkin' John Birch Blues," "Rocks & Gravel" and "Ramblin' Gamblin' Willie." These were deleted and replaced on all subsequent pressings with "Masters Of War," "Girl From North Country," "Talkin' World War III Blues," and "Bob Dylan's Dream." As all known mono copies list the later songs on the label, the record must be played to identify. Rare with a suggested Near Mint value of $8,000-12,000.)

Label & Catalog #		Title	Year	VG+	NM
Columbia CS-8786	(S)	**The Freewheelin' Bob Dylan**	1963	**9,000.00**	Rare

*(Original pressings contain "Let Me Die In My Footsteps," "Talkin'
John Birch Blues," "Rocks & Gravel" and "Ramblin' Gamblin' Willie."
These were deleted and replaced on all subsequent pressings with
"Masters Of War," "Girl From North Country," "Talkin' World War
III Blues," and "Bob Dylan's Dream." The only stereo copy found
lists these songs on the label; refer to the article "The World's Most
Valuable Album" elsewhere in this book for more information.
Rare with a suggested Near Mint value of $15,000-25,000.
The aforementioned copy found in '92 was well-played and sold
in auction for approximately $12,000. Several interested parties
claimed that had the record been nearly mint they would have
bid at least as much as the values suggested above. . .)*

Label & Catalog #		Title	Year	VG+	NM
Columbia CL-1986	(DJ)	**The Freewheelin' Bob Dylan** *(White label)*	1963	**660.00**	Rare

*(Both the label and the timing strip on the cover list the original
deleted tracks but the album plays the replacement tracks.
Near Mint copies have a suggested value of $1,000-2,000.)*

Label & Catalog #		Title	Year	VG+	NM
Columbia CL-1986	(DJ)	**The Freewheelin' Bob Dylan Insert**	1963	**40.00**	**100.00**

*(Some copies of the original promos above were issued with an
approximately 4" x 11" note that reads "NOTICE: Please note that
on Side 1, Band 3 and Band 6 are reversed." This is in reference to
the original track line-up where those songs, "Let Me Die In My
Footsteps" and "A Hard Rain's A-Gonna Fall," respectively, were
transposed on the master after the labels had been printed.)*

Label & Catalog #		Title	Year	VG+	NM
Columbia CL-1986	(DJ)	**The Freewheelin' Bob Dylan** *(White label)*	1963	**420.00**	**700.00**

*(The label lists the original deleted tracks while the timing strip
on the cover lists the replacement tracks. The album, of course,
plays the replacement tracks.)*

Label & Catalog #		Title	Year	VG+	NM
Columbia CL-1986	(DJ)	**The Freewheelin' Bob Dylan** *(White label)*	1963	**300.00**	**500.00**

*(The timing strip on the cover lists the original deleted tracks.
The cover and the labels list, and the album plays, the four
replacement tracks.)*

Label & Catalog #		Title	Year	VG+	NM
Columbia CL-1986	(DJ)	**The Freewheelin' Bob Dylan** *(White label)*	1963	**200.00**	**400.00**

*(The timing strip on the cover lists the replacement tracks.
The cover and the labels also list, and the album plays, the four
replacement tracks.)*

Label & Catalog #		Title	Year	VG+	NM
Columbia CL-1986	(M)	**The Freewheelin' Bob Dylan**	1963	**16.00**	**40.00**

(Original labels read "Guaranteed High Fidelity" on the bottom.)

Label & Catalog #		Title	Year	VG+	NM
Columbia CL-1986	(M)	**The Freewheelin' Bob Dylan**	1967	**12.00**	**30.00**

(The label reads "360 Sound Mono.")

Label & Catalog #		Title	Year	VG+	NM
Columbia CS-8786	(S)	**The Freewheelin' Bob Dylan**	1963	**16.00**	**40.00**

(The label reads "360 Sound Stereo" in black without arrows.)

Label & Catalog #		Title	Year	VG+	NM
Columbia CS-8786	(S)	**The Freewheelin' Bob Dylan**	1965	**12.00**	**30.00**

*(The label reads "360 Sound Stereo" in black with arrows
pointing upwards on both sides.)*

Label & Catalog #		Title	Year	VG+	NM
Columbia CS-8786	(S)	**The Freewheelin' Bob Dylan**	1967	**10.00**	**25.00**

(The label reads "360 Sound Stereo" in white.)

Label & Catalog #		Title	Year	VG+	NM
Columbia CL-2105	(DJ)	**The Times They Are A-Changin'**	1964	**200.00**	**400.00**

(White label promo with timing strip on the cover.)

Label & Catalog #		Title	Year	VG+	NM
Columbia CL-2105	(M)	**The Times They Are A-Changin'**	1964	**16.00**	**40.00**

*(Original labels read "Guaranteed High Fidelity" on the bottom.
Issued with a sheet continuing "11 Outlined Epitaphs.")*

Label & Catalog #		Title	Year	VG+	NM
Columbia CL-2105	(M)	**The Times They Are A-Changin'**	1967	**12.00**	**30.00**

(The label reads "360 Sound Mono.")

Label & Catalog #		Title	Year	VG+	NM
Columbia CS-8905	(S)	**The Times They Are A-Changin'**	1964	**12.00**	**30.00**

*(Original labels read "360 Sound Stereo" in black on the bottom.
Issued with a sheet continuing "11 Outlined Epitaphs.")*

Label & Catalog #		Title	Year	VG+	NM
Columbia CS-8905	(S)	**The Times They Are A-Changin'**	1967	**10.00**	**25.00**

(The label reads "360 Sound Stereo" in white.)

Label & Catalog #		Title	Year	VG+	NM
Columbia CL-2193	(DJ)	**Another Side Of Bob Dylan**	1964	**300.00**	**500.00**

(White label promo with timing strip on the cover.)

Label & Catalog #		Title	Year	VG+	NM
Columbia CL-2193	(M)	**Another Side Of Bob Dylan**	1964	**16.00**	**40.00**

(Original labels read "Guaranteed High Fidelity" on the bottom.)

Label & Catalog #		Title	Year	VG+	NM
Columbia CL-2193	(M)	**Another Side Of Bob Dylan**	1967	**12.00**	**30.00**

(The label reads "360 Sound Mono.")

Label & Catalog #		Title	Year	VG+	NM
Columbia CS-8993	(S)	**Another Side Of Bob Dylan**	1964	**12.00**	**30.00**

(Original labels read "360 Sound Stereo" in black on the bottom.)

Label & Catalog #		Title	Year	VG+	NM
Columbia CS-8993	(S)	**Another Side Of Bob Dylan**	1967	**10.00**	**25.00**

(The label reads "360 Sound Stereo" in white.)

Label & Catalog #		Title	Year	VG+	NM
Columbia CL-2302	(M)	Bob Dylan In Concert	1965	Unreleased	
Columbia CS-9102	(S)	Bob Dylan In Concert	1965	Unreleased	
		(Front cover slicks exist for this cancelled title and have a suggested Near Mint value of $3,000-5,000.)			
Columbia CL-2328	(DJ)	Bringing It All Back Home	1965	200.00	400.00
		(White label promo with timing strip on the cover.)			
Columbia CL-2328	(M)	Bringing It All Back Home	1965	20.00	50.00
		(Original labels read "Guaranteed High Fidelity" on the bottom.)			
Columbia CL-2328	(M)	Bringing It All Back Home	1967	16.00	40.00
		(The label reads "360 Sound Mono.")			
Columbia CS-9128	(S)	Bringing It All Back Home	1965	12.00	30.00
		(Original labels read "360 Sound Stereo" in black on the bottom.)			
Columbia CS-9128	(S)	Bringing It All Back Home	1967	10.00	25.00
		(The label reads "360 Sound Stereo" in white.)			
Columbia CL-2389	(DJ)	Highway 61 Revisited	1965	150.00	300.00
		(White label promo with timing strip on the cover.)			
Columbia CL-2389	(M)	Highway 61 Revisited	1965	20.00	50.00
Columbia CS-9189	(S)	Highway 61 Revisited	1965	80.00	200.00
		(The label reads "360 Sound Stereo" in white. Some copies of the first pressings were issued with an alternate take of "From A Buick 6.")			
Columbia		Highway 61 Revisited Poster	1965	40.00	100.00
		(Album-size ink line drawing of Dylan by Lambert. This may have been included with other Dylan albums during 1965.)			
Columbia CS-9189	(S)	Highway 61 Revisited	1965	10.00	25.00
		(The label reads "360 Sound Stereo" in white.)			
Columbia C2L-41	(DJ)	Blonde On Blonde (2 LPs)	1966	420.00	700.00
		(White label promo with timing strip on the cover.)			
Columbia C2L-41	(M)	Blonde On Blonde (2 LPs)	1966	40.00	100.00
Columbia C2S-41	(S)	Blonde On Blonde (2 LPs)	1966	20.00	50.00
		(The label reads "360 Sound Stereo" in white. Original covers have nine photos on the inside, including one of Claudia Cardinale.)			
Columbia C2S-41	(S)	Blonde On Blonde	1966	12.00	30.00
		(The label reads "360 Sound Stereo" in white. The inside cover has seven rearranged photos, omitting the one of Claudia Cardinale.)			
Columbia KCL-2663	(DJ)	Bob Dylan's Greatest Hits (White label)	1967	40.00	100.00
Columbia KCL-2663	(M)	Bob Dylan's Greatest Hits	1967	20.00	50.00
Columbia KCS-9463	(S)	Bob Dylan's Greatest Hits	1967	10.00	25.00
		(The label reads "360 Sound Stereo" in white. This and most subsequent pressings were issued with a fold-open poster of Dylan by artist Peter Max. These are worth $5-10.)			
Warner/7-Arts. 221567	(DJ)	"The Bob Dylan Whitmark Demos"	1967	See note below	
		(One-sided album in a plain cardboard jacket compiled by Whitmark Publishers to showcase twelve of Dylan's [then] unreleased. Rare with a suggested Near Mint value of $500-1,000.)			
Columbia CL-2804	(DJ)	John Wesley Harding	1968	60.00	150.00
		(White label promo with timing strip on the cover.)			
Columbia CL-2804	(M)	John Wesley Harding	1968	40.00	100.00
Columbia CS-9604	(S)	John Wesley Harding	1968	10.00	25.00
		(The label reads "360 Sound Stereo" in white.)			
Columbia KCS-9825	(S)	Nashville Skyline	1969	10.00	25.00
		(The label reads "360 Sound Stereo" in white.)			
Columbia CQ-32825	(Q)	Nashville Skyline	1973	12.00	30.00
Columbia HE-49825	(S)	Nashville Skyline (Half-speed master)	1975	25.00	75.00
Columbia C2X-30050	(S)	Self Portrait (2 LPs)	1970	40.00	100.00
		(The label reads "360 Sound Stereo" in white.)			
Columbia KC-32460	(S)	Pat Garrett And Billy The Kid (Soundtrack)	1973	6.00	15.00
		(The title on the front cover is in raised black letters.)			
Asylum 7E-1003	(DJ)	Planet Waves (White label)	1974	16.00	40.00
Asylum 7E-1003	(S)	Planet Waves	1974	8.00	20.00
		(With The Band. Issued with a wraparound second cover.)			
Asylum EQ-1003	(Q)	Planet Waves	1974	20.00	50.00
Island AB-201	(S)	Before The Flood (2 LPs with The Band)	1974	16.00	40.00
Asylum AB-201	(DJ)	Before The Flood (2 LPs with The Band)	1974	16.00	40.00
Asylum AB-201	(S)	Before The Flood (2 LPs with The Band)	1974	8.00	20.00
Columbia PC-33235	(DJ)	Blood On The Tracks (Test pressing)	1975	2,000.00	Rare
		(Original test pressings include completely different recordings of "Idiot Wind," "Lily, Rosemary And The Jack Of Hearts," "Tangled Up In Blue," "If You See Her Say Hello" and "You're A Big Girl Now." Near Mint copies have a suggested value of $4,000-6,000.)			

Label & Catalog #		Title	Year	VG+	NM
Columbia PC-33235	(DJ)	**Blood On The Tracks**	1975	16.00	40.00
		(White label promo with timing strip on the cover.)			
Columbia PC-33235	(S)	**Blood On The Tracks**	1975	8.00	20.00
		(First pressing covers have black liner notes on the back.)			
Columbia PC-33235	(S)	**Blood On The Tracks** ("Mural cover")	1976	10.00	25.00
		(Second pressing covers feature a full-cover drawing on the back.)			
Columbia HC-43235	(S)	**Blood On The Tracks** (Half-speed master)	1975	25.00	75.00
Columbia CS2-33682	(DJ)	**The Basement Tapes** (2 LPs)	1975	16.00	40.00
		(White label promo with timing strip on the cover.)			
Columbia PC-33893	(DJ)	**Desire**	1976	12.00	30.00
		(White label promo with timing strip on the cover.)			
Columbia PCQ-33893	(Q)	**Desire**	1976	14.00	35.00
Columbia PC-34349	(DJ)	**Hard Rain**	1976	12.00	30.00
		(White label promo with timing strip on the cover.)			
Columbia AS-422	(DJ)	**Renaldo And Clara**	1976	14.00	35.00
		(Originals have a title sticker on the cover; counterfeits do not.)			
Columbia JC-35453	(DJ)	**Street Legal**	1978	10.00	25.00
		(White label promo with timing strip on the cover.)			
Columbia PC2-36067	(DJ)	**Bob Dylan At Budokan** (2 LPs)	1979	12.00	30.00
		(White label promo with timing strip on the cover.)			
Columbia FC-36120	(DJ)	**Slow Train Coming** (White label)	1979	8.00	20.00
		(White label promo with timing strip on the cover.)			
Columbia AS-798	(DJ)	**Saved** (White label)	1980	10.00	25.00
Columbia AS-1259	(DJ)	**The Dylan London Interview, July 1981**	1981	8.00	20.00
Columbia AS-1471	(DJ)	**Electric Lunch**	1982	6.00	15.00
		(Sampler of material from the two Asylum albums.)			
Columbia C5S-38830	(P)	**Biograph** (5 LPs)	1985	10.00	25.00
Columbia CAS-2222	(DJ)	**Time Passes Slowly: Biograph Sampler**	1985	10.00	25.00
Mobile Fidelity MFSL-114	(S)	**The Times They Are A-Changin'**	1988	6.00	18.00

DYLAN, BOB, & ALAN J. WEBERMAN

Folkways FB-5322	(M)	**Bob Dylan Versus A.J. Weberman**	1977	150.00	300.00
		(This album consists of a porrly taped telephone conversation between A.J. and his hero. . .)			

DYNAMICS, THE

Bolo BLP-8001	(M)	**The Dynamics With Jimmy Hanna**	1963	20.00	50.00

DYNAMICS

Cotillion SD-9009	(S)	**First Landing**	1969	6.00	15.00

DYNATONES, THE

HBR HLP-8509	(M)	**The Fife Piper**	1966	6.00	15.00
HBR HST-9509	(S)	**The Fife Piper**	1966	8.00	20.00

EAGLE

Eagle originally recorded as The Beacon Street Union.

Janus JLS-3011	(S)	**Come Under Nancy's Tent**	1970	6.00	15.00

EAGLES, THE

Asylum SD-5054	(S)	**The Eagles** (Gatefold cover)	1972	5.00	12.00
Asylum EQ-1004	(Q)	**On The Border**	1979	6.00	15.00
Mobile Fidelity MFSL-126	(S)	**Hotel California**	1981	30.00	90.00

At the time of release of Clint's first—and only—collection of tunes, he was coming off his initial success as Rowdy Yates on television's Rawhide. He would suffer through several years of type-casting and no success in Hollywood before jarring the big screens of America as the man-with-no-name in Sergio Leone's "spaghetti westerns." His no-nonsense, tight-lipped demeanor combined with a flair for Old Testament retribution and a complete lack of personal warmth made him the most popular American male sex symbol of the '70s. . . much to the confusion of the testostered portion of the population.

Label & Catalog #		Title	Year	VG+	NM

EAGLIN, "BLIND" SNOOKS
| Folkways FA-2476 | (M) | New Orleans Street Singer | 1959 | 16.00 | 40.00 |
| Bluesville BVLP-1046 | (M) | That's All Right | 1962 | 16.00 | 40.00 |

EARLS, THE
| Old Town LP-104 | (M) | Remember Me Baby | 1963 | 150.00 | 400.00 |
| | | *(Original covers have the catalog number stamped on the front.)* | | | |

EARTH ISLAND
| Philips 600-340 | (S) | We Must Survive | 1970 | 10.00 | 25.00 |

EARTH OPERA
| Elektra EKS-74016 | (S) | Earth Opera | 1968 | 8.00 | 20.00 |
| Elektra EKS-74038 | (S) | The Great American Eagle Tragedy | 1969 | 8.00 | 20.00 |

EARTH QUAKE
| A&M SP-4308 | (S) | Earth Quake | 1971 | 6.00 | 15.00 |
| A&M SP-4337 | (S) | Why Don't You Try Me? | 1972 | 6.00 | 15.00 |

EARTH, WIND & FIRE
Columbia CQ-32194	(Q)	Head To The Sky	1974	8.00	20.00
Columbia CQ-32712	(Q)	Open Our Eyes	1974	8.00	20.00
Columbia FC-035647	(DJ)	Best Of Earth, Wind & Fire *(Picture disc)*	1979	8.00	20.00
Columbia HC-45647	(S)	Best Of Earth, Wind & Fire *(Half-speed)*	1981	13.00	40.00
Columbia HC-45730	(S)	I Am *(Half-speed master)*	1981	10.00	30.00
Columbia HC-47548	(S)	Raise *(Half-speed master)*	1982	10.00	30.00
Columbia HC-48367	(S)	Powerlight *(Half-speed master)*	1982	16.00	50.00
Mobile Fidelity MFSL-159	(S)	That's The Way Of The World	198?	5.00	15.00

EARTHEN VESSEL
| NRS 2587 | (S) | Everlasting Life | 1971 | 60.00 | 150.00 |

EAST OF EDEN
Deram DES-18023	(S)	Mercator Projected	1969	6.00	15.00
Deram DES-18043	(S)	Snafu	1970	6.00	15.00
Harvest SW-806	(S)	East Of Eden	1971	5.00	12.00

EAST SIDE KIDS, THE
| Uni 73032 | (S) | Tiger And The Lamb | 1968 | 8.00 | 20.00 |

EASTFIELD MEADOWS
| V.M.C. 133 | (S) | Eastfield Meadows | 1969 | 8.00 | 20.00 |

EASTWOOD, CLINT
| Cameo C-1056 | (M) | Clint Eastwood Sings Cowboy Favorites | 1963 | 40.00 | 100.00 |
| Cameo CS-1056 | (S) | Clint Eastwood Sings Cowboy Favorites | 1963 | 60.00 | 150.00 |

EASY CHAIR, THE
The Easy Chair features Jeff Simmons.
| Vanco 1004 | (M) | The Easy Chair *(One sided. No cover)* | 1968 | 150.00 | 300.00 |

EASY RIDERS, THE
Columbia CL-990	(M)	Marianne And Other Songs	1957	20.00	50.00
Columbia CL-1302	(M)	Wanderin' Folk Songs	1959	14.00	35.00
Epic LN-24033	(M)	Easy Riders	1962	8.00	20.00
Epic BN-26033	(S)	Easy Riders	1962	12.00	30.00

EASYBEATS, THE
United Arts. UAL-3588	(M)	Friday On My Mind	1967	16.00	40.00
		("Make You Feel Alright" is rechanneled on this album.)			
United Arts. UAS-6588	(S)	Friday On My Mind	1967	20.00	50.00
		("Women" is rechanneled on this album.)			
United Arts. UAS-6667	(S)	Falling Off The Edge Of The World	1968	16.00	40.00
Rare Earth 517	(S)	Easy Ridin'	1970	*Unreleased*	

EBON-KNIGHTS, THE
| Stepheny MF-4001 | (M) | First Date With The Ebon-Knights | 1963 | 500.00 | 1,500.00 |

Label & Catalog #		Title	Year	VG+	NM

EBONY RHYTHM FUNK CAMPAIGN, THE

Uni 73142	(S)	The Ebony Rhythm Funk Campaign	1970	6.00	15.00

EBSEN, BUDDY

Reprise R-6174	(M)	Buddy Ebsen Says Howdy	1965	10.00	25.00
Reprise R9-6174	(S)	Buddy Ebsen Says Howdy	1965	12.00	30.00
Columbia CL-2402	(M)	The Beverly Hillbillies *(TV Soundtrack)*	1965	16.00	40.00
Columbia CS-9202	(S)	The Beverly Hillbillies *(TV Soundtrack)*	1965	20.00	50.00

ECKSTINE, BILLY: *Refer to* GOLDMINE'S PRICE GUIDE TO COLLECTIBLE JAZZ ALBUMS

ECLECTION

Elektra EKS-74023	(S)	Eclection	1968	6.00	15.00

EDDY, DUANE

Jamie JLP-3000	(M)	Have "Twangy" Guitar-Will Travel	1958	30.00	75.00
Jamie JLPS-3000	(S)	Have "Twangy" Guitar-Will Travel	1958	100.00	250.00
		(Yellow label. The title on the cover is in white print. "Lonesome Road," "I Almost Lost My Mind," "Three-30-Blues," "Detour," "Anytime" and "Loving You" are in stereo.)			
Jamie JLPM-3000	(M)	Have "Twangy" Guitar-Will Travel	1959	20.00	50.00
Jamie JLPS-3000	(S)	Have "Twangy" Guitar-Will Travel	1959	30.00	75.00
		(Gold & white label. The title on the cover is in red print. Early pressings have the same stereo content as above. All subsequent stereo pressings are completely rechanneled.)			
Jamie JLPS-3000	(E)	Have "Twangy" Guitar-Will Travel	196?	8.00	20.00
		(Gold & white label with electronic stereo.)			
Jamie JLPM-3006	(M)	Especially For You....	1959	16.00	40.00
Jamie JLPS-3006	(S)	Especially For You....	1959	24.00	60.00
Jamie JLPM-3009	(M)	The "Twangs" The "Thang"	1959	16.00	40.00
Jamie JLPS-3009	(S)	The "Twangs" The "Thang"	1959	24.00	60.00
Jamie JLPM-3011	(M)	Songs Of Our Heritage *(Gatefold cover)*	1960	26.00	65.00
Jamie JLPS-3011	(S)	Songs Of Our Heritage *(Gatefold cover)*	1960	34.00	85.00
Jamie JLPS-3011	(S)	Songs Of Our Heritage *(Blue vinyl)*	1960	80.00	200.00
Jamie JLPS-3011	(S)	Songs Of Our Heritage *(Red vinyl)*	1960	80.00	200.00
		(Original pressings of Jamie 301 on black and colored vinyl above have gatefold covers with a fold-open poster bound to the inside. Subtract 20-30% if the poster has been removed.)			
Jamie JLPM-3011	(M)	Songs Of Our Heritage *(Standard cover)*	1960	12.00	30.00
Jamie JLPS-3011	(S)	Songs Of Our Heritage *(Standard cover)*	1960	16.00	40.00
Jamie JLPM-3014	(M)	$1,000,000 Worth Of Twang	1960	16.00	40.00
Jamie JLPS-3014	(E)	$1,000,000 Worth Of Twang	1960	12.00	30.00
Jamie JLPM-3019	(M)	Girls! Girls! Girls!	1961	12.00	30.00
Jamie JLPS-3019	(S)	Girls! Girls! Girls!	1961	16.00	40.00
Jamie JLPM-3021	(M)	$1,000,000 Worth Of Twang, Volume 2	1962	12.00	30.00
Jamie JLPS-3021	(P)	$1,000,000 Worth Of Twang, Volume 2	1962	16.00	40.00
Jamie JLPM-3022	(M)	Twistin' With Duane Eddy	1962	12.00	30.00
Jamie JLPS-3022	(S)	Twistin' With Duane Eddy	1962	16.00	40.00
		("Rebel Rouser Twist," "Cannon Ball Twist," "Movin' 'N Groovin' Twist," "Ramrod Twist" and "Twisting Up & Down" are rechanneled.)			
Jamie JLPM-3024	(M)	Surfin'/Duane Eddy & The Rebels-In Person	1963	16.00	40.00
Jamie JLPS-3024	(S)	Surfin'/Duane Eddy & The Rebels-In Person	1963	20.00	50.00
Jamie JLPM-3026	(M)	16 Greatest Hits	1964	12.00	30.00
Jamie JLPS-3026	(E)	16 Greatest Hits	1964	8.00	20.00
		— Original Jamie albums above have gold & white labels.—			
RCA Victor LPM-2525	(M)	Twistin' And Twangin'	1962	8.00	20.00
RCA Victor LSP-2525	(S)	Twistin' And Twangin'	1962	12.00	30.00
RCA Victor LPM-2576	(M)	Twangy Guitar, Silky Strings	1962	8.00	20.00
RCA Victor LSP-2576	(S)	Twangy Guitar, Silky Strings	1962	12.00	30.00
RCA Victor LPM-2648	(M)	Dance With The Guitar Man	1962	8.00	20.00
RCA Victor LSP-2648	(S)	Dance With The Guitar Man	1962	12.00	30.00
RCA Victor LPM-2681	(M)	Twang A Country Song	1963	8.00	20.00
RCA Victor LSP-2681	(S)	Twang A Country Song	1963	12.00	30.00
RCA Victor LPM-2700	(M)	Twangin' Up A Storm	1963	8.00	20.00
RCA Victor LSP-2700	(S)	Twangin' Up A Storm	1963	12.00	30.00
		— Original RCA mono albums above have "Long Play" on the bottom of the label; stereo albums have "Living Stereo" on the bottom.—			
RCA Victor LPM-2798	(M)	Lonely Guitar	1964	8.00	20.00
RCA Victor LSP-2798	(S)	Lonely Guitar	1964	12.00	30.00

Label & Catalog #		Title	Year	VG+	NM
RCA Victor LPM-2918	(M)	Water Skiing	1964	8.00	20.00
RCA Victor LSP-2918	(S)	Water Skiing	1964	12.00	30.00
RCA Victor LPM-2993	(M)	Twangin' The Golden Hits	1965	8.00	20.00
RCA Victor LSP-2993	(S)	Twangin' The Golden Hits	1965	12.00	30.00
RCA Victor LPM-3432	(M)	Twangsville	1965	8.00	20.00
RCA Victor LSP-3432	(S)	Twangsville	1965	12.00	30.00
RCA Victor LPM-3477	(M)	The Best Of Duane Eddy	1966	6.00	15.00
RCA Victor LSP-3477	(P)	The Best Of Duane Eddy	1966	8.00	20.00
		— Original RCA albums above have black labels.—			
Colpix CP-490	(M)	Duane A-Go-Go	1965	14.00	35.00
Colpix CPS-490	(S)	Duane A-Go-Go	1965	20.00	50.00
Colpix CP-494	(M)	Duane Eddy Does Bob Dylan	1965	20.00	50.00
Colpix CPS-494	(S)	Duane Eddy Does Bob Dylan	1965	30.00	75.00
Reprise R-6218	(M)	The Biggest Twang Of Them All	1966	8.00	20.00
Reprise RS-6218	(S)	The Biggest Twang Of Them All	1966	10.00	25.00
Reprise R-6240	(M)	The Roaring Twangies	1967	8.00	20.00
Reprise RS-6240	(S)	The Roaring Twangies	1967	10.00	25.00
Sire SASH-3707	(P)	Vintage Years (2 LPs)	1975	10.00	25.00

EDEN, BARBARA

Dot DLP-3795	(M)	Miss Barbara Eden	1967	12.00	30.00
Dot DLP-25795	(S)	Miss Barbara Eden	1967	16.00	40.00

EDEN'S CHILDREN

ABC S-624	(S)	Eden's Children	1968	10.00	25.00
ABC S-652	(S)	Sure Looks Real	1968	8.00	20.00

EDGE, THE

Nose NRS-48003	(S)	The Edge	1970	16.00	40.00

EDMONSON, TRAVIS
Refer to Bud & Travis; The Gateway Singers.

Reprise R-6035	(M)	Travis On His Own	1962	10.00	25.00
Reprise R9-6035	(S)	Travis On His Own	1962	12.00	30.00
Horizon T-1606	(M)	Travis On Cue	1962	8.00	20.00
Horizon ST-1606	(S)	Travis On Cue	1962	10.00	25.00

EDMUNDS, DAVE
Edmunds was formerly a member of Love Sculpture.

MAM 3	(S)	Rockpile (Counterfeits exist)	1972	10.00	25.00
Atlantic PR-320	(DJ)	College Network Interview (Colored label)	1978	12.00	30.00

EDWARDS, JONATHAN & DARLENE

Westminster WGAP-68104	(M)	American Popular Songs	195?	10.00	25.00
Columbia CL-1513	(M)	In Paris	1960	8.00	20.00
Columbia CS-8313	(S)	In Paris	1960	10.00	25.00
RCA Victor LPM-2495	(M)	Sing Along With Jonathan And Darlene	1962	6.00	15.00
RCA Victor LSP-2495	(S)	Sing Along With Jonathan And Darlene	1962	8.00	20.00
Dot DLP-3792	(M)	Songs For Sheiks And Flappers	1967	5.00	12.00
Dot DLP-25792	(S)	Songs For Sheiks And Flappers	1967	6.00	15.00

EDWARDS, TOMMY

Regent MG-6096	(M)	Tommy Edwards Sings	195?	30.00	75.00
Lion L-70120	(M)	Tommy Edwards	1959	12.00	30.00
		(Lion 70120 is a reissue of Regent 6096.)			
MGM E-3732	(M)	It's All In The Game	1959	12.00	30.00
MGM SE-3732	(S)	It's All In The Game	1959	20.00	50.00
MGM E-3760	(M)	For Young Lovers	1959	12.00	30.00
MGM SE-3760	(S)	For Young Lovers	1959	20.00	50.00
		— Original MGM albums above have yellow labels.—			
MGM E-3805	(M)	You Started Me Dreaming	1960	8.00	20.00
MGM SE-3805	(S)	You Started Me Dreaming	1960	12.00	30.00
MGM E-3822	(M)	Step Out Singing	1960	8.00	20.00
MGM SE-3822	(S)	Step Out Singing	1960	12.00	30.00
MGM E-3838	(M)	Tommy Edwards In Hawaii	1960	8.00	20.00
MGM SE-3838	(S)	Tommy Edwards In Hawaii	1960	12.00	30.00
MGM E-3884	(M)	Tommy Edwards' Greatest Hits	1961	8.00	20.00
MGM SE-3884	(S)	Tommy Edwards' Greatest Hits	1961	12.00	30.00

Label & Catalog #		Title	Year	VG+	NM
MGM E-3959	(M)	Golden Country Hits	1961	8.00	20.00
MGM SE-3959	(S)	Golden Country Hits	1961	12.00	30.00
MGM E-4020	(M)	Stardust	1962	8.00	20.00
MGM SE-4020	(S)	Stardust	1962	12.00	30.00
MGM E-4060	(M)	Soft Strings And Two Guitars	1962	8.00	20.00
MGM SE-4060	(S)	Soft Strings And Two Guitars	1962	12.00	30.00
MGM E-4141	(M)	The Very Best Of Tommy Edwards	1963	6.00	15.00
MGM SE-4141	(S)	The Very Best Of Tommy Edwards	1963	8.00	20.00
		— Original MGM albums above have black labels.—			

EIRE APPARENT

Buddah BDS-5031	(S)	Sunrise	1969	10.00	25.00

EL CAMPO JADES, THE

Golden Eagle LP-101	(M)	The El Campo Jades	1966	40.00	100.00

EL DORADOS, THE [THE ELDORADOS]

Vee Jay VJLP-1001	(M)	Crazy Little Mama	1959	250.00	600.00
		(First pressings have maroon labels with a thick silver band. Vee Jay 1001 contains two tracks by The Magnificents.)			
Vee Jay VJLP-1001	(M)	Crazy Little Mama	1960	200.00	500.00
		(Second pressings have maroon labels with a thin silver band.)			
Vee Jay VJLP-1001	(M)	Crazy Little Mama	196?	100.00	250.00
		(Later pressings have black labels.)			
Lost-Nite LLP-20 (10")	(M)	The Eldorados (Red vinyl)	1981	4.00	10.00

ELBERT, DONNIE

King 629	(M)	The Sensational Donnie Elbert Sings	1959	150.00	400.00
All Platinum 3007	(S)	Where Did Our Love Go	1971	6.00	15.00
Deluxe DLP-12003	(S)	Have I Sinned	1971	6.00	15.00
Trip 9524	(S)	Stop In The Name Of Love	1972	6.00	15.00

ELECTRIC FLAG, THE
The original Flag includes Mike Bloomfield, Barry Goldberg and Nick Gravenites.

Sidewalk T-5908	(M)	The Trip (Soundtrack)	1967	12.00	30.00
Sidewalk ST-5908	(S)	The Trip (Soundtrack)	1967	16.00	40.00
Columbia CS-9597	(S)	A Long Time Comin'	1968	8.00	20.00
Columbia CS-9714	(S)	An American Music Band	1968	8.00	20.00
		— Original Columbia albums above have "360 Sound" on the bottom of the label.—			

ELECTRIC INDIAN, THE

United Arts. UAS-6728	(S)	Keem 'O Sabe	1969	5.00	12.00

ELECTRIC JUNKYARD

RCA Victor LSP-4158	(S)	The Electric Junkyard	1969	6.00	15.00

ELECTRIC LIGHT ORCHESTRA, THE (E.L.O.)
E.L.O. features Roy Wood and Jeff Lynne. Refer to The Idle Race; The Move.

Jet/United Arts. LA546	(DJ)	Face The Music (Banded for air-play)	1975	8.00	20.00
Jet/United Arts. LA823	(DJ)	Out Of The Blue (2 LPs. Blue vinyl)	1977	10.00	25.00
Jet SP-123	(DJ)	Ole ELO (Gold vinyl in black & white cover)	1978	30.00	75.00
Jet SP-123	(DJ)	Ole ELO (Gold vinyl & no cover)	1978	20.00	50.00
Jet SP-123	(DJ)	Ole ELO (Red vinyl & no cover)	1978	60.00	150.00
Jet SP-123	(DJ)	Ole ELO (Blue vinyl & no cover)	1978	30.00	75.00
Jet SP-123	(DJ)	Ole ELO (White vinyl & no cover)	1978	30.00	75.00
		("Ole" was first issued promotionally on gold vinyl in a black & white photo cover. It was then issued on gold, red, white and blue vinyl in plain cardboard jackets. U.A. finally issued the album commercially with the same cover as the original gold vinyl LP except in color.)			
Jet HZ-45769	(S)	Discovery (Half-speed master)	1981	10.00	30.00
Jet HZ-46310	(S)	ELO's Greatest Hits (Half-speed master)	1981	13.00	40.00
Jet HZ-47371	(S)	Time (Half-speed master)	1981	10.00	30.00
Jet HZ-48490	(S)	Secret Messages (Half-speed master)	1983	16.00	50.00

ELECTRIC PRUNES, THE

Reprise R-6248	(M)	I Had Too Much To Dream	1967	16.00	40.00
Reprise RS-6248	(S)	I Had Too Much To Dream	1967	20.00	50.00
Reprise R-6262	(M)	Underground	1967	14.00	35.00
Reprise RS-6262	(S)	Underground	1967	16.00	40.00

Label & Catalog #		Title	Year	VG+	NM
Reprise R-6275	(M)	Mass In F Minor	1967	14.00	35.00
Reprise RS-6275	(S)	Mass In F Minor	1967	10.00	25.00
Reprise R-6316	(M)	Release Of An Oath	1968	14.00	35.00
Reprise RS-6316	(S)	Release Of An Oath	1968	10.00	25.00
		— Original Reprise albums above have pink, gold & green labels.—			
Reprise RS-6275	(S)	Mass In F Minor (Brown label)	1969	6.00	15.00
Reprise RS-6342	(S)	Just Good Rock N' Roll	1969	10.00	25.00

ELECTRIC TOILET

Nasco 9004	(S)	In The Hands Of Karma	1970	40.00	100.00

ELECTROMAGNETS, THE
The Electromagnets feature Eric Johnson, formerly of Mariani.

E.C.M. 1001	(S)	The Electromagnets (Green cover)	197?	60.00	150.00
E.C.M. 1001	(S)	The Electromagnets (Red/orange cover)	197?	50.00	125.00

ELEPHANT'S MEMORY
For additional listings refer to John Lennon & Yoko Ono.

Buddah BDS-5033	(S)	Elephant's Memory	1969	6.00	15.00
Buddah BDS-5038	(S)	Songs From "Midnight Cowboy"	1969	6.00	15.00
Metromedia MD-1035	(S)	Take It To The Streets	1970	8.00	20.00
Apple SMAS-3389	(S)	Elephants Memory (Prod. by John & Yoko)	1972	10.00	25.00

ELF

Epic KE-31789	(S)	Elf	1972	10.00	25.00
MGM M3G-4974	(S)	L.A. 59	1974	6.00	15.00
MGM M3G-4994	(S)	Trying To Burn The Sun	1975	6.00	15.00

ELGINS, THE

V.I.P. 400	(M)	Darling Baby	1966	12.00	30.00
V.I.P. S-400	(S)	Darling Baby	1966	16.00	40.00

ELIMINATORS, THE

Liberty LRP-3365	(M)	Liverpool! Dragsters! Cycles! Surfing!	1964	16.00	40.00
Liberty LST-7365	(S)	Liverpool! Dragsters! Cycles! Surfing!	1964	20.00	50.00

ELIZABETH

Vanguard VSD-6501	(S)	Elizabeth	1968	5.00	12.00

ELLEDGE, JIMMY

Little Darlin' SLD-8013	(S)	Funny How Time Slips Away	1968	6.00	15.00
		("Funny How Time Slips Away" is a rerecorded version of the hit.)			

ELLINGTON, HARVEY

Stepheny MF-4010	(M)	I Can't Hide The Blues	1959	40.00	100.00

ELLIOT, "MAMA" CASS
Refer to The Big Three; The Mugwumps; The Mamas & The Papas; Dave Mason & Cass Elliot.

Dunhill DS-50040	(S)	Dream A Little Dream	1968	8.00	20.00
Dunhill DS-50055	(S)	Bubble Gum, Lemonade & Something For Mama	1969	8.00	20.00
Dunhill DS-50071	(S)	Make Your Own Kind Of Music	1970	8.00	20.00
Dunhill DS-50093	(S)	Mama's Big Ones	1970	6.00	15.00
RCA Victor LSP-4619	(S)	Cass Elliot	1971	6.00	15.00
RCA Victor LSP-4753	(S)	The Road Is No Place For A Lady	1972	6.00	15.00
RCA Victor APL1-0303	(S)	Don't Call Me Mama No More	1973	6.00	15.00
		— Original RCA albums above have orange labels.—			

ELLIOT, RAMBLIN' JACK

Prestige Int. PRLP-13016	(M)	The Songs Of Woody Guthrie	1961	12.00	30.00
Prestige Int. PRLP-13033	(M)	Ramblin'	1961	12.00	30.00
Prestige Int. PRLP-13045	(M)	Country Style	1962	12.00	30.00
Prestige Int. PRLP-13065	(M)	At The Second Fret	1962	12.00	30.00
Monitor MF-379	(M)	Ramblin' Cowboy	1962	8.00	20.00
Monitor MF-380	(M)	Sings Woody Guthrie And Jimmie Rodgers	1962	8.00	20.00
Monitor MS-380	(S)	Sings Woody Guthrie And Jimmie Rodgers	1962	10.00	25.00
Vanguard VRS-9151	(M)	Jack Elliott	1964	6.00	15.00
Vanguard VSD-79151	(S)	Jack Elliott	1964	8.00	20.00

Label & Catalog #		Title	Year	VG+	NM
Folklore FRLP-14011	(M)	The Songs Of Woody Guthrie	1964	10.00	25.00
Folklore FRST-14011	(S)	The Songs Of Woody Guthrie	1964	12.00	30.00
		(Folklore 14011 is a reissue of Prestige Int. 13016.)			
Folklore FRLP-14014	(M)	Ramblin'	1964	10.00	25.00
Folklore FRST-14014	(S)	Ramblin'	1964	12.00	30.00
		(Folklore 14014 is a reissue of Prestige Int. 13033.)			
Folklore FRLP-14019	(M)	Hootenanny With Jack Elliott	1964	10.00	25.00
Folklore FRST-14019	(S)	Hootenanny With Jack Elliott	1964	12.00	30.00
Folklore FRLP-14029	(M)	Country Style	1964	10.00	25.00
Folklore FRST-14029	(S)	Country Style	1964	12.00	30.00
Delmark DS-801	(S)	Talking Woody Guthrie	1968	10.00	25.00
Prestige PRST-7453	(S)	Ramblin' Jack Elliot Sings Woody Guthrie	1967	8.00	20.00
Prestige PRST-7721	(S)	Ramblin' Jack Elliot	1969	6.00	15.00
		(Prestige 7721 is a reissue of Folklore 14014.)			
Prestige PRST-7804	(S)	Country Style	1969	6.00	15.00
		(Prestige 7804 is a reissue of Folklore 14029.)			
Reprise RS-6284	(S)	Young Brigham	1968	4.00	10.00
Reprise RS-6387	(S)	Bull Durham Sacks And Railroad Tracks	1970	4.00	10.00
Vanguard VSD-89	(M)	The Essential Ramblin' Jack Elliott	1970	4.00	10.00

ELLIOT, RON
Ron Elliott was formerly a member of the Beau Brummels.

Warner Bros. WS-1833	(S)	Candlestickmaker (With booklet)	1969	10.00	25.00

ELLIS, ANITA: *Refer to* GOLDMINE'S PRICE GUIDE TO COLLECTIBLE JAZZ ALBUMS

ELLIS, DOLAN

Reprise R-6038	(M)	Almost Authentic Folk Songs	1962	6.00	15.00
Reprise R9-6038	(S)	Almost Authentic Folk Songs	1962	8.00	20.00

ELLIS, JIMMY
Jimmy Ellis also recorded as Orion.

Boblo 78-829	(S)	Ellis Sings Elvis By Request	1978	30.00	75.00

ELLIS, SHIRLEY

Congress CGL-3002	(M)	Shirley Ellis In Action	1964	10.00	25.00
Congress CGS-3002	(S)	Shirley Ellis In Action	1964	12.00	30.00
Congress CGL-3003	(M)	The Name Game	1965	10.00	25.00
Congress CGS-3003	(S)	The Name Game	1965	12.00	30.00
Columbia CL-2679	(M)	Sugar, Let's Shing-A-Ling	1967	8.00	20.00
Columbia CS-9479	(S)	Sugar, Let's Shing-A-Ling	1967	6.00	15.00

ELLIS, STEVE, & THE STARFIRES

I.G.L. 105	(M)	The Steve Ellis Songbook	1967	150.00	300.00

ELMER CITY RAMBLING DOGS, THE

Dog Dirt DD-1	(S)	Jam It	1975	10.00	25.00

ELMER GANTRY'S VELVET OPERA

Epic BN-26415	(S)	Elmer Gantry's Velvet Opera	1968	20.00	50.00

EMBERS, THE

J.C.P. Recording 2006	(M)	The Embers Roll Eleven	196?	70.00	175.00
J.C.P. Recording 2009	(M)	Just For The Birds	196?	40.00	100.00
E.E.E. 1069	(S)	The Embers Burn You A New One	197?	12.00	30.00

EMERALD CHOIR, THE

Boat 1017	(S)	Timber Timbre Burn	198?	5.00	12.00

EMERSON, LAKE & PALMER

Atlantic PR-277	(DJ)	Works, Volume 1 (Sampler)	197?	6.00	15.00
Mobile Fidelity MFSL-031	(S)	Pictures At An Exhibition	1980	8.00	25.00

EMERSON'S OLD TIMEY CUSTARD-SUCKIN' BAND

ESP-Disk' 2006	(S)	Emerson's Old Timey Custard-Suckin' Band	196?	12.00	30.00

EMERY, TIM

Ros-Sound 130	(S)	Alias Red Garrett	1978	20.00	50.00

Label & Catalog #		Title	Year	VG+	NM

EMMAUS ROAD BAND, THE
Members of The E.R.B. originally recorded as Maranatha.

(No label)	(S)	This Could Be The Beginning	197?	80.00	200.00

EMMONS, BUDDY
Refer to Longbranch Pennywhistle.

Mercury MG-20843	(M)	Steel Guitar Jazz	1963	30.00	75.00
Mercury SR-60843	(S)	Steel Guitar Jazz	1963	40.00	100.00
Emmons ELP-1001	(M)	Buddy Emmons (The Black Album)	196?	10.00	25.00
Cumberland MGC-29507	(M)	Best Of Western Swing	196?	8.00	20.00

EMMONS, BUDDY, & SHOT JACKSON

Starday SLP-230	(M)	Singing Strings Of Steel And Dobro	196?	20.00	50.00
K-Ark 6028	(M)	Two Aces	196?	8.00	20.00

EMPEROR HUDSON

Hook 100	(M)	The Adventures Of Emperor Hudson	196?	10.00	25.00

END, THE

London PS-560	(S)	Introspection (Produced by Bill Wyman)	1969	20.00	50.00

ENDLE ST. CLOUD

International Arts. 12	(S)	Thank You All Very Much	1968	16.00	40.00

ENGEL, SCOTT, & JOHN STEWART
Refer to Scott Walker; The Walker Brothers.

Tower T-5026	(M)	I Only Came To Dance With You	1966	8.00	20.00
Tower ST-5026	(S)	I Only Came To Dance With You	1966	10.00	25.00

ENNIS, ETHEL

Jubilee 1021	(M)	Lullabies For Losers	1956	16.00	40.00
Capitol T-941	(M)	Changes Of Scenery	1957	12.00	30.00
Capitol T-1078	(M)	Have You Forgotten?	1958	12.00	30.00
Jubilee 5024	(M)	Ethel Ennis Sings	1963	8.00	20.00
RCA Victor LPM-2984	(M)	Eyes For You	1964	6.00	15.00
RCA Victor LSP-2984	(S)	Eyes For You	1964	8.00	20.00

ENO, BRIAN
Formerly a member of Roxy Music. Eno also recorded with Robert Fripp.

Antilles AN-7018	(S)	Evening Star	1973	4.00	10.00
Antilles AN-7030	(S)	Discreet Music	1973	4.00	10.00
Island ILPS-9268	(S)	Here Come The Warm Jets	1973	6.00	15.00
Island ILPS-9309	(S)	Taking Tiger Mountain By Strategy	1974	6.00	15.00
Island ILPS-9351	(S)	Another Green World	1975	8.00	20.00
		(Includes a set of four lithographs.)			
Island ILPS-9351	(S)	Another Green World (Without the lithos)	1975	6.00	15.00
Island ILPS-9478	(S)	Before And After Science	1978	6.00	15.00

ENTWISTLE, JOHN
Mr. Entwistle is a member of The Who.

Decca DL-79183	(S)	Smash Your Head Against The Wall	1971	8.00	20.00
Decca DL-79190	(S)	Whistle Rhymes	1972	8.00	20.00
MCA/Track 321	(S)	Rigor Mortis Sets In	1973	6.00	15.00
MCA/Track 2129	(S)	Mad Dog	1975	6.00	15.00

EPPS, PRESTON

Original Sound OS-8851	(M)	Bongo, Bongo, Bongo	1960	14.00	35.00
Original Sound OSS-8851	(S)	Bongo, Bongo, Bongo	1960	20.00	50.00
		("Bongo Rock" is rechanneled on this album.)			
Top Rank RM-349	(M)	Bongola	1961	14.00	35.00
Top Rank RS-649	(S)	Bongola	1961	20.00	50.00
Original Sound OS-8872	(M)	Surfin' Bongos (With The Bongo Teens)	1963	12.00	30.00
Original Sound OSS-8872	(S)	Surfin' Bongos (With The Bongo Teens)	1963	16.00	40.00

EQUALS, THE

Laurie LP-2045	(M)	Unequalled	1967	10.00	25.00
Laurie SLP-2045	(S)	Unequalled	1967	12.00	30.00
RCA Victor LSP-4078	(S)	Baby Come Back	1968	8.00	20.00
President PTL-1015	(S)	Equal Sensation	1968	8.00	20.00

Label & Catalog #		Title	Year	VG+	NM
President PTL-1020	(S)	The Sensational Equals	1968	8.00	20.00
President PTL-1025	(S)	Equals Supreme	1968	8.00	20.00
President PTL-1030	(S)	Strikeback	1969	8.00	20.00
ERICA					
ESP-Disk' 1099	(S)	You Used To Think	1968	40.00	100.00
ERIK					
Vanguard VRS-9267	(M)	Look Where I Am	1967	6.00	15.00
Vanguard VSD-79267	(S)	Look Where I Am	1967	8.00	20.00
ERIK & THE VIKINGS					
Karate 1401	(M)	Sing Along Rock 'N Roll	1965	8.00	20.00
ESCORTS, THE					
Teo LPM-5000	(M)	The Escorts Bring Down The House	1966	60.00	150.00
ESQUERITA					
Capitol T-1186	(M)	Esquerita	1959	300.00	750.00
ESQUIRES, THE					
Bunky 300	(S)	Get On Up And Get Away	1968	10.00	25.00
ESSEX, THE					
Roulette R-25234	(M)	Easier Said Than Done	1963	14.00	35.00
Roulette SR-25234	(S)	Easier Said Than Done	1963	20.00	50.00
Roulette R-25235	(M)	A Walkin' Miracle	1963	10.00	25.00
Roulette SR-25235	(S)	A Walkin' Miracle	1963	14.00	35.00
Roulette R-25246	(M)	Young And Lively	1964	10.00	25.00
Roulette SR-25246	(S)	Young And Lively	1964	14.00	35.00
ESSEX, DAVID					
Columbia CQ-32560	(Q)	Rock On	1974	6.00	15.00
ESTES, "SLEEPY" JOHN					
Delmark DL-608	(M)	Broke And Hungry	1966	12.00	30.00
Delmark DS-613	(E)	Sleepy John Estes	1969	12.00	30.00
Delmark DS-619	(E)	Electric Sheep	1969	12.00	30.00
ETC.					
Windi WLPS-1011	(S)	Etc. Is The Name Of The Band!	1976	20.00	50.00
ETERNITY'S CHILDREN					
Tower ST-5123	(S)	Eternity's Children	1968	10.00	25.00
Tower ST-5144	(S)	Timeless (Canadian)	1968	12.00	30.00
EUCLID					
Amsterdam AMS-12005	(S)	Heavy Equipment	197?	8.00	20.00
EUPHORIA					
Heritage HTS-35,005	(S)	Euphoria	1969	6.00	15.00
EUPHORIA					
Capitol SKAO-363	(S)	A Gift From Euphoria	1969	60.00	150.00
EUPHORIA					
Rainbow 1003	(S)	Lost In Trance	197?	100.00	250.00
EVANS, DALE					
Ms. Evans also recorded with her hubby, Roy Rogers.					
Capitol T-2772	(M)	It's Real	1967	8.00	20.00
Capitol ST-2772	(S)	It's Real	1967	10.00	25.00
EVANS, PAUL					
Guaranteed GUL-1000	(M)	Fabulous Teens	1960	20.00	50.00
Guaranteed GUS-1000	(S)	Fabulous Teens	1960	30.00	75.00
Carlton TLP-129	(M)	Hear Paul Evans In Your Home Tonight	1961	14.00	35.00
Carlton STLP-129	(S)	Hear Paul Evans In Your Home Tonight	1961	20.00	50.00
		("Seven Little Girls" is rechanneled on this album.)			

Label & Catalog #		Title	Year	VG+	NM
Carlton TLP-130	(M)	Folk Songs Of Many Lands	1961	14.00	35.00
Carlton STLP-130	(S)	Folk Songs Of Many Lands	1961	20.00	50.00
Kapp KL-1346	(M)	21 Years In A Tennessee Jail	1964	8.00	20.00
Kapp KS-3346	(S)	21 Years In A Tennessee Jail	1964	10.00	25.00
Kapp KL-1475	(M)	Another Town, Another Jail	1966	8.00	20.00
Kapp KS-3475	(S)	Another Town, Another Jail	1966	10.00	25.00

EVEN DOZEN JUG BAND, THE

Elektra EKL-246	(M)	The Even Dozen Jug Band	1965	12.00	30.00
Elektra ES-7246	(S)	The Even Dozen Jug Band	1965	20.00	50.00

EVERETT, BETTY
Ms. Everett also recorded with Jerry Butler.

Vee Jay LP-1077	(M)	You're No Good	1964	20.00	50.00
Vee Jay LPS-1077	(S)	You're No Good	1964	30.00	75.00
Vee Jay LP-1077	(M)	It's In His Kiss	1964	14.00	35.00
Vee Jay VJS-1077	(S)	It's In His Kiss	1964	20.00	50.00
		("It's In His Kiss" is a reissue of "You're No Good.")			
Vee Jay LP-1122	(M)	The Very Best Of Betty Everett	1965	8.00	20.00
Vee Jay VJS-1122	(S)	The Very Best Of Betty Everett	1965	12.00	30.00
Sunset SUS-5220	(S)	I Need You So	1968	6.00	15.00
Uni 73048	(S)	There"ll Come A Time	1969	6.00	15.00

EVERGREEN BLUES, THE

Mercury SR-61157	(S)	7 Do 11	1968	6.00	15.00
ABC 669	(S)	Comin' On	1969	6.00	15.00

EVERLY BROTHERS, THE
Of Don and Phil's Cadence repertoire, only "Let It Be Me," "Like Strangers," "Love Of My Life," "Poor Jenny," "Take A Message To Mary," "Til I Kissed You," and "When Will I Be Loved" were released in stereo.

Cadence CLP-3003	(M)	The Everly Brothers	1958	40.00	100.00
Cadence CLP-3106	(M)	Songs Our Daddy Taught Us	1958	40.00	100.00
Cadence CLP-3025	(M)	The Everly Brothers' Best	1959	30.00	75.00
Cadence CLP-3040	(M)	The Fabulous Style Of The Everly Brothers	1960	20.00	50.00
Cadence CLP-25040	(P)	The Fabulous Style Of The Everly Brothers	1960	30.00	75.00
Cadence CLP-3059	(M)	Folk Songs Of The Everly Brothers	1962	30.00	75.00
Cadence CLP-25059	(E)	Folk Songs Of The Everly Brothers	1962	20.00	50.00
Cadence CLP-3062	(M)	15 Everly Hits 15	1963	20.00	50.00
Cadence CLP-25062	(P)	15 Everly Hits 15	1963	30.00	75.00
Warner Bros. PRO-134	(DJ)	It's Everly Time Souvenir Sampler	1960	800.00	600.00
		(10" promotional sampler from their Warner Bros. debut.)			
Warner Bros. W-1381	(M)	It's Everly Time	1960	12.00	30.00
Warner Bros. WS-1381	(S)	It's Everly Time	1960	16.00	40.00
Warner Bros. W-1395	(M)	A Date With The Everly Brothers	1960	16.00	40.00
Warner Bros. WS-1395	(S)	A Date With The Everly Brothers	1960	20.00	50.00
		(Gatefold cover with a sheet of bonus photos.)			
Warner Bros. W-1395	(M)	A Date With The Everly Brothers	1960	12.00	30.00
Warner Bros. WS-1395	(S)	A Date With The Everly Brothers	1960	16.00	40.00
		(Gatefold cover without the bonus photos.)			
Warner Bros. W-1418	(M)	Both Sides Of An Evening	1961	12.00	30.00
Warner Bros. WS-1418	(S)	Both Sides Of An Evening	1961	16.00	40.00
Warner Bros. W-1430	(M)	Instant Party	1962	12.00	30.00
Warner Bros. WS-1430	(S)	Instant Party	1962	16.00	40.00
Warner Bros. W-1471	(M)	The Everly Brothers' Golden Hits	1962	10.00	25.00
Warner Bros. WS-1471	(S)	The Everly Brothers' Golden Hits	1962	14.00	35.00
		— Original Warner mono albums above have grey labels; stereo albums ahve gold labels.—			
Warner Bros. W-1483	(M)	Christmas With The Everly Brothers	1962	16.00	40.00
Warner Bros. WS-1483	(S)	Christmas With The Everly Brothers	1962	20.00	50.00
Warner Bros. W-1513	(M)	Great Country Hits	1963	12.00	30.00
Warner Bros. WS-1513	(S)	Great Country Hits	1963	16.00	40.00
Warner Bros. W-1554	(M)	Very Best Of The Everly Brothers	1964	8.00	20.00
Warner Bros. WS-1554	(S)	Very Best Of The Everly Brothers	1964	12.00	30.00
		(Originally isued with a yellow cover.)			
Warner Bros. W-1554	(M)	The Very Best Of The Everly Brothers	1966	5.00	12.00
Warner Bros. WS-1554	(S)	The Very Best Of The Everly Brothers	1966	6.00	15.00
		(Later pressings have a white cover.)			
Warner Bros. W-1578	(M)	Rock N' Soul	1965	12.00	30.00
Warner Bros. WS-1578	(S)	Rock N' Soul	1965	16.00	40.00

Label & Catalog #		Title	Year	VG+	NM
Warner Bros. W-1585	(M)	Gone, Gone, Gone	1965	12.00	30.00
Warner Bros. WS-1585	(S)	Gone, Gone, Gone	1965	16.00	40.00
Warner Bros. W-1605	(M)	Beat N' Soul	1965	12.00	30.00
Warner Bros. WS-1605	(S)	Beat N' Soul	1965	16.00	40.00
Warner Bros. W-1620	(M)	In Our Image	1966	12.00	30.00
Warner Bros. WS-1620	(S)	In Our Image	1966	16.00	40.00
—Original Warner albums above have grey labels with a black & white logo.—					
Warner Bros. W-1646	(M)	Two Yanks In London	1966	16.00	40.00
Warner Bros. WS-1646	(S)	Two Yanks In London	1966	20.00	50.00
(Although uncredited, the Hollies back up the Everlys throughout this album.)					
Warner Bros. W-1676	(M)	The Hit Sound Of The Everly Brothers	1967	16.00	40.00
Warner Bros. WS-1676	(S)	The Hit Sound Of The Everly Brothers	1967	20.00	50.00
Warner Bros. W-1708	(M)	The Everly Brothers Sing	1967	16.00	40.00
Warner Bros. WS-1708	(S)	The Everly Brothers Sing	1967	20.00	50.00
—Original Warner albums above have gold labels.—					
Warner Bros. WS-1752	(S)	Roots	1968	16.00	40.00
Warner Bros. WS-1858	(S)	The Everly Brothers' Show	1970	8.00	20.00
Harmony HS-11304	(S)	The Everly Brothers	1968	6.00	15.00
Harmony HS-11350	(S)	Christmas With The Everly Brothers	1969	6.00	15.00
Harmony HS-11388	(S)	Chained To A Memory	1970	4.00	10.00
RCA Victor LSP-4781	(S)	Pass The Chicken And Listen	1972	6.00	15.00
RCA Victor LSP-4620	(S)	Stories We Could Tell	1972	6.00	15.00
Passport 4006DJ	(DJ)	Reunion Concert	1983	20.00	50.00

EVERLY, DON

Ode 77005	(S)	Don Everly	1970	6.00	15.00
Ode 77023	(S)	Sunset Towers	1974	5.00	12.00
Hickory AH-44003	(S)	Brother Jukebox	1976	4.00	10.00

EVERLY, PHIL

RCA Victor APL1-0092	(S)	Star Spangled Banner	1973	6.00	15.00
Pye 12104	(S)	Phil's Diner	1975	6.00	15.00
Pye 12121	(S)	Mystic Line	1976	5.00	12.00

EVERY MOTHER'S SON

MGM E-3471	(M)	Every Mother's Son	1967	6.00	15.00
MGM SE-4471	(S)	Every Mother's Son	1967	8.00	20.00
MGM E-4504	(M)	Every Mother's Son's Back	1967	6.00	15.00
MGM SE-4504	(S)	Every Mother's Son's Back	1967	6.00	15.00

EVERPRESENT FULLNESS

White Whale 7132	(S)	Everpresent Fullness	1970	12.00	30.00

EVERYTHING IS EVERYTHING

Vanguard VSD-6512	(S)	Everything Is Everything	1969	10.00	25.00

EVESLAGE, ROBERT

Mark 5208	(M)	Reflecting/Portraits Of Loneliness	196?	20.00	50.00

EXCEPTIONS, THE

Flair 6444	(S)	Rock 'N' Roll Mass	1968	6.00	15.00

EXCITERS, THE

United Arts. UAL-3264	(M)	Tell Him	1963	14.00	35.00
United Arts. UAS-6264	(S)	Tell Him	1963	18.00	45.00
Roulette R-25326	(M)	The Exciters	1966	8.00	20.00
Roulette RS-25326	(S)	The Exciters	1966	12.00	30.00
RCA Victor LSP-4211	(S)	Caviar And Chitlin's	1969	6.00	15.00

EXCURSIONS

No label	(S)	Excursions	197?	60.00	150.00

EYES, THE

World Theatre	(S)	New Gods: Aardvark Thru Zymurgy	1977	300.00	500.00

EYES OF BLUE, THE

Mercury SR-61184	(S)	Crossroads Of Time	1968	8.00	20.00
Mercury SR-61220	(S)	In Fields Of Ardath	1969	8.00	20.00

FABARES, SHELLY

Colpix CLP-426	(M)	Shelly	1962	30.00	75.00
Colpix CST-426	(S)	Shelly	1962	80.00	200.00
Colpix CLP-431	(M)	The Things We Did Last Summer	1962	30.00	75.00
Colpix CST-431	(S)	The Things We Did Last Summer	1962	80.00	200.00
MGM SE-4540	(S)	A Time To Sing (Soundtrack)	1968	10.00	25.00

FABIAN (FABIAN FORTE)

Chancellor CHL-5003	(M)	Hold That Tiger	1959	20.00	50.00
Chancellor CHLS-5003	(S)	Hold That Tiger	1959	30.00	75.00
Chancellor CHL-5005	(M)	The Fabulous Fabian	1959	20.00	50.00
Chancellor CHLX-5005	(S)	The Fabulous Fabian	1959	30.00	75.00
Chancellor CHL-5012	(M)	The Good Old Summertime	1960	16.00	40.00
Chancellor CHLS-5012	(S)	The Good Old Summertime	1960	20.00	50.00
Chancellor CHL-5019	(M)	Rockin' Hot	1961	30.00	75.00
Chancellor CHL-5024	(M)	Fabian's 16 Fabulous Hits	1962	30.00	75.00

FABIAN / FRANKIE AVALON

Chancellor CHL-5009	(M)	The Hit Makers	1960	20.00	50.00
Tele-House CD-2041	(S)	Double Dynamite (2 LPs)	197?	5.00	12.00

FACES, THE: Refer to THE SMALL FACES

FAGEN, DONALD

Warner Bros. 23696	(DJ)	The Nightfly (Quiex II vinyl)	1982	6.00	15.00
Mobile Fidelity MFSL-120	(S)	The Nightfly	1984	6.00	18.00

FAIER, BILLY

Riverside RLP-12-427	(M)	Travelin' Man	195?	10.00	25.00
Riverside RLP-12-	(M)	The Art Of The Five String Banjo	195?	10.00	25.00

FAINE JADE

R.S.V.P. 8002	(S)	Introspection: A Faine Jade Recital	1968	100.00	200.00

FAIRPORT CONVENTION

Cotillion SO-9024	(S)	Fairport Convention	1969	8.00	20.00
A&M SP-4185	(S)	Fairport Convention	1969	6.00	15.00
A&M SP-4206	(S)	Unhalfbricking	1969	6.00	15.00
A&M SP-4257	(S)	Leige And Lief	1970	5.00	12.00
A&M SP-4265	(S)	Full House	1970	5.00	12.00
A&M SP-4319	(S)	Angel Delight	1971	5.00	12.00
A&M SP-4333	(S)	Babbacombe Lee	1972	5.00	12.00
A&M SP-4407	(S)	Nine	1973	5.00	12.00
A&M SP-4386	(S)	Rosie	1973	5.00	12.00
Island ILPS-9313	(S)	Rising For The Moon	1975	5.00	12.00

FAIRWEATHER

Neon 1	(S)	Beginning From An End	1971	6.00	15.00

FAITH

Brown Bag LA085	(S)	Faith	1973	6.00	15.00

(Originally issued as "Limousine" by Limousine.)

FAITH, ADAM

MGM E-3591	(M)	England's Top Singer	1961	16.00	40.00
MGM SE-3591	(S)	England's Top Singer	1961	20.00	50.00
Amy 8005	(M)	Adam Faith	1965	10.00	25.00
Amy S-8005	(S)	Adam Faith	1965	12.00	30.00

The ever-pretty Ms. Fabares was a seasoned entertainment veteran as a member of television's Donna Reed Show when she broke into the recording medium with the dreamy "Johnny Angel," one of the best examples of white teen pop of the rock era. Like many Colpix albums, stereo copies of her two albums are outlandishly rare. Personality collectors should note that Paul Petersen played her brother on the TV series and also signed a recording contract with Colpix.

Label & Catalog #		Title	Year	VG+	NM
FAITHFULL, MARIANNE					
London LL-3423	(M)	Marianne Faithfull	1965	8.00	20.00
London PS-423	(E)	Marianne Faithfull	1965	6.00	15.00
London LL-3452	(M)	Go Away From My World	1965	6.00	15.00
London PS-452	(S)	Go Away From My World	1965	8.00	20.00
		("Summer Nights" is rechanneled.)			
London LL-3482	(M)	Faithfull Forever	1966	6.00	15.00
London PS-482	(S)	Faithfull Forever	1966	8.00	20.00
London PS-547	(S)	Marianne Faithfull's Greatest Hits	1969	6.00	15.00
		("As Tears Go By," "This Little Bird," "Summer Nights," "Come And Stay With Me" and "In My Time Of Sorrow" are rechanneled.)			
Island 90066	(DJ)	A Child's Adventure (Quiex II vinyl)	1983	5.00	12.00
FALCONAIRES, THE					
The Falconaires feature Steve Alaimo, Keith Allison and Mark Lindsay of Paul Revere's Raiders.					
USAF 70-3/4	(S)	Something From The Falconaires	1970	20.00	50.00
FALLEN ANGELS, THE					
Roulette SR-25358	(S)	The Fallen Angels	1968	16.00	40.00
Roulette SR-42011	(S)	It's A Long Way Down	1968	100.00	200.00
FAME, GEORGIE					
Imperial LP-9282	(M)	Yeh, Yeh	1965	10.00	25.00
Imperial LP-12282	(S)	Yeh, Yeh	1965	12.00	30.00
		("Yeh Yeh" is rechanneled on this album.)			
Imperial LP-9331	(M)	Get Away	1966	10.00	25.00
Imperial LP-12331	(E)	Get Away	1966	8.00	20.00
Epic BN-26368	(S)	The Ballad Of Bonnie And Clyde	1968	10.00	25.00
Island ILPS-9293	(S)	Georgie Fame	1975	4.00	10.00
FAMILY					
Reprise RS-6312	(S)	Music In A Doll's House	1968	8.00	20.00
Reprise RS-6340	(S)	Family Entertainment	1969	6.00	15.00
Reprise RS-6384	(S)	A Song For Me	1970	6.00	15.00
United Arts. UAS-5527	(S)	Anyway (Brown label)	1971	6.00	15.00
United Arts. UAS-5562	(S)	Fearless	1971	4.00	10.00
United Arts. UAS-5644	(S)	Bandstand	1972	4.00	10.00
United Arts. LA181	(S)	It's Only A Movie	1973	4.00	10.00
FAMILY DOGG, THE					
Buddah BDS-5100	(S)	The View From Rowland's Head	1972	6.00	15.00
FAMILY TREE, THE					
RCA Victor LSP-3955	(S)	Miss Butters	1968	5.00	12.00
FANKHAUSER, MERRELL					
Refer to Fapardokly; The Impacts; Mu.					
Shamley SS-701	(S)	Things	197?	10.00	25.00
Maui 101	(S)	Merrell Fankhauser	1976	30.00	60.00
FANTASTIC BAGGYS, THE					
The Baggys are the creation of Steve Barri and Phil Sloan.					
Imperial LP-9270	(M)	Tell 'Em I'm Surfin'	1964	40.00	100.00
Imperial LP-12270	(S)	Tell 'Em I'm Surfin'	1964	60.00	150.00
Liberty LN-10192	(S)	Tell 'Em I'm Surfin' (Abridged reissue)	1982	4.00	10.00
FANTASTIC DEE JAY'S, THE					
Stone SLP-4003	(S)	The Fantastic Dee Jay's	196?	660.0	1,000.00
FANTASTIC FOUR, THE					
Soul 717	(P)	Best Of The Fantastic Four	1969	12.00	30.00
Soul 722	(S)	How Sweet He Is	1970	Unreleased	
Westbound 201	(S)	Alvin Stone	1975	6.00	15.00
Westbound 226	(S)	Night People	1976	6.00	15.00
Westbound 306	(S)	Got To Have Your Love	1977	6.00	15.00
Westbound 6108	(S)	B. Y. O. F. (Bring Your Own Funk)	1978	6.00	15.00
FANTASTIC JOHNNY C, THE					
Phil-L.A. 4000	(S)	Boogaloo Down Broadway	1968	20.00	50.00

Label & Catalog #		Title	Year	VG+	NM

FAPARDOKLY
Fapardokly is Merrell Fankhauser.

Label & Catalog #		Title	Year	VG+	NM
U.I.P. 2500	(S)	Fapardokly	1966	100.00	250.00

FAR EAST FAMILY BAND

Muland 7002	(S)	The Cave Down To The Earth	197?	6.00	15.00
Muland 7139	(S)	Parallel World	197?	6.00	15.00

FARINA, RICHARD & MIMI

Vanguard VRS-9174	(M)	Celebrations For A Gray Day	1965	5.00	12.00
Vanguard VSD-79174	(S)	Celebrations For A Gray Day	1965	6.00	15.00
Vanguard VRS-9204	(M)	Reflections In A Crystal Mind	1966	5.00	12.00
Vanguard VSD-79204	(S)	Reflections In A Crystal Mind	1966	6.00	15.00
Vanguard VSD-79263	(S)	Memories	1968	6.00	15.00

FARLOWE, CHRIS (& THE THUNDERBIRDS)

Columbia CL-2593	(M)	The Fabulous Chris Farlowe	1966	12.00	30.00
Columbia CS-9393	(E)	The Fabulous Chris Farlowe	1966	8.00	20.00
Immediate Z12-52010	(S)	Paint It Farlowe	1968	6.00	15.00

FARM

Series-2 F2001	(S)	The Inner Most Limits Of Pure Fun	197?	40.00	100.00
		(Issued with an insert cover.)			

FARM BAND, THE

Mantra 777	(S)	The Farm Band (2 LPs with poster)	197?	14.00	35.00
Farm 1001	(S)	On The Rim Of The Nashville Basin	197?	6.00	15.00
Farm 1013	(S)	Communion	197?	6.00	15.00
		(Farm 1013 credits The Tennessee Farm Band.)			
Farm 1776	(S)	Up In Your Thing	197?	6.00	15.00
		(Farm 1013 credits Stephen & The Farm Band.)			

FARNER, MARK, & DON BREWER
Refer to Grand Funk Railroad; Terry Knight & The Pack.

Quadico 7401	(S)	Monumental Funk	1979	4.00	10.00
Quadico 7401	(S)	Monumental Funk (Picture disc)	1979	6.00	15.00

FARRELL, EILEEN

Columbia CL-1465	(M)	I've Got A Right To Sing The Blues	1960	8.00	20.00
Columbia CS-8256	(S)	I've Got A Right To Sing The Blues	1960	12.00	30.00

FAT

Dream Merchant OU812	(S)	Footloose	1976	10.00	25.00

FAT CITY

ABC/Probe CPLP-4508	(S)	Reincarnation	1969	6.00	15.00
Paramount PAS-6028	(S)	Welcome To Fat City	1972	6.00	15.00

FATHER YOD

Higher Key 3301	(S)	Kohoutek	1973	60.00	150.00
Higher Key 3302	(S)	To Our Children	1973	80.00	200.00
Higher Key 3304	(S)	All Or Nothing At All	1974	60.00	150.00
Higher Key 3306	(S)	The Savage Sons Of Yo Ho Wa	1974	60.00	150.00
Higher Key 3307	(S)	An Aquarian Symphony/Penetration	1974	60.00	150.00
Higher Key 3309	(S)	I'm Gonna Take You Home	1975	60.00	150.00

FAUN

Gregar 7000	(S)	Faun	1969	12.00	30.00

FAYE, ALICE

Columbia CL-3068	(M)	Alice Faye In Hollywood 1934-1937	196?	8.00	20.00
Reprise R-6029	(M)	Alice Faye Sings Her Famous Movie Hits	1962	6.00	15.00
Reprise R9-6029	(S)	Alice Faye Sings Her Famous Movie Hits	1962	8.00	20.00

FAYE, FRANCES: *Refer to* GOLDMINE'S PRICE GUIDE TO COLLECTIBLE JAZZ ALBUMS

FEAR ITSELF

Dot DLP-25942	(S)	Fear Itself	1969	8.00	20.00

Wisconsin's Phil Humphrey and James Sundquist took Jimmie Rodgers' "Mule Skinner Blues" and refitted it into a rock 'n roll hit in 1960. They followed this up with an album that had a limited press run and has been a major collectible for decades. Aside from common black vinyl, there are pressings with non-opaque black vinyl that have a reddish hue when held up to a strong light along with pressings on a lovely translucent blue vinyl. There are rumors of other colored vinyls—red and yellow have been mentioned—circulating but remain unverified at the time of publication. Just a few years ago copies on the Canadian Point label could be had for under $50 at Canadian shows. . . but, as the value for the Soma pressing continues to escalate, the demand for the Canadian pressing has followed suit. Now it, too, is a legitimate three figure album in collectible condition.

Label & Catalog #		Title	Year	VG+	NM
FEATHER					
Magic	(S)	**Feather**	1978	16.00	40.00
FELICE, DEE DEE					
Bethlehem B-1000	(S)	**In The Heat** (Produced by James Brown)	1969	10.00	25.00
FELT					
Nasco 9006	(S)	**Felt**	1971	30.00	75.00
FENDERMEN, THE					
Soma MG-1240	(M)	**Mule Skinner Blues** (Opaque vinyl)	1960	600.00	Rare
		(Near Mint copies have a suggested value of $1,000-1,500.)			
Soma MG-1240	(M)	**Mule Skinner Blues** (Non-opaque vinyl)	1960	1,000.00	Rare
		(When held up to a light, the light will shine through the black vinyl with a reddish brown glow. Rare in any condition with a suggested Near Mint copies have a suggested value of $1,500-2,500.)			
Soma MG-1240	(M)	**Mule Skinner Blues** (Blue vinyl)	1960	2,000.00	Rare
		(Near Mint copies have a suggested value of $3,000-4,000. The possibility remains that other colors may exist.)			
Point P-213	(M)	**Mule Skinner Blues** (Canadian)	1960	150.00	300.00
FERGUSON, JAY					
Jay was formerly a member of SpJo Jo Gunne; Magic; irit.					
Asylum AS-11394	(DJ)	**Jay Ferguson Live**	1978	8.00	20.00
FERLINGHETTI, LAWRENCE					
Fantasy 7002	(M)	**Poetry Readings In The Cellar** (Red vinyl)	1957	30.00	75.00
Fantasy 7004	(M)	**Impeachment Of Eisenhower** (Red vinyl)	1958	30.00	75.00
FERRERS, THE					
Mr. and Mrs. Jose Ferrer. Mrs. Ferrer also recorded under her maiden name, Rosemary Clooney.					
MGM E-3709	(M)	**The Ferrers At Home**	1958	12.00	30.00
FERRIS WHEEL, THE					
Uni 73093	(S)	**The Ferris Wheel**	1970	5.00	12.00
FEVER TREE					
Uni 73024	(S)	**The Fever Tree**	1968	8.00	20.00
Uni 73040	(S)	**Another Time, Another Place**	1968	6.00	15.00
Uni 73067	(S)	**Creation**	1970	6.00	15.00
Uni 73091	(S)	**Angels Die Hard** (Soundtrack)	1970	8.00	20.00
Ampex A-10113	(S)	**For Sale**	1970	6.00	15.00
FIELD, SALLY					
Colgems COL-106	(M)	**Star Of "The Flying Nun"**	1967	8.00	20.00
Colgems COS-106	(S)	**Star Of "The Flying Nun"**	1967	10.00	25.00
FIELDING, JANE: Refer to GOLDMINE'S PRICE GUIDE TO COLLECTIBLE JAZZ ALBUMS					
FIELDS, THE					
Uni 73050	(S)	**The Fields**	1969	6.00	15.00
FIFTH ESTATE, THE					
Jubilee JGM-8005	(M)	**Ding Dong The Witch Is Dead**	1967	8.00	20.00
Jubilee JGS-8005	(S)	**Ding Dong The Witch Is Dead**	1967	10.00	25.00
FIFTY FOOT HOSE					
Limelight 86062	(S)	**Cauldron**	1969	20.00	50.00
FILET OF SOUL					
Mongoloid	(M)	**Freedom**	196?	60.00	150.00
FINCHLEY BOYS, THE					
Golden Throat 200-19	(S)	**Everlasting Tribute**	1971	40.00	100.00
FIRE ESCAPE, THE					
Crescendo GNP-2034	(M)	**Psychotic Reaction** (Red label)	1967	10.00	25.00
Crescendo GNPS-2034	(S)	**Psychotic Reaction** (Red label)	1967	8.00	20.00
Crescendo GNPS-2034	(S)	**Psychotic Reaction** (Blue label)	196?	4.00	10.00

Label & Catalog #		Title	Year	VG+	NM
FIRE TOWN					
Boat 1013	(S)	**In The Heart Of The Heart Country**	1987	5.00	12.00
FIREBALLS, THE [JIMMY GILMER & THE FIREBALLS]					
Top Rank RM-324	(M)	**The Fireballs**	1960	60.00	150.00
Top Rank RM-343	(M)	**Vaquero**	1960	60.00	150.00
Top Rank RS-643	(S)	**Vaquero**	1960	80.00	200.00
Warwick W-2042	(M)	**Here Are The Fireballs**	1961	60.00	150.00
Warwick WST-2042	(S)	**Here Are The Fireballs**	1961	100.00	250.00
Dot DLP-3512	(M)	**Torquay**	1963	14.00	35.00
Dot DLP-25512	(S)	**Torquay**	1963	20.00	50.00
Dot DLP-3545	(M)	**Sugar Shack**	1963	14.00	35.00
Dot DLP-25545	(S)	**Sugar Shack**	1963	20.00	50.00
Dot DLP-3577	(M)	**Buddy's Buddy**	1964	20.00	50.00
Dot DLP-25577	(S)	**Buddy's Buddy**	1964	30.00	75.00
Dot DLP-3643	(M)	**Lucky 'Leven**	1965	10.00	25.00
Dot DLP-25643	(S)	**Lucky 'Leven**	1965	12.00	30.00
Dot DLP-3668	(M)	**Folkbeat**	1965	10.00	25.00
Dot DLP-25668	(S)	**Folkbeat**	1965	12.00	30.00
Dot DLP-3709	(M)	**Campusology**	1966	10.00	25.00
Dot DLP-25709	(S)	**Campusology**	1966	12.00	30.00
Dot DLP-25856	(S)	**Firewater**	1968	8.00	20.00
		("Daisy Petal Pickin'" is rechanneled on this album.)			
Atco SD-33-239	(S)	**Bottle Of Wine**	1968	8.00	20.00
Atco SD-33-275	(S)	**Come On, React!**	1969	8.00	20.00
FIREBIRDS, THE					
Crown CST-589	(S)	**Light My Fire**	1968	30.00	75.00
FIREFLIES, THE					
Taurus S-1002	(S)	**You Were Mine**	1967	150.00	300.00
		(The 1959 hit, "You Were Mine," was rerecorded in stereo.)			
FIRESIGN THEATRE					
Philip Austin, Peter Bergman, David Ossman And Philip Proctor.					
Columbia CL-2719	(M)	**Waiting For The Electrician**	1968	10.00	25.00
Columbia CS-9519	(S)	**Waiting For The Electrician**	1968	6.00	15.00
Columbia CS-9884	(S)	**How Can You Be In Two Places At Once**			
		When You're Not Anywhere At All	1969	6.00	15.00
		— Original Columbia albums above have "360 Sound" on the bottom of the label.—			
Columbia C-30102	(S)	**Don't Crush That Dwarf,**			
		Hand Me The Pliers (With poster)	1970	6.00	15.00
Columbia CQ-30737	(Q)	**I Think We're All Bozos On This Bus**	1971	8.00	20.00
Columbia CQ-33141	(Q)	**Everything You Know Is Wrong**	1974	8.00	20.00
FIRST CHIPS, THE					
Clay Pigeon CPP-SFCV1	(S)	**First Chips, Volume 1**	1972	60.00	150.00
FIRST EDITION, THE					
The First Edition features Kenny Rogers.					
Reprise R-6276	(M)	**The First Edition**	1967	10.00	25.00
Reprise RS-6276	(S)	**The First Edition**	1967	12.00	30.00
Reprise RS-6328	(S)	**The First Edition '69**	1969	6.00	15.00
FIRST FRIDAY					
Webster's Last Word 2895	(S)	**First Friday**	197?	40.00	100.00
FISCHER, WILD MAN					
"Produced" by Frank Zappa.					
Bizarre 2XS-6332	(S)	**An Evening With Wild Man Fischer** (2 LPs)	1969	12.00	30.00
FISHER, AL, & LOU MARKS					
Swan LP-514	(M)	**It's A Beatle (Coo Coo) World**	1964	20.00	50.00
FISHER, CHIP					
RCA Victor LPM-1797	(M)	**Chipper At The Sugar Bowl**	1958	20.00	50.00
RCA Victor LSP-1797	(S)	**Chipper At The Sugar Bowl**	1958	30.00	75.00

Label & Catalog #		Title	Year	VG+	NM
FISHER, EDDIE					
RCA Victor LPM-3025 (10")	(M)	Fisher Sings	1952	20.00	50.00
RCA Victor LPM-3058 (10")	(M)	I'm In The Mood For Love	1952	20.00	50.00
RCA Victor LPM-3065 (10")	(M)	Christmas With Fisher	1952	20.00	50.00
RCA Victor LPM-3122 (10")	(M)	Irving Berlin Favorites	1954	20.00	50.00
RCA Victor LPM-3185 (10")	(M)	May I Sing To You?	1954	20.00	50.00
RCA Victor LPM-3375 (10")	(M)	The Best Of Eddie Fisher	1954	20.00	50.00
RCA Victor LOC-1024	(M)	Academy Award Winners	1955	16.00	40.00
RCA Victor LPM-1097	(M)	I Love You	1955	16.00	40.00
RCA Victor LPM-1180	(M)	I'm In The Mood For Love	1955	16.00	40.00
RCA Victor LPM-1181	(M)	May I Sing To You?	1955	16.00	40.00
RCA Victor LPM-1399	(M)	Bundle Of Joy (Soundtrack)	1956	16.00	40.00
RCA Victor LPM-1548	(M)	Thinking Of You	1957	16.00	40.00
RCA Victor LPM-1647	(M)	As Long As There's Music	1958	16.00	40.00
RCA Victor LSP-1647	(S)	As Long As There's Music	1958	20.00	50.00
Ramrod T-6001	(M)	Scent Of Mystery (Soundtrack)	1960	150.00	300.00
Ramrod ST-6001	(S)	Scent Of Mystery (Soundtrack)	1960	200.00	400.00
RCA Victor LPM-2504	(M)	Eddie Fisher's Greatest Hits	1962	8.00	20.00
RCA Victor LSP-2504	(S)	Eddie Fisher's Greatest Hits	1962	10.00	25.00

— Original RCA mono albums above have "Long Play" on the bottom of the label;
stereo albums have "Living Stereo" on the bottom.—

Ramrod RR-1	(M)	Eddie Fisher At The Winter Garden	1963	8.00	20.00
Ramrod RRS-1	(S)	Eddie Fisher At The Winter Garden	1963	10.00	25.00
Dot DLP-3631	(M)	Eddie Fisher Today!	1965	6.00	15.00
Dot DLP-25631	(S)	Eddie Fisher Today!	1965	8.00	20.00
Dot DLP-3648	(M)	When I Was Young	1965	6.00	15.00
Dot DLP-25648	(S)	When I Was Young	1965	8.00	20.00
Dot DLP-3785	(M)	His Greatest Hits	1966	6.00	15.00
Dot DLP-25785	(S)	His Greatest Hits	1966	8.00	20.00
RCA Victor LPM-3726	(M)	Games That Lovers Play	1966	6.00	15.00
RCA Victor LSP-3726	(S)	Games That Lovers Play	1966	8.00	20.00
RCA Victor LPM-3820	(M)	People Like You	1967	8.00	20.00
RCA Victor LSP-3820	(S)	People Like You	1967	8.00	20.00

— Original RCA albums above have black labels.—

FISHER, KEVIN					
P. Pan P-101	(S)	The First Of Fisher	1977	60.00	150.00
FISHER, MISS TONI					
Signet WP-509	(S)	The Big Hurt	1960	20.00	50.00

("The Big Hurt" is rechanneled on this album.)

FITZGERALD, ELLA: Refer to GOLDMINE'S PRICE GUIDE TO COLLECTIBLE JAZZ ALBUMS

FIVE AMERICANS, THE					
HBR HLP-8503	(M)	I See The Light	1966	6.00	15.00
HBR HST-9503	(S)	I See The Light	1966	8.00	20.00
Abnak AB-2067	(M)	Western Union/Sound Of Love	1967	6.00	15.00
Abnak ABST-2067	(S)	Western Union/Sound Of Love	1967	8.00	20.00
Abnak AB-2069	(M)	Progressions	1967	6.00	15.00
Abnak ABST-2069	(S)	Progressions	1967	8.00	20.00

("Evol-Not Love" is rechanneled on this album.)

Abnak ABST-2071	(P)	Now And Then (2 LPs)	1968	8.00	20.00
FIVE BY FIVE					
Paula LPS-2202	(S)	Next Exit	1969	6.00	15.00
FIVE EMPREES, THE					
Freeport FR-3001	(M)	The Five Emprees	1965	30.00	75.00
Freeport FRS-4001	(S)	The Five Emprees	1965	40.00	100.00
Freeport FR-3001	(M)	Little Miss Sad	1966	20.00	50.00
Freeport FRS-4001	(S)	Little Miss Sad	1966	30.00	75.00

("Little Miss Sad" is a reissue of "The Five Emprees.")

FIVE KEYS, THE					
Aladdin 806	(M)	The Best Of The Five Keys (Maroon label)	1956	750.00	1,500.00

(Note: Copies of Aladdin 806 with a blue label are not known to exist.
Should one be found it would command at least twice the value of the
maroon label.)

Label & Catalog #		Title	Year	VG+	NM
Score LP-4003	(M)	The Five Keys On The Town	1957	250.00	600.00
Capitol T-828	(M)	The Five Keys On Stage	1957	100.00	250.00
		(The cover photo has the first member's hand against his body so that his thumb has a phallic appearance.)			
Capitol T-828	(M)	The Five Keys On Stage	1957	200.00	400.00
		(The cover has the thumb airbrushed out.)			
King 688	(M)	The Five Keys	1960	150.00	300.00
King 692	(M)	Rhythm & Blues Hits Past And Present	1960	150.00	300.00
		— Original King albums above have crownless black labels.—			
Capitol T-1769	(M)	The Fantastic Five Keys	1962	80.00	200.00

FIVE MAN ELECTRICAL BAND, THE

Label & Catalog #		Title	Year	VG+	NM
Capitol ST-165	(S)	The Five Man Electrical Band	1969	8.00	20.00
Lionel 1100	(S)	Goodbyes And Butterflies	1970	6.00	15.00
Lionel 1101	(S)	Coming Of Age	1971	6.00	15.00
Lion LN-1009	(S)	Sweet Paradise	1973	6.00	15.00

FIVE ROYALES, THE

Label & Catalog #		Title	Year	VG+	NM
Apollo LP-488	(M)	The Rockin' 5 Royales (Green label)	1956	750.00	Rare
		(Near Mint copies have a suggested value of $1,500-2,500.)			
Apollo LP-488	(M)	The Rockin' 5 Royales (Yellow label)	1956	See note below	
Apollo LP-488	(M)	The Rockin' 5 Royales (Purple label)	1956	See note below	
		(Copies with yellow purple labels are either later legitimate pressings or counterfeits.)			
King 580	(M)	Dedicated To You	1957	200.00	400.00
King 616	(M)	The 5 Royales Sing For You	1959	100.00	250.00
King 678	(M)	The Five Royales	1960	100.00	250.00
King 955	(M)	24 All Time Hits	1966	40.00	100.00
		— Original King albums above have crownless black labels.—			

FIVE SATINS, THE
Refer to Fred Parris & The Satins.

Label & Catalog #		Title	Year	VG+	NM
Ember ELP-100	(M)	The Five Satins Sing (Red label)	1957	200.00	400.00
		(Original pressings have a red cover with a group photo. All later pressings below have black & gold title covers.)			
Ember ELP-100	(M)	The Five Satins Sing (Blue vinyl)	1957	600.00	Rare
		(Near Mint copies have a suggested value of $1,000-1,600.)			
Ember ELP-100	(M)	The Five Satins Sing (Logs label)	1959	60.00	150.00
Ember ELP-100	(M)	The Five Satins Sing (Black label)	1961	30.00	75.00
Ember ELP-401	(M)	Encore, Volume 2 (Logs label)	1960	60.00	150.00
Ember ELP-401	(M)	Encore, Volume 2 (Black label)	1961	30.00	75.00
Mt. Vernon 108	(M)	The Five Satins Sing	196?	12.00	30.00
Celebrity Show. JB-7671	(M)	The Best Of The Five Satins	1970	10.00	25.00
Lost Nite LLP-8 (10")	(M)	The Five Satins (Red vinyl)	1981	4.00	10.00
Lost Nite LLP-9 (10")	(M)	The Five Satins (Red vinyl)	1981	4.00	10.00

FIVE STAIRSTEPS, THE [THE STAIRSTEPS]

Label & Catalog #		Title	Year	VG+	NM
Windy C 6000	(M)	The Five Stairsteps	1967	8.00	20.00
Windy C S-6000	(S)	The Five Stairsteps	1967	10.00	25.00
Curtom 8002	(S)	Love's Happening	1969	6.00	15.00
Buddah BSD-5008	(S)	Our Family Portrait	1968	6.00	15.00
Buddah BSD-5061	(S)	The Stairsteps	1970	6.00	15.00
Buddah BSD-5068	(S)	Step By Step By Step	1970	6.00	15.00

FLAIRS, THE

Label & Catalog #		Title	Year	VG+	NM
Crown CLP-5356	(M)	The Flairs	1963	20.00	50.00
Crown CST-356	(E)	The Flairs	1963	10.00	25.00

FLAME, THE
Features Blondie Chaplin And Rickie Fataar, later of The Beach Boys.

Label & Catalog #		Title	Year	VG+	NM
Brother BR-2500	(S)	Flame (With poster)	1970	10.00	25.00

FLAMIN' GROOVIES, THE

Label & Catalog #		Title	Year	VG+	NM
Snazz R-2371 (10")	(S)	Sneekers	1969	30.00	75.00
Epic BN-26487	(S)	Supersnazz	1969	16.00	40.00
Kama Sutra KSBS-2021	(S)	Flamingo (Pink label in a gatefold cover)	1970	10.00	25.00
Kama Sutra KSBS-2021	(S)	Flamingo (Blue label)	1972	6.00	15.00
Kama Sutra KSBS-2031	(S)	Teenage Head (Pink label)	1971	10.00	25.00
Kama Sutra KSBS-2031	(S)	Teenage Head (Blue label)	1972	6.00	15.00

Label & Catalog #		Title	Year	VG+	NM
Sire D-7521	(S)	Shake Some Action	1976	6.00	15.00
Buddah BDS-5683	(S)	Still Shakin'	1977	6.00	15.00
Sire SRK-6059	(S)	The Flamin' Groovies Now (12 tracks)	1978	6.00	15.00
Sire SRK-6059	(S)	The Flamin' Groovies Now (14 tracks)	1978	5.00	12.00
Sire SRK-6067	(S)	Jumpin' In The Night	1979	5.00	12.00

FLAMING EMBER

Hot Wax HA-702	(S)	Westbound #9	1970	6.00	15.00
Hot Wax HA-705	(S)	Sunshine	1970	5.00	12.00

FLAMING YOUTH
Flaming Youth features Phil Collins, later of of Genesis.

Uni 73075	(S)	Ark 2	1969	12.00	30.00

FLAMINGOS, THE

Checker LP-1433	(M)	The Flamingos (Black label)	1959	150.00	300.00
Checker LP-1433	(M)	The Flamingos (Blue label)	1965	30.00	75.00
Checker LPS-3005	(E)	The Flamingos (Blue label)	1965	20.00	50.00
End LP-304	(M)	Flamingo Serenade	1959	80.00	200.00
End LPS-304	(S)	Flamingo Serenade	1959	150.00	300.00
		(Original covers correctly list the record as Stereo. "But Not For Me" is rechaneled on this and all subsequent pressings.)			
End STLP-304	(S)	Flamingo Serenade	196?	80.00	200.00
		(Later covers incorrectly read Rechanneled Stereo.)			
End LP-307	(M)	Flamingo Favorites	1960	30.00	75.00
End LPS-307	(E)	Flamingo Favorites	1960	30.00	75.00
End LP-308	(M)	Requestfully Yours	1960	30.00	75.00
End LPS-308	(E)	Requestfully Yours	1960	30.00	75.00
End LP-316	(M)	The Sound Of The Flamingos	1962	30.00	75.00
End LPS-316	(S)	The Sound Of The Flamingos	1962	100.00	250.00
		(Stereo copies read "Stereo" in the upper right corner of the cover.)			
End LPS-316	(E)	The Sound Of The Flamingos	1962	30.00	75.00
Constellation CS-3	(M)	Collectors Showcase: The Flamingos	1964	10.00	25.00
Philips PHM-200-206	(M)	Their Hits-Then And Now	1966	10.00	25.00
Philips PHS-600-206	(S)	Their Hits-Then And Now	1966	14.00	35.00
Chess	(M)	The Flamingos	1975	4.00	10.00
Lost Nite LLP-7 (10")	(M)	The Flamingos (Red vinyl)	1981	4.00	10.00

FLAMINGOS, THE / THE MOONGLOWS

Vee Jay LP-1052	(M)	The Flamingos Meet The Moonglows	1962	40.00	100.00

FLANDERS, TOMMY
Flanders was formerly a member of the Blues Project.

Verve/Forecast FTS-3075	(S)	Moonstone	1970	8.00	20.00

FLARES, THE

Press PR-73001	(M)	Encore Of Foot Stompin' Hits	1961	8.00	20.00
Press PRS-83001	(S)	Encore Of Foot Stompin' Hits	1961	16.00	40.00

FLAT EARTH SOCIETY

Fleetwood 3027	(S)	Waleeco	1968	100.00	250.00

FLATT, LESTER, & EARL SCRUGGS

Columbia CL-1019	(M)	Foggy Mountain Jamboree	1957	20.00	50.00
Mercury MG-20358	(M)	Country Music	1958	16.00	40.00
Mercury MG-20542	(M)	Lester Flatt And Earl Scruggs	1959	20.00	50.00
Mercury MG-20773	(M)	The Original Sound Of Flatt And Scruggs	1963	10.00	25.00
Mercury SR-60773	(E)	The Original Sound Of Flatt And Scruggs	1963	6.00	15.00
Columbia CL-1421	(M)	Songs Of Glory	1960	10.00	25.00
Columbia CS-8221	(S)	Songs Of Glory	1960	12.00	30.00
Columbia CL-1564	(M)	Foggy Mountain Banjo	1961	10.00	25.00
Columbia CS-8364	(S)	Foggy Mountain Banjo	1961	12.00	30.00
Columbia CL-1664	(M)	Songs Of The Famous Carter Family	1961	10.00	25.00
Columbia CS-8464	(S)	Songs Of The Famous Carter Family	1961	12.00	30.00
Columbia CL-1830	(M)	Folk Songs Of Our Land	1962	10.00	25.00
Columbia CS-8630	(S)	Folk Songs Of Our Land	1962	12.00	30.00
		— Original Columbia albums above have three white "eye" logos on each side of the spindle hole.—			
Columbia CL-2045	(M)	Flatt And Scruggs At Carnegie Hall	1963	8.00	20.00
Columbia CS-8845	(S)	Flatt And Scruggs At Carnegie Hall	1963	10.00	25.00

Label & Catalog #		Title	Year	VG+	NM
Columbia CL-2134	(M)	**Live At Vanderbilt University**	1964	8.00	20.00
Columbia CS-8934	(S)	**Live At Vanderbilt University**	1964	10.00	25.00
Columbia CL-2255	(M)	**The Fabulous Sound Of Flatt And Scruggs**	1964	8.00	20.00
Columbia CS-9055	(S)	**The Fabulous Sound Of Flatt And Scruggs**	1964	10.00	25.00
Columbia CL-2354	(M)	**The Versatile**	1965	8.00	20.00
Columbia CS-9154	(S)	**The Versatile**	1965	10.00	25.00
		— Original Columbia albums above have "360 Sound" on the bottom of the label.—			
Starday SLP-365	(M)	**Stars Of The Grand Ole Opry**	1966	10.00	25.00

FLEETWOOD MAC
Over the years Mick Fleetwood and John McVie have hosted a revolving door of members including Peter Green, Jeremy Spencer, Christine McVie, Bob Welch, Lindsay Buckingham and Stevie Nicks.

Epic BN-26402	(S)	**Fleetwood Mac** *(Yellow label)*	1968	10.00	25.00
Epic BN-26446	(S)	**English Rose** *(Yellow label)*	1969	10.00	25.00
Epic KE-30632	(S)	**Black Magic Woman** *(2 LPs)*	1971	8.00	20.00
		(Epic 30632 repackages 26402 and 26445.)			
Epic KE-33740	(S)	**Fleetwood Mac / English Rose** *(2 LPs)*	1974	6.00	15.00
		(Epic 33740 repackages 30632.)			
Reprise RS-6368	(S)	**Then Play On**	1969	8.00	20.00
		(Contains "When You Say" and "My Dream.")			
Reprise RS-6368	(S)	**Then Play On**	1970	5.00	12.00
		("Oh Well" replaces "When You Say" and "My Dream.")			
Reprise RS-6408	(S)	**Kiln House**	1970	6.00	15.00
Reprise RS-6465	(S)	**Future Games** *(Yellow cover)*	1971	8.00	20.00
Reprise RS-6465	(S)	**Future Games** *(Green cover)*	1971	5.00	12.00
Reprise MS-2080	(S)	**Bare Trees** *(With lyric sheet)*	1972	6.00	15.00
Reprise MS-2138	(S)	**Penguin**	1973	5.00	12.00
Reprise MS-2158	(S)	**Mystery To Me** *(With lyric sheet)*	1973	6.00	15.00
		(Side 2 lists "Good Things Come To Those Who Wait.")			
Reprise MS-2158	(S)	**Mystery To Me** *(With lyric sheet)*	1973	5.00	12.00
		(Side 2 lists "For Your Love.")			
Reprise MS-2196	(S)	**Heroes Are Hard To Find**	1974	5.00	12.00
Reprise MS-2225	(S)	**Fleetwood Mac**	1975	5.00	12.00
Sire SASH-3706	(S)	**Vintage Years** *(2 LPs)*	1975	6.00	15.00
Sire SASH-3715	(S)	**Fleetwood Mac In Chicago** *(2 LPs)*	1975	6.00	15.00
		(Sire 3716 reissues the Blue Horizon material with Otis Spann.)			
Sire 2XS-6006	(S)	**Vintage Years** *(2 LPs)*	1977	5.00	12.00
		(Sire 6006 is a reissue of 3705.)			
Sire 2XS-6046	(S)	**The Original Fleetwood Mac** *(2 LPs)*	1977	5.00	12.00
Sire 2XS-6009	(S)	**Fleetwood Mac In Chicago** *(2 LPs)*	1977	5.00	12.00
		(Sire 6009 is a reissue of 3715.)			
Warner Bros. PRO-652	(DJ)	**Rumours** *(Embossed promo cover)*	1976	20.00	50.00
Warner Bros. PRO-866	(DJ)	**Tusk Remix**	1979	6.00	15.00
Warner Bros. PRO	(DJ)	**The Fleetwood Mac Story** *(2 LPs)*	1979	20.00	50.00
Warner Bros. 23607	(DJ)	**Mirage** *(Quiex II vinyl)*	1982	6.00	15.00
Mobile Fidelity MFSL-012	(S)	**Fleetwood Mac**	1980	13.00	40.00
Mobile Fidelity MFSL-119	(S)	**Mirage**	198?	12.00	35.00
Nautilus NR-8	(S)	**Rumours**	1980	8.00	25.00

FLEETWOOD MAC & OTIS SPANN

Blue Horizon BH-66227	(S)	**Blues Jam At Chess**	1969	12.00	30.00
Blue Horizon BH-4802	(S)	**The Biggest Thing Since Colossus**	1970	14.00	35.00
Blue Horizon BH-4803	(S)	**Blues Jam In Chicago, Volume 1**	1970	10.00	25.00
Blue Horizon BH-4803	(S)	**Blues Jam In Chicago, Volume 2**	1970	10.00	25.00
Blue Horizon BH-3801	(S)	**Blues Jam In Chicago** *(2 LPs)*	1970	12.00	30.00

FLEETWOODS, THE

Dolton BLP-2001	(M)	**Mr. Blue**	1959	20.00	50.00
Dolton BST-8001	(S)	**Mr. Blue** *("Mr. Blue" is rechanneled)*	1959	30.00	75.00
Dolton BLP-2002	(M)	**The Fleetwoods**	1960	16.00	40.00
Dolton BST-8002	(S)	**The Fleetwoods**	1960	20.00	50.00
Dolton BLP-2005	(M)	**Softly**	1961	16.00	40.00
Dolton BST-8005	(S)	**Softly** *("Come Softly To Me" is rechanneled)*	1961	20.00	50.00
Dolton BLP-2007	(M)	**Deep In A Dream**	1961	12.00	30.00
Dolton BST-8007	(S)	**Deep In A Dream**	1961	16.00	40.00
Dolton BLP-2011	(M)	**The Best Of The Oldies**	1962	12.00	30.00
Dolton BST-8011	(S)	**The Best Of The Oldies**	1962	16.00	40.00
		— Original Dolton albums above have light blue labels with the fish logo above the spindle hole.—			

Label & Catalog #		Title	Year	VG+	NM
Dolton BLP-2018	(M)	The Fleetwoods' Greatest Hits	1962	8.00	20.00
Dolton BST-8018	(P)	The Fleetwoods' Greatest Hits	1962	12.00	30.00
Dolton BLP-2025	(M)	Goodnight My Love	1963	8.00	20.00
Dolton BST-8025	(S)	Goodnight My Love	1963	12.00	30.00
Dolton BLP-2020	(M)	The Fleetwoods Sing For Lovers By Night	1963	8.00	20.00
Dolton BST-8020	(S)	The Fleetwoods Sing For Lovers By Night	1963	12.00	30.00
Dolton BLP-2030	(M)	Before And After	1965	8.00	20.00
Dolton BST-8030	(S)	Before And After	1965	12.00	30.00
Dolton BLP-2039	(M)	Folk Rock	1965	8.00	20.00
Dolton BST-8039	(S)	Folk Rock	1965	12.00	30.00
— Dolton albums above have dark blue labels with a color logo on the left side.—					
Sunset SUM-5131	(M)	In A Mellow Mood	1966	5.00	12.00
Sunset SUS-1131	(S)	In A Mellow Mood	1966	6.00	15.00

FLEMING, RHONDA
Columbia CL-1080	(M)	Rhonda	1958	20.00	50.00

FLEMONS, WADE
Vee Jay LP-1011	(M)	Wade Flemons (Maroon label)	1959	40.00	100.00
Vee Jay LP-1011	(M)	Wade Flemons (Black label)	196?	20.00	50.00

FLETCHER, SAM
Vault 116	(M)	The Look Of Love, Sound of Soul	1967	6.00	15.00

FLINT, SHELBY
Valiant LP-401	(M)	Shelby Flint (The Quiet Girl)	1961	12.00	30.00
Valiant LPS-401	(S)	Shelby Flint (The Quiet Girl)	1961	16.00	40.00
Valiant LP-403	(M)	Shelby Flint Sings Folk	1962	10.00	25.00
Valiant LPS-403	(S)	Shelby Flint Sings Folk	1962	14.00	35.00
Valiant VL-25003	(M)	Cast Your Fate To The Wind	1966	10.00	25.00
Valiant VLS-25003	(S)	Cast Your Fate To The Wind	1966	14.00	35.00
Mad Satyr MSR-101	(S)	You've Been On My Mind	1982	5.00	12.00

FLINTSTONES, THE
The voices of Barnie, Dino and Bamm Bamm are by Mel Blanc.
Colpix CLP-302	(M)	The Flintstones (TV Soundtrack)	1963	30.00	75.00
HBR HLP-2055	(M)	A Man Called Flintstone (TV Soundtrack)	1966	20.00	50.00

FLIRTATIONS, THE
Deram DES-18028	(S)	Nothing But A Heartache	1969	8.00	20.00

FLO & EDDIE
Mark Volman And Howard Kaylan, formerly members of the Turtles and The Mothers Of Invention.
Reprise MS-2099	(S)	The Phlorescent Leech And Eddie	1972	6.00	15.00
Reprise MS-2141	(S)	Flo And Eddie	1973	6.00	15.00
Columbia PC-33554	(S)	Illegal, Immoral And Fattening	1975	5.00	12.00
Columbia PC-34262	(S)	Moving Targets	1976	5.00	12.00
Epiphany ELP-4010	(S)	Rock Steady With Flo & Eddie	1981	4.00	10.00

FLOATING BRIDGE, THE
Vault 124	(S)	The Floating Bridge	1969	5.00	12.00

FLOATING OPERA, THE
Embryo 730	(S)	The Floating Opera	1971	5.00	12.00

FLOCK, THE
Columbia CS-9911	(S)	The Flock ("360 Sound" label)	1969	8.00	20.00
Columbia C-30007	(S)	Dinosaur Swamps	1970	5.00	12.00
Mercury SRM-1-1035	(S)	Inside Out	1975	4.00	10.00

FLOWERS, PHIL
Guest Star G-1456	(M)	I Am The Greatest	196?	8.00	20.00
Guest Star G-1457	(M)	Phil Flowers Sings A Tribute	196?	8.00	20.00
Mt. Vernon 154	(M)	Rhythm 'N' Blues	196?	10.00	25.00
Dot DLP-25849	(S)	Our Man In Washington	1968	6.00	15.00

FLOYD, EDDIE
Stax 714	(M)	Knock On Wood	1967	10.00	25.00
Stax S-714	(S)	Knock On Wood	1967	12.00	30.00

Label & Catalog #		Title	Year	VG+	NM
Stax STS-2002	(S)	I've Never Found A Girl	1968	8.00	20.00
Stax STS-2011	(S)	Rare Stamps	1969	6.00	15.00
		("Big Bird" and "Things Get Better" are rechanneled on this album.)			
Stax STS-2017	(S)	You've Got To Have Eddie	1969	6.00	15.00
Stax STS-2029	(S)	California Girl	1970	6.00	15.00
Stax STS-2041	(S)	Down To Earth	1971	6.00	15.00
Stax STS-3016	(S)	Baby Lay Your Head Down	1973	5.00	12.00
Stax STS-5512	(S)	Soul Street	1974	5.00	12.00

FLYING BURRITO BROTHERS, THE [THE BURRITO BROTHERS]
Features Chris Hillman and Gram Parsons amongst a cast of thousands.

A&M SD-4175	(S)	The Gilded Palace Of Sin	1969	6.00	15.00
A&M SD-4258	(S)	Burrito Deluxe	1970	5.00	12.00
A&M SD-4295	(S)	Flying Burrito Brothers	1971	5.00	12.00
A&M SD-4343	(S)	The Last Of The Red Hot Burritos	1972	5.00	12.00
		— Original A&M albums above have brown labels.—			
A&M SP-8070	(DJ)	Hot Burrito (Sampler)	1975	20.00	50.00

FLYING MACHINE, THE: *Refer to JAMES TAYLOR*

FLYING MACHINE, THE

Janus JLS-3007	(P)	The Flying Machine	1969	5.00	12.00

FLYNN, ERROL / BASIL RATHBONE

Columbia CL-4162 (10")	(M)	The Three Musketeers / Oliver Twist	195?	14.00	35.00
Columbia CL-674	(M)	The Three Musketeers / Oliver Twist	1955	10.00	25.00
		("Musketeers" is narrated by Flynn, "Twist" by Rathbone.)			

FOGELBERG, DAN

Full Moon PEQ-33499	(Q)	Captured Angel (2 LPs)	1975	8.00	20.00
Full Moon A2S-1335	(DJ)	Interchords (2 LPs)	1982	10.00	25.00
Full Moon HE-45634	(S)	Phoenix (Half-speed master)	1982	5.00	15.00
Full Moon HE-48308	(S)	Greatest Hits (Half-speed master)	1982	5.00	15.00

FOGELBERG, DAN, & TIM WEISBURG

Full Moon HE-45339	(S)	Twin Sons Of Different Mothers (Half-speed)	1982	5.00	15.00

FOGERTY, JOHN
Refer to The Blue Ridge Rangers; Creedence Clearwater Revival; The Golliwogs.

Asylum 7E-1046	(S)	John Fogerty	1975	5.00	12.00
Warner Bros. 25203	(DJ)	Centerfield (Quiex II vinyl)	1985	8.00	20.00
Warner Bros. 25203	(S)	Centerfield (With "Zantz Kant Danz.")	1985	4.00	10.00

FOGERTY, TOM
Refer to Creedence Clearwater Revival; The Golliwogs.

Fantasy F-9407	(S)	Tom Fogerty	1972	6.00	15.00
Fantasy F-9413	(S)	Excalibur	1972	6.00	15.00
Fantasy F-9448	(S)	Zephyr National	1974	5.00	12.00
Fantasy F-9469	(S)	Myopia	1974	5.00	12.00
Fantasy F-9611	(S)	Deal It Out	1981	4.00	10.00

FOGHAT

Bearsville BRK-6977	(DJ)	Stone Blue (Blue vinyl)	1978	6.00	15.00

FOREST

Harvest SKAO-419	(S)	Forest	1970	12.00	30.00

FOLEY, RED

Decca DL-5303 (10")	(M)	Souvenir Album	1951	40.00	100.00
Decca DL-5338 (10")	(M)	Lift Up Your Voice	1951	40.00	100.00
Decca DL-8294	(M)	Souvenir Album	1956	24.00	60.00
Decca DL-8296	(M)	Red Foley Beyond The Sunset	1956	20.00	50.00
Decca DL-8767	(M)	He Walks With Thee	1958	16.00	40.00
Decca DL-8806	(M)	My Keepsake Album	1958	16.00	40.00
Decca DL-8847	(M)	Let's All Sing With Red Foley	1959	16.00	40.00
Decca DL-8903	(M)	Let's All Sing To Him	1959	16.00	40.00
		— Original Decca albums above have black & silver labels.—			
Decca DL-4107	(M)	Red Foley's Golden Favorites	1961	10.00	25.00
Decca DL-74107	(S)	Red Foley's Golden Favorites	1961	12.00	30.00

Label & Catalog #		Title	Year	VG+	NM
Decca DL-4140	(M)	Company's Comin'	1961	10.00	25.00
Decca DL-74140	(S)	Company's Comin'	1961	12.00	30.00
Decca DL-4198	(M)	Songs Of Devotion	1961	10.00	25.00
Decca DL-74198	(S)	Songs Of Devotion	1961	12.00	30.00
Decca DL-4290	(M)	Dear Hearts And Gentle People	1962	8.00	20.00
Decca DL-74290	(S)	Dear Hearts And Gentle People	1962	10.00	25.00
Decca DL-4341	(M)	The Red Foley Show	1963	6.00	15.00
Decca DL-74341	(S)	The Red Foley Show	1963	8.00	20.00
Decca DXB-177	(M)	The Red Foley Story (2 LPs)	1964	6.00	15.00
Decca DXSB-7177	(S)	The Red Foley Story (2 LPs)	1964	8.00	20.00
Decca DL-4603	(M)	Songs Everybody Knows	1965	6.00	15.00
Decca DL-74603	(S)	Songs Everybody Knows	1965	8.00	20.00

— Original Decca albums above have black labels with "Mfrd by Decca" beneath the rainbow.—

Decca DL-4849	(M)	Songs For The Soul	1967	6.00	15.00
Decca DL-74849	(S)	Songs For The Soul	1967	6.00	15.00

FOLEY, RED, & ERNEST TUBB

Decca DL-8298	(M)	Red And Ernie	1956	20.00	50.00

FOLK STRINGERS, THE

Prestige PRLP-7371	(M)	The Folk Stringers	1965	8.00	20.00
Prestige PRST-7371	(S)	The Folk Stringers	1965	10.00	25.00

FOLKNIKS, THE

Hi Fi LP-1017	(M)	The Folkniks	196?	6.00	15.00
Hi Fi SL-1017	(S)	The Folkniks	196?	8.00	20.00

FOLKSINGERS, THE

Elektra EKL-157	(M)	Run Come Here	1958	14.00	35.00

FOLKSTERS, THE

Mercury MG-20749	(M)	New In Folk	1962	6.00	15.00
Mercury SR-60749	(S)	New In Folk	1962	8.00	20.00

FOLKSWINGERS, THE

The Folkswingers feature Glen Campbell.

World Pacific WP-1812	(M)	12 String Guitar	1963	8.00	20.00
World Pacific ST-1812	(S)	12 String Guitar	1963	10.00	25.00
World Pacific ST-1812	(S)	12 String Guitar (Red vinyl)	1963	20.00	50.00
World Pacific WP-1814	(M)	12 String Guitar, Volume 2	1963	8.00	20.00
World Pacific ST-1814	(S)	12 String Guitar, Volume 2	1963	10.00	25.00
World Pacific WP-1846	(M)	Raga Rock	1966	8.00	20.00
World Pacific ST-1846	(S)	Raga Rock	1966	10.00	25.00

FONDA, HENRY

Coral CRL-57308	(M)	Voices Of The 20th Century	1959	16.00	40.00

FONTANA, WAYNE, & THE MINDBENDERS

Fontana MGF-27542	(M)	The Game Of Love	1965	10.00	25.00
Fontana SRF-67542	(E)	The Game Of Love	1965	10.00	25.00

FONTANA, WAYNE

MGM E-4459	(M)	Wayne Fontana	1967	8.00	20.00
MGM SE-4459	(S)	Wayne Fontana	1967	10.00	25.00

FONTANE SISTERS, THE

Dot DLP-3004	(M)	The Fontane Sisters (Maroon label)	1956	16.00	40.00
Dot DLP-3042	(M)	The Fontanes Sing	1957	12.00	30.00
Dot DLP-3531	(M)	Tips Of My Fingers	1963	6.00	15.00
Dot DLP-25531	(S)	Tips Of My Fingers	1963	8.00	20.00

FOOL, THE

Mercury SR-61178	(S)	The Fool	1968	8.00	20.00

FORBES, WALTER

RCA Victor LPM-2472	(M)	Ballads And Bluegrass	1962	6.00	15.00
RCA Victor LSP-2472	(S)	Ballads And Bluegrass	1962	8.00	20.00
RCA Victor LPM-2670	(M)	Folk Song Festival	1963	6.00	15.00
RCA Victor LSP-2670	(S)	Folk Song Festival	1963	8.00	20.00

Label & Catalog #		Title	Year	VG+	NM
FORD, FRANKIE					
Ace LP-1005	(M)	**Let's Take A Sea Cruise**	1959	100.00	250.00
FORD, NEAL, & THE FANATICS					
Hickory LPS-141	(S)	**Neal Ford & The Fanatics**	1968	12.00	30.00
FORD, ROCKY BILL					
Audio Lab AL-1561	(M)	**A New Singing Star**	1960	40.00	100.00
FORD, TENNESSE ERNIE					
Ernie's catalog is primarily gospel and not covered in this edition. Refer to Brenda Lee / Ernie Ford.					
Capitol T-888	(M)	**Ol' Rockin' Ern'** *(Turquoise label)*	1957	20.00	50.00
Capitol T-1539	(M)	**Civil War Songs Of The North**	1961	6.00	15.00
Capitol ST-1539	(S)	**Civil War Songs Of The North**	1961	8.00	20.00
Capitol T-1540	(M)	**Civil War Songs Of The South**	1961	6.00	15.00
Capitol ST-1540	(S)	**Civil War Songs Of The South**	1961	8.00	20.00
FOREIGNER					
Mobile Fidelity MFSL-052	(S)	**Double Vision**	1979	6.00	18.00
FORREST, HELEN: *Refer to* **GOLDMINE'S PRICE GUIDE TO COLLECTIBLE JAZZ ALBUMS**					
FORTUNE, JOHNNY					
Park Avenue P-401	(M)	**Soul Surfer**	1963	30.00	75.00
Park Avenue PS-401	(S)	**Soul Surfer**	1963	40.00	100.00
FORTUNE-TELLER					
R.M.T. 4956	(S)	**Inner-City Scream**	1978	60.00	150.00
FORTUNES, THE					
Press PR7-3002	(M)	**The Fortunes**	1965	14.00	35.00
Press PRS-83002	(S)	**The Fortunes**	1965	20.00	50.00
World Pacific WPS-21904	(S)	**That Same Old Feeling**	1970	6.00	15.00
Capitol ST-647	(S)	**Freedom**	1971	6.00	15.00
Capitol ST-809	(S)	**Here Comes That Rainy Day Feeling Again**	1971	8.00	20.00
FORUM, THE					
Mira MLP-301	(M)	**The River Is Wide**	1967	6.00	15.00
Mira MLPS-301	(S)	**The River Is Wide**	1967	8.00	20.00
		("The River Is Wide" is rechanneled on this album.)			
FORUM QUORUM, THE					
Decca DL-75030	(S)	**The Forum Quorum**	1968	6.00	15.00
FORTY-NINTH PARALLEL, THE					
Maverick MAS-7001	(S)	**The Forty-Ninth Parallel**	1969	70.00	175.00
FOTHERINGAY					
A&M SP-4289	(S)	**Fotheringay**	1970	6.00	15.00
FOUL DOGS, THE					
Rhythm Sound GA-481	(M)	**No. 1**	1966	150.00	300.00
FOUNDATIONS, THE					
Uni 73016	(S)	**Baby, Now That I've Found You**	1968	10.00	25.00
		("Baby, Now That I've Found You" is rechanneled on this album.)			
Uni 73043	(S)	**Build Me Up Buttercup**	1969	10.00	25.00
		(Side 1 is in stereo; side 2 is rechanneled.)			
Uni 73058	(S)	**Digging The Foundations**	1969	10.00	25.00
FOUR ACES, THE					
The lead Ace was Al Alberts.					
Decca DL-5429 (10")	(M)	**The Four Aces**	1952	30.00	75.00
Decca DL-8122	(M)	**The Mood For Love**	1955	20.00	50.00
Decca DL-8191	(M)	**Merry Christmas**	1956	20.00	50.00
Decca DL-8227	(M)	**Sentimental Souvenirs**	1956	20.00	50.00
Decca DL-8228	(M)	**Heart And Soul**	1956	20.00	50.00
Decca DL-8312	(M)	**She Sees All The Hollywood Hits**	1957	20.00	50.00
Decca DL-8424	(M)	**Written On The Wind** *(Soundtrack)*	1957	40.00	100.00

Label & Catalog #		Title	Year	VG+	NM
Decca DL-8567	(M)	Shuffling Along	1957	20.00	50.00
Decca DL-8693	(M)	Hits From Hollywood	1958	20.00	50.00
Decca DL-8766	(M)	The Swingin' Aces	1958	14.00	35.00
Decca DL-78766	(S)	The Swingin' Aces	1958	20.00	50.00
Decca DL-8855	(M)	Hits From Broadway	1959	14.00	35.00
Decca DL-78855	(S)	Hits From Broadway	1959	20.00	50.00
Decca DL-8944	(M)	Beyond The Blue Horizon	1959	14.00	35.00
Decca DL-78944	(S)	Beyond The Blue Horizon	1959	20.00	50.00
		—Original Decca albums above have black & silver labels.—			
Decca DL-4013	(M)	The Golden Hits Of The Four Aces	1960	8.00	20.00
Decca DL-74013	(P)	The Golden Hits Of The Four Aces	1960	10.00	25.00
United Arts. UAL-3337	(M)	Record Oldies	1963	6.00	15.00
United Arts. UAS-6337	(S)	Record Oldies	1963	8.00	20.00
FOUR COINS, THE					
Epic LN-1104	(M)	The Four Coins	1955	20.00	50.00
Epic LN-3445	(M)	The Four Coins In Shangri La	1958	14.00	35.00
MGM E-3944	(M)	Greek Songs	1961	6.00	15.00
MGM SE-3944	(S)	Greek Songs	1961	8.00	20.00
Roulette R-25288	(M)	Greek Songs Mama Never Taught Me	1965	6.00	15.00
Roulette SR-25288	(S)	Greek Songs Mama Never Taught Me	1965	8.00	20.00
FOUR FRESHMEN, THE					
Capitol H-522 (10")	(M)	Voices In Modern	1955	20.00	50.00
Capitol T-522	(M)	Voices In Modern	1955	16.00	40.00
Capitol T-683	(M)	Four Freshmen And Five Trombones	1956	16.00	40.00
Capitol T-743	(M)	Freshmen Favorites	1956	16.00	40.00
Capitol T-763	(M)	Four Freshmen And Five Trumpets	1957	16.00	40.00
Capitol T-844	(M)	Four Freshmen And Five Saxes	1957	16.00	40.00
Capitol T-992	(M)	Voices In Latin	1958	12.00	30.00
Capitol T-1008	(M)	The Four Freshmen In Person	1958	12.00	30.00
Capitol ST-1008	(S)	The Four Freshmen In Person	1958	16.00	40.00
		— Original Capitol albums above have turquoise labels.—			
Capitol T-1074	(M)	Voices In Love	1958	8.00	20.00
Capitol ST-1074	(S)	Voices In Love	1958	12.00	30.00
Capitol T-1103	(M)	Freshmen Favorites, Volume 2	1959	8.00	20.00
Capitol ST-1103	(S)	Freshmen Favorites, Volume 2	1959	12.00	30.00
Capitol T-1189	(M)	Love Lost	1959	8.00	20.00
Capitol ST-1189	(S)	Love Lost	1959	12.00	30.00
Capitol T-1255	(M)	The Four Freshmen And Five Guitars	1960	8.00	20.00
Capitol ST-1255	(S)	The Four Freshmen And Five Guitars	1960	10.00	25.00
Capitol T-1295	(M)	Voices And Brass	1960	8.00	20.00
Capitol ST-1295	(S)	Voices And Brass	1960	10.00	25.00
Capitol T-1378	(M)	First Affair	1960	8.00	20.00
Capitol ST-1378	(S)	First Affair	1960	10.00	25.00
Capitol T-1485	(M)	Freshmen Year	1961	8.00	20.00
Capitol ST-1485	(S)	Freshmen Year	1961	10.00	25.00
Capitol T-1543	(M)	Voices In Fun	1961	8.00	20.00
Capitol ST-1543	(S)	Voices In Fun	1961	10.00	25.00
Capitol T-1640	(M)	The Best Of The Four Freshmen	1962	8.00	20.00
Capitol ST-1640	(S)	The Best Of The Four Freshmen	1962	10.00	25.00
Capitol T-1682	(M)	Stars In Our Eyes	1962	8.00	20.00
Capitol ST-1682	(S)	Stars In Our Eyes	1962	10.00	25.00
		— Original Capitol albums above have black labels with the Capitol logo on the left side.—			
Capitol T-1753	(M)	Swingers	1962	6.00	15.00
Capitol ST-1753	(S)	Swingers	1962	8.00	20.00
Capitol T-1860	(M)	The Four Freshmen In Person, Volume 2	1963	6.00	15.00
Capitol ST-1860	(S)	The Four Freshmen In Person, Volume 2	1963	8.00	20.00
Capitol T-1950	(M)	Got That Feelin'	1963	6.00	15.00
Capitol ST-1950	(S)	Got That Feelin'	1963	8.00	20.00
Capitol T-2067	(M)	Funny How Time Slips Away	1964	6.00	15.00
Capitol ST-2067	(S)	Funny How Time Slips Away	1964	8.00	20.00
Capitol T-2168	(M)	More Four Freshmen And Five Trombones	1964	6.00	15.00
Capitol ST-2168	(S)	More Four Freshmen And Five Trombones	1964	8.00	20.00
		— Original Capitol albums above have black labels with the Capitol logo on top.—			
Liberty LST-7563	(S)	Today Is Tomorrow	1968	6.00	15.00
Liberty LST-7590	(S)	In A Class By Themselves	1969	6.00	15.00

Label & Catalog #		Title	Year	VG+	NM

FOUR JACKS & A JILL

Label & Catalog #		Title	Year	VG+	NM
RCA Victor LSP-4019	(S)	Master Jack	1968	6.00	15.00
RCA Victor LSP-4103	(S)	Fables	1968	6.00	15.00

FOUR KNIGHTS, THE

Label & Catalog #		Title	Year	VG+	NM
Capitol H-345 (10")	(M)	Spotlight Songs	1953	80.00	200.00
Capitol T-345	(M)	Spotlight Songs	1956	40.00	100.00
Coral CRL-57221	(M)	The Four Knights	1959	40.00	100.00
Coral CRL-57309	(M)	Million Dollar Baby	1960	20.00	50.00
Coral CRL-757309	(S)	Million Dollar Baby	1960	30.00	75.00

FOUR LADS, THE

Label & Catalog #		Title	Year	VG+	NM
Columbia CL-6329 (10")	(M)	Stage Show	1954	20.00	50.00
Columbia CL-2545 (10")	(M)	The Four Lads Sing Frank Loesser	1956	20.00	50.00
Columbia CL- 2577 (10")	(M)	Stage Show	1956	20.00	50.00
Columbia CL-861	(M)	The Four Lads With Frankie Laine	1956	16.00	40.00
Columbia CL-912	(M)	On The Sunny Side	1956	16.00	40.00
Columbia CL-950	(M)	The Stingiest Man In Town (Soundtrack)	1956	20.00	50.00
Columbia CL-1045	(M)	The Four Lads Sing Frank Loesser	1957	20.00	50.00
Columbia CL-1235	(M)	The Four Lads' Greatest Hits	1958	12.00	30.00
Columbia CL-1???	(M)	Breezin' Along	1959	10.00	25.00
Columbia CS-8035	(S)	Breezin' Along	1959	12.00	30.00
Columbia CL-1111	(M)	Four On The Aisle	1959	10.00	25.00
Columbia CS-8047	(S)	Four On The Aisle	1959	12.00	30.00
Columbia CL-1299	(M)	The Four Lads Swing Along	1959	10.00	25.00
Columbia CS-8106	(S)	The Four Lads Swing Along	1959	12.00	30.00
Columbia CL-1407	(M)	High Spirits!	1959	10.00	25.00
Columbia CS-8203	(S)	High Spirits!	1959	12.00	30.00
Columbia CL-1502	(M)	Love Affair	1960	6.00	15.00
Columbia CS-8293	(S)	Love Affair	1960	8.00	20.00
Columbia CL-1550	(M)	Everything Goes	1960	6.00	15.00
Columbia CS-8350	(S)	Everything Goes	1960	8.00	20.00
— Original Columbia albums above have three white "eye" logos on each side of the spindle hole.—					
Kapp KL-1224	(M)	Twelve Hits	1961	6.00	15.00
Kapp KS-3224	(S)	Twelve Hits	1961	8.00	20.00
Kapp KL-1254	(M)	Dixieland Doin's	1961	6.00	15.00
Kapp KS-3254	(S)	Dixieland Doin's	1961	8.00	20.00
Dot DLP-3438	(M)	Hits Of The 60's	1962	6.00	15.00
Dot DLP-25438	(S)	Hits Of The 60's	1962	8.00	20.00
Dot DLP-3533	(M)	Oh, Happy Day	1963	6.00	15.00
Dot DLP-25533	(S)	Oh, Happy Day	1963	8.00	20.00
United Arts. UAL-3356	(M)	This Year's Top Movie Hits	1964	6.00	15.00
United Arts. UAS-6356	(S)	This Year's Top Movie Hits	1964	8.00	20.00
United Arts. UAL-3399	(M)	Songs Of World War I	1964	6.00	15.00
United Arts. UAS-6399	(S)	Songs Of World War I	1964	8.00	20.00

FOUR LOVERS, THE
Members Frankie Valli, Nick DeVito and Hank Majewski formed the Four Seasons.

Label & Catalog #		Title	Year	VG+	NM
RCA Victor LPM-1317	(M)	Joyride	1956	500.00	1,000.00

FOUR MOST, THE

Label & Catalog #		Title	Year	VG+	NM
Dawn DLP-1112	(M)	The Four Most Sing	1956	30.00	75.00

FOUR PREPS, THE

Label & Catalog #		Title	Year	VG+	NM
Capitol T-994	(M)	The Four Preps (Turquoise label)	1958	12.00	30.00
Capitol T-1090	(M)	The Things We Did Last Summer	1958	10.00	25.00
Capitol T-1216	(M)	Dancing And Dreaming	1959	8.00	20.00
Capitol ST-1216	(S)	Dancing And Dreaming	1959	12.00	30.00
Capitol T-1291	(M)	Early In The Morning	1960	10.00	25.00
Capitol DT-1291	(E)	Early In The Morning	1960	6.00	15.00
Capitol T-1566	(M)	Four Preps On Campus	1961	8.00	20.00
Capitol ST-1566	(S)	Four Preps On Campus	1961	10.00	25.00
Capitol T-1647	(M)	Campus Encore	1962	8.00	20.00
Capitol ST-1647	(S)	Campus Encore	1962	10.00	25.00
— Original Capitol albums above have black labels with the Capitol logo on the left side.—					
Capitol T-1814	(M)	Campus Confidential	1963	6.00	15.00
Capitol ST-1814	(S)	Campus Confidential	1963	8.00	20.00
Capitol T-1976	(S)	Songs For A Campus Party	1963	6.00	15.00
Capitol ST-1976	(S)	Songs For A Campus Party	1963	8.00	20.00

Frankie Valli, Hank Majewski and Nick and Tommy DeVito scored one hit for RCA Victor as The Four Lovers, 1956's "The Apple Of My Eye"). By the time they signed with the basically black rhythm 'n blues Vee Jay label, Hank and Nick were gone and Bob Gaudio and Nick Massi were in, forming the now classic Four Seasons line-up. With producer and fifth Season Bob Crewe they created a '50s like sound that kept them on the top of the charts from 1962 through 1967, by which time their sound and image had become [temporarily] dated. In fifteen years The Seasons placed nearly two-dozen albums on the best-seller lists and three of their Philips titles received RIAA Gold Records. Vee Jay did not open their books for independent auditing , the exact sales of their successful early albums is unknown. . .

Label & Catalog #		Title	Year	VG+	NM
Capitol T-2169	(S)	How To Succeed In Love	1964	6.00	15.00
Capitol ST-2169	(S)	How To Succeed In Love	1964	8.00	20.00
Capitol T-2708	(S)	The Best Of The Four Preps	1967	5.00	12.00
Capitol ST-2708	(S)	The Best Of The Four Preps	1967	6.00	15.00

— *Original Capitol albums above have black labels with the Capitol logo on top.*—

FOUR SEASONS, THE [FRANKIE VALLI & THE FOUR SEASONS]
Refer to The Beatles; The Four Lovers; Frankie Valli.

Vee Jay LP-1053	(M)	Sherry And 11 Others	1962	12.00	30.00
Vee Jay SR-1053	(P)	Sherry And 11 Others	1962	16.00	40.00
Vee Jay LP-1055	(M)	Four Seasons' Greetings	1963	12.00	30.00
Vee Jay SR-1055	(S)	Four Seasons' Greetings	1963	16.00	40.00
Vee Jay LP-1056	(M)	Big Girls Don't Cry	1963	12.00	30.00
Vee Jay SR-1056	(P)	Big Girls Don't Cry	1963	16.00	40.00
Vee Jay LP-1059	(M)	Ain't That A Shame	1963	10.00	25.00
Vee Jay SR-1059	(P)	Ain't That A Shame	1963	16.00	40.00
Vee Jay LP-1065	(M)	Golden Hits Of The Four Seasons	1963	14.00	35.00
Vee Jay SR-1065	(P)	Golden Hits Of The Four Seasons	1963	20.00	50.00
Vee Jay LP-1082	(M)	Folk-Nanny	1963	10.00	25.00
Vee Jay SR-1082	(S)	Folk-Nanny	1963	16.00	40.00

("Connie-O," "Soon," "Silver Wings" and "Star Maker"
are rechanneled on this album.)

ee Jay LP-1082	(M)	Stay & Other Great Hits	1964	8.00	20.00
Vee Jay SR-1082	(S)	Stay & Other Great Hits	1964	12.00	30.00

("Stay" is a repackage of "Folk-Nanny.")

Vee Jay LP-1088	(M)	More Golden Hits By The Four Seasons	1964	12.00	30.00
Vee Jay SR-1088	(P)	More Golden Hits By The Four Seasons	1964	16.00	40.00

(First pressings includes "Long Lonely Nights.")

Vee Jay LP-1088	(M)	More Golden Hits By The Four Seasons	1965	6.00	15.00
Vee Jay SR-1088	(P)	More Golden Hits By The Four Seasons	1965	8.00	20.00

(Later pressings replace "Nights" with "Apple Of My Eye.")

Vee Jay LP-1121	(M)	We Love Girls	1965	12.00	30.00
Vee Jay SR-1121	(S)	We Love Girls	1965	16.00	40.00
Vee Jay LP-1154	(M)	Recorded Live On Stage	1965	12.00	30.00
Vee Jay SR-1154	(S)	Recorded Live On Stage	1965	16.00	40.00
Philips PHM-200-124	(M)	Dawn (Go Away) & 11 Other Great Songs	1964	8.00	20.00
Philips PHS-600-124	(S)	Dawn (Go Away) & 11 Other Great Songs	1964	10.00	25.00
Philips PHM-200-129	(M)	Born To Wander	1964	8.00	20.00
Philips PHS-600-129	(S)	Born To Wander	1964	10.00	25.00
Philips PHM-200-146	(M)	Rag Doll	1964	8.00	20.00
Philips PHS-600-146	(P)	Rag Doll	1964	10.00	25.00
Philips PHM-200-146	(M)	Rag Doll	1964	8.00	20.00
Philips PHS-600-146	(P)	Rag Doll	1964	10.00	25.00

(Second pressings of Philips 145 have a yellow seal noting "Save
It For Me" on the cover. "Rag Doll" is in mono on this album.)

Philips PHM-200-150	(M)	All The Song Hits Of The Four Seasons	1964	8.00	20.00
Philips PHS-600-150	(S)	All The Song Hits Of The Four Seasons	1964	10.00	25.00
Philips PHM-200-164	(M)	The Four Seasons Entertain You	1965	8.00	20.00
Philips PHS-600-164	(S)	The Four Seasons Entertain You	1965	10.00	25.00

(The cover has an orange seal noting "Bye Bye Baby.")

Philips PHM-200-164	(M)	The Four Seasons Entertain You	1965	8.00	20.00
Philips PHS-600-164	(S)	The Four Seasons Entertain You	1965	10.00	25.00

(Cover has an orange seal noting "Bye Bye Baby" and "Toy Soldier.")

Philips PHM-200-164	(M)	The Four Seasons Entertain You	1965	6.00	15.00
Philips PHS-600-164	(S)	The Four Seasons Entertain You	1965	8.00	20.00

(The cover has a blue seal noting "Bye Bye Baby" and "Toy Soldier.")

Philips PHM-200-193	(M)	Big Hits By Bacharach, David & Dylan	1965	8.00	20.00
Philips PHS-600-193	(S)	Big Hits By Bacharach, David & Dylan	1965	10.00	25.00

(The cover has a medieval motif.)

Philips PHM-200-193	(M)	Big Hits By Bacharach, David & Dylan	1965	12.00	30.00
Philips PHS-600-193	(S)	Big Hits By Bacharach, David & Dylan	1965	16.00	40.00

(The cover features photos of the group.)

Philips PHM-200-196	(M)	Gold Vault Of Hits	1965	8.00	20.00
Philips PHS-600-196	(S)	Gold Vault Of Hits	1965	10.00	25.00

(The title on the cover is in unadorned red print; the group
photo on the back cover features Charlie Calello.)

Label & Catalog #		Title	Year	VG+	NM
Philips PHM-200-196	(M)	Gold Vault Of Hits	1965	6.00	15.00
Philips PHS-600-196	(S)	Gold Vault Of Hits	1965	8.00	20.00
		(The title on the cover is in red print outlined in black; the group photo on the back cover features Charlie Calello.)			
Philips PHM-200-196	(M)	Gold Vault Of Hits	196?	5.00	12.00
Philips PHS-600-196	(S)	Gold Vault Of Hits	196?	6.00	15.00
		(Later pressings the title is red with black trim or solid black; the group photo on the back cover features Joe Long.)			
Philips PHM-200-201	(M)	Working My Way Back To You	1966	8.00	20.00
Philips PHS-600-201	(S)	Working My Way Back To You	1966	10.00	25.00
Philips PHM-200-221	(M)	2nd Gold Vault Of Hits	1966	6.00	15.00
Philips PHS-600-221	(S)	2nd Gold Vault Of Hits	1966	8.00	20.00
Philips PHM-200-222	(M)	Lookin' Back	1966	8.00	20.00
Philips PHS-600-222	(S)	Lookin' Back	1966	10.00	25.00
Philips PHM-200-223	(M)	The Four Seasons' Christmas Album	1966	10.00	25.00
Philips PHS-600-223	(S)	The Four Seasons' Christmas Album	1966	12.00	30.00
Philips PHM-200-243	(M)	New Gold Hits	1967	6.00	15.00
Philips PHS-600-243	(S)	New Gold Hits	1967	8.00	20.00
Philips PHS-2-6501	(P)	Edizone D'Oro (2 LPs)	1969	12.00	30.00
		(The "4" on the cover is in unadorned red on a gold foil. "Rag Doll" is in stereo on all pressings of this album.)			
Philips PHS-2-6501	(P)	Edizone D'Oro (2 LPs)	1969	16.00	40.00
		(The "4" on the cover is twhite or red with black trim on gold foil.)			
Philips PHS-2-6501	(P)	Edizone D'Oro (2 LPs)	1969	16.00	40.00
		(The "4" on the cover is in white print on a gold board.)			
Philips PHS-600290	(S)	Genuine Imitation Life Gazette	1969	10.00	25.00
		(Original covers are yellow newspaper.)			
Philips PHS-600290	(S)	Genuine Imitation Life Gazette	1969	5.00	12.00
		(Later covers are white newspaper.)			
Philips PHS-600341	(S)	Half And Half	1970	6.00	15.00
Sears 609	(S)	Brotherhood Of Man	1970	8.00	20.00
Pickwick SPC-3223	(S)	Brotherhood Of Man	1970	4.00	10.00
		(Pickwick 3223 is a reissue of Sears 609.)			
Longines Sym. 95833	(P)	The Greatest Hits Of Frankie Valli & The Four Seasons (4 LPs)	197?	10.00	25.00
		(The cover reads "As seen on TV.")			
Longines Sym. 95833	(P)	The Greatest Hits Of Frankie Valli & The Four Seasons (4 LPs)	197?	8.00	20.00
		(The cover reads "As seen on TV." and "4 Record Collection.")			
Longines Sym. 95833	(P)	The Greatest Hits Of Frankie Valli & The Four Seasons (4 LPs)	197?	6.00	15.00
		(The cover makes no mention of the TV offer.)			
Motown S-788	(S)	Inside Out	1973	Unreleased	
Sweet Thunder 3	(S)	Reunited Live	198?	10.00	30.00

FOUR TOPS, THE
Refer to The Supremes & The Four Tops.

Workshop 217	(M)	Jazz Impressions	1962	Unreleased	
Motown 622	(M)	The Four Tops	1964	12.00	30.00
Motown MS-622	(S)	The Four Tops	1964	16.00	40.00
Motown 634	(M)	The Four Tops, No. 2	1964	12.00	30.00
Motown MS-634	(S)	The Four Tops, No. 2	1965	16.00	40.00
Motown 647	(M)	The Four Tops On Top	1966	12.00	30.00
Motown MS-647	(S)	The Four Tops On Top	1966	16.00	40.00
Motown 654	(M)	The Four Tops Live	1966	10.00	25.00
Motown MS-654	(S)	The Four Tops Live	1966	12.00	30.00
Motown 657	(M)	The Four Tops On Broadway	1967	8.00	20.00
Motown MS-657	(S)	The Four Tops On Broadway	1967	10.00	25.00
Motown 660	(M)	Reach Out	1967	8.00	20.00
Motown MS-660	(S)	Reach Out	1967	10.00	25.00
Motown 662	(M)	The Four Tops' Greatest Hits	1967	6.00	15.00
Motown MS-662	(S)	The Four Tops' Greatest Hits	1967	8.00	20.00
Motown MS-669	(S)	Yesterday Dreams	1968	6.00	15.00
Motown MS-675	(S)	The Four Tops Now	1969	6.00	15.00
Motown MS-695	(S)	Soul Spin	1969	6.00	15.00
Motown MS-704	(S)	Still Waters Run Deep	1970	6.00	15.00
Motown MS-721	(S)	Changing Times	1970	6.00	15.00
Motown MS-740	(S)	The Four Tops' Greatest Hits, Volume 2	1971	5.00	12.00
Motown MS-748	(S)	Nature Planned It	1972	5.00	12.00

Label & Catalog #		Title	Year	VG+	NM
Dunhill DX-50129	(S)	Keeper Of The Castle	1972	5.00	12.00
Dunhill DX-50144	(S)	Main Street People	1973	5.00	12.00
Dunhill DX-50166	(S)	Meeting Of The Minds	1974	5.00	12.00
Dunhill DX-50188	(S)	Live & In Concert	1974	5.00	12.00
Command QD-40011	(Q)	Keeper Of The Castle	1974	10.00	25.00
Command QD-40012	(Q)	Mainstreet People	1974	10.00	25.00

FOUR TUNES, THE

Jubilee LP-1039	(M)	12 X 4	1957	150.00	500.00

FOURTH WAY, THE

Capitol ST-317	(S)	The Fourth Way	1969	6.00	15.00
Harvest SKAO-423	(S)	Sun And Moon Have Come Together	1970	5.00	12.00
Harvest ST-666	(S)	Werewolf	1971	5.00	12.00

FOWLEY, KIM

Tower T-5080	(M)	Love Is Alive And Well	1967	10.00	25.00
Tower ST-5080	(S)	Love Is Alive And Well	1967	12.00	30.00
Imperial LP-12413	(S)	Born To Be Wild	1968	12.00	30.00
Imperial LP-12423	(S)	Outrageous	1969	12.00	30.00
Imperial LP-12443	(S)	Good Clean Fun	1969	12.00	30.00
Capitol ST-11075	(S)	I'm Bad	1972	4.00	10.00
Capitol ST-11159	(S)	International Heroes	1973	4.00	10.00
Capitol ST-11248	(S)	Automatic	1974	4.00	10.00

FOWLER, WALLY, & THE OAK RIDGE QUARTET

King 702	(M)	Gospel Song Festival	1960	16.00	40.00
Starday SLP-112	(M)	All Night Singing Gospel Concert	1960	12.00	30.00

FOWLKES, DOUG, & THE AIRDALES

Atco 33-145	(M)	Airdale Walk	1962	5.00	12.00
Atco SD-33-145	(S)	Airdale Walk	1962	6.00	15.00

FOX, CURLY, & TEXAS RUBY

Starday SLP-235	(M)	Curly Fox And Texas Ruby	196?	16.00	40.00
Harmony HL-7302	(M)	Travelling Blues	196?	10.00	25.00

FOXX, INEZ & CHARLIE

Symbol SYM-4400	(M)	Mockingbird	1963	40.00	100.00
Sue LP-1037	(M)	Inez And Charlie Foxx	1966	20.00	50.00
Sue LP-1037	(S)	Inez And Charlie Foxx	1966	30.00	75.00
Dynamo D-7000	(M)	Come By Here	1967	6.00	15.00
Dynamo DS-8000	(S)	Come By Here	1967	8.00	20.00
Dynamo D-7002	(M)	Inez And Charlie Foxx's Greatest Hits	1967	6.00	15.00
Dynamo DS-8002	(S)	Inez And Charlie Foxx's Greatest Hits	1967	8.00	20.00
		(Contains rerecorded stereo versions of earlier Symbol material.)			

FRACTION

Angelus WR-5005	(S)	Moon Blood	197?	1,000.00	2,000.00
		(Issued in a die-cut cover with a red cellophane window that allows the moon pictured on the inner sleeve to show through.)			

FRAMPTON, PETER

Peter Frampton formerly recorded with The Herd.

A&M PR-3703	(S)	Frampton Comes Alive *(Picture disc)*	1978	4.00	10.00
A&M SP-4704	(DJ)	I'm In You *(Picture disc)*	1978	6.00	15.00
A&M SP-27200	(DJ)	The Peter Frampton Radio Special	197?	10.00	25.00
Sweet Thunder	(S)	Frampton Comes Alive *(2 LPs. Half-speed)*	198?	35.00	100.00

FRANCIS, CONNIE

MGM E-3686	(M)	Who's Sorry Now?	1958	40.00	100.00
MGM E-3761	(M)	The Exciting Connie Francis	1959	20.00	50.00
MGM SE-3761	(S)	The Exciting Connie Francis	1959	30.00	75.00
		— Original MGM albums above have yellow labels. —			
MGM E-3686	(M)	Who's Sorry Now?	1959	16.00	40.00
MGM SE-3686	(E)	Who's Sorry Now?	1959	10.00	25.00
MGM E-3761	(M)	The Exciting Connie Francis	1959	12.00	30.00
MGM SE-3761	(S)	The Exciting Connie Francis	1959	16.00	40.00

Label & Catalog #		Title	Year	VG+	NM
MGM E-3776	(M)	My Thanks To You	1959	12.00	30.00
MGM SE-3776	(S)	My Thanks To You	1959	16.00	40.00
MGM E-3791	(M)	Italian Favorites	1959	12.00	30.00
MGM SE-3791	(S)	Italian Favorites	1959	16.00	40.00
MGM E-3792	(M)	Christmas In My Heart	1959	12.00	30.00
MGM SE-3792	(S)	Christmas In My Heart	1959	16.00	40.00
MGM E-3793	(M)	Connie's Greatest Hits	1960	14.00	35.00
MGM SE-3793	(E)	Connie's Greatest Hits	1960	10.00	25.00
MGM E-3794	(M)	Rock 'N' Roll Million Sellers	1960	12.00	30.00
MGM SE-3794	(S)	Rock 'N' Roll Million Sellers	1960	16.00	40.00
MGM E-3795	(M)	Country And Western Golden Hits	1960	12.00	30.00
MGM SE-3795	(S)	Country And Western Golden Hits	1960	16.00	40.00
MGM E-3853	(M)	Spanish And Latin American Favorites	1960	10.00	25.00
MGM SE-3853	(S)	Spanish And Latin American Favorites	1960	14.00	35.00
MGM E-3869	(M)	Jewish Favorites	1961	10.00	25.00
MGM SE-3869	(S)	Jewish Favorites	1961	14.00	35.00
MGM E-3871	(M)	More Italian Favorites	1961	10.00	25.00
MGM SE-3871	(S)	More Italian Favorites	1961	14.00	35.00
MGM E-3893	(M)	Songs To A Swinging Band	1961	10.00	25.00
MGM SE-3893	(S)	Songs To A Swinging Band	1961	14.00	35.00
MGM E-3913	(M)	Connie At The Copa	1961	10.00	25.00
MGM SE-3913	(S)	Connie At The Copa	1961	14.00	35.00
MGM E-3942	(M)	More Greatest Hits	1961	10.00	25.00
MGM SE-3942	(S)	More Greatest Hits	1961	14.00	35.00
MGM E-3965	(M)	Never On Sunday	1961	10.00	25.00
MGM SE-3965	(S)	Never On Sunday	1961	14.00	35.00
MGM E-3969	(M)	Folk Song Favorites	1961	10.00	25.00
MGM SE-3969	(S)	Folk Song Favorites	1961	14.00	35.00
MGM E-4013	(M)	Irish Favorites	1962	10.00	25.00
MGM SE-4013	(S)	Irish Favorites	1962	14.00	35.00
MGM E-4022	(M)	Do The Twist With Connie Francis	1962	12.00	30.00
MGM SE-4022	(S)	Do The Twist With Connie Francis	1962	16.00	40.00
MGM E-4022	(M)	Dance Party	196?	10.00	25.00
MGM SE-4022	(S)	Dance Party	196?	12.00	30.00
		("Dance Party" is a repackage of "Do The Twist.")			
MGM L-70126	(M)	Fun Songs For Children	196?	30.00	75.00
MGM E-4023	(M)	Fun Songs For Children	1962	14.00	35.00
MGM E-4048	(M)	Award Winning Motion Picture Hits	1962	10.00	25.00
MGMS E-4048	(S)	Award Winning Motion Picture Hits	1962	12.00	30.00
MGM E-4049	(M)	Second Hand Love And Other Hits	1962	10.00	25.00
MGM SE-4049	(S)	Second Hand Love And Other Hits	1962	12.00	30.00
MGM E-4079	(M)	Country Music, Connie Style	1962	10.00	25.00
MGM SE-4079	(S)	Country Music, Connie Style	1962	12.00	30.00
MGM E-4102	(M)	Modern Italian Hits	1963	10.00	25.00
MGM SE-4102	(S)	Modern Italian Hits	1963	12.00	30.00
MGM E-4123	(M)	Follow The Boys (Soundtrack)	1963	10.00	25.00
MGM SE-4123	(S)	Follow The Boys (Soundtrack)	1963	12.00	30.00
MGM E-4124	(M)	German Favorites	1963	10.00	25.00
MGM SE-4124	(S)	German Favorites	1963	12.00	30.00
MGM E-4145	(M)	Greatest American Waltzes	1963	10.00	25.00
MGM SE-4145	(S)	Greatest American Waltzes	1963	12.00	30.00
MGM E-4161	(M)	Mala Femmina And Big Hits From Italy	1963	10.00	25.00
MGM SE-4161	(S)	Mala Femmina And Big Hits From Italy	1963	12.00	30.00
MGM E-4167	(M)	The Very Best Of Connie Francis	1963	10.00	25.00
MGM SE-4167	(S)	The Very Best Of Connie Francis	1963	12.00	30.00
MGM E-4210	(M)	In The Summer Of His Years	1964	10.00	25.00
MGM SE-4210	(S)	In The Summer Of His Years	1964	12.00	30.00
MGM E-4229	(M)	Looking For Love (Soundtrack)	1964	10.00	25.00
MGM SE-4229	(S)	Looking For Love (Soundtrack)	1964	12.00	30.00
MGM E-4253	(M)	A New Kind Of Connie	1964	10.00	25.00
MGM SE-4253	(S)	A New Kind Of Connie	1964	12.00	30.00
MGM E-4294	(M)	For Mama	1965	10.00	25.00
MGM SE-4294	(S)	For Mama	1965	12.00	30.00
MGM E-4298	(M)	All Time International Hits	1965	10.00	25.00
MGM SE-4298	(S)	All Time International Hits	1965	12.00	30.00
MGM E-4334	(M)	When The Boys Meet The Girls (Sdtk)	1965	5.00	12.00
MGM SE-4334	(S)	When The Boys Meet The Girls (Sdtk)	1965	6.00	15.00
MGM E-4355	(M)	Jealous Heart	1965	10.00	25.00
MGM SE-4355	(S)	Jealous Heart	1965	12.00	30.00

Label & Catalog #		Title	Year	VG+	NM
MGM E-4382	(M)	Movie Greats Of The 60's	1966	10.00	25.00
MGM SE-4382	(S)	Movie Greats Of The 60's	1966	12.00	30.00
MGM E-4399	(M)	Connie's Christmas	1966	10.00	25.00
MGM SE-4399	(S)	Connie's Christmas	1966	12.00	30.00
		(MGM SE-4399 is a repackage of 3792.)			
MGM E-4411	(M)	Live At The Sahara In Las Vegas	1966	10.00	25.00
MGM SE-4411	(S)	Live At The Sahara In Las Vegas	1966	12.00	30.00
MGM E-4448	(M)	Love, Italian Style	1967	10.00	25.00
MGM SE-4448	(S)	Love, Italian Style	1967	12.00	30.00
MGM E-4472	(M)	Connie Francis On Broadway Today	1967	10.00	25.00
MGM SE-4472	(S)	Connie Francis On Broadway Today	1967	12.00	30.00
MGM E-4474	(M)	Grandes Exitos del Cine de los Anos 60	1967	10.00	25.00
MGM SE-4474	(S)	Grandes Exitos del Cine de los Anos 60	1967	12.00	30.00
MGM E-4487	(M)	My Heart Cries For You	1967	10.00	25.00
MGM SE-4487	(S)	My Heart Cries For You	1967	12.00	30.00
		— Original MGM albums above have black labels.—			
MGM E-4522	(M)	Hawaii: Connie	1968	10.00	25.00
MGM SE-4522	(S)	Hawaii: Connie	1968	6.00	15.00
MGM SE-4573	(S)	Connie & Clyde	1968	6.00	15.00
MGM SE-4585	(S)	Connie Francis Sings Bacharach & David	1968	6.00	15.00
MGM ST-91145	(S)	My Best To You *(Capitol Record Club)*	1968	6.00	15.00
MGM SE-4637	(S)	The Wedding Cake	1969	6.00	15.00
MGM SE-4655	(S)	The Songs Of Les Reed	1969	6.00	15.00
MGM GAS-109	(S)	Greatest Golden Groovy Goodies	1970	8.00	20.00
MGM LES-903	(S)	Connie Francis And The Kids Next Door	197?	6.00	15.00
MGM E6PS-2	(S)	A Connie Francis Spectacular *(5 LP box)*	197?	12.00	30.00
Mati-Mor 8002	(M)	Brylcreem Presents "Sing Along With Connie Francis"	195?	4.00	10.00
Metro M-519	(M)	Connie Francis	1964	5.00	12.00
Metro MS-519	(S)	Connie Francis	1964	6.00	15.00
Metro M-538	(M)	Folk Favorites	1965	5.00	12.00
Metro MS-538	(S)	Folk Favorites	1965	6.00	15.00
Metro M-571	(M)	Songs Of Love	1966	5.00	12.00
Metro MS-571	(S)	Songs Of Love	1966	6.00	15.00
Metro M-603	(M)	The Incomparable Connie Francis	1967	5.00	12.00
Metro MS-603	(S)	The Incomparable Connie Francis	1967	6.00	15.00
Sessions SG-60	(S)	Connie	196?	5.00	12.00
Laurie LH-8019	(S)	Connie: Italiano	196?	5.00	12.00
Columbia LV-8098	(S)	Connie: Italiano	196?	5.00	12.00

FRANCIS, CONNIE, & HANK WILLIAMS, JR.

Label & Catalog #		Title	Year	VG+	NM
MGM E-4251	(M)	Great Country Favorites	1964	12.00	30.00
MGM SE-4251	(S)	Great Country Favorites	1964	16.00	40.00

FRANKLIN, ALAN [THE ALAN FRANKLIN EXPLOSION]

Label & Catalog #		Title	Year	VG+	NM
Horne JC-888	(S)	The Blues Climax	1969	50.00	125.00
Aladdin 104049	(S)	Come Home, Baby	1979	20.00	50.00

FRANKLIN, ARETHA

Label & Catalog #		Title	Year	VG+	NM
Columbia CL-1612	(M)	Aretha	1961	12.00	30.00
Columbia CS-8412	(S)	Aretha	1961	16.00	40.00
Columbia CL-1761	(M)	The Electrifying Aretha Franklin	1962	12.00	30.00
Columbia CS-8561	(S)	The Electrifying Aretha Franklin	1962	16.00	40.00
Columbia CL-1876	(M)	The Tender... Swinging Aretha Franklin	1962	12.00	30.00
Columbia CS-8676	(S)	The Tender... Swinging Aretha Franklin	1962	16.00	40.00
		— Original Columbia albums above have three white "eye" logos on each side of the spindle hole.—			
Columbia CL-2079	(M)	Laughing On The Outside	1963	8.00	20.00
Columbia CS-8879	(S)	Laughing On The Outside	1963	10.00	25.00
Columbia CL-2163	(M)	Unforgettable	1964	8.00	20.00
Columbia CS-8963	(S)	Unforgettable	1964	10.00	25.00
Columbia CL-2281	(M)	Runnin' Out Of Fools	1964	8.00	20.00
Columbia CS-9081	(S)	Runnin' Out Of Fools	1964	10.00	25.00
Columbia CL-2351	(M)	Yeah!!!	1965	8.00	20.00
Columbia CS-9151	(S)	Yeah!!!	1965	10.00	25.00
Columbia CL-2521	(M)	Soul Sister	1966	8.00	20.00
Columbia CS-9321	(S)	Soul Sister	1966	10.00	25.00
Columbia CL-2629	(M)	Take It Like You Give It	1967	8.00	20.00
Columbia CS-9429	(S)	Take It Like You Give It	1967	10.00	25.00

Label & Catalog #		Title	Year	VG+	NM
Columbia CL-2673	(M)	**Aretha Franklin's Greatest Hits**	1967	8.00	20.00
Columbia CS-9473	(S)	**Aretha Franklin's Greatest Hits**	1967	10.00	25.00
Columbia CL-2754	(M)	**Take A Look**	1967	8.00	20.00
Columbia CS-9554	(S)	**Take A Look**	1967	10.00	25.00
Columbia CS-9601	(S)	**Aretha Franklin's Greatest Hits, Volume 2**	1968	8.00	20.00
Columbia CS-9776	(S)	**Soft And Beautiful**	1969	8.00	20.00
— Columbia albums above have "360 Sound" on the bottom of the label.—
Atlantic 8139	(M)	**I Never Loved A Man (The Way I Love You)**	1967	10.00	25.00
Atlantic SD-8139	(S)	**I Never Loved A Man (The Way I Love You)**	1967	8.00	20.00
Atlantic 8150	(M)	**Aretha Arrives**	1967	10.00	25.00
Atlantic SD-8150	(S)	**Aretha Arrives**	1967	8.00	20.00
Atlantic 8176	(M)	**Lady Soul**	1968	12.00	30.00
Atlantic SD-8176	(S)	**Lady Soul**	1968	8.00	20.00
Atlantic SD-8186	(S)	**Aretha Now**	1968	8.00	20.00
— Original Stereo Atlantic albums above have green & blue labels.—
Atlantic SD-8207	(S)	**Aretha In Paris**	1968	8.00	20.00
Atlantic SD-8212	(S)	**Soul '69**	1969	8.00	20.00
Atlantic SD-8227	(S)	**Aretha's Gold**	1969	6.00	15.00
Atlantic SD-8248	(S)	**This Girl's In Love With You**	1970	5.00	12.00
Atlantic SD-8265	(S)	**Spirit In The Dark**	1970	5.00	12.00
Atlantic SD-8295	(S)	**Aretha's Greatest Hits**	1971	5.00	12.00
Atlantic SD-7205	(S)	**Live At The Fillmore West**	1971	5.00	12.00
— Original Atlantic albums above have green & orange labels with "1841 Broadway" on the bottom.—
Atlantic QD-7205	(Q)	**Live At The Fillmore West**	1974	10.00	25.00
Atlantic QD-8305	(Q)	**The Best Of Aretha Franklin**	1974	12.00	30.00
FRANKLIN, CAROLYN					
RCA Victor LSP-4160	(S)	**Baby Dynamite**	1969	6.00	15.00
RCA Victor LSP-4317	(S)	**Chain Reaction**	1969	6.00	15.00
RCA Victor LSP-4411	(S)	**I'd Rather Be Lonely**	1970	6.00	15.00
FRANKLIN, ERMA					
Epic LN-3824	(S)	**Her Name Is Erma**	1962	6.00	15.00
Epic BN-619	(S)	**Her Name Is Erma**	1962	8.00	20.00
Brunswick BL-754147	(S)	**Soul Sister**	1969	6.00	15.00
FRANKLIN, PETE					
Bluesville BVLP-1068	(M)	**Guitar Pete's Blues**	1963	16.00	40.00
FRANKS, MICHAEL					
Direct Disk SD-16611	(S)	**Tiger In The Rain**	197?	5.00	15.00
FRANTIC					
Lizard 20103	(S)	**Conception**	197?	6.00	15.00
FRANTIC FREDDIE & THE REFLECTIONS					
Tom Rice	(M)	**Music Power**	1967	80.00	200.00
FRATERNITY OF MAN, THE					
ABC S-647	(S)	**The Fraternity Of Man**	1968	12.00	30.00
Dot DLP-25955	(S)	**Get It On**	1969	12.00	30.00
FRAWLEY, WILLIAM					
Dot DLP-3061	(M)	**The Old Ones**	1957	12.00	30.00
FRAZIER, DALLAS					
Capitol T-2552	(M)	**Elvira**	1966	10.00	25.00
Capitol ST-2552	(S)	**Elvira**	1966	12.00	30.00
Capitol T-2764	(M)	**Tell It Like It Is**	1967	10.00	25.00
Capitol ST-2764	(S)	**Tell It Like It Is**	1967	12.00	30.00
FREAK SCENE, THE					
Columbia CL-2656	(M)	**Psychedelic Psoul**	1967	20.00	50.00
Columbia CS-9456	(S)	**Psychedelic Psoul**	1967	30.00	75.00
FREBERG, STAN					
Capitol T-732	(M)	**Comedy Caravan**	1956	20.00	50.00
Capitol T-777	(M)	**A Child's Garden Of Freberg**	1957	20.00	50.00
— Original Capitol albums above have turquoise labels.—

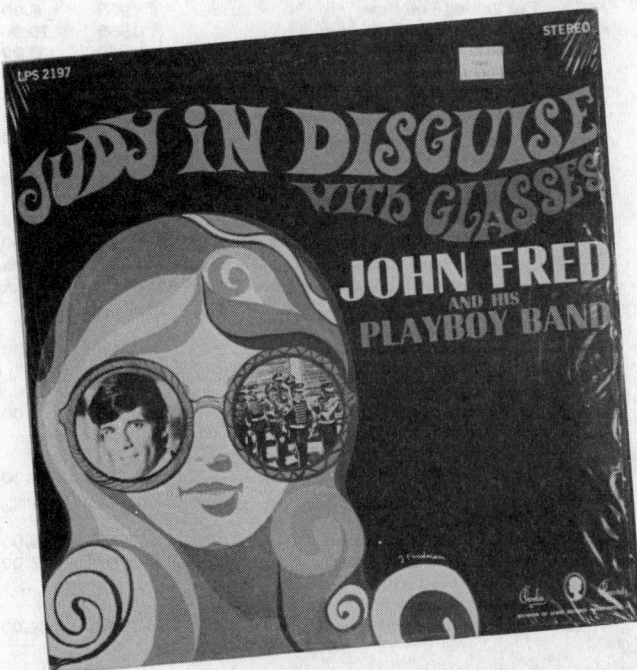

John Fred Gourrier had been a regional success for more than a decade when the ridiculously wonderful "Judy In Disguise (With Glasses)" spoofed Sgt. Pepper on its way to the top of the charts. After the single's unexpected success, Paula 2197, Agnes English, was rechristened, given gear new cover art (a big improvement over the drab original) and sent back out into the field for retail exposure.

Label & Catalog #		Title	Year	VG+	NM
Capitol WBO-1035	(M)	The Best Of The Stan Freberg Show	1958	20.00	50.00
Capitol T-1242	(M)	Stan Freberg With The Original Cast	1959	12.00	30.00
Capitol W-1573	(M)	The United States Of America	1961	8.00	20.00
Capitol SW-1573	(S)	The United States Of America	1961	12.00	30.00
Capitol T-1694	(M)	Face The Funnies	1962	8.00	20.00
Capitol ST-1694	(S)	Face The Funnies	1962	12.00	30.00
		— Original Capitol albums above have black labels with the Capitol logo on the left side.—			
Capitol T-1816	(M)	Madison Avenue Werewolf	1962	8.00	20.00
Capitol J-3264	(M)	Mickey Mouse's Birthday Party	1963	10.00	25.00
Capitol T-2020	(M)	The Best Of Stan Freberg	1964	8.00	20.00
Capitol T-2551	(M)	Underground Show #1	1966	6.00	15.00
Capitol ST-2551	(S)	Underground Show #1	1966	8.00	20.00
		— Original Capitol albums above have black labels with the Capitol logo on top.—			

FRED, JOHN, & HIS PLAYBOY BAND
Paula LP-2191	(M)	John Fred And His Playboys	1966	8.00	20.00
Paula LPS-2191	(S)	John Fred And His Playboys	1966	10.00	25.00
Paula LP-2193	(M)	34:40 Of John Fred And His Playboys	1967	8.00	20.00
Paula LPS-2193	(S)	34:40 Of John Fred And His Playboys	1967	10.00	25.00
Paula LP-2197	(M)	Agnes English	1967	8.00	20.00
Paula LPS-2197	(S)	Agnes English	1967	10.00	25.00
Paula LPS-2197	(S)	Judy In Disguise With Glasses	1968	8.00	20.00
		("Judy" is a repackage of "Agnes.")			
Paula LPS-2201	(S)	Permanently Stated	1968	6.00	15.00
Uni 73077	(S)	Love In My Soul	1970	6.00	15.00

FRED & THE NEW JB'S: *Refer to* FRED WESLEY & THE JB'S

FREDDIE & THE DREAMERS
Tower T-5003	(M)	I'm Telling You Now	1965	10.00	25.00
Tower DT-5003	(E)	I'm Telling You Now	1965	8.00	20.00
Mercury MG-21017	(M)	Freddie & The Dreamers	1965	10.00	25.00
Mercury SR-61017	(E)	Freddie & The Dreamers	1965	8.00	20.00
Mercury MG-21026	(M)	Do The Freddie	1965	8.00	20.00
Mercury SR-61026	(S)	Do The Freddie	1965	10.00	25.00
Mercury MG-21031	(M)	Seaside Swingers *(Soundtrack)*	1965	8.00	20.00
Mercury SR-61031	(S)	Seaside Swingers *(Soundtrack)*	1965	10.00	25.00
Mercury MG-21053	(M)	Frantic Freddie	1965	6.00	15.00
Mercury SR-61053	(S)	Frantic Freddie	1965	8.00	20.00
Mercury MG-21061	(M)	Fun Lovin' Freddie	1966	6.00	15.00
Mercury SR-61061	(S)	Fun Lovin' Freddie	1966	8.00	20.00
Capitol SM-11896	(M)	The Best Of Freddie & The Dreamers	1976	4.00	10.00
		("I'm Telling You Now," "You Were Made For Me", "Over You," "I Just Don't Understand" and "A Little You" are in stereo.)			

FREDRIC
Forte 301	(S)	Phases And Faces	1968	360.00	600.00

FREE BAND, THE
Vanguard VSD-6507	(S)	The Free Band	1969	8.00	20.00

FREE MOVEMENT, THE
Columbia KC-31136	(S)	I've Found Someone Of My Own	1972	6.00	15.00

FREE SPIRITS, THE
ABC 593	(M)	Out Of Sight And Sound	1967	6.00	15.00
ABC S-593	(S)	Out Of Sight And Sound	1967	8.00	20.00

FREEBORNE
Monitor MPS-607	(S)	Peak Impressions	1967	24.00	60.00

FREED, ALAN
MGM E-293 (10")	(M)	The Big Beat	1956	70.00	175.00
Coral CRL-57063	(M)	Rock 'N Roll Dance Party, Volume 1	1956	40.00	100.00
Coral CRL-57115	(M)	Rock 'N Roll Dance Party, Volume 2	1957	40.00	100.00
Coral CRL-57177	(M)	TV Record Hop	1957	40.00	100.00
Coral CRL-57213	(M)	Rock Around The Block	1958	40.00	100.00
Coral CRL-57216	(M)	Alan Freed Presents The King's Henchmen	1958	60.00	150.00
Brunswick BL-54043	(M)	The Alan Freed Rock & Roll Show	1959	50.00	125.00

Label & Catalog #		Title	Year	VG+	NM

FREEMAN, BOBBY

Jubilee JLP-1086	(M)	Do You Wanna Dance?	1959	40.00	100.00
Jubilee JLPS-1086	(S)	Do You Wanna Dance?	1959	60.00	150.00
Jubilee JGM-5010	(M)	Twist With Bobby Freeman	1962	20.00	50.00
Autumn LP-102	(M)	C'mon And S-W-I-M	1964	20.00	50.00
King 930	(M)	The Lovable Style Of Bobby Freeman	1965	16.00	40.00
Josie JM-4007	(M)	Get In The Swim With Bobby Freeman	1965	12.00	30.00
Josie JGS-4007	(E)	Get In The Swim With Bobby Freeman	1965	10.00	25.00

FREEMAN, ERNIE

Imperial LP-9022	(M)	Ernie Freeman Plays Irving Berlin	1957	20.00	50.00
Imperial LP-9030	(M)	Jivin' Around	1957	20.00	50.00
Imperial LP-9057	(M)	Ernie Freeman	1958	20.00	50.00
Imperial LP-9067	(M)	Dark At The Top Of The Stairs	1959	12.00	30.00
Imperial LP-12067	(S)	Dark At The Top Of The Stairs	1959	16.00	40.00
Imperial LP-9081	(M)	Twistin' Time	1960	12.00	30.00
Imperial LP-12081	(S)	Twistin' Time	1960	16.00	40.00
Imperial LP-9193	(M)	The Stripper	1962	10.00	25.00
Imperial LP-12193	(S)	The Stripper	1962	12.00	30.00
Liberty LRP-3283	(M)	Limbo Dance Party	1963	10.00	25.00
Liberty LST-7283	(S)	Limbo Dance Party	1963	12.00	30.00
Liberty LRP-3331	(M)	Comin' Home, Baby	1963	10.00	25.00
Liberty LST-7331	(S)	Comin' Home, Baby	1963	12.00	30.00
Dunhill D-50026	(M)	Hitmaker	1967	5.00	12.00
Dunhill DS-50026	(S)	Hitmaker	1967	6.00	15.00

FREHELY, ACE: Refer to KISS

FREIGHT TRAIN

| Fly-by-Nite LPFBN-1001 | (S) | Just The Beginning | 1971 | 20.00 | 50.00 |

FREY, GLENN
Frey was formerly a member of The Eagles.

| MCA 5501 | (DJ) | The Allnighter (Quiex II vinyl) | 1984 | 6.00 | 15.00 |

FRIAR TUCK

| Mercury MG-21111 | (M) | Friar Tuck & His Psychedelic Guitar | 1967 | 10.00 | 25.00 |
| Mercury SR-61111 | (S) | Friar Tuck & His Psychedelic Guitar | 1967 | 12.00 | 30.00 |

FRIEDMAN, KINKY

Vanguard VSD-79333	(S)	Sold American	1973	6.00	15.00
ABC ABCS-829	(S)	Kinky Friedman	1975	6.00	15.00
Epic PE-34304	(S)	Lasso From El Paso	1976	6.00	15.00

FRIEND & LOVER

| Verve/Forecast FTS-3055 | (S) | Reach Out Of The Darkness | 1968 | 8.00 | 20.00 |

FRIENDS

| Oblivion 3 | (S) | Friends | 1972 | 6.00 | 15.00 |
| Probe 4511 | (S) | From Here To There | 1969 | 6.00 | 15.00 |

FRIENDS OF DISTINCTION, THE

| RCA Victor APD1-0276 | (Q) | Friends Of Distinction's Greatest Hits | 1973 | 6.00 | 15.00 |

FRIENDSOUND
Friendsound is Phil Volk, Drake Levin and Mike Smith of Paul Revere's Raiders. Refer to Brotherhood.

| RCA Victor LSP-4114 | (S) | Joyride | 1969 | 6.00 | 15.00 |

FRIJID PINK

Parrot PAS-71033	(S)	Frijid Pink	1970	10.00	25.00
Parrot PAS-71041	(S)	Frijid Pink Defrosted	1970	10.00	25.00
		(The inner sleeve is a full-color photo of the group.)			
Lion LN-1004	(S)	Earth Omen	1972	8.00	20.00
Fantasy F-9464	(S)	All Pink Inside	1974	6.00	15.00

FRIPP & ENO
Robert Fripp of King Crimson and Brian Eno of Roxy Music.

| Antilles ANM-7001 | (S) | No Pussy Footing | 1973 | 6.00 | 15.00 |

Label & Catalog #		Title	Year	VG+	NM

FRIZZELL, LEFTY
Refer to Carl Smith / Lefty Frizzell / Marty Robbins.

Label & Catalog #		Title	Year	VG+	NM
Columbia HL-9019 (10")	(M)	The Songs Of Jimmie Rodgers	1951	80.00	200.00
Columbia HL-9021 (10")	(M)	Listen To Lefty	1952	80.00	200.00
Columbia CL-1342	(M)	The One And Only Lefty Frizzell	1959	40.00	100.00

— *Original Columbia albums above have three white "eye" logos on each side of the spindle hole.*—

Columbia CL-2169	(M)	Saginaw, Michigan	1964	14.00	35.00
Columbia CS-8969	(S)	Saginaw, Michigan	1964	16.00	40.00
Columbia CL-2386	(M)	The Sad Side Of Love	1965	14.00	35.00
Columbia CS-9186	(S)	The Sad Side Of Love	1965	16.00	40.00
Columbia CL-2488	(M)	Lefty Frizzell's Greatest Hits	1966	14.00	35.00
Columbia CS-9288	(S)	Lefty Frizzell's Greatest Hits	1966	16.00	40.00
Columbia CL-2772	(M)	Puttin' On	1967	20.00	50.00
Columbia CS-9572	(S)	Puttin' On	1967	16.00	40.00

— *Columbia albums above have "360 Sound Mono/Stereo" on the bottom of the label.*—

FROGGIE BEAVER

Froggie Beaver 7301	(S)	From The Pond	1973	12.00	30.00

FROLK HAVEN

LRS RF-6023	(S)	At The Apex Of High	197?	60.00	150.00

FROM BRITAIN WITH BEAT

Modern Sound 544	(M)	From Britain With Beat	196?	30.00	75.00

FROMAN, JANE

RCA Victor LPT-3055 (10")	(M)	Gems From Gershwin	1952	20.00	50.00
Capitol H-309 (10")	(M)	With A Song In My Heart (Soundtrack)	1952	40.00	100.00
Capitol H-310 (10")	(M)	Pal Joey	1952	40.00	100.00
Capitol H-354 (10")	(M)	Yours Alone	1952	20.00	50.00
Capitol T-309	(M)	With A Song In My Heart (Soundtrack)	1955	16.00	40.00
Capitol T-310	(M)	Pal Joey (Soundtrack)	1952	40.00	100.00
Capitol T-726	(M)	Faith	1956	12.00	30.00
Capitol T-889	(M)	Songs At Sunset	1957	12.00	30.00

FROST, THE

Vanguard VSD-6520	(S)	Frost Music	1969	10.00	25.00
Vanguard VSD-6541	(S)	Rock And Roll Music	1969	10.00	25.00
Vanguard VSD-6556	(S)	Through The Eyes Of Music	1970	10.00	25.00

FROST, FRANK, & THE NIGHTHAWKS

Phillips Int. 1975	(M)	Hey Boss Man!	1961	1,000.00	Rare

(*Near Mint copies have a suggested value of $2,000-3,000.*)

FROST, MAX, & THE TROOPERS

Tower ST-5147	(S)	Shape Of Things To Come	1968	20.00	50.00

FRUMMOX

Probe 4511	(S)	From Here To There	1969	6.00	15.00

FRUT

Westbound WB-2005	(S)	Keep On Truckin'	1971	8.00	20.00
Westbound WB-2008	(S)	Spoiled Rotten	1972	8.00	20.00

FUGITIVES, THE

Hideout 1001	(M)	The Fugitives At Dave's Hideout	1968	500.00	1,500.00
Justice JLP-141	(S)	The Fugitives On The Run	1967	100.00	250.00

FUGS, THE [THE VILLAGE FUGS]
The Fugs are Tuli Kupferburg, Ed Sanders and Ken Weaver. The Broadside and ESP albums feature backing by Peter Stampfel and Steve Weber, later The Holy Modal Rounders.

Broadside 304	(M)	The Village Fugs Sing Ballads Of Contemporary Protest (Includes a bonus insert)	1966	80.00	200.00
Broadside 304	(M)	The Village Fugs Sing Ballads Of Contemporary Protest (Without the insert)	1966	60.00	150.00
ESP-Disk' 1018	(M)	The Fugs First Album	1966	16.00	40.00
		(Cover reads "Reissue of Broadside 304.)			
ESP-Disk' 1018	(M)	The Fugs First Album	1966	60.00	150.00
		(Turquoise & black cover with different back cover)			

Label & Catalog #		Title	Year	VG+	NM
ESP-Disk' 1017	(M)	**The Fugs First Album**	196?	12.00	30.00
		(The cover makes no mention of the Broadside original.)			
ESP-Disk' 1017	(M)	**The Fugs First Album**	196?	20.00	50.00
		(Psychedelic wizard cover)			
ESP-Disk' 1028	(S)	**The Fugs**	196?	20.00	50.00
		(Black & white cover with the photos on the back staggered.)			
ESP-Disk' 1028	(S)	**The Fugs**	196?	14.00	35.00
		(Black & white cover with the photos on the back straight.)			
ESP-Disk' 1028	(S)	**The Fugs**	196?	30.00	75.00
		(The cover is a psychedelic color shield.)			
ESP-Disk' 1038	(S)	**Virgin Fugs**	1967	40.00	100.00
		(The cover has a sticker that reads " For Adults Minds Only"			
		and was issued with a poster, a flip book, and stickers.)			
ESP-Disk' 1038	(S)	**Virgin Fugs**	1967	20.00	50.00
		(The cover has a sticker that reads " For Adults Minds Only"			
		without the inserts.)			
ESP-Disk' 1038	(S)	**Virgin Fugs**	1967	20.00	50.00
		("For Adult Minds" is stamped on the back cover.)			
ESP-Disk' 1038	(S)	**Virgin Fugs**	1967	14.00	35.00
		("For Adult Minds" printed on the front cover.)			
ESP-Disk' 2018	(S)	**Fugs 4, Rounders Score**	1967	30.00	75.00
Reprise R-6280	(M)	**Tenderness Junction**	1967	14.00	35.00
Reprise RS-6280	(S)	**Tenderness Junction**	1967	10.00	25.00
Reprise RS-6305	(S)	**It Crawled Into My Hand, Honest**	1968	10.00	25.00
Reprise RS-6359	(S)	**Belle Of Avenue A**	1969	10.00	25.00
Reprise RS-6396	(S)	**Golden Filth**	1970	10.00	25.00
PVC 8914	(S)	**Proto Punk** *(With insert)*	1982	6.00	15.00
Olufsen 5006	(S)	**Refuse To Be Burnt Out**	1985	6.00	15.00
Olufsen 5009	(S)	**Buckets Of Love**	1985	20.00	50.00
		(Banned due to the breast- fondling cover.)			
Olufsen 5011	(S)	**No More Slavery**	1986	3.00	8.00
New Rose 56	(S)	**Refuse To Be Burnt Out**	1985	6.00	15.00
New Rose 79	(S)	**No More Slavery**	1986	6.00	15.00
New Rose 115	(S)	**Star Peace**	1987	6.00	15.00

FULL MOON

Douglas KZ-31904	(S)	**Full Moon**	1972	6.00	15.00

FULLER, BOBBY [THE BOBBY FULLER FOUR]

Mustang M-900	(M)	**KRLA King Of The Wheels**	1965	60.00	150.00
Mustang MS-900	(S)	**KRLA King Of The Wheels**	1965	100.00	250.00
Mustang M-901	(M)	**I Fought The Law**	1966	30.00	75.00
Mustang MS-901	(S)	**I Fought The Law**	1966	100.00	200.00
		(The mono and stereo versions of "I Fought The Law" contain			
		different takes of several songs. Both Mustang 900 and 901			
		have been convincingly counterfeited in mono.)			

FULLER, JERRY

Lin LP-100	(M)	**Teenage Love**	1960	30.00	75.00

FULLER, JESSE

Cavalier 5006 (10")	(M)	**Frisco Bound**	195?	80.00	200.00
Cavalier 6009	(M)	**Frisco Bound**	195?	40.00	100.00
Good Time Jazz 10039	(M)	**The Lone Cat**	1961	12.00	30.00
Good Time Jazz S-10039	(S)	**The Lone Cat**	1961	16.00	40.00
Folklore FRLP-14006	(M)	**San Francisco Bay Blues**	1964	10.00	25.00
Folklore FRST-14006	(S)	**San Francisco Bay Blues**	1964	12.00	30.00
Prestige PRST-7718	(S)	**San Francisco Bay Blues**	1969	6.00	15.00
		(Prestige 7718 is a reissue of Folklore 14006.)			

FULSON, LOWELL [LOWELL FOLSOM]

Kent KLP-5016	(M)	**Lowell Fulson**	1965	16.00	40.00
Kent KLP-5020	(M)	**Lowell Fulson**	1965	16.00	40.00
Kent KLP-520	(M)	**Tramp**	1967	12.00	30.00
Kent KST-520	(S)	**Tramp**	1967	16.00	40.00
Kent KST-531	(S)	**Lowell Fulson Now**	1969	12.00	30.00

FUN & GAMES, THE

Uni 73042	(S)	**Elephant Candy**	1968	8.00	20.00

Label & Catalog #		Title	Year	VG+	NM

FUNKADELIC
Funkadelic, who also recorded as Parliament, is the brainchild of George Clinton.

Westbound 2000	(S)	**Funkadelic**	1970	16.00	40.00
Westbound 2001	(S)	**Free Your Mind And Your Ass Will Follow**	1970	16.00	40.00
Westbound 2007	(S)	**Maggot Brain**	1971	16.00	40.00
Westbound 2020	(S)	**America Eats Its Young**	1972	16.00	40.00
Westbound 2022	(S)	**Cosmic Slop**	1973	16.00	40.00
Westbound 1001	(S)	**Standing On The Verge Of Getting It On**	1974	16.00	40.00
Westbound 1004	(S)	**Funkadelic's Greatest Hits**	1975	16.00	40.00
Westbound 215	(S)	**Let's Take It To The Stage**	1975	16.00	40.00
Westbound 227	(S)	**Tales Of Kidd Funkadelic**	1976	16.00	40.00
Westbound 303	(S)	**The Best Of The Early Years**	1977	16.00	40.00
Warner Bros. BS-2973	(S)	**Hardcore Jollies**	1976	8.00	20.00
Warner Bros. BS-3209	(S)	**One Nation Under A Groove**	1978	8.00	20.00
Warner Bros. BSK-3371	(S)	**Uncle Jam Wants You**	1979	8.00	20.00
Warner Bros. 3BSK-482	(S)	**The Electric Spanking Of War Babies**	1981	8.00	20.00

FUSE
Fuse features Rick Nielson And Tom Peterson, later of Cheap Trick.

Epic BN-26502	(S)	**Fuse** *(Counterfeits exist)*	1970	16.00	40.00

FUSION

Atco SD-33-295	(S)	**Border Town**	1969	6.00	15.00

FUTURE

Shamley 703	(S)	**Down The Country Road**	1969	8.00	20.00

G. T. O. 'S
Girls Together Outrageously were produced by Frank Zappa.

Straight STS-1059	(S)	**Permanent Damage**	1969	40.00	100.00
Reprise RS-6390	(S)	**Permanent Damage**	1970	30.00	75.00
		(Both the Straight and the Reprise releases included a booklet, priced separately below.)			
Stright/Reprise		**Permanent Damage Booklet**	1969	10.00	25.00

GABLES, THE

Fleetwood GAB-1	(M)	**Snake Dance**	196?	150.00	300.00

GABRIEL, PETER
Gabriel was formerly the leader of Genesis.

Direct Disk SD-16615	(S)	**Peter Gabriel**	198?	25.00	75.00
Geffen GHS-2011	(DJ)	**Peter Gabriel** *(Quiex II vinyl)*	1982	6.00	15.00

GABRIEL BONDAGE

Dharma D-804	(S)	**Angel Dust** *(Blue vinyl)*	1973	16.00	40.00

GAINSBOROUGH GALLERY, THE

Evolution 2012	(S)	**Life Is A Song**	1970	5.00	12.00

GALAHADS, THE

Liberty LRP-3371	(M)	**The Galahads**	1964	8.00	20.00
Liberty LST-7371	(S)	**The Galahads**	1964	10.00	25.00

Label & Catalog #		Title	Year	VG+	NM
GALE, SUNNY					
RCA Victor LPM-1277	(M)	Sunny And Blue	1956	16.00	40.00
GALS & PALS					
Fontana MGF-27538	(M)	Gals And Pals	1965	6.00	15.00
Fontana SRS-67538	(S)	Gals And Pals	1965	8.00	20.00
GAME					
Faithful Virtue 2003	(S)	Game	1969	8.00	20.00
Evolution 2021	(S)	Game	1970	5.00	12.00
Evolution 3008	(S)	Long Hot Summer	1970	5.00	12.00
GANDALF					
Capitol ST-121	(S)	Gandalf	1969	60.00	150.00
GANDALF THE GREY					
G.W.R. 7	(S)	The Grey Wizard Am I	196?	150.00	300.00
GANT, CECIL					
Red Mill (No number)	(M)	Cecil Gant (Red vinyl)	1956	150.00	300.00
King 671	(M)	Cecil Gant	1958	60.00	150.00
Sound 601	(M)	The Incomparable Cecil Gant	1958	40.00	100.00
GANTS, THE					
Liberty LRP-3432	(M)	Road Runner	1965	12.00	30.00
Liberty LST-7432	(S)	Road Runner	1965	16.00	40.00
		("Road Runner" is rechanneled on this album.)			
Liberty LRP-3455	(M)	The Gants Galore	1966	12.00	30.00
Liberty LST-7455	(S)	The Gants Galore	1966	16.00	40.00
Liberty LRP-3473	(M)	The Gants Again	1966	12.00	30.00
Liberty LST-7473	(S)	The Gants Again	1966	16.00	40.00
GARAGIOLA, JOE					
Joe was formerly a member of The Pittsburgh Pirates.					
United Arts. UAL-3032	(M)	That Holler Guy	1959	16.00	40.00
United Arts. UAS-6032	(S)	That Holler Guy	1959	20.00	50.00
GARBO, GRETA					
MGM E-4201	(M)	Garbo	1964	16.00	40.00
MGM SE-4201	(E)	Garbo	1964	12.00	30.00
GARCIA, JERRY					
Refer to The Grateful Dead; Old & In The Way; Merl Saunders; Howard Wales.					
Warner Bros. BS-2582	(S)	Garcia	1972	10.00	25.00
Round RX-102	(S)	Garcia	1974	10.00	25.00
Round RX-107	(S)	Reflections	1975	10.00	25.00
United Arts. LA565	(S)	Reflections	1976	8.00	20.00
GARDNER, DON, & DEE DEE FORD					
Fire LP-105	(M)	Need Your Lovin'	1962	100.00	250.00
Sue LP-1044	(M)	Don Gardner & Dee Dee Ford In Sweden	1965	40.00	100.00
GARFUNKEL, ART					
Refer to Simon & Garfunkel.					
Columbia CQ-31474	(Q)	Angel Clare	1974	6.00	15.00
Columbia CQ-33700	(Q)	Breakaway	1975	6.00	15.00
GARLAND, HANK					
Hank also recorded as a member of The Nashville All-Stars.					
Sesac N-3901/2	(M)	Subtle Swing	196?	40.00	100.00
Columbia CL-1572	(M)	Jazz Winds From A New Direction	1961	12.00	30.00
Columbia CS-8372	(S)	Jazz Winds From A New Direction	1961	16.00	40.00
Columbia CL-1913	(M)	The Unforgettable Guitar Of Hank Garland	1962	12.00	30.00
Columbia CS-8713	(S)	The Unforgettable Guitar Of Hank Garland	1962	16.00	40.00
— Original Columbia albums above have six white-on-black "eye" logos around the perimeter of the label.—					
H.G. 1001 LPS	(S)	Jazz In New York	197?	20.00	50.00

Label & Catalog #		Title	Year	VG+	NM

GARLAND, JUDY

Label & Catalog #		Title	Year	VG+	NM
MGM E-501 (10")	(M)	Till's The Clouds Roll By (Soundtrack)	1950	40.00	100.00
MGM E-502 (10")	(M)	Easter Parade (Soundtrack)	1950	40.00	100.00
MGM E-505 (10")	(M)	Words And Music (Soundtrack)	1950	40.00	100.00
MGM E-519 (10")	(M)	Summer Stock (Soundtrack)	1950	40.00	100.00
MGM E-21 (10")	(M)	The Pirate / Summer Stock (Soundtracks)	1951	40.00	100.00
MGM E-82 (10")	(M)	Judy Garland Sings	1951	30.00	75.00
MGM E-3149	(M)	If You Feel Like Singing, Sing	1955	30.00	75.00
MGM E-3227	(M)	Easter Parade (Soundtrack)	1955	30.00	75.00
MGM E-3231	(M)	Till's The Clouds Roll By (Soundtrack)	1955	30.00	75.00
MGM E-3232	(M)	In The Good Old Summertime (Soundtrack)	1955	30.00	75.00
MGM E-3233	(M)	Words And Music (Soundtrack)	1955	30.00	75.00
MGM E-3234	(M)	Summer Stock / The Pirate (Soundtracks)	1955	30.00	75.00
MGM E-3249	(M)	Judy Garland With The MGM Orchestra	1956	30.00	75.00
MGM E-3464	(M)	The Wizard Of Oz (Soundtrack)	1956	50.00	125.00
MGM E-3770	(M)	Till's The Clouds Roll By (Soundtrack)	1959	20.00	50.00
MGM E-3771	(M)	Words & Music / Good News (Soundtracks)	1959	20.00	50.00
— Original MGM albums above have yellow labels.—					
MGM E-3989	(M)	The Star Years	1962	12.00	30.00
MGM E-3996	(M)	The Wizard Of Oz	1962	12.00	30.00
MGM SE-3996	(E)	The Wizard Of Oz	1962	10.00	25.00
MGM E-4005	(M)	The Hollywood Years	1962	12.00	30.00
MGM E-4204	(M)	The Very Best Of Judy Garland	1962	12.00	30.00
— Original MGM albums above have black labels.—					
Metro M-505	(M)	Judy Garland	1965	6.00	15.00
Metro MS-505	(E)	Judy Garland	1965	4.00	10.00
MGM SDP-1	(P)	Golden Years At M-G-M	1969	6.00	15.00
MGM GAS-113	(P)	Judy Garland	1970	6.00	15.00
Capitol T-676	(M)	Miss Show Business	1955	16.00	40.00
Capitol T-734	(M)	Judy	1956	16.00	40.00
Capitol T-835	(M)	Alone	1957	14.00	35.00
— Original Capitol albums above have turquoise labels.—					
Capitol T-1036	(M)	In Love	1958	14.00	35.00
Capitol ST-1036	(S)	In Love	1958	20.00	50.00
Capitol T-1118	(M)	Garland At The Grove	1959	14.00	35.00
Capitol ST-1118	(S)	Garland At The Grove	1959	20.00	50.00
Capitol T-1188	(M)	The Letter (With letter attached to cover)	1959	20.00	50.00
Capitol ST-1188	(S)	The Letter (With letter attached to cover)	1959	30.00	75.00
Capitol T-1188	(M)	The Letter (Without the letter)	1959	12.00	30.00
Capitol ST-1188	(S)	The Letter (Without the letter)	1959	16.00	40.00
Capitol T-1467	(M)	That's Entertainment	1960	10.00	25.00
Capitol ST-1467	(S)	That's Entertainment	1960	14.00	35.00
Capitol WBO-1569	(M)	Judy At Carnegie Hall	1961	10.00	25.00
Capitol SWBO-1569	(S)	Judy At Carnegie Hall	1961	14.00	35.00
— Original Capitol albums above have black labels with the Capitol logo on the left side.—					
Capitol W-1710	(M)	The Garland Touch	1962	10.00	25.00
Capitol SW-1710	(S)	The Garland Touch	1962	12.00	30.00
Capitol W-1861	(M)	I Could Go On Singing (Soundtrack)	1963	20.00	50.00
Capitol SW-1861	(S)	I Could Go On Singing (Soundtrack)	1963	30.00	75.00
Capitol T-1941	(M)	Our Love Letter	1963	10.00	25.00
Capitol ST-1941	(S)	Our Love Letter	1963	12.00	30.00
Capitol T-1999	(M)	The Hits Of Judy Garland	1963	8.00	20.00
Capitol ST-1999	(S)	The Hits Of Judy Garland	1963	10.00	25.00
Capitol W-2062	(M)	Just For Openers	1964	8.00	20.00
Capitol DW-2062	(S)	Just For Openers	1964	10.00	25.00
Capitol TAO-2295	(M)	Live At The London Palladium	1965	6.00	15.00
Capitol STAO-2295	(S)	Live At The London Palladium	1965	8.00	20.00
Capitol STCL-2988	(S)	Deluxe Set	1967	16.00	40.00
— Original Capitol albums above have black labels with the Capitol logo on top.—					
Decca DL-6020 (10")	(M)	Judy At The Palace	1952	30.00	75.00
Decca DL-5152 (10")	(M)	The Wizard Of Oz	1951	50.00	125.00
Decca DL-5412 (10")	(M)	Girl Crazy (Soundtrack)	1953	40.00	100.00
Decca DL-8190	(M)	Judy Garland's Greatest Performances	1955	16.00	40.00
Decca DL-8387	(M)	The Wizard Of Oz	1957	16.00	40.00
Decca DL-8498	(M)	Meet Me In St. Louis / The Harvey Girls (Soundtracks)	1957	60.00	150.00
Decca DL-4199	(M)	The Magic Of Judy Garland	1961	12.00	30.00
Decca DXB-172	(M)	The Best Of Judy Garland (2 LPs)	1964	8.00	20.00
Decca DXSB-172	(S)	The Best Of Judy Garland (2 LPs)	1964	10.00	25.00

Label & Catalog #		Title	Year	VG+	NM
Decca DL-75150	(S)	Judy Garland's Greatest Hits	1970	6.00	15.00
Decca DL-5	(E)	Collectors Items 1936-1945	1970	6.00	15.00
Columbia CL-1101	(M)	A Star Is Born (Soundtrack; boxed set)	1958	54.00	100.00
Columbia CL-1101	(M)	A Star Is Born (Soundtrack)	1958	20.00	50.00
Columbia CL-1940	(M)	A Star Is Born (Soundtrack)	1963	10.00	25.00
Columbia CS-8740	(E)	A Star Is Born (Soundtrack)	1963	6.00	15.00
Colpix CP-507	(M)	Pepe (Soundtrack)	1961	30.00	75.00
Colpix SCP-507	(S)	Pepe (Soundtrack)	1961	50.00	125.00
Warner Bros. B-1479	(M)	Gay Purr-ee (Soundtrack)	1962	20.00	50.00
Warner Bros. BS-1479	(S)	Gay Purr-ee (Soundtrack)	1962	30.00	75.00
ABC 620	(M)	At Home At The Palace	1967	8.00	20.00
ABC S-620	(S)	At Home At The Palace	1967	8.00	20.00
MGM SDP-1	(P)	Golden Years At M-G-M	1969	6.00	15.00
MGM GAS-113	(P)	Judy Garland	1970	6.00	15.00
Decca DL-75150	(S)	Judy Garland's Greatest Hits	1970	6.00	15.00
Decca DL-75	(E)	Collectors Items 1936-1945	1970	6.00	15.00
Mark-56	(S)	Live In San Francisco (Picture disc)	1978	20.00	50.00

GARLAND, JUDY, & LIZA MINELLI

Mobile Fidelity MFSL-048	(S)	Live At The London Palladium	1979	5.00	15.00

GARNER, STU

Revue 202	(M)	To Soul With Love	1967	5.00	12.00
Revue 7-202	(S)	To Soul With Love	1967	6.00	15.00

GARNETT, GALE

RCA Victor LPM-2833	(M)	My Kind Of Folk Songs	1964	8.00	20.00
RCA Victor LSP-2833	(S)	My Kind Of Folk Songs	1964	10.00	25.00
RCA Victor LSP-3305	(M)	Lovin' Place	1965	6.00	15.00
RCA Victor LSP-3305	(S)	Lovin' Place	1965	8.00	20.00
RCA Victor LPM-3325	(M)	The Many Faces Of Gale Garnett	1965	6.00	15.00
RCA Victor LSP-3325	(S)	The Many Faces Of Gale Garnett	1965	8.00	20.00
RCA Victor LPM-3498	(M)	Variety Is The Spice Of Gale Garnett	1966	6.00	15.00
RCA Victor LSP-3498	(S)	Variety Is The Spice Of Gale Garnett	1966	8.00	20.00
RCA Victor LPM-3586	(M)	New Adventures	1966	6.00	15.00
RCA Victor LSP-3586	(S)	New Adventures	1966	8.00	20.00
RCA Victor LPM-3747	(M)	Flying And Rainbows And Love	1967	6.00	15.00
RCA Victor LSP-3747	(S)	Flying And Rainbows And Love	1967	8.00	20.00
Columbia CL-2825	(M)	An Audience With The King Of Wands	1968	8.00	20.00
Columbia CS-9625	(S)	An Audience With The King Of Wands	1968	6.00	15.00
Columbia CS-9760	(S)	Sausalito Heliport	1969	6.00	15.00

GAS MASK

Tonsil 4001	(S)	Gas Mask	1970	8.00	20.00

GASLIGHT SINGERS, THE

Mercury MG-20848	(M)	The Gaslight Singers	1963	6.00	15.00
Mercury SR-60848	(S)	The Gaslight Singers	1963	8.00	20.00
Mercury MG-20923	(M)	Turning It On	1964	6.00	15.00
Mercury SR-60923	(S)	Turning It On	1964	8.00	20.00

GATES, DAVID
Gates was formerly a member of Bread.

Elektra EQ-5066	(Q)	David Gates' First	1973	6.00	15.00

GATES, HEN, & HIS GATERS

Masterseal M-700	(M)	Let's Go Dancing To Rock And Roll	195?	20.00	50.00
Plymouth R12-144	(M)	Rock And Roll	1956	20.00	50.00

GATEWAY SINGERS, THE
The Gateways feature Travis Edmonson.

Decca DL-8413	(M)	Puttin' On The Style	1958	12.00	30.00
Decca DL-8671	(M)	The Gateway Singers At The Hungry i	1958	12.00	30.00
Decca DL-8742	(M)	The Gateway Singers In Hi Fi	1958	12.00	30.00
Warner Bros. W-1295	(M)	The Gateway Singers On The Lot	1959	8.00	20.00
Warner Bros. WS-1295	(S)	The Gateway Singers On The Lot	1959	10.00	25.00
Warner Bros. W-1334	(M)	Wagons West	1960	8.00	20.00
Warner Bros. WS-1334	(S)	Wagons West	1960	10.00	25.00

Label & Catalog #		Title	Year	VG+	NM
MGM E-3905	(M)	Down In The Valley	1961	6.00	15.00
MGM SE-3905	(S)	Down In The Valley	1961	8.00	20.00
MGM E-4154	(M)	Hootenanny	1963	6.00	15.00
MGM SE-4154	(S)	Hootenanny	1963	8.00	20.00

GATEWAY TRIO, THE

Capitol T-1868	(M)	The Mad, Mad, Mad, Mad Gateway Trio	1963	6.00	15.00
Capitol ST-1868	(S)	The Mad, Mad, Mad, Mad Gateway Trio	1963	8.00	20.00
Capitol T-2184	(M)	The Gateway Trio	1964	5.00	12.00
Capitol ST-2184	(S)	The Gateway Trio	1964	6.00	15.00

GATLIN BROTHERS, THE

Columbia HC-48135	(S)	Sure Feels Like Love (Half-soeed master)	198?	25.00	75.00

GAVIN, KEVIN: *Refer to* **GOLDMINE'S PRICE GUIDE TO COLLECTIBLE JAZZ ALBUMS**

GAYE, MARVIN
Marvin also recorded with Diana Ross; Mary Wells.

Tamla 221	(M)	Soulful Moods Of Marvin Gaye	1961	300.00	600.00
Tamla 239	(M)	That Stubborn Kind Of Fella	1963	200.00	400.00
Tamla 242	(M)	On Stage Recorded Live	1963	100.00	200.00
Tamla 251	(M)	When I'm Alone I Cry	1964	60.00	150.00
Tamla 258	(M)	How Sweet It Is To Be Loved By You	1965	16.00	40.00
Tamla TS-258	(S)	How Sweet It Is To Be Loved By You	1965	20.00	50.00
Tamla 259	(M)	Hello Broadway, This Is Marvin	1965	12.00	30.00
Tamla TS-259	(S)	Hello Broadway, This Is Marvin	1965	16.00	40.00
Tamla 261	(M)	Tribute To The Great Nat King Cole	1965	16.00	40.00
Tamla TS-261	(S)	Tribute To The Great Nat King Cole	1965	20.00	50.00
Tamla 266	(M)	Moods Of Marvin Gaye	1966	12.00	30.00
Tamla TS-266	(S)	Moods Of Marvin Gaye	1966	16.00	40.00
Tamla 278	(M)	Marvin Gaye's Greatest Hits, Volume 2	1967	6.00	15.00
Tamla TS-278	(S)	Marvin Gaye's Greatest Hits, Volume 2	1967	8.00	20.00

— Tamla albums above have two side-by-side circles at the top of the label. —

Tamla TS-285	(S)	In The Groove	1968	10.00	25.00
Tamla TS-285	(S)	I Heard It Through The Grapevine	1968	8.00	20.00

("Grapevine" is a repackage of "In The Groove.")

Tamla TS-292	(S)	M. P. G.	1969	8.00	20.00
Tamla TS-293	(S)	Marvin Gaye And His Girls	1969	8.00	20.00

(Duets with Tammi Terrell and Kim Weston.)

Tamla TS-299	(S)	That's The Way Love Is	1970	6.00	15.00
Tamla TS-300	(S)	Marvin Gaye's Super Hits	1970	6.00	15.00
Tamla TS-310	(S)	What's Going On	1971	4.00	10.00
Tamla TS-322	(S)	Trouble Man (Soundtrack)	1972	4.00	10.00
Tamla TS-329	(S)	Let's Get It On	1973	4.00	10.00
Motown M9-791A3	(S)	Anthology (3 LPs)	1974	6.00	15.00
Tamla TS-333	(S)	Marvin Gaye Live!	1974	4.00	10.00
Tamla T6-342S1	(S)	I Want You	1976	4.00	10.00
Tamla T6-348	(S)	Marvin Gaye's Greatest Hits	1976	4.00	10.00
Tamla T7-352R2	(S)	Live (At The London Palladium) (2 LPs)	1977	6.00	15.00
Tamla TS-364	(S)	Hear, My Dear (2 LPs)	1979	6.00	15.00
Tamla TS-374	(S)	In Our Lifetime	1981	4.00	10.00
Columbia HC-48197	(S)	Midnight Love (Half-speed master)	198?	16.00	50.00

GAYE, MARVIN, & TAMI TERRELL

Tamla 277	(M)	United	1967	8.00	20.00
Tamla TS-277	(S)	United	1967	10.00	25.00

— Tamla albums above have two side-by-side circles at the top of the label. —

Tamla TS-284	(S)	You're All I Need	1968	8.00	20.00
Tamla TS-294	(S)	Easy	1969	8.00	20.00
Tamla TS-302	(S)	Greatest Hits	1970	6.00	15.00

GAYE, MARVIN, & KIM WESTON

Tamla T-260	(M)	Side By Side	1965	Unreleased	
Tamla TS-260	(S)	Side By Side	1965	Unreleased	
Tamla 270	(M)	Marvin Gaye And Kim Weston	1966	10.00	25.00
Tamla TS-270	(S)	Marvin Gaye And Kim Weston	1966	12.00	30.00

— Tamla albums above have two side-by-side circles at the top of the label. —

Label & Catalog #		Title	Year	VG+	NM

GAYLE, CRYSTAL

United Artists LA-856	(DJ)	Somebody Loves You (Picture disc)	1978	20.00	50.00
Mobile Fidelity MFSL-043	(S)	We Must Believe In Magic	197?	5.00	15.00
Nautilus NR-36	(S)	When I Dream	198?	5.00	15.00

GAYLORDS, THE

Mercury MG-25198 (10")	(M)	By Request	1955	16.00	40.00
Mercury MG-20075	(M)	Let's Have A Pizza Party	1956	10.00	25.00
Mercury MG-20186	(M)	Italia	1957	10.00	25.00
Mercury MG-20620	(M)	American Hits In Italian	1961	6.00	15.00
Mercury SR-60620	(S)	American Hits In Italian	1961	8.00	20.00
Mercury MG-20695	(M)	The Gaylords At The Shamrock	1962	6.00	15.00
Mercury SR-60695	(S)	The Gaylords At The Shamrock	1962	8.00	20.00
Mercury MG-20742	(M)	Party Style	1963	6.00	15.00
Mercury SR-60742	(S)	Party Style	1963	8.00	20.00
Wing MGW-12139	(M)	Italiano Favorites	1962	5.00	12.00
Wing SRW-16139	(S)	Italiano Favorites	1962	6.00	15.00

GAYNOR, MITZI

Verve MGV-2115	(M)	The Lyrics Of Ira Gershwin	195?	16.00	40.00
Verve MGVS-6014	(S)	Mitzi	195?	16.00	40.00
Armstrong ICPR 3-77	(DJ)	Mitzi Zings Into Spring (One sided)	1977	10.00	25.00

GAUCHOS, THE

ABC-Paramount 506	(M)	The Gauchos Featuring Jim Doval	1965	10.00	25.00
ABC-Paramount S-506	(S)	The Gauchos Featuring Jim Doval	1965	12.00	30.00

GENE & DEBBIE

T.R.X. LPS-1001	(S)	Hear And Now	1968	10.00	25.00

GENESIS

Genesis features Peter Gabriel And Phil Collins.

London PS-643	(S)	From Genesis To Revelation	1969	12.00	30.00
ABC X-816	(S)	Trespass	1970	5.00	12.00
Fam. Charisma CAS-1052	(S)	Nursery Cryme (Pink label)	1971	5.00	12.00
Fam. Charisma CAS-1058	(S)	Foxtrot (Pink label)	1972	5.00	12.00
Mercury SR-61175	(S)	In The Beginning (Red label)	1974	6.00	15.00
		(Mercury 51175 is a repackage of London 643.)			
Mobile Fidelity MFSL-062	(S)	A Trick Of The Tail	1981	13.00	40.00

GENTLE GIANT

Vertigo VE-1005	(S)	Acquiring The Taste	1971	6.00	15.00

GENTLE SOUL

Epic BN-26374	(S)	Gentle Soul	1968	10.00	25.00

GENTRYS, THE

MGM E-4336	(M)	Keep On Dancing	1965	10.00	25.00
MGM SE-4336	(P)	Keep On Dancing	1965	12.00	30.00
MGM E-4346	(M)	Time	1966	10.00	25.00
MGM SE-4346	(S)	Time	1966	12.00	30.00
MGM GAS-127	(S)	The Gentrys	1970	8.00	20.00
Sun 117	(S)	The Gentrys	1970	20.00	50.00

GEORDIE

MGM SE-4903	(S)	Hope You Like It	1973	12.00	30.00

GEORGE, BARBARA

A.F.O. 5001	(M)	I Know (You Don't Love Me Anymore)	1962	80.00	200.00

GERONIMO BLACK

Uni 73132	(S)	Geronimo Black	1972	10.00	25.00
Helios 4405	(S)	Welcome Back	1980	5.00	12.00

GERRY & THE PACEMAKERS

Laurie LLP-2024	(M)	Don't Let The Sun Catch You Crying	1964	14.00	35.00
Laurie SLP-2024	(E)	Don't Let The Sun Catch You Crying	1964	14.00	35.00
Laurie LLP-2027	(M)	Gerry & The Pacemakers' Second Album	1964	14.00	35.00
Laurie SLLP-2027	(E)	Gerry & The Pacemakers' Second Album	1964	14.00	35.00

Label & Catalog #		Title	Year	VG+	NM
Laurie LLP-2030	(M)	I'll Be There	1964	14.00	35.00
Laurie SLLP-2030	(E)	I'll Be There	1964	14.00	35.00
United Arts. UAL-3387	(M)	Ferry Cross The Mersey (Soundtrack)	1965	14.00	35.00
United Arts. UAS-6387	(S)	Ferry Cross The Mersey (Soundtrack)	1965	20.00	50.00
		(Note that three tracks are by George Martin & Orchestra.)			
Laurie LLP-2031	(M)	Gerry & The Pacemakers' Greatest Hits	1965	12.00	30.00
Laurie SLLP-2031	(E)	Gerry & The Pacemakers' Greatest Hits	1965	12.00	30.00
Laurie LLP-2037	(M)	Girl On A Swing	1966	14.00	35.00
Laurie SLP-2037	(E)	Girl On A Swing	1966	14.00	35.00
Capitol SM-11898	(S)	The Best Of Gerry & The Pacemakers	1979	4.00	10.00
		("I Like It," "I'm The One" and "Away From You" are in mono.)			

GHOULS, THE
The Ghouls are a creation of Gary Usher & Co.

Capitol T-2215	(M)	Dracula's Deuce	1965	40.00	100.00
Capitol ST-2215	(S)	Dracula's Deuce	1965	60.00	150.00

GIANT CRAB

Uni 73037	(S)	A Giant Crab Comes Forth	1968	6.00	15.00
Uni 73057	(S)	Cool It, Helios	1969	6.00	15.00

GIBB, ROBIN
Robin Gibb is a member of The Bee Gees.

Atco SD-33-323	(S)	Robin's Reign	1970	8.00	20.00

GIBBS, GEORGIA

Coral CRL-56037 (10")	(M)	Ballin' The Jack	1951	20.00	50.00
Mercury MG-25175 (10")	(M)	Georgia Gibbs Sings Oldies	1953	20.00	50.00
Mercury MG-25199 (10")	(M)	The Man That Got Away	1954	20.00	50.00
Mercury MG-20071	(M)	Music And Memories	1956	16.00	40.00
Mercury MG-20114	(M)	Song Favorites	1956	16.00	40.00
Mercury MG-20170	(M)	Swingin' With Her Nibs	1956	16.00	40.00
Coral CRL-57183	(M)	Her Nibs	1957	12.00	35.00
Epic LN-24059	(M)	Georgia Gibbs' Greatest Hits	1963	6.00	15.00
Epic BN-26059	(S)	Georgia Gibbs' Greatest Hits	1963	8.00	20.00
Imperial LP-9264	(M)	Something's Gotta Give	1964	6.00	15.00
Imperial LP-12264	(S)	Something's Gotta Give	1964	8.00	20.00
Bell 6000	(M)	Call Me	1966	6.00	15.00
Bell 6000	(S)	Call Me	1966	8.00	20.00

GIBSON, BOB

Riverside RLP-12-802	(M)	Offbeat Folk Songs	1957	12.00	30.00
Riverside RLP-12-806	(M)	I Come For To Sing	1957	12.00	30.00
Riverside RLP-12-816	(M)	Carnegie Concert	1958	12.00	30.00
Riverside RLP-12-830	(M)	There's A Meetin' Here Tonight	1958	12.00	30.00
Elektra EKL-177	(M)	Ski Songs	1959	10.00	25.00
Elektra EKS-7177	(S)	Ski Songs	1959	12.00	30.00
Elektra EKL-197	(M)	Yes I See	1961	8.00	20.00
Elektra EKS-7197	(S)	Yes I See	1961	10.00	25.00
Elektra EKL-239	(M)	Where I'm Bound	1963	8.00	20.00
Elektra EKS-7239	(S)	Where I'm Bound	1963	10.00	25.00
Stinson SLP-76	(M)	Folksongs Of Ohio	196?	8.00	20.00

GIBSON, BOB, & BOB CAMP

Elektra EKL-207	(M)	At The Gate Of Horn	1961	8.00	20.00
Elektra EKS-7207	(S)	At The Gate Of Horn	1961	10.00	25.00

GIBSON, DON

Lion 70069	(M)	Songs By Don Gibson	1958	30.00	75.00
RCA Victor LPM-1743	(M)	Oh Lonesome Me	1958	16.00	50.00
RCA Victor LPM-1918	(M)	No One Stands Alone	1959	14.00	35.00
RCA Victor LSP-1918	(S)	No One Stands Alone	1959	20.00	50.00
RCA Victor LPM-2038	(M)	That Gibson Boy	1959	14.00	35.00
RCA Victor LSP-2038	(S)	That Gibson Boy	1959	20.00	50.00
RCA Victor LPM-2184	(M)	Look Who's Blue	1960	14.00	35.00
RCA Victor LSP-2184	(S)	Look Who's Blue	1960	20.00	50.00
RCA Victor LPM-2269	(M)	Sweet Dreams	1960	14.00	35.00
RCA Victor LSP-2269	(S)	Sweet Dreams	1960	20.00	50.00

Label & Catalog #		Title	Year	VG+	NM
RCA Victor LPM-2361	(M)	Girls, Guitars And Gibson	1961	12.00	25.00
RCA Victor LSP-2361	(S)	Girls, Guitars And Gibson	1961	14.00	35.00
RCA Victor LPM-2448	(M)	Some Favorites Of Mine	1962	12.00	25.00
RCA Victor LSP-2448	(S)	Some Favorites Of Mine	1962	14.00	35.00
RCA Victor LPM-2702	(M)	I Wrote A Song	1963	12.00	25.00
RCA Victor LSP-2702	(S)	I Wrote A Song	1963	14.00	35.00

— Original RCA mono albums above have "Long Play" on the bottom of the label;
stereo albums have "Living Stereo" on the bottom.—

RCA Victor LPM-2878	(M)	God Walks These Hills	1964	8.00	20.00
RCA Victor LSP-2878	(S)	God Walks These Hills	1964	10.00	25.00
RCA Victor LPM-3376	(M)	The Best Of Don Gibson	1965	8.00	20.00
RCA Victor LSP-3376	(S)	The Best Of Don Gibson	1965	10.00	25.00
RCA Victor LPM-3470	(M)	Too Much Hurt	1965	8.00	20.00
RCA Victor LSP-3470	(S)	Too Much Hurt	1965	10.00	25.00
RCA Victor LPM-3594	(M)	Don Gibson With Spanish Guitar	1966	8.00	20.00
RCA Victor LSP-3594	(S)	Don Gibson With Spanish Guitar	1966	10.00	25.00
RCA Victor LPM-3680	(M)	Great Country Songs	1966	8.00	20.00
RCA Victor LSP-3680	(S)	Great Country Songs	1966	10.00	25.00
RCA Victor LPM-3843	(M)	All My Love	1967	8.00	20.00
RCA Victor LSP-3843	(S)	All My Love	1967	10.00	25.00
RCA Victor LPM-3974	(M)	The King Of Country Soul	1968	20.00	50.00
RCA Victor LSP-3974	(S)	The King Of Country Soul	1968	8.00	20.00
RCA Victor LSP-4053	(S)	More Country Soul	1968	8.00	20.00

— Original RCA albums above have black labels.—

GIBSON, HARRY

Sutton SSU-313	(M)	Rockin' Rhythm	196?	6.00	15.00

GIBSON, STEVE, & THE RED CAPS

Mercury MG-25115 (10")	(M)	You're Driving Me Crazy	1954	150.00	300.00
Mercury MG-25116 (10")	(M)	Blueberry Hill	1954	150.00	300.00

GILBERT, ANN: Refer to GOLDMINE'S PRICE GUIDE TO COLLECTIBLE JAZZ ALBUMS

GILBERT, JOHN

(No label)	(S)	Mead River	1971	30.00	75.00

GILES, GILES & FRIPP

Deram DES-18019	(S)	Cheerful Insanity	1968	16.00	40.00

GILKYSON, TERRY

Decca DL-5263 (10")	(M)	Folksongs	1950	20.00	50.00
Decca DL-5457 (10")	(M)	Golden Minutes Of Folk Music	1952	20.00	50.00
Kapp KL-1196	(M)	Rollin'	1960	6.00	15.00
Kapp KS-3196	(S)	Rollin'	1960	8.00	20.00
Kapp KL-1327	(M)	Cry Of The Wild Goose	1963	5.00	12.00
Kapp KS-3327	(S)	Cry Of The Wild Goose	1963	6.00	15.00

GILLESPIE, DARLENE

Disneyland WDL-3010	(M)	Darlene Of The Teens	195?	20.00	50.00

GILLEY, MICKEY

Astro 101	(M)	Lonely Wine	1964	150.00	300.00
Paula LP-2195	(M)	Down The Line	1967	16.00	40.00
Paula LPS-2195	(S)	Down The Line	1967	20.00	50.00

GILMER, JIMMY, & THE FIREBALLS: Refer to THE FIREBALLS

GINNY & GALLIONS

Downey DS-1003	(S)	Two Sides Of Ginny And Gallions	1964	14.00	35.00

GINSBERG, ALLEN

Fantasy F-7006	(M)	Howl And Other Poems (Red vinyl)	1959	60.00	150.00
Fantasy F-7006	(M)	Howl And Other Poems (Black vinyl)	1959	30.00	75.00
Atlantic 4001	(M)	Allen Ginsberg Reads Kaddish	1966	10.00	25.00
Verve/Forecast FVS-3083	(M)	Blake's Songs Of Innocence And Experience	1970	8.00	20.00
Fantasy F-7013	(M)	Howl And Other Poems	197?	6.00	15.00

(Fantasy 7013 is a reissue of 7006.)

Label & Catalog #		Title	Year	VG+	NM

GIRARD, CHUCK
Chuck was formerly the lead singer for The Hondells. Refer to Lovesong.

| Good News GNR-001 | (DJ) | The Chuck Girard Radio Special | 1979 | 6.00 | 15.00 |
| Good News 8110 | (S) | Take A Hand *(Picture disc)* | 1979 | 4.00 | 10.00 |

GLACIERS, THE

| Mercury MG-20895 | (M) | From Sea To Ski | 1964 | 8.00 | 20.00 |
| Mercury SR-60895 | (S) | From Sea To Ski | 1964 | 10.00 | 25.00 |

GLAD

| ABC S-655 | (S) | Feelin' Glad | 1969 | 6.00 | 15.00 |

GLASER, TOMPALL (& THE GLASER BROTHERS)

Decca DL-4041	(M)	This Land-Folk Songs	1960	12.00	30.00
Decca DL-74041	(S)	This Land-Folk Songs	1960	16.00	40.00
United Arts. UAL-3540	(M)	The Ballad Of Namu The Killer Whale	1966	6.00	15.00
United Arts. UAS-6540	(S)	The Ballad Of Namu The Killer Whale	1966	8.00	20.00

GLASS FAMILY, THE

| Warner Bros. WS-1776 | (S) | The Glass Family | 1969 | 6.00 | 15.00 |

GLASS HARP, THE

Decca DL-75261	(S)	Glass Harp	1971	6.00	15.00
Decca DL-75306	(S)	Synergy	1971	6.00	15.00
Decca DL-75358	(S)	It Makes Me Glad	1972	8.00	20.00

GLASS PRISM, THE

| RCA Victor LSP-4201 | (S) | Poe Through The Glass Prism | 1969 | 6.00 | 15.00 |
| RCA Victor LSP-4270 | (S) | On Joy And Sorrow | 1970 | 6.00 | 15.00 |

GLAZER, TOM

| Mercury MG-20007 | (M) | Olden Ballads | 1955 | 20.00 | 50.00 |
| Washington 301 | (M) | Tom Glazer Concert | 1959 | 10.00 | 25.00 |

GLAZER, TOM, & THE DO-RE-MI CHILDREN'S CHORUS

Wonderland 1492	(M)	Songs Children Sing In Latin America	1963	8.00	20.00
Kapp KL-1331	(M)	On Top Of Spaghetti	1963	8.00	20.00
Kapp KS-3331	(S)	On Top Of Spaghetti	1963	10.00	25.00

GLENN, DARRELL

| NRC LPA-5 | (M) | Crying In The Chapel | 1959 | 6.00 | 15.00 |
| NRC SLPA-5 | (S) | Crying In The Chapel | 1959 | 8.00 | 20.00 |

GLENN, LLOYD

Swing Time 1901 (10")	(M)	Lloyd Glenn	1954	750.00	Rare
		(Near Mint copies have a suggested value of $1,500-3,000.)			
Aladdin LP-808	(M)	Chica Boo	1956	150.00	400.00
Aladdin LP-808	(M)	Chica Boo *(Red vinyl)*	1956	300.00	750.00
Imperial LP-9176	(M)	Chica Boo	1956	80.00	200.00
Score SLP-4006	(M)	Lloyd Glenn	1957	200.00	400.00
Score SLP-4020	(M)	After Hours	1958	200.00	400.00

GLITTER, GARY

| Bell 1108 | (S) | Gary Glitter | 1972 | 5.00 | 12.00 |

GLITTER BAND, THE
Gary Glitter's former mates.

| Arista 207 | (S) | Makes You Blind | 1976 | 5.00 | 12.00 |

GLORY

| Texas Revolution CFS-2531 | (S) | A Meat Music Sampler | 197? | 20.00 | 50.00 |

GLORY

| Avalanche LA148 | (S) | Glory | 1973 | 10.00 | 25.00 |

GNARLY, PHIL & THE TOUGH GUYS

| Flaming Pie 319 | (S) | Philville | 1987 | 5.00 | 12.00 |

Label & Catalog #		Title	Year	VG+	NM
GO-GO'S, THE					
RCA Victor LPM-2930	(M)	Swim With The Go-Go's	1964	6.00	15.00
RCA Victor LSP-2930	(S)	Swim With The Go-Go's	1964	8.00	20.00
GO ZOO BAND					
Go Go 22170004	(S)	Sounds That Are Happening	196?	6.00	15.00
GOBEL, GEORGE					
Decca DL-4163	(M)	Lonesome George	1962	8.00	20.00
Decca DL-74163	(S)	Lonesome George	1962	10.00	25.00
GODCHAUX, KEITH & DONNA					
Refer to The Grateful Dead; The Heart Of Gold Band.					
Round RX-104	(S)	Keith And Donna	1975	12.00	30.00
GODFREY, ARTHUR					
Columbia CL-1580	(M)	Arthur Godfrey's Greatest Hits	1960	8.00	20.00
Columbia CS-8380	(S)	Arthur Godfrey's Greatest Hits	1960	10.00	25.00
GODMOMA					
Godmoma features William "Bootsy" Collins.					
Elektra 552	(S)	Here	1981	6.00	15.00
GODZ, THE					
ESP-Disk' 1037	(M)	Contact High With The Godz	1967	12.00	30.00
ESP-Disk' 1037	(S)	Contact High With The Godz	1967	12.00	30.00
ESP-Disk' 1047	(S)	Godz 2	1968	12.00	30.00
ESP-Disk' 1077	(S)	Third Testament	1969	12.00	30.00
ESP-Disk' 2017	(S)	Godzundheit	1970	12.00	30.00
GOGGLES, THE					
Audio Fidelity AFS-6244	(S)	The Goggles	1971	6.00	15.00
GOLDBERG, BARRY					
Refer to The Electric Flag.					
Epic LN-24199	(M)	Blowing My Mind	1966	12.00	30.00
Epic BN-26199	(S)	Blowing My Mind	1966	16.00	40.00
Buddah BDS-5012	(S)	The Barry Goldberg Reunion	1968	10.00	25.00
Buddah BDS-5029	(S)	Two Jews Blues	1970	10.00	25.00
Buddah BDS-5051	(S)	Street Man	1970	6.00	15.00
Buddah BDS-5081	(S)	Blast From My Past	1971	6.00	15.00
Record Man 5015	(S)	Barry Goldberg And Friends	1972	6.00	15.00
Atco SD-36-7040	(S)	Barry Goldberg	1974	5.00	12.00
		(Features Bob Dylan on backing vocals/percussion on six tracks.)			
GOLDEBRIARS, THE					
Epic LN-24087	(M)	The Goldebriars	1964	5.00	12.00
Epic BN-26087	(S)	The Goldebriars	1964	6.00	15.00
Epic LN-24114	(M)	Straight Ahead	1964	5.00	12.00
Epic BN-26114	(S)	Straight Ahead	1964	6.00	15.00
GOLDEN DAWN					
International Art. 4	(S)	Power Plant	1968	16.00	40.00
International Art. 4	(S)	Power Plant	1979	6.00	15.00
		(Reissues have "Masterfonics" stamped in the trail-off vinyl.)			
GOLDEN EARRING					
Capitol T-2823	(M)	Winter Harvest	1967	20.00	50.00
Capitol ST-2823	(E)	Winter Harvest	1967	16.00	40.00
Capitol ST-164	(S)	Miracle Mirror	1969	16.00	40.00
Atlantic SD-8244	(S)	Eight Miles High	1969	10.00	25.00
Track 396	(S)	Moontan *(Nude dancer cover)*	1973	8.00	20.00
Capitol ST-11315	(S)	Golden Earring	1974	5.00	12.00
GOLDEN GATE QUARTET, THE					
Mercury MG-25063 (10")	(M)	Spirituals	1950	80.00	200.00
Columbia CL-6102 (10")	(M)	The Golden Gate Spirituals	1953	80.00	200.00
Camden CAL-308	(M)	The Golden Gate Quartet *(Purple label)*	1956	40.00	100.00
Harmony HL-7018	(M)	That Golden Chariot *(Maroon label)*	1957	40.00	100.00

Label & Catalog #		Title	Year	VG+	NM

GOLDENROD
| Chartmaker CSG-1101 | (S) | Goldenrod | 1968 | 50.00 | 125.00 |

GOLDMARK, ANDY
| Warner Bros. BS-2703 | (S) | Andy Goldmark *(Produced by Gary Usher)* | 1973 | 5.00 | 12.00 |

GOLDSBORO, BOBBY
United Arts. UAL-3358	(M)	The Bobby Goldsboro Album	1964	10.00	25.00
United Arts. UAS-6358	(S)	The Bobby Goldsboro Album	1964	12.00	30.00
United Arts. UAL-3381	(M)	I Can't Stop Loving You	1964	10.00	25.00
United Arts. UAS-6381	(S)	I Can't Stop Loving You	1964	12.00	30.00
United Arts. UAL-3425	(M)	Little Things	1965	10.00	25.00
United Arts. UAS-6425	(S)	Little Things	1965	12.00	30.00
United Arts. UAL-3471	(M)	Broomstick Cowboy	1966	8.00	20.00
United Arts. UAS-6471	(S)	Broomstick Cowboy	1966	10.00	25.00
United Arts. UAL-3486	(M)	It's Too Late	1966	8.00	20.00
United Arts. UAS-6486	(S)	It's Too Late	1966	10.00	25.00
United Arts. UAL-3552	(M)	Blue Autumn	1966	8.00	20.00
United Arts. UAS-6552	(S)	Blue Autumn	1966	10.00	25.00
United Arts. UAL-3561	(M)	Solid Goldsboro/Greatest Hits	1967	5.00	12.00
United Arts. UAS-6561	(S)	Solid Goldsboro/Greatest Hits	1967	6.00	15.00
United Arts. UAL-3599	(M)	Romantic, Soulful, Wacky	1967	5.00	12.00
United Arts. UAS-6599	(S)	Romantic, Soulful, Wacky	1967	6.00	15.00
United Arts. UAS-6642	(S)	Honey	1968	6.00	15.00
United Arts. UAS-6657	(S)	Word Pictures	1968	6.00	15.00
United Arts. UAS-6704	(S)	Today	1969	6.00	15.00
United Arts. UAS-6735	(S)	Muddy Mississippi Line	1970	6.00	15.00
United Arts. UAS-5502	(S)	Bobby Goldsboro's Greatest Hits	1970	5.00	12.00
United Arts. UAS-6777	(S)	We Gotta Start Lovin'	1971	5.00	12.00
United Arts. UAS-5516	(S)	Summer (The First Time)	1971	5.00	12.00
Doral	(S)	Doral Presents Bobby Goldboro	1971	8.00	20.00
		(Promotional compilation of previously released material.)			

GOLDSBORO, BOBBY, & DEL REEVES
| United Arts. UAL-3615 | (M) | Our Way Of Life | 1967 | 5.00 | 12.00 |
| United Arts. UAS-6615 | (S) | Our Way Of Life | 1967 | 6.00 | 15.00 |

GOLDTONES, THE
| LaBrea L-8011 | (M) | The Goldtones Featuring Randy Seol | 196? | 20.00 | 50.00 |
| LaBrea LS-8011 | (S) | The Goldtones Featuring Randy Seol | 196? | 30.00 | 75.00 |

GOLLIWOGS, THE
The Golliwogs was an early incarnation of Creedence Clearwater Revival.
| Fantasy F-9474 | (M) | Pre-Creedence | 1975 | 10.00 | 25.00 |

GOOD & PLENTY
| Senate 21001 | (S) | The World Of Good & Plenty | 196? | 10.00 | 25.00 |

GOOD GUYS, THE
The Good Guys is a pseudonym for The Challengers.
| Crescendo GNP-2001 | (M) | Sidewalk Surfing *(Red label)* | 1964 | 8.00 | 20.00 |
| Crescendo GNPS-2001 | (S) | Sidewalk Surfing *(Red label)* | 1964 | 10.00 | 25.00 |

GOOD GUYS, THE
| United Arts. UAL-3370 | (M) | The Good Guys Sing | 1964 | 5.00 | 12.00 |
| United Arts. UAS-6370 | (S) | The Good Guys Sing | 1964 | 6.00 | 15.00 |

GOOD OLD BOYS, THE
| Round 576 | (S) | Pistol Packin' Mama | 1976 | 10.00 | 25.00 |

GOOD RATS, THE
Kapp KS-3580	(S)	The Good Rats	1969	10.00	25.00
Warner Bros. BS-2813	(S)	Tasty	1974	5.00	12.00
Passport SP-20	(DJ)	Rats The Way You Like It-Live	1978	20.00	50.00

GOOD TIMES, THE
| Kama Sutra KLP-8052 | (M) | The Good Times | 1966 | 6.00 | 15.00 |
| Kama Sutra KLPS-8052 | (S) | The Good Times | 1966 | 8.00 | 20.00 |

Label & Catalog #		Title	Year	VG+	NM
GOODIES, THE					
Hip HIS-7002	(S)	**Candy Coated Goodies**	1969	10.00	25.00
GOODING, CYNTHIA					
Ms. Gooding also recorded with Theodore Bikel.					
Elektra EKL-8	(M)	**Mexican Folk Songs**	195?	10.00	25.00
Elektra EKL-17	(M)	**Italian Folk Songs**	195?	10.00	25.00
Elektra EKL-107	(M)	**Faithful Lovers And Other Phenomena**	195?	10.00	25.00
Elektra EKL-131	(M)	**Queen Of Hearts**	195?	10.00	25.00
Riverside RLP-12-830	(M)	**Languages Of Love**	195?	10.00	25.00
GOODMAN, DICKIE					
Refer to Buchanan & Goodman.					
Rori 3301	(M)	**The Many Heads Of Dickie Goodman**	1962	30.00	75.00
Cash 451	(M)	**Mr. Jaws**	1974	10.00	25.00
Comet 69	(M)	**My Son, The Joke**	197?	6.00	15.00
GOODMAN, DODY					
Coral CRL-57196	(M)	**Dody Goodman Sings**	1957	12.00	30.00
GOODTHUNDER					
Elektra EKS7-5041	(S)	**Goodthunder**	1972	6.00	15.00
GORDIAN KNOT, THE					
Verve V-5062	(M)	**Tones**	1968	6.00	15.00
Verve V6-5062	(S)	**Tones**	1968	6.00	15.00
GORDON, HONI: *Refer to* GOLDMINE'S PRICE GUIDE TO COLLECTIBLE JAZZ ALBUMS					
GORDON, ROBERT					
RCA Victor AFL1-3294	(DJ)	**Rock Billy Boogie** (White vinyl)	1979	6.00	15.00
RCA Victor DJL1-3411	(DJ)	**The Essential Robert Gordon**	1979	6.00	15.00
GORDON 'N ROGERS					
Capitol STAO-276	(S)	**Bug In!**	1969	8.00	20.00
GORE, CHARLIE					
Audio Lab AL-1526	(M)	**The Country Gentleman**	1959	40.00	100.00
GORE, LESLEY					
Mercury MG-20805	(M)	**I'll Cry If I Want To**	1963	12.00	30.00
Mercury SR-60805	(S)	**I'll Cry If I Want To**	1963	16.00	40.00
Mercury MG-20849	(M)	**Lesley Gore Sings Of Mixed Up Hearts**	1963	12.00	30.00
Mercury SR-60849	(S)	**Lesley Gore Sings Of Mixed Up Hearts**	1963	16.00	40.00
Mercury MG-20901	(M)	**Boys, Boys, Boys**	1964	12.00	30.00
Mercury SR-60901	(S)	**Boys, Boys, Boys**	1964	16.00	40.00
Mercury MG-20943	(M)	**Girl Talk**	1964	12.00	30.00
Mercury SR-60943	(S)	**Girl Talk**	1964	16.00	40.00
Mercury MG-21024	(M)	**The Golden Hits Of Lesley Gore**	1965	8.00	20.00
Mercury SR-61024	(S)	**The Golden Hits Of Lesley Gore** (12 tracks)	1965	12.00	30.00
		(The stereo "Look Of Love," "You Don't Own Me" and "I Don't Wanna Be A Loser" are different takes than the mono versions.)			
Mercury SR-61024	(S)	**The Golden Hits Of Lesley Gore** (10 tracks)	196?	6.00	15.00
Mercury MG-21042	(M)	**My Town, My Guy And Me**	1965	8.00	20.00
Mercury SR-61042	(S)	**My Town, My Guy And Me**	1965	12.00	30.00
Mercury MG-21066	(M)	**All About Love**	1966	8.00	20.00
Mercury SR-61066	(S)	**All About Love**	1966	12.00	30.00
Mercury MG-21120	(M)	**California Nights**	1967	8.00	20.00
Mercury SR-61120	(S)	**California Nights**	1967	12.00	30.00
Mercury SR-61185	(S)	**The Golden Hits Of Lesley Gore, Volume 2**	1968	8.00	20.00
Wing SRW-16350	(S)	**Girl Talk**	1968	8.00	20.00
		(Wing SRW-16350 is a reissue of Mercury 60943.)			
Wing SRW-16382	(S)	**Love, Love, Love**	1968	8.00	20.00
		(Wing 16382 is a reissue of Mercury 61066.)			
Wing PKW-2-119	(S)	**The Sound Of Young Love** (2 LPs)	1969	12.00	30.00
		(Wing 119 repackages 16350 and 16382.)			
Mowest MW-117L	(S)	**Someplace Else Now**	1972	6.00	15.00
A&M SP-4564	(S)	**Love Me By Name**	1975	6.00	15.00

Label & Catalog #		Title	Year	VG+	NM
GORME, EYDIE					
Ms. Gorme also recorded with Steve Lawrence.					
Coral CRL-57109	(M)	Delight	1957	14.00	35.00
ABC-Paramount 150	(M)	Eydie Gorme	1957	14.00	35.00
ABC-Paramount 192	(M)	Eydie Swings The Blues	1957	14.00	35.00
ABC-Paramount 218	(M)	Eydie Gorme Vamps The Roaring '20s	1958	14.00	35.00
ABC-Paramount 246	(M)	Eydie In Love	1958	14.00	35.00
ABC-Paramount 254	(M)	Showstoppers	1958	10.00	25.00
ABC-Paramount S-254	(S)	Showstoppers	1958	14.00	35.00
ABC-Paramount 273	(M)	Love Is A Season	1958	10.00	25.00
ABC-Paramount S-273	(S)	Love Is A Season	1958	14.00	35.00
ABC-Paramount 307	(M)	Eydie Gorme On Stage	1959	10.00	25.00
ABC-Paramount S-307	(S)	Eydie Gorme On Stage	1959	14.00	35.00
United Arts. UAL-3143	(M)	Come Sing With Me	1961	6.00	15.00
United Arts. UAS-6143	(S)	Come Sing With Me	1961	8.00	20.00
United Arts. UAL-3189	(M)	The Very Best Of Eydie Gorme	1962	6.00	15.00
United Arts. UAS-6189	(S)	The Very Best Of Eydie Gorme	1962	8.00	20.00
Columbia CL-2012	(M)	Blame It On The Bossa Nova	1963	6.00	15.00
Columbia CS-8812	(S)	Blame It On The Bossa Nova	1963	8.00	20.00
Columbia CL-2065	(M)	Let The Good Times Roll	1963	5.00	12.00
Columbia CS-8865	(S)	Let The Good Times Roll	1963	6.00	15.00
Columbia CL-2120	(M)	Gorme Country Style	1964	5.00	12.00
Columbia CS-8920	(S)	Gorme Country Style	1964	6.00	15.00
Columbia CL-2203	(M)	Amor	1964	5.00	12.00
Columbia CS-9003	(S)	Amor	1964	6.00	15.00
Columbia CL-2300	(M)	The Sound Of Music	1965	5.00	12.00
Columbia CS-9100	(S)	The Sound Of Music	1965	6.00	15.00
Columbia CL-2376	(M)	More Amor	1965	5.00	12.00
Columbia CS-9176	(S)	More Amor	1965	6.00	15.00
Columbia CL-2476	(M)	Don't Go To Strangers	1966	5.00	12.00
Columbia CS-9276	(S)	Don't Go To Strangers	1966	6.00	15.00
Columbia CL-2594	(M)	Softly, As I Leave You	1967	5.00	12.00
Columbia CS-9394	(S)	Softly, As I Leave You	1967	6.00	15.00
Columbia CL-2764	(M)	Eydie Gorme's Greatest Hits	1967	5.00	12.00
Columbia CS-9564	(S)	Eydie Gorme's Greatest Hits	1967	6.00	15.00
		— Original Columbia albums above have "360 Sound" labels.—			
GOSDIN BROTHERS, THE					
Vern and Rex Gosdin. Refer to Gene Clark; The Hillmen.					
Capitol ST-2852	(S)	Sounds Of Goodbye	1968	12.00	30.00
GOULDMAN, GRAHAM					
RCA Victor LPM-3954	(M)	Graham Gouldman Thing	1968	30.00	75.00
RCA Victor LSP-3954	(S)	Graham Gouldman Thing	1968	20.00	50.00
GRACEFUL HEAD					
Excelsior	(S)	Graceful Head	198?	40.00	100.00
		(Limited edition pressed from recently unearthed tapes.)			
GRACEN, THELMA: Refer to GOLDMINE'S PRICE GUIDE TO COLLECTIBLE JAZZ ALBUMS					
GRACIOUS					
Gracious features Paul Davis.					
Capitol ST-602	(S)	Gracious	1970	16.00	40.00
GRAHAM CENTRAL STATION					
Warner Bros. BS4-2763	(Q)	Graham Central Station	1975	6.00	15.00
Warner Bros. BS4-2876	(Q)	Ain't No 'Bout-A-Doubt It	1975	6.00	15.00
GRAMMER, BILLY					
Monument MLP-4000	(M)	Travelin' On	1961	10.00	25.00
Monument SLP-14000	(P)	Travelin' On	1961	16.00	40.00
GRAND FUNK RAILROAD					
Mark Farner, Don Brewer, Mel Schacher and Craig Frost. Refer to Terry Knight.					
Capitol ST-307	(S)	On Time	1969	8.00	20.00
Capitol SKAO-406	(S)	Grand Funk	1969	8.00	20.00
Capitol SKAO-471	(S)	Closer To Home	1970	8.00	20.00
Capitol SWBB-633	(S)	Grand Funk/Live Album	1970	8.00	20.00

Label & Catalog #		Title	Year	VG+	NM
Capitol SW-764	(S)	**Survival**	1971	8.00	20.00
Capitol SW-853	(S)	**E Pluribus Funk**	1971	8.00	20.00
		— Original Capitol albums above have green labels.—			
Capitol SMAS-11207	(DJ)	**We're An American Band** (Gold vinyl)	1973	10.00	25.00
Capitol SMAS-11207	(S)	**We're An American Band** (Gold vinyl)	1973	6.00	15.00
		(Both the DJ and stock copies include a sheet of four stickers.)			

GRAND THEFT

No label	(S)	**Grand Theft** (Issued without a cover)	197?	150.00	300.00

GRANDMA'S ROCKERS

Fredlo 6727	(M)	**Homemade Apple Pie**	1967	750.00	1,500.00

GRANICUS

RCA Victor AFL1-0321	(S)	**Granicus**	1973	6.00	15.00

GRANMAX

Panam 1002	(S)	**A Ninth Alive** (White vinyl)	1977	6.00	15.00
Panam 1023	(S)	**Kiss Heaven Goodbye**	1978	6.00	15.00

GRANT, GOGI

Era 20001	(M)	**Suddenly There's Gogi Grant** (Red vinyl)	1956	40.00	100.00
Era 20001	(M)	**Suddenly There's Gogi Grant**	1957	20.00	50.00
RCA Victor LOC-1030	(M)	**The Helen Morgan Story** (Soundtrack)	1957	20.00	50.00
RCA Victor LPM-1717	(M)	**Welcome To My Heart**	1958	14.00	35.00
RCA Victor LPM-1940	(M)	**Torch Time**	1959	10.00	25.00
RCA Victor LSP-1940	(S)	**Torch Time**	1959	14.00	35.00
RCA Victor LPM-1984	(M)	**Kiss Me, Kate**	1959	10.00	25.00
RCA Victor LSP-1984	(S)	**Kiss Me, Kate**	1959	14.00	35.00
Liberty LRP-3144	(M)	**If You Want To Get To Heaven, Shout**	1959	8.00	20.00
Liberty LST-7144	(S)	**If You Want To Get To Heaven, Shout**	1959	10.00	25.00
Era EL-106	(M)	**The Wayward Wind**	1960	16.00	40.00
Charter C-107	(S)	**City Girl In The Country**	1964	6.00	15.00
Charter CS-107	(M)	**City Girl In The Country**	1964	8.00	20.00

GRAPEFRUIT

Dunhill DS-50050	(S)	**Around Grapefruit**	1968	8.00	20.00
RCA Victor LSP-4215	(S)	**Deep water**	1969	6.00	15.00

GRASS ROOTS, THE

Originally a studio concoction of Steve Barri and Phil Sloan (Dunhill 50011), their initial success lead to the formation of a "real" group based around vocalist Rob Grill.

Dunhill D-50011	(M)	**Where Were You When I Needed You?**	1966	20.00	50.00
Dunhill DS-50011	(S)	**Where Were You When I Needed You?**	1966	30.00	75.00
Dunhill D-50020	(M)	**Let's Live For Today**	1967	10.00	25.00
Dunhill DS-50020	(S)	**Let's Live For Today**	1967	12.00	30.00
Dunhill D-50027	(M)	**Feelings**	1968	8.00	20.00
Dunhill DS-50027	(S)	**Feelings**	1968	6.00	15.00
Dunhill DS-50047	(S)	**Golden Grass**	1968	6.00	15.00
Dunhill DS-50052	(S)	**Lovin' Things**	1969	6.00	15.00
Dunhill DS-50067	(S)	**Leavin' It All Behind**	1969	6.00	15.00
Dunhill DS-50087	(S)	**More Golden Grass**	1970	6.00	15.00
Command QD-40013	(Q)	**Their 16 Greatest Hits**	1974	10.00	25.00

GRATEFUL DEAD, THE

Original members were Jerry Garcia, Bill Kreutzmann, Phil Lesh, Ron "Pig Pen" McKernan (died 1973), Bob Weir and lyricist Robert Hunter. Mickey Hart joined in 1967, left 1970 and rejoined 1974. Tom Constanten was a member 1968-70; Keith and Donna Godchaux, 1971-1978; Brent Mydland, 1979 through his death in 1990. Refer to Bob Dylan; Ken Kesey; Kingfish; The Rhythm Devils; Touchstone.

Warner Bros. W-1689	(M)	**The Grateful Dead**	1967	30.00	75.00
Warner Bros. WS-1689	(S)	**The Grateful Dead**	1967	16.00	40.00
		— Original Warner albums above have gold labels.—			
Warner Bros. WS-1689	(S)	**The Grateful Dead**	1968	8.00	20.00
Warner Bros. WS-1749	(S)	**Anthem Of The Sun** (Purple cover)	1968	8.00	20.00
Warner Bros. WS-1749	(S)	**Anthem Of The Sun** (White cover)	197?	20.00	50.00
		(Green label with "WB" logo and remixed by Lesh.)			
Warner Bros. WS-1790	(S)	**Aoxomoxoa**	1969	8.00	20.00
Warner Bros. 2WS-1830	(S)	**Live/Dead** (2 LPs with booklet)	1970	12.00	30.00
		— Original Warner albums above have green labels with a "W7" logo on top.—			

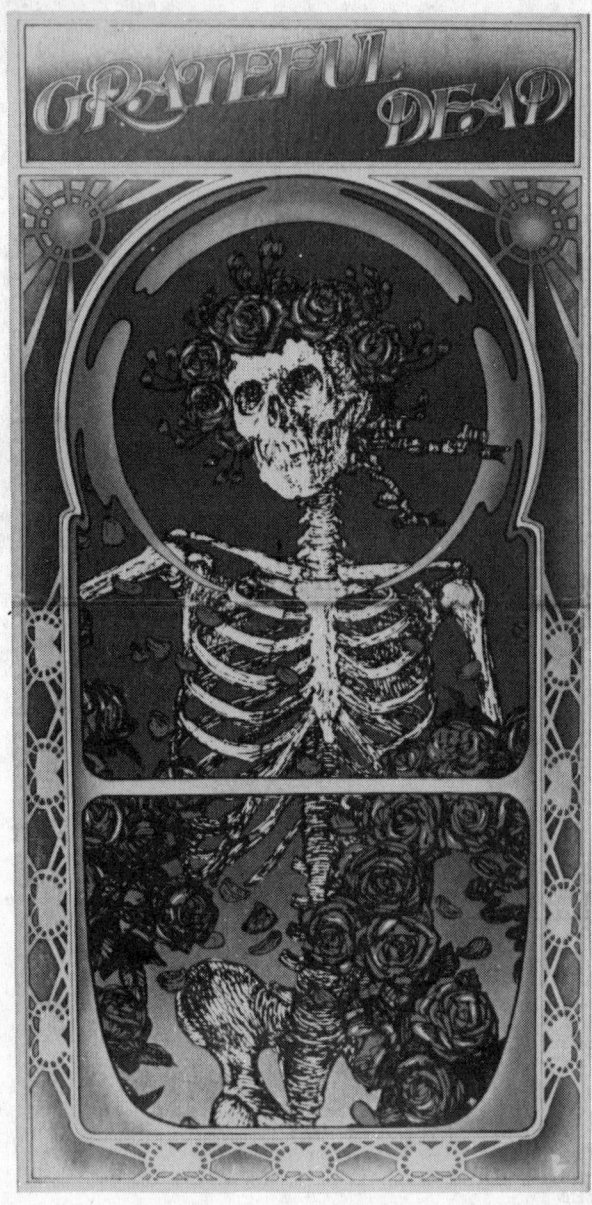

This eponymous live double (Warner Bros. 1935, 1971) is referred to as the "Skull & Roses" album in deference to the beautiful artwork of Alton Kelley, one of the original— and finest— of the San Francisco psychedelic poster artists. While the Dead are the epitome of artists who haven't "sold out" they have nonetheless sold well: two dozen charting albums with eight RIAA Gold Records.

Label & Catalog #		Title	Year	VG+	NM
Warner Bros. WS-1869	(S)	**Workingman's Dead**	1970	6.00	15.00
Warner Bros. WS-1893	(S)	**American Beauty**	1970	6.00	15.00
Warner Bros. 2WS-1935	(S)	**Grateful Dead** (2 LPs)	1971	10.00	25.00
		(First pressing with a "Skull & Roses" sticker on the front.)			
Warner Bros. 2WS-1935	(S)	**Grateful Dead** (2 LPs)	1972	6.00	15.00
		(Without the "Skull & Roses" sticker.)			
Warner Bros. 3WX-2668	(S)	**Europe '72** (3 LPs)	1972	8.00	20.00
		— Original Warner albums above have green labels with a "WB" logo on top.—			
Sunflower SUN-5001	(S)	**Vintage Dead**	1970	8.00	20.00
		(Counterfeits are 1/4" shorter than normal album covers.)			
Sunflower SNF-5004	(S)	**Historic Dead**	1971	8.00	20.00
Pride PRD-0016	(S)	**History Of The Grateful Dead**	1972	10.00	25.00
Verve V6-5093	(S)	**Grateful Dead**	1972		Unreleased
		(As Verve was owned by MGM, this may have been a reissue of			
		the Sunflower material or additional live recordings from 1966.)			
Grateful Dead GD-01	(S)	**Wake Of The Flood** (Green vinyl)	1973	150.00	300.00
		(The green vinyl was issued to members of the fan club.			
		Most of the copies were damaged by local flooding!)			
Grateful Dead GD-01	(S)	**Wake Of The Flood**	1973	10.00	25.00
		(First pressings do not have contributing artists on the back.)			
Grateful Dead GD-01	(S)	**Wake Of The Flood**	1975	6.00	15.00
		(Second pressings have contributing artists listed on the back.)			
Grateful Dead GD-102	(S)	**From The Mars Hotel**	1974	10.00	25.00
Grateful Dead LA-494	(S)	**Blues For Allah**	1975	8.00	20.00
United Arts. SP-114	(DJ)	**For Dead Heads**	1975	12.00	30.00
Grateful Dead LA-620	(S)	**Steal Your Face** (2 LPs)	1976	8.00	20.00
Arista SP-35	(DJ)	**Grateful Dead Sampler**	1977	12.00	30.00
Arista AL-7001	(DJ)	**Terrapin Station** (Banded for air-play)	1977	12.00	30.00
Mobile Fidelity MFSL-014	(S)	**American Beauty**	1978	20.00	60.00
Mobile Fidelity MFSL-172	(S)	**From The Mars Hotel**	1980	12.00	30.00
Direct Disk SD-16619	(S)	**Terrapin Station**	1980	50.00	150.00
Arista A2L-8604	(S)	**Reckoning** (2 LPs)	1981	8.00	20.00
Arista A2L-8606	(S)	**Dead Set** (2 LPs)	1981	5.00	12.00

GRAVENITES, NICK
Refer to Mike Bloomfield & Nick Gravenites; The Electric Flag; Big Brother & The Holding Company

Columbia CS-9899	(S)	**My Labors**	1969	6.00	15.00

GRAVES, TERESA

Kirshner KES-104	(S)	**Teresa Graves**	1970	8.00	20.00

GRAVITY ADJUSTERS EXPANSION BAND

Nocturne NRS-302	(S)	**One**	1973	18.00	200.00

GRAY, BILLY

Decca DL-5567 (10")	(M)	**Dance-O-Rama #7**	1955	100.00	250.00

GRAY, DOBIE
Dobie Gray later recorded with Pollution.

Stripe LPM-2001	(M)	**Look-Dobie Gray**	1963	40.00	100.00
Charger CHR-M-2002	(M)	**Dobie Gray Sings For In Crowders**	1965	20.00	50.00
Charger CHR-S-2002	(S)	**Dobie Gray Sings For In Crowders**	1965	30.00	75.00
Decca DL-75397	(S)	**Drift Away**	1973	5.00	12.00

GRAY, CLAUDE (& THE GRAYMEN)

Mercury MG-20658	(M)	**Songs Of Broken Love Affairs**	1962	6.00	15.00
Mercury SR-60658	(S)	**Songs Of Broken Love Affairs**	1962	8.00	20.00
Mercury MG-20718	(M)	**Country Goes To Town**	1962	6.00	15.00
Mercury SR-60718	(S)	**Country Goes To Town**	1962	8.00	20.00
Decca DL-4882	(M)	**Claude Gray Sings**	1967	6.00	15.00
Decca DL-74882	(S)	**Claude Gray Sings**	1967	6.00	15.00
Decca DL-74963	(S)	**The Easy Way Of Claude Gray**	1968	6.00	15.00

GRAY, DOLORES

Capitol T-897	(M)	**Warm Brandy**	1957	12.00	30.00

GRAYCO, HELEN

Vik LX-1066	(M)	**After Midnight**	1957	10.00	25.00

Label & Catalog #		Title	Year	VG+	NM

GRAYSON, KATHRYN

MGM E-551 (10")	(M)	Kathryn Grayson	1952	20.00	50.00
MGM E-3077 (10")	(M)	Kiss Me Kate (Soundtrack)	1953	40.00	100.00
RCA Victor LOC-3000 (10")	(M)	So This Is Love (Soundtrack)	1953	40.00	100.00
RCA Victor LPM-3105 (10")	(M)	The Desert Song (Soundtrack)	1953	40.00	100.00
MGM E-3257	(M)	Kathryn Grayson Sings	1956	16.00	40.00
Lion L-7055	M)	Kathryn Grayson	1959	10.00	25.00

GREAT SOCIETY, THE
The Great Society features Grace Slick, later of Jefferson Airplane.

| Columbia CS-9624 | (S) | Conspicuous Only In Its Absence | 1968 | 10.00 | 25.00 |
| Columbia CS-9702 | (S) | How It Was | 1968 | 10.00 | 25.00 |

— *Original Columbia albums above have "360 Sound" on the bottom of the label.—*

| Columbia G-30459 | (S) | The Great Society/Collectors Item (2 LPs) | 1971 | 8.00 | 20.00 |
| Harmony KH-30391 | (S) | Somebody To Love | 197? | 6.00 | 15.00 |

GRECO, JULIETTE

| Columbia CL-569 | (M) | Juliette Greco | 1954 | 12.00 | 30.00 |
| Columbia CL-992 | (M) | Greco | 1957 | 12.00 | 30.00 |

GREEK FOUNTAIN RIVER FRONT BAND, THE

| Montel LLP-110 | (M) | The Greek Fountain River Front Band Takes Requests | 1965 | 30.00 | 75.00 |

GREEN

| Atco SD-33-282 | (S) | Green | 1969 | 6.00 | 15.00 |
| Atco SD-33-366 | (S) | To Help Somebody | 1971 | 4.00 | 10.00 |

GREEN, AL

Hot Line 1500	(M)	Back Up Train	1967	10.00	25.00
Hot Line 1500	(S)	Back Up Train	1967	12.00	30.00
Bell 6076	(S)	Al Green	1971	8.00	20.00
Hi SHL-32055	(S)	Green Is Blues	1969	6.00	15.00
Hi SHL-32062	(S)	Al Green Gets Next To You	1971	6.00	15.00
Hi SHL-32070	(S)	Let's Stay Together	1972	6.00	15.00
Hi SHL-32074	(S)	I'm Still In Love With You	1972	6.00	15.00
Hi SHL-32077	(S)	Call Me	1973	6.00	15.00
Hi SHL-32082	(S)	Livin' For You	1973	6.00	15.00
Hi SHL-32087	(S)	Al Green Explores Your Mind	1974	6.00	15.00
Hi SHL-32089	(S)	Al Green's Greatest Hits	1975	6.00	15.00
Hi SHL-32092	(S)	Al Green Is Love	1975	6.00	15.00

— *Original Hi albums above have grey labels.—*

Hi SHL-32097	(S)	Full Of Fire	1976	4.00	10.00
Hi SHL-32103	(S)	Have A Good Time	1976	4.00	10.00
Hi SHL-32105	(S)	Al Green's Greatest Hits, Volume 2	1977	4.00	10.00
Hi SHL-8000	(S)	Tired Of Being Alone	1977	4.00	10.00
Hi SHL-6004	(S)	The Belle Album	1977	4.00	10.00
Hi SHL-6009	(S)	Truth 'N' Time	1978	4.00	10.00

GREEN, LLOYD

Time 2152	(M)	Big Steel Guitar	196?	8.00	20.00
Little Darlin' LD-4002	(M)	Day For Decision	1967	5.00	12.00
Little Darlin' SLD-8002	(S)	Day For Decision	1967	6.00	15.00
Little Darlin' LD-4005	(M)	Hit Sounds	1967	5.00	12.00
Little Darlin' SLD-8005	(S)	Hit Sounds	1967	6.00	15.00
Little Darlin' SLD-8021	(S)	Green Country	1968	6.00	15.00

GREEN, PETER
Green was formerly a member of Fleetwood Mac.

| Reprise RS-6436 | (S) | The End Of The Game | 1971 | 8.00 | 20.00 |

GREEN, VERNON, & THE MEDALLIONS

| Dooto DLT-857 | (M) | Vernon Green & The Medallions | 197? | 12.00 | 30.00 |

GREEN BULLFROG
Green Bullfrog features Richie Blackmore and Jon Lord of Deep Purple.

| Decca DL-75269 | (S) | Green Bullfrog | 1971 | 10.00 | 25.00 |

Label & Catalog #		Title	Year	VG+	NM
GREEN ON RED					
Green On Red 714	(S)	**Green On Red** (Red vinyl)	1981	40.00	100.00
GREEN RIVER BOYS, THE: Refer to GLEN CAMPBELL					
GREENBAUM, NORMAN					
Norman was formerly a member of Dr. West's Medicine Show & Jug Band.					
Gregar GG-101	(E)	**Norman Greenbaum**	1970	8.00	20.00
Reprise RS-6365	(S)	**Spirit In The Sky**	1969	6.00	15.00
Reprise RS-6422	(S)	**Back Home Again**	1969	4.00	10.00
GREENBRIAR BOYS, THE					
The Greenbriar Boys also recorded with Dian James.					
Vanguard VR-9104	(M)	**The Greenbriar Boys**	1962	6.00	15.00
Vanguard VRS-9104	(S)	**The Greenbriar Boys**	1962	8.00	20.00
Vanguard VSD-9159	(M)	**Ragged But Right!**	1964	5.00	12.00
Vanguard VSD-79159	(S)	**Ragged But Right!**	1964	6.00	15.00
Vanguard VSD-9233	(M)	**Better Late Than Never**	1966	5.00	12.00
Vanguard VSD-79233	(S)	**Better Late Than Never**	1966	6.00	15.00
GREENE, BERNIE, & HIS STEREO MAD-MEN					
RCA Victor LPM-1929	(M)	**Musically Mad**	1958	20.00	50.00
RCA Victor LSP-1929	(S)	**Musically Mad**	1958	30.00	75.00
GREENE, DODO: Refer to GOLDMINE'S PRICE GUIDE TO COLLECTIBLE JAZZ ALBUMS					
GREENE, LORNE					
RCA Victor LPM-2661	(M)	**Young At Last**	1963	8.00	20.00
RCA Victor LSP-2661	(S)	**Young At Last**	1963	10.00	25.00
RCA Victor LPM-2843	(M)	**Welcome To The Ponderosa**	1964	8.00	20.00
RCA Victor LSP-2843	(S)	**Welcome To The Ponderosa**	1964	10.00	25.00
RCA Victor SP-33-327	(DJ)	**Palaver With The Man**	1965	20.00	50.00
		(Open-end interview issued with a script.)			
RCA Victor LPM-3302	(M)	**Lorne Greene-The Man**	1965	8.00	20.00
RCA Victor LSP-3302	(S)	**Lorne Greene-The Man**	1965	10.00	25.00
RCA Victor LPM-3409	(M)	**Lorne Greene's American West**	1965	8.00	20.00
RCA Victor LSP-3409	(S)	**Lorne Greene's American West**	1965	10.00	25.00
RCA Victor LPM-3410	(M)	**Have A Happy Holiday**	1965	8.00	20.00
RCA Victor LSP-3410	(S)	**Have A Happy Holiday**	1965	10.00	25.00
RCA Victor LPM-3678	(M)	**Portrait Of The West**	1966	8.00	20.00
RCA Victor LSP-3678	(S)	**Portrait Of The West**	1966	10.00	25.00
GREENHILL, MITCH					
Folklore FRLP-14026	(M)	**Pickin' The City Blues**	1964	6.00	15.00
Folklore FRST-14026	(S)	**Pickin' The City Blues**	1964	8.00	20.00
Prestige PRLP-7438	(M)	**Shepherd Of The Highway**	1966	6.00	15.00
Prestige PRST-7438	(S)	**Shepherd Of The Highway**	1966	8.00	20.00
GREENHILL SINGERS, THE					
United Arts. UAL-3347	(M)	**50 Fabulous Folk Favorites** (2 LPs)	1964	6.00	15.00
United Arts. UAS-6347	(S)	**50 Fabulous Folk Favorites** (2 LPs)	1964	8.00	20.00
GREENSLEEVES, EDDIE					
Cameo C-1031	(M)	**Humorous Folk Songs**	1963	8.00	20.00
Cameo SC-1031	(S)	**Humorous Folk Songs**	1963	10.00	25.00
GREENWICH, ELLIE					
Ms. Greenwich was formerly a member of The Raindrops.					
United Arts. UAS-6648	(S)	**Composes, Produces And Sings**	1968	10.00	25.00
Verve V6-5091	(S)	**Let It Be Written, Let It Be Sung**	1973	6.00	15.00
GREENWOODS, THE					
Decca DL-4496	(M)	**Folk Instrumentals**	1964	5.00	12.00
Decca DL-74496	(S)	**Folk Instrumentals**	1964	6.00	15.00
GREER					
Sugarbush SBS-109	(S)	**Between Two Worlds**	197?	60.00	150.00

Label & Catalog #		Title	Year	VG+	NM
GREGG, BOBBY					
Epic LN-24051	(M)	"Let's Stomp" And "Wild Weekend"	1963	8.00	20.00
Epic BN-26051	(S)	"Let's Stomp" And "Wild Weekend"	1963	12.00	30.00
GRIFFIN, JAMES					
Refer to Bread.					
Reprise R-6091	(M)	**Summer Holiday**	1963	14.00	35.00
Reprise R9-6091	(S)	**Summer Holiday**	1963	20.00	50.00
GRIFFITH, ANDY					
Capitol T-962	(M)	**Just For Laughs**	1958	12.00	30.00
Capitol T-1105	(M)	**Shouts The Blues And Old Time Songs**	1959	12.00	30.00
Capitol T-1215	(M)	**This Here Andy Griffith**	1959	10.00	25.00
Capitol T-1611	(M)	**The Andy Griffith Show**	1961	8.00	20.00
Capitol ST-1611	(S)	**The Andy Griffith Show**	1961	12.00	30.00
Capitol T-2066	(M)	**Andy And Cleopatra**	1964	6.00	15.00
Capitol ST-2066	(S)	**Andy And Cleopatra**	1964	8.00	20.00
GRIFFITH, SHIRLEY					
Bluesvile BVLP-1087	(M)	**The Blues Of Shirley Griffith**	1964	16.00	40.00
GROOM, DEWEY, & THE TEXAS LONGHORNS					
Longhorn LP-004	(M)	**Last Of The Big Bands**	196?	30.00	75.00
GROOTNA					
Grootna features Marty Balin.					
Columbia C-31033	(S)	**Grootna**	1971	6.00	15.00
GROOV-U					
Gateway GLP-3010	(M)	**Groov-U On Campus**	196?	16.00	40.00
GROOVIE GOOLIES, THE					
RCA Victor LSP-4420	(S)	**The Groovie Goolies**	1970	8.00	20.00
GROUNDHOGS, THE					
Cleve CH-82871	(S)	**The Groundhogs With John Lee Hooker**			
		And John Mayall	1968	30.00	75.00
World Pacific WPS-21892	(S)	**Scratching The Surface**	1968	16.00	40.00
Imperial LP-12452	(S)	**Blues Obituary**	1969	16.00	40.00
Liberty LST-7644	(S)	**Thank Christ For The Bomb**	1970	14.00	35.00
United Arts. UAS-5513	(S)	**The Groundhogs Split**	1971	10.00	25.00
United Arts. UAS-5570	(S)	**Who Will Save The World**	1972	10.00	25.00
United Arts. LA008	(S)	**Hogwash**	1973	10.00	25.00
United Arts. LA603	(S)	**Crosscut Saw**	1976	10.00	25.00
United Arts. LA680	(S)	**Black Diamond**	1976	10.00	25.00
GROUNDSTAR					
Stellar SR-2549	(S)	**Forced Landing**	1980	12.00	30.00
GROUP, THE					
RCA Victor LPM-2663	(M)	**The Group**	1963	8.00	20.00
RCA Victor LSP-2663	(S)	**The Group**	1963	10.00	25.00
GROUP, THE					
Bell 6038	(S)	**The Group**	1970	8.00	20.00
GROUP IMAGE, THE					
Community A-101	(S)	**A Mouth In The Clouds**	1968	8.00	20.00
GROUP ONE					
RCA Victor LPM-3524	(M)	**Brothers Go To Mothers And Others**	1966	6.00	15.00
RCA Victor LST-3524	(S)	**Brothers Go To Mothers And Others**	1966	8.00	20.00
GROUP THERAPY					
RCA Victor LSP-3976	(S)	**People Get Ready For Group Therapy**	1968	8.00	20.00
Philips PHS-600-303	(S)	**37 Minutes Of Group Therapy**	1969	6.00	15.00
GROUPIES, THE					
Earth ELPS-1000	(S)	**The Groupies** *(Documentary)*	196?	16.00	40.00

Label & Catalog #		Title	Year	VG+	NM

GROVE, BOBBY

| King 831 | (M) | It Was For You | 1963 | 16.00 | 40.00 |

GROWING CONCERN, THE

| Mainstream 56108 | (M) | Growing Concern | 1968 | 16.00 | 40.00 |
| Mainstream S-6108 | (S) | Growing Concern | 1968 | 16.00 | 40.00 |

GRYPHON
(No label)

| (No label) | (S) | Gryphon | 197? | 24.00 | 60.00 |

GRYPHON

| Bell 1316 | (S) | Red Queen To Gryphon Three | 1974 | 6.00 | 15.00 |

GUARD, DAVE, & THE WHISKEYHILL SINGERS
Dave Guard olater recorded as a member of The Kingston Trio.

Capitol T-1728	(M)	Dave Guard & The Whiskeyhill Singers	1962	12.00	30.00
Capitol ST-1728	(S)	Dave Guard & The Whiskeyhill Singers	1962	16.00	40.00
MGM 1E-5	(M)	How The West Was Won (Soundtrack)	1963	14.00	35.00
MGM S1E-5	(S)	How The West Was Won (Soundtrack)	1963	16.00	45.00

GUESS WHO, THE
The original group was formed by Chad Allan, who left in 1965, and Randy Bachman, who left in 1970. Burton Cummings joined in 1965. Refer to Chad Allan & The Expressions; Brave Belt.

Wand WDS-691	(E)	Born In Canada	1969	10.00	25.00
MGM SE-4645	(S)	The Guess Who	1969	10.00	25.00
RCA Victor LSP-4141	(S)	Wheatfield Soul	1969	10.00	25.00
RCA Victor LSP-4157	(S)	Canned Wheat	1969	8.00	20.00
RCA Victor LSP-4266	(S)	American Woman	1970	6.00	15.00
RCA Victor LSP-4359	(S)	Share The Land	1970	6.00	15.00
RCA Victor LSP-4574	(S)	So Long, Bannatyne	1971	6.00	15.00
RCA Victor LSP-4602	(S)	Rockin'	1972	6.00	15.00
RCA Victor LSP-4779	(S)	Live At The Paramount	1972	12.00	30.00
RCA Victor LSP-4830	(S)	Artificial Paradise (With paper bag)	1972	10.00	25.00
RCA Victor APD1-0130	(Q)	Guess Who No. 10	1973	8.00	20.00
RCA Victor APD1-0269	(Q)	The Best Of The Guess Who, Volume 2	1974	8.00	20.00
RCA Victor APD1-0405	(Q)	Road Food	1974	8.00	20.00
		— Original RCA albums above have orange labels.—			
Pickwick SPC-3246	(S)	Wild One	197?	6.00	15.00
Pickwick ACL-7069	(S)	Wheatfield Soul	1975	6.00	15.00
Hilltak PR-331	(DJ)	Track And Dialogue	1979	10.00	25.00

GUILD, THE
The Guild is a creation of Gary Usher & Co.

| Elektra EKS- | (S) | The Guild | 1972 | 10.00 | 25.00 |

GUITAR, BONNIE

Dot DLP-3069	(M)	Moonlight And Shadows	1957	20.00	50.00
Dot DLP-3151	(M)	Whispering Hope	1958	14.00	35.00
Dot DLP-25151	(S)	Whispering Hope	1958	20.00	50.00
Dot DLP-3335	(M)	Dark Moon	1961	10.00	25.00
Dot DLP-25335	(E)	Dark Moon	1961	8.00	20.00
Dot DLP-3696	(M)	Two Worlds	1966	8.00	20.00
Dot DLP-25696	(S)	Two Worlds	1966	10.00	25.00
Dot DLP-3737	(M)	Miss Bonnie Guitar	1966	8.00	20.00
Dot DLP-25737	(S)	Miss Bonnie Guitar	1966	10.00	25.00
Dot DLP-3746	(M)	Merry Christmas From Bonnie Guitar	1966	8.00	20.00
Dot DLP-25746	(S)	Merry Christmas From Bonnie Guitar	1966	10.00	25.00
Dot DLP-3793	(M)	Award Winner	1967	6.00	15.00
Dot DLP-25793	(S)	Award Winner	1967	8.00	20.00

GUITAR JR.
Refer to Mississippi Fred McDowll / Guitar Jr.

| Goldband 1085 | (M) | Pick Me Up On Your Way Down | 1960 | 10.00 | 25.00 |

GUITAR SLIM
Guitar Slim is a pseudonym for Lee Baker.

| Capitol ST-403 | (S) | Broke And Hungry | 1969 | 8.00 | 20.00 |
| Specialty SP-2120 | (E) | Things That I Used To Do | 1969 | 8.00 | 20.00 |

Label & Catalog #		Title	Year	VG+	NM

GUN
Gun features Adrian and Paul Gurvitz (a.k.a. Paul Curtis). Refer to The Baker-Gurvitz Army.

Epic BN-26468	(S)	**Gun**	1969	8.00	20.00
Epic BN-26551	(S)	**Gunsight**	1970	10.00	25.00

GUNS N' ROSES

Uzi Suicide USR-001	(S)	**Live! Like A Suicide**	1986	40.00	100.00

GUNTER, ARTHUR

Excello 8017	(E)	**Black And Blues**	1971	10.00	25.00

GUTHRIE, ARLO

Reprise R-6267	(M)	**Alice's Restaurant**	1967	8.00	20.00
Reprise RS-6267	(S)	**Alice's Restaurant**	1967	8.00	20.00

— *Original Reprise albums above have green, gold & pink labels.* —

United Arts. UAS-5196	(S)	**Alice's Restaurant** *(Soundtrack)*	1969	6.00	15.00
Reprise MS4-2142	(Q)	**The Last Of The Brooklyn Cowboys**	1973	8.00	20.00

GUTHRIE, JACK

Capitol T-2456	(M)	**Jack Guthrie's Greatest Songs**	1966	6.00	15.00
Capitol ST-2456	(S)	**Jack Guthrie's Greatest Songs**	1966	8.00	20.00

GUTHRIE, WOODY

Folkways FA-2011	(M)	**Talking Dust Bowl**	195?	20.00	50.00
Folkways FC-7015	(M)	**Songs To Grow On**	195?	20.00	50.00
Verve/Folkways FV-9007	(M)	**Bed On The Floor**	1965	12.00	30.00
Verve/Folkways FVS-9007	(E)	**Bed On The Floor**	1965	8.00	20.00
Verve/Folkways FV-9036	(M)	**Bonneville Dam** **& Other Columbia River Songs**	1965	12.00	30.00
Verve/Folkways FVS-9036	(E)	**Bonneville Dam** **& Other Columbia River Songs**	1965	8.00	20.00

GUTHRIE, WOODY, & CISCO HOUSTON

Stinson SLP-32	(M)	**Cowboy Songs**	195?	20.00	50.00
Stinson SLP-44	(M)	**Folksongs**	195?	20.00	50.00
Stinson SLP-53	(M)	**More Songs**	195?	20.00	50.00

GUY, BUDDY

Vanguard VSD-79272	(S)	**A Man And The Blues**	1968	12.00	30.00
Vanguard VSD-79290	(S)	**This Is Buddy Guy**	1968	12.00	30.00
Chess LPS-1527	(S)	**Left My Blues In San Francisco**	1969	10.00	25.00
Blue Thumb BYS-20	(S)	**Buddy And The Juniors**	1970	8.00	20.00
Blue Thumb BYS-20	(S)	**Buddy And The Juniors** *(Colored vinyl)*	1970	16.00	40.00

H. P. LOVECRAFT [LOVECRAFT]

Philips PHM-200-252	(M)	**H. P. Lovecraft**	1967	10.00	25.00
Philips PHS-600-252	(S)	**H. P. Lovecraft**	1967	12.00	30.00
Philips PHS-600-279	(S)	**Lovecraft II**	1968	12.00	30.00
Reprise RS-6419	(S)	**Valley Of The Moon**	1970	8.00	20.00
Mercury SRM-1-1031	(S)	**We Love You**	1976	6.00	15.00

(The Reprise and Mercury albums credit Lovecraft.)

Label & Catalog #		Title	Year	VG+	NM

HA' PENNYS, THE

Fersch FL-1110	(M)	Love Is Not The Same	1968	200.00	400.00

HAGAR, ERNIE

Sage C-42	(M)	Swinging Steel Guitar	195?	20.00	50.00

HAGGARD, MERLE, & THE STRANGERS

Capitol T-2373	(M)	Strangers	1965	10.00	25.00
Capitol ST-2373	(S)	Strangers	1965	12.00	30.00
Capitol T-2585	(M)	Swinging Doors	1966	10.00	25.00
Capitol ST-2585	(S)	Swinging Doors	1966	12.00	30.00
Capitol T-2702	(M)	I'm A Lonesome Fugitive	1967	10.00	25.00
Capitol ST-2702	(S)	I'm A Lonesome Fugitive	1967	12.00	30.00
Capitol T-2789	(M)	Branded Man/I Threw Away The Rose	1967	8.00	20.00
Capitol ST-2789	(S)	Branded Man/I Threw Away The Rose	1967	10.00	25.00
Capitol ST-2848	(S)	Sing Me Back Home	1968	10.00	25.00
Capitol ST-2912	(S)	Legend Of Bonnie & Clyde	1968	8.00	20.00
Capitol SKAO-2951	(S)	Best Of Merle Haggard	1968	8.00	20.00
Capitol ST-2972	(S)	Mama Tried	1969	8.00	20.00
Capitol SKAO-168	(S)	Pride In What I Am	1969	8.00	20.00
Capitol ST-223	(S)	Same Train, A Different Time (2 LPs)	1969	12.00	30.00
		— Original Capitol albums above have black rainbow labels.—			
Capitol ST-319	(S)	Portrait Of Merle Haggard	1969	8.00	20.00
Capitol ST-384	(S)	Okie From Muskogee	1969	6.00	15.00
Capitol ST-451	(S)	The Fighting Side Of Me	1970	6.00	15.00
Capitol ST-638	(S)	Tribute To The Best Damn Fiddle Player	1970	10.00	25.00
Capitol ST-735	(S)	Hag	1971	8.00	20.00
Capitol ST-803	(S)	Land Of Many Churches (2 LPs)	1971	20.00	50.00
Capitol ST-823	(S)	Truly The Best Of Merle Haggard	1971	16.00	40.00
Capitol ST-835	(S)	Someday We'll Look Back	1972	8.00	20.00
		— Original Capitol albums above have green labels.—			

HAGGARD, MERLE, & BONNIE OWENS

Capitol T-2453	(M)	Just Between The Two Of Us	1966	10.00	25.00
Capitol ST-2453	(S)	Just Between The Two Of Us	1966	12.00	30.00

HAGGARD'S STRANGERS, MERLE

Capitol ST-169	(S)	The Instrumental Sound Of The Strangers	1969	10.00	25.00
Capitol ST-445	(S)	Introducing My Friends, The Strangers	1970	8.00	20.00
Capitol ST-590	(S)	Gettin' To Know Merle Haggard's Strangers	1970	8.00	20.00
Capitol ST-796	(S)	Honky Tonkin'	1971	8.00	20.00

HAINES, CONNIE

Coral CRL-56055 (10")	(M)	Connie Haines Sings	1955	14.00	35.00
RCA Victor LPM-2264	(M)	Faith, Hope And Charity	1960	6.00	15.00
RCA Victor LSP-2264	(S)	Faith, Hope And Charity	1960	8.00	20.00
Tops L-1606	(M)	Connie Haines Sings Helen Morgan	1959	6.00	15.00

HALE, CORKY: Refer to GOLDMINE'S PRICE GUIDE TO COLLECTIBLE JAZZ ALBUMS

HALEN, VAN

Warner Bros. 23985	(DJ)	1984 (Quiex II vinyl)	1984	6.00	15.00

HALEY, BILL, & HIS COMETS

Refer to Trini Lopez / Scott Gregory. Note: In the previous edition of this book the pink label promo Decca albums were listed with dramatically inflated prices. A realistic Near Mint value for each is $100-200.

Essex LP-202	(M)	Rock With Bill Haley And The Comets	1955	100.00	400.00
Trans World 202	(M)	Rock With Bill Haley And The Comets	1956	150.00	300.00
		(Transworld 202 is a reissue of Essex 202.)			
Somerset P-4600	(M)	Rock With Bill Haley And The Comets	1957	50.00	150.00
Decca DL-5560 (10")	(M)	Shake, Rattle And Roll	1955	200.00	500.00
Decca DL-8225	(M)	Rock Around The Clock	1956	40.00	100.00
		(Black label with "Decca" on top and "Long Play" on the bottom.)			
Decca DL-78225	(E)	Rock Around The Clock	1958	20.00	50.00
		(Black label with "Decca Stereo" on top.)			
Decca DL-8225	(M)	Rock Around The Clock	1960	16.00	40.00
Decca DL-78225	(E)	Rock Around The Clock	1960	10.00	25.00
		(Black label with "Decca" in a rainbow band across the middle and "Mfrd. by Decca Records Inc New York" beneath the band.)			

While historians have tended to less than understanding of Bill Haley's place in the pantheon of rock 'n roll deities, he remains nonetheless a pivotal figure, the first white artist to be able to sell rhythm 'n blues to a white audience in large numbers. . . and get played on the radio! His Decca albums rarely receive the attention from collectors they deserve and finding them in nearly mint condition may be more difficult that the current market values imply.

Label & Catalog #		Title	Year	VG+	NM
Decca DL-8225	(M)	Rock Around The Clock	1967	6.00	15.00
Decca DL-78225	(E)	Rock Around The Clock	1967	5.00	12.00
		(Black label with "Decca" in a rainbow band across the middle and "Mfrd. by Decca Records. A division of MCA" beneath the band.)			
Decca DL-78225	(E)	Rock Around The Clock	1972	4.00	10.00
		(Black label with "Decca" in a rainbow band across the middle and "Mfrd. by MCA Records" beneath the band.)			
Decca DL-8315	(M)	Music For The Boyfriend	1956	60.00	150.00
Decca DL-8345	(M)	Rock And Roll Stage Show	1956	80.00	200.00
Decca DL-8569	(M)	Rockin' The Oldies	1957	60.00	150.00
Decca DL-8692	(M)	Rockin' Around The World	1958	60.00	150.00
Decca DL-8775	(M)	Rockin' The Joint	1958	60.00	150.00
Decca DL-8821	(M)	Bill Haley's Chicks	1959	40.00	100.00
Decca DL-78821	(S)	Bill Haley's Chicks	1959	60.00	150.00
Decca DL-8964	(M)	Strictly Instrumental	1960	40.00	100.00
Decca DL-78964	(S)	Strictly Instrumental	1960	60.00	150.00

— Original Decca mono albums above have black labels with "Long Play 33 1/3 RPM" on the bottom; stereo albums have black labels with "Decca Stereo" on top.—

Warner Bros. W-1378	(M)	Bill Haley And His Comets	1960	20.00	50.00
Warner Bros. WS-1378	(S)	Bill Haley And His Comets	1960	30.00	75.00
Warner Bros. W-1391	(M)	Bill Haley's Jukebox	1960	20.00	50.00
Warner Bros. WS-1391	(S)	Bill Haley's Jukebox	1960	30.00	75.00
Vocalion VL-3696	(M)	Bill Haley And The Comets	1963	10.00	25.00
Guest Star 1454	(M)	Rock Around The Clock King	1964	10.00	25.00
Guest Star S-1454	(S)	Rock Around The Clock King	1964	6.00	15.00
Decca DL-75027	(S)	Bill Haley's Greatest Hits	1969	8.00	20.00
Kama Sutra KLPS-2104	(S)	Scrapbook/Live At The Bitter End	1970	12.00	30.00
Janus 3035	(S)	Travelin' Band	1970	10.00	25.00
Janus JX25-7003	(S)	Razzle Dazzle (2 LPs)	1971	6.00	15.00
Ambassador 98089	(S)	Bill Haley & His Comets	1970	8.00	20.00
Valiant 1831	(DJ)	Rock 'N' Roll Revival	1970	10.00	25.00
Valiant 1831	(S)	Rock 'N' Roll Revival	1970	8.00	20.00
Warner Bros. WS-1831	(S)	Rock 'N' Roll Revival	1971	6.00	15.00
Decca DXSE-211	(P)	Golden Hits (2 LPs)	1972	6.00	15.00
Crescendo GNP-2077	(DJ)	Rock 'N' Roll	1973	6.00	15.00
Crescendo GNP-2077	(S)	Rock 'N' Roll	1973	5.00	12.00
Crescendo GNP-2097	(DJ)	Rock Around The Country	1976	6.00	15.00
Crescendo GNP-2097	(S)	Rock Around The Country	1976	5.00	12.00
Sun 143	(S)	R-O-C-K	1979	6.00	15.00

HALFNELSON
Halfnelson is Ron and Russell Mael, later of Sparks.

Bearsville BV-2048	(S)	Halfnelson (Reissued as "Sparks")	1971	8.00	20.00

HALL, CONNIE

Decca DL-4217	(M)	Connie Hall	1962	6.00	15.00
Decca DL-74217	(S)	Connie Hall	1962	8.00	20.00

HALL, DARYL, & JOHN OATES

RCA Victor AFL1-2804	(S)	Along The Red Ledge (Red vinyl)	1978	5.00	12.00
RCA Victor DJL1-3832	(DJ)	RCA Special Radio Series (Interview)	1980	4.00	10.00
Mobile Fidelity MFSL-069	(S)	Abandoned Luncheonette	1979	5.00	15.00

HALL, DICKSON [DIXON HALL]

MGM E-329 (10")	(M)	Outlaws Of The Old West	1954	16.00	40.00
MGM E-3263	(M)	Outlaws Of The Old West	1956	10.00	25.00
Kapp KL-1067	(M)	Fabulous Country Hits Way Out West	1957	10.00	25.00
Kapp KL-1464	(M)	24 Fabulous Country Hits	1966	5.00	12.00
Kapp KS-3464	(S)	24 Fabulous Country Hits	1966	6.00	15.00
Epic LN-3427	(M)	25 All-Time Country And Western Hits	1958	10.00	25.00

HALL, JUANITA

Counterpoint 556	(M)	Jaunita Hall Sings The Blues	1958	50.00	100.00
Counterpoint 556	(S)	Jaunita Hall Sings The Blues	1958	60.00	150.00

HALL, LARRY

Strand 1005	(M)	Sandy	1960	30.00	75.00
Strand S-1005	(S)	Sandy	1960	60.00	150.00

Label & Catalog #		Title	Year	VG+	NM

HALLYDAY, JOHNNY

Philips PHM-200-019	(M)	America's Rockin' Hits	1961	30.00	75.00
Philips PHS-600-019	(S)	America's Rockin' Hits	1961	40.00	100.00

HALOS, THE

Warwick W-2046	(M)	The Halos	1962	150.00	350.00

HAMBLEN, STUART
Refer to Webb Pierce / Marvin Rainwater / Stuart Hamblen.

RCA Victor LPM-3265 (10")	(M)	It Is No Secret	1954	20.00	50.00
RCA Victor LPM-1253	(M)	It Is No Secret	1956	12.00	30.00
RCA Victor LPM-1436	(M)	Grand Old Hymns	1957	12.00	30.00
Coral CRL-57254	(M)	Remember Me	1960	10.00	25.00
Columbia CL-1588	(M)	The Spell Of The Yukon	1961	6.00	15.00
Columbia CS-8388	(S)	The Spell Of The Yukon	1961	8.00	20.00
Columbia CL-1769	(M)	Of God I Sing	1962	6.00	15.00
Columbia CS-8569	(S)	Of God I Sing	1962	8.00	20.00

— Original Columbia albums above have three white "eye" logos on each side of the spindle hole.—

HAMILTON, FRANK
Hamilton was formerly a member of The Weavers.

Capitol T-2005	(M)	Sing A Song With The Kingston Trio	1964	10.00	25.00
Capitol ST-2005	(S)	Sing A Song With The Kingston Trio	1964	12.00	30.00

HAMILTON, GEORGE, IV

ABC-Paramount 220	(M)	George Hamilton IV On Campus	1958	14.00	35.00
ABC-Paramount S-220	(S)	George Hamilton IV On Campus	1958	20.00	50.00
ABC-Paramount 251	(M)	Sing Me A Sad Song (A Tribute To Hank Williams)	1958	14.00	35.00
ABC-Paramount S-251	(S)	Sing Me A Sad Song (A Tribute To Hank Williams)	1958	20.00	50.00
ABC-Paramount 461	(M)	Big Fifteen	1963	12.00	30.00
ABC-Paramount S-461	(S)	Big Fifteen	1963	12.00	40.00

("Little Tom," "Even Tho," "Why Don't They Understand," and "One Heart" are rechanneled on this album.)

ABC-Paramount 535	(M)	By George	1966	6.00	15.00
ABC-Paramount S-535	(S)	By George	1966	8.00	20.00
RCA Victor LPM-2373	(M)	To You And Yours From Me And Mine	1961	6.00	15.00
RCA Victor LSP-2373	(S)	To You And Yours From Me And Mine	1961	8.00	20.00
RCA Victor LPM-2778	(M)	Abilene	1963	6.00	15.00
RCA Victor LSP-2778	(S)	Abilene	1963	8.00	20.00
RCA Victor LPM-2972	(M)	Fort Worth, Dallas Or Houston	1964	6.00	15.00
RCA Victor LSP-2972	(S)	Fort Worth, Dallas Or Houston	1964	8.00	20.00
RCA Victor LPM-3371	(M)	Mister Sincerity	1965	6.00	15.00
RCA Victor LSP-3371	(S)	Mister Sincerity	1965	8.00	20.00
RCA Victor LPM-3510	(M)	Coast Country	1966	6.00	15.00
RCA Victor LSP-3510	(S)	Coast Country	1966	8.00	20.00
RCA Victor LPM-3601	(M)	Steel Rail Blues	1966	6.00	15.00
RCA Victor LSP-3601	(S)	Steel Rail Blues	1966	8.00	20.00
RCA Victor LPM-3752	(M)	Folk Country Classics	1967	8.00	20.00
RCA Victor LSP-3752	(S)	Folk Country Classics	1967	6.00	15.00
RCA Victor LPM-3854	(M)	Folksy	1967	8.00	20.00
RCA Victor LSP-3854	(S)	Folksy	1967	6.00	15.00
RCA Victor LPM-3962	(M)	The Gentle Sound Of George Hamilton IV	1968	12.00	30.00
RCA Victor LSP-3962	(S)	The Gentle Sound Of George Hamilton IV	1968	6.00	15.00
RCA Victor LSP-4006	(S)	George Hamilton IV	1968	6.00	15.00

HAMILTON, ROY

Epic LN-1103 (10")	(M)	The Voice Of Roy Hamilton	195?	40.00	100.00
Epic LN-3176	(M)	Roy Hamilton	1955	20.00	50.00
Epic LN-3294	(M)	You'll Never Walk Alone	1956	20.00	50.00
Epic LN-3364	(M)	Golden Boy	1957	20.00	50.00
Epic LN-3628	(M)	Roy Hamilton At His Best	1958	20.00	50.00
Epic LN-3???	(M)	With All My Love	1959	12.00	30.00
Epic BN-518	(S)	With All My Love	1959	16.00	40.00
Epic LN-3???	(M)	Why Fight The Feeling?	1960	10.00	25.00
Epic BN-525	(S)	Why Fight The Feeling?	1960	12.00	30.00
Epic LN-3???	(M)	Come Out Swingin'	1960	10.00	25.00
Epic BN-530	(S)	Come Out Swingin'	1960	12.00	30.00

Label & Catalog #		Title	Year	VG+	NM
Epic LN-3???	(M)	Have Blues, Must Travel	1961	12.00	30.00
Epic BN-535	(S)	Have Blues, Must Travel	1961	12.00	30.00
Epic LN-3???	(M)	Spirituals	1961	10.00	25.00
Epic BN-551	(S)	Spirituals	1961	12.00	30.00
Epic LN-3???	(M)	Soft 'N Warm	1961	10.00	25.00
Epic BN-578	(S)	Soft 'N Warm	1961	12.00	30.00
Epic LN-3775	(M)	You Can Have Her	1961	12.00	30.00
Epic BN-595	(S)	You Can Have Her	1961	16.00	40.00
Epic LN-3???	(M)	Only You	1962	10.00	25.00
Epic BN-610	(S)	Only You	1962	12.00	30.00
Epic LN-24000	(M)	Mr. Rock And Soul	1962	10.00	25.00
Epic BN-26000	(S)	Mr. Rock And Soul	1962	12.00	30.00
Epic LN-24009	(M)	Roy Hamilton's Greatest Hits	1962	8.00	20.00
Epic BN-26009	(S)	Roy Hamilton's Greatest Hits	1962	10.00	25.00

— Original Epic albums above have yellow labels with black spokes along the perimeter.—

HAMILTON, RUSS

Kapp KL-1076	(M)	Rainbow	1957	30.00	75.00

HAMILTON STREETCAR

Dot DLP-25939	(S)	Hamilton Streetcar	1969	6.00	15.00

HAMMER

San Francisco SD-203	(S)	Hammer	1970	8.00	20.00

HAMMOND, JOHN

Vanguard VRS-9153	(M)	Big City Blues	1964	10.00	25.00
Vanguard VSD-79153	(S)	Big City Blues	1964	12.00	30.00
Vanguard VRS-9178	(M)	So Many Roads	1966	12.00	30.00
Vanguard VSD-79178	(S)	So Many Roads	1966	16.00	40.00
Vanguard VRS-9198	(M)	Country Blues	1966	10.00	25.00
Vanguard VSD-79198	(S)	Country Blues	1966	12.00	30.00
Vanguard VRS-9245	(M)	Mirrors	1967	12.00	30.00
Vanguard VSD-79245	(S)	Mirrors	1967	16.00	40.00

(Vanguard 9178 and 9245 feature Levon Helm, Garth Hudson
and Robbie Robertson of The Band.)

Atlantic SD-8206	(S)	Sooner Or Later	1968	8.00	20.00
Atlantic 8152	(M)	I Can Tell	1967	16.00	40.00
Atlantic SD-8152	(S)	I Can Tell	1967	20.00	50.00

(Atlantic 8152 features Robertson, Rick Danko and Bill Wyman.)

Atlantic SD-8251	(S)	Southern Fried	1969	6.00	15.00
Columbia 30458	(S)	Source Point	1970	4.00	10.00
Columbia 30545	(S)	Little Big Man (Soundtrack)	1970	5.00	12.00
Columbia 31318	(S)	I'm Satisfied	1972	4.00	10.00
Capricorn 0153	(S)	Can't Beat The Kid	1975	4.00	10.00

HANGMEN, THE

Monument MLP-8077	(M)	Bitter Sweet	1967	8.00	20.00
Monument SLP-18077	(S)	Bitter Sweet	1967	10.00	25.00

HANKINS, ESCO

Audio Lap AL-1547	(M)	Country Style	1959	40.00	100.00

HAPPENINGS, THE

B.T. Puppy BT-1001	(M)	The Happenings	1966	10.00	25.00
B.T. Puppy BTS-1001	(S)	The Happenings	1966	12.00	30.00
B.T. Puppy BT-1003	(M)	Psycle	1967	10.00	25.00
B.T. Puppy BTS-1003	(S)	Psycle	1967	12.00	30.00
B.T. Puppy BTS-1004	(S)	The Happenings' Golden Hits!	1968	16.00	40.00
Jubilee JGS-8028	(S)	Piece Of Mind	1969	10.00	25.00
Jubilee JGS-8030	(S)	The Happenings' Greatest Hits!	1969	10.00	25.00

HAPPENINGS, THE / THE TOKENS

B.T. Puppy BT-1002	(M)	Back To Back	1967	6.00	15.00
B.T. Puppy BTS-1002	(S)	Back To Back	1967	8.00	20.00

HAPPY DRAGON BAND, THE

Fiddler's Music 1157	(S)	The Happy Dragon Band	1977	40.00	100.00

Label & Catalog #		Title	Year	VG+	NM
HAPSHASH & THE COLOURED COAT					
Imperial LP-12377	(S)	**Hapshash & The Coloured Coat**	1968	12.00	30.00
Imperial LP-12430	(S)	**Western Flyer**	1969	12.00	30.00
HARD STUFF					
Mercury SRM-1-663	(S)	**Bolex Dementia**	1973	6.00	15.00
HARDWATER					
Hardwater originally recorded as The Astronauts.					
Capitol ST-2954	(S)	**Hardwater**	1968	12.00	30.00
HARDIN, TIM					
Verve/Folkways FT-3004	(M)	**Tim Hardin**	1966	80.00	20.00
Verve/Folkways FTS-3004	(S)	**Tim Hardin**	1966	10.00	25.00
Atco 33-210	(M)	**Tim Hardin**	1967	12.00	30.00
Atco SD-33-210	(E)	**Tim Hardin**	1967	6.00	15.00
Verve/Forecast FTS-3022	(S)	**Tim Hardin II**	1967	80.00	20.00
Verve/Forecast FTS-3049	(S)	**Tim Hardin 3/Live In Concert**	1968	80.00	20.00
Verve/Forecast FTS-3064	(S)	**Tim Hardin 4**	1969	6.00	15.00
Verve/Forecast FTS-3078	(S)	**The Best Of Tim Hardin**	1969	6.00	15.00
HARDTIMES, THE					
World Pacific WP-1867	(M)	**Blew Mind**	1968	10.00	25.00
World Pacific ST-1867	(S)	**Blew Mind**	1968	12.00	30.00
HARDY, FRANCOISE					
Four Corners FC-4231	(M)	**Francoise**	196?	10.00	25.00
Four Corners FCS-4231	(S)	**Francoise**	196?	12.00	30.00
Four Corners FC-4238	(M)	**Je Vous Aime**	196?	10.00	25.00
Four Corners FCS-4238	(S)	**Je Vous Aime**	196?	12.00	30.00
Reprise RS-6290	(S)	**Francoise Hardy**	1968	12.00	30.00
HARDY BOYS, THE					
RCA Victor LSP-4217	(S)	**Here Come The Hardy Boys**	1969	8.00	20.00
RCA Victor LSP-4315	(S)	**Wheels**	1970	8.00	20.00
HARLEM-AIRES, THE: *Refer to* **CONNIE BENNETT, BILL SMYTH & THE HARLEM-AIRES**					
HARPER, ARTHUR LEE					
Mr. Harper also recorded as Arthur.					
Nocturne NRS-905	(S)	**Love Is The Revolution**	1975	150.00	300.00
HARPER, ROY					
World Pacific WPS-21888	(S)	**Folkjokeopus**	1969	10.00	25.00
Harvest SKAO-418	(S)	**Flat, Baroque And Berserk**	1970	6.00	15.00
Chrysalis PRO-620	(DJ)	**Introduction To Roy Harper**	1976	12.00	30.00
Chrysalis CHR-1105	(S)	**When An Old Cricketer Leaves The Crease**	1975	4.00	10.00
Chrysalis CHR-1139	(S)	**One Of Those Days In England**	1977	4.00	10.00
HARPER, TONI: *Refer to* **GOLDMINE'S PRICE GUIDE TO COLLECTIBLE JAZZ ALBUMS**					
HARPERS BIZARRE					
Warner Bros. W-1693	(M)	**Feelin' Groovy** *(Gold label)*	1967	6.00	15.00
Warner Bros. WS-1693	(S)	**Feelin' Groovy** *(Gold label)*	1967	8.00	20.00
Warner Bros. WS-1716	(S)	**Anything Goes**	1968	6.00	15.00
Warner Bros. WS-1739	(S)	**Secret Life Of Harpers Bazaar**	1968	6.00	15.00
Warner Bros. WS-1784	(S)	**Harpers Bazaar**	1969	6.00	15.00
Forest Bay BS-7545LP	(S)	**As Time Goes By**	1976	4.00	10.00
HARRIS, DAVE					
Decca DL-4113	(M)	**Dinner Music**			
		For A Pack Of Hungry Cannibals	1961	8.00	20.00
Decca DL7-4113	(S)	**Dinner Music**			
		For A Pack Of Hungry Cannibals	1961	12.00	30.00
HARRIS, EMMYLOU					
Jubilee JGS-8031	(S)	**Gliding Bird** *(Full color cover)*	1969	40.00	100.00
		(Counterfeits have black & white covers.)			
Mobile Fidelity MFSL-015	(S)	**Quarter Moon In A Ten Cent Town**	1979	10.00	30.00

Label & Catalog #		Title	Year	VG+	NM

HARRIS, MAJOR
Major Harris was formerly the lead singer with The Delfonics.

| Atlantic SD-18119 | (S) | **My Way** | 1974 | 8.00 | 20.00 |

HARRIS, PEPPERMINT

| Time 5 | (M) | **Peppermint Harris** | 1962 | 60.00 | 150.00 |

HARRIS, ROLF

| Epic LN-24053 | (M) | **The Original Sun Arise** | 1963 | 16.00 | 40.00 |
| Epic LN-24110 | (M) | **The Court Of King Caractacus** | 1964 | 16.00 | 40.00 |

— Original Epic albums above have yellow labels with "A Product of CBS" on the bottom.—

HARRIS, SHAUN
Harris was formerly a member of The West Coast Pop Art Experimental Band.

| Capitol ST-11168 | (S) | **Shaun Harris** | 1973 | 12.00 | 30.00 |

HARRIS, WYNONIE
Refer to Roy Brown; Amos Milburn.

| King KS-1086 | (E) | **Good Rockin' Blues** | 1970 | 10.00 | 25.00 |

HARRISON, GEORGE
Harrison was formerly a member of The Fab Four. Refer to The Beatles; Jackie Lomax; Bill;y Preston; The Radha Krsna Temple Leon Russell; Ravi Shankar; and Doris Troy.

Apple ST-3350	(S)	**Wonderwall Music**	1969	60.00	150.00
		(Apple labels read "A Subsidiary of Capitol" on the bottom.)			
Apple ST-3350	(S)	**Wonderwall Music**	1969	8.00	20.00
		(Apple labels read "Manufactured by Apple" on the bottom.)			
Zapple ST-3358	(S)	**Electronic Sound**	1969	10.00	25.00
Apple STCH-639	(S)	**All Things Must Pass** *(3 LP box)*	1970	16.00	40.00
		(First pressings have "Mfd. by Apple" on the inside front cover. Issued with a poster and a lyric sheet. Produced by Phil Spector)			
Apple STCH-639	(S)	**All Things Must Pass** *(3 LP box)*	1988	12.00	30.00
		(This reissue has an "S" in the trail-off vinyl.)			
Apple SMAS-3410	(S)	**Living In The Material World**	1973	4.00	10.00
Apple SMAS-3418	(S)	**Dark Horse**	1974	6.00	15.00
Apple SW-3420	(S)	**Extra Texture** *(Die-cut title cover)*	1975	5.00	12.00
Apple SW-3492	(S)	**Somewhere In England**	1981	4.00	10.00
Dark Horse *(No number)*	(DJ)	**Dark Horse Radio Special**	1975	100.00	250.00
Dark Horse PRO-649	(DJ)	**Personal Music Dialogue At 33 & 1/3**	1976	20.00	50.00
Dark Horse 23734	(DJ)	**Gone Troppo** *(Quiex II vinyl)*	1982	8.00	20.00
Dark Horse W1-25643	(S)	**Cloud Nine** *(Columbia Record Club)*	1987	6.00	15.00
Dark Horse R-172348	(S)	**Cloud Nine** *(RCA Record Club)*	1987	6.00	15.00
Dark Horse W1-25726	(S)	**Best Of Dark Horse** *(Columbia Record Club)*	1989	6.00	15.00
Dark Horse R-180307	(S)	**Best Of Dark Horse** *(RCA Record Club)*	1989	6.00	15.00
Capitol STCH-639	(S)	**All Things Must Pass** *(Orange label)*	1976	10.00	25.00
Capitol STCH-639	(S)	**All Things Must Pass** *(Purple label)*	1978	6.00	15.00
Capitol STCH-639	(S)	**All Things Must Pass** *(Black label)*	1983	20.00	50.00
Capitol ST-11578	(S)	**Best Of George Harrison** *(Photo label)*	1976	6.00	15.00
		(Originals do not have the UPC bar code on the back cover.)			
Capitol ST-11578	(S)	**Best Of George Harrison** *(Orange label)*	1976	30.00	75.00
Capitol SN-16217	(S)	**Extra Texture** *(Green label)*	198?	8.00	20.00

HARRISON, GEORGE, & FRIENDS
Features performances by Ravi Shankar, Harrison, Billy Preston, Ringo, Leon Russell, amd Bob Dylan, featuring Badfinger as everybody's band. Produced by Harrison and Phil Spector.

Apple STCX-3385	(S)	**The Concert For Bangla Desh** *(3 LP box)*	1972	10.00	25.00
Capitol SABB-12248	(S)	**The Concert For Bangla Desh** *(2 LPs)*	1982	300.00	500.00
		(Abridged two-album reissue of the original Apple box.)			

HARRISON, NOEL

London LL-3459	(M)	**Noel Harrison**	1965	8.00	20.00
London PS-459	(S)	**Noel Harrison**	1965	10.00	25.00
Reprise R-6321	(M)	**Santa Monica Pier**	1967	6.00	15.00
Reprise RS-6321	(S)	**Santa Monica Pier**	1967	8.00	20.00
Reprise RS-6321	(S)	**The Great Electric Experiment Is Over**	1968	8.00	20.00

HARRISON, WILBERT

| Sphere Sound SR-7000 | (M) | **Kansas City** | 1965 | 40.00 | 100.00 |
| Sphere Sound SSR-7000 | (E) | **Kansas City** | 1965 | 30.00 | 75.00 |

Label & Catalog #		Title	Year	VG+	NM
Sue SSLP-8801	(S)	Let's Work Together	1970	12.00	30.00
Juggernaut ST-8803	(S)	Shoot You Full Of Love	1971	6.00	15.00
Buddah BDS-5092	(S)	Wilbert Harrison	1971	6.00	15.00

HARROW, NANCY: *Refer to GOLDMINE'S PRICE GUIDE TO COLLECTIBLE JAZZ ALBUMS*

HART, MICKEY
Refer to The Diga Rhythm Band; The Grateful Dead; The Heart Of Gold Band.

Warner Bros. BS-2635	(S)	Rolling Thunder *(With insert)*	1972	16.00	40.00

HART, MICKEY, & AIRTO & FLORA PUMIN

Reference Recordings 12	(S)	Dafos *(45 RPM)*	1983	6.00	15.00

HARTFORD, JOHN

RCA Victor LPM-3687	(M)	John Hartford Looks At Life	1967	10.00	25.00
RCA Victor LSP-3687	(S)	John Hartford Looks At Life	1967	6.00	15.00
RCA Victor LPM-3796	(M)	Earthwords And Music	1967	10.00	25.00
RCA Victor LSP-3796	(S)	Earthwords And Music	1967	6.00	15.00
RCA Victor LPM-3884	(M)	The Love Album	1968	20.00	50.00
RCA Victor LSP-3884	(S)	The Love Album	1968	6.00	15.00
RCA Victor LSP-4068	(S)	Gentle On My Mind	1968	6.00	15.00
RCA Victor LSP-4156	(S)	John Hartford	1969	4.00	10.00
RCA Victor LSP-4337	(S)	Iron Mountain Depot	1970	4.00	10.00

HARTLEY BAND, KEEF

Deram DES-18024	(S)	Halfbreed	1969	6.00	15.00
Deram DES-18035	(S)	Battle Of North West Six	1970	6.00	15.00
Deram DES-18047	(S)	Time Is Near	1970	6.00	15.00

HARTMAN, DAN

Blue Sky ASZ-246	(DJ)	Who Is Dan Hartman?	1976	6.00	15.00

HARTMAN, JOHNNY: *Refer to GOLDMINE'S PRICE GUIDE TO COLLECTIBLE JAZZ ALBUMS*

HARUMI

Verve/Forecast FTS-3030	(S)	Harumi	1968	8.00	20.00

HARVEST FLIGHT

Destiny D-3303	(S)	One Way	197?	40.00	100.00

HASKELL, JIMMIE

Capitol T-1915	(M)	Sunset Surf	1963	6.00	15.00
Capitol ST-1915	(S)	Sunset Surf	1963	8.00	20.00
Capitol T-2151	(M)	Teen Love Themes	1964	5.00	12.00
Capitol ST-2151	(S)	Teen Love Themes	1964	6.00	15.00

HASSLES, THE
The Hassles feature Billy Joel.

United Arts. UAS-6631	(S)	The Hassles	1968	8.00	20.00
United Arts. UAS-6699	(S)	The Hour Of The Wolf	1969	8.00	20.00

HATFIELD, BOBBY
Hatfield was formerly one half of The Righteous Brothers.

MGM SE-4727	(S)	Messin' In Muscle Shoals	1971	4.00	10.00

HAVENS, RICHIE

Douglas D-779	(M)	Richie Havens' Record	1966	5.00	12.00
Douglas SD-779	(S)	Richie Havens' Record	1966	6.00	15.00
Douglas D-780	(M)	Electric Havens	1966	5.00	12.00
Douglas SD-780	(S)	Electric Havens	1966	6.00	15.00
Verve/Forecast FT-3006	(M)	Mixed Bag	1966	6.00	15.00
Verve/Forecast FTS-3006	(S)	Mixed Bag	1966	8.00	20.00
Verve/Forecast FTS-3034	(S)	Somethin' Else Again	1968	6.00	15.00
Verve/Forecast FTS-3047	(S)	Richard P. Havens, 1983 *(2 LPs)*	1968	8.00	20.00
Verve/Forecast FTS-3061	(S)	Richie Havens	1969	*Unreleased*	

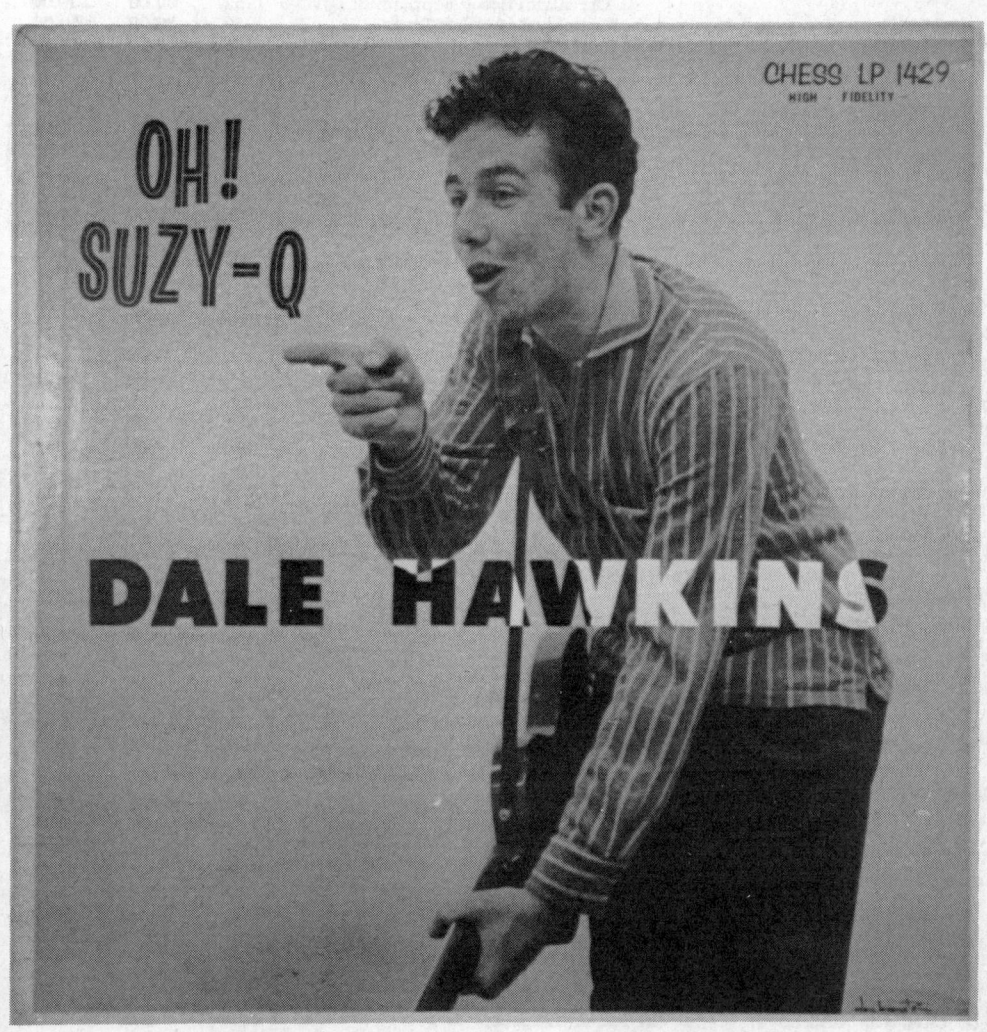

Dale Hawkins' contribution to rock 'n roll history is the perennial favorite, "Suzy-Q," featuring the amazing guitar of James Burton. Like many LPs from the Chess label, the print run for this title was small and copies today—especially in collectible condition—are diminishing. Collectors should note that legitimate second pressings from Europe's EEC are pressed on modern vinyl with the cover art printed on the thin cardboard jacket. Originals were pressed on the thick, old style vinyl and the cover slick is pasted on to the heavy cardboard jacket.

Label & Catalog #		Title	Year	VG+	NM

HAWKINS, DALE

Chess LP-1429	(M)	Oh! Suzie-Q	1958	300.00	*Rare*
		(Near Mint copies have a suggested value of $500-1,000.)			
Roulette R-25175	(M)	Let's All Twist			
		At The Miami Beach Peppermint Lounge	1962	50.00	125.00
Roulette SR-25175	(S)	Let's All Twist			
		At The Miami Beach Peppermint Lounge	1962	80.00	200.00
Bell 6036	(S)	L.A., Memphis And Tyler, Texas	1969	16.00	40.00
Chess 703	(M)	Dale Hawkins	1976	6.00	15.00
		(Outtakes from the '50's Chess sessions.)			

HAWKINS, HAWKSHAW

Refer to Cowboy Copas / Hawkshaw Hawkins.

Gladwynne 2006	(M)	Country Western Cavalcade	195?	50.00	125.00
LaBrea 8020	(M)	Hawkshaw Hawkins	195?	50.00	125.00
King 587	(M)	Hawkshaw Hawkins	1958	30.00	75.00
King 592	(M)	Grand Ole Opry Favorites	1958	30.00	75.00
King 599	(M)	Hawkshaw Hawkins	1959	30.00	75.00
King 808	(M)	The All New Hawkshaw Hawkins	1963	16.00	40.00
King 858	(M)	Taken From Our Vaults, Volume 1	1963	20.00	50.00
King 870	(M)	Taken From Our Vaults, Volume 2	1963	20.00	50.00
King 873	(M)	Taken From Our Vaults, Volume 3	1963	20.00	50.00

HAWKINS, JENNELL

Amazon AM-1001	(M)	The Many Moods Of Jenny	1961	6.00	15.00
Amazon AS-1001	(S)	The Many Moods Of Jenny	1961	8.00	20.00
Amazon AM-1002	(M)	Moments To Remember	1962	6.00	15.00
Amazon AS-1002	(S)	Moments To Remember	1962	8.00	20.00

HAWKINS, RONNIE

The Hawks, a.k.a. The Band, is Ronnie's group on many of the Roulette sides.

Roulette R-25078	(M)	Ronnie Hawkins	1959	40.00	100.00
Roulette SR-25078	(S)	Ronnie Hawkins	1959	60.00	150.00
Roulette SR-25078	(S)	Ronnie Hawkins *(Red vinyl)*	1959	200.00	400.00
Roulette R-25102	(M)	Mr. Dynamo	1960	40.00	100.00
Roulette SR-25102	(S)	Mr. Dynamo	1960	60.00	150.00
Roulette SR-25102	(S)	Mr. Dynamo *(Red vinyl)*	1960	200.00	400.00
Roulette R-25120	(M)	The Folk Ballads Of Ronnie Hawkins	1960	30.00	75.00
Roulette SR-25120	(S)	The Folk Ballads Of Ronnie Hawkins	1960	50.00	125.00
Roulette R-25137	(M)	The Songs Of Hank Williams	1960	30.00	75.00
Roulette SR-25137	(S)	The Songs Of Hank Williams	1960	50.00	125.00
Roulette SR-42045	(S)	The Best Of Ronnie Hawkins & His Band	1970	10.00	25.00

HAWKINS, "SCREAMIN' JAY"

Epic LN-3448	(M)	At Home With Screamin' Jay Hawkins	1958	300.00	*Rare*
		(Near Mint copies have a suggested value of $500-1,000.)			
Epic LN-3457	(M)	I Put A Spell On You	1959	150.00	300.00
Epic BN-26457	(E)	I Put A Spell On You	1969	20.00	50.00
		(Epic 26457 is a reissue of 3457.)			
Philips PHS-600-319	(S)	What That Is	1969	16.00	40.00
Philips PHS-600-336	(S)	Screamin' Jay Hawkins	1970	16.00	40.00
Sounds Of Hawaii 5015	(S)	A Night At Forbidden City	196?	20.00	50.00

HAWKWIND

United Arts. UAS-5519	(S)	In Search Of Space	1971	6.00	15.00
United Arts. UAS-5567	(S)	Hawkwind	1971	6.00	15.00
United Arts. LA001	(S)	Doremi Fasol Latido	1973	5.00	12.00
United Arts. LA120	(S)	Space Ritual Alive	1973	6.00	15.00
United Arts. LA328	(S)	Hall Of The Mountain Grill	1974	5.00	12.00
Atco SD-36-115	(S)	Warrior On The Edge Of Time	1975	4.00	10.00
Sire SRK-6047	(S)	Quark Strangeness And Charm	1978	4.00	10.00

HAWKS, BILLY

Prestige PRLP-7501	(M)	New Genius Of The Blues	1967	8.00	20.00
Prestige PRST-7501	(S)	New Genius Of The Blues	1967	6.00	15.00

HAWN, GOLDIE

Reprise MS-2061	(S)	Goldie	1972	8.00	20.00

Label & Catalog #		Title	Year	VG+	NM

HAYDEN, WILLIE

| Dooto DTL-293 | (M) | Blame It On The Blues | 1960 | 100.00 | Rare |

(Near Mint copies have a suggested value of $200-400.)

HAYES, BILL

| ABC-Paramount 194 | (M) | Bill Hayes Sings The Best Of Disney | 1957 | 14.00 | 35.00 |

HAYES, CATHY

| HiFi R-416 | (M) | It's All Right With Me | 1959 | 10.00 | 25.00 |

HAYES, ISAAC

Enterprise E-100	(M)	Presenting Isaac Hayes	1968	12.00	30.00
Enterprise ES-100	(S)	Presenting Isaac Hayes	1968	12.00	30.00
Enterprise ENS-1001	(S)	Hot Buttered Soul	1969	5.00	12.00
Enterprise ENS-1010	(S)	The Isaac Hayes Movement	1970	5.00	12.00
Enterprise ENS-1014	(S)	To Be Continued	1970	5.00	12.00
Enterprise ENS-5002	(S)	Shaft (2 LPs. Soundtrack)	1971	6.00	15.00
Enterprise ENS-5003	(S)	Black Moses (2 LPs)	1971	6.00	15.00
Atlantic SD-1599	(S)	In The Beginning	1972	6.00	15.00

(Atlantic 1599 is a reissue of Enterprise 100.)

Enterprise ENS-5007	(S)	Joy	1973	5.00	12.00
Enterprise ENS-7504	(S)	Tough Guys	1974	5.00	12.00
Enterprise ENS-7507	(S)	Truck Turner (2 LPs)	1974	6.00	15.00
Enterprise ENS-7510	(S)	The Best Of Isaac Hayes	1975	4.00	10.00

HAYES, MARTHA

| Jubilee 1023 | (M) | A Hayes Named Martha | 1956 | 12.00 | 30.00 |

HAYMARKET SQUARE

| Chaparral 201 | (S) | Magic Lantern | 1968 | 1,000.00 | 1,500.00 |

HAYMES, DICK

Decca DL-5023 (10")	(M)	Dick Haymes Sings	1950	12.00	30.00
Decca DL-5038 (10")	(M)	Little Shamrocks	1950	12.00	30.00
Decca DL-8773	(M)	Little White Lies	1958	8.00	20.00
Hollywood 138	(M)	Look At Me Now	195?	8.00	20.00
Capitol T-713	(M)	Rain Or Shine	1956	8.00	20.00
Capitol T-787	(M)	Moondreams	1956	8.00	20.00
Hallmark 301	(M)	The Name's Haymes	195?	8.00	20.00
Warwick W-2023	(M)	Richard The Lion-Hearted	195?	8.00	20.00

HAYNES, WALTER

| Mercury MG-20715 | (M) | Steel Guitar Sounds | 1962 | 8.00 | 20.00 |
| Mercury SR-60715 | (S) | Steel Guitar Sounds | 1962 | 10.00 | 25.00 |

HAYWARD, JUSTIN, & JOHN LODGE

Hayward and Lodge are members of The Moody Blues.

Threshold THSX-1	(DJ)	Blue Jays (Open-end interview with script)	1975	20.00	50.00
Threshold THS-14	(S)	Blue Jays	1975	4.00	10.00
Mapcity	(S)	Nascence	197?	6.00	15.00

HAZEL, EDDIE

Eddie Hazel is a member of the Parliament/Funkadelic community.

| Warner Bros. 3058 | (S) | Games, Dames And Guitar Thangs | 1977 | 10.00 | 25.00 |

HEAD

| Buddah BDS-5062 | (S) | Head (Issued with a coloring book) | 1970 | 8.00 | 20.00 |

HEAD, JIM, & HIS DEL RAYS

| "HP" 22893 | (M) | Jim Head & His Del Rays | 1964 | 80.00 | 200.00 |

HEAD, ROY

TNT 101	(M)	Roy Head And The Traits	1965	40.00	100.00
Scepter S-532	(M)	Treat Me Right	1965	12.00	30.00
Scepter SS-532	(S)	Treat Me Right	1965	16.00	40.00
Dunhill DS-50080	(S)	Some People	1970	8.00	20.00

HEAD SHOP, THE

| Epic BN-26476 | (S) | The Head Shop | 1969 | 20.00 | 50.00 |

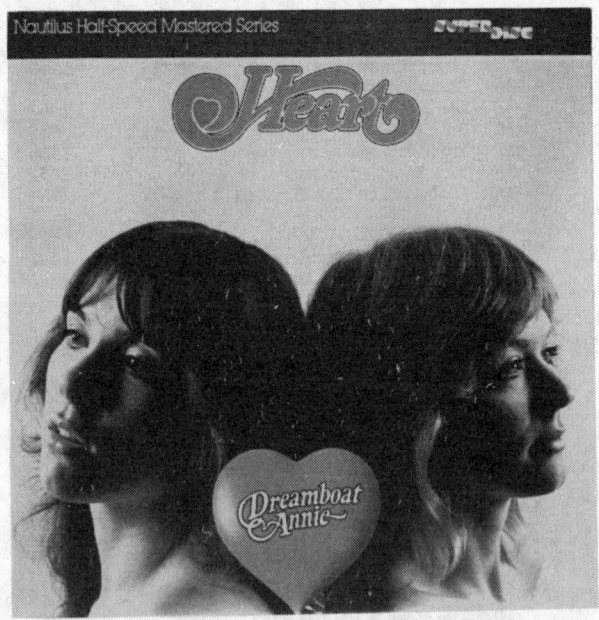

Original pressings of Magazine on Mushroom were issued during a dispute with the band; the album bore a contractual dispute disclaimer on the back notifying the public of the situation. Subsequent pressings have a radically different content and mix (without the disclaimer). When Nautilus began, one of their first selections of their "Super Disc" series was Heart's Dreamboat Annie. The album's success as an audiophile half-speed pressing helped the fledgling company survive the treacherous waters all new corporations endure.

Label & Catalog #		Title	Year	VG+	NM

HEADS, THE

| Liberty LST-7581 | (S) | **Heads Up** | 1968 | 8.00 | 20.00 |

HEADSTONE

| Starr 740539 | (S) | **Still Looking** | 1974 | 60.00 | 150.00 |

HEART

| Look LLP-11000 | (S) | **Heart** | 1969 | 5.00 | 12.00 |
| King KS-1119 | (S) | **Have A Heart** | 1970 | 4.00 | 10.00 |

HEART

Heart features Ann and Nancy Wilson. Refer to Bordersong.

Mushroom MRS-5005	(S)	**Dreamboat Annie**	1976	6.00	15.00
Mushroom MRS-5008	(S)	**Magazine**	1977	8.00	20.00
		(Original pressings have a contractual dispute disclaimer printed on the back cover.)			
Mushroom MRS-5008	(DJ)	**Magazine** *(Picture disc)*	1978	12.00	30.00
Mushroom MRS-1-SP	(S)	**Magazine** *(Picture disc)*	1978	6.00	15.00
Mushroom MRS-2-SP	(S)	**Dreamboat Annie** *(Picture disc)*	1979	8.00	20.00
Columbia AS-884	(DJ)	**Heart** *(Sampler)*	197?	8.00	20.00
Portrait HR-44799	(S)	**Little Queen** *(Half-speed master)*	1981	10.00	30.00
Nautilus NR-3	(S)	**Dreamboat Annie**	1980	12.00	35.00

HEARTBEATS, THE

Roulette R-25107	(M)	**A Thousand Miles Away**	1960	80.00	200.00
Roulette SR-25107	(E)	**A Thousand Miles Away**	1960	50.00	125.00
— *Original Roulette albums above have white labels with four crossed color bars.—*					
Emus ES-12033	(E)	**A Thousand Miles Away**	1980	10.00	25.00
		(Emus 12033 is a reissue of Roulette 25107.)			

HEARTS, THE

The Hearts feature Baby Washington.

| Zells 337 | (M) | **I Feel So Good** | 195? | 200.00 | 400.00 |

HEARTS & FLOWERS

Heart & Flowers features Rick Cunha. Linda Ronstadt supplies backing vocals.

Capitol T-2762	(M)	**Now Is The Time For Hearts And Flowers**	1967	10.00	25.00
Capitol ST-2762	(S)	**Now Is The Time For Hearts And Flowers**	1967	12.00	30.00
Capitol ST-2868	(S)	**Of Horses, Kids And Forgotten Women**	1968	20.00	50.00

HEATHER BLACK

American Playboy 1001	(S)	**Heather Black** *(2 LPs)*	197?	50.00	125.00
American Playboy 1001	(S)	**Heather Black** *(Single LP)*	197?	24.00	60.00
Double Bayou 2000	(S)	**Heather Black**	197?	12.00	30.00

HEATHERTON, JOEY

| MGM SE-4858 | (S) | **The Joey Heatherton Album** | 1972 | 8.00 | 20.00 |

HEAVEN

| W.W. 8701 | (S) | **Heaven** | 197? | 12.00 | 30.00 |

HEAVY BALLOON, THE

| Elephant EVS-104 | (S) | **32,000 Lbs.** | 196? | 14.00 | 35.00 |

HEAVY CRUISER

Family 2706	(S)	**Heavy Cruiser**	1972	6.00	15.00
Family 2712	(S)	**Lucky Dog**	1973	6.00	15.00
Tiger Lily 14034	(S)	**Heavy Cruiser II**	197?	4.00	10.00

HEAVY REGGAE MACHINE, THE

| Reggae 15004 | (S) | **Doin' The Reggae** | 1970 | 6.00 | 15.00 |

HEBB, BOBBY

| Philips PHM-200-212 | (M) | **Sunny** | 1966 | 10.00 | 25.00 |
| Philips PHS-600-212 | (S) | **Sunny** | 1966 | 12.00 | 30.00 |

HELL, RICHARD, & THE VOIDOIDS

Richard Hell is a pseudonym for Richard Lloyd, formerly of Television.

| Sire SR-6037 | (S) | **Blank Generation** | 1977 | 10.00 | 25.00 |

Label & Catalog #		Title	Year	VG+	NM
HELM, LEVON					
Helm was formerly a member of The Band.					
ABC SPPD-4-5	(DJ)	**Levon Helm** *(Picture disc)*	1978	5.00	12.00
HELMS, BOBBY					
Decca DL-8638	(M)	**To My Special Angel**	1957	40.00	100.00
Columbia CL-2060	(M)	**The Best Of Bobby Helms**	1963	10.00	25.00
Columbia CS-8860	(S)	**The Best Of Bobby Helms**	1963	12.00	30.00
Kapp KL-13463	(M)	**I'm The Man**	1966	6.00	15.00
Kapp KS-3463	(M)	**I'm The Man**	1966	8.00	20.00
Kapp KL-1505	(S)	**Sorry My Name Isn't Fred**	1966	6.00	15.00
Kapp KS-3505	(S)	**Sorry My Name Isn't Fred**	1966	8.00	20.00
HELMS, DON					
Smash MGS-27001	(M)	**Steel Guitar Sounds Of Hank Williams**	1963	10.00	25.00
Smash SRS-67001	(S)	**Steel Guitar Sounds Of Hank Williams**	1963	12.00	30.00
Smash MGS-27019	(M)	**Don Helms' Steel Guitar**	1963	8.00	20.00
Smash SRS-67019	(S)	**Don Helms' Steel Guitar**	1963	10.00	25.00
HELP					
Decca DL-75257	(S)	**Help**	1971	10.00	25.00
Decca DL-75304	(S)	**Second Coming**	1971	10.00	25.00
HENDERSON, BILL: *Refer to* GOLDMINE'S PRICE GUIDE TO COLLECTIBLE JAZZ ALBUMS					
HENDERSON, BUGS					
Armadillo LP-78-1	(S)	**The Bugs Henderson Group At Last**	195?	12.00	30.00
HENDERSON, JOE					
Todd MT-2701	(M)	**Snap Your Fingers**	1962	16.00	40.00
Todd ST-2701	(S)	**Snap Your Fingers**	1962	20.00	50.00
Capitol T-1765	(M)	**You'd Be So Nice To Come Home To**	1962	8.00	20.00
Capitol ST-1765	(S)	**You'd Be So Nice To Come Home To**	1962	10.00	25.00
HENDERSON, WILLIE, & THE SOUL EXPLOSIONS					
Brunswick BL7-54163	(S)	**Funky Chicken**	1969	6.00	15.00
Brunswick BL7-54202	(S)	**Dance With The Master**	1970	6.00	15.00
HENDRICKS, JAMES					
Hendricks was formerly a member of the Big Three; The Mugwumps.					
Soul City SCS-92003	(S)	**The Songs Of James Hendricks**	1968	6.00	15.00
MGM SE-4768	(S)	**James Hendricks**	1971	5.00	12.00
HENDRICKS, JON: *Refer to* GOLDMINE'S PRICE GUIDE TO COLLECTIBLE JAZZ ALBUMS					
HENDRIX, JIMI					
Refer to The Isley Brothers; Curtis Knight; Love; Martha Velez.					
Reprise R-6261	(DJ)	**Are You Experienced?** *(White label)*	1967	100.00	250.00
Reprise R-6261	(M)	**Are You Experienced?**	1967	40.00	100.00
Reprise RS-6261	(P)	**Are You Experienced?**	1967	16.00	40.00
Reprise R-6281	(DJ)	**Axis: Bold As Love** *(White label)*	1968	150.00	300.00
Reprise R-6281	(M)	**Axis: Bold As Love**	1968	200.00	400.00
Reprise RS-6281	(S)	**Axis: Bold As Love**	1968	16.00	40.00
— Original Reprise albums have pink, gold & green labels.—					
Reprise RS-6261	(P)	**Are You Experienced?**	1968	8.00	20.00
Reprise RS-6281	(S)	**Axis: Bold As Love**	1968	8.00	20.00
Reprise 2R-6307	(DJ)	**Electric Ladyland** *(2 LPs. Mono)*	1968	500.00	800.00
Reprise 2RS-6307	(DJ)	**Electric Ladyland** *(2 LPs. Stereo)*	1968	50.00	125.00
Reprise 2RS-6307	(S)	**Electric Ladyland** *(2 LPs)*	1968	16.00	40.00
Reprise MS-2025	(DJ)	**Smash Hits** *(White label)*	1969	50.00	125.00
Reprise MS-2025	(P)	**Smash Hits**	1969	16.00	40.00
(Original covers advertised a poster in the lower right corner.)					
Reprise MS-2025		**Smash Hits Poster**	1969	14.00	35.00
—Reprise albums above have brown & orange labels.—					
Capitol STAO-472	(S)	**Band Of Gypsies** *(Green label)*	1970	6.00	15.00
Capitol STAO-472	(S)	**Band Of Gypsies** *(Red label)*	1970	10.00	25.00
Capitol STAO-8-472	(S)	**Band Of Gypsies** *(Record Club)*	1970	10.00	25.00
Reprise MS-2025	(P)	**Smash Hits**	1971	8.00	20.00
Reprise MS-2034	(S)	**The Cry Of Love**	1971	6.00	15.00

Label & Catalog #		Title	Year	VG+	NM
Reprise MS-2040	(S)	**Rainbow Bridge**	1971	10.00	25.00
Reprise MS-2049	(S)	**Hendrix In The West**	1972	10.00	25.00
Reprise MS-2103	(S)	**War Heroes**	1972	8.00	20.00
Reprise MS-2204	(S)	**Crash Landing**	1975	6.00	15.00
Reprise MS-2229	(S)	**Midnight Lightning**	1975	8.00	20.00
Reprise PRO-A-840	(DJ)	**Jimi Hendrix Medley**	1979	30.00	75.00
		—*Reprise albums above have brown labels.*—			
Springboard SPB-4031	(S)	**Jimi Hendrix In Concert**	1972	6.00	15.00
Shout 502	(S)	**In The Beginning**	1972	6.00	15.00
Trip TLP-9500	(S)	**Rare Hendrix**	1972	6.00	15.00
Trip TLP-9501	(S)	**The Roots Of Hendrix**	1972	6.00	15.00
Trip TLP-9523	(S)	**The Genius Of Jimi Hendrix**	1973	6.00	15.00
United Artists LA505	(S)	**The Very Best Of Jimi Hendrix**	1975	6.00	15.00
Crawdaddy 5-1975	(DJ)	**The Jimi Hendrix Interview LP**	1975	80.00	200.00

HENDRIX, JIMI, & LITTLE RICHARD

ALA 1972	(S)	**Friends From The Beginning**	1972	6.00	15.00
Pickwick SPC-3347	(S)	**Jimi Hendrix/Little Richard Together**	1973	6.00	15.00
Everest 296	(S)	**Roots Of Rock**	1974	4.00	10.00

HENDRIX, JIMI / OTIS REDDING

Reprise MS-2029	(S)	**Historic Performances Recorded At The Monterey International Pop Festival**	1970	6.00	15.00

HENDRIX, JIMI, & LONNIE YOUNGBLOOD

Maple 6004	(S)	**Together With Lonnie Youngblood**	1971	10.00	25.00

HENRI, ADRIAN, & ROGER McGOUGH

Epic LN-26336	(M)	**The Incredible New Liverpool Scene**	1967	8.00	20.00
Epic BN-24336	(S)	**The Incredible New Liverpool Scene**	1967	10.00	25.00

HENRY, CLARENCE "FROGMAN"

Argo LP-4009	(M)	**You Always Hurt The One You Love**	1961	50.00	150.00
Roulette SR-42039	(S)	**Alive And Well And Living In New Orleans**	1969	8.00	20.00

HENSKE, JUDY

Elektra EKL-231	(M)	**Judy Henske**	1963	6.00	15.00
Elektra EKS-7231	(S)	**Judy Henske**	1963	8.00	20.00
Mercury MG-21010	(M)	**A Little Bit Of Sunshine, A Little Bit Of Rain**	1965	6.00	15.00
Mercury SR-61010	(S)	**A Little Bit Of Sunshine, A Little Bit Of Rain**	1965	8.00	20.00
Reprise R-6203	(M)	**The Death Defying Judy Henske**	1966	6.00	15.00
Reprise RS-6203	(S)	**The Death Defying Judy Henske**	1966	8.00	20.00

HENSKE & YESTER
Judy Henske and Jerry Yester. Refer to The Lovin' Spoonful; The Modern Folk Quartet.

Straight STS-1052	(S)	**Farewell Aldebaran**	1968	20.00	50.00
Reprise RS-6388	(S)	**Farewell Aldebaran**	1971	10.00	25.00

HENSON, COUSIN HERB, & THE TRADING POST GANG

Tally	(M)	**Herb Henson & The Trading Post Gang**	195?	40.00	100.00

HERD, THE
The Herd features Peter Frampton.

Fontana SRF-67579	(S)	**Lookin' Thru You**	1968	10.00	25.00
		("Understand Me" and "William" are rechanneled on this album.)			

HERE COMES EVERYBODY

Cab 101	(S)	**Here Comes Everybody**	1971	16.00	40.00

HERMAN, PEE WEE

Fatima	(S)	**The Pee Wee Herman Show** *(Picture disc)*	1981	20.00	50.00

HERMAN'S HERMITS

MGM E-4282	(M)	**Introducing Herman's Hermits**	1965	10.00	25.00
MGM SE-4282	(E)	**Introducing Herman's Hermits**	1965	8.00	20.00
		(The front cover reads "Including Their Hit Single I'm Into Something Good." Later copies feature a sticker on the cover that reads "Featuring Mrs. Brown You Have A Lovely Daughter.")			

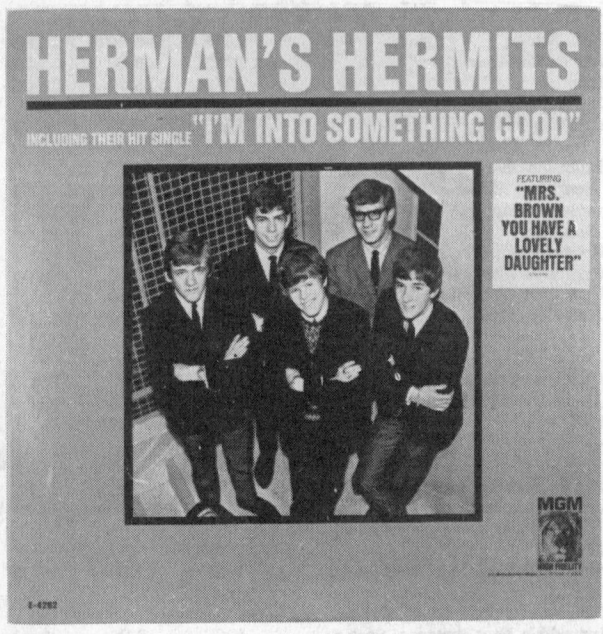

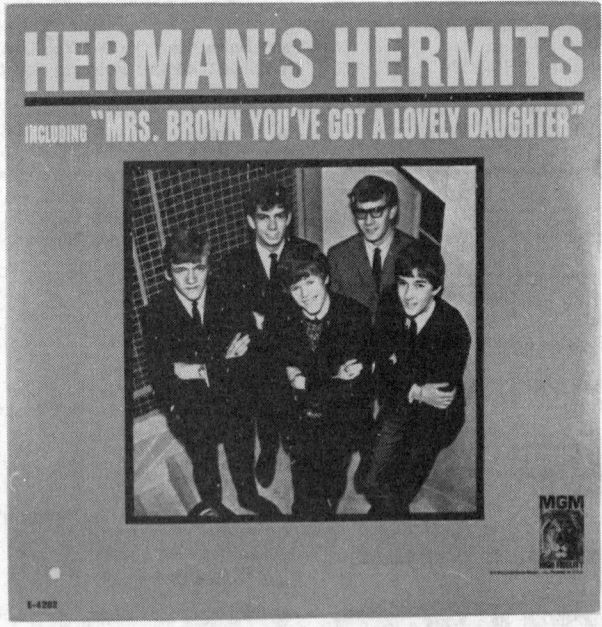

You can argue over The Beatles and The Stones in the beat battle of the world that took place in 1964-65, but on this side of the Atlantic it was Herman's Hermits that fought for chart supremacy with the Fab Four, scoring eighteen straight top 40 hits before their popularity waned in 1967. Each of their ten MGM albums made the charts, five of them achieving RIAA Gold Records. Original pressings of their first MGM album (above) read "Including Their Hit Single I'm Into Something Good" (the copy here has a sticker applied to the cover noting— and mistitling— their next single). After the unexpected success of "Mrs. Brown You've Got A Lovely Daughter," the cover of all subsequent pressings was amended (below).

Label & Catalog #		Title	Year	VG+	NM
MGM E-4282	(M)	Introducing Herman's Hermits	1965	6.00	15.00
MGM SE-4282	(E)	Introducing Herman's Hermits	1965	4.00	10.00
		(Cover reads "Including Mrs. Brown You've... Daughter.")			
MGM E-4295	(M)	On Tour: Their Second Album	1965	6.00	15.00
MGM SE-4295	(E)	On Tour: Their Second Album	1965	4.00	10.00
MGM E-4315	(M)	The Best Of Herman's Hermits	1965	6.00	15.00
MGM SE-4315	(E)	The Best Of Herman's Hermits	1965	4.00	10.00
MGM E-4342	(M)	Hold On! (Soundtrack)	1966	3.50	8.00
MGM SE-4342	(S)	Hold On! (Soundtrack)	1966	4.00	10.00
MGM E-4386	(M)	Both Sides Of Herman's Hermits	1966	4.00	10.00
MGM SE-4386	(E)	Both Sides Of Herman's Hermits	1966	3.50	8.00
MGM E-4416	(M)	Best Of Herman's Hermits, Volume 2	1966	6.00	15.00
MGM SE-4416	(E)	Best Of Herman's Hermits, Volume 2	1966	5.00	12.00
		("Hold On" and "Leanining On A Lamp Post" are in stereo. Issued with a bonus poster.)			
MGM E-4438	(M)	There's A Kind Of Hush All Over The World	1967	5.00	12.00
MGM SE-4438	(E)	There's A Kind Of Hush All Over The World	1967	4.00	10.00
MGM E-4478	(M)	Blaze	1967	4.00	10.00
MGM SE-4478	(S)	Blaze	1967	1.00	5.00
		("Moonshine Man" is rechanneled on this album.)			
MGM E-4505	(M)	The Best Of Herman's Hermits, Volume III	1967	5.00	12.00
MGM SE-4505	(E)	The Best Of Herman's Hermits, Volume III	1967	3.50	8.00
		("Museum," "Mom And Dad," "Last Bus Home" and "Don't Go Out Into The Rain" are in stereo on this album.)			
MGM E-4548	(M)	Mrs. Brown You've Got A Lovely Daughter (Soundtrack)	1968	6.00	15.00
MGM SE-4548	(P)	Mrs. Brown You've Got A Lovely Daughter (Soundtrack)	1968	3.50	8.00
		("Mrs. Brown You've Got A Lovely Daughter" and "There's A Kind Of Hush All Over The World" are rechanneled.)			

HERMON KNIGHTS, THE

Label & Catalog #		Title	Year	VG+	NM
C.O. 2323	(S)	The Hermon Knights	1968	20.00	50.00

HERON, MIKE
Mike Heron was formerly a member of The Incredible String Band.

Label & Catalog #		Title	Year	VG+	NM
Elektra EKS-74093	(S)	Smiling Men With Bad Reputations	1971	6.00	15.00

HESITATIONS, THE

Label & Catalog #		Title	Year	VG+	NM
Kapp KL-1525	(M)	Soul Superman	1967	8.00	20.00
Kapp KS-3525	(S)	Soul Superman	1967	10.00	25.00
Kapp KS-3548	(S)	The New Born Free	1968	8.00	20.00
Kapp KS-3561	(S)	Where We're At	1968	8.00	20.00
Kapp KS-3574	(S)	Solid Gold	1968	6.00	15.00

HESTER, BENNY

Label & Catalog #		Title	Year	VG+	NM
V.M.I. 72001	(S)	Benny Hester	1972	20.00	50.00

HESTER, CAROLYN

Label & Catalog #		Title	Year	VG+	NM
Columbia CL-1796	(M)	Carolyn Hester	1962	12.00	30.00
Columbia CS-8596	(S)	Carolyn Hester	1962	16.00	40.00
		(Bob Dylan plays harmonica on "Swing And Turn Jubilee," "I'll Fly Away" and "Come Back, Baby.")			
Columbia CL-2032	(M)	This Life I'm Living	1963	8.00	20.00
Columbia CS-8832	(S)	This Life I'm Living	1963	10.00	25.00
Columbia Sp. Pro. CS-8832	(S)	This Life I'm Living	196?	5.00	12.00
Dot DLP-3604	(M)	That's My Song	1964	5.00	12.00
Dot DLP-25604	(S)	That's My Song	1964	6.00	15.00
Dot DLP-3649	(M)	Carolyn Hester At The Town Hall	1965	5.00	12.00
Dot DLP-25649	(S)	Carolyn Hester At The Town Hall	1965	6.00	15.00

HI-LITES, THE

Label & Catalog #		Title	Year	VG+	NM
Dandee DLP-206	(M)	For Your Precious Love	195?	300.00	Rare
		(Near Mint copies have a suggested value of $500-1,000.)			

HI-LO'S, THE
Refer to The Reprise Repertory Theatre.

Label & Catalog #		Title	Year	VG+	NM
Starlite 6004 (10")	(M)	The Hi-Lo's	1955	16.00	40.00
Starlite 6005 (10")	(M)	The Hi-Lo's, I Presume	1955	16.00	40.00

Label & Catalog #		Title	Year	VG+	NM
Starlite 7005	(M)	Under Glass	1956	12.00	30.00
Starlite 7006	(M)	Listen To The	1956	12.00	30.00
Starlite 7007	(M)	The Hi-Lo's, I Presume	1956	12.00	30.00
Starlite 7008	(M)	On Hand	1956	12.00	30.00
Kapp KL-1027	(M)	The Hi-Lo's And The Jerry Fielding Band	1956	8.00	20.00
Kapp KL-1184	(M)	Under Glass	1959	8.00	20.00
Kapp KL-1194	(M)	On Hand	1960	8.00	20.00
Columbia CL-952	(M)	Suddenly It's The Hi-Lo's	1957	12.00	30.00
Columbia CL-1023	(M)	Now Hear This	1957	10.00	25.00
Columbia CL-1259	(M)	All That Jazz	1959	8.00	20.00
Columbia CS-8077	(S)	All That Jazz	1959	10.00	25.00
Columbia CL-1416	(M)	Broadway Playbill	1959	8.00	20.00
Columbia CS-8213	(S)	Broadway Playbill	1959	10.00	25.00
Columbia CL-1509	(M)	All Over The Place	1960	8.00	20.00
Columbia CS-8300	(S)	All Over The Place	1960	10.00	25.00
Columbia CL-1723	(M)	This Time It's Love	1962	6.00	15.00
Columbia CS-8523	(S)	This Time It's Love	1962	8.00	20.00
— Original Columbia albums above have three white "eye" logos on each side of the spindle hole.—					
Reprise R-6066	(M)	The Hi-Lo's Happen To Bossa Nova	1963	5.00	12.00
Reprise RS-6066	(S)	The Hi-Lo's Happen To Bossa Nova	1963	6.00	15.00
Omega 11	(S)	The Hi-Lo's In Stereo	196?	8.00	20.00

HI-LO'S, THE, & ROSEMARY CLOONEY

Columbia CL-1006	(M)	Ring Around Rosie	1957	12.00	30.00

HI-TONES, THE

Hi HL-32011	(M)	Raunchy Sounds	1963	5.00	12.00
Hi SHL-32011	(S)	Raunchy Sounds	1963	6.00	15.00

HIBBLER, AL: Refer to GOLDMINE'S PRICE GUIDE TO COLLECTIBLE JAZZ ALBUMS

HICKMAN, DWAYNE

Capitol T-1441	(M)	Dobie!	1960	12.00	30.00
Capitol ST-1441	(S)	Dobie!	1960	16.00	40.00

HICKS, DAN, & HIS HOT LICKS

Epic BN-26464	(S)	Dan Hicks And His Hot Licks (Yellow label)	1969	6.00	15.00
Blue Thumb BTS-29	(S)	Where's The Money	1971	5.00	12.00
Blue Thumb BTS-36	(S)	Striking It Rich (Fold-open cover)	1972	6.00	15.00
Warner Bros. BSK-3158	(S)	It Happened One Bite	1978	4.00	10.00
MCA 51	(S)	Last Train To Hicksville	1980	4.00	10.00

HICKS, JOE

Enterprise ENS-1028	(S)	Mighty	1971	6.00	15.00

HIGGINS, CHUCK

Combo LP-300	(M)	Pachuko Hop	1960	200.00	600.00
		(Original pressing covers feature a delightfully naked woman.)			
Combo LP-300	(M)	Pachuko Hop	1961	100.00	300.00
		(Later pressings feature a photo of a fully attired Higgins.)			

HIGGINS, CHUCK / ROY MILTON

Authentic AUL-223	(M)	Rock 'N' Roll Versus Rhythm And Blues	1959	150.00	300.00

HIGH, MARTHA

Salsoul	(S)	He's My Ding Dong Man	1979	5.00	12.00
		(Produced by James Brown..)			

HIGH TIDE

Liberty LST-7638	(S)	Sea Shanties	1969	10.00	25.00

HIGH TREASON

Abbott ABS-1209	(S)	High Treason	197?	20.00	50.00

HIGHTOWER, DEAN

ABC-Paramount 312	(M)	Guitar-Twangy With A Beat	1959	10.00	25.00
ABC-Paramount S-312	(S)	Guitar-Twangy With A Beat	1959	14.00	35.00

Label & Catalog #		Title	Year	VG+	NM
HIGHTOWER, DONNA					
Capitol T-1133	(M)	Take One	1959	12.00	30.00
Capitol T-1273	(M)	Gee Baby, Ain't I Good To You?	1959	12.00	30.00
HIGHWAY, THE					
(No label)	(S)	The Highway	197?	60.00	150.00
HIGHWAYMEN, THE					
United Arts. UAL-3125	(M)	The Highwaymen	1961	6.00	15.00
United Arts. UAS-6125	(S)	The Highwaymen	1961	8.00	20.00
United Arts. UAL-3168	(M)	Standing Room Only!	1962	6.00	15.00
United Arts. UAS-6168	(S)	Standing Room Only!	1962	8.00	20.00
United Arts. UAL-3225	(S)	Encore!	1962	6.00	15.00
United Arts. UAS-6225	(S)	Encore!	1962	8.00	20.00
United Arts. UAL-3245	(M)	March On, Brothers	1963	6.00	15.00
United Arts. UAS-6245	(M)	March On, Brothers	1963	8.00	20.00
United Arts. UAL-3294	(M)	Hootenanny With The Highwaymen	1963	6.00	15.00
United Arts. UAS-6294	(S)	Hootenanny With The Highwaymen	1963	8.00	20.00
United Arts. UAL-3323	(S)	One More Time	1964	6.00	15.00
United Arts. UAS-6323	(S)	One More Time	1964	8.00	20.00
HILL, GOLDIE					
Decca DL-4034	(M)	Goldie Hill	1960	12.00	30.00
Decca DL-74034	(S)	Goldie Hill	1960	16.00	40.00
Decca DL-4148	(M)	Lonely Heartaches	1961	8.00	20.00
Decca DL-74148	(S)	Lonely Heartaches	1961	12.00	30.00
Decca DL-4219	(M)	According To My Heart	1962	8.00	20.00
Decca DL-74219	(S)	According To My Heart	1962	10.00	25.00
Decca DL-4492	(M)	Country Hit Parade	1964	6.00	15.00
Decca DL-74492	(S)	Country Hit Parade	1964	8.00	20.00
HILL, VINCE					
Tower T-5064	(M)	At The Club	1966	8.00	20.00
HILLMEN, THE					

Members include Chris Hillmen with Vern & Rex Gosdin. Refer to The Byrds; The Gosdin Brothers; The Scottsville Squirrel Barkers.

Together STT-1012	(S)	The Hillmen	1970	20.00	50.00
HILLOW HAMMET					
House Of Fox 2	(S)	Hammer	197?	24.00	60.00
L & BJ 14028	(S)	Hammer	197?	40.00	100.00
HILLTOPPERS, THE					
Dot DLP-3001	(M)	The Hilltoppers	1956	20.00	50.00
Dot DLP-3003	(M)	Tops In Pops	1956	20.00	50.00
Dot DLP-3029	(M)	The Towering Hilltoppers	1957	14.00	35.00
Dot DLP-3073	(M)	The Hilltoppers	1958	14.00	35.00
HINES, MIMI					
Decca DL-8434	(M)	Mimi Hines Is A Happening	1958	8.00	20.00
Decca DL-78434	(S)	Mimi Hines Is A Happening	1958	10.00	25.00
Decca DL-4709	(M)	Mimi Hines Sings	1965	5.00	12.00
Decca DL-74709	(S)	Mimi Hines Sings	1965	6.00	15.00
HINSON, DON, & THE RIGORMORTICIANS					
Capitol T-2219	(M)	Monster Dance Party	1964	10.00	25.00
Capitol ST-2219	(S)	Monster Dance Party	1964	14.00	35.00
HINTON, EDDIE					
Capricorn CPN-0204	(S)	Very Extremely Dangerous	1978	8.00	20.00
HINTON, JOE					
Backbeat B-60	(M)	Funny How Time Slips Away	1965	10.00	25.00
Backbeat B-60	(S)	Funny How Time Slips Away	1965	14.00	35.00
HINTON, SAM					
Decca DL-8108	(M)	Singing Across The Land	1956	14.00	35.00

Label & Catalog #		Title	Year	VG+	NM

HITCHCOCK, ALFRED

Imperial LP-9052	(M)	Music To Be Murdered By	1958	30.00	75.00
Imperial LP-12052	(S)	Music To Be Murdered By	1958	40.00	100.00
Golden Record LP-89	(M)	Ghost Stories For Young People	1962	12.00	30.00

HOBBITS, THE

Decca DL-4290	(M)	Down To Middle Earth	1967	10.00	25.00
Decca DL-74290	(S)	Down To Middle Earth	1967	12.00	30.00
Decca DL-5009	(M)	Men And Doors	1968	8.00	20.00
Decca DL-75009	(S)	Men And Doors	1968	6.00	15.00
Perception	(S)	Return To Middle Earth	1971	12.00	30.00

HOFFMAN, ABBIE

Big Toe 1	(M)	Wake Up, America!	196?	12.00	30.00

HOFFMAN, JEANNIE

Capitol T-2021	(M)	Folk-Type Singer	1964	5.00	12.00
Capitol ST-2021	(S)	Folk-Type Singer	1964	6.00	15.00

HOFNER, ADOLPH

Decca DL-5564 (10")	(M)	Dance-O-Rama #4	1955	100.00	250.00

HOG HEAVEN

Hog Heaven is comprised of members of Tommy James' Shondells.

Roulette SR-42057	(S)	Hog Heaven	1971	6.00	15.00

HOGAN SILAS

Excello EX-8019	(S)	Trouble	1972	8.00	20.00

HOGAN, CLAIRE

MGM E-3349	(M)	Just Imagine	1956	10.00	25.00

HOGAN'S HEROES

Sunset SUM-1137	(M)	The Best Of World War II	196?	6.00	15.00
Sunset SUS-5137	(S)	The Best Of World War II	196?	8.00	20.00

HOGG, ANDREW "SMOKEY"

Time 6	(M)	Smokey Hogg	1962	30.00	75.00
Crown CLP-5226	(M)	Smokey Hogg Sings The Blues	1962	12.00	30.00
Kent LP-5226	(M)	Original Folk Blues	1966	6.00	15.00
United 7745	(M)	Smokey Hogg	1970	4.00	10.00

(Both the Kent and United albums are reissues of Crown 5226.)

HOLDEN, RANDY

Holden was formerly a member of The Other Half; Blue Cheer.

Hobbit 5002	(S)	Population II	1968	30.00	175.00

HOLDEN, RON

Donna DLP-2111	(M)	I Love You So	1960	75.00	150.00
Donna DLPS-2111	(S)	I Love You So	1960	150.00	300.00

HOLIDAY, BILLIE: *Refer to* GOLDMINE'S PRICE GUIDE TO COLLECTIBLE JAZZ ALBUMS

HOLIDAY, JIMMY

Minit LP-24005	(M)	Turning Point	1966	6.00	15.00

HOLLAND, EDDIE

Motown 604	(M)	Eddie Holland	1963	40.00	100.00

HOLLIDAY, JUDY

Columbia OL-5170	(M)	Bells Are Ringing (Original Cast)	1956	12.00	30.00
Columbia CL-1153	(M)	Trouble Is A Man	1958	8.00	20.00
Columbia CS-8041	(S)	Trouble Is A Man	1958	12.00	30.00
Capitol W-1435	(M)	Bells Are Ringing (Soundtrack)	1960	8.00	20.00
Capitol SW-1435	(S)	Bells Are Ringing (Soundtrack)	1960	12.00	30.00

Label & Catalog #		Title	Year	VG+	NM

HOLLIES, THE
Original members include Allan Clarke, Graham Nash, Tony Hicks, Eric Haydock and Donald Rathbone. Rathbone was replaced by Bobby Elliott in 1963; Haydock by Bernie Calvert, 1966; and Nash by Terry Sylvester, 1968. Mikael Rikfors replaced Clarke on "Romany." Refer to The Everly Brothers; Peter Sellers.

Label & Catalog #		Title	Year	VG+	NM
Imperial LP-9265	(M)	Here I Go Again *(Black label with stars)*	1964	40.00	100.00
Imperial LP-12265	(E)	Here I Go Again *(Black & silver label)*	1964	30.00	75.00
Imperial LP-9265	(M)	Here I Go Again	1964	20.00	50.00
Imperial LP-12265	(E)	Here I Go Again	1964	14.00	35.00
Imperial LP-9299	(M)	Hear! Here!	1965	20.00	50.00
Imperial LP-12299	(E)	Hear! Here!	1965	16.00	40.00
Imperial LP-9312	(M)	The Hollies (Beat Group)	1966	12.00	30.00
Imperial LP-12312	(S)	The Hollies (Beat Group)	1966	16.00	40.00
Imperial LP-9330	(M)	Bus Stop	1966	12.00	30.00
Imperial LP-12330	(E)	Bus Stop	1966	8.00	20.00
— Imperial albums above have black, pink & white labels.—					
Imperial LP-9339	(M)	Stop! Stop! Stop!	1966	10.00	25.00
Imperial LP-12339	(S)	Stop! Stop! Stop!	1966	12.00	30.00
Imperial LP-9350	(M)	The Hollies' Greatest Hits	1967	8.00	20.00
Imperial LP-12350	(P)	The Hollies' Greatest Hits	1967	8.00	20.00
Epic LN-24315	(M)	Evolution	1967	8.00	20.00
Epic BN-26315	(S)	Evolution	1967	8.00	20.00
Epic LN-24344	(M)	Dear Eloise / King Midas In Reverse	1967	8.00	20.00
Epic BN-26344	(S)	Dear Eloise / King Midas In Reverse	1967	8.00	20.00
Epic BN-26447	(S)	Words And Music By Bob Dylan	1969	8.00	20.00
Epic BN-26538	(S)	He Ain't Heavy, He's My Brother	1969	8.00	20.00
Epic KE-30255	(S)	Moving Finger	1970	8.00	20.00
Epic KE-30958	(S)	Distant Light	1971	5.00	12.00
Epic KE-31992	(S)	Romany	1972	5.00	12.00
Epic KE-32061	(S)	The Hollies' Greatest Hits	1973	5.00	12.00
— Original Epic albums above have yellow labels.—					
Epic KE-32574	(S)	Hollies	1974	4.00	10.00
Epic PE-33387	(S)	Another Night	1975	4.00	10.00
Epic AS-138	(DJ)	Everything You Always Wanted To Hear	1976	6.00	15.00

HOLLIN'S FERRY
Label & Catalog #		Title	Year	VG+	NM
Port City	(S)	Hollin's Ferry	197?	30.00	75.00

HOLLOWAY, BRENDA
Label & Catalog #		Title	Year	VG+	NM
Tamla 257	(M)	Every Little Bit Hurts	1964	100.00	250.00

HOLLY, BUDDY (& THE CRICKETS)
Refer to The Crickets; Terry Noland; Norman Petty.

Label & Catalog #		Title	Year	VG+	NM
Brunswick BL-54038	(DJ)	The Chirping Crickets *(Yellow label)*	1957	400.00	800.00
Brunswick BL-54038	(M)	The Chirping Crickets	1957	250.00	500.00
Decca DL-8707	(DJ)	That'll Be The Day *(Pink label)*	1958	500.00	1,000.00
Decca DL-8707	(M)	That'll Be The Day	1958	600.00	1,200.00
(Original pressings have black labels with silver print.)					
Decca DL-8707	(M)	That'll Be The Day	196?	100.00	200.00
(Later pressings have a black label with a rainbow band through the center and were pressed on thick vinyl. Counterfeits from the '70s have poor cover reproduction and were pressed on thin vinyl.)					
Coral CRL-57210	(DJ)	Buddy Holly *(Blue label)*	1958	300.00	500.00
Coral CRL-57210	(M)	Buddy Holly	1958	100.00	250.00
Coral CRL-57279	(DJ)	The Buddy Holly Story *(Blue label)*	1959	300.00	500.00
Coral CRL-57279	(M)	The Buddy Holly Story	1959	80.00	200.00
(The print on the back cover is in red and black.)					
Coral CRL-57279	(M)	The Buddy Holly Story	1959	60.00	150.00
Coral CRL-757279	(E)	The Buddy Holly Story	1959	50.00	125.00
(The print on the back cover is in black only.)					
Coral CRL-57326	(DJ)	The Buddy Holly Story, Vol. 2 *(Blue label)*	1959	300.00	500.00
Coral CRL-57326	(M)	The Buddy Holly Story, Vol. 2	1959	60.00	150.00
Coral CRL-57405	(DJ)	Buddy Holly & The Crickets *(Blue label)*	1962	300.00	500.00
Coral CRL-57405	(M)	Buddy Holly & The Crickets	1962	60.00	150.00
Coral CRL-757405	(E)	Buddy Holly & The Crickets	1962	50.00	125.00
(Coral 57405 is a reissue of Brunswick 54038.)					
Coral CRL-57426	(DJ)	Reminiscing *(Blue label)*	1963	180.00	300.00
Coral CRL-57426	(M)	Reminiscing	1963	60.00	150.00
Coral CRL-757426	(E)	Reminiscing	1963	50.00	125.00
— Original Coral albums above have maroon labels.—					

Label & Catalog #		Title	Year	VG+	NM
Coral CRL-57210	(M)	Buddy Holly	1963	40.00	100.00
Coral CRL-57279	(M)	The Buddy Holly Story	1963	30.00	75.00
Coral CRL-757279	(E)	The Buddy Holly Story	1963	20.00	50.00
Coral CRL-57326	(M)	The Buddy Holly Story, Vol. 2	1963	30.00	75.00
Coral CRL-757326	(E)	The Buddy Holly Story, Vol. 2	1963	20.00	50.00
Coral CRL-57426	(M)	Reminiscing	1964	30.00	75.00
Coral CRL-757426	(E)	Reminiscing	1964	20.00	50.00
Coral CRL-57450	(DJ)	Showcase (Yellow label)	1964	100.00	250.00
Coral CRL-57450	(M)	Showcase	1964	40.00	100.00
Coral CRL-757450	(E)	Showcase	1964	30.00	75.00
Coral CRL-57463	(DJ)	Holly In The Hills (Yellow label)	1965	100.00	250.00
Coral CRL-57463	(M)	Holly In The Hills	1965	50.00	125.00
Coral CRL-757463	(E)	Holly In The Hills	1965	40.00	100.00
Coral CXB-8	(DJ)	The Best Of Buddy Holly (Yellow label)	1966	100.00	200.00
Coral CXB-8	(M)	The Best Of Buddy Holly	1966	30.00	75.00
Coral CXSB-8	(E)	The Best Of Buddy Holly	1966	20.00	50.00
Coral CRL-57492	(M)	Buddy Holly's Greatest Hits	1967	30.00	75.00
Coral CRL-757492	(E)	Buddy Holly's Greatest Hits	1967	20.00	50.00
Coral CRL-757504	(DJ)	Giant (Yellow label)	1969	60.00	150.00
Coral CRL-757504	(E)	Giant	1969	20.00	50.00
— Coral albums above have black labels that read "A subsidiary of Decca."—					
Vocalion VL-3811	(M)	The Great Buddy Holly	1967	30.00	75.00
Vocalion VL-73811	(E)	The Great Buddy Holly	1967	20.00	50.00
(Vocalion 3811 is a repackage of "That'll Be The Day.")					
Vocalion VL-73923	(E)	Good Rockin'	1971	40.00	100.00
Decca DXSE-207	(M)	A Rock & Roll Collection (2 LPs)	1972	14.00	35.00
MCA 2-4009	(M)	A Rock & Roll Collection (2 LPs)	1973	10.00	25.00
(Reissue of Decca 207. Original pressings have liner notes.)					
Cricket C001000	(M)	Buddy Holly Live (Volume 1)	197?	8.00	20.00
Cricket C001001	(M)	Buddy Holly Live (Volume 2)	197?	8.00	20.00
Solid Smoke 8002	(M)	A Portrait In Music, Volume 1 (Picture disc)	1979	6.00	15.00
Solid Smoke 8003	(M)	A Portrait In Music, Volume 2 (Picture disc)	1979	6.00	15.00
MCA 6-8000	(M)	The Complete Buddy Holly (6 LP box)	1981	16.00	40.00
HOLLYRIDGE STRINGS, THE					
Capitol T-2116	(M)	The Beatles Songbook	1964	6.00	15.00
Capitol ST-2116	(S)	The Beatles Songbook	1964	8.00	20.00
Capitol T-2156	(M)	The Beach Boys Songbook	1964	6.00	15.00
Capitol T-2156	(S)	The Beach Boys Songbook	1964	8.00	20.00
Capitol T-2199	(M)	The Four Seasons Songbook	1964	5.00	12.00
Capitol ST-2199	(S)	The Four Seasons Songbook	1964	6.00	15.00
Capitol T-2202	(M)	The Beatles Songbook, Volume 2	1964	5.00	12.00
Capitol ST-2202	(S)	The Beatles Songbook, Volume 2	1964	6.00	15.00
Capitol T-2221	(M)	Hits Made Famous By Elvis Presley	1964	8.00	20.00
Capitol ST-2221	(S)	Hits Made Famous By Elvis Presley	1964	10.00	25.00
Capitol T-2310	(M)	The Nat King Cole Songbook	1965	4.00	10.00
Capitol ST-2310	(S)	The Nat King Cole Songbook	1965	5.00	12.00
Capitol T-2429	(M)	The New Beatles Songbook	1966	5.00	12.00
Capitol ST-2429	(S)	The New Beatles Songbook	1966	6.00	15.00
Capitol T-2564	(M)	Oldies But Goodies	1966	4.00	10.00
Capitol ST-2564	(S)	Oldies But Goodies	1966	5.00	12.00
Capitol T-2656	(M)	Strawberry Fields Forever	1967	5.00	12.00
Capitol ST-2656	(S)	Strawberry Fields Forever	1967	6.00	15.00
Capitol T-2749	(M)	The Beach Boys Songbook, Volume 2	1967	8.00	20.00
Capitol ST-2749	(S)	The Beach Boys Songbook, Volume 2	1967	10.00	25.00
Capitol T-2876	(M)	The Beatles Songbook, Volume 4	1968	6.00	15.00
Capitol ST-2876	(S)	The Beatles Songbook, Volume 4	1968	6.00	15.00
Capitol ST-2998	(S)	Hits Of Simon And Garfunkel	1968	4.00	10.00
HOLLYWOOD ARGYLES, THE					
Lute L-9001	(M)	Ally Oop	1960	500.00	1,000.00
HOLLYWOOD PERSUADERS, THE					
Original Sound LPM-5013	(M)	Drums A Go-Go	1965	20.00	50.00
Original Sound LPS-8874	(S)	Drums A Go-Go	1965	30.00	75.00
HOLMAN, EDDIE					
ABC S-701	(S)	I Love You	1969	12.00	30.00

Peter Stampfel and Steve Weber, a.k.a. The Holy Modal Rounders, recorded some of the downright weirdest music of their time (no small claim to fame, given the times), combining an eclectic mix of basically American sounds with their unorthodox folkie sensibilities. They were also responsible for creating the aural backdrop for the early Fugs' albums.

Label & Catalog #		Title	Year	VG+	NM

HOLMBERG, JIM

ESP-Disk' 1098	(S)	MIJ	196?	8.00	20.00

HOLMES, MARVIN, & THE UPTIGHTS

Uni 73046	(S)	Ooh Ooh The Dragon & Other Monsters	1969	8.00	20.00

HOLMES, MARVIN, & JUSTICE

Brown Door MH-6573	(S)	Summer Of '73	1973	10.00	25.00
Brown Door MH-6581	(S)	Honor Thy Father	1975	10.00	25.00

HOLT, WILL

Coral CRL-57114	(M)	The World Of Will Holt	1956	16.00	40.00
Stinson 64	(M)	Songs And Ballads	196?	6.00	15.00

HOLY MACKEREL

Holy Mackerel features Paul Williams.

Reprise RS-6311	(S)	Holy Mackerel	1968	10.00	25.00

HOLY MODAL ROUNDERS, THE

The Rounders are Peter Stampfel and Steve Weber. Refer to The Fugs.

Folklore FRLP-14031	(M)	The Holy Modal Rounders	1964	30.00	75.00
Prestige PRLP-7410	(M)	The Holy Modal Rounders 2 (Blue label)	1966	14.00	35.00
Prestige PRLP-7451	(M)	The Holy Modal Rounders (Blue label)	1966	14.00	35.00
		(Prestige 7451 is a reissue of Folklore 14031.)			
ESP-Disk' 1068	(M)	Indian War Whoop	1967	16.00	40.00
ESP-Disk' 1068	(S)	Indian War Whoop	1967	16.00	40.00
Elektra EKS-74026	(S)	The Moray Eels Eat			
		The Holy Modal Rounders	1968	12.00	30.00
Metromedia MD-1039	(S)	Good Taste Is Timeless	1971	12.00	30.00
Fantasy F-24711	(S)	Stampfel And Weber	1972	6.00	15.00
Prestige PR-7720	(M)	The Holy Modal Rounders	1972	6.00	15.00
		(Prestige 7720 is a reissue of Folklore 14031.)			
Rounder 3004	(S)	Alleged In Their Own Time	1975	6.00	15.00
Rounder 3010	(S)	Have Moicy!	1975	6.00	15.00
Adelphi 1030	(S)	Last Round	1978	6.00	15.00
Rounder 3051	(S)	Going Nowhere Fast	1981	6.00	15.00

HOMBRES, THE

Verve/Forecast FT-3036	(M)	Let It Out	1967	10.00	25.00
Verve/Forecast FTS-3036	(S)	Let It Out	1967	12.00	30.00
Verve/Forecast FTS-3068	(S)	The Hombres	1969	Unreleased	

HOMER

Universal Rec. Art. HS-101	(S)	Grown In U.S.A	197?	150.00	300.00

HOMER & JETHRO

Homer & Jethro are Henry Haynes and Kenny Burns. Refer to The Country All-Stars.

RCA Victor LPM-3112 (10")	(M)	Homer & Jethro Fracture Frank Loesser	1953	50.00	125.00
Audio Lab AL-1513	(M)	Musical Madness	1958	40.00	100.00
King 639	(M)	They Sure Are Corny	1959	30.00	75.00
King 848	(M)	Cornier Than Corn	1963	20.00	50.00
RCA Victor LPM-1412	(M)	Barefoot Ballads	1957	20.00	50.00
RCA Victor LPM-1560	(M)	The Worst Of Homer & Jethro	1957	20.00	50.00
RCA Victor LPM-1880	(M)	Life Can Be Miserable	1958	14.00	35.00
RCA Victor LSP-1880	(S)	Life Can Be Miserable	1958	20.00	50.00
RCA Victor LPM-2181	(M)	At The Country Club	1960	10.00	25.00
RCA Victor LSP-2181	(S)	At The Country Club	1960	12.00	30.00
RCA Victor LPM-2286	(M)	Songs My Mother Never Sang	1961	10.00	25.00
RCA Victor LSP-2286	(S)	Songs My Mother Never Sang	1961	12.00	30.00
RCA Victor LPM-2455	(M)	Zany Songs Of The '30s	1962	10.00	25.00
RCA Victor LSP-2455	(S)	Zany Songs Of The '30s	1962	12.00	30.00
RCA Victor LPM-2459	(M)	Playing It Straight	1962	12.00	30.00
RCA Victor LSP-2459	(S)	Playing It Straight	1962	16.00	40.00
RCA Victor LPM-2492	(M)	Homer & Jethro At The Convention	1962	10.00	25.00
RCA Victor LSP-2492	(S)	Homer & Jethro At The Convention	1962	12.00	30.00
RCA Victor LPM-2674	(M)	Homer & Jethro Go West	1963	10.00	25.00
RCA Victor LSP-2674	(S)	Homer & Jethro Go West	1963	12.00	30.00

— *Original RCA mono albums above have "Long Play" on the bottom of the label;
stereo albums have "Living Stereo" on the bottom.*—

Label & Catalog #		Title	Year	VG+	NM
RCA Victor LPM-2743	(M)	Ooh, That's Corny	1963	8.00	20.00
RCA Victor LSP-2743	(S)	Ooh, That's Corny	1963	10.00	25.00
RCA Victor LPM-2928	(M)	Cornfucius Say	1964	8.00	20.00
RCA Victor LSP-2928	(S)	Cornfucius Say	1964	10.00	25.00
RCA Victor LPM-2954	(M)	Fractured Folk Songs	1964	8.00	20.00
RCA Victor LSP-2954	(S)	Fractured Folk Songs	1964	10.00	25.00
RCA Victor LPM-3357	(M)	Homer & Jethro Sing Tenderly	1965	8.00	20.00
RCA Victor LSP-3357	(S)	Homer & Jethro Sing Tenderly	1965	10.00	25.00
RCA Victor LPM-3462	(M)	The Old Crusty Minstrels	1965	8.00	20.00
RCA Victor LSP-3462	(S)	The Old Crusty Minstrels	1965	10.00	25.00
RCA Victor LPM-3474	(M)	The Best Of Homer & Jethro	1966	8.00	20.00
RCA Victor LSP-3474	(S)	The Best Of Homer & Jethro	1966	10.00	25.00
RCA Victor LPM-3538	(M)	Any News From Nashville	1966	8.00	20.00
RCA Victor LSP-3538	(S)	Any News From Nashville	1966	10.00	25.00
RCA Victor LPM-3673	(M)	Wanted For Murder	1966	8.00	20.00
RCA Victor LSP-3673	(S)	Wanted For Murder	1966	8.00	20.00
RCA Victor LPM-3701	(M)	It Ain't Necessarily Square	1967	10.00	25.00
RCA Victor LSP-3701	(S)	It Ain't Necessarily Square	1967	10.00	25.00
RCA Victor LPM-3822	(M)	Nashville Cats	1967	8.00	20.00
RCA Victor LSP-3822	(S)	Nashville Cats	1967	10.00	25.00
RCA Victor LPM-3877	(M)	Somethin' Stupid	1967	8.00	20.00
RCA Victor LSP-3877	(S)	Somethin' Stupid	1967	10.00	25.00
RCA Victor LPM-3973	(M)	There's Nothing Like An Old Hippie	1968	40.00	100.00
RCA Victor LSP-3973	(S)	There's Nothing Like An Old Hippie	1968	8.00	20.00
RCA Victor LSP-4001	(S)	Cool Crazy Christmas	1968	8.00	20.00
RCA Victor LSP-4024	(S)	Live At Vanderbilt U	1968	8.00	20.00

— *Original RCA albums above have black labels.*—

HOMESICK JAMES

Label & Catalog #		Title	Year	VG+	NM
Prestige PRST-7388	(M)	Blues On The South Side	197?	6.00	15.00
BluesWay BLS-6071	(S)	Ain't Sick No More	1973	5.00	12.00

HONDELLS, THE
The Hondells are a creation of Gary Usher & Co. featuring Chuck Girard.

Label & Catalog #		Title	Year	VG+	NM
Mercury MG-20940	(M)	Go Little Honda	1964	12.00	30.00
Mercury SR-60940	(S)	Go Little Honda	1964	20.00	50.00
Mercury MG-20982	(M)	The Hondells	1965	20.00	50.00
Mercury SR-60982	(S)	The Hondells	1965	30.00	75.00

HONEY & THE BEES

Label & Catalog #		Title	Year	VG+	NM
Josie JOS-4013	(S)	Honey And The Bees	197?	6.00	15.00

HONEYCOMBS, THE

Label & Catalog #		Title	Year	VG+	NM
Vee Jay IN-88001	(M)	Here Are The Honeycombs	1964	20.00	50.00
Vee Jay IN-88001	(E)	Here Are The Honeycombs	1964	16.00	40.00
Interphon IN-88001	(M)	Here Are The Honeycombs	1964	16.00	40.00
Interphon IN-88001	(E)	Here Are The Honeycombs	1964	12.00	30.00

HONEYDREAMERS, THE

Label & Catalog #		Title	Year	VG+	NM
Fantasy 3-207	(M)	The Honeydreamers Sing Gershwin	1956	10.00	25.00
RKO ULP-134	(M)	An Evening With The Honeydreamers	1958	8.00	20.00
Dot DLP-3175	(M)	It's Dark On Observatory Hill	1959	8.00	20.00
Dot DLP-25175	(S)	It's Dark On Observatory Hill	1959	10.00	25.00

HOOKER, D. R.

Label & Catalog #		Title	Year	VG+	NM
On XTL-1029	(S)	The Truth	1972	100.00	200.00
On 40725	(S)	Armaggedon	1979	12.00	30.00

HOOKER, JOHN LEE
John Lee also recorded with Canned Heat; The Groundhogs; Big Maceo Merriweather.

Label & Catalog #		Title	Year	VG+	NM
Vee Jay LP-1007	(M)	I'm John Lee Hooker (Maroon label)	1959	100.00	300.00
Vee Jay LP-1007	(M)	I'm John Lee Hooker (Black label)	1960	40.00	100.00
Vee Jay LP-1023	(M)	Travelin'	1960	30.00	75.00
Vee Jay LP-1033	(M)	The Folk Lore Of John Lee Hooker	1961	14.00	35.00
Vee Jay SR-1033	(S)	The Folk Lore Of John Lee Hooker	1961	20.00	50.00
Vee Jay LP-1043	(M)	Burnin'	1962	14.00	35.00
Vee Jay SR-1043	(S)	Burnin'	1962	30.00	75.00
Vee Jay LP-1049	(M)	The Best Of John Lee Hooker	1962	14.00	35.00
Vee Jay SR-1049	(P)	The Best Of John Lee Hooker	1962	20.00	50.00

Label & Catalog #		Title	Year	VG+	NM
Vee Jay LP-1066	(M)	John Lee Hooker On Campus	1963	14.00	35.00
Vee Jay SR-1066	(S)	John Lee Hooker On Campus	1963	20.00	50.00
Vee Jay LP-1078	(M)	John Lee Hooker At Newport	1964	14.00	35.00
Vee Jay SR-1078	(S)	John Lee Hooker At Newport	1964	20.00	50.00
— Original Vee Jay albums above have black rainbow labels.—					
King 727	(M)	John Lee Hooker Sings The Blues	1960	100.00	Rare
		(Near Mint copies have a suggested value of $250-500.)			
Chess LP-1438	(M)	House Of The Blues	1960	50.00	150.00
Chess LP-1454	(M)	Plays And Sings The Blues	1961	50.00	150.00
Chess LP-1508	(M)	Real Folk Blues	1966	20.00	50.00
Chess LPS-1508	(E)	Real Folk Blues	1966	14.00	35.00
Crown CLP-5157	(M)	The Blues	196?	10.00	25.00
Crown CLP-5295	(M)	Folk Blues	196?	10.00	25.00
Atco 33-151	(M)	Don't Turn Me From Your Door	1963	20.00	50.00
Atco SD-33-151	(E)	Don't Turn Me From Your Door	1967	14.00	35.00
Riverside RLP-12-838	(M)	Folk Blues	196?	14.00	35.00
Verve/Folkways FT-3003	(M)	John Lee Hooker	1965	10.00	25.00
Verve/Folkways FTS-3003	(S)	John Lee Hooker	1965	14.00	35.00
Impulse A-9103	(M)	It Serve You Right To Suffer	1966	12.00	30.00
Impulse AS-9103	(S)	It Serve You Right To Suffer	1966	16.00	40.00
BluesWay BL-6002	(M)	Live At Cafe Au-Go-Go	1966	8.00	20.00
BluesWay BLS-6002	(S)	Live At Cafe Au-Go-Go	1966	10.00	25.00
BluesWay BLS-6012	(S)	Urban Blues	1968	8.00	20.00
BluesWay 6023	(S)	Simply The Truth	1969	8.00	20.00
BluesWay BLS-6038	(S)	If You Miss 'Im	1970	6.00	15.00
BluesWay BLS-6052	(S)	Live At Kabuki Wuki	1973	6.00	15.00
Stax STS-2013	(S)	That's Where It's At	1969	6.00	15.00
Buddah BDS-4002	(P)	The Very Best Of John Lee Hooker	1969	6.00	15.00
Buddah BDS-7506	(S)	Big Band Blues	1969	6.00	15.00
Wand WDS-689	(S)	John Lee Hooker On The Waterfront	1970	6.00	15.00
Specialty SPS-2125	(E)	Alone	1970	6.00	15.00
ABC S-720	(S)	Endless Boogie *(2 LPs)*	1970	8.00	20.00
ABC S-761	(S)	Live At Soledad Prison	1972	4.00	10.00
ABC S-768	(S)	Born In Mississippi, Raised Up In Tennessee	1973	6.00	15.00
ABC XQ-768	(Q)	Born In Mississippi, Raised Up In Tennessee	1973	8.00	20.00
King KS-1085	(E)	Moanin' And Stompin' Blues	1970	6.00	15.00
Jewel 5005	(S)	I Feel Good	1971	6.00	15.00
Kent 559	(S)	John Lee Hooker's Greatest Hits	1971	6.00	15.00
United Arts. UAS-5512	(S)	Coast To Coast Blues Band	1971	6.00	15.00
Fantasy 24706	(S)	Boogie Chillun' *(2 LPs)*	1972	6.00	15.00
United Arts. LA127	(S)	John Lee Hooker's Detroit *(2 LPs)*	1973	6.00	15.00
Chess 2SC-60011	(M)	Mad Man's Blues *(2 LPs)*	1974	6.00	15.00

HOOTCH

Pro-gress PRS-4844	(S)	Hootch	1974	500.00	800.00

HOPE, BOB

Decca DL-4396	(M)	Hope In Russia And Other Places	1963	8.00	20.00
Decca DL-74396	(S)	Hope In Russia And Other Places	1963	10.00	25.00

HOPE, LYNN

Aladdin 707 (10")	(M)	Lynn Hope And His Tenor Sax	1953	200.00	500.00
Aladdin 805	(M)	Lynn Hope And His Tenor Sax	1955	100.00	250.00
Aladdin 820	(M)	Lynn Hope	1957	100.00	250.00
Score LP-4015	(M)	Tenderly	1957	70.00	175.00
King 717	(M)	Maharaja Of The Saxophone	1961	60.00	150.00
Imperial LP-9177	(M)	Tenderly	1962	20.00	50.00
Imperial LP-12177	(S)	Tenderly	1962	30.00	75.00

HOPKIN, MARY

Apple SW-3351	(S)	Postcard *(Produced by Paul McCartney)*	1969	6.00	15.00
Apple SW-53351	(S)	Postcard *(Record club)*	1969	12.00	30.00
		("Those Were The Days" is in stereo on both versions of "Postcard.".)			
Apple SMAS-3381	(S)	Earth Song/Ocean Song	1969	6.00	15.00
Apple SW-3395	(S)	Those Were The Days	1972	14.00	35.00
		("Those Were The Days," "Temma Harbour," "Think About Your Children" and "Knock Knock Who's There?" are in mono.)			
Paramount PAS-5005	(S)	Where's Jack *(Soundtrack)*	1969	16.00	40.00
American Int. STA-1042	(S)	Kidnapped *(Soundtrack)*	1972	10.00	25.00

Legendary country bluesman Sam "Lightnin'" Hopkins rarely saw his picture appear on any of his early albums, as both the Fire and Herald albums here illustrate. The lowly Guest Star label featured this great cover on a rarely seen live album from his home state.

Label & Catalog #		Title	Year	VG+	NM

HOPKINS, LIGHTNIN'

Label & Catalog #		Title	Year	VG+	NM
Fire 104	(M)	Mojo Hand	1960	500.00	800.00
Herald 1012	(M)	Lightnin' And The Blues	1960	300.00	750.00
Score 4022	(M)	Lightnin' Hopkins Strums The Blues	1960	360.00	600.00
Tradition TLP-1035	(M)	Country Blues	1960	20.00	50.00
Tradition TLP-1040	(M)	Autobiography In Blues	1960	20.00	50.00
Time 70004	(M)	Last Of The Great Blues Singers	1960	20.00	50.00
Time 1	(M)	Blues/Folk	1962	20.00	50.00
Time 3	(M)	Blues/Folk, Volume 2	1962	20.00	50.00
Bluesville BVLP-1019	(M)	Lightnin'	1961	20.00	50.00
Bluesville BVLP-1029	(M)	Last Night Blues	1961	20.00	50.00
Bluesville BVLP-1045	(M)	Blues In My Bottle	1962	20.00	50.00
Bluesville BVLP-1057	(M)	Walkin' This Street By Myself	1962	20.00	50.00
Bluesville BVLP-1061	(M)	Lightnin' & Co.	1963	20.00	50.00
Bluesville BVLP-1070	(M)	Smokes Like Lightnin'	1963	20.00	50.00
Bluesville BVLP-1073	(M)	Goin' Away	1963	20.00	50.00
Bluesville BVLP-1081	(M)	Gotta Move Your Baby	1964	16.00	40.00
		(Bluesville 1081 is a reissue of 1029.)			
Bluesville BVLP-1084	(M)	His Greatest Hits	1964	16.00	40.00
Bluesville BVLP-1986	(M)	Down Home Blues	1964	16.00	40.00
Vee Jay LP-1044	(M)	Lightnin' Hopkins	1962	20.00	50.00
Verve V-8453	(M)	Fast Life Woman	1962	20.00	50.00
Imperial LP-9180	(M)	Lightnin' Hopkins On Stage	1962	40.00	100.00
Imperial LP-9211	(M)	Lightnin' Hopkins And The Blues	1962	40.00	100.00
Imperial LP-12211	(S)	Lightnin' Hopkins And The Blues	1962	50.00	125.00
Guest Star G-1458	(M)	"Live" At The Bird Lounge	196?	20.00	50.00
Mt. Vernon 104	(M)	Nothin' But The Blues	196?	10.00	25.00
		(Mt. Vernon 104 is a reissue of Herald 1012.)			
World Pacific WP-1817	(M)	First Meetin'	1963	8.00	20.00
World Pacific ST-1817	(S)	First Meetin'	1963	10.00	25.00
World Pacific ST-1817	(S)	First Meetin' (Red vinyl)	1963	20.00	50.00
Verve/Folkways FV-9000	(M)	The Roots Of Lightnin' Hopkins	1965	10.00	25.00
Verve/Folkways FVS-9000	(S)	The Roots Of Lightnin' Hopkins	1965	12.00	30.00
Verve/Folkways FV-9022	(M)	Lightnin' Strikes	1965	10.00	25.00
Verve/Folkways FVS-9022	(S)	Lightnin' Strikes	1965	12.00	30.00
Verve/Folkways FT-3013	(M)	Something Blue	1967	8.00	20.00
Verve/Folkways FTS-3013	(S)	Something Blue	1967	10.00	25.00
Verve/Folkways FTS-3031	(S)	Lightnin' Strikes	1968	8.00	20.00
		(Folkways 3031 is a reissue of 9022.)			
Folklore PRLP-14021	(M)	Hootin' The Blues	196?	10.00	25.00
Folklore PRST-14021	(S)	Hootin' The Blues	196?	12.00	30.00
Prestige PRLP-7370	(M)	My Life With The Blues (2 LPs)	1965	14.00	35.00
Prestige PRLP-7377	(M)	Soul Blues	1966	8.00	20.00
Prestige PRST-7377	(S)	Soul Blues	1966	10.00	25.00
Prestige PRST-7592	(S)	Lightnin' Hopkins' Greatest Hits	1969	6.00	15.00
		(Prestige 7592 is a reissue of Bluesville 1084.)			
Prestige PRST-7714	(S)	The Best Of Lightnin' Hopkins & His Texas Blues Band	1969	6.00	15.00
Prestige PRST-7806	(S)	Hootin' The Blues	1970	6.00	15.00
		(Prestige 7592 is a reissue of Folklore 14021.)			
Prestige PRST-7811	(S)	The Blues Of Lightnin' Hopkins	1970	6.00	15.00
		(Prestige 7811 is a reissue of Bluesville 1019.)			
International Art. 6	(S)	Free Form Patterns	1968	80.00	200.00
		(With a picture of Hopkins on the cover.)			
International Art. 6	(S)	Free Form Patterns ("Art" cover)	1968	20.00	50.00
Vault 129	(S)	California Mudslide	1969	8.00	20.00
Poppy 60002	(S)	Lightnin'	1969	8.00	20.00
United US-7713	(E)	Lightnin' Hopkins Sings The Blues	196?	6.00	15.00
Everest 241	(S)	Lightnin' Hopkins	1969	6.00	15.00
Jewel 5000	(M)	Blue Lightnin'	1970	6.00	15.00
Jewel 5001	(S)	Talkin' Some Sense	1970	6.00	15.00
Jewel 5002	(S)	Great Electric Show And Dance	1970	6.00	15.00
Mainstream 311	(S)	The Blues	1971	6.00	15.00
Mainstream 326	(S)	Dirty Blues	1971	6.00	15.00
Barnaby Z-30247	(S)	Lightnin' Hopkins In New York	1971	6.00	15.00
Columbia S-31944	(S)	Sounder (Soundtrack)	1972	5.00	12.00

HOPKINS, NICKY

Label & Catalog #		Title	Year	VG+	NM
Columbia KC-32074	(S)	The Tin Man Was A Dreamer	1973	8.00	20.00

Label & Catalog #		Title	Year	VG+	NM

HOPNEY

Illusion CM-1032	(S)	End And Means	197?	80.00	200.00
Illusion CM-1033	(S)	Perils Of Love	197?	100.00	250.00
Illusion CM-1034	(S)	Cosmic Rockout	197?	300.00	500.00

HORN, SHIRLEY: *Refer to* GOLDMINE'S PRICE GUIDE TO COLLECTIBLE JAZZ ALBUMS

HORNE, LENA
Refer to Ella Fitzgerald.

MGM E-545 (10")	(M)	Lena Horne Sings	1952	20.00	50.00
Tops L-910 (10")	(M)	Moanin' Low	195?	14.00	35.00
Tops L-931 (10")	(M)	Lena Horne Sings	195?	14.00	35.00
RCA Victor LPT-3061 (10")	(M)	This Is Lena Horne	1952	20.00	50.00
RCA Victor LPM-1148	(M)	It's Love	1955	20.00	50.00
RCA Victor LPM-1375	(M)	Stormy Weather	1956	20.00	50.00
RCA Victor LOC-1028	(M)	Lena Horne At The Waldorf Astoria	1957	14.00	35.00
RCA Victor LSO-1028	(S)	Lena Horne At The Waldorf Astoria	1957	20.00	50.00
RCA Victor LOC-1036	(M)	Jamaica *(Soundtrack)*	1957	14.00	35.00
RCA Victor LSO-1036	(S)	Jamaica *(Soundtrack)*	1957	20.00	50.00
Jazztone J-1262	(M)	Lena And Ivie	1957	20.00	50.00
Tops L-1502	(M)	Lena Horne	1958	6.00	15.00
Lion L-70050	(M)	I Feel So Smoochie	1959	6.00	15.00
RCA Victor LPM-1879	(M)	Give The Lady What She Wants	1958	14.00	35.00
RCA Victor LSP-1879	(S)	Give The Lady What She Wants	1958	20.00	50.00
RCA Victor LPM-1895	(M)	Songs Of Burke And Van Heusen	1959	14.00	35.00
RCA Victor LSP-1895	(S)	Songs Of Burke And Van Heusen	1959	20.00	50.00
RCA Victor LOC-1507	(M)	Porgy And Bess *(Soundtrack)*	1959	10.00	25.00
RCA Victor LSO-1507	(S)	Porgy And Bess *(Soundtrack)*	1959	14.00	35.00
RCA Victor LPM-2364	(M)	Lena Horne At The Sands	1961	8.00	20.00
RCA Victor LSP-2364	(S)	Lena Horne At The Sands	1961	12.00	30.00
RCA Victor LPM-2465	(M)	On The Blue Side	1962	8.00	20.00
RCA Victor LSP-2465	(S)	On The Blue Side	1962	12.00	30.00

*— Original RCA mono albums above have "Long Play" on the bottom of the label;
stereo albums have "Living Stereo" on the bottom. —*

RCA Victor LPM-2587	(M)	Lovely And Alive	1963	6.00	15.00
RCA Victor LSP-2587	(S)	Lovely And Alive	1963	8.00	20.00
Charter CL-101	(M)	Lena Horne Sings Your Requests	1963	6.00	15.00
Charter CLS-101	(S)	Lena Horne Sings Your Requests	1963	8.00	20.00
Charter CL-106	(M)	Like Latin	1964	6.00	15.00
Charter CLS-106	(S)	Like Latin	1964	8.00	20.00
Movietone 71005	(M)	Once In A Lifetime	196?	6.00	15.00
Movietone 72005	(S)	Once In A Lifetime	196?	8.00	20.00
20th Century TF-4115	(M)	Here's Lena Now	1964	6.00	15.00
20th Century TFS-4115	(S)	Here's Lena Now	1964	8.00	20.00
RCA Victor LOC-1103	(M)	Jamaica *(Soundtrack)*	1965	6.00	15.00
RCA Victor LSO-1103	(S)	Jamaica *(Soundtrack)*	1965	8.00	20.00
United Arts. UAL-3433	(M)	Feelin' Good	1965	6.00	15.00
United Arts. UAS-6433	(S)	Feelin' Good	1965	8.00	20.00
United Arts. UAL-3470	(M)	Lena In Hollywood	1966	6.00	15.00
United Arts. UAS-6470	(S)	Lena In Hollywood	1966	8.00	20.00
United Arts. UAL-3496	(M)	Soul	1966	8.00	20.00
United Arts. UAS-6496	(S)	Soul	1966	8.00	20.00
Mobile Fidelity MFSL-094	(S)	A Lady And Her Music	1980	8.00	25.00

HORNETS, THE

Liberty LRP-3348	(M)	Motorcycles U.S.A.	1963	10.00	25.00
Liberty LST-7348	(S)	Motorcycles U.S.A.	1963	14.00	35.00
Liberty LRP-3364	(M)	Big Drag Boats U.S.A.	1964	20.00	50.00
Liberty LST-7364	(S)	Big Drag Boats U.S.A.	1964	24.00	60.00

HORSES, THE

White Whale WWS-7121	(S)	Horses	1970	8.00	20.00

HORTON, JOHNNY

Briar Int. 104	(M)	Done Rovin'	195?	50.00	125.00
Sesac 1201	(M)	Free And Easy Songs	1959	60.00	150.00
Mercury MG-20478	(M)	The Fantastic Johnny Horton	1959	20.00	50.00
Columbia CL-1362	(M)	The Spectacular Johnny Horton	1960	12.00	30.00
Columbia CS-8167	(S)	The Spectacular Johnny Horton	1960	16.00	40.00

Label & Catalog #		Title	Year	VG+	NM
Columbia CL-1478	(M)	Johnny Horton Makes History	1960	12.00	30.00
Columbia CS-8269	(S)	Johnny Horton Makes History	1960	16.00	40.00
Columbia CL-1596	(M)	Greatest Hits (With bonus photo)	1961	16.00	40.00
Columbia CS-8396	(S)	Greatest Hits (With bonus photo)	1961	20.00	50.00
Columbia CL-1596	(M)	Greatest Hits (Without bonus photo)	1961	12.00	30.00
Columbia CS-8396	(S)	Greatest Hits (Without bonus photo)	1961	16.00	40.00
Columbia CL-1721	(M)	Honky-Tonk Man	1962	12.00	30.00
Columbia CS-8779	(E)	Honky-Tonk Man	1962	6.00	15.00

— Original Columbia albums above have three white "eye" logos on each side of the spindle hole.—

Dot DLP-3221	(M)	Johnny Horton	1962	12.00	30.00
Dot DLP-25221	(E)	Johnny Horton	1962	6.00	15.00
Columbia CL-2299	(M)	I Can't Forget You	1965	10.00	25.00
Columbia CS-9099	(E)	I Can't Forget You	1965	6.00	15.00
Columbia CL-2566	(S)	Johnny Horton On The Louisiana Hayride	1966	8.00	20.00
Columbia CS-9366	(S)	Johnny Horton On The Louisiana Hayride	1966	10.00	25.00
Columbia CS-9940	(S)	Johnny Horton On The Road	1969	6.00	15.00

—Columbia albums above have "360 Sound Mono/Stereo" on the bottom of the label.—

HORTON, ROBERT

Columbia CL-2202	(M)	The Very Thought Of You	1964	6.00	15.00
Columbia CS-9002	(S)	The Very Thought Of You	1964	8.00	20.00
Columbia CL-2408	(M)	The Man Called Shenendoah	1965	10.00	25.00
Columbia CS-9208	(S)	The Man Called Shenendoah	1965	12.00	30.00

HORTON, WALTER "SHAKEY"

Argo LP-4037	(M)	The Soul Of Blues Harmonica	1964	40.00	100.00

HORWITZ, BILL

ESP-Disk' 3020	(S)	Lies, Lies, Lies	1970	6.00	15.00

HOT BUTTER

Musicor MS-3242	(S)	Popcorn (Die-cut shaped cover)	1972	6.00	15.00

HOT DOGGERS, THE
The Hot Doggers feature Bruce Johnston.

Epic LN-24054	(M)	Surfin' USA	1963	50.00	125.00
Epic BN-26054	(S)	Surfin' USA	1963	70.00	175.00

HOT POOP

Hot Poop 3072	(S)	Hot Poop Does Their Own Stuff	1975	30.00	75.00

HOT RODDERS, THE

Crown CLP-5378	(M)	Big Hot Rod	1963	6.00	15.00
Crown CST-378	(S)	Big Hot Rod	1963	8.00	20.00

HOT TUNA
Hot Tuna is Jorma Kaukonen and Jack Casady of Jefferson Airplane.

Grunt BFD1-0820	(Q)	America's Choice	1975	6.00	15.00
Grunt BFD1-1238	(Q)	Yellow Fever	1975	6.00	15.00
Grunt DJL1-2852	(DJ)	The Last Interview (With poster)	1978	8.00	20.00
		(Features a live track by Janis Joplin.)			

HOTLEGS

Capitol ST-587	(S)	Hotlegs Thinks: School Stinks	1971	10.00	25.00

HOTZ, JIMMY

Vision VR-777	(S)	Beyond The Crystal Sea	1980	60.00	150.00

HOUR GLASS, THE
Hour Glass features Duane and Gregg Allman.

Liberty LRP-3536	(M)	The Hour Glass	1967	10.00	25.00
Liberty LST-7536	(S)	The Hour Glass	1967	12.00	30.00
Liberty LST-7555	(S)	The Power Of Love	1968	12.00	30.00
United Artists LA013G2	(S)	The Hour Glass (2 LPs)	1973	6.00	15.00
		(U.A. 013 repackages the two Liberty albums.)			

HOUSE, SON

Columbia CL-2417	(M)	Father Of The Folk Blues	1965	6.00	15.00
Columbia CS-9217	(S)	Father Of The Folk Blues ("360 Sound" label)	1965	8.00	20.00

Label & Catalog #		Title	Year	VG+	NM
HOUSE, SON, & J.D. SHORT					
Verve/Folkways FV-9035	(M)	Blues From The Mississippi Delt	1966	12.00	30.00
Verve/Folkways FVS-9035	(E)	Blues From The Mississippi Delta	1966	8.00	20.00
HOUSE, WALLACE					
Folkways FA-2152	(M)	Ballads Of The Revolution	195?	8.00	20.00
HOUSTON, CISCO					
Houston also recorded with Woody Guthrie.					
Stinson SLP-37	(M)	Traditional Songs Of The Old West	195?	20.00	50.00
Folkways FA-2013	(M)	900 Miles And Other Railroad Ballads	1952	12.00	30.00
Folkways FA-2022	(M)	Cowboy Songs	1952	12.00	30.00
Folkways FA-2042	(M)	Hard Travelin'	1954	12.00	30.00
Folkways FA-2346	(M)	Folk Songs	195?	12.00	30.00
Vanguard VRS-	(M)	The Cisco Special!	195?	12.00	30.00
Verve/Folkways FV-9002	(M)	Passing Through	1965	8.00	20.00
Verve/Folkways FVS-9002	(S)	Passing Through	1965	10.00	25.00
HOUSTON, DAVID (& THE PERSUADERS)					
Epic LN-24112	(M)	New Voice From Nashville	1964	6.00	15.00
Epic BN-26112	(S)	New Voice From Nashville	1964	8.00	20.00
Epic LN-24156	(M)	Twelve Great Country Hits	1965	6.00	15.00
Epic BN-26156	(S)	Twelve Great Country Hits	1965	8.00	20.00
Epic LN-24213	(M)	Almost Persuaded	1966	6.00	15.00
Epic BN-26213	(S)	Almost Persuaded	1966	8.00	20.00
Epic LN-24303	(M)	A Loser's Cathedral	1967	6.00	15.00
Epic BN-26303	(S)	A Loser's Cathedral	1967	8.00	20.00
Epic LN-24320	(M)	Golden Hymns	1967	6.00	15.00
Epic BN-26320	(S)	Golden Hymns	1967	8.00	20.00
Epic LN-24338	(M)	You Mean The World To Me	1967	6.00	15.00
Epic BN-26338	(S)	You Mean The World To Me	1967	8.00	20.00
HOUSTON, DAVID, & TAMMY WYNETTE					
Epic LN-24325	(M)	My Elusive Dreams	1967	6.00	15.00
Epic BN-26325	(S)	My Elusive Dreams	1967	8.00	20.00
HOUSTON, DOLLY					
RKO Unique 107	(M)	Dolly's Lullabye	1957	8.00	20.00
HOUSTON, JOE					
Combo LP-100	(M)	Where Is Joe?	1960	60.00	150.00
Combo LP-400	(M)	Rockin' At The Drive In	1960	60.00	150.00
Modern LMP-1206	(M)	Joe Houston Blows All Night Long	1960	30.00	75.00
Crown CLP-5006	(M)	Joe Houston Rocks & Rolls All Nite Long	1961	12.00	30.00
Crown CLP-5203	(M)	Wild Man Of The Tenor Sax	1962	10.00	25.00
Crown CLP-5313	(M)	Surf Rockin'	1963	10.00	25.00
Crown CST-313	(E)	Surf Rockin'	1963	4.00	10.00
Crown CLP-5319	(M)	Limbo	1963	10.00	25.00
Crown CST-319	(E)	Limbo	1963	4.00	10.00
Tops L-1518	(M)	Rock And Roll	1962	12.00	30.00
HOUSTON, THELMA, & PRESSURE COOKER					
Sheffield Lab 2	(S)	I've Got The Music In Me	1974	8.00	20.00
HOUSTON FEARLESS					
Imperial LP-12421	(S)	Houston Fearless	1969	8.00	20.00
HOWARD, DAVE					
Choreo 5	(M)	I Love Everybody	1961	10.00	25.00
HOWARD, HARLAN					
Capitol T-1631	(M)	Harlan Howard Sings Harlan Howard	1961	16.00	40.00
Capitol ST-1631	(S)	Harlan Howard Sings Harlan Howard	1961	20.00	50.00
Monument MLP-8038	(M)	All-Time Favorite Country Songwriter	1965	10.00	25.00
Monument SLP-18038	(S)	All-Time Favorite Country Songwriter	1965	12.00	30.00
RCA Victor LPM-3729	(M)	Mr. Songwriter	1967	8.00	20.00
RCA Victor LSP-3729	(S)	Mr. Songwriter	1967	10.00	25.00
RCA Victor LPM-3886	(M)	Down To Earth	1968	20.00	50.00
RCA Victor LSP-3886	(S)	Down To Earth	1968	10.00	25.00

While the veneration of the guitar as the prime instrument in the history of rock 'n roll continues to this day, few seem to recall that it was the saxophone of such artists as Joe Houston that was the driving force behind much of the earliest rhythm 'n blues derived rock 'n roll.

Label & Catalog #		Title	Year	VG+	NM

HOWARD, JAN

Wrangler 1005	(M)	Jan Howard	1962	12.00	30.00
Wrangler S-1005	(S)	Jan Howard	1962	16.00	40.00
Capitol T-1779	(M)	Sweet And Sentimental	1962	8.00	20.00
Capitol ST-1779	(S)	Sweet And Sentimental	1962	12.00	30.00
Forum 7G-505	(M)	Jan Howard	196?	12.00	30.00
Decca DL-4793	(M)	Evil On Your Mind	1966	6.00	15.00
Decca DL-74793	(S)	Evil On Your Mind	1966	8.00	20.00
Decca DL-4832	(M)	Bad Seed	1966	6.00	15.00
Decca DL-74832	(S)	Bad Seed	1966	8.00	20.00
Decca DL-4931	(M)	This Is Jan Howard Country	1967	6.00	15.00
Decca DL-74931	(S)	This Is Jan Howard Country	1967	8.00	20.00
Tower T-5068	(M)	Lonely Country	1967	6.00	15.00
Tower ST-5068	(S)	Lonely Country	1967	8.00	20.00
Tower DT-5119	(E)	The Real Me	1968	4.00	10.00
Decca DL-75012	(S)	Count Your Blessings, Woman	1968	4.00	10.00
Decca DL-75130	(S)	Jan Howard	1969	4.00	10.00
Decca DL-75166	(S)	For God And Country	1970	4.00	10.00
Decca DL-75207	(S)	Rock Me Back To Little Rock	1970	4.00	10.00
Decca DL-75333	(S)	Love Is Like A Spinning Wheel	1972	4.00	10.00

HOWL THE GOOD

Rare Earth 537	(S)	Howl The Good	1972	8.00	20.00

HOWLIN' WOLF

Howlin' Wolf is a pseudonym for Chester Burnett. Refer to Bo Diddley.

Chess LP-1434	(M)	Moanin' In The Moonlight	1958	150.00	350.00
Chess LP-1469	(M)	Howlin' Wolf	1962	150.00	300.00
		— Chess albums above have black & silver labels.—			
Chess LP-1502	(M)	The Real Folk Blues	1966	20.00	50.00
Chess LP-1512	(M)	More Real Folk Blues	1967	20.00	50.00
		— Chess albums above have dark blue labels with a color logo on top.—			
Crown CLP-5240	(M)	Howlin' Wolf Sings The Blues	1962	10.00	25.00
Custom CM-2055	(M)	Big City Blues	196?	14.00	35.00
Custom CS-2055	(E)	Big City Blues	196?	8.00	20.00
Kent KLP-526	(M)	Original Folk Blues	1967	6.00	15.00
Kent KST-526	(E)	Original Folk Blues	1967	5.00	12.00
Kent KST-527	(E)	Howlin' Wolf's Twenty Greatest R&B Hits	1967	6.00	15.00
Kent KST-535	(E)	Underground Blues	1967	6.00	15.00
United 7717	(E)	Big City Blues	1969	5.00	12.00
United 7747	(E)	Original Folk Blues	1969	5.00	12.00
Cadet 319	(S)	This Is Howlin' Wolf's New Album	1969	10.00	25.00
Chess LP-1540	(M)	Evil	1969	10.00	25.00
Chess CH-50015	(S)	Live And Cookin'	1972	8.00	20.00
Chess CH-60008	(S)	The London Howlin' Wolf Sessions	1971	8.00	20.00
		(Features Ian Stewart, Charlie Watts and Bill Wyman.)			
Chess CH-50045	(M)	The Back Door Wolf	1974	8.00	20.00
Chess CH-60016	(E)	Howlin' Wolf A.K.A. Chester Burnett (2 LPs)	1972	10.00	25.00
		— Chess albums above have blue & white labels.—			
Chess CH-201	(S)	Howlin' Wolf (2 LPs)	1976	5.00	12.00
Chess CH-418	(S)	Change My Way	1977	5.00	12.00

HUDSON, ROCK

Refer to Doris Day & Rock Hudson

Stanyan 10014	(S)	Rock Gently	1971	10.00	25.00

HUGHES, FREDDIE

Wand WD-664	(M)	Send My Baby Back	1965	6.00	15.00
Wand WDS-664	(S)	Send My Baby Back	1965	8.00	20.00
Brunswick BL-754157	(S)	Baby Boy	1970	5.00	12.00

HUGHES, JIMMY

Vee Jay VJ-1102	(M)	Steal Away	1965	10.00	25.00
Vee Jay SR-1102	(E)	Steal Away	1965	8.00	20.00
Atco 33-209	(M)	Why Not Tonight	1967	8.00	20.00
Atco SD-33-209	(E)	Why Not Tonight	1967	6.00	15.00
Volt VOS-6003	(S)	Something Special	1969	5.00	12.00

Label & Catalog #		Title	Year	VG+	NM

HULLABALOOS, THE

Label & Catalog #		Title	Year	VG+	NM
Roulette R-25297	(M)	England's Newest Singing Sensations	1965	16.00	40.00
Roulette SR-25297	(S)	England's Newest Singing Sensations	1965	20.00	50.00
		("Can't You Tell," "I'm Gonna Love You Too," "Party Doll" and			
		"Why Do Fools Fall In Love" are rechanneled on this album.)			
Roulette R-25310	(M)	The Hullabaloos On Hullabaloo	1965	16.00	40.00
Roulette SR-25310	(S)	The Hullabaloos On Hullabaloo	1965	20.00	50.00
		("Don't Cha Know," "Learning The Game," "Rave On" and			
		"That'll Be The Day" are rechanneled on this album.)			

HUMAN BEINZ, THE / THE MAMMALS

Label & Catalog #		Title	Year	VG+	NM
Gateway GLP-3012	(S)	Nobody But Me	1968	16.00	40.00

HUMAN BEINZ, THE

Label & Catalog #		Title	Year	VG+	NM
Capitol ST-2906	(S)	Nobody But Me	1968	12.00	30.00
Capitol ST-2926	(S)	Evolutions	1968	12.00	30.00

HUMAN ZOO, THE

Label & Catalog #		Title	Year	VG+	NM
Accent ACS-5055	(S)	The Human Zoo	1971	40.00	100.00

HUMBLE PIE

Label & Catalog #		Title	Year	VG+	NM
Immediate 101	(S)	As Safe As Yesterday Is	1968	10.00	25.00
Immediate 027	(S)	Town And Country	1972	6.00	15.00

HUMES, HELEN: Refer to GOLDMINE'S PRICE GUIDE TO COLLECTIBLE JAZZ ALBUMS

HUMPERDINCK, ENGELBERT

Label & Catalog #		Title	Year	VG+	NM
Parrot PA-1012	(M)	Release Me	1967	6.00	15.00
Parrot PAS-71012	(S)	Release Me	1967	8.00	20.00
Parrot PA-1015	(M)	The Last Waltz	1967	6.00	15.00
Parrot PAS-71015	(S)	The Last Waltz	1967	8.00	20.00
Parrot PAS-71022	(S)	A Man Without Love	1968	6.00	15.00
Parrot PAS-71026	(S)	Engelbert	1969	6.00	15.00
Parrot PAS-71030	(S)	Engelbert Humperdinck	1970	6.00	15.00
Epic PAL-35020	(DJ)	Last Of The Romantics (Picture disc)	1978	20.00	50.00

HUNGER

Label & Catalog #		Title	Year	VG+	NM
Public 1006	(S)	Strictly From Hunger	1969	100.00	250.00

HUNT, TOMMY

Hunt was formerly a member of the Flamingos.

Label & Catalog #		Title	Year	VG+	NM
Scepter 506	(M)	I Just Don't Know What To Do With Myself	1962	14.00	35.00
Scepter SS-506	(S)	I Just Don't Know What To Do With Myself	1962	20.00	50.00
Dynamo D-7001	(M)	Tommy Hunt's Greatest Hits	1967	8.00	20.00
Dynamo DS-8001	(S)	Tommy Hunt's Greatest Hits	1967	10.00	25.00
		(Contains rerecordings of Hunt's former glories.)			

HUNTER, IAN

Hunter was formerly a member of Mott The Hoople.

Label & Catalog #		Title	Year	VG+	NM
Columbia 34721	(DJ)	Overnight Angels	1977	6.00	15.00

HUNTER, IVORY JOE

Label & Catalog #		Title	Year	VG+	NM
MGM E-3488	(M)	I Get That Lonesome Feeling	1957	100.00	300.00
Sound 603	(M)	Ivory Joe Hunter	1957	100.00	300.00
King 605	(M)	16 Of His Greatest Hits	1958	150.00	350.00
Atlantic 8008	(M)	Ivory Joe Hunter	1957	80.00	200.00
Atlantic 8015	(M)	The Old & The New	1958	80.00	200.00
		— Original Atlantic albums above have black labels.—			
Atlantic 8008	(M)	Ivory Joe Hunter	1960	40.00	100.00
Atlantic 8015	(M)	The Old & The New	1960	40.00	100.00
		— Atlantic albums above have purple & orange labels.—			
Sage 603	(M)	Ivory Joe Hunter	1959	60.00	150.00
Lion L-70068	(M)	I Need You So	1959	60.00	150.00
Goldisc 403	(M)	The Fabulous Ivory Joe Hunter	1961	30.00	75.00
Smash MGS-27037	(M)	Ivory Joe Hunter's Golden Hits	1963	14.00	35.00
Smash SRS-67037	(S)	Ivory Joe Hunter's Golden Hits	1963	20.00	50.00
Dot DLP-3569	(M)	This Is Ivory Joe Hunter	1964	14.00	35.00
Dot DLP-25569	(S)	This Is Ivory Joe Hunter	1964	20.00	50.00
Strand 1123	(M)	The Artistry Of Ivory Joe Hunter	196?	8.00	20.00

Label & Catalog #		Title	Year	VG+	NM
Epic SE-30348	(S)	The Return Of Ivory Joe Hunter	1971	8.00	20.00
Everest 289	(S)	Ivory Joe Hunter	1974	4.00	10.00
Paramount PAS-6080	(S)	I've Always Been Country	1974	5.00	12.00

HUNTER, LURLEAN: *Refer to* **GOLDMINE'S PRICE GUIDE TO COLLECTIBLE JAZZ ALBUMS**

HUNTER, ROBERT
Refer to The Grateful Dead.

Round RX-101	(S)	Tales Of The Great Rum Runners	1974	12.00	30.00
Round RX-105	(S)	Tiger Rose	1975	12.00	30.00

HUNTER, TAB

Warner Bros. W-1221	(M)	Tab Hunter	1958	12.00	30.00
Warner Bros. WS-1221	(S)	Tab Hunter	1958	16.00	40.00
Warner Bros. W-1292	(M)	When I Fall In Love	1959	12.00	30.00
Warner Bros. WS-1292	(S)	When I Fall In Love	1959	16.00	40.00
Warner Bros. W-1367	(M)	R. F. D. Tab Hunter	1960	12.00	30.00
Warner Bros. WS-1367	(S)	R. F. D. Tab Hunter	1960	16.00	40.00
Dot DLP-3370	(M)	Young Love	1961	8.00	20.00
Dot DLP-25370	(S)	Young Love	1961	12.00	30.00

HUNTER MUSKETT

Bradley 1003	(S)	Hunter Muskett	1969	30.00	75.00

HURT, MISSISSIPPI JOHN

Vanguard VRS-9145	(M)	Blues At Newport	1965	10.00	25.00
Vanguard VSD-79145	(S)	Blues At Newport	1965	12.00	30.00
Vanguard VRS-9220	(M)	Mississippi John Hurt Today	1966	10.00	25.00
Vanguard VSD-79220	(S)	Mississippi John Hurt Today	1966	12.00	30.00
Vanguard VRS-9248	(M)	The Immortal Mississippi John Hurt	1967	10.00	25.00
Vanguard VSD-79248	(S)	The Immortal Mississippi John Hurt	1967	12.00	30.00

HURVITZ, SANDY

Verve V6-5064	(S)	Sandy's Album Is Here At Last	1969	10.00	25.00
		(Produced by Frank Zappa.)			

HUSKY, FERLIN
Husky also recorded as Simon Crum.

Capitol T-718	(M)	Songs Of The Home And Heart	1956	30.00	75.00
Capitol T-880	(M)	Boulevard Of Broken Dreams	1957	20.00	50.00
Capitol T-976	(M)	Sittin' On A Rainbow	1959	20.00	50.00
— Original Capitol albums above have turquoise labels.—					
King 647	(M)	Country Tunes Sung From The Heart	1959	30.00	75.00
King 728	(M)	Easy Livin'	1960	30.00	75.00
Capitol T-1204	(M)	Born To Lose	1959	12.00	40.00
Capitol T-1280	(M)	Ferlin's Favorites	1960	12.00	40.00
Capitol T-1383	(M)	Gone	1960	12.00	40.00
Capitol T-1546	(M)	Walkin' And Hummin'	1961	10.00	25.00
Capitol ST-1546	(S)	Walkin' And Hummin'	1961	12.00	30.00
Capitol T-1633	(M)	Memories Of Home	1961	10.00	25.00
Capitol ST-1633	(S)	Memories Of Home	1961	12.00	30.00
— Original Capitol albums above have black labels with the Capitol logo on the side.—					
Capitol T-1720	(M)	Some Of My Favorites	1962	6.00	15.00
Capitol ST-1720	(S)	Some Of My Favorites	1962	8.00	20.00
Capitol T-1885	(M)	The Heart And Soul Of Ferlin Husky	1963	6.00	15.00
Capitol ST-1885	(S)	The Heart And Soul Of Ferlin Husky	1963	8.00	20.00
Capitol T-1991	(M)	The Hits Of Ferlin Husky	1963	8.00	20.00
Capitol DT-1991	(E)	The Hits Of Ferlin Husky	1963	5.00	12.00
Capitol T-2101	(M)	By Request	1964	6.00	15.00
Capitol ST-2101	(S)	By Request	1964	8.00	20.00
Capitol T-2305	(M)	True, True Lovin'	1965	6.00	15.00
Capitol ST-2305	(S)	True, True Lovin'	1965	8.00	20.00
Capitol T-2439	(M)	Songs Of Music City, U.S.A.	1966	6.00	15.00
Capitol ST-2439	(S)	Songs Of Music City, U.S.A.	1966	8.00	20.00
Capitol T-2548	(M)	I Could Sing All Night	1966	6.00	15.00
Capitol ST-2548	(S)	I Could Sing All Night	1966	8.00	20.00
Capitol T-2705	(M)	What Am I Gonna Do Now?	1967	6.00	15.00
Capitol ST-2705	(S)	What Am I Gonna Do Now?	1967	8.00	20.00

Label & Catalog #		Title	Year	VG+	NM
Capitol T-2793	(M)	Christmas All Year Long	1967	6.00	15.00
Capitol ST-2793	(S)	Christmas All Year Long	1967	8.00	20.00
Capitol ST-2870	(S)	Just For You	1968	6.00	15.00
Capitol ST-2913	(S)	Where No One Stands Alone	1968	6.00	15.00

— Original Capitol albums above have black labels with the Capitol logo on top.—

HUTTO, J. B., & THE HAWKS
Delmark DL-617	(S)	Hawk Squat	1972	8.00	20.00
Delmark DL-636	(S)	Sidewinder	1973	8.00	20.00

HUTTON, BETTY
Capitol H-256 (10")	(M)	Square In The Social Circle	1950	16.00	40.00
MGM E-509 (10")	(M)	Annie Get Your Gun (Soundtrack)	1950	40.00	100.00
RCA LPM-3097 (10")	(M)	Somebody Loves Me (Soundtrack)	1952	40.00	100.00
Capitol L-547 (10")	(M)	Satins And Spurs (TV Soundtrack)	1954	50.00	125.00
MGM E-3227	(M)	Annie Get Your Gun (Soundtrack)	1955	16.00	40.00
Warner Bros. W-1267	(M)	At The Saints And Sinners Ball	1959	5.00	12.00
Warner Bros. WS-1267	(S)	At The Saints And Sinners Ball	1959	6.00	15.00

HUTTON, DANNY
Danny Hutton was a member of Three Dog Night.
MGM SE-4664	(S)	Pre-Dog Night	1970	10.00	25.00

HUTTON, JUNE
Capitol T-643	(M)	Afterglow	1955	12.00	30.00
Venise 10017	(M)	Dream	195?	12.00	30.00
Tops L-1608	(M)	June Hutton In Hi-Fi	1959	8.00	20.00

HYLAND, BRIAN
Kapp KL-1202	(M)	The Bashful Blonde	1960	16.00	40.00
Kapp KS-3202	(S)	The Bashful Blonde	1960	20.00	50.00
ABC-Paramount 400	(M)	Let Me Belong To You	1961	12.00	30.00
ABC-Paramount S-400	(S)	Let Me Belong To You	1961	16.00	40.00
ABC-Paramount 431	(M)	Sealed With A Kiss	1962	12.00	30.00
ABC-Paramount S-431	(S)	Sealed With A Kiss	1962	16.00	40.00

("Sealed With A Kiss" is rechanneled on this album.)

ABC-Paramount 463	(M)	Country Meets Folk	1964	10.00	25.00
ABC-Paramount S-463	(S)	Country Meets Folk	1964	14.00	35.00
Philips PHM-200-136	(M)	Here's To Our Love	1964	6.00	15.00
Philips PHS-600-136	(S)	Here's To Our Love	1964	8.00	20.00
Philips PHM-200-158	(M)	Rockin' Folk	1965	6.00	15.00
Philips PHS-600-158	(S)	Rockin, Folk	1965	8.00	20.00
Philips PHM-200-217	(M)	The Joker Went Wild	1966	6.00	15.00
Philips PHS-600-217	(S)	The Joker Went Wild	1966	8.00	20.00
Dot DLP-25926	(S)	Tragedy	1969	5.00	12.00
Dot DLP-25954	(S)	Stay And Love Me All Summer	1969	5.00	12.00
Uni 73097	(S)	Brian Hyland	1971	5.00	12.00

("Gypsy Woman" is rechanneled on this album.)

Private Stock PS-7003	(S)	In A State Of Bayou	1977	4.00	10.00

IAN, JANIS
Verve V-5027	(M)	Society's Child	1967	8.00	20.00
Verve VS-5027	(S)	Society's Child	1967	10.00	25.00

Label & Catalog #		Title	Year	VG+	NM
Verve/Forecast FT-3017	(M)	Society's Child	1967	6.00	15.00
Verve/Forecast FTS-3017	(S)	Society's Child	1967	8.00	20.00
Verve/Forecast FTS-3024	(S)	For All The Seasons Of Your Mind	1967	6.00	15.00
Verve/Forecast FTS-3048	(S)	The Secret Life Of J. Eddy Fink	1968	6.00	15.00
Verve/Forecast FTS-3063	(S)	Who Really Cares?	1969	6.00	15.00
— Original Forecast albums above have brown labels.—					
Columbia PCQ-33394	(Q)	Between The Lines	1975	6.00	15.00
Columbia PCQ-33919	(Q)	Aftertones	1976	6.00	15.00
Columbia PCQ-34440	(Q)	Miracle Row	1977	6.00	15.00

IAN & SYLVIA

Vanguard VRS-9133	(M)	Four Strong Winds	1963	6.00	15.00
Vanguard VSD-79133	(S)	Four Strong Winds	1963	8.00	20.00
Vanguard VRS-9154	(M)	Northern Journey	1964	6.00	15.00
Vanguard VSD-79154	(S)	Northern Journey	1964	8.00	20.00
Vanguard VRS-9175	(M)	Early Morning Rain	1965	6.00	15.00
Vanguard VSD-79175	(S)	Early Morning Rain	1965	8.00	20.00
Vanguard VRS-9215	(M)	Play One More	1966	6.00	15.00
Vanguard VSD-79215	(S)	Play One More	1966	8.00	20.00
Vanguard VRS-9241	(M)	So Much For Dreaming	1967	6.00	15.00
Vanguard VSD-79241	(S)	So Much For Dreaming	1967	8.00	20.00
MGM E-4388	(M)	Lovin' Sound	1967	6.00	15.00
MGM SE-4388	(S)	Lovin' Sound	1967	8.00	20.00
MGM SE-4550	(S)	Full Circle	1968	6.00	15.00
Vanguard VSD-79269	(S)	Ian And Sylvia	1968	6.00	15.00
Vanguard VSD-79284	(S)	Nashville	1968	6.00	15.00
Ampex 10103	(S)	The Great Speckled Bird	1970	6.00	15.00

IAN & THE ZODIACS

Philips PHM-200-176	(M)	Ian And The Zodiacs	1965	16.00	40.00
Philips PHS-600-176	(S)	Ian And The Zodiacs	1965	20.00	50.00

ICE MAN'S BAND, THE
Jerry Butler's band sans the Man.

Mercury SRM-1-648	(S)	Introducing The Ice Man's Band	1972	6.00	15.00

ID, THE

RCA Victor LPM-3805	(M)	The Inner Sounds Of The Id	1967	12.00	30.00
RCA Victor LSP-3805	(S)	The Inner Sounds Of The Id	1967	10.00	25.00
		("The Rake" is rechanneled on this album.)			
Aura 1000	(S)	Where Are We Going?	1976	12.00	30.00

IDES OF MARCH, THE

Warner Bros. WS-1863	(S)	Vehicle	1970	5.00	12.00
Warner Bros. WS-1896	(S)	Common Bond	1971	4.00	10.00

IDLE, ERIC, & NEIL INNES
Refer to The Rutles.

Passport PPSD-98018	(S)	The Rutland Weekend Television Songbook	1976	10.00	25.00

IDLE RACE, THE
The Idle Race features Jeff Lynne. Refer to The Electric Light Orchestra; The Move.

Liberty LST-7603	(S)	Birthday Party	1969	16.00	40.00
		("Sitting In My Tree" is in mono on this album.)			
Sunset SLS-50381	(S)	Birthday Party	1972	8.00	20.00

IF

Capitol ST-539	(S)	If	1969	8.00	20.00
Capitol SW-676	(S)	If 2	1970	8.00	20.00
Capitol SMAS-820	(S)	If 3	1971	8.00	20.00
Metromedia BML1-057	(S)	Waterfall	1972	5.00	12.00
Metromedia BML1-074	(S)	Double Diamond	1973	5.00	12.00
Capitol ST-11299	(S)	Not Just Another Bunch Of Pretty Faces	1974	4.00	10.00
Capitol ST-11344	(S)	Tea-Break Over-Back On Your 'Eads!	1974	4.00	10.00

IFIELD, FRANK
Refer to The Beatles.

Vee Jay LP-1054	(M)	I Re-mem-ber You	1963	12.00	30.00
Vee Jay SR-1054	(S)	I Re-mem-ber You	1963	20.00	50.00

The Impalas were an integrated group from Brooklyn made up of three white guys—Tony Carlucci, Lenny Renda and Richard Wagner—backing black lead singer Joe Frazier. Their huge hit, "Sorry (I Ran All The Way Home)," spawned their sole album outing, which is one of the most valuable of the early stereo albums in the field.

Label & Catalog #		Title	Year	VG+	NM
Capitol Int. T-10356	(M)	I'm Confessin'	196?	6.00	15.00
Capitol Int. ST-10356	(S)	I'm Confessin'	196?	8.00	20.00
Hickory LPM-132	(M)	The Best Of Frank Ifield	196?	8.00	20.00
Hickory LPS-132	(S)	The Best Of Frank Ifield	196?	12.00	30.00
Hickory LPM-136	(M)	Tale Of Two Cities	196?	8.00	20.00
Hickory LPS-136	(S)	Tale Of Two Cities	196?	12.00	30.00
Hickory LPM-144	(M)	Rockin' Lover	196?	8.00	20.00
Hickory LPS-144	(S)	Rockin' Lover	196?	12.00	30.00

IKETTES, THE
The Ikettes backed Ike & Tina Turner during the '60s.

Modern M-102	(M)	Soul Hits	1965	8.00	20.00
Modern MST-102	(S)	Soul Hits	1965	12.00	30.00

ILL WIND

ABC S-641	(S)	Flashes	1968	12.00	30.00

ILLINOIS SPEED PRESS, THE

Columbia CS-9792	(S)	Illinois Speed Press	1969	6.00	15.00
Columbia CS-9976	(S)	Duet	1970	6.00	15.00

ILLUSION

Sinergia SR-7654	(S)	Illusion	1974	30.00	75.00

ILLUSTRATION

Janus 3010	(S)	Illustration	1969	10.00	25.00

ILMO SMOKEHOUSE

Beautiful Sound 3002	(S)	Ilmo Smokehouse	1971	14.00	35.00
Roulette SR-3002	(S)	Ilmo Smokehouse	1971	6.00	15.00

IMMIGRANTS, THE

Justice JLP	(M)	The Immigrants '66	1966	100.00	250.00

IMPACS, THE

King 886	(M)	Impact!	1964	30.00	75.00
King KS-886	(S)	Impact!	1964	50.00	125.00
King 916	(M)	Weekend With The Impacs	1964	30.00	75.00
King KS-916	(S)	Weekend With The Impacs	1964	50.00	125.00

IMPACTS, THE
The Impacts feature Merrel Fankhauser.

Del-Fi DFLP-1234	(M)	Wipe Out	1963	14.00	35.00
Del-Fi DFS-1234	(S)	Wipe Out	1963	20.00	50.00

IMPALA SYNDROME, THE

Parallax 4002	(S)	The Impala Syndrome	1970	12.00	30.00

IMPALAS, THE

Cub 8003	(M)	Sorry (I Ran All The Way Home)	1959	200.00	400.00
Cub S-8003	(S)	Sorry (I Ran All The Way Home)	1959	360.00	600.00

IMPRESSIONS, THE
The Impressions feature Curtis Mayfield. Refer to Jerry Butler.

ABC-Paramount 450	(M)	The Impressions	1963	10.00	25.00
ABC-Paramount S-450	(S)	The Impressions	1963	12.00	30.00
ABC-Paramount 468	(M)	Never Ending Impressions	1964	10.00	25.00
ABC-Paramount S-468	(S)	Never Ending Impressions	1964	12.00	30.00
ABC-Paramount 493	(M)	Keep On Pushing	1964	8.00	20.00
ABC-Paramount S-493	(S)	Keep On Pushing	1964	10.00	25.00
ABC-Paramount 505	(M)	People Get Ready	1965	8.00	20.00
ABC-Paramount S-505	(S)	People Get Ready	1965	10.00	25.00
ABC-Paramount 515	(M)	The Impressions' Greatest Hits	1965	6.00	15.00
ABC-Paramount S-515	(S)	The Impressions' Greatest Hits	1965	8.00	20.00
ABC-Paramount 523	(M)	One By One	1965	6.00	15.00
ABC-Paramount S-523	(S)	One By One	1965	8.00	20.00
ABC-Paramount 545	(M)	Ridin' High	1966	8.00	20.00
ABC-Paramount S-545	(S)	Ridin' High	1966	10.00	25.00

Label & Catalog #		Title	Year	VG+	NM
ABC-Paramount 606	(M)	The Fabulous Impressions	1967	8.00	20.00
ABC-Paramount S-606	(S)	The Fabulous Impressions	1967	8.00	20.00
ABC-Paramount S-635	(S)	We're A Winner	1968	6.00	15.00
ABC-Paramount S-654	(S)	The Best Of The Impressions	1968	5.00	12.00
ABC-Paramount S-669	(S)	The Versatile Impressions	1969	5.00	12.00
ABC-Paramount S-727	(S)	16 Greatest Hits	1970	5.00	12.00
Curtom CRS-8001	(S)	This Is My Country	1968	6.00	15.00
Curtom CRS-8004	(S)	Best Impressions (Curtis, Sam & Fred)	1969	6.00	15.00
Curtom CRS-8006	(S)	Check Out Your Mind	1970	5.00	12.00
Curtom CRS-8012	(S)	Times Have Changed	1972	5.00	12.00
Curtom CRS-8016	(S)	Preacher Man	1973	5.00	12.00
Curtom CRS-8019	(S)	Finally Got Myself Together	1974	5.00	12.00
Curtom CRS-8602	(S)	Three The Hard Way (Soundtrack)	1974	5.00	12.00
Curtom CRS-5003	(S)	First Impressions	1975	4.00	10.00
Curtom CRS-5009	(S)	Loving Power	1976	4.00	10.00
Cotillion SD-9912	(S)	It's About Time	1976	4.00	10.00

IN-SECT, THE

Camden CAL-909	(M)	Introducing The In-Sect	1965	16.00	40.00
Camden CAS-909	(S)	Introducing The In-Sect	1965	20.00	50.00

INCORPORATED THANG BAND, THE
The Thangs are members of the Parliament/Funkadelic community.

Warner Bros. 925617	(S)	Lifestyles Of The Roach And Famous	1988	4.00	10.00

INCREDIBLE STRING BAND, THE
The Incredible String Band was Mike Heron and Robin Williamson.

Elektra EKL-322	(M)	The Incredible String Band	1967	6.00	15.00
Elektra EKS-7322	(S)	The Incredible String Band	1967	8.00	20.00
Elektra EKL-4010	(M)	The 5,000 Spirits	1967	6.00	15.00
Elektra EKS-74010	(S)	The 5,000 Spirits	1967	8.00	20.00
Elektra EKS-4021	(M)	The Hangman's Beautiful Daughter	1968	6.00	15.00
Elektra EKS-74021	(S)	The Hangman's Beautiful Daughter	1968	8.00	20.00
Elektra EKS-74036	(S)	Wee Tam	1969	8.00	20.00
Elektra EKS-74037	(S)	The Big Huge	1969	8.00	20.00
		—Original Elektra albums above have brown labels.—			
Elektra EKS-74057	(S)	Changing Horses	1969	6.00	15.00
Elektra EKS-74061	(S)	I Looked Up	1970	6.00	15.00
Decca DL-79181	(S)	Taking Off (Soundtrack)	1971	16.00	40.00
Elektra EKS-2002	(S)	"U" (2 LPs)	1971	6.00	15.00
Elektra EKS-2004	(S)	Relics Of The Incredible String Band (2 LPs)	1971	6.00	15.00
Elektra EKS-74112	(S)	Liquid Acrobat As Regards The Air	1972	4.00	10.00
Reprise MS-2122	(S)	Earthspan	1972	4.00	10.00
Reprise MS-2198	(S)	Hard Rope And Silver Twine	1974	4.00	10.00
Reprise MS-2129	(S)	No Ruinous Feud	1973	4.00	10.00

INCREDIBLES, THE

Audio Arts AAS-7000	(S)	Heart And Soul	1970	8.00	20.00

INDEPENDENTS, THE

Wand WDS-694	(S)	The First Time We Met	1972	6.00	15.00
Wand WDS-696	(S)	The Independents	1973	6.00	15.00
Wand WDS-699	(S)	Discs Of Gold	1974	6.00	15.00

INDEX, THE
Members of The Index later recorded as Just Us.

D. C. (No number)	(M)	The Index	1968	*See note below*	
		(The price here is for an original record in an original cover, both featuring "New York Mining Disaster." Rare with suggested values in collectible condition of $1,500-3,000.)			
D. C. (No number)	(M)	The Index	1968	1,000.00	1,500.00
		(The price here is for an original record featuring "New York Mining Disaster" in a second pressing cover listing "Fire Eyes.")			
D. C. (No number)	(M)	The Index	1968	800.00	1,200.00
		(The price here is for a second pressing record in a second pressing cover, both featuring "Fire Eyes.")			

INDIAN SUMMER

RCA/Neon NE-3	(S)	Indian Summer	1971	8.00	20.00

Label & Catalog #		Title	Year	VG+	NM
INFLUENCE					
ABC S-630	(S)	Influence	1968	8.00	20.00
INGMANN, JORGEN					
Mercury MG-20200	(M)	Swinging Guitar	1956	30.00	75.00
Mercury MG-20292	(M)	Swing Softly	1956	30.00	75.00
Atco 33-130	(M)	Apache	1961	16.00	40.00
Atco 33-139	(M)	The Many Guitars Of Jorgen Ingmann	1962	16.00	40.00
United Arts. Int. 15549	(S)	Movie Themes	1968	6.00	15.00
United Arts. UAS-6785	(S)	El Condor Pasa	1970	6.00	15.00
INGRAM, LUTHER					
Koko KOS-2201	(S)	I've Been Here All The Time	1971	5.00	12.00
Koko KOS-2202	(S)	If Loving You Is Wrong (With bonus photo)	1972	6.00	15.00
Koko KOS-2202	(S)	If Loving You Is Wrong (Without photo)	1972	5.00	12.00
INK SPOTS, THE					
Waldorf Music 33-144 (10")	(M)	The Ink Spots	195?	30.00	75.00
Waldorf Music 33-152 (10")	(M)	The Ink Spots	195?	30.00	75.00
Waldorf Music 33-W2A	(M)	America's Favorite Music	195?	30.00	75.00
		(Collects all th songs on the two 10" albums plus eight others.)			
Decca DL-5056 (10")	(M)	The Ink Spots, Volume 1	1950	20.00	50.00
Decca DL-5071 (10")	(M)	The Ink Spots, Volume 2	1950	20.00	50.00
Decca DL-5333 (10")	(M)	Precious Memories	1951	20.00	50.00
Decca DL-5541 (10")	(M)	Street Of Dreams	1954	20.00	50.00
Decca DL-8154	(M)	The Ink Spots	1955	16.00	40.00
Decca DL-8232	(M)	Time Out For Tears	1956	16.00	40.00
Decca DL-8768	(M)	Torch Time	1958	16.00	40.00
Decca DL-4297	(M)	Our Golden Favorites	1962	6.00	15.00
Decca DXB-182	(M)	The Best Of The Ink Spots (2 LPs)	1965	8.00	20.00
Decca DXSB-182	(P)	The Best Of The Ink Spots (2 LPs)	1965	6.00	15.00
Grand Award 328	(M)	The Ink Spots' Greatest, Volume 1	1956	10.00	25.00
Grand Award 354	(M)	The Ink Spots' Greatest, Volume 2	1956	10.00	25.00
King LP-535	(M)	Something Old, Something New	1958	100.00	250.00
King LP-642	(M)	Songs That Will Live Forever	1959	100.00	175.00
Tops L-1561	(M)	The Ink Spots In Hi-Fi	1958	8.00	20.00
Colortone 4901	(M)	The Ink Spots	1958	30.00	75.00
Colortone 4947	(M)	The Ink Spots (Volume 2)	1959	30.00	75.00
Grand LP-328	(M)	The Ink Spots' Greatest	1959	10.00	25.00
Grand LP-354	(M)	The Ink Spots' Greatest, Volume 2	1959	10.00	25.00
Verve V-6096	(M)	The Ink Spots' Favorites	1960	10.00	25.00
Verve VS-606	(S)	The Ink Spots' Favorites	1960	16.00	40.00
Crown CLP-5142	(M)	The Ink Spots	196?	6.00	15.00
Crown CLP-5144	(M)	The Ink Spots' Greatest Hits	196?	8.00	20.00
Crown CST-144	(E)	The Ink Spots' Greatest Hits	196?	4.00	10.00
Crown CST-144	(E)	The Ink Spots' Greatest Hits (Red vinyl)	196?	16.00	40.00
Crown CLP-5217	(M)	The Sensational Ink Spots	196?	8.00	20.00
Crown CST-217	(E)	The Sensational Ink Spots	196?	4.00	10.00
Crown CST-217	(E)	The Sensational Ink Spots (Red vinyl)	196?	16.00	40.00
Mayfair 9685S	(M)	In The Spotlight (Yellow vinyl)	196?	16.00	40.00
Vocalion VL-3606	(M)	Sincerely Yours	1964	6.00	15.00
Vocalion VL-3725	(M)	Lost In A Dream	1965	6.00	15.00
Vocalion VL-73725	(E)	Lost In A Dream	1965	4.00	10.00
INNOCENCE, THE					
The Innocence is Pete Anders and Vinnie Poncia.					
Kama Sutra KLP-8059	(M)	The Innocence	1967	6.00	15.00
Kama Sutra KLPS-8059	(S)	The Innocence	1967	10.00	25.00
INNOCENTS, THE					
The Innocents also recorded with Kathy Young.					
Indigo 503	(DJ)	Innocently Yours	1961	250.00	750.00
		(Advance copies designated as promos were issued in plain white covers with "The Innocents" printed in blue letters on the front.)			
Indigo 503	(M)	Innocently Yours	1961	60.00	150.00
INSECT TRUST, THE					
Capitol SKAO-109	(S)	The Insect Trust	1968	16.00	40.00
Atco SD-33-313	(S)	Hoboken Saturday Night	1970	14.00	35.00

Label & Catalog #		Title	Year	VG+	NM

INTERNATIONAL SUBMARINE BAND, THE
The I.S.B. features Gram Parsons.

| L.H.I. 12001 | (S) | **Safe At Home** *(Multi-color label)* | 1968 | 40.00 | 100.00 |

(Originals have multi-color labels; counterfeits have white labels.
"Safe At Home" was reissued on Shiloh as "Gram Parsons.")

INTRIGUES, THE

| Yew YS-777 | (S) | **In A Moment** | 1970 | 16.00 | 40.00 |

INTRUDERS, THE

Gamble 5001	(M)	**The Intruders Are Together**	1967	8.00	20.00
Gamble KZ-5001	(P)	**The Intruders Are Together**	1967	10.00	25.00
Gamble KZ-5004	(P)	**Cowboys To Girls**	1968	8.00	20.00
Gamble KZ-5005	(P)	**The Intruders' Greatest Hits**	1969	6.00	15.00
Gamble KZ-5008	(S)	**When We Get Married**	1970	6.00	15.00

INVADERS, THE

| Justice JLP-125 | (M) | **On The Right Track** | 196? | 100.00 | 250.00 |

INVADERS, THE

| Duane 1006 | (M) | **Spacing Out** | 1968 | 40.00 | 100.00 |

INVICTAS, THE

| Sahara 101 | (M) | **The Invictas A-Go-Go** | 1965 | 40.00 | 100.00 |

IRON BUTTERFLY

Atco 33-227	(M)	**Heavy**	1967	10.00	25.00
Atco SD-33-227	(S)	**Heavy**	1967	8.00	20.00
Atco 33-250	(M)	**In-A-Gadda-Da-Vida**	1968	14.00	35.00
Atco SD-33-250	(S)	**In-A-Gadda-Da-Vida**	1968	10.00	25.00

— Original Atco stereo albums above have purple & brown labels.—

Atco SD-33-227	(S)	**Heavy**	1969	5.00	12.00
Atco SD-33-250	(S)	**In-A-Gadda-Da-Vida**	1969	5.00	12.00
Atco SD-33-280	(S)	**Ball**	1969	5.00	12.00
Atco SD-33-318	(S)	**Iron Butterfly Live**	1970	5.00	12.00
Atco SD-33-339	(S)	**Metamorphosis**	1970	5.00	12.00
Atco SD-33-318	(S)	**Evolution/The Best Of Iron Butterfly Live**	1971	5.00	12.00

— Atco albums above yellow labels with "Atlantic Recording Co." on the bottom.—

IRON MAIDEN

| Capitol SEAX-12219 | (S) | **Number Of The Beast** *(Picture disc)* | 19?? | 20.00 | 50.00 |
| Capitol SEAX-12306 | (S) | **Piece Of Mind** *(Picture disc)* | 19?? | 20.00 | 50.00 |

(Contains one bonus track, "Cross Eyed Mary.")

IRONMEN, THE

| Reggae 15003 | (S) | **Reggae Thing** | 1970 | 6.00 | 15.00 |

ISLEY BROTHERS, THE
Refer to Jimi Hendrix / The Isley Brothers.

RCA Victor LPM-2156	(M)	**Shout!**	1959	30.00	75.00
RCA Victor LSP-2156	(S)	**Shout!**	1959	50.00	125.00
Wand WD-653	(M)	**Twist And Shout**	1962	20.00	50.00
Wand WDS-653	(S)	**Twist And Shout**	1962	30.00	75.00
United Arts. UAL-6313	(M)	**The Famous Isley Brothers**	1963	12.00	30.00
United Arts. UAS-6313	(S)	**The Famous Isley Brothers**	1963	16.00	40.00
Scepter SC-552	(M)	**Take Some Time Out For The Isley Brothers**	1966	6.00	15.00
Scepter SCS-552	(S)	**Take Some Time Out For The Isley Brothers**	1966	8.00	20.00
Tamla T-269	(M)	**This Old Heart Of Mine**	1966	6.00	15.00
Tamla TS-269	(S)	**This Old Heart Of Mine**	1966	8.00	20.00
Tamla 275	(M)	**Soul On The Rocks**	1967	6.00	15.00
Tamla TS-275	(S)	**Soul On The Rocks**	1967	6.00	15.00
Tamla TS-287	(S)	**Doin' Their Thing**	1969	6.00	15.00
Sunset SUS-5257	(S)	**The Isley Brothers Do Their Thing**	1969	6.00	15.00
Camden ACL1-0126	(S)	**Rock On, Brother**	1973	4.00	10.00

(Camden 0126 is a repackage of RCA Victor 2156.)

T-Neck TNS-3001	(S)	**It's Our Thing**	1969	5.00	12.00
T-Neck TNS-3002	(S)	**The Brothers Isley**	1969	5.00	12.00
T-Neck TNS-3003	(S)	**The Brothers Isley**	1969	5.00	12.00

Label & Catalog #		Title	Year	VG+	NM
T-Neck TNS-3004	(S)	Live At Yankee Stadium (2 LPs)	1969	6.00	15.00
		(The first side is The Isleys; side 2 is The Edwin Hawkins Singers; side 3 is The Brooklyn Bridge; and side 4, various artists.)			
T-Neck TNS-3005	(S)	Dave "Baby" Cortez The Isley Brothers Way	1970	5.00	12.00
T-Neck TNS-3006	(S)	Get Into Something	1970	5.00	12.00
T-Neck TNS-3007	(S)	In The Beginning (With Jimi Hendrix)	1971	6.00	15.00
T-Neck TNS-3008	(S)	Givin' It Back	1971	5.00	12.00
T-Neck TNS-3009	(S)	Brother, Brother, Brother	1972	5.00	12.00
T-Neck TNS-3010	(S)	The Isley Brothers Live (2 LPs)	1973	6.00	15.00
T-Neck TNS-3011	(S)	The Isley Brothers' Greatest Hits	1973	5.00	12.00
T-Neck ZQ-32453	(Q)	3 + 3	1974	8.00	20.00
T-Neck ZQ-33070	(Q)	The Isley Brothers Live It Up	1974	8.00	20.00
T-Neck PZQ-33536	(Q)	The Heat Is On	1975	8.00	20.00
T-Neck PZQ-33809	(Q)	Harvest For The World	1976	8.00	20.00
T-Neck A5Z-137	(DJ)	Everything You Always Wanted To Hear	1976	6.00	15.00
T-Neck PZQ-34432	(Q)	Go For Your Guns	1977	8.00	20.00

ISLEY BROTHERS, THE / MARVIN & JOHNNY
Crown CLP-5352	(M)	The Isley Brothers And Marvin & Johnny	196?	10.00	25.00
Crown CST-352	(E)	The Isley Brothers And Marvin & Johnny	196?	4.00	10.00

ISAACS, BUD
Jabs 101	(M)	The Best Of Bud Isaacs	195?	80.00	200.00

IT'S A BEAUTIFUL DAY
Columbia CS-9768	(S)	It's A Beautiful Day	1969	16.00	40.00
		(Originally issued on Columbia's "360 Sound" label. The long rumored "naked maiden" cover is just that, a rumor.)			
Columbia CS-9768	(S)	It's A Beautiful Day (Red & gold label)	1970	6.00	15.00
Columbia CS-1058	(S)	Marrying Maiden	1970	8.00	20.00
Columbia C-30734	(S)	Choice Quality Stuff/Anytime	1971	8.00	20.00
Columbia KC-31338	(S)	Live At Carnegie Hall	1972	8.00	20.00
Columbia KC-32181	(S)	It's A Beautiful Day Today	1973	8.00	20.00
San Fran. Sound 11790	(S)	It's A Beautiful Day (Half-speed master)	1985	10.00	30.00

ITALIAN ASPHALT & PAVEMENT CO., THE
Colossus 5000	(S)	Dupree's Gold	1970	6.00	15.00

IVES, BURL
Columbia CL-6058 (10")	(M)	Return Of The Wayfaring Stranger	195?	12.00	30.00
Columbia CL-6109 (10")	(M)	Wayfaring Stranger	195?	12.00	30.00
Columbia CL-6144 (10")	(M)	More Folksongs	195?	12.00	30.00
Decca DL-5013 (10")	(M)	Ballads And Folk Songs, Volume 1	1950	12.00	30.00
Decca DL-5080 (10")	(M)	Ballads And Folk Songs, Volume 2	1950	12.00	30.00
Decca DL-5093 (10")	(M)	Ballads Folk And Country Songs	1950	12.00	30.00
Decca DL-5428 (10")	(M)	Christmas Day In The Morning	1952	12.00	30.00
Decca DL-5467 (10")	(M)	Folk Songs Dramatic And Dangerous	1953	12.00	30.00
Decca DL-5490 (10")	(M)	Women: Folk Songs About The Fair	1954	12.00	30.00
Columbia CL-628	(M)	Wayfaring Stranger	1955	8.00	20.00
Columbia CL-980	(M)	Burl Ives Sings Songs For All Ages	1957	8.00	20.00
Decca DL-8080	(M)	Coronation Concert	1956	8.00	20.00
Decca DL-8125	(M)	Men	1956	8.00	20.00
Decca DL-8245	(M)	Down To The Sea In Ships	1956	8.00	20.00
Decca DL-8246	(M)	Women	1956	8.00	20.00
Decca DL-8247	(M)	In The Quiet Of Night	1956	8.00	20.00
Decca DL-8248	(M)	Burl Ives Sings For Fun	1956	8.00	20.00
Decca DL-8391	(M)	Christmas Eve With Ives	1957	8.00	20.00
Decca DL-8444	(M)	Songs Of Ireland	1958	8.00	20.00
Decca DL-8587	(M)	Captain Burl Ives' Ark	1958	8.00	20.00
Decca DL-8749	(M)	Australian Folk Songs	1958	8.00	20.00
Decca DL-4815	(M)	Rudolph The Red-Nosed Reindeer	1966	12.00	30.00
Decca DL-74815	(S)	Rudolph The Red-Nosed Reindeer (TV Soundtrack)	1966	16.00	40.00
Columbia CL-2570	(M)	Children's Favorites	1966	4.00	10.00
Columbia CS-9370	(S)	Children's Favorites	1966	5.00	12.00

Label & Catalog #		Title	Year	VG+	NM

IVEYS, THE
The Iveys later recorded as Badfinger.

Apple SAPCOR-8S	(S)	**Maybe Tomorrow** *(Italian. Green label)*	*1968*	**500.00**	**1,000.00**
		(Copies of this album with a black label are counterfeits. This album was also issued in several other countries, including Japan and West Germany.)			

IVORY

Tetragrammaton T-104	(S)	**Ivory**	*1968*	**8.00**	**20.00**
Playboy 115	(S)	**Ivory**	*1973*	**5.00**	**12.00**

IVORY, JACKIE

Atco 33-178	(M)	**Soul Discovery**	*1965*	**8.00**	**20.00**
Atco SD-33-178	(S)	**Soul Discovery**	*1965*	**10.00**	**25.00**

IVORY LIBRARY

Dairyland	(S)	**Ivory Library**	*1985*	**5.00**	**12.00**

IVY LEAGUE, THE

Cameo C-2000	(M)	**Tossing And Turning**	*1965*	**10.00**	**25.00**
Cameo CS-2000	(E)	**Tossing And Turning**	*1965*	**8.00**	**20.00**

IVY LEAGUE TRIO, THE

Coral CRL-57399	(M)	**On And Off Campus**	*1962*	**6.00**	**15.00**
Coral CRL-757399	(S)	**On And Off Campus**	*1962*	**8.00**	**20.00**
Coral CRL-57404	(M)	**Folk Songs Bare And Well Done**	*1962*	**6.00**	**15.00**
Coral CRL-757404	(S)	**Folk Songs Bare And Well Done**	*1962*	**8.00**	**20.00**
Reprise R-6087	(M)	**Folk Ballads From The World Of Edgar Allan Poe**	*1963*	**6.00**	**15.00**
Reprise R-96087	(S)	**Folk Ballads From The World Of Edgar Allan Poe**	*1963*	**8.00**	**20.00**

J. A. BLUEZY

Apollo Music ERK-0782	(S)	**At The Delta Lady**	*1980*	**30.00**	**75.00**

J. GEILS BAND

Atlantic QD-7260	(Q)	**Bloodshot**	*1973*	**8.00**	**20.00**
Atlantic QD-7286	(Q)	**Ladies Invited**	*1973*	**8.00**	**20.00**
Atlantic QD-18107	(Q)	**Nightmares**	*1974*	**8.00**	**20.00**
Atlantic SD-7260	(S)	**Bloodshot** *(Red vinyl)*	*1973*	**6.00**	**15.00**
EMI 17006	(DJ)	**Sanctuary** *(Picture disc)*	*1979*	**6.00**	**15.00**
Nautilus NR-25	(S)	**Love Stinks**	*198?*	**5.00**	**15.00**
Nautilus NR-25	(S)	**Love Stinks** *(DBX encoded)*	*198?*	**6.00**	**18.00**

J.K. & CO.

White Whale WWS-7117	(S)	**Suddenly One Summer**	*1969*	**6.00**	**15.00**

J. TEAL BAND, THE

Mother Cleo MCPLP-7721	(S)	**The J. Teal Band Cooks**	*1977*	**24.00**	**60.00**

J'S & JAMIE, THE

Columbia CL-2005	(M)	**Hey, Look Us Over**	*1963*	**6.00**	**15.00**
Columbia CS-8805	(S)	**Hey, Look Us Over**	*1963*	**8.00**	**20.00**

Label & Catalog #		Title	Year	VG+	NM
Columbia CL-2149	(M)	The Remarkable J's With Jamie	1964	6.00	15.00
Columbia CS-8949	(S)	The Remarkable J's With Jamie	1964	8.00	20.00

JACKIE & ROY: *Refer to* **GOLDMINE'S PRICE GUIDE TO COLLECTIBLE JAZZ ALBUMS**

JACKS, THE
The Jacks also recorded as The Cadets. Refer to Aaron Collins.

RPM LRP-3006	(M)	Jumpin' With The Jacks	1956	500.00	1,500.00
Crown CLP-5021	(M)	Jumpin' With The Jacks	1960	60.00	150.00
Crown CLP-5372	(M)	Jumpin' With The Jacks	1962	40.00	100.00
Crown CST-372	(E)	Jumpin' With The Jacks	1962	20.00	50.00

JACKSON, BULL MOOSE

Audio Lab LP-1524	(M)	Bull Moose Jackson	1959	100.00	250.00

JACKSON, CHUCK

Wand WD-650	(M)	I Don't Want To Cry	1961	16.00	40.00
Wand WDS-650	(S)	I Don't Want To Cry	1961	20.00	50.00
Wand WD-654	(M)	Any Day Now	1962	16.00	40.00
Wand WDS-654	(S)	Any Day Now	1962	20.00	50.00
Wand WD-655	(M)	Encore	1963	12.00	30.00
Wand WDS-655	(S)	Encore	1963	16.00	40.00
Wand WD-658	(M)	Chuck Jackson On Tour	1964	12.00	30.00
Wand WDS-658	(S)	Chuck Jackson On Tour	1964	16.00	40.00
Wand WD-667	(M)	Mr. Everything	1965	12.00	30.00
Wand WDS-667	(S)	Mr. Everything	1965	16.00	40.00
Wand WD-673	(M)	A Tribute To Rhythm & Blues	1966	12.00	30.00
Wand WDS-673	(S)	A Tribute To Rhythm & Blues	1966	16.00	40.00
Wand WD-676	(M)	A Tribute To Rhythm & Blues, Volume 2	1966	12.00	30.00
Wand WDS-676	(S)	A Tribute To Rhythm & Blues, Volume 2	1966	16.00	40.00
Wand WD-680	(M)	Dedicated To The King!!	1966	12.00	30.00
Wand WDS-680	(S)	Dedicated To The King!!	1966	16.00	40.00
Wand WD-683	(M)	Chuck Jackson's Greatest Hits	1967	8.00	20.00
Wand WDS-683	(S)	Chuck Jackson's Greatest Hits	1967	10.00	25.00
Motown MS-667	(S)	Chuck Jackson Arrives	1968	8.00	20.00
Motown MS-687	(S)	Goin' Back To Chuck Jackson	1969	8.00	20.00
ABC X-798	(S)	Through All Times	1973	6.00	15.00
Scepter 5100	(S)	A Tribute To Burt Bacharach	1972	6.00	15.00
All Platinum AP-3014	(S)	Needing You, Wanting You	1976	6.00	15.00

JACKSON, CHUCK, & MAXINE BROWN

Wand WD-669	(M)	Saying Something	1965	12.00	30.00
Wand WDS-669	(S)	Saying Something	1965	16.00	40.00
Wand WD-678	(M)	Hold On, We're Coming	1966	12.00	30.00
Wand WDS-678	(S)	Hold On, We're Coming	1966	16.00	40.00

JACKSON, CHUCK, & TAMMI TERRELL

Wand LP-682	(M)	The Early Show	1967	12.00	30.00
Wand WDS-682	(S)	The Early Show	1967	16.00	40.00

JACKSON, DEON

Atco 33-188	(M)	Love Makes The World Go Round	1966	12.00	30.00
Atco SD-33-188	(S)	Love Makes The World Go Round	1966	16.00	40.00

JACKSON, J. J.

Calla C-1101	(M)	But It's Alright/I Dig Girls	1967	8.00	20.00
Calla CS-1101	(S)	But It's Alright/I Dig Girls	1967	10.00	25.00
Warner Bros. WS-1797	(S)	The Great J.J. Jackson	1969	6.00	15.00
Perception 3	(S)	J.J. Jackson's Dilemma	1969	6.00	15.00

JACKSON, JACKIE
Jackie is a member of The Jacksons.

Motown M-785	(S)	Jackie Jackson	1973	5.00	12.00

JACKSON, JERMAINE
Jermaine is a member of The Jacksons.

Motown M-752	(S)	Jermaine	1972	5.00	12.00
Motown M-775	(S)	Come Into My Life	1973	5.00	12.00

Label & Catalog #		Title	Year	VG+	NM

JACKSON, JOE
| Mobile Fidelity MFSL-080 | (S) | **Night And Day** | 1979 | 5.00 | 15.00 |

JACKSON, LIL' SON
| Imperial LP-9142 | (M) | **Rockin' And Rollin'** | 1961 | 100.00 | 250.00 |

JACKSON, MICHAEL
Michael was a member of The Jacksons.
Motown M-747	(S)	**Got To Be There**	1972	6.00	15.00
Motown M-755	(S)	**Ben** (Soundtrack)	1972	6.00	15.00
Motown M-767	(S)	**Music And Me**	1973	5.00	12.00
Motown M-825	(S)	**Forever Michael**	1975	5.00	12.00
Motown 6099ML	(S)	**14 Greatest Hits** (Picture disc)	1984	2.00	10.00
Epic HE-47545	(S)	**Off The Wall** (Half-speed master)	1982	15.00	45.00
Epic HE-48112	(S)	**Thriller** (Half-speed master)	1982	15.00	45.00
Epic 8E8-38867	(S)	**Thriller** (Picture disc)	1983	2.00	10.00
Epic 9E9-44043	(S)	**Bad** (Picture disc)	1987	2.00	10.00

JACKSON, STONEWALL
Columbia CL-1391	(M)	**The Dynamic Stonewall Jackson**	1959	12.00	30.00
Columbia CS-8186	(S)	**The Dynamic Stonewall Jackson**	1959	16.00	40.00
Columbia CL-1770	(M)	**Sadness In A Song**	1962	8.00	20.00
Columbia CS-8570	(S)	**Sadness In A Song**	1962	10.00	25.00
— Original Columbia albums above have three white "eye" logos on each side of the spindle hole.—					
Columbia CL-2059	(M)	**I Love A Song**	1963	6.00	15.00
Columbia CS-8859	(S)	**I Love A Song**	1963	8.00	20.00
Columbia CL-2278	(M)	**Trouble And Me**	1965	6.00	15.00
Columbia CS-9078	(S)	**Trouble And Me**	1965	8.00	20.00
Columbia CL-2377	(M)	**Stonewall Jackson's Greatest Hits**	1965	6.00	15.00
Columbia CS-9177	(S)	**Stonewall Jackson's Greatest Hits**	1965	8.00	20.00
Columbia CL-2509	(M)	**All's Fair In Love 'N' War**	1966	6.00	15.00
Columbia CS-9309	(S)	**All's Fair In Love 'N' War**	1966	8.00	20.00
Columbia CL-2674	(M)	**Help Stamp Out Loneliness**	1967	6.00	15.00
Columbia CS-9474	(S)	**Help Stamp Out Loneliness**	1967	8.00	20.00
Columbia CL-2762	(M)	**Stonewall Jackson Country**	1967	8.00	20.00
Columbia CS-9562	(S)	**Stonewall Jackson Country**	1967	6.00	15.00
Columbia CL-2869	(M)	**Nothing Takes The Place Of Loving You**	1968	12.00	30.00
Columbia CS-9669	(S)	**Nothing Takes The Place Of Loving You**	1968	6.00	15.00
—Columbia albums above have "360 Sound" on the bottom of the label.—					

JACKSON, WALTER
OKeh OKM-12107	(M)	**It's All Over**	1965	6.00	15.00
OKeh OKS-14107	(S)	**It's All Over**	1965	8.00	20.00
OKeh OKM-12108	(M)	**Welcome Home**	1965	6.00	15.00
OKeh OKS-14108	(S)	**Welcome Home**	1965	8.00	20.00
OKeh OKM-12120	(M)	**Speak Her Name**	1967	6.00	15.00
OKeh OKS-14120	(S)	**Speak Her Name**	1967	8.00	20.00
OKeh OKS-14128	(S)	**Walter Jackson's Greatest Hits**	1969	6.00	15.00

JACKSON, WANDA (& THE PARTY TIMERS)
Capitol T-1041	(M)	**Wanda Jackson**	1958	80.00	200.00
Capitol T-1384	(M)	**Rockin' With Wanda!**	1960	200.00	400.00
		("Rockin'" is a collection of her earlier rockabilly singles.			
		Reissued on Capitol's Starline label, listed below.)			
Capitol T-1384	(M)	**Rockin' With Wanda!** (Gold Starline label)	1962	80.00	200.00
Capitol T-1384	(M)	**Rockin' With Wanda!** (Black Starline label)	1963	30.00	75.00
Capitol T-1511	(M)	**There's A Party Goin' On**	1961	60.00	150.00
Capitol ST-1511	(S)	**There's A Party Goin' On**	1961	80.00	200.00
Capitol T-1596	(M)	**Right Or Wrong**	1961	16.00	40.00
Capitol ST-1596	(S)	**Right Or Wrong**	1961	20.00	50.00
— Original Capitol albums above have black labels with the Capitol logo on the side.—					
Decca DL-4224	(M)	**Lovin' Country Style**	1962	20.00	50.00
Capitol T-1776	(M)	**Wonderful Wanda**	1962	10.00	25.00
Capitol ST-1776	(S)	**Wonderful Wanda**	1962	12.00	30.00
Capitol T-1911	(M)	**Love Me Forever**	1963	10.00	25.00
Capitol ST-1911	(S)	**Love Me Forever**	1963	12.00	30.00
Capitol T-2030	(M)	**Two Sides Of Wanda Jackson**	1964	12.00	30.00
Capitol ST-2030	(S)	**Two Sides Of Wanda Jackson**	1964	16.00	40.00

Purty Miss Wanda Jackson was one of the hottest rocking white gals of the '50s, although her biggest hit, a great version of Elvis' "Let's Have A Party," occurred in 1960. Both Rockin' With Wanda *and* There's A Party Going On *are quintessential female rock 'n roll albums. Like many rockabilly artists, when commercial success didn't materialize with rock 'n roll, she turned to country music in the early '60s.*

Label & Catalog #		Title	Year	VG+	NM
Capitol T-2306	(M)	Blues In My Heart	1964	12.00	30.00
Capitol ST-2306	(S)	Blues In My Heart	1964	16.00	40.00
Capitol T-2438	(M)	Wanda Jackson Sings Country Songs	1966	10.00	25.00
Capitol ST-2438	(S)	Wanda Jackson Sings Country Songs	1966	12.00	30.00
Capitol T-2606	(M)	Salutes The Country Music Hall Of Fame	1966	6.00	15.00
Capitol ST-2606	(S)	Salutes The Country Music Hall Of Fame	1966	8.00	20.00
Capitol T-2704	(M)	Reckless Love Affair	1967	6.00	15.00
Capitol ST-2704	(S)	Reckless Love Affair	1967	8.00	20.00
Capitol T-2812	(M)	You'll Always Have My Love	1967	6.00	15.00
Capitol ST-2812	(S)	You'll Always Have My Love	1967	8.00	20.00
Capitol T-2883	(M)	The Best Of Wanda Jackson	1967	6.00	15.00
Capitol ST-2883	(S)	The Best Of Wanda Jackson	1967	6.00	15.00
Capitol ST-2976	(S)	Cream Of The Crop	1968	6.00	15.00
— Original Capitol albums above have black labels with the Capitol logo on top. —					
Capitol ST-129	(S)	The Many Moods Of Wanda Jackson	1969	6.00	15.00
Capitol ST-238	(S)	The Happy Side Of Wanda Jackson	1969	6.00	15.00
Capitol ST-345	(S)	Wanda Jackson In Person	1969	6.00	15.00
Capitol ST-434	(S)	Wanda Jackson Country!	1970	5.00	12.00
Capitol ST-554	(S)	A Woman Lives For Love	1970	5.00	12.00
Capitol ST-669	(S)	I've Gotta Sing	1971	5.00	12.00

JACKSON FIVE, THE [THE JACKSONS]
The Jacksons feature Jackie, Jermaine and Michael Jackson.

Label & Catalog #		Title	Year	VG+	NM
Motown MS-700	(S)	Diana Ross Presents The Jackson Five	1970	10.00	25.00
Motown MS-709	(S)	ABC	1970	8.00	20.00
Motown MS-713	(S)	Christmas Won't Be The Same This Year	1970	8.00	20.00
Motown MS-718	(S)	The Jackson Five's Third Album	1970	6.00	15.00
Motown MS-735	(S)	Maybe Tomorrow	1971	6.00	15.00
Motown M-741	(S)	The Jackson Five's Greatest Hits	1971	6.00	15.00
Motown M-742	(S)	Goin' Back To Indiana	1971	4.00	10.00
Motown M-750	(S)	Looking Through The Windows	1972	4.00	10.00
Motown M-761	(S)	Skywriter	1973	4.00	10.00
Motown M-780	(S)	Dancing Machine	1974	4.00	10.00
Motown M-783	(S)	Get It Together	1973	4.00	10.00
Motown M-829	(S)	Moving Violation	1975	4.00	10.00
Motown M57-868	(S)	Anthology (2 LPs)	1976	5.00	12.00
Epic PAL-34835	(DJ)	Goin' Places (Picture disc)	1978	6.00	15.00
Epic HE-46424	(S)	Triumph (Half-speed master)	1981	13.00	40.00
Epic 8E8-39576	(S)	Victory (Picture disc)	1984	4.00	10.00

JACKSON HEIGHTS

Label & Catalog #		Title	Year	VG+	NM
Mercury SR-61331	(S)	King Progress	1970	10.00	25.00
Verve V6-5089	(S)	Jackson Heights	1973	8.00	20.00

JACOBS, HANK

Label & Catalog #		Title	Year	VG+	NM
Sue LP-1023	(M)	So Far Away	1964	40.00	100.00

JADE

Label & Catalog #		Title	Year	VG+	NM
Gar 11311	(S)	The Faces Of Jade	196?	20.00	50.00

JADE STONE & LUV

Label & Catalog #		Title	Year	VG+	NM
Jade JS-4351	(S)	Mosaics-Pieces Of Stone	1977	50.00	125.00

JADES, THE

Label & Catalog #		Title	Year	VG+	NM
Jarrett 21517	(M)	Live At The Disc A-Go-Go	196?	50.00	125.00

JAGGER, MICK
Mick Jagger is a member of The Rolling Stones.

Label & Catalog #		Title	Year	VG+	NM
United Arts. UAS-5213	(S)	Ned Kelly (Soundtrack)	1970	6.00	15.00
Warner Bros. BS-1846	(S)	Performance (Soundtrack)	1970	10.00	25.00
Warner Bros. BS-2554	(S)	Performance (Soundtrack)	1972	6.00	15.00

JAGGERZ, THE

Label & Catalog #		Title	Year	VG+	NM
Kama Sutra KSBS-2017	(S)	We Went To Different Schools Together	1970	5.00	12.00

JAIM

Label & Catalog #		Title	Year	VG+	NM
Ethereal 1001	(S)	Prophesy Fulfilled	1970	20.00	50.00

Label & Catalog #		Title	Year	VG+	NM
JALOPY FIVE, THE					
Modern Sound M-525	(M)	Draggin' & Surfin'	196?	20.00	50.00
Modern Sound MS-525	(S)	Draggin' & Surfin'	196?	24.00	60.00
Modern Sound M-536	(M)	Draggin' & Surfin'	196?	20.00	50.00
Modern Sound MS-536	(S)	Draggin' & Surfin'	196?	24.00	60.00
Modern Sound M-561	(M)	I Love That West Coast Sound	1965	10.00	25.00
Modern Sound MS-561	(S)	I Love That West Coast Sound	1965	12.00	30.00
JAMAICAN ALL STARS, THE					
Atlantic 8098	(M)	Jamaica Ska	1964	6.00	15.00
Atlantic SD-8098	(S)	Jamaica Ska	1964	8.00	20.00
JAMES, DIAN, & THE GREENBRIAR BOYS					
Refer to The Greenbriar Boys.					
Elektra EKL-233	(M)	Dian & The Greenbriar Boys	1963	6.00	15.00
Elektra EKS-7233	(S)	Dian & The Greenbriar Boys	1963	8.00	20.00
JAMES, ELMORE					
Crown CLP-5168	(M)	Blues After Hours	1961	30.00	75.00
Sphere Sound SR-7002	(M)	The Sky Is Crying	1965	20.00	50.00
Sphere Sound SSR-7002	(S)	The Sky Is Crying	1965	30.00	75.00
Sphere Sound SR-7008	(M)	I Need You	1966	20.00	50.00
Sphere Sound SSR-7008	(S)	I Need You	1966	30.00	75.00
Kent KLP-5022	(M)	Original Folk Blues	1964	16.00	40.00
Kent KLP-9001	(M)	Anthology Of The Blues Legend	196?	10.00	25.00
Kent KLP-9010	(M)	The Resurrection Of Elmore James	196?	10.00	25.00
Chess 1537	(S)	Whose Muddy Shoes	1969	10.00	25.00
Bell 6037	(S)	Elmore James	1969	10.00	25.00
United 7716	(S)	Blues In My Heart, Rhythm In My Soul	1969	4.00	10.00
United 7743	(M)	Original Folk Blues	1969	4.00	10.00
United 7787	(M)	The Resurrection Of Elmore James	1969	4.00	10.00
JAMES, ETTA					
Kent KLP-5000	(M)	Miss Etta James	196?	20.00	50.00
Kent KLP-5000	(M)	Miss Etta James (Red vinyl)	196?	50.00	125.00
Crown CLP-5209	(M)	Miss Etta James	1961	30.00	75.00
		(Original pressings have a framed picture of Etta on the cover.)			
Crown CLP-5209	(M)	Miss Etta James	196?	12.00	30.00
		Later pressings have a generic white cover with "Miss Etta James.")			
Crown CLP-5250	(M)	Twist With Etta James	1962	12.00	30.00
Argo LP-4003	(M)	At Last	1961	12.00	30.00
Argo LPS-4003	(S)	At Last	1961	16.00	40.00
Argo LP-4011	(M)	The Second Time Around	1961	12.00	30.00
Argo LPS-4011	(S)	The Second Time Around	1961	16.00	40.00
Argo LP-4013	(M)	Etta James	1962	12.00	30.00
Argo LPS-4013	(S)	Etta James	1962	16.00	40.00
		("Spoonful" and "If I Can't Have You" are rechanneled on this album.)			
Argo LP-4018	(M)	Etta James Sings For Lovers	1962	12.00	30.00
Argo LPS-4018	(S)	Etta James Sings For Lovers	1962	16.00	40.00
Argo LP-4025	(M)	Top Ten	1963	12.00	30.00
Argo LPS-4025	(S)	Top Ten	1963	16.00	40.00
Argo LP-4032	(M)	Etta James Rocks The House	1964	40.00	100.00
Argo LPS-4032	(S)	Etta James Rocks The House	1964	60.00	150.00
Argo LP-4040	(M)	The Queen Of Soul	1965	12.00	30.00
Argo LPS-4040	(S)	The Queen Of Soul	1965	16.00	40.00
Cadet LPS-4003	(S)	At Last	1969	6.00	15.00
Cadet LPS-4011	(S)	The Second Time Around	1969	6.00	15.00
Cadet LPS-4013	(P)	Etta James	1969	6.00	15.00
Cadet LPS-4018	(S)	Etta James Sings For Lovers	1969	6.00	15.00
Cadet LPS-4025	(S)	Top Ten	1969	6.00	15.00
Cadet LPS-4032	(S)	Etta James Rocks The House	1969	6.00	15.00
Cadet LPS-4040	(S)	The Queen Of Soul	1969	6.00	15.00
Chess 2CH-60004	(P)	Peaches (2 LPs)	1971	6.00	15.00
Chess CH-50042	(S)	Etta James	1973	4.00	10.00
Chess 2CH-60029	(S)	Come A Little Bit Closer (2 LPs)	1974	6.00	15.00
JAMES, JIMMY, & THE VAGABONDS					
Atco 33-222	(M)	The New Religion	1967	6.00	15.00
Atco SD-33-222	(S)	The New Religion	1967	8.00	20.00

Joan Carmeglio Babbo, Miss Joni James in the world of entertainment, was a successful pop singer with more than a dozen nationally charted hits in the '50s. Oddly, not a single one of her many albums for MGM made the best-seller lists and are consequently highly sought after by pop vocal collectors.

Label & Catalog #		Title	Year	VG+	NM

JAMES, JONI

Label & Catalog #		Title	Year	VG+	NM
MGM E-222 (10")	(M)	Let There Be Love	1955	40.00	100.00
MGM E-234 (10")	(M)	Award Winning Album	1955	40.00	100.00
MGM E-272 (10")	(M)	Little Girl Blue	1955	40.00	100.00
MGM E-3328	(M)	In The Still Of The Night	1956	30.00	75.00
MGM E-3240	(M)	When I Fall In Love	1956	30.00	75.00
MGM E-3346	(M)	Award Winning Album	1956	30.00	75.00
MGM E-3347	(M)	Little Girl Blue	1956	30.00	75.00
MGM E-3348	(M)	Let There Be Love	1956	30.00	75.00
MGM E-3449	(M)	Songs By Victor Young And Frank Loesser	1956	30.00	75.00
MGM E-3468	(M)	Merry Christmas From Joni	1957	30.00	75.00
MGM E-3528	(M)	Give Us This Day	1957	30.00	75.00
MGM E-3533	(M)	Songs By Kern & Warren	1957	30.00	75.00
MGM E-3602	(M)	Among My Souvenirs	1958	20.00	50.00
MGM SE-3602	(S)	Among My Souvenirs	1958	30.00	75.00
MGM E-3623	(M)	Ti Voglio Bene	1958	20.00	50.00
MGM SE-3623	(S)	Ti Voglio Bene	1958	30.00	75.00
MGM E-3702	(M)	Award Winning Album, Volume 2	1958	20.00	50.00
MGM SE-3702	(S)	Award Winning Album, Volume 2	1958	30.00	75.00
MGM E-3718	(M)	Je T'aime (I Love You)	1958	20.00	50.00
MGM SE-3718	(S)	Je T'aime (I Love You)	1958	30.00	75.00
MGM E-3739	(M)	Songs Of Hank Williams	1959	20.00	50.00
MGM SE-3739	(S)	Songs Of Hank Williams	1959	30.00	75.00
MGM E-3749	(M)	Irish Favorites	1959	20.00	50.00
MGM SE-3749	(S)	Irish Favorites	1959	30.00	75.00
MGM E-3755	(M)	100 Strings And Joni	1959	20.00	50.00
MGM SE-3755	(S)	100 Strings And Joni	1959	30.00	75.00

— Original MGM albums above have yellow labels.—

Label & Catalog #		Title	Year	VG+	NM
MGM E-3772	(M)	Joni James Swings Sweet	1959	16.00	40.00
MGM SE-3772	(S)	Joni James Swings Sweet	1959	20.00	50.00
MGM E-3800	(M)	Joni James At Carnegie Hall	1959	16.00	40.00
MGM SE-3800	(S)	Joni James At Carnegie Hall	1959	20.00	50.00
MGM E-3837	(M)	I'm In The Mood For Love	1960	12.00	30.00
MGM SE-3837	(S)	I'm In The Mood For Love	1960	16.00	40.00
MGM E-3839	(M)	100 Strings And Joni On Broadway	1960	12.00	30.00
MGM SE-3839	(S)	100 Strings And Joni On Broadway	1960	16.00	40.00
MGM E-3840	(M)	Joni James Sings Hollywood	1960	12.00	30.00
MGM SE-3840	(S)	Joni James Sings Hollywood	1960	16.00	40.00
MGM E-3885	(M)	More Joni Hits	1960	12.00	30.00
MGM SE-3885	(P)	More Joni Hits	1960	16.00	40.00
MGM E-3892	(M)	100 Voices, 100 Strings	1960	12.00	30.00
MGM SE-3892	(S)	100 Voices, 100 Strings	1960	16.00	40.00
MGM E-3958	(M)	Folk Songs By Joni James	1961	12.00	30.00
MGM SE-3958	(S)	Folk Songs By Joni James	1961	16.00	40.00
MGM E-3987	(M)	The Mood Is Swinging	1961	12.00	30.00
MGM SE-3987	(S)	The Mood Is Swinging	1961	16.00	40.00
MGM E-3990	(M)	The Mood Is Romance	1961	12.00	30.00
MGM SE-3990	(S)	The Mood Is Romance	1961	16.00	40.00
MGM E-3991	(M)	The Mood Is Blue	1961	12.00	30.00
MGM SE-3991	(S)	The Mood Is Blue	1961	16.00	40.00
MGM E-4053	(M)	I Feel A Song Comin' On	1962	12.00	30.00
MGM SE-4053	(S)	I Feel A Song Comin' On	1962	16.00	40.00
MGM E-4054	(M)	I'm Your Girl	1962	12.00	30.00
MGM SE-4054	(S)	I'm Your Girl	1962	16.00	40.00
MGM E-4088	(M)	After Hours	1962	12.00	30.00
MGM SE-4088	(S)	After Hours	1962	16.00	40.00
MGM E-4101	(M)	Country Girl Style	1962	12.00	30.00
MGM SE-4101	(S)	Country Girl Style	1962	16.00	40.00
MGM E-4151	(M)	The Very Best Of Joni James	1963	10.00	25.00
MGM SE-4151	(S)	The Very Best Of Joni James	1963	14.00	35.00
MGM E-4158	(M)	Something For The Boys	1963	10.00	25.00
MGM SE-4158	(S)	Something For The Boys	1963	14.00	35.00
MGM E-4182	(M)	Three O' Clock In The Morning	1963	10.00	25.00
MGM SE-4182	(S)	Three O' Clock In The Morning	1963	14.00	35.00
MGM E-4200	(M)	My Favorite Things	1963	10.00	25.00
MGM SE-4200	(S)	My Favorite Things	1963	14.00	35.00
MGM E-4208	(M)	Italianissime!	1963	10.00	25.00
MGM E-4208	(S)	Italianissime!	1963	14.00	35.00

Label & Catalog #		Title	Year	VG+	NM
MGM E-4248	(M)	Put On A Happy Face	1964	10.00	25.00
MGM SE-4248	(S)	Put On A Happy Face	1964	14.00	35.00
MGM E-4255	(M)	Joni James Sings The Gershwins	1964	10.00	25.00
MGM SE-4255	(S)	Joni James Sings The Gershwins	1964	14.00	35.00
MGM E-4263	(M)	Beyond The Reef	1964	10.00	25.00
MGM SE-4263	(S)	Beyond The Reef	1964	14.00	35.00
MGM E-4286	(M)	Bossa Nova Style	1965	10.00	25.00
MGM SE-4286	(S)	Bossa Nova Style	1965	14.00	35.00

— Original MGM albums above have black labels.—

JAMES, LEONARD

Decca DL-8772	(M)	Boppin' And A Strollin'	1958	20.00	50.00

JAMES, NICKY
James was formerly a member of Rare Bird.

Threshold 10	(S)	Every Home Should Have One	1972	5.00	12.00
Threshold 19	(DJ)	Thunderthroat	1976	8.00	20.00

JAMES, SKIP

Vanguard VSR-9219	(M)	Skip James Today!	1966	10.00	25.00
Vanguard VSD-79219	(S)	Skip James Today!	1966	12.00	30.00
Vanguard VSD-79273	(S)	Devil Got My Woman	1968	8.00	20.00

JAMES, SONNY

Capitol T-779	(M)	The Southern Gentleman	1957	24.00	60.00
Capitol T-867	(M)	Sonny	1957	24.00	60.00
Capitol T-988	(M)	Honey	1958	24.00	60.00
Capitol T-1178	(M)	This Is Sonny James	1959	16.00	40.00

— Original Capitol albums above have turquoise labels.—

Dot DLP-3462	(M)	Young Love	1962	8.00	20.00
Dot DLP-25462	(S)	Young Love	1962	12.00	30.00
Capitol T-2017	(M)	The Minute You're Gone	1964	6.00	15.00
Capitol ST-2017	(S)	The Minute You're Gone	1964	8.00	20.00
Capitol T-2209	(M)	You're The Only World I Know	1965	6.00	15.00
Capitol ST-2209	(S)	You're The Only World I Know	1965	8.00	20.00
Capitol T-2317	(M)	I'll Keep Holding On	1965	6.00	15.00
Capitol ST-2317	(S)	I'll Keep Holding On	1965	8.00	20.00
Capitol T-2415	(M)	Behind The Tear	1965	6.00	15.00
Capitol ST-2415	(S)	Behind The Tear	1965	8.00	20.00
Capitol T-2500	(M)	True Love's A Blessing	1966	6.00	15.00
Capitol ST-2500	(S)	True Love's A Blessing	1966	8.00	20.00
Capitol T-2561	(M)	Till The Last Leaf Shall Fall	1966	6.00	15.00
Capitol ST-2561	(S)	Till The Last Leaf Shall Fall	1966	8.00	20.00
Capitol T-2589	(M)	My Christmas Dream	1966	6.00	15.00
Capitol ST-2589	(S)	My Christmas Dream	1966	8.00	20.00
Capitol T-2615	(M)	The Best Of Sonny James	1966	6.00	15.00
Capitol ST-2615	(P)	The Best Of Sonny James	1966	8.00	20.00
Capitol T-2703	(M)	Need You	1967	8.00	20.00
Capitol ST-2703	(S)	Need You	1967	6.00	15.00
Capitol T-2788	(M)	I'll Never Find Another You	1967	8.00	20.00
Capitol ST-2788	(S)	I'll Never Find Another You	1967	6.00	15.00
Capitol T-2884	(M)	A World Of Our Own	1968	12.00	30.00
Capitol ST-2884	(S)	A World Of Our Own	1968	6.00	15.00
Capitol ST-2937	(S)	Heaven Says Hello	1968	6.00	15.00

— Original Capitol albums above have black labels with the Capitol logo on top.—

JAMES, TOMMY, & THE SHONDELLS
Members of The Shondells also recordeed as Hog Heaven.

Roulette R-25336	(M)	Hanky Panky	1966	8.00	20.00
Roulette SR-25336	(S)	Hanky Panky	1966	10.00	25.00

("Hanky Panky" is rechanneled on this album.)

Roulette R-25344	(M)	It's Only Love	1967	8.00	20.00
Roulette SR-25344	(S)	It's Only Love	1967	8.00	20.00
Roulette R-25353	(M)	I Think We're Alone Now	1967	8.00	20.00
Roulette SR-25353	(S)	I Think We're Alone Now *(Photo cover)*	1967	12.00	30.00
Roulette SR-25353	(S)	I Think We're Alone Now *(Footprint cover)*	1968	8.00	20.00

("I Think We're Alone Now" is rechanneled on this album.)

Roulette SR-25355	(P)	Something Special!	1968	8.00	20.00
Roulette SR-25357	(S)	Gettin' Together	1968	8.00	20.00

Label & Catalog #		Title	Year	VG+	NM
Roulette SR-42012	(P)	**Mony Mony**	1968	8.00	20.00
Roulette SR-42023	(S)	**Crimson And Clover**	1968	8.00	20.00
Roulette SR-42030	(S)	**Cellophane Symphony**	1969	6.00	15.00
Roulette SR-42040	(P)	**The Best Of Tommy James & The Shondells**	1969	4.00	10.00
Roulette SR-42044	(S)	**Travelin'**	1970	4.00	10.00
JAMES, TOMMY					
Roulette SR-42051	(S)	**Tommy James**	1970	4.00	10.00
Roulette SR-3001	(S)	**Christian Of The World**	1971	4.00	10.00
Roulette SR-3007	(S)	**My Head, My Bed, My Red Guitar**	1972	4.00	10.00
JAMME					
Dunhill DS-50072	(S)	**Jamme**	1970	8.00	20.00
JAN & DEAN					
Jan Berry and Dean Torrence.					
Dore LP-101	(M)	**Jan & Dean** *(Light blue label)*	1960	80.00	200.00
		(Issued with a bonus photo, priced separately below.)			
Dore LP-101		**Jan & Dean Bonus Photo**	1960	60.00	150.00
Liberty LRP-3248	(M)	**Jan & Dean's Golden Hits**	1962	16.00	40.00
Liberty LST-7248	(S)	**Jan & Dean's Golden Hits**	1962	20.00	50.00
		("Baby Talk," "We Go Together," "Heart And Soul"			
		and "Jenny Lee" are rechanneled.)			
Liberty LRP-3294	(M)	**Jan & Dean Take Linda Surfing**	1963	20.00	50.00
Liberty LST-7294	(S)	**Jan & Dean Take Linda Surfing**	1963	30.00	75.00
		(The Beach Boys provide backing on "Surfin'" and "Surfin' Safari.")			
Liberty LRP-3314	(M)	**Surf City**	1963	12.00	30.00
Liberty LST-7314	(S)	**Surf City**	1963	16.00	40.00
Liberty LRP-3339	(M)	**Drag City**	1963	16.00	40.00
Liberty LST-7339	(S)	**Drag City**	1963	20.00	50.00
		(The Beach Boys provide backing on "Little Deuce Coupe..")			
L-J 101	(M)	**Jan & Dean With The Soul Surfers**	1963	8.00	20.00
Inter. Award AKS-250	(M)	**Jan & Dean & The Satellites**	196?	6.00	15.00
Liberty LRP-3361	(M)	**Dead Man's Curve/New Girl In School**	1964	16.00	40.00
Liberty LST-7361	(S)	**Dead Man's Curve/New Girl In School**	1964	20.00	50.00
		(The cover photo is black & white with pink overtones.)			
Liberty LRP-3361	(M)	**Dead Man's Curve/New Girl In School**	1964	12.00	30.00
Liberty LST-7361	(S)	**Dead Man's Curve/New Girl In School**	1964	16.00	40.00
		(The cover photo is full color.)			
Liberty LRP-3361	(M)	**New Girl In School/Dead Man's Curve**	1964	12.00	30.00
Liberty LST-7361	(S)	**New Girl In School/Dead Man's Curve**	1964	16.00	40.00
Liberty LRP-3368	(M)	**Ride The Wild Surf** *(Soundtrack)*	1964	12.00	30.00
Liberty LST-7368	(S)	**Ride The Wild Surf** *(Soundtrack)*	1964	16.00	40.00
Liberty LRP-3377	(M)	**Little Old Lady From Pasadena**	1964	12.00	30.00
Liberty LST-7377	(S)	**Little Old Lady From Pasadena**	1964	16.00	40.00
Coca-Cola TX-98	(DJ)	**Jan & Dean Swing The Jingle**	1965	300.00	500.00
		(Both sides contain the same five cuts, ranging from ten			
		to 90 seconds in length. Issued with a color cover.)			
Liberty LRP-3403	(M)	**Command Performance**	1965	12.00	30.00
Liberty LST-7403	(S)	**Command Performance**	1965	14.00	35.00
Liberty LRP-3414	(M)	**Jan & Dean's Pop Symphony No.1**	1965	30.00	75.00
Liberty LST-7414	(S)	**Jan & Dean's Pop Symphony No.1**	1965	50.00	125.00
Liberty LRP-3417	(M)	**Jan & Dean's Golden Hits, Volume 2**	1965	10.00	25.00
Liberty LST-7417	(S)	**Jan & Dean's Golden Hits, Volume 2**	1965	12.00	30.00
Liberty LRP-3431	(M)	**Folk 'N' Roll**	1965	10.00	25.00
Liberty LST-7431	(S)	**Folk 'N' Roll**	1965	12.00	30.00
Liberty LRP-3441	(M)	**Filet Of Soul**	1966	8.00	20.00
Liberty LST-7441	(S)	**Filet Of Soul**	1966	10.00	25.00
Liberty LRP-3444	(M)	**Jan & Dean Meet Batman**	1966	16.00	40.00
Liberty LST-7444	(S)	**Jan & Dean Meet Batman**	1966	20.00	50.00
Liberty LRP-3458	(M)	**Popsicle**	1966	12.00	30.00
Liberty LST-7458	(S)	**Popsicle**	1966	12.00	30.00
Liberty LRP-3460	(M)	**Jan & Dean's Golden Hits, Volume 3**	1966	8.00	20.00
Liberty LST-7460	(S)	**Jan & Dean's Golden Hits, Volume 3**	1966	10.00	25.00
Sunset SUM-1156	(M)	**Jan & Dean**	196?	5.00	12.00
Sunset SUS-5156	(S)	**Jan & Dean**	196?	6.00	15.00
Columbia CL-2661	(M)	**Save For A Rainy Day**	1967	*Unreleased*	
Columbia CS-9461	(S)	**Save For A Rainy Day**	1967	*Unreleased*	

Label & Catalog #		Title	Year	VG+	NM
J&D 101	(M)	Save For A Rainy Day	1967	100.00	250.00
		(J&D 101 is a "reissue" of the album inteneded for Columbia above.)			
United Arts. UAS-9961	(P)	The Jan & Dean Anthology Album (2 LPs)	1971	10.00	25.00
United Arts. UA-341	(P)	Gotta Take That One Last Ride (2 LPs)	1971	6.00	15.00
Deadman's Curve	(M)	Live At The Keystone Berkeley	1981	20.00	50.00
		(Authorized private pressing taken from an audience tape.			
		Originally issued in plain jackets with front and back cover inserts.)			
Deadman's Curve	(M)	Live At The Keystone Berkeley	1981	10.00	25.00
		(Reissued with the front and backs pasted on.)			
JANIS, JOHNNY					
ABC-Paramount 140	(M)	For The First Time	1956	20.00	50.00
Columbia CL-1674	(M)	The Start Of Something New	1961	6.00	15.00
Columbia CS-8474	(S)	The Start Of Something New	1961	8.00	20.00
Monument MLP-8036	(M)	Once In A Blue Moon	1965	6.00	15.00
Monument SLP-18036	(S)	Once In A Blue Moon	1965	8.00	20.00
JANSSEN, DAVID					
Epic LN-24150	(M)	Hidden Island	1965	8.00	20.00
Epic BN-26150	(S)	Hidden Island	1965	10.00	25.00
JASPER WRATH					
Sunflower SNF-5003	(S)	Jasper Wrath (With insert)	1971	10.00	25.00
JAY, BOB, & THE HAWKS					
Warner Bros. W-1562	(M)	Everybody's Doing The Watusi	1964	5.00	12.00
Warner Bros. WS-1562	(S)	Everybody's Doing The Watusi	1964	6.00	15.00
Warner Bros. W-1563	(M)	Everybody's Doing The Ska	1964	5.00	12.00
Warner Bros. WS-1563	(S)	Everybody's Doing The Ska	1964	6.00	15.00
Warner Bros. W-1564	(M)	Everybody's Doing The Monkey	1964	5.00	12.00
Warner Bros. WS-1564	(S)	Everybody's Doing The Monkey	1964	6.00	15.00
JAY & THE AMERICANS					
United Arts. UAL-3222	(M)	She Cried	1962	12.00	30.00
United Arts. UAS-6222	(S)	She Cried	1962	16.00	40.00
United Arts. UAL-3300	(M)	At The Cafe Wha?	1963	12.00	30.00
United Arts. UAS-6300	(S)	At The Cafe Wha?	1963	16.00	40.00
United Arts. UAL-3407	(M)	Come A Little Bit Closer	1964	10.00	25.00
United Arts. UAS-6407	(S)	Come A Little Bit Closer	1964	12.00	30.00
United Arts. UAL-3417	(M)	Blockbusters	1965	10.00	25.00
United Arts. UAS-6417	(S)	Blockbusters	1965	12.00	30.00
United Arts. UAL-3453	(M)	Jay & The Americans' Greatest Hits	1965	6.00	15.00
United Arts. UAS-6453	(P)	Jay & The Americans' Greatest Hits	1965	8.00	20.00
United Arts. UAL-3474	(M)	Sunday And Me	1966	6.00	15.00
United Arts. UAS-6474	(S)	Sunday And Me	1966	8.00	20.00
United Arts. UAL-3534	(M)	Livin' Above Your Head	1966	6.00	15.00
United Arts. UAS-6534	(S)	Livin' Above Your Head	1966	8.00	20.00
United Arts. UAL-3555	(M)	Jay & The Americans' Greatest Hits, Vol. 2	1966	6.00	15.00
United Arts. UAS-6555	(S)	Jay & The Americans' Greatest Hits, Vol. 2	1966	8.00	20.00
United Arts. UAL-3562	(M)	Try Some Of This	1967	6.00	15.00
United Arts. UAS-6562	(S)	Try Some Of This	1967	8.00	20.00
		— Original U.A. albums above have black labels.—			
United Arts. UAS-6671	(S)	Sands Of Time	1969	6.00	15.00
United Arts. UAS-6719	(S)	Wax Museum	1970	6.00	15.00
United Arts. UAS-6751	(S)	Wax Museum, Volume 2	1970	6.00	15.00
		(U.A. 6751 is a reissue of 6671.)			
United Arts. UAS-6762	(S)	Capture The Moment	1970	6.00	15.00
Doral	(S)	Doral Presents Jay & The Americans	1971	8.00	20.00
		(Promotional compilation of previously released material.)			
JAY & THE TECHNIQUES					
Smash MGS-27095	(M)	Apples, Peaches, Pumpkin Pie	1967	8.00	20.00
Smash SRS-67095	(S)	Apples, Peaches, Pumpkin Pie	1967	10.00	25.00
Smash SRS-67102	(S)	Love Lost And Found	1968	10.00	25.00
JAYE, JERRY					
Hi HL-12038	(M)	My Girl Josephine	1967	5.00	12.00
Hi SHL-32038	(S)	My Girl Josephine	1967	6.00	15.00

Label & Catalog #		Title	Year	VG+	NM
JAYNETTES, THE					
Tuff LP-13	(M)	**Sally Go Round The Roses**	1963	100.00	250.00
JB'S, THE [JB'S INTERNATIONAL]					
The JB's are James Brown's backing group and were produced by JB. Refer to Fred Wesley.					
People PE-5601	(S)	**Food For Thought**	1972	6.00	15.00
Polydor PD-6153	(S)	**Disco Fever**	1978	6.00	15.00
		(Polydor 6153 credits The JB's International.)			
Drive DR-111	(S)	**Groove Machine**	1979	6.00	15.00
JEFFERSON					
Janus JLS-3006	(S)	**Baby, Take Me In Your Arms**	1969	10.00	25.00
JEFFERSON, BLIND LEMON					
Riverside 1014 (10")	(M)	**The Folk Blues Of Blind Lemon Jefferson**	1953	80.00	200.00
Riverside 1053 (10")	(M)	**Penitentiary Blues**	1955	80.00	200.00
Riverside RLP-12-125	(M)	**Classic Folk Blues**	1957	30.00	75.00
Riverside RLP-12-126	(M)	**Blind Lemon Jefferson**	1957	30.00	75.00
JEFFERSON, EDDIE: *Refer to* **GOLDMINE'S PRICE GUIDE TO COLLECTIBLE JAZZ ALBUMS**					
JEFFERSON AIRPLANE					

The original group (RCA Victor 3584) was founder Marty Balin with Signe Andersson, Jack Casady, Paul Kantner, Jorma Kaukonen and Alexander Spence. Andersson and Spence left in 1966, replaced by Grace Slick, formerly of The Great Society, and Spencer Dryden, replaced in 1970 by Joey Covington and then John Barbata (1972). "Papa" John Creach joined in 1970. In 1971 Balin left his group in disgust and, by 1974, what's left of the Airplane became (shudder) Jefferson Starship. Refer to Hot Tuna; Moby Grape.

Label & Catalog #		Title	Year	VG+	NM
RCA Victor LPM-3584	(M)	**Jefferson Airplane Takes Off!**	1965	1,000.00	Rare
		(LPM-3584 was originally issued with "Runnin' Round This World,"			
		deleted from all subsequent pressings, and a version of "Let Me In"			
		deemed risqué, which was rerecorded for subsequent pressings.			
		Near Mint copies have a suggested value of $2,000-3,000.			
		Stereo copies are not known to exist.)			
RCA Victor LPM-3584	(M)	**Jefferson Airplane Takes Off!**	1966	12.00	30.00
RCA Victor LSP-3584	(S)	**Jefferson Airplane Takes Off!**	1966	10.00	25.00
RCA Victor LPM-3766	(M)	**Surrealistic Pillow**	1967	20.00	50.00
RCA Victor LSP-3766	(S)	**Surrealistic Pillow**	1967	10.00	25.00
RCA Victor LCO-1511	(M)	**After Bathing At Baxter's**	1967	12.00	30.00
RCA Victor LOS-1511	(S)	**After Bathing At Baxter's**	1967	10.00	25.00
RCA Victor LSP-4058	(S)	**Crown Of Creation**	1968	12.00	30.00
— *Original RCA albums above have black labels with Nipper on top.—*					
RCA Victor LSP-3584	(S)	**Jefferson Airplane Takes Off!**	1969	6.00	15.00
RCA Victor LSP-3766	(S)	**Surrealistic Pillow**	1969	6.00	15.00
RCA Victor LOS-1511	(S)	**After Bathing At Baxter's**	1969	6.00	15.00
RCA Victor LSP-4058	(S)	**Crown Of Creation**	1969	6.00	15.00
RCA Victor LSP-4133	(S)	**Bless Its Pointed Little Head**	1969	6.00	15.00
RCA Victor LSP-4238	(S)	**Volunteers**	1969	6.00	15.00
— *RCA albums above have orange labels on non-flexible vinyl.—*					
RCA Victor APD1-0320	(Q)	**Volunteers**	1973	20.00	50.00
		("Volunteers," "We Can Be Together," "Wooden Ships" and			
		"Hey Frederick" are alternate takes from the stereo album.)			
RCA Victor LSP-4459	(S)	**The Worst Of Jefferson Airplane**	1970	4.00	10.00
		(Custom black label.)			
Grunt FTR-1001	(S)	**Bark** *(Issued in a brown paper bag)*	1971	6.00	15.00
Grunt FTR-1007	(S)	**Long John Silver**	1972	4.00	10.00
Grunt BFL1-0147	(S)	**Thirty Seconds Over Winterland**	1973	4.00	10.00
Grunt CYL1-0437	(S)	**Early Flight**	1974	4.00	10.00
Mobile Fidelity MFSL-148	(S)	**Crown Of Creation**	1989	5.00	15.00
JEFFERSON STARSHIP					
Refer to Paul Kantner & The Jefferson Starship.					
Grunt BFD1-0717	(Q)	**Dragonfly**	1974	8.00	20.00
Grunt BFD1-0999	(Q)	**Red Octopus**	1975	8.00	20.00
Grunt BFD1-1557	(Q)	**Spitfire**	1976	8.00	20.00
Grunt CYL1-3363	(S)	**Gold** *(Picture disc)*	1976	4.00	10.00
JEFFREY, JOE					
Wand WDS-686	(S)	**My Pledge Of Love**	1969	14.00	35.00

Label & Catalog #		Title	Year	VG+	NM

JELLY BEAN BANDITS, THE

Mainstream 56103	(M)	Jelly Bean Bandits	1967	14.00	35.00
Mainstream S-6103	(S)	Jelly Bean Bandits	1967	20.00	50.00

JELLYBREAD

Blue Horizon BH-4801	(S)	First Slice	1970	8.00	20.00

JELLYROLL

Kapp KS-3626	(S)	Jellyroll	1971	8.00	20.00

JENNINGS, WAYLON

Bat 1001	(M)	Waylon Jennings At JD's	1964	300.00	500.00
Sounds 1001	(M)	Waylon Jennings At JD's	1964	80.00	200.00
RCA Victor LPM-3523	(M)	Folk Country	1966	12.00	30.00
RCA Victor LSP-3523	(S)	Folk Country	1966	16.00	40.00
RCA Victor LPM-3620	(M)	Leavin' Town	1966	12.00	30.00
RCA Victor LSP-3620	(S)	Leavin' Town	1966	16.00	40.00
RCA Victor LPM-3660	(M)	Waylon Sings Ol' Harlan	1967	16.00	40.00
RCA Victor LSP-3660	(S)	Waylon Sings Ol' Harlan	1967	20.00	50.00
RCA Victor LPM-3736	(M)	Nashville Rebel (Soundtrack)	1967	12.00	30.00
RCA Victor LSP-3736	(S)	Nashville Rebel (Soundtrack)	1967	10.00	25.00
RCA Victor LPM-3825	(M)	Love Of The Common People	1967	12.00	30.00
RCA Victor LSP-3825	(S)	Love Of The Common People	1967	10.00	25.00
RCA Victor LPM-3918	(M)	Hangin' On	1968	40.00	100.00
RCA Victor LSP-3918	(S)	Hangin' On	1968	10.00	25.00
RCA Victor LSP-4023	(S)	Only The Greatest	1968	10.00	25.00
		— Original RCA albums above have black labels.—			
A&M SP-4238	(S)	Don't Think Twice	1969	16.00	40.00
RCA Victor LSP-4085	(S)	Jewels	1968	8.00	20.00
RCA Victor LSP-4137	(S)	Just To Satisfy You	1969	8.00	20.00
RCA Victor LSP-4180	(S)	Country-Folk	1969	8.00	20.00
RCA Victor LSP-4260	(S)	Waylon	1970	8.00	20.00
RCA Victor LSP-4341	(S)	The Best Of Waylon Jennings	1970	8.00	20.00
RCA Victor LSP-4418	(S)	Singer Of Sad Songs	1970	8.00	20.00
		— Original RCA albums above have orange labels on non-flexible vinyl.—			
RCA Victor LSP-4487	(S)	The Taker/Tulsa	1971	6.00	15.00
RCA Victor LSP-4567	(S)	Cedartown, Georgia	1971	6.00	15.00
RCA Victor LSP-4647	(S)	Good Hearted Woman	1972	6.00	15.00
RCA Victor SPS-570	(DJ)	Get Into Waylon Jennings	1972	20.00	50.00
RCA Victor LSP-4651	(S)	Ladies Love Outlaws	1972	6.00	15.00
RCA Victor LSP-4854	(S)	Lonesome, On'ry And Mean	1973	6.00	15.00
		— Original RCA albums above have orange labels.—			
RCA Victor CPL1-3406	(S)	Greatest Hits (Picture disc)	1979	4.00	10.00

JENSEN, KRIS

Hickory MH-110	(M)	Torture	1962	20.00	50.00

JESSE & THE BANDITS

Re-Car 2001	(M)	Top Teen Hits	1965	50.00	125.00

JETHRO TULL

Reprise RS-6336	(S)	This Was	1969	8.00	20.00
Reprise RS-6360	(S)	Stand Up (Gatefold cover)	1969	8.00	20.00
Reprise RS-6400	(S)	Benefit	1970	6.00	15.00
Reprise MS-2035	(S)	Aqualung	1971	6.00	15.00
Reprise MS-2072	(DJ)	Thick As A Brick (Air-play sampler)	1972	12.00	30.00
Reprise MS-2072	(S)	Thick As A Brick (With booklet)	1972	6.00	15.00
Reprise MS-2106	(S)	Living In The Past (With booklet)	1972	6.00	15.00
Chrysalis CHR-1040	(DJ)	A Passion Play (Edited for airplay)	1973	10.00	25.00
Chrysalis CHR-1040	(S)	A Passion Play (With booklet)	1973	6.00	15.00
Chrysalis CH4-1044	(Q)	Aqualung	1973	12.00	30.00
Chrysalis CH4-1067	(Q)	War Child	1974	12.00	30.00
Mobile Fidelity MFSL-061	(S)	Aqualung	1980	25.00	75.00
Mobile Fidelity MFSL-092	(S)	The Broadsword And The Beast	1982	7.00	20.00
Mobile Fidelity MFSL-187	(S)	Thick As A Brick	1982	7.00	20.00

JETSONS, THE

Colpix CP-213	(M)	The Jetsons (TV Soundtrack)	196?	80.00	200.00
HBR HLP-2037	(M)	First Family On The Moon	196?	30.00	75.00

Label & Catalog #		Title	Year	VG+	NM
JIM & JEAN					
Philips PHM-200-182	(M)	Jim And Jean	1965	6.00	15.00
Philips PHS-600-182	(S)	Jim And Jean	1965	8.00	20.00
Verve/Folkways FT-3001	(M)	Changes	1966	5.00	12.00
Verve/Folkways FTS-3001	(S)	Changes	1966	6.00	15.00
Verve/Folkways FT-3015	(M)	People World	1967	5.00	12.00
Verve/Folkways FTS-3015	(S)	People World	1967	6.00	15.00
JIM & JESSIE (& THE VIRGINIA BOYS)					
Epic LN-24031	(M)	Bluegrass Special	1963	6.00	15.00
Epic BN-26031	(S)	Bluegrass Special	1963	8.00	20.00
Epic LN-24074	(M)	Bluegrass Classics	1963	6.00	15.00
Epic BN-26074	(S)	Bluegrass Classics	1963	8.00	20.00
Epic LN-24107	(M)	The Old Country Church	1964	6.00	15.00
Epic BN-26107	(S)	The Old Country Church	1964	8.00	20.00
Epic LN-24144	(M)	Y'All Come	1964	6.00	15.00
Epic BN-26144	(S)	Y'All Come	1964	8.00	20.00
Epic LN-24176	(M)	Berry Pickin' In The Country	1965	6.00	15.00
Epic BN-26176	(S)	Berry Pickin' In The Country	1965	8.00	20.00
Epic LN-24204	(M)	Sing Unto Him A New Song	1966	6.00	15.00
Epic BN-26204	(S)	Sing Unto Him A New Song	1966	8.00	20.00
Epic LN-24314	(M)	Diesel On My Tail	1967	6.00	15.00
Epic BN-26314	(S)	Diesel On My Tail	1967	8.00	20.00
Epic BN-26394	(S)	All-Time Great Country Instrumentals	1968	6.00	15.00
Epic BN-26425	(S)	Saluting The Louvin Brothers	1969	6.00	15.00
Epic BN-26513	(S)	We Like Trains	1970	6.00	15.00
JIMMY G & THE TACKHEADS					
Jimmy and The 'Heads are members of the Parliament/Funkadelic community.					
Capitol ST-12392	(S)	Federation Of Tackheads	1985	4.00	10.00
JIVE FIVE, THE					
United Arts. UAL-3455	(M)	The Jive Five	1965	12.00	30.00
United Arts. UAS-6455	(S)	The Jive Five	1965	16.00	40.00
Ambient Sound 37717	(S)	Here We Are	1982	5.00	12.00
JO JO GUNNE					
Jo Jo features Jay Ferguson of Spirit.					
Asylum SD-5053	(S)	Jo Jo Gunne	1972	6.00	15.00
Asylum SD-5065	(S)	Bite Down Hard	1973	6.00	15.00
Asylum SD-5071	(S)	Jumpin' The Gunne *(Gatefold cover)*	1973	6.00	15.00
Asylum SD-5071	(S)	Jumpin' The Gunne	1974	4.00	10.00
Asylum 7E-1022	(S)	So Where Is The Show	1974	4.00	10.00
JOE & EDDIE					
Crescendo GNP-86	(M)	There's A Meetin' Here Tonight	1964	8.00	20.00
Crescendo GNPS-86	(S)	There's A Meetin' Here Tonight	1964	10.00	25.00
Crescendo GNP-96	(M)	Coast To Coast	1964	8.00	20.00
Crescendo GNPS-96	(S)	Coast To Coast	1964	10.00	25.00
Crescendo GNP-99	(M)	Joe And Eddie	1964	8.00	20.00
Crescendo GNPS-99	(S)	Joe And Eddie	1964	10.00	25.00
Crescendo GNP-2005	(M)	Tear Down The Walls	1965	8.00	20.00
Crescendo GNPS-2005	(S)	Tear Down The Walls	1965	10.00	25.00
Crescendo GNP-2007	(M)	Joe And Eddie Live In Hollywood	1965	6.00	15.00
Crescendo GNPS-2007	(S)	Joe And Eddie Live In Hollywood	1965	8.00	20.00
Crescendo GNP-2014	(M)	Walkin' Down The Line	1965	6.00	15.00
Crescendo GNPS-2014	(S)	Walkin' Down The Line	1965	8.00	20.00
Crescendo GNP-2021	(M)	The Magic Of Their Singing	1966	6.00	15.00
Crescendo GNPS-2021	(S)	The Magic Of Their Singing	1966	8.00	20.00
Crescendo GNP-2032	(M)	The Best Of Joe And Eddie	1967	6.00	15.00
Crescendo GNPS-2032	(S)	The Best Of Joe And Eddie	1967	8.00	20.00
JOEL, BILLY					
Billy Joel originally recorded with The Hassles; Attila.					
Family Prod. 2700	(S)	Cold Spring Harbor	1971	20.00	50.00
		(Originals have color labels; counterfeits have white labels.)			
Columbia CQ-32544	(Q)	Piano Man	1974	8.00	20.00
Columbia PCQ-33146	(Q)	Streetlife Serenade	1974	8.00	20.00
Columbia PCQ-33848	(Q)	Turnstiles	1976	8.00	20.00

Label & Catalog #		Title	Year	VG+	NM
Columbia AS-326	(DJ)	**Souvenir**	1976	10.00	30.00
Columbia HC-34987	(S)	**The Stranger** (Half-speed master)	1981	13.00	40.00
Columbia HC-44987	(S)	**The Stranger** (Half-speed master)	1982	8.00	25.00
Columbia HC-45609	(S)	**52nd Street** (Half-speed master)	1982	8.00	25.00
Columbia HC-47461	(S)	**Songs In The Attic** (Half-speed master)	1982	8.00	25.00
Columbia HC-48837	(S)	**An Innocent Man** (Half-speed master)	1983	12.00	35.00
Columbia AS-1433	(DJ)	**Billy Joel Interview**	1982	6.00	15.00

JOHN, ELTON

Viking 105	(S)	**The Games** (Soundtrack)	1970	80.00	200.00
Uni 73090	(S)	**Elton John** (With booklet)	1970	8.00	20.00
Uni 73096	(S)	**Tumbleweed Connection** (With booklet)	1971	8.00	20.00
Uni 93090	(S)	**Elton John** (With booklet)	1971	6.00	15.00
Uni 93096	(S)	**Tumbleweed Connection** (With booklet)	1971	6.00	15.00
Uni 93105	(S)	**11-17-70**	1971	5.00	12.00
Uni 93120	(S)	**Madman Across The Water** (With booklet)	1971	6.00	15.00
Uni 93135	(S)	**Honky Chateau**	1972	5.00	12.00
Paramount DJ-1	(DJ)	**Friends** (Open-end interview)	1971	80.00	200.00
Paramount PAS-6004	(S)	**Friends** (Soundtrack)	1971	10.00	25.00
MCA 2100	(S)	**Don't Shoot Me, I'm Only The Piano Player** (Solid black label with a lyric book.)	1972	6.00	15.00
MCA 2142	(DJ)	**Capt. Fantastic & The Brown Dirt Cowboy** (Brown vinyl. All copies are autographed by Elton and Bernie.)	1979	150.00	300.00
MCA L33-1995	(DJ)	**A Single Man** (Picture disc)	1979	16.00	40.00
MCA 14591	(S)	**A Single Man** (Picture disc)	1979?	4.00	10.00
Nautilus NR-43	(S)	**Greatest Hits**	198?	35.00	100.00
Direct Disk 10003	(S)	**Goodbye Yellow Brick Road** (2 LPs)	1980	12.00	35.00
Geffen GHS-24031	(DJ)	**Breaking Hearts** (Quiex II vinyl)	1984	6.00	15.00
Mobile Fidelity MFSL-160	(S)	**Goodbye Yellow Brick Road** (2 LPs)	1990	8.00	25.00

JOHN, LITTLE WILLIE

King 395-564	(M)	**Fever** (Original covers are brown with a nurse holding a thermometer.)	1956	250.00	750.00
King 595-564	(M)	**Fever** (Later covers are white with "Fever" in large colored letters.)	1957	100.00	300.00
King 395-596	(M)	**Talk To Me**	1958	80.00	200.00
King 603	(M)	**Mister Little Willie John**	1958	80.00	200.00
King 691	(M)	**Action**	1960	40.00	100.00
King 739	(M)	**Sure Things**	1961	40.00	100.00
King 767	(M)	**The Sweet, The Hot, The Teenage Beat**	1961	40.00	100.00
King 802	(M)	**Come On And Join Little Willie John**	1962	40.00	100.00
King 895	(M)	**These Are My Favorite Songs**	1964	30.00	75.00
King K-949	(M)	**Little Willie Sings All Originals**	1966	20.00	50.00
King KS-949	(S)	**Little Willie Sings All Originals**	1966	40.00	100.00
		— King albums above have crownless black labels.—			
King KS-1081	(M)	**Free At Last** ("Leave My Kitten Alone" and "Free At last" are in stereo on this LP.)	1970	16.00	40.00
BluesWay BLS-6069	(P)	**Free At Last**	1970	10.00	25.00

JOHN STREET ROCKETS, THE

Confidential SCR-5001	(S)	**Rot And Roll The Hard Way**	1979	20.00	50.00

JOHN'S CHILDREN

White Whale WWS-7128	(S)	**Orgasm**	1970	60.00	150.00

JOHNNIE & JOE

Ambient Sound 38345	(S)	**Kingdom Of Love**	1982	5.00	12.00

JOHNNY & JACK

RCA Victor LPM-1587	(M)	**The Tennessee Mountain Boys**	1957	14.00	35.00
RCA Victor LPM-2017	(M)	**Hits By Johnny And Jack**	1959	14.00	35.00
Decca DL-4308	(M)	**Smiles And Tears**	1962	6.00	15.00
Decca DL-74308	(S)	**Smiles And Tears**	1962	8.00	20.00

JOHNNY & THE BLUE BEATS

Winsor R-1001	(M)	**Smile**	196?	10.00	25.00
Winsor RL-1001	(S)	**Smile**	196?	12.00	30.00

Label & Catalog #		Title	Year	VG+	NM
JOHNNY & THE HURRICANES					
Warwick W-2007	(M)	Johnny & The Hurricanes	1959	50.00	125.00
Warwick WST-2007	(S)	Johnny & The Hurricanes	1959	80.00	200.00
		("Red River Rock" is rechanneled on this album.)			
Warwick W-2010	(M)	Stormsville	1960	50.00	125.00
Warwick WST-2010	(S)	Stormsville	1960	80.00	200.00
Big Top 12-1302	(M)	Big Sound Of Johnny & The Hurricanes	1960	50.00	125.00
Big Top ST-1302	(S)	Big Sound Of Johnny & The Hurricanes	1960	80.00	200.00
Attila 1030	(M)	Live At The Star Club	1962	60.00	150.00
JOHNSON, BETTY					
Atlantic 8017	(M)	Betty Johnson	1958	20.00	50.00
Atlantic 8027	(M)	Songs You Heard When You Fell In Love	1959	20.00	50.00
JOHNSON, BLIND WILLIE					
Folkways F-3585	(M)	Blues	1959	20.00	50.00
JOHNSON, BUBBER					
King 395-569	(M)	Come Home	1957	80.00	200.00
King 624	(M)	Sings Sweet Love Songs	1959	50.00	125.00
JOHNSON, BUDDY					
Wing MGW-12005	(M)	Rock 'N' Roll Stage Show	1956	40.00	100.00
Mercury MG-20072	(M)	Buddy Johnson Wails	1958	30.00	75.00
Mercury MG-20209	(M)	Rock 'N' Roll	1958	30.00	75.00
Mercury MG-20322	(M)	Walkin'	1958	30.00	75.00
JOHNSON, BUDDY & ELLA					
Mercury MG-20347	(M)	Swing Me	1958	30.00	75.00
Roulette R-25085	(M)	Go Ahead And Rock And Roll	1959	30.00	75.00
Roulette SR-25085	(S)	Go Ahead And Rock And Roll	1959	50.00	125.00
JOHNSON, CANDY					
Canjo LP-1001	(M)	The Candy Johnson Show	1964	10.00	25.00
Canjo LP-1002	(M)	Bikini Beach	1964	10.00	25.00
JOHNSON, LONNIE					
King 395-520	(M)	Lonesome Road	1958	600.00	Rare
		(Near Mint copies have a suggested value of $1,200-2,000.)			
Bluesville BVLP-1007	(M)	Blues By Lonnie	1960	20.00	50.00
Bluesville BVLP-1011	(M)	Blues And Ballads	1960	20.00	50.00
Bluesville BVLP-1024	(M)	Losing Game	1961	20.00	50.00
Bluesville BVLP-1062	(M)	Another Night To Cry	1963	20.00	50.00
King K-958	(M)	Lonnie Johnson 24 Twelve Bar Blues	1966	30.00	75.00
King KS-958	(S)	Lonnie Johnson 24 Twelve Bar Blues	1966	40.00	100.00
King KS-1083	(S)	Tomorrow Night	1970	10.00	25.00
Prestige PRST-7724	(S)	The Blues Of Lonnie Johnson	1969	8.00	20.00
JOHNSON, LONNIE, & VICTORIA SPIVEY					
Lonnie Johnson also recorded with Victoria Spivey.					
Bluesville BVLP-1044	(M)	Idle Hours	1961	20.00	50.00
Bluesville BVLP-1054	(M)	Woman Blues	1962	20.00	50.00
JOHNSON, LOU					
Cotillion SD-9008	(S)	Sweet Southern Soul	1969	6.00	15.00
Volt VOS-6016	(S)	With You In Mind	1971	6.00	15.00
JOHNSON, MARV					
United Arts. UAL-3081	(M)	Marvelous Marv Johnson	1960	30.00	75.00
United Arts. UAS-6081	(P)	Marvelous Marv Johnson	1960	40.00	100.00
United Arts. UAL-3118	(M)	More Marv Johnson	1960	30.00	75.00
United Arts. UAS-6118	(P)	More Marv Johnson	1960	40.00	100.00
United Arts. UAL-3187	(M)	I Believe	1962	20.00	50.00
United Arts. UAS-6187	(S)	I Believe	1962	30.00	75.00
JOHNSON, OLLIE					
RCA Victor LPM-1369	(M)	A Bit Of The Blues	1957	16.00	40.00

Label & Catalog #		Title	Year	VG+	NM

JOHNSON, PETE
Pete Johnson also recorded with Hadda Brooks; Joe Turner.

| Savoy MG-14018 | (M) | **Pete's Blues** | 196? | 14.00 | 35.00 |

JOHNSON, PETE / HADDA BROOKS

| Crown CLP-5058 | (M) | **Boogie** | 196? | 8.00 | 20.00 |

JOHNSON, ROBERT

Columbia CL-1654	(M)	**King Of The Delta Blues Singers**	1961	40.00	100.00
		(The label has six white-on-black "eye" logos around the perimeter.)			
Columbia CL-1654	(M)	**King Of The Delta Blues Singers**	1963	12.00	30.00
		(The label reads "Guaranteed High Fidelity" on the bottom.)			
Columbia CL-1654	(M)	**King Of The Delta Blues Singers**	1965	10.00	25.00
		(The label has "360 Sound Mono" on the bottom.)			
Columbia CL-1654	(M)	**King Of The Delta Blues Singers**	1970	6.00	15.00
		(The label has "Columbia" in gold around the perimeter.)			
Columbia C-30034	(M)	**King Of The Delta Blues Singers, Volume 2**	1970	6.00	15.00

JOHNSTON, BRUCE
Refer to The Beach Boys; The Catalinas; The De-Fenders; The Hot Doggers; The Rip Chords; The Vettes.

Del-Fi DFLP-1228	(M)	**Surfers' Pajama Party**	1963	20.00	50.00
Del-Fi DFST-1228	(S)	**Surfers' Pajama Party**	1963	30.00	75.00
Columbia CL-2057	(M)	**Surfin' 'Round The World**	1963	60.00	150.00
Columbia CS-8857	(S)	**Surfin' 'Round The World**	1963	80.00	200.00
Columbia KC-34459	(S)	**Going Public** *(Produced by Gary Usher)*	1976	6.00	15.00

JOHNSTONS, THE

Tetragrammaton 110	(S)	**Both Sides Now**	1969	6.00	15.00
Vanguard VSD-6572	(S)	**Colours Of The Dawn**	1971	5.00	12.00
Mercury SRM-1-640	(S)	**The Johnstons**	1972	5.00	12.00

JOKER'S MEMORY

| M.S. 11843 | (S) | **Joker's Memory** *(Canadian)* | 1975 | 40.00 | 100.00 |

JOLLIVER ARKANSAS

| Bell 6031 | (S) | **Home** | 1969 | 6.00 | 15.00 |

JONES, ANN, & HER AMERICAN SWEETHEARTS

| Audio Lab AL-1521 | (M) | **Ann Jones & Her American Sweethearts** | 195? | 40.00 | 100.00 |
| Audio Lab AL-1556 | (M) | **Hit And Run** | 195? | 40.00 | 100.00 |

JONES, BRIAN
Brian Jones was formerly a member of The Rolling Stones.

| Roll. Stones RSR-49100 | (DJ) | **Pipes Of Pan At Joujouka** *(With inserts)* | 1971 | 16.00 | 40.00 |
| Roll. Stones RSR-49100 | (S) | **Pipes Of Pan At Joujouka** *(With inserts)* | 1971 | 20.00 | 50.00 |

JONES, CURTIS

| Bluesville BVLP-1022 | (M) | **Trouble Blues** | 1961 | 20.00 | 50.00 |
| Delmar DL-605 | (M) | **Lonesome Bedroom Blues** | 1963 | 16.00 | 40.00 |

JONES, DAVY
Davy Jones was a member of The Monkees.

Colpix CP-493	(M)	**David Jones**	1965	10.00	25.00
Colpix SCP-493	(S)	**David Jones**	1965	16.00	40.00
Bell 6067	(S)	**Davy Jones**	1971	8.00	20.00

JONES, DEAN

Valiant LP-407	(M)	**Introducing Dean Jones**	1962	10.00	25.00
Valiant LPS-407	(S)	**Introducing Dean Jones**	1962	12.00	30.00
Dot DLP-25890	(S)	**The Names Of My Sorrow**	1968	6.00	15.00

JONES, ETTA

King 395-544	(M)	**Etta Jones Sings**	1958	100.00	200.00
		(The cover has an iridescent background.)			
King 395-544	(M)	**Etta Jones Sings**	1958	150.00	300.00
		(The cover has a plain background.)			
King 707	(M)	**Etta Jones Sings**	1960	40.00	100.00
		(Black crownless label. King 707 is a reissue of 544.)			

Label & Catalog #		Title	Year	VG+	NM
Prestige PRLP-7186	(M)	Don't Go To Strangers	1960	16.00	40.00
Prestige PRST-7186	(S)	Don't Go To Strangers	1960	12.00	30.00
Prestige PRLP-7194	(M)	Something Nice	1961	16.00	40.00
Prestige PRLP-7204	(M)	So Warm (Etta Jones & Strings)	1961	16.00	40.00
Prestige PRST-7204	(S)	So Warm (Etta Jones & Strings)	1961	12.00	30.00
Prestige PRLP-7214	(M)	From The Heart	1961	12.00	30.00
Prestige PRST-7214	(S)	From The Heart	1961	10.00	25.00
Prestige PRLP-7241	(M)	Lonely And Blue	1962	12.00	30.00
Prestige PRST-7241	(S)	Lonely And Blue	1962	10.00	25.00
Prestige PRLP-7272	(M)	Love Shout	1963	12.00	30.00
Prestige PRST-7272	(S)	Love Shout	1963	10.00	25.00
Prestige PRLP-7284	(M)	Hollar!	1963	12.00	30.00
Prestige PRST-7284	(S)	Hollar!	1963	10.00	25.00

— Original Prestige mono albums above have yellow labels with a Bergenfield, NJ address; stereo albums have silver labels.—

Roulette R-25329	(M)	Etta Jones Sings	1965	8.00	20.00
Roulette SR-25329	(S)	Etta Jones Sings	1965	6.00	15.00
Prestige PRLP-7443	(M)	Etta Jones' Greatest Hits	1967	8.00	20.00
Prestige PRST-7443	(E)	Etta Jones' Greatest Hits	1967	6.00	15.00

— Original Prestige albums above have blue labels.—

JONES, GEORGE
Refer to The Jones Boys; Dolly Parton.

Starday SLP-101	(M)	The Grand Ole Opry's New Star	1958	600.00	Rare

(Near Mint copies have a suggested value of $600-1,200.)

Starday SLP-102	(M)	Hillbilly Hit Parade	1958	100.00	250.00

(This is actually a various artists album but features six tracks by George and so is listed here.)

Starday SLP-125	(M)	The Crown Prince Of Country Music	1960	50.00	100.00
Starday SLP-150	(M)	His Greatest Hits	1962	20.00	50.00
Starday SLP-151	(M)	The Fabulous Country Music Sound Of George Jones	1962	20.00	50.00
Starday SLP-335	(M)	George Jones	1965	12.00	30.00
Starday SLP-344	(M)	Long Live King George	1965	12.00	30.00
Starday SLP-366	(M)	The George Jones Story (With bonus photo)	1966	20.00	50.00
Starday SLP-366	(M)	The George Jones Story (Without photo)	1966	12.00	30.00
Starday SLP-401	(M)	Song Book & Picture Album (With book)	1967	20.00	50.00
Starday SLP-401	(M)	Song Book & Picture Album (Without book)	1967	12.00	30.00
Starday SLP-440	(M)	The Golden Country Hits Of George Jones	1969	10.00	25.00
Mercury MG-20306	(M)	14 Country Favorites	1957	50.00	100.00
Mercury MG-20462	(M)	Country Church Time	1959	75.00	150.00
Mercury MG-20477	(M)	White Lightning And Other Favorites	1959	50.00	100.00
Mercury MG-20596	(M)	George Jones Salutes Hank Williams	1960	20.00	50.00
Mercury SR-60596	(S)	George Jones Salutes Hank Williams	1960	30.00	75.00
Mercury MG-20621	(M)	George Jones' Greatest Hits	1961	12.00	30.00
Mercury SR-60621	(S)	George Jones' Greatest Hits	1961	16.00	40.00
Mercury MG-20624	(M)	Country And Western Hits	1961	12.00	30.00
Mercury SR-60624	(S)	Country And Western Hits	1961	16.00	40.00
Mercury MG-20694	(M)	From The Heart	1962	12.00	30.00
Mercury SR-60694	(S)	From The Heart	1962	16.00	40.00
Mercury MG-20793	(M)	The Novelty Side Of George Jones	1963	20.00	50.00
Mercury SR-60793	(S)	The Novelty Side Of George Jones	1963	30.00	75.00
Mercury MG-20836	(M)	The Ballad Side Of George Jones	1963	12.00	30.00
Mercury SR-60836	(S)	The Ballad Side Of George Jones	1963	16.00	40.00

— Original Mercury albums above have black labels.—

Mercury MG-20906	(M)	Blue And Lonesome	1964	10.00	25.00
Mercury SR-60906	(S)	Blue And Lonesome	1964	12.00	30.00
Mercury MG-20937	(M)	Country & Western #1 Male Singer	1964	10.00	25.00
Mercury SR-60937	(S)	Country & Western #1 Male Singer	1964	12.00	30.00
Mercury MG-20990	(M)	Heartaches And Tears	1965	10.00	25.00
Mercury SR-60990	(S)	Heartaches And Tears	1965	12.00	30.00
Mercury MG-21029	(M)	Singing The Blues	1965	10.00	25.00
Mercury SR-61029	(S)	Singing The Blues	1965	12.00	30.00
Mercury MG-21048	(M)	George Jones' Greatest Hits, Volume 2	1965	10.00	25.00
Mercury SR-61048	(S)	George Jones' Greatest Hits, Volume 2	1965	12.00	30.00

— Original Mercury albums above have red labels.—

United Arts. UAL-3193	(M)	The New Favorites Of George Jones	1962	10.00	25.00
United Arts. UAS-6193	(S)	The New Favorites Of George Jones	1962	12.00	30.00

Label & Catalog #		Title	Year	VG+	NM
United Arts. UAL-3218	(M)	The Hits Of His Country Cousins	1962	10.00	25.00
United Arts. UAS-6218	(S)	The Hits Of His Country Cousins	1962	12.00	30.00
United Arts. UAL-3219	(M)	Homecoming In Heaven	1962	10.00	25.00
United Arts. UAS-6219	(S)	Homecoming In Heaven	1962	12.00	30.00
United Arts. UAL-3220	(M)	My Favorites Of Hank Williams	1962	12.00	30.00
United Arts. UAS-6220	(S)	My Favorites Of Hank Williams	1962	16.00	40.00
United Arts. UAL-3221	(M)	George Jones Sings Bob Wills	1962	16.00	40.00
United Arts. UAS-6221	(S)	George Jones Sings Bob Wills	1962	20.00	50.00
United Arts. UAL-3270	(M)	I Wish Tonight Would Never End	1963	10.00	25.00
United Arts. UAS-6270	(S)	I Wish Tonight Would Never End	1963	12.00	30.00
United Arts. UAL-3291	(M)	The Best Of George Jones	1963	8.00	20.00
United Arts. UAS-6291	(S)	The Best Of George Jones	1963	10.00	25.00
United Arts. UAL-3338	(M)	More New Favorites	1964	12.00	30.00
United Arts. UAS-6338	(S)	More New Favorites	1964	16.00	40.00
United Arts. UAL-3364	(M)	George Jones Sings Like The Dickens	1964	16.00	40.00
United Arts. UAS-6364	(S)	George Jones Sings Like The Dickens	1964	20.00	50.00
United Arts. UAL-3388	(M)	I Get Lonely In A Hurry	1964	8.00	20.00
United Arts. UAS-6388	(S)	I Get Lonely In A Hurry	1964	12.00	30.00
United Arts. UAL-3408	(M)	Trouble In Mind	1965	10.00	25.00
United Arts. UAS-6408	(S)	Trouble In Mind	1965	12.00	30.00
United Arts. UAL-3422	(M)	The Race Is On	1965	10.00	25.00
United Arts. UAS-6422	(S)	The Race Is On	1965	12.00	30.00
United Arts. UAL-3442	(M)	King Of Broken Hearts	1965	10.00	25.00
United Arts. UAS-6442	(S)	King Of Broken Hearts	1965	12.00	30.00
United Arts. UAL-3457	(M)	The Great George Jones	1966	10.00	25.00
United Arts. UAS-6457	(S)	The Great George Jones	1966	12.00	30.00
United Arts. UAL-3532	(M)	George Jones' Golden Hits, Volume 1	1966	6.00	15.00
United Arts. UAS-6532	(S)	George Jones' Golden Hits, Volume 1	1966	8.00	20.00
United Arts. UAL-3558	(M)	The Young George Jones	1967	10.00	25.00
United Arts. UAS-6558	(S)	The Young George Jones	1967	8.00	20.00
United Arts. UAL-3566	(M)	George Jones' Golden Hits, Volume 1	1967	10.00	25.00
United Arts. UAS-6566	(S)	George Jones' Golden Hits, Volume 1	1967	8.00	20.00
		— Original U.A. albums above have black labels.—			
Musicor M-2060	(M)	New Country Hits	1965	10.00	25.00
Musicor MS-3060	(S)	New Country Hits	1965	14.00	35.00
Musicor M-2061	(M)	Old Brush Arbors	1966	10.00	25.00
Musicor MS-3061	(S)	Old Brush Arbors	1966	14.00	35.00
Musicor M-2088	(M)	Love Bug	1966	10.00	25.00
Musicor MS-3088	(S)	Love Bug	1966	14.00	35.00
Musicor P2-5094	(M)	Country Heart	1966	10.00	25.00
Musicor P2S-5094	(S)	Country Heart	1966	14.00	35.00
Musicor M-2099	(M)	I'm A People	1966	8.00	20.00
Musicor MS-3099	(S)	I'm A People	1966	10.00	25.00
Musicor M-2106	(M)	We Found Heaven Right Here On Earth	1966	8.00	20.00
Musicor MS-3106	(S)	We Found Heaven Right Here On Earth	1966	10.00	25.00
Musicor M-2116	(M)	George Jones' Greatest Hits	1967	8.00	20.00
Musicor MS-3116	(S)	George Jones' Greatest Hits	1967	8.00	20.00
Musicor M-2119	(M)	Walk Through This World With Me	1967	10.00	25.00
Musicor MS-3119	(S)	Walk Through This World With Me	1967	8.00	20.00
Musicor M-2124	(M)	Cup Of Loneliness	1967	10.00	25.00
Musicor MS-3124	(S)	Cup Of Loneliness	1967	8.00	20.00
Musicor M-2128	(M)	Hits By George	1967	10.00	25.00
Musicor MS-3128	(S)	Hits By George	1967	8.00	20.00
Musicor MS-3149	(S)	The Songs Of Dallas Frazier	1968	8.00	20.00
Musicor MS-3158	(S)	If My Heart Had Windows	1968	8.00	20.00
Musicor MS-3159	(S)	The Musical Loves, Life And Sorrows Of America's Great Country Star	1968	10.00	25.00
Musicor MS-3169	(S)	My Country	1969	8.00	20.00
Musicor MS-3177	(S)	I'll Share My World With You	1969	6.00	15.00
Musicor MS-3181	(S)	Where Grass Won't Grow	1969	6.00	15.00
Musicor MS-3188	(S)	Will You Visit Me On Sunday?	1970	6.00	15.00
Musicor MS-3191	(S)	The Best Of George Jones	1970	6.00	15.00
Musicor MS-3194	(S)	With Love	1971	6.00	15.00
Musicor MS-3203	(S)	The Best Of Sacred Music	1971	6.00	15.00
Musicor MS-3204	(S)	The Great Songs Of Leon Payne	1971	6.00	15.00
		— Original Musicor albums above have black labels.—			

Label & Catalog #		Title	Year	VG+	NM
JONES, GEORGE, & MELBA MONTGOMERY					
United Arts. UAL-3301	(M)	What's In Our Hearts	1963	10.00	25.00
United Arts. UAS-6301	(S)	What's In Our Hearts	1963	12.00	30.00
United Arts. UAL-3352	(M)	Bluegrass Hootenanny	1964	10.00	25.00
United Arts. UAS-6352	(S)	Bluegrass Hootenanny	1964	12.00	30.00
United Arts. UAL-3472	(M)	Blue Moon Of Kentucky	1966	8.00	20.00
United Arts. UAS-6420	(S)	Blue Moon Of Kentucky	1966	10.00	25.00
Musicor M-3046	(M)	Mr. Country And Western	1965	10.00	25.00
Musicor MS-3046	(S)	Mr. Country And Western	1965	12.00	30.00
Musicor M-3079	(M)	Famous Country Duets	1965	6.00	15.00
Musicor MS-3079	(S)	Famous Country Duets	1965	8.00	20.00
Musicor M-3109	(M)	Close Together As You And Me	1966	6.00	15.00
Musicor MS-3109	(S)	Close Together As You And Me	1966	8.00	20.00
Musicor M-3127	(M)	Let's Get Together/Boy Meets Girl	1967	10.00	25.00
Musicor MS-3127	(S)	Let's Get Together/Boy Meets Girl	1967	8.00	20.00
JONES, GEORGE; MELBA MONTGOMERY & GENE PITNEY					
Musicor M-3079	(M)	Famous Country Duets	1965	6.00	15.00
Musicor MS-3079	(S)	Famous Country Duets	1965	8.00	20.00
JONES, GEORGE, & GENE PITNEY					
Musicor M-2044	(M)	For The First Time! Two Great Singers	1965	6.00	15.00
Musicor MS-3044	(S)	For The First Time! Two Great Singers	1965	8.00	20.00
Musicor M-2044	(M)	Recorded In Nashville	1965	6.00	15.00
Musicor MS-3044	(S)	Recorded In Nashville	1965	8.00	20.00
Musicor M-3065	(M)	It's Country Time Again!	1965	6.00	15.00
Musicor MS-3065	(S)	It's Country Time Again!	1965	8.00	20.00
JONES, GEORGE, & MARGE SINGLETON					
Mercury MG-20747	(M)	Duets Country Style	1962	10.00	25.00
Mercury SR-60747	(S)	Duets Country Style	1962	12.00	30.00
JONES, GRANPA					
Granpa also recorded as a member of The Brown's Ferry Four.					
King 554	(M)	Granpa Jones Sings His Greatest Hits	1958	30.00	75.00
King 625	(M)	Strictly Country Tunes	1959	30.00	75.00
King 809	(M)	Rollin' Along With Granpa Jones	1963	24.00	60.00
King 822	(M)	16 Sacred Gospel Songs	1963	24.00	60.00
King 845	(M)	Do You Remember?	1963	24.00	60.00
King 888	(M)	The Other Side Of Granpa Jones	1964	20.00	50.00
Decca DL-4364	(M)	An Evening With Granpa Jones	1963	8.00	20.00
Monument MLP-4006	(M)	Granpa Jones Makes The Rafters Ring	1962	10.00	25.00
Monument SLP-14006	(S)	Granpa Jones Makes The Rafters Ring	1962	12.00	30.00
Monument MLP-8001	(M)	Yodeling Hits	1963	10.00	25.00
Monument SLP-18001	(S)	Yodeling Hits	1963	12.00	30.00
Monument MLP-8021	(M)	Real Folk Songs	1964	10.00	25.00
Monument SLP-18021	(S)	Real Folk Songs	1964	12.00	30.00
Monument MLP-8041	(M)	Remembers The Brown's Ferry Four	1966	10.00	25.00
Monument SLP-18041	(S)	Remembers The Brown's Ferry Four	1966	12.00	30.00
Monument SLP-18083	(S)	Everybody's Grandpa	1968	8.00	20.00
King 1042	(M)	The Living Legend Of Country Music	1969	6.00	15.00
JONES, JIM, & THE CHAUNTEYS					
Sunglow SLP-113	(S)	Soul Clap	196?	10.00	25.00
JONES, JIMMY					
MGM E-3847	(M)	Good Timin'	1960	40.00	100.00
MGM SE-3847	(E)	Good Timin'	1960	60.00	150.00
		("I Just Go For You" is in stereo on this album.)			
JONES, JOE					
Roulette R-25143	(M)	You Talk Too Much	1961	20.00	50.00
Roulette SR-25143	(E)	You Talk Too Much	1961	16.00	40.00
JONES, LINDA					
Loma 5907	(S)	Hypnotized	1967	10.00	25.00
Turbo 7007	(S)	Your Precious Love	196?	10.00	25.00

Label & Catalog #		Title	Year	VG+	NM
JONES, PAUL					
Paul Jones was formerly a member of Manfred Mann.					
Universal 3005	(M)	**Privilege** *(Soundtrack)*	1967	8.00	20.00
Universal 73005	(S)	**Privilege** *(Soundtrack)*	1967	8.00	20.00
Capitol T-2795	(M)	**Songs From The Film "Privilege"**	1967	10.00	25.00
Capitol ST-2795	(S)	**Songs From The Film "Privilege"**	1967	8.00	20.00
London XPS-605	(S)	**Crucifix In A Horseshoe**	1971	4.00	10.00
JONES, RICKIE LEE					
Mobile Fidelity MFSL-089	(S)	**Rickie Lee Jones**	1980	50.00	150.00
Mobile Fidelity MFQR-089	(S)	**Rickie Lee Jones** *(UHQR test pressing)*	1980	250.00	750.00
JONES, RUFUS					
Cameo C-1076	(M)	**Five On Eight**	1964	10.00	25.00
Cameo SC-1076	(S)	**Five On Eight**	1964	16.00	40.00
JONES, SPIKE					
RCA Victor LPT-18 (10")	(M)	**Spike Jones Plays The Charleston**	1952	80.00	200.00
RCA Victor LPM-3054 (10")	(M)	**Bottoms Up**	1952	40.00	100.00
RCA Victor LPM-3128 (10")	(M)	**Spike Jones Murders Carmen**	1953	40.00	100.00
Verve V-2021	(M)	**Let's Sing A Song For Christmas**	1956	30.00	75.00
Verve V-4005	(M)	**Dinner Music For People Who Aren't Very Hungry**	1957	30.00	75.00
Verve V-8564	(M)	**35 Reasons Why Christmas Can Be Fun**	1958	20.00	50.00
Liberty LRP-3140	(M)	**Omnibust**	1959	20.00	50.00
Liberty LST-7140	(S)	**Omnibust**	1959	30.00	75.00
Liberty LST-7140	(S)	**Omnibust** *(Red vinyl)*	1959	60.00	150.00
Liberty LRP-3154	(M)	**60 Years Of Music America Hates Best**	1959	20.00	50.00
Liberty LST-7154	(S)	**60 Years Of Music America Hates Best**	1959	30.00	75.00
Warner Bros. B-1332	(M)	**Spike Jones In Hi Fi**	1960	14.00	35.00
Warner Bros. WS-1332	(S)	**Spike Jones In Stereo**	1960	20.00	50.00
Liberty LRP-3338	(M)	**Washington Square**	1963	12.00	30.00
Liberty LST-7338	(S)	**Washington Square**	1963	16.00	40.00
Liberty LRP-3349	(M)	**Spike Jones' New Band**	1963	12.00	30.00
Liberty LST-7349	(S)	**Spike Jones' New Band**	1963	16.00	40.00
Liberty LRP-3401	(M)	**Hank Williams Hits**	1965	12.00	30.00
Liberty LST-7401	(S)	**Hank Williams Hits**	1965	16.00	40.00
RCA Victor LPM-2224	(M)	**Thank You, Music Lovers**	1960	20.00	50.00
RCA Victor LOC-3235	(M)	**Spike Jones Is Murdering The Classics**	1965	12.00	30.00
RCA Victor LSC-3235	(E)	**Spike Jones Is Murdering The Classics**	1965	10.00	25.00
RCA Victor LPM-3849	(M)	**The Best Of Spike Jones**	1967	10.00	25.00
RCA Victor LSP-3849	(E)	**The Best Of Spike Jones**	1967	8.00	20.00
MGM SE-4731	(S)	**Let's Sing A Song For Christmas**	1970	8.00	20.00
JONES, STAN					
Buena Vista BV-3306	(M)	**Ghost Riders In The Sky**	1961	14.00	35.00
Buena Vista BV-3315	(M)	**Creakin' Leather**	1962	14.00	35.00
Disneyland WDL-3015	(M)	**Creakin' Leather**	196?	6.00	15.00
JONES, TOM					
Parrot PA-61004	(M)	**It's Not Unusual**	1965	6.00	15.00
Parrot PAS-71004	(S)	**It's Not Unusual**	1965	8.00	20.00
Parrot PA-61006	(M)	**What's New Pussycat?**	1965	6.00	15.00
Parrot PAS-71006	(S)	**What's New Pussycat?**	1965	8.00	20.00
United Arts. UAL-4132	(M)	**Thunderball** *(Soundtrack)*	1965	5.00	12.00
United Arts. UAS-5132	(S)	**Thunderball** *(Soundtrack)*	1965	6.00	15.00
Parrot PA-61007	(M)	**A-Tomic Jones**	1966	6.00	15.00
Parrot PAS-71007	(S)	**A-Tomic Jones**	1966	8.00	20.00
Kapp KL-1476	(M)	**Promise Her Anything** *(Soundtrack)*	1966	8.00	20.00
Kapp KS-3476	(S)	**Promise Her Anything** *(Soundtrack)*	1966	12.00	30.00
Parrot PA-1009	(M)	**Green, Green Grass Of Home**	1967	8.00	20.00
Parrot PAS-71009	(S)	**Green, Green Grass Of Home**	1967	6.00	15.00
Parrot PA-1014	(M)	**Tom Jones Live!**	1967	8.00	20.00
Parrot PAS-71014	(S)	**Tom Jones Live!**	1967	6.00	15.00
Parrot PAS-71019	(S)	**The Tom Jones Fever Zone**	1968	6.00	15.00
Parrot 71025	(S)	**Help Yourself**	1969	6.00	15.00
Parrot 71028	(S)	**This Is Tom Jones**	1969	6.00	15.00
Parrot 71031	(S)	**Live In Las Vegas**	1969	6.00	15.00

— Original Parrot albums above read "Distributed by London" on the bottom of the label.—

Label & Catalog #		Title	Year	VG+	NM

JONES BOYS, THE
George Jones' boys.

Label & Catalog #		Title	Year	VG+	NM
Musicor M-2017	(M)	Country & Western Songbook	1964	12.00	30.00
Musicor MS-3017	(S)	Country & Western Songbook	1964	16.00	40.00
Musicor MS-3182	(S)	My Boys, The Jones Boys	1970	8.00	20.00

JOPLIN, JANIS
Janis was formerly a member of Big Brother & The Holding Company. Refer to Hot Tuna.

Columbia CS-9913	(S)	I Got Dem Ol' Kozmic Blues Again! ("360 Sound" label)	1969	6.00	15.00
Columbia KC-31160	(S)	Janis Joplin In Concert (2 LPs)	1972	5.00	12.00
Columbia CQ-30322	(Q)	Pearl	1974	8.00	20.00
Mobile Fidelity MFSL-154	(S)	Pearl (Test pressing)	1974	100.00	300.00

JORDAN, KING

Coral CRL-57372	(M)	Phantom Guitar	1962	8.00	20.00
Coral CRL-757372	(S)	Phantom Guitar	1962	10.00	25.00

JORDAN, LOUIS

Score SLP-4007	(M)	Go Blow Your Horn	1957	80.00	200.00
Mercury MG-20242	(M)	Somebody Up There Digs Me	1957	50.00	125.00
Mercury MG-20331	(M)	Man, We're Wailin'	1958	50.00	125.00
Decca DL-8551	(M)	Let The Good Times Roll	1958	40.00	100.00

JORDAN, SHEILA: Refer to GOLDMINE'S PRICE GUIDE TO COLLECTIBLE JAZZ ALBUMS

JORDANAIRES, THE
The Jordanaires backed Elvis on virtually everything he recorded from 1956-1966.

RCA Victor LPM-3081 (10")	(M)	Beautiful City	1953	40.00	100.00
Decca DL-8681	(M)	Peace In The Valley	1957	20.00	50.00
Sesac 1401	(M)	Of Rivers And Plains	195?	30.00	75.00
Capitol T-1011	(M)	Heavenly Spirit	1958	16.00	40.00
Capitol T-1167	(M)	Gloryland	1959	16.00	40.00
Capitol T-1311	(M)	Land Of Jordan	1960	14.00	35.00
Capitol ST-1311	(S)	Land Of Jordan	1960	16.00	40.00
Capitol T-1742	(M)	Spotlight On The Jordanaires	1962	10.00	25.00
Capitol ST-1742	(S)	Spotlight On The Jordanaires	1962	12.00	30.00
Capitol T-1559	(M)	To God Be The Glory	1961	8.00	20.00
Capitol ST-1559	(S)	To God Be The Glory	1961	10.00	25.00
Columbia CL-2214	(M)	This Land	1964	6.00	15.00
Columbia CS-9014	(S)	This Land	1964	8.00	20.00
Columbia CL-2458	(M)	Big Country Hits	1966	6.00	15.00
Columbia CS-9258	(S)	Big Country Hits	1966	8.00	20.00

JOSEFUS

Hookah 330	(S)	Dead Man	1969	80.00	200.00
Mainstream 6127	(S)	Josefus	1970	20.00	50.00

JOSEPH

Scepter 674	(S)	Stoned Age Man	1970	16.00	40.00

JOSHUA FOX

Tetragrammaton 125	(S)	Joshua Fox	1968	8.00	20.00

JOSIE & THE PUSSYCATS
Cheryl Ladd is the voice of Josie.

Capitol ST-665	(S)	Josie And The Pussycats	1970	60.00	150.00

JOURNEY

Columbia AS-914	(DJ)	Journey	1975	6.00	15.00
Columbia PCQ-33904	(Q)	Look Into The Future	1976	5.00	12.00
Columbia AS-1606	(DJ)	A Candid Conversation	197?	6.00	15.00
Columbia HC-46339	(S)	Departure (Half-speed master)	1981	7.00	20.00
Columbia HC-47408	(S)	Escape (Half-speed master)	1981	7.00	20.00
Columbia HC-4912	(S)	Infinity (Half-speed master)	1981	7.00	20.00
Columbia HC-47998	(S)	Dream After Dream (Half-speed master)	1982	7.00	20.00
Mobile Fidelity MFSL-144	(S)	Escape	1986	50.00	150.00

Label & Catalog #		Title	Year	VG+	NM

JOURNEYMEN, THE
The Journeymen are John Phillips, Scott McKenzie and Dick Weissman.

Capitol T-1629	(M)	The Journeymen	1961	12.00	30.00
Capitol ST-1629	(S)	The Journeymen	1961	16.00	40.00
Capitol T-1951	(M)	New Directions In Folk Music	1963	10.00	25.00
Capitol ST-1951	(S)	New Directions In Folk Music	1963	12.00	30.00

JOY

Paula LPS-2217	(S)	Thunderfoot	1972	6.00	15.00

JOY OF COOKING

Capitol ST-661	(S)	Joy Of Cooking	1970	6.00	15.00

JOYFUL NOISE

RCA Victor LSP-3963	(S)	Joyful Noise	1968	6.00	15.00

JOYOUS NOISE

Capitol SMAS-844	(S)	Joyous Noise	1971	6.00	15.00

JUDAS PRIEST

Columbia 9C9-39926	(S)	Great Vinyl And Concert Hits (Picture disc)	1984	4.00	10.00
Columbia AS-99-1543	(DJ)	Screaming For Vengeance (Picture disc)	1984	8.00	20.00
		(Mispressing plays Neil Diamond's "Heartlight" album.)			
Columbia AS-99-1543	(DJ)	Screaming For Vengeance (Picture disc)	1984	5.00	12.00

JUICY LUCY

Atco SD-33-325	(S)	Juicy Lucy	1970	6.00	15.00
Atco SD-33-345	(S)	Lie Back And Enjoy It	1970	6.00	15.00
Atco SD-33-367	(S)	Get A Whiff Of This	1971	6.00	15.00

JULIAN, DON

Amazon 1009	(M)	Greatest Oldies	1963	24.00	60.00

JULY

Epic BN-26416	(E)	July	1969	50.00	125.00

JUPITER

Jupiter 1005	(S)	Multiple Choice	1980	16.00	40.00

JUST IV

Liberty LRP-3340	(M)	First Twelve Sides	1964	6.00	15.00
Liberty LST-7340	(S)	First Twelve Sides	1964	8.00	20.00

JUST US
Just Us features former members of The Index.

Valord AR-2634	(S)	The U.S.A. From The Air	197?	40.00	100.00

JUSTICE, JIMMY

Kapp KL-1308	(M)	Justice For All	1964	10.00	25.00
Kapp KS-3308	(S)	Justice For All	1964	14.00	35.00

JUSTIS, BILL

Phillips Int. 1950	(M)	Cloud Nine	1959	200.00	400.00
Smash MGS-27021	(M)	Twelve Big Instrumental Hits	1962	6.00	15.00
Smash SRS-67021	(S)	Twelve Big Instrumental Hits	1962	8.00	20.00
Smash MGS-27030	(M)	Twelve More Big Instrumental Hits	1962	6.00	15.00
Smash SRS-67030	(S)	Twelve More Big Instrumental Hits	1962	8.00	20.00
Smash MGS-27036	(M)	Twelve Top Tunes	1963	6.00	15.00
Smash SRS-67036	(S)	Twelve Top Tunes	1963	8.00	20.00
Smash MGS-27043	(M)	Twelve Other Instrumental Hits	1964	6.00	15.00
Smash SRS-67043	(S)	Twelve Other Instrumental Hits	1964	8.00	20.00
Smash MGS-27047	(M)	Dixieland Folk Style	1964	6.00	15.00
Smash SRS-67047	(S)	Dixieland Folk Style	1964	8.00	20.00
Smash MGS-27065	(M)	More Instrumental Hits	1965	6.00	15.00
Smash SRS-67065	(S)	More Instrumental Hits	1965	8.00	20.00
Smash MGS-27077	(M)	A Taste Of Honey	1966	6.00	15.00
Smash SRS-67077	(S)	A Taste Of Honey	1966	8.00	20.00

K. O. BOSSY

Toga TSTLP-2003	(S)	K. O. Bossy	197?	12.00	30.00

K-DOE, ERNIE
Ernie K-Doe is a pseudonym for Ernest Kador.

Minit LP-0002	(M)	Mother-In-Law	1961	70.00	175.00
Janus JLS-3030	(S)	Ernie K-Doe	1971	6.00	15.00

KAHN, SAJID

Colgems COS-114	(S)	Sajid	1969	6.00	15.00

KAILUA, PRINCE, & THE TROPICAL ISLANDERS
Prince Kailua is a pseudonym for Roy Smeck.

Epic LN-24055	(M)	Hawaii's Greatest Hits	1963	6.00	15.00
Epic BN-26055	(S)	Hawaii's Greatest Hits	1963	8.00	20.00

KAK

Epic BN-26429	(S)	Kak	1969	60.00	150.00

KALABASH CORP., THE

Uncle Bill KB-3114	(S)	The Kalabash Corp.	197?	30.00	75.00

KALB, DANNY, & STEFAN GROSSMAN
Kalb and Grossman were former members of The Blues Project.

Cotillion SD-90007	(S)	Crosscurrents	1969	6.00	15.00

KALEIDOSCOPE

Epic LN-24304	(M)	Side Trips	1967	12.00	30.00
Epic BN-26304	(S)	Side Trips	1967	16.00	40.00
Epic LN-24333	(M)	Beacon From Mars	1967	16.00	40.00
Epic BN-26333	(S)	Beacon From Mars	1967	20.00	50.00
Epic BN-26467	(S)	Incredible Kaleidoscope	1969	10.00	25.00
Epic BN-26508	(S)	Bernice	1970	8.00	20.00
Pacific Arts 102	(S)	When Scopes Collide	1978	4.00	10.00

KALIN TWINS, THE

Decca DL-8812	(M)	The Kalin Twins	1959	40.00	100.00

KALLEN, KITTY
Refer to Ann-Margret / Kitty Kallen / Della Reese.

Mercury MG-25206 (10")	(M)	Pretty Kitty Kallen Sings	1955	20.00	50.00
Decca DL-8397	(M)	It's A Lonesome Old Town	1958	16.00	40.00
Vocalion VL-3679	(M)	Little Things Mean A Lot	1959	10.00	25.00
Columbia CL-1404	(M)	If I Give My Heart To You	1960	6.00	15.00
Columbia CS-8204	(S)	If I Give My Heart To You	1960	8.00	20.00
Columbia CL-1662	(M)	Honky Tonk Angel	1961	6.00	15.00
Columbia CS-8462	(S)	Honky Tonk Angel	1961	8.00	20.00
RCA Victor LPM-2640	(M)	My Coloring Book	1963	6.00	15.00
RCA Victor LSP-2640	(S)	My Coloring Book	1963	8.00	20.00

KAMMERZELL

Artco-Alpha 50-1209	(S)	Hot For Your Love	1979	30.00	75.00

KANGAROO
Kangaroo features Barbara Keith.

MGM SE-4586	(S)	Kangaroo	1968	6.00	20.00

TRIBAL VILLAGE ● DEC. 1969 ●
Toronto, Ontario

"...Bent Wind Is A Young Group With A Lot Of Potential And With Direction And Work, Will Make It..."

Goldmine **● DEC. 1983 ●**
Iola, Wisconsin

"...Goes To Show There's A Lot More To Canadian Music Than Just Neil Young & The Maple Leaf Forever..."

"...Many Well Written Songs Performed By Some Of The Best Musicians Ever To Record In This Vein..."

CANADIAN RECORDS ● 1987
● Montreal, Quebec

"...Bent Wind Made A Legendary Album That Has Become The Most Sought After Of All Canadian L.P.'s..."

The Bulletin Board September 27, 1991

The Fourth Line is..."YOU WILL by BENT WIND

Marty Roth's 2nd album is a great follow up to his 1st (**"SUSSEX"**) which goes for up to $4000 US in Europe. It's well considered to be in the top 5 Psychedelic records ever produced in Canada.

Goldmine, Iola, Wisconsin, 1991

The Top 100 Most Valuable Albums

27. THE BEATLES United Artists UAL-3366	(M)	**A Hard Day's Night** (White label promo)	*1964*	**$1,800.00**
28. THE BEATLES Vee Jay DXS-30	(S)	**The Beatles Vs. The Four Seasons** (2 LPs with poster)	*1964*	**$1,700.00**
29. THE PATRON SAINTS No label	(M)	**Fohhoh Bohob**	*1969*	*** $1,600.00**
30. BENT WIND Trend T-1015	(S)	**Sussex**	*196?*	*** $1,500.00**

Goldmine

BENT WIND Trend T-1015	(S)	**Sussex**	*196?*	*See note below*
		(Rare, Estimated near mint value $1,000-$2,000.)		

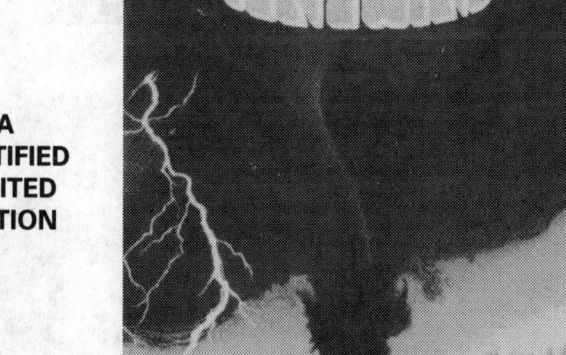

Seems like only a few years ago the psych collectors all but frowned on anything on a major label, but as more collectors began reaching a saturation point in their pursuit of the rarer—and far more expensive—private pressings, they did what all others do—expanded the parameters of acceptability. In the past few years quite a few such albums have jumped into the three figure range, including the highly sought-after Kak, shown here without the normally ubiquitous cut-out markings so many of these late '60s titles that didn't sell always have...

Label & Catalog #		Title	Year	VG+	NM
KANNIBAL KOMIX					
Colossus CS-1004	(S)	**Kannibal Komix**	1970	6.00	20.00
KANSAS					
Kirshner AS-555	(DJ)	**Two For The Show** (Album sampler)	1978	40.00	100.00
Kirshner HZ-44224	(S)	**Leftoverture** (Half-speed master)	1982	12.00	35.00
Kirshner HZ-44929	(S)	**Point Of Know Return** (Half-speed master)	1982	13.00	40.00
Kirshner JZ-44929	(DJ)	**Point Of Know Return** (Picture disc)	1982	20.00	50.00
Kirshner HZ-46008	(S)	**Monolith** (Half-speed master)	1982	16.00	50.00
Kirshner HZ-48002	(S)	**Vinyl Confessions** (Half-speed master)	1982	10.00	30.00
KANSAS CITY JAMMERS, THE					
(No label)	(S)	**Got Good (If You Get It)**	197?	20.00	50.00
KANTNER, PAUL, & THE JEFFERSON STARSHIP					
RCA Victor LSP-4448	(DJ)	**Blows Against The Empire** (Clear vinyl)	1970	100.00	250.00
RCA Victor LSP-4448	(S)	**Blows Against The Empire** (Orange label)	1970	6.00	15.00
KANTNER, PAUL, & GRACE SLICK					
Kantner and Slick are members of The Jefferson Airplane.					
Grunt FTR-1002	(S)	**Sunfighter** (With booklet)	1971	6.00	15.00
Grunt BXL1-0148	(S)	**Baron Von Tollbooth And The Chrome Nun**	1973	4.00	10.00
KARLOFF, BORIS					
Cricket CR-32	(M)	**Tales Of Mystery And Imagination**	1959	12.00	30.00
Mercury MG-20815	(M)	**Tales Of The Frightened, Volume 1**	1963	14.00	35.00
Mercury SR-60815	(S)	**Tales Of The Frightened, Volume 1**	1963	16.00	40.00
Mercury MG-20816	(M)	**Tales Of The Frightened, Volume 2**	1963	14.00	35.00
Mercury SR-60816	(S)	**Tales Of The Frightened, Volume 2**	1963	16.00	40.00
MGM E-901	(M)	**How The Grinch Stole Christmas** (TV Sdtk)	1966	10.00	25.00
MGM SE-901	(S)	**How The Grinch Stole Christmas** (TV Sdtk)	1966	14.00	35.00
Decca DL-4833	(M)	**An Evening With Karloff And His Friends**	1967	8.00	20.00
Decca DL-74833	(S)	**An Evening With Karloff And His Friends**	1967	10.00	25.00
KASENETZ-KATZ SUPER CIRCUS, THE					
Buddah BDS-5020	(S)	**The Kasenetz-Katz Super Circus**	1968	1.50	8.00
KATZ, FRED					
Warner Bros. W-1277	(M)	**Folk Songs For Far Out Folks**	1959	8.00	20.00
Warner Bros. WS-1277	(S)	**Folk Songs For Far Out Folks**	1959	10.00	25.00
KAUFMANN, BOB					
L.H.I. 12002	(S)	**Trip Through A Blown Mind**	1967	16.00	40.00
KAUKONEN, JORMA					
Refer to The Jefferson Airplane; The Jefferson Starship; Hot Tuna.					
Grunt BFL1-0209	(S)	**Quah**	1973	4.00	10.00
Relix 2027	(S)	**Quah** (Picture disc)	1987	4.00	10.00
KAY, JOHN, & SPARROW					
Sparrow as an early incarnation of Steppenwolf; the tracks on this album were recorded in 1966-67.					
Columbia CS-9758	(S)	**John Kay & Sparrow** ("360 Sound" label)	1970	8.00	20.00
KAYE, MARY					
Decca DL-8238	(M)	**The Mary Kaye Trio**	1956	12.00	30.00
Decca DL-8454	(M)	**Music On A Silver Platter**	1957	12.00	30.00
Decca DL-8650	(M)	**You Don't Know What Love Is**	1958	12.00	30.00
Warner Bros. W-1263	(M)	**Jackpot**	1959	8.00	20.00
Warner Bros. WS-1263	(S)	**Jackpot**	1959	10.00	25.00
KAYE, THOMAS JEFFERSON					
Dunhill DSX-50142	(S)	**First Grade**	1974	6.00	15.00
KEACK, ALEX					
Crown CLP-5315	(M)	**For Surfers Only/Surfer's Paradise**	1963	6.00	15.00
Crown CST-315	(S)	**For Surfers Only/Surfer's Paradise**	1963	8.00	20.00

Label & Catalog #		Title	Year	VG+	NM

KEEN, SPEEDY
Speedy was formerly a member of Thunderclap Newton.

Track/MCA 331	(S)	**Previous Convictions**	1973	6.00	15.00
Island ILPS-9338	(S)	**Y' Know Wot I Mean**	1975	4.00	10.00

KEITH

Mercury MG-21102	(M)	**98.6/Ain't Gonna Lie**	1967	6.00	15.00
Mercury SR-61102	(S)	**98.6/Ain't Gonna Lie**	1967	8.00	20.00
Mercury MG-21129	(M)	**Out Of Crank**	1967	6.00	15.00
Mercury SR-61129	(S)	**Out Of Crank**	1967	8.00	20.00
RCA Victor LSP-4143	(S)	**The Adventures Of Keith**	1969	6.00	15.00

KEITH, BARBARA
Ms. Keith also recorded with Kangaroo.

Verve/Forecast FTS-3062	(S)	**Barbara Keith**	1970	8.00	20.00
Warner Bros. MS-2087	(S)	**Barbara Keith**	1972	20.00	50.00

KEITH & ROONEY

Folklore FRLP-14002	(M)	**Living On The Mountain**	1964	8.00	20.00
Folklore FRST-14002	(S)	**Living On The Mountain**	1964	10.00	25.00

KELLER, JERRY

Kapp KL-1178	(M)	**Here Comes Jerry Keller**	1960	14.00	35.00
Kapp KS-3178	(S)	**Here Comes Jerry Keller**	1960	20.00	50.00

KELLY, BEVERLY: *Refer to* GOLDMINE'S PRICE GUIDE TO COLLECTIBLE JAZZ ALBUMS

KELLY, PAUL

Happy Tiger 1015	(S)	**Stealing In The Name Of The Lord**	1970	6.00	15.00

KELTNER, JIM, & RON TUTT

Sheffield Lab	(S)	**The Sheffield Drum Record** *(Direct-to-disc)*	198?	10.00	30.00

KENNEDY, JERRY
Refer to Tom & Jerry.

Smash MGS-27004	(M)	**Dancing Guitars Rock Elvis' Hits**	1962	12.00	30.00
Smash SRS-67004	(S)	**Dancing Guitars Rock Elvis' Hits**	1962	16.00	40.00
Smash MGS-27024	(M)	**The Golden Standards**	1963	10.00	25.00
Smash SRS-67024	(S)	**The Golden Standards**	1963	12.00	30.00
Smash MGS-27066	(M)	**From Nashville To Soulville**	1965	10.00	25.00
Smash SRS-67066	(S)	**From Nashville To Soulville**	1965	12.00	30.00

KENNEDY, MIKE
Mike Kennedy was formerly a member of Los Bravos.

ABC X-754	(S)	**Louisiana**	1972	6.00	15.00

KENNEY, BEVERLY

Roost 2206	(M)	**Beverly Kenney Sings For Jimmy Smith**	1956	16.00	40.00
Roost 2212	(M)	**Come Swing With Me**	1956	16.00	40.00
Roost 2218	(M)	**Beverly Kenney With Jimmy Jones**			
		And The Basie-Ites	1956	16.00	40.00
Decca DL-8743	(M)	**Beverly Kenney Sings For Playboys**	1958	12.00	30.00
Decca DL-8850	(M)	**Born To Be Blue**	1959	12.00	30.00
Decca DL-8948	(M)	**Like Yesterday**	1959	12.00	30.00
Decca DL-78948	(S)	**Like Yesterday**	1959	16.00	40.00

KENNY & THE KASUALS

Mark LP-5000	(M)	**The Impact Sound Of Kenny & The Kasuals**			
		Live At The Studio Club	1966	300.00	500.00
Mark LP-5000	(M)	**The Impact Sound Of Kenny & The Kasuals**			
		Live At The Studio Club	1977	20.00	50.00
Mark LP-6000	(M)	**Teen Dreams** *(Red vinyl)*	1978	100.00	250.00
		(Mark 6000 is a signed, numbered edition of 200 copies.)			
Mark LP-7000	(S)	**Garage Kings**	1979	20.00	50.00

KENTUCKY COLONELS, THE
The Colonels feature Clarence White, later of The Byrds.

World Pacific T-1821	(M)	**Appalachian Swing**	1964	16.00	40.00
World Pacific ST-1821	(S)	**Appalachian Swing**	1964	20.00	50.00

Label & Catalog #		Title	Year	VG+	NM

KEROUAC, JACK

Dot DLP-3154	(M)	Poetry For The Beat Generation	1959	See note below	
		(Pressed in minute quantities and then deleted. A copy in collectible condition has a suggested value of $2,000-5,000.)			
Hanover HML-5000	(M)	Poetry For The Beat Generation	1959	150.00	300.00
Hanover HML-5006	(M)	Blues And Haikus	1959	150.00	300.00
Verve MGV-15005	(M)	Readings On The Beat Generation	1959	100.00	250.00

KESEY, KEN

| Sound City 27690 | (M) | The Acid Test (With the Grateful Dead) | 1967 | 150.00 | 300.00 |

KEYMEN, THE

| ABC-Paramount 258 | (M) | Dance With Dick Clark | 1958 | 12.00 | 30.00 |
| ABC-Paramount S-258 | (S) | Dance With Dick Clark | 1958 | 16.00 | 40.00 |

KEYMEN, THE

| Goldust LPS-153 | (S) | The Keymen Live | 196? | 20.00 | 50.00 |

KICKSTANDS, THE
The Kickstands are a creation of Gary Usher & Co.

| Capitol T-2078 | (M) | Black Boots And Bikes | 1964 | 20.00 | 50.00 |
| Capitol ST-2078 | (S) | Black Boots And Bikes | 1964 | 30.00 | 75.00 |

KILGORE, MERLE

| Starday SLP-251 | (M) | There's Gold In Them Thar Hills | 196? | 12.00 | 30.00 |
| Wing MGW-12316 | (M) | The Tall Man | 196? | 8.00 | 20.00 |

KILLING FLOOR
Killing Floor features Rory Gallagher.

| Sire SES-97019 | (S) | Killing Floor | 1970 | 20.00 | 50.00 |

KING, ALBERT

King 852	(M)	Big Blues	1963	100.00	250.00
Stax ST-723	(M)	Born Under A Bad Sign	1967	14.00	35.00
Stax STS-723	(S)	Born Under A Bad Sign	1967	20.00	50.00
Stax STS-2003	(S)	Live Wire/Blues Power	1968	8.00	20.00
King KS-1060	(S)	Travelin' To California	1969	8.00	20.00
Atlantic SD-8213	(S)	King Of The Blues Guitar	1969	8.00	20.00
Stax STS-2010	(S)	Years Gone By	1969	6.00	15.00
Stax STS-2015	(S)	King Does The King's Thing	1969	8.00	20.00
Stax STS-2040	(S)	Love Joy	1971	6.00	15.00
Stax STS-3009	(S)	I'll Play The Blues For You	1972	5.00	12.00
Stax 5505	(S)	I Wanna Get Funky	1974	5.00	12.00

KING, ALBERT, & OTIS RUSH

| Chess LPS-1538 | (S) | Door To Door | 1969 | 10.00 | 25.00 |

KING, ANNA

| Smash MGS-27059 | (M) | Back To Soul (Produced by James Brown) | 1964 | 10.00 | 25.00 |
| Smash SRS-67059 | (S) | Back To Soul (Produced by James Brown) | 1964 | 12.00 | 30.00 |

KING, B. B.
Refer to Bobby Bland / B. B. King.

Crown CLP-5020	(M)	Singin' The Blues	1960	12.00	30.00
Crown CLP-5063	(M)	The Blues	1960	12.00	30.00
Crown CLP-5115	(M)	B. B. King Wails	1960	12.00	30.00
Crown CST-147	(E)	B. B. King Wails	1960	4.00	10.00
Crown CST-147	(E)	B. B. King Wails (Red vinyl)	1960	30.00	75.00
Crown CLP-5119	(M)	B. B. King Sings Spirituals	1960	12.00	30.00
Crown CST-152	(M)	B. B. King Sings Spirituals	1960	4.00	10.00
Crown CST-152	(M)	B. B. King Sings Spirituals (Red vinyl)	1960	30.00	75.00
Crown CLP-5143	(M)	The Great B. B. King	1961	12.00	30.00
Crown CLP-5167	(M)	King Of The Blues	1961	12.00	30.00
Crown CST-195	(E)	King Of The Blues	1961	4.00	10.00
Crown CST-195	(E)	King Of The Blues (Red vinyl)	1961	30.00	75.00
Crown CLP-5188	(M)	My Kind Of Blues	1961	12.00	30.00
Crown CLP-5230	(M)	More B. B. King	1962	12.00	30.00
Crown CLP-5248	(M)	Twist With B. B. King	1962	12.00	30.00
Crown CLP-5286	(M)	Easy Listening Blues	1962	12.00	30.00

Label & Catalog #		Title	Year	VG+	NM
Crown CLP-5309	(M)	Blues In My Heart	1962	12.00	30.00
Crown CST-309	(E)	Blues In My Heart	1962	4.00	10.00
Crown CLP-5359	(M)	B. B. King	1963	12.00	30.00
Crown CST-359	(E)	B. B. King	1963	4.00	10.00
Galaxy 202	(M)	The Best Of B. B. King	1963	10.00	25.00
Galaxy 8202	(S)	The Best Of B. B. King	1963	10.00	25.00
ABC-Paramount 456	(M)	Mr. Blues	1963	10.00	25.00
ABC-Paramount S-456	(S)	Mr. Blues	1963	12.00	30.00
ABC-Paramount 509	(M)	Live At The Regal	1965	16.00	40.00
ABC-Paramount S-509	(S)	Live At The Regal	1965	20.00	50.00
ABC-Paramount 528	(M)	Confessin' The Blues	1965	10.00	25.00
ABC-Paramount S-528	(S)	Confessin' The Blues	1965	12.00	30.00
Kent KLP-5012	(M)	Rock Me Baby	1964	5.00	12.00
Kent KST-512	(S)	Rock Me Baby	1964	6.00	15.00
Kent KLP-5013	(M)	Let Me Love You	1965	5.00	12.00
Kent KST-513	(S)	Let Me Love You	1965	6.00	15.00
Kent KLP-5015	(M)	B. B. King Live On Stage	1965	5.00	12.00
Kent KST-515	(S)	B. B. King Live On Stage	1965	6.00	15.00
Kent KLP-5016	(M)	The Soul Of B. B. King	1966	5.00	12.00
Kent KST-516	(S)	The Soul Of B. B. King	1966	6.00	15.00
Kent KST-517	(S)	Pure Soul	1966	6.00	15.00
Kent KLP-5021	(M)	The Jungle	1967	5.00	12.00
Kent KST-521	(S)	The Jungle	1967	6.00	15.00
Kent KLP-5029	(M)	Boss Of The Blues	1968	5.00	12.00
Kent KST-529	(S)	Boss Of The Blues	1968	6.00	15.00
Kent KST-533	(S)	From The Beginning	1969	4.00	10.00
Kent KST-535	(S)	Underground Blues	1969	4.00	10.00
Kent KST-539	(S)	The Incredible Soul Of B. B. King	1970	4.00	10.00
Kent KST-548	(S)	Turn On With B. B. King	1971	4.00	10.00
Kent KST-552	(S)	Greatest Hits, Volume 1	1971	4.00	10.00
Kent KST-561	(S)	Better Than Ever	1971	4.00	10.00
Kent KST-563	(S)	Doing My Thing, Lord	1971	4.00	10.00
Kent KST-565	(S)	B. B. King Live	1972	4.00	10.00
Kent KST-568	(S)	The Original Sweet Sixteen	1972	4.00	10.00
Kent 9011	(S)	B. B. King Anthology	197?	4.00	10.00
Custom CM-2049	(M)	I Love You So	196?	4.00	10.00
Custom CM-2046	(M)	Blues For Me	196?	4.00	10.00
Custom CM-2052	(M)	The Soul Of B. B. King	196?	4.00	10.00
BluesWay BL-6001	(S)	Blues Is King	1967	8.00	20.00
BluesWay BLS-6001	(S)	Blues Is King	1967	8.00	20.00
BluesWay BLS-6011	(S)	Blues On Top Of Blues	1968	8.00	20.00
BluesWay BLS-6016	(S)	Lucille	1968	8.00	20.00
BluesWay BLS-6022	(S)	His Best/The Electric B. B. King	1968	6.00	15.00
BluesWay BLS-6031	(S)	Live And Well	1969	6.00	15.00
BluesWay BLS-6037	(S)	Completely Well	1969	6.00	15.00
BluesWay BLS-6050	(S)	Back In The Alley	1970	6.00	15.00
ABC D-713	(S)	Indianola Mississippi Seeds	1970	6.00	15.00
ABC D-723	(S)	Live In Cook County Jail	1971	6.00	15.00
ABC D-724	(S)	Live At The Regal	1971	6.00	15.00
		(ABC 724 is a reissue of ABC-Paramount 509.)			
ABC D-730	(S)	B. B. King In London	1971	6.00	15.00
ABC D-743	(S)	L. A. Midnight	1972	6.00	15.00
ABC X-759	(S)	Guess Who?	1972	6.00	15.00
ABC X-767	(S)	B. B. King's Greatest Hits	1973	4.00	10.00
ABC D-794	(S)	To Know You Is To Love You	1973	4.00	10.00
ABC D-825	(S)	Friends	1974	4.00	10.00
ABC D-898	(S)	Lucille Talks Back	1975	4.00	10.00
ABC D-977	(S)	King Size	1977	4.00	10.00
ABC D-1061	(S)	Midnight Believer	1978	4.00	10.00
Direct Disk SD-16616	(S)	Midnight Believer	1980	10.00	30.00

KING, BEN E.
Ben E. King was formerly a member of The Drifters.

Atco SD-33-133	(M)	Spanish Harlem	1961	30.00	75.00
Atco SD-33-133	(S)	Spanish Harlem	1961	40.00	100.00
		— Original Atco albums above have yellow "harp" labels. —			
Atco SD-33-137	(M)	Ben E. King Sings For Soulful Lovers	1962	16.00	40.00
Atco SD-33-137	(S)	Ben E. King Sings For Soulful Lovers	1962	20.00	50.00

Label & Catalog #		Title	Year	VG+	NM
Atco SD-33-142	(M)	Don't Play That Song	1962	16.00	40.00
Atco SD-33-142	(S)	Don't Play That Song	1962	20.00	50.00
Atco SD-33-165	(M)	Ben E. King's Greatest Hits	1964	12.00	30.00
Atco SD-33-165	(S)	Ben E. King's Greatest Hits	1964	16.00	40.00
Atco SD-33-174	(M)	Seven Letters	1965	12.00	30.00
Atco SD-33-174	(S)	Seven Letters	1965	16.00	40.00

KING, CAROLE
Refer to City; The Cookies / Little Eva / Carole King.

Ode S-88013	(S)	Carole King Music *(Textured cover)*	1973	5.00	12.00
Ode SQ-88013	(Q)	Carole King Music	1974	8.00	20.00
Epic/Ode HE-44946	(S)	Tapestry *(Half-speed master)*	1980	25.00	75.00

KING, CLAUDE

Columbia CL-1810	(M)	Meet Claude King	1962	10.00	25.00
Columbia CS-8610	(S)	Meet Claude King	1962	16.00	40.00

— Original Columbia albums above have six eye logos around the perimeter of the label.—

Columbia CL-2415	(M)	Tiger Woman	1965	8.00	20.00
Columbia CS-9215	(S)	Tiger Woman	1965	10.00	25.00

KING, FREDDIE

King 762	(M)	Freddie King Sings The Blues	1961	40.00	100.00
King 773	(M)	Let's Hide Away And Dance Away	1961	40.00	100.00
King 821	(M)	Bossa Nova And Blues	1962	40.00	100.00
King 856	(M)	Freddie King Goes Surfin'	1963	20.00	50.00
King 856	(S)	Freddie King Goes Surfin'	1963	30.00	75.00
King 928	(M)	A Bonanza Of Instrumentals	1965	14.00	35.00
King 928	(S)	A Bonanza Of Instrumentals	1965	20.00	50.00
King 964	(M)	24 Vocals And Instrumentals	1966	10.00	25.00
King KS-1059	(S)	Hide Away	1969	6.00	15.00
Cotillion SD-9004	(S)	Freddie King Is A Blues Master	1969	5.00	12.00
Cotillion SD-9016	(S)	My Feeling For The Blues	1970	5.00	12.00
Shelter SW-8905	(S)	Getting Ready	1971	5.00	12.00
Shelter SW-8913	(S)	Texas Cannonball	1972	5.00	12.00
Shelter SW-8919	(S)	Woman Across The River	1973	5.00	12.00

KING, FREDDIE, & LULA REED & SONNY THOMPSON

King 777	(M)	Boy-Girl-Boy	1962	40.00	100.00

KING, JONATHAN

Parrot PA-61013	(M)	Or Then Again	1967	16.00	40.00
Parrot PAS-71013	(S)	Or Then Again	1967	20.00	50.00

("Where The Sun Has Never Shown" is rechanneled on this album.)

UK S-53101	(S)	Bubble Rock Is Here To Stay	1972	8.00	20.00
UK S-53104	(S)	Pandora's Box	1973	8.00	20.00

KING, MORGANA

EmArcy MG-36079	(M)	For You, For Me, Forever More	1956	30.00	75.00
Mercury MG-20231	(M)	Morgana King Sings The Blues	1958	20.00	50.00
Camden CAL-543	(M)	The Greatest Songs Ever Swung	1959	10.00	25.00
United Arts. UAL-3020	(M)	Let Me Love You	1960	12.00	30.00
United Arts. UAS-6020	(S)	Let Me Love You	1960	16.00	40.00
United Arts. UAL-3028	(M)	Folk Songs Ala King	1960	12.00	30.00
United Arts. UAS-6028	(S)	Folk Songs Ala King	1960	16.00	40.00
Ascot ALM-13014	(M)	The Winter Of My Discontent	1965	10.00	25.00
Ascot ALS-16014	(S)	The Winter Of My Discontent	1965	12.00	30.00
Ascot ALM-13019	(M)	The End Of A Love Affair	1965	10.00	25.00
Ascot ALS-16019	(S)	The End Of A Love Affair	1965	12.00	30.00
Ascot ALM-13020	(M)	Everybody Loves Saturday Night	1965	10.00	25.00
Ascot ALS-16020	(S)	Everybody Loves Saturday Night	1965	12.00	30.00
Reprise R-6205	(M)	Wild Is Love	1966	8.00	20.00
Reprise RS-6205	(S)	Wild Is Love	1966	10.00	25.00
Reprise R-6257	(M)	Gemini Changes	1967	8.00	20.00
Reprise RS-6257	(S)	Gemini Changes	1967	8.00	20.00
Verve V-5061	(M)	I Know How It Feels	1968	8.00	20.00
Verve V6-5061	(S)	I Know How It Feels	1968	8.00	20.00

Label & Catalog #		Title	Year	VG+	NM
KING, PEE WEE					
RCA Victor LPM-3028 (10")	(M)	Pee Wee King	1954	40.00	100.00
RCA Victor LPM-3071 (10")	(M)	Western Hits	1954	40.00	100.00
RCA Victor LPM-3109 (10")	(M)	Waltzes	1955	40.00	100.00
RCA Victor LPM-3280 (10")	(M)	Swing West	1955	40.00	100.00
RCA Victor LPM-1237	(M)	Swing West	1955	20.00	50.00
Longhorn 1236	(M)	The Legendary Pee Wee King	1967	10.00	25.00
KING, PEGGY					
Columbia CL-2549 (10")	(M)	Wish Upon A Star	1955	14.00	35.00
Columbia CL-713	(M)	Girl Meets Boy	1955	10.00	25.00
Imperial LP-9026	(M)	Peggy King	1959	8.00	20.00
Imperial LP-12026	(S)	Peggy King	1959	12.00	30.00

KING, TEDDI: *Refer to* GOLDMINE'S PRICE GUIDE TO COLLECTIBLE JAZZ ALBUMS

KING, TYLER, & THE TWISTEENS					
Startime TW-100	(M)	Twistin' Time	1961	8.00	20.00
KING CRIMSON					

King Crimson features Robert Fripp.

Label & Catalog #		Title	Year	VG+	NM
Atlantic SD-8245	(S)	In The Court Of The Crimson King	1969	6.00	15.00
Atlantic SD-8266	(S)	In The Wake Of Poseidon	1970	6.00	15.00
Atlantic SD-8278	(S)	Lizard	1971	6.00	15.00
Atlantic SD-7212	(S)	Islands	1972	6.00	15.00

—Atlantic albums above have green & orange labels with a Broadway address on the bottom.—

Mobile Fidelity MFSL-075	(S)	In The Court Of The Crimson King	1980	20.00	60.00
KING CURTIS					
Atco 33-113	(M)	Have Tenor Sax, Will Blow	1959	30.00	75.00
Atco SD-33-113	(S)	Have Tenor Sax, Will Blow	1959	40.00	100.00
New Jazz NJLP-8237	(M)	The New Scene Of King Curtis	1960	30.00	75.00
Prestige PRLP-7222	(M)	Soul Meeting	1962	20.00	50.00
Prestige PRST-7222	(S)	Soul Meeting	1962	30.00	75.00
Everest LPBR-5121	(M)	Azure	1961	20.00	50.00
Everest SDBR-1121	(S)	Azure	1961	30.00	75.00
Tru-Sound TS-15001	(M)	Trouble In Mind	1961	20.00	50.00
Tru-Sound STS-15001	(S)	Trouble In Mind	1961	30.00	75.00
Tru-Sound TS-15009	(M)	Doin' The Dixie Twist	1962	20.00	50.00
Tru-Sound STS-15009	(S)	Doin' The Dixie Twist	1962	30.00	75.00
Tru-Sound TS-15008	(M)	It's Party Time	1962	20.00	50.00
Tru-Sound STS-15008	(S)	It's Party Time	1962	30.00	75.00
RCA Victor LPM-2492	(M)	Arthur Murray's Music For Dancing: The Twist!	1962	10.00	25.00
RCA Victor LSM-2492	(S)	Arthur Murray's Music For Dancing: The Twist!	1962	12.00	30.00
Capitol T-1756	(M)	Country Soul	1963	12.00	30.00
Capitol ST-1756	(S)	Country Soul	1963	16.00	40.00
Capitol T-2095	(M)	Soul Serenade	1964	12.00	30.00
Capitol ST-2095	(S)	Soul Serenade	1964	16.00	40.00
Capitol T-2341	(M)	Hits Made Famous By Sam Cooke	1965	12.00	30.00
Capitol ST-2341	(S)	Hits Made Famous By Sam Cooke	1965	16.00	40.00
Capitol ST-2858	(S)	The Best Of King Curtis	1968	10.00	25.00
Atco 33-189	(M)	That Lovin' Feeling	1966	10.00	25.00
Atco SD-33-189	(S)	That Lovin' Feeling	1966	12.00	30.00
Atco 33-198	(M)	Live At Small's Paradise	1966	10.00	25.00
Atco SD-33-198	(S)	Live At Small's Paradise	1966	12.00	30.00
Atco 33-211	(M)	The Great Memphis Hits	1967	10.00	25.00
Atco SD-33-211	(S)	The Great Memphis Hits	1967	12.00	30.00
Atco 33-231	(M)	King Size Soul	1967	10.00	25.00
Atco SD-33-231	(S)	King Size Soul	1967	12.00	30.00
Atco SD-33-247	(S)	Sweet Soul	1968	8.00	20.00
Atco SD-33-266	(S)	The Best Of King Curtis	1968	8.00	20.00
Atco SD-33-293	(S)	Instant Groove	1969	8.00	20.00
Atco SD-33-338	(S)	Get Ready	1970	8.00	20.00
Atco SD-33-359	(S)	Live At Fillmore West	1971	6.00	15.00
Atco SD-33-385	(S)	Everybody's Talkin'	1972	6.00	15.00
Prestige PRST-7709	(S)	The Best Of King Curtis	1969	8.00	20.00

(Prestige 7709 reissues Tru-Sound material.)

Label & Catalog #		Title	Year	VG+	NM
Prestige PRST-7789	(S)	Soul	1969	8.00	20.00
Prestige PRST-7833	(S)	Soul Meeting	1969	8.00	20.00
		(Prestige 7833 is a reissue of 7222.)			
Prestige PRST-8237	(S)	The New Scene	1969	8.00	20.00

KING PINS, THE

King 865	(M)	It Won't Be This Way Always	1963	50.00	125.00

KING HANNIBAL

Aware 1001	(S)	Truth	1973	6.00	20.00

KING'S HENCHMEN, THE: *Refer to ALAN FREED*

KINGDOM

Specialty 2135	(S)	Kingdom	1970	40.00	100.00

KINGFISH
Kingfish features Bob Weir of The Grateful Dead.

Round RX-108	(S)	Kingfish	1976	6.00	15.00
Jet LA732-G	(S)	Live 'N' Kickin'	1977	4.00	10.00

KINGSMEN, THE

Wand WD-657	(M)	The Kingsmen In Person	1964	8.00	20.00
Wand WDS-657	(P)	The Kingsmen In Person	1964	10.00	25.00
Wand WD-659	(M)	More Great Sounds	1964	8.00	20.00
Wand WDS-659	(S)	More Great Sounds	1964	10.00	25.00
		(Originally issued with "Death Of An Angel")			
Wand WD-659	(M)	More Great Sounds	1964	6.00	15.00
Wand WDS-659	(S)	More Great Sounds	196?	8.00	20.00
		("Death Of An Angel" replaced by an uncredited instrumental)			
Wand WD-662	(M)	The Kingsmen, Volume 3	1965	6.00	15.00
Wand WDS-662	(S)	The Kingsmen, Volume 3	1965	8.00	20.00
Wand WD-670	(M)	The Kingsmen On Campus	1965	6.00	15.00
Wand WDS-670	(S)	The Kingsmen On Campus	1965	8.00	20.00
Wand WD-674	(M)	15 Great Hits	1966	6.00	15.00
Wand WDS-674	(P)	15 Great Hits	1966	8.00	20.00
Wand WD-675	(M)	Up And Away	1966	6.00	15.00
Wand WDS-675	(S)	Up And Away	1966	8.00	20.00
Wand WD-681	(M)	The Kingsmen's Greatest Hits	1967	5.00	12.00
Wand WDS-681	(P)	The Kingsmen's Greatest Hits	1967	6.00	15.00

KINGSTON TRIO, THE
Members include Bob Shane, Nick Reynolds and Dave Guard, later replaced by John Stewart.

Capitol T-996	(M)	The Kingston Trio	1958	20.00	50.00
		—Original Capitol albums above have turquoise labels.—			
Capitol T-996	(M)	The Kingston Trio	1958	14.00	35.00
Capitol T-1107	(M)	From The Hungry i	1959	14.00	35.00
Capitol ST-1183	(S)	Stereo Concert	1959	16.00	40.00
Capitol T-1199	(M)	The Kingston Trio At Large	1959	10.00	25.00
Capitol ST-1199	(S)	The Kingston Trio At Large	1959	14.00	35.00
Capitol T-1258	(M)	Here We Go Again	1959	10.00	25.00
Capitol ST-1258	(S)	Here We Go Again	1959	14.00	35.00
Capitol T-1352	(M)	Sold Out	1960	10.00	25.00
Capitol ST-1352	(S)	Sold Out	1960	14.00	35.00
Capitol T-1407	(M)	String Along	1960	10.00	25.00
Capitol ST-1407	(S)	String Along	1960	14.00	35.00
Capitol T-1446	(M)	The Last Month Of The Year	1960	10.00	25.00
Capitol ST-1446	(S)	The Last Month Of The Year	1960	14.00	35.00
Capitol T-1474	(M)	Make Way!	1961	10.00	25.00
Capitol ST-1474	(S)	Make Way!	1961	14.00	35.00
Capitol T-1564	(M)	Goin' Places	1961	10.00	25.00
Capitol ST-1564	(S)	Goin' Places	1961	14.00	35.00
Capitol T-1612	(M)	Encores	1961	10.00	25.00
Capitol DT-1612	(E)	Encores	1961	8.00	20.00
Capitol T-1642	(M)	Close Up	1961	10.00	25.00
Capitol ST-1642	(S)	Close Up	1961	14.00	35.00
		—Original Capitol albums above have black labels with the logo on the left side.—			
Capitol T-1658	(M)	College Concert	1962	8.00	20.00
Capitol ST-1658	(S)	College Concert	1962	10.00	25.00

Label & Catalog #		Title	Year	VG+	NM
Capitol T-1705	(M)	Best Of The Kingston Trio	1962	6.00	15.00
Capitol ST-1705	(S)	Best Of The Kingston Trio	1962	8.00	20.00
Capitol T-1747	(M)	Something Special	1962	8.00	20.00
Capitol ST-1747	(S)	Something Special	1962	10.00	25.00
Capitol T-1809	(M)	New Frontier	1962	8.00	20.00
Capitol ST-1809	(S)	New Frontier	1962	10.00	25.00
Capitol T-1871	(M)	Kingston Trio #16	1963	8.00	20.00
Capitol ST-1871	(S)	Kingston Trio #16	1963	10.00	25.00
Capitol T-1935	(M)	Sunny Side!	1963	8.00	20.00
Capitol ST-1935	(S)	Sunny Side!	1963	10.00	25.00
Capitol T-2011	(M)	Time To Think	1963	10.00	25.00
Capitol ST-2011	(S)	Time To Think	1963	12.00	30.00
Capitol T-2081	(M)	Back In Town	1964	8.00	20.00
Capitol ST-2081	(S)	Back In Town	1964	10.00	25.00
Capitol TCL-2180	(M)	The Folk Era (3 LPs with booklet)	1964	16.00	40.00
Capitol STCL-2180	(S)	The Folk Era (3 LPs with booklet)	1964	20.00	50.00
Capitol T-2280	(M)	Best Of The Kingston Trio, Volume 2	1965	6.00	15.00
Capitol ST-2280	(S)	Best Of The Kingston Trio, Volume 2	1965	8.00	20.00
Capitol T-2614	(M)	Best Of The Kingston Trio, Volume 3	1966	6.00	15.00
Capitol ST-2614	(S)	Best Of The Kingston Trio, Volume 3	1966	8.00	20.00
— Original Capitol albums above have black labels with the logo on top.—					
Capitol DT-996	(E)	The Kingston Trio	1969	6.00	15.00
Decca DL-4613	(M)	The Kingston Trio: Nick-Bob-John	1965	12.00	30.00
Decca DL-74613	(S)	The Kingston Trio: Nick-Bob-John	1965	14.00	35.00
Decca DL-4656	(M)	Stay Awhile	1965	12.00	30.00
Decca DL-74656	(S)	Stay Awhile	1965	14.00	35.00
Decca DL-4694	(M)	Somethin' Else	1965	12.00	30.00
Decca DL-74694	(S)	Somethin' Else	1965	14.00	35.00
Decca DL-4758	(M)	Children In The Morning	1966	14.00	35.00
Decca DL-74758	(S)	Children In The Morning	1966	16.00	40.00
Tetragrammaton 5101	(S)	Once Upon A Time	1969	10.00	25.00
Longines SYS-5507	(P)	The World Needs A Melody	1973	8.00	20.00
Longines SYS-5569-5574	(P)	American Gold (6 LPs)	1973	20.00	50.00
Nautilus NR-2	(S)	Aspen Gold	1979	7.00	20.00

KINKS, THE

The original Kinks were Ray and Dave Davies, Mick Avory and Pete Quaife, replaced by John Dalton in '66.

Label & Catalog #		Title	Year	VG+	NM
Reprise R-6143	(M)	You Really Got Me	1965	16.00	40.00
Reprise RS-6143	(S)	You Really Got Me	1965	20.00	50.00
Reprise R-6158	(M)	Kinks Size	1965	20.00	50.00
Reprise RS-6158	(E)	Kinks Size	1965	16.00	40.00
Reprise R-6173	(M)	Kinda Kinks	1965	20.00	50.00
Reprise RS-6173	(E)	Kinda Kinks	1965	16.00	40.00
Reprise R-6184	(M)	Kinks' Kinkdom	1965	20.00	50.00
Reprise RS-6184	(E)	Kinks' Kinkdom	1965	16.00	40.00
Reprise R-6197	(M)	Kink Kontroversy	1966	16.00	40.00
Reprise RS-6197	(E)	Kink Kontroversy	1966	14.00	35.00
Reprise R-6217	(M)	The Kinks' Greatest Hits	1966	10.00	25.00
Reprise RS-6217	(E)	The Kinks' Greatest Hits	1966	8.00	20.00
Reprise R-6228	(M)	Face To Face	1967	12.00	30.00
Reprise RS-6228	(P)	Face To Face	1967	10.00	25.00
Reprise R-6260	(M)	Live Kinks	1967	12.00	30.00
Reprise RS-6260	(S)	Live Kinks	1967	10.00	25.00
Reprise R-6279	(M)	Something Else By The Kinks	1968	60.00	150.00
Reprise RS-6279	(S)	Something Else By The Kinks	1968	10.00	25.00
Reprise RS-6327	(S)	The Village Green Preservation Society	1969	10.00	25.00
Reprise RS-6366	(S)	Arthur	1969	10.00	25.00
— Original Reprise albums above have multi-color labels.—					
Reprise RS-6143	(P)	You Really Got Me	1969	5.00	12.00
Reprise RS-6217	(E)	The Kinks' Greatest Hits	1969	5.00	12.00
Reprise RS-6228	(E)	Face To Face	1969	5.00	12.00
Reprise RS-6260	(S)	Live Kinks	1969	5.00	12.00
Reprise RS-6279	(S)	Something Else By The Kinks	1969	5.00	12.00
Reprise RS-6327	(S)	The Village Green Preservation Society	1969	5.00	12.00
Reprise RS-6366	(S)	Arthur	1969	5.00	12.00
Reprise RS-6423	(S)	Lola Vs. The Powerman	1969	5.00	12.00
Reprise RS-6454	(P)	The Kink Kronikles (2 LPs)	1972	5.00	12.00
Reprise MS-2127	(P)	The Great Lost Kinks Album	1973	20.00	50.00
— Reprise albums above have brown labels.—					

Label & Catalog #		Title	Year	VG+	NM
RCA Victor LSP-4644	(S)	**Muswell Hillbillies**	1971	10.00	25.00
RCA Victor VPS-6065	(S)	**Everybody's In Show Biz** (2 LPs)	1972	6.00	15.00
RCA Victor LPL1-5002	(S)	**Preservation, Act 1**	1973	5.00	12.00
RCA Victor CPL2-5040	(S)	**Preservation, Act 2** (2 LPs)	1974	6.00	15.00
RCA Victor APL1-5081	(S)	**Soap Opera**	1975	5.00	12.00
		— Original RCA albums above orange labels.—			
Pye 505	(M)	**The History Of British Pop Music**	1975	4.00	10.00
Pye 509	(M)	**The History Of British Pop Music, Volume 2**	1976	4.00	10.00
Mobile Fidelity MFSL-070	(S)	**Misfits**	1981	5.00	15.00
		—Special/Promotional Releases—			
Reprise PRO-328	(P)	**God Save The Kinks Box**	1969	200.00	400.00
		(Boxed set includes a postcard, a decal, a bag of grass, a Unio Jack pin, a letter, Kinks consumer guide, a "God Save The Kinks" button and an album, also priced separately below.)			
Reprise PRO-328	(P)	**Then, Now And In Between**	1969	20.00	50.00
		(Issued as part of the "God Save The Kinks" box above.)			
Arista SP-69	(S)	**Low Budget Radio Interview**	1979	16.00	40.00
MCA 17281	(S)	**A Look At "Think Visual"** (Plain jacket)	1986	16.00	40.00

KIRBY STONE FOUR, THE

Label & Catalog #		Title	Year	VG+	NM
Columbia CL-1211	(M)	**Baubles, Bangles And Beads**	1958	10.00	25.00
Columbia CL-1297	(M)	**The Go Sound Of The Kirny Stone Four**	1959	10.00	25.00
Tops L-1582	(M)	**The Kirby Stone Four**	1959	8.00	20.00

KISS

The original Kiss consisted of Peter Criss, Ace Freheye, Gene Simmons and Paul Stanley. Criss was replaced by Eric Carr in 1981 while Frehely was replaced by Vinnie Vincent in 1982.

Label & Catalog #		Title	Year	VG+	NM
Casablanca NBLP-9001	(DJ)	**Kiss** (White label)	1974	50.00	125.00
Casablanca NBLP-9001	(S)	**Kiss**	1974	20.00	50.00
Casablanca NBLP-7001	(S)	**Kiss**	1974	10.00	25.00
Casablanca NBLP-7006	(S)	**Hotter Than Hell**	1974	10.00	25.00
Casablanca NBLP-7016	(S)	**Dressed To Kill** (Embossed cover)	1975	10.00	25.00
Casablanca NBLP-7020	(S)	**Alive!**	1975	10.00	25.00
Casablanca NBLP-7025	(S)	**Destroyer**	1976	10.00	25.00
		— Original Casablanca albums above have blue/grey with a smoking man on the left.—			
Casablanca NBLP-7001	(S)	**Kiss**	1976	6.00	15.00
Casablanca NBLP-7006	(S)	**Hotter Than Hell**	1976	6.00	15.00
Casablanca NBLP-7016	(S)	**Dressed To Kill**	1976	6.00	15.00
Casablanca NBLP-7020	(S)	**Alive!**	1976	6.00	15.00
Casablanca NBLP-7025	(S)	**Destroyer**	1976	6.00	15.00
Casablanca NBLP-7032	(S)	**Kiss: The Originals**	1976	50.00	125.00
		(Issued with a bonus booklet, four Kiss cards and a Kiss Army sticker. Repackages 7001, 7006 and 7016.)			
Casablanca NBLP-7032	(S)	**Kiss: The Originals** (Without inserts)	1976	40.00	100.00
Casablanca NBLP-7037	(DJ)	**Rock And Roll Over Special Edition**	1976	16.00	40.00
Casablanca NBLP-7037	(S)	**Rock And Roll Over**	1976	6.00	15.00
		— Casablanca albums above have labels with a desert scene with three camels and "Casablanca" on top.—			
Casablanca NBLP-7001	(S)	**Kiss**	1977	5.00	12.00
Casablanca NBLP-7006	(S)	**Hotter Than Hell**	1977	5.00	12.00
Casablanca NBLP-7016	(S)	**Dressed To Kill**	1977	5.00	12.00
Casablanca NBLP-7020	(S)	**Alive!**	1977	5.00	12.00
Casablanca NBLP-7025	(S)	**Destroyer**	1977	5.00	12.00
Casablanca NBLP-7032	(S)	**Kiss: The Originals** (Includes inserts)	1977	40.00	100.00
Casablanca NBLP-7032	(S)	**Kiss: The Originals** (Without inserts)	1977	30.00	75.00
Casablanca NBLP-7037	(S)	**Rock And Roll Over**	1977	5.00	12.00
Casablanca NBLP-7057	(S)	**Love Gun** (Includes a punchout sheet)	1977	10.00	25.00
Casablanca NBLP-7057	(S)	**Love Gun** (Without the punchout sheet)	1977	5.00	12.00
Casablanca NBLP-7076	(S)	**Alive II** (Includes booklet and "tattoos.")	1977	10.00	25.00
Casablanca NBLP-7076	(S)	**Alive II** (Without the booklet and "tattoos.")	1977	5.00	12.00
Casablanca NBLP-7100	(S)	**Double Platinum** (2 LPs)	1978	12.00	30.00
		(Issued with a bonus cardboard platinum album award.)			
Casablanca NBLP-7100	(S)	**Double Platinum** (2 LPs without the bonus)	1978	8.00	20.00
Casablanca NBLP-7120	(S)	**Gene Simmons** (Includes poster)	1978	10.00	25.00
Casablanca NBLP-7120	(S)	**Gene Simmons** (Without poster)	1978	6.00	15.00
Casablanca NBLP-7122	(S)	**Gene Simmons** (Picture disc)	1978	12.00	30.00
Casablanca NBLP-7121	(S)	**Ace Frehley** (Includes poster)	1978	10.00	25.00
Casablanca NBLP-7121	(S)	**Ace Frehley** (Without poster)	1978	6.00	15.00
Casablanca NBLP-7121	(S)	**Ace Frehley** (Picture disc)	1978	12.00	30.00

Label & Catalog #		Title	Year	VG+	NM
Casablanca NBLP-7122	(S)	**Peter Criss** (Includes poster)	1978	10.00	25.00
Casablanca NBLP-7122	(S)	**Peter Criss** (Without poster)	1978	6.00	15.00
Casablanca NBLP-7122	(S)	**Peter Criss** (Picture disc)	1978	12.00	30.00
Casablanca NBLP-7123	(S)	**Paul Stanley** (Includes poster)	1978	10.00	25.00
Casablanca NBLP-7123	(S)	**Paul Stanley** (Without poster)	1978	6.00	15.00
Casablanca NBLP-7123	(S)	**Paul Stanley** (Picture disc)	1978	12.00	30.00
Casablanca NBLP-7152	(S)	**Dynasty** (Includes poster)	1979	6.00	15.00
Casablanca NBLP-7152	(S)	**Dynasty** (Without poster)	1979	4.00	10.00
Casablanca NBLP-7225	(S)	**Unmasked** (Includes poster)	1980	6.00	15.00
Casablanca NBLP-7225	(S)	**Unmasked** (Without poster)	1980	4.00	10.00
		— Casablanca albums above have labels with a desert scene with a film crew and "Manufactured by Casablanca" on the bottom.—			
Casablanca NBLP-7001	(S)	**Kiss**	1981	4.00	10.00
Casablanca NBLP-7006	(S)	**Hotter Than Hell**	1981	4.00	10.00
Casablanca NBLP-7016	(S)	**Dressed To Kill**	1981	4.00	10.00
Casablanca NBLP-7020	(S)	**Alive!**	1981	4.00	10.00
Casablanca NBLP-7025	(S)	**Destroyer**	1981	4.00	10.00
Casablanca NBLP-7037	(S)	**Rock And Roll Over**	1981	4.00	10.00
Casablanca NBLP-7057	(S)	**Love Gun**	1981	4.00	10.00
Casablanca NBLP-7076	(S)	**Alive II**	1981	4.00	10.00
Casablanca NBLP-7100	(S)	**Double Platinum**	1981	4.00	10.00
Casablanca NBLP-7152	(S)	**Dynasty**	1981	4.00	10.00
Casablanca NBLP-7225	(S)	**Unmasked**	1981	4.00	10.00
		(Includes a paper inner sleeve with lyrics on it.)			
Casablanca NBLP-7261	(S)	**Music From The Elder** (Soundtrack)	1981	14.00	35.00
		(Includes a paper inner sleeve with lyrics on it.)			
Casablanca NBLP-7270	(S)	**Creatures Of The Night**	1982	8.00	20.00
		— Casablanca albums above have labels with a desert scene with a film crew and "Manufactured by Polygram" on the bottom.—			
Mercury 814 297-1	(S)	**Lick It Up**	1983	4.00	10.00
Mercury 822 495-1	(S)	**Animalize**	1984	4.00	10.00
Mercury 824 154-1	(S)	**Creatures Of The Night**	1984	4.00	10.00
Mercury 826 099-1	(S)	**Asylum**	1985	4.00	10.00
Mercury 832 626-1	(S)	**Crazy Nights**	1987	4.00	10.00
Mercury 832 903-1	(S)	**Crazy Nights** (Picture disc)	1987	4.00	10.00
Mercury 836 427-1	(S)	**Smashes, Thrashes And Hits**	1988	4.00	10.00
Mercury 836 8871-	(S)	**Smashes, Thrashes And Hits** (Picture disc)	1988	6.00	15.00
Mercury 838 913-1	(S)	**Hot In The Shade**	1989	4.00	10.00
		— Special Promotional Albums—			
Casablanca Kiss-76	(DJ)	**Special Album For Their Summer Tour**	1978	20.00	50.00
Casablanca NB 20128	(DJ)	**A Taste Of Platinum**	1978	16.00	40.00
Casablanca NB 20137	(DJ)	**Solo Album Sampler**	1978	16.00	40.00
Mercury 792	(DJ)	**First Kiss, Last Licks**	1990	16.00	40.00
KIT KATS, THE					
Jamie LPM-3029	(M)	**It's Just A Matter Of Time**	1966	20.00	50.00
Jamie LPS-3029	(E)	**It's Just A Matter Of Time**	1966	16.00	40.00
Jamie LPM-3032	(M)	**Do Their Thing Live**	1967	16.00	40.00
Jamie LPS-3032	(S)	**Do Their Thing Live**	1967	20.00	50.00
KITCHEN CINQ, THE					
L.H.I. 12000	(M)	**Everything But The Kitchen Cinq**	1967	10.00	25.00
L.H.I. 12000	(S)	**Everything But The Kitchen Cinq**	1967	12.00	30.00
KITT, EARTHA					
RCA Victor LOC-1008	(M)	**New Faces Of 1952** (Original Cast)	1952	20.00	50.00
RCA Victor LPM-3062 (10")	(M)	**Songs**	1953	20.00	50.00
RCA Victor LPM-3187 (10")	(M)	**That Bad Eartha**	1953	20.00	50.00
RCA Victor LPM-1109	(M)	**Down To Eartha**	1955	12.00	30.00
RCA Victor LPM-1183	(M)	**That Bad Eartha**	1955	12.00	30.00
RCA Victor LPM-1300	(M)	**Thursday's Child**	1956	12.00	30.00
RCA Victor LPM-1661	(M)	**St. Louis Blues**	1958	8.00	20.00
RCA Victor LSP-1661	(S)	**St. Louis Blues**	1958	12.00	30.00
Kapp KL-1162	(M)	**The Fabulous Eartha Kitt**	1959	8.00	20.00
Kapp KS-3046	(S)	**The Fabulous Eartha Kitt**	1959	10.00	25.00
Kapp KL-1192	(M)	**Eartha Kitt Revisited**	1960	8.00	20.00
Kapp KS-3192	(S)	**Eartha Kitt Revisited**	1960	10.00	25.00
MGM E-4009	(M)	**Bad But Beautiful**	1962	6.00	15.00
MGM SE-4009	(S)	**Bad But Beautiful**	1962	8.00	20.00

Label & Catalog #		Title	Year	VG+	NM

KLUGMAN: *Refer to* TONY RANDALL & JACK KLUGMAN

KNICKERBOCKERS, THE
Challenge LP-12664	(M)	Sing And Sync Along With Lloyd Thaxton	1965	40.00	100.00
Challenge CH-621	(M)	Jerk And Twine Time	1965	60.00	150.00
Challenge CH-622	(M)	Lies	1966	30.00	75.00
Challenge CHS-622	(S)	Lies	1966	40.00	100.00

KNIGHT, CHRIS, & MAUREEN McCORMICK
| Paramount PAS-6062 | (S) | Chris Knight And Maureen McCormick | 1973 | 10.00 | 25.00 |

KNIGHT, CURTIS, & JIMI HENDRIX
Knight's group features a young Jimi Hendrix on guitar.
Capitol T-2856	(M)	Get That Feeling	1967	12.00	30.00
Capitol ST-2856	(S)	Get That Feeling	1967	10.00	25.00
Capitol T-2894	(M)	Flashing	1968	16.00	40.00
Capitol ST-2894	(S)	Flashing	1968	10.00	25.00

KNIGHT, FREDERICK
| Stax STS-3011 | (S) | I've Been Lonely So Long | 1973 | 6.00 | 15.00 |

KNIGHT, GLADYS, & THE PIPS
Fury 1003	(M)	Letter Full Of Tears	1962	100.00	250.00
Maxx 3000	(M)	Gladys Knight & The Pips	1964	30.00	75.00
Sphere Sound SR-7006	(M)	Gladys Knight & The Pips	1965	20.00	50.00
Sphere Sound SSR-7006	(E)	Gladys Knight & The Pips	1965	16.00	40.00
Bell 6013	(S)	Tastiest Hits	1968	6.00	15.00
Bell 1323	(S)	In The Beginning	1969	6.00	15.00
Soul 706	(M)	Everybody Needs Love	1967	8.00	20.00
Soul SS-706	(S)	Everybody Needs Love	1967	10.00	25.00
Soul SS-707	(S)	Feelin' Bluesy	1968	8.00	20.00
Soul SS-711	(S)	Silk And Soul	1968	8.00	20.00
Soul SS-713	(S)	The Nitty Gritty	1969	6.00	15.00
Soul SS-723	(S)	Gladys Knight & The Pips' Greatest Hits	1970	6.00	15.00
Soul SS-730	(S)	All In A Night's Work	1971	5.00	12.00
Soul SS-731	(S)	If I Were Your Woman	1971	5.00	12.00
Soul SS-736	(S)	Standing Ovation	1972	5.00	12.00
Soul SS-737	(S)	Neither One Of Us	1973	5.00	12.00
Soul SS-739	(S)	All I Need Is Time	1973	5.00	12.00
Soul SS-741	(S)	Knight Time	1974	5.00	12.00
Soul SS-744	(S)	A Little Knight Music	1975	5.00	12.00

KNIGHT, JEAN
| Stax STS-2045 | (S) | Mr. Big Stuff | 1971 | 6.00 | 15.00 |

KNIGHT, LONNIE
| Symposium 2004 | (S) | Family In The Wind | 1974 | 6.00 | 15.00 |
| Flashlight 3002 | (S) | Song For A City Mouse | 1975 | 6.00 | 15.00 |

KNIGHT, ROBERT
| Sound Stage-7 SSM-7000 | (M) | Everlasting Love | 1967 | 12.00 | 30.00 |
| Sound Stage-7 SM-17000 | (S) | Everlasting Love | 1967 | 16.00 | 40.00 |

KNIGHT, SONNY
| Aura AR-3001 | (M) | If You Want This Love | 1964 | 8.00 | 20.00 |
| Aura AS-3001 | (S) | If You Want This Love | 1964 | 10.00 | 25.00 |

KNIGHT, TERRY, & THE PACK
The Pack features Mark Farner and Don Brewer, later of Grand Funk Railroad.
Lucky Eleven LE-8000	(M)	Terry Knight & The Pack	1966	10.00	25.00
Lucky Eleven LES-8000	(S)	Terry Knight & The Pack	1966	12.00	30.00
Lucky Eleven LE-8001	(S)	Reflections	1966	10.00	25.00
Lucky Eleven LES-8001	(S)	Reflections	1966	12.00	30.00
Cameo C-2007	(M)	Reflections	1967	6.00	15.00
Cameo CS-2007	(S)	Reflections	1967	8.00	20.00
Abkco AB-4217	(S)	Mark, Don And Terry 1966-67 (2 LPs)	1972	5.00	12.00

Label & Catalog #		Title	Year	VG+	NM

KNIGHTS, THE
The Knights are a creation of Gary Usher & Co.

Capitol T-2189	(M)	Hot Rod High	1964	80.00	200.00
Capitol DT-2189	(E)	Hot Rod High	1964	100.00	250.00

KNIGHTS, THE

Ace MG-200854	(M)	Across The Road	1966	60.00	150.00
Ace MG-201303	(M)	The Knights 1967	1967	50.00	125.00

KNIGHTS, THE

Justice JLP-156	(S)	On The Move	196?	100.00	250.00

KNOCKOUTS, THE

Tribute 1202	(M)	Go Ape With The Knockouts	1964	40.00	100.00

KNOWBODY ELSE

Hip HIS-7003	(S)	Knowbody Else	1969	8.00	20.00

KNOTTS, DON

United Arts. UAL-4090	(M)	Don Knotts	1961	8.00	20.00
United Arts. UAS-5090	(S)	Don Knotts	1961	10.00	25.00

KNOX, BUDDY

Roulette R-25003	(M)	Buddy Knox *(Black label)*	1957	60.00	150.00
Liberty LRP-3251	(M)	Buddy Knox's Golden Hits	1962	12.00	30.00
Liberty LSP-7251	(P)	Buddy Knox's Golden Hits	1962	16.00	40.00
		(Contains rerecorded versions of the Roulette material.)			
United Arts. UAS-6689	(S)	Gypsy Man	1969	10.00	25.00

KNOX, BUDDY, & JIMMY BOWEN

Roulette R-25048	(M)	Buddy Knox & Jimmy Bowen *(Black label)*	1958	60.00	150.00

KOALA, THE

Capitol SKAO-176	(S)	The Koala	1969	8.00	20.00

KODAKS, THE / THE STARLITES

Sphere Sound SR-7005	(M)	The Kodaks Vs. The Starlites	1965	60.00	150.00

KEORNER, "SPIDER" JOHN

Elektra EKL-290	(M)	Spider Blues	1965	8.00	20.00
Elektra EKS-7290	(S)	Spider Blues	1965	10.00	25.00
Elektra EKS-74041	(S)	Running, Jumping, Standing Still	1969	8.00	20.00

KOERNER, JOHN; DAVE RAY & TONY GLOVER

Elektra EKL-240	(M)	Blue Rags And Hollers	1963	10.00	25.00
Elektra EKS-7240	(S)	Blue Rags And Hollers	1963	12.00	30.00
Elektra EKL-267	(M)	Lots More Blues Rags And Hollers	1964	10.00	25.00
Elektra EKS-7267	(S)	Lots More Blues Rags And Hollers	1964	12.00	30.00
Elektra EKL-305	(M)	The Return Of Koerner, Ray & Glover	1966	8.00	20.00
Elektra EKS-7305	(S)	The Return Of Koerner, Ray & Glover	1966	10.00	25.00

KOKI, SAM, & THE PARADISE ISLANDERS

Kapp KL-1321	(M)	Surfin' At Waikiki	1963	6.00	15.00
Kapp KS-3321	(S)	Surfin' At Waikiki	1963	8.00	20.00

KOLE, JERRY, & THE STROKERS
Jerry Kole is a pseudonym for Jerry Cole. Refer to Ritchie Valens / Jerry Kole.

Crown CLP-5385	(M)	Hot Rod Alley	1963	10.00	25.00
Crown CST-385	(S)	Hot Rod Alley	1963	12.00	30.00

KOOL & THE GANG

De-Lite DSR-2003	(S)	Kool & The Gang	1969	10.00	25.00
De-Lite MK-48	(DJ)	History Of Kool & The Gang	1979	6.00	15.00

KOOPER, AL
Refer to Blood, Sweat & Tears; Mike Bloomfield & Al Kooper; The Blues Project.

Columbia CS-9718	(S)	I Stand Alone	1969	5.00	12.00
Columbia CS-9855	(S)	You Never Know Who Your Friends Are	1969	5.00	12.00
Columbia CS-9951	(S)	Kooper Session	1969	5.00	12.00

Label & Catalog #		Title	Year	VG+	NM
Columbia KC-33031	(S)	Easy Does It (2 LPs)	1970	6.00	15.00
United Arts. UAS-5209	(S)	The Landlord (Soundtrack)	1970	6.00	15.00
KOPPERFIELD					
Kopperdisc 5014N5	(S)	Tales Untold	1974	200.00	400.00
KORNER, ALEXIS					
Warner Bros. 2XS-1966	(S)	Bootleg Him (2 LPs with Charlie Watts)	1972	10.00	25.00
Warner Bros. BS-2647	(S)	Accidently Borne In New Orleans	1972	5.00	12.00
Columbia PC-33427	(S)	Get Off Of My Cloud (With Keith Richards)	1975	6.00	15.00
KOTTKE, LEO					
Oblivion 1	(S)	Live At The Scholar Coffee House	197?	10.00	25.00
Symposium 2001	(S)	Circle 'Round The Sun	1970	6.00	15.00
KRABER, TONY					
Mercury MG-20008	(M)	The Old Chisolm Trail	1955	12.00	30.00
KRACKER					
Primo PS-001	(S)	Kracker	1978	12.00	30.00
KRAL, IRENE: Refer to Goldmine's Price Guide To Collectible Albums					
KRAMER, BILLY J., & THE DAKOTAS					
Imperial LP-9267	(M)	Little Children (Black label with stars)	1964	16.00	40.00
Imperial LP-12267	(P)	Little Children (Black & silver label)	1964	20.00	50.00
Imperial LP-9267	(M)	Little Children	1964	12.00	30.00
Imperial LP-12267	(P)	Little Children	1964	16.00	40.00
Imperial LP-9273	(M)	I'll Keep You Satisfied/From A Window	1964	12.00	30.00
Imperial LP-12273	(S)	I'll Keep You Satisfied/From A Window	1964	16.00	40.00
		("I'll Keep You Satisfied," "Sugar Babe," "I'll Be On My Way," "From A Window," "Second To None," and "The Cruel Surf" are rechanneled.)			
Imperial LP-9291	(M)	Trains And Boats And Planes	1965	14.00	35.00
Imperial LP-12291	(E)	Trains And Boats And Planes	1965	10.00	25.00
		— Imperial albums above have black & pink labels.—			
Capitol SM-11897	(M)	The Best Of Billy J., Kramer & The Dakotas	1979	5.00	12.00
		("Trains And Boats And Planes" and "From A Window" are stereo.)			
KRAZY KATS, THE					
Damon 12478	(S)	Movin' Out	196?	30.00	75.00
KREED					
Visions Of Sound 71-56	(S)	This Is Kreed	1971	360.00	600.00
KRISTOFFERSON, KRIS					
Monument SLP-18139	(S)	Kristofferson	1970	6.00	15.00
Monument ZQ-30679	(Q)	The Silver-Tongued Devil And I	1972	6.00	15.00
Monument ZQ-31909	(Q)	Jesus Was A Capricorn	1972	6.00	15.00
Monument PZQ-32914	(Q)	Spooky Lady's Sideshow	1974	6.00	15.00
KRISTYL					
(No label)	(M)	Kristyl	196?	150.00	300.00
KUBAN, BOB, & THE IN-MEN					
Musicland LP-3500	(M)	Look Out For The Cheater	1966	12.00	30.00
Musicland SLP-3500	(S)	Look Out For The Cheater	1966	16.00	40.00
KUPFERBERG, TULI					
Tuli was formerly a member of The Fugs.					
ESP-Disk' 1035	(M)	No Deposit No Return	1967	12.00	30.00
ESP-Disk' 1035	(M)	No Deposit No Return (Gold vinyl)	1967	16.00	40.00
Shimmy Disc	(S)	Tuli And Friends	1989	4.00	10.00
KUSTOM KINGS, THE					
Smash MGS-27051	(M)	Kustom City, U.S.A.	1964	40.00	100.00
Smash SRS-67051	(S)	Kustom City, U.S.A.	1964	60.00	150.00

Label & Catalog #		Title	Year	VG+	NM
KWESKIN, JIM, & THE JUG BAND					
Vanguard VRS-9163	(M)	**Jug Band Music**	1966	8.00	20.00
Vanguard VSD-79163	(S)	**Jug Band Music**	1966	10.00	25.00
Vanguard VRS-9234	(M)	**See Reverse Side For Title**	1966	8.00	20.00
Vanguard VSD-79234	(S)	**See Reverse Side For Title**	1966	10.00	25.00
Reprise R-6266	(M)	**Garden Of Joy**	1967	8.00	20.00
Reprise RS-6266	(S)	**Garden Of Joy**	1967	10.00	25.00
Vanguard VSD-13/14	(S)	**Greatest Hits** (2 LPs)	1970	6.00	15.00

Label & Catalog #		Title	Year	VG+	NM
LaBELLE (PATTI LaBELLE)					
Epic PEQ-33579	(Q)	**Phoenix**	1975	6.00	15.00
LaBELLE, PATTI & THE BLUEBELLES [THE BLUEBELLES]					
Newtown 631	(M)	**Sweethearts Of The Apollo**	1963	150.00	300.00
Newtown 632	(M)	**Sleigh Bells, Jingle Bells And Blue Bells**	1963	100.00	250.00
Parkway 7043	(M)	**The Bluebelles On Stage** (With bonus single)	1965	60.00	150.00
Parkway 7043	(M)	**The Bluebelles On Stage** (Without single)	1965	50.00	125.00
Atlantic 8101	(M)	**Dreamer**	1965	12.00	30.00
Atlantic SD-8101	(S)	**Dreamer**	1965	16.00	40.00
Atlantic 8119	(M)	**Over The Rainbow**	1966	12.00	30.00
Atlantic SD-8119	(S)	**Over The Rainbow**	1966	16.00	40.00
LADD, CHERYL					
Refer to Josie & The Pussycats.					
Capitol SW-11808	(S)	**Cheryl Ladd**	1978	6.00	15.00
LaFARGE, PETER [PETER LaFORGE]					
Verve/Folkways FV-9004	(M)	**Women Blues**	1965	8.00	20.00
Verve/Folkways FVS-9004	(S)	**Women Blues**	1965	10.00	25.00
LAINE, DENNY					
Denny Laine was an original member of The Moody Blues.					
Wizard/Reprise-MS-2180	(S)	**Ah, Laine!**	1972	6.00	15.00
Capitol ST-11588	(DJ)	**Holly Days** (Produced by Paul McCartney)	1976	20.00	50.00
		(Original copies were issued as advanced promos in plain cardboard jackets with a 1976 copyright date on the label.)			
Capitol ST-11588	(M)	**Holly Days** (Produced by Paul McCartney)	1977	6.00	15.00
Takoma 71034	(S)	**Japanese Tears**	1983	5.00	12.00
LAINE, FRANKIE					
Refer to The Four Lads; Jo Stafford & Frankie Laine.					
Mercury MG-25007 (10")	(M)	**Favorites**	1949	20.00	50.00
Mercury MG-25024 (10")	(M)	**Songs From The Heart**	1950	20.00	50.00
Mercury MG-25025 (10")	(M)	**Frankie Laine**	1950	20.00	50.00
Mercury MG-25026 (10")	(M)	**Frankie Laine**	1950	20.00	50.00
Mercury MG-25027 (10")	(M)	**Frankie Laine**	1950	20.00	50.00
Mercury MG-25097 (10")	(M)	**Mr. Rhythm Sings**	1951	20.00	50.00
Mercury MG-25082 (10")	(M)	**Christmas Favorites**	1951	20.00	50.00
Mercury MG-25124 (10")	(M)	**Listen To Laine**	1952	20.00	50.00
Mercury MG-20069	(M)	**Songs By Frankie Laine**	1956	14.00	35.00
Mercury MG-20080	(M)	**That's My Desire**	1957	14.00	35.00
Mercury MG-20083	(M)	**Frankie Laine Sings For Us**	1957	14.00	35.00
Mercury MG-20085	(M)	**Concert Date**	1957	14.00	35.00

Label & Catalog #		Title	Year	VG+	NM
Mercury MG-20105	(M)	With All My Heart	1957	14.00	35.00
Mercury MG-20587	(M)	Frankie Laine's Golden Hits	1960	10.00	25.00
Wing MGW-12158	(M)	Singing The Blues	1963	8.00	20.00
Wing SRW-16158	(E)	Singing The Blues	1963	5.00	12.00
Columbia CL-6200 (10")	(M)	One For My Baby	1952	14.00	35.00
Columbia CL-6278 (10")	(M)	Mr. Rhythm	1954	14.00	35.00
Columbia CL-2504 (10")	(M)	Lover's Laine	1955	14.00	35.00
Columbia CL-2548 (10")	(M)	One For My Baby	1955	14.00	35.00
Columbia CL-625	(M)	Command Performance	1956	14.00	35.00
Columbia CL-808	(M)	Jazz Spectacular	1956	12.00	30.00
Columbia CL-975	(M)	Rockin'	1957	12.00	30.00
Columbia CL-1116	(M)	Foreign Affair	1958	12.00	30.00
Columbia CL-1231	(M)	Frankie Laine's Greatest Hits	1959	10.00	25.00
Columbia CL-1224	(M)	Torchin'	1960	6.00	15.00
Columbia CS-8024	(S)	Torchin'	1960	8.00	20.00
Columbia CL-1287	(M)	Reunion In Rhythm	1961	6.00	15.00
Columbia CS-8087	(S)	Reunion In Rhythm	1961	8.00	20.00
Columbia CL-1319	(M)	You Are My Love	1961	6.00	15.00
Columbia CS-8119	(S)	You Are My Love	1961	8.00	20.00
Columbia CL-1388	(M)	Frankie Laine, Balladeer	1961	6.00	15.00
Columbia CS-8188	(S)	Frankie Laine, Balladeer	1961	8.00	20.00
Columbia CL-1615	(M)	Hell Bent For Leather!	1961	6.00	15.00
Columbia CS-8415	(S)	Hell Bent For Leather!	1961	8.00	20.00
Columbia CL-1696	(M)	Deuces Wild	1962	6.00	15.00
Columbia CS-8496	(S)	Deuces Wild	1962	8.00	20.00

— *Original Columbia albums above have three white "eye" logos on each side of the spindle hole.* —

Columbia CL-1829	(M)	Call Of The Wild	1962	6.00	15.00
Columbia CS-8629	(S)	Call Of The Wild	1962	8..00	20.00
Columbia CL-1836	(M)	Frankie Laine's Greatest Hits	1962	6.00	15.00
Columbia CS-8636	(S)	Frankie Laine's Greatest Hits	1962	8..00	20.00
Columbia CL-1962	(M)	Wanderlust	1963	6.00	15.00
Columbia CS-8762	(S)	Wanderlust	1963	8..00	20.00
Capitol T-2277	(M)	I Believe	1965	5.00	12.00
Capitol ST-2277	(S)	I Believe	1965	6.00	15.00
Tower T-5092	(M)	Memory Laine	1967	5.00	12.00
Tower ST-5092	(S)	Memory Laine	1967	6.00	15.00
ABC-Paramount 604	(M)	I'll Take Care Of Your Cares	1967	5.00	12.00
ABC-Paramount S-604	(S)	I'll Take Care Of Your Cares	1967	6.00	15.00
ABC-Paramount 608	(M)	I Want Someone To Love	1967	5.00	12.00
ABC-Paramount S-608	(S)	I Want Someone To Love	1967	6.00	15.00
ABC-Paramount S-628	(S)	To Each His Own	1968	5.00	12.00

LAKE, GREG

Sweet Thunder 11	(S)	Greg Lake	198?	7.00	20.00

LAMB

Fillmore F-30003	(S)	Sign Of Change	1970	6.00	15.00
Warner Bros. WS-1920	(S)	Cross Between	1971	6.00	15.00
Warner Bros. WS-1952	(S)	Bring Out The Sun	1972	6.00	15.00

LAMBERT, DAVE / LAMBERT, HENDRICKS & BAVAN / LAMBERT, HENDRICKS & ROSS: *Refer to* GOLDMINE'S PRICE GUIDE TO COLLECTIBLE JAZZ ALBUMS

LAMEGO, DANNY, & HIS JUMPIN' JACKS

Forget-Me-Not 105A	(M)	The Big Weekend	1964	40.00	100.00

LAMOUR, DOROTHY

Decca DL-5115 (10")	(M)	Favorite Hawaiian Songs	1950	30.00	75.00
Design 45	(M)	The Road To Romance	195?	14.00	35.00

LANCE, MAJOR

OKeh OKM-12105	(M)	The Monkey Time	1963	10.00	25.00
OKeh OKS-14105	(S)	The Monkey Time	1963	12.00	30.00

("Monkey Time" and "Mama Didn't Know" are rechanneled.)

OKeh OKM-12106	(M)	Um, Um, Um, Um, Um, Um	1964	10.00	25.00
OKeh OKS-14106	(P)	Um, Um, Um, Um, Um, Um	1964	12.00	30.00
OKeh OKM-12110	(M)	Major Lance's Greatest Hits	1965	10.00	25.00
OKeh OKS-14110	(S)	Major Lance's Greatest Hits	1965	12.00	30.00

("Monkey Time" is rechanneled on this album.)

Label & Catalog #		Title	Year	VG+	NM

LANCELOT LINK

| ABC S-715 | (S) | Lancelot Link & The Evolution Revolution | 1970 | 10.00 | 25.00 |

LANCERS, THE

| Trend TL-1009 (10") | (M) | The Lancers | 1954 | 16.00 | 40.00 |
| Coral CRL-57100 | (M) | Dixieland Ball | 1957 | 10.00 | 25.00 |

LANCERS, THE

| Imperial LP-9023 | (M) | Concerts In Contrasts | 1969 | 12.00 | 30.00 |
| Imperial LP-12023 | (S) | Concerts In Contrasts | 1969 | 16.00 | 40.00 |

LANCHESTER, ELSA

| HiFi R-405 | (M) | Songs For A Smoke Filled Room | 195? | 10.00 | 25.00 |

LANE, VICKI

| RCA Victor LPM-2056 | (M) | I Swing For You | 1959 | 12.00 | 30.00 |

LANGDON, DORY

| Verve V-2101 | (M) | Leprechauns Are Upon Me | 195? | 8.00 | 20.00 |

LARKS, THE
The Larks feature Don Julian.

Money MY-1102	(M)	The Jerk	1965	10.00	25.00
Money MS-1102	(S)	The Jerk	1965	12.00	30.00
Money MY-1107	(M)	Soul Kaleidoscope	1966	10.00	25.00
Money MS-1107	(S)	Soul Kaleidoscope	1966	12.00	30.00
Money MY-1110	(M)	Superslick	1967	10.00	25.00
Money MS-1110	(S)	Superslick	1967	12.00	30.00

LaROSA, JULIUS

RCA Victor LPM-1299	(M)	Julius LaRosa	1956	16.00	40.00
Cadence CLP-1007	(M)	Julius LaRosa	1957	12.00	30.00
Roulette R-25054	(M)	Love Songs A LaRosa	1959	8.00	20.00
Roulette SR-25054	(S)	Love Songs A LaRosa	1959	12.00	30.00
Roulette R-25083	(M)	On The Sunny Side	1960	8.00	20.00
Roulette SR-25083	(S)	On The Sunny Side	1960	10.00	25.00
Forum S-16012	(M)	Just Say I Love Her	1960	6.00	15.00
Forum SF-16012	(S)	Just Say I Love Her	1960	8.00	20.00
Kapp KL-1245	(M)	The New Julie LaRosa	1961	6.00	15.00
Kapp KS-3245	(S)	The New Julie LaRosa	1961	8.00	20.00
MGM E-4398	(M)	You're Gonna Hear From Me	1966	5.00	12.00
MGM SE-4398	(S)	You're Gonna Hear From Me	1966	6.00	15.00

LAST DAYS, THE

| (No label) | (S) | The Last Days | 197? | 20.00 | 50.00 |

LAST POETS, THE

Juggernaut 8802	(S)	Right On	1971	8.00	20.00
Douglas Z-30583	(S)	This Is Madness	1971	8.00	20.00
Douglas Z-30811	(S)	Last Poets	1971	10.00	25.00

LAST RITUAL

| Capitol SKAO-206 | (S) | The Last Ritual | 1969 | 5.00 | 12.00 |

LAST WORDS, THE

| Atco SD-33-235 | (S) | The Last Words | 1968 | 6.00 | 15.00 |

LAUGHTON, CHARLES

| Capitol TBO-1650 | (M) | The Story Teller | 1962 | 8.00 | 20.00 |
| Capitol STBO-1650 | (S) | The Story Teller | 1962 | 10.00 | 25.00 |

LAUPER, CYNDI

| Portrait 9R9-39610 | (S) | She's So Unusual (Picture disc) | 1983 | 4.00 | 10.00 |

LAUREN, ROD

| RCA Victor LPM-2176 | (M) | I'm Rod Lauren | 1961 | 8.00 | 20.00 |
| RCA Victor LSP-2176 | (S) | I'm Rod Lauren | 1961 | 12.00 | 30.00 |

Annie Laurie had been singing rhythm 'n blues for more than a decade when she hit the pop charts in 1957 with "It Hurts To Be In Love" for DeLuxe. The album of the same name appeared on the King subsidiary Audio Lab, where, like virtually everything else on that label, it is almost impossible to find today.

Label & Catalog #		Title	Year	VG+	NM

LAURIE, ANNIE

Audio Lab AL-1510	(M)	...It Hurts To Be In Love!	195?	100.00	300.00
Palace 793	(M)	Annie Laurie	1964	20.00	50.00

LAURIE SISTERS, THE

Camden CAL-545	(M)	Hits Of The Great Girl Groups	1960	8.00	20.00
Camden CAS-545	(S)	Hits Of The Great Girl Groups	1960	12.00	30.00

LAWRENCE, CAROL

Chancellor CHL-5015	(M)	Tonight At 8:30	1960	5.00	12.00
Chancellor CHLS-5015	(S)	Tonight At 8:30	1960	6.00	15.00
Choreo A-2	(M)	This Heart Of Mine	196?	6.00	15.00
Cameo S-1077	(M)	An Evening With Carol Lawrence	1964	5.00	12.00
Cameo SC-1077	(S)	An Evening With Carol Lawrence	1964	6.00	15.00

LAWRENCE, GERTRUDE

Decca DL-5418 (10")	(M)	Souvenir Album	1952	16.00	40.00
RCA Victor LPM-1156	(M)	Noel And Gertie	1955	12.00	30.00
Decca DL-8673	(M)	A Remembrance	1958	12.00	30.00
Audio Fidelity AF-709	(M)	The Star	195?	12.00	30.00

LAWRENCE, STEVE

Coral CRL-57050	(M)	About That Girl	1956	12.00	30.00
Coral CRL-57182	(M)	Songs	1957	12.00	30.00
Coral CRL-57204	(M)	Here's Steve Lawrence	1958	12.00	30.00
Coral CRL-57268	(M)	All About Love	1959	8.00	20.00
Coral CRL-757268	(S)	All About Love	1959	12.00	30.00
Coral CRL-57434	(M)	Songs Everybody Knows	1963	10.00	25.00
Coral CRL-757434	(S)	Songs Everybody Knows	1963	12.00	30.00
King 395-593	(M)	Steve Lawrence	1959	10.00	50.00
ABC-Paramount 290	(M)	Swing Softly With Me	1959	10.00	25.00
ABC-Paramount S-290	(S)	Swing Softly With Me	1959	12.00	30.00
ABC-Paramount 392	(M)	The Best Of Steve Lawrence	1960	8.00	20.00
ABC-Paramount S-392	(S)	The Best Of Steve Lawrence	1960	10.00	25.00
United Arts. UAL-3098	(M)	The Steve Lawrence Sound	1960	6.00	15.00
United Arts. UAS-6098	(S)	The Steve Lawrence Sound	1960	8.00	20.00
United Arts. UAL-3150	(M)	Portrait Of My Love	1961	6.00	15.00
United Arts. UAS-6150	(S)	Portrait Of My Love	1961	8.00	20.00
United Arts. UAL-3190	(M)	The Very Best Of Steve Lawrence	1962	6.00	15.00
United Arts. UAS-6190	(S)	The Very Best Of Steve Lawrence	1962	8.00	20.00
United Arts. UAL-3265	(M)	People Will Say We're In Love	1963	6.00	15.00
United Arts. UAS-6265	(S)	People Will Say We're In Love	1963	8.00	20.00
Columbia CL-1870	(M)	Come Waltz With Me	1962	6.00	15.00
Columbia CS-8670	(S)	Come Waltz With Me	1962	8.00	20.00
Columbia CL-1953	(M)	Winners	1963	5.00	12.00
Columbia CS-8753	(S)	Winners	1963	6.00	15.00
Columbia CL-2052	(M)	Swinging West	1964	5.00	12.00
Columbia CS-8852	(M)	Swinging West	1964	6.00	15.00
Columbia CL-2419	(M)	The Steve Lawrence Show	1965	5.00	12.00
Columbia CS-9219	(S)	The Steve Lawrence Show	1965	6.00	15.00
Columbia KOL-2440	(S)	What Makes Sammy Run? (Soundtrack)	1965	8.00	20.00
Columbia KOS-9240	(S)	What Makes Sammy Run? (Soundtrack)	1965	10.00	25.00

LAWRENCE, STEVE, & EYDIE GORME

ABC-Paramount 300	(M)	We Got Us	1960	8.00	20.00
ABC-Paramount S-300	(S)	We Got Us	1960	10.00	25.00
ABC-Paramount 311	(M)	Steve & Eydie Sing The Golden Hits	1960	8.00	20.00
ABC-Paramount S-311	(S)	Steve & Eydie Sing The Golden Hits	1960	10.00	25.00
ABC-Paramount 469	(M)	Our Best To You	1964	8.00	20.00
ABC-Paramount S-469	(S)	Our Best To You	1964	10.00	25.00
United Arts. UAL-4509	(M)	Cozy	1961	8.00	20.00
United Arts. UAS-8509	(S)	Cozy	1961	10.00	25.00
United Arts. UAL-4518	(M)	Two On The Aisle	1963	8.00	20.00
United Arts. UAS-8518	(S)	Two On The Aisle	1963	10.00	25.00
United Arts. UAL-3191	(M)	The Very Best Of Eydie & Steve	1962	8.00	20.00
United Arts. UAS-6191	(S)	The Very Best Of Eydie & Steve	1962	10.00	25.00
Columbia CL-2021	(M)	At The Movies	1963	5.00	12.00
Columbia CS-8821	(S)	At The Movies	1963	6.00	15.00

Label & Catalog #		Title	Year	VG+	NM
Columbia CL-2262	(M)	**That Holiday Feeling**	1964	5.00	12.00
Columbia CS-9062	(S)	**That Holiday Feeling**	1964	6.00	15.00
Columbia CL-2636	(M)	**Together On Broadway**	1967	5.00	12.00
Columbia CS-9436	(S)	**Together On Broadway**	1967	6.00	15.00
Calendar KOM-1001	(M)	**Golden Rainbow** (Soundtrack)	1968	12.00	30.00
Calendar KOS-1001	(S)	**Golden Rainbow** (Soundtrack)	1968	8.00	20.00
RCA Victor LSP-4115	(S)	**What It Was, Was Love** (Soundtrack)	1969	6.00	15.00

LAWSON, DEE: *Refer to* GOLDMINE'S PRICE GUIDE TO COLLECTIBLE JAZZ ALBUMS

LAY, SAM

Blue Thumb BTS-14	(S)	**Sam Lay In Bluesland**	1968	10.00	25.00

LAYTON, EDDIE

Mercury MG-20814	(M)	**Folk Sounds**	1963	6.00	15.00
Mercury SR-60814	(S)	**Folk Sounds**	1963	8.00	20.00

LAZAR, BILLY

Scarlett 100	(M)	**Surfin' Around**	1963	40.00	100.00

LAZARUS

Amazon 1001	(S)	**Lazarus**	1970	8.00	20.00

LAZARUS, KEN

Steady 100	(S)	**Reggae's Greatest Hits**	1970	6.00	15.00
Steady 102	(S)	**Scorcher**	1970	6.00	15.00
Steady 105	(S)	**Reggae's Greatest Hits, Volume 2**	1970	6.00	15.00

LAZY LESTER

Excello LP-8006	(M)	**True Blues**	1966	10.00	25.00

LAZY SMOKE

Onyx 6903	(M)	**Corridor Of Faces**	196?	660.00	1,000.00

LEA, BARBARA: *Refer to* GOLDMINE'S PRICE GUIDE TO COLLECTIBLE JAZZ ALBUMS

LEACH, CURTIS

Longhorn 003	(M)	**Indescribable**	1965	20.00	50.00

LEADBELLY
Leadbelly was a nickname for Huddie Ledbetter.

Folkways 4 (10")	(M)	**Leadbelly**	1950	20.00	50.00
Folkways 14 (10")	(M)	**Leadbelly**	1950	20.00	50.00
Folkways 24 (10")	(M)	**Leadbelly**	1950	20.00	50.00
Folkways 43 (10")	(M)	**Leadbelly**	1950	20.00	50.00
Folkways 2004 (10")	(M)	**Take This Hammer**	1951	20.00	50.00
Folkways 2013 (10")	(M)	**Huddie Ledbetter**	1951	20.00	50.00
Folkways 2014 (10")	(M)	**Rock Island Line**	1951	20.00	50.00
Folkways 2024 (10")	(M)	**Leadbelly's Legacy**	1951	20.00	50.00
Stinson SLP-17 (10")	(M)	**Leadbelly Memorial** (Red vinyl)	1951	30.00	75.00
Stinson SLP-19 (10")	(M)	**Leadbelly Memorial** (Red vinyl)	1951	30.00	75.00
Stinson SLP-39 (10")	(M)	**Leadbelly Plays Party Songs** (Red vinyl)	1951	30.00	75.00
Stinson SLP-41 (10")	(M)	**More Party Songs** (Red vinyl)	1951	30.00	75.00
Stinson SLP-48 (10")	(M)	**Leadbelly Memorial** (Red vinyl)	1951	30.00	75.00
Stinson SLP-51 (10")	(M)	**Leadbelly Memorial**	1951	16.00	40.00
Stinson SLP-72 (10")	(M)	**Leadbelly Memorial**	1951	16.00	40.00
Allegro 4027 (10")	(M)	**Sinful Songs**	195?	100.00	250.00
Capitol H-369 (10")	(M)	**Leadbelly**	1952	100.00	250.00
Capitol T-1821	(M)	**Leadbelly (Huddie Ledbetter's Best)**	1962	20.00	50.00
Capitol DT-1891	(E)	**Leadbelly (Huddie Ledbetter's Best)**	1962	16.00	40.00
Folkways FA-2941	(M)	**Leadbelly's Last Sessions, Part 1**	1963	12.00	30.00
Folkways FA-2942	(M)	**Leadbelly's Last Sessions, Part 2**	1963	12.00	30.00
Folkways FA-3106	(M)	**Leadbelly Sings Folk Songs**	1964	12.00	30.00
Verve/Folkways FV-9001	(M)	**Take This Hammer**	1965	10.00	25.00
Verve/Folkways FVS-9001	(E)	**Take This Hammer**	1965	6.00	15.00
Verve/Folkways FT-9021	(M)	**Keep Your Hands Off Her**	1965	10.00	25.00
Verve/Folkways FTS-9021	(E)	**Keep Your Hands Off Her**	1965	6.00	15.00
Verve/Folkways FT-3019	(M)	**From The Last Sessions**	1967	10.00	25.00
Verve/Folkways FTS-3019	(E)	**From The Last Sessions**	1967	6.00	15.00

Label & Catalog #		Title	Year	VG+	NM
RCA Victor LPV-505	(M)	**Midnight Special**	1964	20.00	50.00
Elektra EKL-301-2	(M)	**Library Of Congress Recordings** (2 LPs)	1966	10.00	25.00
Columbia 30035	(M)	**Legendary Performances**			
		Never Before Released	1970	4.00	10.00
Fantasy F-24715	(M)	**Leadbelly** (2 LPs)	1973	8.00	20.00
Playboy 119	(M)	**Leadbelly**	1973	4.00	10.00
Olympic 7103	(M)	**The Legendary Leadbelly**	1973	4.00	10.00
Sutton SU-278	(M)	**Ballads Of Beautiful Women And Bad Men**		4.00	10.00

LEADBELLY / JOSH WHITE / SONNY TERRY

Label & Catalog #		Title	Year	VG+	NM
Tradition 2093	(M)	**Legend Of Leadbelly,**			
		Josh White And Sonny Terry	1969	6.00	15.00

LEARY, TIMOTHY

Label & Catalog #		Title	Year	VG+	NM
Broadside 601	(M)	**The Psychedelic Experience**	1966	30.00	75.00
Pixie CA-1069	(M)	**L.S.D.**	1966	30.00	75.00
ESP-Disk' 1027	(M)	**Turn On, Tune In, Drop Out**	1966	20.00	50.00
Mercury MG-21131	(M)	**Turn On, Tune In, Drop Out** (Soundtrack)	1967	16.00	40.00
Mercury SR-61131	(S)	**Turn On, Tune In, Drop Out** (Soundtrack)	1967	20.00	50.00
Douglas 1	(M)	**You Can Be Anyone This Time Around**	196?	40.00	100.00
		(Featuring Jimi Hendrix on guitar.)			

LEASEBREAKERS, THE

Label & Catalog #		Title	Year	VG+	NM
United Arts. UAL-3423	(M)	**The Leasebreakers**	1965	5.00	12.00
United Arts. UAS-6423	(S)	**The Leasebreakers**	1965	6.00	15.00

LEATHERCOATED MINDS, THE
The Minds feature J.J. Cale.

Label & Catalog #		Title	Year	VG+	NM
Viva V-36003	(M)	**Trip Down Sunset Strip**	1967	12.00	30.00
Viva VS-36003	(S)	**Trip Down Sunset Strip**	1967	16.00	40.00

LEAVES, THE

Label & Catalog #		Title	Year	VG+	NM
Mira LP-3005	(M)	**Hey Joe**	1966	16.00	40.00
Mira LPS-3005	(S)	**Hey Joe**	1966	20.00	50.00
		(Previous listings of this album on Surrey were erroneous.)			
Capitol T-2638	(M)	**All The Good That's Happening**	1967	10.00	25.00
Capitol ST-2638	(S)	**All The Good That's Happening**	1967	12.00	30.00

LED ZEPPELIN

Label & Catalog #		Title	Year	VG+	NM
Atlantic SD-8216	(DJ)	**Led Zeppelin** (White label. Mono)	1968	80.00	200.00
Atlantic SD-8216	(DJ)	**Led Zeppelin** (White label. Stereo)	1968	60.00	150.00
Atlantic SD-8216	(S)	**Led Zeppelin** (Purple & brown label)	1968	80.00	200.00
		(Atlantic 8215 was erroneously pressed with an Atco-style label.			
		These may have been the first pressings and are very rare.)			
Atlantic SD-8216	(S)	**Led Zeppelin** (Green & orange label)	1968	80.00	200.00
		(Issued with a laminated cover manufactured for export.)			
Atlantic SD-8216	(S)	**Led Zeppelin** (Green & orange label)	1968	8.00	20.00
Atlantic SD-8236	(DJ)	**Led Zeppelin II** (White label. Mono)	1969	80.00	200.00
Atlantic SD-8236	(DJ)	**Led Zeppelin II** (White label. Stereo)	1969	60.00	150.00
Atlantic SD-8236	(S)	**Led Zeppelin II**	1969	8.00	20.00
Atlantic SD-7201	(DJ)	**Led Zeppelin III** (White label. Mono)	1970	80.00	200.00
Atlantic SD-7201	(DJ)	**Led Zeppelin III** (White label. Stereo)	1970	60.00	150.00
Atlantic SD-7201	(S)	**Led Zeppelin III**	1970	6.00	15.00
Atlantic SD-7208	(DJ)	**Led Zeppelin IV** (White label. Stereo)	1971	60.00	150.00
Atlantic SD-7208	(S)	**Led Zeppelin IV**	1971	4.00	10.00
Atlantic SD-7255	(DJ)	**Houses Of The Holy** (White label. Mono)	1973	150.00	300.00
Atlantic SD-7255	(DJ)	**Houses Of The Holy** (White label. Stereo)	1973	80.00	200.00
Atlantic SD-7255	(S)	**Houses Of The Holy**	1973	4.00	10.00
— Original Atlantic albums above have green & orange labels with "1841 Broadway" on the bottom.—					
Mobile Fidelity MFSL-065	(S)	**Led Zeppelin II**	1980	25.00	75.00

LED ZEPPELIN / DUSTY SPRINGFIELD

Label & Catalog #		Title	Year	VG+	NM
Atlantic SP-135	(DJ)	**Led Zeppelin / Dusty Springfield**	1969	60.00	150.00
		(Album sampler with one side devoted to each artist; this is			
		known among Zep collectors as "Climb Aboard Led Zeppelin.")			

LEE, ADA

Label & Catalog #		Title	Year	VG+	NM
Atco 33-132	(M)	**Ada Lee Comes On**	1961	6.00	15.00
Atco SD-33-132	(S)	**Ada Lee Comes On**	1961	8.00	20.00

Label & Catalog #		Title	Year	VG+	NM

LEE, ARTHUR
Mr. Lee was formerly a member of Love.

Label & Catalog #		Title	Year	VG+	NM
A&M SP-4356	(S)	**Vindicator**	1972	6.00	15.00

LEE, BRENDA

Label & Catalog #		Title	Year	VG+	NM
Decca DL-8873	(M)	**Grandma, What Great Songs You Sang**	1959	16.00	40.00
Decca DL-78873	(S)	**Grandma, What Great Songs You Sang** *(Black label with silver print.)*	1959	20.00	50.00
Decca DL-4039	(M)	**Brenda Lee**	1960	12.00	30.00
Decca DL-74039	(S)	**Brenda Lee**	1960	16.00	40.00
Decca DL-4082	(M)	**This Is Brenda**	1960	12.00	30.00
Decca DL-74082	(S)	**This Is Brenda**	1960	16.00	40.00
Decca DL-4104	(M)	**Emotions**	1961	10.00	25.00
Decca DL-74104	(S)	**Emotions**	1961	12.00	30.00
Decca DL-4176	(M)	**All The Way**	1961	10.00	25.00
Decca DL-74176	(S)	**All The Way**	1961	12.00	30.00
Decca DL-4216	(M)	**Sincerely, Brenda Lee**	1962	10.00	25.00
Decca DL-74216	(S)	**Sincerely, Brenda Lee**	1962	12.00	30.00
Decca DL-4326	(M)	**That's All**	1962	8.00	20.00
Decca DL-74326	(S)	**That's All**	1962	10.00	25.00
Decca DL-4370	(M)	**All Alone Am I**	1963	8.00	20.00
Decca DL-74370	(S)	**All Alone Am I**	1963	10.00	25.00
Decca DL-4439	(M)	**Let Me Sing**	1963	8.00	20.00
Decca DL-74439	(S)	**Let Me Sing**	1963	10.00	25.00
Decca DL-4509	(M)	**By Request**	1964	8.00	20.00
Decca DL-74509	(S)	**By Request**	1964	10.00	25.00
Decca DL-4583	(M)	**Merry Christmas From Brenda Lee**	1964	8.00	20.00
Decca DL-74583	(S)	**Merry Christmas From Brenda Lee**	1964	10.00	25.00
Decca DL-4626	(M)	**Top Teen Hits**	1965	8.00	20.00
Decca DL-74626	(S)	**Top Teen Hits**	1965	10.00	25.00
Decca DL-4661	(M)	**The Versatile Brenda Lee**	1965	6.00	15.00
Decca DL-74661	(S)	**The Versatile Brenda Lee**	1965	8.00	20.00
Decca DL-4684	(M)	**Too Many Rivers**	1965	6.00	15.00
Decca DL-74684	(S)	**Too Many Rivers**	1965	8.00	20.00
Decca DL-4755	(M)	**Bye, Bye Blues**	1966	6.00	15.00
Decca DL-74755	(S)	**Bye, Bye Blues**	1966	8.00	20.00
Decca DL-4757	(M)	**Ten Golden Years** *(Gatefold cover)*	1966	8.00	20.00
Decca DL-74757	(S)	**Ten Golden Years** *(Gatefold cover)*	1966	10.00	25.00
Decca DL-4825	(M)	**Coming On Strong**	1966	6.00	15.00
Decca DL-74825	(S)	**Coming On Strong**	1966	8.00	20.00

— Original Decca albums above have black labels with "Mfrd by Decca" beneath the rainbow.—

Label & Catalog #		Title	Year	VG+	NM
Decca DL-4941	(M)	**Reflections In Blue**	1967	6.00	15.00
Decca DL-74941	(S)	**Reflections In Blue**	1967	6.00	15.00
Decca DL-74955	(S)	**For The First Time**	1968	6.00	15.00
Decca DL-75111	(S)	**Johnny One Time**	1969	6.00	15.00
Decca DL-75232	(S)	**Memphis Portrait**	1970	6.00	15.00
Vocalion VL-3795	(M)	**Here's Brenda Lee**	1967	5.00	12.00
Vocalion VL-73795	(S)	**Here's Brenda Lee**	1967	6.00	15.00
Vocalion VL-73890	(S)	**Let It Be Me**	1970	5.00	12.00

LEE, BRENDA / TENNESSEE ERNIE FORD

Label & Catalog #		Title	Year	VG+	NM
Decca MG-9226	(M)	**The Show For Christmas Seals**	1962	12.00	30.00
Decca MG-79226	(S)	**The Show For Christmas Seals**	1962	16.00	40.00

LEE, DICKEY

Label & Catalog #		Title	Year	VG+	NM
Smash MGS-27020	(M)	**Tales Of Patches**	1962	12.00	30.00
Smash SRS-67020	(S)	**Tales Of Patches**	1962	16.00	40.00
TCF Hall T-9001	(M)	**Laurie And The Girl From Peyton Place**	1965	6.00	15.00
TCF Hall ST-9001	(S)	**Laurie And The Girl From Peyton Place**	1965	8.00	20.00

LEE, JULIA: *Refer to* **GOLDMINE'S PRICE GUIDE TO COLLECTIBLE JAZZ ALBUMS**

LEE, KATIE

Label & Catalog #		Title	Year	VG+	NM
Specialty 5000	(M)	**Spicy Songs For Cool Knights**	195?	10.00	25.00

LEE, KUI

Label & Catalog #		Title	Year	VG+	NM
Columbia CL-2603	(M)	**The Extraordinary Kui Lee**	1966	6.00	15.00
Columbia CS-9403	(S)	**The Extraordinary Kui Lee**	1966	8.00	20.00

Label & Catalog #		Title	Year	VG+	NM

LEE, MICHELE

Label & Catalog #		Title	Year	VG+	NM
Columbia OL-5800	(M)	Bravo Giovanni! (Soundtrack)	1962	6.00	15.00
Columbia OS-2200	(S)	Bravo Giovanni! (Soundtrack)	1962	8.00	20.00
Columbia CL-2486	(M)	A Taste Of The Fantastic	1967	6.00	15.00
Columbia CS-9286	(S)	A Taste Of The Fantastic	1967	6.00	15.00
Columbia CS-9682	(S)	L. David Sloane	1968	6.00	15.00

LEE, PEGGY
Ms. Lee also recorded with Doris Day.

Label & Catalog #		Title	Year	VG+	NM
Columbia CL-6033 (10")	(M)	Benny Goodman And Peggy Lee	1949	20.00	50.00
Decca DL-5482 (10")	(M)	Black Coffee	1953	30.00	75.00
Capitol H-151 (10")	(M)	Rendezvous With Peggy Lee	1952	30.00	75.00
Capitol H-204 (10")	(M)	My Best To You	1952	20.00	50.00
Decca DL-5539 (10")	(M)	Song In Intimate Style	1953	20.00	50.00
Decca DL-5557 (10")	(M)	The Lady And The Tramp (Soundtrack)	1955	50.00	125.00
Decca DL-8083	(M)	White Christmas (Soundtrack)	1954	30.00	75.00
Decca DL-8166	(M)	Songs From Pete Kelly's Blues (Soundtrack)	1955	24.00	60.00
Decca DL-8358	(M)	Black Coffee	1956	20.00	50.00
Decca DL-8411	(M)	Dream Street	1956	16.00	40.00
Decca DL-8462	(M)	The Lady And The Tramp (Soundtrack)	1957	40.00	100.00
Decca DL-8591	(M)	Sea Shells	1958	16.00	40.00
Decca DL-8816	(M)	Miss Wonderful	1959	16.00	40.00
—Original Decca albums above have black & silver labels.—					
Decca DL-4478	(M)	Lover	1964	6.00	15.00
Decca DL-74478	(E)	Lover	1964	5.00	12.00
Decca DL-4461	(M)	The Fabulous Peggy Lee	1964	6.00	15.00
Decca DL-74461	(E)	The Fabulous Peggy Lee	1964	5.00	12.00
Decca DXB-164	(M)	The Best Of Peggy Lee (2 LPs)	1964	10.00	25.00
Decca DXSB-164	(E)	The Best Of Peggy Lee (2 LPs)	1964	8.00	20.00
Capitol T-151	(M)	Rendezvous With Peggy Lee	1954	12.00	30.00
Capitol T-204	(M)	My Best To You	1954	12.00	30.00
Capitol T-864	(M)	The Man I Love	1957	12.00	30.00
		(Capitol 864 was conducted by Frank Sinatra.)			
Capitol T-975	(M)	Jump For Joy	1957	12.00	30.00
—Original Capitol albums above have turquoise labels.—					
Capitol T-1049	(M)	Things Are Swingin'	1959	8.00	20.00
Capitol ST-1049	(S)	Things Are Swingin'	1959	10.00	25.00
Capitol T-1131	(M)	I Like Men	1959	8.00	20.00
Capitol ST-1131	(S)	I Like Men	1959	10.00	25.00
Capitol T-1219	(M)	Beauty And The Beat	1960	8.00	20.00
Capitol ST-1219	(S)	Beauty And The Beat	1960	10.00	25.00
—Original Capitol albums above have black labels with the logo on the left side.—					
Capitol T-1290	(M)	Latin Ala Lee!	1960	6.00	15.00
Capitol ST-1290	(S)	Latin Ala Lee!	1960	8.00	20.00
Capitol T-1366	(M)	All Aglow Again	1960	6.00	15.00
Capitol ST-1366	(S)	All Aglow Again	1960	8.00	20.00
Capitol T-1401	(M)	Pretty Eyes	1960	6.00	15.00
Capitol ST-1401	(S)	Pretty Eyes	1960	8.00	20.00
Capitol T-1423	(M)	Christmas Carousel	1960	6.00	15.00
Capitol ST-1423	(S)	Christmas Carousel	1960	8.00	20.00
Capitol T-1520	(M)	Basin Street East	1960	6.00	15.00
Capitol ST-1520	(S)	Basin Street East	1960	8.00	20.00
Capitol T-1671	(M)	Blue Cross Country	1961	6.00	15.00
Capitol ST-1671	(S)	Blue Cross Country	1961	8.00	20.00
Capitol T-1630	(M)	If You Go	1961	6.00	15.00
Capitol ST-1630	(S)	If You Go	1961	8.00	20.00
Capitol T-1743	(M)	Bewitching Lee	1962	8.00	20.00
Capitol DT-1743	(E)	Bewitching Lee	1962	6.00	15.00
		(Capitol 1743 is a reissue of 151 and 204.)			
Capitol T-1772	(M)	Sugar 'N' Spice	1962	6.00	15.00
Capitol ST-1772	(S)	Sugar 'N' Spice	1962	8.00	20.00
Capitol T-1850	(M)	Mink Jazz	1963	8.00	20.00
Capitol ST-1850	(S)	Mink Jazz	1963	10.00	25.00
Capitol T-1857	(M)	I'm A Woman	1963	5.00	12.00
Capitol ST-1857	(S)	I'm A Woman	1963	6.00	15.00
Capitol T-1969	(M)	In Love Again	1963	5.00	12.00
Capitol ST-1969	(S)	In Love Again	1963	6.00	15.00
Capitol T-2096	(M)	In The Name Of Love	1964	5.00	12.00
Capitol ST-2096	(S)	In The Name Of Love	1964	6.00	15.00

Label & Catalog #		Title	Year	VG+	NM
Capitol T-2320	(M)	Pass Me By	1965	5.00	12.00
Capitol ST-2320	(S)	Pass Me By	1965	6.00	15.00
Capitol T-2388	(M)	Then Was Then Now Is Now	1965	5.00	12.00
Capitol ST-2388	(S)	Then Was Then Now Is Now	1965	6.00	15.00
Capitol T-2475	(M)	Big Spender	1966	5.00	12.00
Capitol ST-2475	(S)	Big Spender	1966	6.00	15.00
Capitol T-2732	(M)	Extra Special	1967	6.00	15.00
Capitol ST-2732	(S)	Extra Special	1967	5.00	12.00
Capitol T-2781	(M)	Something Groovy	1967	6.00	15.00
Capitol ST-2781	(S)	Something Groovy	1967	5.00	12.00
Capitol ST-2887	(S)	The Hits Of Peggy Lee	1968	5.00	12.00

— Original Capitol albums above have black labels with the logo on top.—

Capitol ST-386	(M)	Is That All There Is?	1969	4.00	10.00

LEE, PINKY

Decca DL-8421	(M)	The Surprise Party	1957	20.00	50.00

LEE, WILMA, & STONEY COOPER

Hickory 100	(M)	There's A Big Wheel	1960	16.00	40.00
Hickory 106	(M)	Family Favorites	1960	16.00	40.00

LEFT BANKE, THE

Smash MGS-27088	(M)	Walk Away Renee/Pretty Ballerina	1967	20.00	50.00
Smash SRS-67088	(P)	Walk Away Renee/Pretty Ballerina	1967	16.00	40.00
Smash SRS-67113	(P)	Left Banke, Too	1968	16.00	40.00

(Both stereo albums have been poorly counterfeited.)

LEGEND

Bell 6027	(S)	Legend	1969	16.00	40.00

LEGEND

Megaphone 101	(S)	Legend	1970	30.00	75.00

LEGEND

Empire 11186	(S)	From The Fjords (With insert)	1979	150.00	300.00

LEGENDS, THE

Columbia CL-1707	(M)	Hit Sounds Of Today's Smash Hit Combos	1961	12.00	30.00
Columbia CS-8507	(S)	Hit Sounds Of Today's Smash Hit Combos	1961	16.00	40.00

LEGENDS, THE

Ermine 101	(M)	The Legends Let Loose	1963	50.00	125.00
Capitol T-1925	(M)	The Legends Let Loose	1963	20.00	50.00
Capitol ST-1925	(S)	The Legends Let Loose	1963	20.00	50.00

LEHRER, TOM

Rivoli 4 (10")	(M)	Song Satires	1954	20.00	50.00
Lehrer 101 (10")	(M)	Songs By Tom Lehrer	1954	20.00	50.00
Lehrer TL-101	(M)	Songs By Tom Lehrer	1958	12.00	30.00
Lehrer TL-202	(M)	An Evening Wasted With Tom Lehrer	1958	8.00	20.00
Lehrer TL-202S	(S)	An Evening Wasted With Tom Lehrer	1958	12.00	30.00
Lehrer TL-102	(M)	More Of Tom Lehrer	1958	8.00	20.00
Lehrer TL-102S	(M)	More Of Tom Lehrer	1958	12.00	30.00

(Lehrer 102 contains the same live tracks as Lehrer 202 with
Tom's spoken commentary and the audience sounds edited out.)

Reprise R-6179	(M)	That Was The Year That Was	1965	6.00	15.00
Reprise RS-6179	(S)	That Was The Year That Was	1965	8.00	20.00
Reprise R-6199	(M)	An Evening Wasted With Tom Lehrer	1966	6.00	15.00
Reprise RS-6199	(S)	An Evening Wasted With Tom Lehrer	1966	8.00	20.00

LEIBER, JERRY

Kapp KL-1127	(M)	Scooby-Doo	1959	20.00	50.00

LEIBER, JERRY, & MIKE STOLLER: Refer to ELVIS PRESLEY

LEIBER & STOLLER BIG BAND

Atlantic 8047	(M)	Yakety Yak	1960	16.00	40.00
Atlantic SD-8047	(S)	Yakety Yak	1960	20.00	50.00

Label & Catalog #		Title	Year	VG+	NM
LEMMON, JACK					
Epic LN-3491	(M)	**A Twist Of Lemmon**	1959	12.00	30.00
Epic BN-3491	(S)	**A Twist Of Lemmon**	1959	16.00	40.00
Epic LN-3551	(M)	**Music From "Some Like It Hot"**	1959	12.00	30.00
Epic BN-3551	(S)	**Music From "Some Like It Hot"**	1959	16.00	40.00
Riverside RLP-12-849	(M)	**Jack Lemmon Reads**			
		E.B. White's "Here Is New York"	196?	10.00	25.00
Capitol T-1943	(M)	**Piano Selections From "Irma La Douce"**	1963	10.00	25.00
Capitol ST-1943	(S)	**Piano Selections From "Irma La Douce"**	1963	12.00	30.00
LEMON PIPERS, THE					
Refer to 1910 Fruitgum Co. / The Lemon Pipers.					
Buddah BD-5009	(M)	**Green Tambourine**	1968	8.00	20.00
Buddah BDS-5009	(S)	**Green Tambourine**	1968	10.00	25.00
Buddah BDS-5016	(S)	**Jungle Marmalade**	1968	8.00	20.00
LEN & JUDY					
Prestige PRLP-7355	(M)	**Folk Songs Sweet, Bitter Sweet**	1964	6.00	15.00
Prestige PRST-7355	(S)	**Folk Songs Sweet, Bitter Sweet**	1964	8.00	20.00
LENNON, JOHN (& THE PLASTIC ONO BAND)					
Refer to The Beatles; Elephant's Memory; Nilsson; Yoko Ono; David Peel.					
United Arts. FLP-671010	(DJ)	**How I Won The War** *(Radio spots)*	1965	300.00	500.00
		(The listed values are based on the assumption that John is not present on the spots. Should he indeed prove to be on the record, the values would likely double. . .)			
Apple SW-3362	(S)	**Live Peace In Toronto**	1969	12.00	30.00
		(Apple label reads "A Subsidiary of Capitol" on the bottom and credits The Plastic Ono Band. Issued with a 16 page 1970 calendar.)			
Apple SW-3362	(S)	**Live Peace In Toronto**	1969	8.00	20.00
		(Apple label reads "Manufactured by Apple" on the bottom and credits The Plastic Ono Band. Issued with a 16 page 1970 calendar.)			
Apple SW-3372	(S)	**John Lennon/Plastic Ono Band**	1970	8.00	20.00
Apple SW-3379	(S)	**Imagine**	1971	8.00	20.00
		(Original Apple label reads "Manufactured by Apple" on the bottom. Issued wth poster and a postcard.)			
Apple SW-3379	(S)	**Imagine**	1971	4.00	10.00
		(Original Apple label reads "Manufactured by Apple" on the bottom. Without the poster and postcard.)			
Apple SW-3379	(S)	**Imagine**	1974	8.00	20.00
		(Apple label with an "All Rights Reserved" disclaimer. Issued wth poster and a postcard.)			
Apple SW-3379	(S)	**Imagine**	1974	4.00	10.00
		(Apple label with an "All Rights Reserved" disclaimer. Without the poster and postcard.)			
Apple SW-3414	(S)	**Mind Games**	1973	8.00	20.00
Apple SW-3416	(S)	**Walls And Bridges** *(With book)*	1974	8.00	20.00
Apple SK-3419	(S)	**Rock 'N' Roll**	1975	8.00	20.00
Apple SW-3421	(S)	**Shaved Fish**	1975	6.00	15.00
Adam VIII 8018	(S)	**Roots: John Lennon Sings**			
		The Great Rock & Roll Hits	1975	500.00	1,000.00
		(Originals must have "A-8018" hand- etched on the label. Original covers have the art printed on the cardboard and the song titles on the ads on the back cover for "20 Solid Gold Hits" are legible. Copies with pasted on slicks, illegible print on the back ads, or print on the spine of the cover that reads "John Lennon Sings The Greatest Rock & Roll Hits" are counterfeits)			
Capitol SW-3414	(S)	**Mind Games** *(Purple label)*	1978	12.00	30.00
Capitol SK-3419	(S)	**Rock 'N' Roll** *(Purple label)*	1978	12.00	30.00
Capitol SW-3362	(S)	**Live Peace In Toronto 1969** *(Black label)*	1988	10.00	25.00
Capitol SW-3379	(S)	**Imagine** *(Black label)*	1983	6.00	15.00
Geffen GHSP-2023	(DJ)	**The John Lennon Collection** *(Quiex II vinyl)*	1982	20.00	50.00
Geffen GHSP-2023	(S)	**The John Lennon Collection**	1982	5.00	12.00
Mobile Fidelity MFSL-153	(S)	**Imagine**	1984	10.00	25.00
Capitol R-144136	(S)	**Menlove Ave.** *(RCA Record Club)*	1986	10.00	25.00
Capitol R-144497	(S)	**Live In New York City** *(RCA Record Club)*	1986	6.00	15.00
Capitol SV-512451	(S)	**Live In New York City** *(Columbia Rec. Club)*	1986	6.00	15.00

LENNON, JOHN, & YOKO ONO

Label & Catalog #		Title	Year	VG+	NM
Apple T-5001	(S)	**Two Virgins: Unfinished Music No. 1**	1968	60.00	150.00
		(Issued in a brown paper outer sleeve that is the same size as the album jacket and opens on the right. Originals have glossy labels with "MR" machine-stamped in the trail-off vinyl. Reissued in 1985 with non-glossy labels; these are worth $10-15.)			
Zapple ST-3357	(S)	**Unfinished Music #2: Life With The Lions**	1969	10.00	25.00
Apple 3361	(S)	**Wedding Album**	1969	60.00	150.00
		(Boxed set contains photos, postcard, poster of wedding photos, poster of lithographs, a booklet of press clippings, duplicate of marriage certificate, a "bagism" bag.)			
Apple SVBB-3392	(DJ)	**Some Time In New York City** (2 LPs)	1972	500.00	800.00
		(White label promo)			
Apple SVBB-3392	(S)	**Some Time In New York City** (2 LPs)	1972	12.00	30.00
		(Label credits John & Yoko/Plastic Ono Band With Elephant's Memory And Invisible Strings. Issued with a bonus photo and a petiton to the government to allow John to stay in the U.S.)			
Capitol SVBB-3392	(S)	**Some Time In New York City**	1978	10.00	25.00
		(Purple label in a double pocket, gatefold jacket.)			
Capitol SVBB-3392	(S)	**Some Time In New York City**	1978	100.00	250.00
		(Purple label in a single pocket, gatefold jacket.)			
Geffen GHS-2001	(S)	**Double Fantasy**	1980	8.00	20.00
		(Off-white labels with no print along the perimeter.)			
Geffen GHS-2001	(S)	**Double Fantasy** (Black label)	1986	12.00	30.00
Geffen GHS-2001	(S)	**Double Fantasy** (Columbia Record Club)	1980	6.00	15.00
Geffen R-104689	(S)	**Double Fantasy** (RCA Record Club)	1980	6.00	15.00
Nautilus NR-47	(DJ)	**Double Fantasy**	1980	200.00	400.00
		(Issued in a plain white jacket with a nautilus seashell.)			
Nautilus NR-47	(S)	**Double Fantasy** (Includes a poster)	1980	16.00	50.00
Nautilus NR-47	(S)	**Double Fantasy** (Alternate cover)	1980	*See note below*	
		(This alternate cover has yellowish markings added to the background and a red heart drawn on Yoko's chest. There is one known copy and no transactions; the suggested Near Mint value of $1,000-3,000 is made with reservations. . .)			
Capitol C1-91425	(S)	**Double Fantasy**	1989	6.00	15.00
Capitol C1-591425	(S)	**Double Fantasy** (Columbia Record Club)	1989	16.00	40.00
Polydor 817-160-1	(S)	**Milk And Honey** (Green vinyl)	1984	60.00	150.00
Polydor 817-160-1	(S)	**Milk And Honey** (Gold vinyl)	1984	40.00	100.00
		(These are unauthorized pressings done by a Polydor company employee "after hours." Issued without a cover.)			
Polydor 817-160-1	(S)	**Milk And Honey** (Columbia Record Club)	1984	20.00	50.00
Silhouette SM-10012	(DJ)	**Reflections And Poetry** (2 LPs with poster)	1984	20.00	50.00
Silhouette SM-10012	(S)	**Reflections And Poetry** (2 LPs with poster)	1984	5.00	12.00
LENOIR, J.B.					
Chess LP-	(M)	**Natural Man**	1963	20.00	50.00
Polydor 24-4011	(S)	**J.B. Lenoir**	1970	6.00	15.00
LEORME					
Peters Int. 9008	(S)	**Beyond Leng**	1974	6.00	15.00
LESTER, BOBBY, & THE MOONGLOWS: *Refer to* THE MOONGLOWS					
LESTER, KETTY					
Era EL-108	(M)	**Love Letters**	1963	16.00	40.00
Era ES-108	(S)	**Love Letters**	1963	20.00	50.00
RCA Victor LPM-2945	(M)	**Soul Of Me**	1964	8.00	20.00
RCA Victor LSP-2945	(S)	**Soul Of Me**	1964	10.00	25.00
RCA Victor LPM-3326	(M)	**Where Is Love**	1965	8.00	20.00
RCA Victor LSP-3326	(S)	**Where Is Love**	1965	10.00	25.00
Tower T-5029	(M)	**When A Woman Loves A Man**	1967	6.00	15.00
Tower ST-5029	(S)	**When A Woman Loves A Man**	1967	8.00	20.00
LETTERMEN, THE					
Refer to Sonny & Cher.					
Capitol T-1669	(M)	**A Song For Young Love**	1962	6.00	15.00
Capitol ST-1669	(S)	**A Song For Young Love**	1962	8.00	20.00
Capitol T-1711	(M)	**Once Upon A Time**	1962	6.00	15.00
Capitol ST-1711	(S)	**Once Upon A Time**	1962	8.00	20.00
Capitol T-1761	(M)	**Jim, Tony, Bob**	1962	6.00	15.00

Label & Catalog #		Title	Year	VG+	NM
Capitol T-1761	(M)	Jim, Tony, Bob	1962	6.00	15.00
Capitol ST-1761	(S)	Jim, Tony, Bob	1962	8.00	20.00
Capitol T-1829	(M)	College Standards	1963	6.00	15.00
Capitol ST-1829	(S)	College Standards	1963	8.00	20.00
Capitol T-1936	(M)	The Lettermen In Concert	1963	5.00	12.00
Capitol ST-1936	(S)	The Lettermen In Concert	1963	6.00	15.00
Capitol T-2013	(M)	A Lettermen Kind Of Love	1964	5.00	12.00
Capitol ST-2013	(S)	A Lettermen Kind Of Love	1964	6.00	15.00
Capitol T-2083	(M)	The Lettermen Look At Love	1964	5.00	12.00
Capitol ST-2083	(S)	The Lettermen Look At Love	1964	6.00	15.00
Capitol T-2142	(M)	She Cried	1964	5.00	12.00
Capitol ST-2142	(S)	She Cried	1964	6.00	15.00
Capitol T-2270	(M)	Portrait Of My Love	1965	5.00	12.00
Capitol ST-2270	(S)	Portrait Of My Love	1965	6.00	15.00
Capitol T-2213	(M)	You'll Never Walk Alone	1965	5.00	12.00
Capitol ST-2213	(S)	You'll Never Walk Alone	1965	6.00	15.00
Capitol T-2359	(M)	The Hit Sounds Of The Lettermen	1965	5.00	12.00
Capitol ST-2359	(S)	The Hit Sounds Of The Lettermen	1965	6.00	15.00
Capitol T-2428	(M)	More Hit Sounds Of The Lettermen	1966	5.00	12.00
Capitol ST-2428	(S)	More Hit Sounds Of The Lettermen	1966	6.00	15.00
Capitol T-2496	(M)	A New Song For Young Love	1966	5.00	12.00
Capitol ST-2496	(S)	A New Song For Young Love	1966	6.00	15.00
Capitol T-2554	(M)	The Best Of The Lettermen	1966	5.00	12.00
Capitol ST-2554	(S)	The Best Of The Lettermen	1966	6.00	15.00
Capitol T-2587	(M)	For Christmas This Year	1966	5.00	12.00
Capitol ST-2587	(S)	For Christmas This Year	1966	6.00	15.00
Capitol T-2633	(M)	Warm	1967	6.00	15.00
Capitol ST-2633	(S)	Warm	1967	6.00	15.00
Capitol T-2711	(M)	Spring!!	1967	6.00	15.00
Capitol ST-2711	(S)	Spring!!	1967	6.00	15.00
Capitol T-2758	(M)	The Lettermen!! And Live!	1967	6.00	15.00
Capitol ST-2758	(S)	The Lettermen!! And Live!	1967	6.00	15.00
Capitol T-2865	(M)	Goin' Out Of My Head	1968	8.00	20.00
Capitol ST-2865	(S)	Goin' Out Of My Head	1968	5.00	12.00
—Original Capitol albums above have black labels with the logo on top.—					
Capitol SPRO-6218/9	(DJ)	The Lettermen At The Waldorf	196?	12.00	30.00

LEVIATHAN

Mach XMA-12501	(S)	Leviathan	1974	14.00	35.00

LEWIS, BARBARA

Atlantic 8086	(M)	Hello Stranger	1963	14.00	35.00
Atlantic SD-8086	(S)	Hello Stranger	1963	20.00	50.00
Atlantic 8090	(M)	Snap Your Fingers	1964	14.00	35.00
Atlantic SD-8090	(S)	Snap Your Fingers	1964	20.00	50.00
Atlantic 8110	(M)	Baby, I'm Yours	1965	10.00	25.00
Atlantic SD-8110	(S)	Baby, I'm Yours	1965	14.00	35.00
Atlantic 8118	(M)	It's Magic	1966	8.00	20.00
Atlantic SD-8118	(S)	It's Magic	1966	10.00	25.00
Atlantic SD-8173	(S)	Workin' On A Groovy Thing	1968	8.00	20.00
Atlantic SD-8286	(S)	The Best Of Barbara Lewis	1971	8.00	20.00

LEWIS, BOBBY

Beltone 4000	(M)	Tossin' And Turnin'	1961	70.00	175.00

LEWIS, FURRY

Bluesville BVLP-1036	(M)	Back On My Feet Again	1961	20.00	50.00
Bluesville BVLP-1037	(M)	Done Changed My Mind	1961	20.00	50.00
Prestige PRST-7810	(S)	Back On My Feet Again	1970	6.00	15.00
(Prestige 7810 is a reissue of Bluesville 1036.)					
Adelphi 1007	(S)	On The Road Again	1970	6.00	15.00
Ampex A-10140	(S)	Live At The Gaslight	1971	8.00	20.00
Fantasy F-24709	(S)	Shake 'Em On Down (2 LPs)	1972	6.00	15.00

LEWIS, GARY (& THE PLAYBOYS)

Liberty LRP-3408	(M)	This Diamond Ring	1965	8.00	20.00
Liberty LST-7408	(S)	This Diamond Ring	1965	10.00	25.00
Liberty LRP-3419	(M)	A Session With Gary Lewis	1965	6.00	15.00
Liberty LST-7419	(S)	A Session With Gary Lewis	1965	8.00	20.00

Label & Catalog #		Title	Year	VG+	NM
Liberty LRP-3428	(M)	Everybody Loves A Clown	1965	6.00	15.00
Liberty LST-7428	(S)	Everybody Loves A Clown	1965	8.00	20.00
Liberty LRP-3435	(M)	She's Just My Style	1966	6.00	15.00
Liberty LST-7435	(S)	She's Just My Style	1966	8.00	20.00
Liberty LRP-3452	(M)	Hits Again!	1966	6.00	15.00
Liberty LST-7452	(S)	Hits Again!	1966	8.00	20.00
Liberty LRP-3468	(M)	Gary Lewis' Golden Greats	1966	6.00	15.00
Liberty LST-7468	(S)	Gary Lewis' Golden Greats	1966	8.00	20.00
Liberty LRP-3487	(M)	You Don't Have To Paint Me A Picture	1967	6.00	15.00
Liberty LST-7487	(S)	You Don't Have To Paint Me A Picture	1967	8.00	20.00
Liberty LRP-3519	(M)	New Directions	1967	6.00	15.00
Liberty LST-7519	(S)	New Directions	1967	8.00	20.00
Liberty LRP-3524	(M)	Listen	1967	6.00	15.00
Liberty LST-7524	(S)	Listen	1967	8.00	20.00
Liberty LST-7568	(S)	Gary Lewis Now!	1968	6.00	15.00
Liberty LST-7589	(S)	More Golden Greats	1968	6.00	15.00
Liberty LST-7606	(S)	Close Cover Before Playing	1969	6.00	15.00
Liberty LST-7623	(S)	Rhythm Of The Rain	1969	6.00	15.00
Liberty LST-7633	(S)	I'm On The Right Road Now	1969	6.00	15.00

LEWIS, HUEY, & THE NEWS

Label & Catalog #		Title	Year	VG+	NM
Mobile Fidelity MFSL-181	(S)	Sports	198?	5.00	15.00

LEWIS, JERRY

Label & Catalog #		Title	Year	VG+	NM
Decca DL-8410	(M)	Jerry Lewis Just Sings	1956	30.00	75.00
Decca DL-8595	(M)	More Jerry Lewis	1956	30.00	75.00
Decca DL-8936	(M)	Big Songs For Little People	1959	20.00	50.00
Decca DL-78936	(S)	Big Songs For Little People	1969	30.00	75.00
Dot DLP-8001	(M)	Cinderfella (Soundtrack)	1960	20.00	50.00
Dot DLP-8001	(M)	Cinderfella (Soundtrack. Colored vinyl)	1960	40.00	100.00
Dot DLP-38001	(S)	Cinderfella (Soundtrack)	1960	30.00	75.00
Dot DLP-38001	(S)	Cinderfella (Soundtrack. Colored vinyl)	1960	60.00	150.00
Capitol J-3267	(M)	Nagger	1963	12.00	30.00
Vocalion VL-3781	(M)	Jerry Lewis Sings For Children	196?	6.00	15.00
Vocalion VL-73781	(S)	Jerry Lewis Sings For Children	196?	8.00	20.00

LEWIS, JERRY LEE

For additional listings refer to Johnny Cash / Jerry Lee Lewis.

Label & Catalog #		Title	Year	VG+	NM
Sun SLP-1230	(M)	Jerry Lee Lewis	1958	80.00	200.00
Sun SLP-1265	(DJ)	Jerry Lee's Greatest (White label)	1961	250.00	750.00
Sun SLP-1265	(M)	Jerry Lee's Greatest	1961	100.00	250.00
Design DLP-165	(M)	Rockin' With Jerry Lee Lewis	1963	10.00	25.00
Design DSP-165	(E)	Rockin' With Jerry Lee Lewis	1963	8.00	20.00
Smash MGS-27040	(M)	The Golden Hits Of Jerry Lee Lewis	1964	10.00	25.00
Smash SRS-67040	(S)	The Golden Hits Of Jerry Lee Lewis	1964	14.00	35.00
Smash SRS-67040	(S)	The Golden Rock Hits Of Jerry Lee Lewis	1969	6.00	15.00
		("Golden Rock Hits" is a reissue of "Golden Hits.")			
Smash MGS-27056	(M)	The Greatest Live Show On Earth	1964	30.00	75.00
Smash SRS-67056	(S)	The Greatest Live Show On Earth	1964	40.00	100.00
Smash MGS-27063	(M)	The Return Of Rock	1965	14.00	35.00
Smash SRS-67063	(S)	The Return Of Rock	1965	20.00	50.00
Smash MGS-27071	(M)	Country Songs For City Folks	1965	6.00	15.00
Smash SRS-67071	(S)	Country Songs For City Folks	1965	10.00	25.00
Smash SRS-67071	(S)	All Country	1969	6.00	15.00
		("All Country" is a reissue of "Country Songs For City Folks.")			
Smash MGS-27079	(M)	Memphis Beat	1966	8.00	20.00
Smash SRS-67079	(S)	Memphis Beat	1966	12.00	30.00
Smash MGS-27086	(M)	By Request	1966	8.00	20.00
Smash SRS-67086	(S)	By Request	1966	12.00	30.00
Smash MGS-27097	(M)	Soul My Way	1967	12.00	30.00
Smash SRS-67097	(S)	Soul My Way	1967	16.00	40.00
Smash SRS-67104	(S)	Another Place, Another Time	1968	6.00	15.00
Smash SRS-67112	(S)	She Still Comes Around	1968	6.00	15.00
Smash SRS-67117	(S)	Country Music Hall Of Fame Hits, Volume 1	1969	6.00	15.00
Smash SRS-67118	(S)	Country Music Hall Of Fame Hits, Volume 2	1969	6.00	15.00
Smash SRS-67128	(S)	She Even Woke Me Up To Say Goodbye	1970	6.00	15.00
Smash SRS-67131	(S)	The Best Of Jerry Lee Lewis	1970	6.00	15.00

Not only one of the great rock 'n rollers, nor merely one of the great country 'n westerners (sic), Mr. Lewis is one of the great American singers... period. While Jerry Lee has yet to receive an RIAA Gold Record, he has placed twenty albums on the charts, although the Sun material had to wait until Shelby Singleton's repackages in 1969 to see the best-seller lists. Collectors should note that a rare white label promo exists for Sun 1265, Jerry Lee's Greatest (below) that commands big buckaroos...

Label & Catalog #		Title	Year	VG+	NM
Wing MGW-12340	(M)	The Return Of Rock	1967	5.00	12.00
Wing SRW-16340	(S)	The Return Of Rock	1967	6.00	15.00
		(Wing 12/16340 is an abridged reissue of Smash 2/67063.)			
Wing SRW-16340	(S)	In Demand	1968	6.00	15.00
		("In Demand" is a reissue of "The Return Of Rock.")			
Wing SRW-16406	(S)	Unlimited	1968	6.00	15.00
Wing PKW2-125	(S)	The Legend Of Jerry Lee Lewis (2 LPs)	1969	10.00	25.00
		(Wing 125 is a repackage of 16340 and 16405.)			
Sun LP-102	(E)	Original Golden Hits, Volume 1	1969	5.00	12.00
Sun LP-103	(E)	Original Golden Hits, Volume 2	1969	5.00	12.00
Sun LP-107	(E)	Rockin' Rhythm & Blues	1969	5.00	12.00
Sun LP-108	(E)	The Golden Cream Of The Country	1969	5.00	12.00
Sun LP-114	(E)	A Taste Of Country	1970	5.00	12.00
Sun LP-124	(E)	Monsters	1971	5.00	12.00
Sun LP-128	(E)	Original Golden Hits, Volume 3	1971	5.00	12.00
Sun LP-145	(E)	Roots	1971	5.00	12.00
		(The Sun 100 series collects material from 1957-60.)			
Sears SPS-610	(E)	Hound Dog	1971	8.00	20.00
Mercury SR-61278	(S)	Live At The International	1970	6.00	15.00
Mercury SR-61318	(S)	In Loving Memories	1971	10.00	25.00
Mercury SR-61323	(S)	There Must Be More To Love Than This	1971	6.00	15.00
Mercury SR-61343	(S)	Touching Home (Drawing cover)	1971	10.00	25.00
Mercury SR-61343	(S)	Touching Home (Photo cover)	1971	6.00	15.00
Mercury SR-61346	(S)	Would You Take Another Chance On Me	1971	6.00	15.00
Mercury SR-61366	(S)	Who's Gonna Play This Old Piano	1972	5.00	12.00
Mercury SRM-1-637	(S)	The Killer Rocks On	1972	8.00	20.00
Mercury SRM-1-677	(S)	Sometimes A Memory Ain't Enough	1972	5.00	12.00
Mercury SRM-1-690	(S)	Southern Roots	1972	5.00	12.00
Mercury MK-3	(DJ)	Southern Roots Radio Special	1972	20.00	50.00
Mercury SRM-1-710	(S)	I-40 Country	1973	8.00	20.00
Mercury SRM-2-803	(S)	The Session (2 LPs)	1973	10.00	25.00
Mercury SRM-1-1030	(S)	Boogie Woogie Country Man	1975	5.00	12.00
Mercury SRM-1-1064	(S)	Odd Man In	1975	5.00	12.00
Mercury SRM-1-1109	(S)	Country Class	1976	5.00	12.00
Mercury SRM-1-5004	(S)	Country Memories	1977	5.00	12.00
Mercury SRM-1-5006	(S)	The Best Of Jerry Lee Lewis, Volume 2	1978	5.00	12.00
Mercury SRM-1-5010	(S)	Jerry Lee Lewis Keeps Rockin'	1978	5.00	12.00

LEWIS, JERRY LEE, & LINDA GAIL LEWIS

Smash SRS-67126	(S)	Together	1969	6.00	15.00

LEWIS, LINDA GAIL

Smash SRS-67119	(S)	Two Sides Of Linda Gail Lewis	1969	6.00	15.00

LEWIS, KATHERINE HANDY

Folkways FG-3540	(M)	W.C. Handy Blues	196?	10.00	25.00

LEWIS, MEADE LUX: *Refer to* GOLDMINE'S PRICE GUIDE TO COLLECTIBLE JAZZ ALBUMS

LEWIS, SHARI

RCA Victor LBY-1006	(M)	Fun In Shariland	1954	30.00	75.00
Golden GLP-39	(M)	Hi, Kids!	1962	12.00	30.00

LEWIS, SMILEY

Imperial LP-9141	(M)	I Hear You Knocking	1961	200.00	400.00

LEWIS & CLARKE EXPEDITION

Colgems COM-105	(M)	The Lewis And Clarke Expedition	1967	8.00	20.00
Colgems COS-105	(S)	The Lewis And Clarke Expedition	1967	10.00	25.00

LIBERMAN, JEFFREY

Librah 1545	(S)	Jeffrey Liberman	1975	30.00	75.00
Librah 6969	(S)	Solitude Within	1975	40.00	100.00
Librah 12157	(S)	Synergy	1978	40.00	100.00

LIC

Big Dog BD-1001	(S)	Just A Taste	1979	20.00	50.00

Label & Catalog #		Title	Year	VG+	NM
LT. GARCIA'S MAGIC MUSIC BOX					
Kama Sutra KLPS-8071	(S)	Cross The Border	1968	6.00	15.00
LIGHTCRUST DOUGHBOYS, THE					
Audio Lab LP-1525	(M)	The Lightcrust Doughboys	1959	50.00	125.00
LIGHTFOOT, GORDON					
United Arts. UAL-3487	(M)	Lightfoot	1965	6.00	15.00
United Arts. UAS-6487	(S)	Lightfoot	1965	8.00	20.00
United Arts. UAL-3587	(M)	The Way I Feel	1967	6.00	15.00
United Arts. UAS-6587	(S)	The Way I Feel	1967	8.00	20.00
Reprise MS4-2177	(Q)	Sundown	1974	6.00	15.00
Reprise MS4-2206	(Q)	Cold On The Shoulder	1975	6.00	15.00
Mobile Fidelity MFSL-018	(S)	Sundown	1979	12.00	35.00
LIGHTHOUSE					
RCA Victor LSP-4173	(S)	Lighthouse	1969	6.00	15.00
RCA Victor LSP-4241	(S)	Suite Feeling	1969	6.00	15.00
RCA Victor LSP-4325	(S)	Peacing It All Together	1970	6.00	15.00
Evolution 3007	(S)	One Fine Morning	1971	5.00	12.00
LIGHTNIN' SLIM					
Excello 8000	(M)	Rooster Blues	1960	60.00	150.00
Excello 8004	(M)	Lightnin' Slim's Bell Ringer	1965	30.00	75.00
Excello S-8004	(M)	Lightnin' Slim's Bell Ringer	1967	12.00	30.00
		(While the cover states rechanneled stereo the disc plays mono!)			
Excello 8018	(S)	High And Low Down	1971	6.00	15.00
Excello 8023	(S)	London Gumbo	1972	6.00	15.00
LIGHTNING					
P.I.P. 6807	(S)	Lightning	1971	12.00	30.00
LILLIE, BEATRICE					
Liberty Music 1002 (10")	(M)	Thirty Minutes With Beatrice	1952	20.00	50.00
Decca DL-5453 (10")	(M)	Souvenir Album	1953	16.00	40.00
London LL-1373	(M)	An Evening With Beatrice Lillie	1957	10.00	25.00
LILLY BROTHERS, THE					
Folklore FRLP-14010	(M)	Bluegrass Breakdown	1964	8.00	20.00
Folklore FRST-14010	(S)	Bluegrass Breakdown	1964	10.00	25.00
Folklore FRLP-14035	(M)	Country Songs	1964	8.00	20.00
Folklore FRST-14035	(S)	Country Songs	1964	10.00	25.00
LIMELITERS, THE					
The Limeliters feature Glenn Yarbrough.					
Elektra EKL-180	(M)	The Limeliters	1960	6.00	15.00
Elektra EKS-7180	(S)	The Limeliters	1960	8.00	20.00
RCA Victor LPM-2272	(M)	Tonight: In Person	1961	6.00	15.00
RCA Victor LSP-2272	(S)	Tonight: In Person	1961	8.00	20.00
RCA Victor LPM-2393	(M)	The Slightly Fabulous Limeliters	1961	6.00	15.00
RCA Victor LSP-2393	(S)	The Slightly Fabulous Limeliters	1961	8.00	20.00
RCA Victor LPM-2445	(M)	The Limeliters Sing Out!	1962	6.00	15.00
RCA Victor LSP-2445	(S)	The Limeliters Sing Out!	1962	8.00	20.00
RCA Victor LPM-2512	(M)	Through Children's Eyes	1962	6.00	15.00
RCA Victor LSP-2512	(S)	Through Children's Eyes	1962	8.00	20.00
RCA Victor LPM-2547	(M)	Folk Matinee	1962	6.00	15.00
RCA Victor LSP-2547	(S)	Folk Matinee	1962	8.00	20.00
RCA Victor LPM-2588	(M)	Makin' A Joyful Noise	1963	6.00	15.00
RCA Victor LSP-2588	(S)	Makin' A Joyful Noise	1963	8.00	20.00
RCA Victor LPM-2609	(M)	Our Men In San Francisco	1963	6.00	15.00
RCA Victor LSP-2609	(S)	Our Men In San Francisco	1963	8.00	20.00
RCA Victor LPM-2671	(M)	Fourteen 14K Folk Songs	1963	6.00	15.00
RCA Victor LSP-2671	(S)	Fourteen 14K Folk Songs	1963	8.00	20.00
		— Original RCA mono albums above have "Long Play" on the bottom of the label;			
		stereo albums have "Living Stereo" on the bottom.—			
RCA Victor LPM-2844	(M)	More Of Everything	1964	5.00	12.00
RCA Victor LSP-2844	(S)	More Of Everything	1964	6.00	15.00
RCA Victor LPM-2889	(M)	The Best Of The Limeliters	1964	5.00	12.00
RCA Victor LSP-2889	(S)	The Best Of The Limeliters	1964	6.00	15.00

Label & Catalog #		Title	Year	VG+	NM
RCA Victor LPM-2906	(M)	Leave It To The Limeliters	1964	5.00	12.00
RCA Victor LSP-2906	(S)	Leave It To The Limeliters	1964	6.00	15.00
RCA Victor LPM-2907	(M)	London Concert	1965	5.00	12.00
RCA Victor LSP-2907	(S)	London Concert	1965	6.00	15.00
RCA Victor LPM-3385	(M)	The Limeliters Look At Love In Depth	1965	5.00	12.00
RCA Victor LSP-3385	(S)	The Limeliters Look At Love In Depth	1965	6.00	15.00

— Original RCA albums above have black labels.—

LINCOLN, ABBEY: *Refer to* **GOLDMINE'S PRICE GUIDE TO COLLECTIBLE JAZZ ALBUMS**

LINCOLN, PHILAMORE

Epic BN-26497	(S)	North Wind Blew South	1970	8.00	20.00

LINCOLN STREET EXIT

Mainstream S-6126	(S)	Drive It	1970	12.00	30.00

LIND, BOB

Verve/Forecast FT-3005	(M)	Elusive Bob Lind	1966	8.00	20.00
Verve/Forecast FTS-3005	(S)	Elusive Bob Lind	1966	10.00	25.00
World Pacific WP-1841	(M)	Don't Be Concerned	1966	8.00	20.00
World Pacific ST-21841	(S)	Don't Be Concerned	1966	10.00	25.00
World Pacific WP-1851	(M)	Photographs Of Feeling	1966	8.00	20.00
World Pacific ST-21851	(S)	Photographs Of Feeling	1966	10.00	25.00
Capitol ST-780	(S)	Since There Were Circles	1971	5.00	12.00

LINDE, DENNIS

Intrepid 74004	(M)	Linde Manor	1966	10.00	25.00

LINDEN, KATHY

Felsted 7501	(M)	That Certain Boy	1958	30.00	75.00

LINN COUNTY

Mercury SR-61181	(S)	Proud Flesh Soothseer	1968	8.00	20.00
Mercury SR-61218	(S)	Fever Shot	1969	8.00	20.00
Philips PHS-600-326	(S)	Till The Break Of Dawn	1970	6.00	15.00

LINTON, SHERWOOD, & THE COTTON KINGS

Re-Car 2108	(S)	Sherwood Linton & The Cotton Kings	1968	30.00	75.00

LIPSCOMB, MANCE

Reprise R-2012	(M)	Trouble In Mind	1961	10.00	25.00
Reprise R9-2012	(S)	Trouble In Mind	1961	14.00	35.00

LIPTON, PEGGY

Ode Z12-44006	(S)	Peggy Lipton	1968	10.00	25.00

LIQUID SMOKE

Avco Embassy AVE-33005	(S)	Liquid Smoke	196?	10.00	25.00

LIQUIDATORS, THE

Reggae 15002	(S)	Super Reggae	1970	6.00	15.00

LISTENING

Vanguard VSD-6504	(S)	Listening	1968	10.00	25.00

LITE STORM

Beverly Hills 1135	(S)	Lite Storm Warning	1973	16.00	40.00

LITTER, THE

Warick UR-5M-1940	(M)	Distortions	1967	200.00	400.00
Hexagon HX-681	(S)	$100 Fine	1968	150.00	300.00
Probe CPLP-4504	(S)	Emerge	1969	12.00	30.00

LITTLE ANTHONY (& THE IMPERIALS)
Little Anthony is Anthony Guardine. Refer to The Chantels.

End 303	(M)	We Are Little Anthony & The Imperials	1959	100.00	250.00
End 311	(M)	Shades Of The 40's	1960	80.00	200.00
DCP DCL-3801	(M)	I'm On The Outside Looking In	1964	8.00	20.00
DCP DCS-6801	(S)	I'm On The Outside Looking In	1964	10.00	25.00

After all but inventing rock 'n roll music (along with Chuck, Fats, countless vocal and instrumental groups, and the white kid with the sideburns) for Specialty Records, the flamboyant (ho ho) Richard Penniman opted for the ministry, intending to give his life over to the non-secular service of the Lord. As we all know, he has made several comeback attempts. . . In a career certainly divined in Heaven, Richard is currently one of the hottest stars in the field of children's music (praise the aforementioned Lord); his recording of "Itsy Bitsy Spider" not only cuts all comers but remains, after an entire year, my daughter Ananda's absolute faverave of all time (er, she's four).

Label & Catalog #		Title	Year	VG+	NM
DCP DCL-3808	(M)	Goin' Out Of My Head	1965	8.00	20.00
DCP DCS-6808	(S)	Goin' Out Of My Head	1965	10.00	25.00
DCP DCL-3809	(M)	Best Of Little Anthony & The Imperials	1966	8.00	20.00
DCP DCS-6809	(S)	Best Of Little Anthony & The Imperials	1966	10.00	25.00
Roulette R-25294	(M)	Greatest Hits	1965	8.00	20.00
Roulette SR-25294	(S)	Greatest Hits	1965	10.00	25.00
Veep VP-13510	(M)	I'm On The Outside Looking In	1966	6.00	15.00
Veep VPS-16510	(S)	I'm On The Outside Looking In	1966	8.00	20.00
Veep VP-13513	(M)	Payin' Our Dues	1966	6.00	15.00
Veep VPS-16513	(S)	Payin' Our Dues	1966	8.00	20.00
Veep VP-13514	(M)	Reflections	1967	6.00	15.00
Veep VPS-16514	(S)	Reflections	1967	8.00	20.00
Veep VP-13516	(M)	Movie Grabbers	1967	6.00	15.00
Veep VPS-16516	(S)	Movie Grabbers	1967	8.00	20.00
Veep VPS-16519	(S)	The Best Of Little Anthony, Volume 2	1968	6.00	15.00
United Arts. UAS-6720	(S)	Out Of Sight, Out Of Mind	1969	8.00	20.00
Sunset SUS-5287	(S)	Little Anthony & The Imperials	1970	6.00	15.00
United Arts. LA026	(S)	Legendary Masters (2 LPs)	1973	10.00	25.00

LITTLE BOY BLUES

Fontana MGF-27578	(M)	In The Woodland Of Weir	1967	10.00	25.00
Fontana SRF-67578	(S)	In The Woodland Of Weir	1967	12.00	30.00

LITTLE CAESAR & THE ROMANS

Del-Fi DFLP-1218	(M)	Memories Of Those Oldies But Goodies	1961	80.00	200.00

LITTLE ESTHER: Refer to ESTHER PHILLIPS

LITTLE EVA
Little Eva is Eva Boyd. Refer to The Cookies / Little Eva / Carole King.

Dimension DLP-6000	(M)	L-L-L-L-Loco-Motion	1962	40.00	100.00
Dimension DLPS-6000	(E)	L-L-L-L-Loco-Motion	1962	50.00	125.00
		(First pressings do not contain "Keep Your Hands Off Of My Baby.")			
Dimension DLP-6000	(M)	L-L-L-L-Loco-Motion	1962	60.00	150.00
Dimension DLPS-6000	(E)	L-L-L-L-Loco-Motion	1962	70.00	175.00
		(Later pressings contain "Keep Your Hands Off Of My Baby.")			

LITTLE FEAT
The Feat were formed and led by Lowell George.

Mobile Fidelity MFSL-013	(S)	Waiting For Columbus (2 LPs)	1978	25.00	75.00
Nautilus NR-24	(S)	Time Loves A Hero	198?	20.00	60.00

LITTLE JOE

Brunswick BL7-54135	(S)	Little Joe Sure Can Sing	1968	8.00	20.00

LITTLE MILTON
Little Milton is a pseudonym for Milton Campbell.

Checker 2995	(M)	We're Gonna Make It (Black label)	1965	20.00	50.00
Checker 3002	(M)	Little Milton Sings Big Blues	1966	14.00	35.00
Checker 3011	(S)	Grits Ain't Groceries	1969	8.00	20.00
Checker 3012	(S)	If Walls Could Talk	1970	6.00	15.00
Chess CH-50013	(S)	Little Milton's Greatest Hits	1972	4.00	10.00

LITTLE RICHARD (PENNIMAN)
Refer to Canned Heat; Jimi Hendrix / Little Richard.

Camden CAL-420	(M)	Little Richard	1956	50.00	150.00
Specialty 100	(M)	Here's Little Richard	1957	150.00	400.00
Specialty 2100	(M)	Here's Little Richard	1957	50.00	150.00
Specialty SP-2103	(M)	Little Richard	1957	50.00	150.00
Specialty SP-2104	(M)	The Fabulous Little Richard	1958	50.00	150.00
Specialty SP-2113	(E)	Grooviest 17 Original Hits	1968	8.00	20.00
Specialty SP-2136	(M)	Well Alright!	1970	8.00	20.00
		("Poor Boy Paul," "Bama-Lama Bama-Loo," "Annie Is Back"			
		and "Shakle A Hand" are in stereo on this album.)			
		— Original Specialty albums above have black & gold labels.—			
20th Century FXG-5010	(M)	Little Richard Sings Gospel	1959	20.00	50.00
20th Century SGM-5010	(S)	Little Richard Sings Gospel	1959	30.00	75.00
Mercury MG-20656	(M)	It's Real	1961	14.00	35.00
Mercury SR-60656	(S)	It's Real	1961	20.00	50.00

Label & Catalog #		Title	Year	VG+	NM
Crown CLP-5362	(M)	Little Richard Sings Freedom Songs	1963	8.00	20.00
Crown CST-362	(E)	Little Richard Sings Freedom Songs	1963	4.00	10.00
Coral CRL-57446	(M)	Coming Home	1963	12.00	30.00
Coral CRL-757446	(S)	Coming Home	1963	16.00	40.00
Specialty SP-2111	(M)	Little Richard's Biggest Hits	1963	16.00	40.00
Wing MGW-122288	(M)	King Of The Gospel Singers	1964	8.00	20.00
Wing SRW-162288	(S)	King Of The Gospel Singers	1964	10.00	25.00
Vee Jay LP-1107	(M)	Little Richard Is Back	1964	10.00	25.00
Vee Jay SR-1107	(S)	Little Richard Is Back	1964	16.00	40.00
Vee Jay LP-1124	(M)	Little Richard's Greatest Hits	1965	10.00	25.00
Vee Jay SR-1124	(S)	Little Richard's Greatest Hits	1965	16.00	40.00
Vee Jay VJS-2-100	(S)	Little Richard's Gold (2 LPs)	196?	10.00	25.00
Modern 100	(M)	His Greatest Hits/Recorded Live	196?	6.00	15.00
Modern 1000	(S)	His Greatest Hits/Recorded Live	196?	6.00	15.00
Modern 103	(M)	The Wild And Frantic Little Richard	196?	6.00	15.00
Modern 1003	(S)	The Wild And Frantic Little Richard	196?	6.00	15.00
Dynasty DYS-730	(S)	Talkin' 'Bout Soul	196?	6.00	15.00
Custom 2061	(M)	Little Richard Sings Spirituals	196?	6.00	15.00
OKeh OKM-12121	(M)	Greatest Hits Recorded Live	1967	6.00	15.00
OKeh OKS-14121	(S)	Greatest Hits Recorded Live	1967	8.00	20.00
OKeh OKM-12117	(M)	The Explosive Little Richard	1967	6.00	15.00
OKeh OKS-14117	(S)	The Explosive Little Richard	1967	8.00	20.00
Roulette RS-42007	(S)	Forever Yours	1968	6.00	15.00
Buddah BDS-7501	(S)	Little Richard	1969	8.00	20.00
Kama Sutra NSBS-2023	(S)	Little Richard	1970	8.00	20.00
Reprise RS-6406	(S)	The Rill Thing	1970	6.00	15.00
Reprise RS-6462	(S)	The King Of Rock And Roll	1971	6.00	15.00
Reprise MS-2107	(S)	The Second Coming	1972	6.00	15.00
Epic EG-3042	(S)	Cast A Long Shadow	1971	6.00	15.00
Scepter 18020	(S)	The Best Of Little Richard	1971	6.00	15.00
Audio Encores 1002	(S)	Little Richard	1980	10.00	25.00

LITTLE RIVER BAND, THE

Mobile Fidelity MFSL-036	(S)	First Under The Wire	197?	5.00	15.00

LITTLE WALTER
Refer to Bo Diddley.

Chess LP-1428	(M)	The Best Of Little Walter	1958	100.00	400.00
Chess LPS-1535	(S)	Hate To See You Go	1969	10.00	25.00
Chess 2CH-60014	(S)	Boss Blues Harmonica (2 LPs)	1972	6.00	15.00

LIVELY ONES, THE

Del-Fi DFLP-1226	(M)	Surf-Rider	1963	12.00	30.00
Del-Fi DFST-1226	(S)	Surf-Rider	1963	16.00	40.00
Del-Fi DFLP-1231	(M)	Surf Drums	1963	12.00	30.00
Del-Fi DFST-1231	(S)	Surf Drums	1963	16.00	40.00
Del-Fi DFLP-1237	(M)	This Is Surf City	1963	12.00	30.00
Del-Fi DFST-1237	(S)	This Is Surf City	1963	16.00	40.00
Del-Fi DFLP-1238	(M)	Great Surf Hits	1963	12.00	30.00
Del-Fi DFST-1238	(S)	Great Surf Hits	1963	16.00	40.00
Del-Fi DFLP-1240	(M)	Surfin' South Of The Border	1964	12.00	30.00
Del-Fi DFST-1240	(S)	Surfin' South Of The Border	1964	16.00	40.00
MGM E-4449	(M)	Bugalu Party	1967	6.00	15.00
MGM SE-4449	(S)	Bugalu Party	1967	8.00	20.00

LIVERPOOL BEATS, THE

Rondo 2026	(M)	The New Merseyside Sound	1964	20.00	50.00
		(This was also released on Design credited to The Beats.)			

LIVERPOOL FIVE, THE
Refer to The Astronauts / The Liverpool Five.

RCA Victor LPM-3583	(M)	Arrive	1966	10.00	25.00
RCA Victor LSP-3583	(S)	Arrive	1966	12.00	30.00
RCA Victor LPM-3682	(M)	Out Of Sight	1967	10.00	25.00
RCA Victor LSP-3682	(S)	Out Of Sight	1967	12.00	30.00

LIVERPOOL KIDS, THE
While the cover credits The Liverpool Lads, the label lists the artists as The Schoolboys.

Palace 777	(M)	Beatle Mash	1964	12.00	30.00

Label & Catalog #		Title	Year	VG+	NM

LIVERPOOL LADS, THE
This album features The Liverpool Lads in the studio overdubbed by crowd noise from a Beatles concert!

Lloyds ER-MC-Ltd.	(M)	The Great American Tour:			
		1965 Live Beatlemania Concert	1965	300.00	500.00

LIVERPOOL SCENE, THE

RCA Victor LSP-4189	(S)	Amazing Adventures	1969	8.00	20.00
RCA Victor LSP-4267	(S)	Bread On The Night	1970	8.00	20.00

LIVERPOOLS, THE

Wyncote W-9001	(M)	Beatlemania In The U.S.A.	1964	8.00	20.00
Wyncote WS-9001	(S)	Beatlemania In The U.S.A.	1964	10.00	25.00
Wyncote W-9061	(M)	The Hit Sounds From England	1964	8.00	20.00
Wyncote WS-9061	(S)	The Hit Sounds From England	1964	10.00	25.00

LIVIN' BLUES

Dwarf 2003	(S)	Dutch Treat	1971	12.00	30.00

LOADING ZONE, THE

RCA Victor LSP-3959	(S)	The Loading Zone	1968	10.00	25.00
Umbrella US-101	(S)	One For All	1970	30.00	75.00

LOCKLIN, HANK
Refer to Hank Snow / Hank Locklin / Porter Wagoner.

RCA Victor LPM-1673	(M)	Foreign Love	1958	20.00	50.00
RCA Victor LPM-2291	(M)	Please Help Me, I'm Falling	1960	14.00	35.00
RCA Victor LSP-2291	(S)	Please Help Me, I'm Falling	1960	20.00	50.00
King 672	(M)	The Best Of Hank Locklin	1961	20.00	50.00
King 738	(M)	Encores	1961	20.00	50.00
RCA Victor LPM-2464	(M)	Happy Journey	1962	10.00	25.00
RCA Victor LSP-2464	(S)	Happy Journey	1962	12.00	30.00
RCA Victor LPM-2597	(M)	A Tribute To Roy Acuff	1962	10.00	25.00
RCA Victor LSP-2597	(S)	A Tribute To Roy Acuff	1962	12.00	30.00
RCA Victor LPM-2680	(M)	The Ways Of Love	1963	10.00	25.00
RCA Victor LSP-2680	(S)	The Ways Of Love	1963	12.00	30.00

— Original RCA mono albums above have "Long Play" on the bottom of the label. Stereo albums have "Living Stereo" on the bottom.—

RCA Victor LPM-2801	(M)	Irish Songs, Country Style	1964	6.00	15.00
RCA Victor LSP-2801	(S)	Irish Songs, Country Style	1964	8.00	20.00
RCA Victor LPM-2997	(M)	Hank Locklin Sings Hank Williams	1964	6.00	15.00
RCA Victor LSP-2997	(S)	Hank Locklin Sings Hank Williams	1964	8.00	20.00
RCA Victor LPM-3391	(M)	Hank Locklin Sings Eddy Arnold	1965	6.00	15.00
RCA Victor LSP-3391	(S)	Hank Locklin Sings Eddy Arnold	1965	8.00	20.00
RCA Victor LPM-3465	(M)	Once Over Lightly	1965	6.00	15.00
RCA Victor LSP-3465	(S)	Once Over Lightly	1965	8.00	20.00
RCA Victor LPM-3559	(M)	The Best Of Hank Locklin	1966	8.00	20.00
RCA Victor LSP-3559	(S)	The Best Of Hank Locklin	1966	8.00	20.00

("Fraulein," "Send Me The Pillow You Dream On," "Geisha Girl" and "It's A Little More Like Heaven" are rechanneled.)

RCA Victor LPM-3588	(M)	The Girls Get Prettier	1966	6.00	15.00
RCA Victor LSP-3588	(S)	The Girls Get Prettier	1966	8.00	20.00
RCA Victor LPM-3656	(M)	The Gloryland Way	1966	6.00	15.00
RCA Victor LSP-3656	(S)	The Gloryland Way	1966	8.00	20.00
RCA Victor LPM-3770	(M)	Send Me The Pillow You Dream On	1967	10.00	25.00
RCA Victor LSP-3770	(S)	Send Me The Pillow You Dream On	1967	8.00	20.00
RCA Victor LPM-3841	(M)	Nashville Women	1967	10.00	25.00
RCA Victor LSP-3841	(S)	Nashville Women	1967	8.00	20.00
RCA Victor LPM-3946	(M)	Country Hall Of Fame	1968	40.00	100.00
RCA Victor LSP-3946	(S)	Country Hall Of Fame	1968	8.00	20.00

— Original RCA Victor albums above have black labels.—

LOFGREN, NILS
Refer to Crazy Horse; Grin.

A&M SP-8362	(DJ)	Authorized Bootleg *(Counterfeits exist)*	1976	16.00	40.00

LOGGINS, KENNY

Columbia AS-946	(DJ)	Kenny Loggins *(Radio sampler)*	1981	6.00	15.00
Columbia HC-45387	(S)	Nightwatch *(Half-speed master)*	1981	7.00	20.00

Okay, she's gorgeous. Yeah, she married a biggie in the biz. And her covers are rather exploitational. Nonetheless, Ms. London's early recordings are sultry, sensuous; slow dance music for late at night that beat even Johnny's Greatest Hits for intimacy. . .

Label & Catalog #		Title	Year	VG+	NM

LOGGINS & MESSINA
Kenny Loggins and Jim Messina.

Columbia CQ-32540	(Q)	Full Sail	1974	6.00	15.00
Columbia PCQ-33578	(Q)	Native Sons	1976	6.00	15.00
Columbia HC-44388	(S)	Best Of Friends *(Half-speed master)*	1982	8.00	25.00
Direct Disk SD-16606	(S)	Full Sail	197?	7.00	20.00

LOGSDON, JIMMIE

King 843	(M)	Howdy, Neighbors	1963	12.00	30.00

LOLLIPOP SHOPPE, THE
The Lollipop Shoppe features Nik Pascal Raicevic.

Tower ST-5128	(S)	Angels From Hell *(Soundtrack)*	1968	12.00	30.00
Uni 73019	(S)	The Lollipop Shoppe	1968	16.00	40.00

LOMAX, ALAN

Kapp KL-1316	(M)	Raise A Ruckus And Have A Hootenanny	1963	6.00	15.00
Kapp KS-3316	(S)	Raise A Ruckus And Have A Hootenanny	1963	8.00	20.00
Tradition TLP-1029	(M)	Texas Folk Songs	196?	8.00	20.00

LOMAX, JACKIE

Apple ST-3354	(S)	Is This What You Want	1969	8.00	20.00
		(Produced by George Harrison.)			
Warner Bros. WS-1914	(S)	Home Is In My Head	1971	4.00	10.00
Warner Bros. BS-2591	(S)	Three	1972	4.00	10.00

LONDON, JULIE

Liberty LRP-3006	(M)	Julie Is Her Name	1955	16.00	40.00
Liberty LST-7027	(S)	Julie Is Her Name	1958	20.00	50.00
Liberty LST-7027	(S)	Julie Is Her Name *(Blue vinyl)*	1958	50.00	125.00
Liberty LST-7027	(S)	Julie Is Her Name *(Red vinyl)*	1958	50.00	125.00
Liberty LRP-3012	(M)	Lonely Girl	1956	16.00	40.00
Liberty SL-9002	(M)	Calendar Girl *(Fold-open cover)*	1956	30.00	75.00
Liberty LRP-3043	(M)	About The Blues	1957	16.00	40.00
Liberty LST-7012	(S)	About The Blues	1958	20.00	50.00
Liberty LRP-3060	(M)	Make Love To Me	1957	16.00	40.00
Liberty LRP-3096	(M)	Julie	1957	16.00	40.00
Liberty LST-7004	(S)	Julie	1958	20.00	50.00
Liberty LRP-3100	(M)	Julie Is Her Name, Volume 2	1958	16.00	40.00
Liberty LST-7100	(S)	Julie Is Her Name, Volume 2	1958	20.00	50.00
Liberty LRP-3105	(M)	London By Night	1958	16.00	40.00
Liberty LRP-3119	(M)	Swing Me An Old Song	1959	16.00	40.00
Liberty LST-7119	(S)	Swing Me An Old Song	1959	20.00	50.00
Liberty LRP-3130	(M)	Your Number Please...	1959	16.00	40.00
Liberty LST-7130	(S)	Your Number Please...	1959	20.00	50.00

— Original Liberty mono albums above have turquoise labels; stereo albums have black & silver labels.—

Liberty LRP-3152	(M)	Julie...At Home	1959	12.00	30.00
Liberty LST-7152	(S)	Julie...At Home	1959	16.00	40.00
Liberty LRP-3164	(M)	Around Midnight	1960	12.00	30.00
Liberty LST-7164	(S)	Around Midnight	1960	16.00	40.00
Liberty LRP-3171	(M)	Send For Me	1960	12.00	30.00
Liberty LST-7171	(S)	Send For Me	1960	16.00	40.00
Liberty LRP-3192	(M)	Whatever Julie Wants	1961	10.00	25.00
Liberty LST-7192	(S)	Whatever Julie Wants	1961	12.00	30.00
Liberty LRP-3203	(M)	Sophisticated Lady	1962	10.00	25.00
Liberty LST-7203	(S)	Sophisticated Lady	1962	12.00	30.00
Liberty LRP-3231	(M)	Love Letters	1962	10.00	25.00
Liberty LST-7231	(S)	Love Letters	1962	12.00	30.00
Liberty LRP-3249	(S)	Love On The Rocks	1962	10.00	25.00
Liberty LST-7249	(S)	Love On The Rocks	1962	12.00	30.00
Liberty LRP-3278	(M)	Latin In A Satin Mood	1963	10.00	25.00
Liberty LST-7278	(S)	Latin In A Satin Mood	1963	12.00	30.00
Liberty LRP-3291	(M)	Julie's Golden Greats	1963	8.00	20.00
Liberty LST-7291	(S)	Julie's Golden Greats	1963	10.00	25.00
Liberty LRP-3300	(M)	The End Of The World	1963	8.00	20.00
Liberty LST-7300	(S)	The End Of The World	1963	10.00	25.00
Liberty LRP-3324	(M)	The Wonderful World Of Julie London	1963	8.00	20.00
Liberty LST-7324	(S)	The Wonderful World Of Julie London	1963	10.00	25.00

Label & Catalog #		Title	Year	VG+	NM
Liberty LRP-3342	(M)	Julie London	1964	8.00	20.00
Liberty LST-7342	(S)	Julie London	1964	10.00	25.00
Liberty LRP-3375	(M)	In Person At The Americana	1964	6.00	15.00
Liberty LST-7375	(S)	In Person At The Americana	1964	8.00	20.00
Liberty LRP-3392	(M)	Our Fair Lady	1965	6.00	15.00
Liberty LST-7392	(S)	Our Fair Lady	1965	8.00	20.00
Liberty LRP-3434	(M)	All Through The Night	1965	6.00	15.00
Liberty LST-7434	(S)	All Through The Night	1965	8.00	20.00
Liberty LRP-3416	(M)	Feeling Good	1966	6.00	15.00
Liberty LRP-3416	(M)	Feeling Good	1966	8.00	20.00
Liberty LRST-7478	(S)	For The Night People	1966	6.00	15.00
Liberty LST-7478	(S)	For The Night People	1966	8.00	20.00
Liberty LRP-3493	(M)	Nice Girls Don't Stay For Breakfast	1967	6.00	15.00
Liberty LST-7493	(S)	Nice Girls Don't Stay For Breakfast	1967	8.00	20.00
Liberty LRP-3516	(S)	Feeling Good	1967	6.00	15.00
Liberty LST-7516	(S)	Feeling Good	1967	8.00	20.00

— Original Liberty albums above have black labels with a gold & white logo on the side.—

LONDON, LAURIE

Capitol T-1016	(M)	Laurie London	1958	12.00	30.00

LONE RANGER, THE

Decca DL-8578	(M)	The Adventures Of The Lone Ranger	1958	40.00	100.00

LONESOME VALLEY SINGERS, THE

Diplomat D-2622	(M)	Song Of The Gragsters	196?	12.00	30.00
Diplomat DS-2622	(S)	Song Of The Gragsters	196?	16.00	40.00

LONG, BARBARA

Savoy MG-12161	(M)	Soul	1961	10.00	25.00

LONG, SHORTY

Soul SS-709	(S)	Here Comes The Judge	1968	6.00	15.00
Soul SS-719	(S)	The Prime Of Shorty Long	1969	6.00	15.00

LONGBRANCH PENNYWHISTLE
Members include J.D. Souther, Glen Frey, James Burton, Ry Cooder, Doug Kershaw; Buddy Emmons.

Amos AAS-7007	(S)	Longbranch Pennywhistle	1969	16.00	40.00

LONZO & OSCAR

Starday SLP-119	(M)	America's Greatest Country Comedians	1960	12.00	30.00
Starday SLP-244	(M)	Country Music Time	1963	10.00	25.00

LOOSE

Necturne 906	(S)	Freaky Billie, The Wheelie King	1970	12.00	30.00

LOPEZ, TRINI

King 863	(M)	Teenage Love Songs	1963	20.00	50.00
King 877	(M)	More Of Trini Lopez	1964	20.00	50.00

LOPEZ, TRINI / SCOTT GREGORY
This album includes early, rare tracks by Bill Haley a.k.a. Scott Gregory.

Guest Star GS-1499	(M)	Trini Lopez And Scott Gregory	1964	20.00	50.00
Guest Star GSS-1499	(E)	Trini Lopez And Scott Gregory	1964	8.00	20.00

LORBER, ALAN

MGM SE-4647	(S)	The Changing Times Of Bob Dylan	1969	6.00	15.00

LORD, BOBBY

Harmony HL-7322	(M)	Bobby Lord's Best	1964	12.00	30.00

LORD SITAR

Capitol ST-3916	(S)	Lord Sitar	1968	12.00	30.00

LORD SUTCH

Cotillion SD-9015	(S)	Lord Sutch And His Heavy Friends	1972	12.00	30.00
Cotillion SD-9049	(S)	Hands Of Jack The Ripper	1972	12.00	30.00

Boccaccio '70 was issued on RCA Victor International, a specialist label used for foreign produced recordings, many of which are quite rare. This one is desirable for, among other attributes, the stunning cover and the very evident attributes of the Misses Loren, Schneider and Ekberg. The Columbia album is taken from the 1964 TV Special in which Sophia takes the viewer on a tour of her native Roma. These are among the few albums on which Ms. Loren actually sings, although she appears on the covers of many others—especially soundtracks.

Label & Catalog #		Title	Year	VG+	NM

LOREN, DONNA

Capitol T-2323	(M)	Beach Blanket Bingo	1965	12.00	30.00
Capitol ST-2323	(S)	Beach Blanket Bingo	1965	16.00	40.00

LOREN, SOPHIA
Ms. Loren also recorded with Peter Sellers.

Columbia CL-1222	(M)	Houseboat (Soundtrack)	1958	80.00	200.00
RCA Victor Int. FOC-5	(M)	Boccaccio '70 (Soundtrack)	1962	20.00	50.00
RCA Victor Int. FSO-5	(S)	Boccaccio '70 (Soundtrack)	1962	30.00	75.00

(Although the cover pictures Romy Schneider and Anita Ekberg with Ms. Loren, neither of them appear on the record.)

Columbia OL-6310	(M)	Sophia Loren In Rome (TV Soundtrack)	1964	10.00	25.00
Columbia OS-2710	(S)	Sophia Loren In Rome (TV Soundtrack)	1964	12.00	30.00
Mace MXX-10020	(S)	The Poems Of Salvatore Di Giacomo	196?	6.00	15.00

LOS BRAVOS
Los Bravos features Mike Kennedy.

Press PR-73003	(M)	Black Is Black	1966	12.00	30.00

(Features the original single version of "Black Is Black.")

Press PAS-83003	(E)	Black Is Black	1966	10.00	25.00
Parrot PAS-71021	(S)	Bring A Little Lovin	1968	12.00	30.00

LOS LOBOS [LOS LOBOS DEL ESTE DE LOS ANGELES]

Pan American 101	(S)	Si Se Puede!	1976	100.00	200.00
New Vista 1001	(S)	Just Another Band From East L.A.	1978	200.00	400.00

LOST & FOUND

International Art. 3	(S)	Everybody's Here	1968	16.00	40.00
International Art. 3	(S)	Everybody's Here	1979	6.00	15.00

(Reissues have "Masterfonics" stamped in the trail-off vinyl.)

Tempo 7064	(S)	Number Two	1973	See note below	

(The existence of this record is in doubt.)

LOST NATION

Rare Earth RS-518	(S)	Paradise Lost	1970	8.00	20.00

LOTHAR & THE HAND PEOPLE

Capitol ST-2997	(S)	Presenting Lothar & The Hand People	1968	16.00	40.00
Capitol ST-247	(S)	Space Hymn	1969	16.00	40.00

LOUDERMILK, JOHN D.

RCA Victor LPM-2434	(M)	Language Of Love	1961	8.00	20.00
RCA Victor LSP-2434	(S)	Language Of Love	1961	10.00	25.00
RCA Victor LPM-2539	(M)	Twelve Sides Of Loudermilk	1962	8.00	20.00
RCA Victor LSP-2539	(S)	Twelve Sides Of Loudermilk	1962	10.00	25.00

— Original RCA mono albums above have "Long Play" on the bottom of the label; stereo albums have "Living Stereo" on the bottom.—

RCA Victor LPM-3497	(M)	A Bizarre Collection Of... Unusual Songs	1965	10.00	25.00
RCA Victor LSP-3497	(S)	A Bizarre Collection Of... Unusual Songs	1965	12.00	30.00
RCA Victor LPM-3807	(M)	Suburban Attitudes In Country Verse	1967	6.00	15.00
RCA Victor LSP-3807	(S)	Suburban Attitudes In Country Verse	1967	6.00	15.00
RCA Victor LSP-4040	(S)	Country Love Songs	1968	6.00	15.00
RCA Victor LSP-4097	(S)	The Open Mind Of John D. Loudermilk	1968	6.00	15.00

LOUDON, DOROTHY

Coral CRL-57265	(M)	Live At The Blue Angel	1959	6.00	15.00
Coral CRL-757265	(S)	Live At The Blue Angel	1959	10.00	25.00

LOUIE & THE LOVERS

Epic KE-30026	(S)	Rise	1970	6.00	15.00

LOUISE, TINA

Concert Hall	(M)	It's Time For Tina	1957	150.00	300.00
Urania ULM-2005	(M)	It's Time For Tina	1958	80.00	200.00
Urania ULS-2005	(S)	It's Time For Tina	1958	150.00	300.00

(Urania 2005 is a reissue of the Concert hall album.)

LOUISIANA HONEY DRIPPERS, THE

Prestige Int. PRLP-13035	(M)	Bluegrass	1961	12.00	30.00

Label & Catalog #		Title	Year	VG+	NM
LOUISIANA RED					
Roulette R-25200	(M)	The Lowdown Back Porch Blues	1963	14.00	35.00
Atco SD-33-389	(S)	Louisiana Red Sings The Blues	1972	6.00	15.00
LOUVIN, CHARLIE					
Capitol T-2208	(M)	Less And Less	1965	6.00	15.00
Capitol ST-2208	(S)	Less And Less	1965	8.00	20.00
Capitol T-2437	(M)	The Many Moods Of Charlie Louvin	1966	6.00	15.00
Capitol ST-2437	(S)	The Many Moods Of Charlie Louvin	1966	8.00	20.00
Capitol T-2482	(M)	Lonesome Is Me	1966	6.00	15.00
Capitol ST-2482	(S)	Lonesome Is Me	1966	8.00	20.00
Capitol T-2689	(M)	I'll Remember Always	1967	6.00	15.00
Capitol ST-2689	(S)	I'll Remember Always	1967	6.00	15.00
Capitol T-2787	(M)	I Forgot To Cry	1967	6.00	15.00
Capitol ST-2787	(S)	I Forgot To Cry	1967	6.00	15.00
Capitol ST-2958	(S)	Will You Visit Me On Sundays	1968	6.00	15.00
LOUVIN, IRA					
Capitol T-2413	(M)	The Unforgettable Ira Louvin	1965	10.00	25.00
Capitol ST-2413	(S)	The Unforgettable Ira Louvin	1965	12.00	30.00
LOUVIN BROTHERS, THE					
Charlie and Ira Louvin.					
MGM E-3426	(M)	The Louvin Brothers	1956	80.00	200.00
Capitol T-769	(M)	Tragic Songs Of Life	1956	50.00	100.00
Capitol T-825	(M)	Nearer My God To Thee	1957	40.00	100.00
Capitol T-910	(M)	Ira And Charlie	1958	40.00	100.00
— Original Capitol albums above have turquoise labels.—					
Capitol T-1061	(M)	The Family Who Prays	1958	30.00	75.00
Capitol T-1106	(M)	Country Love Ballads	1959	30.00	75.00
Capitol T-1277	(M)	Satan Is Real	1960	30.00	75.00
Capitol T-1385	(M)	My Baby's Gone	1960	30.00	75.00
Capitol T-1449	(M)	A Tribute To The Delmore Brothers	1960	30.00	75.00
Capitol T-1547	(M)	Encore	1961	20.00	50.00
Capitol T-1616	(M)	Country Christmas	1961	20.00	50.00
Capitol ST-1616	(S)	Country Christmas	1961	30.00	75.00
— Original Capitol albums above have black labels with the logo on the left side.—					
Capitol T-1721	(M)	Weapon Of Prayer	1962	16.00	40.00
Capitol ST-1721	(S)	Weapon Of Prayer	1962	20.00	50.00
Capitol T-1834	(M)	Keep Your Eyes On Jesus	1963	16.00	40.00
Capitol ST-1834	(S)	Keep Your Eyes On Jesus	1963	20.00	50.00
Capitol T-2091	(M)	The Louvin Brothers Sing And Play Their Current Hits	1964	12.00	30.00
Capitol ST-2091	(S)	The Louvin Brothers Sing And Play Their Current Hits	1964	16.00	40.00
Capitol T-2331	(M)	Thank God For My Christian Home	1965	12.00	30.00
Capitol ST-2331	(S)	Thank God For My Christian Home	1965	16.00	40.00
Capitol T-2827	(M)	The Great Roy Acuff Songs	1967	12.00	30.00
Capitol ST-2827	(S)	The Great Roy Acuff Songs	1967	16.00	40.00
Tower T-5038	(M)	Two Different Worlds	1966	12.00	30.00
Tower DT-5038	(E)	Two Different Worlds	1966	8.00	20.00
Tower DT-5122	(E)	Country Heart And Soul	1968	10.00	25.00
LOVE					
Love was the brainchild of Arthur Lee.					
Elektra EKL-4001	(M)	Love	1966	16.00	40.00
Elektra EKS-74001	(S)	Love	1966	10.00	25.00
Elektra EKL-4005	(M)	Da Capo	1966	16.00	40.00
Elektra EKS-74005	(S)	Da Capo	1966	10.00	25.00
Elektra EKL-4013	(M)	Forever Changes	1967	16.00	40.00
Elektra EKS-74013	(S)	Forever Changes	1967	8.00	20.00
— Original Elektra albums above have brown labels.—					
Elektra EKS-74049	(S)	Four Sail	1969	6.00	15.00
Elektra EKS-74058	(S)	Revisited	1970	6.00	15.00
Blue Thumb BTS-9000	(S)	Out Here *(2 LPs)*	1969	8.00	20.00
		(Features Jimi Hendrix on one track.)			
Blue Thumb BTS-8822	(S)	False Start	1970	6.00	15.00

Quick: Name the only '60s group to provide complete, original soundtracks for two virtually unknown film directors, Woody Allen and Francis Ford Coppola. . .

Label & Catalog #		Title	Year	VG+	NM

LOVE EXCHANGE, THE

| Tower ST-5115 | (S) | The Love Exchange | 1968 | 8.00 | 20.00 |

LOVE GENERATION, THE

Imperial LP-9351	(M)	The Love Generation	1967	5.00	12.00
Imperial LP-12351	(S)	The Love Generation	1967	6.00	15.00
Imperial LP-12364	(S)	A Generation Of Love	1968	5.00	12.00
Imperial LP-12408	(S)	Montage	1968	5.00	12.00

LOVE IS A HEART-ON

| Heavy | (S) | Love Is A Heart-On | 1970 | 100.00 | 250.00 |

LOVE SCULPTURE

Love Sculpture features Dave Edmunds.

| Rare Earth RS-505 | (S) | Blues Helping | 1969 | 16.00 | 40.00 |
| Parrot PAS-71035 | (S) | Forms And Feeling | 1970 | 10.00 | 25.00 |

LOVECRAFT: Refer to H.P. LOVECRAFT

LOVELITES, THE

| Uni 73081 | (S) | The Lovelites | 1970 | 6.00 | 15.00 |

LOVETTE, EDDIE

| Steady 101 | (S) | Eddie Lovette Sings Reggae | 1970 | 8.00 | 20.00 |

LOVIN' SPOONFUL, THE

The original Spoonful were Steve Boone, Joe Butler, John Sebastian and Zal Yanovsky, replaced in 1967 by Jerry Yester, formerly of The Modern Folk Quartet. By 1969 Boone was the only original member left.

Kama Sutra KLP-8050	(M)	Do You Believe In Magic?	1965	10.00	25.00
Kama Sutra KLPS-8050	(S)	Do You Believe In Magic?	1965	12.00	30.00
Kama Sutra ST-90597	(S)	Do You Believe In Magic? (Capitol Rec. Club)	1965	16.00	40.00
Kama Sutra KLP-8051	(M)	Daydream	1966	10.00	25.00
Kama Sutra KLPS-8051	(S)	Daydream	1966	12.00	30.00
Kama Sutra KLP-8053	(M)	What's Up, Tiger Lily? (Soundtrack)	1966	8.00	20.00
Kama Sutra KLPS-8053	(S)	What's Up, Tiger Lily? (Soundtrack)	1966	10.00	25.00
Kama Sutra KLP-8054	(M)	Hums Of The Lovin' Spoonful	1966	10.00	25.00
Kama Sutra KLPS-8054	(S)	Hums Of The Lovin' Spoonful	1966	12.00	30.00
Kama Sutra KLP-8056	(M)	The Best Of The Lovin' Spoonful	1967	8.00	20.00
Kama Sutra KLPS-8056	(S)	The Best Of The Lovin' Spoonful	1967	10.00	25.00
		(Includes four full-color glossy photos of the Spoonful and a sticker on the cover noting these bonuses.)			
Kama Sutra KLP-8056	(M)	The Best Of The Lovin' Spoonful	1967	6.00	15.00
Kama Sutra KLPS-8056	(S)	The Best Of The Lovin' Spoonful	1967	8.00	20.00
		(Without the bonus photos.)			
Kama Sutra KLP-8058	(M)	You're A Big Boy Now	1967	6.00	15.00
Kama Sutra KLPS-8058	(S)	You're A Big Boy Now	1967	8.00	20.00
Kama Sutra KLPS-8061	(S)	Everything's Playing	1968	6.00	15.00
Kama Sutra KLPS-8064	(S)	The Best Of The Lovin' Spoonful, Volume 2	1968	6.00	15.00
Kama Sutra KOPS-750-2	(S)	24 Karat Hits (2 LPs)	1968	10.00	25.00
Kama Sutra KLPS-8073	(S)	Revelations: Revolution '69	1969	10.00	25.00
Kama Sutra KLPS-2011	(S)	The John Sebastian Songbook	1970	6.00	15.00
Kama Sutra KSBS-2013	(S)	The Very Best Of The Lovin' Spoonful	1970	6.00	15.00
Kama Sutra KLPS-2029	(S)	Once Upon A Time	1971	6.00	15.00

LOWE, JIM

Mercury MG-20246	(M)	The Door Of Fame	1957	40.00	100.00
Dot DLP-3051	(M)	Songs They Sang Behind The Green Door	1957	60.00	150.00
Dot DLP-25051	(E)	Songs They Sang Behind The Green Door	195?	40.00	100.00
Dot DLP-3114	(M)	Wicked Women	1958	40.00	100.00

LOWE, NICK

| Columbia AS-1408 | (DJ) | An Interrogation Of Nick Lowe | 1982 | 6.00 | 15.00 |

LOWE & STRAUSS

| Riverside RS-7541 | (M) | Folk Music For People Who Hate Folk Music | 1963 | 6.00 | 15.00 |
| Riverside RS9-7541 | (S) | Folk Music For People Who Hate Folk Music | 1963 | 8.00 | 20.00 |

LRY

| Congress/Crow 8031002 | (S) | The LRY Record | 1968 | 40.00 | 100.00 |

Label & Catalog #		Title	Year	VG+	NM
LUCAS, NICK					
Cavalier 5003 (10")	(M)	Tiptoe Thru The Tulips	1955	12.00	30.00
Decca DL-8653	(M)	Painting The Clouds With Sunshine	1957	20.00	50.00
LUCIFER					
Uni 73111	(S)	Black Mass By Lucifer	1971	6.00	15.00
Invictus ST-7309	(S)	Lucifer	1971	6.00	15.00
LULU					
Epic LN-24339	(M)	To Sir With Love	1967	10.00	25.00
Epic BN-26339	(S)	To Sir With Love	1967	12.00	30.00
		("Morning Dew" and "Let's Pretend" are rechanneled on this album.)			
Parrot PA-61016	(M)	From Lulu With Love	1967	10.00	25.00
Parrot PAS-71016	(S)	From Lulu With Love	1967	12.00	30.00
Atco SD-33-310	(S)	New Routes	1970	6.00	15.00
Atco SD-33-330	(S)	Melody Fair	1970	6.00	15.00
Epic BN-26536	(S)	It's Lulu	1970	6.00	15.00
Chelsea CHL-518	(S)	Heaven And Earth And The Stars	1977	10.00	25.00
		(Features two tracks arranged and produced by David Bowie.)			
Chelsea BCL1-0144	(S)	Lulu	1973	6.00	15.00
LULU BELLE & SCOTTY					
Super 6201	(M)	Lulu Belle & Scotty	1963	20.00	50.00
Starday SLP-206	(M)	The Sweethearts Of Country Music	1963	12.00	30.00
Starday SLP-285	(M)	Down Memory Lane	1964	12.00	30.00
Starday SLP-351	(M)	Lulu Belle & Scotty	1965	12.00	30.00
LUMAN, BOB					
Warner Bros. W-1396	(M)	Let's Think About Livin'	1960	20.00	50.00
Warner Bros. WS-1396	(S)	Let's Think About Livin'	1960	30.00	75.00
Hickory LPM-124	(M)	Livin' Lovin' Sounds	1965	10.00	25.00
Hickory LPS-124	(S)	Livin' Lovin' Sounds	1965	12.00	30.00
LUMBEE					
Radnor 2003	(S)	Overdose (Includes a bonus game)	197?	30.00	75.00
Radnor 2003	(S)	Overdose (Without the game)	197?	20.00	50.00
LUND, GARRETT					
(No label)	(S)	Almost Grown (With insert)	1975	150.00	300.00
LUNDY, PAT					
Columbia CS-9588	(S)	Soul Ain't Nothin' But The Blues	1968	6.00	15.00
LUTCHER, NELLIE					
Capitol H-232 (10")	(M)	Real Gone	1950	20.00	50.00
Capitol T-232	(M)	Real Gone	1955	16.00	40.00
Epic 1108 (10")	(M)	Whee! Nellie	1955	20.00	50.00
Liberty LRP-3014	(M)	Our New Nellie	1956	10.00	25.00
LYMON, FRANKIE, & THE TEENAGERS [THE TEENAGERS]					
Gee GLP-701	(DJ)	The Teenagers Featuring Frankie Lymon (White label promo.)	1957	500.00	1,000.00
Gee GLP-701	(M)	The Teenagers Featuring Frankie Lymon (First pressings have a red label.)	1957	150.00	300.00
Gee GLP-701	(M)	The Teenagers Featuring Frankie Lymon (Second pressings have a grey label.)	1961	60.00	150.00
Gee GLPS-701	(E)	The Teenagers Featuring Frankie Lymon	1961	40.00	100.00
Roulette R-25013	(M)	The Teenagers At The London Palladium	1958	80.00	200.00
Roulette R-25036	(M)	Rock And Roll	1958	80.00	200.00
Guest G-1406	(M)	Frankie Lymon Dance Party	1959	16.00	40.00
Guest GS-1406	(S)	Frankie Lymon Dance Party	1959	20.00	50.00
		(This is actually a various artists compilation.)			
Roulette R-25250	(M)	Jerry Blavatt Presents The Teenagers	1964	40.00	100.00
LYNN, BARBARA					
Jamie JLP-3023	(M)	You'll Lose A Good Thing	1962	10.00	25.00
Jamie JLPS-3023	(E)	You'll Lose A Good Thing	1962	14.00	35.00
Atlantic SD-8171	(S)	Here Is Barbara Lynn	1968	6.00	15.00

Label & Catalog #		Title	Year	VG+	NM

LYNN, DONNA

Capitol T-2085	(M)	Java Jones	1964	6.00	15.00
Capitol ST-2085	(S)	Java Jones	1964	8.00	20.00

LYNN, JUDY

United Arts. UAL-3226	(M)	Judy Lynn Sings At The Golden Nugget	1962	5.00	12.00
United Arts. UAS-6226	(S)	Judy Lynn Sings At The Golden Nugget	1962	6.00	15.00
United Arts. UAL-3288	(M)	Here Is Our Gal Judy Lynn	1963	5.00	12.00
United Arts. UAS-6288	(S)	Here Is Our Gal Judy Lynn	1963	6.00	15.00
United Arts. UAL-3390	(M)	The Judy Lynn Show	1964	5.00	12.00
United Arts. UAS-6390	(S)	The Judy Lynn Show	1964	6.00	15.00
United Arts. UAL-3342	(M)	Country And Western Girl Singer	1964	5.00	12.00
United Arts. UAS-6342	(S)	Country And Western Girl Singer	1964	6.00	15.00
United Arts. UAL-3443	(M)	The Judy Lynn Show, Act 2	1965	5.00	12.00
United Arts. UAS-6443	(S)	The Judy Lynn Show, Act 2	1965	6.00	15.00
United Arts. UAL-3461	(M)	The Best Of Judy Lynn	1966	5.00	12.00
United Arts. UAS-6461	(S)	The Best Of Judy Lynn	1966	6.00	15.00
Musicor M-3096	(M)	The Judy Lynn Show Plays Again	1966	5.00	12.00
Musicor MS-3096	(S)	The Judy Lynn Show Plays Again	1966	6.00	15.00
Musicor M-3112	(M)	Honey Stuff	1966	5.00	12.00
Musicor MS-3112	(S)	Honey Stuff	1966	6.00	15.00
Musicor M-3126	(M)	Golden Nuggets	1967	5.00	12.00
Musicor MS-3126	(S)	Golden Nuggets	1967	6.00	15.00
Columbia CS-9879	(S)	Judy Lynn Sings At Caesar's Place	1969	5.00	12.00

LYNN, LORETTA

Decca DL-4457	(M)	Loretta Lynn Sings	1963	16.00	40.00
Decca DL-74457	(S)	Loretta Lynn Sings	1963	20.00	50.00
Decca DL-4541	(M)	Before I'm Over You	1964	12.00	30.00
Decca DL-74541	(S)	Before I'm Over You	1964	16.00	40.00
Decca DL-4620	(M)	Songs From My Heart	1965	12.00	30.00
Decca DL-74620	(S)	Songs From My Heart	1965	16.00	40.00
Decca DL-4665	(M)	Blue Kentucky Girl	1965	12.00	30.00
Decca DL-74665	(S)	Blue Kentucky Girl	1965	16.00	40.00
Decca DL-4695	(M)	Hymns	1965	10.00	25.00
Decca DL-74695	(S)	Hymns	1965	12.00	30.00
Decca DL-4744	(M)	I Like 'Em Country	1966	10.00	25.00
Decca DL-74744	(S)	I Like 'Em Country	1966	12.00	30.00
Decca DL-4783	(M)	You Ain't Woman Enough	1966	10.00	25.00
Decca DL-74783	(S)	You Ain't Woman Enough	1966	12.00	30.00
Decca DL-4817	(M)	A Country Christmas	1966	10.00	25.00
Decca DL-74817	(S)	A Country Christmas	1966	12.00	30.00

— Original Decca albums above have black labels with "Mfrd. by Decca" beneath the rainbow. —

Decca DL-4842	(M)	Don't Come Home Drinkin'	1967	6.00	15.00
Decca DL-74842	(S)	Don't Come Home Drinkin'	1967	8.00	20.00
Decca DL-4930	(M)	Singin' With Feelin'	1967	8.00	20.00
Decca DL-74930	(S)	Singin' With Feelin'	1967	8.00	20.00
Decca DL-74928	(S)	Who Says God Is Dead?	1968	8.00	20.00
Decca DL-74997	(S)	Fist City	1968	8.00	20.00
Decca DL-75000	(S)	Loretta Lynn's Greatest Hits	1968	8.00	20.00
Decca DL-75084	(S)	Your Squaw Is On The Warpath	1969	16.00	40.00
		(Originally issued with "Barney.")			
Decca DL-75084	(S)	Your Squaw Is On The Warpath	1969	6.00	15.00
Decca DL-75113	(S)	A Woman Of The World	1969	6.00	15.00
Decca DL-75163	(S)	Wings Upon Your Horns	1970	6.00	15.00
Decca DL-75198	(S)	Loretta Lynn Writes 'Em And Sings 'Em	1970	6.00	15.00
Decca DL-75253	(S)	Coal Miner's Daughter	1971	8.00	20.00
Decca DL-75282	(S)	I Wanna Be Free	1971	6.00	15.00
Decca DL-75310	(S)	You're Lookin' At Country	1971	6.00	15.00
Decca DL-75334	(S)	One's On The Way	1972	6.00	15.00
Decca DL-75351	(S)	God Bless America Again	1972	6.00	15.00
Decca DL-75381	(S)	Here I Am Again	1972	6.00	15.00
MCA PRO-1934	(DJ)	Loretta Lynn	1974	16.00	40.00
MCA 35013	(DJ)	Allis-Chambers Presents Loretta Lynn	1978	16.00	40.00
MCA 35018	(DJ)	Crisco Presents Loretta Lynn	1979	16.00	40.00

LYNN, LORETTA, & ERNEST TUBB

Decca DL-4639	(M)	Mr & Mrs Used To Be	1965	10.00	25.00
Decca DL-74639	(S)	Mr & Mrs Used To Be	1965	12.00	30.00

Label & Catalog #		Title	Year	VG+	NM
Decca DL-4872	(M)	Singin' Again	1967	8.00	20.00
Decca DL-74872	(S)	Singin' Again	1967	8.00	20.00
Decca DL-75115	(S)	If We Put Our Heads Together	1969	6.00	15.00

LYNYRD SKYNYRD
| MCA 3029 | (S) | Street Survivors | 1977 | 8.00 | 20.00 |
| | | *(Original covers picture the group in flames.)* | | | |

MABON, WILLIE
| Chess LP-1439 | (M) | Willie Mabon *(Black label)* | 1958 | 150.00 | 300.00 |

MacARTHUR
| R.P.C. | (S) | MacArthur | 1970 | 200.00 | 400.00 |
| Bay Music | (S) | MacArthur II | 1982 | 50.00 | 125.00 |

MacBEE, HAMMER
| Folklore FRLP-14008 | (M) | Cumberland Moonshiner | 1964 | 8.00 | 20.00 |
| Folklore FRST-14008 | (S) | Cumberland Moonshiner | 1964 | 10.00 | 25.00 |

MACEO
Maceo Parker from James Brown's band.
| People PE-6601 | (S) | Us *(Produced by James Brown)* | 1973 | 6.00 | 15.00 |

MACEO & ALL THE KING'S MEN
Maceo Parker from James Brown's band.
| House Of Fox LP-1 | (S) | Doing Their Own Thing | 197? | 10.00 | 25.00 |

MacCOLL, EWAN
Riverside RLP-12-632	(M)	Bad Lads And Hard Cases	195?	12.00	30.00
Riverside RLP-12-642	(M)	Bless 'Em All	195?	12.00	30.00
Riverside RLP-12-652	(M)	Champions And Sporting Blades	195?	12.00	30.00

MacDONALD, JEANETTE, & NELSON EDDY
| RCA Victor LPM-1738 | (M) | Favorites In Hi-Fi | 1959 | 12.00 | 30.00 |

MACK, LONNIE
Fraternity SF-1014	(M)	The Wham Of That Memphis Man	1963	30.00	75.00
Fraternity SSF-1014	(S)	The Wham Of That Memphis Man	1963	60.00	150.00
Elektra EKS-74050	(S)	Whatever's Right	1969	8.00	20.00
Elektra EKS-74040	(S)	Glad I'm In The Band	1969	8.00	20.00
Elektra EKS-74077	(M)	For Collectors Only	1970	8.00	20.00
Elektra EKS-74012	(S)	The Hills Of Indiana	1971	8.00	20.00

MacKAY, RABBIT
| Uni 73026 | (S) | Bug Cloth | 1968 | 5.00 | 12.00 |
| Uni 73064 | (S) | Passing Through | 1969 | 5.00 | 12.00 |

MacKENZIE, GISELE
Vik LX-1055	(M)	Gisele MacKenzie	1956	16.00	40.00
Vik LX-1075	(M)	Mam' Selle Gisele	1956	16.00	40.00
Vik LX-1099	(M)	Christmas With Gisele	1957	16.00	40.00
RCA Victor LPM-1790	(M)	Gisele	1958	12.00	30.00
RCA Victor LSP-1790	(S)	Gisele	1958	16.00	40.00

Label & Catalog #		Title	Year	VG+	NM
RCA Victor LPM-2006	(M)	Christmas With Gisele	1959	12.00	30.00
RCA Victor LSP-2006	(S)	Christmas With Gisele	1959	16.00	40.00
Everest LPBR-5069	(M)	In Person At The Empire Room	196?	5.00	12.00
Everest SDBR-1069	(S)	In Person At The Empire Room	196?	8.00	20.00

MACON, UNCLE DAVE

Decca DL-4760	(M)	Uncle Dave Macon	1966	8.00	20.00
Decca DL-74760	(S)	Uncle Dave Macon	1966	10.00	25.00

MacRAE, GORDON
Refer to Jane Powell; Jo Stafford.

Capitol H-231 (10")	(M)	Songs	1950	16.00	40.00
MGM E-104 (10")	(M)	Prisoner Of Love (Soundtrack)	1952	16.00	40.00
Capitol L-334 (10")	(M)	Roberta (Studio Cast)	1952	16.00	40.00
Capitol L-335 (10")	(M)	Merry Widow (Studio Cast)	1952	16.00	40.00
Capitol L-351 (10")	(M)	Desert Song (Studio Cast)	1953	20.00	50.00
Capitol L-407 (10")	(M)	Student Prince (Studio Cast)	1953	16.00	40.00
Capitol H-422 (10")	(M)	By The Light Of The Silvery Moon (Sdtk)	1953	20.00	50.00
Capitol L-530 (10")	(M)	The Red Mill (Soundtrack)	1954	16.00	40.00
Capitol T-219	(M)	New Moon / Vagabond King (Soundtrack)	1952	12.00	30.00
Capitol T-384	(M)	The Desert Song / Roberta (Soundtrack)	1953	16.00	40.00
Capitol T-428	(M)	Memory Songs (With Jo Stafford)	1954	16.00	40.00
Capitol T-437	(M)	Merry Widow / The Student Prince (Sdtk)	1954	16.00	40.00
Capitol T-537	(M)	Romantic Ballads	1955	14.00	35.00
Capitol T-551	(M)	The Red Mill / Naughty Marietta (Sdtk)	1954	16.00	40.00
Capitol SAO-595	(M)	Oklahoma (Soundtrack)	1955	8.00	20.00
Capitol T-681	(M)	Operetta Favorites	1956	12.00	30.00
Capitol W-694	(M)	Carousel (Soundtrack)	1956	12.00	30.00
Capitol T-765	(M)	The Best Things In Life Are Free	1956	12.00	30.00
Capitol T-834	(M)	Cowboy's Lament	1957	12.00	30.00
Capitol T-875	(M)	Motion Picture Soundstage	1957	12.00	30.00
Capitol T-980	(M)	Gordon MacRae In Concert	1958	12.00	30.00
Capitol T-1050	(M)	This Is Gordon MacRae	1958	12.00	30.00

MAD DOG

Fish Head	(S)	Mad Dog	1975	16.00	40.00

MAD FABLE

Magic MAD-101	(S)	Get Off!	1977	40.00	100.00

MAD LADS, THE

Volt 414	(M)	The Mad Lads In Action	1966	6.00	15.00
Volt 414	(S)	The Mad Lads In Action	1966	8.00	20.00
Volt VOS-6005	(S)	The Mad Mad Mad Mad Mad Lads	1969	6.00	15.00
Volt VOS-6020	(S)	A New Beginning	1973	5.00	12.00

MAD RIVER

Capitol ST-2985	(S)	Mad River	1968	20.00	50.00
Capitol ST-185	(S)	Paradise Bar And Grill	1969	16.00	40.00
		(Counterfeits of 185—perhaps 2985—exist.)			

MADDOX, ROSE

Columbia CL-1159	(M)	Precious Memories	1958	20.00	50.00
Capitol T-1312	(M)	The One Rose	1960	16.00	35.00
Capitol ST-1312	(S)	The One Rose	1960	20.00	50.00
Capitol T-1437	(M)	Glorybound Train	1960	16.00	35.00
Capitol ST-1437	(S)	Glorybound Train	1960	20.00	50.00
Capitol T-1548	(M)	A Big Bouquet Of Roses	1961	16.00	35.00
Capitol ST-1548	(S)	A Big Bouquet Of Roses	1961	20.00	50.00
Capitol T-1779	(M)	Rose Maddox Sing Bluegrass	1962	16.00	40.00
Capitol ST-1779	(S)	Rose Maddox Sing Bluegrass	1962	20.00	50.00
Capitol T-1993	(M)	Alone With You	1963	12.00	30.00
Capitol ST-1993	(S)	Alone With You	1963	16.00	40.00
Starday SLP-463	(M)	Rosie	196?	12.00	30.00

MADDOX BROTHERS, THE, & ROSE [MADDOX]

King 669	(M)	A Collection Of Standard Sacred Songs	1956	50.00	125.00
King 677	(M)	The Maddox Brothers And Rose	1961	30.00	75.00
King 752	(M)	I'll Write Your Name In The Sand	1961	30.00	75.00

Label & Catalog #		Title	Year	VG+	NM

MADIGAN, BETTY

MGM E-3448	(M)	Am I Blue?	1957	10.00	25.00
Coral CRL-57192	(M)	The Jerome Kern Songbook	1958	10.00	25.00

MADONNA

Sire 25157	(DJ)	Like A Virgin (White vinyl)	1984	16.00	40.00
Sire	(S)	True Blue (Picture disc)	1986	30.00	75.00
Sire	(S)	True Blue (Clear vinyl)	1986	60.00	150.00

(Both the picture disc and clear vinyl "True Blue" albums above were manufactured domestically for export to Hong Kong.)

MADRIGAL

(No label)	(S)	Madrigal	196?	200.00	400.00

MAESTRO, JOHNNY

Johnny Maestro was formerly the lead singer for The Crests; The Brooklyn Bridge.

Buddah BDS-5091	(P)	The Johnny Maestro Story (With inserts)	1971	16.00	40.00

MAGI

Uncle Dirty 6102-N13	(S)	Win Or Lose	1975	80.00	200.00

MAGIC

Armadillo 8031	(S)	Enclosed	1970	80.00	200.00

MAGIC

Magic features Jay Ferguson.

Rare Earth 527	(S)	Magic	1971	8.00	20.00

MAGIC FERN, THE

Piccadilly PIC-	(S)	The Magic Fern	1980	20.00	50.00

MAGIC LANTERNS, THE

Atlantic SD-8217	(S)	Shame Shame	1969	8.00	20.00

MAGIC SAM

Delmark DL-615	(S)	West Side Soul	1968	16.00	40.00
Delmark DL-620	(S)	Black Magic	1969	16.00	40.00

MAGIC SAND

Uni 73094	(S)	Magic Sand	1971	5.00	12.00

MAGNIFICENT MEN, THE

Capitol T-2678	(M)	The Magnificent Men	1967	5.00	12.00
Capitol ST-2678	(S)	The Magnificent Men	1967	6.00	15.00
Capitol T-2775	(M)	The Magnificent Men "Live!"	1967	5.00	12.00
Capitol ST-2775	(S)	The Magnificent Men "Live!"	1967	6.00	15.00
Capitol T-2846	(M)	World Of Soul	1968	6.00	15.00
Capitol ST-2846	(S)	World Of Soul	1968	5.00	12.00
Mercury SR-61252	(S)	Better Than A Ten Cent Movie	1970	4.00	10.00

MAHAL, TAJ

Columbia CS-9579	(S)	Taj Mahal	1968	8.00	20.00
Columbia CS-9698	(S)	Natch'l Blues	1969	6.00	15.00
Columbia GP-18	(S)	Giant Step (2 LPs)	1969	8.00	20.00

— Original Columbia albums above have "360 Sound" on the bottom of the label.—

Crystal Clear	(S)	Live And Direct (Direct-to-disc)	198?	6.00	15.00

MAHOGANY RUSH

Nine 936	(S)	Maxoom	1972	20.00	50.00
20th Century S-451	(S)	Child Of Novelty	1973	6.00	15.00
20th Century S-463	(S)	Maxoom	1975	6.00	15.00
20th Century S-482	(S)	Strange Universe	1975	6.00	15.00

MAIDA

Audio Fidelity 6136	(M)	Maida Sings Folk	1965	5.00	12.00
Audio Fidelity SD-6136	(S)	Maida Sings Folk	1965	6.00	15.00

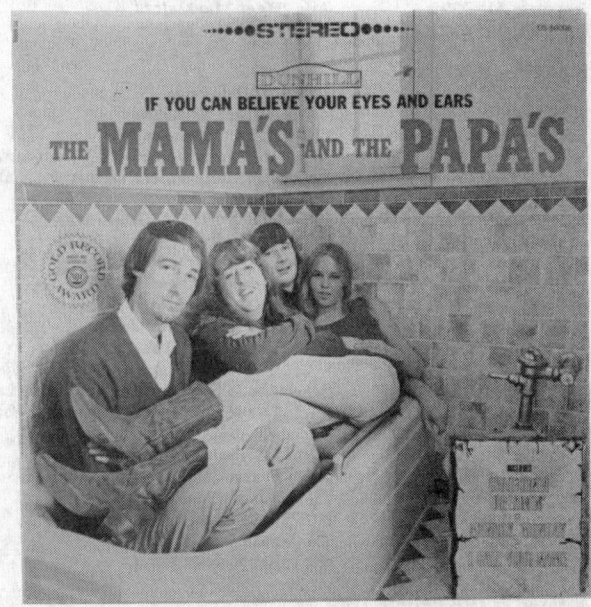

The original pressings of If You Can Believe Your Eyes And Ears *plainly featured a toilet in the lower right corner (above), a normal fixture in most every bathroom in the Western World. For some reason, this was deemed potentially offensive and the cover was pulled and amended (below). The Record Club version (not shown) went even further, placing a generous black border around the front cover, making the whole cover art unnecessary. Their first four albums hit the charts big-time and received RIAA Gold Records.*

Label & Catalog #		Title	Year	VG+	NM
MAIN ATTRACTION, THE					
Tower ST-5177	(S)	**And Now**	1968	8.00	20.00
MAINER, J. E.					
King 765	(M)	**Variety Album**	1961	16.00	40.00
MAINER, WADE					
King 769	(M)	**Soulful Sacred Songs**	1961	16.00	40.00
MAINER'S MOUNTAINEERS					
King 666	(M)	**Good Old Mountain Music**	195?	16.00	40.00
MAIZE, JOE (& HIS CORDSMEN)					
Decca DL-8590	(M)	**Presenting Joe Maize & His Cordsmen**	1958	16.00	40.00
Decca DL-8817	(M)	**Hawaiian Dreams**	1959	12.00	30.00
Decca DL-4555	(M)	**Isle Of Dreams**	1965	8.00	20.00
Decca DL-74555	(S)	**Isle Of Dreams**	1965	10.00	25.00
MAJIC SHIP					
Bel Ami BA-711	(S)	**Majic Ship**	1968	150.00	300.00
MAIDEN, SIDNEY					
Bluesville BVLP-1035	(M)	**Trouble**	1961	16.00	40.00
MAILER, NORMAN					
Prestige PRST-7682	(S)	**Norman Mailer Reads Norman Mailer**	1968	8.00	20.00
MAIYEROS, THE / THE INSTINCTS					
TCS 3952	(S)	**The Loving Sandwich**	1969	200.00	400.00
MAJORS, THE					
Imperial LP-9222	(M)	**Meet The Majors**	1963	40.00	100.00
Imperial LP-12222	(P)	**Meet The Majors**	1963	150.00	300.00
MAKEBA, MIRIAM					
Ms. Makeba also recorded with Harry Belafonte.					
RCA Victor LPM-2267	(M)	**Miriam Makeba**	1960	8.00	20.00
RCA Victor LSP-2267	(S)	**Miriam Makeba**	1960	10.00	25.00
Kapp KL-1274	(M)	**The Many Voices Of Miriam Makeba**	1962	6.00	15.00
Kapp KS-3274	(S)	**The Many Voices Of Miriam Makeba**	1962	8.00	20.00
RCA Victor LPM-2750	(M)	**The World Of Miriam Makeba**	1963	6.00	15.00
RCA Victor LSP-2750	(S)	**The World Of Miriam Makeba**	1963	8.00	20.00
RCA Victor LPM-2845	(M)	**The Voice Of Africa**	1964	6.00	15.00
RCA Victor LSP-2845	(S)	**The Voice Of Africa**	1964	8.00	20.00
RCA Victor LPM-3321	(M)	**Makeba Sings**	1965	6.00	15.00
RCA Victor LSP-3321	(S)	**Makeba Sings**	1965	8.00	20.00
RCA Victor LPM-3512	(M)	**The Magic Of Makeba**	1966	6.00	15.00
RCA Victor LSP-3512	(S)	**The Magic Of Makeba**	1966	8.00	20.00
		— Original RCA albums above have black labels.—			
Mercury MG-21082	(M)	**The Magnificent Miriam Makeba**	1966	5.00	12.00
Mercury SR-61082	(S)	**The Magnificent Miriam Makeba**	1966	6.00	15.00
Mercury MG-261095	(M)	**All About Miriam**	1966	5.00	12.00
Mercury SR-61095	(S)	**All About Miriam**	1966	6.00	15.00
Reprise R-6253	(M)	**Miriam Makeba In Concert!**	1967	5.00	12.00
Reprise RS-6253	(S)	**Miriam Makeba In Concert!**	1967	6.00	15.00
Reprise R-6274	(M)	**Pata Pata**	1967	5.00	12.00
Reprise RS-6274	(S)	**Pata Pata**	1967	6.00	15.00
Reprise RS-6381	(S)	**Keep Me In Mind**	1970	5.00	12.00
MAMAS & THE PAPAS, THE					
The Mamas were Michelle Phillips and Cass Elliott; the Papas were John Phillips and Denny Doherty.					
Dunhill D-50006	(M)	**If You Can Believe Your Eyes And Ears**	1966	40.00	100.00
Dunhill DS-50006	(S)	**If You Can Believe Your Eyes And Ears**	1966	40.00	100.00
		(First pressing covers plainly show the toilet in the lower right corner. On all subsequent pressings a scroll with the titles of the album's hit singles has been placed over the toilet.)			
Dunhill D-50006	(M)	**If You Can Believe Your Eyes And Ears**	1966	8.00	20.00
Dunhill DS-50006	(S)	**If You Can Believe Your Eyes And Ears**	1966	6.00	15.00
		(The toilet on the cover is concealed by a scroll.)			

Label & Catalog #		Title	Year	VG+	NM
Dunhill DS-50006	(S)	If You Can Believe Your Eyes And Ears	1968	20.00	50.00
		(Some later pressings have a black border on all four sides of			
		the cover, eliminating all but the faces of the four members.			
		The label reads "A Subsidiary of ABC" on the bottom.)			
Dunhill D-50010	(M)	The Mamas & The Papas	1966	8.00	20.00
Dunhill DS-50010	(S)	The Mamas & The Papas	1966	6.00	15.00
Dunhill D-50014	(M)	The Mamas & The Papas Deliver	1967	8.00	20.00
Dunhill DS-50014	(S)	The Mamas & The Papas Deliver	1967	6.00	15.00
		— Original Dunhill albums above read "Dist. by ABC-Paramount" on the bottom of the label.—			
Dunhill D-50025	(M)	Farewell To The First Golden Era	1967	6.00	15.00
Dunhill DS-50025	(S)	Farewell To The First Golden Era	1967	6.00	15.00
Dunhill DS-50031	(S)	The Papas And The Mamas	1968	8.00	20.00
		— Original Dunhill albums above read "A Subsidiary of ABC Records" on the bottom of the label.—			
Dunhill DS-50032	(S)	Book Of Songs	1968	6.00	15.00
Dunhill DS-50038	(S)	Golden Era, Volume 2	1968	6.00	15.00
Dunhill DS-50073	(S)	A Gathering Of Flowers *(2 LP box)*	1970	10.00	25.00
Dunhill DSX-50100	(S)	Monterey International Pop Festival	1970	5.00	12.00
Dunhill DSX-50106	(S)	People Like Us	1971	4.00	10.00
		— Original Dunhill albums above have black labels with "Dunhill/ABC" on top			
		and "Dunhill Records is a subsidiary" on the bottom.—			
Dunhill DSX-50145	(S)	20 Golden Hits *(2 LPs)*	1973	6.00	15.00

MANCHESTER, MELISSA

Label & Catalog #		Title	Year	VG+	NM
Arista AQ-4031	(Q)	Melissa	1975	6.00	15.00
Arista AQ-4067	(Q)	Better Days And Happy Endings	1976	6.00	15.00
Mobile Fidelity MFSL-028	(S)	Melissa	1979	5.00	15.00
Nautilus NR-33	(S)	Don't Cry Out Loud	198?	5.00	15.00

MANCHESTERS, THE

The Manchesters is a pseudonym for The Chartbusters and the albums include both Beatles covers and The Chartbusters' singles! Note that all three albums below are the same and that the first listing does not credit the artist on the cover or label.

Label & Catalog #		Title	Year	VG+	NM
Diplomat D-2307	(M)	Beatlerama	1964	6.00	15.00
Diplomat DS-2307	(B)	Beatlerama	1964	8.00	20.00
Diplomat D-2307	(M)	Beatlerama, Volume 1	1964	6.00	15.00
Diplomat DS-2307	(B)	Beatlerama, Volume 1	1964	8.00	20.00
Guest Star G-2307	(M)	Beatlerama, Volume 1	1964	6.00	15.00
Guest Star GS-2307	(S)	Beatlerama, Volume 1	1964	8.00	20.00

MANDEL, HARVEY

Label & Catalog #		Title	Year	VG+	NM
Philips PHS-600-281	(S)	Cristo Redentor	1968	10.00	25.00
Philips PHS-600-306	(S)	Righteous	1969	10.00	25.00
Philips PHS-600-325	(S)	Games Guitars Play	1969	10.00	25.00
Janus JLS-3017	(S)	Baby Batter	1970	6.00	15.00

MANDRAKE MEMORIAL

Label & Catalog #		Title	Year	VG+	NM
Poppy PYS-40,002	(S)	Mandrake Memorial	1968	12.00	30.00
Poppy PYS-40,003	(S)	Medium	1969	12.00	30.00
Poppy PYS-40,006	(S)	Puzzle	1970	12.00	30.00

MANFRED MANN

Label & Catalog #		Title	Year	VG+	NM
Ascot ALM-13015	(M)	The Manfred Mann Album	1964	16.00	40.00
Ascot ALS-16015	(P)	The Manfred Mann Album	1964	20.00	50.00
Ascot ALM-13018	(M)	The Five Faces Of Manfred Mann	1965	16.00	40.00
Ascot ALS-16018	(P)	The Five Faces Of Manfred Mann	1965	20.00	50.00
Ascot ALM-13021	(M)	My Little Red Book Of Winners	1965	16.00	40.00
Ascot ALS-16021	(S)	My Little Red Book Of Winners	1965	20.00	50.00
Ascot ALM-13024	(M)	Mann Made	1966	16.00	40.00
Ascot ALS-16024	(S)	Mann Made	1966	20.00	50.00
United Arts. UAL-94	(DJ)	Manfred Mann Interview	1966	80.00	200.00
		(Promotional interview issued in a plain cardboard jacket.)			
United Arts. UAL-3549	(M)	Pretty Flamingo	1966	12.00	30.00
United Arts. UAS-6549	(P)	Pretty Flamingo	1966	16.00	40.00
United Arts. UAL-3551	(M)	Manfred Mann's Greatest Hits	1966	10.00	25.00
United Arts. UAS-6551	(P)	Manfred Mann's Greatest Hits	1966	12.00	30.00
United Arts. UAS-5177	(S)	Charge Of The Light Brigade *(Soundtrack)*	1968	16.00	40.00
Mercury SR-61159	(E)	Up The Junction *(Soundtrack)*	1968	8.00	20.00
Mercury SR-61168	(S)	The Mighty Quinn	1968	8.00	20.00

Label & Catalog #		Title	Year	VG+	NM

MANHATTAN STRINGS, THE

Tower T-5067	(M)	Hits Made Famous By The Monkees	1967	8.00	20.00
Tower ST-5067	(S)	Hits Made Famous By The Monkees	1967	10.00	25.00

MANHATTAN TRANSFER, THE

Mobile Fidelity MFSL-1-022	(S)	Live (Original Master Recording)	1978	8.00	25.00

MANHATTANS, THE

Carnival CLP-101	(M)	Dedicated To You	1964	40.00	100.00
Carnival CLPS-101	(S)	Dedicated To You	1964	100.00	250.00
Carnival CLP-102	(M)	For You And Yours	1965	40.00	100.00
Carnival CLPS-102	(S)	For You And Yours	1965	60.00	150.00
Deluxe DLP-12000	(S)	With These Hands	1971	6.00	15.00
Deluxe DLP-12004	(S)	A Million To One	1972	6.00	15.00
Columbia PCQ-34450	(Q)	It Feels So Good	1977	6.00	15.00

MANILOW, BARRY

Bell 1129	(S)	Barry Manilow I (Original cover)	1972	8.00	20.00
Bell 1314	(S)	Barry Manilow II	1973	6.00	15.00
Arista AQ-4016	(Q)	Barry Manilow II	1974	6.00	15.00
Arista AQ-6060	(Q)	Tryin' To Get That Feeling	1975	6.00	15.00
Mobile Fidelity MFSL-097	(S)	Barry Manilow!	1979	5.00	15.00

MANN, BARRY

ABC-Paramount 399	(M)	Who Put The Bomp	1963	30.00	75.00
ABC-Paramount S-399	(S)	Who Put The Bomp	1963	40.00	100.00

MANN, CARL

Phillips Int. 1960	(M)	Like Mann	1960	300.00	500.00

MANN, SHADOW

Tomorrow's TPS-69001	(S)	Come Live With Me	1974	20.00	50.00

MANSFIELD, JAYNE

20th Century	(M)	Jayne Mansfield Busts Up Las Vegas	195?	30.00	75.00
MGM E-4204	(M)	Shakespeare, Tchaikovsky And Me	1964	14.00	35.00
MGM SE-4204	(S)	Shakespeare, Tchaikovsky And Me	1964	20.00	50.00

MANSON, CHARLES

Awareness	(M)	Lie: The Love And Terror Cult	1970	100.00	250.00
ESP-Disk' 2003	(M)	Lie: The Love And Terror Cult	1970	40.00	100.00

MAPHIS, JOE

Maphis also recorded with Merle Travis.

Columbia CL-1005	(M)	Fire On The Strings	1957	30.00	75.00

— Original Columbia albums above have six white-on-black "eye" logos around the perimeter of the label.—

MacGregor MGR-1205	(M)	King Of The Strings	196?	30.00	75.00
Starday SLP-316	(M)	King Of The Strings	1966	16.00	40.00
Starday SLP-322	(M)	Golden Gospel	1966	12.00	30.00
Starday SLP-373	(M)	Country Guitar Goes To The Jimmy Dean Show	1966	16.00	40.00
Mosrite MA-400	(M)	The New Sound Of Joe Maphis	196?	16.00	40.00

MAPHIS, JOE & ROSE LEE

Capitol T-1778	(M)	With The Blue Ridge Mountain Boys	1962	12.00	30.00
Capitol ST-1778	(S)	With The Blue Ridge Mountain Boys	1962	16.00	40.00
Starday SLP-286	(S)	Mr. And Mrs. Country Music	1964	10.00	25.00

MAPHIS, ROSE LEE

Columbia CL-1598	(M)	Rose Lee Maphis	1961	10.00	25.00
Columbia CS-8398	(S)	Rose Lee Maphis	1961	14.00	35.00

— Original Columbia albums above have six white-on-black "eye" logos around the perimeter of the label.—

MAR-KEYS, THE

Atlantic 8055	(M)	Last Night	1961	12.00	30.00
Atlantic SD-8055	(E)	Last Night	1966	10.00	25.00
Atlantic 8062	(M)	Do The Pop-Eye With The Mar-Kays	1962	12.00	30.00
Atlantic SD-8062	(E)	Do The Pop-Eye With The Mar-Keys	1966	10.00	25.00

In 1963 Margaret Battavio became the youngest female singer to top the charts when the fifteen year old hit with the precocious "I Will Follow Him." (Um, first she became Little Peggy March. . .)

Label & Catalog #		Title	Year	VG+	NM
Stax ST-707	(M)	**Great Memphis Sound**	1966	12.00	30.00
Stax STS-707	(E)	**Great Memphis Sound**	1966	8.00	20.00
Stax STS-2025	(S)	**Damifiknew**	1969	6.00	15.00
Stax STS-2036	(S)	**Memphis Experience**	1971	6.00	15.00
MAR-KEYS, THE, & BOOKER T. & THE M.G.'S					
Stax ST-720	(M)	**Back To Back**	1967	6.00	15.00
Stax STS-720	(S)	**Back To Back**	1967	8.00	20.00
MARAIS & MIRANDA					
Decca DL-8711	(M)	**Sundown Songs**	1958	10.00	25.00
Decca DL-9087	(M)	**Songs Of Spirit And Humor**	1959	8.00	20.00
Decca DL-79087	(S)	**Songs Of Spirit And Humor**	1959	10.00	25.00
Decca DL-9026	(M)	**Marais & Miranda In Person, Volume 1**	1959	8.00	20.00
Decca DL-79026	(S)	**Marais & Miranda In Person, Volume 1**	1959	10.00	25.00
Decca DL-9027	(M)	**Marais & Miranda In Person, Volume 2**	1959	8.00	20.00
Decca DL-79027	(S)	**Marais & Miranda In Person, Volume 2**	1959	10.00	25.00
MARANATHA					
Members of Maranatha later recorded as The Emmaus Road Band.					
(No label)	(S)	**Soon**	197?	80.00	200.00
MARATHONS, THE					
Arvee A-428	(M)	**Peanut Butter**	1961	50.00	125.00
MARAUDERS, THE					
No label	(M)	**The Marauders Check In**	1964	24.00	60.00
No label	(M)	**Maraudin' '65**	1965	24.00	60.00
MARBLE PHROGG, THE					
Derrick 8868	(S)	**The Marble Phrogg**	1968	200.00	400.00
MARCELS, THE					
Colpix CP-416	(M)	**Blue Moon** *(Gold Label)*	1961	30.00	75.00
Colpix CSP-416	(S)	**Blue Moon** *(Gold Label)*	1961	80.00	200.00
Colpix CP-416	(M)	**Blue Moon** *(Blue Label)*	196?	16.00	40.00
Colpix CSP-416	(S)	**Blue Moon** *(Blue Label)*	196?	40.00	100.00
MARCH, LITTLE PEGGY					
RCA Victor LPM-2732	(M)	**I Will Follow Him**	1963	10.00	25.00
RCA Victor LSP-2732	(S)	**I Will Follow Him**	1963	14.00	35.00
RCA Victor LPM-3408	(M)	**In Our Fashion**	1965	14.00	35.00
RCA Victor LSP-3408	(S)	**In Our Fashion**	1965	16.00	45.00
RCA Victor LPM-3883	(M)	**No Foolin'**	1968	20.00	50.00
RCA Victor LSP-3883	(S)	**No Foolin'**	1968	10.00	25.00
MARCHAN, BOBBY					
Sphere Sound SR-7004	(M)	**There's Something On Your Mind**	1964	60.00	150.00
Sphere Sound SSR-7004	(S)	**There's Something On Your Mind**	1964	80.00	200.00
MARCUS					
NR 10788	(S)	**From The House Of Trax**	1979	660.00	1,000.00
MARESCA, ERNIE					
Seville SV-77001	(M)	**Shout! Shout! Knock Yourself Out**	1962	40.00	100.00
Seville SV-87001	(S)	**Shout! Shout! Knock Yourself Out**	1962	60.00	150.00
MARIANI					
Mariani features Eric Johnson, later of The Electromagnets.					
Sonobeat 1001	(M)	**Perpetuum Mobile** *(Issued without a cover)*	196?	1,000.00	2,000.00
MARKETTS, THE [THE MAR-KETTS]					
Liberty LRP-3226	(M)	**Surfer's Stomp**	1962	16.00	40.00
Liberty LST-7226	(S)	**Surfer's Stomp**	1962	20.00	50.00
Liberty LRP-3226	(M)	**The Surfing Scene**	1963	12.00	30.00
Liberty LST-7226	(S)	**The Surfing Scene**	1963	16.00	40.00
		("Surfing Scene" is a reissue of "Surfer's Stomp.")			
Warner Bros. T-1509	(M)	**The Marketts Take To Wheels**	1963	12.00	30.00
Warner Bros. ST-1509	(S)	**The Marketts Take To Wheels**	1963	16.00	40.00

Label & Catalog #		Title	Year	VG+	NM
Warner Bros. T-1537	(M)	Out Of Limits	1964	10.00	25.00
Warner Bros. ST-1537	(S)	Out Of Limits	1964	12.00	30.00
Warner Bros. T-1642	(M)	Batman Theme	1966	10.00	25.00
Warner Bros. ST-1642	(S)	Batman Theme	1966	12.00	30.00
World Pacific WP-1870	(M)	Sun Power	1967	6.00	15.00
World Pacific ST-1870	(S)	Sun Power	1967	8.00	20.00
Mercury SRM-1-679	(S)	AM, FM, Etc.	1973	6.00	15.00

MARKLEY

Forward 1007	(S)	Markley: A Group	1969	12.00	30.00

MARKS, GUY

ABC-Paramount 549	(M)	Hollywood Sings	1966	5.00	12.00
ABC-Paramount S-549	(S)	Hollywood Sings	1966	6.00	15.00
ABC-Paramount 648	(M)	Loving You Has Made Me Bananas	1967	6.00	15.00
ABC-Paramount S-648	(S)	Loving You Has Made Me Bananas	1967	8.00	20.00

MARKS, J., & SHIPEN LEBZELTER

Columbia 7193	(S)	Rock And Other Four Letter Words (2 LPs)	1968	12.00	30.00

MARLBOROS, THE

Justice JLP-	(S)	The Marlboros	1969	40.00	100.00

MARLENE [MARLENE VERPLANCK]

Savoy MG-12058	(M)	I Think Of You With Every Breath I Take	1956	30.00	75.00
Mounted 108	(M)	A Breath Of Fresh Air	1963	12.00	30.00

MARLEY, BOB, & THE WAILERS
For additional listings refer to Johnny Nash.

Island ILPS-9256	(S)	Burnin'	1975	6.00	15.00
Island ILPS-9281	(S)	Natty Dread	1975	6.00	15.00
Island ILPS-9329	(S)	Catch A Fire	1975	20.00	50.00
		(The cover is shaped like a cigarette lighter with a hinge that allows the top to flip open.)			
Island ILPS-9329	(S)	Catch A Fire *(Standard cover)*	1975	6.00	15.00
Island ILPS-9376	(S)	Bob Marley Live	1976	6.00	15.00
Island ILPS-9383	(S)	Rastaman Vibration	1976	40.00	100.00
		(Issued promotionally in a burlap box with a press kit.)			
Island ILPS-9383	(S)	Rastaman Vibration	1976	6.00	15.00
		— Original Island albums above have black labels with an "i" on the bottom. —			

MARLOWE, MARION: *Refer to* **FESS PARKER**

MARMALADE

Epic BN-26553	(S)	The Best Of Marmalade	1970	8.00	20.00
London PS-575	(P)	Reflections Of My Life	1970	8.00	20.00

MARSHALL, CHUCK, & THE TWIST STARS

Decca DL-4267	(M)	Twist To Songs Everybody Knows	1962	5.00	12.00
Decca DL7-4267	(S)	Twist To Songs Everybody Knows	1962	6.00	15.00

MARSHALL, JACK, & THE NEWPORT BEACH LITTLE THEATER SURFING GROUP

Capitol T-1939	(M)	My Son The Surf Nut	1963	8.00	20.00
Capitol ST-1939	(S)	My Son The Surf Nut	1963	10.00	25.00

MARSHMALLOW WAY

United Arts. UAS-6708	(S)	Marshmallow Way	1969	6.00	15.00

MARTHA & THE VANDELLAS
Martha is Ms. Martha Reeves.

Gordy 902	(M)	Come And Get These Memories	1963	60.00	150.00
Gordy GS-902	(S)	Come And Get These Memories	1963	80.00	200.00
Gordy 907	(M)	Heat Wave	1963	40.00	100.00
Gordy 907	(E)	Heat Wave	1963	40.00	100.00
		(Copies of Gordy 907 issued in covers with "Stereo" on the top are rechanneled stereo.)			
Gordy GS-907	(S)	Heat Wave	1963	100.00	300.00
		(Copies of Gordy 907 issued in mono covers with a black "Stereo" sticker are real stereo.)			

Label & Catalog #		Title	Year	VG+	NM
Gordy 915	(M)	**Dance Party**	1965	12.00	30.00
Gordy GS-915	(S)	**Dance Party**	1965	16.00	40.00
Gordy 917	(M)	**Martha & The Vandellas' Greatest Hits**	1966	6.00	15.00
Gordy GS-917	(S)	**Martha & The Vandellas' Greatest Hits**	1966	8.00	20.00
Gordy 920	(M)	**Watchout!**	1967	6.00	15.00
Gordy GS-920	(S)	**Watchout!**	1967	8.00	20.00
Gordy 925	(M)	**Martha & The Vandellas' Live!**	1967	6.00	15.00
Gordy GS-925	(S)	**Martha & The Vandellas' Live!**	1967	8.00	20.00
Gordy GS-926	(S)	**Ridin' High**	1968	6.00	15.00
Gordy GS-944	(S)	**Sugar 'N Spice**	1969	6.00	15.00
Gordy GS-952	(S)	**Natural Resources**	1970	6.00	15.00
Gordy GS-958	(S)	**Black Magic**	1972	6.00	15.00
Motown 778	(S)	**Anthology** (2 LPs)	1974	6.00	15.00

MARTIN, BENNY

Label & Catalog #		Title	Year	VG+	NM
Starday SLP-131	(M)	**Country Music's Sensational Entertainer**	1961	20.00	50.00

MARTIN, DEAN
Refer to The Reprise Repertory Theatre.

Label & Catalog #		Title	Year	VG+	NM
Capitol L-401 (10")	(M)	**The Stooge** (Soundtrack)	1953	40.00	100.00
Capitol T-401	(M)	**The Stooge** (Soundtrack)	1953	20.00	50.00
Capitol T-576	(M)	**Swingin' Down Yonder**	1955	12.00	30.00
Capitol T-849	(M)	**Pretty Baby**	1957	12.00	30.00
Capitol T-1047	(M)	**This Is Martin**	1958	12.00	30.00
		— Original Capitol albums above have turquoise labels—			
Capitol T-1150	(M)	**Sleep Warm**	1959	8.00	20.00
Capitol ST-1150	(S)	**Sleep Warm**	1959	12.00	30.00
		(Capitol 1150 conducted by Frank Sinatra.)			
Capitol T-1285	(M)	**Winter Romance**	1959	8.00	20.00
Capitol ST-1285	(S)	**Winter Romance**	1959	12.00	30.00
Capitol W-1435	(M)	**Bells Are Ringing** (Soundtrack)	1960	14.00	35.00
Capitol SW-1435	(S)	**Bells Are Ringing** (Soundtrack)	1960	20.00	50.00
Capitol T-1442	(M)	**This Time I'm Swingin'**	1961	6.00	15.00
Capitol ST-1442	(S)	**This Time I'm Swingin'**	1961	8.00	20.00
Capitol W-1580	(M)	**Dean Martin**	1961	6.00	15.00
Capitol SW-1580	(S)	**Dean Martin**	1961	8.00	20.00
Capitol T-1659	(M)	**Dino**	1962	6.00	15.00
Capitol ST-1659	(S)	**Dino**	1962	8.00	20.00
Capitol T-1702	(M)	**Cha Cha De Amor**	1962	6.00	15.00
Capitol ST-1702	(S)	**Cha Cha De Amor**	1962	8.00	20.00
		— Original Capitol albums above have black labels with the logo on the left side.—			
Capitol T-2212	(M)	**Hey Brother, Pour The Wine**	1964	6.00	15.00
Capitol DT-2212	(E)	**Hey Brother, Pour The Wine**	1964	5.00	12.00
Capitol T-2297	(M)	**Dean Martin Sings, Sinatra Conducts**	1965	6.00	15.00
Capitol ST-2297	(S)	**Dean Martin Sings, Sinatra Conducts**	1965	8.00	20.00
Capitol T-2333	(M)	**Southern Style**	1965	6.00	15.00
Capitol DT-2333	(E)	**Southern Style**	1965	5.00	12.00
Capitol TT-2343	(M)	**Holiday Cheer**	1965	5.00	12.00
Capitol STT-2343	(S)	**Holiday Cheer**	1965	6.00	15.00
Capitol T-2601	(M)	**The Best Of Dean Martin**	1966	5.00	12.00
Capitol DT-2601	(E)	**The Best Of Dean Martin**	1966	4.00	10.00
Capitol TCL-2815	(M)	**Deluxe Set** (3 LPs)	1967	10.00	25.00
Capitol DTCL-2815	(P)	**Deluxe Set** (3 LPs)	1967	8.00	20.00
Capitol DT-2941	(E)	**Favorites**	1968	6.00	15.00
		— Original Capitol albums above have black labels with the logo on top.—			
Tower T-5006	(M)	**Lush Years**	1965	6.00	15.00
Tower ST-5006	(S)	**Lush Years**	1965	8.00	20.00
Tower T-5018	(M)	**Relaxin'**	1966	6.00	15.00
Tower ST-5018	(S)	**Relaxin'**	1966	8.00	20.00
Tower T-5036	(M)	**Happy In Love**	1966	6.00	15.00
Tower ST-5036	(S)	**Happy In Love**	1966	8.00	20.00
Reprise R-6021	(M)	**French Style**	1962	6.00	15.00
Reprise RS-6021	(S)	**French Style**	1962	5.00	12.00
Reprise R-6054	(M)	**Dino Latino**	1963	6.00	15.00
Reprise RS-6054	(S)	**Dino Latino**	1963	5.00	12.00
Reprise R-6061	(M)	**Country Style**	1963	6.00	15.00
Reprise RS-6061	(S)	**Country Style**	1963	6.00	15.00
Reprise R-6085	(M)	**Dean "Tex" Martin Rides Again**	1963	8.00	20.00
Reprise RS-6085	(S)	**Dean "Tex" Martin Rides Again**	1963	6.00	15.00

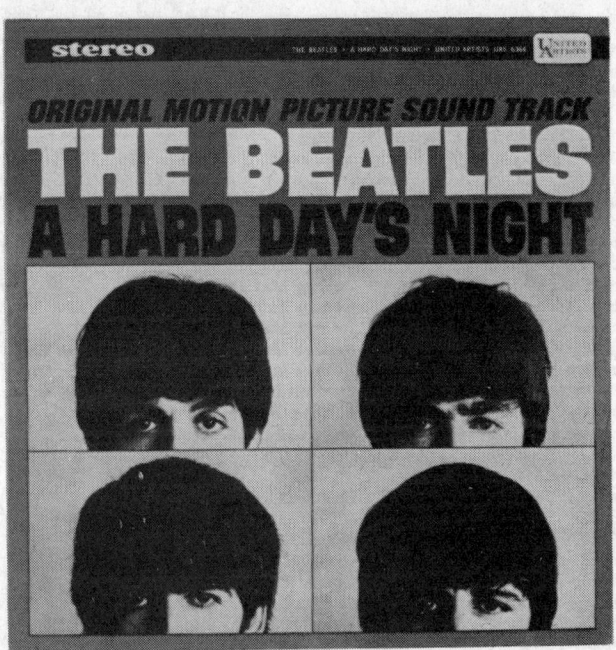

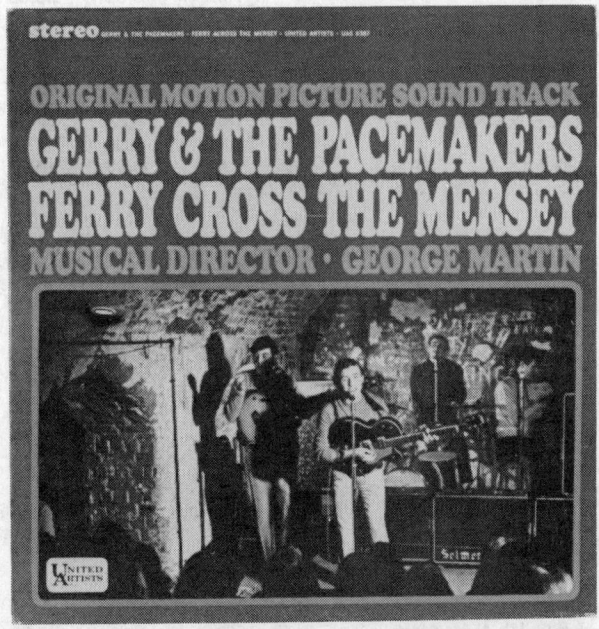

Producer, arranger, conductor and musician. . . George Martin played a pivotal role in the British Invasion for his sympathetic handling of the greatest rock 'n roll band of all time, The Beatles. His contributions to the soundtracks of two of the finest rock/pop movies of the decade, A Hard Day's Night and Ferry Cross The Mersey (listed under The Beatles and Gerry & The Pacemakers, respectively) were perfectly incidental and are all too overlooked.

Label & Catalog #		Title	Year	VG+	NM

MARTIN, DEWEY
Dewey Martin was formerly a member of The Buffalo Springfield.

Uni 73088	(S)	**Dewey Martin And Medicine Ball**	1970	6.00	15.00

MARTIN, GEORGE (& HIS ORCHESTRA)
Mr. Martin was the "fifth" Beatle, producer of their work, 1962-1969. Martin's scores for the "A Hard Day's Night," "Help!" and "Yellow Submarine" soundtracks are listed under The Beatles while "Ferry Cross The Mersey" is under Gerry & The Pacemakers..

United Arts. UAL-3377	(M)	**Off The Beatle Track**	1964	20.00	50.00
United Arts. UAS-6377	(S)	**Off The Beatle Track**	1964	30.00	75.00
United Arts. UAL-3420	(M)	**George Martin**	1965	12.00	30.00
United Arts. UAS-6420	(S)	**George Martin**	1965	16.00	40.00
United Arts. UAL-3448	(M)	**George Martin Plays "Help"**	1965	16.00	40.00
United Arts. UAS-6448	(S)	**George Martin Plays "Help"**	1965	20.00	50.00
United Arts. UAL-3539	(M)	**George Martin Salutes The Beatle Girls**	1966	16.00	40.00
United Arts. UAS-6539	(S)	**George Martin Salutes The Beatle Girls**	1966	20.00	50.00
United Arts. UAL-3647	(M)	**London By George**	1967	10.00	25.00
United Arts. UAS-6647	(S)	**London By George**	1967	12.00	30.00
United Arts. LA100	(S)	**Live And Let Die** (Soundtrack)	1973	6.00	15.00

MARTIN, GRADY

Decca DL-5566 (10")	(M)	**Dance-O-Rama #6**	1955	100.00	250.00

MARTIN, JIMMY (& THE SUNNY MOUNTAIN BOYS)

Decca DL-4016	(M)	**Good 'N' Country**	1960	8.00	20.00
Decca DL-74016	(S)	**Good 'N' Country**	1960	10.00	25.00
Decca DL-4285	(M)	**Country Music Time**	1962	8.00	20.00
Decca DL-74285	(S)	**Country Music Time**	1962	10.00	25.00
Decca DL-4360	(M)	**This World Is Not My Home**	1963	8.00	20.00
Decca DL-74360	(S)	**This World Is Not My Home**	1963	10.00	25.00
Decca DL-4536	(M)	**Widow Maker**	1964	6.00	15.00
Decca DL-74536	(S)	**Widow Maker**	1964	8.00	20.00
Decca DL-4643	(M)	**Sunny Side Of The Mountain**	1965	6.00	15.00
Decca DL-74643	(S)	**Sunny Side Of The Mountain**	1965	8.00	20.00
Decca DL-4769	(M)	**Mr. Good 'N' Country Music**	1966	6.00	15.00
Decca DL-74769	(S)	**Mr. Good 'N' Country Music**	1966	8.00	20.00
Decca DL-4891	(M)	**Big Country Instrumentals**	1967	6.00	15.00
Decca DL-74891	(S)	**Big Country Instrumentals**	1967	8.00	20.00
Decca DL-74996	(S)	**Tennessee**	1968	6.00	15.00
Decca DL-75116	(S)	**Free Born Man**	1969	6.00	15.00

MARTIN, MARTY
Marty later recorded as Boxcar Willie.

A.H.M.C. 118	(S)	**Marty Martin Sings Country Music**	197?	20.00	50.00

MARTIN, MARY

Decca DL-7027 (10")	(M)	**The Ford 50th Anniversary Show**	195?	14.00	35.00
Disneyland 3031	(M)	**A Musical Love Story**	195?	10.00	25.00
Disneyland 3038	(M)	**Hi Ho**	195?	10.00	25.00

MARTIN & NEIL
Vince Martin & Fed Neil.

Elektra EKL-248	(M)	**Tear Down The Walls**	1965	20.00	50.00
Elektra EKS-7248	(S)	**Tear Down The Walls**	1965	24.00	60.00

MARTINEZ, TONY

Del Fi DFLP-1205	(M)	**The Many Sides Of Pepino**	1959	10.00	25.00
Del Fi DFLP-1205S	(S)	**The Many Sides Of Pepino**	1959	14.00	35.00

MARTINO, AL

20th Century SF-3025	(M)	**Al Martino**	1959	12.00	30.00
20th Century SF-3032	(M)	**Sing Along With Al Martino**	1959	8.00	20.00
20th Century SFX-3032	(S)	**Sing Along With Al Martino**	1959	12.00	30.00
20th Century TF-4168	(M)	**Al Martino Sings**	1962	6.00	15.00
20th Century TFS-4168	(S)	**Al Martino Sings**	1962	8.00	20.00
20th Century TF-5009	(M)	**Love Notes**	1963	6.00	15.00
20th Century TFS-5009	(S)	**Love Notes**	1963	8.00	20.00
Capitol T-1774	(M)	**The Exciting Voice Of Al Martino**	1962	5.00	12.00
Capitol ST-1774	(S)	**The Exciting Voice Of Al Martino**	1962	6.00	15.00

Label & Catalog #		Title	Year	VG+	NM
Capitol T-1807	(M)	The Italian Voice Of Al Martino	1962	5.00	12.00
Capitol ST-1807	(S)	The Italian Voice Of Al Martino	1962	6.00	15.00
Capitol T-1914	(M)	I Love You Because	1963	5.00	12.00
Capitol ST-1914	(S)	I Love You Because	1963	6.00	15.00
Capitol T-1975	(M)	Painted, Tainted Rose	1963	5.00	12.00
Capitol ST-1975	(S)	Painted, Tainted Rose	1963	6.00	15.00
Capitol T-2040	(M)	Living A Lie	1964	5.00	12.00
Capitol ST-2040	(S)	Living A Lie	1964	6.00	15.00
Capitol T-2107	(M)	I Love You More And More Every Day	1964	5.00	12.00
Capitol ST-2107	(S)	I Love You More And More Every Day	1964	6.00	15.00
Capitol T-2165	(M)	Merry Christmas	1964	5.00	12.00
Capitol ST-2165	(S)	Merry Christmas	1964	6.00	15.00
Capitol T-2200	(M)	We Could	1965	5.00	12.00
Capitol ST-2200	(S)	We Could	1965	6.00	15.00
Capitol T-2312	(M)	Somebody Else Is Taking My Place	1965	5.00	12.00
Capitol ST-2312	(S)	Somebody Else Is Taking My Place	1965	6.00	15.00
Capitol T-2362	(M)	My Cherie	1965	5.00	12.00
Capitol ST-2362	(S)	My Cherie	1965	6.00	15.00
Capitol T-2435	(M)	Spanish Eyes	1966	5.00	12.00
Capitol ST-2435	(S)	Spanish Eyes	1966	6.00	15.00
Capitol T-2528	(M)	Think I'll Go Somewhere And Cry Myself To Sleep	1966	5.00	12.00
Capitol ST-2528	(S)	Think I'll Go Somewhere And Cry Myself To Sleep	1966	6.00	15.00
Capitol T-2592	(M)	This Is Love	1966	5.00	12.00
Capitol ST-2592	(S)	This Is Love	1966	6.00	15.00
Capitol T-2654	(M)	This Love For You	1967	5.00	12.00
Capitol ST-2654	(S)	This Love For You	1967	6.00	15.00
Capitol T-2733	(M)	Daddy's Little Girl	1967	5.00	12.00
Capitol ST-2733	(S)	Daddy's Little Girl	1967	6.00	15.00
Capitol T-2780	(M)	Mary In The Morning	1967	5.00	12.00
Capitol ST-2780	(S)	Mary In The Morning	1967	6.00	15.00
Capitol ST-2843	(S)	This Is Al Martino	1968	5.00	12.00
Capitol ST-2908	(S)	Love Is Blue	1968	5.00	12.00
Capitol ST-2946	(S)	The Best Of Al Martino	1968	5.00	12.00

— Original Capitol albums above have black labels with the logo on top.—

MARVELETTES, THE

Tamla 228	(M)	Please Mr. Postman	1961	300.00	500.00
Tamla 229	(M)	The Marvelettes Sing Hits Of '62	1962	600.00	1,200.00
		(Original covers are white with a large "M" and a "62" inside a circle.)			
Tamla 229	(M)	The Marvelettes Sing Hits Of '62	1962	250.00	500.00
		(Later covers are black with the titles of the hits inside circles.)			
Tamla 231	(M)	Playboy	1962	250.00	500.00

— Original Tamla albums above have a disc over-lapping a globe at the top of the label.—

Tamla 228	(M)	Please Mr. Postman	1963	80.00	200.00
Tamla 229	(M)	The Marvelettes Sing Hits Of '62	1963	80.00	200.00
Tamla 231	(M)	Playboy	1963	80.00	200.00
Tamla 237	(M)	The Marvelous Marvelettes	1963	80.00	200.00
Tamla 243	(M)	On Stage	1963	30.00	75.00
Tamla 253	(M)	The Marvelettes' Greatest Hits	1966	6.00	15.00
Tamla TS-253	(S)	The Marvelettes' Greatest Hits	1966	8.00	20.00
Tamla 274	(M)	The Marvelettes	1967	6.00	15.00
Tamla TS-274	(S)	The Marvelettes	1967	8.00	20.00
Tamla TS-286	(S)	Sophisticated Soul	1968	6.00	15.00
Tamla TS-288	(S)	The Marvelettes In Full Bloom	1969	6.00	15.00
Tamla TS-305	(S)	Return Of The Marvelettes	1970	6.00	15.00

— Tamla albums above have two side-by-side circles at the top of the label.—

Motown M7-827	(S)	Anthology (2 LPs)	1975	6.00	15.00

MARVELOWS, THE

ABC-Paramount S-643	(S)	The Mighty Marvelows	1968	12.00	30.00

MARVIN & JOHNNY
For additional listings refer to The Isley Brothers / Marvin & Johnny.

Crown CLP-5381	(M)	Marvin & Johnny	1963	10.00	25.00
Crown CST-381	(E)	Marvin & Johnny	1963	4.00	10.00

Label & Catalog #		Title	Year	VG+	NM
MARX, BILL					
Vee Jay LP-3035	(M)	My Son The Folk Singer	1963	6.00	15.00
Vee Jay SR-3035	(S)	My Son The Folk Singer	1963	10.00	25.00
MARX, GROUCHO					
Decca DL-5405 (10")	(M)	Hooray For Captain Spaulding	1952	100.00	250.00
A&M SP-3515	(M)	An Evening With Groucho	1972	6.00	15.00
A&M SP-3515	(M)	An Evening With Groucho (Picture disc)	1972	4.00	10.00
MARX, HARPO					
RCA Victor LPM-27 (10")	(M)	Harp By Harpo	1951	60.00	150.00
Mercury MG-20232	(M)	Harpo In Hi-Fi	1957	20.00	50.00
Mercury SR-60232	(S)	Harpo In Hi-Fi	1957	30.00	75.00
Mercury MG-20363	(M)	Harpo At Work	1959	20.00	50.00
Mercury SR-60016	(S)	Harpo At Work	1959	30.00	75.00
RCA Victor LPM-2720	(M)	Harp By Harpo	1963	20.00	50.00
RCA Victor LSP-2720	(E)	Harp By Harpo	1963	16.00	40.00
MARX BROTHERS, THE					
The Marx Brothers were Chico, Groucho, Harpo and Zeppo.					
Decca DL-79168	(E)	The Marx Brothers	1969	8.00	20.00
MARY BUTTERWORTH					
Custom Fidelity	(M)	Mary Butterworth	1968	150.00	300.00
MASKED MARAUDERS, THE					
Reprise/Deity RS-6378	(S)	The Masked Marauders	1969	8.00	20.00
MASON, BARBARA					
Arctic ALP-1000	(M)	Yes, I'm Ready	1965	10.00	25.00
Arctic ALPS-1000	(S)	Yes, I'm Ready	1965	12.00	30.00
Arctic ALPS-1004	(S)	Oh, How It Hurts	1968	8.00	20.00
MASON, DAVE					
Dave Mason was formerly a member of Traffic.					
Blue Thumb BTS-19	(S)	Alone Together (Multi-colored vinyl)	1970	8.00	20.00
Blue Thumb BTS-19	(S)	Alone Together (Black vinyl)	1971	16.00	40.00
Blue Thumb BTS-34	(S)	Headkeeper	1972	6.00	15.00
Blue Thumb BTS-54	(S)	Dave Mason Is Alive	1973	6.00	15.00
Columbia PCQ-31721	(Q)	It's Like You Never Left	1974	6.00	15.00
Columbia PCQ-33096	(Q)	Dave Mason	1974	6.00	15.00
Columbia PCQ-33698	(Q)	Split Coconut	1976	6.00	15.00
MASON, DAVE, & CASS ELLIOT					
Blue Thumb BTS-25	(S)	Dave Mason And Cass Elliot	1969	12.00	30.00
Blue Thumb BTS-8825	(S)	Dave Mason And Cass Elliot	1971	6.00	15.00
		(Blue Thumb 8825 is a reissue of 25.)			
MASON, LINDA					
RIC R-1005	(M)	How Many Seas Must A White Dove Sail?	1964	6.00	15.00
MASON PROFFIT					
Happy Tiger HT-1009	(S)	Wanted! Mason Profitt	1970	6.00	15.00
Happy Tiger HT-1019	(S)	Movin' Toward Happiness	1971	6.00	15.00
MATCHBOX WHOOPEE BAND, CAPTAIN					
ESP-Disk' 3009	(S)	Smoke Dreams	1973	6.00	15.00
MATHIS, JOHNNY					
Columbia CL-887	(M)	Johnny Mathis	1957	20.00	50.00
Columbia CL-1028	(M)	Wonderful, Wonderful	1957	14.00	35.00
Columbia CL-1078	(M)	Warm	1957	14.00	35.00
Columbia CL-1090	(M)	Wild Is The Wind (Soundtrack)	1957	80.00	200.00
Columbia CL-1119	(M)	Good Night, Dear Lord	1958	14.00	35.00
Columbia CL-1133	(M)	Johnny's Greatest Hits	1958	14.00	35.00
Columbia CL-1165	(M)	Swing Softly	1958	14.00	35.00
Columbia CL-1194	(M)	A Certain Smile (Soundtrack)	1958	80.00	200.00
Columbia CL-1195	(M)	Merry Christmas	1958	14.00	35.00
Columbia CL-1270	(M)	Open Fire, Two Guitars	1959	14.00	35.00

Label & Catalog #		Title	Year	VG+	NM
Columbia CL-1344	(M)	More Johnny's Greatest Hits	1959	10.00	25.00
Columbia CL-1351	(M)	Heavenly	1959	6.00	15.00
Columbia CS-8151	(S)	Heavenly	1959	8.00	20.00
Columbia CL-1419	(M)	Faithfully	1960	6.00	15.00
Columbia CS-8219	(S)	Faithfully	1960	8.00	20.00
Columbia CL-1526	(M)	Johnny's Moods	1960	6.00	15.00
Columbia CS-8326	(S)	Johnny's Moods	1960	8.00	20.00
Columbia C2L-803	(M)	The Rhythms And Ballads Of Broadway	1960	8.00	20.00
Columbia C2S-803	(S)	The Rhythms And Ballads Of Broadway	1960	10.00	25.00
Columbia CL-1623	(M)	I'll Buy You A Star	1961	6.00	15.00
Columbia CS-8423	(S)	I'll Buy You A Star	1961	8.00	20.00
Columbia CL-1644	(M)	Portrait Of Johnny (With bonus portrait)	1961	8.00	20.00
Columbia CS-8444	(S)	Portrait Of Johnny (With bonus portrait)	1961	10.00	25.00
Columbia CL-1644	(M)	Portrait Of Johnny (Without the portrait)	1961	6.00	15.00
Columbia CS-8444	(S)	Portrait Of Johnny (Without the portrait)	1961	8.00	20.00
Columbia CL-1711	(M)	Live It Up!	1962	6.00	15.00
Columbia CS-8511	(S)	Live It Up!	1962	8.00	20.00

— Original Columbia albums above have three white "eye" logos on each side of the spindle hole. —

Label & Catalog #		Title	Year	VG+	NM
Columbia CL-1834	(M)	Johnny's Greatest Hits	1962	6.00	15.00
Columbia CS-8634	(E)	Johnny's Greatest Hits	1962	4.00	10.00
Columbia CL-1915	(M)	Rapture	1962	4.00	10.00
Columbia CS-8715	(S)	Rapture	1962	5.00	12.00
Columbia CL-2016	(M)	Johnny's Newest Hits	1963	5.00	12.00
Columbia CS-8816	(S)	Johnny's Newest Hits	1963	6.00	15.00
Columbia CL-2044	(M)	Johnny	1963	4.00	10.00
Columbia CS-8844	(S)	Johnny	1963	5.00	12.00
Columbia CL-2098	(M)	Romantically	1963	4.00	10.00
Columbia CS-8898	(S)	Romantically	1963	5.00	12.00
Columbia CL-2143	(M)	I'll Search My Heart And Other Great Hits	1964	4.00	10.00
Columbia CS-8943	(S)	I'll Search My Heart And Other Great Hits	1964	5.00	12.00
Columbia C2L-834	(M)	The Great Years	1964	4.00	10.00
Columbia C2S-834	(S)	The Great Years	1964	5.00	12.00
Columbia CL-2223	(M)	The Ballads Of Broadway	1964	4.00	10.00
Columbia CS-9023	(S)	The Ballads Of Broadway	1964	5.00	12.00
Columbia CL-2224	(M)	The Rhythms Of Broadway	1964	4.00	10.00
Columbia CS-9024	(S)	The Rhythms Of Broadway	1964	5.00	12.00
Columbia CL-2246	(M)	Wonderful! Wonderful!	1964	5.00	12.00
Columbia CS-9046	(E)	Wonderful! Wonderful!	1964	3.20	8.00

— Original Columbia albums above have "360 Sound Mono/Stereo" on the bottom of the label. —

Label & Catalog #		Title	Year	VG+	NM
Mercury MG-20837	(M)	The Sound Of Christmas	1964	4.00	12.00
Mercury SR-60837	(S)	The Sound Of Christmas	1964	5.00	15.00
Mercury MG-20890	(M)	Tender Is The Night	1964	4.00	12.00
Mercury SR-60890	(S)	Tender Is The Night	1964	5.00	15.00
Mercury MG-20913	(M)	The Wonderful World Of Make Believe	1964	4.00	12.00
Mercury SR-60913	(S)	The Wonderful World Of Make Believe	1964	5.00	15.00
Mercury MG-20942	(M)	This Is Love	1964	4.00	12.00
Mercury SR-60942	(S)	This Is Love	1964	5.00	15.00
Mercury MG-20988	(M)	Johnny Mathis Ole	1964	4.00	12.00
Mercury SR-60988	(S)	Johnny Mathis Ole	1964	5.00	15.00
Mercury MG-20991	(M)	Love Is Everything	1965	4.00	12.00
Mercury SR-60991	(S)	Love Is Everything	1965	5.00	15.00
Mercury MG-21041	(M)	The Sweetheart Tree	1965	4.00	12.00
Mercury SR-61041	(S)	The Sweetheart Tree	1965	5.00	15.00
Mercury MG-21073	(M)	The Shadow Of Your Smile	1966	4.00	12.00
Mercury SR-61073	(S)	The Shadow Of Your Smile	1966	5.00	15.00
Mercury MG-21091	(M)	So Nice	1966	4.00	12.00
Mercury SR-61091	(S)	So Nice	1966	5.00	15.00
Mercury MG-21107	(M)	Johnny Mathis Sings	1967	4.00	12.00
Mercury SR-61107	(S)	Johnny Mathis Sings	1967	5.00	15.00
Columbia CQ-30740	(Q)	You've Got A Friend	1971	6.00	15.00
Columbia CQ-30979	(Q)	Johnny Mathis In Person	1972	6.00	15.00
Columbia CQ-31626	(Q)	Song Sung Blue	1972	6.00	15.00
Columbia CQ-32114	(Q)	Me And Mrs Jones	1973	6.00	15.00
Columbia CQ-32435	(Q)	I'm Coming Home	1973	6.00	15.00
Columbia CQ-33420	(Q)	When Will I See You Again	1975	6.00	15.00
Mobile Fidelity MFSL-171	(S)	Heavenly	198?	7.00	20.00

MATRIX

Label & Catalog #		Title	Year	VG+	NM
Rare Earth R-542L	(S)	Matrix	1972	6.00	15.00

Label & Catalog #		Title	Year	VG+	NM
MATTHEWS, DAVE					
People 3000	(S)	**Grodeck Whipperjenny**	1970	20.00	50.00
MAUDS, THE					
Mercury MG-21135	(M)	**The Mauds Hold On**	1967	6.00	15.00
Mercury SR-61135	(S)	**The Mauds Hold On**	1967	8.00	20.00
MAXWELL, DIANE					
Challenge CHL-607	(M)	**Almost Seventeen**	1959	10.00	25.00
Challenge CHS-2501	(S)	**Almost Seventeen**	1959	14.00	35.00
MAY, BILLY					
Capitol T-562	(M)	**Sorta May**	1955	12.00	30.00
MAY BLITZ					
Paramount PAS-5020	(S)	**May Blitz**	1970	8.00	20.00
MAYA, CANTA					
Roulette R-25052	(M)	**A Long, Long Kiss**	1958	8.00	20.00

MAYALL, JOHN [JOHN MAYALL'S BLUESBREAKERS]
Refer to the Groundhogs; Mick Taylor.

London LL-3492	(M)	**Blues Breakers With Eric Clapton**	1967	8.00	20.00
London PS-492	(S)	**Blues Breakers With Eric Clapton**	1967	8.00	20.00
London LL-3502	(M)	**A Hard Road**	1967	8.00	20.00
London PS-502	(S)	**A Hard Road**	1967	6.00	15.00
London PS-529	(S)	**Crusade**	1968	6.00	15.00
London PS-534	(S)	**The Blues Alone**	1968	6.00	15.00
London PS-537	(S)	**Bare Wires**	1968	6.00	15.00
London PS-545	(S)	**Blues From Laurel Canyon**	1969	6.00	15.00
London PS-562	(S)	**Looking Back**	1969	6.00	15.00
London PS-570	(S)	**The Diary Of A Band**	1970	5.00	12.00
London PS-589	(S)	**Live In Europe**	1971	5.00	12.00
London 2PS-600	(S)	**Thru The Years** (2 LPs)	1971	6.00	15.00
London 2BP-618	(S)	**Down The Line** (2 LPs)	1973	5.00	12.00
Polydor 24-4004	(S)	**The Turning Point**	1969	5.00	12.00
Polydor 24-4010	(S)	**Empty Rooms**	1970	5.00	12.00
Polydor 24-4022	(S)	**U.S.A. Union**	1970	5.00	12.00
Polydor 25-3002	(S)	**Back To The Roots** (2 LPs)	1971	6.00	15.00
Mobile Fidelity MFSL-183	(S)	**Blues Breakers With Eric Clapton**	198?	7.00	20.00

MAYER, NATHANIEL					
Fortune 8014	(M)	**Going Back To The Village Of Love** *(Purple labels on thick vinyl.)*	1962	60.00	150.00
Fortune 8014	(M)	**Going Back To The Village Of Love** *(Yellow labels on thick vinyl.)*	196?	20.00	50.00
Fortune 8014	(M)	**Going Back To The Village Of Love** *(Bluish purple labels on thin vinyl.)*	197?	6.00	15.00

MAYFIELD, CURTIS
Curtis Mayfield was a founding member of The Impressions.

Curtom CRS-8005	(S)	**Curtis**	1970	4.00	10.00
Curtom CRS-8008	(S)	**Curtis Mayfield Live** (2 LPs)	1971	5.00	12.00
Curtom CRS-8009	(S)	**Roots**	1971	4.00	10.00
Curtom CRS-8014	(S)	**Superfly** (Soundtrack)	1972	4.00	10.00
Curtom CRS-8015	(S)	**Back To The World**	1973	4.00	10.00
Curtom CRS-8018	(S)	**Curtis Mayfield In Chicago**	1973	4.00	10.00
Curtom CRS-SP	(DJ)	**Rapping** (Interview)	1973	6.00	15.00

MAYFIELD, PERCY					
Tangerine TRC-1505	(M)	**My Jug And I**	1966	6.00	15.00
Tangerine TRCS-1505	(S)	**My Jug And I**	1966	8.00	20.00
Tangerine TRC-1510	(M)	**Bought Blues**	1967	6.00	15.00
Tangerine TRCS-1510	(S)	**Bought Blues**	1967	8.00	20.00
Brunswick BL7-54145	(S)	**Walking On A Tightrope**	1969	6.00	15.00
Specialty SPS-2186	(E)	**The Best Of Percy Mayfield**	1970	6.00	15.00
RCA Victor LSP-4269	(S)	**Percy Mayfield Sings Percy Mayfield**	1970	6.00	15.00
RCA Victor LSP-4444	(S)	**Weakness Is A Thing Called Man**	1970	6.00	15.00
RCA Victor LSP-4558	(S)	**Blues And Then Some**	1971	6.00	15.00

MAYSA

Label & Catalog #		Title	Year	VG+	NM
United Arts. UAL-3034	(M)	The Sound Of Love	1959	8.00	20.00
United Arts. UAS-6034	(S)	The Sound Of Love	1959	10.00	25.00

MAZANTI

Mazanti Music	(S)	Philosopher	1979	40.00	100.00

MAZE

M.T.A. 5012	(S)	Armageddon	1971	40.00	100.00

MC-5, THE [THE MOTOR CITY FIVE]

Elektra EKS-74042	(S)	Kick Out The Jams (Brown label)	1969	30.00	75.00
		(Original pressings open side one with the anthem, "Kick out the jams, motherfuckers!" and feature liner notes on the back cover.)			
Elektra EKS-74042	(S)	Kick Out The Jams	1969	16.00	40.00
		(Later pressings replace the expletive with "Kick out the jams, brothers and sisters" and delete the liner notes.)			
Atlantic SD-8247	(S)	Back In The U.S.A.	1970	16.00	40.00
Atlantic SD-8285	(S)	High Time	1971	16.00	40.00

McAULIFFE, LEON (& HIS CIMMARON BOYS)

Sesac 1601	(M)	Points West	195?	60.00	150.00
Sesac 1602	(M)	Just A Minute	195?	40.00	100.00
Dot DLP-3139	(M)	Take Off	1958	24.00	60.00
Cimarron 202	(M)	Swingin' Western Strings	1960	24.00	60.00
ABC-Paramount 394	(M)	Cozy Inn	1961	14.00	35.00
ABC-Paramount S-394	(S)	Cozy Inn	1961	20.00	50.00
Starday SLP-171	(M)	Mr. Western Swing	1962	16.00	40.00
Starday SLP-280	(M)	Swinging West	1962	16.00	40.00
Starday SLP-309	(M)	Swingin' Western Strings	1962	16.00	40.00
Capitol T-2016	(M)	The Dancin'est Band Around	1964	12.00	30.00
Capitol ST-2016	(S)	The Dancin'est Band Around	1964	16.00	40.00
Capitol T-2148	(M)	Everybody Dance! Everybody Swing!	1964	12.00	30.00
Capitol ST-2148	(S)	Everybody Dance! Everybody Swing!	1964	16.00	40.00
Dot DLP-3689	(M)	Golden Country Hits	1966	24.00	60.00
Dot DLP-25689	(E)	Golden Country Hits	1966	20.00	50.00

McCALL, MARY ANN: *Refer to* **GOLDMINE'S PRICE GUIDE TO COLLECTIBLE JAZZ ALBUMS**

McCALL, TOUSSAINT

Ronn 7527	(M)	Nothing Can Take The Place Of You	1967	12.00	30.00
Ronn 7527S	(S)	Nothing Can Take The Place Of You	1967	16.00	40.00
		("Nothing Can Take The Place Of You" and "Shimmy" are rechanneled on this album.)			

McCARTNEY, PAUL (& WINGS)

Albums may be credited to Paul McCartney, Paul & Linda McCartney, Paul McCartney & Wings, or Wings. Refer to The Beatles; The Crickets; Mary Hopkin; Denny Laine; Percy Thrillington. Note: After the fall of Apple, all of Mac's albums were reissued by Capitol, often with several label variations. When Paul moved to Columbia, he took his catalog with him and all of the Apple and Capitol albums were reissued first on Columbia's regular line (with a "JC" prefix) and then on their budget line ("PC"). Those reissues and variations that have significant value are listed below.

Warner Bros. PRO (10")	(DJ)	The Family Way (Radio spots)	1967	150.00	300.00
London M-76007	(M)	The Family Way (Soundtrack)	1967	30.00	75.00
London MS-82007	(S)	The Family Way (Soundtrack)	1967	40.00	100.00
		(Original covers have front and back slicks adhered to cardboard; labels are flat. Counterfeit covers are printed on posterboard and the labels are glossy.)			
Apple STAO-3363	(S)	McCartney	1970	14.00	40.00
		(Apple label with "A Subsidiary of Capitol" on the bottom. Counterfeits have inferior reproductions of the labels and cover.)			
Apple STAO-3363	(S)	McCartney	1970	8.00	20.00
		(Apple label with "Manufactured by Apple" on the bottom.)			
Apple SMAS-3363	(S)	McCartney	1975	12.00	30.00
		(Apple label with "All Rights Reserved" disclaimer.)			
Apple SPRO-6210	(DJ)	Brung To Ewe By	1971	200.00	400.00
		(Radio spots for "Ram." Originals have even spacing between the tracks; counterfeits are uneven.)			

Label & Catalog #		Title	Year	VG+	NM
Apple MAS-3375	(M)	**Ram**	1971	**1,000.00**	*Rare*
		(Mono pressing issued to radio stations in standard stereo cover.			
		Near Mint copies have a suggested value of $2,000-3,000.)			
Apple SMAS-3375	(S)	**Ram**	1971	**16.00**	**40.00**
		(Apple label with "A Subsidiary of Capitol" on the bottom.)			
Apple SMAS-3375	(S)	**Ram**	1971	**6.00**	**15.00**
		(Apple label with "Manufactured by Apple" on the bottom.			
		Apple is unsliced on one side while sliced on the other.)			
Apple SMAS-3375	(S)	**Ram**	1971	**10.00**	**25.00**
		(Apple label with "Manufactured by Apple" on the bottom.			
		Apple is unsliced on both sides.)			
Apple SMAS-3375	(S)	**Ram**	1975	**30.00**	**75.00**
		(Apple label with "All Rights Reserved" disclaimer.)			
Apple SW-3386	(S)	**Wild Life**	1971	**6.00**	**15.00**
Apple SMAL-3409	(S)	**Red Rose Speedway** *(With booklet)*	1973	**6.00**	**15.00**
Apple SO-3415	(S)	**Band On The Run** *(With poster)*	1973	**6.00**	**15.00**
Capitol SMAS-3363	(S)	**McCartney** *(Black label)*	197?	**8.00**	**20.00**
Capitol SMAS-3375	(S)	**Ram**	197?	**8.00**	**20.00**
		(Black label with "Manufactured by McCartney Music" on top.)			
Capitol SMAS-3375	(S)	**Ram**	197?	**6.00**	**15.00**
		(Black label with "Manufactured by MPL" on top.)			
Capitol SMAS-3375	(S)	**Ram**	197?	**12.00**	**30.00**
		(Black label with "Manufactured by Capitol" at the top.)			
Capitol SMAS-3375	(S)	**Ram**	197?	**6.00**	**15.00**
Capitol SW-3386	(S)	**Wild Life**	197?	**8.00**	**20.00**
		(Black label with "Manufactured by McCartney Music" on top.)			
Capitol SW-3386	(S)	**Wild Life**	197?	**6.00**	**15.00**
		(Black label with "Manufactured by MPL" on top.)			
Capitol SMAL-3409	(S)	**Red Rose Speedway** *(With booklet)*	197?	**8.00**	**20.00**
		(Black label with "Manufactured by McCartney Music" on top.)			
Capitol SMAL-3409	(S)	**Red Rose Speedway** *(With booklet)*	197?	**6.00**	**15.00**
		(Black label with "Manufactured by MPL" on top.)			
Capitol PRO-2955/56	(DJ)	**Band On The Run Radio Interview**	1973	**300.00**	**600.00**
		(White label with a script and two photos in a plain cardboard jacket..			
		Counterfeits have yellow labels.)			
Capitol SO-3415	(S)	**Band On The Run** *(With poster)*	1973	**12.00**	**30.00**
		(Black label with "Manufactured by Capitol" at the top.)			
Capitol SO-3415	(S)	**Band On The Run** *(With poster)*	197?	**8.00**	**20.00**
		(Custom photo label with "Manufactured by MPL.")			
Capitol SO-3415	(S)	**Band On The Run** *(With poster)*	197?	**6.00**	**15.00**
		(Black label with "Manufactured by MPL" at the top.)			
Capitol SEAX-11901	(S)	**Band On The Run** *(Picture disc)*	1975	**14.00**	**35.00**
Capitol SMAS-11419	(S)	**Venus And Mars** *(With inserts)*	1975	**5.00**	**12.00**
		(Includes two posters and two stickers.)			
Capitol SW-11525	(DJ)	**Wings At The Speed Of Sound**	1976	**80.00**	**200.00**
Capitol SW-11525	(S)	**Wings At The Speed Of Sound**	1976	**3.50**	**8.00**
Columbia C3X-37990	(S)	**Wings Over America**	1976	**16.00**	**40.00**
Columbia JC-36482	(S)	**Band On The Run**	1981	**16.00**	**40.00**
		(The front cover has the "MPL" logo in lower left corner.)			
Columbia PC-36482	(S)	**Band On The Run**	1984	**6.00**	**15.00**
Columbia HC-46482	(S)	**Band On The Run** *(Half-speed master)*	1981	**16.00**	**50.00**
Columbia FC-36057	(DJ)	**Back To The Egg**	1979	**16.00**	**40.00**
Columbia PC-36057	(S)	**Back To The Egg**	1979	**10.00**	**25.00**
Columbia FC-36511	(DJ)	**McCartney II** *(White label)*	1980	**12.00**	**30.00**
Columbia FC-36511	(S)	**McCartney II** *(With "Coming Up" single)*	1980	**6.00**	**15.00**
Columbia PC-36511	(S)	**McCartney II**	1984	**16.00**	**40.00**
Columbia AS2-821	(DJ)	**The McCartney Interview** *(2 LPs)*	1980	**12.00**	**30.00**
		(Originals have white labels with black print in a glossy cover.			
		Counterfeits have blank white labels.)			
Columbia PC-37990	(S)	**Wings Over America** *(3 LPs)*	1980	**16.00**	**40.00**
Capitol C1-94778	(S)	**Tripping The Live Fantastic** *(3 LPs)*	1990	**20.00**	**50.00**
Capitol C1-94778	(S)	**Highlight! Tripping The Live Fantastic**	1990	**10.00**	**25.00**
		(Capitol Record Club single album sampler.)			

McCOY, CHARLIE

Monument ZQ-32749	(Q)	**Fastest Harp In The South**	1974	**6.00**	**15.00**
Monument ZQ-32922	(Q)	**Nashville Hit Man**	1974	**6.00**	**15.00**

Gene McDaniels scored a half-dozen r&b based pop hits in the early '60s. A fine singer, he is generally overlooked because he is a black pop singer, a genre that attracts neither black nor white collectors. . .

Label & Catalog #		Title	Year	VG+	NM

McCOY, VAN

Columbia CL-2497	(M)	Night Time Is Lonely Time	1966	6.00	15.00
Columbia CS-9297	(S)	Night Time Is Lonely Time	1966	8.00	20.00
Buddah BDS-5103	(S)	Soul Improvisations	1972	6.00	15.00

McCOYS, THE

Bang BLP-212	(M)	Hang On Sloopy	1965	12.00	30.00
Bang BLPS-212	(S)	Hang On Sloopy	1965	16.00	40.00
		("Hang On Sloopy" is rechanneled on this album.)			
Bang BLP-213	(M)	You Make Me Feel So Good	1966	12.00	30.00
Bang BLPS-213	(S)	You Make Me Feel So Good	1966	16.00	40.00
Mercury SR-61163	(S)	Infinite McCoys	1968	6.00	15.00
Mercury SR-61207	(S)	Human Ball	1969	6.00	15.00

McCRACKLIN, JIMMY

Chess 1464	(M)	Jimmy McCracklin Sings	1961	30.00	75.00
Crown CLP-5244	(M)	Twist With Jimmy McCracklin	1962	10.00	25.00
Imperial LP-9285	(M)	Every Night, Every Day	1965	8.00	20.00
Imperial LP-12285	(S)	Every Night, Every Day	1965	10.00	25.00
Imperial LP-9297	(M)	Think	1965	8.00	20.00
Imperial LP-12297	(S)	Think	1965	10.00	25.00
Imperial LP-9306	(M)	My Answer	1966	8.00	20.00
Imperial LP-12306	(S)	My Answer	1966	10.00	25.00
Imperial LP-9316	(M)	New Soul Of Jimmy McCracklin	1966	8.00	20.00
Imperial LP-12316	(S)	New Soul Of Jimmy McCracklin	1966	10.00	25.00
Minit LP-4009	(M)	The Best Of Jimmy McCracklin	1967	8.00	20.00
Minit LP-24009	(S)	The Best Of Jimmy McCracklin	1967	8.00	20.00
Minit LP-24011	(S)	Let's Get Together	1968	8.00	20.00
Minit LP-24017	(S)	Stinger Man	1969	8.00	20.00
Stax STS-2047	(S)	Yesterday Is Gone	1972	6.00	15.00

McCULLOCH, DANNY

Danny was formerly a member of The Animals.

| Verve/Forecast FTS-3058 | (S) | Danny McCulloch | 1968 | 8.00 | 20.00 |
| Capitol ST-174 | (S) | Wings Of A Man | 1969 | 8.00 | 20.00 |

McCURDY, ED

Riverside RLP-12-180	(M)	The Legend Of Robin Hood	195?	8.00	20.00
Riverside RLP-12-601	(M)	The Ballad Record	195?	8.00	20.00
Riverside RLP-12-807	(M)	Bar Room Ballads	195?	8.00	20.00
Elektra EKL-24	(M)	Sin Songs, Pro And Con	195?	8.00	20.00
Elektra EKL-108	(M)	Blood, Booze 'N Bones	195?	8.00	20.00
Elektra EKL-112	(M)	Songs Of The Old West	195?	8.00	20.00
Elektra EKL-170	(M)	When Dalliance Was In Flower	195?	8.00	20.00
Tradition TLP-1003	(M)	A Ballad Singer's Choice	195?	8.00	20.00
Tradition TLP-1027	(M)	Children's Songs	195?	8.00	20.00
Dawn DLP-1127	(M)	The Folk Singer	195?	8.00	20.00
By-Line 1	(M)	Frankie And Johnny	195?	8.00	20.00

McDANIELS, GENE

Liberty LRP-3146	(M)	In Times Like These	1960	12.00	30.00
Liberty LST-7146	(S)	In Times Like These	1960	16.00	40.00
Liberty LST-7146	(S)	In Times Like These (Blue vinyl)	1960	30.00	75.00
Liberty LRP-3175	(M)	Sometimes I'm Happy, Sometimes I'm Blue	1960	10.00	25.00
Liberty LST-7175	(S)	Sometimes I'm Happy, Sometimes I'm Blue	1960	12.00	30.00
Liberty LRP-3191	(M)	100 Lbs. Of Clay	1961	10.00	25.00
Liberty LST-7191	(S)	100 Lbs. Of Clay	1961	12.00	30.00
Liberty LRP-3204	(M)	Gene McDaniels Sings Movie Memories	1962	10.00	25.00
Liberty LST-7204	(S)	Gene McDaniels Sings Movie Memories	1962	12.00	30.00
Liberty LRP-3215	(M)	Tower Of Strength	1962	10.00	25.00
Liberty LST-7215	(S)	Tower Of Strength	1962	12.00	30.00
Liberty LRP-3258	(M)	Hit After Hit	1962	8.00	20.00
Liberty LST-7258	(S)	Hit After Hit	1962	10.00	25.00
Liberty LRP-3275	(M)	Spanish Lace	1963	8.00	20.00
Liberty LST-7275	(S)	Spanish Lace	1963	10.00	25.00
Liberty LRP-3311	(M)	The Wonderful Word Of Gene McDaniels	1963	6.00	15.00
Liberty LST-7311	(S)	The Wonderful Word Of Gene McDaniels	1963	8.00	20.00
Sunset SUM-1122	(M)	Facts Of Life	1967	5.00	12.00
Sunset SUS-5122	(S)	Facts Of Life	1967	6.00	15.00

Label & Catalog #		Title	Year	VG+	NM

McDONALD, "COUNTRY" JOE: *Refer to* **COUNTRY JOE (McDONALD)**

McDONALD, KATHY

Capitol ST-11224	(S)	Insane Asylum	1974	12.00	30.00

McDONALD, MARIE

RCA Victor LPM-1585	(M)	The Body Sings!	1957	20.00	50.00

McDONALD, MICHAEL

Mobile Fidelity MFSL-149	(S)	If That's What It Takes	198?	5.00	15.00

McDONALD, SKEETS

Capitol T-1040	(M)	Goin' Steady With The Blues	1958	30.00	75.00
Capitol T-1179	(M)	The Country's Best	1959	20.00	50.00
Columbia CL-2170	(M)	Call Me Skeets!	1964	12.00	30.00
Columbia CS-8970	(S)	Call Me Skeets!	1964	16.00	40.00
Fortune 3001	(S)	Tattooed Lady	1969	16.00	40.00

McDOWELL, "MISSISSIPPI" FRED

Sire SASH 97018	(S)	Mississippi Fred McDowell In London	1970	12.00	30.00
Everest 253	(S)	Mississippi Fred McDowell	1971	8.00	20.00
Capitol ST-403	(S)	I Do Not Play No Rock & Roll	1973	10.00	25.00
Just Sunshine JSS-4	(S)	Mississippi Fred McDowell 1904-1972	1973	6.00	15.00

McDOWELL, "MISSISSIPPI" FRED / GUITAR JR.

Capitol SAT-403	(DJ)	I Do Not Play No Rock & Roll *(Picture disc)*	1973	30.00	75.00

McDUFF, BROTHER JACK: *Refer to* **GOLDMINE'S PRICE GUIDE TO COLLECTIBLE JAZZ ALBUMS**

McGHEE, BROWNIE: *Refer to* **SONNY TERRY & BROWNIE McGHEE**

McGHEE, STICKS, & JOHN LEE HOOKER

Audio Lab AL-1520	(M)	Highway Of Blues	1959	80.00	200.00

McGOVERN, PATTY

Atlantic 1245	(M)	Patty McGovern With Thomas Talbert	1956	16.00	40.00

McGUINN, ROGER
Roger was formerly a member of The Byrds.

Columbia AS-353	(DJ)	The Roger McGuinn Airplay Anthology	1977	16.00	40.00
		(Compilation of Byrds and solo material.)			

McGUINNESS-FLINT

Capitol SMAS-625	(S)	McGuinness-Flint	1970	6.00	15.00
Capitol ST-794	(S)	Happy Birthday, Ruthy Baby	1971	6.00	15.00

McGUIRE, BARRY
Barry McGuire was formerly a member of The New Christy Minstrels.

Horizon WP-1608	(M)	Barry Here And Now	1962	6.00	15.00
Horizon ST-1608	(S)	Barry Here And Now	1962	8.00	20.00
Horizon WP-1636	(M)	The Barry McGuire Album	1963	6.00	15.00
Horizon ST-1636	(S)	The Barry McGuire Album	1963	8.00	20.00
Dunhill D-50003	(M)	Eve Of Destruction	1966	10.00	25.00
Dunhill DS-50003	(S)	Eve Of Destruction	1966	12.00	30.00
Dunhill D-50005	(M)	This Precious Time	1966	8.00	20.00
Dunhill DS-50005	(S)	This Precious Time	1966	10.00	25.00
Dunhill DS-50033	(S)	The World's Last Private Citizen	1968	8.00	20.00
Ode SP-77004	(S)	McGuire And The Doctor	1970	6.00	15.00

McGUIRE, PHYLLIS

ABC 552	(M)	Phyllis McGuire Sings	1966	5.00	12.00
ABC S-552	(S)	Phyllis McGuire Sings	1966	5.00	15.00

McGUIRE SISTERS, THE

Coral CRL-56123 (10")	(M)	By Request	1955	20.00	50.00
Coral CRL-57097	(M)	Children's Holiday	1956	14.00	35.00
Coral CRL-57026	(M)	Do You Remember When?	1956	14.00	35.00
Coral CRL-57028	(M)	S'Wonderful	1956	14.00	35.00
Coral CRL-57033	(M)	He	1956	14.00	35.00

Label & Catalog #		Title	Year	VG+	NM
Coral CRL-57052	(M)	Sincerely	1956	14.00	35.00
Coral CRL-57134	(M)	Teenage Party	1957	14.00	35.00
Coral CRL-57145	(M)	When The Lights Are Low	1957	14.00	35.00
Coral CRL-57180	(M)	Musical Magic	1957	12.00	30.00
Coral CRL-57217	(M)	Sugartime	1958	12.00	30.00
Coral CRL-57225	(M)	Greetings From The McGuire Sisters	1958	12.00	30.00
Coral CRL-57296	(M)	May You Always	1959	8.00	20.00
Coral CRL-757296	(S)	May You Always	1959	12.00	30.00
Coral CRL-57303	(M)	In Harmony With Him	1959	8.00	20.00
Coral CRL-757303	(S)	In Harmony With Him	1959	12.00	30.00
Coral CRL-57337	(M)	His And Her's	1960	8.00	20.00
Coral CRL-757337	(S)	His And Her's	1960	12.00	30.00
Coral CRL-57349	(M)	Our Golden Favorites	1961	8.00	20.00
Coral CRL-57385	(M)	Just For Old Times Sake	1961	8.00	20.00
Coral CRL-757385	(S)	Just For Old Times Sake	1961	12.00	30.00
Coral CRL-57398	(M)	Subways Are For Sleeping	1961	6.00	15.00
Coral CRL-757398	(S)	Subways Are For Sleeping	1961	8.00	20.00
Coral CRL-57415	(M)	Songs Everybody Knows	1962	6.00	15.00
Coral CRL-757415	(S)	Songs Everybody Knows	1962	8.00	20.00
— Original Coral albums above have maroon & silver labels.—					
Coral CRL-57443	(M)	Showcase	1964	5.00	12.00
Coral CRL-757443	(S)	Showcase	1964	6.00	15.00
Coral CXB-6	(M)	The Best Of The McGuire Sisters	1966	5.00	12.00
Coral CXSB-6	(S)	The Best Of The McGuire Sisters	1966	6.00	15.00
ABC-Paramount 530	(S)	The McGuire Sisters Today	1966	5.00	12.00
ABC-Paramount S-530	(S)	The McGuire Sisters Today	1966	6.00	15.00

McINTYRE, KEN

United Arts. UAL-3336	(M)	Way, Way Out	1964	5.00	12.00
United Arts. UAS-6336	(S)	Way, Way Out	1964	6.00	15.00

McKAY, SCOTTY

Ace LP-1017	(M)	Tonight In Person	1961	30.00	75.00

McKENZIE, SCOTT
Scott McKenzie formerly recorded as a member of The Journeymen.

Ode Z12-44001	(M)	The Voice Of Scott McKenzie	1967	8.00	20.00
Ode Z12-44002	(S)	The Voice Of Scott McKenzie	1967	10.00	25.00
Ode SP-77007	(S)	Stained Glass Morning	1970	6.00	15.00

McKINLEY, WILSON
Wilson McKinley also recorded as a California Poppy Picker.

Voice of Elijah 29005/6	(S)	Heaven's Gonna Be A Blast!	197?	60.00	150.00
Voice of Elijah 29077/8	(S)	Spirit Of Elijah	197?	100.00	250.00
No label	(S)	Wilson McKinley On Stage	197?	60.00	150.00

McKUEN, ROD / JULIE MEREDITH / TAK SHINDO

Imperial LP-9036	(M)	The Yellow Unicorn	1958	16.00	40.00
Imperial LP-12036	(S)	The Yellow Unicorn	1958	20.00	50.00

McKUEN, ROD

Liberty LRP-3011	(M)	Lazy Afternoon	1956	16.00	40.00
Decca DL-8714	(M)	Summer Love (Soundtrack)	1958	50.00	125.00
Decca DL-8882	(M)	Anywhere I Wander	1958	8.00	20.00
Decca DL-78882	(S)	Anywhere I Wander	1958	12.00	30.00
Decca DL-8946	(M)	Alone After Dark	1958	8.00	20.00
Decca DL-78946	(S)	Alone After Dark	1958	12.00	30.00
Hi Fi R-419	(M)	Beatsville	1959	6.00	15.00
Hi Fi SR-419	(S)	Beatsville	1959	8.00	20.00
Jubilee J-5013	(M)	Mr. Oliver Twist	1962	5.00	12.00
Jubilee SJ-5013	(S)	Mr. Oliver Twist	1962	6.00	15.00
Horizon T-1612	(M)	New Sounds In Folk Music	1963	5.00	12.00
Horizon ST-1612	(S)	New Sounds In Folk Music	1963	6.00	15.00
In 1003	(M)	Seasons In The Sun	1964	5.00	12.00
In S-1003	(S)	Seasons In The Sun	1964	6.00	15.00
Capitol T-2079	(M)	Rod McKuen Sings Rod McKuen	1964	5.00	12.00
Capitol ST-2079	(S)	Rod McKuen Sings Rod McKuen	1964	6.00	15.00
Tradition 2063	(M)	A San Francisco Hippie Trip	1967	8.00	20.00

Label & Catalog #		*Title*	*Year*	*VG+*	*NM*

McLAIN, DENNY
Denny was formerly a member of the Detroit Tigers.

| Capitol ST-2881 | (S) | Denny McLain At The Organ | 1968 | 12.00 | 30.00 |
| Capitol ST-204 | (S) | Denny McLain In Las Vegas | 1969 | 10.00 | 25.00 |

McLEAN, DON

| Mediarts 41-4 | (S) | Tapestry | 1970 | 6.00 | 15.00 |
| Millenium DJL1-3933 | (DJ) | RCA Special Radio Series *(With insert)* | 197? | 4.00 | 10.00 |

McLUHAN, MARSHALL

| Columbia CL-2701 | (M) | The Medium Is The Message | 1967 | 10.00 | 25.00 |
| Columbia CS-9501 | (S) | The Medium Is The Message | 1967 | 12.00 | 30.00 |

McNAIR, BARBARA

Warner Bros. W-1541	(M)	I Enjoy Being A Girl	1964	6.00	15.00
Warner Bros. WS-1541	(S)	I Enjoy Being A Girl	1964	8.00	20.00
Warner Bros. W-1570	(M)	Livin' End	1964	6.00	15.00
Warner Bros. WS-1570	(S)	Livin' End	1964	8.00	20.00
Motown 644	(M)	Here I Am	1966	6.00	15.00
Motown S-644	(S)	Here I Am	1966	8.00	20.00
Motown S-680	(S)	The Real Barbara McNair	1969	6.00	15.00

McNEELY, BIG JAY

Federal 295-96 (10")	(M)	Big Jay McNeely	1954	600.00	Rare
		(Near Mint copies have a suggested value of $1,200-2,000.)			
Savoy MG-15045 (10")	(M)	A Rhythm And Blues Concert	1955	300.00	500.00
Federal 395-530	(M)	Big Jay McNeely In 3-D	1956	300.00	500.00
King 395-530	(M)	Big Jay McNeely In 3-D	1956	150.00	300.00
King 650	(M)	Big Jay McNeely In 3-D	1959	50.00	125.00
		(King 530 and 650 are reissues of Federal 530.)			
Warner Bros. W-1523	(M)	Big Jay McNeely	1963	20.00	50.00
Warner Bros. WS-1523	(S)	Big Jay McNeely	1963	30.00	75.00

McPHATTER, CLYDE
Clyde was formerly the lead singer for Billy Ward & The Dominoes; The Drifters.

Atlantic 8024	(M)	Love Ballads	1958	150.00	300.00
Atlantic 8031	(M)	Clyde	1959	150.00	300.00
		— Original Atlantic albums above have black labels.—			
Atlantic 8024	(M)	Love Ballads	1960	80.00	200.00
Atlantic 8031	(M)	Clyde	1960	80.00	200.00
Atlantic 8077	(M)	The Best Of Clyde McPhatter	1963	60.00	150.00
		—Atlantic albums above have orange & purple labels.—			
MGM E-3775	(M)	Let's Start Over Again	1959	30.00	75.00
MGM SE-3775	(S)	Let's Start Over Again	1959	40.00	100.00
MGM E-3866	(M)	Clyde McPhatter's Greatest Hits	1960	16.00	40.00
MGM SE-3866	(S)	Clyde McPhatter's Greatest Hits	1960	20.00	50.00
Mercury MG-20597	(M)	Ta Ta	1960	12.00	30.00
Mercury SR-60597	(S)	Ta Ta	1960	16.00	40.00
Mercury MG-20655	(M)	Golden Blues Hits	1962	12.00	30.00
Mercury SR-60655	(S)	Golden Blues Hits	1962	16.00	40.00
Mercury MG-20711	(M)	Lover Please	1962	12.00	30.00
Mercury SR-60711	(S)	Lover Please	1962	16.00	40.00
Mercury MG-20750	(M)	Rhythm And Soul	1962	12.00	30.00
Mercury SR-60750	(S)	Rhythm And Soul	1962	16.00	40.00
Wing MGW-12224	(M)	May I Sing For You?	1962	8.00	20.00
Wing SRW-16224	(S)	May I Sing For You?	1962	10.00	25.00
Mercury MG-20783	(M)	Clyde McPhatter's Greatest Hits	1963	12.00	30.00
Mercury SR-60783	(S)	Clyde McPhatter's Greatest Hits	1963	16.00	40.00
Mercury MG-20902	(M)	Songs Of The Big City	1964	12.00	30.00
Mercury SR-60902	(S)	Songs Of The Big City	1964	16.00	40.00
Mercury MG-20915	(M)	Live At The Apollo	1964	12.00	30.00
Mercury SR-60915	(S)	Live At The Apollo	1964	16.00	40.00
Decca DL-75231	(S)	Welcome Home	1970	10.00	25.00

McRAE, CARMEN
Ms. McRae also recorded with Sammy Davis, Jr.

Bethlehem 1023 (10")	(M)	Carmen McRae	1954	16.00	40.00
Decca DL-8173	(M)	By Special Request	1955	12.00	30.00
Decca DL-8267	(M)	Torchy	1955	12.00	30.00

Label & Catalog #		Title	Year	VG+	NM
Decca DL-8347	(M)	Blue Moon	1956	16.00	40.00
Decca DL-8583	(M)	After Glow	1957	12.00	30.00
Decca DL-8662	(M)	Mad About The Man	1957	16.00	40.00
Decca DL-8738	(M)	Carmen For Cool Ones	1958	12.00	30.00
Decca DL-8815	(M)	Birds Of A Feather	1958	16.00	40.00
Kapp KL-1117	(M)	Book Of Ballads	1958	8.00	20.00
Kapp KS-1117S	(S)	Book Of Ballads	1960	8.00	20.00
Kapp KL-1135	(M)	When You're Away	1959	8.00	20.00
Kapp KS-3018	(S)	When You're Away	1960	8.00	20.00
Kapp KL-1169	(M)	Something To Swing About	1959	8.00	20.00
Kapp KS-3053	(S)	Something To Swing About	1960	8.00	20.00
Columbia CL-1609	(M)	Tonight's The Night	1961	5.00	12.00
Columbia CS-8409	(S)	Tonight's The Night	1961	6.00	15.00
Columbia CL-1730	(M)	Lover Man	1962	5.00	12.00
Columbia CS-8530	(S)	Lover Man	1962	6.00	15.00
Columbia CL-1943	(M)	Something Wonderful	1962	5.00	12.00
Columbia CS-8743	(S)	Something Wonderful	1962	6.00	15.00
Time 52104	(M)	Live At Sugar Hill	1963	5.00	12.00
Time 2104	(S)	Live At Sugar Hill	1963	6.00	15.00
Focus 334	(M)	Bittersweet	1965	5.00	12.00
Focus 334	(S)	Bittersweet	1965	6.00	15.00
Mainstream 56028	(M)	Second To None	1965	5.00	12.00
Mainstream S-6028	(S)	Second To None	1965	6.00	15.00
Mainstream 56044	(M)	Haven't We Met?	1965	5.00	12.00
Mainstream S-6044	(S)	Haven't We Met?	1965	6.00	15.00

McTELL, RAPLH
| Capitol ST-240 | (S) | Eight Frames A Second | 1969 | 8.00 | 20.00 |
| 20th Century T-486 | (S) | Streets Of London | 1975 | 6.00 | 15.00 |

McTELL, "BLIND" WILLIE
Melodeon 7323	(M)	1940	1956	80.00	200.00
Bluesville BVLP-1040	(M)	Last Session	1962	24.00	60.00
Prestige PRST-7809	(E)	Last Session	1969	6.00	15.00

(Prestige 7809 is a reissue of Bluesville 1040.)

McVIE, CHRISTINE
Refer to Chickenshack; Fleetwood Mac.
| Sire 7522 | (S) | The Legendary Christine Perfect Album | 1976 | 6.00 | 15.00 |
| Warner Bros. 25059 | (DJ) | Christine McVie (Quiex II vinyl) | 1984 | 6.00 | 15.00 |

MEAT LOAF
Refer to Stoney & Meatloaf
| Epic E99-34974 | (S) | Bat Out Of Hell (Picture disc) | 1979 | 6.00 | 15.00 |
| Epic HE-44974 | (S) | Bat Out Of Hell (Half-speed master) | 1981 | 8.00 | 25.00 |

MECKI MARK MEN, THE
| Limelight LS-86054 | (S) | The Mecki Mark Men | 1968 | 10.00 | 25.00 |
| Limelight LS-86068 | (S) | Running In The Summer Night | 1969 | 10.00 | 25.00 |

MEDIUM
| Gamma GS-503 | (S) | Medium | 196? | 80.00 | 200.00 |

MEDLEY, BILL
Mr. Medley is one half of The Righteous Brothers. Refer to Sonny & Cher.
MGM SE-4583	(S)	Bill Medley 100%	1968	6.00	15.00
MGM SE-4603	(S)	Soft And Soulful	1969	6.00	15.00
MGM SE-4640	(S)	Someone Is Standing Outside	1969	6.00	15.00
MGM SE-4702	(S)	Nobody Knows	1970	6.00	15.00
MGM SE-4741	(S)	Gone	1970	6.00	15.00
Paramount 6005	(S)	The Hard Ride (Soundtrack)	1971	5.00	12.00
A&M SP-3505	(S)	A Song For You	1971	5.00	12.00
A&M SP-3517	(S)	Smile	1973	5.00	12.00

MEL & TIM
Mel Hardin and Tim McPherson.
Bamboo BMS-8001	(S)	Good Guys Only Win In The Movies	1970	8.00	20.00
Stax STS-3007	(S)	Starting All Over Again	1972	8.00	20.00
Stax STS-5501	(S)	Mel And Tim	1974	8.00	20.00

Label & Catalog #		Title	Year	VG+	NM

MELACHRINO, GEORGE
| RCA Victor LPM-1045 | (M) | Christmas In High Fidelity | 1955 | 10.00 | 25.00 |
| RCA Victor LPM-1676 | (M) | Under Western Skies | 1957 | 10.00 | 25.00 |

MELCHER, TERRY
| Reprise 2185 | (S) | Terry Melcher | 1974 | 6.00 | 15.00 |

MELLENCAMP, JOHN COUGAR [JOHN COUGAR]
| MCA 2225 | (S) | Chestnut Street Incident | 1977 | 10.00 | 25.00 |
| Riva | (DJ) | The Kid Inside (Picture disc) | 198? | 16.00 | 40.00 |

MELLO-LARKS, THE
| Epic LN-1106 (10") | (M) | The Mello-Larks & Jamie | 1955 | 20.00 | 50.00 |
| Camden CAL-530 | (M) | Just For A Lark | 1959 | 16.00 | 40.00 |

MELLO-KINGS, THE
| Herald H-1013 | (M) | Tonight-Tonight | 1960 | 300.00 | 500.00 |

MELLOMEN, THE
| Columbia CL-6338 | (M) | White Christmas (Soundtrack) | 1954 | 12.00 | 30.00 |

MELTON, BARRY
Formerly a member of Country Joe & The Fish.
| Vanguard VSD-6551 | (S) | Bright Sun Is Shining | 1970 | 6.00 | 15.00 |
| Columbia KC-31279 | (S) | Melton, Levy And The Dey Brothers | 1972 | 5.00 | 12.00 |

MELTZER, DAVID & TINA
Refer to Serpent Power.
| Vanguard VSD-6519 | (S) | Poet Song | 1969 | 8.00 | 20.00 |

MELVIN, HAROLD, & THE BLUENOTES
| Philadelphia Int. PQ-32407 | (Q) | Black And Blue | 1974 | 8.00 | 20.00 |
| Philadelphia Int. PZ-33808 | (Q) | Wake Up Everybody | 1975 | 8.00 | 20.00 |

MEMPHIS SLIM
Memphis Slim is a pseudonym for Peter Chapman. Refer to Willie Dixon.
Vee Jay VJLP-1012	(M)	Memphis Slim At The Gate Of The Horn	1959	40.00	100.00
Chess LP-1455	(M)	Memphis Slim (Black label)	1961	40.00	100.00
Chess LP-1510	(M)	Real Folk Blues	1966	16.00	40.00
United Arts. UAL-3137	(M)	Broken Soul Blues	1961	16.00	40.00
United Arts. UAS-6137	(S)	Broken Soul Blues	1961	20.00	50.00
Bluesville BVLP-1018	(M)	Just Blues	1961	16.00	40.00
Bluesville BVLP-1031	(M)	No Strain	1961	16.00	40.00
Bluesville BVLP-1053	(M)	All Kinds Of Blues	1962	16.00	40.00
Bluesville BVLP-1075	(M)	Steady Rollin' Blues	1963	16.00	40.00
Candid 8023	(M)	Tribute To Big Bill Broonzy	1961	16.00	40.00
Candid 9023	(S)	Tribute To Big Bill Broonzy	1961	20.00	50.00
Candid 8024	(M)	Memphis Slim, U.S.A.	1962	16.00	40.00
Candid 9024	(S)	Memphis Slim, U.S.A.	1962	20.00	50.00
Battle BM-6118	(M)	Alone With My Friends	1963	12.00	30.00
King LP-885	(M)	Memphis Slim	1964	20.00	50.00
Scepter SM-535	(M)	Self Portrait	1966	10.00	25.00
Strand SLS-1046	(S)	The World's Foremost Blues Singer	196?	8.00	20.00
Jubilee 8003	(S)	Legend Of The Blues	1967	6.00	15.00
Everest 215	(S)	Memphis Slim	1968	6.00	15.00
Buddah BDS-7505	(S)	Mother Earth	1969	6.00	15.00
King KS-1082	(S)	Messin' Around With The Blues	1970	6.00	15.00
Jewell 5004	(S)	Born With The Blues	1971	4.00	10.00
Warner Bros. WS-1899	(S)	Blue Memphis	1971	6.00	15.00
Warner Bros. BS-2646	(S)	South Side Reunion	1972	6.00	15.00
Fantasy 24705	(S)	Raining The Blues (2 LPs)	1972	5.00	12.00

MEMPHIS SOUL BAND, THE
| Minit 24028 | (S) | Soul Cowboy | 1970 | 6.00 | 15.00 |

MEMPHIS WILLIE B.
| Bluesville BVLP-1034 | (M) | Introducing Memphis Willie B. | 1961 | 16.00 | 40.00 |
| Bluesville BVLP-1048 | (M) | Hard Working Man Blues | 196s | 16.00 | 40.00 |

Label & Catalog #		Title	Year	VG+	NM
MEN AT WORK					
Epic PAL-37978	(DJ)	**Business As Usual** (Picture disc)	1983	16.00	40.00
Epic HE-47978	(S)	**Business As Usual** (Half-speed master)	1982	5.00	15.00
Epic HE-48660	(S)	**Cargo** (Half-speed master)	1982	5.00	15.00
MENDES, SERGIO					
Mobile Fidelity MFSL-118	(S)	**Brazil '66**	198?	12.00	35.00
MERCER, MABEL: *Refer to* GOLDMINE'S PRICE GUIDE TO COLLECTIBLE JAZZ ALBUMS					
MERCHANTS OF DREAM, THE					
Capitol ST-102	(S)	**Soul Knight**	1968	6.00	15.00
MERCURY, ERIC					
Avco Embassy 33001	(S)	**Electric Black Man**	1969	6.00	15.00
Enterprise ENS-1020	(S)	**Funky Rock**	1972	6.00	15.00
Enterprise ENS-1021	(S)	**Funky Sound Nurtured In the Fertile Soil of Memphis**	1972	6.00	15.00
Enterprise ENS-1033	(S)	**Love Is Taking Over**	1973	6.00	15.00
MERCY					
Sundi SRLP-803	(S)	**Love Can Make You Happy**	1969	6.00	15.00
Warner Bros. WS-1799	(S)	**Love Can Make You Happy**	1969	5.00	12.00
MERKIN					
Windi 1004	(S)	**Music From Merkin Manor**	1972	150.00	300.00
MERRILL, HELEN: *Refer to* GOLDMINE'S PRICE GUIDE TO COLLECTIBLE JAZZ ALBUMS					
MERRIWEATHER, BIG MACEO, & JOHN LEE HOOKER					
Fortune 3002	(M)	**Big Maceo Merriweather & John Lee Hooker**	196?	50.00	125.00
MERRY-GO-ROUND, THE					
The Merry-Go-Round features Emitt Rhodes.					
A&M LP-132	(M)	**The Merry-Go-Round**	1967	16.00	40.00
A&M SP-4132	(S)	**The Merry-Go-Round**	1967	20.00	50.00
MERRYWEATHER [NEIL MERRYWEATHER]					
Capitol SKAO-220	(S)	**Merryweather**	1969	6.00	15.00
Capitol STBB-278	(S)	**Word Of Mouth**	1969	6.00	15.00
RCA Victor LSP-4442	(S)	**Ivar Avenue Reunion**	1970	6.00	15.00
RCA Victor LSP-4485	(S)	**Vacuum Cleaner**	1971	6.00	15.00
Kent KST-546	(S)	**Neil Merryweather And The Boers**	1972	8.00	20.00
MERSEYBEATS, THE [THE MERSEYBEATS OF LIVERPOOL]					
Arc International	(M)	**Mersey Hits**	1964	16.00	40.00
Arc International 834	(M)	**England's Best Sellers**	1964	16.00	40.00
MERSEYBOYS, THE					
Vee Jay VJ-1101	(M)	**15 Greatest Songs Of The Beatles**	1964	30.00	75.00
Vee Jay VJS-1101	(S)	**15 Greatest Songs Of The Beatles**	1964	60.00	150.00
MESMERIZING EYE, THE					
Smash MGS-27090	(M)	**Psychedelia/A Musical Light Show**	1967	8.00	20.00
Smash SRS-67090	(S)	**Psychedelia/A Musical Light Show**	1967	10.00	25.00
MESSENGERS, THE					
Rare Earth RS-509	(S)	**The Messengers**	1969	8.00	20.00
MESSINA, JIM, & HIS JESTERS					
Refer to The Buffalo Springfield; Loggins & Messina.					
Audio Fidelity DFM-3037	(M)	**The Dragsters**	1964	20.00	50.00
Audio Fidelity DFS-7037	(S)	**The Dragsters**	1964	30.00	75.00
Thimble TLP-3	(S)	**Jim Messina**	197?	6.00	15.00
		(Thimble 3 is a reissue of the Audio Fidelity album.)			
METERS, THE					
Josie JOS-4010	(S)	**The Meters**	1969	20.00	50.00
Josie JOS-4011	(S)	**Look-Ka Py Py**	1970	20.00	50.00

Label & Catalog #		Title	Year	VG+	NM
Josie JOS-4012	(S)	Struttin'	1970	20.00	50.00
Reprise MS-2076	(S)	Cabbage Alley	1972	10.00	25.00
Reprise MS-2200	(S)	Rejuvenation	1972	10.00	25.00
Virgo 12002	(S)	Best Of The Meters	1975	6.00	15.00
Island 9250	(S)	Cissy Strut	1975	6.00	15.00
Warner Bros. B-3042	(S)	New Directions	1977	6.00	15.00

METHUSELAH
| Elektra EKS-70452 | (S) | Matthew, Mark, Luke And John | 1969 | 6.00 | 15.00 |

METOYER, HERB
| Verve/Folkways FV-9012 | (M) | Something New | 1965 | 6.00 | 15.00 |
| Verve/Folkways FVS-9012 | (S) | Something New | 1965 | 8.00 | 20.00 |

METRONOMES, THE
| Strand 3002 | (M) | The Standard Hits | 196? | 12.00 | 30.00 |
| Strand S-3002 | (S) | The Standard Hits | 196? | 16.00 | 40.00 |

METROTONES, THE
| Columbia 6341 (10") | (M) | Tops In Rock And Roll | 1955 | 100.00 | 250.00 |

MFSB
| Phila. Inter. PZQ-32707 | (Q) | Love Is The Message | 1974 | 6.00 | 15.00 |
| Phila. Inter. PZQ-33845 | (Q) | Philadelphia Freedom | 1975 | 6.00 | 15.00 |

MICAH
| Sterling World ST-1001 | (S) | I'm Only One Man | 197? | 80.00 | 200.00 |

MICHAELANGELO
| Guinn 1050 | (S) | Michaelangelo | 1975 | 500.00 | 800.00 |

MICHAELS, LEE
A&M LP-140	(M)	Carnival Of Life	1967	6.00	15.00
A&M SP-4140	(S)	Carnival Of Life	1967	6.00	15.00
A&M SP-4152	(S)	Recital	1968	6.00	15.00
A&M SP-4199	(S)	Lee Michaels	1969	6.00	15.00
A&M SP-4249	(S)	Barrel	1970	5.00	12.00
A&M SP-4302	(S)	5th	1971	5.00	12.00
A&M SP-4336	(S)	Space And First Takes	1972	5.00	12.00
A&M SP-3518	(S)	Live (2 LPs)	1973	6.00	15.00

— Original A&M albums above have brown labels.—
| Columbia CQ-32275 | (Q) | Nice Day For Something | 1973 | 6.00 | 15.00 |
| Columbia | (DJ) | Lee Michaels In Hawaii | 1975 | 10.00 | 25.00 |

MICKEY & SYLVIA
Mickey Baker and Sylvia Vanderpool.
| Vik LX-1102 | (M) | New Sounds | 1957 | 200.00 | 400.00 |
| Camden CAL-863 | (M) | Love Is Strange | 1965 | 20.00 | 50.00 |

(Camden 863 is a reissue of Vik 1102.)
| RCA Victor APM1-0327 | (M) | Do It Again | 1973 | 6.00 | 15.00 |

(RCA 0327 is a reissue of Vik 1102.)

MICO WAVE
Mico Wave is a member of William "Bootsy" Collins' band.
| Columbia 40909 | (S) | Cookin' From The Inside Out!!! | 1987 | 4.00 | 10.00 |

MIDAS TOUCH, THE
| Decca DL-75151 | (S) | Midas Touch | 1969 | 6.00 | 15.00 |
| Decca DL-75240 | (S) | Color My World With Love | 1970 | 5.00 | 12.00 |

MIDLER, BETTE
| Atlantic QD-7238 | (Q) | The Divine Miss M | 1973 | 6.00 | 15.00 |

MIGHTY BABY
| Head LPS-025 | (S) | Mighty Baby | 1969 | 24.00 | 60.00 |

MIGHTY SPARROW
| Warner Bros. BS-2771 | (S) | Hot And Sweet | 1974 | 6.00 | 15.00 |

Label & Catalog #		Title	Year	VG+	NM

MILBURN, AMOS

| Aladdin 704 (10") | (M) | Rockin' The Boogie (Red vinyl) | 1955 | 1,500.00 | Rare |

(Red vinyl copies of Aladdin 704 were issued in blue covers. Near Mint copies have a suggested value of $3,000-5,000.)

| Aladdin 704 (10") | (M) | Rockin' The Boogie | 1955 | 1,000.00 | Rare |

(Black vinyl copies of Aladdin 704 were issued in brown covers. Near Mint copies have a suggested value of $2,000-3,000.)

| Aladdin 810 | (M) | Rockin' The Boogie | 1958 | | See note below |

(Contrary to previous listings, this 12" album does not exist.)

Score LP-4012	(M)	Let's Have A Party	1957	200.00	600.00
Imperial LP-9176	(M)	Million Sellers	1962	150.00	350.00
Motown 608	(M)	The Blues Boss	1963	660.00	Rare

(Near Mint copies have a suggested value of $1,000-2,000.)

MILBURN, AMOS / WYNONIE HARRIS / CROWN PRINCE WATERFORD

| Aladdin 703 (10") | (M) | Party After Hours (Red vinyl) | 1955 | 1,500.00 | Rare |

(Near Mint copies have a suggested value of $2,000-4,000.)

| Aladdin 703 (10") | (M) | Party After Hours | 1955 | 1,000.00 | Rare |

(Near Mint copies have a suggested value of $1,500-2,500.)

MILES, BUDDY [BUDDY MILES EXPRESS]

| Mercury SR-61196 | (S) | Expressway To Your Skull | 1968 | 6.00 | 15.00 |
| Mercury SR-61222 | (S) | Electric Church | 1969 | 6.00 | 15.00 |

— Original Mercury albums above have red labels with twelve logos around the perimeter.—

MILES, JACKIE

| Imperial LP-9154 | (M) | 120 Pounds Dripping Wet | 1961 | 8.00 | 20.00 |

MILES, LIZZIE: Refer to GOLDMINE'S PRICE GUIDE TO COLLECTIBLE JAZZ ALBUMS

MILES, LONG GONE

| World Pacific WP-1820 | (M) | Country Born | 1964 | 10.00 | 25.00 |
| World Pacific ST-1820 | (S) | Country Born | 1964 | 12.00 | 30.00 |

MILKWOOD

| A&M SP-4226 | (S) | Under Milkwood | 1969 | 6.00 | 15.00 |

MILKWOOD

| Paramount PAS-6046 | (S) | How's The Weather? | 1973 | 12.00 | 30.00 |

MILLARD & DYCE

| Kaymar KS-7-265 | (S) | Open | 1973 | 24.00 | 60.00 |

MILLENIUM

Millenium features Curt Boetcher with Gary Usher as e.xecutive producer:

| Columbia CS-9663 | (S) | Begin | 1968 | 8.00 | 20.00 |

MILLER, CLARENCE "BIG"

United Arts. UAL-3047	(M)	Did You Ever Hear The Blues?	1959	16.00	40.00
United Arts. UAS-6047	(S)	Did You Ever Hear The Blues?	1959	16.00	40.00
Columbia CL-1611	(M)	Revelation And The Blues	1961	12.00	30.00
Columbia CS-8411	(S)	Revelation And The Blues	1961	12.00	30.00
Columbia CL-1808	(M)	Big Miller Sings, Twists, Shouts & Preaches	1962	12.00	30.00
Columbia CS-8608	(S)	Big Miller Sings, Twists, Shouts & Preaches	1962	12.00	30.00

— Original Columbia albums above have six white-on-black "eye" logo around the perimeter of the label.—

MILLER, FRANKIE

Starday SLP-134	(M)	Country Music's Great New Star	1961	50.00	125.00
Starday SLP-199	(M)	The True Country Style Of Frankie Miller	1962	40.00	100.00
Audio Lab AL-1562	(M)	The Fine Country Singing Of Frankie Miller	1963	80.00	200.00
Starday SLP-339	(M)	Blackland Farmer	1965	24.00	60.00

MILLER, JODY

Capitol T-1913	(M)	Wednesday's Child Is Full Of Woe	1963	6.00	15.00
Capitol ST-1913	(S)	Wednesday's Child Is Full Of Woe	1963	8.00	20.00
Capitol T-2349	(M)	Queen Of The House	1965	6.00	15.00
Capitol ST-2349	(S)	Queen Of The House	1965	8.00	20.00
Capitol T-2414	(M)	Home Of The Brave	1965	6.00	15.00
Capitol ST-2414	(S)	Home Of The Brave	1965	8.00	20.00

Label & Catalog #		Title	Year	VG+	NM
Capitol T-2446	(M)	The Great Hits Of Buck Owens	1966	6.00	15.00
Capitol ST-2446	(S)	The Great Hits Of Buck Owens	1966	8.00	20.00
Capitol ST-2996	(S)	The Nashville Sound Of Jody Miller	1969	6.00	15.00

MILLER, MICKEY

Folkways FA-2393	(M)	American Folk Songs	1959	12.00	30.00

MILLER, NED

Fabor FLP-1001	(M)	From A Jack To A King	1963	20.00	50.00
Fabor FLP-1001	(M)	From A Jack To A King (Colored vinyl)	1963	60.00	150.00
Capitol T-2330	(M)	Ned Miller Sings The Songs Of Ned Miller	1965	8.00	20.00
Capitol ST-2330	(S)	Ned Miller Sings The Songs Of Ned Miller	1965	10.00	25.00
Capitol T-2414	(M)	The Best Of Ned Miller	1966	6.00	15.00
Capitol ST-2414	(S)	The Best Of Ned Miller	1966	8.00	20.00
Capitol T-2586	(M)	Teardrop Lane	1967	8.00	20.00
Capitol ST-2586	(S)	Teardrop Lane	1967	8.00	20.00
Capitol ST-2914	(S)	In The Name Of Love	1968	6.00	15.00

MILLER, ROGER

Camden CAL-851	(M)	Roger Miller	1964	5.00	12.00
Camden CAS-851	(S)	Roger Miller	1964	6.00	15.00
Camden CAL-903	(M)	The One And Only Roger Miller	1965	5.00	12.00
Camden CAS-903	(S)	The One And Only Roger Miller	1965	6.00	15.00
Starday SLP-318	(M)	Wild-Child Roger Miller	1965	12.00	30.00
Starday SLP-318	(M)	The Country Side Of Roger Miller	1965	12.00	30.00
Smash MGS-27049	(M)	Roger And Out	1964	6.00	15.00
Smash SRS-67049	(S)	Roger And Out	1964	8.00	20.00
Smash MGS-27049	(M)	Dang Me And The New Hit Chug-A-Lug	1964	6.00	15.00
Smash SRS-67049	(S)	Dang Me And The New Hit Chug-A-Lug	1964	8.00	20.00
Smash MGS-27061	(M)	The Return Of Roger Miller	1965	6.00	15.00
Smash SRS-67061	(S)	The Return Of Roger Miller	1965	8.00	20.00
Smash MGS-27068	(M)	The Third Time Around	1965	6.00	15.00
Smash SRS-67068	(S)	The Third Time Around	1965	8.00	20.00
Smash MGS-27073	(M)	Golden Hits	1965	6.00	15.00
Smash SRS-67073	(S)	Golden Hits	1965	8.00	20.00
Smash MGS-27075	(M)	Words And Music	1966	6.00	15.00
Smash SRS-67075	(S)	Words And Music	1966	8.00	20.00
Smash MGS-27092	(M)	Walkin' In The Sunshine	1967	6.00	15.00
Smash SRS-67092	(S)	Walkin' In The Sunshine	1967	8.00	20.00
Smash MGS-27096	(M)	Waterhole #3 (Soundtrack)	1967	6.00	15.00
Smash SRS-67096	(S)	Waterhole #3 (Soundtrack)	1967	8.00	20.00
Smash SRS-67103	(S)	A Tender Look At Love	1968	6.00	15.00
Smash SRS-67123	(S)	Roger Miller	1969	6.00	15.00
Smash SRS-67129	(S)	Roger Miller 1970	1970	6.00	15.00

MILLER, STEVE [THE STEVE MILLER BAND]
Refer to Chuck Berry.

Capitol SKAO-2920	(S)	Children Of The Future	1968	10.00	25.00
Capitol ST-2984	(S)	Sailor	1968	10.00	25.00
Capitol STBB-177	(S)	Children Of The Future / Sailor (2 LPs)	1969	12.00	30.00
Capitol ST-184	(S)	Brave New World	1969	10.00	25.00
		— Original Capitol albums above have black rainbow labels.—			
Capitol SKAO-2920	(S)	Children Of The Future	1970	6.00	15.00
Capitol ST-2984	(S)	Sailor	1970	6.00	15.00
Capitol STBB-177	(S)	Children Of The Future / Sailor (2 LPs)	1968	8.00	20.00
Capitol ST-184	(S)	Brave New World	1970	6.00	15.00
Capitol ST-436	(S)	Number Five	1970	6.00	15.00
Capitol ST-331	(S)	Your Saving Grace	1970	6.00	15.00
		— Capitol albums above have green labels.—			
Capitol SEAX-11903	(S)	Book Of Dreams (Picture disc)	1978	4.00	10.00
Capitol SOO-11872	(DJ)	Greatest Hits 1974-78 (Blue vinyl)	1978	12.00	30.00
Mobile Fidelity MFSL-021	(S)	Fly Like An Eagle	1976	12.00	35.00

MILLER, STEVE / QUICKSILVER MESSENGER SERVICE / THE BAND

Capitol STCR-288	(S)	Steve Miller Band / Quicksilver Messenger Service / The Band (3 LP box)	1969	16.00	40.00
		(This boxed set contains three lime green label albums: "Sailor," "Quicksilver Messenger Service" and "Music From Big Pink.")			

Label & Catalog #		Title	Year	VG+	NM

MILLS, ALAN

Folkways FC-7021	(M)	Folk Songs For Young Folk	195?	12.00	30.00
Folkways FA-2312	(M)	Songs Of The Sea	195?	12.00	30.00
Folkways FA-3001	(M)	O Canada	196?	12.00	30.00

MILLS, HAYLEY
Refer to Annette & Hayley Mills.

Disneyland ST-1960	(M)	Pollyanna (Soundtrack)	1960	20.00	50.00
Buena Vista BV-3311	(M)	Let's Get Together	1962	12.00	30.00
Buena Vista STER-3311	(S)	Let's Get Together	1962	16.00	40.00
Disneyland ST-3916	(M)	In Search Of The Castaways (Soundtrack)	1962	40.00	100.00
Disneyland ST-3916	(S)	In Search Of The Castaways (Soundtrack)	1962	60.00	150.00
Buena Vista BV-4025	(M)	Summer Magic (Soundtrack)	1963	30.00	75.00
Buena Vista STER-4025	(S)	Summer Magic (Soundtrack)	1963	50.00	125.00
Mainstream 56090	(M)	Gypsy Girl (Soundtrack)	1966	14.00	35.00
Mainstream S-6090	(S)	Gypsy Girl (Soundtrack)	1966	20.00	50.00

MILLS BROTHERS, THE

Decca DL-5050 (10")	(M)	Barber Shop Ballads	1950	20.00	50.00
Decca DL-5051 (10")	(M)	Barber Shop Ballads	1950	20.00	50.00
Decca DL-5102 (10")	(M)	Souvenir Album	1950	20.00	50.00
Decca DL-5337 (10")	(M)	Wonderful Words	1951	20.00	50.00
Decca DL-5506 (10")	(M)	Meet The Mills Brothers	1954	20.00	50.00
Decca DL-5509 (10")	(M)	Louis Armstrong And The Mills Brothers	1954	20.00	50.00
Decca DL-5516 (10")	(M)	Four Boys And A Guitar	1954	20.00	50.00
Decca DL-8148	(M)	Souvenir Album	1955	12.00	30.00
Decca DL-8209	(M)	Singin' And Swingin'	1956	12.00	30.00
Decca DL-8219	(M)	Memory Lane	1956	12.00	30.00
Decca DL-8491	(M)	One Dozen Roses	1957	12.00	30.00
Decca DL-8664	(M)	The Mills Brothers In Hi-Fi	1958	12.00	30.00
Decca DL-8827	(M)	Glow With The Mills Brothers	1959	12.00	30.00
Decca DL-8890	(M)	Barber Shop Harmony	1959	12.00	30.00
Decca DL-8892	(M)	Harmonizin' With The Mills Brothers	1959	12.00	30.00
		—Original Decca albums above have black & silver labels.—			
Decca DXB-193	(M)	The Best Of The Mills Brothers	1965	8.00	20.00
Decca DXSB-193	(P)	The Best Of The Mills Brothers	1965	8.00	20.00
Dot DLP-3103	(M)	Mmmm, The Mills Brothers	1958	8.00	20.00
Dot DLP-25103	(S)	Mmmm, The Mills Brothers	1958	12.00	30.00
Dot DLP-3157	(M)	The Mills Brothers' Great Hits	1958	8.00	20.00
Dot DLP-25157	(S)	The Mills Brothers' Great Hits	1958	12.00	30.00
Dot DLP-25157	(S)	The Mills Brothers' Great Hits (Blue vinyl)	1958	24.00	60.00
Dot DLP-3208	(M)	Great Barbershop Hits	1959	8.00	20.00
Dot DLP-25208	(S)	Great Barbershop Hits	1959	12.00	30.00
Dot DLP-3232	(M)	Merry Christmas	1959	8.00	20.00
Dot DLP-25232	(S)	Merry Christmas	1959	12.00	30.00
Dot DLP-3237	(M)	The Mills Brothers Sing	1960	8.00	20.00
Dot DLP-25237	(S)	The Mills Brothers Sing	1960	12.00	30.00
Dot DLP-3308	(M)	Great Hits, Volume 2	1961	6.00	15.00
Dot DLP-25308	(S)	Great Hits, Volume 2	1961	8.00	20.00
Dot DLP-3338	(M)	Yellow Bird	1961	6.00	15.00
Dot DLP-25338	(S)	Yellow Bird	1961	8.00	20.00
Dot DLP-3363	(M)	San Antonio Rose	1961	6.00	15.00
Dot DLP-25363	(S)	San Antonio Rose	1961	8.00	20.00
Dot DLP-3368	(M)	Great Hawaiian Hits	1961	6.00	15.00
Dot DLP-25368	(S)	Great Hawaiian Hits	1961	8.00	20.00
Dot DLP-3465	(M)	The Beer Barrel Polka And Other Hits	1962	5.00	12.00
Dot DLP-25465	(S)	The Beer Barrel Polka And Other Hits	1962	6.00	15.00
Dot DLP-3508	(M)	The End Of The World	1963	5.00	12.00
Dot DLP-25508	(S)	The End Of The World	1963	6.00	15.00
Dot DLP-3565	(M)	Gems By The Mills Brothers	1964	5.00	12.00
Dot DLP-25565	(S)	Gems By The Mills Brothers	1964	6.00	15.00
Dot DLP-3568	(M)	Hymns We Love	1964	5.00	12.00
Dot DLP-25568	(S)	Hymns We Love	1964	6.00	15.00
Dot DLP-3592	(M)	Say Si Si And Other Great Latin Hits	1964	5.00	12.00
Dot DLP-25592	(S)	Say Si Si And Other Great Latin Hits	1964	6.00	15.00
Hamilton HL-12116	(M)	The Mills Brothers Sing For You	1964		12.00
Hamilton HS-12116	(S)	The Mills Brothers Sing For You	1964	5.00	12.00
Dot DLP-3652	(M)	Ten Years Of Hits 1954-1964	1965	5.00	12.00
Dot DLP-25652	(S)	Ten Years Of Hits 1954-1964	1965	6.00	15.00

Label & Catalog #		Title	Year	VG+	NM
Dot DLP-3699	(M)	These Are The Mills Brothers	1966	5.00	12.00
Dot DLP-25699	(S)	These Are The Mills Brothers	1966	6.00	15.00
Dot DLP-3744	(M)	That Country Feeling	1966	5.00	12.00
Dot DLP-25744	(S)	That Country Feeling	1966	6.00	15.00
Dot DLP-3783	(M)	The Mills Brothers Live	1967	5.00	12.00
Dot DLP-25783	(S)	The Mills Brothers Live	1967	6.00	15.00
Dot DLP-25809	(S)	Fortuosity	1968	6.00	15.00
Dot DLP-25838	(S)	The Board Of Directors	1968	6.00	15.00
Dot DLP-25872	(S)	My Shy Violet	1968	6.00	15.00
Dot DLP-25927	(S)	Dream	1969	6.00	15.00

MILTON, ROY
Refer to Chuck Higgins / Roy Milton.

Kent 554	(M)	The Great Roy Milton	1963	20.00	50.00

MIMMS, GARNET, & THE ENCHANTERS

United Arts. UAL-3305	(M)	Cry Baby And 11 Other Hits	1963	16.00	40.00
United Arts. UAS-6305	(S)	Cry Baby And 11 Other Hits	1963	20.00	50.00
United Arts. UAL-3396	(M)	As Long As I Have You	1964	12.00	30.00
United Arts. UAS-6396	(S)	As Long As I Have You	1964	16.00	40.00
United Arts. UAL-3498	(M)	I'll Take Good Care Of You	1966	12.00	30.00
United Arts. UAS-6498	(S)	I'll Take Good Care Of You	1966	16.00	40.00

MIND EXPANDERS, THE

Dot DLP-3773	(M)	What's Happening	1967	20.00	50.00
Dot DLP-25773	(S)	What's Happening	1967	30.00	75.00

MIND GARAGE

RCA Victor LSP-4218	(S)	Mind Garage	1969	8.00	20.00
RCA Victor LSP-4319	(S)	Mind Garage Again!	1970	8.00	20.00

MINDBENDERS, THE
The Mindbenders originally recorded with Wayne Fontana.

Fontana MGF-27554	(M)	A Groovy Kind Of Love	1966	16.00	40.00
Fontana SRF-67554	(E)	A Groovy Kind Of Love	1966	12.00	30.00
		(First pressings include "Don't Cry No More.")			
Fontana MGF-27554	(M)	A Groovy Kind Of Love	1966	14.00	35.00
Fontana SRF-67554	(E)	A Groovy Kind Of Love	1966	1000	25.00
		(Later pressings include "Ashes To Ashes.")			

MINEO, SAL

Epic LN-3405	(M)	Sal	1958	40.00	100.00

MINNELLI, LIZA
Refer to Judy Garland & Liza Minnelli.

Cadence CE-4012	(M)	Best Foot Forward (Soundtrack)	1963	20.00	50.00
Cadence CLP-24012	(S)	Best Foot Forward (Soundtrack)	1963	30.00	75.00
Capitol T-2174	(M)	Liza! Liza!	1964	6.00	15.00
Capitol ST-2174	(S)	Liza! Liza!	1964	8.00	20.00
Capitol T-2271	(M)	It Amazes Me	1965	6.00	15.00
Capitol ST-2271	(S)	It Amazes Me	1965	8.00	20.00
Capitol TAO-2295	(M)	Live At The London Palladium	1965	8.00	20.00
Capitol STAO-2295	(S)	Live At The London Palladium	1965	10.00	25.00
Capitol T-2448	(M)	There Is A Time	1966	6.00	15.00
Capitol ST-2448	(S)	There Is A Time	1966	8.00	20.00
RCA Victor LOC-1111	(M)	Flora The Red Menace (Soundtrack)	1965	20.00	50.00
RCA Victor LSO-1111	(S)	Flora The Red Menace (Soundtrack)	1965	30.00	75.00
A&M SP-4141	(S)	Liza Minnelli	1969	6.00	15.00
A&M SP-4164	(S)	Come Saturday Morning	1969	6.00	15.00
Columbia CQ-32149	(Q)	The Singer	1973	6.00	15.00

MINSTRELS THREE, THE

Wing MGW-12264	(M)	Hootenanny Hits	1963	5.00	12.00
Wing SRW-16264	(S)	Hootenanny Hits	1963	6.00	15.00

MINT TATTOO

Dot DLP-25918	(S)	Mint Tattoo	1969	12.00	30.00

MIRACLES, THE: Refer to SMOKEY ROBINSON & THE MIRACLES

Label & Catalog #		Title	Year	VG+	NM

MIRACLES, THE

| Columbia PCQ-24460 | (Q) | Love Crazy | 1977 | 6.00 | 15.00 |

MIRTHRANDER

| Mirth Music | (S) | For You, The Old Woman | 1976 | 40.00 | 100.00 |

MR. ED

| Colpix CP-209 | (M) | Mr. Ed, The Talking Horse | 196? | 60.00 | 150.00 |
| Golden LP-88 | (M) | Straight From The Horse's Mouth | 1962 | 70.00 | 175.00 |

MR. FLOOD'S PARTY

| Cotillion SD-9003 | (S) | Mr. Flood's Party | 1969 | 6.00 | 15.00 |

MR. GASSER & THE WEIRDOS

Mr. Gasser is a pseudonym for Ed "Big Daddy" Roth. The Weirdos are a creation of Gary Usher & Co.

Capitol T-2010	(M)	Hot Rod Hootenanny	1963	20.00	50.00
Capitol ST-2010	(S)	Hot Rod Hootenanny	1963	30.00	75.00
Capitol T-2057	(M)	Rods N' Ratfinks (With ratfink decal)	1963	30.00	60.00
Capitol ST-2057	(S)	Rods N' Ratfinks (With ratfink decal)	1963	42.50	85.00
Capitol T-2057	(M)	Rods N' Ratfinks (Without decal)	1963	20.00	50.00
Capitol ST-2057	(S)	Rods N' Ratfinks (Without decal)	1963	30.00	75.00
Capitol T-2114	(M)	Surfink!	1964	30.00	60.00
Capitol ST-2114	(S)	Surfink!	1964	42.50	85.00
		(Includes the a bonus single "Santa Barbara" / "Midnight Run" by The Super Stocks in a pocket on the cover.			
Capitol T-2114	(M)	Surfink! (Without bonus single)	1964	20.00	50.00
Capitol ST-2114	(S)	Surfink! (Without bonus single)	1964	30.00	75.00

MR. GREENJEANS

| Harmony HL-9538 | (M) | Mama Goose And Papa Gander | 1963 | 10.00 | 25.00 |

MR. MAGOO

Mr. Magoo's voice was supplied by Jim Backus.

| RCA Victor LPM-1362 | (M) | MaGoo In Hi Fi | 1956 | 20.00 | 50.00 |

MRS. MILLER

Capitol T-2494	(M)	Mrs. Miller's Greatest Hits	1966	8.00	20.00
Capitol ST-2494	(S)	Mrs. Miller's Greatest Hits	1966	10.00	25.00
Capitol T-2579	(M)	Will Success Spoil Mrs. Miller?	1966	8.00	20.00
Capitol ST-2579	(S)	Will Success Spoil Mrs. Miller?	1966	10.00	25.00
Capitol T-2734	(M)	The Country Soul Of Mrs. Miller	1967	8.00	20.00
Capitol ST-2734	(S)	The Country Soul Of Mrs. Miller	1967	10.00	25.00
Amaret 5000	(S)	Mrs. Miller Does Her Thing	1969	10.00	25.00

MITCHELL, BILLY

| Smash MGS-27027 | (M) | This Is Billy Mitchell | 1963 | 6.00 | 15.00 |
| Smash SRS-67027 | (S) | This Is Billy Mitchell | 1963 | 8.00 | 20.00 |

MITCHELL, CHAD [CHAD MITCHELL TRIO]

Kapp KL-1262	(M)	Mighty Day On Campus	1962	8.00	20.00
Kapp KS-3262	(S)	Mighty Day On Campus	1962	10.00	25.00
Kapp KL-1281	(M)	At The Bitter End	1962	8.00	20.00
Kapp KS-3281	(S)	At The Bitter End	1962	10.00	25.00
Kapp KL-1313	(M)	Blowin' In The Wind	1963	8.00	20.00
Kapp KS-3313	(S)	Blowin' In The Wind	1963	10.00	25.00
Kapp KL-1334	(M)	The Best Of The Chad Mitchell Trio	1963	6.00	15.00
Kapp KS-3334	(S)	The Best Of The Chad Mitchell Trio	1963	8.00	20.00
Colpix CP-411	(M)	The Chad Mitchell Trio Arrives	1963	8.00	20.00
Colpix SCP-411	(S)	The Chad Mitchell Trio Arrives	1963	12.00	30.00
Colpix CP-463	(M)	In Concert	1964	8.00	20.00
Colpix SCP-463	(S)	In Concert	1964	12.00	30.00
Mercury MG-20838	(M)	Singin' Our Mind	1963	6.00	15.00
Mercury SR-60838	(S)	Singin' Our Mind	1963	8.00	20.00
Mercury MG-20891	(M)	Reflecting	1964	6.00	15.00
Mercury SR-60891	(S)	Reflecting	1964	8.00	20.00
Mercury MG-20944	(M)	The Slightly Irreverent Mitchell Trio	1964	6.00	15.00
Mercury SR-60944	(S)	The Slightly Irreverent Mitchell Trio	1964	8.00	20.00
Mercury MG-20992	(M)	Typical American Boys	1965	6.00	15.00
Mercury SR-60992	(S)	Typical American Boys	1965	8.00	20.00

The mid-'60s was an interesting time for the recording industry as they attempted to exploit fads from other forms, such as the fascination with horror movies monsters. This series played upon the then popular custom-car creations and related cartoon work of Ed "Big Daddy" Roth, who also supplied the cover art and the voice of Mr. Gasser. Roth also bestowed the ever lovable "Ratfink" on American lore.

Label & Catalog #		Title	Year	VG+	NM
Mercury MG-21049	(M)	That's The Way It's Gonna Be	1965	6.00	15.00
Mercury SR-61049	(S)	That's The Way It's Gonna Be	1965	8.00	20.00
Mercury MG-21067	(M)	Violets Of Dawn	1966	6.00	15.00
Mercury SR-61067	(S)	Violets Of Dawn	1966	8.00	20.00
Warner Bros. W-1706	(M)	A Feeling Of Love	1967	8.00	20.00
Warner Bros. WS-1706	(S)	A Feeling Of Love	1967	6.00	15.00
Bell 6028	(S)	Chad	1969	6.00	15.00

MITCHELL, GUY

Columbia CL-6231 (10")	(M)	Songs Of Open Spaces	1953	20.00	50.00
Columbia CL-6282 (10")	(M)	Red Garters (Soundtrack)	1954	40.00	100.00
Columbia CL-1211	(M)	A Guy In Love	1959	12.00	30.00
Columbia CS-8011	(S)	A Guy In Love	1959	16.00	40.00
Columbia CL-1226	(M)	Guy Mitchell's Greatest Hits	1959	14.00	35.00
Columbia CL-1552	(M)	Sunshine Guitar	1960	10.00	25.00
Columbia CS-8352	(S)	Sunshine Guitar	1960	14.00	35.00

— Original Columbia albums above have three white "eye" logos on each side of the spindle hole.—

MITCHELL, JONI

Asylum EQ-1001	(Q)	Court And Spark	1974	8.00	20.00
Asylum EQ-1051	(Q)	The Hissing Of Summer Lawns	1975	8.00	20.00
Nautilus NR-11	(S)	Court And Spark	1980	30.00	90.00
Geffen 2019	(DJ)	Wild Things Run Fast (Quiex II vinyl)	198?	10.00	25.00

MITCHELL, WILLIE

Hi HL-32010	(M)	Sunrise Serenade	1963	8.00	20.00
Hi SHL-32010	(E)	Sunrise Serenade	1963	6.00	15.00
Hi HL-32021	(M)	Hold It	1964	6.00	15.00
Hi SHL-32021	(S)	Hold It	1964	8.00	20.00
Hi HL-32026	(M)	It's Dance Time	1965	6.00	15.00
Hi SHL-32026	(S)	It's Dance Time	1965	8.00	20.00
Hi HL-32029	(M)	Driving Beat	1966	8.00	15.00
Hi SHL-32029	(S)	Driving Beat	1966	8.00	20.00
Hi HL-32034	(M)	Hit Sound Of Willie Mitchell	1967	6.00	15.00
Hi SHL-32034	(S)	Hit Sound Of Willie Mitchell	1967	6.00	15.00
Hi HL-32039	(M)	Ooh Baby, You Turn Me On	1967	6.00	15.00
Hi HL-32039	(S)	Ooh Baby, You Turn Me On	1967	6.00	15.00
Hi SHL-32042	(S)	Willie Mitchell Live	1968	6.00	15.00
Hi SHL-32045	(S)	Solid Soul	1968	6.00	15.00
Hi SHL-32048	(S)	On Top	1969	6.00	15.00
Hi SHL-32050	(S)	Soul Bag	1969	6.00	15.00
Hi SHL-32056	(S)	The Many Moods Of Willie Mitchell	1971	6.00	15.00
Hi SHL-32058	(S)	Robbin's Nest	1970	6.00	15.00

MITCHUM, ROBERT

Capitol T-853	(M)	Calypso Is Like So	1957	40.00	100.00
Monument MLP-8086	(M)	That Man, Robert Mitchum, Sings	1967	8.00	20.00
Monument SLP-18086	(S)	That Man, Robert Mitchum, Sings	1967	10.00	25.00

MIXTURES, THE

Linda 3301	(M)	Stompin' At The Rainbow	1962	20.00	50.00

MOB, THE

Colossus CS-1006	(S)	The Mob	1971	6.00	15.00

MOBY GRAPE

Moby Grape was Alexander "Skip" Spence, Bob Mosley, Jerry Miller, Peter Lewis and Don Stephenson.

Columbia CL-2698	(M)	Moby Grape	1967	16.00	40.00
Columbia CS-9498	(S)	Moby Grape	1967	16.00	40.00
		("360 Sound" label. The cover features Don Stephenson "giving the finger." Issued with a poster, priced separately below.)			
Columbia 26/9498		Moby Grape Bonus Poster #1	1967	8.00	20.00
		(The poster also features Stephenson "giving the finger.")			
Columbia CL-2698	(M)	Moby Grape	1967	8.00	20.00
Columbia CS-9498	(S)	Moby Grape	1967	8.00	20.00
		(Second pressings have "360 Sound" labels and the offending member airbrushed. Issued with a poster, priced separately below.)			
Columbia 26/9498		Moby Grape Bonus Poster #2	1967	3.60	8.00
		(The second poster has Stephenson's finger airbrushed out.)			

Label & Catalog #		Title	Year	VG+	NM
Columbia CS-9498	(S)	Moby Grape	1970	6.00	15.00
		(Third pressings have red labels with gold print. Price includes poster #2.)			
Columbia CS-9613	(S)	Wow	1968	8.00	20.00
Columbia MGS-1	(S)	Grape Jam	1968	4.00	10.00
		("Grape Jam" was issued as bonus album with "Wow.")			
Columbia CS-9696	(S)	Moby Grape '69	1969	8.00	20.00
Columbia CS-9912	(S)	Truly Fine Citizen	1969	6.00	15.00
— Original Columbia albums above have "360 Sound" on the bottom of the label. —					
Columbia AS-341098	(S)	Great Grape	1972	4.00	10.00
Harmony KH-30392	(M)	Omaha	1971	4.00	10.00
Reprise RS-6460	(S)	20 Granite Creek	1971	5.00	12.00
Escape ESA1A	(S)	Live Grape (Marble vinyl)	1978	5.00	12.00
San Francisco 04805	(S)	Moby Grape (Half speed master)	1983	6.00	18.00
San Francisco 04801	(S)	Wow/Grape Jam (Half speed master)	1983	8.00	25.00
San Francisco 04830	(S)	Moby Grape '84 (Picture disc)	1984	8.00	20.00

MOD & THE ROCKERS

Justice JLP-153	(M)	Mod & The Rockers Now!	196?	200.00	400.00

MODERN FOLK QUARTET, THE
The MFQ features Jerry Yester. Refer to Henske & Yester; The Lovin' Spoonful.

Warner Bros. W-1511	(M)	Modern Folk Quartet	1963	12.00	30.00
Warner Bros. WS-1511	(S)	Modern Folk Quartet	1963	16.00	40.00
Warner Bros. W-1546	(M)	Changes	1964	12.00	30.00
Warner Bros. WS-1546	(S)	Changes	1964	16.00	40.00

MODERN LOVERS, THE: *Refer to* JONATHAN RICHMAN

MODLIN, DAN, & DAVE SCOTT

700 West 760715	(S)	The Train Don't Stop Here Anymore	1976	60.00	150.00

MODUGNO, DOMENICO

Decca DL-8808	(M)	Nel Blu Dipinti Blu	1958	20.00	50.00
Decca DL-4133	(M)	Viva Italia	1961	12.00	30.00

MOLLY HATCHET

Epic PJE-35347	(DJ)	Molly Hatchet (Picture disc)	1979	10.00	25.00
Epic AS-99-694	(DJ)	Flirtin' With Disaster (Picture disc)	1979	8.00	20.00
Epic AS-99-884	(DJ)	Beatin' The Odds (Picture disc)	1980	6.00	15.00
Epic AS-99-1320	(DJ)	Take No Prisoners (Picture disc)	1981	5.00	12.00

MOM'S APPLIE PIE

Brown Bag 14200	(S)	Mom's Apple Pie	1972	4.00	10.00
		(Original covers feature a vagina in mom's apple pie.)			
Brown Bag 14200	(S)	Mom's Apple Pie	1972	6.00	15.00
		(Later covers replace the vagina with a barbed wire wall!)			

MOMENTS, THE

Stang ST-1003	(S)	Not On The Outside, But On The Inside Strong	1969	12.00	30.00
Stang ST-1003	(S)	A Moment With The Moments	1970	8.00	20.00
Stang ST-1004	(S)	Greatest Hits	1971	8.00	20.00
Stang ST-1006	(S)	Live At The New York State Women's Prison	1971	8.00	20.00
Stang ST-1009	(S)	The Other Side Of The Moments	1972	8.00	20.00
Stang ST-1015	(S)	Live At The Miss Black America Contest	1972	8.00	20.00
Stang ST-1019	(S)	The Best Of The Moments	1973	6.00	15.00
Stang ST-1022	(S)	My Thing	1974	6.00	15.00
Stang ST-1023	(S)	Those Sexy Moments	1974	6.00	15.00
Stang ST-1026	(S)	Look At Me	1975	6.00	15.00
Stang ST-1034	(S)	Sharp	1978	6.00	15.00

MONDAY BLUES

Vault 133	(S)	The Phil Spector Song Book	1970	8.00	20.00

MONICA, CORBETT

Dot DLP-3303	(M)	For Laughs	1960	16.00	40.00

Label & Catalog #		Title	Year	VG+	NM

MONITORS, THE

| Soul SS-714 | (S) | Greetings, We're The Monitors | 1969 | 8.00 | 20.00 |

MONKEES, THE
The Monkees were Michael Nesmith, Micky Dolenz, Peter Tork and Davy Jones.

Colgems COM-101	(M)	The Monkees	1966	16.00	45.00
Colgems COS-101	(S)	The Monkees	1966	20.00	60.00
		(Originally issued erroneously listing "Papa Jean's Blues.")			
Colgems COM-101	(M)	The Monkees	1966	12.00	35.00
Colgems COS-101	(S)	The Monkees	1966	16.00	45.00
		(Reissued correctly listing "Papa Gene's Blues.")			
Colgems COM-102	(DJ)	More Of The Monkees *(Clear vinyl)*	1967	300.00	500.00
Colgems COM-102	(M)	More Of The Monkees	1967	12.00	40.00
Colgems COS-102	(S)	More Of The Monkees	1967	16.00	50.00
Colgems COM-103	(M)	Headquarters	1967	20.00	50.00
Colgems COS-103	(S)	Headquarters	1967	16.00	40.00
Colgems COM-104	(M)	Pisces, Aquarius, Capricorn & Jones	1967	20.00	50.00
Colgems COS-104	(S)	Pisces, Aquarius, Capricorn & Jones	1967	16.00	40.00
— *Original Colgems albums above read "TM of Colgems Records" at the top of the label.—*					
Colgems COS-101	(S)	The Monkees	1968	12.00	30.00
Colgems COS-102	(S)	More Of The Monkees	1968	12.00	30.00
Colgems COS-103	(S)	Headquarters	1968	16.00	40.00
		(The back cover has a photo of Mike, Pete and Mickey with beards.)			
Colgems COS-104	(S)	Pisces, Aquarius, Capricorn & Jones	1968	12.00	30.00
— *Colgems albums above do not have "TM of Colgems Records" on the label.—*					
Colgems COM-109	(M)	The Birds, The Bees And The Monkees	1968	80.00	200.00
Colgems COS-109	(S)	The Birds, The Bees And The Monkees	1968	12.00	30.00
Colgems COSO-5008	(S)	Head	1968	20.00	50.00
Colgems COS-113	(S)	Instant Replay	1969	16.00	40.00
Colgems COS-115	(S)	The Monkees' Greatest Hits	1969	12.00	30.00
Colgems COS-117	(S)	The Monkees Present	1969	16.00	40.00
Colgems COS-119	(S)	Changes	1970	50.00	125.00
Colgems SCOS-1001	(S)	A Barrel Full Of Monkees *(2 LPs)*	1971	40.00	100.00
— *Colgems albums above delete "TM of Colgems Records" from the label.—*					
RCA Victor PRS-329	(S)	The Monkees' Golden Hits	1972	40.00	100.00
Bell 6081	(S)	Refocus	1973	20.00	50.00
Arista AL-4089	(S)	The Monkees' Greatest Hits	1976	6.00	15.00
		(Arista 4089 is a reissue of Bell 6081.)			
RCA/Pair DPL2-0188	(S)	The Monkees *(2 LPs)*	1976	14.00	35.00
Rhino RNLP-144	(S)	The Birds, The Bees And The Monkees	1984	12.00	30.00
		(First pressings issued with an alternate take of "Valleri."			
		There is an "RE-1" etched in the trail-off vinyl.)			

MONRO, MATT

London LL-1611	(M)	Blue And Sentimental	1957	12.00	30.00
Warwick 2045	(M)	My Kind Of Girl	1961	14.00	35.00
Liberty LRP-3240	(M)	Matt Monro	1962	6.00	15.00
Liberty LST-7240	(S)	Matt Monro	1962	8.00	20.00
United Arts. UAL-4114	(M)	From Russia With Love *(Soundtrack)*	1964	5.00	12.00
United Arts. UAS-5114	(S)	From Russia With Love *(Soundtrack)*	1964	6.00	15.00
Liberty LRP-3356	(M)	From Russia With Love	1964	6.00	15.00
Liberty LST-7356	(S)	From Russia With Love	1964	8.00	20.00
Liberty LRP-3402	(M)	Walk Away	1965	6.00	15.00
Liberty LST-7402	(S)	Walk Away	1965	8.00	20.00
Liberty LRP-3423	(M)	All My Loving	1965	6.00	15.00
Liberty LST-7423	(S)	All My Loving	1965	8.00	20.00
Liberty LRP-3437	(M)	Yesterday	1966	6.00	15.00
Liberty LST-7437	(S)	Yesterday	1966	8.00	20.00
Liberty LRP-3459	(M)	Matt Monro's Best	1966	6.00	15.00
Liberty LST-7459	(S)	Matt Monro's Best	1966	8.00	20.00
MGM E-4368	(M)	Born Free *(Soundtrack)*	1966	6.00	15.00
MGM SE-4368	(S)	Born Free *(Soundtrack)*	1966	6.00	15.00
Columbia OL-6660	(M)	The Quiller Memorandum *(Soundtrack)*	1966	40.00	100.00
Columbia OS-3060	(S)	The Quiller Memorandum *(Soundtrack)*	1966	50.00	125.00
Capitol T-2730	(M)	Invitation To The Movies/Born Free	1967	5.00	12.00
Capitol ST-2730	(S)	Invitation To The Movies/Born Free	1967	6.00	15.00
Decca DL-79160	(S)	A Matter Of Innocence *(Soundtrack)*	1968	20.00	50.00
Colgems COSO-5009	(S)	The Southern Star *(Soundtrack)*	1969	40.00	100.00
Paramount PAS-5007	(S)	The Italian Job *(Soundtrack)*	1969	14.00	35.00

Label & Catalog #		Title	Year	VG+	NM

MONROE, BILL (& HIS BLUEGRASS BOYS)

Label & Catalog #		Title	Year	VG+	NM
Decca DL-8731	(M)	Knee Deep In Bluegrass	1958	20.00	50.00
Decca DL-78731	(S)	Knee Deep In Bluegrass	1958	30.00	75.00
Decca DL-8769	(M)	I Saw The Light	1959	20.00	50.00
Decca DL-78769	(S)	I Saw The Light	1959	30.00	75.00

— Original Decca albums above have black & silver labels.—

Decca DL-4080	(M)	Mr. Bluegrass	1960	12.00	30.00
Decca DL-74080	(S)	Mr. Bluegrass	1960	14.00	35.00
Decca DL-4266	(M)	Bluegrass Ramble	1962	8.00	20.00
Decca DL-74266	(S)	Bluegrass Ramble	1962	10.00	25.00
Decca DL-4327	(M)	My All Time Country Favorites	1962	8.00	20.00
Decca DL-74327	(S)	My All Time Country Favorites	1962	10.00	25.00
Decca DL-4382	(M)	Bluegrass Special	1963	8.00	20.00
Decca DL-74382	(S)	Bluegrass Special	1963	10.00	25.00
Decca DL-4537	(M)	I'll Meet You In Church Sunday Morning	1964	6.00	15.00
Decca DL-74537	(S)	I'll Meet You In Church Sunday Morning	1964	8.00	20.00
Decca DL-4601	(M)	Bluegrass Instrumentals	1965	6.00	15.00
Decca DL-74601	(S)	Bluegrass Instrumentals	1965	8.00	20.00
Decca DL-4780	(M)	The High Lonesome Sound Of Bill Monroe	1966	6.00	15.00
Decca DL-74780	(S)	The High Lonesome Sound Of Bill Monroe	1966	8.00	20.00

— Original Decca albums above have black labels with "Mfd by Decca" beneath the rainbow.—

Decca DL-4896	(M)	Bluegrass Time	1967	6.00	15.00
Decca DL-74896	(S)	Bluegrass Time	1967	8.00	20.00
Decca DL-75010	(E)	Bill Monroe's Greatest Hits	1968	4.00	10.00
Decca DL-75135	(S)	A Voice From On High	1969	6.00	15.00
Decca DL-75213	(S)	Kentucky Bluegrass	1970	6.00	15.00
Decca DL-75281	(S)	Country Music Hall Of Fame	1971	6.00	15.00
Decca DL-75348	(S)	Uncle Pen	1972	6.00	15.00
Harmony HL-7290	(M)	The Great Bill Monroe	1961	8.00	20.00
Harmony HL-7315	(M)	Bill Monroe's Best	1964	6.00	15.00
Harmony HL-7338	(M)	Original Blue Grass Sound	1965	6.00	15.00
Camden CAL-719	(M)	Father Of Bluegrass Music	1962	8.00	20.00
Camden CAL-774	(M)	Early Bluegrass	1963	8.00	20.00
Vocalion VL-3702	(M)	Bill Monroe Sings Country Songs	1964	6.00	15.00

MONROE, MARILYN

MGM E-208 (10")	(M)	Gentlemen Prefer Blondes (Soundtrack)	1953	80.00	200.00
MGM E-3231	(M)	Gentlemen Prefer Blondes (Soundtrack)	1955	40.00	100.00

("Blondes" also features Ms. Jane Russell.)

United Arts. UAL-4030	(M)	Some Like It Hot (Soundtrack)	1959	20.00	50.00
United Arts. UAS-5030	(S)	Some Like It Hot (Soundtrack)	1959	30.00	75.00

(This soundtrack was released simultaneously on U.A. credited to Sweet Sue & Her Society Syncopaters.)

Columbia CL-1527	(M)	Let's Make Love (Soundtrack)	1960	20.00	50.00
Columbia CS-8327	(S)	Let's Make Love (Soundtrack)	1960	30.00	75.00
20th Century FXG-5000	(M)	Marilyn	1959	40.00	100.00
20th Century SXG-5000	(E)	Marilyn	1959	30.00	75.00

(Issued with a full color poster, priced separately below.)

20th Century 5000		Marilyn Poster	1959	30.00	75.00
Ascot ALM-13008	(M)	Marilyn Monroe	1964	16.00	40.00
Ascot ALS-16008	(S)	Marilyn Monroe	1964	20.00	50.00
Ascot US-13500	(M)	Some Like It Hot (Soundtrack)	1964	8.00	20.00
Ascot US-16500	(S)	Some Like It Hot (Soundtrack)	1964	12.00	30.00
Movietone 1016	(M)	The Unforgettable Marilyn Monroe	1967	10.00	25.00
Movietone 72016	(E)	The Unforgettable Marilyn Monroe	1967	8.00	20.00
20th Century T-901	(E)	Remember Marilyn	1972	10.00	25.00

(20th Century Fox 901 is a reissue of 5000.)

MONROE, VAUGHN

RCA Victor LPM-1799	(M)	There I Sing, Swing It Again	1958	8.00	20.00
RCA Victor LSP-1799	(S)	There I Sing, Swing It Again	1958	12.00	30.00
Dot DLP-3431	(M)	His Greatest Hits	1962	5.00	12.00
Dot DLP-25431	(S)	His Greatest Hits	1962	6.00	15.00
Dot DLP-3470	(M)	Great Themes Of Famous Bands And Great Singers	1962	5.00	12.00
Dot DLP-25470	(S)	Great Themes Of Famous Bands And Great Singers	1962	6.00	15.00

Label & Catalog #		Title	Year	VG+	NM

MONROE BROTHERS, THE
Bill and Charlie Monroe.

Camden CAL-774	(M)	Early Bluegrass Music	1963	8.00	20.00
Camden CAS-774	(E)	Early Bluegrass Music	1963	6.00	15.00
Decca DL-75066	(S)	The Monroe Brothers	1969	6.00	15.00

MONTAGE
Montage features Steve Martin of The Left Banke.

Laurie SLP-2049	(S)	Montage	1969	6.00	15.00

MONTANA, PATSY

Sims LP-122	(M)	The New Sound Of Patsy Montana	1964	20.00	50.00

MONTANA, SLIM
Montana Slim is a pseudonym for Wilf Carter.

Camden CAL-527	(M)	Wilf Carter/Montana Slim	1958	14.00	35.00
Camden CAL-668	(M)	Reminiscin'	1962	8.00	20.00
Camden CAL-846	(M)	32 Wonderful Years	1965	8.00	20.00
Decca DL-8917	(M)	I'm Ragged But I'm Right	1959	20.00	50.00
Decca DL-4092	(S)	The Dynamite Trail	1960	20.00	50.00
Starday SLP-300	(M)	Wilf Carter As Montana Slim	1964	14.00	35.00

MONTEZ, CHRIS
Refer to The Chantels.

Monogram M-100	(M)	Let's Dance And Have Some Kinda' Fun!!!	1963	100.00	300.00
A&M LP-115	(M)	The More I See You/Call Me	1966	8.00	20.00
A&M SP-4115	(S)	The More I See You/Call Me	1966	10.00	25.00
		("Call Me" is rechanneled on this album.)			
A&M LP-120	(M)	Time After Time	1966	5.00	12.00
A&M SP-4120	(S)	Time After Time	1966	6.00	15.00
A&M LP-128	(M)	Foolin' Around	1967	5.00	12.00
A&M SP-4128	(S)	Foolin' Around	1967	6.00	15.00
A&M LP-157	(M)	Watch What Happens	1967	5.00	12.00
A&M SP-4157	(S)	Watch What Happens	1967	6.00	15.00

MONTGOMERY, "LITTLE BROTHER"
For the bullk of Little Brother's catalog refer to Goldmine's Price Guide To Collectible Jazz Albums

Bluesville BVLP-1012	(M)	Tasty Blues	1960	16.00	40.00
Prestige PRST-7807	(S)	Tasty Blues	1969	6.00	15.00
		(Prestige 7807 is a reissue of Bluesville 1012.)			

MONTGOMERY, MARIAN: *Refer to GOLDMINE'S PRICE GUIDE TO COLLECTIBLE JAZZ ALBUMS*

MONTGOMERY, MELBA
Ms. Montgomery also recorded with George Jones; Gene Pitney.

United Arts. UAL-3341	(M)	#1 Country & Western Girl Singer	1964	6.00	15.00
United Arts. UAS-6341	(S)	#1 Country & Western Girl Singer	1964	8.00	20.00
United Arts. UAL-3369	(M)	Down Home	1964	6.00	15.00
United Arts. UAS-6369	(S)	Down Home	1964	8.00	20.00
United Arts. UAL-3391	(M)	I Can't Get Used To Being Lonely	1964	6.00	15.00
United Arts. UAS-6391	(S)	I Can't Get Used To Being Lonely	1964	8.00	20.00
Musicor M-2074	(M)	Country Girl	1966	5.00	12.00
Musicor MS-3074	(S)	Country Girl	1966	6.00	15.00
Musicor M-2097	(M)	The Hallelujah Road	1966	5.00	12.00
Musicor MS-3097	(S)	The Hallelujah Road	1966	6.00	15.00
Musicor M-2113	(M)	Melba Toast	1966	5.00	12.00
Musicor MS-3113	(S)	Melba Toast	1966	6.00	15.00
Musicor M-2114	(M)	Don't Keep Me Lonely Too Long	1966	5.00	12.00
Musicor MS-3114	(S)	Don't Keep Me Lonely Too Long	1966	6.00	15.00
Musicor M-2129	(M)	I'm Just Living	1967	5.00	12.00
Musicor MS-3129	(S)	I'm Just Living	1967	6.00	15.00

MOODY, CLYDE

King 891	(M)	The Best Of Clyde Moody	1964	16.00	40.00

MOODY BLUES
The Moodys on the first LP were Graeme Edge, Denny Laine, Mike Pinder, Ray Thomas and Clint Warwick. Laine and Warwick were replaced by Justin Hayward and John Lodge.

Label & Catalog #		Title	Year	VG+	NM
London LL-3428	(M)	Go Now/Moody Blues #1	1965	20.00	50.00
London PS-428	(E)	Go Now/Moody Blues #1	1965	10.00	25.00
Deram DES-18012	(S)	Days Of Future Passed	1968	8.00	20.00
Deram DES-18017	(S)	In Search Of The Lost Chord	1968	8.00	20.00
Deram DES-18025	(S)	On The Threshold Of A Dream	1969	8.00	20.00
Deram DES-18051	(E)	In The Beginning	1970	5.00	12.00

— Original Deram albums above have the "London" logo beneath Deram at the top of the label.—

Threshold THS-1	(S)	To Our Children's Children's Children	1969	6.00	15.00

(White & blue label reads "Distributed by London.")

Threshold THS-3	(S)	A Question Of Balance	1970	5.00	12.00
Threshold THX-100	(DJ)	Special Interview Kit *(Includes script)*	1971	40.00	100.00
Threshold THS-5	(S)	Every Good Boy Deserves Favour	1971	5.00	12.00
Threshold THS-7	(S)	Seventh Sojourn	1972	5.00	12.00

— Original Threshold albums above have white labels with a purple logo on top.—

Threshold THS-2-12/13	(S)	This Is The Moody Blues *(2 LPs)*	1974	4.00	10.00
London PS-708	(DJ)	Octave *(Blue vinyl)*	1978	10.00	25.00
Mobile Fidelity MFSL-042	(S)	Days Of Future Passed	1980	16.00	50.00
Mobile Fidelity MFSL-151	(S)	Seventh Sojourn	1984	13.00	40.00
Nautilus NR-21	(S)	On The Threshold Of A Dream	198?	25.00	75.00
Nautilus NR-21	(S)	On The Threshold Of A Dream *(DBX)*	198?	30.00	90.00

MOOLAH
Annuit Septus M-1	(S)	Whoa, Ye Demons Possessed	1974	40.00	100.00

MOON, KEITH
Keith Moon was formerly a member of The Who.

MCA 2136	(S)	Two Sides Of The Moon	1975	16.00	40.00

MOONDOG
Epic LN-1002 (10")	(M)	Moondog And His Friends	1954	80.00	200.00
Prestige PRLP-7042	(M)	Moondog	1956	40.00	100.00
Prestige PRLP-7069	(M)	More Moondog	1956	40.00	100.00
Prestige PRLP-7099	(M)	The Story Of Moondog	1957	40.00	100.00

— Original Prestige albums above have yellow labels with a W 50th St, NY, address.—

Columbia MS-7335	(S)	Moondog	1970	6.00	15.00
Columbia KC-30897	(S)	Moondog II	1971	6.00	15.00

MOONEY, JOE: *Refer to* GOLDMINE'S PRICE GUIDE TO COLLECTIBLE JAZZ ALBUMS

MOONEY, RALPH, & JAMES BURTON
Capitol T-2872	(M)	Corn Pickin' And Slick Slidin'	1967	16.00	40.00
Capitol ST-2872	(S)	Corn Pickin' And Slick Slidin'	1967	20.00	50.00

MOONGLOWS, THE
Refer to The Flamingos / The Moonglows.

Chess LP-1430	(M)	Look, It's The Moonglows	1959	200.00	400.00
Chess LP-1471	(M)	The Best Of Bobby Lester & The Moonglows	1962	80.00	200.00
Constellation CS-2	(M)	The Moonglows: Collectors Showcase	1964	12.00	30.00
RCA Victor LSP-4722	(S)	The Return Of The Moonglows	1972	6.00	15.00
Chess ACRR-701	(S)	The Moonglows	197?	6.00	15.00

MOONLIGHTERS
Century 29132	(M)	An Evening With The Moonlighters	197?	6.00	15.00

MOORE, ADA: *Refer to* GOLDMINE'S PRICE GUIDE TO COLLECTIBLE JAZZ ALBUMS

MOORE, BOBBY, & THE RHYTHM ACES
Checker LP-3000	(M)	Searching For My Love	1966	8.00	20.00
Checker LPS-3000	(E)	Searching For My Love	1966	6.00	15.00

MOORE, BOB, & HIS ORCHESTRA
Monument MLP-4005	(M)	Mexico And Other Great Hits!	1961	10.00	25.00
Monument SLP-4005	(M)	Mexico And Other Great Hits!	1961	14.00	35.00
Hickory LP-131	(M)	Viva Bob Moore	1966	6.00	15.00
Hickory LPS-131	(S)	Viva Bob Moore	1966	8.00	20.00

A retelling of the Faust fable, Bedazzled *teamed the comedy team of the bumbling Moore with the suave Peter Cook; at one point in the film Cook's mephistophelian character adapts a persona that accurately predicts the David Bowie cool of the '70s. Moore, a talented musician, composed the scores for both* Bedazzled *and its follow-up,* 30 Is A Dangerous Age, Cynthia!

Label & Catalog #		Title	Year	VG+	NM
Monument MLP-8008	(M)	Mexico	1967	6.00	15.00
Monument SLP-18008	(S)	Mexico	1967	8.00	20.00

MOORE, DANNY

Everest LPBR-1211	(M)	Folk Songs From Here And There	1963	6.00	15.00
Everest SDBR-1211	(S)	Folk Songs From Here And There	1963	8.00	20.00

MOORE, DEBBY: Refer to GOLDMINE'S PRICE GUIDE TO COLLECTIBLE JAZZ ALBUMS

MOORE, DUDLEY

Atlantic 1403	(M)	"Beyond The Fringe" And All That Jazz	1962	10.00	25.00
London MS-82009	(S)	Bedazzled (Soundtrack)	1968	18.00	40.00
London MS-82010	(S)	30 Is A Dangerous Age, Cynthia (Sdtk.)	1968	12.00	30.00

MOORE, GATEMOUTH

King 684	(M)	Gatemouth Moore Sings The Blues	1960	1,000.00	Rare
		(Near Mint copies have a suggested value of $2,000-3,000.)			

MOORE, LATTIE

Audio Lab AL-1555	(M)	The Best Of Lattie Moore	1960	50.00	125.00
Audio Lab AL-1573	(M)	Country Side	1962	40.00	100.00
Derbytown 102	(M)	Lattie Moore	196?	8.00	20.00

MOORE, MARILYN: Refer to GOLDMINE'S PRICE GUIDE TO COLLECTIBLE JAZZ ALBUMS

MOORE, SCOTTY
Scotty was formerly a member of Elvis, Scotty & Bill.

Epic LN-24103	(M)	The Guitar That Changed The World	1964	20.00	50.00
Epic BN-26103	(S)	The Guitar That Changed The World	1964	30.00	75.00

MOORE, SHELLY: Refer to GOLDMINE'S PRICE GUIDE TO COLLECTIBLE JAZZ ALBUMS

MORENO, RITA

Strand 1039	(M)	Rita Moreno Sings	195?	16.00	40.00
Wynne 103	(M)	Warm, Wonderful And Wild	195?	16.00	40.00

MORGAN, GEORGE

Columbia CL-1044	(M)	Morgan, By George	1957	16.00	40.00
Columbia CL-1831	(M)	Golden Memories	1961	6.00	15.00
Columbia CS-8431	(S)	Golden Memories	1961	8.00	20.00
Columbia CL-2111	(M)	Tender Lovin' Care	1964	5.00	12.00
Columbia CS-8911	(S)	Tender Lovin' Care	1964	6.00	15.00
Columbia CL-2197	(M)	Slippin' Around	1964	5.00	12.00
Columbia CS-8997	(S)	Slippin' Around	1964	6.00	15.00
Columbia CL-2333	(M)	Red Roses For A Blue Lady	1965	5.00	12.00
Columbia CS-9133	(S)	Red Roses For A Blue Lady	1965	6.00	15.00

MORGAN, JANE

Kapp KL-1023	(M)	Jane Morgan	1956	12.00	30.00
Kapp KL-1066	(M)	Fascination	1957	12.00	30.00
Kapp KS-3017	(M)	Fascination	195?	12.00	30.00
Kapp KL-1098	(M)	Jane Morgan	1958	12.00	30.00
Kapp KL-1105	(M)	The Day The Rain Came	1958	12.00	30.00
Kapp KL-1105S	(S)	The Day The Rain Came	1958	12.00	30.00
Kapp KL-1129	(M)	Jane In Spain	1959	10.00	25.00
Kapp KS-3014	(S)	Jane In Spain	1959	10.00	25.00
Kapp KL-1191	(M)	Ballads Of Lady Jane	1960	6.00	15.00
Kapp KS-3191	(S)	Ballads Of Lady Jane	1960	8.00	20.00
Kapp KL-1239	(M)	Second Time Around	1961	6.00	15.00
Kapp KS-3239	(S)	Second Time Around	1961	8.00	20.00
Kapp KL-1246	(M)	The Great Golden Hits	1961	6.00	15.00
Kapp KS-3246	(S)	The Great Golden Hits	1961	8.00	20.00
Kapp KL-1247	(M)	Big Hits From Broadway	1961	6.00	15.00
Kapp KS-3247	(S)	Big Hits From Broadway	1961	8.00	20.00
Kapp KL-1250	(M)	Love Makes The World Go 'Round	1961	6.00	15.00
Kapp KS-3250	(S)	Love Makes The World Go 'Round	1961	8.00	20.00
Kapp KL-1268	(M)	Jane Morgan At The Cocoanut Grove	1962	6.00	15.00
Kapp KS-3268	(S)	Jane Morgan At The Cocoanut Grove	1962	8.00	20.00

Label & Catalog #		Title	Year	VG+	NM
Kapp KL-1296	(M)	What Now My Love	1962	6.00	15.00
Kapp KS-3296	(S)	What Now My Love	1962	8.00	20.00
Kapp KL-1329	(M)	Jane Morgan's Greatest Hits	1963	5.00	12.00
Kapp KS-3329	(S)	Jane Morgan's Greatest Hits	1963	6.00	15.00
Colpix CP-497	(M)	The Jane Morgan Album	1966	6.00	15.00
Colpix SCP-497	(S)	The Jane Morgan Album	1966	10.00	25.00
Epic LN-24166	(M)	In My Style	1965	5.00	12.00
Epic BN-26166	(S)	In My Style	1965	6.00	15.00
Epic LN-24190	(M)	Today's Hits... Tomorrow's Golden Favorites	1966	5.00	12.00
Epic BN-26190	(S)	Today's Hits... Tomorrow's Golden Favorites	1966	6.00	15.00
Epic LN-24211	(M)	Fresh Flavor	1966	5.00	12.00
Epic BN-26211	(S)	Fresh Flavor	1966	6.00	15.00

MORGAN, JAYE P.

Label & Catalog #		Title	Year	VG+	NM
RCA Victor LPM-1155	(M)	Jaye P. Morgan	1955	20.00	50.00
MGM E-3774	(M)	Slow And Easy	1959	12.00	30.00
MGM SE-3774	(S)	Slow And Easy	1959	16.00	40.00
MGM E-3830	(M)	Up North	1960	10.00	25.00
MGM SE-3830	(S)	Up North	1960	12.00	30.00
MGM E-3867	(M)	Down South	1960	10.00	25.00
MGM SE-3867	(S)	Down South	1960	12.00	30.00
MGM E-3940	(M)	That Country Sound	1961	10.00	25.00
MGM SE-3940	(S)	That Country Sound	1961	12.00	30.00

MORGEN

Label & Catalog #		Title	Year	VG+	NM
Probe CPLP-4507	(M)	Morgen (With insert)	1969	40.00	100.00

MOREL, TERRY

Label & Catalog #		Title	Year	VG+	NM
Bethlehem 47	(M)	Songs Of A Woman In Love	1955	16.00	40.00

MORLY GREY

Label & Catalog #		Title	Year	VG+	NM
Starshine 69000	(M)	The Only Truth (With poster)	1968	200.00	400.00

MORNING

Label & Catalog #		Title	Year	VG+	NM
Vault 138	(S)	Morning	1970	8.00	20.00
Fantasy 9402	(S)	Struck Like Silver	1972	6.00	15.00

MORNING DEW

Label & Catalog #		Title	Year	VG+	NM
Roulette R-41045	(M)	Morning Dew	1967	20.00	50.00
Roulette RS-41045	(S)	Morning Dew	1967	40.00	100.00

MORNING GLORY

Label & Catalog #		Title	Year	VG+	NM
Fontana MGF-27573	(M)	Two Suns Worth	1967	6.00	15.00
Fontana SRF-67573	(S)	Two Suns Worth	1967	8.00	20.00

MORNINGLORY

Label & Catalog #		Title	Year	VG+	NM
Toya STLP-003	(S)	Growing	1972	14.00	35.00

MORRISEY, PAT: *Refer to* GOLDMINE'S PRICE GUIDE TO COLLECTIBLE JAZZ ALBUMS

MORRISON, VAN

Van The Man was formerly lead singer for Them.

Label & Catalog #		Title	Year	VG+	NM
Bang BLP-218	(M)	Blowin' Your Mind	1967	12.00	30.00
Bang BLPS-218	(S)	Blowin' Your Mind	1967	12.00	30.00
		(Originally issued with the complete version of "Brown-Eyed Girl" with the line "Making love in the green grass.")			
Bang BLPS-218	(S)	Blowin' Your Mind	1968	10.00	25.00
		(Reissued with a censored version of "Brown-Eyed Girl" that deletes "Making love in the green grass.")			
		— Original Bang albums above have red & white labels.—			
Bang BLPS-218	(S)	Blowin' Your Mind	1970	4.00	10.00
Bang BLPS-222	(S)	The Best Of Van Morrison	1970	8.00	20.00
Bang BLPS-400	(S)	T.B. Sheets	1973	6.00	15.00
		— Original Bang albums above have yellow labels.—			
Warner Bros. WS-1768	(S)	Astral Weeks	1968	6.00	15.00
Warner Bros. WS-1835	(S)	Moondance	1970	6.00	15.00
		— Original Warner albums above have green labels with a "W7" on top.—			
Warner Bros. WBMS-102	(DJ)	Live At The Roxy	1978	16.00	40.00
Direct Disk SD-16604	(S)	Moondance	1981	16.00	50.00

These two albums by Buddy Morrow, whose trombone is familiar to fans of Johnny Carson's "Tonight Show," are included here for their content: Jazzy big band interpretations of popular televison scores of the late '50s and early '60s.

Label & Catalog #		Title	Year	VG+	NM

MORROW, BUDDY

RCA Victor LPM-2042	(M)	Impact	1959	8.00	20.00
RCA Victor LSP-2042	(S)	Impact	1959	12.00	30.00
RCA Victor LPM-2180	(M)	Double Impact	1960	8.00	20.00
RCA Victor LSP-2180	(S)	Double Impact	1960	12.00	30.00

MORSE, ELLA MAE

Capitol H-513 (10")	(M)	Barrelhouse Boogie And The Blues	1954	150.00	300.00
Capitol T-513	(M)	Barrelhouse Boogie And The Blues	1955	60.00	150.00
Capitol T-898	(M)	Morse Code	1957	30.00	75.00
Capitol T-1802	(M)	Hits Of Ella Mae Morse And Freddie Slack	1962	16.00	40.00
Capitol ST-1802	(S)	Hits Of Ella Mae Morse And Freddie Slack	1962	20.00	50.00

MORTIMER

| Philips PHS-600-267 | (S) | Mortimer | 1968 | 8.00 | 20.00 |

MOREY STORE BAND, THE

| Sound Machine SMS-49007 | (S) | Cry For The Dreamer | 197? | 40.00 | 100.00 |

MOSER, J., & THE HOTS

| Moco FIT-003 | (S) | For Life | 1975 | 20.00 | 50.00 |

MOSLEY, BOB
Bob Mosley was a former member of Moby Grape.

| Reprise RS-2068 | (S) | Bob Mosley | 1972 | 8.00 | 20.00 |

MOSS, GENE

| RCA Victor LPM-2977 | (M) | Dracula's Greatest Hits | 1964 | 10.00 | 25.00 |
| RCA Victor LSP-2977 | (S) | Dracula's Greatest Hits | 1964 | 12.00 | 30.00 |

MOTHER EARTH
Mother Earth features Tracy Nelson.

Mercury SR-61194	(S)	Living With The Animals	1968	8.00	20.00
Mercury SR-61226	(S)	Make A Joyful Noise	1969	6.00	15.00
Mercury SR-61230	(S)	Tracy Nelson Country	1969	6.00	15.00
Mercury SR-61270	(S)	Satisfied	1970	6.00	15.00
Reprise RS-6431	(S)	Bring Me Home	1971	6.00	15.00

MOTHERLODE

| Buddah BDS-5046 | (S) | When I Die | 1969 | 6.00 | 15.00 |
| Buddah BDS-5108 | (S) | Tapped Out | 1972 | 4.00 | 10.00 |

MOTHERS OF INVENTION, THE: *Refer to FRANK ZAPPA*

MOTLEY CRUE

Leathur LR-123	(S)	Too Fast For Love (White letter cover)	1981	40.00	100.00
Leathur LR-123	(S)	Too Fast For Love (Red letter cover)	1981	30.00	75.00
Elektra 60395	(S)	Helter Skelter (Picture disc)	1984	10.00	25.00

MOTIONS, THE

| Philips PHS-600-317 | (S) | Electric Baby | 1969 | 8.00 | 20.00 |

MOTT THE HOOPLE [MOTT]
Mott The Hoople features Ian Hunter.

Atlantic SD-8272	(S)	Mad Shadows	1970	6.00	15.00
Atlantic SD-8258	(S)	Mott The Hoople	1970	6.00	15.00
Atlantic SD-8284	(S)	Wildlife	1971	6.00	15.00
Atlantic SD-8304	(S)	Brain Capers	1972	6.00	15.00
Atlantic SD-7297	(S)	Rock And Roll Queen	1974	4.00	10.00
Columbia PCQ-32871	(Q)	The Hoople	1974	8.00	20.00

MOUNT RUSHMORE

| Dot DLP-25898 | (S) | High On Mount Rushmore | 1968 | 6.00 | 15.00 |
| Dot DLP-25934 | (S) | Mount Rushmore '69 | 1969 | 6.00 | 15.00 |

MOUNTAIN BUS

| Good 101 | (S) | Sundance | 1971 | 60.00 | 150.00 |

While Frank Zappa has had a long and distinctive career, for collectors—and, more than likely historians—it was his early work with the original Mothers [Of Invention] for Verve Records that will maintain his reputation as a rock genius. . . Absolutely Free was a collage of iconoclastic noises with appropriate cover art. Many fans were made aware of this odd group through ads buried in the back of comic books in the mid-'60s. Due to the fact that all aspects of creativity were the [all but] exclusive domain of Zappa, and due to the fluidity of the group's line-up through the years, the original albums on Verve, although clearly credited to The Mothers Of Invention as a group, are listed under Frank Zappa, along with his solo work and his other Mothers.

Label & Catalog #		Title	Year	VG+	NM

MOUNTAIN RAMBLERS, THE

| Atlantic 1347 | (M) | Blue Ridge Mountain Music | 1962 | 14.00 | 35.00 |

MOUSEKETEERS, THE

| Disneyland T-3918 | (M) | How To Be A Mouseketeer | 1962 | 10.00 | 25.00 |
| Disneyland ST-3918 | (S) | How To Be A Mouseketeer | 1962 | 14.00 | 35.00 |

MOUZOKIS

| British Main 90069 | (S) | Magic Tube | 1972 | 40.00 | 100.00 |

MOVE, THE

A&M SP-4259	(S)	Shazam	1969	16.00	40.00
A&M SP-3181	(S)	Shazam	1982	6.00	15.00
Capitol ST-658	(S)	Looking On	1971	10.00	25.00
Capitol ST-811	(S)	Message From The Country	1971	8.00	20.00
United Arts. UAS-5666	(S)	Split Ends	1973	8.00	20.00
A&M SP-3625	(P)	Best Of The Move/First Move (2 LPs)	1974	8.00	20.00

MOVING SIDEWALKS
The Sidewalks featured Billy Gibbons, later of ZZ Top.

| Tantara 6919 | (S) | Flash | 1968 | 80.00 | 200.00 |

MOYA, MONTE, & THE SURFERS

| Everest EDBR-1212 | (M) | Percussionata | 1963 | 5.00 | 12.00 |
| Everest SBDR-1212 | (S) | Percussionata | 1963 | 6.00 | 15.00 |

MU
Mu is a creation of Merrell Fankhauser.

| CAS 300 | (S) | Mu (With insert) | 1972 | 16.00 | 40.00 |

MUDDY WATERS
Muddy Waters is a pseudonym for McKinley Morganfield. Refer to Bo Diddley.

Chess LP-1427	(M)	The Best Of Muddy Waters	1957	150.00	350.00
Chess LP-1444	(M)	Muddy Waters Sings Big Bill	1960	100.00	250.00
Chess LP-1449	(M)	Muddy Waters At Newport	1963	60.00	150.00
Chess LP-1483	(M)	Folk Singer	1964	30.00	75.00
		— Original Chess albums above have black & silver labels.—			
Chess LP-1501	(M)	The Real Folk Blues Of Muddy Waters	1965	16.00	40.00
Chess LPS-1501	(S)	The Real Folk Blues Of Muddy Waters	1965	30.00	75.00
Chess LP-1507	(M)	Muddy, Brass And Blues	1966	14.00	35.00
Chess LPS-1507	(S)	Muddy, Brass And Blues	1966	20.00	50.00
Chess LP-1511	(M)	More Real Folk Blues	1966	14.00	35.00
Chess LPS-1511	(S)	More Real Folk Blues	1966	20.00	50.00
Chess LP-1533	(M)	Blues From Big Bill's Copacabana	1967	12.00	30.00
Chess LPS-1533	(S)	Blues From Big Bill's Copacabana	1967	14.00	35.00
Cadet Concept 314	(S)	Electric Mud	1968	8.00	20.00
Cadet Concept 320	(S)	After The Rain	1969	8.00	20.00
Chess LPS-1539	(S)	Sail On	1969	10.00	25.00
Chess LPS-1553	(S)	They Call Me Muddy Waters	1971	6.00	15.00
Chess 2CH-60006	(S)	McKinley Morganfield			
		A.K.A. Muddy Waters (2 LPs)	1971	10.00	25.00
Chess CH-50012	(S)	Muddy Waters Live	1972	6.00	15.00
Chess CH-60013	(S)	The London Muddy Waters Sessions	1972	8.00	20.00
		— Original Chess albums above have blue labels.—			
Chess CH-50023	(S)	Can't Get No Grindin'	1973	8.00	20.00
Chess CH-60026	(S)	London Revisited	1974	6.00	15.00
Chess CH-60031	(S)	Unk In Funk	1974	6.00	15.00
Chess CH-50033	(S)	Fathers And Sons (2 LPs)	1975	12.00	30.00
		(Original covers have pockets that open on the inside.)			
Chess CH-50033	(S)	Fathers And Sons (2 LPs)	1976	8.00	20.00
		(Later covers have pockets that open normally on the outside.)			

MUELLER, BILL, & THE BRAT

| Brat CT-3301 | (S) | No Place Like Home | 1979 | 30.00 | 75.00 |

MUGWUMPS
The Mugwumps were Cass Elliot, Denny Doherty, Jim Hendricks and Zal Yanovsky.

| Warner Bros. W-1697 | (M) | The Mugwumps | 1967 | 10.00 | 25.00 |
| Warner Bros. WS-1697 | (S) | The Mugwumps | 1967 | 12.00 | 30.00 |

Label & Catalog #		Title	Year	VG+	NM
MULDAUER, GEOFF					
Folklore FRLP-14004	(M)	Sleepy Man Blues	1964	16.00	40.00
Folklore FRST-14004	(S)	Sleepy Man Blues	1964	20.00	50.00
Prestige PRST-7727	(S)	Sleepy Man Blues	1969	10.00	25.00
		(Prestige 7727 is a reissue of Folklore 14004.)			
MULLICAN, MOON					
Coral CRL-57235	(M)	Moon Over Mullican	1958	200.00	500.00
Sterling ST-601	(M)	I'll Sail My Ship Alone	1958	60.00	150.00
King 555	(M)	His All-Time Greatest Hits	1958	60.00	150.00
King 628	(M)	16 Of His Favorite Tunes	1959	50.00	125.00
King 681	(M)	The Many Moods Of Moon Mullican	1960	50.00	125.00
King 937	(M)	24 Of His Favorite Tunes	1965	16.00	40.00
Audio Lab AL-1568	(M)	Instrumentals	1962	60.00	150.00
Spar SP-3005	(M)	Mister Honky Tonk Man	196?	40.00	100.00
Starday SLP-135	(M)	Playin' And Singin'	1963	40.00	100.00
Starday SLP-267	(M)	Mister Piano Man	1964	20.00	50.00
Starday SLP-398	(M)	The Unforgettable Moon Mullican	1967	16.00	40.00
Kapp KS-3600	(S)	Showcase	1968	16.00	40.00
Hilltop JS-6033	(S)	Good Times Gonna Roll Again	196?	12.00	30.00
MUMY, BILL					
"BB" 103	(S)	Bill Mumy	1980	10.00	25.00
MUNSTERS, THE					
Decca DL-4588	(M)	The Munsters *(TV Soundtrack)*	1964	30.00	75.00
Decca DL-74588	(S)	The Munsters *(TV Soundtrack)*	1964	40.00	100.00
Golden LP-139	(M)	At Home With The Munsters	1964	30.00	75.00
MURE, BILLY					
United Arts. UAL-3031	(M)	Bandstand Record Hop	1959	10.00	25.00
United Arts. UAS-6031	(S)	Bandstand Record Hop	1959	16.00	40.00
MGM E-4131	(M)	Teen Bossa Nova	1963	8.00	20.00
MGM SE-4131	(S)	Teen Bossa Nova	1963	10.00	25.00
MURPHEY, MICHAEL					
Epic PEQ-33851	(Q)	Swans Against The Sun	1975	6.00	15.00
MURPHY, MARK					
Decca DL-8390	(M)	Meet Mark Murphy	1956	16.00	40.00
Decca DL-8632	(M)	Let Yourself Go	1958	12.00	30.00
Capitol T-1177	(M)	This Could Be The Start Of Something	1959	8.00	20.00
Capitol ST-1177	(S)	This Could Be The Start Of Something	1959	10.00	25.00
Capitol T-1299	(M)	Hip Parade	1960	6.00	15.00
Capitol ST-1299	(S)	Hip Parade	1960	8.00	20.00
Capitol T-1458	(M)	Playing The Field	1960	6.00	15.00
Capitol ST-1458	(S)	Playing The Field	1960	8.00	20.00
Riverside RLP-395	(M)	Rah!	1961	6.00	15.00
Riverside RS-9395	(S)	Rah!	1961	8.00	20.00
Riverside RLP-441	(M)	That's How I Love The Blues	1962	6.00	15.00
Riverside RS-9441	(S)	That's How I Love The Blues	1962	8.00	20.00
Fontana MGF-27537	(M)	A Swingin' Singin' Affair	1965	6.00	15.00
Fontana SRF-67537	(S)	A Swingin' Singin' Affair	1965	8.00	20.00
MURPHY, ROSE					
Royale 1835 (10")	(M)	Rose Murphy And Quartette	195?	12.00	30.00
Verve V-2070	(M)	Not Cha-Cha, But Chi-Chi	1957	10.00	25.00
United Arts. UAL-12025	(M)	Jazz, Joy And Happiness	195?	10.00	25.00
United Arts. UAS-15025	(S)	Jazz, Joy And Happiness	195?	12.00	30.00
MURRAY, ANNE					
Capitol 11743	(DJ)	Let's Keep It That Way *(Picture disc)*	1978	20.00	50.00
MUSIC ASYLUM					
United Arts. UAS-6778	(S)	Commit Thyself	1970	6.00	15.00
MUSIC EMPORIUM, THE					
Sentinal 69001	(S)	The Music Emporium	1969	1,200.00	1,750.00

Label & Catalog #		Title	Year	VG+	NM
MUSIC EXPLOSION, THE					
Laurie LLP-2040	(M)	**A Little Bit O' Soul**	1967	6.00	15.00
Laurie SLLP-2040	(S)	**A Little Bit O' Soul**	1967	8.00	20.00
MUSIC MACHINE, THE					
Refer to Bonniwell's Music Machine.					
Original Sound 5015	(M)	**Turn On The Music Machine**	1966	10.00	25.00
Original Sound 8875	(S)	**Turn On The Music Machine**	1966	20.00	50.00
MUSICAL THEATRE					
Metromedia 1015	(S)	**Revolutionary Revelation**	1969	5.00	12.00
MUSSELWHITE, CHARLIE					
Crystal Clear	(S)	**Time's Gettin' Tougher Than Tough**	198?	6.00	15.00
MUSSO, VIDO					
Crown CLP-5029	(M)	**Teenage Dance Party**	1958	10.00	25.00
MUSTANGS, THE					
Providence PLP-001	(M)	**Dartell Stomp**	1963	20.00	50.00
MUTHA GOOSE					
Alpha Omega 264-01	(S)	**Mutha Goose I**	197?	60.00	150.00
MYERS, DAVE					
Del-Fi DFLP-1239	(M)	**Hangin' Twenty**	1963	12.00	30.00
Del-Fi DFST-1239	(S)	**Hangin' Twenty**	1963	20.00	50.00
		(Del-Fi 1239 is credited to Dave Myers & The Surftones.)			
Carole CAR-8002	(M)	**Greatest Racing Themes**	1966	14.00	35.00
		(Carole 8002 is credited to The Dave Myers Effect.)			
MYSTIC ASTROLOGIC CRYSTAL BAND, THE					
Carole 8001	(M)	**Mystic Astrologic Crystal Band**	1967	10.00	25.00
Carole S-8001	(S)	**Mystic Astrologic Crystal Band**	1967	12.00	30.00
Carole S-8003	(S)	**Clip Out, Put On Book**	1968	12.00	30.00
MYSTIC MOODS ORCHESTRA, THE					
Mobile Fidelity MFSL-001	(S)	**Emotions**	1979	12.00	35.00
Mobile Fidelity MFSL-002	(S)	**Cosmic Force**	1979	12.00	35.00
Mobile Fidelity MFSL-003	(S)	**Stormy Weekend**	1979	12.00	35.00
MYSTIC NUMBER NATIONAL BANK, THE					
Probe CPLPS-4501	(S)	**The Mystic Number National Bank**	1969	6.00	15.00
MYSTIC SIVA					
V.O. 19713	(S)	**Mystic Siva**	1970	200.00	400.00

NAGLE, RON					
Warner Bros. WS-1902	(S)	**Bad Rice**	1970	8.00	20.00
NANTOS, NICK, & THE FIREBALLERS					
Summit 4114	(M)	**Guitars On Fire**	197?	5.00	12.00

Label & Catalog #		Title	Year	VG+	NM
NAPOLEON XIV					
Warner Bros. W-1661	(M)	They're Coming To Take Me Away Ha-Haaa!	1966	30.00	75.00
Warner Bros. WS-1661	(S)	They're Coming To Take Me Away Ha-Haaa!	1966	60.00	150.00
NARZ, JACK					
Dot DLP-3244	(M)	Sing The Folk Songs With Jack Narz	1959	5.00	12.00
Dot DLP-25244	(S)	Sing The Folk Songs With Jack Narz	1959	6.00	15.00
NASH, JOHNNY					
ABC-Paramount 244	(M)	Johnny Nash	1958	12.00	30.00
ABC-Paramount S-244	(S)	Johnny Nash	1958	16.00	40.00
ABC-Paramount 276	(M)	Quiet Hour	1959	12.00	30.00
ABC-Paramount S-276	(S)	Quiet Hour	1959	16.00	40.00
ABC-Paramount 299	(M)	I Got Rhythm	1959	12.00	30.00
ABC-Paramount S-299	(S)	I Got Rhythm	1959	16.00	40.00
ABC-Paramount 344	(M)	Let's Get Lost	1960	10.00	25.00
ABC-Paramount S-344	(S)	Let's Get Lost	1960	12.00	30.00
ABC-Paramount 383	(M)	Studio Time	1961	10.00	25.00
ABC-Paramount S-383	(S)	Studio Time	1961	12.00	30.00
Argo LP-4038	(M)	Composer's Choice	1964	6.00	15.00
Argo LPS-4038	(S)	Composer's Choice	1964	8.00	20.00
Jad JS-1207	(S)	Hold Me Tight	1968	6.00	15.00
Jad JS-1001	(S)	Prince Of Peace	1969	6.00	15.00
Jad JS-1006	(S)	Folk Soul	1969	6.00	15.00
Epic KE-31607	(S)	I Can See Clearly Now (Yellow label)	1972	6.00	15.00
		(Although uncredited, Nash is backed by Bob Marley & The Wailers.)			
Epic KE-32158	(S)	My Merry-Go-Round	1973	4.00	10.00
Epic KE-32828	(S)	Celebrate Life	1974	4.00	10.00
NASHVILLE ALL-STARS, THE					
The All-Stars feature Chet Atkins, Gary Burton and Hank Garland.					
RCA Victor LPM-2302	(M)	After The Riot At Newport	1960	12.00	30.00
RCA Victor LSP-2302	(S)	After The Riot At Newport	1960	16.00	40.00
NASHVILLE TEENS, THE					
London LL-3407	(M)	Tobacco Road	1964	30.00	75.00
London PS-407	(E)	Tobacco Road	1964	20.00	50.00
NAZZ, THE					
The Nazz features Todd Rundgren.					
SGC 5001	(S)	Nazz	1968	16.00	40.00
SGC 5002	(S)	Nazz Nazz (Red vinyl)	1969	16.00	40.00
		(Orange & red label with a blue SGC logo.)			
SGC 5002	(S)	Nazz Nazz (Red vinyl)	1969	20.00	50.00
		(Orange & red label with a purple SGC logo.)			
SGC 5002	(S)	Nazz Nazz (Black vinyl)	1970	30.00	75.00
SGC 5004	(S)	Nazz III	1971	16.00	40.00
		(Poorly reproduced counterfeits of each of the Nazz albums exist.)			
NEGATIVE SPACE					
Evil 1001	(M)	Hard, Heavy, Mean	196?	300.00	500.00
		(Heavy cardboard cover with the title in blue print on the front. Counterfeits have flimsy covers with black print.)			
NEIGHB'RHOOD CHILDR'N, THE					
Acta 8005	(M)	The Neighb'rhood Childr'n	1968	12.00	30.00
Acta 38005	(S)	The Neighb'rhood Childr'n	1968	16.00	40.00
NEIL, FRED					
Refer to Martin & Neil.					
Elektra EKL-293	(M)	Bleecker And MacDougal	1965	12.00	30.00
Elektra EKS-7293	(S)	Bleecker And MacDougal (Gold label)	1965	16.00	40.00
Elektra EKS-7293	(S)	Bleecker And MacDougal (Red label)	1969	8.00	20.00
Capitol T-2665	(M)	Fred Neil	1966	10.00	25.00
Capitol ST-2665	(S)	Fred Neil	1966	12.00	30.00
		(Original covers have a full color photo of Neil on the back cover.)			
Capitol ST-2665	(S)	Fred Neil	196?	6.00	15.00
		(Later pressings have a black & white photo the back cover.)			

Label & Catalog #		Title	Year	VG+	NM
Capitol T-2862	(M)	Fred Neil: Sessions	1967	6.00	15.00
Capitol ST-2862	(S)	Fred Neil: Sessions	1967	8.00	20.00

NELSON, PORTIA

Label & Catalog #		Title	Year	VG+	NM
Columbia CL-4722 (10")	(M)	Love Songs For A Late Evening	195?	12.00	30.00
Dolphin 4	(M)	Autumn Leaves	195?	10.00	25.00

NELSON, RICK [RICKY NELSON]

Label & Catalog #		Title	Year	VG+	NM
Verve V-2083	(M)	Teen Time	1957	100.00	250.00
		(This is actually a various artists album containing Ricky's first three sides for Verve but, as it gets its hefty value from the great shot of Ricky on the cover, it is listed here.)			
Imperial LP-9048	(M)	Ricky	1957	40.00	100.00
Imperial LP-9050	(M)	Ricky Nelson	1958	40.00	100.00
Imperial LP-9061	(M)	Ricky Sings Again	1959	40.00	100.00
Imperial LP-9082	(M)	Songs By Ricky	1959	30.00	75.00
Imperial LP-9122	(M)	More Songs By Ricky	1960	30.00	75.00
Imperial LP-12059	(S)	More Songs By Ricky	1960	40.00	100.00
Imperial LP-12059	(DJ)	More Songs By Ricky *(Blue vinyl)*	1960	500.00	800.00
		(Issued with a poster, priced separately below.)			
Imperial LP-12059		More Songs By Ricky Bonus Poster	1960	60.00	150.00
Imperial LP-9152	(M)	Rick Is 21	1961	16.00	40.00
Imperial LP-12071	(S)	Rick Is 21	1961	30.00	75.00
Imperial LP-9167	(M)	Album Seven By Rick	1962	16.00	40.00
Imperial LP-12082	(S)	Album Seven By Rick	1962	30.00	75.00
Imperial LP-9218	(M)	Best Sellers	1963	16.00	40.00
Imperial LP-9232	(M)	Million Sellers	1963	16.00	40.00
Imperial LP-9223	(M)	It's Up To You	1963	16.00	40.00
Imperial LP-9244	(M)	A Long Vacation	1963	12.00	30.00
Imperial LP-12244	(E)	A Long Vacation	1963	10.00	25.00
Imperial LP-9251	(M)	Rick Nelson Sings For You	1964	12.00	30.00
Imperial LP-12251	(E)	Rick Nelson Sings For You	1964	10.00	25.00
		— Original Imperial mono albums above have black labels with stars on top; stereo albums have black labels with silver print.—			
Imperial LP-9048	(M)	Ricky	1966	8.00	20.00
Imperial LP-9218	(M)	Best Sellers	1966	8.00	20.00
Imperial LP-12218	(E)	Best Sellers	1966	5.00	12.00
Imperial LP-9232	(M)	Million Sellers	1966	8.00	20.00
Imperial LP-12232	(E)	Million Sellers	1966	5.00	12.00
		— Imperial albums above have black & green labels.—			
Decca DL-4419	(M)	For Your Sweet Love	1963	12.00	30.00
Decca DL-74419	(S)	For Your Sweet Love	1963	16.00	40.00
Decca DL-4479	(M)	Rick Nelson Sings For You	1963	12.00	30.00
Decca DL-74479	(S)	Rick Nelson Sings For You	1963	16.00	40.00
Decca DL-4559	(M)	The Very Thought Of You	1964	12.00	30.00
Decca DL-74559	(S)	The Very Thought Of You	1964	16.00	40.00
Decca DL-4608	(M)	Spotlight On Rick	1964	12.00	30.00
Decca DL-74608	(S)	Spotlight On Rick	1964	16.00	40.00
Decca DL-4660	(M)	Best Always	1965	12.00	30.00
Decca DL-74660	(S)	Best Always	1965	16.00	40.00
Decca DL-4678	(M)	Love And Kisses	1965	12.00	30.00
Decca DL-74678	(S)	Love And Kisses	1965	16.00	40.00
Decca DL-4779	(M)	Bright Lights And Country Music	1966	12.00	30.00
Decca DL-74779	(S)	Bright Lights And Country Music	1966	16.00	40.00
Decca DL-4827	(M)	Country Fever	1967	12.00	30.00
Decca DL-74827	(S)	Country Fever	1967	16.00	40.00
Decca DL-4836	(M)	On The Flip Side *(TV Soundtrack)*	1967	12.00	30.00
Decca DL-74836	(S)	On The Flip Side *(TV Soundtrack)*	1967	16.00	40.00
		("On The Flip Side" also stars Joannie Sommers.)			
		— Original Decca albums above have black labels with "Mfrd by Decca" beneath the rainbow.—			
Decca DL-4944	(M)	Another Side Of Rick	1967	12.00	30.00
Decca DL-74944	(S)	Another Side Of Rick	1967	16.00	40.00
Decca DL-75014	(S)	Perspective	1968	16.00	40.00
Decca DL-75162	(S)	Rick Nelson In Concert *(Gatefold cover)*	1970	8.00	20.00
Decca DL-75236	(S)	Rick Sings Nelson *(With poster)*	1970	10.00	25.00
Decca DL-75297	(S)	Rudy The Fifth	1971	6.00	15.00
Decca DL-75391	(S)	Garden Party	1972	6.00	15.00
Sunset SUM-4118	(M)	Ricky Nelson	1966	6.00	15.00
Sunset SUS-5118	(P)	Ricky Nelson	1966	8.00	20.00

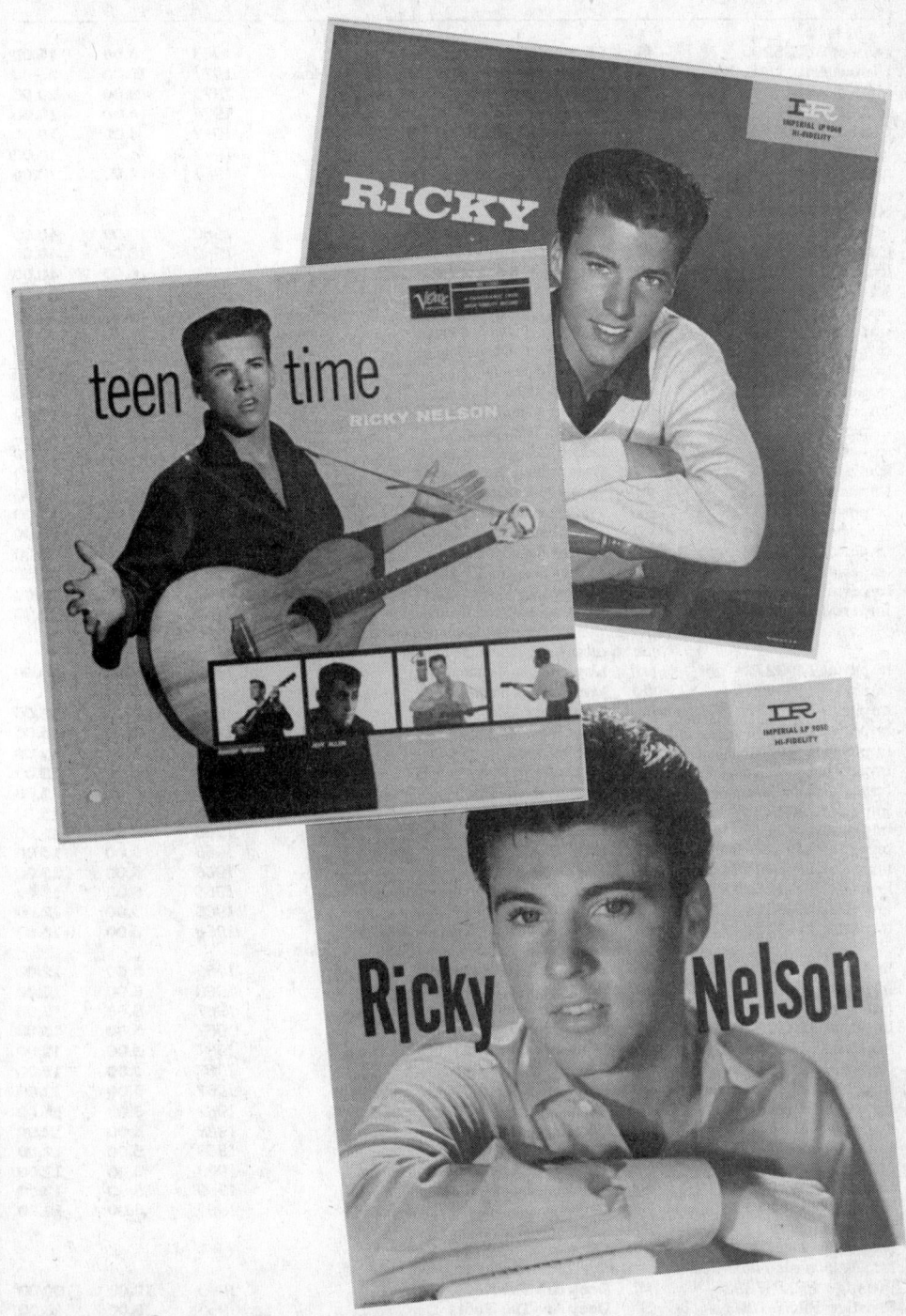

First: Ricky's first released album was Imperial 9048, Ricky. His second released album, Teen Time, containing all of his recordings for his original label, was not his album at all but a various artists compilation packaged to look like his album (it does contain all three of his 1957 Verve sides: "I'm Walking," "A Teenage Romance," and "You're My One And Only Love," hits all). His third released album, really his second real album, was Imperial 9050, Ricky Nelson. Does that answer everyone's questions?

Label & Catalog #		Title	Year	VG+	NM
Sunset SUS-5205	(S)	I Need You	1968	6.00	15.00
United Arts. UAS-960	(M)	Legendary Masters (2 LPs. Brown label)	1971	10.00	25.00
MCA 2-4004	(S)	Rick Nelson Country (2 LPs)	1973	8.00	20.00
MCA 383	(S)	Windfall	1974	4.00	10.00
Capitol SOO-12109	(S)	Playing To Win	197?	4.00	10.00
Epic KE-34420	(S)	Intakes	1977	4.00	10.00
Epic 3E-36868	(S)	Four You	1981	4.00	10.00

NELSON, SANDY

Label & Catalog #		Title	Year	VG+	NM
Imperial LP-9105	(M)	Sandy Nelson Plays Teen Beat	1960	16.00	40.00
Imperial LP-9136	(M)	He's A Drummer Boy	1962	16.00	40.00
Imperial LP-9159	(M)	Let There Be Drums	1962	16.00	40.00
Imperial LP-9168	(M)	Drums Are My Beat	1962	8.00	20.00
Imperial LP-12083	(P)	Drums Are My Beat	196?	10.00	25.00
Imperial LP-9189	(M)	Drummin' Up A Storm	1962	8.00	20.00
Imperial LP-12189	(S)	Drummin' Up A Storm	1962	10.00	25.00
Imperial LP-9202	(M)	Golden Hits	1962	8.00	20.00
Imperial LP-12202	(P)	Golden Hits	1962	10.00	25.00
Imperial LP-9203	(M)	On The Wild Side	1962	8.00	20.00
Imperial LP-12203	(S)	On The Wild Side	1962	10.00	25.00
Imperial LP-9204	(M)	Compelling Percussion	1962	8.00	20.00
Imperial LP-12204	(S)	Compelling Percussion	1962	10.00	25.00
Imperial LP-9215	(M)	Teenage House Party	1962	12.00	30.00
Imperial LP-9224	(M)	The Best Of The Beats	1963	6.00	15.00
Imperial LP-12224	(S)	The Best Of The Beats	1963	8.00	20.00
Imperial LP-9249	(M)	Sandy Nelson Plays	1963	6.00	15.00
Imperial LP-12249	(S)	Sandy Nelson Plays	1963	8.00	20.00
Imperial LP-9258	(M)	Be True To Your School	1963	6.00	15.00
Imperial LP-12258	(S)	Be True To Your School	1963	8.00	20.00

— Original Imperial mono albums above have black labels with stars on top; stereo albums have black labels with silver print.—

Label & Catalog #		Title	Year	VG+	NM
Imperial LP-9272	(M)	Live! In Las Vegas	1964	8.00	20.00
Imperial LP-12272	(E)	Live! In Las Vegas	1964	6.00	15.00
Imperial LP-9278	(M)	Teen Beat '65	1965	5.00	12.00
Imperial LP-12278	(S)	Teen Beat '65	1965	6.00	15.00
Imperial LP-9283	(M)	Drum Discotheque	1965	5.00	12.00
Imperial LP-12283	(S)	Drum Discotheque	1965	6.00	15.00
Imperial LP-9287	(M)	Drums A Go-Go	1965	5.00	12.00
Imperial LP-12287	(S)	Drums A Go-Go	1965	6.00	15.00
Imperial LP-9298	(M)	Boss Beat	1966	5.00	12.00
Imperial LP-12298	(S)	Boss Beat	1966	6.00	15.00
Imperial LP-9305	(M)	The In Beat	1966	5.00	12.00
Imperial LP-12305	(S)	The In Beat	1966	6.00	15.00
Imperial LP-9314	(M)	Superdrums	1966	5.00	12.00
Imperial LP-12314	(S)	Superdrums	1966	6.00	15.00

— Imperial albums above have black & pink labels.—

Label & Catalog #		Title	Year	VG+	NM
Imperial LP-9329	(M)	Beat That #!!@* Drum	1966	5.00	12.00
Imperial LP-12329	(S)	Beat That #!!@* Drum	1966	6.00	15.00
Imperial LP-9340	(M)	Cheetah Beat	1967	5.00	12.00
Imperial LP-12340	(S)	Cheetah Beat	1967	6.00	15.00
Imperial LP-9345	(M)	The Beat Goes On	1967	5.00	12.00
Imperial LP-12345	(S)	The Beat Goes On	1967	6.00	15.00
Imperial LP-9362	(M)	Soul Drums	1967	5.00	12.00
Imperial LP-12362	(S)	Soul Drums	1967	6.00	15.00
Imperial LP-12367	(S)	Boogaloo Beat	1968	5.00	12.00
Imperial LP-12400	(S)	Rock And Roll Revival	1968	5.00	12.00
Imperial LP-12424	(S)	Rebirth Of The Beat	1969	5.00	12.00
Imperial LP-12439	(S)	Manhattan Spiritual	1969	5.00	12.00
Imperial LP-12451	(S)	Groovy	1969	5.00	12.00

NELSON, TRACY

Ms. Nelson also recorded as a member of Earth Opera.

Label & Catalog #		Title	Year	VG+	NM
Prestige PRLP-7393	(M)	Deep Are The Roots	1965	12.00	30.00
Prestige PRST-7393	(S)	Deep Are The Roots	1965	16.00	40.00
Prestige PRST-7726	(S)	Deep Are The Roots	1969	10.00	25.00
		(Prestige 7726 is a reissue of 7393.)			
Reprise MS-2054	(S)	Mother Earth	1972	4.00	10.00

Label & Catalog #		Title	Year	VG+	NM
NELSON, WILLIE					
Liberty LRP-3238	(M)	**And Then I Wrote**	1962	16.00	40.00
Liberty LST-7238	(S)	**And Then I Wrote**	1962	20.00	50.00
Liberty LRP-3308	(M)	**Here's Willie Nelson**	1963	16.00	40.00
Liberty LST-7308	(S)	**Here's Willie Nelson**	1963	20.00	50.00
RCA Victor LPM-3418	(M)	**Country Willie: His Own Songs**	1965	10.00	25.00
RCA Victor LSP-3418	(S)	**Country Willie: His Own Songs**	1965	12.00	30.00
RCA Victor LPM-3528	(M)	**Country Favorites, Willie Nelson Style**	1966	10.00	25.00
RCA Victor LSP-3528	(S)	**Country Favorites, Willie Nelson Style**	1966	12.00	30.00
RCA Victor LPM-3659	(M)	**Live Country Music Concert**	1966	10.00	25.00
RCA Victor LSP-3659	(S)	**Live Country Music Concert**	1966	12.00	30.00
RCA Victor LPM-3748	(M)	**Make Way For Willie Nelson**	1967	12.00	30.00
RCA Victor LSP-3748	(S)	**Make Way For Willie Nelson**	1967	10.00	25.00
RCA Victor LPM-3858	(M)	**The Party's Over**	1967	12.00	30.00
RCA Victor LSP-3858	(S)	**The Party's Over**	1967	10.00	25.00
RCA Victor LPM-3937	(M)	**Texas In My Soul**	1968	40.00	100.00
RCA Victor LSP-3937	(S)	**Texas In My Soul**	1968	10.00	25.00
		— Original RCA Victor albums above have black labels.—			
RCA Victor LSP-4057	(S)	**Good Times**	1968	6.00	15.00
RCA Victor LSP-4111	(S)	**My Own Peculiar Way**	1969	6.00	15.00
RCA Victor LSP-4294	(S)	**Both Sides Now**	1970	6.00	15.00
RCA Victor LSP-4404	(S)	**Laying My Burdens Down**	1970	6.00	15.00
		— Original RCA Victor albums above have orange labels on non-flexible vinyl.—			
RCA Victor LSP-4489	(S)	**Willie Nelson And Family**	1971	5.00	12.00
RCA Victor LSP-4568	(S)	**Yesterday's Wine**	1971	5.00	12.00
RCA Victor LSP-4653	(S)	**The Words Don't Fit The Picture**	1971	5.00	12.00
RCA Victor LSP-4760	(S)	**The Willie Way**	1972	5.00	12.00
		— Original RCA Victor albums above have orange labels.—			
Columbia PAL-35305	(DJ)	**Stardust** *(Picture disc)*	1978	12.00	30.00
Columbia HC-43482	(S)	**Red Headed Stranger** *(Half-speed master)*	1982	10.00	30.00
Columbia HC-45305	(S)	**Stardust** *(Half-speed master)*	1982	25.00	75.00
Columbia HC-47951	(S)	**Always On My Mind** *(Half-speed master)*	1982	13.00	40.00
Columbia HC-48248	(S)	**Tougher Than Leather** *(Half-speed master)*	1983	13.00	40.00
Columbia CX-38258	(DJ)	**Always On My Mind** *(Picture disc)*	1983	13.00	40.00
Columbia 9C9-39943	(S)	**Always On My Mind** *(Picture disc)*	1983	4.00	10.00
Columbia XSM-171010	(DJ)	**Willie Nelson And Family** *(Picture disc)*	1983	6.00	15.00
NEON PHILHARMONIC					
Warner Bros. WS-1769	(S)	**Moth Confesses**	1969	8.00	20.00
Warner Bros. WS-1804	(S)	**Neon Philharmonic**	1969	6.00	15.00
NEP-TUNES, THE					
Family FLP-152	(M)	**Surfer's Holiday**	1963	14.00	35.00
Family SFLP-552	(S)	**Surfer's Holiday**	1963	20.00	50.00
NERVOUS KATS, THE					
Emma	(M)	**The Nervous Kats**	196?	40.00	100.00
NESMITH, MICHAEL					
Nesmith was formerly a member of The Monkees. Refer to Wichita Train Whistle.					
RCA Victor LSP-4371	(S)	**Magnetic South**	1970	12.00	30.00
RCA Victor LSP-4415	(S)	**Loose Salute**	1970	10.00	25.00
RCA Victor LSP-4497	(S)	**Nevada Fighter**	1971	10.00	25.00
RCA Victor LSP-4563	(S)	**Tantamount To Treason**	1971	10.00	25.00
RCA Victor LSP-4696	(S)	**And The Hits Just Keep On Comin'**	1972	10.00	25.00
Pacific Arts 7-101	(S)	**The Prison** *(Box with booklet)*	1978	16.00	40.00
Pacific Arts 7-101	(S)	**The Prison** *(Standard cover)*	1978	8.00	20.00
Pacific Arts 7-106	(S)	**Michael Nesmith Compilation**	1978	8.00	20.00
Pacific Arts 7-107	(S)	**From A Radio Engine To The Photon Wing**	1978	8.00	20.00
Pacific Arts 7-116	(S)	**And The Hits Just Keep On Comin'**	1978	8.00	20.00
Pacific Arts 7-117	(S)	**Pretty Much Your Standard Ranch Stash**	1978	8.00	20.00
Pacific Arts 7-118	(S)	**Live At The Palais**	1978	8.00	20.00
Pacific Arts 7-130	(S)	**Infinite Rider On The Big Dogma**	1979	8.00	20.00
Pacific Arts	(DJ)	**The Michael Nesmith Radio Special**	1979	16.00	40.00
NETHERWORLD					
R.E.M. 4441	(S)	**Netherworld**	1981	30.00	75.00

One of the most interesting of all cover designs is The New Tweedy Brothers, a six-sided "cube" printed with a silver foil finish. This finish and the size of the jacket make the likelihood of finding it in Near Mint condition extremely difficult. A copy such as the one above, with its dog-eared corners, is better than what many collectors have had to settle for to fit this record into their collection.

Label & Catalog #		Title	Year	VG+	NM
NEVILLE, AARON					
Par-Lo LP-1	(M)	Tell It Like It Is	1967	20.00	50.00
Par-Lo LP-1	(S)	Tell It Like It Is	1967	60.00	150.00
Minit LP-40007	(M)	Like It 'Tis	1967	10.00	25.00
Minit LP-40007	(E)	Like It 'Tis	1967	8.00	20.00
NEW BIRTH					
RCA Victor APD1-0285	(Q)	It's Been A Long Time	1974	6.00	15.00
NEW COLONY SIX, THE					
Sentar LP-101	(M)	Breakthrough	1966	200.00	400.00
Sentar ST-3001	(M)	Colonization	1967	12.00	30.00
Sentar SST-3001	(S)	Colonization	1967	16.00	40.00
Mercury SR-61165	(S)	Revelations	1968	8.00	20.00
Mercury SR-61228	(S)	Attacking A Straw Man	1969	8.00	20.00
NEW DAWN					
Hoot GR70-4569	(M)	There's A New Dawn	1969	200.00	400.00
NEW DIMENSIONS, THE					
Sutton SU-331	(M)	Deuces And Eights	1963	14.00	35.00
Sutton SSU-331	(S)	Deuces And Eights	1963	20.00	50.00
Sutton SU-332	(M)	Surf 'N' Bongos	1963	10.00	25.00
Sutton SSU-332	(S)	Surf 'N' Bongos	1963	16.00	40.00
Sutton SU-336	(M)	Soul Surf	1964	10.00	25.00
Sutton SSU-336	(S)	Soul Surf	1964	16.00	40.00
NEW HIGH, A					
Tempo Two T-2	(S)	Dallas, 1971	1972	20.00	50.00
NEW HOPE					
Jamie LPS-3034	(S)	To Understand Is To Love	1970	8.00	20.00
NEW LEGION ROCK SPECTACULAR, THE					
Spectacular SPLP-7777	(S)	Wild Ones!	197?	30.00	75.00
NEW LOST CITY RAMBLERS, THE					

The NLCR were John Cohen, Mike Seeger and Tom Paley, replaced by Tracy Schwarz in 1962.

Folkways FA-2395	(M)	The New Lost City Ramblers, Volume 1	1960	12.00	30.00
Folkways FA-2396	(M)	The New Lost City Ramblers, Volume 2	1960	12.00	30.00
Folkways FA-2397	(M)	The New Lost City Ramblers, Volume 3	1960	12.00	30.00
Folkways FA-2398	(M)	The New Lost City Ramblers, Volume 4	1960	12.00	30.00
Folkways FA-2399	(M)	The New Lost City Ramblers, Volume 5	1960	12.00	30.00
Folkways FA-2491	(M)	The New Lost City Ramblers	1964	10.00	25.00
Folkways FA-2492	(M)	String Band Instrumentals	1964	10.00	25.00
Folkways FA-2494	(M)	Songs Of The New Lost City Ramblers	1965	10.00	25.00
Folkways FA-2496	(M)	Rural Delivery No. 1	1965	10.00	25.00
Folkways FA-5264	(M)	Songs Of The Depression	1965	10.00	25.00
Verve/Folkways FV-9003	(M)	Rural Delivery No. 1	1965	6.00	15.00
Verve/Folkways FVS-9003	(S)	Rural Delivery No. 1	1965	8.00	20.00
Verve/Folkways FT-3018	(M)	Remembrances	1967	6.00	15.00
Verve/Folkways FTS-3018	(S)	Remembrances	1967	8.00	20.00
NEW RIDERS OF THE PURPLE SAGE, THE					
Columbia CQ-32450	(Q)	Adventures Of Panama Red	1974	6.00	15.00
Relix 2025	(S)	Vintage NRPS (Picture disc)	1987	2.00	10.00
NEW STRANGERS, THE					
Folklore FRLP-14027	(M)	Meet The New Strangers	1964	8.00	20.00
Folklore FRST-14027	(S)	Meet The New Strangers	1964	10.00	25.00
NEW TWEEDY BROTHERS, THE					
Ridon 234	(S)	The New Tweedy Brothers	196?	500.00	Rare
		(Issued in an oversized, hexagonal cover designed to look like an acid laced sugar cube, only a few of which exist today! Near Mint copies have a suggested value of $1,000-1,500.)			
Ridon 234	(S)	The New Tweedy Brothers (Without cover)	196?	150.00	300.00

Label & Catalog #		Title	Year	VG+	NM

NEW VAUDEVILLE BAND, THE

Label & Catalog #		Title	Year	VG+	NM
Fontana MGF-27560	(M)	Winchester Cathedral	1966	6.00	15.00
Fontana SRF-67560	(S)	Winchester Cathedral	1966	8.00	20.00
		("Winchester Cathedral," "Lili Marlene," "A Nightingale Sang In Berkeley Square," "Your Love Ain't What It Used To Be" and "That's All For Now, Sugar Baby" are rechanneled.)			
Fontana MGF-27688	(M)	The New Vaudeville Band On Tour	1967	6.00	15.00
Fontana SRF-67588	(P)	The New Vaudeville Band On Tour	1967	8.00	20.00
		("Thoroughly Modern Millie," "Peek-A-Boo," "Shirl;," "Sadie Moonshine" and "Amy" are rechanneled on this album.)			
RCA Victor LSP-4080	(S)	The Bliss Of Mrs. Blossom (Soundtrack)	1968	8.00	20.00

NEW WAVE, THE

Label & Catalog #		Title	Year	VG+	NM
Canterbury CLPS-1501	(S)	The New Wave	1967	6.00	15.00

NEW YORK DOLLS, THE

Both Dolls albums were originally issued with custom dolls labels and inner sleeves.

Label & Catalog #		Title	Year	VG+	NM
Mercury SRM-1-675	(S)	New York Dolls	1973	16.00	40.00
Mercury SRM-1-1001	(S)	Too Much, Too Soon	1974	16.00	40.00
—Original Mercury albums above have custom "doll" labels and inner sleeves.—					
Mercury SRM-1-675	(S)	New York Dolls	197?	6.00	15.00
Mercury SRM-1-1001	(S)	Too Much, Too Soon	197?	6.00	15.00

NEW YORK ROCK & ROLL ENSEMBLE, THE [THE NEW YORK ROCK ENSEMBLE]

The Ensemble features Michael Kamen.

Label & Catalog #		Title	Year	VG+	NM
Atco SD-33-240	(S)	New York Rock & Roll Ensemble	1968	6.00	15.00
Atco SD-33-294	(S)	Faithful Friends	1969	6.00	15.00
Atco SD-33-312	(S)	Reflections	1970	6.00	15.00
Columbia KC-30033	(S)	Roll Over	1970	5.00	12.00
Columbia KC-31317	(S)	Freedomburger	1972	5.00	12.00

NEWBEATS, THE

Larry Henley, Dean Mathis and Mark Mathis.

Label & Catalog #		Title	Year	VG+	NM
Hickory LP-120	(M)	Bread And Butter	1964	30.00	75.00
Hickory LPS-120	(S)	Bread And Butter	1964	See note below	
		(There is some doubt as to the existence of this stereo pressing.)			
Hickory DT-90701	(E)	Bread And Butter (Capitol Record Club)	1964	30.00	75.00
Hickory LP-122	(M)	Big Beat Sounds By The Newbeats	1965	20.00	50.00
Hickory LPS-122	(S)	Big Beat Sounds By The Newbeats	1965	30.00	75.00
Hickory LP-128	(M)	Run Baby Run	1965	20.00	50.00
Hickory LPS-128	(S)	Run Baby Run	1965	30.00	75.00

NEWMAN, BOB

Label & Catalog #		Title	Year	VG+	NM
Audio Lab AL-1536	(M)	The Kentucky Colonel	195?	30.00	75.00

NEWMAN, JIMMY C.

Label & Catalog #		Title	Year	VG+	NM
MGM E-3777	(M)	This Is Jimmy Newman	1959	8.00	20.00
MGM SE-3777	(S)	This Is Jimmy Newman	1959	10.00	25.00
MGM E-4045	(M)	Songs By Jimmy Newman	1962	6.00	15.00
MGM SE-4045	(S)	Songs By Jimmy Newman	1962	8.00	20.00
Decca DL-4221	(M)	Jimmy Newman	1962	5.00	12.00
Decca DL-74221	(S)	Jimmy Newman	1962	6.00	15.00
Decca DL-4398	(M)	Folk Songs Of The Bayou Country	1963	5.00	12.00
Decca DL-74398	(S)	Folk Songs Of The Bayou Country	1963	6.00	15.00
Decca DL-4748	(M)	Artificial Rose	1966	5.00	12.00
Decca DL-74748	(S)	Artificial Rose	1966	6.00	15.00
Decca DL-4781	(M)	Jimmy Newman Sings Country Songs	1966	5.00	12.00
Decca DL-74781	(S)	Jimmy Newman Sings Country Songs	1966	6.00	15.00
Dot DLP-3390	(M)	A Fallen Star	1966	6.00	15.00
Dot DLP-25390	(E)	A Fallen Star	1966	5.00	12.00
Dot DLP-3736	(M)	Country Crossroads	1966	5.00	12.00
Dot DLP-25736	(S)	Country Crossroads	1966	6.00	15.00

NEWMAN, PHYLLIS

Label & Catalog #		Title	Year	VG+	NM
London SES-97002	(S)	Those Were The Days	1969	8.00	20.00

NEWMAN, RANDY

Label & Catalog #		Title	Year	VG+	NM
Epic LN-24147	(M)	Peyton Place (TV Soundtrack)	1965	16.00	40.00
Epic BN-26147	(S)	Peyton Place (TV Soundtrack)	1965	20.00	50.00

Label & Catalog #		Title	Year	VG+	NM
Reprise RS-6286	(S)	**Randy Newman**	1968	8.00	20.00
		(Full color cover of Newman in the clouds.)			
Reprise RS-6286	(S)	**Randy Newman**	1969	6.00	15.00
		(Black & white close-up cover.)			
Reprise RS-6373	(S)	**12 Songs**	1970	6.00	15.00
Reprise PRO	(DJ)	**Randy Newman Live**	1970	10.00	25.00
		(Initially issued only as a promo to radio stations.)			
Reprise RS-6459	(S)	**Randy Newman Live**	1971	4.00	10.00
Reprise MS-2064	(S)	**Sail Away** *(With poster)*	1972	6.00	15.00
		(Original covers do not list the song titles on the back.)			
Reprise MS4-2193	(Q)	**Good Old Boys**	1974	6.00	15.00
NEWTON-JOHN, OLIVIA					
Kirshner	(S)	**Toomorrow** *(U.K. Soundtrack)*	1971	40.00	100.00
Sire 97012	(S)	**Toomorrow** *(U.K. Soundtrack)*	1971	40.00	100.00
Uni 73117	(S)	**If Not For You**	1971	16.00	40.00
MCA 3067	(S)	**Totally Hot** *(Picture disc)*	1979	8.00	20.00
MCA 16011	(S)	**Physical** *(Half-speed master)*	1981	8.00	25.00
Mobile Fidelity MFSL-40	(S)	**Totally Hot!**	1981	5.00	15.00
NEXT MORNING, THE					
Calla SC-2002	(S)	**The Next Morning**	1972	40.00	100.00
NICE, THE					
Immediate Z12-52004	(S)	**Thoughts of Emerlist Davjack**	1968	8.00	20.00
Immediate Z12-52020	(S)	**Ars Longa Vita Brevis**	1969	8.00	20.00
Immediate Z12-52022	(S)	**The Nice**	1969	8.00	20.00
Immediate Z12-52026	(S)	**Nice**	1971	8.00	20.00
Mercury SR-61295	(S)	**Five Bridges**	1970	6.00	15.00
Mercury SR-61324	(S)	**Elegy**	1971	6.00	15.00
Sire SASH-3710	(S)	**The Immediate Story** *(2 LPs)*	1975	6.00	15.00
NICHOLAS BROTHERS, THE					
Mercury MG-20355	(M)	**We Do Sing, Too**	195?	8.00	20.00
NICHOLS, MIKE, & ELAINE MAY					
Mercury MG-20376	(M)	**Improvisations To Music**	1959	16.00	40.00
Mercury OCM-2200	(M)	**An Evening With Mike Nichols & Elaine May**	1960	12.00	30.00
Mercury OCS-6200	(S)	**An Evening With Mike Nichols & Elaine May**	1960	16.00	40.00
Mercury MG-20680	(M)	**Examine Doctors**	1962	8.00	20.00
Mercury SR-60680	(S)	**Examine Doctors**	1962	10.00	25.00
Mercury MG-20997	(M)	**The Best Of Mike Nichols & Elaine May**	1965	6.00	15.00
Mercury SR-60997	(S)	**The Best Of Mike Nichols & Elaine May**	1965	8.00	20.00
NICHOLS, NICHELLE					
Ms Nichols was formerly a member of the U.S.S. Enterprise.					
Epic LN-24351	(M)	**Down To Earth**	1968	16.00	40.00
Epic BN-26351	(S)	**Down To Earth**	1968	20.00	50.00
NICKEL BAG, THE					
Kama Sutra KLPS-8066	(S)	**Doing Their Love Thing**	1968	8.00	20.00
NICKS, STEVIE					
Refer to Buckingham/Nicks; Fleetwood Mac.					
Mobile Fidelity MFSL-121	(S)	**Bella Donna**	1982	15.00	45.00
NICO					
Nico originally recorded with The Velvet Underground.					
Verve V-5032	(M)	**Chelsea Girl**	1967	12.00	30.00
Verve V6-5032	(S)	**Chelsea Girl**	1967	16.00	40.00
Elektra EKS-74029	(S)	**The Marble Index**	1968	10.00	25.00
Reprise RS-6424	(S)	**Desert Shore**	1970	8.00	20.00
Island ILPS-9311	(S)	**The End**	1975	6.00	15.00
NIGHT OWLS, THE					
Valmor 79	(M)	**Twisting The Oldies**	1962	20.00	50.00

Label & Catalog #		Title	Year	VG+	NM
NIGHT SHADOWS, THE					
Spectrum	(S)	The Square Root Of Two	1968	600.00	1,000.00
Hottrax 1414	(S)	The Square Root Of Two	1968	60.00	150.00
Hottrax 1430	(S)	Live At The Spot	1981	10.00	25.00
NIGHTCAPS, THE					
Vandan VRLP-8124	(M)	Wine, Wine, Wine	196?	60.00	150.00
NIGHTCRAWLERS, THE					
Kapp KL-1520	(M)	The Little Black Egg	1967	30.00	75.00
Kapp KS-3520	(E)	The Little Black Egg	1967	20.00	50.00
NIGHTHAWKS, THE					
Aladdin LP-101	(M)	Rock And Roll (Thick vinyl)	1974	100.00	250.00
NIELSEN, GERTRUDE					
Decca DL-5138 (10")	(M)	Gertrude Nielsen	1951	14.00	35.00
NILES, JOHN JACOB					
Camden CAL-219	(M)	American Folk And Gambling Songs	195?	8.00	20.00
Camden CAL-245	(M)	American Folk Songs	195?	8.00	20.00
Camden CAL-330	(M)	50th Anniversary Album	196?	6.00	15.00
Boone Tolliver BTR-22	(M)	American Folk Love Songs	196?	8.00	20.00
Boone Tolliver BTR-23	(M)	Ballads	196?	8.00	20.00
Tradition TRP-1023	(M)	I Wonder As I Wander	196?	6.00	15.00
NILSSON [HARRY NILSSON]					
Tower T-5095	(M)	Spotlight On Nilsson	1967	6.00	15.00
Tower ST-5095	(S)	Spotlight On Nilsson	1967	8.00	20.00
Tower T-5165	(M)	Spotlight On Nilsson	1967	5.00	12.00
Tower DT-5165	(E)	Spotlight On Nilsson	1967	4.00	10.00
		(Tower 5165 is a reissue of 5095.)			
RCA Victor LPM-3874	(M)	Pandemonium Shadow Show	1967	12.00	30.00
RCA Victor LSP-3874	(S)	Pandemonium Shadow Show	1967	8.00	20.00
RCA Victor	(DJ)	The True One	1967	60.00	150.00
		(Boxed set includes a copy of LPM-3874, two black & white glossy photos, a button, poster, stickers and bios.)			
RCA Victor LPM-3956	(M)	Aerial Ballet	1968	40.00	100.00
RCA Victor LSP-3956	(S)	Aerial Ballet	1968	8.00	20.00
		— Original RCA albums above have black labels.—			
RCA Victor LSO-1152	(S)	Skidoo (Soundtrack)	1968	10.00	25.00
United Arts. UAS-5198	(S)	Midnight Cowboy (Soundtrack)	1969	6.00	15.00
RCA Victor LSP-3956	(S)	Aerial Ballet	1969	6.00	15.00
RCA Victor LSP-4197	(S)	Harry	1969	6.00	15.00
RCA Victor LSP-4289	(S)	Nilsson Sings Newman	1969	8.00	20.00
RCA Victor LSP-4417	(S)	The Point (TV Soundtrack with booklet)	1971	8.00	20.00
		— Original RCA albums above have orange labels on non-flexible vinyl.—			
Musicor MS-2505	(S)	Early Times	1970	5.00	12.00
RCA Victor LSP-4543	(S)	Aerial Pandemonium Ballet	1971	5.00	12.00
		(RCA 4548 is a compilation of remixed tracks from 3874 and 3956 with additional vocals.)			
RCA SPS-33-567	(DJ)	Scatalogue (With insert)	197?	60.00	150.00
RCA Victor LSP-4515	(S)	Nilsson Schmilsson	1971	5.00	12.00
RCA Victor LSP-4717	(S)	Son Of Schmilsson	1972	5.00	12.00
RCA Victor APL1-0097	(S)	A Little Touch Of Schmilsson In The Night	1973	5.00	12.00
Rapple ABL1-0220	(S)	Son Of Dracula (Soundtrack)	1974	5.00	12.00
RCA Victor CPL1-0570	(S)	Pussy Cats (With John Lennon)	1974	8.00	20.00
RCA Victor APD1-0570	(Q)	Pussy Cats (With John Lennon)	1974	12.00	30.00
RCA Victor APD1-0817	(Q)	Duit On Mon Dei	1975	6.00	15.00
RCA Victor APD1-1031	(Q)	Sandman	1976	6.00	15.00
		— Original RCA albums above have orange labels.—			
NIMOY, LEONARD					
Mr. Nimoy was formerly a member of the U.S.S. Enterprise.					
Dot DLP-3794	(M)	Mr. Spock's Music From Outer Space	1967	20.00	50.00
Dot DLP-25794	(S)	Mr. Spock's Music From Outer Space	1967	24.00	60.00
Dot DLP-3835	(M)	Two Sides Of Leonard Nimoy	1968	16.00	40.00
Dot DLP-25835	(S)	Two Sides Of Leonard Nimoy	1968	12.00	30.00
Dot DLP-25883	(S)	The Way I Feel	1968	12.00	30.00

Label & Catalog #		Title	Year	VG+	NM
Dot DLP-25910	(S)	The Touch Of Leonard Nimoy	1969	12.00	30.00
Dot DLP-25966	(S)	The New World Of Leonard Nimoy	1969	16.00	40.00
Paramount 1030	(S)	Outer Space/Inner Mind	1970	12.00	30.00
Pickwick SPC-3199	(S)	Space Odyssey	197?	10.00	25.00
Sears SPS-491	(S)	Leonard Nimoy	197?	10.00	25.00
Caedmon TC-1520	(S)	H.G. Wells' "War Of The Worlds"	1976	16.00	40.00
NINA & FREDERIK					
Atco 33-119	(M)	Introducing The Fabulous Nina & Frederik	1960	8.00	20.00
Atco SD-33-119	(S)	Introducing The Fabulous Nina & Frederik	1960	10.00	25.00
Atco 33-154	(M)	Where Have All The Flowers Gone?	1963	8.00	20.00
Atco SD-33-154	(S)	Where Have All The Flowers Gone?	1963	10.00	25.00
Atco 33-217	(M)	Lovers Of The World Unite	1967	6.00	15.00
Atco SD-33-217	(S)	Lovers Of The World Unite	1967	8.00	20.00
1910 FRUITGUM COMPANY, THE					
Buddah BDS-5010	(S)	Simon Says	1968	6.00	15.00
Buddah BDS-5022	(S)	1, 2, 3 Red Light	1968	5.00	12.00
Buddah BDS-5036	(S)	Indian River	1969	4.00	10.00
Buddah BDS-5043	(S)	Hard Ride	1969	4.00	10.00
Buddah BDS-5057	(S)	Goody, Goody, Gumdrops	1969	4.00	10.00
1910 FRUITGUM COMPANY, THE / THE LEMON PIPERS					
Buddah BDS-5015	(S)	Checkmate	1968	4.00	10.00
98% AMERICAN MOM & APPLE PIE 1929 CRASH BAND, THE					
L.H.I. 12001	(S)	The 98% American Mom & Apple Pie Crash Band	1967	6.00	15.00
NINTH CREATION					
Rite Track RKA-01M	(S)	Bubble Gum	196?	6.00	15.00
NIRVANA					
Bell 6015	(S)	The Story Of Simon Simopath	1968	10.00	25.00
Bell 6024	(S)	All Of Us	1969	10.00	25.00
Metromedia 1018	(S)	Nirvana	1970	10.00	25.00
NITTY GRITTY DIRT BAND, THE [THE DIRT BAND]					
Liberty LRP-3501	(M)	The Nitty Gritty Dirt Band	1967	10.00	25.00
Liberty LST-7501	(S)	The Nitty Gritty Dirt Band	1967	12.00	30.00
Liberty LRP-3516	(M)	Ricochet	1967	10.00	25.00
Liberty LST-7516	(S)	Ricochet	1967	12.00	30.00
Liberty LST-7540	(S)	Rare Junk	1968	10.00	25.00
Liberty LST-7611	(S)	Alive	1969	8.00	20.00
Liberty LST-7642	(S)	Uncle Charlie & His Dog Teddy	1970	6.00	15.00
Liberty LST-7642	(DJ)	Uncle Charlie & His Dog Teddy Promo Pack	1970	30.00	75.00
United Arts. UAS-5553	(S)	All The Good Times	1971	4.00	10.00
United Arts. UAS-9801	(S)	Will The Circle Be Unbroken (3 LPs)	1972	5.00	12.00
United Arts. SP-117	(DJ)	The Nitty Gritty Dirt Band Interview	1975	8.00	20.00
United Arts. LA469	(DJ)	A Programmers Guide To Dream	1975	12.00	30.00
NITZSCHE, JACK					
Reprise R-6101	(M)	The Lonely Surfer	1963	30.00	75.00
Reprise RS-6101	(S)	The Lonely Surfer	1963	50.00	125.00
Reprise R-6115	(M)	Dance To The Hits Of The Beatles	1964	16.00	40.00
Reprise RS-6115	(S)	Dance To The Hits Of The Beatles	1964	20.00	50.00
Reprise R-6200	(M)	Chopin '66	1966	8.00	20.00
Reprise RS-6200	(S)	Chopin '66	1966	10.00	25.00
Reprise MS-2092	(S)	St. Giles Cripplegate	1972	8.00	20.00
NOBLES, CLIFF, & COMPANY					
Phil L.A. Of Soul 4001	(S)	The Horse	1968	20.00	50.00
Moon Shot 601	(S)	Pony The Horse	1969	10.00	25.00
NOLAND, TERRY					
Brunswick BL-54041	(M)	Terry Noland (With Buddy Holly on guitar)	1958	250.00	500.00
NOMADDS, THE					
Radex MLP-6521	(M)	The Nomadds	1965	150.00	300.00

Label & Catalog #		Title	Year	VG+	NM

NOONAN, STEVE

Elektra EKS-74017	(S)	Steve Noonan	1968	6.00	15.00

NORDINE, KEN

Decca DL-8550	(M)	Concert In The Sky	1957	20.00	50.00
Dot DLP-3075	(M)	Word Jazz	1957	20.00	50.00
Dot DLP-3096	(M)	Son Of Word Jazz	1958	14.00	35.00
Dot DLP-25096	(S)	Son Of Word Jazz	1958	20.00	50.00
Dot DLP-3115	(M)	Love Words	1958	14.00	35.00
Dot DLP-25115	(S)	Love Words	1958	20.00	50.00
Dot DLP-3142	(M)	My Baby	1958	14.00	35.00
Dot DLP-25142	(S)	My Baby	1958	20.00	50.00
Dot DLP-3196	(M)	Next!	1959	14.00	35.00
Dot DLP-25196	(S)	Next!	1959	20.00	50.00
Dot DLP-3301	(M)	Word Jazz, Volume 2	1960	14.00	35.00
Dot DLP-25301	(S)	Word Jazz, Volume 2	1960	20.00	50.00
Hamilton HLP-102	(M)	The Voice Of Love	1964	6.00	15.00
Hamilton HLS-102	(S)	The Voice Of Love	1964	8.00	20.00
Philips PHM-200-224	(M)	Colors	1966	10.00	25.00
Philips PHS-600-224	(S)	Colors	1966	14.00	35.00
Philips PHM-200-258	(M)	Twink	1967	10.00	25.00
Philips PHS-600-258	(S)	Twink	1967	14.00	35.00
Dot DLP-25880	(S)	Classic Collection/Best Of Word Jazz	1968	10.00	25.00
Snail	(S)	Stare With Your Ears	1979	6.00	15.00

NORMA JEAN

Norma Jean also recorded with Porter Wagoner.

RCA Victor LPM-2961	(M)	Let's Go All The Way	1964	6.00	15.00
RCA Victor LSP-2961	(S)	Let's Go All The Way	1964	8.00	20.00
RCA Victor LPM-3449	(M)	Pretty Miss Norma Jean	1965	6.00	15.00
RCA Victor LSP-3449	(S)	Pretty Miss Norma Jean	1965	8.00	20.00
RCA Victor LPM-3541	(M)	Please Don't Hurt Me	1966	6.00	15.00
RCA Victor LSP-3541	(S)	Please Don't Hurt Me	1966	8.00	20.00
RCA Victor LPM-3664	(M)	A Tribute To Kitty Wells	1966	6.00	15.00
RCA Victor LSP-3664	(S)	A Tribute To Kitty Wells	1966	8.00	20.00
RCA Victor LPM-3700	(M)	Norma Jean Sings Porter Wagoner	1967	10.00	25.00
RCA Victor LSP-3700	(S)	Norma Jean Sings Porter Wagoner	1967	8.00	20.00
RCA Victor LPM-3836	(M)	Jackson Ain't A Very Big Town	1967	10.00	25.00
RCA Victor LSP-3836	(S)	Jackson Ain't A Very Big Town	1967	8.00	20.00
RCA Victor LPM-3910	(M)	Heaven's Just A Prayer Away	1968	20.00	50.00
RCA Victor LSP-3910	(S)	Heaven's Just A Prayer Away	1968	6.00	15.00
		— Original RCA albums above have black labels.—			

NORMAN, LARRY

Larry was formerly a member of People.

Capitol ST-446	(S)	Upon This Rock	1969	16.00	40.00
Impact HWS-3121	(S)	Upon This Rock	1970	6.00	15.00
		(Impact 3121 is a reissue of Capitol 446.)			
One Way JC-7937	(S)	Street Level	1970	20.00	50.00
One Way JC-900	(S)	Bootleg *(Gatefold cover)*	1971	16.00	40.00
One Way JC-900	(S)	Bootleg *(Regular cover)*	1971	12.00	30.00
MGM SE-4942	(S)	So Long Ago / The Garden	1973	12.00	30.00
Verve V6-5092	(S)	Only Visiting This Planet *(Tri-fold cover)*	1972	10.00	25.00
Verve V6-5092	(S)	Only Visiting This Planet *(Gatefold cover)*	1972	12.00	30.00
Solid Rock SRA-2001	(S)	In Another Land	1976	6.00	15.00
Sunrise AB-777	(S)	Streams Of White Light	1977	8.00	20.00
Street Level 888-5	(S)	Only Visiting This Planet	1978	4.00	10.00
		(Street Level 888-5 is a reissue of Verve 5092.)			
Solid Rock SRA-2007	(S)	Something New Under The Sun	1981	6.00	15.00
Phydeaux BONE 777-6	(S)	Almost / So Long Ago / The Garden	1981	4.00	10.00
		(Phydeaux 777-6 is a reissue of MGM 4942.)			

NORTH, JAY

Kem LP-27	(M)	Look Who's Singing!	195?	30.00	75.00
Colpix CP-204	(M)	The Misadventures Of Dennis The Menace	196?	50.00	125.00
		(TV Soundtrack)			

NORTHERN FRONT, THE

(No label)	(M)	The Furniture Store	196?	30.00	75.00

Label & Catalog #		Title	Year	VG+	NM
NOSY PARKER					
(No label)	(S)	**Nosy Parker**	1975	80.00	200.00
NOTES FROM THE UNDERGROUND					
Vanguard VSD-6502	(S)	**Notes From The Underground**	1970	10.00	25.00
NOVA LOCAL, THE					
Decca DL-74977	(S)	**Nova 1**	1968	14.00	35.00
NOVELLS, THE					
Mother's MLPS-73	(S)	**That Did It!**	197?	12.00	30.00
NRBQ [THE NEW RHYTHM & BLUES QUINTET]					
Refer to Carl Perkins; Wildweeds.					
Columbia CS-9858	(S)	**NRBQ** *("360 Sound" label)*	1969	8.00	20.00
Kama Sutra KSBS-2045	(S)	**Scraps**	1972	8.00	20.00
Kama Sutra KSBS-2065	(S)	**Workshop**	1973	12.00	30.00
Annuit Coeptis 1001	(S)	**Scraps/Workshop** *(2 LPs)*	1976	6.00	15.00
Mercury SRM-1-3712	(S)	**NRBQ At Yankee Stadium**	1978	6.00	15.00
Red Rooster 101	(S)	**All Hopped Up**	1977	6.00	15.00
Red Rooster 3029	(S)	**All Hopped Up**	1979	4.00	10.00
Red Rooster 3030	(S)	**Kick Me Hard**	1979	4.00	10.00
Red Rooster 3048	(S)	**Tiddly Winks**	1980	4.00	10.00
Red Rooster 3055	(S)	**Scraps**	1982	4.00	10.00
Red Rooster 3066	(S)	**Tapdancin' Bats**	1983	4.00	10.00
Bearsville 23187	(S)	**Grooves In Orbit**	1983	4.00	10.00
NUCLEUS					
Mainstream S-6120	(S)	**Nucleus**	1969	6.00	15.00
NUGENT, TED					
Nugent was formerly a member of The Amboy Dukes.					
DiscReet DS-2181	(S)	**Call Of The Wild**	1974	5.00	12.00
Epic PEQ-34121	(Q)	**Free For All**	1976	6.00	15.00
Epic AS-99-607	(DJ)	**State Of Shock** *(Picture disc)*	1979	6.00	15.00
NUTTY SQUIRRELS, THE					
Hanover HML-8014	(M)	**The Nutty Squirrels**	1960	12.00	30.00
Columbia CL-1589	(M)	**Bird Watching**	1961	10.00	25.00
Columbia CS-8389	(S)	**Bird Watching**	1961	12.00	30.00
MGM E-4272	(M)	**A Hard Day's Night**	1964	10.00	25.00
MGM SE-4272	(S)	**A Hard Day's Night**	1964	12.00	30.00
NYE, LOUIS					
Riverside 842	(M)	**Heigh-Ho, Madison Avenue**	196?	8.00	20.00
Signature SM-2004	(M)	**Man On The Street**	196?	8.00	20.00
United Arts. UAL-4089	(M)	**Here's Nye In You Eye**	196?	8.00	20.00
NYRO, LAURA					
Verve/Folkways FT-3020	(M)	**More Than A New Discovery**	1967	12.00	30.00
Verve/Folkways FTS-3020	(S)	**More Than A New Discovery**	1967	16.00	40.00
		(The back cover has liner notes.)			
Verve/Forecast FT-3020	(M)	**First Songs**	1968	8.00	20.00
Verve/Forecast FTS-3020	(S)	**First Songs**	1968	8.00	20.00
		(Forecast 3020 is a reissue of Folkways 3020. Back cover has lyrics.)			
Verve/Forecast FTS-3029	(S)	**Laura Nyro**	1968	*Unreleased*	
Columbia CL-2826	(M)	**Eli And The 13th Confession**	1968	12.00	30.00
Columbia CS-9626	(S)	**Eli And The 13th Confession**	1968	6.00	15.00
Columbia CS-9737	(S)	**New York Tendaberry** *(Includes a booklet)*	1969	8.00	20.00
Columbia CS-9737	(S)	**New York Tendaberry** *(Without booklet)*	1969	6.00	15.00
		— Original Columbia albums above have "360 Sound" on the bottom of the label.—			
Columbia KC-30259	(S)	**Christmas And The Beads Of Sweat**	1970	4.00	10.00
Columbia KC-30987	(S)	**Gonna Take A Miracle**	1971	4.00	10.00
Columbia KC-31410	(S)	**The First Songs**	1971	4.00	10.00
Columbia JG-34331	(DJ)	**Seasons Of Light** *(2 LPs)*	1976	20.00	50.00
		(Issued in a plain cardboard jacket. This album was edited down to a single LP for commercial release in 1977.)			

O' BRIEN, HUGH

ABC-Paramount 203	(M)	Wyatt Earp Sings	1957	30.00	75.00

O' CONNELL, HELEN

Vik LX-1093	(M)	Green Eyes	1957	16.00	40.00
Cameo C-1045	(M)	An Era Reborn	1963	6.00	15.00
Cameo CS-1045	(S)	An Era Reborn	1963	8.00	20.00

O' DAY, ANITA: *Refer to* GOLDMINE'S PRICE GUIDE TO COLLECTIBLE JAZZ ALBUM

O' DAY, MOLLY

Harmony HL-7299	(M)	The Unforgettable Molly O' Day	1963	8.00	20.00
Harmony HS-7299	(S)	The Unforgettable Molly O' Day	1963	6.00	15.00
Starday SLP-367	(M)	The Living Legend Of Country Music	1966	12.00	30.00

O' DELL, MAC

Audio Lab AL-1544	(M)	Hymns For The Country Folk	1960	40.00	100.00

O' HARA, MAUREEN

Columbia CL-1750	(M)	Her Favorite Irish Songs	1961	16.00	40.00
Columbia CS-8550	(S)	Her Favorite Irish Songs	1961	20.00	50.00

O' JAYS, THE

Imperial LP-9290	(M)	Comin' Through	1965	16.00	40.00
Imperial LP-12290	(S)	Comin' Through	1965	20.00	50.00
Minit LP-4008	(M)	Soul Sounds	1967	12.00	30.00
Minit LP-24008	(S)	Soul Sounds	1967	16.00	40.00
Bell 6014	(S)	Back On Top	1968	6.00	15.00
Sunset SUS-5222	(S)	Full Of Soul	1968	6.00	15.00
		(Sunset 5522 is a reissue of Imperial 12290.)			
United Arts. UAS-5655	(P)	The O' Jays' Greatest Hits	1972	4.00	10.00
Bell 6082	(S)	The O' Jays	1973	4.00	10.00
Stang 1024	(S)	The O' Jays Meet The Moments	1974	4.00	10.00
Kory 1006	(S)	The O' Jays	1977	4.00	10.00
Philadelphia Int. ASZ-140	(DJ)	Everything You Always Wanted To Hear	197?	5.00	12.00
Phila. Inter. PZQ-32408	(Q)	Ship Ahoy	1974	6.00	15.00
Phila. Inter. PZQ-32953	(Q)	The O' Jays Live In London	1974	6.00	15.00
Phila. Inter. PZQ-33807	(Q)	Family Reunion	1975	6.00	15.00

O' KAYSIONS, THE

ABC S-664	(S)	Girl Watcher	1968	16.00	40.00
		("Girl Watcher" is rechanneled on this album.)			

O' KEEFE, DANNY

Danny O' Keefe originally recorded with Calliope.

Cotilion SD-9036	(S)	Danny O' Keefe	1970	6.00	15.00

OAK RIDGE BOYS, THE [THE OAK RIDGE QUARTET]

Cadence CLP-3019	(M)	The Oak Ridge Quartet	1959	30.00	75.00
Warner Bros. W-1497	(M)	The Oak Ridge Boys	1963	10.00	25.00
Warner Bros. WS-1497	(S)	The Oak Ridge Boys	1963	12.00	30.00
Warner Bros. W-1521	(M)	Folk Minded Spirituals	1963	10.00	25.00
Warner Bros. WS-1521	(S)	Folk Minded Spirituals	1963	12.00	30.00
Skylite M-6020	(M)	The Oak Ridge Boys Sing For You	1964	10.00	25.00
Skylite M-6030	(M)	I Wouldn't Take Nothing For My Journey Now	1965	8.00	20.00
Skylite S-6030	(S)	I Wouldn't Take Nothing For My Journey Now	1965	10.00	25.00

Label & Catalog #		Title	Year	VG+	NM
Starday SLP-356	(M)	The Sensational Oak Ridge Boys	1965	10.00	25.00
Skylite M-6040	(M)	The Solid Gospel Sound Of The Oak Ridge Boys	1966	8.00	20.00
Skylite S-6040	(S)	The Solid Gospel Sound Of The Oak Ridge Boys	1966	10.00	25.00
Skylite M-6045	(M)	River Of Love	1967	8.00	20.00
Skylite S-6045	(S)	River Of Love	1967	10.00	25.00
United Arts. UAL-3554	(M)	The Oak Ridge Boys At Their Best	1966	8.00	20.00
United Arts. UAS-6554	(S)	The Oak Ridge Boys At Their Best	1966	10.00	25.00
Columbia PC-33935	(S)	The Oak Ridge Boys	1976	6.00	15.00
MCA 51247	(DJ)	Sail Away (Picture disc)	1979	20.00	50.00

OBJECTS, THE
(No label)	(S)	Live At The Greatwood Cafe	1980	24.00	60.00

OBOLER, ARCH
Capitol T-1763	(M)	Drop Dead! An Exercise In Horror	1962	6.00	15.00
Capitol ST-1763	(S)	Drop Dead! An Exercise In Horror	1962	8.00	20.00

OCHS, PHIL
Elektra EKL-269	(M)	All The News That's Fit To Sing	1964	10.00	25.00
Elektra EKS-7269	(S)	All The News That's Fit To Sing	1964	12.00	30.00
Elektra EKL-287	(M)	I Ain't Marching Anymore	1965	10.00	25.00
Elektra EKS-7287	(S)	I Ain't Marching Anymore	1965	12.00	30.00
Elektra EKL-310	(M)	Phil Ochs In Concert	1965	10.00	25.00
Elektra EKS-7310	(S)	Phil Ochs In Concert	1965	12.00	30.00
A&M LP-133	(M)	Pleasures Of The Harbor	1967	8.00	20.00
A&M SP-4133	(S)	Pleasures Of The Harbor	1967	8.00	20.00
A&M SP-4148	(S)	Tape From California	1968	8.00	20.00
A&M SP-4181	(S)	Rehearsals For Retirement	1969	8.00	20.00
A&M SP-4253	(S)	Phil Ochs' Greatest Hits	1970	8.00	20.00
—Original A&M albums above have brown labels.—					
A&M SP-4599	(S)	Chords Of Fame (2 LPs)	1976	6.00	15.00

OCTOBER COUNTRY
Epic BN-26381	(S)	October Country	1968	8.00	20.00

ODA
Loud A0011	(S)	Oda	1974	200.00	400.00

ODETTA
Fantasy 3-15 (10")	(M)	Odetta And Lary	1955	16.00	40.00
Fantasy F-3252	(M)	Odetta (Dark red vinyl)	1957	20.00	50.00
Fantasy F-3252	(M)	Odetta	1958	12.00	30.00
Tradition TRP-1010	(M)	Ballads And Blues	1956	12.00	30.00
Tradition TRP-1025	(M)	Odetta At The Gate Of Horn	1957	12.00	30.00
Vanguard VRS-9059	(M)	My Eyes Have Seen	1960	6.00	15.00
Vanguard VSD-72046	(S)	My Eyes Have Seen	1960	8.00	20.00
Vanguard VRS-9066	(M)	Ballads For Americans	1960	6.00	15.00
Vanguard VSD-72057	(S)	Ballads For Americans	1960	8.00	20.00
Vanguard VRS-9076	(M)	Odetta At Carnegie Hall	1961	6.00	15.00
Vanguard VSD-72072	(S)	Odetta At Carnegie Hall	1961	8.00	20.00
Vanguard VRS-2079	(M)	Christmas Spirituals	1961	6.00	15.00
Vanguard VSD-72079	(S)	Christmas Spirituals	1961	8.00	20.00
Riverside RLP-417	(M)	Odetta And The Blues	1962	6.00	15.00
Riverside RS-9417	(S)	Odetta And The Blues	1962	8.00	20.00
Vanguard VRS-2109	(M)	Odetta At Town Hall	1962	6.00	15.00
Vanguard VSD-72109	(S)	Odetta At Town Hall	1962	8.00	20.00
Vanguard VRS-2153	(M)	One Grain Of Sand	1963	6.00	15.00
Vanguard VSD-72153	(S)	One Grain Of Sand	1963	8.00	20.00
Vanguard VRS-3003	(M)	Odetta At Carnegie Hall	1964	5.00	12.00
Vanguard VSD-73003	(S)	Odetta At Carnegie Hall	1964	6.00	15.00
RCA Victor LPM-2573	(M)	Sometimes I Feel Like Crying	1962	6.00	15.00
RCA Victor LSP-2573	(S)	Sometimes I Feel Like Crying	1962	8.00	20.00
RCA Victor LPM-2643	(M)	Odetta Sings Folk Songs	1963	6.00	15.00
RCA Victor LSP-2643	(S)	Odetta Sings Folk Songs	1963	8.00	20.00
RCA Victor LPM-2792	(M)	It's A Mighty World	1964	6.00	15.00
RCA Victor LSP-2792	(S)	It's A Mighty World	1964	8.00	20.00

Label & Catalog #		Title	Year	VG+	NM
RCA Victor LPM-2923	(M)	Odetta Sings Of Many Things	1964	6.00	15.00
RCA Victor LSP-2923	(S)	Odetta Sings Of Many Things	1964	8.00	20.00
RCA Victor LPM-3324	(M)	Odetta Sings Dylan	1965	8.00	20.00
RCA Victor LSP-3324	(S)	Odetta Sings Dylan	1965	10.00	25.00
RCA Victor LPM-3457	(M)	Odetta In Japan	1966	6.00	15.00
RCA Victor LSP-3457	(S)	Odetta In Japan	1966	8.00	20.00
		— Original RCA albums above have black labels. —			
Verve/Forecast FV-3014	(M)	Give Me Your Hand	1967	6.00	15.00
Verve/Forecast FVS-3014	(S)	Give Me Your Hand	1967	8.00	20.00
Verve/Forecast FVS-3050	(S)	Odetta	1968	Unreleased	
Riverside 3007	(S)	Odetta Sings The Blues	1968	6.00	15.00
Fantasy 3252	(M)	Odetta And Larry	196?	6.00	15.00
Polydor 24-4048	(S)	Odetta Sings	1970	5.00	12.00

ODOM, ANDREW

BluesWay BLS-6055	(S)	Father Down The Road	197?	6.00	15.00

ODYSSEY

Organic ORG-1	(M)	Odyssey	196?	500.00	800.00

OHIO EXPRESS, THE

Cameo C-20,000	(M)	Beg, Borrow And Steal	1968	12.00	30.00
Cameo CS-20,000	(S)	Beg, Borrow And Steal	1968	16.00	40.00
Buddah BDS-5018	(S)	The Ohio Express	1968	6.00	15.00
Buddah BDS-5021	(S)	Salt Water Taffy	1968	6.00	15.00
Buddah BDS-5026	(S)	Chewy Chewy	1969	6.00	15.00
Buddah BDS-5037	(S)	Mercy	1969	6.00	15.00
Buddah BDS-5058	(P)	The Very Best Of The Ohio Express	1970	6.00	15.00

OHIO PLAYERS, THE

Capitol ST-192	(S)	Observations In Time	1969	12.00	30.00
Westbound 2015	(S)	Pain	1972	8.00	20.00
Westbound 2017	(S)	Pleasure	1973	8.00	20.00
Westbound 2021	(S)	Ecstasy	1973	8.00	20.00
Westbound 1003	(S)	Climax	1974	8.00	20.00
Westbound 1005	(S)	The Ohio Players' Greatest Hits	1975	6.00	15.00
Westbound 211	(S)	Rattlesnake	1975	6.00	15.00

OLAY, RUTH: *Refer to GOLDMINE'S PRICE GUIDE TO COLLECTIBLE JAZZ ALBUM*

OLD & IN THE WAY
Features Jerry Garcia of The Grateful Dead.

Round RX-103	(S)	Old And In The Way	1975	10.00	25.00

OLDFIELD, MIKE

Virgin HE-44116	(S)	Tubular Bells (Half-speed master)	198?	10.00	25.00

OLDHAM ORCHESTRA, ANDREW

London LL-3457	(M)	The Rolling Stones Songbook	1965	30.00	75.00
London PS-457	(S)	The Rolling Stones Songbook	1965	40.00	100.00
Parrot PA-61003	(M)	East Meets West	1965	20.00	50.00
Parrot PAS-71003	(S)	East Meets West	1965	30.00	75.00

OLENN, JOHNNY

Liberty LRP-3029	(M)	Just Rollin' With Johnny Olenn	1957	150.00	300.00

OLIVER & THE TWISTERS

Colpix CP-423	(M)	Look Who's Twistin' Everybody	1961	16.00	40.00

OLYMPICS, THE

Arvee A-423	(M)	Doin' The Hully Gully	1960	70.00	175.00
Arvee A-424	(M)	Dance By The Light Of The Moon	1961	50.00	125.00
Arvee A-429	(M)	Party Time	1961	50.00	125.00
Tri-Disc 1001	(M)	Do The Bounce	1963	20.00	50.00
Mirwood M-7003	(M)	Something Old, Something New	1966	12.00	30.00
Mirwood MS-7003	(S)	Something Old, Something New	1966	16.00	40.00
		(Conttains rerecorded versions of earlier hits.)			

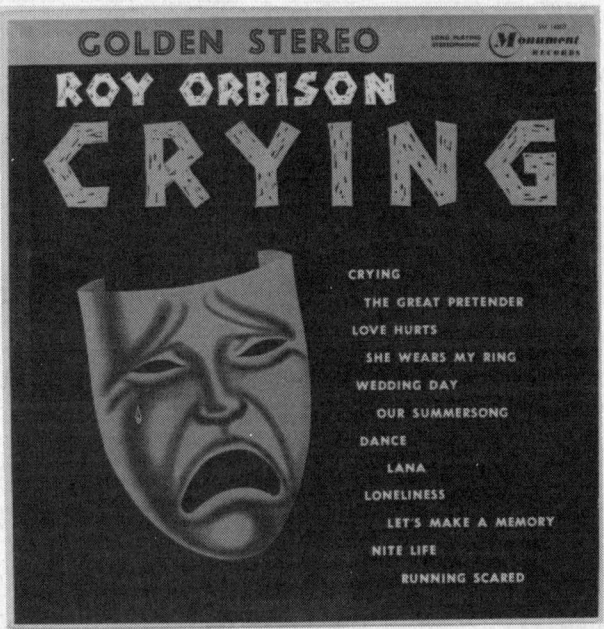

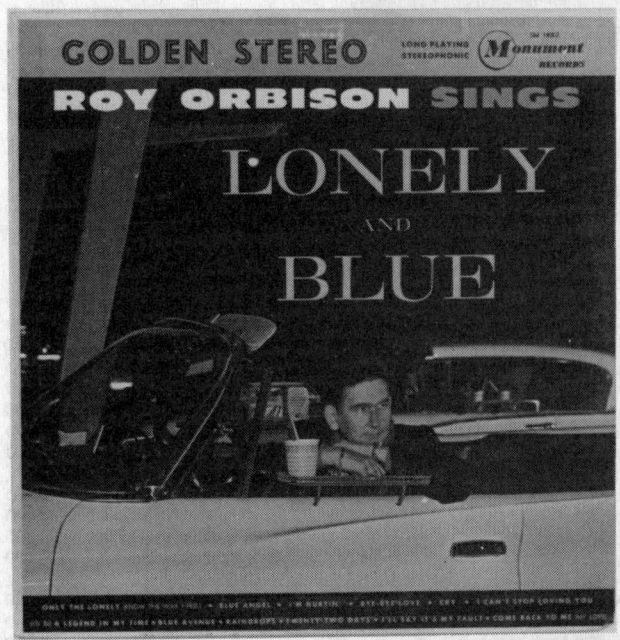

Stereo copies of Roy's first two Monument albums (creatively produced by Fred Foster and impeccably engineered by Bill Porter) have been difficult to find for decades. The recent interest paid them by the audiophile community, where they are often revered as the finest stereo pop recordings ever made, have pushed the prices way above their mono counterparts. Never a big seller during his life (only nine of his albums made the charts), he received a solitary RIAA Gold Record for his 1962 Greatest Hits compilation. In the wake of his death in 1989 two albums on Virgin, a hits package and his final studio recordings, Mystery Girl, *both went gold.*

Label & Catalog #		Title	Year	VG+	NM

OMNIBUS

| United Arts. UAS-6743 | (S) | Omnibus | 1970 | 6.00 | 15.00 |

ON THE SEVENTH DAY

| Mercury SR-61248 | (S) | On The Seventh Day | 1970 | 6.00 | 15.00 |

ONE

| Village | (S) | Creation Earth (With posters) | 1977 | 20.00 | 50.00 |

ONE

| Grunt FTR-1008 | (S) | Come | 1972 | 6.00 | 15.00 |

ONES, THE

| Ashwood House 1105 | (S) | The Ones | 196? | 500.00 | 1,000.00 |

ONO, YOKO

Ms. Ono also recorded with her husband, John Lennon, who co-produced her first three albums. Refer to Elephant's Memory; David Peel.

Apple SW-3373	(S)	Plastic Ono Band	1971	6.00	15.00
Apple SVBB-3380	(S)	Fly (2 LPs with poster)	1971	12.00	30.00
Apple SVBB-3380	(S)	Fly (2 LPs without poster)	1971	8.00	20.00
Apple SVBB-3399	(S)	Approximately Infinite Universe	1972	8.00	20.00
Apple SW-3412	(S)	Feeling The Space	1973	6.00	15.00

OPEN WINDOW

| Vanguard VSD-6515 | (S) | The Open Window | 1969 | 6.00 | 15.00 |

ORANG-UTAN

| Bell 6054 | (S) | Orang-Utan | 1971 | 16.00 | 40.00 |

ORANGE COLORED SKY

| Uni 73031 | (S) | Orange Colored Sky | 1968 | 12.00 | 30.00 |

ORANGE GROVE

| Somerset 34000 | (S) | Crystal Blue Persuasion | 1969 | 6.00 | 15.00 |

ORANGE WEDGE: Refer to WEDGE

ORBACH, JERRY

| MGM E-4056 | (M) | Off Broadway | 1962 | 6.00 | 15.00 |
| MGM SE-4056 | (S) | Off Broadway | 1962 | 8.00 | 20.00 |

ORBISON, ROY

For additional listing refer to Jerry Lee Lewis / Johnny Cash / Roy Orbison.

Sun SLP-1260	(M)	Roy Orbison At The Rockhouse	1961	300.00	500.00
Sun 113	(E)	The Original Sun Sound Of Roy Orbison	1969	8.00	20.00
Monument M-4002	(M)	Lonely And Blue	1961	40.00	100.00
Monument SM-14002	(S)	Lonely And Blue	1961	150.00	300.00
Monument M-4007	(M)	Crying	1962	30.00	75.00
Monument SM-14007	(S)	Crying	1962	80.00	200.00
Monument M-4009	(M)	Roy Orbison's Greatest Hits	1962	14.00	35.00
Monument SM-14009	(S)	Roy Orbison's Greatest Hits	1962	20.00	50.00
— Original Monument albums above have copper & white swirl labels.—					
Monument MLP-8000	(M)	Roy Orbison's Greatest Hits	1963	12.00	30.00
Monument SLP-18000	(S)	Roy Orbison's Greatest Hits	1963	16.00	40.00
Monument MLP-8003	(M)	In Dreams	1963	30.00	75.00
Monument SLP-18003	(S)	In Dreams	1963	60.00	150.00
— Original Monument albums above have rainbow & white swirl labels.—					
Monument MLP-8023	(M)	Early Orbison	1964	12.00	30.00
Monument SLP-18023	(S)	Early Orbison	1964	20.00	50.00
Monument MLP-8024	(M)	More Of Roy Orbison's Greatest Hits	1964	12.00	30.00
Monument SLP-18024	(S)	More Of Roy Orbison's Greatest Hits	1964	16.00	40.00
("It's Over" is in stereo on this album.)					
Monument MLP-8035	(M)	Orbisongs	1965	10.00	25.00
Monument SLP-18035	(S)	Orbisongs	1965	14.00	35.00
Monument MLP-8045	(M)	The Very Best Of Roy Orbison	1966	10.00	25.00
Monument SLP-18045	(S)	The Very Best Of Roy Orbison	1966	14.00	35.00
("It's Over" is rechanneled on this album.)					

— Original Monument albums above have green labels with a gold perimeter.—

Label & Catalog #		Title	Year	VG+	NM
Spectrum DLP-164	(M)	Orbiting With Roy Orbison	196?	6.00	15.00
Spectrum DLPS-164	(E)	Orbiting With Roy Orbison	196?	4.00	10.00
MGM E-4308	(M)	There Is Only One Roy Orbison	1965	8.00	20.00
MGM SE-4308	(S)	There Is Only One Roy Orbison	1965	10.00	25.00
MGM E-4322	(M)	The Orbison Way	1965	8.00	20.00
MGM SE-4322	(S)	The Orbison Way	1965	10.00	25.00
MGM E-4379	(M)	The Classic Roy Orbison	1966	8.00	20.00
MGM SE-4379	(S)	The Classic Roy Orbison	1966	10.00	25.00
MGM E-4424	(M)	Roy Orbison Sings Don Gibson	1966	8.00	20.00
MGM SE-4424	(S)	Roy Orbison Sings Don Gibson	1966	10.00	25.00
MGM E-4514	(M)	Cry Softly, Lonely One	1967	8.00	20.00
MGM SE-4514	(S)	Cry Softly, Lonely One	1967	10.00	25.00
MGM SE-4475	(S)	The Fastest Guitar Alive (Soundtrack)	1968	10.00	25.00
MGM SE-4636	(S)	The Many Moods Of Roy Orbison	1969	6.00	15.00
MGM SE-4659	(S)	The Great Songs Of Roy Orbison	1970	6.00	15.00
MGM SE-4683	(S)	Hank Williams The Roy Orbison Way	1970	8.00	20.00
MGM SE-4835	(S)	Roy Orbison Sings	1972	6.00	15.00
MGM SE-4867	(S)	Memphis	1972	6.00	15.00
MGM SE-4934	(S)	Milestones	1973	6.00	15.00
Monument KZG-31484	(S)	All-Time Greatest Hits (2 LPs)	1972	10.00	25.00
		("It's Over" is rechanneled on this album.)			
Mercury SRM-1-1045	(S)	I'm Still In Love With You	1975	5.00	12.00
Monument MG-7600	(S)	Regeneration	1976	5.00	12.00
Monument MP-8600	(S)	All-Time Greatest Hits (2 LPs)	1977	6.00	15.00
		("It's Over" is rechanneled on this album.)			
Monument MC-6619	(S)	Roy Orbison's Greatest Hits	1977	5.00	12.00
Monument MC-6620	(S)	In Dreams	1977	5.00	12.00
Monument MC-6621	(S)	More Of Roy Orbison's Greatest Hits	1977	5.00	12.00
		("It's Over" is in stereo on this album.)			
Monument MC-6622	(S)	The Very Best Of Roy Orbison	1977	5.00	12.00
		("It's Over" is rechanneled on this album.)			
Candlelite P2-12946	(S)	The Living Legend Of Roy Orbison (2 LPs)	197?	6.00	15.00

ORCHIDS, THE

| Roulette R-25169 | (M) | Twistin' At The Roundtable | 1962 | 10.00 | 25.00 |
| Roulette SR-25169 | (S) | Twistin' At The Roundtable | 1962 | 12.00 | 30.00 |

OREGON

| Vanguard 40031 | (Q) | Distant Hills | 1974 | 6.00 | 15.00 |

ORIENT EXPRESS, THE

| Mainstream 6117 | (S) | The Orient Express | 1969 | 16.00 | 40.00 |

ORIGINAL SURFARIS, THE

| Diplomat DS-2309 | (M) | Wheels-Shorts-Hot Rods | 1963 | 10.00 | 25.00 |
| Diplomat DS-2309 | (S) | Wheels-Shorts-Hot Rods | 1963 | 14.00 | 35.00 |

ORIGINALS, THE

Soul SS-716	(S)	Baby, I'm For Real	1969	8.00	20.00
Soul SS-724	(S)	Portrait Of The Originals	1970	8.00	20.00
Soul SS-729	(S)	Naturally Together	1970	8.00	20.00
Soul SS-734	(S)	Definitions	1973	6.00	15.00
Soul SS-740	(S)	The Game Called	1973	6.00	15.00
Soul SS-743	(S)	California Sunset	1974	Unreleased	

ORIOLES, THE
Refer to The Cadillacs; Sonny Til & The Orioles.

| Parker PLP-816 | (M) | Modern Sounds Of The Orioles | 1962 | 30.00 | 75.00 |
| Parker PLP-816S | (S) | Modern Sounds Of The Orioles | 1962 | 80.00 | 200.00 |

ORION

| Sun Int. 1012 | (S) | Orion Reborn (Coffin cover. Gold vinyl) | 1978 | 6.00 | 15.00 |

ORION, P.J., & THE MAGNATES

| Magnate 122459 | (M) | P.J. Orion And The Magnates | 196? | 50.00 | 125.00 |

ORLANDO, TONY

| Epic LN-611 | (M) | Bless You And 11 Other Great Hits | 1961 | 12.00 | 30.00 |
| Epic BN-611 | (S) | Bless You And 11 Other Great Hits | 1961 | 16.00 | 40.00 |

Label & Catalog #		Title	Year	VG+	NM
ORLONS, THE					
Cameo C-1020	(M)	The Wah Watusi	1962	20.00	50.00
Cameo C-1033	(M)	All The Hits	1962	20.00	50.00
Cameo C-1041	(M)	South Street	1963	20.00	50.00
Cameo C-1054	(M)	Not Me	1963	20.00	50.00
Cameo C-1061	(M)	Biggest Hits	1963	20.00	50.00
Cameo C-1073	(M)	Down Memory Lane	1963	20.00	50.00
ORLONS, THE / THE DOVELLS					
Cameo C-1067	(M)	Golden Hits Of The Orlons & The Dovells	1963	20.00	50.00
ORPHAN EGG					
Carole CARS-8004	(S)	Orphan Egg	1968	16.00	40.00
American Inter. ST-A-1033	(S)	The Cycle Savages (Soundtrack)	1970	16.00	40.00
ORPHANN					
O.M.I. M-70021	(S)	Up For Adoption	1977	30.00	75.00
ORPHEUS					
MGM SE-4524	(S)	Orpheus	1968	8.00	20.00
MGM SE-4569	(S)	Ascending	1968	8.00	20.00
MGM SE-4599	(S)	Joyful	1969	8.00	20.00
OSBORNE, JIMMY					
Audio Lab AL-1527	(M)	Singing Songs He Wrote	1959	30.00	75.00
King 730	(M)	The Legendary Jimmy Osborne	1961	16.00	40.00
King 782	(M)	Golden Harvest, Volume 3	1962	16.00	40.00
King 892	(M)	The Very Best Of Jimmy Osborne	1964	16.00	40.00
OSBORNE, MARY: Refer to GOLDMINE'S PRICE GUIDE TO COLLECTIBLE JAZZ ALBUMS					
OSBORNE BROTHERS, THE					
MGM E-3734	(M)	Country Pickin' And Hillside Singin'	1959	16.00	40.00
MGM E-4018	(M)	Blue Grass Music	1959	12.00	30.00
Decca DL-4602	(M)	Voices In Bluegrass	1965	6.00	15.00
Decca DL-74602	(S)	Voices In Bluegrass	1965	8.00	20.00
Decca DL-4767	(M)	Up This Hill And Down	1966	6.00	15.00
Decca DL-74767	(S)	Up This Hill And Down	1966	8.00	20.00
Decca DL-4903	(M)	Modern Sounds Of Bluegrass Music	1967	6.00	15.00
Decca DL-74903	(S)	Modern Sounds Of Bluegrass Music	1967	8.00	20.00
Decca DL-74993	(S)	Yesterday, Today & The Osborne Brothers	1968	6.00	15.00
OSBOURNE, OZZY					
Jet AS-99-1372	(DJ)	Diary Of A Madman (Picture disc)	1981	8.00	20.00
Epic 8Z8-37640	(EP)	Mr. Crowley Live (Picture disc)	1981	4.00	10.00
OSMOND, MARIE					
MGM SE-4910	(S)	Paper Roses	1973	8.00	20.00
OSMOND BROTHERS, THE					
The Osmonds feature Donny Osmond.					
MGM E-4146	(M)	Songs We Sang On The Andy Williams Show	1963	10.00	25.00
MGM SE-4146	(S)	Songs We Sang On The Andy Williams Show	1963	12.00	30.00
MGM E-4187	(M)	We Sing You A Merry Christmas	1963	10.00	25.00
MGM SE-4187	(S)	We Sing You A Merry Christmas	1963	12.00	30.00
MGM E-4235	(M)	All-Time Hymn Favorites	1964	8.00	20.00
MGM SE-4235	(S)	All-Time Hymn Favorites	1964	10.00	25.00
MGM E-4291	(M)	The New Sound Of The Osmond Brothers	1965	8.00	20.00
MGM SE-4291	(S)	The New Sound Of The Osmond Brothers	1965	10.00	25.00
Metro M-543	(M)	We Sing You A Merry Christmas	1965	5.00	12.00
Metro MS-543	(S)	We Sing You A Merry Christmas	1965	6.00	15.00
		(Metro 543 is a reissue of MGM 4137.)			
OSMOSIS					
RCA Victor LSP-4369	(S)	Osmosis	1970	8.00	20.00
OSWALD, LEE HARVEY					
Truth 22-65	(M)	Lee Harvey Oswald Speaks	1967	40.00	100.00
Inca 1001	(M)	Self Portrait In Red	1967	40.00	100.00

Label & Catalog #		Title	Year	VG+	NM

OTHER HALF, THE

"7/2"	(M)	The Other Half	196?	200.00	400.00

(Original covers open on the left; counterfeits open on the right.
Counterfeit's vinyl shows blue when held up to a light.)

OTHER HALF, THE

The Other Half features Randy Holden, later of Blue Cheer.

Acta 8004	(M)	The Other Half	1968	16.00	40.00
Acta 38004	(S)	The Other Half	1968	20.00	50.00

OTIS, JOHNNY

Refer to Mel Williams.

Dig 104	(M)	Rock And Roll Hit Parade, Volume 1	1957	250.00	500.00

(Original covers are yellow; counterfeits are gold.)

Capitol T-940	(M)	The Johnny Otis Show	1958	60.00	150.00
Kent KST-534	(S)	Cold Shot	1968	10.00	25.00
Epic BN-26524	(S)	Cuttin' Up	1970	10.00	25.00
Epic EG-30473	(S)	Live At Monterey	1971	10.00	25.00
Savoy 2230	(S)	Original Johnny Otis Show (2 LPs)	1978	6.00	15.00
Savoy 2252	(S)	Original Johnny Otis Show, Vol. 2 (2 LPs)	1980	6.00	15.00

OTIS, SHUGGIE

Epic BN-26511	(S)	Here Comes Shuggie Otis	1970	6.00	15.00
Epic KE-30752	(S)	Freedom Flight	1971	6.00	15.00
Epic KE-33059	(S)	Inspiration Information	1974	4.00	10.00

OUTLAW BLUES BAND, THE

BluesWay BLS-6021	(S)	The Outlaw Blues Band	1968	10.00	25.00

OUTLAWS, THE

Direct Disk SD-16617	(S)	Outlaws	198?	8.00	25.00

OUTSIDERS, THE

Capitol T-2501	(M)	Time Won't Let Me	1966	10.00	25.00
Capitol ST-2501	(S)	Time Won't Let Me	1966	12.00	30.00
Capitol T-2568	(M)	Album #2	1966	8.00	20.00
Capitol ST-2568	(S)	Album #2 ("Respectable" is rechanneled)	1966	10.00	25.00
Capitol T-2636	(M)	In	1967	8.00	20.00
Capitol ST-2636	(S)	In	1967	8.00	20.00
Capitol T-2745	(M)	Happening Live	1967	10.00	25.00
Capitol ST-2745	(S)	Happening Live	1967	8.00	20.00

OWEN, REG

RCA Victor LPM-1906	(M)	I'll Sing You 1,000 Love Songs	1958	8.00	20.00
RCA Victor LPM-1908	(M)	Girls Were Made To Take Care Of Boys	1958	8.00	20.00
RCA Victor LPM-1914	(M)	Cuddle Up A Little Closer	1959	6.00	15.00
RCA Victor LSP-1914	(S)	Cuddle Up A Little Closer	1959	8.00	20.00
Decca DL-8859	(M)	Under Paris Skies	1959	6.00	15.00
Decca DL-78859	(S)	Under Paris Skies	1959	8.00	20.00

OWEN-B

C. B. 19210	(S)	Owen-B	197?	24.00	60.00

OWENS, BONNIE (& THE STRANGERS)

Refer to Merle Haggard.

Capitol T-2403	(M)	Don't Take Advantage Of Me	1965	10.00	25.00
Capitol ST-2403	(S)	Don't Take Advantage Of Me	1965	12.00	30.00
Capitol T-2660	(M)	All Of Me Belongs To You	1967	10.00	25.00
Capitol ST-2660	(S)	All Of Me Belongs To You	1967	12.00	30.00
Capitol ST-2861	(S)	Somewhere Between	1968	10.00	25.00
Capitol ST-195	(S)	Lead Me On	1969	10.00	25.00
Capitol ST-341	(S)	Hifi To Cry By	1969	10.00	25.00
Capitol ST-557	(S)	Mother's Favorite Hymns	1970	10.00	25.00

OWENS, BUCK (& THE BUCKAROOS)

LaBrea 8017	(M)	Buck Owens	1961	40.00	100.00
Starday SLP-172	(M)	Fabulous Country Music Sound	1962	20.00	50.00
Starday SLP-324	(M)	Country Hit Maker #1	196?	16.00	40.00
Starday SLP-324	(M)	Fabulous Country Music Sound	196?	16.00	40.00

Label & Catalog #		Title	Year	VG+	NM
Capitol T-1482	(M)	Buck Owens Sings Harlan Howard	1961	16.00	40.00
Capitol ST-1482	(S)	Buck Owens Sings Harlan Howard	1961	20.00	50.00
Capitol T-1489	(M)	Under Your Spell Again	1961	16.00	40.00
Capitol DT-1489	(E)	Under Your Spell Again	1961	10.00	25.00
Capitol T-1777	(M)	You're For Me	1962	16.00	40.00
Capitol ST-1777	(S)	You're For Me	1962	20.00	50.00
Capitol T-1879	(M)	On The Bandstand	1963	16.00	40.00
Capitol ST-1879	(S)	On The Bandstand	1963	20.00	50.00
Capitol T-1989	(M)	Buck Owens Sings Tommy Collins	1963	16.00	40.00
Capitol ST-1989	(S)	Buck Owens Sings Tommy Collins	1963	20.00	50.00
Capitol T-2105	(M)	The Best Of Buck Owens	1964	8.00	20.00
Capitol ST-2105	(S)	The Best Of Buck Owens	1964	10.00	25.00
Capitol T-2135	(M)	Together Again	1964	8.00	20.00
Capitol ST-2135	(S)	Together Again	1964	10.00	25.00
Capitol T-2186	(M)	I Don't Care	1964	8.00	20.00
Capitol ST-2186	(S)	I Don't Care	1964	10.00	25.00
Capitol T-2283	(M)	I've Got A Tiger By The Tail	1965	8.00	20.00
Capitol ST-2283	(S)	I've Got A Tiger By The Tail	1965	10.00	25.00
Capitol T-2353	(M)	Before You Go	1965	8.00	20.00
Capitol ST-2353	(S)	Before You Go	1965	10.00	25.00
Capitol T-2367	(M)	The Instrumental Hits	1965	8.00	20.00
Capitol ST-2367	(S)	The Instrumental Hits	1965	10.00	25.00
Capitol T-2396	(M)	Christmas With Buck Owens	1965	8.00	20.00
Capitol ST-2396	(S)	Christmas With Buck Owens	1965	10.00	25.00
Capitol T-2443	(M)	Roll Out The Red Carpet	1966	8.00	20.00
Capitol ST-2443	(S)	Roll Out The Red Carpet	1966	10.00	25.00
Capitol T-2497	(M)	Dust On Mother's Bible	1966	8.00	20.00
Capitol ST-2497	(S)	Dust On Mother's Bible	1966	10.00	25.00
Capitol SPRO-2980	(DJ)	Minute Masters (Radio sampler)	1966	20.00	50.00
Capitol T-2556	(M)	Carnegie Hall Concert	1966	8.00	20.00
Capitol ST-2556	(S)	Carnegie Hall Concert	1966	10.00	25.00
Capitol T-2640	(M)	Open Up Your Heart	1967	8.00	20.00
Capitol ST-2640	(S)	Open Up Your Heart	1967	10.00	25.00
Capitol T-2715	(M)	Buck Owens & His Buckaroos In Japan	1967	8.00	20.00
Capitol ST-2715	(S)	Buck Owens & His Buckaroos In Japan	1967	10.00	25.00
Capitol T-2760	(M)	Your Tender Loving Care	1967	8.00	20.00
Capitol ST-2760	(S)	Your Tender Loving Care	1967	10.00	25.00
Capitol ST-2841	(S)	It Takes People Like You	1968	10.00	25.00
Capitol ST-2897	(S)	The Best Of Buck Owens, Volume 2	1968	10.00	25.00
Capitol ST-2902	(S)	A Night On The Town	1968	10.00	25.00
Capitol ST-2962	(S)	Sweet Rosie Jones	1968	10.00	25.00
Capitol ST-2977	(S)	Christmas Shopping	1968	10.00	25.00
Capitol ST-2994	(S)	The Guitar Player	1968	10.00	25.00
Capitol ST-131	(S)	I've Got You On My Mind Again	1969	8.00	20.00
Capitol SKAO-145	(S)	The Best Of Buck Owens, Volume 3	1969	8.00	20.00
Capitol ST-212	(S)	Tall Dark Stranger	1969	8.00	20.00
Capitol ST-232	(S)	Live At The London Palladium	1969	8.00	20.00
— Original Capitol albums above have black labels with the Capitol logo on top.—					
Capitol SWBB-257	(S)	Close-Up (2 LPs)	1969	8.00	20.00
Capitol ST-413	(S)	Big In Vegas (The Buck Owens Show)	1969	8.00	20.00
Capitol ST-439	(S)	Your Mother's Prayer	1970	8.00	20.00
Capitol ST-476	(S)	Kansas City Song	1970	8.00	20.00
Capitol STBB-486	(S)	A Merry "Hee Haw" Christmas (2 LPs)	1970	10.00	25.00
Capitol STBB-532	(E)	My Heart Skips A Beat / Under Your Spell Again (2 LPs)	1970	8.00	20.00
Capitol ST-574	(S)	Buck Owens (3 LPs)	1970	10.00	25.00
Capitol ST-628	(S)	I Wouldn't Live In New York City	1970	8.00	20.00
Capitol ST-685	(S)	Bridge Over Troubled Water	1971	8.00	20.00
Capitol ST-795	(S)	Ruby	1971	8.00	20.00
Capitol ST-830	(S)	The Best Of Buck Owens, Volume 4	1971	8.00	20.00
Capitol ST-860	(S)	The Songs Of Merle Haggard	1972	8.00	20.00

OXFORD, VERNON

Label & Catalog #		Title	Year	VG+	NM
RCA Victor LPM-3704	(M)	Woman, Let Me Sing You A Song	1967	8.00	20.00
RCA Victor LSP-3704	(S)	Woman, Let Me Sing You A Song	1967	10.00	25.00

OZ KNOZZ

Label & Catalog #		Title	Year	VG+	NM
Ozone 02-1000	(S)	Ruff Mix	1975	80.00	200.00

One of the most successful series of the early television era, The Ozzie & Harriet Show had previously been a successful radio series for years in which the audience had followed the birth and growth of the young family. Like many TV comedies then and now, the portrait of the husband/father was somewhat harried, though not quite as bumbling as was the norm. Of course, the whole show and the family's enviable success was masterminded by Ozzie Nelson, a former big band leader who was, by all accounts, a creative man and a delightful individual. The album here is one the rare personality LPs of the '50s. And, of course, national TV exposure was a great assist to the fledgling recording career of their youngest son, Ricky Nelson.

Label & Catalog #		Title	Year	VG+	NM

OZZIE & HARRIET (NELSON)

Imperial LP-9049	(M)	The Ozzie And Harriet Show *(TV Sdtk)*	1957	60.00	150.00
Sunset SUM-1146	(M)	Ozzie And Harriet Sing	1967	12.00	30.00
Sunset SUS-5146	(E)	Ozzie And Harriet Sing	1967	8.00	20.00
		(Sunset 1145 is a reissue of Imperial 9049.)			

P. FUNK ALL-STARS, THE
The Pure Funk All-Stars are members of the Parliament/Funkadelic community.

Epic 39168	(S)	Urban Dancefloor Guerilla	1983	8.00	20.00

P. H. PHACTOR

Piccadilly PIC-3343	(S)	P.H. Factor	1980	24.00	60.00

PABLO CRUISE

Mobile Fidelity MFSL-029	(S)	A Place In The Sun	1979	5.00	15.00
Nautilus NR-6	(S)	Lifeline	198?	5.00	15.00
Nautilus NR-28	(S)	Worlds Away	198?	5.00	15.00

PACE, JOHNNY: *Refer to* GOLDMINE'S PRICE GUIDE TO COLLECTIBLE JAZZ ALBUMS

PAGE, JIMMY
Refer to Cartoone; Led Zepplin; The Yardbirds.

Springboard SPB-4038	(S)	Special Early Works	1972	10.00	25.00

PAGE, PATTI

Mercury MG-25059 (10")	(M)	Songs	1950	16.00	40.00
Mercury MG-25101 (10")	(M)	Folksong Favorites	1951	16.00	40.00
Mercury MG-25109 (10")	(M)	Christmas	1951	16.00	40.00
Mercury MG-25154 (10")	(M)	Tennessee Waltz	1952	16.00	40.00
Mercury MG-25185 (10")	(M)	Patti Sings For Romance	1954	16.00	40.00
Mercury MG-25187 (10")	(M)	Song Souvenirs	1954	16.00	40.00
Mercury MG-25196 (10")	(M)	Just Patti	1954	16.00	40.00
Mercury MG-25197 (10")	(M)	Patti's Songs	1954	16.00	40.00
Mercury MG-25209 (10")	(M)	And I Thought About You	1954	16.00	40.00
Mercury MG-25210 (10")	(M)	So Many Memories	1954	16.00	40.00
EmArcy MG-36074	(M)	In The Land Of Hi Fi	1956	14.00	35.00
EmArcy MG-36116	(M)	The East Side	1957	12.00	30.00
EmArcy SR-60014	(S)	The East Side	1959	14.00	35.00
EmArcy MG-36136	(M)	The West Side	1957	12.00	30.00
EmArcy SR-60113	(S)	The West Side	1959	14.00	35.00
Mercury MG-20076	(M)	Romance On The Range	1955	12.00	30.00
Mercury MG-20093	(M)	Christmas With Patti Page	1956	12.00	30.00
Mercury MG-20095	(M)	Page I	1955	12.00	30.00
Mercury MG-20096	(M)	Page II	1955	12.00	30.00
Mercury MG-20097	(M)	Page III	1955	12.00	30.00
Mercury MG-20098	(M)	You Go To My Head	1955	12.00	30.00
Mercury MG-20099	(M)	Music For Two In Love	1955	12.00	30.00
Mercury MG-20100	(M)	The Voices Of Patti Page	1955	12.00	30.00
Mercury MG-20101	(M)	Page IV	1955	12.00	30.00
Mercury MG-20102	(M)	My Song	1955	12.00	30.00
Mercury MG-20318	(M)	The Waltz Queen	1957	12.00	30.00
Mercury SR-60049	(S)	The Waltz Queen	1959	14.00	35.00

Label & Catalog #		Title	Year	VG+	NM
Mercury MG-20387	(M)	Let's Get Away From It All	1957	12.00	30.00
Mercury SR-60010	(S)	Let's Get Away From It All	1959	14.00	35.00
Mercury MG-20388	(M)	I've Heard That Song Before	1958	12.00	30.00
Mercury SR-60011	(S)	I've Heard That Song Before	1959	14.00	35.00
Mercury MG-20398	(M)	Patti Page On Camera	1959	12.00	30.00
Mercury SR-60025	(S)	Patti Page On Camera	1959	14.00	35.00
Mercury MG-20417	(M)	Three Little Words	1960	12.00	30.00
Mercury SR-60037	(S)	Three Little Words	1960	14.00	35.00
Mercury MG-20405	(M)	Indiscretion	1959	12.00	30.00
Mercury SR-60059	(S)	Indiscretion	1959	14.00	35.00
Mercury MG-20406	(M)	I'll Remember April	1959	12.00	30.00
Mercury SR-60081	(S)	I'll Remember April	1959	14.00	35.00
Mercury MG-20226	(M)	Manhattan Tower	1956	12.00	30.00
Mercury MG-20573	(M)	Just A Closer Walk With Thee	1960	12.00	30.00
Mercury SR-60233	(S)	Just A Closer Walk With Thee	1960	14.00	35.00
Mercury MG-20599	(M)	Sings And Stars In "Elmer Gantry"	1960	8.00	20.00
Mercury SR-60260	(M)	Sings And Stars In "Elmer Gantry"	1960	12.00	30.00
Mercury MG-20495	(M)	Patti Page's Golden Hits	1961	6.00	15.00
Mercury SR-60495	(S)	Patti Page's Golden Hits	1961	8.00	20.00
Mercury MG-20615	(M)	Country & Western Golden Hits	1961	6.00	15.00
Mercury SR-60615	(S)	Country & Western Golden Hits	1961	8.00	20.00
Mercury MG-20689	(M)	Go On Home	1962	6.00	15.00
Mercury SR-60689	(S)	Go On Home	1962	8.00	20.00
Mercury MG-20712	(M)	Golden Hits Of The Boys	1962	6.00	15.00
Mercury SR-60712	(S)	Golden Hits Of The Boys	1962	8.00	20.00
Mercury MG-20758	(M)	Patti Page On Stage	1963	6.00	15.00
Mercury SR-60758	(S)	Patti Page On Stage	1963	8.00	20.00
Mercury MG-20794	(M)	Patti Page's Golden Hits, Volume 2	1963	5.00	12.00
Mercury SR-60794	(S)	Patti Page's Golden Hits, Volume 2	1963	6.00	15.00
Mercury MG-20819	(M)	The Singing Rage	1963	5.00	12.00
Mercury SR-60819	(S)	The Singing Rage	1963	6.00	15.00
Mercury MG-20909	(M)	Blue Dream Street	1964	5.00	12.00
Mercury SR-60909	(S)	Blue Dream Street	1964	6.00	15.00

— Original Mercury albums above have black labels with silver print. —

PAISLEYS, THE

Audio City 70	(S)	Cosmic Mind At Play	196?	60.00	150.00

PALANCE, JACK

Warner Bros. WS-1865	(S)	Palance	1970	12.00	30.00

PALEY, TOM

Tom Paley also recorded with The New Lost City Ramblers.

Elektra EKL-12	(M)	Folk Songs From The South Appalachian Mountains	1956	16.00	40.00

PALEY, TOM, & PEGGY SEEGER

Elektra EKL-295	(M)	Tom Paley And Peggy Seeger	1965	6.00	15.00
Elektra EKS-7295	(S)	Tom Paley And Peggy Seeger	1965	8.00	20.00

PALMER, BRUCE

Palmer was formerly a member of The Buffalo Springfield.

Verve/Forecast FTS-3086	(S)	The Cycle Is Complete	1970	8.00	20.00

PALMER, EARL

Liberty LRP-3201	(M)	Drumsville	1961	8.00	20.00
Liberty LST-7201	(S)	Drumsville	1961	10.00	25.00
Liberty LRP-3227	(M)	Percolator Twist	1962	8.00	20.00
Liberty LST-7227	(S)	Percolator Twist	1962	10.00	25.00

PALMER, ROBERT

Island PRO-819	(DJ)	Secrets (Picture disc)	1979	8.00	20.00

PANDORA

(No label)	(S)	Pandora (10" flexidisc)	198?	20.00	50.00

PANICS, THE

Chancellor CHL-5026	(M)	Panicsville	1962	8.00	20.00
Chancellor CHLS-5026	(S)	Panicsville	1962	10.00	25.00

Label & Catalog #		Title	Year	VG+	NM
Phillips PHM-200-159	(M)	Discotheque Dance Party	1964	5.00	12.00
Phillips PHS-600-159	(S)	Discotheque Dance Party	1964	6.00	15.00
PAPA DOO RUN RUN					
Telarc	(S)	California Project	198?	6.00	15.00
PARAGONS, THE / THE JESTERS					
Jubilee JLP-1098	(M)	The Paragons Meet The Jesters	1959	100.00	250.00
Jubilee JLP-1098	(M)	The Paragons Meet The Jesters	1959	500.00	800.00
		(Multi-color vinyl)			
Winley LP-6003	(M)	War! The Jesters Vs. The Paragons	195?	100.00	250.00
PARAGONS, THE / THE HARPTONES					
Musicnote M-8001	(M)	The Paragons Vs. The Harptones	1964	14.00	35.00
PARAMOR, NORRIE					
Capitol Int. 10025	(M)	In London, In Love	1956	12.00	30.00
PARIS, JACKIE: Refer to GOLDMINE'S PRICE GUIDE TO COLLECTIBLE JAZZ ALBUMS					
PARIS, PRISCILLA					
Priscilla also recorded with her sisters as The Paris Sisters.					
Happy Tiger HT-1002	(S)	Priscilla Loves Billy	1969	6.00	15.00
PARIS SISTERS, THE					
Sidewalk T-5906	(M)	The Hits Of The Paris Sisters	1967	40.00	100.00
Reprise R-6250	(M)	Everything Under The Sun	1967	20.00	50.00
Reprise RS-6250	(S)	Everything Under The Sun	1967	30.00	75.00
PARKER, FESS					
Columbia CL-576	(M)	TV Sweethearts (With Marion Marlowe)	1955	30.00	75.00
Columbia CL-666	(M)	Davy Crockett	1955	30.00	75.00
Disneyland WDA-3007	(M)	Three Adventures Of Davy Crockett	195?	16.00	40.00
Disneyland WDA-3602	(M)	Yarns And Songs	195?	16.00	40.00
Disneyland 1336	(M)	Cowboy And Indian Songs	195?	14.00	35.00
RCA Victor LPM-2973	(M)	Fess Parker Sings	1964	8.00	20.00
RCA Victor LSP-2973	(S)	Fess Parker Sings	1964	12.00	30.00
PARKER, GRAHAM, & THE RUMOUR					
Arista SP-63	(DJ)	Live Sparks	1979	12.00	30.00
PARKER, JACY					
Verve V-8424	(M)	Spotlight On Jacy Parker	1962	6.00	15.00
Verve V6-8424	(S)	Spotlight On Jacy Parker	1962	8.00	20.00
PARKER, LITTLE JUNIOR					
Duke DLP-72	(S)	Blues Consolidated (With Bobby Bland)	1961	40.00	100.00
Duke DLP-76	(M)	Driving Wheel	1962	30.00	75.00
Mercury MG-21101	(M)	Like It Is	1967	8.00	20.00
Mercury SR-61101	(S)	Like It Is	1967	10.00	25.00
Minit 24024	(S)	Blues Man	1969	8.00	20.00
Blue Rock SRB-64004	(S)	Honey-Drippin' Blues	1969	6.00	15.00
Capitol ST-64	(S)	The Outside Man	1970	6.00	15.00
United Arts. UAS-6823	(S)	I Tell Stories Sad And True	1971	5.00	12.00
BluesWay BLS-6066	(S)	Sometime Tomorrow	1973	5.00	12.00
Duke DLP-83	(M)	The Best Of Junior Parker	1974	5.00	12.00
PARKER, LITTLE JUNIOR, & JIMMY McGRIFF					
Capitol ST-569	(S)	Dudes Doin' Business	1971	6.00	15.00
United Arts. UAS-6814	(S)	100 Proof Black Magic	1971	6.00	15.00
PARKER, ROBERT					
Nola LP-1001	(M)	Barefootin'	1966	16.00	40.00
PARKS, VAN DYKE					
Warner Bros. WS-2727	(S)	Song Cycle (Gold Label)	1968	10.00	25.00
Warner Bros. WS-2727	(S)	Song Cycle (Green Label)	1969	6.00	15.00
Warner Bros. BS-2589	(S)	Discover America	1972	8.00	20.00
Warner Bros. BS-2878	(S)	Clang Of The Yankee Reaper	1975	6.00	15.00

Label & Catalog #		Title	Year	VG+	NM

PARLET
Parlet is a member of the Parliament/Funkadelic community.

Casablanca 7094	(S)	Pleasure Principle	1978	6.00	15.00
Casablanca 7146	(S)	Invasion Of The Body Snatchers	1979	6.00	15.00
Casablanca 7224	(S)	Play Me Or Trade Me	1980	6.00	15.00

PARLIAMENT
Parliament, who also recorded as Funkadelic, is the brainchild of George Clinton.

Invictus 7302	(S)	Osmium	1970	40.00	100.00
Casablanca NBLP-9003	(S)	Up For The Down Stroke	1974	12.00	30.00
Casablanca NBLP-7002	(S)	Up For The Down Stroke	1975	10.00	25.00
Casablanca NBLP-7014	(S)	Chocolate City	1975	10.00	25.00
Casablanca NBLP-7022	(S)	Mothership Connection	1976	10.00	25.00
Casablanca NBLP-7034	(S)	The Clones Of Dr. Funkenstein	1976	10.00	25.00
Casablanca NBLP-7053	(S)	Parliament Live/P. Funk Earth Tour	1977	10.00	25.00
Casablanca NBLP-7084	(S)	Funkentelechy Vs. The Placebo Syndrome	1977	10.00	25.00
Casablanca NBLP-7125	(S)	Motor-Booty Affair	1978	10.00	25.00
Casablanca NBLP-7125	(S)	Motor Booty Affair (Picture disc)	1979	12.00	30.00
Casablanca NBLP-7195	(S)	Gloryhallastoopid	1979	10.00	25.00
Casablanca NBLP-7249	(S)	Trombipulation	1980	10.00	25.00
Casablanca 822367	(S)	Parliament's Greatest Hits	1984	4.00	10.00

PARRIS, FRED, & THE SATINS

Elektra E1-60152	(S)	Fred Parris & The Satins	1982	6.00	15.00

PARRISH, PAUL

Music Factory MFS-12,001	(S)	The Forest Of My Mind	196?	6.00	15.00
Warner Bros. WS-1930	(S)	Songs	1971	5.00	12.00
ABC 1013	(DJ)	Song For A Young Girl (Picture disc)	1979	4.00	10.00

PARRISH & GURVITZ
Paul Parrish and Adrian Gurvitz. Refer to The Baker-Gurvitz Army.

Decca DL-75336	(S)	Parrish And Gurvitz	1972	6.00	15.00

PARSONS, ALAN [ALAN PARSONS PROJECT]

Arista SP-68	(DJ)	Audio Guide To The Alan Parsons Project	1979	16.00	40.00
		(Boxed set of four Project albums with a special double-album set of Parson's work with other artists.)			
Arista SP-140	(DJ)	Audio Guide To The Alan Parsons Project	1979	20.00	50.00
		(Boxed set of six Project albums with a special double-album set of Parson's work with other artists.)			
Mobile Fidelity MFSL-084	(S)	I, Robot	1980	8.00	25.00
Mobile Fidelity MFQR-084	(S)	I, Robot (Ultra High Quality Record. in a box)	1982	16.00	50.00
Arista PD-8263	(DJ)	Vulture Culture	1985	6.00	15.00

PARTON, DOLLY
Dolly also recorded with Porter Wagoner.

Monument MLP-8085	(M)	Hello, I'm Dolly	1967	12.00	30.00
Monument SLP-18085	(S)	Hello, I'm Dolly	1967	16.00	40.00
Monument SLP-18136	(S)	As Long As I Love	1970	6.00	15.00
Monument KZG-31913	(S)	The World Of Dolly	1972	6.00	15.00
RCA Victor LPM-3949	(M)	Just Because I'm A Woman	1968	40.00	100.00
RCA Victor LSP-3949	(S)	Just Because I'm A Woman	1968	12.00	30.00
		— Original RCA albums above have black labels with Nipper on top.—			
RCA Victor LSP-3949	(S)	Just Because I'm A Woman	1969	8.00	20.00
RCA Victor LSP-4099	(S)	In The Good Old Days			
		(When Times Were Bad)	1969	8.00	20.00
RCA Victor LSP-4188	(S)	My Blue Ridge Mountain Boy	1969	8.00	20.00
RCA Victor LSP-4288	(S)	The Fairest Of Them All	1970	8.00	20.00
RCA Victor LSP-4387	(S)	A Real Live Dolly	1970	8.00	20.00
RCA Victor LSP-4396	(S)	Golden Streets Of Glory	1970	8.00	20.00
		— Original RCA albums above have orange labels on non-flexible vintl.—			
RCA Victor LSP-4449	(S)	The Best Of Dolly Parton	1971	6.00	15.00
RCA Victor LSP-4507	(S)	Joshua	1971	6.00	15.00
RCA Victor LSP-4603	(S)	Coat Of Many Colors	1971	6.00	15.00
RCA Victor LSP-4686	(S)	Touch Your Woman	1972	6.00	15.00
RCA Victor LSP-4752	(S)	My Favorite Song Writer: Porter Wagoner	1972	6.00	15.00
RCA Victor LSP-4762	(S)	Dolly Parton Sings	1972	6.00	15.00
		— Original RCA albums above have orange labels.—			

Label & Catalog #		Title	Year	VG+	NM
RCA Victor APD1-0033	(Q)	My Tennessee Mountain Home	1973	6.00	15.00
RCA Victor CPL1-1343	(S)	Great Balls Of Fire (Picture disc)	1979	4.00	10.00
RCA Victor 812	(DJ)	HBO Presents Dolly Parton (Picture disc)	1983	5.00	12.00

PARTON, DOLLY, & GEORGE JONES

Starday SLP-429	(E)	Dolly Parton And George Jones	1968	16.00	40.00

PARTON, DOLLY, & FAYE TUCKER

Somerset SF-19700	(S)	Hits Made Famous By Country Queens	1963	12.00	30.00

PARTRIDGE FAMILY, THE
The Partridge Family features David Cassidy.

Bell 6050	(S)	Album	1970	8.00	20.00
Bell 6059	(S)	Up To Date	1971	6.00	15.00
		(Issued with a 12" x 20" Partridge Family school book cover, priced separately below.)			
Bell 6059		Up To Date Book Cover	1971	6.00	15.00
Bell 6064	(S)	Sound Magazine	1971	6.00	15.00
Bell 6066	(S)	A Christmas Card (With card)	1971	10.00	25.00
Bell 6066	(S)	A Christmas Card (Without card)	1971	6.00	15.00
Bell 6072	(S)	Shopping Bag (With bag)	1972	10.00	25.00
Bell 6072	(S)	Shopping Bag (Without bag)	1972	6.00	15.00
Bell 1107	(S)	At Home With Their Greatest Hits	1972	6.00	15.00
Bell 1111	(S)	The Partridge Family Notebook	1972	6.00	15.00
Bell 1122	(S)	Crossword Puzzle	1973	6.00	15.00
Bell 1137	(S)	Bulletin Board	1973	6.00	15.00
Bell 1319	(S)	The World Of The Partridge Family (2 LPs)	1974	8.00	20.00
Laurie House H-8014	(S)	The Partridge Family (2 LPs)	197?	12.00	30.00

PASSING CLOUDS

Pete 1106	(S)	Hawks And Doves	1969	6.00	15.00

PASTEL SIX, THE

Zen 1001	(M)	Cinnamon Cinder	1963	24.00	60.00

PATRON SAINTS, THE

(No label)	(M)	Fohhoh Bohob	1969	800.00	1,200.00

PATTO
Mike Patto Of Spooky Tooth.

Island SW-9322	(S)	Roll 'Em, Smoke 'Em Put Another Line Out	197?	12.00	30.00
Vertigo VEL-1001	(S)	Patto	1971	5.00	12.00
Vertigo VEL-1008	(S)	Hold Your Fire	1972	5.00	12.00

PATTON, JIMMY

Stereophonic LP-1002	(S)	Take 30 Minutes With Jimmy Patton	196?	50.00	125.00
Sourdough 127	(M)	Blue Darlin'	1965	20.00	50.00
Sims 127	(M)	Blue Darlin'	1965	16.00	40.00
Moon 101	(M)	Make Room For The Blues	1966	20.00	50.00

PAUL, BILLY

Neptune 201	(S)	Ebony Woman	1970	6.00	15.00
Gamble 5002	(S)	Feelin' Good At The Cadillac Club	197?	6.00	15.00
Phila. Inter. ZQ-31793	(Q)	360 Degrees Of Billy Paul	1972	6.00	15.00
Phila. Inter. ZQ-32409	(Q)	War Of The Gods	1973	6.00	15.00
Phila. Inter. ZQ-32952	(Q)	Billy Paul Live In Europe	1974	6.00	15.00

PAUL, LES, & MARY FORD

Decca DL-5018 (10")	(M)	Hawaiian Paradise	1949	40.00	100.00
Decca DL-5376 (10")	(M)	Galloping Guitars	1952	40.00	100.00
Capitol H-226 (10")	(M)	New Sound, Volume 1	1950	30.00	75.00
Capitol H-286 (10")	(M)	New Sound, Volume 2	1951	30.00	75.00
Capitol H-356 (10")	(M)	Bye Bye Blues	1952	30.00	75.00
Capitol H-416 (10")	(M)	The Hit Makers	1953	30.00	75.00
Capitol H-577 (10")	(M)	Les & Mary	1955	30.00	75.00
Capitol T-226	(M)	New Sound, Volume 1	1955	20.00	50.00
Capitol T-286	(M)	New Sound, Volume 2	1955	20.00	50.00
Capitol T-356	(M)	Bye Bye Blues	1955	20.00	50.00

Label & Catalog #		Title	Year	VG+	NM
Capitol T-416	(M)	The Hitmakers	1955	20.00	50.00
Capitol T-577	(M)	Les And Mary	1955	20.00	50.00
Capitol T-802	(M)	Time To Dream	1957	20.00	50.00
Capitol T-1476	(M)	The Hits Of Les And Mary	1960	10.00	25.00
Capitol DT-1476	(E)	The Hits Of Les And Mary	1960	8.00	20.00
Columbia CL-1276	(M)	Lover's Luau	1959	8.00	20.00
Columbia CL-1688	(M)	Warm And Wonderful	1962	10.00	25.00
Columbia CS-8488	(S)	Warm And Wonderful	1962	8.00	20.00
Columbia CL-1821	(M)	Bouquet Of Roses	1962	8.00	20.00
Columbia CS-8621	(S)	Bouquet Of Roses	1962	10.00	25.00

— Original Columbia albums above have three white "eye" logos on each side of the spindle hole.—

Columbia CL-1928	(M)	Swingin' South	1963	6.00	15.00
Columbia CS-8728	(S)	Swingin' South	1963	8.00	20.00

PAUL & PAULA

Phillips PHM-200-078	(M)	Paul And Paula Sing For Young Lovers	1963	10.00	25.00
Phillips PHS-600-078	(S)	Paul And Paula Sing For Young Lovers	1963	14.00	35.00
Phillips PHM-200-089	(M)	We Go Together	1963	10.00	25.00
Phillips PHS-600-089	(S)	We Go Together	1963	14.00	35.00
Phillips PHM-200-101	(M)	Holiday For Teens	1963	10.00	25.00
Phillips PHS-600-101	(S)	Holiday For Teens	1963	14.00	35.00

PAUPERS, THE

Verve/Forecast FT-3026	(M)	Magic People	1967	6.00	15.00
Verve/Forecast FTS-3026	(S)	Magic People	1967	6.00	15.00
Verve/Forecast FTS-3051	(S)	Ellis Island	1968	6.00	15.00

PAVLOV'S DOG

ABC-Paramount D-866	(S)	Pampered Menial	1975	6.00	15.00

PAXTON, SANDY

Elektra EKL-148	(M)	The Many Sides Of Sandy Paxton	195?	8.00	20.00

PAXTON, TOM

Elektra EKL-277	(M)	Ramblin' Boy	1964	5.00	12.00
Elektra EKS-7277	(S)	Ramblin' Boy	1964	6.00	15.00
Elektra EKL-298	(M)	Ain't That News	1965	5.00	12.00
Elektra EKS-7298	(S)	Ain't That News	1965	6.00	15.00
Elektra EKL-317	(M)	Outward Bound	1966	5.00	12.00
Elektra EKS-7317	(S)	Outward Bound	1966	6.00	15.00
Elektra EKS-74019	(S)	Morning Again	1968	5.00	12.00
Elektra EKS-74043	(S)	Things I Notice Now	1969	5.00	12.00
Elektra EKS-74066	(S)	Tom Paxton 6	1970	5.00	12.00

PAYNE, FREDA

Impulse A-53	(M)	After The Lights Go Down Low	1964	10.00	25.00
Impulse AS-53	(S)	After The Lights Go Down Low	1964	12.00	30.00
MGM E-4370	(M)	How Do You Say I Don't Love You Anymore	1966	6.00	15.00
MGM SE-4370	(S)	How Do You Say I Don't Love You Anymore	1966	8.00	20.00
MGM GAS-128	(S)	Freda Payne	1970	6.00	15.00
Invictus ST-7301	(S)	Band Of Gold	1970	6.00	15.00
Invictus ST-7307	(S)	Contact	1971	6.00	15.00
Invictus ST-9804	(S)	The Best Of Freda Payne	1972	6.00	15.00

PAYNE, LEON

Starday SLP-231	(M)	Leon Payne	1963	30.00	75.00
Starday SLP-236	(M)	Americana	1963	20.00	50.00

PAYCHECK, JOHNNY

Little Darlin' LD-8001	(M)	Johnny Paycheck At Carnegie Hall	1966	5.00	12.00
Little Darlin' SLD-8001	(S)	Johnny Paycheck At Carnegie Hall	1966	6.00	15.00
Little Darlin' LD-8003	(M)	The Lovin' Machine	1966	5.00	12.00
Little Darlin' SLD-8003	(S)	The Lovin' Machine	1966	6.00	15.00
Little Darlin' LD-8004	(M)	Gospeltime In My Fashion	1967	5.00	12.00
Little Darlin' SLD-8004	(S)	Gospeltime In My Fashion	1967	6.00	15.00
Little Darlin' LD-8006	(M)	Johnny Paycheck Sings Jukebox Charlie	1967	5.00	12.00
Little Darlin' SLD-8006	(S)	Johnny Paycheck Sings Jukebox Charlie	1967	6.00	15.00
Little Darlin' SLD-8010	(S)	Country Soul	1968	5.00	12.00
Little Darlin' SLD-8023	(S)	Wherever You Are	1969	5.00	12.00

Label & Catalog #		Title	Year	VG+	NM

PEACE, JOE
| (No label) | (S) | **Finding Peace Of Mind** | 1972 | 40.00 | 100.00 |

PEACHES & HERB
Date TE-3004	(M)	Let's Fall In Love	1967	8.00	20.00
Date TES-4004	(S)	Let's Fall In Love	1967	10.00	25.00
Date TE-3005	(M)	For Your Love	1967	8.00	20.00
Date TES-4005	(S)	For Your Love	1967	10.00	25.00
Date TES-4007	(S)	Peaches And Herbs' Golden Duets	1968	8.00	20.00
Date TES-4012	(S)	Peaches And Herbs' Greatest Hits	1968	8.00	20.00

PEANUT BUTTER CONSPIRACY, THE
The Conspiracy Columbia albums were produced by Gary Usher.
Columbia CL-2654	(M)	Peanut Butter Conspiracy Is Spreading	1967	10.00	25.00
Columbia CS-9495	(S)	Peanut Butter Conspiracy Is Spreading	1967	12.00	30.00
Columbia CL-2790	(M)	The Great Conspiracy	1968	12.00	30.00
Columbia CS-9590	(S)	The Great Conspiracy	1968	12.00	30.00
Challenge 2000	(M)	For Children Of All Ages	1969	12.00	30.00

PEARL, MINNIE
Starday SLP-224	(M)	Howdee	1963	10.00	25.00
Starday SLP-380	(M)	America's Beloved Minnie Pearl	1965	10.00	25.00
Starday SLP-397	(M)	The Country Music Story	1966	10.00	25.00
Nashville NLP-2043	(M)	Lookin' For A Feller	196?	8.00	20.00
Nashville NLPS-2043	(S)	Lookin' For A Feller	196?	10.00	25.00

PEARLS BEFORE SWINE
Pearls features Tom Rapp, formerly of The Yett-Men.
ESP-Disk' 1054	(M)	One Nation Under Ground	1967	16.00	40.00
ESP-Disk' 1054	(S)	One Nation Under Ground	1967	12.00	30.00
		(First pressing covers are brown with a white border on two sides.)			
ESP-Disk' 1054	(S)	One Nation Under Ground	196?	10.00	25.00
		(Second pressing covers are brown without the border.)			
ESP-Disk' 1054	(S)	One Nation Under Ground	196?	8.00	20.00
		(Third pressing covers are black & white.)			
ESP-Disk' 1054	(S)	One Nation Under Ground	196?	6.00	15.00
		(Fourth pressing covers are in full color.)			
ESP-Disk' 1075	(S)	Balaklava	1968	8.00	20.00
Reprise MS-6364	(S)	These Things Too	1969	6.00	15.00
Reprise MS-6405	(S)	The Use Of Ashes	1970	6.00	15.00
Reprise MS-6442	(S)	City Of Gold	1971	6.00	15.00
Reprise MS-6467	(S)	Beautiful Lies You Could Live In	1971	6.00	15.00

PECK, GREGORY
| Decca DL-8009 | (M) | Lullabye Of Christmas | 1966 | 6.00 | 15.00 |
| Decca DL-78009 | (S) | Lullabye Of Christmas | 1966 | 8.00 | 20.00 |

PEDDLERS, THE
| DJM 408 | (S) | Goodbye Gemini (Soundtrack) | 1971 | 8.00 | 20.00 |

PEDICIN, MIKE
| Apollo LP-484 | (M) | Musical Medicine | 1957 | 50.00 | 125.00 |

PEEBLES, ANN
Hi SHL-32059	(S)	Part Time Love	1970	6.00	15.00
Hi SHL-32065	(S)	Straight From The Heart	1972	6.00	15.00
Hi SHL-32079	(S)	I Can't Stand The Rain	1974	6.00	15.00
Hi SHL-32091	(S)	Tellin' It	1975	6.00	15.00
Hi 6002	(S)	If This Is Heaven	197?	5.00	12.00
Hi 6007	(S)	Handwriting Is On The Wall	197?	5.00	12.00
Hi 8009	(S)	Straight From The Heart	197?	5.00	12.00

PEEL, DAVID (& THE LOWER EAST SIDE)
Elektra EKS-74032	(S)	Have A Marijuana	1968	10.00	25.00
Elektra EKS-74069	(S)	The American Revolution	1970	8.00	20.00
Apple SW-3391	(S)	The Pope Smokes Dope	1972	30.00	75.00
		(Apple 3391 produced by John & Yoko.)			

Label & Catalog #		Title	Year	VG+	NM

PEELS, THE

Karate 5402	(M)	**Juanita Banana**	1966	30.00	75.00

PENDERGRASS, TEDDY

Phila. Inter. JZ-30595	(DJ)	**Life Is A Song Worth Singing** (Picture disc)	1978	6.00	15.00
Phila. Inter. JE-47491	(S)	**It's Time For Love** (Half-speed master)	1981	6.00	18.00

PEERCE, JAN

Vanguard VRS-9166	(M)	**On 2nd Avenue**	1965	5.00	12.00
Vanguard VSD7-9166	(S)	**On 2nd Avenue**	1965	6.00	15.00

PENGUINS, THE

Dootone DTL-204	(M)	**Best In Rhythm 'N Blues** (Red vinyl)	1957	500.00	Rare

(Original pressings are on red vinyl with flat maroon labels. Actually a various artists album, because all of side one is by The Penguins it is referred to as the "first Penguins album." Rare in collectible condition, although lesser copies are available for $100-150. Near Mint copies have a suggested value of $1,200-2,000.)

Dootone DTL-204	(M)	**Best In Rhythm 'N Blues**	1959	60.00	150.00

(Later pressings are on black vinyl with glossy maroon labels. Counterfeits have black & white covers and multi-color labels.)

Dooto DTL-242	(M)	**The Cool Cool Penguins**	1959	150.00	400.00

(Original pressings have yellow & red labels.)

Dooto DTL-242	(M)	**The Cool Cool Penguins**	196?	50.00	125.00

(Later pressings have multi-color labels. Counterfeits have maroon Dootone labels and black & white covers.)

PENNY, HANK

Audio Lab AL-1508	(M)	**Hank Penny Sings**	195?	50.00	125.00

PENNYWHISTLERS, THE

Verve/Folkways FV-9034	(M)	**Songs From Everywhere**	1965	6.00	15.00
Verve/Folkways FVS-9034	(S)	**Songs From Everywhere**	1965	8.00	20.00

PENTANGLE, THE

Reprise RS-6315	(S)	**The Pentangle**	1968	6.00	15.00
Reprise 2RS-6334	(S)	**Sweet Child** (2 LPs)	1969	8.00	20.00
Reprise RS-6372	(S)	**Basket Of Light**	1969	6.00	15.00

— Original Reprise albums above have brown & orange labels.—

PEOPLE

People features Larry Norman.

Capitol ST-2924	(S)	**I Love You**	1968	16.00	40.00
Capitol ST-151	(S)	**Both Sides Of People**	1969	16.00	40.00
Paramount PAS-5013	(S)	**There Are People And There Are People**	1970	10.00	25.00

PEPPER, JIM

Embryo SD-7312	(S)	**Pepper's Pow Wow**	196?	24.00	60.00

PEPPERMINT RAINBOW, THE

Decca DL-75129	(S)	**Will You Be Staying After Sunday**	1969	6.00	15.00

PEPPERMINT, DANNY

Carlton LP-20001	(M)	**Danny Peppermint**	1962	6.00	15.00
Carlton LP-20001	(S)	**Danny Peppermint**	1962	8.00	20.00

PEPPERMINT TROLLEY COMPANY, THE

Acta 8007	(M)	**The Peppermint Trolley Company**	1968	8.00	20.00
Acta 38007	(S)	**The Peppermint Trolley Company**	1968	10.00	25.00

PERKINS, CARL

Sun LP-1225	(M)	**The Dance Album Of Carl Perkins**	1957	360.00	600.00
Sun SLP-1225	(M)	**Teen Beat (The Best Of Carl Perkins)**	1961	300.00	500.00

("Teen Beat" is a repackage of "Dance Album.")

Columbia CL-1234	(M)	**Whole Lotta Shakin'**	1958	150.00	300.00
Design DLP-611	(M)	**Tennessee**	1963	12.00	30.00
Design SDLP-611	(E)	**Tennessee**	1963	8.00	20.00

(Contains material by other artists.)

Label & Catalog #		Title	Year	VG+	NM
Sun LP-112	(E)	Blue Suede Shoes	1969	6.00	15.00
		(Reissue of material recorded 1956-57.)			
Columbia CS-9833	(S)	Carl Perkins' Greatest Hits	1969	8.00	20.00
Columbia CS-9931	(S)	On Top	1969	8.00	20.00
Columbia CS-9981	(S)	Boppin' The Blues (With NRBQ)	1970	8.00	20.00
		— Original Columbia albums above have "360 Sound" labels.—			
Harmony HKH-31179	(S)	Brown Eyed Handsome Man	1972	4.00	10.00
Harmony HKH-31185	(S)	Carl Perkins	1972	4.00	10.00
Harmony HKH-31192	(S)	The Greatest Hits Of Carl Perkins	1972	4.00	10.00
Mercury SRM-1-691	(S)	My Kind Of Country	1973	4.00	10.00
Sunnyvale 330-903	(M)	The Sun Story, Volume 3: Carl Perkins	1977	4.00	10.00
Jet LA856H	(S)	Ol' Blue Suede's Back	1978	4.00	10.00
Suede 002	(S)	Live At Austin City Limits	1981	4.00	10.00
PERKINS, TONY					
Epic LN-3394	(M)	Tony Perkins	1957	16.00	40.00
RCA Victor LPM-1679	(M)	From My Heart	1958	16.00	40.00
RCA Victor LPM-1853	(M)	On A Rainy Afternoon	1958	16.00	40.00
RCA Victor LSP-1853	(S)	On A Rainy Afternoon	1958	24.00	60.00
PERRINE, PEP					
Hideout 1003	(M)	Pep Perrine Live And In Person	196?	60.00	150.00
PERSUADERS, THE					
Saturn SAT-5000	(M)	Surfer's Nightmare	1963	60.00	150.00
Saturn SATS-5000	(S)	Surfer's Nightmare	1963	80.00	200.00
PERSUADERS, THE					
Atco SD-36-7021	(S)	The Persuaders	1973	6.00	15.00
Atco SD-36-7046	(S)	Best Thing That Ever Happened To Me	1974	6.00	15.00
PERSUASIONS, THE					
Catamount CATA-905	(S)	Stardust	197?	20.00	50.00
Straight STS-6394	(S)	Acappella	1970	12.00	30.00
Capitol ST-791	(S)	We Came To Play	1971	8.00	20.00
Capitol ST-872	(S)	Street Corner Symphony	1972	8.00	20.00
Capitol ST-11101	(S)	Spread The Word	1972	6.00	15.00
MCA 326	(S)	We Still Ain't Got No Band	1973	4.00	10.00
A&M SD-3656	(S)	I Just Want To Sing With My Friends	1974	4.00	10.00
A&M SD-3635	(S)	More Than Before	1974	4.00	10.00
Elektra 7E-1099	(S)	Chirpin'	1977	4.00	10.00
PETER & GORDON					
Peter Asher and Gordon Waller.					
Capitol T-2115	(M)	A World Without Love	1964	8.00	20.00
Capitol ST-2115	(S)	A World Without Love	1964	10.00	25.00
Capitol T-2220	(M)	I Don't Want To See You Again	1964	8.00	20.00
Capitol ST-2220	(S)	I Don't Want To See You Again	1964	10.00	25.00
Capitol T-2324	(M)	I Go To Pieces	1965	8.00	20.00
Capitol ST-2324	(S)	I Go To Pieces	1965	10.00	25.00
Capitol T-2368	(M)	True Love Ways	1965	8.00	20.00
Capitol ST-2368	(S)	True Love Ways	1965	10.00	25.00
Capitol T-2430	(M)	Peter & Gordon Sing The Hits Of Nashville	1966	12.00	30.00
Capitol ST-2430	(S)	Peter & Gordon Sing The Hits Of Nashville	1966	16.00	40.00
Capitol T-2477	(M)	Woman	1966	8.00	20.00
Capitol ST-2477	(S)	Woman ("Woman" is rechanneled)	1966	10.00	25.00
Capitol T-2549	(M)	The Best Of Peter & Gordon	1966	6.00	15.00
Capitol ST-2549	(S)	The Best Of Peter & Gordon	1966	8.00	20.00
		(Black Starline label.. "Woman" is rechanneled on this album.)			
Capitol ST-2549	(S)	The Best Of Peter & Gordon	196?	6.00	15.00
		(Red & white Starline label. "Woman" is rechanneled on this album.)			
Capitol T-2664	(M)	Lady Godiva	1967	8.00	20.00
Capitol ST-2664	(S)	Lady Godiva	1967	10.00	25.00
Capitol T-2729	(M)	A Knight In Rusty Armour	1967	8.00	20.00
Capitol ST-2729	(S)	A Knight In Rusty Armour	1967	10.00	25.00
Capitol T-2747	(M)	In London For Tea	1967	10.00	25.00
Capitol ST-2747	(S)	In London For Tea	1967	8.00	20.00
Capitol T-2882	(M)	Hot, Cold And Custard	1968	16.00	40.00
Capitol ST-2882	(S)	Hot, Cold And Custard	1968	12.00	30.00

Label & Catalog #		Title	Year	VG+	NM

PETER, PAUL & MARY
Peter Yarrow, Paul Stookey & Mary Travers.

Label & Catalog #		Title	Year	VG+	NM
Warner Bros. W-1449	(M)	Peter, Paul And Mary	1962	8.00	20.00
Warner Bros. WS-1449	(S)	Peter, Paul And Mary	1962	10.00	25.00
Warner Bros. W-1473	(M)	Moving	1962	8.00	20.00
Warner Bros. WS-1473	(S)	Moving	1962	10.00	25.00
Warner Bros. W-1507	(M)	In The Wind	1963	8.00	20.00
Warner Bros. WS-1507	(S)	In The Wind	1963	10.00	25.00
Warner Bros. W2-1555	(M)	Peter, Paul And Mary In Concert	1964	8.00	20.00
Warner Bros. W2S-1555	(S)	Peter, Paul And Mary In Concert	1964	10.00	25.00
Warner Bros. W-1589	(M)	A Song Will Rise	1965	8.00	20.00
Warner Bros. WS-1589	(S)	A Song Will Rise	1965	10.00	25.00
Warner Bros. W-1615	(M)	See What Tomorrow Brings	1965	8.00	20.00
Warner Bros. WS-1615	(S)	See What Tomorrow Brings	1965	10.00	25.00

— Original Warner mono albums above have grey labels; stereo albums ahve gold labels.—

Label & Catalog #		Title	Year	VG+	NM
Warner Bros. W-1648	(M)	The Peter, Paul And Mary Album	1966	6.00	15.00
Warner Bros. WS-1648	(S)	The Peter, Paul And Mary Album	1966	8.00	20.00
Warner Bros. W-1700	(M)	Album 1700	1967	6.00	15.00
Warner Bros. WS-1700	(S)	Album 1700	1967	8.00	20.00

— Original Warner albums above have gold labels.—

Label & Catalog #		Title	Year	VG+	NM
Warner Bros. WS-1751	(S)	Late Again	1968	4.00	10.00
Warner Bros. WS-1785	(S)	Peter, Paul And Mommy	1969	4.00	10.00
Warner Bros. BS-2552	(S)	Ten Years Together	1970	4.00	10.00

PETERS, BROCK

Label & Catalog #		Title	Year	VG+	NM
United Arts. UAL-3041	(M)	Sing'a Man	1959	10.00	25.00
United Arts. UAS-6041	(S)	Sing'a Man	1959	14.00	35.00
United Arts. UAL-3062	(M)	Brock Peters At The Villlage Gate	1959	10.00	25.00
United Arts. UAS-6062	(S)	Brock Peters At The Villlage Gate	1959	14.00	35.00

PETERSEN, PAUL

Label & Catalog #		Title	Year	VG+	NM
Colpix CP-429	(M)	Lollipops And Roses	1962	20.00	50.00
Colpix SCP-429	(S)	Lollipops And Roses	1962	30.00	75.00
Colpix CP-442	(M)	My Dad	1963	20.00	50.00
Colpix SCP-442	(S)	My Dad	1963	30.00	75.00

PETERSON, RAY

Label & Catalog #		Title	Year	VG+	NM
RCA Victor LPM-2297	(M)	Tell Laura I Love Her	1960	30.00	75.00
RCA Victor LSP-2297	(S)	Tell Laura I Love Her	1960	50.00	125.00
MGM E-4250	(M)	The Very Best Of Ray Peterson	1964	10.00	25.00
MGM SE-4250	(S)	The Very Best Of Ray Peterson	1964	12.00	30.00
MGM E-4277	(M)	The Other Side Of Ray Peterson	1965	10.00	25.00
MGM SE-4277	(S)	The Other Side Of Ray Peterson	1965	12.00	30.00
Uni 73078	(S)	The Best Of Ray Peterson	1969	8.00	20.00
		(Contains rerecordings of earlier material.)			
Decca DL-75307	(S)	Ray Peterson Country	1971	8.00	20.00

PETTY TRIO, NORMAN

Label & Catalog #		Title	Year	VG+	NM
Vik LX-1073	(M)	Corsage	1957	30.00	75.00
Columbia CL-1092	(M)	Moondreams	1958	80.00	200.00
		(Features Buddy Holly on guitar on the title track.)			
Top Rank RS-639	(S)	Petty For Your Thoughts	1960	14.00	35.00

PETTY, TOM (& THE HEARTBREAKERS)

Label & Catalog #		Title	Year	VG+	NM
Shelter SRL-52006	(S)	Tom Petty & The Heartbreakers	1976	8.00	20.00
		(Yellow label. Issued with a sheet of black & white photos of TP.)			
Shelter/ABC TP-12677	(DJ)	Official Live 'Leg	1976	16.00	40.00
		(One-sided. Convincing counterfeits exist.)			
Shelter/ABC DA-52029	(DJ)	You're Gonna Get It! *(Red vinyl)*	1978	10.00	25.00
MCA 8021	(DJ)	Pack Up The Plantation *(Sampler)*	1985	6.00	15.00

PHANTOM'S DIVINE COMEDY, THE

Label & Catalog #		Title	Year	VG+	NM
Capitol ST-11313	(S)	Part One	1974	24.00	60.00

PHAPHNER

Label & Catalog #		Title	Year	VG+	NM
Dragon LP-101	(S)	Overdrive	197?	1,300.00	2,000.00

PHARAOHS, THE

Label & Catalog #		Title	Year	VG+	NM
Scarab 001	(S)	Awakening	1972	6.00	15.00

Label & Catalog #		Title	Year	VG+	NM
PHILLIPS, BILL					
Harmony HL-7309	(M)	**Bill Phillips' Best**	1964	8.00	20.00
Decca DL-4792	(M)	**Put It Off Until Tomorrow**	1966	8.00	20.00
Decca DL-74792	(S)	**Put It Off Until Tomorrow**	1966	10.00	25.00
PHILLIPS, ESTHER [LITTLE ESTHER]					
King LP-622	(M)	**Down Memory Lane With Little Esther**	1959	1,000.00	*Rare*
		(Near Mint copies have a suggested value of $1,500-2,500.)			
Lenox 227	(M)	**Release Me**	1962	30.00	75.00
Lenox 227	(S)	**Release Me**	1962	60.00	150.00
Atlantic 8102	(M)	**And I Love Him**	1965	12.00	30.00
Atlantic SD-8102	(S)	**And I Love Him**	1965	16.00	40.00
Atlantic 8122	(M)	**Esther**	1966	12.00	30.00
Atlantic SD-8122	(S)	**Esther**	1966	16.00	40.00
Atlantic 8130	(M)	**The Country Side Of Esther Phillips**	1966	12.00	30.00
Atlantic SD-8130	(S)	**The Country Side Of Esther Phillips**	1966	16.00	40.00
		(Atlantic 8130 is a repackage of Lenox 227.)			
Atlantic SD-1565	(S)	**Burnin'**	1970	6.00	15.00
Kudu 05	(S)	**From A Whisper To A Scream**	1972	4.00	10.00
Kudo 09	(S)	**Alone Again Naturally**	1972	4.00	10.00
Kudo 14	(S)	**Black-Eyed Blues**	1973	4.00	10.00
Kudu 18	(S)	**Performance**	1974	4.00	10.00
Kudo 23	(S)	**Esther Phillips And Joe Beck**	1975	4.00	10.00
Kudo 28	(S)	**For All We Know** *(With Joe Beck)*	1976	4.00	10.00
Kudo 31	(S)	**Capricorn Princess**	1976	4.00	10.00
Atlantic SD-1680	(S)	**Confession The Blues**	1976	4.00	10.00
PHILLIPS, GENE					
Crown CLP-5375	(S)	**Gene Phillips And The Rockers**	1963	10.00	25.00
Crown CST-375	(E)	**Gene Phillips And The Rockers**	1963	4.00	10.00
PHILLIPS, JOHN					
Mr. Phillips was formerly a member of The Journeymen; The Mamas & The Papas.					
Dunhill DS-50077	(S)	**John Phillips/Wolf King Of L.A.**	1970	6.00	15.00
20th Century 4210	(DJ)	**Myra Breckinridge** *(Soundtrack)*	1970	300.00	500.00
MGM 1SE-28ST	(S)	**Brewster McCloud** *(Soundtrack)*	1970	6.00	15.00
PHILLIPS, MICHELLE					
Ms. Phillips was formerly a member of The Mamas & The Papas.					
A&M SP-4651	(S)	**Victim Of Romance**	1977	4.00	10.00
PHILLIPS, STU					
Capitol T-2356	(M)	**Feels Like Lovin'**	1965	5.00	12.00
Capitol ST-2356	(S)	**Feels Like Lovin'**	1965	6.00	15.00
RCA Victor LPM-3619	(M)	**Singing Stu Phillips**	1966	5.00	12.00
RCA Victor LSP-3619	(S)	**Singing Stu Phillips**	1966	6.00	15.00
RCA Victor LPM-3717	(M)	**Grass Roots Country**	1966	5.00	12.00
RCA Victor LSP-3717	(S)	**Grass Roots Country**	1966	6.00	15.00
RCA Victor LSP-4012	(S)	**Our Last Rendezvous**	1968	5.00	12.00
PHILLIPS, WARREN, & THE ROCKETS					
Members of The Rockets later recorded as Foghat.					
Parrot PAS-71044	(S)	**Rocked Out**	1970	12.00	30.00
London 50018	(S)	**Barefoot Days**	1979	4.00	10.00
PHILOSOPHERS, THE					
Philo Spectrum LP-1001	(S)	**After Sundown**	1970	40.00	100.00
PHLUPH					
Verve V-5054	(M)	**Phluph**	1968	10.00	25.00
Verve V6-5054	(S)	**Phluph**	1968	10.00	25.00
PIANO RED					
Piano Red also recorded as Dr. Feelgood.					
Groove LG-1001	(M)	**Jump Man, Jump**	1956	200.00	400.00
Groove LG-1002	(M)	**Piano Red In Concert**	1956	250.00	500.00

Label & Catalog #		Title	Year	VG+	NM
PICKETT, BOBBY "BORIS" (& THE CRYPT KICKERS)					
Garpax GP-67001	(M)	The Monster Mash	1962	40.00	100.00
Garpax SGP-67001	(S)	The Monster Mash	1962	60.00	150.00
Parrott XPAS-71063	(E)	The Original Monster Mash	1973	10.00	25.00
		(Parrot 71063 is a reissue of Garpax 67001.)			
PICKETT, WILSON					
Double-L DL-2300	(M)	It's Too Late	1963	16.00	40.00
Double-L SDL-8300	(S)	It's Too Late	1963	20.00	50.00
		("R 'n B Special" is rechanneled on this album.)			
Wand WD-672	(M)	Great Wilson Pickett Hits	196?	12.00	30.00
Wand WDS-672	(E)	Great Wilson Pickett Hits	196?	10.00	25.00
Atlantic 8114	(M)	In The Midnight Hour	1965	16.00	40.00
Atlantic SD-8114	(E)	In The Midnight Hour	1965	12.00	30.00
Atlantic 8129	(M)	The Exciting Wilson Pickett	1966	16.00	40.00
Atlantic SD-8129	(E)	The Exciting Wilson Pickett	1966	12.00	30.00
Atlantic 8138	(M)	The Wicked Pickett	1967	16.00	40.00
Atlantic SD-8138	(E)	The Wicked Pickett	1967	12.00	30.00
Atlantic 8145	(M)	The Sound Of Wilson Pickett	1967	16.00	40.00
Atlantic SD-8145	(P)	The Sound Of Wilson Pickett	1967	12.00	30.00
Atlantic 8151	(M)	The Best Of Wilson Pickett	1967	10.00	25.00
Atlantic SD-8151	(E)	The Best Of Wilson Pickett	1967	8.00	20.00
Atlantic SD-8175	(S)	I'm In Love	1968	8.00	20.00
Atlantic SD-8183	(S)	Midnight Mover	1968	8.00	20.00
Atlantic SD-8215	(S)	Hey Jude	1869	8.00	20.00
Atlantic SD-8250	(S)	Right On	1970	8.00	20.00
Atlantic SD-8270	(S)	Wilson Pickett In Philadelphia	1970	8.00	20.00
Atlantic SD-8290	(S)	The Best Of Wilson Pickett, Volume 2	1971	6.00	15.00
Atlantic SD-8300	(S)	Don't Knock My Love	1971	6.00	15.00
Atlantic SD-2501	(P)	Wilson Pickett's Greatest Hits	1973	5.00	12.00
RCA Victor LSP-4858	(S)	Tonight I'm My Biggest Audience	1973	4.00	10.00
RCA Victor APL1-0312	(S)	Miz Lena's Boy	1973	4.00	10.00
RCA Victor APL1-0495	(S)	Pickett In The Picket	1974	4.00	10.00
RCA Victor APL1-0856	(S)	Join Me And Let's Be Free	1975	4.00	10.00
PIERCE, WEBB					
Decca DL-5536 (10")	(M)	That Wondering Boy	1953	40.00	100.00
Decca DL-8129	(M)	Webb Pierce	1955	20.00	50.00
Decca DL-8295	(M)	That Wondering Boy	1956	20.00	50.00
Decca DL-8728	(M)	Just Imagination	1957	16.00	40.00
Decca DL-8889	(M)	Bound For The Kingdom	1959	10.00	25.00
Decca DL-78889	(S)	Bound For The Kingdom	1959	16.00	40.00
Decca DL-8899	(M)	Webb!	1959	10.00	25.00
Decca DL-78899	(S)	Webb!	1959	16.00	40.00
		—Original Decca albums above have black & silver labels.—			
King 648	(M)	The One And Only Webb Pierce	1959	20.00	50.00
Decca DL-4015	(M)	Webb With A Beat	1960	8.00	20.00
Decca DL-74015	(S)	Webb With A Beat	1960	10.00	25.00
Decca DL-4079	(M)	Walking The Streets	1960	8.00	20.00
Decca DL-74079	(S)	Walking The Streets	1960	10.00	25.00
Decca DL-4110	(M)	Golden Favorites	1961	8.00	20.00
Decca DL-74110	(E)	Golden Favorites	1961	4.00	10.00
Decca DL-4144	(M)	Fallen Angel	1961	6.00	15.00
Decca DL-74144	(S)	Fallen Angel	1961	8.00	20.00
Decca DL-4218	(M)	Hideaway Heart	1962	6.00	15.00
Decca DL-74218	(S)	Hideaway Heart	1962	8.00	20.00
Decca DL-4294	(M)	Cross Country	1962	6.00	15.00
Decca DL-74294	(S)	Cross Country	1962	8.00	20.00
Decca DL-4358	(M)	I've Got A New Heartache	1963	6.00	15.00
Decca DL-74358	(S)	I've Got A New Heartache	1963	8.00	20.00
Decca DL-4384	(M)	Bow Thy Head	1963	6.00	15.00
Decca DL-74384	(S)	Bow Thy Head	1963	8.00	20.00
Decca DXB-181	(M)	The Webb Pierce Story *(2 LPs with booklet)*	1964	10.00	25.00
Decca DXSB-181	(S)	The Webb Pierce Story *(2 LPs with booklet)*	1964	10.00	25.00
Decca DL-4486	(M)	Sands Of Gold	1964	6.00	15.00
Decca DL-74486	(S)	Sands Of Gold	1964	8.00	20.00
Decca DL-4604	(M)	Memory No. 1	1965	6.00	15.00
Decca DL-74604	(S)	Memory No. 1	1965	8.00	20.00

Label & Catalog #		Title	Year	VG+	NM
Decca DL-4659	(M)	**Country Music Time**	1965	6.00	15.00
Decca DL-74659	(S)	**Country Music Time**	1965	8.00	20.00
Decca DL-4739	(M)	**Sweet Memories**	1966	6.00	15.00
Decca DL-74739	(S)	**Sweet Memories**	1966	8.00	20.00
Decca DL-4782	(M)	**Webb's Choice**	1966	6.00	15.00
Decca DL-74782	(S)	**Webb's Choice**	1966	8.00	20.00
— Original Decca albums above have black labels with "Mfrd by Decca" beneath the rainbow.—					
Decca DL-4844	(M)	**Where'd Ya Stay Last Night?**	1967	6.00	15.00
Decca DL-74844	(S)	**Where'd Ya Stay Last Night?**	1967	6.00	15.00
Decca DL-74964	(S)	**Fool, Fool, Fool**	1968	6.00	15.00
Decca DL-74999	(S)	**Webb Pierce's Greatest Hits**	1968	6.00	15.00
Decca DL-75071	(S)	**Saturday Night**	1969	6.00	15.00
Decca DL-75132	(S)	**Webb Pierce Sings This Thing**	1969	6.00	15.00
Decca DL-75168	(S)	**Love Ain't Never Gonna Be No Better**	1970	6.00	15.00
Decca DL-75210	(S)	**Merry-Go-Round World**	1970	6.00	15.00
Decca DL-75280	(S)	**Webb Pierce Road Show**	1971	6.00	15.00
Decca DL-75393	(S)	**I'm Gonna Be A Swinger**	1972	6.00	15.00

PIERCE, WEBB / MARVIN RAINWATER / STUART HAMBLEN

Audio Lab AL-1563	(M)	**Sing For You**	195?	30.00	75.00

PIKE, PETE

Audio Lab AL-1559	(M)	**Pete Pike**	1960	20.00	50.00

PINK FLOYD

Pink Floyd is Nick Mason, Roger Waters, Roger Wright and Syd Barrett, who was replaced by David Gilmour in 1968.

Tower T-5093	(DJ)	**Piper At The Gates Of Dawn** (White label)	1967	80.00	200.00
Tower T-5093	(M)	**Piper At The Gates Of Dawn** (Orange label)	1967	60.00	150.00
Tower ST-5093	(S)	**Piper At The Gates Of Dawn** (Orange label)	1967	20.00	50.00
Tower ST-5093	(S)	**Piper At The Gates Of Dawn** (Striped label)	1968	30.00	75.00
Tower ST-5131	(DJ)	**A Saucerful Of Secrets** (White label)	1968	40.00	100.00
Tower ST-5131	(S)	**A Saucerful Of Secrets** (Orange label)	1968	20.00	50.00
Tower ST-5131	(S)	**A Saucerful Of Secrets** (Striped label)	1968	30.00	75.00
Tower ST-5169	(DJ)	**More** (Soundtrack. White label)	1968	40.00	100.00
Tower ST-5169	(S)	**More** (Soundtrack)	1968	20.00	50.00
Harvest 388	(S)	**Ummagumma** (2 LPs)	1969	16.00	40.00
		(Original covers have a copy of the "Gigi" soundtrack album leaning against the wall in the lower foreground.)			
Harvest 388	(S)	**Ummagumma** (2 LPs)	1969	16.00	40.00
		(The cover has a copy of "Ummagumma" leaning against the wall.)			
Harvest 388	(S)	**Ummagumma** (2 LPs)	197?	6.00	15.00
		(The cover has a blank cover leaning against the wall.)			
Harvest SMAS-382	(S)	**Atom Heart Mother**	1970	8.00	20.00
Harvest SW-759	(S)	**Relics**	1971	6.00	15.00
Harvest SMAS-832	(S)	**Meddle**	1971	6.00	15.00
Harvest ST-11078	(S)	**Obscured By Clouds** (Soundtrack)	1972	6.00	15.00
Harvest SMAS-11163	(S)	**The Dark Side Of The Moon**	1973	5.00	12.00
Harvest SABB-11257	(S)	**Nice Pair** (2 LPs)	1973	6.00	15.00
		(Repackages material from Tower 5098, 5131 and Harvest 388.)			
Capitol SPRO-8116	(DJ)	**Pink Floyd Tour '75**	1975	30.00	75.00
Capitol SEAX-11902	(S)	**The Dark Side Of The Moon** (Picture disc)	1978	12.00	30.00
Columbia PC-33453	(S)	**Wish You Were Here**	1975	4.00	10.00
Columbia PCQ-33453	(Q)	**Wish You Were Here**	1975	16.00	40.00
Columbia AP-1	(DJ)	**Animals** (With insert)	1977	12.00	30.00
Columbia PCQ-34474	(Q)	**Animals**	1977	16.00	40.00
Columbia HC-33453	(S)	**Wish You Were Here** (Half-speed master)	1981	20.00	60.00
Columbia HC-43453	(S)	**Wish You Were Here** (Half-speed master)	1982	15.00	45.00
Columbia H2C-46183	(S)	**The Wall** (2 LPs. Half-speed master)	1983	50.00	150.00
Columbia HC-47680	(S)	**Collection Of Great Dance Songs**	1983	16.00	50.00
		(Half-speed master)			
Columbia AS-	(DJ)	**Off The Wall**	1983	30.00	75.00
Columbia AS-1636	(DJ)	**Final Cut** (Banded for airplay)	1983	8.00	20.00
Mobile Fidelity MFSL-017	(S)	**The Dark Side Of The Moon**	1977	16.00	40.00
Mobile Fidelity MFQR-017	(S)	**The Dark Side Of The Moon**	1982	120.00	360.00
		(Ultra High Quality Recording in a box.)			
Mobile Fidelity MFSL-197	(S)	**Meddle**	198?	10.00	30.00

PINK PUZZ: *Refer to* **PAUL REVERE & THE RAIDERS**

Label & Catalog #		Title	Year	VG+	NM
PIPKINS, THE					
Capitol ST-483	(S)	**Gimme Dat Ding**	1970	6.00	15.00
PIRANHAS, THE					
Custom Fidelity 1452	(S)	**Somethin' Fishy**	1969	60.00	150.00
PISANI, FRANK					
Dellwood DLD-56010	(S)	**Sky**	1977	40.00	100.00
PITNEY, GENE					
Gene also recorded with George Jones.					
Musicor MM-2001	(M)	**The Many Sides Of Gene Pitney**	1962	20.00	50.00
Musicor MS-3001	(E)	**The Many Sides Of Gene Pitney**	1962	16.00	40.00
		— Original Musicor albums above have brown labels.—			
Musicor MM-2001	(M)	**The Many Sides Of Gene Pitney**	1962	12.00	30.00
Musicor MS-3001	(E)	**The Many Sides Of Gene Pitney**	1962	10.00	25.00
Musicor MM-2003	(M)	**Only Love Can Break A Heart**	1962	10.00	25.00
Musicor MS-3003	(S)	**Only Love Can Break A Heart**	1962	12.00	30.00
Musicor MM-2004	(M)	**Gene Pitney Sings Just For You**	1963	10.00	25.00
Musicor MS-3004	(S)	**Gene Pitney Sings Just For You**	1963	12.00	30.00
Musicor MM-2005	(M)	**Gene Pitney Sings World-Wide Winners**	1963	10.00	25.00
Musicor MS-3005	(E)	**Gene Pitney Sings World-Wide Winners**	1963	12.00	30.00
		("Only Love Can Break A Heart," "If I Didn't Have A Dime," "The Man Who Shot Liberty Valance," "Tower Tall" and "Half Heaven-Half Heartache" are in stereo on this album.)			
Musicor MM-2006	(M)	**Blue Gene**	1963	10.00	25.00
Musicor MS-3006	(S)	**Blue Gene**	1963	12.00	30.00
Musicor MM-2007	(M)	**The Fair Young Ladies Of Folkland**	1964	10.00	25.00
Musicor MS-3007	(S)	**The Fair Young Ladies Of Folkland**	1964	12.00	30.00
Musicor MM-2008	(M)	**Gene Pitney's Big Sixteen**	1964	8.00	20.00
Musicor MS-3008	(S)	**Gene Pitney's Big Sixteen**	1964	10.00	25.00
		("Town Without Pity" and "Take Me Tonight" are rechanneled.)			
		— Musicor albums above have black labels with "Distributed by United Artists."—			
Musicor MM-2015	(M)	**Gene Italiano**	1964	8.00	20.00
Musicor MS-3015	(S)	**Gene Italiano**	1964	10.00	25.00
Musicor MM-2019	(M)	**It Hurts To Be In Love**	1964	8.00	20.00
Musicor MS-3019	(P)	**It Hurts To Be In Love**	1964	10.00	25.00
Musicor MM-2043	(M)	**Gene Pitney's More Big Sixteen, Volume 2**	1965	8.00	20.00
Musicor MS-3043	(S)	**Gene Pitney's More Big Sixteen, Volume 2**	1965	10.00	25.00
		("It Hurts To Be In Love," "Today's Teardrops," "Hello, Mary Lou," "Every Breath I Take" and "I Laughed So Hard I Cried" are re-channeled on this album.)			
Musicor MM-2056	(M)	**I Must Be Seeing Things**	1965	8.00	20.00
Musicor MS-3056	(S)	**I Must Be Seeing Things**	1965	10.00	25.00
Musicor MM-2069	(M)	**Looking Through The Eyes Of Love**	1965	8.00	20.00
Musicor MS-3069	(S)	**Looking Through The Eyes Of Love**	1965	10.00	25.00
Musicor MM-2072	(M)	**Gene Pitney Espanol**	1965	8.00	20.00
Musicor MS-3072	(S)	**Gene Pitney Espanol**	1965	10.00	25.00
Musicor MM-2085	(M)	**Big Sixteen, Volume 3**	1966	8.00	20.00
Musicor MS-3085	(S)	**Big Sixteen, Volume 3**	1966	10.00	25.00
Musicor MM-2095	(M)	**Backstage I'm Lonely**	1966	8.00	20.00
Musicor MS-3095	(S)	**Backstage I'm Lonely**	1966	10.00	25.00
Musicor MM-2100	(M)	**Messumo Mi Puo Giudicare**	1966	8.00	20.00
Musicor MS-3100	(S)	**Messumo Mi Puo Giudicare**	1966	10.00	25.00
Musicor MM-2101	(M)	**The Gene Pitney Show**	1966	8.00	20.00
Musicor MS-3101	(S)	**The Gene Pitney Show**	1966	10.00	25.00
Musicor MM-2102	(M)	**Greatest Hits Of All Time**	1966	8.00	20.00
Musicor MS-3102	(P)	**Greatest Hits Of All Time**	1966	10.00	25.00
		("Town Without Pity," "Every Breath I Take" and "It Hurts To Be In Love" are rechanneled this album.)			
Musicor MM-2104	(M)	**The Country Side Of Gene Pitney**	1966	8.00	20.00
Musicor MS-3104	(S)	**The Country Side Of Gene Pitney**	1966	10.00	25.00
Musicor MM-2108	(M)	**Young And Warm And Wonderful**	1966	8.00	20.00
Musicor MS-3108	(S)	**Young And Warm And Wonderful**	1966	10.00	25.00
Musicor MM-2117	(M)	**Just One Smile**	1967	8.00	20.00
Musicor MS-3117	(S)	**Just One Smile**	1967	10.00	25.00
Musicor MM-2134	(M)	**Golden Greats**	1967	8.00	20.00
Musicor MS-3134	(P)	**Golden Greats**	1967	10.00	25.00
Musicor M2S-3148	(P)	**The Gene Pitney Story** *(2 LPs)*	1968	10.00	25.00

Label & Catalog #		Title	Year	VG+	NM
Musicor MS-3161	(S)	Gene Pitney Sings Burt Bacharach	1968	8.00	20.00
Musicor MS-3164	(S)	She's A Heartbreaker	1968	10.00	25.00
Musicor P2S-5025	(P)	This Is Gene Pitney (2 LPs. Record Club)	1968	10.00	25.00
Musicor MS-3174	(S)	The Greatest Hits Of Gene Pitney	1969	6.00	15.00
		("I Wanna Love My Life Away," "Something's Gotten Hold Of My Heart," "Nessuno Mi Puo Giudicare" and "Louisiana Mama" are rechanneled on this album.)			
Musicor MS-3183	(S)	This Is Gene Pitney	1970	6.00	15.00
Musicor MS-3206	(S)	Ten Years After	1971	6.00	15.00
Musicor MS-3250	(P)	The Golden Hits Of Gene Pitney	1971	6.00	15.00
— Original Musicor albums above have black labels.—					
Music Disc MDS-1005	(S)	Town Without Pity	1969	4.00	10.00
Music Disc MDS-1008	(S)	Twenty Four Hours From Tulsa	1969	4.00	10.00
Music Disc MDS-1014	(S)	Baby, I Need Your Lovin'	1969	4.00	10.00

PIXIES, THE

Elektra PR-8127	(DJ)	The Pixies Live (One sided)	1989	20.00	50.00

PIXIES THREE, THE

Mercury MG-20912	(M)	Party With The Pixies Three	1964	40.00	100.00
Mercury SR-60912	(P)	Party With The Pixies Three	1964	60.00	150.00

PLAIN JANE

Hobbit 5000	(S)	Plain Jane	1969	10.00	25.00

PLANT & SEE

White Whale S-7120	(S)	Plant And See	1969	8.00	20.00

PLASTER CASTERS, THE

Bluestime 9001	(S)	The Plaster Casters Blues Band	197?	10.00	25.00

PLATTERS, THE

The original Platters feature Tony Williams.

Federal 295-549	(M)	The Platters	1955	See note below	
		(Contrary to previous reports, this 10" album does not exist.)			
King 395-549	(M)	The Platters	1955	300.00	500.00
King 651	(M)	Only You (Repackage of King 549)	1959	200.00	400.00
Mercury MG-20146	(M)	The Platters	1956	50.00	100.00
Mercury MG-20216	(M)	The Platters, Volume 2	1956	40.00	100.00
Mercury MG-20298	(M)	Flying Platters	1957	40.00	100.00
Mercury MG-20366	(M)	Flying Platters Around The World	1959	16.00	40.00
Mercury SR-60043	(S)	Flying Platters Around The World	1959	30.00	75.00
Mercury MG-20410	(M)	Remember When?	1959	16.00	40.00
Mercury SR-60087	(S)	Remember When?	1959	30.00	75.00
Mercury MG-20472	(M)	Encore Of Golden Hits	1960	12.00	30.00
Mercury SR-60243	(P)	Encore Of Golden Hits	1960	16.00	40.00
Mercury MG-20481	(M)	Reflections	1960	12.00	30.00
Mercury SR-60160	(S)	Reflections	1960	16.00	40.00
Mercury MG-20589	(M)	Life Is Just A Bowl Of Cherries	1960	12.00	30.00
Mercury SR-60254	(S)	Life Is Just A Bowl Of Cherries	1960	16.00	40.00
Mercury MG-20591	(M)	More Encore Of Golden Hits	1960	12.00	30.00
Mercury SR-60252	(S)	More Encore Of Golden Hits	1960	16.00	40.00
Mercury MG-20613	(M)	Encore Of Broadway Golden Hits	1961	12.00	30.00
Mercury SR-60613	(S)	Encore Of Broadway Golden Hits	1961	16.00	40.00
Mercury MG-20669	(M)	Song For The Lonely	1962	12.00	30.00
Mercury SR-60669	(S)	Song For The Lonely	1962	16.00	40.00
Mercury MG-20759	(M)	Moonlight Memories	1963	12.00	30.00
Mercury SR-60759	(S)	Moonlight Memories	1963	16.00	40.00
Mercury MG-20782	(M)	The Platters Present All-Time Movie Hits	1963	12.00	30.00
Mercury SR-60782	(S)	The Platters Present All-Time Movie Hits	1963	16.00	40.00
Mercury MG-20808	(M)	The Platters Sing Latino	1963	12.00	30.00
Mercury SR-60808	(S)	The Platters Sing Latino	1963	16.00	40.00
Mercury MG-20841	(M)	Christmas With The Platters	1963	12.00	30.00
Mercury SR-60841	(S)	Christmas With The Platters	1963	16.00	40.00
Mercury MG-20893	(M)	Encore Of Golden Hits Of The Groups	1964	12.00	30.00
Mercury SR-60893	(S)	Encore Of Golden Hits Of The Groups	1964	16.00	40.00
Mercury MG-20933	(M)	10th Anniversary Album	1964	10.00	25.00
Mercury SR-60933	(S)	10th Anniversary Album	1964	12.00	30.00
— Original Mercury albums above have black & silver labels.—					

Label & Catalog #		Title	Year	VG+	NM
Mercury MG-20983	(M)	The New Soul Of The Platters	1965	8.00	20.00
Mercury SR-60983	(S)	The New Soul Of The Platters	1965	10.00	25.00
Wing MGW-12112	(M)	Encores	1962	5.00	12.00
Wing SRW-16112	(S)	Encores	1962	6.00	15.00
Wing MGW-12226	(M)	Flying Platters	1963	5.00	12.00
Wing SRW-16226	(S)	Flying Platters	1963	6.00	15.00
Wing MGW-12272	(M)	Reflections	1964	5.00	12.00
Wing SRW-16272	(S)	Reflections	1964	6.00	15.00
Wing MGW-12346	(M)	10th Anniversary Album	1965	5.00	12.00
Wing SRW-16346	(S)	10th Anniversary Album	1965	6.00	15.00
Musicor MM-2091	(M)	I Love You 1,000 Times	1966	6.00	15.00
Musicor MS-3091	(S)	I Love You 1,000 Times	1966	8.00	20.00
Musicor MM-2111	(M)	The Platters Have The Magic Touch	1966	6.00	15.00
Musicor MS-3111	(S)	The Platters Have The Magic Touch	1966	8.00	20.00
Musicor MM-2125	(M)	Going Back To Detroit	1967	6.00	15.00
Musicor MS-3125	(S)	Going Back To Detroit	1967	8.00	20.00
Musicor MM-2141	(M)	New Golden Hits Of The Platters	1967	6.00	15.00
Musicor MS-3141	(S)	New Golden Hits Of The Platters	1967	8.00	20.00
Musicor MS-3156	(S)	Sweet, Sweet Lovin'	1968	8.00	20.00
Musicor MS-3171	(S)	I Get The Sweetest Feeling	1968	8.00	20.00
Musicor MS-3185	(S)	Singing The Great Hits Our Way	1969	8.00	20.00
Music Disc MDS-1002	(S)	Only You	1969	8.00	20.00
Musicor MS-3251	(S)	The Golden Hits Of The Platters	1973	2.00	10.00
Chicago Fire 7401	(S)	Live In Chicago	1974	6.00	15.00
Ram	(S)	Reborn	1978	6.00	15.00

PLAYBACKS, THE

| Round LP-1111 | (M) | Greatest Of The Latest | 196? | 30.00 | 75.00 |

PLAYERS, THE

| Minit 4006 | (M) | He'll Be Back | 1966 | 8.00 | 20.00 |
| Minit 24006 | (S) | He'll Be Back | 1966 | 10.00 | 25.00 |

PLAYMATES, THE

Roulette R-25001	(M)	Calypso	1958	8.00	20.00
Roulette SR-25001	(S)	Calypso	1958	10.00	25.00
Roulette R-25043	(M)	At Play With The Playmates	1958	8.00	20.00
Roulette SR-25043	(S)	At Play With The Playmates	1958	10.00	25.00
Roulette R-25059	(M)	Rock And Roll Record Hop	1959	8.00	20.00
Roulette SR-25059	(S)	Rock And Roll Record Hop	1959	10.00	25.00
Roulette R-25068	(M)	Cuttin' Capers	1959	8.00	20.00
Roulette SR-25068	(S)	Cuttin' Capers	1959	10.00	25.00
Roulette R-25084	(M)	Broadway Show Stoppers	1959	8.00	20.00
Roulette SR-25084	(S)	Broadway Show Stoppers	1959	10.00	25.00
Forum F-16001	(M)	The Playmates Visit West Of The Indies	1960	6.00	15.00
Forum SF-16001	(S)	The Playmates Visit West Of The Indies	1960	8.00	20.00
Roulette R-25139	(M)	Wait For Me	1961	6.00	15.00
Roulette SR-25139	(S)	Wait For Me	1961	8.00	20.00

PLEASURE FAIR, THE

| Uni 3009 | (M) | The Pleasure Fair | 1967 | 6.00 | 15.00 |
| Uni 73009 | (S) | The Pleasure Fair | 1967 | 8.00 | 20.00 |

PLIMSOULS, THE

| Beat BE-1001 | (S) | Zero Hour | 1980 | 10.00 | 25.00 |
| Planet P-13 | (S) | The Plimsouls | 1981 | 8.00 | 20.00 |

PLUS

| Probe CPLP-4513 | (S) | The Seven Deadly Sins | 1969 | 6.00 | 15.00 |

POCO

Poco's original line-up included Richie Furay and Jim Messina of The Buffalo Springfield.

Epic BN-26460	(S)	Pickin' Up The Pieces (Yellow label)	1969	6.00	15.00
Epic EQ-30209	(Q)	Deliverin'	1971	6.00	15.00
Epic EQ-32354	(Q)	Crazy Eyes	1973	6.00	15.00
Epic PEQ-33192	(Q)	Cantamos	1974	6.00	15.00
Mobile Fidelity MFSL-020	(S)	Legend (Original Master Recording)	1978	8.00	25.00

Label & Catalog #		Title	Year	VG+	NM
POINT, THE					
(No label)	(S)	**The Point** (10" on white vinyl)	1981	30.00	75.00
POLICE					
A&M SP-3735	(S)	**Synchronicity** (Brown & grey cover)	1983	12.00	30.00
A&M SP-3735	(S)	**Synchronicity** (Black & white cover)	1983	20.00	50.00
A&M SP-3735	(S)	**Synchronicity** (Blue, red & yellow cover)	1983	5.00	12.00
		(Non-opaque vinyl; light will shine through with a purple glow.)			
Nautilus NR-19	(S)	**Zenyatta Mondatta**	198?	7.00	20.00
Nautilus NR-40	(S)	**Ghost In The Machine**	198?	8.00	25.00
Nautilus NR-40	(S)	**Ghost In The Machine** (DBX)	198?	10.00	30.00

POLK, LUCY ANN: *Refer to* GOLDMINE'S PRICE GUIDE TO COLLECTIBLE JAZZ ALBUMS

POLLUTION					
Pollution features Dobie Gray.					
Prophecy SD-6051	(S)	**Pollution**	1971	12.00	30.00
Prophecy SD-6057	(S)	**Pollution II**	1972	12.00	30.00
PONCE, PONCIE					
Warner Bros. W-1453	(M)	**Poncie Ponce Sings**	1962	8.00	20.00
Warner Bros. WS-1453	(S)	**Poncie Ponce Sings**	1962	10.00	25.00
PONTY, JEAN LUC					
World Pacific WPS-20172	(S)	**King Kong/Ponty Plays Zappa**	1970	10.00	25.00
		(Although uncredited, Zappa produces and plays guitar.)			
POOBAH					
Peppermint	(S)	**Let Me In**	1969	200.00	400.00
Peppermint	(S)	**U.S. Rock**	1969	60.00	150.00
Peppermint	(S)	**Steamroller**	1969	60.00	150.00

POOLE, BILLIE: *Refer to* GOLDMINE'S PRICE GUIDE TO COLLECTIBLE JAZZ ALBUMS

POOLE, BRIAN, & THE TREMELOES					
Audio Fidelity AF-2151	(M)	**Brian Poole Is Here**	1966	12.00	30.00
Audio Fidelity AFS-6151	(S)	**Brian Poole Is Here**	1966	16.00	40.00
Audio Fidelity AF-2177	(M)	**The Tremeloes Are Here**	1967	10.00	25.00
Audio Fidelity AFS-6177	(S)	**The Tremeloes Are Here**	1967	12.00	30.00
		(These are the same album with different titles.)			
POOR BOYS, THE					
Rare Earth 519	(S)	**Ain't Nothin' In Our Pocket But Love**	1970	6.00	15.00
POPCORN BLIZZARD, THE					
De-Lite DE-2004	(S)	**Explode!**	1968	14.00	35.00
POPPIES, THE					
Epic LN-24200	(M)	**Lullaby Of Love**	1966	5.00	12.00
Epic BN-24200	(S)	**Lullaby Of Love**	1966	6.00	15.00
PORTER, PEPPER					
First American FA-7756	(S)	**Invasion**	197?	10.00	25.00
POWELL, DICK					
Decca DL-8837	(S)	**Song Book**	1958	20.00	50.00
Dot DLP-3421	(M)	**Themes From Original TV Soundtracks**	1962	12.00	30.00
Dot DLP-25421	(S)	**Themes From Original TV Soundtracks**	1962	16.00	40.00
Columbia C2L-44	(M)	**Dick Powell In Hollywood** (2 LPs)	1966	8.00	20.00
Columbia C2S-44	(S)	**Dick Powell In Hollywood** (2 LPs)	1966	10.00	25.00
POWELL, JANE					
Refer to Gordon MacRae; Marilyn Monroe.					
Columbia CL-2034 (10")	(M)	**Romance**	1949	40.00	100.00
Columbia CL-2045 (10")	(M)	**A Date With Jane Powell**	1949	40.00	100.00
Columbia ML-4148	(M)	**Alice In Wonderland**	1950	40.00	100.00
MGM E-508 (10")	(M)	**Nancy Goes To Rio** (Soundtrack)	1950	40.00	100.00
MGM E-530 (10")	(M)	**Two Weeks With Love** (Soundtrack)	1950	40.00	100.00
MGM E-543 (10")	(M)	**Royal Wedding** (Soundtrack)	1951	40.00	100.00

Label & Catalog #		Title	Year	VG+	NM
MGM E-86 (10")	(M)	**Rich, Young And Pretty** *(Soundtrack)*	1951	40.00	100.00
Mercury MG-25202	(M)	**Athena** *(Soundtrack)*	1954	80.00	200.00
MGM E-224 (10")	(M)	**7 Brides For 7 Brothers** *(Soundtrack)*	1954	40.00	100.00
MGM E-3233	(M)	**Two Weeks With Love** *(Soundtrack)*	1955	20.00	50.00
MGM E-3236	(M)	**Rich, Young And Pretty** *(Soundtrack)*	1955	20.00	50.00
MGM E-3451	(M)	**Something Wonderful**	1957	16.00	40.00
Verve V-2023	(M)	**Can't We Be Friends?**	1956	14.00	35.00

POWER & THE MAJESTY, THE

Label & Catalog #		Title	Year	VG+	NM
Mobile Fidelity MFSL-004	(S)	**The Power And The Majesty**	1979	13.00	40.00
		(Thunder storm and railroad sound effects.)			

POWERS OF BLUE, THE

Label & Catalog #		Title	Year	VG+	NM
M.T.A. 1002	(M)	**Flipout**	1967	6.00	15.00
M.T.A. 5002	(S)	**Flipout**	1967	8.00	20.00

PRADO ORCHESTRA, PEREZ

Label & Catalog #		Title	Year	VG+	NM
RCA Victor LPM-1196	(M)	**Mambo By The King**	1956	20.00	50.00
RCA Victor LPM-1459	(M)	**Latin Satin**	1956	20.00	50.00
RCA Victor LPM-1556	(M)	**Perez**	1959	16.00	40.00
RCA Victor LPM-1883	(M)	**Dilo**	1959	16.00	40.00
RCA Victor LPM-2028	(M)	**Pops And Prado**	1959	16.00	40.00
RCA Victor LPM-2104	(M)	**Big Hits By Prado**	1959	16.00	40.00
RCA Victor LSP-2104	(P)	**Big Hits By Prado**	1959	20.00	50.00
RCA Victor LPM-2524	(M)	**The Twist Goes Latin**	1962	10.00	25.00
RCA Victor LSP-2524	(S)	**The Twist Goes Latin**	1962	12.00	30.00
RCA Victor LPM-2308	(M)	**Rockambo**	1961	10.00	25.00
RCA Victor LSP-2308	(S)	**Rockambo**	1961	12.00	30.00
RCA Victor LPM-2610	(M)	**Our Man In Latin America**	1963	10.00	25.00
RCA Victor LSP-2610	(S)	**Our Man In Latin America**	1963	12.00	30.00
RCA Victor LPM-3732	(M)	**The Best Of Perez Prado**	1967	12.00	30.00
RCA Victor LSP-3732	(S)	**The Best Of Perez Prado**	1967	8.00	20.00

PREMIERS, THE

Label & Catalog #		Title	Year	VG+	NM
Warner Bros. W-1565	(M)	**Farmer John**	1964	12.00	30.00
Warner Bros. WS-1565	(S)	**Farmer John**	1964	16.00	40.00

PRESLEY, ELVIS

Elvis Aron Presley is the single most collectible artist in all of recorded music. With few exceptions, each of Elvis' albums remained in print since release through the vinyl era. For this third edition, the listings were expanded for those albums issued prior to 1965 to include each of the mono and stereo label variations for RCA's classic black label with Nipper on top listening to "his master's voice."

Beginning with LPM-4088 and continuing through 4445, original pressings have orange labels and were pressed on thick, non-flexible vinyl. These were reissued with identical labels but on flimsy, flexible vinyl in 1971-73. Similarly, Camden CAS-2304 through 2428 were pressed on the non-flexible vinyl and also reissued on the flexible vinyl. The flexible of the RCA and the Camden reissues are worth 50-60% of the non-flexible prices. (Each of the Camden titles were reissued by Pickwick when it took over the line in 1975. These Pickwick reissues have little collector value.)

RCA switched to a babypoo brown label in 1975 and back to a "new" black label, with Nipper in the upper right, in the late '70s. The values for these vary dramatically and are not listed here; for more information on where to acquire data for these records, refer to the main introduction of this book.

Very few records prior to the early 1960s were factory sealed; a shrink-wrapped Presley LP prior to 2231 must be a re-seal. During the 1960s, it was common practice for RCA to have millions of covers printed at once (saving money on a per unit cost) and then using the jackets as the demand arose. Consequently, it's possible that a first pressing jacket could as easily hold a second or third pressing record as a first. So, as a rule of thumb, mono covers prior to 2756 could conceivably hold a first ("Long Play" at the bottom of the label), second ("Mono") or third ("Monaural") pressing album. Any sealed mono album after 2756 must hold a first pressing album with the "Monaural" label.

With stereo albums, there are some first pressing covers that only held original LPs, and there are some stereo jackets that were printed in the mid '60s and used into the 1970s. Albums initially issued from 1969-70 (4088 through 4460) found sealed can be determined by attempting to carefully "bend" the record: If the disc inside is non-flexible, it's an original. But, if the disc is flexible, it may be any number of pressings.

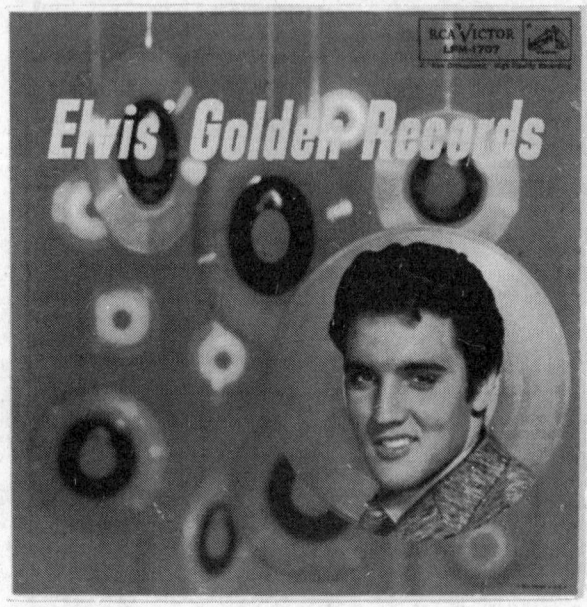

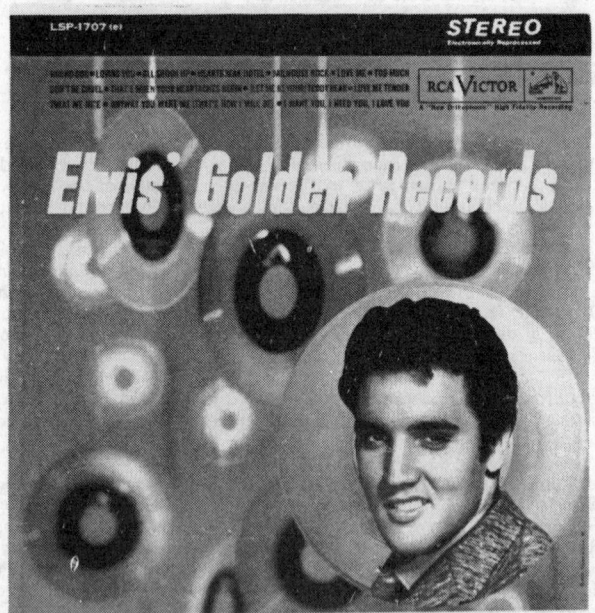

Original pressings of Elvis' Golden Records from the '50s had the title in light blue print (above); later pressings (below) changed the print to white print and added the song titles in a black border at the cover's top. As for Elvis' golden records, during his career RCA Victor released over 70 catalog albums of studio recording, hit packages (including two boxed sets of four LPs each), soundtracks and live outings plus ten budget compilations. Of these, 75 made the charts and 36 received RIAA Gold Records during his career. An additional eight releases have gone gold since his death.

Certain Elvis albums that only saw a single pressing with the original prefix (APL1-0283 and APL1-0388) are reasonably safe bets as being original. These "safe bets," both mono and stereo, generally command little more than twice the listed Near Mint value. Otherwise, the wise Elvis investor is better off seeing what he is buying.

While the listings here are more than adequate for most dealers and collectors to assess their acquisitions, they may be less than so for the completist. For the true Elvis collector, or the dealer who caters to such collectors' needs, I recommend my own A Touch Of Gold: The American Record Collectors Price Guide To Elvis Presley Records & Memorabilia. This book is 8 1/2" x 11" with 350 pages containing nearly 5,000 listings covering singles, EPs, LPs, tapes, compact discs, sheet music and RCA released memorabilia. A Touch Of Gold is available for $20.00 (includes postage and handling) from: White Dragon Press, 33309 Santiago Road, Suite 16, Acton, CA 91350.

Everything Elvis released in the '50s was cut "live" in the studio in mono. (Although during January 1957, when RCA's regular back-up tape machine was inoperative, they used one of their new two-track recorders on Elvis. The binaural results are available on Stereo 57 (Essential Elvis, Volume 2). All other appearances of Elvis' '50s recordings on stereo albums are [hideously] rechanneled. This includes several tracks first issued in the '60s: "Tomorrow Night," "When It Rains, It Really Pours," "Ain't That Loving You, Baby" and "Your Cheatin' Heart."

The following soundtrack songs were released in mono: "In My Way," "Forget Me Never," "I Slipped, I Stumbled, I Fell," and the single versions of "Wild In The Country" and "Lonely Man" (from Wild In The Country, 1960); "Follow That Dream," "What A Wonderful Life," "I'm Not The Marrying Kind," "A Whistling Tune," and "Sound Advice" (from Follow That Dream, 1961); "King Of The Whole Wide World," "This Is Living," "Riding The Rainbow," "Home Is Where The Heart Is," "I Got Lucky," and "A Whistling Tune" (from Kid Galahad, 1961); "Mama" (from Girls, Girls, Girls, 1962): and "Stay Away" and "Stay Away, Joe" (from Stay Away, Joe, 1967).

The sessions held in NBC's Burbank studios in June 1968, used as the basis for the '68 TV Special, were recorded in mono. Aside from the soundtrack from the special (LPM-4088), these astounding recordings have been scattered to the wind on various and sundry compilations, primarily the "Legendary Performer" series.

Section 1. lists those albums issued by RCA Victor. The albums originally issued on the classic RCA black label with Nipper on top are followed through their many black label permutations. Reissues from 1968-1970 first appeared on stiff, non-flexible vinyl; these are worth approximately $25-40. They were then reissued in the early '70s with the same orange label on the flimsily flexible vinyl common to the time; these are worth $15-30. This was followed by a light brown label ($10-20) and, finally, the "new" black label where Nipper is in the upper right ($10-15). These albums often are the staples of used-shops and are not listed, although many are difficult to find for the Presley completist.

Section 2. collects albums were issued promotionally that are entirely Elvis. Any RCA promotional sampler with an Elvis track has some value; several are listed in the Various Artists section of this book. Section 3. lists RCA's Camden budget subsidiary. Section 4. lists albums issued through the RCA Record Club Releases or leased to such mail-order outlets as Reader's Digest and Candlelite Music.

Finally, the Presley completist will often pay extraordinary prices for anything with Elvis on it. Hence, virtually any various artist album with at least one Elvis track will have some value to these collectors. Several of these—those with exceptional value—are noted in the RCA Victor section of the Various Artists chapter at the end of the book.

1. RCA Victor 1955-1977

Label & Catalog #		Title	Year	VG+	NM
RCA Victor LPM-1254	(M)	**Elvis Presley**	1956	100.00	250.00
		(Black label with "Long Play" on the bottom. Original pressings have "Elvis" on the cover in pale pink letters.)			
RCA Victor LPM-1254	(M)	**Elvis Presley**	1956	60.00	150.00
		(Black label with "Long Play" on the bottom. On the cover of this and all subsequent pressings, "Elvis" is in dark pink letters.)			
RCA Victor LPM-1254	(M)	**Elvis Presley**	1963	24.00	60.00
		(Black label with "Mono" on the bottom.)			
RCA Victor LPM-1254	(M)	**Elvis Presley**	1965	20.00	50.00
		(Black label with "Monaural" on the bottom.)			
RCA Victor LSP-1254	(E)	**Elvis Presley**	1962	24.00	60.00
		(Black label with a silver "RCA Victor" on top and "Stereo Electronically Reprocessed" on the bottom.)			

Label & Catalog #		Title	Year	VG+	NM
RCA Victor LSP-1254	(E)	**Elvis Presley** *(Black label with a white "RCA Victor" on top and "Stereo Electronically Reprocessed" on the bottom.)*	1965	16.00	40.00
RCA Victor LPM-1382	(M)	**Elvis** *(Black label with "Long Play" on the bottom. Original pressings have color ads for other albums along the border of the back cover.)*	1956	80.00	200.00
RCA Victor LPM-1382	(M)	**Elvis** *(Black label with "Long Play" on the bottom without the ads.)*	1956	60.00	150.00
RCA Victor LPM-1382	(M)	**Elvis** *(Black label with "Long Play" on the bottom. The label prefixes each track with "Band 1" through "Band 6.")*	1956	300.00	500.00
RCA Victor LPM-1382	(M)	**Elvis** *(Black label with "Long Play" on the bottom. Some later pressings contain an alternate take of "Old Shep." The matrix number in the trail-off vinyl ends with either "17S" or "19S.")*	1956	600.00	1,200.00
RCA Victor LPM-1382	(M)	**Elvis** *(Black label with "Mono" on the bottom.)*	1963	24.00	60.00
RCA Victor LPM-1382	(M)	**Elvis** *(Black label with "Monaural" on the bottom.)*	1965	20.00	50.00
RCA Victor LSP-1382	(E)	**Elvis** *(Black label with a silver "RCA Victor" on top and "Stereo Electronically Reprocessed" on the bottom.)*	1962	24.00	60.00
RCA Victor LSP-1382	(E)	**Elvis** *(Black label with a white "RCA Victor" on top and "Stereo Electronically Reprocessed" on the bottom.)*	1965	16.00	40.00
RCA Victor LPM-1515	(M)	**Loving You** *(Black label with "Long Play" on the bottom.)*	1957	60.00	150.00
RCA Victor LPM-1515	(M)	**Loving You** *(Black label with "Mono" on the bottom.)*	1963	24.00	60.00
RCA Victor LPM-1515	(M)	**Loving You** *(Black label with "Monaural" on the bottom.)*	1965	20.00	50.00
RCA Victor LSP-1515	(E)	**Loving You** *(Black label with a silver "RCA Victor" on top and "Stereo Electronically Reprocessed" on the bottom.)*	1962	24.00	60.00
RCA Victor LSP-1515	(E)	**Loving You** *(Black label with a white "RCA Victor" on top and "Stereo Electronically Reprocessed" on the bottom.)*	1965	16.00	40.00
RCA Victor LOC-1035	(M)	**Elvis' Christmas Album** *(Some copies had a special "gift certificate" sticker on the cover.)*	1957	500.00	1,000.00
RCA Victor LOC-1035	(M)	**Elvis' Christmas Album** *(Without the "gift certificate" sticker.)*	1957	250.00	500.00
RCA Victor LPM-1707	(M)	**Elvis' Golden Records** *(Black label with "Long Play" on the bottom. Original pressings have the title on the front cover in blue print.)*	1958	60.00	150.00
RCA Victor LPM-1707	(M)	**Elvis' Golden Records** *(Black label with "Long Play" on the bottom. Later pressings have the title in blue print with "RE" on the back.)*	1959	40.00	100.00
RCA Victor LPM-1707	(M)	**Elvis' Golden Records** *(Black label with "Mono" on the bottom.)*	1963	24.00	60.00
RCA Victor LPM-1707	(M)	**Elvis' Golden Records** *(Black label with "Monaural" on the bottom.)*	1965	20.00	50.00
RCA Victor LSP-1707	(E)	**Elvis' Golden Records** *(Black label with a silver "RCA Victor" on top and "Stereo Electronically Reprocessed" on the bottom.)*	1962	24.00	60.00
RCA Victor LSP-1707	(E)	**Elvis' Golden Records** *(Black label with a white "RCA Victor" on top and "Stereo Electronically Reprocessed" on the bottom.)*	1965	16.00	40.00
RCA Victor LPM-1884	(M)	**King Creole** *(Black label with "Long Play" on the bottom. Issued with a bonus photo, priced separately below.)*	1958	60.00	150.00
RCA Victor LPM-1884		**King Creole Bonus Photo**	1958	60.00	150.00
RCA Victor LPM-1884	(M)	**King Creole** *(Black label with "Mono" on the bottom.)*	1963	24.00	60.00
RCA Victor LPM-1884	(M)	**King Creole** *(Black label with "Monaural" on the bottom.)*	1965	20.00	50.00
RCA Victor LSP-1884	(E)	**King Creole** *(Black label with a silver "RCA Victor" on top and "Stereo Electronically Reprocessed" on the bottom.)*	1962	24.00	60.00

Label & Catalog #		Title	Year	VG+	NM
RCA Victor LSP-1884	(E)	**King Creole** *(Black label with a white "RCA Victor" on top and "Stereo Electronically Reprocessed" on the bottom.)*	1965	16.00	40.00
RCA Victor LPM-1951	(M)	**Elvis' Christmas Album** *(Black label with "Long Play" on the bottom. RCA 1951 is a reissue of 1035.)*	1958	40.00	100.00
RCA Victor LPM-1951	(M)	**Elvis' Christmas Album**	1958	40.00	100.00
RCA Victor LPM-1951	(M)	**Elvis' Christmas Album** *(Black label with "Mono" on the bottom.)*	1963	24.00	60.00
RCA Victor LPM-1951	(M)	**Elvis' Christmas Album** *(Black label with "Monaural" on the bottom.)*	1965	20.00	50.00
RCA Victor LSP-1951	(E)	**Elvis' Christmas Album** *(Black label with a white "RCA Victor" on top and "Stereo Electronically Reprocessed" on the bottom.)*	1965	16.00	40.00
RCA Victor LPM-1990	(M)	**For LP Fans Only** *(Black label with "Long Play" on the bottom.*	1959	60.00	150.00
RCA Victor LPM-1990	(M)	**For LP Fans Only**	1959	60.00	150.00
RCA Victor LPM-1990	(M)	**For LP Fans Only** *(Black label with "Mono" on the bottom.)*	1963	24.00	60.00
RCA Victor LPM-1990	(M)	**For LP Fans Only** *(Black label with "Monaural" on the bottom.)*	1965	20.00	50.00
RCA Victor LSP-1990	(E)	**For LP Fans Only** *(Black label with a white "RCA Victor" on top and "Stereo Electronically Reprocessed" on the bottom.)*	1965	16.00	40.00
RCA Victor LPM-2011	(M)	**A Date With Elvis** *(Black label with "Long Play" on the bottom. Issued in a gatefold jacket without song titles and a 1960 calendar on the back.)*	1959	80.00	200.00
RCA Victor LPM-2011	(M)	**A Date With Elvis** *(Black label with "Long Play" on the bottom. Issued in a gatefold jacket without song titles and a 1960 calendar on the back. A red sticker reads "Never Before On LP" and lists the songs.)*	1959	150.00	300.00
RCA Victor LPM-2011	(M)	**A Date With Elvis** *(Black label with "Mono" on the bottom.)*	1963	24.00	60.00
RCA Victor LPM-2011	(M)	**A Date With Elvis** *(Black label with "Monaural" on the bottom.)*	1965	20.00	50.00
RCA Victor LSP-2011	(E)	**A Date With Elvis** *(Black label with a white "RCA Victor" on top and "Stereo Electronically Reprocessed" on the bottom.)*	1965	16.00	40.00
RCA Victor LPM-2075	(M)	**Elvis' Gold Records, Volume 2** *(Black label with "Long Play" on the bottom.)*	1960	60.00	150.00
RCA Victor LPM-2075	(M)	**Elvis' Gold Records, Volume 2** *(Black label with "Mono" on the bottom.)*	1963	24.00	60.00
RCA Victor LPM-2075	(M)	**Elvis' Gold Records, Volume 2** *(Black label with "Monaural" on the bottom.)*	1965	20.00	50.00
RCA Victor LSP-2075	(E)	**Elvis' Gold Records, Volume 2** *(Black label with a silver "RCA Victor" on top and "Stereo Electronically Reprocessed" on the bottom.)*	1962	24.00	60.00
RCA Victor LSP-2075	(E)	**Elvis' Gold Records, Volume 2** *(Black label with a white "RCA Victor" on top and "Stereo Electronically Reprocessed" on the bottom.)*	1965	16.00	40.00
RCA Victor LPM-2231	(M)	**Elvis Is Back!** *(Gatefold cover) (Black label with "Long Play" on the bottom. First pressings have no song titles printed on the cover; a yellow sticker affixed to the front lists the contents. Original pressings list "The Girl Next Door" on both the label and the sticker.)*	1960	50.00	125.00
RCA Victor LPM-2231	(M)	**Elvis Is Back!** *(Gatefold cover) (Black label with "Long Play" on the bottom. Second pressings have no song titles printed on the cover; a yellow sticker affixed to the front lists the contents. This and all subsequent pressings list the song as "The Girl Next Door Went A-Walking.")*	1960	50.00	125.00
RCA Victor LPM-2231	(M)	**Elvis Is Back!** *(Gatefold cover) (Black label with "Long Play" on the bottom. Third pressings have the song titles printed on the front cover.)*	1960	40.00	100.00
RCA Victor LPM-2231	(M)	**Elvis Is Back!** *(Gatefold cover) (Black label with "Mono" on the bottom.)*	1963	24.00	60.00
RCA Victor LPM-2231	(M)	**Elvis Is Back!** *(Gatefold cover) (Black label with "Monaural" on the bottom.)*	1965	20.00	50.00

Label & Catalog #		Title	Year	VG+	NM
RCA Victor LSP-2231	(S)	**Elvis Is Back!** *(Gatefold cover)* *(Black label with "Living Stereo" on the bottom. First pressings have no song titles printed on the cover; a yellow sticker affixed to the front lists the contents. Original pressings list "The Girl Next Door" on both the label and the sticker.)*	1960	60.00	150.00
RCA Victor LSP-2231	(S)	**Elvis Is Back!** *(Gatefold cover)* *(Black label with "Living Stereo" on the bottom. Second pressings have no song titles printed on the cover; a yellow sticker affixed to the front lists the contents. This and all subsequent pressings list the song as "The Girl Next Door Went A-Walking.")*	1960	60.00	150.00
RCA Victor LSP-2231	(S)	**Elvis Is Back!** *(Gatefold cover)* *(Black label with "Living Stereo" on the bottom. Third pressings have the song titles printed on the front cover.)*	1960	50.00	125.00
RCA Victor LSP-2231	(S)	**Elvis Is Back!** *(Gatefold cover)* *(Black label with "Stereo" on the bottom.)*	1965	20.00	50.00
RCA Victor LSP-2231	(S)	**Elvis Is Back!** *(Brown label on green vinyl)*	1977	300.00	500.00
RCA Victor LPM-2256	(M)	**G.I. Blues** *(Black label with "Long Play" on the bottom.)*	1960	20.00	50.00
RCA Victor LPM-2256	(M)	**G.I. Blues** *(Black label with "Long Play" on the bottom and a heart shaped sticker on the cover advertising "Wooden Heart.)*	1960	40.00	100.00
RCA Victor LPM-2256	(M)	**G.I. Blues** *(Black label with "Mono" on the bottom.)*	1963	24.00	60.00
RCA Victor LPM-2256	(M)	**G.I. Blues** *(Black label with "Monaural" on the bottom.)*	1965	20.00	50.00
RCA Victor LSP-2256	(S)	**G.I. Blues** *(Black label with "Living Stereo" on the bottom.)*	1960	30.00	75.00
RCA Victor LSP-2256	(S)	**G.I. Blues** *(Black label with "Living Stereo" on the bottom and a heart shaped sticker on the cover advertising "Wooden Heart.)*	1960	50.00	125.00
RCA Victor LSP-2256	(S)	**G.I. Blues** *(Black label with "Stereo" on the bottom.)*	1963	20.00	50.00
RCA Victor LPM-2328	(M)	**His Hand In Mine** *(Black label with "Long Play" on the bottom.)*	1961	24.00	60.00
RCA Victor LPM-2328	(M)	**His Hand In Mine** *(Black label with "Mono" on the bottom.)*	1963	20.00	50.00
RCA Victor LPM-2328	(M)	**His Hand In Mine** *(Black label with "Monaural" on the bottom.)*	1965	16.00	40.00
RCA Victor LSP-2328	(S)	**His Hand In Mine** *(Black label with "Living Stereo" on the bottom.)*	1961	40.00	100.00
RCA Victor LSP-2328	(S)	**His Hand In Mine** *(Black label with "Stereo" on the bottom.)*	1963	20.00	50.00
RCA Victor LPM-2370	(M)	**Something For Everybody** *(Black label with "Long Play" on the bottom. Original pressings advertise Elvis' Compact-33s on the back.)*	1961	24.00	60.00
RCA Victor LPM-2370	(M)	**Something For Everybody** *(Black label with "Mono" on the bottom.)*	1963	20.00	50.00
RCA Victor LPM-2370	(M)	**Something For Everybody** *(Black label with "Monaural" on the bottom.)*	1965	16.00	40.00
RCA Victor LSP-2370	(S)	**Something For Everybody** *(Black label with "Living Stereo" on the bottom. Original pressings advertise Elvis' Compact-33s on the back.)*	1961	40.00	100.00
RCA Victor LSP-2370	(S)	**Something For Everybody** *(Black label with "Stereo" on the bottom.)*	1963	20.00	50.00
RCA Victor LPM-2426	(M)	**Blue Hawaii** *(Black label with "Long Play" on the bottom.)*	1961	24.00	60.00
RCA Victor LPM-2426	(M)	**Blue Hawaii** *(Black label with "Long Play" on the bottom. The cover has a red sticker that reads "Contains the Twist Special Rock-A-Hula Baby.")*	1961	40.00	100.00
RCA Victor LPM-2426	(M)	**Blue Hawaii** *(Black label with "Mono" on the bottom.)*	1963	20.00	50.00
RCA Victor LPM-2426	(M)	**Blue Hawaii** *(Black label with "Monaural" on the bottom.)*	1965	16.00	40.00
RCA Victor LSP-2426	(S)	**Blue Hawaii** *(Black label with "Living Stereo" on the bottom.)*	1961	24.00	60.00
RCA Victor LSP-2426	(S)	**Blue Hawaii** *(Black label with "Living Stereo" on the bottom. The cover has a red sticker that reads "Contains the Twist Special Rock-A-Hula Baby.")*	1961	50.00	125.00

Label & Catalog #		Title	Year	VG+	NM
RCA Victor LSP-2426	(S)	**Blue Hawaii**	1963	20.00	50.00
		(Black label with "Stereo" on the bottom.)			
RCA Victor LPM-2523	(M)	**Pot Luck With Elvis**	1962	24.00	60.00
		(Black label with "Long Play" on the bottom.)			
RCA Victor LPM-2523	(M)	**Pot Luck With Elvis**	1963	20.00	50.00
		(Black label with "Mono" on the bottom.)			
RCA Victor LPM-2523	(M)	**Pot Luck With Elvis**	1965	16.00	40.00
		(Black label with "Monaural" on the bottom.)			
RCA Victor LSP-2523	(S)	**Pot Luck With Elvis**	1962	40.00	100.00
		(Black label with "Living Stereo" on the bottom.)			
RCA Victor LSP-2523	(S)	**Pot Luck With Elvis**	1963	20.00	50.00
		(Black label with "Stereo" on the bottom.)			
RCA Victor LPM-2621	(M)	**Girls! Girls! Girls!**	1962	24.00	60.00
		(Black label with "Long Play" on the bottom.			
		Issued with a bonus calendar, priced separately below.)			
RCA Victor LPM-2621	(M)	**Girls! Girls! Girls!**	1963	20.00	50.00
		(Black label with "Mono" on the bottom.)			
RCA Victor LPM-2621	(M)	**Girls! Girls! Girls!**	1965	16.00	40.00
		(Black label with "Monaural" on the bottom.)			
RCA Victor LSP-2621	(S)	**Girls! Girls! Girls!**	1962	30.00	75.00
		(Black label with "Living Stereo" on the bottom.			
		Issued with a bonus calendar, priced separately below.)			
RCA Victor LSP-2621	(S)	**Girls! Girls! Girls!**	1963	20.00	50.00
		(Black label with "Stereo" on the bottom.)			
RCA Victor LPM/LSP-2621		**Girls! Girls! Girls! Bonus Calendar #1**	1962	40.00	100.00
		(1963 calendar with ads for Elvis' EPs and LPs on the back)			
RCA Victor LPM/LSP-2621		**Girls! Girls! Girls! Bonus Calendar #2**	1962	50.00	125.00
		(1963 calendar with ads for Elvis' 45s on the back)			
RCA Victor LPM/LSP-2621		**Girls! Girls! Girls! Bonus Calendar #3**	1962	150.00	300.00
		(1963 calendar with Col. Parker as Santa Claus on the back)			
RCA Victor LPM-2697	(M)	**It Happened At The World's Fair**	1963	24.00	60.00
		(Black label with "Long Play" on the bottom.			
		Issued with a bonus photo, priced separately below.)			
RCA Victor LSP-2697	(S)	**It Happened At The World's Fair**	1963	30.00	75.00
		(Black label with "Living Stereo" on the bottom.			
		Issued with a bonus photo, priced separately below.)			
RCA Victor LPM/LSP-2697		**It Happened At The World's Fair Bonus Photo**	1963	60.00	150.00
RCA Victor LPM-2756	(M)	**Fun In Acapulco**	1963	20.00	50.00
		(Black label with "Mono" on the bottom.)			
RCA Victor LPM-2756	(M)	**Fun In Acapulco**	1965	16.00	40.00
		(Black label with "Monaural" on the bottom.)			
RCA Victor LSP-2756	(S)	**Fun In Acapulco**	1963	20.00	50.00
		(Black label with "Stereo" on the bottom.)			
RCA Victor LPM-2765	(M)	**Elvis' Golden Records, Volume 3**	1963	20.00	50.00
		(Black label with "Mono" on the bottom.			
		Issued with a bonus booklet, priced separately below.)			
RCA Victor LPM-2765	(M)	**Elvis' Golden Records, Volume 3**	1963	16.00	40.00
		(Black label with "Monaural" on the bottom.)			
RCA Victor LSP-2765	(S)	**Elvis' Golden Records, Volume 3**	1963	20.00	50.00
		(Black label with "Stereo" on the bottom.			
		Issued with a bonus booklet, priced separately below.)			
RCA Victor LPM/LSP-2765		**Elvis' Golden Records, Volume 3 Bonus**	1963	16.00	40.00
		("Elvis Full Color Picture Folio Plus Special Giant Size Pin-Up			
		Picture Inside. Halve the value if the pin-up is pulled out.)			
RCA Victor LPM-2894	(M)	**Kissin' Cousins**	1964	20.00	50.00
		(Black label with "Mono" on the bottom. The cover has			
		a small black & white photo of the cast on the right.)			
RCA Victor LPM-2894	(M)	**Kissin' Cousins**	1964	40.00	100.00
		(Black label with "Mono" on the bottom. The cover			
		does not have the small black & white photo.)			
RCA Victor LPM-2894	(M)	**Kissin' Cousins**	1965	16.00	40.00
		(Black label with "Monaural" on the bottom.)			
RCA Victor LSP-2894	(S)	**Kissin' Cousins**	1964	20.00	50.00
		(Black label with "Stereo" on the bottom. The cover has			
		a small black & white photo of the cast on the right.)			
RCA Victor LSP-2894	(S)	**Kissin' Cousins**	1964	40.00	100.00
		(Black label with "Stereo" on the bottom. The cover			
		does not have the small black & white photo.)			

Label & Catalog #		Title	Year	VG+	NM
RCA Victor LPM-2999	(M)	Roustabout	1964	24.00	60.00
		(Black label with "Mono" on the bottom.)			
RCA Victor LPM-2999	(M)	Roustabout	1965	16.00	40.00
		(Black label with "Monaural" on the bottom.)			
RCA Victor LSP-2999	(S)	Roustabout	1964	200.00	400.00
		(Black label with a silver "RCA Victor" and "Stereo" on the bottom.)			
RCA Victor LSP-2999	(S)	Roustabout	1965	20.00	50.00
		(Black label with a white "RCA Victor" and "Stereo" on the bottom.)			
RCA Victor LPM-3338	(M)	Girl Happy	1965	20.00	50.00
RCA Victor LSP-3338	(S)	Girl Happy	1965	20.00	50.00
		(Black label with "Stereo" on the bottom.)			
RCA Victor LPM-3450	(M)	Elvis For Everyone	1965	20.00	50.00
RCA Victor LSP-3450	(S)	Elvis For Everyone	1965	16.00	40.00
		(Black label with "Stereo" on the bottom.)			
RCA Victor LPM-3468	(M)	Harum Scarum	1965	16.00	40.00
RCA Victor LSP-3468	(S)	Harum Scarum	1965	16.00	40.00
		(Black label with "Stereo" on the bottom. Both mono and stereo were issued with a bonus photo, priced separately below.)			
RCA Victor LPM/LSP-3468		Harum Scarum Bonus Photo	1965	12.00	30.00
RCA Victor LPM-3553	(M)	Frankie And Johnny	1966	16.00	40.00
RCA Victor LSP-3553	(S)	Frankie And Johnny	1966	16.00	40.00
		(Black label with "Stereo" on the bottom. Both mono and stereo were issued with a bonus photo, priced separately below.)			
RCA Victor LPM/LSP-3553		Frankie And Johnny Bonus Photo	1966	12.00	30.00
RCA Victor LPM-3643	(M)	Paradise Hawaiian Style	1966	16.00	40.00
RCA Victor LSP-3643	(S)	Paradise Hawaiian Style	1966	16.00	40.00
		(Black label with "Stereo" on the bottom.)			
RCA Victor LPM-3702	(M)	Spinout	1966	16.00	40.00
RCA Victor LSP-3702	(S)	Spinout	1966	16.00	40.00
		(Black label with "Stereo" on the bottom. Both mono and stereo were issued with a bonus photo, priced separately below.)			
RCA Victor LPM/LSP-3702		Spinout Bonus Photo	1966	12.00	30.00
RCA Victor LPM-3758	(M)	How Great Thou Art	1967	20.00	50.00
		(Black label with "Mono Dynagroove" on the bottom.)			
RCA Victor LSP-3758	(S)	How Great Thou Art	1967	16.00	40.00
		(Black label with "Stereo Dynagroove" on the bottom.)			
RCA Victor LSP-3758	(S)	How Great Thou Art	1967	12.00	30.00
		("Stereo Dynagroove" label with an RIAA Gold Record Award notification printed on the back cover.)			
RCA Victor LPM-3787	(M)	Double Trouble	1967	16.00	40.00
RCA Victor LSP-3787	(S)	Double Trouble	1967	16.00	40.00
		(Black label with "Stereo" on the bottom. Both mono and stereo original pressings have a printed announcement for the bonus photo, priced separately below, on the cover.)			
RCA Victor LPM/LSP-3787		Double Trouble Bonus Photo	1967	12.00	30.00
RCA Victor LPM-3787	(M)	Double Trouble	1967	16.00	40.00
RCA Victor LSP-3787	(S)	Double Trouble	1967	16.00	40.00
		(Black label with "Stereo" on the bottom. Both mono and stereo second pressings delete the bonus photo announcement.)			
RCA Victor LPM-3893	(M)	Clambake	1967	80.00	200.00
RCA Victor LSP-3893	(S)	Clambake	1967	16.00	40.00
		(Black label with "Stereo" on the bottom. Both mono and stereo were issued with a bonus photo, priced separately below.)			
RCA Victor LPM/LSP-3893		Clambake Bonus Photo	1967	12.00	30.00
RCA Victor LPM-3921	(M)	Elvis' Gold Records, Volume 4	1968	660.00	1,000.00
RCA Victor LSP-3921	(S)	Elvis' Gold Records, Volume 4	1968	16.00	40.00
		(Black label with "Stereo" on the bottom. Both mono and stereo version were issued with a bonus photo, priced separately below.)			
RCA Victor LPM/LSP-3921		Elvis' Gold Records, Volume 4 Bonus Photo	1968	50.00	100.00
RCA Victor LPM-3989	(M)	Speedway	1968	660.00	1,000.00
RCA Victor LSP-3989	(S)	Speedway	1968	16.00	40.00
		(Black label with "Stereo" on the bottom. Both mono and stereo were issued with a bonus photo, priced separately below. Contains one track by Nancy Sinatra.)			
RCA Victor LPM/LSP-3989		Speedway Bonus Photo	1968	14.00	35.00
RCA Victor LPM-4088	(M)	Elvis (NBC TV Special)	1968	8.00	20.00
		(Original pressings have orange labels on non-flexible vinyl. Approximately half of this album is stereo.)			

Label & Catalog #		Title	Year	VG+	NM
RCA Victor LPM-4088	(M)	**Elvis (NBC TV Special)**	1971	**4.00**	**10.00**
		(Second pressings have orange labels on extremely flexible vinyl.)			
RCA Victor PRS-279	(S)	**Singer Presents Elvis**			
		Singing Flaming Star & Others	1968	**10.00**	**25.00**
		(Available through Singer Sewing Centers in the latter quarter of 1968 in preparation for the Singer sponsored NBC TV Special. With the purchase of an album the fan was rewarded with several bonuses, priced separately below. "Tiger Man" is in mono on this album. This album was reissued as Elvis' first Camden budget LP.)			
RCA Victor PRS-279		**Singer Presents Elvis Bonus #1**	1968	**30.00**	**75.00**
		(32 page booklet listing all of the stations carrying the TV Special.)			
RCA Victor PRS-279		**Singer Presents Elvis Bonus #2**	1968	**8.00**	**20.00**
		(Full color photo with Elvis in-print catalog on the back and an ad for the TV Special on the bottom.)			
RCA Victor PRS-279		**Singer Presents Elvis Bonus #3**	1968	**6.00**	**15.00**
		(Full color photo with the catalog on the back but without the ad.)			
RCA Victor PRS-279		**Singer Presents Elvis Bonus #4**	1968	**6.00**	**15.00**
		(A 4" x 6" "ticket" inviting the customer to watch the TV Special.)			
RCA Victor LSP-4155	(S)	**From Elvis In Memphis**	1969	**8.00**	**20.00**
		(Original pressings have orange labels on non-flexible vinyl. Issued with a bonus photo, priced separately below.)			
RCA Victor LSP-4155		**From Elvis In Memphis Bonus Photo**	1969	**6.00**	**15.00**
RCA Victor LSP-4155	(S)	**From Elvis In Memphis**	1971	**4.00**	**10.00**
		(Second pressings have orange labels on extremely flexible vinyl.)			
RCA Victor LSP-6020	(S)	**From Memphis To Vegas** *(2 LPs)*	1969	**10.00**	**25.00**
		(Original pressings have orange labels on non-flexible vinyl. Issued with two bonus photos, priced separately below.)			
RCA Victor LSP-6020		**From Memphis To Vegas Bonus Photo**	1969	**6.00**	**15.00**
		(Issued with two photos; the price is for either one.)			
RCA Victor (No number)		**International Hotel Presents Elvis, 1969**	1969	**1,000.00**	Rare
		(Box given to attendees of Elvis' opening show in Vegas includes a copy of LPM-4088; a copy of LSP-4155; three photos; an Elvis Record Catalog; and a letter from Elvis and the Colonel. Rare with a suggested Near Mint value of $1,500-2,600 of which at least 80% is for the box alone.)			
RCA Victor (No number)		**International Hotel Presents Elvis, 1970**	1970	**1,000.00**	Rare
		(Box given to attendees of Elvis' opening show in Vegas includes a copy of LSP-6020; a copy of "Kentucky Rain;" one photo; an Elvis Record Catalog; a wallet calendar; a hotel menu; a photo album; and a letter from Elvis and the Colonel. Rare with a suggested Near Mint value of $1,500-2,600 of which at least 80% is for the box alone.)			
RCA Victor LSP-4362	(S)	**On Stage-February, 1970**	1970	**8.00**	**20.00**
		(Original pressings have orange labels on non-flexible vinyl.)			
RCA Victor LSP-4362	(S)	**On Stage-February, 1970**	1971	**4.00**	**10.00**
		(Second pressings have orange labels on extremely flexible vinyl.)			
RCA Victor LPM-6401	(M)	**Worldwide 50 Gold Award Hits** *(4 LP box)*	1970	**24.00**	**60.00**
		(Original pressings have orange labels on non-flexible vinyl. Issued with a bonus book, priced separately below.)			
RCA Victor LPM-6401		**Worldwide 50 Gold Award Hits Bonus Book**	1970	**10.00**	**25.00**
RCA Victor LPM-6401	(M)	**Worldwide 50 Gold Award Hits** *(4 LP box)*	1971	**10.00**	**25.00**
		(Second pressings have orange labels on extremely flexible vinyl.)			
RCA Victor LSP-4428	(S)	**Elvis In Person At The International Hotel**	1970	**8.00**	**20.00**
		(Original pressings have orange labels on non-flexible vinyl.)			
RCA Victor LSP-4428	(S)	**Elvis In Person At The International Hotel**	1971	**4.00**	**10.00**
		(Second pressings have orange labels on extremely flexible vinyl.)			
RCA Victor LSP-4429	(S)	**Back In Memphis**	1970	**8.00**	**20.00**
		(Original pressings have orange labels on non-flexible vinyl.)			
RCA Victor LSP-4429	(S)	**Back In Memphis**	1971	**4.00**	**10.00**
		(Second pressings have orange labels on extremely flexible vinyl.)			
RCA Victor LSP-4445	(S)	**That's The Way It Is**	1970	**10.00**	**25.00**
		(Original pressings have orange labels on non-flexible vinyl.)			
RCA Victor LSP-4445	(S)	**That's The Way It Is**	1971	**4.00**	**10.00**
		(Second pressings have orange labels on extremely flexible vinyl.)			
RCA Victor LSP-4460	(S)	**Elvis Country**	1971	**8.00**	**20.00**
		(Original pressings have orange labels on non-flexible vinyl. Issued with a bonus photo, priced separately below.)			
RCA Victor LSP-4460		**Elvis Country Bonus Photo**	1971	**6.00**	**15.00**

Label & Catalog #		Title	Year	VG+	NM
RCA Victor LSP-4460	(S)	**Elvis Country**	1971	4.00	10.00
		(Second pressings have orange labels on extremely flexible vinyl.)			
RCA Victor LSP-4460	(S)	**Elvis Country** *(Brown label on blue vinyl)*	1977	300.00	500.00
RCA Victor LSP-4530	(S)	**Love Letters From Elvis**	1971	16.00	40.00
		(Original pressings have orange labels with the RCA logo at top of the front cover.)			
RCA Victor LSP-4530	(S)	**Love Letters From Elvis**	1971	14.00	35.00
		(Second pressings have orange labels with the RCA logo in the lower right corner of the cover.)			
RCA Victor LPM-6402	(M)	**The Other Sides: Worldwide Gold Award Hits, Volume 2** *(4 LP box.)*	1971	16.00	40.00
		(Original pressings have orange labels with printed ads on the cover for two bonuses, priced separately below.)			
RCA Victor LPM-6402		**The Other Sides Bonus #1**	1971	6.00	15.00
		(Full color fold-open poster of a painting of a jumpsuited Elvis.)			
RCA Victor LPM-6402		**The Other Sides Bonus Envelope**	1971	6.00	15.00
		(Small envelope holds a piece of cloth from Elvis' wardrobe.)			
RCA Victor LSP-4579	(S)	**The Wonderful World Of Christmas**	1971	10.00	25.00
		(Orange label issued with a bonus photo, priced separately below.)			
RCA Victor LSP-4579		**The Wonderful World Of Christmas Photo**	1971	6.00	15.00
RCA Victor LSP-4671	(S)	**Elvis Now** *(Orange label)*	1972	8.00	20.00
RCA Victor LSP-4671	(S)	**Elvis Now** *(Brown label on green vinyl)*	1977	300.00	500.00
RCA Victor LSP-4690	(S)	**He Touched Me** *(Orange label)*	1972	8.00	20.00
RCA SPS-33-571-1	(DJ)	**Recorded At Madison Square Garden**	1972	100.00	250.00
		(2 LPs banded for air-play and issued in a plain white cover.)			
RCA Victor LSP-4776	(S)	**Recorded At Madison Square Garden** *(Orange label)*	1972	6.00	15.00
RCA Victor VPSX-6089	(Q)	**Aloha From Hawaii Via Satellite** *(2 LPs)*	1973	1,000.00	Rare
		(RCA provided the Van Camp Co., sponsors of the "Aloha" TV Special, with advance copies of this album, to which Chicken of the Sea tuna stickers were affixed and used promotionally. Rare with a suggested Near Mint value of $1,500-2,500.)			
RCA Victor VPSX-6089	(Q)	**Aloha From Hawaii Via Satellite** *(2 LPs)*	1973	10.00	25.00
		(Dark orange label with a dark "Quadradisc" on top and "RCA" on the bottom.)			
RCA Victor APL1-0283	(S)	**Elvis (Featuring "Fool")**	1973	16.00	40.00
RCA Victor APL1-0388	(S)	**Raised On Rock/For Ol' Times Sake** *(Orange label)*	1973	8.00	20.00
RCA Victor APL1-0388	(S)	**Raised On Rock/For Ol' Times Sake** *(Brown label)*	1975	6.00	15.00
RCA Victor CPL1-0341	(P)	**A Legendary Performer, Volume 1**	1974	8.00	20.00
		(Custom black label. The cover has a die-cut circular window. Issued with a booklet, included in the price.)			
RCA Victor CPL1-0341	(P)	**A Legendary Performer, Volume 1**	1974	300.00	500.00
		(Picture disc manufactured surreptitiously by pressing plant employees. There were at least 24 different pictures used.)			
RCA Victor CPL1-0475	(S)	**Good Times** *(Orange label)*	1974	10.00	25.00
RCA Victor DJL1-0606	(DJ)	**Live On Stage In Memphis** *(White label)*	1974	100.00	250.00
RCA Victor CPL1-0606	(S)	**Live On Stage In Memphis** *(Orange label)*	1974	6.00	15.00
RCA Victor APD1-0606	(Q)	**Live On Stage In Memphis** *(Orange label)*	1974	80.00	200.00
Boxcar *(No number)*	(M)	**Having Fun On Stage**	1974	80.00	200.00
RCA Victor CPM1-0818	(M)	**Having Fun On Stage** *(Orange label)*	1974	8.00	20.00
RCA Victor CPM1-0818	(M)	**Having Fun On Stage** *(Brown label)*	1975	6.00	15.00
RCA Victor APL1-0873	(S)	**Promised Land** *(Orange label)*	1975	20.00	50.00
RCA Victor APL1-0873	(S)	**Promised Land** *(Brown label)*	1975	6.00	15.00
RCA Victor APL1-0873	(S)	**Promised Land** *(Brown label on blue vinyl)*	1977	300.00	500.00
RCA Victor APD1-0873	(Q)	**Promised Land** *(Orange label)*	1975	80.00	200.00
RCA Victor APD1-0873	(Q)	**Promised Land** *(Black label)*	1975	30.00	75.00
RCA Victor APL1-1039	(S)	**Elvis Today** *(Orange label)*	1975	20.00	50.00
RCA Victor APL1-1039	(S)	**Elvis Today** *(Brown label)*	1975	6.00	15.00
RCA Victor APD1-1039	(Q)	**Elvis Today** *(Orange label)*	1975	80.00	200.00
RCA Victor APD1-1039	(Q)	**Elvis Today** *(Black label)*	1975	30.00	75.00
RCA Victor CPL1-1349	(P)	**A Legendary Performer, Volume 2**	1976	8.00	20.00
		(Custom black label. The cover has a die-cut circular window. Issued with a booklet, included in the price.)			
RCA Victor APM1-1675	(M)	**The Sun Sessions** *(Brown label)*	1976	6.00	15.00
RCA Victor APM1-1675	(M)	**The Sun Sessions** *(Brown label on blue vinyl)*	1977	300.00	500.00
RCA Victor APL1-1506	(S)	**From Elvis Presley Boulevard** *(Brown label)*	1976	6.00	15.00

Label & Catalog #		Title	Year	VG+	NM
RCA Victor AFL1-2428	(S)	**Moody Blue** (Gold vinyl)	1977	600.00	1,000.00
RCA Victor AFL1-2428	(S)	**Moody Blue** (Green vinyl)	1977	600.00	1,000.00
RCA Victor AFL1-2428	(S)	**Moody Blue** (Red vinyl)	1977	600.00	1,000.00
RCA Victor AFL1-2428	(S)	**Moody Blue** (White vinyl)	1977	600.00	1,000.00
RCA Victor AFL1-2428	(S)	**Moody Blue** (Purple-on-white vinyl)	1977	900.00	1,500.00
RCA Victor AFL1-2428	(S)	**Moody Blue** (Red-on-white vinyl)	1977	900.00	1,500.00
RCA Victor AFL1-2428	(S)	**Moody Blue** (Yellow-on-white vinyl)	1977	900.00	1,500.00
RCA Victor AFL1-2428	(S)	**Moody Blue** (Black vinyl)	1977	100.00	250.00

(RCA had printed 250,000 copies of AFL1-2428 on blue vinyl and had switched to basic black— when Elvis died. All subsequent pressings were on blue vinyl. Hence there are literally millions of blue copies— worth about $5— and very few black.)

RCA Victor CPL1-3078	(P)	**A Legendary Performer, Volume 3** (Picture disc)	1979	8.00	20.00
RCA Victor CPL1-3078	(P)	**A Legendary Performer, Volume 3**	1979	8.00	20.00

(Custom black label. The cover has a die-cut circular window. Issued with a booklet, included in the price.)

RCA Victor CPL8-3699	(P)	**Elvis Aron Presley** (8 LP box with book)	1980	24.00	60.00
RCA Victor CPL1-4848	(P)	**A Legendary Performer, Volume 4**	1980	5.00	12.00

(Custom black label. The cover has a die-cut circular window. Issued with a booklet, included in the price.)

RCA Victor CPM6-5172	(P)	**A Golden Celebration** (6 LP box with photo)	1984	12.00	30.00
Mobile Fidelity MFSL-059	(S)	**From Elvis In Memphis**	1980	12.00	35.00

2. Promotional Releases

MGM (No number)	(DJ)	**Jailhouse Rock Interview** (Red vinyl)	1957	500.00	1,000.00

(Dick Simmons interviews Jerry Leiber and Mike Stoller on working with Elvis. Issued in a plain cardboard jacket.)

RCA Victor SP-33-461	(M)	**Special Palm Sunday Programming**	1967	500.00	1,000.00

(Religious radio program issued without a cover.)

RCA Victor UNMR-5697	(M)	**Special Christmas Programming**	1967	500.00	1,000.00

(Seasonal radio program issued without a cover.)

RCA Victor DJL1-3455	(S)	**Pure Elvis**	1979	150.00	300.00
RCA Victor DJL1-3729	(P)	**Elvis Aron Presley In-Store Sampler**	1980	60.00	150.00
RCA Victor DJL1-3780	(P)	**Elvis Aron Presley Radio Station Sampler**	1980	80.00	200.00
RCA Victor FJ-1981	(M)	**Felton Jarvis Talks About Elvis**	1981	40.00	100.00

(issued with script sheets in a plain cardboard jacket.)

3. RCA Camden, 1969-1973

Camden CAS-2304	(S)	**Elvis Sings Flaming Star**	1969	8.00	20.00

(Original pressings are on non-flexible vinyl. Camden 2304 is a reissue of RCA PRS 279.)

Camden CAS-2304	(S)	**Elvis Sings Flaming Star**	1971	4.00	10.00

(Second pressings have blue labels on extremely flexible vinyl.)

Camden CAS-2408	(S)	**Let's Be Friends**	1970	8.00	20.00

(Original pressings are on non-flexible vinyl.)

Camden CAS-2408	(S)	**Let's Be Friends**	1971	4.00	10.00

(Second pressings have blue labels on extremely flexible vinyl.)

Camden CAS-2440	(S)	**Almost In Love**	1970	8.00	20.00

(Original pressings are on non-flexible vinyl with "Stay Away, Joe.")

Camden CAS-2440	(S)	**Almost In Love**	1971	6.00	15.00

(Second pressings are on extremely flexible vinyl with "Stay Away.")

Camden CAL-2428	(M)	**Elvis' Christmas Album**	1970	8.00	20.00

(Original pressings are on non-flexible vinyl. "If Every Day Was Like Christmas" is in stereo on this album.)

Camden CAL-2428	(M)	**Elvis' Christmas Album**	1971	4.00	10.00

(Second pressings have blue labels on extremely flexible vinyl.)

Camden CALX-2472	(M)	**You'll Never Walk Alone**	1971	5.00	12.00

("You'll Never Walk Alone," "Who Am I?," "Let Us Pray" and "We Call On Him" are in stereo on this album.)

Camden CAL-2518	(M)	**C'mon Everybody**	1971	5.00	12.00
Camden CAL-2533	(S)	**I Got Lucky**	1971	5.00	12.00
Camden CAS-2567	(S)	**Elvis Sings Hits From His Movies, Volume 1**	1972	5.00	12.00

Label & Catalog #		Title	Year	VG+	NM
Camden CAS-2595	(S)	**Elvis Sings Burning Love**	1972	10.00	25.00
		(Original pressings have a star on the front cover advertising the bonus photo, priced separately below.)			
Camden CAS-2595		**Elvis Sings Burning Love Bonus Photo**	1972	20.00	50.00
Camden CAS-2595	(S)	**Elvis Sings Burning Love**	1972	5.00	12.00
		(Later pressing covers do not mention the bonus photo.)			
Camden CAS-2611	(S)	**Separate Ways**	1973	5.00	12.00
		(Issued with a bonus photo, priced separately below.)			
Camden CAS-2611		**Separate Ways Bonus Photo**	1973	8.00	10.00

4. RCA Record Club Releases & Miscellaneous Mail Order Releases

Label & Catalog #		Title	Year	VG+	NM
RCA Victor R-213690	(M)	**Worldwide Gold Award Hits, Parts 1 & 2**	1974	14.00	35.00
		(Record Club. 2 LPs with orange labels.)			
RCA Victor R-214657	(M)	**Worldwide Gold Award Hits, Parts 3 & 4**	1978	6.00	15.00
		(Record Club. 2 LPs with black labels.)			
RCA Victor R-233299	(P)	**Country Classics** *(Record Club. 2 LPs)*	1978	6.00	15.00
RCA Victor R-234340	(P)	**From Elvis With Love** *(Record Club. 2 LPs)*	1978	6.00	15.00
RCA Victor R-244047	(P)	**Legendary Concert Performances**	1978	6.00	15.00
		(Record Club. 2 LPs)			
RCA Victor R-244069	(P)	**Country Memories** *(Record Club. 2 LPs)*	1980	6.00	15.00
RCA Victor DPL2-0056	(E)	**Elvis** *(2 LPs on blue labels)*	1973	12.00	30.00
		(Special TV mail-order compilation.)			
RCA Victor DPL2-0056	(E)	**Elvis Commemorative Album**	1978	12.00	30.00
		(Gold vinyl reissue of 0056, "Elvis.")			
RCA Victor DPL2-0168	(P)	**Elvis In Hollywood** *(2 LPs on blue labels)*	1976	10.00	25.00
		(Special TV mail-order compilation issued with a bonus book.)			
RCA Victor DML5-0263	(P)	**The Elvis Presley Story** *(5 LPs)*	1977	12.00	30.00
		(Issued with a bonus album, "Elvis-His Songs Of Inspiration," priced separately below.)			
RCA Victor DML1-0264	(P)	**Elvis-His Songs Of Inspiration**	1977	6.00	15.00
RCA Victor DML5-0347	(P)	**Memories Of Elvis** *(5 LPs)*	1978	12.00	30.00
		(Issued with a bonus album, "The Greatest Show On Earth," priced separately below.)			
RCA Victor DML1-0348	(P)	**The Greatest Show On Earth**	1978	6.00	15.00
RCA Victor DML6-0412	(P)	**The Legendary Recordings**			
		Of Elvis Presley *(6 LPs)*	1980	16.00	40.00
		(Issued with a bonus book and print, included in the price, and an album, "Greatest Moments In Music," priced separately below.)			
RCA Victor DML1-0413	(P)	**Greatest Moments In Music**	1980	6.00	15.00
RCA Victor DVL1-0461	(P)	**The Legendary Magic Of Elvis Presley**	1980	6.00	15.00
RCA Victor RD4A-0101	(P)	**Elvis! His Greatest Hits** *(8 LPs)*	1982	100.00	250.00
RCA Victor RD4A-0102	(P)	**Elvis! His Greatest Hits** *(7 LPs)*	1982	20.00	50.00
		(Issued with a bonus book and print, included in the price, and an album, "Inspirational Favorites," priced separately below.)			
RCA Victor RD4A-181	(P)	**Elvis Sings Inspirational Favorites**	1982	6.00	15.00
RCA Victor RB4-191	(P)	**The Legend Lives On** *(7 LPs)*	1984	16.00	40.00
RCA Victor SVL2-0710	(M)	**Fifty Years/Fifty Hits** *(3 LPs)*	1985	6.00	15.00
RCA Victor RDA-242D	(P)	**Elvis Sings Country Favorites**	1985	20.00	50.00
		(Issued as a bonus album with Reader's Digest's various artists boxed set "The Great Country Entertainers.")			
RCA Victor DVM1-0704	(M)	**Elvis (One Night With You)**	1985	12.00	30.00
		(Issued with a bonus poster, priced separately below.)			
RCA Victor DVM1-0704		**Elvis (One Night With You) Bonus Poster**	1985	4.00	10.00
RCA Victor DVL2-0728	(P)	**His Songs Of Faith And Inspiration** *(2 LPs)*	1985	6.00	15.00
RCA Victor DSVL2-0824	(P)	**Good Rockin' Tonight** *(2 LPs)*	1985	4.00	10.00
RCA Victor DJM1-0835	(M)	**An Audio Self Portrait**	1985	20.00	50.00
RCA Victor 6313-1-R	(M)	**Elvis Talks** *(Rissue of DJM1-0835)*	1988	10.00	25.00

5. Miscellaneous Label Albums

Label & Catalog #		Title	Year	VG+	NM
Sun Inter. 1001	(M)	**The Sun Years** *('50s Sun label)*	1977	20.00	50.00
Sun Inter. 1001	(M)	**The Sun Years** *('70s Sun label)*	1977	6.00	15.00
Starday SD-995	(M)	**Interviews With Elvis**	1977	12.00	30.00
Green Valley GV-2001	(M)	**Exclusive Live Press Conference** *(2 LPs)*	1977	10.00	25.00
		(Originally issued in a soft cardboard jacket.)			

Label & Catalog #		Title	Year	VG+	NM
Green Valley GV-2001	(M)	Exclusive Live Press Conference (2 LPs)	1977	6.00	15.00
		(Later issued in a standard hard cardboard jacket.)			
Green Valley GV-2002	(M)	Elvis Speaks To You (2 LPs)	1977	10.00	25.00
		(Originally issued in a gatefold jacket with a bonus photo.)			
Green Valley GV-2002	(M)	Elvis Speaks To You (2 LPs)	1977	6.00	15.00
		(Later issued in a single pocket jacket with a bonus photo.)			
Silhouette 1001/2	(M)	Personally Elvis (2 LPs with EP silhouette)	1979	14.00	35.00
Silhouette 1001/2	(M)	Personally Elvis (2 LPs without silhouette)	1979	10.00	25.00
HALW 00001	M)	The First Years (Pink label)	1979	6.00	15.00
Mavenco (No number)	(M)	Elvis, Scotty & Bill	1988	6.00	15.00
Mavenco (No number)	(M)	Elvis, Scotty & Bill (Pink vinyl)	1988	20.00	50.00
		(Includes a copy of Elvis' management contract with Scotty Moore.)			

PRESLEY, ELVIS / THE SILVER BEATLES

Label & Catalog #		Title	Year	VG+	NM
United Dist. UDL-2382	(M)	Lightning Strikes Twice	1981	20.00	50.00
		(Side 1 contains early live Elvis while side two features The Beatles' Decca audition tapes.)			

PRESTON, BILLY
Refer to George Harrison & Friends.

Label & Catalog #		Title	Year	VG+	NM
Derby LPM-701	(M)	16 Year Old Soul	1963	30.00	75.00
Vee Jay LP-1123	(M)	The Most Exciting Organ Ever	1965	12.00	30.00
Vee Jay LPS-1123	(S)	The Most Exciting Organ Ever	1965	20.00	50.00
Exodus EX-304	(M)	Early Hits Of 1965	1965	8.00	20.00
Exodus EX-304	(S)	Early Hits Of 1965	1965	10.00	25.00
Capitol T-2532	(M)	Wildest Organ In Town	1966	8.00	20.00
Capitol ST-2532	(S)	Wildest Organ In Town	1966	10.00	25.00
Buddah BDS-7502	(S)	Billy Preston	1969	6.00	15.00
Apple ST-3359	(S)	That's The Way God Planned It	1969	20.00	50.00
		(Original covers feature a close-up of Mr. Preston's face. Apple label with "A Subsidiary of Capitol" on the bottom. Produced by George Harrison.)			
Apple ST-3359	(S)	That's The Way God Planned It	1969	16.00	40.00
		(Original covers feature a close-up of Mr. Preston's face. Apple label with "Manufactured by Apple" on the bottom.)			
Apple ST-3359	(S)	That's The Way God Planned It	1969	8.00	20.00
		(Later covers feature multiple images of Preston. Apple label with "A Subsidiary of Capitol" on the bottom.)			
Apple ST-3359	(S)	That's The Way God Planned It	1969	6.00	15.00
		(Later covers feature multiple images of Preston. Apple label with "A Subsidiary of Capitol" on the bottom.)			
Apple ST-3370	(S)	Encouraging Words	1970	8.00	20.00
		(Produced by George Harrison)			
A&M SP-3507	(S)	I Wrote A Simple Song	1971	4.00	10.00
		(Features George Harrison on lead guitar.)			

PRESTON, DON

Label & Catalog #		Title	Year	VG+	NM
A&M SP-4155	(S)	Bluse	1969	6.00	15.00
A&M SP-4174	(S)	Hot Air Through A Straw	1969	6.00	15.00

PRESTON, JOHNNY

Label & Catalog #		Title	Year	VG+	NM
Mercury MG-20592	(M)	Running Bear	1960	30.00	75.00
Mercury SR-60250	(P)	Running Bear	1960	40.00	100.00
Mercury MG-20609	(M)	Come Rock With Me	1961	20.00	50.00
Mercury SR-60609	(P)	Come Rock With Me	1961	30.00	75.00

PRETENDERS, THE

Label & Catalog #		Title	Year	VG+	NM
Warner Bros. WBMS-121	(DJ)	The Pretenders Live	198?	16.00	40.00
Nautilus NR-38	(S)	The Pretenders	198?	7.00	20.00
Sire 23980	(DJ)	Learning To Crawl (Quiex II vinyl)	198?	8.00	20.00

PRETTY THINGS, THE

Label & Catalog #		Title	Year	VG+	NM
Fontana MGF-27544	(M)	The Pretty Things	1966	40.00	100.00
Fontana SRF-67544	(P)	The Pretty Things	1966	30.00	75.00
Rare Earth RS-506	(S)	S.F. Sorrow	1969	20.00	50.00
Rare Earth RS-515	(S)	Parachute	1970	10.00	25.00
Rare Earth R-459R2	(S)	Real Pretty (2 LPs)	1976	6.00	15.00
		(Rare Earth 549 repackges 506 and 515.)			

Label & Catalog #		Title	Year	VG+	NM
Sire SASH-3713	(E)	The Vintage Years (2 LPs)	1976	6.00	15.00
Warner Bros. BS-2680	(S)	Freeway Madness	1973	4.00	10.00
Swan Song 8411	(S)	Silk Torpedo	1975	4.00	10.00

PRICE, ALAN
Price was formerly a member of the original Animals.

Parrot PA-1018	(M)	The Price Is Right	1968	12.00	30.00
Parrot PAS-71018	(S)	The Price Is Right	1968	10.00	25.00
		("I Put A Spell On You" and "Shame" are rechanneled on this album.)			
Warner Bros. DS-2710	(S)	O Lucky Man (Soundtrack)	1973	6.00	15.00

PRICE, LLOYD

Specialty SP-2105	(M)	Lloyd Price	1959	40.00	100.00
ABC-Paramount 277	(M)	The Exciting Lloyd Price	1959	20.00	50.00
ABC-Paramount S-277	(S)	The Exciting Lloyd Price	1959	30.00	75.00
ABC-Paramount 297	(M)	Mr. Personality	1959	20.00	50.00
ABC-Paramount S-297	(S)	Mr. Personality	1959	30.00	75.00
ABC-Paramount 315	(M)	Mr. Personality Sings The Blues	1960	20.00	50.00
ABC-Paramount S-315	(S)	Mr. Personality Sings The Blues	1960	30.00	75.00
ABC-Paramount 324	(M)	Mr. Personality's 15 Hits	1960	12.00	30.00
ABC-Paramount S-324	(E)	Mr. Personality's 15 Hits	1960	10.00	25.00
ABC-Paramount 346	(M)	The Fantastic Lloyd Price	1960	12.00	30.00
ABC-Paramount S-346	(E)	The Fantastic Lloyd Price	1960	10.00	25.00
ABC-Paramount 366	(M)	Lloyd Price Sings The Million Sellers	1961	10.00	25.00
ABC-Paramount S-366	(S)	Lloyd Price Sings The Million Sellers	1961	14.00	35.00
ABC-Paramount 382	(M)	Cookin' With Lloyd Price	1961	10.00	25.00
ABC-Paramount S-382	(S)	Cookin' With Lloyd Price	1961	14.00	35.00
Double-L D-2301	(M)	The Lloyd Price Orchestra	1963	8.00	20.00
Double-L SDL-8301	(S)	The Lloyd Price Orchestra	1963	10.00	25.00
Double-L D-2303	(M)	Misty	1963	8.00	20.00
Double-L SDL-8303	(S)	Misty	1963	10.00	25.00
Monument MLP-8032	(M)	Lloyd Swings For Sammy	1965	8.00	20.00
Monument SMP-18032	(S)	Lloyd Swings For Sammy	1965	10.00	25.00
Jad 1002	(S)	Lloyd Price Now	1969	6.00	15.00
ABC-Paramount X-763	(P)	Lloyd Price's 16 Greatest Hits	1972	5.00	12.00
ABC-Paramount 30006	(P)	The ABC Collection	1976	5.00	12.00

PRICE, RAY

Columbia CL-1015	(M)	Ray Price Sings Heart Songs	1957	20.00	50.00
Columbia CL-1148	(M)	Talk To Your Heart	1958	16.00	40.00
Columbia CL-1494	(M)	Faith	1960	12.00	30.00
Columbia CS-8285	(S)	Faith	1960	16.00	40.00
Columbia CL-1566	(M)	Ray Price's Greatest Hits	1961	12.00	30.00
Columbia CL-1758	(M)	San Antonio Rose	1962	8.00	20.00
Columbia CS-8556	(S)	San Antonio Rose	1962	12.00	30.00
		— Original Columbia albums above have three white "eye" logos on each side of the spindle hole.—			
Columbia CL-1971	(M)	Night Life	1963	6.00	15.00
Columbia CS-8771	(S)	Night Life	1963	8.00	20.00
Columbia CL-1976	(M)	Greatest Western Hits, Volume 1	1963	6.00	15.00
Columbia CS-8776	(S)	Greatest Western Hits, Volume 1	1963	8.00	20.00
Columbia CL-2189	(M)	Love Life	1964	6.00	15.00
Columbia CS-8989	(S)	Love Life	1964	8.00	20.00
Columbia CL-2289	(M)	Burning Memories	1965	6.00	15.00
Columbia CS-9089	(S)	Burning Memories	1965	8.00	20.00
Columbia CL-2339	(M)	Western Strings	1965	8.00	20.00
Columbia CS-9139	(S)	Western Strings	1965	10.00	25.00
Columbia CL-2382	(M)	The Other Woman	1965	6.00	15.00
Columbia CS-9182	(S)	The Other Woman	1965	8.00	20.00
Columbia CL-2528	(M)	Another Bridge To Burn	1966	6.00	15.00
Columbia CS-9328	(S)	Another Bridge To Burn	1966	8.00	20.00
Columbia CL-2606	(M)	Touch My Heart	1967	8.00	20.00
Columbia CS-9406	(S)	Touch My Heart	1967	6.00	15.00
Columbia CL-2670	(M)	Ray Price's Greatest Hits, Volume 2	1967	8.00	20.00
Columbia CS-9470	(S)	Ray Price's Greatest Hits, Volume 2	1967	6.00	15.00
Columbia CL-2677	(M)	Danny Boy	1967	8.00	20.00
Columbia CS-9477	(S)	Danny Boy	1967	6.00	15.00
Columbia CL-2806	(M)	Take Me As I Am	1968	12.00	30.00
Columbia CS-9606	(S)	Take Me As I Am	1968	6.00	15.00

Label & Catalog #		Title	Year	VG+	NM
Columbia CS-9733	(S)	She Wears My Ring	1968	6.00	15.00
Columbia CS-9822	(S)	Sweetheart Of The Year	1969	6.00	15.00
Columbia CS-9861	(S)	Ray Price's Christmas Album	1969	6.00	15.00
Columbia CS-9918	(S)	You Wouldn't Know Love	1970	6.00	15.00
— Original Columbia albums above have "360 Sound" on the bottom of the label.—					
Columbia CQ-30106	(Q)	For The Good Times	1970	6.00	15.00

PRICE, RAY / LEFTY FRIZZELL / CARL SMITH
Columbia CL-1976	(M)	Greatest Western Hits, Volume 1	1963	5.00	12.00
Columbia CS-8776	(S)	Greatest Western Hits, Volume 1	1963	6.00	15.00

PRICE, RUTH: *Refer to* GOLDMINE'S PRICE GUIDE TO COLLECTIBLE JAZZ ALBUMS

PRICE, SAM
Savot MG-14004	(M)	Rock With Sam Price	1956	60.00	150.00

PRICE, VINCENT
Columbia ML-5668	(M)	America The Beautiful	1961	10.00	25.00
Dot DLP-3195	(M)	Gallery	1962	10.00	25.00
Dot DLP-25195	(S)	Gallery	1962	12.00	30.00
Capitol SWBB-342	(S)	Witchcraft/Magic (2 LPs)	1969	10.00	25.00
Co-Star CS-110	(S)	Vincent Price	1977	5.00	12.00

PRIDE, CHARLEY
RCA Victor LPM-3645	(M)	Country Charley Pride	1966	6.00	15.00
RCA Victor LSP-3645	(S)	Country Charley Pride	1966	8.00	20.00
RCA Victor LPM-3775	(M)	The Pride Of Country Music	1967	8.00	20.00
RCA Victor LSP-3775	(S)	The Pride Of Country Music	1967	6.00	15.00
RCA Victor LPM-3895	(M)	The Country Way	1967	8.00	20.00
RCA Victor LSP-3895	(S)	The Country Way	1967	6.00	15.00
RCA Victor LPM-3952	(M)	Make Mine Country	1968	12.00	50.00
RCA Victor LSP-3952	(S)	Make Mine Country	1968	6.00	15.00
RCA Victor LSP-4041	(S)	Songs Of Pride-Charley, That Is	1968	6.00	15.00
— RCA albums above have black labels with Nipper on top.—					
RCA Victor APD1-0217	(Q)	Sweet Country	1973	6.00	15.00
RCA Victor APD1-0397	(Q)	Amazing Love	1973	6.00	15.00
RCA Victor APD1-0757	(Q)	Pride Of America	1974	6.00	15.00
RCA Victor APD1-1038	(Q)	Charley	1975	6.00	15.00
RCA Victor APD1-1241	(Q)	The Happiness Of Having You	1975	6.00	15.00
RCA Victor APD1-1359	(Q)	Sunday Morning With Charley Pride	1976	6.00	15.00

PRIMA, LOUIS
Mercury MG-25142 (10")	(M)	Louis Prima Plays	1953	30.00	75.00
Capitol T-755	(M)	The Wildest	1956	20.00	50.00
Capitol T-836	(M)	Call Of The Wildest	1957	20.00	50.00
Capitol T-908	(M)	The Wildest Show At Tahoe	1957	20.00	50.00
Capitol T-1010	(M)	Las Vegas Prima Style	1958	14.00	35.00
Capitol T-1132	(M)	Strictly Prima	1959	14.00	35.00
Capitol T-1723	(M)	The Wildest Comes Home	1962	10.00	25.00
Capitol ST-1723	(S)	The Wildest Comes Home	1962	12.00	30.00
Columba CL-1206	(M)	Breakin' It Up	1958	14.00	35.00
Rondo 842	(M)	Louis Prima	1959	14.00	35.00
Dot DLP-3262	(M)	His Greatest Hits	1960	6.00	15.00
Dot DLP-25262	(S)	His Greatest Hits	1960	8.00	20.00
Dot DLP-3352	(M)	Wonderland By Night	1961	6.00	15.00
Dot DLP-25352	(S)	Wonderland By Night	1961	8.00	20.00
Dot DLP-3410	(M)	Doin' The Twist	1961	6.00	15.00
Dot DLP-25410	(S)	Doin' The Twist	1961	8.00	20.00

PRIMA, LOUIS, & KEELY SMITH
Capitol T-1160	(M)	Hey Boy, Hey Girl (Soundtrack)	1959	20.00	50.00
Dot DLP-3210	(M)	Louis And Keely	1959	14.00	35.00
Dot DLP-25210	(S)	Louis And Keely	1959	20.00	50.00
Dot DLP-3263	(M)	Together	1960	10.00	25.00
Dot DLP-25263	(S)	Together	1960	14.00	35.00
Capitol T-1531	(M)	The Hits Of Louis And Keely	1961	10.00	25.00
Capitol ST-1531	(S)	The Hits Of Louis And Keely	1961	12.00	30.00

Label & Catalog #		Title	Year	VG+	NM
PRIMEVAL					
700 West 740105	(S)	**Smokin' Bats At Campton's**	1974	50.00	125.00
PRINCE					
Warner Bros. 25110	(DJ)	**Purple Rain** (Purple vinyl)	1984	12.00	30.00
Warner Bros. 25677DJ	(S)	**The Black Album** (2 LPs)	1987	2,500.00	Rare
		(Two 45 rpm promos containing the complete unreleased album. Near Mint copies have a suggested value of $4,000-6,000.)			
Warner Bros. 25677	(S)	**The Black Album**	1987	1,500.00	Rare
		(A completed album withdrawn by the artist prior to release. Near Mint copies have a suggested value of $3,000-5,000.)			
PRINCE BUSTER					
RCA Victor LPM-3792	(M)	**Ten Commandments**	1967	10.00	25.00
RCA Victor LSP-3792	(S)	**Ten Commandments**	1967	14.00	35.00
PRINZ, FREDDIE					
Columbia PC-33562	(S)	**Looking Good**	197?	6.00	15.00
PROBE					
Eborp SS-21396-01	(S)	**Direction**	197?	150.00	300.00
PROBY, P.J.					
Liberty LRP-3406	(M)	**Somewhere / Go Go P. J. Proby**	1965	10.00	25.00
Liberty LST-7406	(S)	**Somewhere / Go Go P. J. Proby**	1965	12.00	30.00
Liberty LRP-3421	(M)	**P. J. Proby**	1965	10.00	25.00
Liberty LST-7421	(S)	**P. J. Proby**	1965	12.00	30.00
Liberty LRP-3497	(M)	**Enigma**	1967	10.00	25.00
Liberty LST-7497	(S)	**Enigma**	1967	12.00	30.00
Liberty LRP-3515	(M)	**Phenomenon**	1967	10.00	25.00
Liberty LST-7515	(S)	**Phenomenon**	1967	10.00	25.00
Liberty LRP-3561	(M)	**What's Wrong With My World?**	1968	12.00	30.00
Liberty LST-7561	(S)	**What's Wrong With My World?**	1968	10.00	25.00
PROCOL HARUM					
Deram DE-16008	(M)	**Procol Harum** (Includes a poster)	1967	30.00	75.00
Deram DES-18008	(E)	**Procol Harum** (Includes a poster)	1967	20.00	50.00
Deram DE-16008	(M)	**Procol Harum** (Without the poster)	1967	20.00	50.00
Deram DES-18008	(E)	**Procol Harum** (Without the poster)	1967	10.00	25.00
A&M SP-4151	(S)	**Shrine On Brightly**	1968	8.00	20.00
A&M SP-4179	(S)	**A Salty Dog**	1969	6.00	15.00
A&M SP-4261	(S)	**Home**	1970	6.00	15.00
A&M SP-4294	(S)	**Broken Barricades** (Gatefold cover)	1971	6.00	15.00
		— Original A&M albums above have brown labels.—			
A&M SP-8503	(DJ)	**Procol Harum Lives**	197?	16.00	40.00
Sweet Thunder 15	(S)	**Grand Hotel**	198?	13.00	40.00
PROCTOR, PHIL, & PETER BERGMAN					
Proctor and Bergman are members of The Firesign Theatre.					
Columbia KC-32199	(S)	**TV Or Not TV**	1973	6.00	15.00
PROFESSOR LONGHAIR (HENRY ROLAND BYRD)					
Atlantic SD-7225	(M)	**New Orleans Piano**	1972	10.00	25.00
Harvest SW-11790	(S)	**Live On The Queen Mary**	1978	6.00	15.00
Atlantic SD-2-4001	(S)	**The Last Mardi Gras** (2 LPs)	1982	6.00	15.00
Nighthawk 108	(M)	**Mardi Gras In New Orleans**	1982	4.00	10.00
PROOF					
Proof Prod.	(S)	**Proof**	197?	200.00	400.00
PROVINE, DOROTHY					
Warner Bros. W-1394	(M)	**The Roaring '20's**	1961	8.00	20.00
Warner Bros. WS-1394	(S)	**The Roaring '20's**	1961	10.00	25.00
Warner Bros. W-1419	(M)	**The Vamp Of The Roaring '20's**	1961	8.00	20.00
Warner Bros. WS-1419	(S)	**The Vamp Of The Roaring '20's**	1961	10.00	25.00
PRYOR, RICHARD					
Partee PBS-2404	(S)	**That Nigger's Crazy**	1974	6.00	15.00

Label & Catalog #		Title	Year	VG+	NM

PRYSOCK, ARTHUR: *Refer to* GOLDMINE'S PRICE GUIDE TO COLLECTIBLE JAZZ ALBUMS

PRYSOCK, RED

Mercury MG-20086	(M)	Rock 'N' Roll	1955	80.00	200.00
Mercury MG-20106	(M)	Battle Royal	1956	50.00	125.00
Mercury MG-20188	(M)	Swing Softly Red	1956	50.00	125.00
Mercury MG-20211	(M)	Fruit Boots	1957	50.00	125.00
Mercury MG-20307	(M)	The Beat	1959	20.00	50.00
Mercury SR-60307	(S)	The Beat	1959	30.00	75.00

PUGSLEY MUNION

J&S SLP-0001	(S)	Just Like You	196?	30.00	75.00

PUCKETT, GARY (& THE UNION GAP)

Columbia CS-9612	(S)	Woman, Woman	1968	6.00	15.00
Columbia CS-9664	(S)	Young Girl	1968	6.00	15.00
Columbia CS-9715	(S)	Incredible	1968	6.00	15.00
Columbia CS-9935	(S)	New Album	1969	6.00	15.00

— Columbia albums above have "360 Sound" labels.—

PUFF

MGM SE-4622	(S)	Puff	1969	6.00	15.00

PULLEN, WHITEY

Crown CLP-5332	(M)	Whitey Pullen	1963	10.00	25.00
Crown CLST-32	(E)	Whitey Pullen	1963	4.00	10.00

PURIFY, JAMES & BOBBY

Bell 6003	(M)	James And Bobby Purify	1967	8.00	20.00
Bell 6003	(S)	James And Bobby Purify	1967	8.00	20.00
Bell 6010	(M)	The Pure Sound Of The Purifys	1967	8.00	20.00
Bell 6010	(S)	The Pure Sound Of The Purifys	1967	8.00	20.00

PURPLE GANG, THE

Sire/London SES-97006	(S)	The Purple Gang Strikes	1969	8.00	20.00

PURSELL, BILL

Columbia CL-1972	(M)	Our Winter Love	1963	6.00	15.00
Columbia CS-8972	(S)	Our Winter Love	1963	8.00	20.00

PYRAMIDS, THE

Best LPM-1001	(M)	The Original Penetration	1964	80.00	200.00

(Original pressings contain "Walkin' The Dog.")

Best BR-16501	(M)	The Original Penetration	1964	60.00	150.00
Best BRS-36501	(E)	The Original Penetration	1964	40.00	100.00

(Later pressings replace "Walkin'" with "Road Runnah.")

QUARTERMASS

Harvest SKAO-314	(S)	Quartermass	1970	8.00	20.00

QUATTLEBAUM, DOUG

Bluesville BVLP-1065	(M)	Softee Man Blues	1963	16.00	40.00

Label & Catalog #		Title	Year	VG+	NM

QUATRO, SUZI

Bell 1302	(S)	Suzi Quatro	1974	8.00	20.00
Bell 1313	(S)	Quatro	1974	8.00	20.00
Bell 4035	(S)	Your Mama Won't Like Me	1975	6.00	15.00
RSO 3044	(S)	If You Knew Suzi	1978	4.00	10.00
Dreamland 15006	(S)	Rock Hard	1980	4.00	10.00

QUEEN

Elektra EKS7-5064	(S)	Queen	1973	12.00	30.00
		("Queen" is embossed in gold on the cover.)			
Elektra EQ-5064	(Q)	Queen	1973	16.00	40.00
Elektra EKS7-5082	(S)	Queen 2	1974	6.00	15.00
Mobile Fidelity MFSL-067	(S)	Night At The Opera	1980	25.00	75.00

QUEEN ANNE'S LACE

Coral CRL-757509	(S)	Queen Anne's Lace	1969	6.00	15.00

QUEEN'S NECTARINE MACHINE

ABC ABCS-666	(S)	Mystic Powers Of Roving Tarot Gamble	1969	6.00	15.00

QUEENSRYCHE

EMI SPRO-1436	(DJ)	Operation Mindcrime (Picture disc)	1988	20.00	50.00
EMI SPRO-9869	(DJ)	Speaking In Digital (Interview)	198?	16.00	40.00

QUESTION MARK & THE MYSTERIANS

Cameo C-2004	(M)	96 Tears	1966	20.00	50.00
Cameo CS-2004	(E)	96 Tears	1966	16.00	40.00
Cameo C-2006	(M)	Action	1967	16.00	40.00
Cameo SC-2006	(E)	Action	1967	12.00	30.00

QUICKSILVER MESSENGER SERVICE [QUICKSILVER]

Original members were John Cippolina, Gary Duncan, Greg Elmore and David Freiberg. Later members include Nicky Hopkins and co-founder Dino Valenti. Refer to The Steve Miller Band; Rocky Sullivan.

Capitol ST-2904	(S)	Quicksilver Messenger Service	1968	12.00	30.00
Capitol ST-120	(S)	Happy Trails	1969	10.00	25.00
		— Original Capitol albums above have black rainbow labels.—			
Capitol ST-2904	(S)	Quicksilver Messenger Service	1969	6.00	15.00
Capitol ST-120	(S)	Happy Trails	1969	6.00	15.00
Capitol ST-391	(S)	Shady Grove	1969	6.00	15.00
Capitol ST-498	(S)	Just For Love	1970	6.00	15.00
Capitol ST-630	(S)	What About Me?	1970	6.00	15.00
Capitol ST-819	(S)	Quicksilver	1971	6.00	15.00
		— Capitol albums above have green labels.—			

R. E. O. SPEEDWAGON

Epic AS-410	(DJ)	Live Again	1978	8.00	20.00
Epic AS-643	(DJ)	Nine Lives	1979	8.00	20.00
Epic HE-45082	(S)	You Can Tune A Piano But You Can't Tuna Fish (Half-speed master)	1982	8.00	25.00
Epic HE-46844	(S)	Hi Infidelity (Half-speed master)	1982	7.00	20.00
Epic HE-48100	(S)	Good Trouble (Half-speed master)	1982	7.00	20.00

Label & Catalog #		Title	Year	VG+	NM
R.P.S.					
Mars/Mid-America	(S)	R.P.S.	197?	30.00	75.00
RABBLE, THE					
Roulette R	(M)	The Rabble	196?	40.00	100.00
Roulette SR	(S)	The Rabble	196?	60.00	150.00
RADHA KRSNA TEMPLE, THE					
Produced by George Harrison.					
Apple SKAO-3376	(S)	Radha Krsna Temple	1971	8.00	20.00
RAEBURN, BOYD					
Columbia CL-889	(M)	Dance Spectacular	1956	20.00	50.00
Columbia CL-957	(M)	Fraternity Rush	1957	20.00	50.00
Columbia CL-1073	(M)	Teen Rock	1957	20.00	50.00
— Original Columbia albums above have six eye logos around the perimeter of the label.—					
RAFFERTY, GERRY					
Mobile Fidelity MFSL-058	(S)	City To City	1978	10.00	30.00
RAICEVIC, NIK PASCAL [NIK PASCAL]					
Nik was formerly a member of The Lollipop Shoppe.					
Narco 102	(S)	Beyond The End Eternity	1971	8.00	20.00
Narco 666	(S)	Sixth Ear	1972	8.00	20.00
Narco 321	(S)	Magnetic Web	1973	8.00	20.00
Narco 123	(S)	Zero Gravity	1975	8.00	20.00
RAIDERS, THE					
Liberty LRP-3225	(M)	Twistin' The Country Classics	1962	10.00	25.00
Liberty LST-7225	(S)	Twistin' The Country Classics	1962	12.00	30.00
RAIDERS, THE: *Refer to* PAUL REVERE & THE RAIDERS					
RAIN					
Project-3 5072	(S)	Rain	1970	6.00	15.00
RAIN					
Whazoo USR-3049	(S)	Live, Christmas Night *(No cover)*	1969	40.00	100.00
RAINBOW PROMISE, THE					
New Wine LPS-251-01	(S)	The Rainbow Promise	196?	150.00	300.00
RAINBOW RANCH GANG, THE					
Cumberland MGC-29531	(M)	We're Moving On	106?	10.00	25.00
RAINDROPS, THE					
The Raindrops feature Jeff Barry and Ellie Greenwich.					
Jubilee J-5023	(M)	The Raindrops	1963	40.00	100.00
Jubilee SJ-5023	(S)	The Raindrops	1963	100.00	250.00
RAINWATER, MARVIN					
Refer to Webb Pierce / Marvin Rainwater / Stuart Hamblen.					
MGM E-3534	(M)	Songs By Marvin Rainwater *(Yellow label)*	1957	80.00	200.00
MGM E-3721	(M)	With A Heart, With A Beat *(Yellow label)*	1958	50.00	125.00
MGM E-4046	(M)	Gonna Find Me A Bluebird *(Black label)*	1962	30.00	75.00
RAINY DAZE					
Uni 3002	(M)	That Acapulco Gold	1967	6.00	15.00
Uni 73002	(S)	That Acapulco Gold	1967	8.00	20.00
RAITT, JOHN					
Capitol T-583	(M)	Highlights Of Broadway	1955	12.00	30.00
Capitol T-714	(M)	Mediterranean Magic	1956	12.00	30.00
Capitol T-1058	(M)	Under Open Skies	1958	12.00	30.00
Capitol ST-1058	(S)	Under Open Skies	1958	16.00	40.00
RAM, BUCK					
Mercury MG-20392	(M)	The Magic Touch	1960	8.00	20.00
Mercury SR-60067	(S)	The Magic Touch	1960	12.00	30.00

Label & Catalog #		Title	Year	VG+	NM

RAMBEAU, EDDIE

DynoVoice 9001	(M)	Concrete And Clay	1965	6.00	15.00
DynoVoice DS-9001	(S)	Concrete And Clay	1965	8.00	20.00

RAMBLERS THREE, THE

MGM E-4072	(M)	Make Way For The Ramblers Three	1962	6.00	15.00
MGM SE-4072	(S)	Make Way For The Ramblers Three	1962	8.00	20.00

RAMJET, RODGER

Camden CAL-1075	(M)	Rodger Ramjet & The American Eagles (TV)	1966	14.00	35.00
Camden CAS-1075	(S)	Rodger Ramjet & The American Eagles (TV)	1966	20.00	50.00

RAMONES

Sire SASD-7520	(S)	Ramones	1976	6.00	15.00
Sire SA-7528	(S)	Ramones Leave Home	1977	10.00	25.00
		(Original pressings contain "Carbona Not Glue.")			
Sire SR-6020	(S)	Ramones	1977	5.00	12.00
		(Sire 6020 is a reissue of 7520.)			
Sire SR-6031	(S)	Ramones Leave Home	1977	5.00	12.00
		(Sire 6031 is a reissue of 7528 and replaces "Carbona Not Glue" with "Sheena Is A Punk Rocker.")			
Sire SR-6042	(S)	Rocket To Russia	1977	5.00	12.00
Sire SRK-6063	(S)	Road To Ruin	1978	5.00	12.00
Sire SRK-6077	(S)	End Of The Century (Prod. by Phil Spector)	1980	5.00	12.00
Sire 3571	(S)	Pleasant Dreams	1981	5.00	12.00
Sire 23800	(S)	Subterranean Jungle	1983	4.00	10.00
Sire 25187	(S)	Too Tough To Die	1984	4.00	10.00

RANDALL, TONY

Imperial LP-9090	(M)	Tony Randall	1960	10.00	25.00
Imperial LP-12090	(S)	Tony Randall	1960	12.00	30.00
Mercury MG-21108	(M)	Vo, Vo, De, Oh, Doe	1967	6.00	15.00
Mercury SR-61108	(S)	Vo, Vo, De, Oh, Doe	1967	8.00	20.00
Mercury MG-21178	(M)	Warm And Wavery	1967	6.00	15.00
Mercury SR-61178	(S)	Warm And Wavery	1967	8.00	20.00

RANDALL, TONY, & JACK KLUGMAN

London XPS-903	(S)	The Odd Couple Sings	1973	8.00	20.00

RANDAZZO, TEDDY

Randazzo was formerly a member of The Three Chuckles.

Vik LX-1121	(M)	I'm Confessin'	195?	20.00	50.00
ABC-Paramount 352	(M)	Journey To Love	1961	12.00	30.00
ABC-Paramount S-352	(S)	Journey To Love	1961	16.00	40.00
ABC-Paramount 421	(M)	Teddy Randazzo Twists	1962	12.00	30.00
ABC-Paramount S-421	(S)	Teddy Randazzo Twists	1962	16.00	40.00
Roulette R-25168	(M)	Hey, Let's Twist (Soundtrack)	1962	12.00	30.00
Roulette SR-25168	(S)	Hey, Let's Twist (Soundtrack)	1962	16.00	40.00
Colpix CP-445	(M)	Big Wide World	1963	10.00	25.00
Colpix SCP-445	(S)	Big Wide World	1963	16.00	40.00

RANDOLPH, BOOTS

RCA Victor LPM-2165	(M)	Yakety Sax	1960	16.00	40.00
RCA Victor LSP-2165	(S)	Yakety Sax	1960	20.00	50.00
		— Original RCA mono albums above have black labels with "Long Play" on the bottom; stereo albums have "Living Stereo" on the bottom.—			
Monument MLP-8002	(M)	Yakety Sax	1963	8.00	20.00
Monument SLP-18002	(S)	Yakety Sax	1963	10.00	25.00
Monument MLP-8015	(M)	Hip Boots	1964	6.00	15.00
Monument SLP-18015	(S)	Hip Boots	1964	8.00	20.00
Monument MLP-8029	(M)	12 Monstrous Sax Hits	1965	6.00	15.00
Monument SLP-18029	(S)	12 Monstrous Sax Hits	1965	8.00	20.00
Monument MLP-8037	(M)	More Yakety Sax	1965	6.00	15.00
Monument SLP-18037	(S)	More Yakety Sax	1965	8.00	20.00
Monument MLP-8042	(M)	The Fantastic Boots Randolph	1966	6.00	15.00
Monument SLP-18042	(S)	The Fantastic Boots Randolph	1966	8.00	20.00
Monument MLP-8066	(M)	Boots With Strings	1966	6.00	15.00
Monument SLP-18066	(S)	Boots With Strings	1966	8.00	20.00

Label & Catalog #		Title	Year	VG+	NM
Monument MLP-8082	(M)	Boots Randolph With The Knightsbridge Strings	1967	6.00	15.00
Monument SLP-18082	(S)	Boots Randolph With The Knightsbridge Strings	1967	8.00	20.00
Monument SLP-18092	(S)	Sunday Sax	1968	6.00	15.00
Monument SLP-18099	(S)	The Sound Of Boots	1968	6.00	15.00
Monument SLP-18111	(S)	With Love/Seductive Sax	1969	6.00	15.00
Monument SLP-18127	(S)	Boots And Stockings	1969	6.00	15.00
Monument SLP-18128	(S)	Yakety Revisited	1969	6.00	15.00
Monument SLP-18144	(S)	Hip Boots 1970	1970	6.00	15.00
Monument SLP-18147	(S)	Boots With Brass	1970	6.00	15.00

RANEY, WAYNE

Label & Catalog #		Title	Year	VG+	NM
King 588	(M)	Songs From The Hills	1958	30.00	75.00
Starday SLP-124	(M)	Wayne Raney And The Raney Family	1960	16.00	40.00
Starday SLP-279	(M)	Don't Try To Be What You Ain't	1962	16.00	40.00

RANGER, ANDY

Label & Catalog #		Title	Year	VG+	NM
Dot DLP-3028	(M)	Singing From "The Song That Never Ends"	1956	30.00	75.00

RANDY & THE RAINBOWS

Label & Catalog #		Title	Year	VG+	NM
Ambient Sound 37715	(S)	C'mon Let's Go	1982	5.00	12.00

RARE BIRD
Rare Bird features Nicky James.

Label & Catalog #		Title	Year	VG+	NM
Probe 24-4514	(S)	Rare Bird	1970	8.00	20.00
ABC 716	(S)	As Your Mind Flies By	1972	6.00	15.00

RARE EARTH

Label & Catalog #		Title	Year	VG+	NM
Verve V6-5066	(S)	Dreams/Answers	1968	8.00	20.00
Rare Earth 6-507	(S)	Get Ready (Shape cover)	1969	14.00	35.00
Rare Earth 6-507	(S)	Get Ready (Square cover)	1969	8.00	20.00
Rare Earth 6-510	(S)	Generation (Soundtrack)	1970	Unreleased	
Rare Earth 6-514	(S)	Ecology	1970	8.00	20.00
Rare Earth 6-520	(S)	One World	1970	8.00	20.00
Rare Earth 6-534	(S)	Rare Earth In Concert (2 LPs)	1970	8.00	20.00

RASCALS, THE [THE YOUNG RASCALS]
The Rascals—The Young Rascals through 1967—were Eddie Brigati, Felix Cavaliere, Gene Cornish and Dino Danelli. Brigati left in 1970 followed by Cornish in 1971; they were replaced by Buzzy Feiten, Robert Popwell and Ann Sutton for the Columbia albums.

Label & Catalog #		Title	Year	VG+	NM
Atlantic 8123	(M)	The Young Rascals	1966	12.00	30.00
Atlantic SD-8123	(S)	The Young Rascals	1966	10.00	25.00
Atlantic 8134	(M)	Collections	1967	12.00	30.00
Atlantic SD-8134	(S)	Collections	1967	10.00	25.00
Atlantic 8148	(M)	Groovin'	1967	12.00	30.00
Atlantic SD-8148	(S)	Groovin'	1967	10.00	25.00
Atlantic 8169	(M)	Once Upon A Dream	1968	12.00	30.00
Atlantic SD-8169	(S)	Once Upon A Dream	1968	8.00	20.00
—Original Atlantic stereo albums above have green & blue labels.—					
Atlantic SD-8190	(S)	Time Peace/The Rascals' Greatest Hits	1968	6.00	15.00
—Atlantic albums above have purple & gold labels.—					
Atlantic SD-8190	(S)	Time Peace/The Rascals' Greatest Hits	1969	4.00	10.00
Atlantic ST-137	(DJ)	Freedom Suite (Sampler)	1969	16.00	40.00
Atlantic SD-2-091	(S)	Freedom Suite (2 LPs)	1969	10.00	25.00
Atlantic SD-8246	(S)	See	1970	4.00	10.00
Atlantic SD-8276	(S)	Search And Nearness	1971	4.00	10.00
—Atlantic albums above have green & orange labels with a Broadway address on the bottom.—					
Columbia 30462	(S)	Peaceful World (2 LPs)	1971	8.00	20.00
Columbia 31103	(S)	The Island Of Real	1972	6.00	15.00

RASPBERRIES, THE
The Raspberries feature Eric Carmen.

Label & Catalog #		Title	Year	VG+	NM
Capitol ST-11036	(S)	Raspberries	1972	8.00	20.00
Capitol ST-11123	(S)	Fresh Raspberries (Shape cover)	1972	12.00	30.00
Capitol SMAS-11220	(S)	Side Three	1973	10.00	25.00
Capitol ST-11329	(S)	Starting Over	1974	8.00	20.00
Capitol ST-11524	(S)	Raspberries' Best	1976	4.00	10.00

Label & Catalog #		Title	Year	VG+	NM
RASPUTIN & THE MONKS					
Trans-Radio 968	(S)	Sun Of My Soul	197?	6.00	15.00
RATHBONE, BASIL					
Refer to Errol Flynn.					
Columbia ML-4038 (10")	(M)	Peter And The Wolf / Treasure Island	195?	20.00	50.00
Columbia ML-4072 (10")	(M)	Sinbad The Sailor / Oliver Twist	195?	20.00	50.00
Columbia CL-673	(M)	Treasure Island / Robin Hood	1955	16.00	40.00
Decca DL-9109	(M)	Rudyard Kipling's Jungle Books	196?	8.00	20.00
RATIONALS, THE					
Crewe CR-1334	(S)	The Rationals	1968	10.00	25.00
RATTLES, THE					
Refer to The Searchers / The Rattles.					
Mercury MG-21127	(M)	The Rattles' Greatest Hits	1967	30.00	75.00
Mercury SR-61127	(E)	The Rattles' Greatest Hits	1967	20.00	50.00
RAVEN					
Owl	(M)	Back To Ohio Blues	196?	200.00	400.00
RAVEN					
Discovery 36133	(M)	Live At The Inferno	1967	30.00	75.00
Columbia CS-9903	(S)	Raven	1969	6.00	15.00
RAVENS, THE					
Regent MG-6062	(M)	Write Me A Letter *(Green label)*	195?	100.00	200.00
Regent MG-6062	(M)	Write Me A Letter *(Red label)*	196?	20.00	50.00
RAW					
Coral CRL7-57515	(S)	Raw Holly	1971	12.00	30.00
RAY, DIANE					
Mercury MG-20903	(M)	The Exciting Years	1964	12.00	30.00
Mercury SR-60903	(S)	The Exciting Years	1964	16.00	40.00
RAY, JAMES					
Caprice LP-1002	(M)	If You Gotta Make A Fool Of Somebody	1962	16.00	40.00
Caprice SLP-1002	(S)	If You Gotta Make A Fool Of Somebody	1962	24.00	60.00
RAY, JOHNNY					
Columbia CL-6199 (10")	(M)	Johnnie Ray	1951	30.00	75.00
Columbia CL-2510 (10")	(M)	I Cry For You	1955	30.00	75.00
Epic LN-1120 (10")	(M)	Johnnie Ray	1955	30.00	75.00
Columbia CL-961	(M)	Johnnie Ray Sings The Big Beat	1957	16.00	40.00
Columbia CL-1093	(M)	At The Desert Inn In Las Vegas	1959	16.00	40.00
Columbia CL-1225	(M)	'Til Morning	1959	12.00	30.00
Columbia CL-1227	(M)	Johnnie Ray's Greatest Hits	1959	12.00	30.00
Columbia CL-1385	(M)	On The Trail	1959	12.00	30.00
— Original Columbia albums above have three white "eye" logos on each side of the spindle hole.—					
Liberty LRP-3221	(M)	Johnnie Ray	1962	8.00	20.00
Liberty LST-7221	(S)	Johnnie Ray	1962	12.00	30.00
RAY, WADE					
ABC-Paramount 539	(M)	A Ray Of Country	1966	6.00	15.00
ABC-Paramount S-539	(S)	A Ray Of Country	1966	8.00	20.00
RAYBURN, MARGE					
Liberty LRP-3126	(M)	Margie	1959	6.00	15.00
Liberty LST-7126	(S)	Margie	1959	10.00	25.00
RAYE, JERRY, & FENWICK					
DeVille LP-101	(M)	The Many Sides Of Jerry Raye & Fenwick	1969	40.00	100.00
RAYE, MARTHA					
Discovery 3010 (10")	(M)	Martha Raye Sings	1951	14.00	35.00
Epic LG-3061	(M)	Here's Martha Raye	1954	12.00	30.00

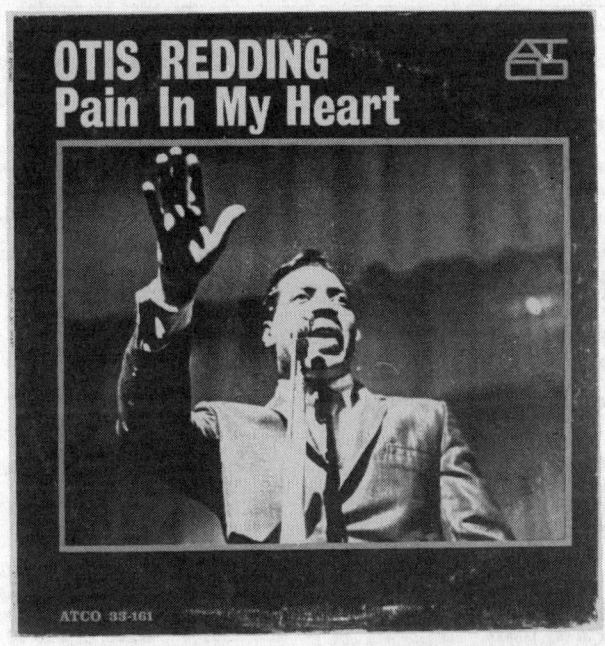

Otis Redding's first album, Pain In My Heart, recorded by Volt and released on Atco, is one of the rarest soul albums by a major artist of the '60s. And, while the stereo version is both a later release, 1967 or so, and in rechanneled stereo, it is harder to find than the mono original. Prior to his tragic death in an airplane crash in 1967—an accident that also took the lives of four members of his backing group, The Bar-Kays—eight of his albums had made the charts. Dock Of The Bay was his last album issued on Volt prior to that company's entire catalog switching over to Atco.

Label & Catalog #		Title	Year	VG+	NM
RAYNE					
(No label)	(S)	**Rayne**	1979	300.00	500.00
REBS, THE					
Fredlo 6830	(M)	**1968 A.D. Breakthrough**	1968	100.00	250.00
REBECCA & THE SUNNYBROOK FARMERS					
Musicor MS-3176	(S)	**Rebecca & The Sunnybrook Farmers**	1969	6.00	15.00
RED CRAYOLA					
International Art.	(S)	**Parable Of Arable**	1968	12.00	30.00
International Art.	(S)	**Parable Of Arable**	1979	6.00	15.00
International Art.	(S)	**God Bless The Crayon**	1968	12.00	30.00
International Art.	(S)	**God Bless The Crayon**	1979	6.00	15.00
		(Reissues have "Masterfonics" stamped in the trail-off vinyl.)			
REDBONE					
Epic EQ-33053	(Q)	**Beaded Dreams Through Turquoise Eyes**	1974	6.00	15.00
REDD, VI					
United Arts. UAL-14106	(M)	**Bird Call**	1962	8.00	20.00
United Arts. UAS-15106	(S)	**Bird Call**	1962	10.00	25.00
Atco 33-157	(M)	**Lady Soul**	1963	8.00	20.00
Atco SD-33-157	(S)	**Lady Soul**	1963	10.00	25.00
REDDING, OTIS					
Refer to Jimi Hendrix / Otis Redding.					
Atco 33-161	(M)	**Pain In My Heart**	1964	60.00	150.00
Atco SD-33-161	(E)	**Pain In My Heart**	1967	80.00	200.00
Volt 411	(M)	**Soul Ballads**	1965	20.00	50.00
Volt S-411	(E)	**Soul Ballads**	1967	30.00	75.00
		(Note: As Volt did not record in stereo until 1965, Otis' first two albums above were reissued in minute press runs in electronically rechanneled stereo several years after the initial mono release. As the press runs were small they are quite rare.)			
Volt 412	(M)	**Otis Blue/Otis Redding Sings Soul**	1965	16.00	40.00
Volt S-412	(S)	**Otis Blue/Otis Redding Sings Soul**	1965	20.00	50.00
		("Respect" and "Old Man Trouble" were rerecorded in stereo.)			
Volt 413	(M)	**The Soul Album**	1966	16.00	40.00
Volt S-413	(P)	**The Soul Album**	1966	20.00	50.00
Volt 415	(M)	**Dictionary Of Soul**	1966	16.00	40.00
Volt S-415	(S)	**Dictionary Of Soul**	1966	20.00	50.00
Volt 416	(M)	**Live In Europe**	1967	12.00	30.00
Volt S-416	(S)	**Live In Europe**	1967	16.00	40.00
Volt 418	(M)	**The History Of Otis Redding**	1967	12.00	30.00
Volt S-418	(P)	**The History Of Otis Redding**	1967	16.00	40.00
Volt S-419	(P)	**The Dock Of The Bay**	1968	12.00	30.00
Atco SD-33-248	(S)	**Soul Ballads**	1968	8.00	20.00
		(Atco 248 is a reissue of Volt 411.)			
Atco SD-33-249	(S)	**Dictionary Of Soul**	1968	8.00	20.00
		(Atco 249 is a reissue of Volt 4195)			
Atco SD-33-252	(S)	**The Immortal Otis Redding**	1968	8.00	20.00
Atco SD-33-261	(P)	**The History Of Otis Redding**	1968	8.00	20.00
		(Atco 261 is a reissue of Volt 418.)			
Atco SD-33-265	(S)	**In Person At The Whiskey A Go Go**	1968	8.00	20.00
Atco SD-33-284	(S)	**Otis Blue/Otis Redding Sings Soul**	1969	8.00	20.00
		(Atco 284 is a reissue of Volt 412.)			
Atco SD-33-286	(S)	**Live In Europe**	1969	8.00	20.00
		(Atco 286 is a reissue of Volt 415.)			
Atco SD-33-288	(S)	**The Dock Of The Bay**	1969	8.00	20.00
		(Atco 288 is a reissue of Volt 419.)			
Atco SD-33-289	(S)	**Love Man**	1969	8.00	20.00
Atco SD-33-333	(S)	**Tell The Truth**	1970	8.00	20.00
Atco SD-2-801	(S)	**The Best Of Otis Redding** (2 LPs)	1972	8.00	20.00
Atlantic 7 81762-2	(P)	**The Otis Redding Story** (4 LPs)	1987	8.00	20.00
REDDING, OTIS, & CARLA THOMAS					
Stax 716	(M)	**King And Queen**	1967	16.00	40.00
Stax S-716	(S)	**King And Queen**	1967	20.00	50.00

Label & Catalog #		Title	Year	VG+	NM

REED, JERRY

Label & Catalog #		Title	Year	VG+	NM
RCA Victor LPM-3756	(M)	The Unbelievable Guitar And Voice Of Jerry Reed	1967	8.00	20.00
RCA Victor LSP-3756	(S)	The Unbelievable Guitar And Voice Of Jerry Reed	1967	6.00	15.00
RCA Victor LPM-3978	(M)	Nashville Underground	1968	20.00	50.00
RCA Victor LSP-3978	(S)	Nashville Underground	1968	6.00	15.00
RCA Victor LSP-4069	(S)	Alabama Wild Man	1968	6.00	15.00

— Original RCA Victor albums above have black labels with Nipper on top.—

Label & Catalog #		Title	Year	VG+	NM
RCA Victor APD1-0238	(Q)	Lord, Mr. Ford	1973	6.00	15.00

REED, JIMMY

Label & Catalog #		Title	Year	VG+	NM
Vee Jay LP-1004	(M)	I'm Jimmy Reed (Maroon label)	1958	80.00	200.00
Vee Jay LP-1004	(M)	I'm Jimmy Reed (Black label)	196?	30.00	75.00
Vee Jay LP-1008	(M)	Rockin' With Reed (Maroon label)	1959	50.00	200.00
Vee Jay LP-1008	(M)	Rockin' With Reed (Black label)	196?	30.00	75.00
Vee Jay LP-1022	(M)	Found Love	1960	16.00	40.00
Vee Jay LP-1025	(M)	Now Appearing	1960	16.00	40.00
Vee Jay 2LP-1035	(M)	Jimmy Reed At Carnegie Hall (2 LPS)	1961	12.00	30.00
Vee Jay 2SR-1035	(P)	Jimmy Reed At Carnegie Hall (2 LPS)	1961	16.00	40.00
Vee Jay LP-1039	(M)	The Best Of Jimmy Reed	1962	8.00	20.00
Vee Jay SR-1039	(P)	The Best Of Jimmy Reed	1962	12.00	30.00
Vee Jay LP-1050	(M)	Just Jimmy Reed	1962	12.00	30.00
Vee Jay LPS-1050	(S)	Just Jimmy Reed	1962	16.00	40.00
Vee Jay LP-1067	(M)	T'Ain't No Big Thing	1963	12.00	30.00
Vee Jay LPS-1067	(S)	T'Ain't No Big Thing	1963	16.00	40.00
Vee Jay LP-1072	(M)	The Best Of The Blues	1963	12.00	30.00
Vee Jay LP-1073	(M)	The 12 String Guitar Blues	1963	10.00	25.00
Vee Jay SR-1073	(S)	The 12 String Guitar Blues	1963	12.00	30.00
Vee Jay LP-1080	(M)	More Of The Best Of Jimmy Reed	1964	10.00	25.00
Vee Jay SR-1080	(P)	More Of The Best Of Jimmy Reed	1964	12.00	30.00
Vee Jay LP-1095	(M)	Jimmy Reed At Soul City	1964	10.00	25.00
Vee Jay VJ-8501	(M)	The Legend, The Man	1965	10.00	25.00
Vee Jay VJS-8501	(S)	The Legend, The Man	1965	12.00	30.00

— Original Vee Jay albums above have black labels with a rainbow border.—

Label & Catalog #		Title	Year	VG+	NM
BluesWay BL-6004	(M)	The New Jimmy Reed Album	1967	8.00	20.00
BluesWay BLS-6004	(S)	The New Jimmy Reed Album	1967	8.00	20.00
BluesWay BL-6009	(M)	Soulin'	1967	8.00	20.00
BluesWay BLS-6009	(S)	Soulin'	1967	8.00	20.00
BluesWay BLS-6013	(S)	Big Boss Man	1968	8.00	20.00
BluesWay BLS-6024	(S)	Down In Virginia	1969	6.00	15.00
BluesWay BLS-6054	(S)	I Ain't From Chicago	1973	5.00	12.00
BluesWay BLS-6067	(S)	The Ultimate Jimmy Reed	1973	5.00	12.00
BluesWay BLX-6073	(P)	Jimmy Reed At Carnegie Hall (2 LPs)	1973	6.00	15.00

REED, LOU

Label & Catalog #		Title	Year	VG+	NM
RCA Victor LSP-4701	(S)	Lou Reed (Orange label)	1972	6.00	15.00
RCA Victor LSP-4807	(S)	Transformer (Orange label)	1972	5.00	12.00
RCA Victor APL1-0207	(S)	Berlin (Orange label with booklet)	1973	5.00	12.00
RCA Victor CPL22-1101	(S)	Metal Machine Music	1973	20.00	50.00
RCA Victor APD2-1101	(Q)	Metal Machine Music	1973	60.00	150.00
RCA Victor DJL1-4266	(DJ)	Special Radio Series, Vol. XVII (Interview)	1980	8.00	20.00
RCA Victor DJL1-4267	(DJ)	Blue Mask Interview Album	1980	8.00	20.00
Direct Disk	(DJ)	The Bells (Test pressing)	198?	50.00	150.00

REED, LUCY

Label & Catalog #		Title	Year	VG+	NM
Fantasy 3-212	(M)	The Singing Reed (Red vinyl)	1956	30.00	75.00
Fantasy 3-212	(M)	The Singing Reed	1956	20.00	50.00
Fantasy 3243	(M)	This Is Lucy Reed	1957	20.00	50.00

REED, LULA

For additional listings refer to Freddie King & Lula Reed.

Label & Catalog #		Title	Year	VG+	NM
King 604	(M)	Blue And Moody	1959	750.00	1,500.00

REED, SUSAN

Label & Catalog #		Title	Year	VG+	NM
Columbia ML-54368	(M)	Folk Songs	195?	10.00	25.00
RCA Victor LXA-3019	(M)	I Know My Love	195?	10.00	25.00
Elektra EKL-116	(M)	Folk Songs	195?	8.00	20.00
Elektra EKL-126	(M)	Susan Reed Sings Old Airs	195?	8.00	20.00

Label & Catalog #		Title	Year	VG+	NM

REESE, DELLA
Refer to Ann-Margret / Kitty Kallen / Della Reese.

Jubilee JLP-1026	(M)	Melancholy Baby	1957	12.00	30.00
Jubilee JLP-1071	(M)	A Date With Della Reese	1958	8.00	20.00
Jubilee SDJLP-1071	(S)	A Date With Della Reese	1958	12.00	30.00
Jubilee JLP-1083	(M)	Amen	1958	8.00	20.00
Jubilee SDJLP-1083	(S)	Amen	1958	12.00	30.00
Jubilee JLP-1095	(M)	The Story Of The Blues	1958	8.00	20.00
Jubilee SDJLP-1095	(S)	The Story Of The Blues	1958	12.00	30.00
Jubilee JLP-1109	(M)	What Do You Know About Love?	1959	8.00	20.00
Jubilee SDJLP-1109	(S)	What Do You Know About Love?	1959	12.00	30.00
Jubilee JLP-1116	(M)	And That Reminds Me	1959	8.00	20.00
Jubilee SDJLP-1116	(S)	And That Reminds Me	1959	12.00	30.00
RCA Victor LPM-2157	(M)	Della	1960	8.00	20.00
RCA Victor LSP-2157	(S)	Della	1960	12.00	30.00
RCA Victor LPM-2204	(M)	Della By Starlight	1960	8.00	20.00
RCA Victor LSP-2204	(S)	Della By Starlight	1960	12.00	30.00
RCA Victor LPM-2280	(M)	Della Della Cha-Cha-Cha	1961	8.00	20.00
RCA Victor LSP-2280	(S)	Della Della Cha-Cha-Cha	1961	12.00	30.00
RCA Victor LPM-2391	(M)	Special Delivery	1961	8.00	20.00
RCA Victor LSP-2391	(S)	Special Delivery	1961	12.00	30.00
RCA Victor LPM-2419	(M)	Classic Della	1961	8.00	20.00
RCA Victor LSP-2419	(S)	Classic Della	1961	12.00	30.00
RCA Victor LPM-2568	(M)	Della Reese On Stage	1962	8.00	20.00
RCA Victor LSP-2568	(S)	Della Reese On Stage	1962	12.00	30.00

— Original RCA mono albums above have "Long Play" on the bottom of the label; stereo albums have "Living Stereo" on the bottom.—

RCA Victor LPM-2711	(M)	Waltz With Me	1963	5.00	12.00
RCA Victor LSP-2711	(S)	Waltz With Me	1963	6.00	15.00
RCA Victor LPM-2872	(M)	Della Reese At Basin Street East	1964	5.00	12.00
RCA Victor LSP-2872	(S)	Della Reese At Basin Street East	1964	6.00	15.00
ABC-Paramount S-524	(S)	C'mon And Hear Della Reese	1966	5.00	12.00
ABC-Paramount S-524	(S)	C'mon And Hear Della Reese	1966	6.00	15.00
ABC-Paramount S-540	(S)	I Like It Like Dat!	1966	5.00	12.00
ABC-Paramount S-540	(S)	I Like It Like Dat!	1966	6.00	15.00
ABC-Paramount S-569	(S)	Della Reese Live	1967	5.00	12.00
ABC-Paramount S-569	(S)	Della Reese Live	1967	6.00	15.00
ABC-Paramount S-589	(S)	One More Time!	1967	5.00	12.00
ABC-Paramount S-589	(S)	One More Time!	1967	6.00	15.00

REEVES, DEL
Del also recorded with Bobby Goldsboro.

United Arts. UAL-3441	(M)	Girl On The Billboard	1965	5.00	12.00
United Arts. UAS-6441	(S)	Girl On The Billboard	1965	6.00	15.00
United Arts. UAL-3458	(M)	Doodle-Oo-Doo-Doo	1965	5.00	12.00
United Arts. UAS-6458	(S)	Doodle-Oo-Doo-Doo	1965	6.00	15.00
United Arts. UAL-3468	(M)	Del Reeves Sings Jim Reeves	1966	5.00	12.00
United Arts. UAS-6468	(S)	Del Reeves Sings Jim Reeves	1966	6.00	15.00
United Arts. UAL-3488	(M)	Special Delivery	1966	5.00	12.00
United Arts. UAS-6488	(S)	Special Delivery	1966	6.00	15.00
United Arts. UAL-3528	(M)	Santa's Boy	1966	5.00	12.00
United Arts. UAS-6528	(S)	Santa's Boy	1966	6.00	15.00
United Arts. UAL-3530	(M)	Gettin' Any Feed For Your Chickens?	1966	5.00	12.00
United Arts. UAS-6530	(S)	Gettin' Any Feed For Your Chickens?	1966	6.00	15.00
United Arts. UAL-3571	(M)	Struttin' My Stuff	1967	6.00	15.00
United Arts. UAS-6571	(S)	Struttin' My Stuff	1967	6.00	15.00
United Arts. UAL-3595	(M)	Six Of One, Half-A-Dozen Of The Other	1967	6.00	15.00
United Arts. UAS-6595	(S)	Six Of One, Half-A-Dozen Of The Other	1967	6.00	15.00
United Arts. UAL-3612	(M)	The Little Church In The Dell	1967	6.00	15.00
United Arts. UAS-6612	(S)	The Little Church In The Dell	1967	6.00	15.00
United Arts. UAL-3635	(M)	The Best Of Del Reeves	1967	6.00	15.00
United Arts. UAS-6635	(S)	The Best Of Del Reeves	1967	6.00	15.00
United Arts. UAS-6643	(S)	Running Wild	1968	6.00	15.00

REEVES, JIM

Abbott LP-5001	(M)	Jim Reeves Sings	1956	600.00	Rare
		(Near Mint copies have a suggested value of $1,000-1,600 .)			
RCA Victor LPM-1256	(M)	Singing Down The Lane	1956	60.00	150.00
RCA Victor LPM-1410	(M)	Bimbo	1957	30.00	75.00

Label & Catalog #		Title	Year	VG+	NM
RCA Victor LPM-1576	(M)	Jim Reeves	1957	20.00	50.00
RCA Victor LPM-1685	(M)	Girls I Have Known	1958	16.00	40.00
RCA Victor LPM-1950	(M)	God Be With You	1958	12.00	30.00
RCA Victor LSP-1950	(S)	God Be With You	1958	20.00	50.00
RCA Victor LPM-2001	(M)	Songs To Warm Your Heart	1959	12.00	30.00
RCA Victor LSP-2001	(S)	Songs To Warm Your Heart	1959	16.00	40.00
RCA Victor LPM-2216	(M)	The Intimate Jim Reeves	1960	8.00	20.00
RCA Victor LSP-2216	(S)	The Intimate Jim Reeves	1960	12.00	30.00
RCA Victor LPM-2223	(M)	He'll Have To Go	1960	12.00	30.00
RCA Victor LSP-2223	(E)	He'll Have To Go	1962	6.00	15.00
RCA Victor LPM-2284	(M)	Tall Tales And Short Tempers	1961	8.00	20.00
RCA Victor LSP-2284	(S)	Tall Tales And Short Tempers	1961	12.00	30.00
RCA Victor LPM-2339	(M)	Talkin' To Your Heart	1961	8.00	20.00
RCA Victor LSP-2339	(S)	Talkin' To Your Heart	1961	12.00	30.00
RCA Victor LPM-2487	(M)	A Touch Of Velvet	1962	8.00	20.00
RCA Victor LSP-2487	(S)	A Touch Of Velvet	1962	12.00	30.00
RCA Victor LPM-2552	(M)	We Thank Thee	1962	8.00	20.00
RCA Victor LSP-2552	(S)	We Thank Thee	1962	12.00	30.00
RCA Victor LPM-2605	(M)	Gentleman Jim	1963	8.00	20.00
RCA Victor LSP-2605	(S)	Gentleman Jim	1963	12.00	30.00
RCA Victor LPM-2704	(M)	The International Jim Reeves	1963	8.00	20.00
RCA Victor LSP-2704	(S)	The International Jim Reeves	1963	12.00	30.00

— Original RCA mono albums above have "Long Play" on the bottom of the label; stereo albums have "Living Stereo" on the bottom.—

Label & Catalog #		Title	Year	VG+	NM
RCA Victor LPM-2758	(M)	Twelve Songs Of Christmas	1963	6.00	15.00
RCA Victor LSP-2758	(S)	Twelve Songs Of Christmas	1963	8.00	20.00
RCA Victor LPM-2780	(M)	Kimberley Jim (Soundtrack)	1964	6.00	15.00
RCA Victor LSP-2780	(S)	Kimberley Jim (Soundtrack)	1964	8.00	20.00
RCA Victor LPM-2854	(M)	Moonlight And Roses	1964	6.00	15.00
RCA Victor LSP-2854	(S)	Moonlight And Roses	1964	8.00	20.00
RCA Victor LPM-2890	(M)	The Best Of Jim Reeves	1964	6.00	15.00
RCA Victor LSP-2890	(P)	The Best Of Jim Reeves	1964	8.00	20.00
RCA Victor LPM-2968	(M)	The Jim Reeves Way	1965	6.00	15.00
RCA Victor LSP-2968	(S)	The Jim Reeves Way	1965	8.00	20.00
RCA Victor LPM-3427	(M)	Up Through The Years	1965	6.00	15.00
RCA Victor LSP-3427	(S)	Up Through The Years	1965	8.00	20.00
RCA Victor SP-33-479	(DJ)	Something Special For Disc Jockeys	1966	50.00	125.00
RCA Victor LPM-3482	(M)	The Best Of Jim Reeves, Volume 2	1966	6.00	15.00
RCA Victor LSP-3482	(P)	The Best Of Jim Reeves, Volume 2	1966	8.00	20.00
RCA Victor LPM-3542	(M)	Distant Drums	1966	6.00	15.00
RCA Victor LSP-3542	(S)	Distant Drums	1966	8.00	20.00
RCA Victor LPM-3709	(M)	Yours Sincerely, Jim Reeves	1966	6.00	15.00
RCA Victor LSP-3709	(S)	Yours Sincerely, Jim Reeves	1966	8.00	20.00
RCA Victor LPM-3793	(M)	The Blue Side Of Lonesome	1967	10.00	25.00
RCA Victor LSP-3793	(S)	The Blue Side Of Lonesome	1967	8.00	20.00
RCA Victor LPM-3903	(M)	My Cathedral	1967	10.00	25.00
RCA Victor LSP-3903	(S)	My Cathedral	1967	8.00	20.00
RCA Victor LPM-3987	(M)	A Touch Of Sadness	1968	20.00	50.00
RCA Victor LSP-3987	(S)	A Touch Of Sadness	1968	8.00	20.00
RCA Victor LSP-4062	(S)	Jim Reeves On Stage	1968	8.00	20.00

— Original RCA albums above have black labels.—

| RCA Victor LSP-4112 | (S) | Jim Reeves And Some Friends | 1969 | 6.00 | 15.00 |
| RCA Victor LSP-4187 | (S) | The Best Of Jim Reeves, Volume 3 | 1969 | 6.00 | 15.00 |

— Original RCA albums above have orange labels on non-flexible vinyl.—

RCA Victor LSP-4475	(S)	Jim Reeves Writes You A Record	1971	4.00	10.00
RCA Victor LSP-4528	(S)	Something Special	1972	4.00	10.00
RCA Victor LSP-4646	(S)	My Friend	1972	4.00	10.00
RCA Victor LSP-4749	(S)	Missing You	1972	4.00	10.00
RCA Victor APL1-0039	(S)	Am I That Easy To Forget (With photo)	1973	5.00	12.00

— Original RCA albums above have orange labels.—

RCA Victor DML5-0587	(S)	Golden Record Collection (5 LPs)	1974	16.00	40.00
RCA Victor APL1-1224	(S)	I Love You Because (With bonus photo)	1976	5.00	12.00
RCA Victor RD4-210	(S)	The Unforgettable Jim Reeves (6 LPs)	1976	16.00	40.00

REFLECTIONS, THE

| Golden World 300 | (M) | (Just Like) Romeo And Juliet | 1964 | 30.00 | 75.00 |

Label & Catalog #		Title	Year	VG+	NM

REGENTS, THE

Gee GLP-708	(M)	Barbara Ann	1961	40.00	100.00
Gee SGLP-708	(S)	Barbara Ann	1961	80.00	200.00
		("Barbara Ann" and "I'm So Lonely" are rechanneled on this album.)			
Gee SGLP-708	(S)	Barbara Ann	197?	10.00	25.00
		(Reissue from Publishers Central Bureau licensed through			
		Roulette Records, as noted on the back cover.)			
Capitol KAO-2153	(M)	Live At The AM/PM Discotheque	1964	20.00	50.00
Capitol SKAO-2153	(S)	Live At The AM/PM Discotheque	1964	30.00	75.00

REID, IRENE: *Refer to* GOLDMINE'S PRICE GUIDE TO COLLECTIBLE JAZZ ALBUMS

REID, TERRY

Epic BN-26427	(S)	Bang Bang, You're Terry Reid (Yellow label)	1968	8.00	20.00
Epic BN-26477	(S)	Move Over For... Terry Reid (Yellow label)	1968	8.00	20.00
Epic BN-26477	(S)	Terry Reid (Yellow label)	1969	6.00	15.00
		("Terry Reid" is a reissue of "Move Over For...")			

REJOICE

Dunhill DS-50049	(S)	Rejoice	1969	6.00	15.00

RELAYER

H.S.R. LSR-1006	(S)	Relayer	1979	24.00	60.00

RELATIVELY CLEAN RIVERS

Pacific PC-17601	(S)	Relatively Clean Rivers	1976	80.00	200.00

REMAINS, THE

Epic LN-24214	(M)	The Remains	1966	50.00	100.00
Epic BN-26214	(S)	The Remains	1966	100.00	200.00

REMINGTON, HERBIE

"D" 7002	(M)	Herbie Remington Plays The Steel	195?	30.00	75.00
"D" 7005	(M)	Aloha Hawaii	195?	30.00	75.00
United Arts. UAL-3167	(M)	Steel Guitar Holiday	1961	10.00	25.00
United Arts. UAS-6167	(E)	Steel Guitar Holiday	1961	6.00	15.00
		(United Arts. 3/6167 is a repackage of "D" 7002.)			

RENAISSANCE
Elektra 74068 features Keith Relf and Jim McCarty of The Yardbirds.

Elektra EKS-74068	(S)	Renaissance	1969	8.00	20.00
Mobile Fidelity MFSL-099	(S)	Scheherezade	1980	15.00	45.00

RENAISSANCE SOCIETY, THE

HBR HLP-8504	(S)	Baroque 'N Stones	1969	8.00	20.00

RENAY, DIANE

20th Century TF-3133	(M)	Navy Blue	1964	30.00	75.00
20th Century TFS-3133	(P)	Navy Blue	1964	60.00	150.00
		("Man Of Mystery," "Navy Blue," "Sooner Or Later" and			
		"Unbelievable Guy" are rechanneled on this album.)			

RENO & SMILEY

King 550	(M)	Sacred Songs	1958	30.00	75.00
King 579	(M)	Folk Ballads And Instrumentals	1958	30.00	75.00
King 621	(M)	Good Old Country Ballads	1959	30.00	75.00
King 646	(M)	A Variety Of Country Songs	1959	30.00	75.00
King 693	(M)	Hymns Sacred And Gospel	1959	30.00	75.00
King 701	(M)	Country Songs	1959	30.00	75.00
King 756	(M)	Folk Songs Of The Civil War	1961	30.00	75.00

REPARATA & THE DELRONS

World Artists WAM-2006	(M)	Whenever A Teenager Cries	1965	16.00	40.00
World Artists WAS-3006	(S)	Whenever A Teenager Cries	1965	20.00	50.00
Avco Embassy AVE-33008	(S)	Rock And Roll Revolution	1970	6.00	15.00

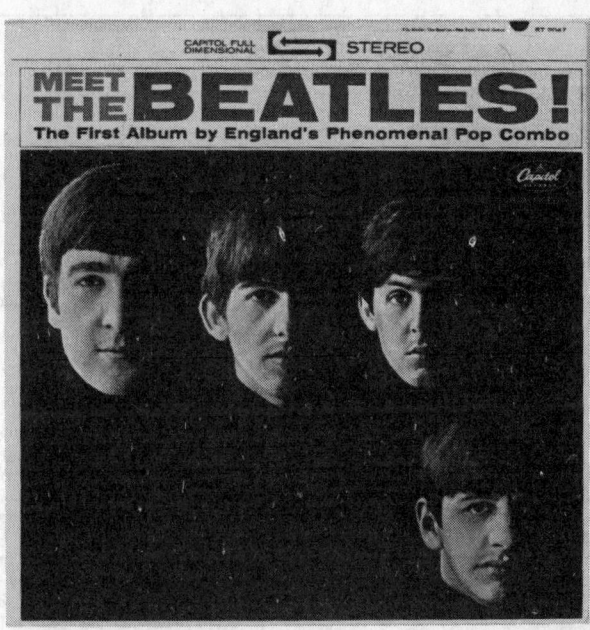

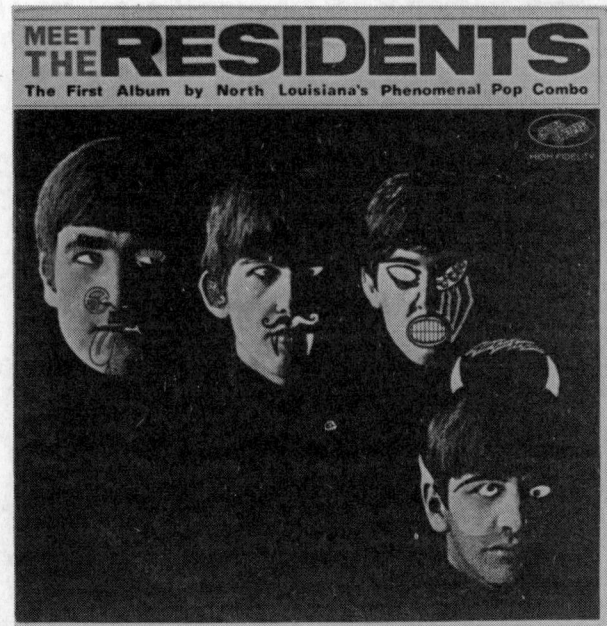

The Bay Area's most well-known unknown group began their lengthy career with a bit of a problem with their first album. It seems that the powers-that-be at Capitol Records took a dim view of the group's icon-oclastic alteration of their client's legendary album cover art and convinced Ralph Records to cease and desist. A new cover was substituted, the record was remixed and sent out to the marketplace. . .

Label & Catalog #		Title	Year	VG+	NM

REPRISE REPERTORY THEATRE, THE
Rosemary Clooney, Bing Crosby, Sammy Davis, Jr., the Hi-Lo's, Dean Martin, the McGuire Sisters, Debbie Reynolds, Allan Sherman, Dinah Shore, Frank Sinatra, Keely Smith and Jo Stafford.

Label & Catalog #		Title	Year	VG+	NM
Reprise F-2015	(M)	Finian's Rainbow	1964	12.00	30.00
Reprise FS-2015	(S)	Finian's Rainbow	1964	16.00	40.00
Reprise F-2016	(M)	Guys And Dolls	1964	12.00	30.00
Reprise FS-2016	(S)	Guys And Dolls	1964	16.00	40.00
Reprise F-2017	(M)	Kiss Me, Kate	1964	12.00	30.00
Reprise FS-2017	(S)	Kiss Me, Kate	1964	16.00	40.00
Reprise F-2018	(M)	South Pacific	1964	12.00	30.00
Reprise FS-2018	(S)	South Pacific	1964	16.00	40.00
Reprise F-2019	(M)	The Reprise Repertory Theatre (4 LP box)	1964	70.00	175.00
Reprise FS-2019	(S)	The Reprise Repertory Theatre (4 LP box)	1964	100.00	250.00

RESIDENTS, THE

Ralph RR-0274	(M)	Meet The Residents	1974	150.00	300.00
		(Back cover reads "First Pressing-1,000 Discs-February, 1974.")			
Ralph RR-0677	(S)	Meet The Residents	1977	10.00	25.00
		(Remixed reissue with non-litigative cover art, this pressing has a split "a" in the Ralph logo on the back cover.)			
Ralph RR-0677	(S)	Meet The Residents (Picture disc)	1985	10.00	25.00
Ralph RR-1075	(S)	Third Reich 'N' Roll	1976	20.00	50.00
		(Back cover reads "First Pressing-1,000 Copies.")			
Ralph RR-1276	(S)	Fingerprince	1976	20.00	50.00
		(Textured chocolate-brown cover states "First Pressing December 1976" on the back)			
Ralph RR-1276	(S)	Fingerprince	1977	6.00	15.00
		(Second pressing has a slick, light brown cover.)			
Ralph RR-0278	(S)	Duck Stab/Buster And Glen	1978	4.00	10.00
Ralph RR-1174	(S)	Not Available (Maroon & purple label)	1978	10.00	25.00
Ralph DJ-7901	(DJ)	Please Do Not Steal It!	1979	10.00	25.00
Ralph ESK-7906	(S)	Eskimo (White vinyl)	1980	10.00	25.00
Ralph ESK-7906	(S)	Eskimo	1980	4.00	10.00
Ralph ESK-7906	(S)	Eskimo (Picture disc)	1983	6.00	15.00
Ralph RZ-8006	(S)	Diskomo	1980	6.00	15.00
Ralph RZ-8052	(S)	Commercial Album	1980	6.00	15.00
		(Back cover has incorrect song listings.)			
Ralph RZ-8052	(S)	Commercial Album	1980	4.00	10.00
		(Back cover has correct song listings.)			
Ralph RZ-8152	(S)	Mark Of The Mole (Brown vinyl)	1981	20.00	50.00
Ralph RZ-8152	(S)	Mark Of The Mole	1981	4.00	10.00
Ralph RZ-8522	(S)	Intermission	1982	4.00	10.00
Ralph RZ-0001	(S)	The Mole Show	1983	12.00	30.00
Ralph RZ-0001	(S)	The Mole Show (Picture disc)	1983	10.00	25.00
Ralph RZ-8402	(S)	George And James	1984	10.00	25.00
		(The matrix number in the trail-off vinyl is #"RZ-8402-A Re-1.")			
Ralph RZ-8402	(S)	George And James (Clear vinyl)	1984	10.00	25.00
Ralph RZ-8452	(S)	Vileness Fats (Red vinyl)	1984	10.00	25.00
Ralph RR-0677	(S)	Meet The Residents (Picture disc)	1985	10.00	25.00
Episode ED-21	(S)	Census Taker (Soundtrack)	1985	20.00	50.00

RESTIVO, JOHNNY

RCA Victor LPM-2149	(M)	Oh, Johnny	1959	16.00	40.00
RCA Victor LSP-2149	(S)	Oh, Johnny	1959	20.00	50.00

REVELLS, THE
The Revells are a creation of Gary Usher & Co.

Reprise R-6160	(M)	The Go Sound Of The Slots	1965	30.00	75.00
Reprise RS-6160	(S)	The Go Sound Of The Slots	1965	40.00	100.00

REVELS, THE

Impact LPM-1	(M)	Revels On A Rampage	1964	150.00	300.00

REVENGERS, THE

Metro M-565	(M)	Batman And Other Supermen	1966	12.00	30.00
Metro MS-565	(S)	Batman And Other Supermen	1966	16.00	40.00

Label & Catalog #		Title	Year	VG+	NM

REVERE, PAUL, & THE RAIDERS [THE RAIDERS]
Revolving around Revere and Mark Lindsay were various Raiders, including the "classic" line-up (1965-67) with Phil Volk, Michael Smith and Drake Levin and later members Jim Valley, Freddy Weller and Keith Allison. By late '67 the albums were recorded mainly by studio musicians under Lindsay's guidance. Refer to Brotherhood; The Falconaires; Friendsound.

Label & Catalog #		Title	Year	VG+	NM
Gardena LP-G1000	(M)	Like, Long Hair	1961	200.00	400.00
Sande S-1001	(M)	Paul Revere & The Raiders	1963	150.00	300.00
Jerden JRL-7004	(M)	In The Beginning	1966	16.00	40.00
Jerden JRS-7004	(E)	In The Beginning	1966	12.00	30.00
		(Jerden 7004 is a repackage of Sande 1001.)			
Columbia CL-2307	(M)	Here They Come!	1965	14.00	35.00
		(Label reads "Guaranteed High Fidelity" on the bottom.)			
Columbia CS-9107	(P)	Here They Come!	1965	20.00	50.00
		(Label reads "360 Sound Stereo" in black on the bottom.)			
Columbia Cl-2307	(M)	Here They Come!	1965	10.00	25.00
		(Label reads "360 Sound Mono" on the bottom.)			
Columbia CS-9107	(P)	Here They Come!	1965	14.00	35.00
		(Label reads "360 Sound Stereo" in white on the bottom.)			
Columbia CL-2451	(M)	Just Like Us!	1966	8.00	20.00
Columbia CS-9251	(P)	Just Like Us!	1966	10.00	25.00
Columbia CS-9308	(M)	Midnight Ride	1966	8.00	20.00
Columbia CS-9308	(P)	Midnight Ride	1966	10.00	25.00
Columbia CL-2595	(M)	The Spirit Of '67	1966	8.00	20.00
Columbia CS-9395	(P)	The Spirit Of '67	1966	10.00	25.00
Columbia 62963	(S)	Good Thing	196?	*See note below*	
		(Recently unearthed, this album is ten of the tracks from "Spirit Of '67" with two older tracks. Its origins are unknown although it has a '60s type label and was manufactured in the U.S.)			
Columbia KCL-2662	(M)	Greatest Hits *(With photo booklet)*	1967	8.00	20.00
Columbia KCS-9462	(P)	Greatest Hits *(With photo booklet)*	1967	8.00	20.00
Columbia KCL-2662	(M)	Greatest Hits *(Without booklet)*	1967	6.00	15.00
Columbia KCS-9462	(P)	Greatest Hits *(Without booklet)*	1967	6.00	15.00
Columbia CL-2721	(M)	Revolution!	1967	8.00	20.00
Columbia CS-9521	(S)	Revolution! *("Him Or Me" is rechanneled)*	1967	6.00	15.00
Columbia CL-755	(M)	Christmas Past... And Present	1967	8.00	20.00
Columbia CS-9555	(S)	Christmas Past... And Present	1967	8.00	20.00
Columbia CL-2805	(M)	Goin' To Memphis	1968	6.00	15.00
Columbia CS-9605	(S)	Goin' To Memphis	1968	5.00	12.00
Columbia CS-9665	(S)	Something Happening	1968	6.00	15.00
Columbia CS-9753	(S)	Hard 'N' Heavy (With Marshmallow)	1969	12.00	30.00
		(The cover photo is in black and white.)			
Columbia CS-9753	(S)	Hard 'N' Heavy (With Marshmallow)	1969	6.00	15.00
		(The cover photo is colored.)			
Columbia (No number)	(DJ)	Pink Puzz	1969	*See note below*	
		(In an attempt to gain a portion of the FM market that condemned the group as teenyboppers, Lindsay compiled ten tracks from the group's 1967-68 albums and issued it to stations as an "advance copy" of a new album by a new group, Pink Puzz. Whether this album exists as an acetate or a test pressing is unknown at the time of publication.)			
Columbia CS-9905	(S)	Alias Pink Puzz	1969	6.00	15.00
Columbia GP-12	(P)	Paul Revere & The Raiders (2 LPs)	1969	6.00	15.00
		(Columbia GP-12 repackages "Spirit Of '67" and "Revolution.")			

— Original Columbia albums above have "360 Sound" on the bottom of the label.—

Label & Catalog #		Title	Year	VG+	NM
Sears SPS-493	(E)	Paul Revere & The Raiders	1969	20.00	50.00
		(Sears 493 is a repackage of Sande 1001.)			
Pickwick SPC-3176	(E)	Paul Revere & The Raiders	1970	4.00	10.00
		(Pickwick 3175 is a repackage of Sande 1001.)			
Raider/America RA-682	(S)	Special Edition Featuring Michael Bradley	1982	6.00	15.00
Hitbound	(S)	Paul Revere Rides Again	1983	5.00	12.00
No label	(S)	Still Live	1984	6.00	15.00
No label	(S)	Generic Rock Album	1984	6.00	15.00

REVOLUTIONARY BLUES BAND, THE

Coral CRL-757506	(S)	The Revolutionary Blues Band	1969	6.00	15.00

REXROTH, KENNETH

Fantasy 7008	(M)	Poetry & Jazz At The Blackhawk *(Red vinyl)*	195?	40.00	100.00
Fantasy 7008	(M)	Poetry & Jazz At The Blackhawk	195?	20.00	50.00

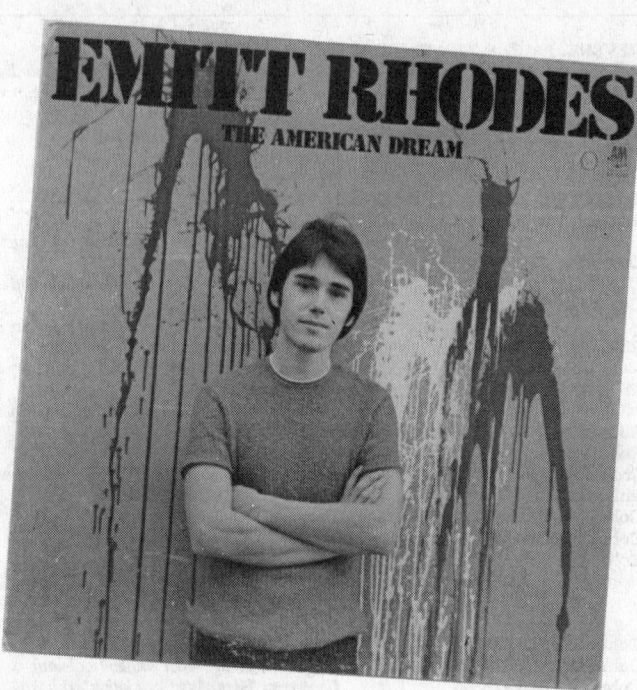

Emitt Rhodes' first solo album was initially issued with the "splattered paint" cover featuring "Saturday Night" (above). Subsequent pressings have a "portrait cover" and replace the aforementioned song with a newly recorded version of The Merry-Go-Round's "You're A Very Lovely Woman."

Label & Catalog #		Title	Year	VG+	NM

REY, ALVINO

Label & Catalog #		Title	Year	VG+	NM
Capitol T-808	(M)	Aloha	1957	12.00	30.00
Capitol T-1085	(M)	Swinging Fling	1958	8.00	20.00
Capitol ST-1085	(S)	Swinging Fling	1958	12.00	30.00
Capitol T-1262	(M)	Ping Pong	1960	8.00	20.00
Capitol ST-1262	(S)	Ping Pong	1960	12.00	30.00
Capitol T-1395	(M)	That Lonely Feeling	1960	8.00	20.00
Capitol ST-1395	(S)	That Lonely Feeling	1960	12.00	30.00
Decca DL-8403	(M)	My Reverie	1958	8.00	20.00
Dot DLP-3391	(M)	His Greatest Hits	1961	6.00	15.00
Dot DLP-25391	(S)	His Greatest Hits	1961	8.00	20.00
Dot DLP-3448	(M)	As I Remember Hawaii	1962	6.00	15.00
Dot DLP-25448	(S)	As I Remember Hawaii	1962	8.00	20.00

REYNOLDS, DEBBIE
Refer to The Reprise Repertory Theatre.

Label & Catalog #		Title	Year	VG+	NM
MGM E-530 (10")	(M)	Two Weeks With Love (Soundtrack)	1950	40.00	100.00
MGM E-113 (10")	(M)	Singing In The Rain (Soundtrack)	1952	40.00	100.00
MGM E-190 (10")	(M)	I Love Melvin (Soundtrack)	1953	40.00	100.00
Mercury MG-25202	(M)	Athena (Soundtrack)	1954	80.00	200.00
MGM E-3233	(M)	Two Weeks With Love (Soundtrack)	1955	20.00	50.00
MGM E-3236	(M)	Singing In The Rain / Rich Young And Pretty	1955	16.00	40.00
RCA Victor LPM-1339	(M)	A Bundle Of Joy (Soundtrack)	1956	30.00	75.00
Coral CRL-57159	(M)	Tammy And The Bachelor (Soundtrack)	1957	80.00	200.00
Columbia CL-1337	(M)	Say One For Me (Soundtrack)	1959	30.00	75.00
Columbia CS-8137	(S)	Say One For Me (Soundtrack)	1959	40.00	100.00
Dot DLP-3191	(M)	Debbie	1959	12.00	30.00
Dot DLP-25191	(S)	Debbie	1959	16.00	40.00
Dot DLP-3295	(M)	Am I That Easy To Forget?	1960	12.00	30.00
Dot DLP-25295	(S)	Am I That Easy To Forget?	1960	16.00	40.00
Dot DLP-25295	(S)	Am I That Easy To Forget? (Blue vinyl)	1960	30.00	75.00
Dot DLP-3298	(M)	Fine And Dandy	1960	8.00	20.00
Dot DLP-25298	(S)	Fine And Dandy	1960	12.00	30.00
Dot DLP-3492	(M)	Tammy	1963	8.00	20.00
Dot DLP-25492	(S)	Tammy	1963	12.00	30.00
MGM 1E-5	(M)	How The West Was Won (Soundtrack)	1963	14.00	35.00
MGM S1E-5	(S)	How The West Was Won (Soundtrack)	1963	18.00	45.00
MGM E-4232	(M)	The Unsinkable Molly Brown (Soundtrack)	1964	6.00	15.00
MGM SE-4232	(S)	The Unsinkable Molly Brown (Soundtrack)	1964	8.00	20.00
MGM 1E-7	(M)	The Singing Nun (Soundtrack)	1966	8.00	20.00
MGM S1E-7	(S)	The Singing Nun (Soundtrack)	1966	12.00	30.00
United Arts. UAL-4163	(M)	Divorce American Style (Soundtrack)	1967	8.00	20.00
United Arts. UAS-5163	(S)	Divorce American Style (Soundtrack)	1967	12.00	30.00
Paramount 1008	(S)	Charlotte's Web (Soundtrack)	1973	6.00	15.00
Columbia KC-32266	(S)	Irene (Soundtrack)	1973	12.00	30.00
MGM SE-3806	(S)	From Debbie With Love	197?	6.00	15.00
A.V.I. AVL-1033	(S)	And Then I Sing	197?	6.00	15.00

REYS, RITA

Label & Catalog #		Title	Year	VG+	NM
Columbia CL-903	(M)	The Cool Sound Of Rita Reys	1956	16.00	40.00
Epic LN-3522	(M)	Her Name Is Rita Reys	1957	16.00	40.00
Dawn LP-1125	(M)	New Voices	195?	16.00	40.00

RHINOCEROUS

Label & Catalog #		Title	Year	VG+	NM
Elektra EKS-74030	(S)	Rhinocerous	1968	8.00	20.00
Elektra EKS-74056	(S)	Satin Chickens	1969	6.00	15.00
Elektra EKS-74075	(S)	Better Times Are Coming	1970	6.00	15.00

RHODES, EMITT
Emitt Rhodes was the leader of The Merry-Go-Round.

Label & Catalog #		Title	Year	VG+	NM
A&M SP-4254	(S)	American Dream	1970	12.00	30.00
		(Originally issued with "Saturday Night.")			
A&M SP-4254	(S)	American Dream	1970	12.00	30.00
		(Second pressings feature "You're A Very Lovely Woman.")			

RHODES, TODD

Label & Catalog #		Title	Year	VG+	NM
King 295-88 (10")	(M)	Todd Rhodes Playing His Greatest Hits	1954	150.00	500.00
King 658	(M)	Dance Music	1960	100.00	300.00

Label & Catalog #		Title	Year	VG+	NM

RHYTHM DEVILS, THE
The Rhythm Devils are Mickey Hart and Bill Kreutzmann of The Grateful Dead.

Passport PB-9844	(S)	The Rhythm Devils Play River Music	1980	8.00	20.00

RHYTHM ROCKERS, THE

Challenge CHL-617	(M)	Soul Surfin'	1963	30.00	75.00

RICH, CHARLIE

Philips Int. 1970	(M)	Lonely Weekends	1960	150.00	400.00
Groove G-1000	(M)	Charlie Rich	1964	40.00	100.00
Groove GS-1000	(S)	Charlie Rich	1964	100.00	250.00
RCA Victor LPM-3352	(M)	That's Rich	1965	16.00	40.00
RCA Victor LSP-3352	(S)	That's Rich	1965	20.00	50.00
RCA Victor LPM-3537	(M)	Big Boss Man	1966	16.00	40.00
RCA Victor LSP-3537	(S)	Big Boss Man	1966	20.00	50.00
Smash MGS-27070	(M)	The Many Sides Of Charlie Rich	1965	10.00	25.00
Smash SRS-67070	(S)	The Many Sides Of Charlie Rich	1965	12.00	30.00
Smash MGS-27078	(M)	The Best Years	1966	10.00	25.00
Smash SRS-67078	(S)	The Best Years	1966	12.00	30.00
Hi HL-32037	(M)	Charlie Rich Sings Country And Western	1967	8.00	20.00
Hi SHL-32037	(S)	Charlie Rich Sings Country And Western	1967	10.00	25.00
Epic AS-50	(DJ)	Charlie Rich (Sampler)	1972	12.00	30.00
Epic EQ-31933	(Q)	The Best Of Charlie Rich	1972	8.00	20.00
Epic EQ-32247	(Q)	Behind Closed Doors	1973	8.00	20.00
Epic EQ-32531	(Q)	Very Special Love Songs	1974	8.00	20.00
Epic PEQ-33250	(Q)	The Silver Fox	1974	8.00	20.00
Epic PEQ-33455	(Q)	Every Time You Touch Me	1975	8.00	20.00
Epic AS-139	(DJ)	Everything You Always Wanted To Hear	1976	8.00	20.00

RICHARD, CLIFF (& THE SHADOWS)
Refer to The Shadows.

ABC-Paramount 321	(M)	Cliff Sings	1960	16.00	40.00
ABC-Paramount S-321	(S)	Cliff Sings	1960	20.00	50.00
ABC-Paramount 391	(M)	Listen To Cliff	1961	16.00	40.00
ABC-Paramount S-391	(S)	Listen To Cliff	1961	20.00	50.00
Dot DLP-3474	(M)	Wonderful To Be Young (Soundtrack)	1962	16.00	40.00
Dot DLP-25474	(S)	Wonderful To Be Young (Soundtrack)	1962	20.00	50.00
Epic LN-24063	(M)	Summer Holiday (Soundtrack)	1963	20.00	50.00
Epic BN-26063	(S)	Summer Holiday (Soundtrack)	1963	35.00	70.00
Epic LN-24089	(M)	It's All In The Game	1964	10.00	25.00
Epic BN-26089	(S)	It's All In The Game	1964	12.00	30.00
Epic LN-24115	(M)	Cliff Richard In Spain	1964	10.00	25.00
Epic BN-26115	(S)	Cliff Richard In Spain	1964	12.00	30.00
Epic LN-24145	(M)	Swinger's Paradise (Soundtrack)	1965	12.00	30.00
Epic BN-26145	(S)	Swinger's Paradise (Soundtrack)	1965	16.00	40.00
Uni (No number)	(S)	Two A Penny (Soundtrack)	1971	20.00	50.00
Light LS-5530	(S)	Two A Penny (Soundtrack)	1971	8.00	20.00

RICHARD, CYRIL

Riverside RLP-406	(M)	Alice In Wonderland	1961	12.00	30.00

RICHARD & JIM

Capitol T-2058	(M)	Folk Songs And Country Sounds	1964	5.00	12.00
Capitol ST-2058	(S)	Folk Songs And Country Sounds	1964	6.00	15.00
Capitol T-2287	(M)	Two Boys From Alabama	1965	5.00	12.00
Capitol ST-2287	(S)	Two Boys From Alabama	1965	6.00	15.00
Folklore 5	(M)	Richard And Jim	196?	4.00	10.00

RICHARDS, ANN

Capitol T-1087	(M)	I'm Shooting High	1959	12.00	30.00
Capitol ST-1087	(M)	I'm Shooting High	1959	16.00	40.00
Capitol T-1406	(M)	The Many Moods Of Ann Richards	1960	10.00	25.00
Capitol ST-1406	(S)	The Many Moods Of Ann Richards	1960	12.00	30.00
Capitol T-1495	(M)	Two Much	1961	10.00	25.00
Capitol ST-1495	(S)	Two Much	1961	12.00	30.00
Atco 33-136	(M)	Ann, Man!	1961	10.00	25.00
Atco SD-33-136	(S)	Ann, Man!	1961	12.00	30.00
Vee Jay LP-1070	(M)	Live... At The Losers	1963	10.00	25.00
Vee Jay SR-1070	(M)	Live... At The Losers	1963	16.00	40.00

Label & Catalog #		Title	Year	VG+	NM

RICHARDS, TRUDY

| Capitol T-838 | (M) | Crazy In Love | 1957 | 12.00 | 30.00 |

RICHARDS, WARREN S.
Warren S. later recorded as Bill Spooner with The Tubes.

| Cotillion SD-9013 | (S) | Warren S. Richards Jr. | 1970 | 20.00 | 50.00 |

RICHMAN, JONATHAN, & THE MODERN LOVERS

Home Of The Hits HH-1910	(S)	The Modern Lovers	1975	20.00	50.00
Beserkley BX-0048	(S)	Jonathan Richman & The Modern Lovers	1976	14.00	35.00
Beserkley BZ-0050	(S)	The Modern Lovers	1976	14.00	35.00
Beserkley PZ-34800	(S)	Rock 'N' Roll With The Modern Lovers	1977	8.00	20.00
Beserkley JBZ-0055	(S)	Modern Lovers 'Live'	1978	8.00	20.00
Beserkley JBZ-0060	(S)	Back In Your Life *(Distributed by Playboy)*	1979	8.00	20.00
Beserkley BZ-0060	(S)	Back In Your Life *(Distributed by Elektra)*	1980	6.00	15.00
Mohawk SCALP-0002	(S)	The Original Modern Lovers	1981	8.00	20.00
Sire 23939	(S)	Jonathan Sings!	1983	6.00	15.00

RICKS, JIMMY
Mr. Ricks was formerly a member of The Ravens.

Signature 1032	(DJ)	Jimmy Ricks	1961	100.00	200.00
Signature 1032	(M)	Jimmy Ricks	1961	150.00	300.00
Mainstream 56050	(M)	Vibrations	1965	12.00	30.00
Mainstream S-6050	(S)	Vibrations	1965	16.00	40.00
Jubilee JGS-8021	(M)	Tell Her You Love Her	1969	10.00	25.00

RIDDLE, NELSON

| 20th Century TF-4180 | (M) | Batman *(TV Soundtrack)* | 1966 | 20.00 | 50.00 |
| 20th Century TFS-4180 | (S) | Batman *(TV Soundtrack)* | 1966 | 30.00 | 75.00 |

RIGHTEOUS BROTHERS, THE
The brothers righteous are Bobby Hatfield and Bill Medley.

Moonglow MLP-1001	(M)	Right Now!	1963	12.00	30.00
Moonglow MSP-1001	(S)	Right Now!	1963	16.00	40.00
Moonglow MLP-1002	(M)	Some Blue-Eyed Soul	1964	12.00	30.00
Moonglow MSP-1002	(S)	Some Blue-Eyed Soul	1964	16.00	40.00
Moonglow MLP-1003	(M)	This Is New!	1965	12.00	30.00
Moonglow MSP-1003	(S)	This Is New!	1965	16.00	40.00
Moonglow MLP-1004	(M)	The Best Of The Righteous Brothers	1966	10.00	25.00
Moonglow MSP-1004	(S)	The Best Of The Righteous Brothers	1966	12.00	30.00
Philles PHLP-4007	(M)	You've Lost That Loving Feelin'	1965	8.00	20.00
Philles PHLP-ST-4007	(P)	You've Lost That Loving Feelin'	1965	12.00	30.00
Philles PHLP-4008	(M)	Just Once In My Life	1965	8.00	20.00
Philles PHLP-ST-4008	(P)	Just Once In My Life	1965	12.00	30.00
Philles PHLP-4009	(M)	Back To Back	1966	6.00	15.00
Philles PHLP-ST-4009	(P)	Back To Back	1966	8.00	20.00

(Portions of Philles 4007 and 4009 were produced by Phil Spector.)

Verve V-5001	(M)	Soul And Inspiration	1966	6.00	15.00
Verve V6-5001	(S)	Soul And Inspiration	1966	8.00	20.00
Verve V-5004	(S)	Go Ahead And Cry	1966	6.00	15.00
Verve V6-5004	(S)	Go Ahead And Cry	1966	8.00	20.00
Verve V-5010	(M)	Sayin' Somethin'	1967	6.00	15.00
Verve V6-5010	(S)	Sayin' Somethin'	1967	6.00	15.00
Verve V-5020	(M)	The Righteous Brothers' Greatest Hits	1967	6.00	15.00
Verve V6-5020	(P)	The Righteous Brothers' Greatest Hits	1967	6.00	15.00
Verve V-5031	(M)	Souled Out	1967	6.00	15.00
Verve V6-5031	(S)	Souled Out	1967	4.00	10.00
Verve V-5051	(M)	Standards	1968	6.00	15.00
Verve V6-5051	(S)	Standards	1968	4.00	10.00
Verve V-5058	(M)	One For The Road	1968	6.00	15.00
Verve V6-5058	(S)	One For The Road	1968	4.00	10.00
Verve V6-5071	(S)	Greatest Hits, Vol. 2	1969	6.00	15.00
Verve V6-5076	(S)	Re-Birth	1969	6.00	15.00
MGM SE-102	(S)	The Righteous Brothers	1970	5.00	12.00
MGM SE-4885	(S)	The History Of The Righteous Brothers	1973	4.00	10.00

RILEY, BILLY LEE

| Mercury MG-20974 | (M) | Beatlemania Harmonica | 1964 | 10.00 | 25.00 |
| Mercury SR-60974 | (S) | Beatlemania Harmonica | 1964 | 12.00 | 30.00 |

Label & Catalog #		Title	Year	VG+	NM

RINCON SURFSIDE BAND, THE
The Rincons are a creation of Steve Barri and Phil Sloan. Refer to The Grass Roots; The Fantastic Baggys.

Dunhill D-50001	(M)	**Surfing Songbook**	1965	50.00	125.00
Dunhill DS-50001	(S)	**Surfing Songbook**	1965	70.00	175.00

RIOPELLE, JERRY

Capitol ST-732	(S)	**Jerry Riopelle**	1971	6.00	15.00
Capitol ST-863	(S)	**Second Album**	1971	6.00	15.00
ABC X-827	(S)	**Saving Grace**	1974	5.00	12.00
ABC D-886	(S)	**Take A Chance**	1975	5.00	12.00

RIP CHORDS, THE
The Rip Chords are a creation of Bruce Johnston and Terry Melcher & Co.

Columbia CL-2151	(M)	**Hey, Little Cobra (& Other Hot Rod Hits)**	1964	12.00	30.00
Columbia CS-8951	(S)	**Hey, Little Cobra (& Other Hot Rod Hits)**	1964	16.00	40.00
Columbia CL-2216	(M)	**Three Window Coupe**	1964	20.00	50.00
Columbia CS-9016	(S)	**Three Window Coupe**	1964	30.00	75.00
		(Originally issued with a borderless, full view cover.)			
Columbia Sp. Prod. CS-9016	(S)	**Three Window Coupe**	196?	8.00	20.00
		(Special Products reissue with a black border on the cover.)			

RIPPERTON, MINNIE

Epic PEQ-3345	(Q)	**Adventures In Paradise**	1975	6.00	15.00

RISERS, THE

Imperial LP-9269	(M)	**She's A Bad Motorcycle**	1964	12.00	30.00
Imperial LP-12269	(S)	**She's A Bad Motorcycle**	1964	16.00	40.00

RISING STORM, THE

Remnant BBA-3571	(M)	**Calm Before The Rising Storm**	1968	500.00	800.00
Arf Arf 007	(S)	**Back In Anover Again**	1983	40.00	100.00
		(Limited pressing of 1,000 numbered copies.)			

RITCHIE, JEAN

Elektra EKL-2	(M)	**Traditional Songs Of Her Kentucky Mountain Home**	195?	12.00	30.00
Elektra EKL-125	(M)	**Kentucky Mountain Songs**	195?	12.00	30.00
Westminster WP-6037	(M)	**Songs From Kentucky**	195?	12.00	30.00
Riverside RLP-12-620	(M)	**Saturday Night And Sunday, Too**	195?	12.00	30.00
Riverside RLP-12-646	(M)	**Songs From Kentucky**	195?	12.00	30.00
Folkways FC-7054	(M)	**Southern Mountain Children's Songs And Games**	195?	10.00	25.00
Folkways FC-2316	(M)	**The Ritchie Family Of Kentucky**	195?	10.00	25.00
Prestige Int. PRLP-13003	(M)	**The Best Of Jean Ritchie**	1961	10.00	25.00
Folklore FRLP-14009	(M)	**The Best Of Jean Ritchie**	1964	8.00	20.00
Folklore FRST-14009	(E)	**The Best Of Jean Ritchie**	1964	6.00	15.00
		(Folklore 14004 is a reissue of Prestige 13003.)			
Verve/Folkways FVS-9026	(M)	**Jean Ritchie At Folk City** *(With Doc Watson)*	1965	8.00	20.00
Verve/Folkways FVS-9026	(M)	**Jean Ritchie At Folk City** *(With Doc Watson)*	1965	10.00	25.00

RITCHIE, JEAN, & OSCAR BRAND

Riverside RLP-12-646	(M)	**Riddle Me This**	195?	12.00	30.00

RITTER, TEX

Capitol H-4004 (10")	(M)	**Cowboy Favorites**	1949	50.00	125.00
Capitol T-971	(M)	**Songs From The Western Screen**	1958	30.00	75.00
		— Original Capitol albums above have turquoise labels.—			
Capitol T-1100	(M)	**Psalms**	1959	20.00	50.00
Capitol T-1292	(M)	**Blood On The Saddle**	1960	12.00	30.00
Capitol ST-1292	(S)	**Blood On The Saddle**	1960	16.00	40.00
Capitol W-1562	(M)	**The Lincoln Hymns**	1961	12.00	30.00
Capitol SW-1562	(S)	**The Lincoln Hymns**	1961	16.00	40.00
Capitol T-1623	(M)	**Hillbilly Heaven**	1961	12.00	30.00
Capitol ST-1623	(S)	**Hillbilly Heaven**	1961	16.00	40.00
		— Original Capitol albums above have black labels with the logo on the left side.—			
Capitol T-1757	(M)	**Stan Kenton / Tex Ritter**	1962	10.00	25.00
Capitol ST-1757	(S)	**Stan Kenton / Tex Ritter**	1962	12.00	30.00
Capitol T-1910	(M)	**Border Affair**	1963	8.00	20.00
Capitol ST-1910	(S)	**Border Affair**	1963	10.00	25.00

Label & Catalog #		Title	Year	VG+	NM
Capitol T-2402	(M)	The Friendly Voice Of Tex Ritter	1965	8.00	20.00
Capitol ST-2402	(S)	The Friendly Voice Of Tex Ritter	1965	10.00	25.00
Capitol T-2595	(M)	The Best Of Tex Ritter	1966	6.00	15.00
Capitol ST-2595	(S)	The Best Of Tex Ritter	1966	8.00	20.00
Capitol T-2743	(M)	Sweet Land Of Liberty	1967	8.00	20.00
Capitol ST-2743	(S)	Sweet Land Of Liberty	1967	6.00	15.00
Capitol T-2786	(M)	Just Beyond The Moon	1967	8.00	20.00
Capitol ST-2786	(S)	Just Beyond The Moon	1967	6.00	15.00
Capitol T-2890	(M)	Bump Tiddil Dee Bum Bum!	1968	12.00	30.00
Capitol ST-2890	(S)	Bump Tiddil Dee Bum Bum!	1968	6.00	15.00
Capitol ST-2974	(S)	Tex Ritter's Wild West	1968	6.00	15.00
Capitol ST-213	(S)	Chuck Wagon Days	1969	6.00	15.00

— Original Capitol albums above have black labels with the logo on top. —

RIVERA, LUIS, & DOC BAGBY

Label & Catalog #		Title	Year	VG+	NM
King 631	(M)	Battle Of The Organs	196?	20.00	50.00

RIVERS, JOHNNY

Label & Catalog #		Title	Year	VG+	NM
Capitol T-2161	(M)	The Sensational Johnny Rivers	1964	8.00	20.00
Capitol ST-2161	(S)	The Sensational Johnny Rivers	1964	10.00	25.00
United Arts. UAL-3386	(M)	Go Johnny, Go	1964	6.00	15.00
United Arts. UAS-6386	(S)	Go Johnny, Go	1964	8.00	20.00
Unart 20007	(M)	The Great Johnny Rivers	1965	5.00	12.00
Unart 20007	(S)	The Great Johnny Rivers	1965	6.00	15.00
		(Unart 20007 is a reissue of United Arts. 3/6386.)			
Imperial LP-9264	(M)	Johnny Rivers At The Whiskey A-Go-Go	1964	7.00	35.00
		(Original mono pressing labels are black with stars on top.)			
Imperial LP-12264	(S)	Johnny Rivers At The Whiskey A-Go-Go	1964	20.00	50.00
		(Original stereo labels are black with silver print.)			
Imperial LP-9264	(M)	Johnny Rivers At The Whiskey A-Go-Go	1964	8.00	20.00
Imperial LP-12264	(S)	Johnny Rivers At The Whiskey A-Go-Go	1964	10.00	25.00
Imperial LP-9274	(M)	Here We A-Go-Go Again	1964	8.00	20.00
Imperial LP-12274	(S)	Here We A-Go-Go Again	1964	10.00	25.00
Imperial LP-9280	(M)	Johnny Rivers In Action	1965	8.00	20.00
Imperial LP-12280	(S)	Johnny Rivers In Action	1965	10.00	25.00
Imperial LP-9284	(M)	Meanwhile Back At The Whiskey A-Go-Go	1965	8.00	20.00
Imperial LP-12284	(S)	Meanwhile Back At The Whiskey A-Go-Go	1965	10.00	25.00
Imperial LP-9293	(M)	Johnny Rivers Rocks The Folk	1965	8.00	20.00
Imperial LP-12293	(S)	Johnny Rivers Rocks The Folk	1965	10.00	25.00
Imperial LP-9307	(M)	And I Know You Wanna Dance	1966	8.00	20.00
Imperial LP-12307	(S)	And I Know You Wanna Dance	1966	10.00	25.00
Imperial LP-9324	(M)	Johnny Rivers' Golden Hits	1966	6.00	15.00
Imperial LP-12324	(S)	Johnny Rivers' Golden Hits	1966	8.00	20.00

— Original Imperial albums above have black & pink labels. —

Label & Catalog #		Title	Year	VG+	NM
Imperial LP-9334	(M)	Changes	1966	6.00	15.00
Imperial LP-12334	(S)	Changes	1966	8.00	20.00
Imperial LP-9341	(M)	Rewind	1967	6.00	15.00
Imperial LP-12341	(S)	Rewind	1967	8.00	20.00
Imperial LP-9372	(M)	Realization	1968	8.00	20.00
Imperial LP-12372	(S)	Realization	1968	6.00	15.00
Imperial LP-12427	(S)	A Touch Of Gold	1969	6.00	15.00
Imperial LP-16001	(S)	Slim Slo Rider	1969	6.00	15.00
Pickwick PC-3022	(M)	Johnny Rivers	196?	2.00	10.00
Pickwick SPC-3022	(S)	Johnny Rivers	196?	2.00	10.00
Sears SPS-417	(S)	Mr. Teenage	1968	10.00	25.00
Sears SPS-487	(S)	Groovin'	1968	6.00	30.00
Sunset SUS-5251	(S)	The Early Years	1968	4.00	20.00
		(Sunset 5251 is a reissue of United Arts. 3/6386.)			

RIVERS, MAVIS

Label & Catalog #		Title	Year	VG+	NM
Capitol T-1408	(M)	The Simple Life	1960	8.00	20.00
Capitol ST-1408	(S)	The Simple Life	1960	10.00	25.00
Reprise R-2002	(M)	Mavis	1961	6.00	15.00
Reprise R9-2002	(S)	Mavis	1961	8.00	20.00
Reprise R-2009	(M)	Swing Along	1961	6.00	15.00
Reprise R9-2009	(S)	Swing Along	1961	8.00	20.00
Reprise R-6074	(M)	Mavis Rivers Meets Shorty Rogers	1962	6.00	15.00
Reprise RS-6074	(S)	Mavis Rivers Meets Shorty Rogers	1962	8.00	20.00

Label & Catalog #		Title	Year	VG+	NM
RIVIERAS, THE					
Riviera 701	(M)	**Campus Party**	1964	60.00	150.00
U.S.A. 102	(M)	**Let's Have A Party**	1964	40.00	100.00
RIVINGTONS, THE					
Liberty LRP-3282	(M)	**Doin' The Bird**	1963	40.00	100.00
Liberty LST-7282	(S)	**Doin' The Bird**	1963	60.00	150.00
ROAD, THE					
Kama Sutra KSBS-8075	(S)	**The Road**	1969	6.00	15.00
Kama Sutra KSBS-2012	(S)	**The Road**	1970	5.00	12.00
Kama Sutra KSBS-2032	(S)	**Cognition**	1970	5.00	12.00
ROAD					
Natural Resources 105L	(S)	**Road**	1972	5.00	12.00
ROAD RUNNERS, THE					
The Road Runners are a creation of Gary Usher & Co.					
London LL-3381	(M)	**The New Mustang (& Other Hot Rod Hits)**	1964	40.00	100.00
London PS-381	(S)	**The New Mustang (& Other Hot Rod Hits)**	1964	60.00	150.00
ROBBINS, MARTY					
Refer to Carl Smith.					
Columbia CL-2601 (10")	(M)	**Rock 'N Roll 'N Robbins**	1956	500.00	800.00
Columbia CL-976	(M)	**The Song Of Robbins**	1957	40.00	100.00
Columbia CL-1087	(M)	**Song Of The Islands**	1957	50.00	125.00
Columbia CL-1189	(M)	**Marty Robbins**	1958	30.00	75.00
Columbia CL-1325	(M)	**Marty's Greatest Hits**	1959	30.00	75.00
Columbia CL-1349	(M)	**Gunfighter Ballads And Trail Songs**	1959	12.00	30.00
Columbia CS-8158	(S)	**Gunfighter Ballads And Trail Songs**	1959	16.00	40.00
Columbia CL-1481	(M)	**More Gunfighter Ballads And Trail Songs**	1960	8.00	20.00
Columbia CS-8272	(S)	**More Gunfighter Ballads And Trail Songs**	1960	12.00	30.00
Columbia CL-1558	(M)	**The Alamo** (Soundtrack)	1960	8.00	20.00
Columbia CS-8358	(S)	**The Alamo** (Soundtrack)	1960	12.00	30.00
Columbia CL-1635	(M)	**More Greatest Hits**	1961	8.00	20.00
Columbia CS-8435	(S)	**More Greatest Hits**	1961	12.00	30.00
Columbia CL-1666	(M)	**Just A Little Sentimental**	1961	8.00	20.00
Columbia CS-8466	(S)	**Just A Little Sentimental**	1961	12.00	30.00
— Original Columbia albums above have six white-on-black "eye" logos around the perimeter of the label.—					
Columbia CL-1801	(M)	**Marty After Midnight**	1962	20.00	50.00
Columbia CS-8601	(S)	**Marty After Midnight**	1962	30.00	75.00
Columbia CS-8639	(E)	**Marty's Greatest Hits**	1962	10.00	25.00
		(This stereo reissue has "Ain't I The Lucky One," "The Hanging Tree," and "The Blues Country Style" in stereo.)			
Columbia CL-1855	(M)	**Portrait Of Marty**	1962	14.00	35.00
Columbia CS-8655	(S)	**Portrait Of Marty**	1962	20.00	50.00
		(Issued with a bonus photo, priced separately below.)			
Columbia		**Portrait Of Marty Bonus Photo**	1962	12.00	30.00
Columbia CL-1918	(M)	**Devil Woman**	1962	10.00	25.00
Columbia CS-8718	(S)	**Devil Woman**	1962	14.00	35.00
Columbia CL-2040	(M)	**Hawaii's Calling Me**	1963	12.00	30.00
Columbia CS-8840	(S)	**Hawaii's Calling Me**	1963	16.00	40.00
Columbia CL-2072	(M)	**Return Of The Gunfighter**	1963	8.00	20.00
Columbia CS-8872	(S)	**Return Of The Gunfighter**	1963	12.00	30.00
Columbia CL-2176	(M)	**Island Woman**	1964	12.00	30.00
Columbia CS-8976	(S)	**Island Woman**	1964	16.00	40.00
Columbia CL-2220	(M)	**R.F.D. Marty Robbins**	1964	12.00	30.00
Columbia CS-9020	(S)	**R.F.D. Marty Robbins**	1964	16.00	40.00
Columbia CL-2304	(M)	**Turn The Lights Down Low**	1965	8.00	20.00
Columbia CS-9104	(S)	**Turn The Lights Down Low**	1965	12.00	30.00
Columbia CL-2448	(M)	**What God Has Done**	1965	6.00	15.00
Columbia CS-9248	(S)	**What God Has Done**	1965	8.00	20.00
Columbia CL-2527	(M)	**The Drifter**	1966	6.00	15.00
Columbia CS-9327	(S)	**The Drifter**	1966	8.00	20.00
Columbia CLP-445	(M)	**Bend In The River** (Special Products)	1966	12.00	30.00
Columbia CLS-445	(P)	**Bend In The River** (Special Products)	1966	16.00	40.00
Columbia DL-237	(M)	**Saddle Tramp** (Record Club)	1966	6.00	15.00
Columbia DS-237	(S)	**Saddle Tramp** (Record Club)	1966	8.00	20.00

Label & Catalog #		Title	Year	VG+	NM
Columbia CL-2621	(M)	The Song Of Robbins	1967	12.00	30.00
Columbia CS-9421	(E)	The Song Of Robbins	1967	8.00	20.00
		(Columbia 26/9421 is a reissue of 976.)			
Columbia CL-2625	(M)	Song Of The Islands	1967	12.00	30.00
Columbia CS-9425	(E)	Song Of The Islands	1967	8.00	20.00
		(Columbia 26/9425 is a reissue of 1087.)			
Columbia CL-2645	(M)	My Kind Of Country	1967	12.00	30.00
Columbia CS-9445	(S)	My Kind Of Country	1967	8.00	20.00
Columbia CL-2725	(M)	Tonight Carmen	1967	12.00	30.00
Columbia CS-9525	(S)	Tonight Carmen	1967	8.00	20.00
Columbia CL-2735	(M)	Christmas With Marty Robbins	1967	20.00	5.00
Columbia CS-9535	(S)	Christmas With Marty Robbins	1967	12.00	30.00
Columbia CL-2817	(M)	By The Time I Get To Phoenix	1968	20.00	50.00
Columbia CS-9617	(S)	By The Time I Get To Phoenix	1968	8.00	20.00
Columbia CS-9725	(S)	I Walk Alone	1968	6.00	15.00
Columbia CSP-445	(S)	Bend In The River (Record Club)	1968	20.00	50.00
Columbia STS-2016	(E)	The Heart Of Marty Robbins (2 LPs)	1969	20.00	50.00
Columbia CS-9811	(S)	It's A Sin	1969	10.00	25.00
Columbia GP-15	(S)	Marty's Country	1969	6.00	15.00
Columbia CS-9978	(S)	My Woman, My Woman, My Wife	1970	6.00	15.00
— Original Columbia albums above have "360 Sound" on the bottom of the label.—					
Columbia C-30316	(S)	El Paso	1970	6.00	15.00
Columbia KC-30324	(S)	Country Hymns	1970	6.00	15.00
Columbia G-30811	(P)	The World Of Marty Robbins (2 LPs)	1971	8.00	20.00
Columbi P-11311	(S)	By The Time I Get To Phoenix	1971	6.00	15.00
Columbia KC-30571	(S)	Marty's Greatest Hits, Volume 3	1971	6.00	15.00
Columbia KC-30816	(S)	Marty Robbins Today	1971	6.00	15.00
Columbia KC-31341	(S)	Bound For Old Mexico	1971	6.00	15.00
Columbia KC-31361	(S)	All-Time Greatest Hits (2 LPs)	1972	6.00	15.00
Columbia KC-31628	(S)	I've Got A Woman's Love	1972	8.00	20.00
Columbia P5S-5812	(S)	Marty (5 LP box)	1972	16.00	40.00
Columbia C-10980	(S)	Christmas With Mrty Robbins	1970	6.00	15.00
Columbia C-11087	(S)	The Joy Of Christmas	1972	6.00	15.00
Artco LPC-110	(S)	The Best Of Marty Robbins	1973	8.00	20.00
Columbi P-12416	(P)	Marty Robbins' Own Favorites	1974	6.00	15.00
Columbia C-32586	(S)	Have I Told You Lately That I Love You	1974	6.00	15.00

ROBBS, THE

Mercury MG-21130	(M)	The Robbs	1967	10.00	25.00
Mercury SR-61130	(S)	The Robbs	1967	12.00	30.00

ROBERTS, JOAN

Quality 719-26 (10")	(M)	Joan Roberts Sings	195?	14.00	35.00

ROBERTS, PERNELL

RCA Victor LPM-2662	(M)	Come All Ye Fair And Tender Ladies	1963	10.00	25.00
RCA Victor LSP-2662	(S)	Come All Ye Fair And Tender Ladies	1963	14.00	35.00

ROBERTSON, DALE

RCA Victor LPM-2158	(M)	His Album Of Western Classics	1960	30.00	75.00
RCA Victor LSP-2158	(S)	His Album Of Western Classics	1960	50.00	125.00

ROBERTSON, DON

RCA Victor LPM-3348	(M)	Heart On My Sleeve	1965	6.00	15.00
RCA Victor LSP-3348	(S)	Heart On My Sleeve	1965	8.00	20.00

ROBINS, THE

Whippet WLP-703	(M)	Rock 'N' Roll With The Robins	1958	300.00	500.00
Crescendo GNPS-9034	(E)	The Best Of The Robins	1975	6.00	15.00

ROBINSON, ANDY

Philips PHS-600-289	(S)	Patterns Of Reality	1969	6.00	15.00

ROBINSON, CARSON

MGM E-3594	(M)	Life Get's Tee-jus, Don't It	1958	16.00	40.00

ROBINSON, FLOYD

RCA Victor LPM-2162	(M)	Floyd Robinson	1960	20.00	50.00
RCA Victor LSP-2162	(S)	Floyd Robinson	1960	30.00	75.00

Label & Catalog #		Title	Year	VG+	NM

ROBINSON, SMOKEY, & THE MIRACLES [THE MIRACLES]
Tamla 220-254 simply credit The Miracles. The Miracles who recorded for Tamla from 1974 on are a different group.

Label & Catalog #		Title	Year	VG+	NM
Tamla 220	(M)	Hi! We're The Miracles	1961	300.00	500.00
Tamla 223	(M)	Cookin' With The Miracles	1962	300.00	500.00
Tamla 230	(M)	I'll Try Something New	1962	300.00	500.00
		— Original Tamla albums above have a disc over-lapping a globe at the top of the label.—			
Tamla 236	(M)	Christmas With The Miracles	1963	150.00	300.00
Tamla 238	(M)	The Fabulous Miracles	1963	150.00	300.00
Tamla 238	(M)	You've Really Got A Hold On Me	1963	60.00	150.00
		(Repackage of "The Fabulous Miracles.")			
Tamla 241	(M)	The Miracles On Stage	1963	60.00	150.00
Tamla 245	(M)	Doin' Mickey's Monkey	1963	60.00	150.00
Tamla T-245	(S)	Doin' Mickey's Monkey	1963	80.00	200.00
Tamla 2-254	(M)	Greatest Hits From The Beginning (2 LPs)	1965	20.00	50.00
Tamla T-2-254	(P)	Greatest Hits From The Beginning (2 LPs)	1965	14.00	35.00
		(The first disc of 254 is rechanneled; the second is stereo.)			
Tamla 267	(M)	Going To A Go-Go	1965	10.00	25.00
Tamla T-267	(S)	Going To A Go-Go	1965	12.00	30.00
Tamla 271	(M)	Away We A Go-Go	1966	8.00	20.00
Tamla T-271	(S)	Away We A Go-Go	1966	10.00	25.00
Tamla 276	(M)	Make It Happen	1967	8.00	20.00
Tamla T-276	(S)	Make It Happen	1967	10.00	25.00
Tamla T-276	(S)	Tears Of A Clown	1970	8.00	20.00
		("Tears Of A Clown" is a repackage of "Make It Happen.")			
Tamla T-280	(S)	Greatest Hits, Volume 2	1968	8.00	20.00
		— Tamla albums above have two side-by-side circles at the top of the label.—			
Tamla T-289	(S)	Live!	1969	6.00	15.00
Tamla T-290	(S)	Special Occasion	1968	6.00	15.00
Tamla T-295	(S)	Time Out	1969	6.00	15.00
Tamla T-297	(S)	Four In Blue	1969	6.00	15.00
Tamla T-301	(S)	What Love Has Joined Together	1970	6.00	15.00
Tamla T-306	(S)	A Pocketful Of Miracles	1970	6.00	15.00
Tamla T-307	(S)	The Season For Miracles	1970	6.00	15.00
Tamla T-312	(S)	One Dozen Roses	1971	6.00	15.00
Tamla T-318	(S)	Flying High Together	1972	6.00	15.00
Tamla T-320	(P)	The Miracles 1957-1972 (2 LPs)	1973	6.00	15.00
Motown 793	(P)	Anthology (3 LPs)	1974	6.00	15.00

ROBINSON, SUGAR CHILE

Label & Catalog #		Title	Year	VG+	NM
Capitol T-589	(M)	Boogie Woogie	1955	60.00	150.00

ROBINSON, SUGAR RAY: *Refer to GOLDMINE'S PRICE GUIDE TO COLLECTIBLE JAZZ ALBUMS*

ROCHE, BETTY: *Refer to GOLDMINE'S PRICE GUIDE TO COLLECTIBLE JAZZ ALBUMS*

ROCK-A-TEENS, THE

Label & Catalog #		Title	Year	VG+	NM
Roulette R-25109	(M)	Woo-Hoo	1960	50.00	125.00
Roulette SR-25109	(S)	Woo-Hoo	1960	70.00	175.00
		("Woo-Hoo" is rechanneled on this album.)			

ROCK, THE

Label & Catalog #		Title	Year	VG+	NM
LeeMo (No number)	(M)	The Rock Shop	1969	80.00	200.00

ROCK & ROLL REVIVAL, THE

Label & Catalog #		Title	Year	VG+	NM
Dunhill DS-50059	(S)	Great Oldies Done Hear And Now	1969	8.00	20.00

ROCK CANDY

Label & Catalog #		Title	Year	VG+	NM
MGM SE-4703	(S)	Rock Candy	1970	8.00	20.00

ROCKET 88
Rocket 88 is a creation of Charlie Watts of The Rolling Stones.

Label & Catalog #		Title	Year	VG+	NM
Atlantic 19293	(S)	Rocket 88	1981	4.00	10.00

ROCKETS, THE
The Rockets feature Ralph Molina and Danny Talbot, later of Crazy Horse.

Label & Catalog #		Title	Year	VG+	NM
White Whale WWS-7116	(S)	The Rockets	1968	16.00	40.00

Label & Catalog #		Title	Year	VG+	NM
ROCKIN' FOO					
Hobbit HB-5001	(S)	Rockin' Foo	1969	8.00	20.00
Uni 73115	(S)	Rockin' Foo	1971	6.00	15.00
ROCKIN' REBELS, THE					
Swan SLP-509	(M)	Wild Weekend	1963	80.00	200.00
ROCKY FELLERS, THE					
Scepter SP-512	(M)	Killer Joe	1963	10.00	25.00
Scepter SPS-512	(S)	Killer Joe	1963	20.00	50.00
ROD & THE COBRAS					
Somerset SF-20500	(M)	Drag Race At Surf City	1964	10.00	25.00
Somerset SS-20500	(S)	Drag Race At Surf City	1964	12.00	30.00
RODERICK, JUDY					
Columbia CL-2153	(M)	Ain't Nothin' But The Blues	1964	6.00	15.00
Columbia CS-8953	(S)	Ain't Nothin' But The Blues	1964	8.00	20.00
Vanguard VRS-9197	(M)	Woman Blue	1964	6.00	15.00
Vanguard VSD-79197	(S)	Woman Blue	1964	8.00	20.00
RODGERS, JIMMIE					
RCA Victor LPT-3037 (10")	(M)	Memorial Album, Volume 1	1952	80.00	200.00
RCA Victor LPT-3038 (10")	(M)	Memorial Album, Volume 2	1952	80.00	200.00
RCA Victor LPT-3039 (10")	(M)	Memorial Album, Volume 3	1952	80.00	200.00
RCA Victor LPT-3073 (10")	(M)	Travelin' Blues	1952	80.00	200.00
RCA Victor LPM-1232	(M)	Never No Mo' Blues/Memorial Album	1955	40.00	100.00
RCA Victor LPM-1640	(M)	Train Whistle Blues	1957	40.00	100.00
RCA Victor LPM-2112	(M)	My Rough And Rowdy Ways	1960	20.00	50.00
RCA Victor LPM-2213	(M)	Jimmie The Kid	1961	20.00	50.00
RCA Victor LPM-2531	(M)	Country Music Hall Of Fame	1962	20.00	50.00
RCA Victor LPM-2634	(M)	The Short But Brilliant Life Of Jimmie Rodgers	1963	20.00	50.00
— Original RCA albums above have "Long Play" on the bottom of the label.—					
RCA Victor LPM-2865	(M)	My Time Ain't Long	1964	10.00	25.00
RCA Victor LPM-3315	(M)	Best Of The Legendary Jimmie Rodgers	1965	10.00	25.00
RCA Victor LSP-3315	(E)	Best Of The Legendary Jimmie Rodgers	1965	6.00	15.00
— Original RCA albums above have black labels.—					
RODGERS, JIMMIE					
Roulette R-25020	(M)	Folk Songs And Readings	1958	16.00	40.00
Roulette R-25026	(M)	The Long Hot Summer (Soundtrack)	1958	20.00	50.00
Roulette R-25033	(M)	Number One Ballads	1958	16.00	40.00
Roulette R-25042	(M)	Jimmie Rodgers Sings Folk Songs	1958	16.00	40.00
— Original Roulette albums above have black labels.—					
Roulette R-25057	(M)	His Golden Year	1959	12.00	35.00
Roulette R-25071	(M)	TV Favorites	1959	10.00	25.00
Roulette SR-25071	(S)	TV Favorites	1959	16.00	40.00
Roulette R-25081	(M)	Twilight On The Trail	1959	10.00	25.00
Roulette SR-25081	(S)	Twilight On The Trail	1959	16.00	40.00
Roulette R-25095	(M)	It's Christmas Once Again	1959	10.00	25.00
Roulette SR-25095	(S)	It's Christmas Once Again	1959	16.00	40.00
Roulette R-25103	(M)	When The Spirit Moves You	1960	10.00	25.00
Roulette SR-25103	(S)	When The Spirit Moves You	1960	12.00	30.00
Roulette R-25128	(M)	At Home With Jimmie Rodgers	1960	10.00	25.00
Roulette SR-25128	(S)	At Home With Jimmie Rodgers	1960	12.00	30.00
Roulette R-25150	(M)	The Folk Song World Of Jimmie Rodgers	1961	10.00	25.00
Roulette SR-25150	(S)	The Folk Song World Of Jimmie Rodgers	1961	12.00	30.00
Roulette R-25160	(M)	The Best Of Jimmie Rodgers Folk Songs	1961	10.00	25.00
Roulette SR-25160	(S)	The Best Of Jimmie Rodgers Folk Songs (Red vinyl)	1961	100.00	250.00
Roulette SR-25160	(S)	The Best Of Jimmie Rodgers Folk Songs	1961	12.00	30.00
Roulette R-25179	(M)	15 Million Sellers	1962	6.00	15.00
Roulette SR-25179	(P)	15 Million Sellers	1962	10.00	25.00
— Original Roulette albums above have white labels.—					
Roulette R-25199	(M)	Folk Songs	1963	6.00	15.00
Roulette SR-25199	(S)	Folk Songs	1963	10.00	25.00
Dot DLP-3453	(M)	No One Will Ever Know	1962	6.00	15.00
Dot DLP-25453	(S)	No One Will Ever Know	1962	8.00	20.00

Label & Catalog #		Title	Year	VG+	NM
Dot DLP-3496	(M)	Folk Concert	1963	6.00	15.00
Dot DLP-25496	(S)	Folk Concert	1963	8.00	20.00
Dot DLP-3502	(M)	My Favorite Hymns	1963	6.00	15.00
Dot DLP-25502	(S)	My Favorite Hymns	1963	8.00	20.00
Dot DLP-3525	(M)	Honeycomb And Kisses Sweeter Than Wine	1963	6.00	15.00
Dot DLP-25525	(S)	Honeycomb And Kisses Sweeter Than Wine	1963	8.00	20.00
Dot DLP-3???	(M)	Town And Country	1963	6.00	15.00
Dot DLP-25???	(S)	Town And Country	1963	8.00	20.00
Dot DLP-3???	(M)	The World I Used To Know	1964	6.00	15.00
Dot DLP-25???	(S)	The World I Used To Know	1964	8.00	20.00
Dot DLP-3579	(M)	Twelve Great Hits	1964	6.00	15.00
Dot DLP-25579	(S)	Twelve Great Hits	1964	8.00	20.00
Dot DLP-3614	(M)	Deep Purple	1965	6.00	15.00
Dot DLP-25614	(S)	Deep Purple	1965	8.00	20.00
Dot DLP-3657	(M)	Christmas With Jimmie Rodgers	1965	6.00	15.00
Dot DLP-25657	(S)	Christmas With Jimmie Rodgers	1965	8.00	20.00
Dot DLP-3687	(M)	Nashville Sound	1966	6.00	15.00
Dot DLP-25687	(S)	Nashville Sound	1966	8.00	20.00
Dot DLP-3710	(M)	Country Music 1966	1966	6.00	15.00
Dot DLP-25710	(S)	Country Music 1966	1966	8.00	20.00
Dot DLP-3717	(M)	It's Over	1966	6.00	15.00
Dot DLP-25717	(S)	It's Over	1966	8.00	20.00
Dot DLP-3780	(M)	Love Me, Please Love Me	1967	8.00	20.00
Dot DLP-25780	(S)	Love Me, Please Love Me	1967	8.00	20.00
Dot DLP-3815	(M)	Golden Hits/15 Hits Of Jimmie Rodgers	1967	6.00	15.00
Dot DLP-25815	(S)	Golden Hits/15 Hits Of Jimmie Rodgers	1967	6.00	15.00
A&M LP-130	(M)	Child Of Clay	1967	6.00	15.00
A&M SP-4130	(S)	Child Of Clay	1967	5.00	12.00
A&M SP-4242	(S)	Troubled Times	1970	4.00	10.00

ROE, TOMMY

ABC-Paramount 432	(M)	Sheila	1962	16.00	40.00
ABC-Paramount S-432	(S)	Sheila	1962	20.00	50.00
ABC-Paramount 467	(M)	Something For Everybody	1964	10.00	25.00
ABC-Paramount S-467	(S)	Something For Everybody	1964	12.00	30.00
ABC-Paramount 575	(M)	Sweet Pea	1966	10.00	25.00
ABC-Paramount S-575	(S)	Sweet Pea	1966	12.00	30.00
ABC-Paramount 594	(M)	It's Now Winter's Day	1967	8.00	20.00
ABC-Paramount S-594	(S)	It's Now Winter's Day	1967	10.00	25.00
ABC 610	(M)	Phantasy	1967	6.00	15.00
ABC S-610	(S)	Phantasy	1967	8.00	20.00
ABC S-683	(S)	Dizzy	1969	8.00	20.00
ABC S-700	(S)	12 In A Roe/A Collection Of Greatest Hits	1969	6.00	15.00
		("Everybody," "Party Girl" and "Carol" are rechanneled.)			
ABC S-714	(S)	We Can Make Music	1970	5.00	12.00
ABC S-732	(S)	Beginnings	1971	5.00	12.00
ABC X-762	(S)	16 Greatest Hits	1972	4.00	10.00

ROE, TOMMY / BOBBY LEE

Crown CLP-5323	(M)	Tommy Roe And Bobby Lee	1963	8.00	20.00
Crown CST-323	(E)	Tommy Roe And Bobby Lee	1963	4.00	10.00

ROGERS, EILEEN

Columbia CL-1229	(M)	Blue Swing	1959	8.00	20.00
Columbia CS-8029	(S)	Blue Swing	1959	12.00	30.00

ROGERS, GINGER

Decca DL-5040 (10")	(M)	Alice In Wonderland	195?	30.00	75.00
Citel CLP-201	(M)	Hello, Ginger!	195?	20.00	50.00

ROGERS, KENNY

Kenny also recorded with The First Edition.

Jolly Rogers 5001	(S)	Backroads (Picture disc)	1975	40.00	100.00
United Artists LA934	(DJ)	The Gambler (Picture disc)	1978	20.00	50.00
Mobile Fidelity MFSL-044	(S)	The Gambler	1979	5.00	15.00
Mobile Fidelity MFSL-049	(S)	Greatest Hits	1979	5.00	15.00
Liberty SLL-8344	(DJ)	HBO Presents Kenny Rogers (Picture disc)	1983	4.00	10.00

Label & Catalog #		Title	Year	VG+	NM

ROGERS, ROY (& DALE EVANS)

Label & Catalog #		Title	Year	VG+	NM
RCA Victor LPT-3041 (10")	(M)	Roy Rogers Souvenir Album	1952	80.00	200.00
RCA Victor LPT-3168 (10")	(M)	Hymns Of Faith	1954	40.00	100.00
RCA Victor LPM-1439	(M)	Sweet Hour Of Prayer	1957	20.00	50.00
Golden A-1978	(M)	16 Great Songs Of The Old West	195?	20.00	50.00
Bluebird LBY-1022	(M)	Jesus Loves Me	1959	14.00	35.00
Capitol T-1745	(M)	The Bible Tells Me So	1962	16.00	40.00
Capitol ST-1745	(S)	The Bible Tells Me So	1962	20.00	50.00
Camden CAL-1054	(M)	Pecos Bill	1964	10.00	25.00
Camden CAL-1074	(M)	Lore Of The West	1966	10.00	25.00
Capitol T-2818	(M)	Christmas Is Always	1967	12.00	30.00
Capitol ST-2818	(S)	Christmas Is Always	1967	12.00	30.00
Camden CAL-1097	(M)	Peter Cottontail And His Friends	1968	6.00	15.00
Capitol ST-594	(S)	The Country Side Of Roy Rogers	1970	6.00	15.00
Capitol ST-785	(S)	A Man From Duck Run	1971	6.00	15.00
Capitol ST-11020	(S)	Take A Little Love And Pass It On	1972	5.00	12.00
20th Century 467	(S)	Happy Trails To You	1975	5.00	12.00

ROKES, THE

Label & Catalog #		Title	Year	VG+	NM
RCA Victor Int. FPM-185	(M)	Che Mondo Strano	1968	10.00	25.00

ROLLING STONES, THE

The original recording group consisted of Mick Jagger, Brian Jones, Keith Richards, Charlie Watts and Bill Wyman with unofficial member, keyboardist Ian Stewart. Jones left in 1969 (he died shortly thereafter) and was replaced by Mick Taylor, who left in 1972. Ron Wood took over good in 1976. Refer to Howlin' Wolf; Alexis Korner; Rocket 88.

With the [inexplicable] exceptions of "Look What You've Done" on "December's Children," the material on the Stones' first five studio albums have not been issued in stereo in this country. And, excepting singles lifted from albums issued since 1966, all of their non-LP singles through 1966 have only appeared in rechanneled stereo. These recordings were almost certainly done on multi-track equipment.

Label & Catalog #		Title	Year	VG+	NM
London LL-3375	(DJ)	The Rolling Stones (White label)	1964	800.00	Rare
		(Near Mint copies have a suggested value of $1,200-1,600.)			
London LL-3375	(M)	The Rolling Stones	1964	60.00	150.00
		(Issued with a bonus photo, which is advertised in the lower left corner of the front cover. The photo is priced separately below.)			
London LL-3375		The Rolling Stones Bonus Photo	1964	80.00	200.00
London LL-3402	(M)	12 X 5	1964	80.00	200.00
London LL-3420	(M)	The Rolling Stones, Now!	1965	80.00	200.00
London LL-3429	(M)	Out Of Our Heads	1965	80.00	200.00

— London albums above have maroon labels with the London/ffrr" logo and "Made in England by the Decca Group" at the top.—

Label & Catalog #		Title	Year	VG+	NM
London LL-3375	(M)	The Rolling Stones	1964	24.00	60.00
London PS-375	(E)	The Rolling Stones	1965	10.00	25.00
London LL-3402	(M)	12 X 5 (Blue vinyl)	1964	3,000.00	Rare
		(Near Mint copies have a suggested value of $5,000-10,000.)			
London LL-3402	(M)	12 X 5	1964	24.00	60.00
London PS-402	(E)	12 X 5	1965	10.00	25.00
London LL-3420	(M)	The Rolling Stones, Now!	1965	24.00	60.00
London PS-420	(E)	The Rolling Stones, Now!	1965	10.00	25.00
London LL-3429	(M)	Out Of Our Heads	1965	24.00	60.00
London PS-429	(E)	Out Of Our Heads	1965	10.00	25.00
London LL-3451	(M)	December's Children	1965	24.00	60.00
London PS-451	(E)	December's Children	1965	10.00	25.00

— London mono albums above have maroon labels with a silver "London" on top; stereo albums above have blue labels with a silver "London" on top.—

Label & Catalog #		Title	Year	VG+	NM
I.N.S. Radio 1003	(M)	It's Here Luv!!	1965	100.00	250.00
		(Originals are on thick vinyl with crisp printing on the cover.)			
London LL-3375	(M)	The Rolling Stones	1965	16.00	40.00
London PS-375	(E)	The Rolling Stones	1966	4.00	10.00
London LL-3402	(M)	12 X 5	1965	16.00	40.00
London PS-402	(E)	12 X 5	1966	4.00	10.00
London LL-3420	(M)	The Rolling Stones, Now!	1965	16.00	40.00
London PS-420	(E)	The Rolling Stones, Now!	1966	4.00	10.00
London LL-3429	(M)	Out Of Our Heads	1965	16.00	40.00
London PS-429	(E)	Out Of Our Heads	1966	4.00	10.00
London LL-3451	(M)	December's Children	1965	16.00	40.00
London PS-451	(E)	December's Children	1966	4.00	10.00

Label & Catalog #		Title	Year	VG+	NM
London NP-1	(M)	**High Tide And Green Grass (Big Hits)**	1966	See note below	
		(The original front cover design had the title on one line in radically different type. These were rejected and replaced. Suggested values in collectible condition are $1,000-3,000.)			
London NP-1	(M)	**High Tide And Green Grass (Big Hits)**	1966	16.00	40.00
London NPS-1	(E)	**High Tide And Green Grass (Big Hits)**	1966	4.00	10.00
London LL-3476	(M)	**Aftermath**	1966	16.00	40.00
London PS-476	(S)	**Aftermath**	1966	4.00	10.00
London LL-4493	(M)	**Got Live If You Want It**	1966	16.00	40.00
London PS-493	(P)	**Got Live If You Want It**	1966	4.00	10.00
London LL-499	(M)	**Between The Buttons**	1967	16.00	40.00
London PS-499	(S)	**Between The Buttons**	1967	4.00	10.00
London LL-509	(M)	**Flowers**	1967	16.00	40.00
London PS-509	(P)	**Flowers**	1967	4.00	10.00
London NP-2	(M)	**Their Satanic Majesties Request** (3-D cover)	1967	80.00	200.00
London NPS-2	(S)	**Their Satanic Majesties Request** (3-D cover)	1967	16.00	40.00
London NPS-2	(S)	**Their Satanic Majesties Request** (2-D cover)	1967	6.00	15.00
London PS-539	(S)	**Beggar's Banquet**	1968	6.00	15.00
		(First pressings credit all songs to Jagger-Richard.)			
London PS-539	(S)	**Beggar's Banquet**	1968	4.00	10.00
		(Later pressings credit Rev. Wilkins as writer of "Prodigal Son.")			
London NPS-3	(S)	**Through The Past, Darkly**	1969	4.00	10.00
London NPS-3	(DJ)	**Through The Past, Darkly (Big Hits, Vol. 2)**	1969	See note below	
		(Picture disc. London pressed up fifteen prototypes to test the viability of a commercial picture disc. Seven copies had the front cover of "High Tide & Green Grass" on both sides; eight copies had Ten Years After's "Sssh" on one side. Suggested values in collectible condition are $2,000-4,000.)			
London RSD-1	(DJ)	**The Rolling Stones/The Promotional Album**	1969	600.00	1,000.00
		(Counterfeits are common.)			
London NPS-4	(S)	**Let It Bleed** (Includes poster)	1969	8.00	20.00
London NPS-4	(S)	**Let It Bleed** (Without poster)	1969	4.00	10.00
London NPS-5	(S)	**Get Your Ya-Ya's Out!**	1970	4.00	10.00
London 2PS-606/7	(P)	**Hot Rocks 1964-1971** (2 LPs)	1971	5.00	12.00
London 2PS-626/7	(P)	**More Hot Rocks** (2 LPs)	1972	5.00	12.00

— London mono albums above have maroon labels with a maroon "London" on top in a silver box;
— stereo albums above have deep blue labels with a blue "London" on top in a silver box.—

Abkco DVL2-0268	(P)	**The Rolling Stones' Greatest Hits** (2 LPs.)	1975	12.00	30.00
Abkco ANA-1	(P)	**Metamorphosis**	1975	4.00	10.00
Abkco MPD-1	(S)	**Songs Of The Rolling Stones**	1975	150.00	300.00
		(Cover photo has a shot of the group in a field.)			
Abkco MPD-1	(S)	**Songs Of The Rolling Stones**	1975	600.00	Rare
		(Orange cover with a shot taken from the "Rock & Roll Circus." Near Mint copies have a suggested value of $1,000-1,500.)			
Roll. Stones COC 59100	(DJ)	**Sticky Fingers** (White label. Mono)	1971	150.00	300.00
Roll. Stones COC 59100	(DJ)	**Sticky Fingers** (White label. Stereo)	1971	80.00	200.00
Roll. Stones COC 59100	(S)	**Sticky Fingers** (Zipper cover)	1971	4.00	10.00
Roll. Stones PRB-164	(DJ)	**Interview With Mick Jagger** (White label)	1971	80.00	200.00
Roll. Stones PRB-164	(DJ)	**Interview With Mick Jagger** (Yellow label)	1971	60.00	150.00
Roll. Stones COC-39100	(DJ)	**Jamming With Edward** (White label)	1972	20.00	50.00
Roll. Stones COC-39100	(S)	**Jamming With Edward**	1972	6.00	15.00
Roll. Stones COC-2-2900	(S)	**Exile On Main Street** (2 LPs)	1972	6.00	15.00
		(Fold-out jacket with pockets that open on the inside. Includes a tear-sheet of postcards.)			
Rolling Stones COC 59101	(S)	**Goat's Head Soup**	1973	4.00	10.00
		(Issued with a goat's head bonus photo.)			
Rolling Stones COC 39108	(S)	**Some Girls**	1978	4.00	10.00
		(Original covers have die-cut face-holes for the inner sleeve, which includes Farrah Fawcett and Lucille Ball. There are at least nine variations on the colors used on this cover.)			
Roll. Stones COC 39113	(S)	**Still Life** (Picture disc)	1982	16.00	40.00
Mobile Fidelity MFSL-060	(S)	**Sticky Fingers**	1980	14.00	35.00
Mobile Fidelity MFSL-087	(S)	**Some Girls**	1982	14.00	35.00
Mobile Fidelity RC-1	(P)	**The Rolling Stones** (11 LP box)	1984	100.00	300.00

ROMANCERS, THE

Selma 1245	(S)	**Do The Slauson**	1963	8.00	20.00
Selma 1501	(S)	**Let's Do The Swim**	1963	8.00	20.00

Label & Catalog #		Title	Year	VG+	NM

ROMEOS, THE

Mark-II 1001	(M)	**Precious Memories**	1967	10.00	25.00

ROMNEY, HUGH

Mr. Romney later claimed fame in the counter-culture as Digger deluxe "Wavy Gravy."

World Pacific WP-1805	(M)	**Third Stream Humor**	1962	10.00	25.00
World Pacific ST-1805	(M)	**Third Stream Humor**	1962	14.00	35.00

RONETTES, THE

The Ronettes feature Veronica Bennett, a.k.a. Ronnie Spector. Philles 4006 was produced by Phil Spector.

Colpix CLP-486	(DJ)	**The Ronettes Featuring Veronica**	1965	150.00	300.00
Colpix CLP-486	(M)	**The Ronettes Featuring Veronica**	1965	60.00	150.00
Colpix CST-486	(S)	**The Ronettes Featuring Veronica**	1965	100.00	200.00
		(First pressings are on a gold label.)			
Colpix CLP-486	(M)	**The Ronettes Featuring Veronica**	196?	40.00	100.00
Colpix CST-486	(S)	**The Ronettes Featuring Veronica**	196?	60.00	150.00
		(Second pressings are on a blue label.)			
Philles PHLP-4006	(M)	**Presenting The Fabulous Ronettes**	1965	100.00	250.00
		(First pressings are mono only on a blue label.)			
Philles PHLP-4006	(M)	**Presenting The Fabulous Ronettes**	1965	60.00	150.00
Philles PHLP-ST-4006	(S)	**Presenting The Fabulous Ronettes**	1965	200.00	400.00
		(Yellow label with red print.)			
Philles ST-	(S)	**Presenting The Fabulous Ronettes**	1965	150.00	300.00
		(Capitol Record Club. Yellow label with black print.)			

RONNIE & THE DEADBEATS

Check 103	(M)	**Groovin' With Ronnie & The Deadbeats**	197?	8.00	20.00

RONNY & THE DAYTONAS

Mala 4001	(M)	**G. T. O.**	1964	60.00	150.00
Mala 4002	(M)	**Sandy**	1966	16.00	40.00
Mala 4002S	(S)	**Sandy**	1966	30.00	75.00

RONNIE & THE POMONA CASUALS

Donna 2112	(M)	**Everybody Jerk**	1965	12.00	30.00

RONSTADT, LINDA, & THE STONE PONEYS

Capitol T-2666	(M)	**The Stone Poneys**	1967	10.00	25.00
Capitol ST-2666	(S)	**The Stone Poneys**	1967	12.00	30.00
Capitol T-2763	(M)	**Evergreen, Volume II**	1967	10.00	25.00
Capitol ST-2763	(S)	**Evergreen, Volume II**	1967	12.00	30.00
Capitol ST-2863	(S)	**Linda Ronstadt, Stone Poneys & Friends**	1968	16.00	40.00

RONSTADT, LINDA

Capitol ST-208	(S)	**Hand Sown**	1969	6.00	15.00
Capitol ST-407	(S)	**Silk Purse**	1970	6.00	15.00
Capitol SMAS-635	(S)	**Linda Ronstadt**	1972	6.00	15.00
		— Original Capitol albums above have green labels.—			
Asylum DP-401	(S)	**Living In The U.S.A.** *(Picture disc)*	1978	4.00	10.00
Mobile Fidelity MFSL-158	(S)	**What's New?**	198?	10.00	30.00
Nautilus NR-26	(S)	**Simple Dreams**	198?	16.00	50.00

ROOFTOP SINGERS, THE

Vanguard VRS-2136	(M)	**Walk Right In**	1963	5.00	12.00
Vanguard VSD-72136	(S)	**Walk Right In**	1963	6.00	15.00
Vanguard VRS-9134	(M)	**Goodtime**	1964	5.00	12.00
Vanguard VSD-79134	(S)	**Goodtime**	1964	6.00	15.00
Vanguard VRS-9190	(M)	**Rainy River**	1965	5.00	12.00
Vanguard VSD-79190	(S)	**Rainy River**	1965	6.00	15.00

ROONEY, MICKEY

RCA Victor LPM-1520	(M)	**Mickey Rooney Sings George M. Cohan**	1957	20.00	50.00

ROSE GARDEN, THE

Atco SD-33-225	(S)	**The Rose Garden**	1968	6.00	15.00

ROSE MARIE

Kapp KRL-2500	(M)	**Songs For Single Girls**	1964	6.00	15.00
Kapp KRS-4500	(S)	**Songs For Single Girls**	1964	8.00	20.00

Label & Catalog #		Title	Year	VG+	NM

ROSIE
Rosalie Hamlin of Rosie & The Originals.

Brunswick BL-54102	(M)	Lonely Blue Nights	1961	50.00	125.00
Brunswick BL7-54102	(S)	Lonely Blue Nights	1961	70.00	175.00

ROSS, ANNIE: *Refer to* GOLDMINE'S PRICE GUIDE TO COLLECTIBLE JAZZ ALBUMS

ROSS, DIANA

Motown M7-923	(DJ)	The Boss (Gold vinyl)	1979	8.00	20.00
Nautilus NR-37	(S)	Diana	1981	5.00	15.00

ROSS, DIANA / NEIL DIAMOND

MCA SM-734727	(S)	It's Happening! Diana Ross-Neil Diamond	1972	30.00	75.00

ROSS, MISS JACKIE

Chess LP-1489	(M)	In Full Bloom	196?	12.00	30.00
Chess LPS-1489	(S)	In Full Bloom	196?	16.00	40.00

ROSS, JOE E.
Mr. Ross also recorded as Officer Gunther Toody.

Roulette R-25281	(M)	Love Songs From A Cop	1964	6.00	15.00
Roulette SR-25281	(S)	Love Songs From A Cop	1964	8.00	20.00

ROTARY CONNECTION, THE

Cadet Concept LPS-312	(S)	Rotary Connection	1968	8.00	20.00
Cadet Concept LPS-317	(S)	Aladdin	1968	8.00	20.00
Cadet Concept LPS-318	(S)	Peace	1969	8.00	20.00
Cadet Concept LPS-322	(S)	Songs	1969	8.00	20.00
Cadet Concept LPS-329	(S)	Dinner Music	1970	8.00	20.00

ROTH, LILLIAN

Epic LN-3206	(M)	I'll Cry Tomorrow	195?	14.00	35.00
Tops L-1567	(M)	Lillian Roth Sings	1958	10.00	25.00

ROUGH TRADE

True North APHT-5010	(S)	For Those Who Think Young (Half-speed)	198?	10.00	30.00

ROUND ROBIN

Domain 101	(M)	Greatest Hits, Slauson Style	1964	10.00	25.00
Challenge LP-620	(M)	Lloyd Thaxton Presents The Land Of 1,000 Dances Featuring Round Robin	1965	8.00	20.00

ROUTERS, THE

Warner Bros. W-1490	(M)	Let's Go With The Routers	1963	8.00	20.00
Warner Bros. WS-1490	(S)	Let's Go With The Routers	1963	10.00	25.00
Warner Bros. W-1524	(M)	1963's Great Instrumental Hits	1964	10.00	25.00
Warner Bros. WS-1524	(S)	1963's Great Instrumental Hits	1964	12.00	30.00
Warner Bros. W-1559	(M)	Charge!	1964	6.00	15.00
Warner Bros. WS-1559	(S)	Charge!	1964	8.00	20.00
Warner Bros. W-1595	(M)	Go Go Go With The Chuck Berry Songbook	1965	6.00	15.00
Warner Bros. WS-1595	(S)	Go Go Go With The Chuck Berry Songbook	1965	8.00	20.00

ROWLES, JIMMY

Capitol T-1831	(M)	Kinda Groovy	1963	6.00	15.00
Capitol ST-1831	(S)	Kinda Groovy	1963	8.00	20.00

ROXX

Sit On It & Spin	(S)	Get Your Roxx Off	1976	20.00	50.00

ROXY MUSIC
The original Roxy Music featured Brian Eno and Brian Ferry.

Reprise MS-2114	(S)	Roxy Music	1972	12.00	30.00
Warner Bros. BS-2969	(S)	For Your Pleasure	1973	12.00	30.00
Atco SD-33-106	(S)	Country Life (Nearly naked ladies cover)	1975	10.00	25.00
Atco SD-38114	(S)	Manifesto (Picture disc)	1979	6.00	15.00

ROYAL, BILLY JOE

Columbia CL-2403	(M)	Down In The Boondocks	1965	8.00	20.00
Columbia CS-9203	(S)	Down In The Boondocks	1965	10.00	25.00

Label & Catalog #		Title	Year	VG+	NM
Columbia CL-2781	(M)	Billy Joe Royal	1967	8.00	20.00
Columbia CS-9581	(S)	Billy Joe Royal	1967	10.00	25.00
Columbia CS-9974	(S)	Cherry Hill Park	1969	8.00	20.00

ROYAL GUARDSMEN, THE

Laurie LLP-2038	(M)	Snoopy Vs. The Red Baron	1967	10.00	25.00
Laurie SLLP-2038	(S)	Snoopy Vs. The Red Baron	1967	12.00	30.00
Laurie LLP-2039	(M)	The Return Of The Red Baron	1967	10.00	25.00
Laurie SLLP-2039	(S)	The Return Of The Red Baron	1967	12.00	30.00
Laurie LLP-2042	(M)	Snoopy And His Friends	1967	12.00	30.00
Laurie SLLP-2042	(S)	Snoopy And His Friends	1967	16.00	40.00
		(Issued with a "Merry Snoopy's Christmas" tear-off sheet attached to the back cover.)			
Laurie LLP-2042	(M)	Snoopy And His Friends *(Without sheet)*	1967	8.00	20.00
Laurie SLLP-2042	(S)	Snoopy And His Friends *(Without sheet)*	1967	10.00	25.00
Laurie SLLP-2046	(S)	Snoopy For President	1968	10.00	25.00

ROYAL PLAYBOYS, THE

Waldorf 33-136 (10")	(M)	Spirituals And Jubilees	195?	60.00	150.00

ROYALETTES, THE

MGM E-4332	(M)	It's Gonna Take A Miracle	1965	6.00	15.00
MGM SE-4332	(S)	It's Gonna Take A Miracle	1965	8.00	20.00
MGM E-4366	(M)	The Elegant Sound Of The Royalettes	1966	6.00	15.00
MGM SE-4366	(S)	The Elegant Sound Of The Royalettes	1966	8.00	20.00

RUBBER BAND, THE

GRT 10007	(S)	The Jimi Hendrix Songbook	1969	6.00	15.00
GRT 10010	(S)	The Cream Songbook	1969	6.00	15.00
GRT 10015	(S)	The Beatles Songbook	1969	6.00	15.00

RUBBER MEMORY

R.P.C. 69401	(M)	Welcome	1969	500.00	*Rare*
		(Near Mint copies have a suggested value of $800-1,400.)			

RUBEN & THE JETS

Mercury SRM-1-659	(S)	For Real *(Produced by Frank Zappa)*	1973	6.00	15.00

RUBY & THE ROMANTICS

Kapp KL-1323	(M)	Our Day Will Come	1963	12.00	30.00
Kapp KS-3323	(S)	Our Day Will Come	1963	16.00	40.00
Kapp KL-1341	(M)	Till Then	1963	10.00	25.00
Kapp KS-3341	(S)	Till Then	1963	12.00	30.00
Kapp KL-1458	(M)	Greatest Hits Album	1966	8.00	20.00
Kapp KS-3458	(S)	Greatest Hits Album	1966	10.00	25.00
Kapp KL-1526	(M)	Ruby And The Romantics	1967	8.00	20.00
Kapp KS-3526	(S)	Ruby And The Romantics	1967	10.00	25.00
ABC S-638	(S)	More Than Yesterday	1968	8.00	20.00

RUFFIN, DAVID

David Ruffin was formerly a member of The Temptations.

Motown MS-685	(S)	My Whole World Ended	1969	8.00	20.00
Motown MS-696	(S)	Feelin' Good	1969	6.00	15.00
Motown M-618	(S)	Me 'N' Rock 'N' Roll	1974	5.00	12.00
Motown M-762	(S)	David Ruffin	1973	5.00	12.00

RUFFIN, JIMMY

Soul 704	(M)	Jimmy Ruffin Sings Top 10	1967	6.00	15.00
Soul S-704	(S)	Jimmy Ruffin Sings Top 10	1967	8.00	20.00
Soul S-708	(S)	Ruff 'N Ready	1969	6.00	15.00

RUFFIN, JIMMY & DAVID

Soul S-728	(S)	I Am My Brother's Keeper	1970	6.00	15.00

RUFUS

Command QD-40023	(Q)	Rufusized	1975	6.00	15.00
Command QD-40024	(Q)	Rags To Rufus	1975	6.00	15.00
ABC AA-1049	(DJ)	Street Player *(Picture disc)*	1979	5.00	12.00
ABC AA-1049	(DJ)	Numbers *(Picture disc)*	1979	5.00	12.00

Label & Catalog #		Title	Year	VG+	NM

RUMBLERS, THE

Downey DLP-1001	(M)	Boss!	1963	50.00	125.00
Downey DLPS-1001	(S)	Boss!	1963	60.00	150.00
Dot DLP-3509	(M)	Boss!	1963	12.00	30.00
Dot DLP-25509	(S)	Boss!	1963	16.00	40.00

RUNAWAYS, THE
The Runaways feature Joan Jett.

Mercury SRM-1-1090	(S)	The Runaways	1976	6.00	15.00
Mercury SRM-1-1126	(S)	Queens Of Noise	1977	6.00	15.00
Mercury SRM-1-3705	(S)	Waitin' For The Night	1977	6.00	15.00

RUNDGREN, TODD
Mr. Rundgren was formerly a member of The Nazz.

Ampex 10105	(S)	Runt *(With "Say No More")*	1970	40.00	100.00
Ampex 10105	(S)	Runt *(Without "Say No More")*	1970	20.00	50.00
Ampex 10116	(S)	Ballad Of Todd Rundgren	1971	20.00	50.00
		(Counterfeits of both Ampex albums are plentiful.)			
Bearsville 10105	(S)	Runt	1972	8.00	20.00
Bearsville 21066	(DJ)	Something/Anything *(2 LPs)*	1972	150.00	300.00
		(One album is on blue vinyl, the other, red.)			
Bearsville 524	(DJ)	The Todd Rundgren Radio Show	1973	60.00	150.00
Bearsville 597	(DJ)	Banded Radio Interview	1974	40.00	100.00
Bearsville 788	(DJ)	Todd Rundgren Radio Sampler	1979	20.00	50.00

RUSH

| Mercury MK-32 | (DJ) | Everything Your Listener Ever Wanted... | 1975 | 40.00 | 100.00 |
| Mercury SRP-1300 | (S) | Hemispheres *(Picture disc)* | 1979 | 10.00 | 25.00 |

RUSH, MERILEE, & THE TURNABOUTS

Bell 6020	(M)	Angel Of The Morning	1968	6.00	15.00
Bell 6020	(S)	Angel Of The Morning	1968	6.00	15.00
		("Angel Of The Morning" is rechanneled on this album.)			

RUSH, OTIS
Refer to Albert King & Otis Rush.

Blue Horizion BM-4602	(S)	Blues Masters, Volume 2	1968	10.00	25.00
Blue Horizion BM-4805	(S)	Chicago Blues	1970	10.00	25.00
Cotillion SD-9006	(S)	Mourning In The Morning	1969	8.00	20.00

RUSH, TOM

Folklore FRLP-14003	(M)	Got A Mind To Ramble	1964	10.00	25.00
Folklore FRST-14003	(M)	Got A Mind To Ramble	1964	12.00	30.00
Prestige PRLP-7374	(M)	Folk Songs And Blues	1965	6.00	15.00
Prestige PRST-7374	(S)	Folk Songs And Blues	1965	8.00	20.00
Elektra EKL-288	(M)	Tom Rush	1965	5.00	12.00
Elektra EKS-7288	(S)	Tom Rush	1965	6.00	15.00
Elektra EKL-308	(M)	Take A Little Walk With Me	1966	5.00	12.00
Elektra EKS-7308	(S)	Take A Little Walk With Me	1966	6.00	15.00
Elektra EKS-74018	(S)	The Circle Game	1968	4.00	10.00
Prestige PRST-7536	(M)	Got A Mind To Ramble	1969	6.00	15.00
		(Prestige 7536 is a reissue of Folklore 14003.)			
Ly Cornu SA-70-2	(S)	Tom Rush At The Unicorn	1970	8.00	20.00

RUSHING, JIMMY

Vanguard VRS-8011 (10")	(M)	Jimmy Rushing Sings The Blues	1954	30.00	60.00
Vanguard VRS-8505	(M)	Listen To The Blues	1955	20.00	50.00
Vanguard VRS-8513	(M)	If This Ain't The Blues	1957	20.00	50.00
Vanguard VDS-2008	(S)	If This Ain't The Blues	1958	16.00	40.00
Vanguard VRS-8518	(M)	Going To Chicago	1957	20.00	50.00
		(Vanguard 8518 is a reissue of 8011.)			
Jazztone J-1244	(M)	Listen To The Blues	1957	20.00	50.00
		(Jazztone 1244 is a reissue of Vanguard 8505.)			
Columbia CL-778	(M)	Cat Meets Chick *(With Ada Moore)*	1956	16.00	40.00
Columbia CL-963	(M)	The Jazz Odyssey Of James Rushing, Esq.	1957	16.00	40.00
Columbia CL-1152	(M)	Little Jimmy Rushing And The Big Brass	1958	12.00	30.00
Columbia CS-8060	(S)	Little Jimmy Rushing And The Big Brass	1959	14.00	35.00
Columbia CL-1401	(M)	Rushing Lullabies	1959	12.00	30.00
Columbia CS-8196	(S)	Rushing Lullabies	1959	14.00	35.00

When the desirable Ms. Russell captured the attention of movie viewers throughout America in the '50s, it was often overlooked that the brunette beauty was a good actress and comedienne of exceptional intelligence. Of course, exploiting her beauty wasn't confined to the silver screen, as her MGM debut above so amply illustrates.

Label & Catalog #		Title	Year	VG+	NM
Columbia CL-1553	(M)	Brubeck And Rushing	1960	10.00	25.00
Columbia CS-8353	(S)	Brubeck And Rushing	1960	12.00	30.00
Columbia CL-1605	(M)	Jimmy Rushing And The Smith Girls	1961	10.00	25.00
Columbia CS-8405	(S)	Jimmy Rushing And The Smith Girls	1961	12.00	30.00
— Original Columbia albums above have six white-on-black "eye" logos around the perimeter of the label.—					
Colpix CP-446	(M)	Five Feet Of Soul	1963	12.00	30.00
Colpix SCP-446	(S)	Five Feet Of Soul	1963	20.00	50.00
— Original Colpix albums above have gold labels.—					
BluesWay BL-3005	(M)	Everyday I Have The Blues	1967	8.00	20.00
BluesWay BLS-6005	(S)	Everyday I Have The Blues	1967	6.00	15.00
BluesWay BLS-6107	(S)	Livin' The Blues	1968	6.00	15.00

RUSHING, JIMMY / JACK DUPREE

Audio Lab AL-1512	(M)	Two Shades Of Blue	1959	60.00	150.00

RUSKIN-SPEAR, ROGER
Ruskin-Spear was formerly a member of The Bonzo Dog Band.

United Arts. LA097	(S)	Electric Shocks	1973	10.00	25.00

RUSSELL, CONNIE

United Arts. UAL-3022	(M)	Don't Smoke In Bed	1959	10.00	25.00
United Arts. UAS-6022	(S)	Don't Smoke In Bed	1959	12.00	30.00

RUSSELL, JANE
Refer to Marilyn Monroe.

Mercury MG-25182 (10")	(M)	The French Line (Soundtrack)	1954	50.00	125.00
Coral CRL-57158	(M)	Make A Joyful Noise Unto The Lord	1957	20.00	50.00
MGM E-3715	(M)	Jane Russell	1959	20.00	50.00
MGM SE-3715	(S)	Jane Russell	1959	30.00	75.00

RUSSELL, KURT

Capitol SKAO-492	(S)	Kurt Russell	1970	8.00	20.00

RUSSELL, LEON
Refer to George Harrison & Friends.

Shelter SHE-1001	(S)	Leon Russell (Features George and Ringo)	1970	4.00	10.00

RUSTIX

Rare Earth RS-508	(S)	Bedlam	1969	6.00	15.00
Rare Earth RS-513	(S)	Come On, People	1969	6.00	15.00

RUTLES, THE
The Rutles feature Neil Innes of The Bonzo Dog Band and Eric Idle.

Warner Bros. PRO-723	(DJ)	Meet The Rutles (Gold vinyl sampler)	1978	10.00	25.00
Warner Bros. H-3151	(S)	Meet The Rutles (With booklet)	1978	10.00	25.00

RYAN, BUCK, & SMITTY IRVIN

Monument MLP-8031	(M)	Ballads And Bluegrass	1965	5.00	12.00
Monument SLP-18031	(S)	Ballads And Bluegrass	1965	6.00	15.00

RYAN, CHARLIE

King 751	(M)	Hot Rod Lincoln	1961	60.00	150.00
Hilltop JM-6006	(M)	Hot Rod Lincoln Drags Again	1964	20.00	50.00
Hilltop JS-6006	(E)	Hot Rod Lincoln Drags Again	1964	16.00	40.00
Pickwick K-417	(M)	Hot Rod Lincoln	196?	10.00	25.00
Pickwick KS-417	(E)	Hot Rod Lincoln	196?	6.00	15.00

RYDELL, BOBBY

Cameo C-1006	(M)	We Got Love	1959	20.00	50.00
Cameo C-1007	(M)	Bobby Sings	1960	16.00	40.00
Cameo C-1009	(M)	Biggest Hits (Fold-open cover with insert)	1961	16.00	40.00
Cameo C-1010	(M)	Bobby Rydell Salutes The "Great Ones"	1961	16.00	40.00
Cameo SC-1010	(S)	Bobby Rydell Salutes The "Great Ones"	1961	20.00	50.00
Cameo C-1011	(M)	Rydell At The Copa	1961	16.00	40.00
Cameo SC-1011	(S)	Rydell At The Copa	1961	24.00	60.00
Cameo C-1019	(M)	All The Hits	1962	16.00	40.00
Cameo C-1028	(M)	Biggest Hits, Volume 2	1962	16.00	40.00
Cameo C-1040	(M)	All The Hits, Volume 2	1963	16.00	40.00
Cameo SC-1040	(P)	All The Hits, Volume 2	1963	24.00	60.00

Label & Catalog #		Title	Year	VG+	NM
Cameo C-1043	(M)	Bye Bye Birdie	1963	12.00	30.00
Cameo C-1055	(M)	Wild (Wood) Days	1963	12.00	30.00
Cameo CS-1055	(S)	Wild (Wood) Days	1963	16.00	40.00
Cameo C-1070	(M)	The Top Hits Of '63	1964	12.00	30.00
Cameo CS-1070	(S)	The Top Hits Of '63	1964	16.00	40.00
Cameo C-1080	(M)	Forget Him	1964	12.00	30.00
Cameo CS-1080	(E)	Forget Him	1964	12.00	30.00
Cameo C-2001	(M)	16 Golden Hits	1965	8.00	20.00
Cameo CS-2001	(E)	16 Golden Hits	1965	8.00	20.00
Cameo C-4017	(M)	An Era Reborn	196?	6.00	15.00
Cameo CS-4017	(S)	An Era Reborn	196?	8.00	20.00
Capitol T-2281	(M)	Somebody Loves You	1965	6.00	15.00
Capitol ST-2281	(S)	Somebody Loves You	1965	8.00	20.00

RYDELL, BOBBY, & CHUBBY CHECKER

Cameo C-1013	(M)	Bobby Rydell / Chubby Checker	1961	12.00	30.00
Cameo C-1063	(M)	Chubby Checker And Bobby Rydell	1963	12.00	30.00

RYDER, MITCH (& THE DETROIT WHEELS)

New Voice 2000	(M)	Take A Ride	1966	10.00	25.00
New Voice S-2000	(S)	Take A Ride	1966	12.00	30.00
New Voice 2002	(M)	Breakout!!!	1966	10.00	25.00
New Voice S-2002	(S)	Breakout!!!	1966	12.00	30.00
		(Originally issued without "Devil With A Blue Dress.")			
New Voice 2002	(M)	Breakout!!!	1966	8.00	20.00
New Voice S-2002	(S)	Breakout!!!	1966	10.00	25.00
		(Later pressings include "Devil With A Blue Dress.")			
New Voice 2003	(M)	Sock It To Me!	1967	10.00	25.00
New Voice S-2003	(S)	Sock It To Me!	1967	12.00	30.00
New Voice 2004	(M)	All Mitch Ryder Hits!	1967	8.00	20.00
New Voice S-2004	(S)	All Mitch Ryder Hits!	1967	10.00	25.00
DynoVoice 1901	(M)	What Now My Love	1967	5.00	12.00
DynoVoice 31901	(S)	What Now My Love	1967	6.00	15.00
New Voice S-2005	(S)	Mitch Ryder Sings The Hits	1968	8.00	20.00
Dot DLP-25963	(S)	The Detroit-Memphis Experiment	1969	8.00	20.00

SABRAS, THE [BEZALEL & THE SABRAS]

Tikva 122	(M)	The Sabras	196?	150.00	300.00

SACCO, LOU CHRISTIE: *Refer to* **LOU CHRISTIE**

SACRED MUSHROOM, THE

Parallax P-4001	(S)	The Sacred Mushroom	1969	30.00	75.00

SAGE & SEER

Stylist SA-600	(S)	Sage & Seer	197?	60.00	150.00

SAGITTARIUS
Sagittarius features Curt Boetcher.

Columbia CS-9644	(S)	Present Tense *(Produced by Gary Usher)*	1968	12.00	30.00
Together STT-1002	(S)	The Blue Marble	1969	16.00	40.00

Label & Catalog #		Title	Year	VG+	NM

SAHL, MORT
Refer to Jonathan Winters / Shelly Berman / Mort Sahl.

MGV-15002	(M)	**Mort Sahl, Iconoclast**	1959	8.00	20.00
MGV-15004	(M)	**Mort Sahl 1960, or Look Forward In Anger**	1959	8.00	20.00
MGV-15006	(M)	**A Way Of Life**	1959	8.00	20.00
MGV-15012	(M)	**Mort Sahl At The Hungry i**	1960	8.00	20.00
MGV-15021	(M)	**The Next President**	1960	8.00	20.00

— Original Verve albums above have black labels with "Verve Records, Inc." on the bottom.—

V-15049	(M)	**Great Moments**	1964	6.00	15.00

SAHM, DOUG
Doug Sahm is Sir Doug of The Sir Douglas Quintet.

Atlantic SD-7254	(S)	**Doug Sahm & Band** (With Bob Dylan)	1973	6.00	15.00
Warner Bros. BS-2810	(S)	**Groover's Paradise**	1974	10.00	25.00
Takoma TAK-7075	(S)	**Hell Of A Spell**	1980	4.00	10.00

ST. ANTHONY'S FIRE

Zonk	(M)	**St. Anthony's Fire**	1968	200.00	400.00

ST. CLAIRE, BETTY: *Refer to* GOLDMINE'S PRICE GUIDE TO COLLECTIBLE JAZZ ALBUMS

ST. JOHN GREEN

Flick Disc FLS-45001	(S)	**St. John Green**	1968	8.00	20.00

ST. LOUIS, JIMMY

Bluesville BVLP-1028	(M)	**Goin' Down Blues**	1961	16.00	40.00

ST. LOUIS HOUNDS, THE

(No label)	(S)	**The St. Louis Hounds**	197?	60.00	150.00

ST. PETERS, CRISPIAN

Jamie JLPM-3027	(M)	**The Pied Piper**	1966	16.00	40.00
Jamie JLPS-3027	(E)	**The Pied Piper**	1966	12.00	30.00

SAINT STEVEN

Probe CPLP-4506	(S)	**Over The Hills**	1970	6.00	15.00

SAINTE-MARIE, BUFFY

Vanguard VRS-9142	(M)	**It's My Way**	1964	6.00	15.00
Vanguard VSD-79142	(S)	**It's My Way**	1964	8.00	20.00
Vanguard VRS-9171	(M)	**Many A Mile**	1965	6.00	15.00
Vanguard VSD-79171	(S)	**Many A Mile**	1965	8.00	20.00
Vanguard VRS-9211	(M)	**Little Wheel Spin And Spin**	1966	6.00	15.00
Vanguard VSD-79211	(S)	**Little Wheel Spin And Spin**	1966	8.00	20.00
Vanguard VRS-9250	(M)	**Fire And Fleet And Candlelight**	1967	6.00	15.00
Vanguard VSD-79250	(S)	**Fire And Fleet And Candlelight**	1967	8.00	20.00
Vanguard VSD-79280	(S)	**I'm Gonna Be A Country Girl Again**	1968	6.00	15.00
Vanguard VSD-79300	(S)	**Illuminations**	1969	6.00	15.00
Vanguard VSD-3	(S)	**The Best Of Buffy Sainte-Marie** (2 LPs)	1970	5.00	12.00
Vanguard VSD-79311	(S)	**She Used To Wanna Be A Ballerina**	1971	5.00	12.00
Vanguard VSD-7????	(S)	**Moonshot**	1972	5.00	12.00
Vanguard 40003	(Q)	**Moonshot**	1972	6.00	15.00
Vanguard VSD-79330	(S)	**Quiet Places**	1973	5.00	12.00
Vanguard 40020	(Q)	**Quiet Places**	1973	6.00	15.00
Vanguard VSD-79340	(S)	**Native North American Child: An Odyssey**	1974	5.00	12.00
Vanguard 40027	(Q)	**Native North American Child: An Odyssey**	1974	6.00	15.00

SAKAMOTO, KYU

Capitol Int. T-10349	(M)	**Sukiyaki**	1963	10.00	25.00
Capitol Int. DT-10349	(E)	**Sukiyaki**	1963	8.00	20.00

SALES, SOUPY

Reprise R-6010	(M)	**The Soupy Sales Show**	1961	12.00	30.00
Reprise R-96010	(S)	**The Soupy Sales Show**	1961	16.00	40.00
Reprise R-6052	(M)	**Up In The Air**	1962	12.00	30.00
Reprise R-96052	(S)	**Up In The Air**	1962	16.00	40.00
ABC-Paramount 503	(M)	**Spy With A Pie**	1965	10.00	25.00
ABC-Paramount S-503	(S)	**Spy With A Pie**	1965	12.00	30.00

Label & Catalog #		Title	Year	VG+	NM
ABC-Paramount 517	(M)	Soupy Sez Do The Mouse	1965	10.00	25.00
ABC-Paramount S-517	(S)	Soupy Sez Do The Mouse	1965	12.00	30.00
Motown MS-686	(S)	A Bag Of Soup	1969	10.00	25.00
5274	(S)	Still Soupy After All These Years	1981	4.00	10.00

SALEM MASS

Salem Mass SM-101	(S)	Witch Burning	1972	80.00	200.00

SALLOOM, SINCLAIR, & THE MOTHER BEAR

Cadet Concept 316	(S)	Sinclair Salloom And The Mother Bear	1968	5.00	12.00

SALLYANGIE
Sallyangie is Sally and Mike Oldfield.

Warner Bros. WS-1783	(S)	Children Of The Sun	1969	10.00	25.00

SALVATION

ABC S-623	(S)	Salvation	1968	8.00	20.00
ABC S-653	(S)	Gypsy Carnival Caravan	1968	8.00	20.00

SAM & DAVE
Sam Moore and Dave Prater.

Stax 708	(M)	Hold On I'm Comin'	1966	16.00	40.00
Stax 708	(S)	Hold On I'm Comin'	1966	20.00	50.00
		("I Take What I Want" is rechanneled on this album.)			
Roulette R-25323	(M)	Sam And Dave	1966	12.00	30.00
Roulette SR-25323	(S)	Sam And Dave	1966	16.00	40.00
		(Half of the tracks on this album are rechanneled.)			
Stax 712	(M)	Double Dynamite	1966	12.00	30.00
Stax 712	(S)	Double Dynamite	1966	16.00	40.00
Stax 725	(M)	Soul Men	1967	8.00	20.00
Stax 725	(S)	Soul Men	1967	12.00	30.00
Atlantic SD-8205	(S)	I Thank You	1968	8.00	20.00
Atlantic SD-8218	(S)	The Best Of Sam And Dave	1969	6.00	15.00
United Arts. LA262	(S)	Back At 'Cha!	1974	6.00	15.00
United Arts. LA524	(S)	Back At 'Cha!	1975	4.00	10.00
Gusto 0045	(S)	Sweet And Funky Gold	197?	4.00	10.00

SAM APPLE PIE

Sire SES-97020	(S)	Sam Apple Pie	1969	6.00	15.00

SAM THE SHAM & THE PHARAOHS

MGM E-4297	(M)	Wooly Bully	1965	12.00	30.00
MGM SE-4297	(S)	Wooly Bully	1965	16.00	40.00
MGM E-4314	(M)	Their Second Album	1965	10.00	25.00
MGM SE-4314	(S)	Their Second Album	1965	12.00	30.00
MGM E-4347	(M)	On Tour	1966	10.00	25.00
MGM SE-4347	(S)	On Tour	1966	12.00	30.00
MGM E-4407	(M)	Lil' Red Riding Hood	1966	10.00	25.00
MGM SE-4407	(S)	Lil' Red Riding Hood	1966	12.00	30.00
MGM E-4422	(M)	The Best Of Sam The Sham	1967	10.00	25.00
MGM SE-4422	(S)	The Best Of Sam The Sham	1967	12.00	30.00
MGM E-4479	(M)	Nefertiti	1967	8.00	20.00
MGM SE-4479	(S)	Nefertiti	1967	10.00	25.00
MGM SE-4479	(S)	Sam The Sham Revue	1968	8.00	20.00
		("Sam The Sham Revue" is a repackage of "Nefertiti.")			
MGM SE-4526	(S)	Ten Of Pentacles	1968	10.00	25.00

SAMUDIO, SAM

Atlantic SD-8271	(S)	Hard And Heavy	1971	6.00	15.00

SANDALS, THE [THE SANDELLS]

World Pacific WP-1818	(M)	Scrambler	1964	16.00	40.00
World Pacific ST-1818	(S)	Scrambler	1964	20.00	50.00
World Pacific ST-1818	(S)	Scrambler (Red vinyl)	1964	40.00	100.00
		(World Pacific 1818 is credited to The Sandells.)			
World Pacific WP-1832	(M)	The Endless Summer (Soundtrack)	1966	8.00	20.00
World Pacific ST-1832	(S)	The Endless Summer (Soundtrack)	1966	10.00	25.00
		(World Pacific 1832 is a repackage of W.P. 1818.)			

Label & Catalog #		Title	Year	VG+	NM
World Pacific WPS-21884	(S)	The Last Of The Ski Bums *(Soundtrack)*	1969	8.00	20.00
		(Orange cover with three skiers' silhouettes.)			
World Pacific WPS-21884	(S)	The Last Of The Ski Bums *(Soundtrack)*	1969	8.00	20.00
		(Blue cover with cartoon skiers in a VW bus.)			

SANDERS, ED
Mr. Sanders was formerly a member of The Fugs.

Reprise RS-6374	(S)	Sanders' Truckstop	1969	12.00	30.00
Reprise MS-2105	(S)	Beer Cans On The Moon	1972	8.00	20.00

SANDERS, FELICIA

Columbia CL-654	(M)	Felicia Sanders At The Blue Angel	1955	14.00	35.00
Columbia CL-713	(M)	Girl Meets Boy	1955	14.00	35.00
Decca DL-8762	(M)	That Certain Feeling	1958	10.00	25.00
Decca DL-78762	(S)	That Certain Feeling	1958	14.00	35.00
Time 2007	(M)	The Songs Of Kurt Weill	1963	6.00	15.00
Time 52007	(S)	The Songs Of Kurt Weill	1963	8.00	20.00
Time 2110	(M)	Felicia Sanders	1964	5.00	12.00
Time 52110	(S)	Felicia Sanders	1964	6.00	15.00

SANDERS, GEORGE

ABC-Paramount 231	(M)	The George Sanders Touch	1958	10.00	25.00
ABC-Paramount S-231	(S)	The George Sanders Touch	1958	12.00	30.00

SANDS, TOMMY
Refer to Annette & Tommy Sands.

Capitol T-848	(M)	Steady Date With Tommy Sands	1957	30.00	75.00
Capitol T-929	(M)	Sing Boy Sing *(Soundtrack)*	1958	30.00	75.00
		— *Original Capitol albums above turquoise labels.*—			
Capitol T-1081	(M)	Sands Storm	1959	20.00	50.00
Capitol T-1109	(M)	Teenage Rock	1959	20.00	50.00
Capitol T-1123	(M)	This Thing Called Love	1959	12.00	30.00
Capitol ST-1123	(S)	This Thing Called Love	1959	16.00	40.00
Capitol T-1239	(M)	When I'm Thinking Of You	1960	12.00	30.00
Capitol ST-1239	(S)	When I'm Thinking Of You	1960	16.00	40.00
Capitol T-1364	(M)	Sands At The Sands	1960	12.00	30.00
Capitol ST-1364	(S)	Sands At The Sands	1960	16.00	40.00
Capitol T-1426	(M)	Dream With Me	1961	12.00	30.00
Capitol ST-1426	(S)	Dream With Me	1961	16.00	40.00

SANDY COAST: *Refer to* **VANITY FARE**

SANELLA, ANDY, & HIS IMPERIAL HAWAIIANS

SeSac H-101/2	(M)	Hawaii	195?	24.00	60.00

SANTANA

Columbia CS-9781	(S)	Santana *("360 Sound" label)*	1969	8.00	20.00
Columbia KC-30130	(S)	Abraxas *(With poster)*	1970	6.00	15.00
Columbia CQ-30130	(Q)	Abraxas	1974	8.00	20.00
Columbia CQ-31610	(Q)	Caravanserai	1974	8.00	20.00
Columbia PCQ-32445	(Q)	Welcome	1974	8.00	20.00
Columbia PCQ-32900	(Q)	Illuminations	1974	8.00	20.00
Columbia PCQ-32964	(Q)	Santana	1974	8.00	20.00
Columbia PCQ-33050	(Q)	Greatest Hits	1974	8.00	20.00
Columbia PCQ-33135	(Q)	Borboletta	1974	8.00	20.00
Columbia PCQ-33576	(Q)	Amigos	1976	8.00	20.00
Columbia PCQ-34423	(Q)	Festival	1977	8.00	20.00
Columbia HC-40130	(S)	Abraxas *(Half-speed master)*	1981	25.00	75.00
Columbia HC-47158	(S)	Zebop! *(Half-speed master)*	1981	12.00	35.00

SANTO & JOHNNY
Santo and Johnny Farina.

Canad. Am. CALP-1001	(M)	Santo & Johnny	1959	30.00	75.00
Canad. Am. SCALP-1001	(S)	Santo & Johnny	1959	40.00	100.00
		("All Night Diner," "Sleepwalk" and "Slave Girl" are rechanneled.)			
Canad. Am. CALP-1002	(M)	Encore	1960	16.00	40.00
Canad. Am. SCALP-1002	(S)	Encore	1960	20.00	50.00
		("Tear Drop" is rechanneled on this album.)			

Label & Catalog #		Title	Year	VG+	NM
Canad. Am. CALP-1004	(M)	Hawaii	1961	12.00	30.00
Canad. Am. SCALP-1004	(S)	Hawaii	1961	16.00	40.00
Canad. Am. CALP-1006	(M)	Come On In	1962	12.00	30.00
Canad. Am. SCALP-1006	(S)	Come On In	1962	16.00	40.00
Canad. Am. CALP-1011	(M)	Off Shore	1963	12.00	30.00
Canad. Am. SCALP-1011	(S)	Off Shore	1963	16.00	40.00
Canad. Am. CALP-1014	(M)	In The Still Of The Night	1963	12.00	30.00
Canad. Am. SCALP-1014	(S)	In The Still Of The Night	1963	16.00	40.00
		("Sleep Walk" and "Tear Drop" are rechanneled on this album.)			
Canad. Am. CALP-1016	(M)	Wish You Were Here	1964	12.00	30.00
Canad. Am. SCALP-1016	(S)	Wish You Were Here	1964	16.00	40.00
Canad. Am. CALP-1017	(M)	The Beatles' Greatest Hits	1964	16.00	40.00
Canad. Am. SCALP-1017	(S)	The Beatles' Greatest Hits	1964	20.00	50.00
Canad. Am. CALP-1018	(M)	Mucho	1965	12.00	30.00
Canad. Am. SCALP-1018	(S)	Mucho	1965	16.00	40.00
Imperial LP-9363	(M)	Brilliant Guitar Sounds	1967	6.00	15.00
Imperial LP-12363	(S)	Brilliant Guitar Sounds	1967	8.00	20.00
Imperial LP-12366	(S)	Golden Guitars	1968	8.00	20.00
Imperial LP-12418	(S)	On The Road Again	1968	8.00	20.00

SAPPHIRES, THE

Swan LP-513	(M)	Who Do You Love	1964	50.00	125.00

SAPPHIRE THINKERS, THE

Hobbit HB-5003	(S)	From Within	1969	8.00	20.00

SARSTEDT, PETER

World Pacific WPS-21895	(S)	Where Do You Go To, My Lovely?	1969	6.00	15.00
World Pacific WPS-21899	(S)	As Though It Were A Movie	1969	6.00	15.00

SATAN & THE DECIPLES

Goldband 7750	(S)	Underground	1969	14.00	35.00

SATANS, THE

(No label)	(M)	Raisin' Hell	1962	100.00	250.00

SATINS FOUR, THE, & THE CINNAMON ANGELS

B.T. Puppy BTS-1010	(S)	Mixed Soul	1970	60.00	150.00

SAUNDERS, MERL, & JERRY GARCIA

Fantasy F-79002	(S)	Live At The Keystone	1973	6.00	15.00
Fantasy F-9421	(S)	Fire Up (With Tom Fogerty)	1973	6.00	15.00

SAUNDERS, MERL

Fantasy F-8421	(S)	Heavy Turbulence	1972	6.00	15.00
Crystal Clear	(S)	Do I Move You? (Direct-to-disc)	198?	6.00	15.00

SAUVAGE, KATHERINE

Epic LN-3489	(M)	The Songs Of Kurt Weill	195?	16.00	40.00

SAVAGE GRACE

Reprise RS-6399	(S)	Savage Grace	1970	6.00	15.00
Reprise RS-6484	(S)	Savage Grace 2	1971	6.00	15.00

SAVAGE RESURRECTION, THE

Mercury SR-61156	(S)	The Savage Resurrection	1968	6.00	15.00

SAVAGE ROSE

Polydor 24-6001	(S)	In The Plain (Gatefold cover)	1969	8.00	20.00
Polydor 24-6001	(S)	In The Plain (Standard cover)	1970	5.00	12.00
Gregar GG-103	(S)	Your Daily Gift	1970	5.00	12.00
Gregar GG-104	(S)	Refugee	1971	5.00	12.00

SAVAGE SONS OF YO HO WA, THE: *Refer to* FATHER YOD

SAVAGES, THE

Duane 1047	(M)	Live And Wild	1966	60.00	150.00

Label & Catalog #		Title	Year	VG+	NM
SAVITT, BUDDY					
Mr. Savitt has backed all of the Cameo/Parkway artists at one time or another.					
Parkway P-7012	(M)	The Most Heard Sax In The World	1962	40.00	100.00
SAVOY BROWN					
Parrot PAS-71024	(S)	Getting To The Point	1968	8.00	20.00
Parrot PAS-71027	(S)	Blue Matter	1969	8.00	20.00
Parrot PAS-71029	(S)	A Step Further	1969	8.00	20.00
Parrot PAS-71036	(S)	Raw Sienna	1970	8.00	20.00
Parrot PAS-71042	(S)	Looking In	1970	8.00	20.00
Parrot PAS-71047	(S)	Street Corner Talking	1971	8.00	20.00
		— Parrot albums above read "Distributed by London" on the label.—			
Parrot PAS-71052	(S)	Hellbound Train	1972	6.00	15.00
Parrot PAS-71057	(S)	Lion's Share	1972	6.00	15.00
Parrot PAS-71059	(S)	Jack The Toad	1973	6.00	15.00
SAXONS, THE					
Mirrosonic AS-1017	(M)	Love Minus Zero	1966	30.00	75.00
SAWBUCK					
Fillmore 2-31248	(S)	Sawbuck	1972	6.00	15.00
SCAFFOLD					
Bell 6018	(S)	Thank U Very Much	1968	14.00	35.00
SCAGGS, BOZ					
Boz was formerly a member of the Steve Miller Band.					
Columbia A2S-71-4	(DJ)	KSAN Live Concert *(2 LPs)*	1974	20.00	50.00
		(Issued in a plain cardboard jacket.)			
Columbia AS-203	(DJ)	The Boz Scaggs Sampler	1976	6.00	15.00
Columbia HC-43920	(S)	Silk Degrees *(Half-speed master)*	1981	7.00	20.00
SCAMPS, THE					
Project 8002	(M)	Teen Dance And Sing Along Party	1962	16.00	40.00
SCHILLER, LAWRENCE					
Capitol TAO-2574	(M)	LSD	1966	16.00	40.00
Capitol STAO-2574	(S)	LSD	1966	20.00	50.00
Capitol PRO-4153	(DJ)	Open-End Interview With Dr. Sidney Cohen	1966	40.00	100.00
		(An interview with the "expert" quoted in charge of the LSD album.)			
Capitol KAO-2630	(M)	Why Did Lenny Bruce Die?	1967	10.00	25.00
Capitol SKAO-2630	(S)	Why Did Lenny Bruce Die?	1967	12.00	30.00
Capitol KAO-2652	(M)	Homosexuality In The American Male	1967	10.00	25.00
Capitol SKAO-2652	(S)	Homosexuality In The American Male	1967	12.00	30.00
SCHLAMME, MARTHA					
Vanguard VRS-9011	(M)	Raisins And Almonds			
		And Other Jewish Folk Songs	195?	8.00	20.00
SCHLOSS, DANNY					
Verve/Forecast FTS-3040	(S)	Dreams And Illusions	1968	6.00	15.00
SCHOOLBOYS, THE: *Refer to* THE LIVERPOOL KIDS					
SCHORY, DICK [DICK SCHORY'S NEW PERCUSSION ENSEMBLE]					
RCA Victor LPM-1866	(M)	Music For Bang, Barroom And Harp	1958	10.00	25.00
RCA Victor LSP-1866	(S)	Music For Bang, Barroom And Harp	1958	40.00	100.00
RCA Victor LPM-2125	(M)	Music To Break Any Mood	1960	8.00	20.00
RCA Victor LSP-2125	(S)	Music To Break Any Mood	1960	30.00	75.00
SCHROECK, ARTIE					
Verve V-5034	(M)	Spoonful Of Lovin'	1968	6.00	15.00
Verve V6-5034	(S)	Spoonful Of Lovin'	1968	8.00	20.00
SCOOBY DOO					
Peter Pan 203	(S)	Scooby Doo *(Picture disc)*	1982	4.00	10.00
SCORPION					
Tower ST-5171	(S)	Scorpion	1969	20.00	50.00

Label & Catalog #		Title	Year	VG+	NM
SCOTT, ALLAN					
Tower ST-5164	(S)	**When I Needed A Woman**	1969	6.00	15.00
SCOTT, BOBBY: *Refer to* GOLDMINE'S PRICE GUIDE TO COLLECTIBLE JAZZ ALBUMS					
SCOTT, CLIFORD: *Refer to* GOLDMINE'S PRICE GUIDE TO COLLECTIBLE JAZZ ALBUMS					
SCOTT, FREDDIE					
Colpix CP-461	(M)	**Freddie Scott Sings** (Gold label)	1964	20.00	50.00
Colpix SCP-461	(S)	**Freddie Scott Sings** (Gold label)	1964	40.00	100.00
Colpix CP-461	(M)	**Freddie Scott Sings** (Blue label)	1965	12.00	30.00
Colpix SCP-461	(E)	**Freddie Scott Sings** (Blue label)	1965	8.00	20.00
Columbia CL-2258	(M)	**Everything I Have Is Yours**	1964	8.00	20.00
Columbia CS-9058	(S)	**Everything I Have Is Yours**	1964	10.00	25.00
Columbia CL-2660	(M)	**Lonely Man**	1967	6.00	15.00
Columbia CS-9460	(S)	**Lonely Man**	1967	8.00	20.00
Shout SLP-501	(M)	**Are You Lonely For Me**	1967	6.00	15.00
Shout SLPS-501	(S)	**Are You Lonely For Me**	1967	8.00	20.00
Probe CPLP-4517	(S)	**I Shall Be Released**	1970	6.00	15.00
SCOTT, HAZEL: *Refer to* GOLDMINE'S PRICE GUIDE TO COLLECTIBLE JAZZ ALBUMS					
SCOTT, JACK					
Carlton LP-12-107	(M)	**Jack Scott**	1959	40.00	100.00
Carlton STLP-12-107	(S)	**Jack Scott**	1959	150.00	300.00
		(The cover has "Stereo" in felt-like letters pasted vertically along the left side. "My True Love" and "Leroy" are rechanneled on this and each subsequent pressing below.)			
Carlton STLP-12-107	(S)	**Jack Scott**	1959	100.00	250.00
		(The cover has "Stereo" in felt-like letters across the top.)			
Carlton STLP-12-107	(S)	**Jack Scott**	1959	100.00	200.00
		(The cover has "Stereo" printed across the top.)			
Carlton LP-12-122	(M)	**What Am I Living For**	1959	40.00	100.00
Carlton STLP-12-122	(S)	**What Am I Living For**	1959	100.00	200.00
		("What Am I Living For" is rechanneled on this album.)			
Top Rank RM-319	(M)	**I Remember Hank Williams**	1960	40.00	100.00
Top Rank RS-619	(S)	**I Remember Hank Williams**	1960	80.00	200.00
Top Rank RM-326	(M)	**What In The World's Come Over You?**	1960	40.00	100.00
Top Rank RS-626	(S)	**What In The World's Come Over You?**	1960	80.00	200.00
Top Rank RM-348	(M)	**The Spirit Moves Me**	1961	40.00	100.00
Top Rank RS-648	(S)	**The Spirit Moves Me**	1961	80.00	200.00
Jade 33-202	(M)	**Great Scott**	196?	40.00	100.00
Sesac 4201	(DJ)	**Soul Stirring**	196?	60.00	150.00
Capitol T-2035	(M)	**Burning Bridges** (Black label)	1964	30.00	75.00
Capitol ST-2035	(S)	**Burning Bridges** (Black label)	1964	60.00	150.00
Capitol ST-2035	(S)	**Burning Bridges** (Green label)	1964	20.00	50.00
SCOTT, JIMMY: *Refer to* GOLDMINE'S PRICE GUIDE TO COLLECTIBLE JAZZ ALBUMS					
SCOTT, LINDA					
Canad. Am. CALP-1005	(M)	**Starlight, Starbright**	1961	20.00	50.00
Canad. Am. SCALP-1005	(S)	**Starlight, Starbright**	1961	30.00	75.00
Canad. Am. CALP-1007	(M)	**Great Scott!! Her Greatest Hits**	1962	20.00	50.00
Canad. Am. SCALP-1007	(S)	**Great Scott!! Her Greatest Hits**	1962	30.00	75.00
Congress 3001	(M)	**Linda**	1962	12.00	30.00
Congress S-3001	(S)	**Linda**	1962	16.00	40.00
Kapp KL-1424	(M)	**Hey, Look At Me Now**	1965	10.00	25.00
Kapp KS-3424	(S)	**Hey, Look At Me Now**	1965	12.00	30.00
SCOTT, LIZABETH					
Vik 1130	(M)	**Lizabeth**	195?	20.00	50.00
SCOTT, PATRICIA					
ABC-Paramount 301	(M)	**Once Around The Clock**	1959	8.00	20.00
ABC-Paramount S-301	(S)	**Once Around The Clock**	1959	12.00	30.00

Label & Catalog #		Title	Year	VG+	NM
SCOTTSVILLE SQUIRREL BARKERS, THE					
The Barkers feature Chris Hillman. Refer to The Hillmen; The Byrds.					
Crown CLP-5346	(M)	**Blue-Grass Favorites**	1963	16.00	40.00
Crown CST-346	(S)	**Blue-Grass Favorites**	1963	20.00	50.00
SCRAMBLERS, THE					
Diplomat D-2316	(M)	**Motorcycle Scramble**	1964	6.00	15.00
Diplomat DS-2316	(S)	**Motorcycle Scramble**	1964	8.00	20.00
Wyncote W-9048	(M)	**Little Honda**	1964	6.00	15.00
Wyncote WS-9048	(S)	**Little Honda**	1964	8.00	20.00
Crown CLP-5384	(M)	**Cycle Psychos**	1964	5.00	12.00
Crown CST-384	(S)	**Cycle Psychos**	1964	6.00	15.00
SCRUGGS, EARL					
Refer to Flatt & Scruggs.					
Folkways FA-2314	(M)	**American Banjo Scruggs Style**	195?	8.00	20.00
SEA, JOHNNY					
Philips PHM-200-139	(M)	**World Of A Country Boy**	1964	8.00	20.00
Philips PHS-600-139	(S)	**World Of A Country Boy**	1964	10.00	25.00
Philips PHM-200-194	(M)	**Live At The Bitter End**	1965	8.00	20.00
Philips PHS-600-194	(S)	**Live At The Bitter End**	1965	10.00	25.00
Warner Bros. B-1659	(M)	**Day For Decision**	1966	6.00	15.00
Warner Bros. BS-1659	(S)	**Day For Decision**	1966	8.00	20.00
MGM E-4506	(M)	**What Am I Bid?** *(Soundtrack)*	1967	6.00	15.00
MGM SE-4506	(S)	**What Am I Bid?** *(Soundtrack)*	1967	8.00	20.00
SEALS & CROFTS					
T.A. 5001	(S)	**Seals And Crofts**	1969	8.00	20.00
T.A. 5004	(S)	**Down Home**	1970	8.00	20.00
Warner Bros. BS4-2629	(Q)	**Summer Breeze**	1974	6.00	15.00
Warner Bros. BS4-2699	(Q)	**Diamond Girl**	1973	6.00	15.00
Warner Bros. WS4-2761	(Q)	**Unborn Child**	1974	6.00	15.00
Warner Bros. BS4-2848	(Q)	**I'll Play For You**	1975	6.00	15.00
Nautilus NR-10	(S)	**Summer Breeze**	197?	8.00	25.00
SEARCH PARTY					
Century 32013	(S)	**Montgomery Chapel**	197?	500.00	1,000.00
SEARCHERS, THE					
Mercury MG-20914	(M)	**Hear! Hear!**	1964	30.00	75.00
Mercury SR-60914	(E)	**Hear! Hear!**	1964	20.00	50.00
		(First pressing covers merely note the album's title.)			
Mercury MG-20914	(M)	**Hear! Hear!**	1964	20.00	50.00
Mercury SR-60914	(E)	**Hear! Hear!**	1964	16.00	40.00
		(Second pressing covers have a sticker reading "Live From The Star Club" affixed to the front.)			
Mercury MG-20914	(M)	**Hear! Hear!**	1964	16.00	40.00
Mercury SR-60914	(E)	**Hear! Hear!**	1964	12.00	30.00
		(Third pressing covers have "Live From The Star Club" printed on the front.)			
Kapp KL-1363	(M)	**Meet The Searchers**	1964	12.00	30.00
Kapp KS-3363	(S)	**Meet The Searchers**	1964	16.00	40.00
Kapp KL-1409	(M)	**This Is Us**	1964	12.00	30.00
Kapp KS-3409	(S)	**This Is Us**	1964	16.00	40.00
Kapp KL-1409	(M)	**This Is Us**	1964	10.00	25.00
Kapp KS-3409	(S)	**This Is Us**	1964	14.00	35.00
		(Later pressings have a "Love Potion No. 9" sticker on the cover.)			
Kapp KL-1412	(M)	**The New Searchers LP**	1965	12.00	30.00
Kapp KS-3412	(S)	**The New Searchers LP**	1965	16.00	40.00
		("What Have They Done To The Rain" is rechanneled on this album.)			
Kapp KL-1449	(M)	**The Searchers No. 4**	1965	12.00	30.00
Kapp KS-3449	(S)	**The Searchers No. 4**	1965	16.00	40.00
Kapp KL-1477	(M)	**Take Me For What I'm Worth**	1966	12.00	30.00
Kapp KS-3477	(S)	**Take Me For What I'm Worth**	1966	16.00	40.00
SEARCHERS, THE / THE RATTLES					
Mercury MG-20994	(M)	**The Searchers Meet The Rattles**	1965	30.00	75.00
Mercury SR-60994	(E)	**The Searchers Meet The Rattles**	1965	20.00	50.00

SEASTONES
Seastones features Jerry Garcia, Micky Hart and Phil Lesh of The Grateful Dead.

Label & Catalog #		Title	Year	VG+	NM
Round RX-106	(S)	**Seastones**	1975	10.00	25.00

SEATRAIN
Seatrain was formed by Roy Blumenfeld and Andy Kulberg of The Blues Project.

A&M SP-4171	(S)	**Seatrain**	1969	6.00	15.00
Capitol SMAS-650	(S)	**Seatrain**	1971	6.00	15.00
Capitol SMAS-829	(S)	**Marblehead Messenger**	1972	6.00	15.00

SEBASTIAN, JOHN
Mr. Sebastian was formerly a member of The Lovin' Spoonful.

MGM SE-4654	(S)	**John B. Sebastian**	1969	5.00	12.00
Reprise RS-6379	(S)	**John B. Sebastian** (With insert)	1969	5.00	12.00
Reprise MS-2036	(S)	**Cheapo-Cheapo Productions Presents Real Live John Sebastian**	1971	5.00	12.00
Reprise MS-2041	(S)	**The Four Of Us**	1971	5.00	12.00

SEDAKA, NEIL

RCA Victor LPM-2035	(M)	**Rock With Sedaka**	1959	20.00	50.00
RCA Victor LSP-2035	(S)	**Rock With Sedaka**	1959	30.00	75.00
RCA Victor LPM-2317	(M)	**Circulate**	1960	12.00	30.00
RCA Victor LSP-2317	(S)	**Circulate**	1960	16.00	40.00
RCA Victor LPM-2421	(M)	**Little Devil And His Other Hits**	1961	12.00	30.00
RCA Victor LSP-2421	(S)	**Little Devil And His Other Hits**	1961	16.00	40.00
RCA Victor LPM-2627	(M)	**Neil Sedaka Sings His Greatest Hits**	1962	10.00	25.00
RCA Victor LSP-2627	(S)	**Neil Sedaka Sings His Greatest Hits**	1962	14.00	35.00

— Original RCA mono albums above have "black labels with Long Play" on the bottom; stereo albums have have black labels with "Living Stereo" on the bottom.—

SEEDS, THE

Crescendo GNP-2023	(M)	**The Seeds**	1966	12.00	30.00
Crescendo GNPS-2023	(S)	**The Seeds**	1966	8.00	20.00
		("Pushin' Too Hard" is rechanneled on this album.)			
Crescendo GNP-2033	(M)	**A Web Of Sound**	1966	12.00	30.00
Crescendo GNPS-2033	(S)	**A Web Of Sound**	1966	8.00	20.00
Crescendo GNP-2038	(M)	**Future** (With three inserts)	1967	16.00	40.00
Crescendo GNPS-2038	(S)	**Future** (With three inserts)	1967	12.00	30.00
Crescendo GNP-2038	(M)	**Future** (Without inserts)	1967	12.00	30.00
Crescendo GNPS-2038	(S)	**Future** (Without inserts)	1967	8.00	20.00
Crescendo GNP-2040	(M)	**Full Spoon of Seedy Blues**	1967	12.00	30.00
Crescendo GNPS-2040	(S)	**Full Spoon of Seedy Blues**	1967	8.00	20.00
Crescendo GNP-2043	(M)	**Raw And Alive**	1967	12.00	30.00
Crescendo GNPS-2043	(S)	**Raw And Alive**	1967	8.00	20.00

— Original GNP albums above have red labels.—

SEEGER, PEGGY
Ms. Seeger also recorded with Tom Paley. Refer to The Seegers.

Riverside RLP-12-655	(M)	**Peggy Seeger**	195?	10.00	25.00
Folkways FA-	(M)	**Songs Of Courting And Complaint**	195?	10.00	25.00
Prestige Int. PRLP-13005	(M)	**The Best Of Peggy Seeger**	1961	12.00	30.00
Prestige Int. PRLP-13058	(M)	**For You And Me**	1962	12.00	30.00
Prestige Int. PRLP-13061	(M)	**A Lover's Garland** (With Ewan MacColl)	1962	12.00	30.00
Folklore FRLP-14016	(M)	**The Best Of Peggy Seeger**	1961	8.00	20.00
Folklore FRST-14016	(E)	**The Best Of Peggy Seeger**	1961	6.00	15.00
		(Folklore 1406 is a reissue of Prestige 13005.)			
Tradition TLP-2059	(M)	**Manchester Angel**	196?	6.00	15.00

SEEGER, PETE
Pete was formerly a member of The Weavers. Refer to Big Bill Broonzy; The Seegers.

Folkways FP-3 (10")	(M)	**Darling Corey**	1950	20.00	50.00
Stinson SLP-52 (10")	(M)	**Lincoln Brigade**	1953	20.00	50.00
Stinson SLP-57 (10")	(M)	**Pete Seeger In Concert**	1953	20.00	50.00
Stinson SLP-90	(M)	**Pete**	195?	20.00	50.00
Folkways 43 (10")	(M)	**Pete Seeger Sampler**	1955	20.00	50.00
Folkways 85-1	(M)	**Talking Union**	1955	12.00	30.00
Folkways 85-2	(M)	**Peter Seeger Sings**	1956	12.00	30.00
Folkways 85-3	(M)	**Love Songs**	1956	12.00	30.00

Label & Catalog #		Title	Year	VG+	NM
Folkways FPH-	(M)	Champlain Valley Song Bag	195?	12.00	30.00
Folkways FH-	(M)	American Industrial Ballads	195?	12.00	30.00
Folkways FH-5285	(M)	Talking Union	195?	12.00	30.00
Folkways FH-5412	(M)	Pete Seeger At Carnegie Hall	195?	12.00	30.00
Folkways FA-2003 (10")	(M)	Darling Corey	1957	12.00	30.00
Folkways FA-2005 (10")	(M)	Seegers	1957	12.00	30.00
Folkways 7053 (10")	(M)	American Christmas Songs	1957	12.00	30.00
Folkways FA-2043	(M)	Pete Seeger Sampler	1958	12.00	30.00
Folkways FA-2045	(M)	Goofing Off Suite	1958	12.00	30.00
Folkways FA-	(M)	Ballads	1958	12.00	30.00
Folkways FA-2175/6	(M)	Frontier Ballads (2 LPs)	1958	12.00	30.00
Folkways FA-2319	(M)	American Favorite Ballads, Volume 1	1958	12.00	30.00
Folkways FA-2320	(M)	American Favorite Ballads, Volume 2	1959	12.00	30.00
Folkways FA-2321	(M)	American Favorite Ballads, Volume 3	1959	12.00	30.00
Folkways FA-2351	(M)	Pete Seeger At Carnegie Hall	1959	12.00	30.00
Folkways FA-2452	(M)	With Voices Together We Sing	1963	10.00	25.00
Folkways FA-2453	(M)	Love Songs For Friends And Foes	1963	10.00	25.00
Folkways FA-2454	(M)	Rainbow Design	1963	10.00	25.00
Folkways FA-2456	(M)	Broadsides	1964	10.00	25.00
Folkways FN-2501	(M)	Gazette	1964	10.00	25.00
Folkways FN-2512	(M)	Hootenanny At Carnegie Hall	1964	10.00	25.00
Folkways FI-8303	(M)	How To Play The Five String Banjo	196?	10.00	25.00
Columbia CL-1101	(M)	We Shall Overcome	1958	16.00	40.00
Columbia CL-1648	(M)	Story Songs	1961	10.00	25.00
Columbia CS-8448	(S)	Story Songs	1961	12.00	30.00
Columbia CL-1916	(M)	In Person At The Bitter End	1962	10.00	25.00
Columbia CS-8716	(S)	In Person At The Bitter End	1962	12.00	30.00
— Original Columbia albums above have three white "eye" logos on each side of the spindle hole.—					
Columbia CL-1947	(M)	Children's Concert At Town Hall	1963	6.00	15.00
Columbia CS-8747	(S)	Children's Concert At Town Hall	1963	8.00	20.00
Columbia CL-2257	(M)	I Can See A New Day	1964	6.00	15.00
Columbia CS-9057	(S)	I Can See A New Day	1964	8.00	20.00
Columbia CL-2334	(M)	Strangers And Cousins	1965	6.00	15.00
Columbia CS-9134	(S)	Strangers And Cousins	1965	8.00	20.00
Columbia CL-2432	(M)	God Bless The Grass	1965	6.00	15.00
Columbia CS-9232	(S)	God Bless The Grass	1965	8.00	20.00
Columbia CL-2503	(M)	Dangerous Songs	1966	6.00	15.00
Columbia CS-9303	(S)	Dangerous Songs	1966	8.00	20.00
Columbia CL-2616	(M)	Pete Seeger's Greatest Hits	1967	5.00	12.00
Columbia CS-9416	(S)	Pete Seeger's Greatest Hits	1967	6.00	15.00
Columbia CL-2705	(M)	Waist Deep In The Big Muddy	1967	6.00	15.00
Columbia CS-9505	(S)	Waist Deep In The Big Muddy	1967	6.00	15.00
Columbia CS-9717	(S)	Pete Seeger Now	1968	6.00	15.00
Columbia CS-9873	(S)	Young Vs. Old	1969	6.00	15.00
— Original Columbia albums above have "360 Sound" on the bottom of the label.—					
Philips PHM-2-300	(M)	The Story Of The Nativity (2 LPs)	1963	8.00	20.00
Philips PHS-2-300	(S)	The Story Of The Nativity (2 LPs)	1963	10.00	25.00
Broadside BR-302	(M)	Broadside Ballads	1963	8.00	20.00
Capitol W-2172	(M)	Folk Songs By Pete Seeger	1964	8.00	20.00
Capitol DW-2172	(E)	Folk Songs By Pete Seeger	1964	5.00	12.00
Verve/Folkways FV-9008	(M)	Pete Seeger & Big Bill Broonzy In Concert	1965	8.00	20.00
Verve/Folkways FVS-9008	(S)	Pete Seeger & Big Bill Broonzy In Concert	1965	10.00	25.00
Verve/Folkways FV-9009	(M)	Pete Seeger On Campus	1965	8.00	20.00
Verve/Folkways FVS-9009	(S)	Pete Seeger On Campus	1965	10.00	25.00
Verve/Folkways FV-9013	(M)	Recorded Live At The Village Gate	1965	8.00	20.00
Verve/Folkways FVS-9013	(S)	Recorded Live At The Village Gate	1965	10.00	25.00
Verve/Folkways FV-9020	(M)	Little Boxes And Other Broadsides	1965	8.00	20.00
Verve/Folkways FVS-9020	(S)	Little Boxes And Other Broadsides	1965	10.00	25.00
Capitol T-2718	(M)	Freight Train	1967	8.00	20.00
Capitol DT-2718	(E)	Freight Train	1967	5.00	12.00
Everest LPBR-2414	(M)	Pete Seeger And Sonny Terry	196?	8.00	20.00
Everest LPBR-2451	(M)	Pete Seeger At The Village Gate	196?	6.00	15.00
Columbia OS-3540	(S)	Tell Me That You Love Me, Junie Moon (Soundtrack)	1970	6.00	15.00
Columbia C-30739	(S)	Rainbow Race	1971	4.00	10.00
Columbia KG-31949	(S)	The World Of Pete Seeger (2 LPs)	1972	4.00	10.00

SEEGER, PETE, & FRANK HAMILTON

Folkways FA-2439	(M)	Nonesuch And Other Folk Tunes	1959	8.00	20.00

Label & Catalog #		Title	Year	VG+	NM
SEEGERS, THE					
Prestige PRLP-7375	(M)	Pete, Peggy & Mike Seeger (2 LPs)	1965	8.00	20.00
Prestige PRST-7375	(S)	Pete, Peggy & Mike Seeger (2 LPs)	1965	10.00	25.00
SEEKERS, THE					
Marvel 2060	(M)	The Seekers	1965	6.00	15.00
Marvel 3060	(S)	The Seekers	1965	8.00	20.00
Capitol T-2319	(M)	The New Seekers	1965	5.00	12.00
Capitol ST-2319	(S)	The New Seekers	1965	6.00	15.00
Capitol T-2369	(M)	A World Of Our Own	1965	5.00	12.00
Capitol ST-2369	(S)	A World Of Our Own	1965	6.00	15.00
Capitol T-2431	(M)	Georgy Girl	1966	5.00	12.00
Capitol ST-2431	(S)	Georgy Girl	1966	6.00	15.00
SEGAL, GEORGE					
Philips PHM-200-242	(M)	The Yama Yama Man	1967	6.00	15.00
Philips PHS-600-242	(S)	The Yama Yama Man	1967	8.00	20.00
SEGER, BOB					
Capitol ST-172	(S)	Ramblin' Gamblin' Man	1969	12.00	30.00
Capitol ST-236	(S)	Noah	1969	20.00	50.00
Capitol SKAO-499	(S)	Mongrel (Fold-open cover)	1970	10.00	25.00
Capitol ST-731	(S)	Brand New Morning	1971	20.00	50.00
Palladium P-1006	(S)	Smokin' O.P.'s	1972	12.00	30.00
Reprise MS-2109	(S)	Smokin' O.P.'s	1972	8.00	20.00
Reprise MS-2126	(S)	Back In '72	1973	8.00	20.00
Reprise MS-2184	(S)	Seven	1974	8.00	20.00
Capitol SPRO-8433	(DJ)	"Live" Bullet	1976	16.00	40.00
Capitol ST-11557	(DJ)	Night Moves (Picture disc)	1978	14.00	35.00
Capitol SEAX-11904	(S)	Stranger In Town (Picture disc)	1979	14.00	35.00
Mobile Fidelity MFSL-034	(S)	Night Moves	1980	10.00	30.00
Mobile Fidelity MFSL-127	(S)	Against The Wind	1983	8.00	25.00
SELAH JUBILEE QUARTET, THE					
Remington 1023 (10")	(M)	Spirituals	195?	50.00	125.00
SELLERS, BROTHER JOHN					
Vanguard VRS-8005 (10")	(M)	Brother John Sellers	1954	20.00	50.00
Vanguard VRS-9036	(M)	Blues And Folksongs	195?	12.00	30.00
SELLERS, BROTHER JOHN, & MICKEY BAKER					
Monitor 505	(M)	Big Beat Up The River	1959	20.00	50.00
SELLERS, MAXINE					
Folklore FRLP-14032	(M)	Folk Songs	1964	6.00	15.00
Folklore FRST-14032	(S)	Folk Songs	1964	8.00	20.00
SELLERS, PETER					
For additional listings refer to Ringo Starr & Peter Sellers.					
Angel 35884	(M)	The Best Of Peter Sellers	1960	12.00	30.00
Angel 35884	(S)	The Best Of Peter Sellers	1960	16.00	40.00
United Arts. UAL-4148	(M)	After The Fox (Soundtrack)	1966	10.00	25.00
United Arts. UAS-5148	(S)	After The Fox (Soundtrack)	1966	12.00	30.00
		(The Hollies back Sellers on "After The Fox," which is rechanneled.)			
Warner Bros. W-1711	(M)	The Bobo (Soundtrack)	1967	12.00	30.00
Warner Bros. WS-1711	(S)	The Bobo (Soundtrack)	1967	16.00	40.00
SELLERS, PETER, & SOPHIA LOREN					
Angel 35910	(M)	Peter Sellers And Sophia Loren	1961	12.00	30.00
Angel 35910	(S)	Peter Sellers And Sophia Loren	1961	16.00	40.00
SENOR SOUL					
Double Shot 5004	(S)	Funky Favorites	1968	6.00	15.00
Double Shot 5005	(S)	It's Your Thing	1969	6.00	15.00
SENSATIONS, THE					
The Sensations feature Yvonne Baker.					
Argo LP-4022	(M)	Let Me In/Music, Music, Music	1963	150.00	400.00

A pseudonym for Ross Bagdasarian, Seville scored several novelty hits in the late '50s, including the chart-topping "Witch Doctor." By Christmas of that year he teamed up with The Chipmunks—Alvin, Theodore and Simon—for a string of hits for Liberty. He recorded under his real name, again for Liberty, in 1966. (The resurrected Chipmunks of the '70s and the '80s were under the direction of his son.)

Label & Catalog #		Title	Year	VG+	NM
SENTINALS, THE					
Del-Fi DFLP-1232	(M)	Big Surf	1963	14.00	35.00
Del-Fi DFST-1232	(S)	Big Surf	1963	20.00	50.00
Del-Fi DFLP-1241	(M)	Surfer Girl	1963	14.00	35.00
Del-Fi DFST-1241	(S)	Surfer Girl	1963	20.00	50.00
Sutton SU-338	(M)	Vegas Go-Go	1964	10.00	25.00
Sutton SSU-338	(S)	Vegas Go-Go	1964	14.00	35.00
SERENDIPITY SINGERS, THE					
Philips PHM-200-115	(M)	The Serendipity Singers	1964	5.00	12.00
Philips PHS-600-115	(S)	The Serendipity Singers	1964	6.00	15.00
Philips PHM-200-134	(M)	The Many Sides Of The Serendipity Singers	1964	5.00	12.00
Philips PHS-600-134	(S)	The Many Sides Of The Serendipity Singers	1964	6.00	15.00
Philips PHM-200-151	(M)	Take Your Shoes Off	1965	5.00	12.00
Philips PHS-600-151	(S)	Take Your Shoes Off	1965	6.00	15.00
Philips PHM-200-180	(M)	We Belong Together	1965	5.00	12.00
Philips PHS-600-180	(S)	We Belong Together	1965	6.00	15.00
Philips PHM-200-190	(M)	Love, Lies And Flying Festoons	1965	5.00	12.00
Philips PHS-600-190	(S)	Love, Lies And Flying Festoons	1965	6.00	15.00
Mercury SR-16352	(S)	The Serendipity Singers	1968	5.00	12.00
SERFS, THE					
Capitol SKAO-207	(S)	Earlybird Cafe	1969	4.00	10.00
SERPENT POWER					
Serpent Power features David and Tina Meltzer.					
Vanguard VRS-9252	(M)	Serpent Power	1967	8.00	20.00
Vanguard VSD-79252	(S)	Serpent Power	1967	10.00	25.00
SEVENTH SONS, THE					
ESP-Disk' 1078	(S)	The Seventh Sons	1967	8.00	20.00
SEVILLE, DAVID					
David Seville is a pseudonym for Ross Bagdasarian, the creator of The Chipmunks.					
Liberty LRP-3073	(M)	The Music Of David Seville	1957	50.00	125.00
Liberty LRP-3092	(M)	The Witch Doctor	1958	50.00	125.00
SEWARD, ALEC					
Bluesville BVLP-1076	(M)	Creepin' Blues	1963	16.00	40.00
SEX PISTOLS, THE					
Warner Bros. BSK-3147	(S)	Never Mind The Bollocks, Here Come The Sex Pistols	1977	8.00	20.00
		(With custom label and inner sleeve.)			
SHACKLEFORDS, THE					
Mercury MG-20806	(M)	You Ain't Heard Nothing Yet	1963	6.00	15.00
Mercury SR-60806	(S)	You Ain't Heard Nothing Yet	1963	8.00	20.00
Capitol T-2450	(M)	The Shacklefords	1966	5.00	12.00
Capitol ST-2450	(S)	The Shacklefords	1966	6.00	15.00
SHADES OF BLUE, THE					
Impact IM-101	(M)	Happiness Is The Shades Of Blue	1966	12.00	30.00
Impact IM-1001	(S)	Happiness Is The Shades Of Blue	1966	16.00	40.00
SHADES OF JOY					
Fontana SRF-67592	(S)	Shades Of Joy	1969	6.00	15.00
SHADOWFAX					
Passport 98013	(S)	Watercourse Way	1976	6.00	15.00
SHADOWS, THE					
The Shadows also recorded with Cliff Richard.					
Atlantic 8089	(M)	Surfing With The Shadows	1963	30.00	75.00
Atlantic SD-8089	(S)	Surfing With The Shadows	1963	40.00	100.00
Atlantic 8097	(M)	The Shadows Know	1964	16.00	40.00
Atlantic SD-8097	(S)	The Shadows Know	1964	20.00	50.00

Label & Catalog #		Title	Year	VG+	NM

SHADOWS OF KNIGHT, THE

Dunwich 666	(M)	Gloria	1966	16.00	40.00
Dunwich S-666	(S)	Gloria	1966	20.00	50.00
Dunwich 667	(M)	Back Door Men	1966	16.00	40.00
Dunwich S-667	(S)	Back Door Men	1966	20.00	50.00
Super-K SKS-6002	(S)	The Shadows Of Knight	1969	12.00	30.00

SHADRACK CHAMELEON

| No label | (S) | Shadrack Chameleon | 1972 | 80.00 | 200.00 |

SHAGGS, THE

| MCM 6311 | (S) | Wink | 1967 | 150.00 | 300.00 |

SHAGGS, THE

| Third World 3001 | (S) | Philosophy Of The World | 197? | *See note below* | |

(Suggested values in collectible condition are $1,000-2,000.)

SHAKERS, THE

Audio Fidelity 2155	(M)	The Break It All	1966	16.00	40.00
Audio Fidelity S-2155	(S)	The Break It All *(Silver label)*	1966	20.00	50.00
Audio Fidelity S-2155	(S)	The Break It All *(Brown label)*	197?	10.00	25.00

SHAKEY JAKE

Bluesville BVLP-1008	(M)	Good Times	1960	16.00	40.00
Bluesville BVLP-1027	(M)	Mouth Harp Blues	1961	16.00	40.00
World Pacific WPS-21886	(S)	Blues Makers	196?	6.00	15.00

SHANGRI-LAS, THE

Red Bird 20-101	(M)	Leader Of The Pack	1965	60.00	150.00
Red Bird 20-104	(M)	The Shangri-Las '65	1965	60.00	150.00
Red Bird 20-104	(M)	I Can Never Go Home Anymore	1966	30.00	75.00

("I Can Never Go Home Anymore" is a repackage of "'65" replacing "Sophisticated Boom Boom" with the title hit.)

Mercury MG-21099	(M)	The Shangri-Las' Golden Hits	1966	16.00	40.00
Mercury SR-61099	(P)	The Shangri-Las' Golden Hits	1966	20.00	50.00
Post 4000	(S)	The Shangri-Las Sing	196?	10.00	25.00

SHANKAR, L.

| Zappa SRZ-1-1602 | (S) | Touch Me There *(Produced by Frank Zappa)* | 1979 | 10.00 | 25.00 |

SHANKAR, RAVI

Refer to George Harrison & Friends.

| Apple SWAO-3384 | (S) | Raga *(Sdtk produced by George Harrison)* | 1971 | 8.00 | 20.00 |
| Apple SVBB-3396 | (S) | Ravi Shankar In Concert *(2 LPs)* | 1973 | 16.00 | 40.00 |

SHANNON, DEL

Big Top 12-3003	(M)	Runaway	1961	60.00	150.00
Big Top 12-3003	(S)	Runaway	1961	600.00	1,200.00
Big Top 12-1308	(M)	Little Town Flirt	1963	60.00	150.00
Big Top 12-1308	(S)	Little Town Flirt	1963	500.00	1,000.00

(Stereo copies are not identified on the cover or label so they must be listened to, although an "S" may be etched in the trail-off vinyl.)

Amy 8003	(M)	Handy Man	1964	16.00	40.00
Amy S-8003	(S)	Handy Man	1964	20.00	50.00
Amy 8004	(M)	Del Shannon Sings Hank Williams	1965	16.00	40.00
Amy S-8004	(S)	Del Shannon Sings Hank Williams	1965	20.00	50.00
Amy 8006	(M)	1,661 Seconds	1965	20.00	50.00
Amy S-8006	(S)	1,661 Seconds	1965	30.00	75.00
Liberty LRP-3453	(M)	This Is My Bag	1966	10.00	25.00
Liberty LST-7453	(S)	This Is My Bag	1966	12.00	30.00
Liberty LRP-3479	(M)	Total Commitment	1966	12.00	30.00
Liberty LST-7479	(S)	Total Commitment	1966	16.00	40.00
Liberty LRP-3539	(DJ)	Further Adventures Of Charles Westover	1968	12.00	30.00
Liberty LRP-3539	(M)	Further Adventures Of Charles Westover	1968	16.00	40.00
Liberty LST-7539	(S)	Further Adventures Of Charles Westover	1968	24.00	60.00
Dot DLP-3834	(M)	The Best Of Del Shannon	1967	16.00	40.00
Dot DLP-25834	(E)	The Best Of Del Shannon	1967	12.00	30.00
Post 9000	(E)	Del Shannon Sings	196?	12.00	30.00

When Dione LaRue signed with Cameo as Dee Dee Sharp in 1962, she helped spearhead the Philly Invasion with four straight top 10 dance hits, including the song that derailed the twist, "Mashed Potato Time." Her albums sold minimally and, like many titles on the Cameo/Parkway imprint, stereo pressings are very hard to find. Many are listed in this edition for the first time, including Songs Of Faith (below).

Label & Catalog #		Title	Year	VG+	NM
United Arts. LA151	(S)	Del Shannon Live In England	1973	8.00	20.00
Sire SHAH-3708-2	(P)	The Vintage Years (2 LPs)	1975	10.00	25.00
SHANNON, HUGH					
Atlantic 406 (10")	(M)	Hugh Shannon Sings	195?	20.00	50.00
SHAPIRO, HELEN					
Epic LN-24075	(M)	A Teenager In Love	1963	8.00	20.00
Epic BN-26075	(S)	A Teenager In Love	1963	10.00	25.00
SHARKEY					
Fireworks 1234	(S)	Signposts	1975	6.00	15.00
SHARP, DEE DEE					
Cameo C-1018	(M)	It's Mashed Potato Time	1962	20.00	50.00
Cameo C-1022	(M)	Songs Of Faith	1962	20.00	50.00
Cameo SC-1022	(S)	Songs Of Faith	1962	30.00	75.00
Cameo C-1032	(M)	All The Hits	1962	20.00	50.00
Cameo SC-1032	(S)	All The Hits	1962	30.00	75.00
Cameo C-1050	(M)	Do The Bird	1963	20.00	50.00
Cameo SC-1050	(S)	Do The Bird	1963	30.00	75.00
Cameo C-1062	(M)	Biggest Hits	1963	20.00	50.00
Cameo C-1074	(M)	Down Memory Lane	1963	20.00	50.00
Cameo C-2002	(M)	18 Golden Hits	1964	20.00	50.00
Cameo SC-2002	(P)	18 Golden Hits	1964	30.00	75.00
SHARP, DEE DEE, & CHUBBY CHECKER					
Cameo C-1029	(M)	Down To Earth	1962	20.00	50.00
Cameo SC-1029	(S)	Down To Earth	1962	30.00	75.00
SHARPE, MIKE					
Liberty LRP-3507	(M)	Spooky Sound Of Mike Sharpe	1967	5.00	12.00
Liberty LST-7507	(S)	Spooky Sound Of Mike Sharpe	1967	6.00	15.00
Liberty LST-7615	(S)	Mystic Light	1969	5.00	12.00
SHARPE, RAY					
Award LMP-711	(M)	Welcome Back, Linda Lou	1964	60.00	150.00
SHATNER, WILLIAM					
William Shatner was formerly a member of The U.S.S. Enterprise.					
Decca DL-5043	(M)	Transformed Man	1968	16.00	40.00
Decca DL-75043	(S)	Transformed Man	1968	20.00	50.00
Caedmon TC-1508	(S)	Isaac Asimov's "Foundation"	1976	12.00	30.00
Lemli 00001	(S)	William Shatner "Live"	1977	16.00	40.00
Century-21 2476/7	(DJ)	Interview With The Star Of "Big Bad Mama" (Issued without a cover.)	1974	30.00	75.00
SHAW, SANDIE					
Reprise R-6166	(M)	Sandi Shaw	1965	16.00	40.00
Reprise RS-6166	(E)	Sandi Shaw	1965	12.00	30.00
Reprise R-6191	(M)	Me	1966	12.00	30.00
Reprise RS-6191	(S)	Me	1966	16.00	40.00
SHEILA					
Philips PHM-200-144	(M)	The Ya Ya Girl	1964	5.00	12.00
Philips PHS-600-144	(S)	The Ya Ya Girl	1964	6.00	15.00
SHELDON, ERNIE, & THE VILLAGERS					
Columbia CL-1515	(M)	Big Men, Bold And Bad	1960	6.00	15.00
Columbia CS-8315	(S)	Big Men, Bold And Bad	1960	8.00	20.00
SHELTON, ROSCOE					
Excello LP-8002	(M)	Roscoe Shelton Sings	1961	200.00	500.00
Sound Stage-7 500	(S)	Music In His Soul, Soul In His Music	196?	20.00	50.00
SHEP & THE LIMELITES					
Hull 1001	(M)	Our Anniversary	1962	350.00	750.00
Roulette R-25350	(M)	Our Anniversary	1967	30.00	75.00
Roulette RS-25350	(E)	Our Anniversary	1967	20.00	50.00

Label & Catalog #		Title	Year	VG+	NM

SHEPARD, JEAN (& THE SECOND FIDDLES)

Label & Catalog #		Title	Year	VG+	NM
Capitol T-728	(M)	Songs Of A Love Affair *(Turquoise label)*	1956	24.00	60.00
Capitol T-1126	(M)	Lonesome Love	1959	16.00	40.00
Capitol T-1253	(M)	This Is Jean Shepard	1959	16.00	40.00
Capitol T-1525	(M)	Got You On My Mind	1961	12.00	30.00
Capitol ST-1525	(S)	Got You On My Mind	1961	16.00	40.00
Capitol T-1663	(M)	Heartaches And Tears	1962	12.00	30.00
Capitol ST-1663	(S)	Heartaches And Tears	1962	16.00	40.00

—Original Capitol albums above have black labels with the logo on the left side.—

Label & Catalog #		Title	Year	VG+	NM
Capitol T-1922	(M)	The Best Of Jean Shepard	1963	6.00	15.00
Capitol ST-1922	(P)	The Best Of Jean Shepard	1963	8.00	20.00
Capitol T-2187	(M)	Lighthearted And Blue	1964	6.00	15.00
Capitol ST-2187	(S)	Lighthearted And Blue	1964	8.00	20.00
Capitol T-2416	(M)	It's A Man Everytime	1965	6.00	15.00
Capitol ST-2416	(S)	It's A Man Everytime	1965	8.00	20.00
Capitol T-2537	(M)	I'll Take The Dog	1966	6.00	15.00
Capitol ST-2537	(S)	I'll Take The Dog	1966	8.00	20.00
Capitol T-2547	(M)	Many Happy Hangovers	1966	6.00	15.00
Capitol ST-2547	(S)	Many Happy Hangovers	1966	8.00	20.00
Capitol T-2690	(M)	Heart, We Did All That We Could	1967	8.00	20.00
Capitol ST-2690	(S)	Heart, We Did All That We Could	1967	6.00	15.00
Capitol T-2765	(M)	Your Forevers Don't Last Very Long	1967	8.00	20.00
Capitol ST-2765	(S)	Your Forevers Don't Last Very Long	1967	6.00	15.00
Capitol T-2871	(M)	Heart To Heart	1968	10.00	25.00
Capitol ST-2871	(S)	Heart To Heart	1968	6.00	15.00
Capitol T-2966	(M)	A Real Good Woman	1968	10.00	25.00
Capitol ST-2966	(S)	A Real Good Woman	1968	6.00	15.00

— Original Capitol albums above have black labels with the logo on top.—

SHEPHARD, JEAN

Label & Catalog #		Title	Year	VG+	NM
Abbott 5003	(M)	Into The Unknown With Jazz	1956	40.00	100.00
Elektra EKL-172	(M)	Jean Shephard And Other Foibles	195?	20.00	50.00

SHEPHERD, CYBIL

Label & Catalog #		Title	Year	VG+	NM
Paramount PAS-1018	(S)	Cybil Does It To Cole Porter *(Gatefold cover)*	1972	10.00	25.00
Paramount PAS-1018	(S)	Cybil Does It To Cole Porter *(Regular cover)*	197?	6.00	15.00

SHEPPARDS, THE

Label & Catalog #		Title	Year	VG+	NM
Constellation CS-4	(M)	The Sheppards	1964	30.00	75.00

SHERMAN, ALLAN

Label & Catalog #		Title	Year	VG+	NM
Warner Bros. W-1475	(M)	My Son, The Folk Singer	1962	6.00	15.00
Warner Bros. WS-1475	(S)	My Son, The Folk Singer	1962	8.00	20.00
Warner Bros. W-1487	(M)	My Son, The Celebrity	1963	6.00	15.00
Warner Bros. WS-1487	(S)	My Son, The Celebrity	1963	8.00	20.00
Warner Bros. W-1501	(M)	My Son, The Nut	1963	6.00	15.00
Warner Bros. WS-1501	(S)	My Son, The Nut	1963	8.00	20.00
Warner Bros. W-1539	(M)	Allan In Wonderland	1964	6.00	15.00
Warner Bros. WS-1539	(S)	Allan In Wonderland	1964	8.00	20.00
Warner Bros. W-1569	(M)	For Swingin' Lovers Only	1964	6.00	15.00
Warner Bros. WS-1569	(S)	For Swingin' Lovers Only	1964	8.00	20.00
Warner Bros. W-1604	(M)	My Name Is Allan	1965	6.00	15.00
Warner Bros. WS-1604	(S)	My Name Is Allan	1965	8.00	20.00

— Original Warner mono albums above have grey labels; stereo albums have gold labels.—

Label & Catalog #		Title	Year	VG+	NM
RCA Victor LPM-2773	(M)	Peter And The Commissar	1964	5.00	12.00
RCA Victor LSP-2773	(S)	Peter And The Commissar	1964	6.00	15.00

SHERRIL, BILLY

Label & Catalog #		Title	Year	VG+	NM
Epic LN-24232	(M)	Classical Country	1967	6.00	15.00
Epic BN-26232	(S)	Classical Country	1967	6.00	15.00

SHERRYS, THE

Label & Catalog #		Title	Year	VG+	NM
Guyden GLP-503	(M)	At The Hop With The Sherry's	1962	80.00	200.00

SHIGETA, JAMES

Label & Catalog #		Title	Year	VG+	NM
Choreo A-7	(M)	We Speak The Same Language	196?	10.00	25.00
Choreo AS-7	(S)	We Speak The Same Language	196?	12.00	30.00

Passaic, New Jersey's Shirley Alston, Micki Harris, Doris Kenner and Beverly Lee can claim to have influenced, among many others, Brian Wilson, John Lennon and John Phillips. This classic "girl group" scored one hit after another from 1958 through 1963, after which their success petered out. Their first album (above) contained at least two standards and is among the most collectible of girl group albums. Each of their first half-dozen albums were issued in mono only; they were mixed into stereo and issued in 1965-66. While the stereo versions are therefore second pressings, they are considerably harder to find and generally command a higher value than the original monos.

Label & Catalog #		Title	Year	VG+	NM
SHILOH					
Shiloh features Don Henley, later of The Eagles.					
Amos AAS-7015	(S)	Shiloh	196?	16.00	40.00
SHINES, JOHNNY					
Blue Horizon BM-4607	(M)	Blues Masters	197?	6.00	15.00
Chess LP-411	(S)	Drop Down Mama	197?	6.00	15.00
SHIP, THE					
Elektra EKS-75036	(S)	The Ship (Produced by Gary Usher)	1972	10.00	25.00
SHIRELLES, THE					
Scepter SRM-501	(M)	Tonight's The Night	1961	40.00	100.00
		(Red label with silver scroll logo on top.)			
Scepter SPS-501	(S)	Tonight's The Night	1965	40.00	100.00
Scepter SRM-502	(M)	The Shirelles Sing To Trumpets & Strings	1961	30.00	75.00
Scepter SPS-502	(S)	The Shirelles Sing To Trumpets & Strings	1965	40.00	100.00
Scepter SRM-504	(M)	Baby It's You	1962	20.00	50.00
Scepter SPS-504	(S)	Baby It's You	1965	30.00	75.00
Scepter SRM-505	(M)	A Twist Party (With King Curtis)	1962	16.00	40.00
Scepter SPS-505	(S)	A Twist Party (With King Curtis)	1965	20.00	50.00
Scepter SRM-507	(M)	The Shirelles' Greatest Hits	1963	16.00	40.00
Scepter SPS-507	(P)	The Shirelles' Greatest Hits	1965	20.00	50.00
		("Dedicated To The One I Love" is rechanneled on this album.)			
Scepter SRM-511	(M)	Foolish Little Girl	1963	12.00	30.00
Scepter SPS-511	(S)	Foolish Little Girl	1965	16.00	40.00
Scepter SRM-514	(M)	It's A Mad, Mad, Mad, Mad, World	1963	10.00	25.00
Scepter SPS-514	(S)	It's A Mad, Mad, Mad, Mad, World	1963	14.00	35.00
Scepter SRM-516	(M)	The Shirelles Sing The Golden Oldies	1964	10.00	25.00
Scepter SPS-516	(S)	The Shirelles Sing The Golden Oldies	1964	14.00	35.00
Scepter SRM-560	(M)	The Shirelles' Greatest Hits, Volume 2	1967	8.00	20.00
Scepter SPS-560	(S)	The Shirelles' Greatest Hits, Volume 2	1967	10.00	25.00
		("Please Be My Boy Friend" is rechanneled on this album.)			
Scepter SRM-562	(M)	Spontaneous Combustion	1967	8.00	20.00
Scepter SPS-562	(S)	Spontaneous Combustion	1967	10.00	25.00
— Original Scepter albums above have orange labels with a black oval-like center.—					
Pricewise P-4001	(S)	Swing The Most	196?	10.00	25.00
Pricewise P-4002	(S)	Here And Now	196?	10.00	25.00
Scepter SPS-2-599	(P)	Remember When	1972	6.00	15.00
SHIRLEY & LEE					
Shirley Goodman and Leonard Lee.					
Aladdin 807	(M)	Let The Good Times Roll	1956	400.00	800.00
Score SLP-4023	(M)	Let The Good Times Roll	1957	300.00	600.00
Warwick W-2028	(M)	Let The Good Times Roll	1961	50.00	125.00
Warwick WST-2028	(S)	Let The Good Times Roll	1961	80.00	200.00
		(New recordings with a rerecorded title tune.)			
Imperial LP-9179	(M)	Let The Good Times Roll	1962	100.00	250.00
United Arts. LA-026-G	(P)	Legendary Masters (2 LPs. Canadian)	1974	20.00	50.00
SHIVA'S HEADBAND					
Armadillo	(S)	Coming To A Head	1969	60.00	150.00
Capitol ST-538	(S)	Take Me To The Mountains	1970	20.00	50.00
Ape 1001	(S)	Psychedelic Yesterday	1981	10.00	25.00
SHOCKING BLUE, THE					
Colossus CS-1000	(S)	The Shocking Blue	1970	10.00	25.00
		("Venus" and "Send Me A Postcard" are rechanneled.)			
SHONDELLS, THE					
La Louisiane 109	(M)	The Shondells At The Saturday Hop	1964	50.00	125.00
SHORE, DINAH					
Refer to The Reprise Repertory Theatre.					
Columbia CL-6004 (10")	(M)	Dinah Shore Sings	1949	16.00	40.00
Columbia CL-6069 (10")	(M)	Reminiscing	1949	16.00	40.00
Columbia JL-8503	(M)	Bongo / Land Of The Lost	1950	16.00	40.00
RCA Victor LOC-1000 (10")	(M)	Call Me Madam	1950	40.00	100.00
RCA Victor LPM-39 (10")	(M)	Two Tickets To Broadway	1951	20.00	50.00

Label & Catalog #		Title	Year	VG+	NM
RCA Victor LPM-3006 (10")	(M)	Aaron Slick From Punkin Crick (Sdtk)	1952	40.00	100.00
RCA Victor LPM-3103 (10")	(M)	Dinah Shore Sings The Blues	1953	14.00	35.00
RCA Victor LPM-3214 (10")	(M)	The Dinah Shore TV Show	1954	14.00	35.00
RCA Victor LPM-1154	(M)	Holding Hands At Midnight	1955	14.00	35.00
RCA Victor LPM-1214	(M)	Bouquet Of Blues	1956	10.00	25.00
RCA Victor LPM-1719	(M)	Moments Like These	1958	10.00	25.00

— Original RCA mono albums above have "black labels with Long Play" on the bottom; stereo albums have have black labels with "Living Stereo" on the bottom.—

Capitol T-1247	(M)	Dinah, Yes Indeed	1959	6.00	15.00
Capitol ST-1247	(S)	Dinah, Yes Indeed	1959	8.00	20.00
Capitol T-1296	(M)	Somebody Loves Me	1959	6.00	15.00
Capitol ST-1296	(S)	Somebody Loves Me	1959	8.00	20.00
Capitol T-1354	(M)	Dinah Sings Some Blues With Red	1960	6.00	15.00
Capitol ST-1354	(S)	Dinah Sings Some Blues With Red	1960	8.00	20.00
Capitol T-1422	(M)	Dinah Sings/Previn Plays	1960	6.00	15.00
Capitol ST-1422	(S)	Dinah Sings/Previn Plays	1960	8.00	20.00
Capitol T-1655	(M)	Dinah Down Home	1962	6.00	15.00
Capitol ST-1655	(S)	Dinah Down Home	1962	8.00	20.00
Capitol T-1704	(M)	Fabulous Hits Newly Recorded	1962	6.00	15.00
Capitol ST-1704	(S)	Fabulous Hits Newly Recorded	1962	8.00	20.00

— Original Capitol albums above have black labels with the logo on the left side.—

Capitol Custom (No #)	(S)	My Very Best To You	1964	10.00	25.00
Decca DL-75094	(S)	Country Feelin'	1969	5.00	12.00

SHORT, BOBBY: *Refer to* GOLDMINE'S PRICE GUIDE TO COLLECTIBLE JAZZ ALBUMS

SHORT, J. D.: *Refer to* SON HOUSE & J. D. SHORT

SHORT CROSS

Grizzly S16-013	(S)	Arising	197?	50.00	125.00

SHORTY
Shorty features Georgie Fame.

Epic BN-26563	(S)	Shorty	1970	4.00	10.00

SICKNICKS, THE

Amy 2	(M)	Sick # 2	196?	12.00	30.00

SIDEKICKS, THE

RCA Victor LPM-3712	(M)	Fifi The Flea	1966	8.00	20.00
RCA Victor LSP-3712	(S)	Fifi The Flea	1966	10.00	25.00

SIEGEL-SCHWALL BAND, THE

Vanguard VRS-9235	(M)	The Siegel-Schwall Band	1966	8.00	20.00
Vanguard VSD-79235	(S)	The Siegel-Schwall Band	1966	10.00	25.00
Vanguard VSD-79249	(M)	The Siegel-Schwall Band Say	1967	8.00	20.00
Vanguard VSD-79249	(S)	The Siegel-Schwall Band Say	1967	10.00	25.00
Vanguard VSD-79289	(S)	Shake!	1968	8.00	20.00
Vanguard VSD-6562	(S)	Siegel-Schwall '70	1970	8.00	20.00

SIGLER, BUNNY

Parkway P-50000	(M)	Let The Good Times Roll	1967	10.00	25.00
Parkway PS-50000	(S)	Let The Good Times Roll	1967	12.00	30.00

SIGNATURES, THE

Whippet W-702	(M)	Their Voices And Instruments	1957	30.00	75.00
Warner Bros. W-1250	(M)	The Signatures Sing In	1959	8.00	20.00
Warner Bros. WS-1250	(S)	The Signatures Sing In	1959	12.00	30.00
Warner Bros. W-1353	(M)	Prepare To Flip!	1959	8.00	20.00
Warner Bros. WS-1353	(S)	Prepare To Flip!	1959	12.00	30.00

SILHOUETTES, THE

Goodway GLP-100	(M)	The Silhouettes 1958-1968/Get A Job	1968	150.00	300.00

SILK

ABC ABCS-694	(S)	Smooth As Raw Silk	1969	5.00	12.00

This little gem was commissioned by the Hawk Model Company, manufacturer of plastic model kits, as a promotional one-shot. Vocals are credited to The Surfers and The Weird-ohs, both accompanied by Shary Richards, with production credit to Jimmie Haskell and Gary Usher. The illustrations above show the front and back cover of the album. Usher took the creations to Mercury where he released one album as the former and recorded an unreleased album as the latter.

Label & Catalog #		Title	Year	VG+	NM
SILKIE, THE					
Fontana MGF-27548	(M)	**You've Got To Hide Your Love Away**	1965	20.00	50.00
Fontana SRF-67548	(E)	**You've Got To Hide Your Love Away**	1965	16.00	40.00
		(Full color cover.)			
Fontana MGF-27548	(M)	**You've Got To Hide Your Love Away**	1965	16.00	40.00
Fontana SRF-67548	(E)	**You've Got To Hide Your Love Away**	1965	12.00	30.00
		(Black & white cover with a violet tone.)			
SILLY SURFERS, THE / THE WEIRD-OHS					

Issued by the Hawk Model Co., The Surfers and The Weird-Ohs are Gary Usher & Co. projects. The tracks on this album were later used by Gary to create individual albums by The Surfers and The Weird-Ohs.

Label & Catalog #		Title	Year	VG+	NM
Hairy 101	(DJ)	**Music To Make Models By**	1964	50.00	125.00
SILLY SURFERS, THE					

The Surfers are a creation of Gary Usher & Co.

Label & Catalog #		Title	Year	VG+	NM
Mercury MG-20977	(M)	**Sounds Of The Silly Surfers**	1965	14.00	35.00
Mercury SR-60977	(S)	**Sounds Of The Silly Surfers**	1965	20.00	50.00
SILVER					
Grammie Fonics 8322	(S)	**Children Of The Lord**	1975	40.00	100.00
SILVER APPLES					
Kapp KS-3562	(S)	**Silver Apples**	1968	10.00	25.00
Kapp KS-3584	(S)	**Contact**	1969	10.00	25.00
SILVER BEATLES, THE: *Refer to* **PRESLEY, ELVIS / THE SILVER BEATLES**					
SILVER METRE					
National General NG-2000	(S)	**Silver Metre**	1970	6.00	15.00
SILVERMAN, JERRY					
Audio Video 101	(M)	**Folk Blues**	195?	10.00	25.00
SILVERSTEIN, SHEL					
Elektra EKL-176	(M)	**Hairy Jazz**	1959	30.00	75.00
Elektra EKS-7176	(S)	**Hairy Jazz**	1959	40.00	100.00
Atlantic 8072	(M)	**Inside Folk Songs**	1963	14.00	35.00
Atlantic SD-8072	(S)	**Inside Folk Songs**	1963	20.00	50.00
Cadet LP-4052	(M)	**I'm So Good I Don't Have To Brag!**	1965	6.00	15.00
Cadet LPS-4052	(S)	**I'm So Good I Don't Have To Brag!**	1965	8.00	20.00
Cadet LP-4054	(M)	**Drain My Brain**	1966	10.00	25.00
Cadet LPS-4054	(S)	**Drain My Brain**	1966	12.00	30.00
RCA Victor LSP-4192	(S)	**A Boy Named Sue**	1969	8.00	20.00
SIMMONS, "JUMPIN'" GENE					
Hi HL-2018	(M)	**Jumpin' Gene Simmons**	1964	14.00	35.00
Hi SHL-32018	(S)	**Jumpin' Gene Simmons**	1964	20.00	50.00
SIMMONS, GENE: *Refer to* **KISS**					
SIMMONS, JEFF					

Mr. Simmons was formerly a member of The Easy Chair.

Label & Catalog #		Title	Year	VG+	NM
Straight STS-1057	(S)	**Lucille Has Messed Up My Mind**	1969	20.00	50.00
Reprise STS-1057	(S)	**Lucille Has Messed Up My Mind**	1970	10.00	25.00
SIMON, CARLY					

Ms. Simon was formerly of The Simon Sisters.

Label & Catalog #		Title	Year	VG+	NM
Decca DL-79181	(S)	**Taking Off** *(Soundtrack)*	1971	6.00	15.00
Elektra EQ-4082	(Q)	**Carly Simon**	1973	8.00	20.00
Elektra EQ-5049	(Q)	**No Secrets**	1973	8.00	20.00
Elektra EQ-1002	(Q)	**Hotcakes**	1974	8.00	20.00
Elektra EQ-1033	(Q)	**Playing Possum**	1975	8.00	20.00
Elektra EQ-1064	(Q)	**Another Passenger**	1975	8.00	20.00
Elektra EQ-1048	(Q)	**The Best Of Carly Simon**	1977	8.00	20.00
Direct Disk SD-16608	(S)	**Boys In The Trees**	198?	7.00	20.00
SIMON, JOE					
Sound Stage-7 5003	(M)	**Pure Soul**	1967	8.00	20.00
Sound Stage-7 15003	(S)	**Pure Soul**	1967	10.00	25.00

Carly Simon began her career as a sort of folk pop duo with sister Lucy, making the charts briefly in 1964 with the folkie favorite "Winkin', Blinkin' And Nod." She resurrected her career as a sort of yuppie princess singer-songwriter, although her biggest hit, "You're So Vain," was pop at its best with backing vocals from Mick Jagger. It appeared on No Secrets, below in its rather rare quadraphonic incarnation. Each of her albums has made the charts with six receiving RIAA Gold Records through 1990.

Label & Catalog #		Title	Year	VG+	NM
Sound Stage-7 15004	(S)	No Sad Songs	1968	10.00	25.00
Sound Stage-7 15005	(S)	Simon Sings	1969	10.00	25.00
Sound Stage-7 15006	(S)	The Chokin' Kind	1969	10.00	25.00
Buddah BDS-7512	(S)	Joe Simon	1969	8.00	20.00
Sound Stage 7 15008	(S)	Better Than Ever	1969	8.00	20.00
Sound Stage 7 15009	(S)	The Best Of Joe Simon	1970	6.00	15.00
Sound Stage 7 KZ-31916	(S)	Greatest Hits	1972	6.00	15.00

SIMON, PAUL

Label & Catalog #		Title	Year	VG+	NM
E.B. Marks	(DJ)	The Earely Songs Of Paul Simon	1972	100.00	250.00
		(Collection of publishers demos from the pre-S&G period. Issued with a booklet and sheet music.)			
Columbia CQ-30750	(Q)	Paul Simon	1974	8.00	20.00
Columbia CQ-32280	(Q)	There Goes Rhymin' Simon	1974	8.00	20.00
Columbia PCQ-33540	(Q)	Still Crazy After All These Years	1975	8.00	20.00
Columbia HC-43540	(S)	Still Crazy After All These Years *(Half-speed)*	1981	16.00	50.00
Columbia HC-45032	(S)	Greatest Hits, Etc. *(Half-speed master)*	1981	16.00	50.00
Warner Bros. 23942	(DJ)	Hearts And Bones *(Quiex II vinyl)*	198?	6.00	15.00

SIMON & GARFUNKEL
Paul Simon and Art Garfunkel.

Label & Catalog #		Title	Year	VG+	NM
Columbia CL-2249	(M)	Wednesday Morning 3 A.M.	1964	12.00	30.00
Columbia CS-9049	(S)	Wednesday Morning 3 A.M.	1964	10.00	25.00
Columbia CL-2469	(M)	Sounds Of Silence	1966	12.00	30.00
Columbia CS-9269	(S)	Sounds Of Silence	1966	10.00	25.00
Pickwick SPC-3059	(S)	The Hit Sounds Of Simon & Garfunkel	1966	20.00	50.00
		(Compilation of S&G's earlier incarnation as Tom & Jerry.)			
Columbia CL-2563	(M)	Parsley, Sage, Rosemary & Thyme	1966	12.00	30.00
Columbia CS-9363	(S)	Parsley, Sage, Rosemary & Thyme	1966	8.00	20.00
Columbia KCL-2729	(M)	Bookends *(With poster)*	1968	20.00	50.00
Columbia KCS-9529	(S)	Bookends *(With poster)*	1968	12.00	30.00
Columbia KCL-2729	(M)	Bookends *(Without poster)*	1968	16.00	40.00
Columbia KCS-9529	(S)	Bookends *(Without poster)*	1968	8.00	20.00
Columbia OS-3180	(S)	The Graduate *(Soundtrack)*	1968	6.00	15.00
		— Original Columbia albums above have "360 Sound" on the bottom of the label.—			
Columbia CQ-30995	(Q)	Bridge Over Troubled Water	1971	12.00	30.00
Columbia HC-41350	(S)	Greatest Hits *(Half-speed master)*	1982	7.00	20.00
Columbia HC-49914	(S)	Bridge Over Troubled Water *(Half-speed)*	1982	7.00	20.00
Sears 435	(S)	Simon & Garfunkel	1969	10.00	25.00
		(Sears 435 is a reissue of Pickwick 3059.)			
Mobile Fidelity MFSL-173	(S)	Bridge Over Troubled Water	198?	7.00	20.00

SIMON & ILANA

Label & Catalog #		Title	Year	VG+	NM
Coral CRL-57409	(M)	The Wonderful World Of Folk Music	1962	6.00	15.00
Coral CRL-757409	(S)	The Wonderful World Of Folk Music	1962	8.00	20.00

SIMON SISTERS, THE
Carly and Lucy Simon.

Label & Catalog #		Title	Year	VG+	NM
Kapp KL-1359	(M)	Winkin,' Blinkin' And Nod	1964	12.00	30.00
Kapp KS-3359	(S)	Winkin,' Blinkin' And Nod	1964	16.00	40.00
Kapp KL-1397	(M)	Cuddlebug	1964	12.00	30.00
Kapp KS-3397	(S)	Cuddlebug	1964	16.00	40.00
Columbia CC-24506	(S)	The Lobster Quadrille *(With booklet)*	1969	6.00	15.00
Columbia CR-21539	(S)	The Simon Sisters Sing For Children	1973	4.00	10.00
		(Columbia 21539 is a remixed repackage of 24506.)			

SIMONE, NINA

Label & Catalog #		Title	Year	VG+	NM
Bethlehem BCP-6028	(M)	Little Girl Blue	1958	20.00	50.00
Bethlehem BCP-6028	(S)	Little Girl Blue	1958	40.00	100.00
Bethlehem BCP-6041	(M)	Nina Simone And Her Friends	1959	16.00	40.00
Bethlehem BCP-6028	(M)	The Original Nina Simone	1961	10.00	25.00
Bethlehem BCPS-6028	(S)	The Original Nina Simone	1961	16.00	40.00
		(Reissue of Nina's first album with the same catalogue number.)			
Colpix CP-407	(M)	The Amazing Nina Simone	1959	8.00	20.00
Colpix SCP-407	(S)	The Amazing Nina Simone	1959	12.00	30.00
Colpix CP-409	(M)	Nina At Town Hall	1959	8.00	20.00
Colpix SCP-409	(S)	Nina At Town Hall	1959	12.00	30.00
Colpix CP-412	(M)	Nina Simone At Newport	1960	8.00	20.00
Colpix SCP-412	(S)	Nina Simone At Newport	1960	12.00	30.00

Label & Catalog #		Title	Year	VG+	NM
Colpix CP-419	(M)	Forbidden Fruit	1961	8.00	20.00
Colpix SCP-419	(S)	Forbidden Fruit	1961	12.00	30.00
Colpix CP-421	(M)	Nina Simone At The Village Gate	1961	8.00	20.00
Colpix SCP-421	(S)	Nina Simone At The Village Gate	1961	12.00	30.00
Colpix CP-425	(M)	Nina Simone Sings Ellington	1962	8.00	20.00
Colpix SCP-425	(S)	Nina Simone Sings Ellington	1962	12.00	30.00
Colpix CP-443	(M)	Nina's Choice	1963	8.00	20.00
Colpix SCP-443	(S)	Nina's Choice	1963	12.00	30.00
Colpix CP-455	(M)	Nina Simone At Carnegie Hall	1963	8.00	20.00
Colpix SCP-455	(S)	Nina Simone At Carnegie Hall	1963	12.00	30.00
Colpix CP-465	(M)	Folksy Nina	1964	8.00	20.00
Colpix SCP-465	(S)	Folksy Nina	1964	12.00	30.00
Colpix CP-496	(M)	Nina With Strings	1966	8.00	20.00
Colpix SCP-496	(S)	Nina With Strings	1966	12.00	30.00
— Original Colpix albums above have gold labels.—					
Philips PHM-200-135	(M)	Nina Simone In Concert	1964	5.00	12.00
Philips PHS-600135	(S)	Nina Simone In Concert	1964	6.00	15.00
Philips PHM-200-148	(M)	Blues: Ballads	1964	5.00	12.00
Philips PHS-600-148	(S)	Blues: Ballads	1964	6.00	15.00
Philips PHM-200-172	(M)	I Put A Spell On You	1965	5.00	12.00
Philips PHS-600-172	(S)	I Put A Spell On You	1965	6.00	15.00
Philips PHM-200-187	(M)	Pastel Blues	1965	5.00	12.00
Philips PHS-600-187	(S)	Pastel Blues	1965	6.00	15.00
Philips PHM-200-202	(M)	Let It All Out	1966	5.00	12.00
Philips PHS-600-202	(S)	Let It All Out	1966	6.00	15.00
Philips PHM-200-207	(M)	Wild Is The Wind	1966	5.00	12.00
Philips PHS-600-207	(S)	Wild Is The Wind	1966	6.00	15.00
Philips PHM-200-219	(M)	The High Priestess Of Soul	1967	5.00	12.00
Philips PHS-600-219	(S)	The High Priestess Of Soul	1967	6.00	15.00
RCA Victor LPM-3789	(M)	Nina Simone Sings The Blues	1966	5.00	12.00
RCA Victor LSP-3789	(S)	Nina Simone Sings The Blues	1966	6.00	15.00
RCA Victor LPM-3837	(M)	Silk And Soul	1967	8.00	20.00
RCA Victor LSP-3837	(S)	Silk And Soul	1967	6.00	15.00
— Original RCA albums above have black labels with Nipper on top.—					
RCA Victor LSP-4065	(S)	Nuff Said	1968	5.00	12.00
RCA Victor LSP-4248	(S)	Black Gold	1970	5.00	12.00
RCA Victor LSP-4347	(S)	The Best Of Nina Simone	1970	5.00	12.00
RCA Victor LSP-4536	(S)	Here Comes The Sun	1972	5.00	12.00

SIMPSON, CAROLE: Refer to GOLDMINE'S PRICE GUIDE TO COLLECTIBLE JAZZ ALBUMS

SIMPSON, FRANK

Audio Lab AL-1552	(M)	Four Star Hits	1960	40.00	100.00

SIMPSON, MIKE, & THE RAUNCH HANDS

Mercury MG-20697	(M)	Dixie Twist	1962	6.00	15.00
Mercury SR-60697	(S)	Dixie Twist	1962	8.00	20.00

SIMPSON, RED

Portland 1003	(M)	Hello, I'm A Truck	1965	30.00	75.00
Capitol T-2468	(M)	Roll Truck, Roll	1966	8.00	20.00
Capitol ST-2468	(S)	Roll Truck, Roll	1966	10.00	25.00
Capitol T-2569	(M)	The Man Behind The Badge	1966	6.00	15.00
Capitol ST-2569	(S)	The Man Behind The Badge	1966	8.00	20.00
Capitol T-2691	(M)	Truck Drivin' Fool	1967	8.00	20.00
Capitol ST-2691	(S)	Truck Drivin' Fool	1967	6.00	15.00
Capitol T-2829	(M)	A Bakersfield Dozen	1967	8.00	20.00
Capitol ST-2829	(S)	A Bakersfield Dozen	1967	6.00	15.00
Capitol ST-881	(S)	I'm A Truck	1971	6.00	15.00

SIMS, FRANKIE LEE

Specialty SPS-2124	(M)	Lucy Mae Blues	1969	14.00	35.00

SIN SAY SHUNS, THE

Venett V-940	(M)	I'll Be There	196?	14.00	35.00
Venett VS-940	(S)	I'll Be There	196?	20.00	50.00

Label & Catalog #		Title	Year	VG+	NM

SINATRA, FRANK, & TOMMY DORSEY

The RCA albums below collect many of FS's earliest recordings as vocalist for Tommy Dorsey's orchestsra.

Label & Catalog #		Title	Year	VG+	NM
RCA Victor LPT-10 (10")	(M)	Getting Sentimental	1949	16.00	40.00
RCA Victor LPT-15 (10")	(M)	Tommy Dorsey All-Time Hits	1949	16.00	40.00
RCA Victor LPT-3005 (10")	(M)	This Is Tommy Dorsey	1954	16.00	40.00
RCA Victor LPT-3063 (10")	(M)	Fabulous Frankie	1955	16.00	40.00
RCA Victor LPM-1229	(M)	Yes Indeed	1956	12.00	30.00
RCA Victor LPM-1432	(M)	Tribute To Dorsey, Volume 1	1956	12.00	30.00
RCA Victor LPM-1433	(M)	Tribute To Dorsey, Volume 2	1956	12.00	30.00
RCA Victor LPM-1569	(M)	Frankie And Tommy	1957	12.00	30.00
RCA Victor LPM-1632	(M)	We Three	1957	12.00	30.00
RCA Victor LPM-1643	(M)	Having A Wonderful Time	1957	12.00	30.00
RCA Victor LPM-6003	(M)	The Sentimental Gentleman (2 LPs)	1958	20.00	50.00
— Original RCA Victor albums have "Long Play" on the bottom of the label.—					
RCA Victor LPV-583	(M)	This Love of Mine	1965	6.00	15.00
RCA Victor VPM-6038	(M)	This Is Tommy Dorsey, Volume 1 (2 LPs)	1974	6.00	15.00
RCA Victor VPM-6039	(M)	This Is Tommy Dorsey, Volume 2 (2 LPs)	1974	6.00	15.00

SINATRA, FRANK

Refer to Peggy Lee; Dean Martin; The Reprise Repertory Theater.

Label & Catalog #		Title	Year	VG+	NM
Columbia CL-6001 (10")	(M)	The Voice Of Frank Sinatra	1949	20.00	50.00
Columbia CL-6019 (10")	(M)	Christmas Songs By Sinatra	1949	20.00	50.00
Columbia CL-6059 (10")	(M)	Frankly Sentimental Sinatra	1949	20.00	50.00
Columbia CL-6087 (10")	(M)	Songs By Sinatra, Volume 1	1950	20.00	50.00
Columbia CL-6096 (10")	(M)	Dedicated To You	1950	20.00	50.00
Columbia CL-6143 (10")	(M)	Sing And Dance With Frank Sinatra	1950	20.00	50.00
Columbia CL-6212 (10")	(M)	This Is My Best	1953	20.00	50.00
Columbia CL-6254 (10")	(M)	Requested By You	1953	20.00	50.00
Columbia CL-6290 (10")	(M)	I've Got A Crush On You	1954	20.00	50.00
Columbia CL-6339 (10")	(M)	Young At Heart (Sdtk with Doris Day)	1954	30.00	75.00
Columbia CL-2521 (10")	(M)	Get Happy	1955	16.00	40.00
Columbia CL-2530 (10")	(M)	Boys And Girls Together	1955	16.00	40.00
Columbia CL-2539 (10")	(M)	I've Got A Crush On You	1955	16.00	40.00
Columbia CL-2542 (10")	(M)	Christmas With Sinatra	1955	16.00	40.00
Columbia ML-4271	(M)	Conducts The Music Of Alec Wilder	1955	14.00	35.00
Columbia CL-606	(M)	Frankie	1955	10.00	25.00
— Original Columbia albums above have labels with "Long LP Playing" on the bottom.—					
Columbia CL-743	(M)	The Voice	1955	8.00	20.00
Columbia CL-884	(M)	Conducts The Music Of Alec Wilder	1956	10.00	25.00
Columbia CL-902	(M)	That Old Feeling	1956	8.00	20.00
Columbia CL-953	(M)	Adventures Of The Heart	1957	8.00	20.00
Columbia CL-1032	(M)	Christmas Dreaming	1957	8.00	20.00
Columbia CL-1130	(M)	The Frank Sinatra Story In Music, Volume 1	1958	8.00	20.00
Columbia CL-1131	(M)	The Frank Sinatra Story In Music, Volume 2	1958	8.00	20.00
Columbia C2L-6	(M)	The Frank Sinatra Story In Music (2 LPs)	1958	10.00	25.00
Columbia CL-1136	(M)	Put Your Dreams Away	1958	8.00	20.00
Columbia CL-1241	(M)	Love Is A Kick	1958	8.00	20.00
Columbia CL-1297	(M)	The Broadway Kick	1959	8.00	20.00
Columbia CL-1359	(M)	Come Back To Sorrento	1959	8.00	20.00
Columbia CL-1448	(M)	Reflections	1960	16.00	40.00
— Original Columbia albums above have three white "eye" logos on each side of the spindle hole.—					
Columbia CL-2474	(M)	Greatest Hits: The Early Years	1965	6.00	15.00
Columbia CS-9274	(E)	Greatest Hits: The Early Years	1965	5.00	12.00
Columbia CL-2572	(M)	Greatest Hits: The Early Years, Volume 2	1966	6.00	15.00
Columbia CS-9372	(E)	Greatest Hits: The Early Years, Volume 2	1966	5.00	12.00
Columbia C3L-42	(M)	The Essential Frank Sinatra (3 LPs)	1966	40.00	100.00
Columbia C3S-42	(E)	The Essential Frank Sinatra (3 LPs)	1966	20.00	50.00
Columbia CL-2739	(M)	The Essential Frank Sinatra, Volume 1	1967	12.00	30.00
Columbia CS-9539	(E)	The Essential Frank Sinatra, Volume 1	1967	6.00	15.00
Columbia CL-2740	(M)	The Essential Frank Sinatra, Volume 2	1967	12.00	30.00
Columbia CS-9540	(E)	The Essential Frank Sinatra, Volume 2	1967	6.00	15.00
Columbia CL-2741	(M)	The Essential Frank Sinatra, Volume 3	1967	12.00	30.00
Columbia CS-9541	(E)	The Essential Frank Sinatra, Volume 3	1967	6.00	15.00
Columbia CL-2913	(M)	Frank Sinatra In Hollywood 1943-1949	1968	1400	35.00
— Original Columbia albums above have "360 Sound" on the bottom of the label.—					
Columbia C6X-40343	(M)	The Voice: The Columbia Years 1943-1952 (6 LPs)	1986	20.00	50.00
Columbia C2X-40897	(M)	Hello Young Lovers (2 LPs)	1987	10.00	25.00
Columbia C-44236	(M)	Rarities	1988	5.00	12.00

Label & Catalog #		Title	Year	VG+	NM
Capitol H-488 (10")	(M)	Songs For Young Lovers	1954	20.00	50.00
Capitol H-528 (10")	(M)	Swing Easy	1954	20.00	50.00
Capitol H1-581 (10")	(M)	In The Wee Small Hours (Part 1)	1955	20.00	50.00
Capitol H2-581 (10")	(M)	In The Wee Small Hours (Part 2)	1955	20.00	50.00
Capitol T-528	(M)	Swing Easy	1954	12.00	30.00
Capitol W-581	(M)	In The Wee Small Hours	1955	12.00	30.00
Capitol W-587	(M)	Swing Easy / Songs For Young Lovers	1955	12.00	30.00
Capitol W-653	(M)	Songs For Swingin' Lovers	1956	12.00	30.00
Capitol W-735	(M)	Conducts Tone Poems Of Color	1956	12.00	30.00
Capitol W-750	(M)	High Society (Soundtrack)	1956	12.00	30.00
Capitol SW-750	(S	High Society (Soundtrack)	1956	20.00	50.00
Capitol T-768	(M)	This Is Sinatra!	1956	12.00	30.00
Capitol W-789	(M)	Close To You	1957	12.00	30.00
Capitol W-803	(M)	A Swingin' Affair	1957	12.00	30.00
— Original Capitol albums above have turquoise or grey labels with "Long Playing" on the bottom.—					
Capitol W-855	(M)	Where Are You?	1957	10.00	25.00
Capitol SW-855	(S)	Where Are You?	1957	14.00	35.00
Capitol W-894	(M)	A Jolly Christmas From Frank Sinatra	1957	10.00	25.00
Capitol W-912	(M)	Pal Joey (Soundtrack)	1957	10.00	25.00
Capitol W-920	(M)	Come Fly With Me	1958	10.00	25.00
Capitol SW-920	(S)	Come Fly With Me	1958	14.00	35.00
Capitol W-982	(M)	This Is Sinatra, Volume 2	1958	10.00	25.00
— Original Capitol albums above have turquoise or grey labels with "Long Playing High Fidelity" on the bottom.—					
Capitol W-1053	(M)	Frank Sinatra Sings For Only The Lonely	1958	8.00	20.00
Capitol SW-1053	(S)	Frank Sinatra Sings For Only The Lonely	1958	10.00	25.00
Capitol W-1069	(M)	Come Dance With Me!	1959	8.00	20.00
Capitol SW-1069	(S)	Come Dance With Me!	1959	10.00	25.00
Capitol W-1164	(M)	Look To Your Heart	1959	8.00	20.00
Capitol W-1221	(M)	No One Cares	1959	8.00	20.00
Capitol SW-1221	(S)	No One Cares	1959	10.00	25.00
Capitol W-1301	(M)	Can-Can (Soundtrack)	1960	8.00	20.00
Capitol SW-1301	(S)	Can-Can (Soundtrack)	1960	12.00	30.00
Capitol W-1417	(M)	Nice 'N' Easy	1960	8.00	20.00
Capitol SW-1417	(S)	Nice 'N' Easy	1960	10.00	25.00
Capitol W-1429	(M)	Swing Easy	1960	8.00	20.00
Capitol W-1432	(M)	Songs For Young Lovers	1960	8.00	20.00
Capitol W-1491	(M)	Sinatra's Swingin' Session!!!	1961	8.00	20.00
Capitol SW-1491	(S)	Sinatra's Swingin' Session!!!	1961	10.00	25.00
Capitol W-1538	(M)	All The Way	1961	8.00	20.00
Capitol SW-1538	(S)	All The Way	1961	10.00	25.00
Capitol W-1594	(M)	Come Swing With Me!	1961	8.00	20.00
Capitol SW-1594	(S)	Come Swing With Me!	1961	10.00	25.00
Capitol W-1676	(M)	Point Of No Return	1962	8.00	20.00
Capitol SW-1676	(S)	Point Of No Return	1962	10.00	25.00
— Original Capitol albums above have black labels with the logo on the left side.—					
Capitol W-1729	(M)	Sinatra Sings... Of Love And Things	1962	5.00	12.00
Capitol W-1729	(S)	Sinatra Sings... Of Love And Things	1962	8.00	20.00
Capitol TCO-1762	(M)	The Great Years (3 LPs)	1962	12.00	30.00
Capitol STCO-1762	(P)	The Great Years (3 LPs)	1962	16.00	40.00
Capitol W-1825	(M)	Frank Sinatra Sings Rodgers And Hart	1963	8.00	20.00
Capitol DW-1825	(E)	Frank Sinatra Sings Rodgers And Hart	1963	5.00	12.00
Capitol T-1919	(M)	Tell Her You Love Her	1963	8.00	20.00
Capitol DT-1919	(E)	Tell Her You Love Her	1963	5.00	12.00
Capitol W-1984	(M)	The Select Johnny Mercer	1963	8.00	20.00
Capitol DW-1984	(E)	The Select Johnny Mercer	1963	5.00	12.00
Capitol T-2036	(M)	The Great Hits Of Frank Sinatra	1964	6.00	15.00
Capitol DT-2036	(E)	The Great Hits Of Frank Sinatra	1964	5.00	12.00
Capitol T-2123	(M)	The Select Harold Arlen	1964	16.00	40.00
(Issued in Australia, Canada and Great Britain only.)					
Capitol W-2301	(M)	The Select Cole Porter	1965	8.00	20.00
Capitol DW-2301	(E)	The Select Cole Porter	1965	5.00	12.00
Capitol PRO-2974/5	(DJ)	Minute Masters	1965	16.00	40.00
Capitol T-2602	(M)	Forever Frank	1966	8.00	20.00
Capitol DT-2602	(E)	Forever Frank	1966	5.00	12.00
Capitol T-2700	(M)	The Movie Songs	1967	8.00	20.00
Capitol DT-2700	(E)	The Movie Songs	1967	5.00	12.00
Capitol TFL-2814	(M)	Deluxe Set (3 LP box)	1968	16.00	40.00
Capitol DTFL-2814	(E)	Deluxe Set (3 LP box)	1968	12.00	30.00

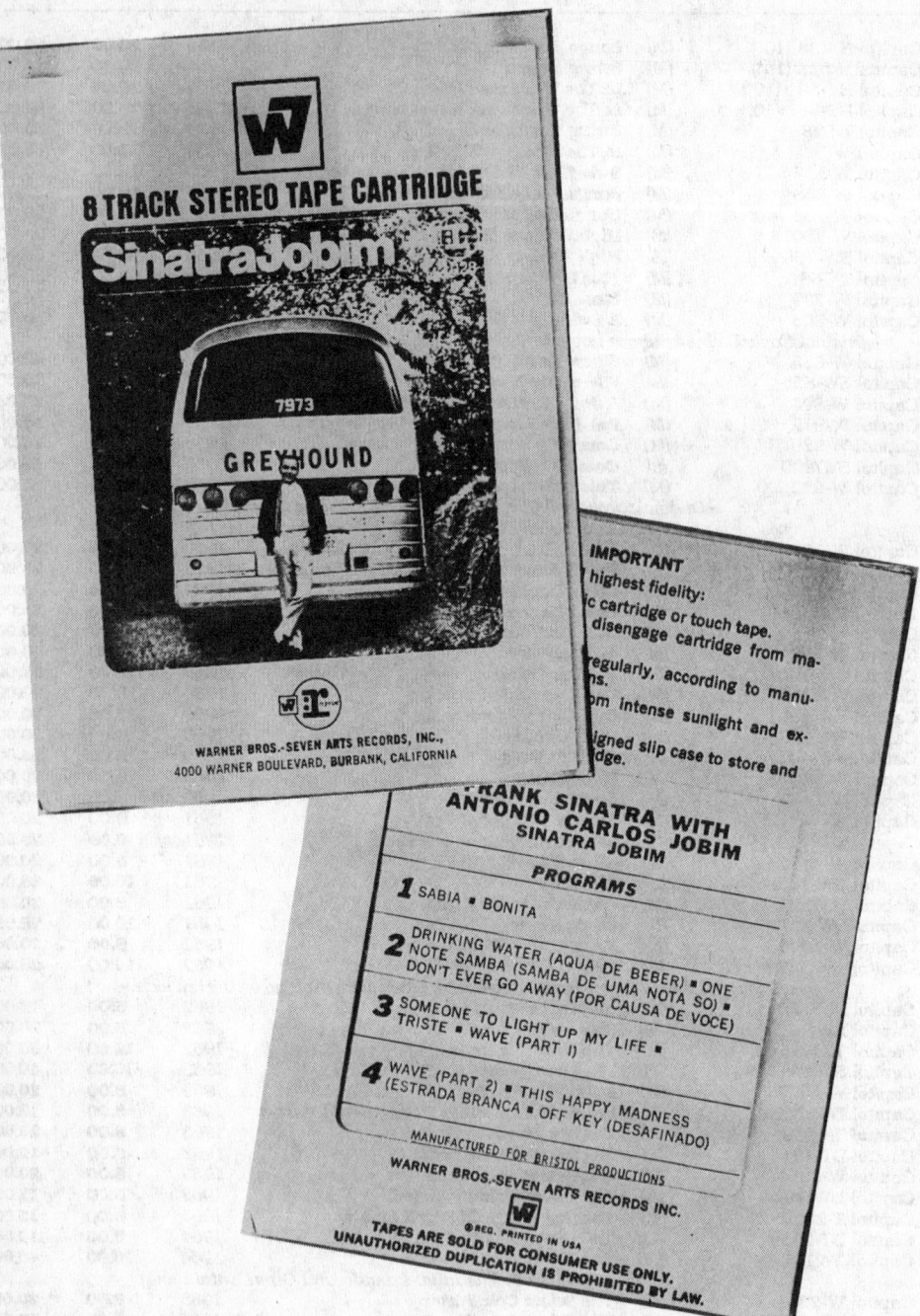

After Frank Sinatra's second collaboration with Antonio Carlos Jobim was cancelled, a collector came up with a Reprise memo instructing the destruction of all but three copies of the 3,500 eight-track tapes that had been manufactured. While this memo indicates that copies of this tape should be rare indeed, whether or not to assume the orders were carried out completely is up the the reader. Nonetheless, this is the only commercial form that this title is known to exist in, as it never got past the test pressing stage on vinyl. The owner of this copy wouldn't part with it "for at least $5,000. . ."

Label & Catalog #		Title	Year	VG+	NM
Capitol DKAO-2950	(E)	The Best Of Frank Sinatra	1969	4.00	10.00
		— Original Capitol albums above have black labels with the logo on top. —			
Capitol DWBB-254	(E)	Close-Up (2 LPs)	1969	5.00	12.00
Capitol DKAO-374	(E)	Frank Sinatra's Greatest	1969	4.00	10.00
Capitol STBB-50074	(E)	My One And Only Love (2 LPs)	1971	5.00	12.00
Capitol SMAS-94408	(E)	The Cole Porter Song Book (Record Club)	1974	6.00	15.00
Capitol C1-94777	(P)	The Capitol Years (5 LP box)	1990	30.00	75.00
Reprise F-1001	(M)	Ring-A-Ding-Ding!	1961	8.00	20.00
Reprise FS-1001	(S)	Ring-A-Ding-Ding!	1961	6.00	15.00
Reprise F-1002	(M)	Swing Along With Me	1961	8.00	20.00
Reprise FS-1002	(S)	Swing Along With Me	1961	6.00	15.00
Reprise F-1003	(M)	I Remember Tommy	1961	8.00	20.00
Reprise FS-1003	(S)	I Remember Tommy	1961	6.00	15.00
Reprise F-1004	(M)	Sinatra And Strings	1962	8.00	20.00
Reprise FS-1004	(S)	Sinatra And Strings	1962	6.00	15.00
Reprise F-1005	(M)	Sinatra And Swingin' Brass	1962	8.00	20.00
Reprise FS-1005	(S)	Sinatra And Swingin' Brass	1962	6.00	15.00
Reprise F-1007	(M)	All Alone	1962	8.00	20.00
Reprise FS-1007	(S)	All Alone	1962	6.00	15.00
Reprise R-6045	(M)	Conducts Music From Pictures	1962	8.00	20.00
Reprise R-96045	(S)	Conducts Music From Pictures	1962	6.00	15.00
Colpix CP-516	(M)	The Victors (Soundtrack)	1963	20.00	50.00
Colpix SCP-516	(S)	The Victors (Soundtrack)	1963	30.00	75.00
Reprise F-1008	(M)	Sinatra-Basie	1963	10.00	25.00
Reprise FS-1008	(S)	Sinatra-Basie	1963	6.00	15.00
Reprise F-1009	(M)	The Concert Sinatra	1963	10.00	25.00
Reprise FS-1009	(S)	The Concert Sinatra	1963	6.00	15.00
Reprise F-1010	(M)	Sinatra's Sinatra	1963	10.00	25.00
Reprise FS-1010	(S)	Sinatra's Sinatra	1963	6.00	15.00
Reprise R-6116	(M)	Greatest Hits From The Greatest Films	1964	10.00	25.00
Reprise RS-6116	(S)	Greatest Hits From The Greatest Films	1964	6.00	15.00
Reprise F-1011	(M)	Days Of Wine And Roses	1964	10.00	25.00
Reprise FS-1011	(S)	Days Of Wine And Roses	1964	6.00	15.00
Reprise F-1012	(M)	It Might As Well Be Swing	1964	10.00	25.00
Reprise FS-1012	(S)	It Might As Well Be Swing	1964	6.00	15.00
Reprise F-1013	(M)	Softly, As I Leave You	1964	10.00	25.00
Reprise FS-1013	(S)	Softly, As I Leave You	1964	6.00	15.00
Reprise R-6167	(M)	Sinatra '65	1965	10.00	25.00
Reprise RS-6167	(S)	Sinatra '65	1965	6.00	15.00
Reprise F-1014	(M)	September Of My Years	1965	10.00	25.00
Reprise FS-1014	(S)	September Of My Years	1965	6.00	15.00
Reprise F-1015	(M)	My Kind Of Broadway	1965	10.00	25.00
Reprise FS-1015	(S)	My Kind Of Broadway	1965	6.00	15.00
Reprise 2F/FS-1016	(M)	A Man And His Music Slipcase	1965	40.00	100.00
		(A limited number of stock copies were issued in a blue slipcase with an embossed silver front, which included a four page booklet. The price above is for the slipcase with the booklet; add the value of the mono or stereo albums below for a complete set price. Also, some cases had Sinatra's signed card attached to it; this is worth an additional $100.)			
Reprise 2F-1016	(M)	A Man And His Music (2 LPs)	1965	12.00	30.00
Reprise 2FS-1016	(S)	A Man And His Music (2 LPs)	1965	8.00	20.00
Reprise PRO-3004	(DJ)	A Man And His Music, Part II: Frank Sinatra CBS Television Special	1965	40.00	100.00
		(Promotional album for Budweiser's corporate use.)			
Reprise F-1017	(M)	Strangers In The Night	1966	10.00	25.00
Reprise FS-1017	(S)	Strangers In The Night	1966	6.00	15.00
Reprise F-1018	(M)	Moonlight Sinatra	1966	10.00	25.00
Reprise FS-1018	(S)	Moonlight Sinatra	1966	6.00	15.00
Reprise 2F-1019	(M)	Sinatra At The Sands (2 LPs)	1966	12.00	30.00
Reprise 2FS-1019	(S)	Sinatra At The Sands (2 LPs)	1966	8.00	20.00
Reprise F-1020	(M)	That's Life	1966	10.00	25.00
Reprise FS-1020	(S)	That's Life	1966	6.00	15.00
Reprise F-1021	(M)	Francis Albert Sinatra And Antonio Carlos Jobim	1967	10.00	25.00
Reprise FS-1021	(S)	Francis Albert Sinatra And Antonio Carlos Jobim	1967	6.00	15.00
Reprise F-1022	(M)	The World We Knew	1967	10.00	25.00
Reprise FS-1022	(S)	The World We Knew	1967	5.00	12.00

How Ms. Sinatra's new label, RCA Victor, failed to title this two-LP collection Nancy's Back *is beyond me.*

Label & Catalog #		Title	Year	VG+	NM
Reprise F-1023	(M)	The Frank Sinatra Christmas Album	1967	Unreleased	
Reprise FS-1023	(S)	The Frank Sinatra Christmas Album	1967	Unreleased	
Reprise F-1024	(M)	Francis A. And Edward K.	1968	10.00	25.00
Reprise FS-1024	(S)	Francis A. And Edward K.	1968	6.00	15.00
Reprise FS-1025	(S)	Frank Sinatra's Greatest Hits	1968	4.00	10.00
— Original Reprise albums have pink, gold & green labels.—					
Reprise FS-1026	(S)	The Sinatra Family Wish You A			
		Merry Christmas (With Nancy Sinatra)	1968	5.00	12.00
Reprise FS-1027	(S)	Cycles	1969	4.00	10.00
Reprise FS-1028	(S)	Sinatra Jobim	1969	See note below	
(Although Reprise 1028 was deleted prior to release, a handful of vinyl test pressings and commercial 8-track tapes exist. Suggested values in collectible condition are $1,000-5,000.)					
Reprise FS-1029	(S)	My Way	1969	6.00	15.00
Reprise FS-1030	(S)	A Man Alone	1970	4.00	10.00
Reprise FS-1031	(S)	Watertown	1970	6.00	15.00
Reprise FS-1032	(S)	Frank Sinatra's Greatest Hits, Volume 2	1971	4.00	10.00
Reprise FS-1033	(S)	Sinatra And Company	1971	4.00	10.00
Reprise FS-1034	(S)	Sinatra's Greatest, Volume 3	1972	4.00	10.00
Reprise FS-2155	(S)	Ol' Blue Eyes Is Back	1973	6.00	15.00
Reprise FS-42155	(Q)	Ol' Blue Eyes Is Back	1973	6.00	15.00
Reprise FS-42195	(Q)	Some Nice Things I've Missed	1974	6.00	15.00
Reprise FS-2195	(S)	Some Nice Things I've Missed	1974	4.00	10.00
Reprise FS-2207	(S)	The Main Event Live	1974	6.00	15.00
Reprise 3FS-2300	(S)	Trilogy (3 LPs)	1981	8.00	20.00
Reprise FS-2305	(S)	She Shot Me Down	1982	4.00	10.00
Q-Wesr 25145	(S)	L.A. Is My Lady	1984	4.00	10.00
Mobile Fidelity MFSL-086	(S)	Nice 'N' Easy	1980	7.00	20.00
Mobile Fidelity MFSL-135	(S)	A Jolly Christmas	1980	7.00	20.00
Mobile Fidelity SC-1	(P)	Sinatra (16 LP box)	1984	100.00	300.00

SINATRA, FRANK, & BING CROSBY

Label & Catalog #		Title	Year	VG+	NM
Reprise F-2020	(M)	America, I Hear You Singing	1964	12.00	30.00
Reprise FS-2020	(S)	America, I Hear You Singing	1964	8.00	20.00
Reprise F-2021	(M)	Robin And The Seven Hoods	1964	12.00	30.00
Reprise FS-2021	(S)	Robin And The Seven Hoods	1964	8.00	20.00
Reprise F-2022	(M)	Twelve Songs Of Christmas	1964	12.00	30.00
Reprise FS-2022	(S)	Twelve Songs Of Christmas	1964	8.00	20.00

SINATRA, NANCY
Ms. Sinatra also appears on Elvis Presley's "Speedway" soundtrack.

Label & Catalog #		Title	Year	VG+	NM
Reprise R-6202	(M)	Boots	1966	10.00	25.00
Reprise RS-6202	(S)	Boots	1966	12.00	30.00
Reprise R-6207	(M)	How Does That Grab You?	1966	6.00	15.00
Reprise RS-6207	(S)	How Does That Grab You?	1966	8.00	20.00
Reprise R-6221	(M)	Nancy In London	1966	5.00	12.00
Reprise RS-6221	(S)	Nancy In London	1966	6.00	15.00
Reprise R-6239	(M)	Sugar	1966	5.00	12.00
Reprise RS-6239	(S)	Sugar	1966	6.00	15.00
United Arts. UAL-4155	(M)	You Only Live Twice (Soundtrack)	1967	5.00	12.00
United Arts. UAS-5155	(S)	You Only Live Twice (Soundtrack)	1967	6.00	15.00
Reprise R-6251	(M)	Country, My Way	1967	4.00	10.00
Reprise RS-6251	(S)	Country, My Way	1967	5.00	12.00
Reprise R-6277	(M)	Movin' With Nancy	1968	6.00	15.00
Reprise RS-6277	(S)	Movin' With Nancy	1968	4.00	10.00
Reprise RS-6333	(S)	Nancy	1969	6.00	15.00
Reprise RS-6409	(S)	Nancy's Greatest Hits	1970	8.00	20.00
RCA Victor VPS-6078	(S)	This Is Nancy Sinatra (2 LPs)	1972	16.00	40.00
RCA Victor LSP-4774	(S)	Woman	1972	8.00	20.00
Rhino RNLP-70227	(S)	Boots: Nancy Sinatra's All-Time Hits	1986	4.00	10.00

SINATRA, NANCY, & LEE HAZLEWOOD

Label & Catalog #		Title	Year	VG+	NM
Reprise R-6273	(M)	Nancy And Lee	1968	8.00	20.00
Reprise RS-6273	(S)	Nancy And Lee	1968	6.00	15.00
RCA Victor LSP-4645	(S)	Nancy And Lee Again	1972	8.00	20.00
Rhino R1-70166	(S)	Fairy Tales & Fantasies	1989	4.00	10.00

SINATRA, NANCY, & MEL TILLIS

Label & Catalog #		Title	Year	VG+	NM
Elektra 5E-549	(S)	Mel And Nancy	1981	4.00	10.00

Label & Catalog #		Title	Year	VG+	NM

SING ALONG WITH THE BEATLES
While photos of the Fab Four are on the gatefold over, the album contains anonymous "Instrumental Background Re-creations of Their Big Hits."

Tower KAO-5000	(M)	Sing A Song With The Beatles	1965	30.00	75.00
Tower DKAO-5000	(E)	Sing A Song With The Beatles	1965	50.00	125.00

SINGLETON, MARGE

United Arts. UAL-3459	(M)	Crying Time	1966	5.00	12.00
United Arts. UAS-6459	(S)	Crying Time	1966	6.00	15.00
Ashley 3003	(M)	Country Music With Soul	1967	6.00	15.00
Ashley 3003	(S)	Country Music With Soul	1967	6.00	15.00

SIR DOUGLAS QUINTET, THE
Refer to Doug Sahm.

Tribe TR-37001	(M)	The Best Of The Sir Douglas Quintet	1966	16.00	40.00
Tribe TRS-47001	(E)	The Best Of The Sir Douglas Quintet	1966	16.00	40.00
Smash SRS-67108	(S)	Honkey Blues	1968	12.00	30.00
Smash SRS-67115	(S)	Mendocino	1969	10.00	25.00
Smash SRS-67130	(S)	Together After Five	1970	10.00	25.00
Philips PHS-600-344	(S)	1+1+1=4	1970	10.00	25.00
Philips PHS-600-353	(S)	The Return Of Doug Saldana	1971	10.00	25.00
Mercury SRM-1-655	(S)	Rough Edges	1972	12.00	30.00
Atlantic SD-7267	(S)	Texas Tornado	1973	5.00	12.00
Dot 2057	(S)	Texas Rock For Country Rollers	1976	6.00	15.00
R&M UDL-2343	(E)	The Tracker	1981	5.00	12.00

(R&M 2343 is a repackage of the Tribe material.)

SIR LANCELOT

Mercury MG-25159 (10")	(M)	Calypso	1952	16.00	40.00

SIR LORD BALTIMORE

Mercury SR-61328	(S)	Kingdom Come	1970	10.00	25.00
Mercury SRM-1-613	(S)	Sir Lord Baltimore	1971	10.00	25.00

SIZEMORE, ASHER, & LITTLE JIMMIE

Decca DL-4785	(M)	Mountain Ballads And Old Hymns	1966	5.00	12.00
Decca DL-74785	(S)	Mountain Ballads And Old Hymns	1966	6.00	15.00

SKIFFLERS, THE

Perfect P-14015	(M)	Folk Songs	1960	6.00	15.00
Perfect PS-14015	(S)	Folk Songs	1960	8.00	20.00
Harmony HL-7307	(M)	Hootenanny	1964	5.00	12.00

SKINNER, CORNELIA & OTIS

Camden CAL-190	(M)	Cornelia Skinner With Otis Skinner	195?	10.00	25.00

SKINNER, JIMMIE

Mercury MG-20352	(M)	Songs That Make The Juke Box Play	1957	30.00	75.00
Decca DL-4132	(M)	Country Singer	1961	12.00	30.00
Decca DL-74132	(S)	Country Singer	1961	16.00	40.00
Mercury MG-20700	(M)	Jimmie Skinner Sings Jimmie Rodgers	1962	12.00	30.00
Mercury MG-60700	(S)	Jimmie Skinner Sings Jimmie Rodgers	1962	16.00	40.00
Starday SLP-240	(M)	The Kentucky Colonel	1963	12.00	30.00
Wing MGW-12277	(M)	Country Blues	1964	6.00	15.00
Wing SRW-16277	(S)	Country Blues	1964	8.00	20.00

SKIP & THE CREATIONS

Justice JLP-	(S)	Mobam	196?	150.00	300.00

SKIP-JACKS, THE

RCA Victor LPM-2200	(M)	Sweet, Hot And Blue	1960	5.00	12.00
RCA Victor LSP-2200	(S)	Sweet, Hot And Blue	1960	6.00	15.00

SKULL SNAPS, THE

G.S.F. 1011	(S)	The Skull Snaps	1973	6.00	15.00

SKUNKS, THE

Teen Town TTLP-101	(S)	Gettin' Started	196?	20.00	50.00

Label & Catalog #		Title	Year	VG+	NM
SKY, PATRICK					
Vanguard VRS-9179	(M)	Patrick Sky	1965	5.00	12.00
Vanguard VSD7-9179	(S)	Patrick Sky	1965	6.00	15.00
SKYLARKS, THE					
Decca DL-8083	(M)	White Christmas (Soundtrack)	1950	24.00	60.00
SKYLINERS, THE					
Calico LP-1000	(M)	The Skyliners (Yellow & blue label)	1959	150.00	400.00
Calico LP-1000	(M)	The Skyliners (Blue label)	196?	20.00	50.00
Original Sound OS-8873	(M)	Since I Don't Have You	1963	14.00	35.00
Original Sound OSS-8873	(S)	Since I Don't Have You	1963	20.00	50.00
		("Since I Don't Have You," "One Night, One Night" and This I Swear" are rechanneled on this album.)			
Kama Sutra KSBS-2026	(S)	Once Upon A Time	1971	8.00	20.00

SLACK, FREDDIE: Refer to GOLDMINE'S PRICE GUIDE TO COLLECTIBLE JAZZ ALBUMS

SLADE [AMBROSE SLADE]					
Fontana SRF-67598	(DJ)	Ballzy (White label)	1969	20.00	50.00
Fontana SRF-67598	(S)	Ballzy	1969	24.00	60.00
		(Fontana 67598 credits Ambrose Slade.)			
Cotillion SD-9035	(S)	Play It Loud	1970	8.00	20.00
Polydor PD-5508	(S)	Slade Alive!	1972	6.00	15.00
Polydor PD-5524	(S)	Slayed	1973	6.00	15.00
Reprise MS-2173	(S)	Sladest	1973	6.00	15.00
Warner Bros. BS-2770	(S)	Stomp Your Hands, Clap Your Feet	1974	5.00	12.00
Warner Bros. BS-2865	(S)	Slade In Flame	1975	5.00	12.00
Warner Bros. BS-2936	(S)	Nobody's Fools	1976	5.00	12.00
SLEDGE, PERCY					
Atlantic 8125	(M)	When A Man Loves A Woman	1966	16.00	40.00
Atlantic SD-8125	(E)	When A Man Loves A Woman	1966	12.00	30.00
Atlantic 8132	(M)	Warm And Tender Soul	1966	16.00	40.00
Atlantic SD-8132	(E)	Warm And Tender Soul	1966	12.00	30.00
Atlantic 8146	(M)	The Percy Sledge Way	1967	12.00	30.00
Atlantic SD-8146	(S)	The Percy Sledge Way	1967	16.00	40.00
Atlantic SC-8180	(S)	Take Time To Know Her	1968	20.00	50.00
		("I Love Everything About You" is rechanneled on this album.)			
Atlantic SD-8210	(S)	The Best Of Percy Sledge	1969	16.00	40.00
		("When A Man Loves A Woman," "Warm And Tender Love," "Baby Help Me" and "It Tears Me Up" are rechanneled on this album.)			
Capricorn 0147	(S)	I'll Be Your Everything	1974	6.00	15.00
SLEEPY HOLLOW					
Family Prod. 2708	(S)	Sleepy Hollow	1973	6.00	15.00
SLICK, GRACE					
Refer to The Great Society; The Jefferson Airplane; The Jefferson Starship; Paul Kantner.					
Grunt	(DJ)	Manhole (Banded for air-play)	1973	6.00	15.00
RCA Victor DJL1-3601	(DJ)	Through The Hoop With Grace Slick	1980	6.00	15.00
RCA Victor DJL1-3922	(DJ)	The Grace Slick Interview	1981	6.00	15.00
RCA Victor DJL1-3923	(DJ)	RCA Special Radio Series (Interview)	1981	6.00	15.00
SLIM HARPO					
Excello LP-8003	(M)	Raining In My Heart	1961	60.00	150.00
		(First pressings have a red & white drawing cover.)			
Excello LPS-8003	(M)	Raining In My Heart	1967	12.00	30.00
		(Later pressing covers read "Electronic Stereo," although the record plays mono.)			
Excello LP-8005	(M)	Baby, Scratch My Back	1966	30.00	75.00
		(First pressings have a green & white drawing cover.)			
Excello LPS-8005	(M)	Baby, Scratch My Back	1967	12.00	30.00
		(Later pressing covers read "Electronic Stereo," although the record plays mono.)			
Excello LPS-8008	(M)	Tip On In	1968	12.00	30.00
Excello LPS-8010	(M)	The Best Of Slim Harpo	1969	12.00	30.00
Excello LPS-8013	(M)	Slim Harpo Knew The Blues	1970	12.00	30.00

Label & Catalog #		Title	Year	VG+	NM
SLIM JIM					
Soma 1225	(M)	**Slim Jim Sings** (Black label)	1958	20.00	50.00
SLOAN, P.F.					
Refer to The Fantastic Baggys; The Grass Roots.					
Dunhill D-50004	(M)	**Songs Of Our Times**	1965	10.00	25.00
Dunhill DS-50004	(S)	**Songs Of Our Times**	1965	12.00	30.00
Dunhill D-50007	(S)	**Twelve More Times**	1966	10.00	25.00
Dunhill DS-50007	(S)	**Twelve More Times**	1966	12.00	30.00
Atco SD-33-268	(S)	**Measure Of Pleasure**	1968	12.00	30.00
Mums KZ-31260	(S)	**Raised On Records**	1972	10.00	25.00

SLOANE, CAROL: *Refer to* GOLDMINE'S PRICE GUIDE TO COLLECTIBLE JAZZ ALBUMS

SLY & THE FAMILY STONE [SLY]

Label & Catalog #		Title	Year	VG+	NM
Epic LN-24324	(M)	**A Whole New Thing**	1967	12.00	30.00
Epic BN-26324	(S)	**A Whole New Thing**	1967	10.00	25.00
Epic BN-26371	(S)	**Dance To The Music**	1968	8.00	20.00
		("*Dance To The Music*" is a repackage of "*A Whole New Thing.*")			
Epic BN-26397	(S)	**Life**	1968	8.00	20.00
Epic BN-26456	(S)	**Stand!**	1969	8.00	20.00
Epic KE-30325	(P)	**Sly & The Family Stone's Greatest Hits**	1970	8.00	20.00
		("*Everybody Is A Star,*" "*Hot Fun In The Summertime,*" and "*Thank You*" are rechanneled on this album.)			
Epic KE-30986	(S)	**There's A Riot Goin' On**	1971	6.00	15.00
		— Original Epic albums above have yellow labels.—			
Epic EQ-30325	(Q)	**Sly & The Family Stone's Greatest Hits**	1973	30.00	75.00
		("*Everybody Is A Star,*" "*Hot Fun In The Summertime,*" and "*Thank You*" are remixed from the multi-tracks on this album.)			
Epic KE-32134	(S)	**Fresh**	1973	6.00	15.00
Epic PE-32930	(S)	**Small Talk**	1974	6.00	15.00
Epic PEQ-32930	(Q)	**Small Talk**	1974	12.00	30.00
Epic PE-33835	(S)	**High On You**	1975	6.00	15.00
Epic PEQ-33835	(Q)	**High On You**	1975	12.00	30.00
Epic PE-34348	(S)	**Heard You Missed Me**	1975	4.00	10.00
Epic AS-264	(DJ)	**Everything You Always Wanted To Hear**	1976	10.00	25.00

SMALL, MILLIE

Label & Catalog #		Title	Year	VG+	NM
Smash MGS-27055	(M)	**My Boy Lollipop**	1964	20.00	50.00
Smash SRS-67055	(E)	**My Boy Lollipop**	1964	16.00	40.00

SMALL FACES, THE [THE FACES]
Features Steve Marriott, Ronnie Lane, Kenny Jones and Ian McLagen. The Warners and Mercury albums include Rod Stewart and Ron Wood.

Label & Catalog #		Title	Year	VG+	NM
Immediate Z12-52-002	(S)	**There Are But Four Small Faces**	1968	20.00	50.00
		(Original covers are full color; counterfeits are green & white.)			
Immediate Z12-52-008	(S)	**Ogden's Nut Gone Flake** (Round cover)	1968	20.00	50.00
Immediate 4225	(S)	**Ogden's Nut Gone Flake** (Regular cover)	1973	8.00	20.00
Warner Bros. PRO	(DJ)	**First Step Box**	1970	*See note below*	
		(Promotional box contains a copy of the album, a badge, a sheet of cutouts with a pair of scissors, and a complete press kit with photos, etc. Rare as a plynth with suggested values in collectible condition of $200-400.)			
Warner Bros. WS-1851	(S)	**First Step**	1970	8.00	20.00
Warner Bros. WS-1892	(S)	**Long Player**	1971	5.00	12.00
Warner Bros. BS-2574	(S)	**A Nod Is As Good As A Wink**	1971	5.00	12.00
Warner Bros. BS-2665	(S)	**Ooh La La**	1973	5.00	12.00
Pride 0001	(E)	**Early Faces**	1972	5.00	12.00
Pride 0014	(P)	**The History Of The Small Faces**	1973	5.00	12.00
MGM M3F-4955	(S)	**Archetypes**	1974	6.00	15.00
Sire SASH 3709	(S)	**The Immediate Story** (2 LPs)	197?	6.00	15.00

SMART SET, THE

Label & Catalog #		Title	Year	VG+	NM
Warner Bros. W-1203	(M)	**A New Experience In Vocal Styles**	1958	8.00	20.00

Label & Catalog #		Title	Year	VG+	NM

SMECK, ROY
Smeck also recorded as Prince Kailua.

"X" LPX-3012 (10")	(M)	South Of The Border	195?	40.00	100.00
"X" LPA-3016 (10")	(M)	Christmas In Hawaii	195?	40.00	100.00
Coral CRL-56013 (10")	(M)	Drifting And Dreaming	195?	20.00	50.00
Decca DL-5458 (10")	(M)	Memory Lane	1953	20.00	50.00
Decca DL-5473 (10")	(M)	Songs Of The Range	1953	20.00	50.00
Decca DL-8674	(M)	Memories Of You	1958	12.00	30.00
ABC-Paramount 119	(M)	South Seas Serenade	1956	8.00	20.00
ABC-Paramount 174	(M)	Melodies With Memories	1957	8.00	20.00
ABC-Paramount 234	(M)	Hi Fi Paradise	1958	8.00	20.00
ABC-Paramount 330	(M)	The Haunting Hawaiian Guitar	1960	6.00	15.00
ABC-Paramount S-330	(S)	The Haunting Hawaiian Guitar	1960	8.00	20.00
ABC-Paramount-379	(M)	His Singing Guitar & Paradise Serenaders	1961	6.00	15.00
ABC-Paramount S-379	(S)	His Singing Guitar & Paradise Serenaders	1961	8.00	20.00
ABC-Paramount 412	(M)	Stringing Along	1962	6.00	15.00
ABC-Paramount S-412	(S)	Stringing Along	1962	8.00	20.00
ABC-Paramount 452	(M)	The Many Guitar Moods Of Roy Smeck	1963	6.00	15.00
ABC-Paramount S-452	(S)	The Many Guitar Moods Of Roy Smeck	1963	8.00	20.00
Kapp KL-1491	(M)	Hawaiian Guitar Hits	1966	5.00	12.00
Kapp KS-3491	(M)	Hawaiian Guitar Hits	1966	6.00	15.00

SMILE

Pickwick SPC-3288	(S)	Smile	1973	12.00	30.00

SMITH
Smith feature Gayle McCormack

Dunhill DS-50056	(S)	A Group Called Smith	1969	6.00	15.00
Dunhill DS-50081	(S)	Minus-Plus	1969	6.00	15.00

SMITH, AL

Bluesville BVLP-1001	(M)	Hear My Blues	1960	20.00	50.00
Bluesville BVLP-1013	(M)	Midnight Special	1960	16.00	40.00
Bluesville BVLP-1069	(M)	Blues Shout	1963	16.00	40.00
		(Bluesville 1069 is a reissue of 1001.)			

SMITH, "FIDDLIN'" ARTHUR

Starday SLP-202	(M)	Rare Old Time Fiddle Tunes	1962	16.00	40.00

SMITH, ARTHUR "GUITAR BOOGIE" (& HIS CRACKERJACKS)

MGM E-236 (10")	(M)	Foolish Questions	1954	40.00	100.00
MGM E-533 (10")	(M)	Fingers On Fire	1955	40.00	100.00
MGM E-3301	(M)	Specials	1955	30.00	75.00
MGM E-3525	(M)	Fingers On Fire	1957	30.00	75.00
		— Original MGM albums above have yellow labels.—			
Starday SLP-173	(M)	Mister Guitar	1962	12.00	30.00
Starday SLP-186	(M)	Arthur Smith And The Crossroads Quartet	1962	12.00	30.00
Starday SLP-216	(M)	Arthur Guitar Boogie Smith Goes To Town	1963	12.00	30.00
Starday SLP-241	(M)	In Person	1963	12.00	30.00
Starday SLP-266	(M)	Down Home	1964	12.00	30.00
Starday SLP-415	(M)	The Guitars Of Arthur Smith	1968	6.00	15.00
ABC Paramount ABC-441	(M)	Arthur Guitar Smith And Voices	1963	6.00	15.00
ABC Paramount ABCS-441	(S)	Arthur Guitar Smith And Voices	1963	8.00	20.00
Folkways FA-2379	(M)	Old Timers Of The Grand Ole Opry	1964	6.00	15.00
Hamilton HLP-12134	(M)	The Arthur Smith Show	1964	5.00	12.00
Hamilton HLPS-12134	(S)	The Arthur Smith Show	1964	6.00	15.00
Dot DLP-3600	(M)	Original Guitar Boogie	1964	8.00	20.00
Dot DLP-25600	(S)	Original Guitar Boogie	1964	10.00	25.00
Dot DLP-3636	(M)	Great Country And Western Hits	1965	5.00	12.00
Dot DLP-25636	(S)	Great Country And Western Hits	1965	6.00	15.00
Dot DLP-3642	(M)	Singing On The Mountain	1965	5.00	12.00
Dot DLP-25642	(S)	Singing On The Mountain	1965	6.00	15.00
Dot DLP-3769	(M)	A Tribute To Jim Reeves	1966	5.00	12.00
Dot DLP-25769	(S)	A Tribute To Jim Reeves	1966	6.00	15.00

SMITH, BOB

Kent KST-551	(S)	The Visit *(2 LPs with poster)*	1969	30.00	75.00
Kent KST-551	(S)	The Visit *(2 LPs without poster)*	1969	20.00	50.00

Label & Catalog #		Title	Year	VG+	NM

SMITH, BUSTER: *Refer to* GOLDMINE'S PRICE GUIDE TO COLLECTIBLE JAZZ ALBUMS

SMITH, CARL

Label & Catalog #		Title	Year	VG+	NM
Columbia HL-9023 (10")	(M)	Sentimental Songs	195?	30.00	75.00
Columbia HL-9026 (10")	(M)	Softly And Tenderly	195?	30.00	75.00
Columbia HL-2579 (10")	(M)	Carl Smith	1956	30.00	75.00
Columbia CL-959	(M)	Sunday Down South	1957	20.00	50.00
Columbia CL-1022	(M)	Smith's The Name	1957	20.00	50.00
Columbia CL-1172	(M)	Let's Live A Little	1958	16.00	40.00
Columbia CL-1532	(M)	The Carl Smith Touch	1960	8.00	20.00
Columbia CS-8332	(S)	The Carl Smith Touch	1960	10.00	25.00
Columbia CL-1740	(M)	Easy To Please	1962	8.00	20.00
Columbia CS-8540	(S)	Easy To Please	1962	10.00	25.00

— Original Columbia albums above have three white-on-black "eye" logos on each side of the spindle hole.—

Label & Catalog #		Title	Year	VG+	NM
Columbia CL-1937	(M)	Carl Smith's Greatest Hits	1962	8.00	20.00
Columbia CS-8737	(P)	Carl Smith's Greatest Hits	1962	8.00	20.00
Columbia CL-2091	(M)	Tall, Tall Gentleman	1963	6.00	15.00
Columbia CS-8891	(S)	Tall, Tall Gentleman	1963	8.00	20.00
Columbia CL-2173	(M)	There Stands The Glass	1964	6.00	15.00
Columbia CS-8973	(S)	There Stands The Glass	1964	8.00	20.00
Columbia CL-2293	(M)	I Want To Live And Love	1965	6.00	15.00
Columbia CS-9093	(S)	I Want To Live And Love	1965	8.00	20.00
Columbia CL-2358	(M)	Kisses Don't Lie	1965	6.00	15.00
Columbia CS-9158	(S)	Kisses Don't Lie	1965	8.00	20.00
Columbia CL-2501	(M)	Man With A Plan	1966	6.00	15.00
Columbia CS-9301	(S)	Man With A Plan	1966	8.00	20.00
Columbia CL-2610	(M)	The Country Gentleman	1967	8.00	20.00
Columbia CS-9410	(S)	The Country Gentleman	1967	8.00	20.00
Columbia CL-2687	(M)	The Country Gentleman Sings	1967	8.00	20.00
Columbia CS-9487	(S)	The Country Gentleman Sings	1967	8.00	20.00
Columbia CL-2822	(M)	Deep Water	1968	8.00	20.00
Columbia CS-9622	(S)	Deep Water	1968	6.00	15.00
Columbia CS-9688	(S)	Country On My Mind	1968	6.00	15.00
Columbia CS-9786	(S)	Faded Love And Winter Roses	1969	6.00	15.00
Columbia CS-9807	(S)	Carl Smith's Greatest Hits, Volume 2	1969	5.00	12.00
Columbia CS-9870	(S)	A Tribute To Roy Acuff	1969	5.00	12.00
Columbia CS-9898	(S)	I Love You Because	1970	5.00	12.00

— Original Columbia albums above have "360 Sound" on the bottom of the label.—

SMITH, CARL / LEFTY FRIZZELL / MARTY ROBBINS

Label & Catalog #		Title	Year	VG+	NM
Columbia CL-2544 (10")	(M)	Carl, Lefty And Marty	1956	80.00	200.00

SMITH, CONNIE

Label & Catalog #		Title	Year	VG+	NM
RCA Victor LPM-3341	(M)	The Other Side Of Connie Smith	1965	8.00	20.00
RCA Victor LSP-3341	(S)	The Other Side Of Connie Smith	1965	10.00	25.00
RCA Victor LPM-3444	(M)	Cute 'N Country	1965	8.00	20.00
RCA Victor LSP-3444	(S)	Cute 'N Country	1965	10.00	25.00
RCA Victor LPM-3520	(M)	Miss Smith Goes To Nashville	1966	8.00	20.00
RCA Victor LSP-3520	(S)	Miss Smith Goes To Nashville	1966	10.00	25.00
RCA Victor LPM-3589	(M)	Great Sacred Songs	1966	6.00	15.00
RCA Victor LSP-3589	(S)	Great Sacred Songs	1966	8.00	20.00
RCA Victor LPM-3628	(M)	Born To Sing	1966	6.00	15.00
RCA Victor LSP-3628	(S)	Born To Sing	1966	8.00	20.00
RCA Victor LPM-3768	(M)	Connie Smith Sings Bill Anderson	1967	6.00	15.00
RCA Victor LSP-3768	(S)	Connie Smith Sings Bill Anderson	1967	8.00	20.00
RCA Victor LPM-3848	(M)	The Best Of Connie Smith	1967	6.00	15.00
RCA Victor LSP-3848	(S)	The Best Of Connie Smith	1967	8.00	20.00
RCA Victor LPM-3889	(M)	Soul Of Country Music	1968	20.00	50.00
RCA Victor LSP-3889	(S)	Soul Of Country Music	1968	8.00	20.00
RCA Victor LSP-4002	(S)	I Love Charley Brown	1968	8.00	20.00

— Original RCA albums above have black labels with Nipper on top.—

SMITH, HUEY "PIANO"

Label & Catalog #		Title	Year	VG+	NM
Ace LP-1004	(M)	Having A Good Time	1959	100.00	300.00
Ace LP-1015	(M)	For Dancing	1961	80.00	200.00
Ace LP-1027	(M)	Twas The Night Before Christmas	1962	80.00	200.00
Ace LP-2021	(M)	Rock 'N' Roll Revival	1971	8.00	20.00

Label & Catalog #		Title	Year	VG+	NM

SMITH, HURICANE

Capitol ST-11139	(S)	Hurricane Smith	1972	6.00	15.00

SMITH, JENNIE

RCA Victor LPM-1523	(M)	Jennie	1957	14.00	35.00
Columbia CL-1242	(M)	Love Among The Young	1958	10.00	25.00

SMITH, KEELY
Keely Smith also recorded with Louis Prima. Refer to The Reprise Repertory Theatre.

Capitol W-914	(M)	I Wish You Love (Turquoise label)	1957	16.00	40.00
Capitol T-1073	(M)	Politely	1958	12.00	30.00
Capitol ST-1073	(S)	Politely	1958	16.00	40.00
Capitol T-1145	(M)	Swingin' Pretty	1959	12.00	30.00
Capitol ST-1145	(S)	Swingin' Pretty	1959	16.00	40.00
— Original Capitol albums above have black labels with the logo on the left side.—					
Dot DLP-3241	(M)	Be My Love	1961	10.00	25.00
Dot DLP-25241	(S)	Be My Love	1961	12.00	30.00
Dot DLP-3387	(M)	Dearly Beloved	1961	10.00	25.00
Dot DLP-25387	(S)	Dearly Beloved	1961	12.00	30.00
Dot DLP-3345	(M)	A Keely Christmas	1961	10.00	25.00
Dot DLP-25345	(S)	A Keely Christmas	1961	12.00	30.00
Dot DLP-3415	(M)	Because You're Mine	1962	10.00	25.00
Dot DLP-25415	(S)	Because You're Mine	1962	12.00	30.00
Dot DLP-3423	(M)	Twist With Keely Smith	1962	10.00	25.00
Dot DLP-25423	(S)	Twist With Keely Smith	1962	12.00	30.00
Reprise R-6086	(M)	Little Girl Blue, Little Girl New	1963	10.00	25.00
Reprise R-96086	(S)	Little Girl Blue, Little Girl New	1963	12.00	30.00
Reprise R-6142	(M)	The Lennon-McCartney Songbook	1964	10.00	25.00
Reprise R-96142	(S)	The Lennon-McCartney Songbook	1964	12.00	30.00

SMITH, LaVERGNE: *Refer to* GOLDMINE'S PRICE GUIDE TO COLLECTIBLE JAZZ ALBUMS

SMITH, MICHAEL

Storyville 4014	(S)	Reflection On Progress	1972	4.00	10.00

SMITH, OSBORNE: *Refer to* GOLDMINE'S PRICE GUIDE TO COLLECTIBLE JAZZ ALBUMS

SMITH, RAY

Judd JLPA-701	(M)	Travelin' With Ray	1960	300.00	500.00
"T" 56062	(M)	The Best Of Ray Smith	196?	40.00	100.00
		("T" 56062 is a reissue of Judd 701.)			
Columbia CL-1937	(M)	Ray Smith's Greatest Hits	1963	10.00	25.00
		(The label reads "Guaranteed High Fidelity" on the bottom.)			
Columbia CS-8737	(S)	Ray Smith's Greatest Hits	1963	12.00	30.00
		(The label reads "360 Sound Stereo" in black on the bottom.)			
Wix 1000	(S)	I'm Gonna Rock Some More	197?	4.00	10.00

SMITH, RAY / PAT CUPP

Crown CLP-5364	(M)	Ray Smith And Pat Cupp	1963	12.00	30.00
Crown CST-364	(E)	Ray Smith And Pat Cupp	1963	5.00	12.00

SMITH, ROBERT CURTIS

Bluesville BVLP-1064	(M)	Clarksdale Blues	1963	16.00	40.00

SMITH, ROGER

Warner Bros. W-1305	(M)	Beach Romance	1959	10.00	25.00
Warner Bros. WS-1305	(S)	Beach Romance	1959	14.00	35.00

SMITH, TAB

United LP-001 (10")	(M)	Music Styled By Tab Smith	1955	50.00	125.00
United LP-003 (10")	(M)	Red, Hot And Cool Blues	1955	50.00	125.00

SMITH, WARREN

Liberty LRP-3199	(M)	The First Country Collection	1961	20.00	50.00
Liberty LST-7199	(S)	The First Country Collection	1961	30.00	75.00

SMITH, WHISPERING

Excello 8020	(S)	Whispering Smith	197?	6.00	15.00

Label & Catalog #		Title	Year	VG+	NM
SMOKE, THE					
Sidewalk ST-5912	(S)	The Smoke	1968	16.00	40.00
Tower ST-5912	(S)	The Smoke	1968	16.00	40.00
SMOKE, THE					
Uni 73052	(S)	The Smoke	1969	8.00	20.00
Uni 73065	(S)	At Georges Coffee Shop	1970	8.00	20.00
SMOKESTACK LIGHTNIN'					
Bell 6026	(S)	Off The Wall	1969	6.00	15.00
SMOKEY BABE					
Bluesville BVLP-1063	(M)	Hottest Brand Going	1963	16.00	40.00
Folk-Lyric FL-108	(M)	Smokey Babe	196?	6.00	15.00
SMOTHERS, DICK					
Mercury MG-21134	(M)	Saturday Night At The World	1966	4.00	10.00
Mercury SR-61134	(S)	Saturday Night At The World	1966	5.00	12.00
SMOTHERS, SMOKEY					
King 779	(M)	The Backporch Blues	1962	250.00	750.00
SMOTHERS BROTHERS, THE					
Dick and Tom Smothers.					
Mercury MG-20611	(M)	Songs And Comedy	1961	6.00	15.00
Mercury SR-60611	(S)	Songs And Comedy	1961	8.00	20.00
Mercury MG-20675	(M)	The Two Sides Of The Smothers Brothers	1962	6.00	15.00
Mercury SR-60675	(S)	The Two Sides Of The Smothers Brothers	1962	8.00	20.00
Mercury MG-20777	(M)	Think Ethnic!	1963	6.00	15.00
Mercury SR-60777	(S)	Think Ethnic!	1963	8.00	20.00
Mercury MG-20862	(M)	Curb Your Tongue, Knave!	1963	6.00	15.00
Mercury SR-60862	(S)	Curb Your Tongue, Knave!	1963	8.00	20.00
Mercury MG-20904	(M)	It Must Have Been Something I Said	1964	6.00	15.00
Mercury SR-60904	(S)	It Must Have Been Something I Said	1964	8.00	20.00
Mercury MG-20948	(M)	Tour De Farce: American History	1964	6.00	15.00
Mercury SR-60948	(S)	Tour De Farce: American History	1964	8.00	20.00
Mercury MG-20989	(M)	Aesop's Fables	1965	6.00	15.00
Mercury SR-60989	(S)	Aesop's Fables	1965	8.00	20.00
Mercury MG-21051	(M)	Mom Always Liked You Best!	1965	6.00	15.00
Mercury SR-61051	(S)	Mom Always Liked You Best!	1965	8.00	20.00
Mercury MG-21064	(M)	The Smothers Brothers Play It Straight	1965	6.00	15.00
Mercury SR-61064	(S)	The Smothers Brothers Play It Straight	1965	8.00	20.00
Mercury MG-21089	(M)	Golden Hits, Volume 2	1966	6.00	15.00
Mercury SR-61089	(S)	Golden Hits, Volume 2	1966	8.00	20.00
SNAKEFINGER					
Ralph SN-7909	(S)	Chewing Hides The Sound	1980	6.00	15.00
Ralph SN-8053	(S)	Green Pastures	1981	6.00	15.00
Ralph SN-8203	(S)	Manual Of Errors	1982	6.00	15.00
SNAKEGRINDER					
Alligator Shoes 40004	(S)	Snakegrinder & The Shredded Field Mice	1977	50.00	125.00
SNELL, TONY					
ESP-Disk' 3004	(S)	Medieval And Latter Day Lays	197?	6.00	15.00
SNOW, HANK					
RCA Victor LPT-3026 (10")	(M)	Country Classics	1952	60.00	150.00
RCA Victor LPT-3070 (10")	(M)	Hank Snow Sings	1952	60.00	150.00
RCA Victor LPT-3131 (10")	(M)	Hank Snow Salutes Jimmie Rodgers	1953	60.00	150.00
RCA Victor LPT-3267 (10")	(M)	Hank Snow's Country Guitar	1954	60.00	150.00
RCA Victor LPM-1113	(M)	Just Keep A-Movin'	1955	30.00	75.00
RCA Victor LPM-1156	(M)	Old Doc Brown & Other Narrations	1955	30.00	75.00
RCA Victor LPM-1233	(M)	Country Classics	1955	30.00	75.00
RCA Victor LPM-1419	(M)	Country And Western Jamboree	1957	30.00	75.00
RCA Victor LPM-1435	(M)	Hank Snow's Country Guitar	1957	30.00	75.00
RCA Victor LPM-1638	(M)	Hank Snow Sings Sacred Songs	1958	20.00	50.00
RCA Victor LPM-1861	(M)	When Tragedy Struck	1958	30.00	75.00
School Of Music 1149	(M)	The Guitar *(With booklet)*	1958	100.00	250.00

Label & Catalog #		Title	Year	VG+	NM
RCA Victor LPM-2043	(M)	Hank Snow Sings Jimmie Rodgers Songs	1959	20.00	50.00
RCA Victor LSP-2043	(S)	Hank Snow Sings Jimmie Rodgers Songs	1959	30.00	75.00
RCA Victor LSP-2285	(M)	Souvenirs	1961	12.00	30.00
RCA Victor LSP-2285	(S)	Souvenirs	1961	16.00	40.00
RCA Victor LPM-2458	(M)	Big Country Hits	1961	12.00	30.00
RCA Victor LSP-2458	(S)	Big Country Hits	1961	16.00	40.00
RCA Victor LPM-2675	(M)	I've Been Everywhere	1963	10.00	25.00
RCA Victor LSP-2675	(S)	I've Been Everywhere	1963	14.00	35.00
RCA Victor LPM-2705	(M)	Railroad Man	1963	10.00	25.00
RCA Victor LSP-2705	(S)	Railroad Man	1963	14.00	35.00

— Original RCA mono albums above have "black labels with Long Play" on the bottom; stereo albums have black labels with "Living Stereo" on the bottom.—

RCA Victor LPM-2812	(M)	More Hank Snow Souvenirs	1964	10.00	25.00
RCA Victor LSP-2812	(S)	More Hank Snow Souvenirs	1964	12.00	30.00
RCA Victor LPM-2901	(M)	Songs Of Tragedy	1964	10.00	25.00
RCA Victor LSP-2901	(S)	Songs Of Tragedy	1964	12.00	30.00
RCA Victor LPM-3317	(M)	Your Favorite Country Hits	1965	10.00	25.00
RCA Victor LSP-3317	(S)	Your Favorite Country Hits	1965	12.00	30.00
RCA Victor LPM-3378	(M)	Gloryland March	1965	12.00	30.00
RCA Victor LSP-3378	(S)	Gloryland March	1965	16.00	40.00
RCA Victor LPM-3471	(M)	Heartbreak Trail	1965	10.00	25.00
RCA Victor LSP-3471	(S)	Heartbreak Trail	1965	12.00	30.00
RCA Victor LPM-3478	(M)	The Best Of Hank Snow	1966	8.00	20.00
RCA Victor LSP-3478	(S)	The Best Of Hank Snow	1966	10.00	25.00
RCA Victor LPM-3548	(M)	The Guitar Stylings Of Hank Snow	1966	12.00	30.00
RCA Victor LSP-3548	(S)	The Guitar Stylings Of Hank Snow	1966	16.00	40.00
RCA Victor LPM-3595	(M)	Gospel Train	1966	12.00	30.00
RCA Victor LSP-3595	(S)	Gospel Train	1966	16.00	40.00
RCA Victor LPM-6014	(M)	This Is My Story (2 LPs)	1966	16.00	40.00
RCA Victor LSP-6014	(S)	This Is My Story (2 LPs)	1966	20.00	50.00
RCA Victor LPM-3737	(M)	Snow In Hawaii	1967	16.00	40.00
RCA Victor LSP-3737	(S)	Snow In Hawaii	1967	12.00	30.00
RCA Victor LPM-3826	(M)	Christmas With Hank Snow	1967	16.00	40.00
RCA Victor LSP-3826	(S)	Christmas With Hank Snow	1967	12.00	30.00
RCA Victor LPM-3857	(M)	Spanish Fireball	1967	16.00	40.00
RCA Victor LSP-3857	(S)	Spanish Fireball	1967	12.00	30.00
RCA Victor LPM-3965	(M)	Hits, Hits And More Hits	1968	40.00	100.00
RCA Victor LSP-3965	(S)	Hits, Hits And More Hits	1968	8.00	20.00
RCA Victor LSP-4032	(S)	Tales Of The Yukon	1968	12.00	30.00

— Original RCA albums above have black labels.—

RCA Victor LSP-4122	(S)	Snow In All Seasons	1969	10.00	25.00
RCA Victor LSP-4166	(S)	Hits Covered By Snow	1969	8.00	20.00
RCA Victor LSP-4306	(S)	In Memory Of Jimmie Rodgers	1970	8.00	20.00
RCA Victor LSP-4379	(S)	Cure For The Blues	1970	8.00	20.00

— Original RCA albums above have orange labels on non-flexible vinyl.—

RCA Victor LSP-4501	(S)	Tracks And Trains	1971	6.00	15.00
RCA Victor LSP-4601	(S)	Award Winners	1971	6.00	15.00
RCA Victor LSP-4708	(S)	The Jimmie Rodgers Story	1972	6.00	15.00
RCA Victor LSP-4798	(S)	The Best Of Hank Snow, Volume 2	1972	6.00	15.00

— Original RCA albums above have orange labels.—

Camden CAL-514	(M)	The Singing Stranger	1959	8.00	20.00
Camden CAL-680	(M)	The Southern Cannonball	1961	8.00	20.00
Camden CAL-722	(M)	The One And Only Hank Snow	1962	8.00	20.00
Camden CAL-782	(M)	The Last Ride	1963	8.00	20.00

— Original Camden albums above have purple & blue labels.—

Camden CAL-836	(M)	Old And Great Songs By Hank Snow	1964	5.00	12.00
Camden CAS-836	(S)	Old And Great Songs By Hank Snow	1964	6.00	15.00
Camden CAL-910	(M)	The Highest Bidder & Other Favorites	1965	5.00	12.00
Camden CAS-910	(S)	The Highest Bidder & Other Favorites	1965	6.00	15.00
Camden CAL-964	(M)	Travelin' Blues	1966	5.00	12.00
Camden CAS-964	(S)	Travelin' Blues	1966	6.00	15.00
Camden CAL-2160	(M)	My Early Country Favorites	1967	5.00	12.00
Camden CAS-2160	(S)	My Early Country Favorites	1967	6.00	15.00
Camden CAS-2257	(S)	My Nova Scotia Home	1968	6.00	15.00

— Original Camden albums above have light & dark blue abels.—

RCA Victor RDA-216	(P)	I'm Movin' On (6 LP box with booklet)	197?	40.00	100.00
RCA Victor DPL2-0134	(P)	The Living Legend (2 LPs)	1978	40.00	100.00

(RCA albums above have orange label.)

Label & Catalog #		Title	Year	VG+	NM

SNOW, HANK, & CHET ATKINS

RCA Victor LPM-2952	(M)	**Reminiscing**	1964	10.00	25.00
RCA Victor LSP-2952	(S)	**Reminiscing**	1964	12.00	30.00
		— Original RCA albums above have black labels.—			
RCA Victor LSP-4254	(S)	**By Special Request**	1970	8.00	20.00
		— Original RCA albums above have orange labels on non-flexible vinyl.—			

SNOW, HANK, & ANITA CARTER

RCA Victor LPM-2580	(M)	**Together Again**	1962	12.00	30.00
RCA Victor LSP-2580	(S)	**Together Again**	1962	16.00	40.00
		— Original RCA albums above have black labels.—			

SNOW, HANK / HANK LOCKLIN / PORTER WAGONER

| RCA Victor LPM-2723 | (M) | **Three Country Gentlemen** | 1963 | 6.00 | 15.00 |
| RCA Victor LSP-2723 | (S) | **Three Country Gentlemen** | 1963 | 8.00 | 20.00 |

SOFT MACHINE

Probe 4500	(S)	**The Soft Machine**	1968	14.00	35.00
		(The cover is a "machine" with movable parts.)			
Probe 4500	(S)	**The Soft Machine** (Standard cover)	1969	8.00	20.00
Probe 4505	(S)	**Soft Machine, Volume 2**	1969	8.00	20.00
Columbia G-30339	(S)	**Soft Machine Third** (2 LPs)	1970	6.00	15.00
Columbia KC-30754	(S)	**Soft Machine Fourth**	1971	4.00	10.00
Columbia KC-31604	(S)	**Soft Machine 5**	1972	4.00	10.00
Columbia KG-32260	(S)	**Soft Machine Six**	1973	4.00	10.00
Columbia KC-32716	(S)	**Soft Machine Seven**	1973	4.00	10.00
Command 964	(S)	**Soft Machine** (2 LPs)	1973	6.00	15.00

SOMMER, ELKE

| MGM E-4321 | (M) | **Love In Any Language** | 1966 | 6.00 | 15.00 |
| MGM SE-4321 | (S) | **Love In Any Language** | 1966 | 8.00 | 20.00 |

SOMMERS, JOANIE
Refer to Rick Nelson.

Warner Bros. W-1346	(M)	**Positively The Most**	1960	16.00	40.00
Warner Bros. WS-1346	(S)	**Positively The Most**	1960	20.00	50.00
Warner Bros. B-1348	(M)	**Behind Closed Doors**			
		At A Recording Session	1960	40.00	100.00
		(Boxed set includes one album and a booklet.)			
Warner Bros. W-1412	(M)	**Joanie Sommers**	1961	12.00	30.00
Warner Bros. WS-1412	(S)	**Joanie Sommers**	1961	16.00	40.00
Warner Bros. W-1436	(M)	**For Those Who Think Young**	1962	12.00	30.00
Warner Bros. WS-1436	(S)	**For Those Who Think Young**	1962	16.00	40.00
Warner Bros. W-1470	(M)	**Johnny Get Angry**	1962	16.00	40.00
Warner Bros. WS-1470	(S)	**Johnny Get Angry**	1962	20.00	50.00
Warner Bros. W-1474	(M)	**Let's Talk About Love**	1962	10.00	25.00
Warner Bros. WS-1474	(S)	**Let's Talk About Love**	1962	12.00	30.00
Warner Bros. W-1504	(M)	**Sommer's Seasons**	1964	10.00	25.00
Warner Bros. WS-1504	(S)	**Sommer's Seasons**	1964	12.00	30.00
Warner Bros. W-1575	(M)	**Softly, The Brazilian Sound**	1965	10.00	25.00
Warner Bros. WS-1575	(S)	**Softly, The Brazilian Sound**	1965	12.00	30.00
		— Original Warner albums above have grey labels.—			
Columbia CL-2495	(M)	**Come Alive**	1966	6.00	15.00
Columbia CS-9295	(S)	**Come Alive**	1966	8.00	20.00
Discovery DS-887	(S)	**Dream** (With Bob Florence)	1983	6.00	15.00

SONICS, THE

Etiquette ALB-024	(M)	**Here Are The Sonics!!!**	1965	60.00	150.00
Etiquette ALBS-024	(S)	**Here Are The Sonics!!!**	1965	150.00	300.00
Etiquette ALB-027	(M)	**The Sonics Boom**	1966	60.00	150.00
Etiquette ALBS-027	(E)	**The Sonics Boom**	1966	40.00	100.00
		— Original Etiquette albums above have purple labels.—			
Etiquette ALBS-024	(S)	**Here Are The Sonics!!!**	197?	16.00	40.00
Etiquette ALBS-027	(E)	**The Sonics Boom**	197?	16.00	40.00
		— Etiquette albums above have red labels.—			
Jerden JRL-7007	(M)	**Introducing The Sonics**	1967	60.00	150.00
Jerden JRS-7007	(E)	**Introducing The Sonics**	1967	40.00	100.00
Buckshot BSR-001	(S)	**Explosives**	1974	20.00	50.00
First American FA-7715	(M)	**Original Northwest Punk**	1977	6.00	15.00

Label & Catalog #		Title	Year	VG+	NM
First American FA-7719	(M)	**Unreleased**	1980	6.00	15.00
First American FA-7779	(M)	**Fire And Ice**	1981	4.00	10.00

SONICS, THE / THE WAILERS / THE GALAXIES
| Etiquette ALB-02 | (M) | **Merry Christmas** | 1965 | 150.00 | 300.00 |

SONNY [SONNY BONO]
| Atco 33-229 | (M) | **Inner Views** | 1967 | 5.00 | 12.00 |
| Atco SD-33-229 | (S) | **Inner Views** | 1967 | 6.00 | 15.00 |

SONNY & CHER
Sonny Bono and Cher.
| Reprise R-6177 | (M) | **Baby Don't Go** | 1965 | 12.00 | 30.00 |
| Reprise RS-6177 | (S) | **Baby Don't Go** | 1965 | 16.00 | 40.00 |

(This LP credits Sonny & Cher & Friends and includes their sides as Caesar & Cleo along with The Blendells, The Lettermen and Bill Medley. "Baby Don't Go," "La-La-La-La-La," "Walkin' The Quetzal," "When" and "Their Hearts Were Full Of Spring" are rechanneled.)

Atco 33-177	(M)	**Look At Us**	1965	8.00	20.00
Atco SD-33-177	(S)	**Look At Us**	1965	10.00	25.00
Atco 33-183	(M)	**The Wondrous World Of Sonny & Cher**	1966	6.00	15.00
Atco SD-33-183	(S)	**The Wondrous World Of Sonny & Cher**	1966	8.00	20.00
Atco 33-203	(M)	**In Case You're In Love**	1967	5.00	12.00
Atco SD-33-203	(S)	**In Case You're In Love**	1967	6.00	15.00
Atco 33-214	(M)	**Good Times** *(Soundtrack)*	1967	5.00	12.00
Atco SD-33-214	(S)	**Good Times** *(Soundtrack)*	1967	6.00	15.00
Atco 33-219	(M)	**The Best Of Sonny & Cher**	1967	5.00	12.00
Atco SD-33-219	(S)	**The Best Of Sonny & Cher**	1967	6.00	15.00

("What Now My Love," "A Beautiful Story," "But You're Mine" and "Laugh At Me" are rechanneled on this album.)

Atco A2-5178	(M)	**Sonny & Cher's Greatest Hits** *(2 LPs)*	1967	8.00	20.00
Atco A2S-5178	(S)	**Sonny & Cher's Greatest Hits** *(2 LPs)*	1967	6.00	15.00
Atco SD-2-804	(S)	**The Two Of Us** *(2 LPs)*	1972	6.00	15.00

(Atco 804 repackages 177 and 203.)

SONNY & THE DEMONS
| United Arts. UAL-3316 | (M) | **Drag Kings** | 1964 | 14.00 | 35.00 |
| United Arts. UAS-6316 | (S) | **Drag Kings** | 1964 | 20.00 | 50.00 |

SONNY TERRY & BROWNIE McGHEE
Saunders Terrell and Walter Brown McGhee recorded together since 1939. The albums below may credit Sonny Terry or Brownie McGhee or both. Refer to Big Bill Broonzy; Leadbelly / Josh White / Sonny Terry.
Stinson 55 (10")	(M)	**Blues**	1950	60.00	150.00
Folkways 2006 (10")	(M)	**Washboard Band**	1950	50.00	100.00
Folkways 2028 (10")	(M)	**Get On Board**	1951	50.00	100.00
Folkways 2030 (10")	(M)	**Brownie McGhee Blues**	1951	50.00	100.00
Folkways 2035 (10")	(M)	**Harmonica**	1952	50.00	100.00
Elektra EKL-14 (10")	(M)	**Folk Blues**	195?	50.00	100.00
Sharp 2003	(M)	**Down Home Blues**	195?	60.00	150.00
Columbia OL-5240	(M)	**Simply Heavenly** *(Soundtrack)*	1957	50.00	100.00
Riverside RLP-644	(M)	**Sonny Terry and His Mouth Harp**	195?	12.00	30.00
Roulette R-25074	(M)	**The Folk Songs Of Sonny & Brownie**	1959	16.00	40.00
Roulette SR-25074	(S)	**The Folk Songs Of Sonny & Brownie**	1959	20.00	50.00
World Pacific WP-1294	(M)	**Blues Is A Story**	1960	12.00	30.00
World Pacific ST-1294	(S)	**Blues Is A Story**	1960	16.00	40.00
World Pacific WP-1296	(M)	**Way Down South Summit Meetin'**	1960	12.00	30.00
World Pacific ST-1296	(S)	**Way Down South Summit Meetin'**	1960	16.00	40.00
Bluesville BVLP-1002	(M)	**Down Home Blues**	1960	16.00	40.00
Bluesville BVLP-1005	(M)	**Blues & Folk**	1960	16.00	40.00
Bluesville BVLP-1020	(M)	**Blues All Around My Head**	1961	16.00	40.00
Bluesville BVLP-1025	(M)	**Sonny's Story**	1961	16.00	40.00
Bluesville BVLP-1033	(M)	**Blues In My Soul**	1961	16.00	40.00
Bluesville BVLP-1042	(M)	**Brownie's Blues**	1962	16.00	40.00
Bluesville BVLP-1058	(M)	**At The 2nd Fret**	1962	16.00	40.00
Bluesville BVLP-1059	(M)	**Sonny Is King**	1963	16.00	40.00
Verve MGV-3008	(M)	**Blues Is My Companion**	1961	12.00	30.00
Verve MGV6-3008	(S)	**Blues Is My Companion**	1961	16.00	40.00
Washington W-702	(M)	**Talkin' 'Bout The Blues**	1961	16.00	40.00

Saunders Terrell and Walter Brown McGhee teamed up in those hoary days of isolationalist America (pre-WWII) and played together through four decades. Like many folk and blues musicians, they were never tied down to one label by an exclusive contract and consequently appeared on sundry labels, often at the same time. While albums may credit Sonny or Brownie only, generally the other was always on hand for each session.

Label & Catalog #		Title	Year	VG+	NM
Folkways F-2327	(M)	**Blues And Folksongs**	1961	12.00	30.00
Folkways FS-2327	(S)	**Blues And Folksongs**	1961	16.00	40.00
Folkways F-2421	(M)	**Traditional Blues, Volume 1**	1961	12.00	30.00
Folkways FS-2421	(S)	**Traditional Blues, Volume 1**	1961	16.00	40.00
Folkways F-2422	(M)	**Traditional Blues, Volume 2**	1961	12.00	30.00
Folkways FS-2422	(S)	**Traditional Blues, Volume 2**	1961	16.00	40.00
Fantasy F-3254	(M)	**Sonny Terry & Brownie McGhee** (Red vinyl)	1961	30.00	75.00
Fantasy F-3254	(M)	**Sonny Terry & Brownie McGhee**	1961	12.00	30.00
Fantasy F-3296	(M)	**Just A Closer Walk With Thee** (Red vinyl)	1962	30.00	75.00
Fantasy F-3296	(M)	**Just A Closer Walk With Thee**	1962	12.00	30.00
Fantasy F-3317	(M)	**Blues & Shouts** (Red vinyl)	1962	30.00	75.00
Fantasy F-3317	(M)	**Blues & Shouts**	1962	12.00	30.00
Fantasy F-3340	(M)	**Sonny & Brownie At Sugar Hill** (Red vinyl)	1962	30.00	75.00
Fantasy F-3340	(M)	**Sonny & Brownie At Sugar Hill**	196?	12.00	30.00
Fantasy FS-8091	(S)	**Sonny & Brownie At Sugar Hill** (Blue vinyl)	1962	30.00	75.00
Fantasy FS-8091	(S)	**Sonny & Brownie At Sugar Hill**	1962	12.00	30.00
Folklore FRLP-14013	(M)	**Down Home Blues**	1964	10.00	25.00
Folklore FRST-14013	(S)	**Down Home Blues**	1964	12.00	30.00
		(Folklore 14013 is a reissue of Bluesville 1002.)			
Verve/Folkways FV-9010	(M)	**Get Together**	1965	10.00	25.00
Verve/Folkways FVS-9010	(S)	**Get Together**	1965	12.00	30.00
Verve/Folkways FV-9019	(M)	**Guitar Highway**	1965	10.00	25.00
Verve/Folkways FVS-9019	(S)	**Guitar Highway**	1965	12.00	30.00
Smash MGS-27067	(M)	**Brownie McGhee At The Bunkhouse**	1965	12.00	30.00
Smash SRS-67067	(S)	**Brownie McGhee At The Bunkhouse**	1965	16.00	40.00
Mainstream MS-6049	(M)	**Hometown Blues**	1965	8.00	20.00
Mainstream MS-6049	(S)	**Hometown Blues**	1965	10.00	25.00
Everest 206	(S)	**Sonny Terry**	1968	6.00	15.00
Everest 242	(S)	**Brownie McGhee & Sonny Terry**	1969	6.00	15.00
Fontana SGF-67599	(S)	**Where The Blues Begin**	1969	8.00	20.00
Prestige PRLP-7715	(S)	**Best Of Sonny Terry & Brownie McGhee**	1969	6.00	15.00
Prestige PRLP-7802	(S)	**Sonny Is King**	1970	6.00	15.00
		(Prestige 7802 is a reissue of Bluesville 1059.)			
Prestige PRLP-7803	(S)	**Live! At The 2nd Fret**	1970	6.00	15.00
		(Prestige 7803 is a reissue of Bluesville 1058.)			
BluesWay BLS-6028	(S)	**Long Way From Home**	1969	6.00	15.00
BluesWay BLS-6059	(S)	**Couldn't Believe My Eyes**	1970	6.00	15.00
Brut 6002	(S)	**The Book Of Numbers** (Soundtrack)	1973	6.00	15.00
Olympic 7108	(S)	**Hootin' & Hollerin'**	1973	4.00	10.00
Savoy 12218	(S)	**Down Home Blues**	1973	4.00	10.00
A&M SP-34379	(S)	**Sonny & Brownie**	1973	5.00	12.00
Fantasy 24708	(S)	**Back To New Orleans** (2 LPs)	1972	6.00	15.00
Fantasy 24721	(S)	**Midnight Special** (2 LPs)	1977	4.00	10.00
Fantasy 24723	(S)	**California Blues** (2 LPs)	1981	4.00	10.00

SONS OF CHAMPLIN

Capitol SWBB-200	(S)	**Loosen Up Naturally** (2 LPs)	1969	See note below	
		("First-state scratch cover." Original LPs were issued with several four-letter words as part of the graffiti in the cover art. Capitol recalled the albums and had the offending expletives scratched off by hand! Covers with the foul language intact are very rare with no values known at this time.)			
Capitol SWBB-200	(S)	**Loosen Up Naturally** (2 LPs)	1969	20.00	50.00
		("Second-state scratch cover." The foul language scratched off of the cover.)			
Capitol SWBB-200	(S)	**Loosen Up Naturally** (2 LPs)	1969	8.00	20.00
		("Third-state scratch cover." Later pressings had the nasties airbrushed off of the cover.)			
		— Original Capitol albums above have black rainbow labels.—			
Capitol SKAO-322	(S)	**The Sons**	1969	6.00	15.00
Capitol ST-675	(S)	**Follow Your Heart**	1971	6.00	15.00
		— Original Capitol albums above have green labels.—			

SONS OF HEROES

MCA 39010	(S)	**Sons Of Heroes** (With Bill Wyman)	1983	8.00	20.00

SONS OF THE PIONEERS, THE

RCA Victor LPM-3032 (10")	(M)	**Cowboy Classics**	1952	40.00	100.00
RCA Victor LPM-3095 (10")	(M)	**Cowboy Hymns And Spirituals**	1952	40.00	100.00

Label & Catalog #		Title	Year	VG+	NM
RCA Victor LPM-3162 (10")	(M)	**Western Classics**	1953	40.00	100.00
RCA Victor LPM-1130	(M)	**Favorite Cowboy Songs**	1955	20.00	50.00
RCA Victor LPM-1431	(M)	**How Great Thou Art**	1957	20.00	50.00
RCA Victor LPM-1483	(M)	**One Man's Songs**	1957	20.00	50.00
RCA Victor LPM-2118	(M)	**Cool Water**	1960	8.00	20.00
RCA Victor LSP-2118	(S)	**Cool Water**	1960	12.00	30.00
RCA Victor LPM-2356	(M)	**Lure Of The West**	1961	8.00	20.00
RCA Victor LSP-2356	(S)	**Lure Of The West**	1961	12.00	30.00
RCA Victor LPM-2456	(M)	**Tumbleweed Trails**	1962	8.00	20.00
RCA Victor LSP-2456	(S)	**Tumbleweed Trails**	1962	12.00	30.00
RCA Victor LPM-2603	(M)	**Our Men Out West**	1963	8.00	20.00
RCA Victor LSP-2603	(S)	**Our Men Out West**	1963	12.00	30.00
RCA Victor LPM-2652	(M)	**Hymns Of The Cowboy**	1963	8.00	20.00
RCA Victor LSP-2652	(S)	**Hymns Of The Cowboy**	1963	12.00	30.00

— Original RCA mono albums above have black labels with "Long Play" on the bottom; stereo albums have have black labels with "Living Stereo" on the bottom.—

RCA Victor LPM-2737	(M)	**Trail Dust**	1963	6.00	15.00
RCA Victor LSP-2737	(S)	**Trail Dust**	1963	8.00	20.00
RCA Victor LPM-2855	(M)	**Country Fare**	1964	6.00	15.00
RCA Victor LSP-2855	(S)	**Country Fare**	1964	8.00	20.00
RCA Victor LPM-2957	(M)	**Down Memory Trail**	1964	6.00	15.00
RCA Victor LSP-2957	(S)	**Down Memory Trail**	1964	8.00	20.00
RCA Victor LPM-3351	(M)	**Legends Of The West**	1965	6.00	15.00
RCA Victor LSP-3351	(S)	**Legends Of The West**	1965	8.00	20.00
RCA Victor LPM-3476	(M)	**The Best Of The Sons Of The Pioneers**	1966	6.00	15.00
RCA Victor LSP-3476	(S)	**The Best Of The Sons Of The Pioneers**	1966	8.00	20.00
RCA Victor LPM-3554	(M)	**The Songs Of Bob Nolan**	1966	6.00	15.00
RCA Victor LSP-3554	(S)	**The Songs Of Bob Nolan**	1966	8.00	20.00
RCA Victor LPM-3714	(M)	**Campfire Favorites**	1967	10.00	25.00
RCA Victor LSP-3714	(S)	**Campfire Favorites**	1967	8.00	20.00
RCA Victor LPM-3964	(M)	**South Of The Border**	1968	15.00	75.00
RCA Victor LSP-3964	(S)	**South Of The Border**	1968	8.00	20.00

— Original RCA albums above have black labels.—

RCA Victor LSP-4119	(S)	**Tumbling Tumbleweeds**	1969	6.00	15.00
RCA Victor LSP-4194	(S)	**Visit The South Seas**	1969	6.00	15.00

— Original RCA albums above have orange labels on non-flexible vinyl.—

SONS OF THE PURPLE SAGE

Waldorf 143 (10")	(M)	**Songs Of the Golden West**	1955	24.00	60.00

SOPHOMORES, THE

Seeco CELP-451	(M)	**The Sophomores**	196?	50.00	150.00

(This is not the "doo wop" group of the '50s but an early soul group.)

SOPWITH CAMEL, THE

Kama Sutra KLP-8060	(M)	**The Sopwith Camel**	1967	12.00	30.00
Kama Sutra KLPS-8060	(S)	**The Sopwith Camel**	1967	14.00	35.00
Kama Sutra KSBS-2063	(S)	**The Sopwith Camel In "Hello, Hello"**	1973	10.00	25.00
		Kama Sutra 2063 is a reissue of 8060.)			
Reprise MS-2108	(S)	**The Miraculous Hump Returns**	1973	8.00	20.00

SORKIN, DAN

Mercury MG-20681	(M)	**Folk Singing One**	1963	5.00	12.00
Mercury SR-60681	(S)	**Folk Singing One**	1963	6.00	15.00

SORRELL, FRANK

Coral CRL-57234	(M)	**Frank Sorrell And His Four Guitars**	1958	12.00	30.00

SOTHERN, ANN

Craftsmen C-8061	(M)	**It's Ann Sothern Time!**	195?	12.00	30.00
Tops L-1611	(M)	**Ann Sothern Sings**	1958	8.00	20.00

SOUL, JIMMY
Refer to Bobby Bland / Jimmy Soul.

S.P.Q.R. E-16001	(M)	**If You Wanna Be Happy**	1963	30.00	75.00
Spin-O-Rama SP-123	(M)	**Jimmy Soul And The Belmonts**	1963	8.00	20.00
Spin-O-Rama SPS-123	(E)	**Jimmy Soul And The Belmonts**	1963	4.00	10.00

Label & Catalog #		Title	Year	VG+	NM

SOUL SISTERS, THE

| Sue LP-1022 | (M) | I Can't Stand It (Orange label) | 1964 | 200.00 | 400.00 |
| Sue STLP-1022 | (S) | I Can't Stand It (Orange label) | 1964 | 300.00 | 600.00 |

SOUL STIRRERS, THE
The Stirrers lead singers included Sam Cooke and Johnny Taylor.

Specialty SPS-2106	(M)	The Soul Stirrers Featuring Sam Cooke	1959	12.00	30.00
Specialty SPS-2116	(E)	The Gospel Soul Of Sam Cooke, Volume 1	1969	6.00	15.00
Specialty SPS-2113	(S)	Two Sides Of Sam Cooke	1969	8.00	20.00

(Original pressings feature an untitled rehearsal track at the end of the second side. "He's My Guide" and "The Last Mile Of The Way" are in mono with added stereo backing on this album.)

Specialty SPS-2128	(E)	The Gospel Soul Of Sam Cooke, Volume 2	1970	6.00	15.00
Specialty SPS-2137	(E)	The Original Soul Stirrers	1970	6.00	15.00
Specialty SPS-2146	(S)	That's Heaven To Me	1972	4.00	10.00
Specialty SPS-2150	(S)	Going Back To The Lord Again	1972	4.00	10.00
Specialty SPS-2166	(S)	Gospel Soul	1972	4.00	10.00
Checker 10063	(S)	A Tribute To Sam Cooke	1971	4.00	10.00

SOUL SURVIVORS

| Crimson LP-502 | (M) | When The Whistle Blows Anything Goes | 1967 | 10.00 | 25.00 |
| Crimson LP-502 | (S) | When The Whistle Blows Anything Goes | 1967 | 12.00 | 30.00 |

("Expressway To Your Heart" and "A Change Is Gonna Come" are rechanneled on this album.)

| Atco SD-33-277 | (S) | Take Another Look | 1969 | 10.00 | 25.00 |

SOUND SYMPOSIUM, THE

| Dot DLP-25871 | (S) | Paul Simon Interpreted | 1969 | 6.00 | 15.00 |
| Dot DLP-25952 | (S) | Bob Dylan Interpreted | 1969 | 10.00 | 25.00 |

SOUNDS OF OUR TIME, THE

| Capitol T-2817 | (M) | Music Of The Flower Children | 1967 | 6.00 | 15.00 |
| Capitol ST-2817 | (S) | Music Of The Flower Children | 1967 | 8.00 | 20.00 |

SOUP

| Arf Arm 1 | (S) | Soup (Insert cover) | 1970 | 40.00 | 100.00 |
| Big Tree BTS-2007 | (S) | The Soup Album | 1971 | 8.00 | 20.00 |

SOUTH, JOE (& THE BELIEVERS)
Refer to Billy Joe Royal.

Capitol ST-108	(S)	Introspect (Black label)	1968	10.00	25.00
Capitol ST-108	(S)	Introspect	1969	6.00	15.00
Capitol ST-235	(S)	Games People Play	1969	6.00	15.00
Capitol ST-392	(S)	Don't It Make You Want To Go Home	1969	6.00	15.00
Capitol ST-450	(S)	Joe South's Greatest Hits	1970	6.00	15.00
Capitol ST-637	(S)	So The Seeds Are Growing	1971	6.00	15.00
Capitol ST-845	(S)	Joe South	1972	6.00	15.00

— Original Capitol albums above have green labels.—

| Capitol ST-1074 | (S) | Look Inside | 1972 | 6.00 | 15.00 |
| Island ILPS-9328 | (S) | Midnight Rainbows | 1975 | 4.00 | 10.00 |

SOUTH CENTRAL AVENUE MUNICIPAL BLUES BAND

| BluesWay BL-6018 | (S) | The Soul Of Bonnie And Clyde | 1968 | 6.00 | 15.00 |

SOUTH 40

| Metrobeat MBS-1000 | (S) | Live At The Someplace Else | 1968 | 14.00 | 35.00 |

SOUTH PAW

| Bad Man RHBP-318 | (S) | South Paw | 1980 | 20.00 | 50.00 |

SOUTHERN, JERI: *Refer to* GOLDMINE'S PRICE GUIDE TO COLLECTIBLE JAZZ ALBUMS

SOUTHWEST F. O. B.

| Hip HIS-7001 | (S) | Smell Of Incense | 1969 | 12.00 | 30.00 |

SOUTHWIND

Venture VTS-4002	(S)	Southwind	1969	5.00	12.00
Blue Thumb BTS-13	(S)	Ready To Ride	1969	5.00	12.00
Blue Thumb BTS-26	(S)	What A Place To Land	1970	5.00	12.00

Label & Catalog #		Title	Year	VG+	NM
SOVINE, RED					
MGM E-3465	(M)	Red Sovine	1957	30.00	75.00
Starday SLP-132	(M)	The One And Only Red Sovine	1961	16.00	40.00
Starday SLP-197	(M)	The Golden Country Ballads Of The 1960s	1962	16.00	40.00
Decca DL-4445	(M)	Red Sovine	1964	8.00	20.00
Decca DL-74445	(S)	Red Sovine	1964	10.00	25.00
Decca DL-4736	(M)	Country Music Time	1966	6.00	15.00
Decca DL-74736	(S)	Country Music Time	1966	8.00	20.00
Starday SLP-341	(M)	Little Rosa	1966	6.00	15.00
Starday SLP-341	(S)	Little Rosa	1966	8.00	20.00
Starday SLP-363	(M)	Giddy-Up Go	1966	6.00	15.00
Starday SLP-363	(S)	Giddy-Up Go	1966	8.00	20.00
Starday SLP-383	(M)	Town And Country Action	1966	6.00	15.00
Starday SLP-383	(S)	Town And Country Action	1966	8.00	20.00
Starday SLP-396	(M)	The Nashville Sound Of Red Sovine	1967	6.00	15.00
Starday SLP-396	(S)	The Nashville Sound Of Red Sovine	1967	8.00	20.00
Starday SLP-405	(M)	I Didn't Jump The Fence	1967	6.00	15.00
Starday SLP-405	(S)	I Didn't Jump The Fence	1967	8.00	20.00
Starday SLP-414	(M)	Phantom 309	1967	6.00	15.00
Starday SLP-414	(S)	Phantom 309	1967	8.00	20.00
SOXX, BOBB B., & THE BLUE JEANS					
Philles PHLP-4002	(DJ)	Zip A Dee Doo Dah (White label)	1963	400.00	800.00
Philles PHLP-4002	(M)	Zip A Dee Doo Dah	1963	150.00	300.00
SPACE					
Hand 5167	(S)	Space	1969	10.00	25.00
SPACE ARK					
Color World CW-1001	(S)	Space Ark	197?	6.00	15.00
SPACE OPERA					
Epic KE-32117	(S)	Space Opera	1973	5.00	12.00
SPACEMEN, THE					
Roulette MG-25275	(M)	Rockin' In The 25th Century	1964	10.00	25.00
Roulette SR-25275	(S)	Rockin' In The 25th Century	1964	12.00	30.00
Roulette MG-25322	(M)	Music For Batman And Robin	1966	12.00	30.00
Roulette SR-25322	(S)	Music For Batman And Robin	1966	16.00	40.00
SPANDAU BALLET					
Mobile Fidelity MFSL-152	(S)	True	198?	5.00	15.00
SPANIELS, THE					
Vee Jay LP-1002	(M)	Goodnite, It's Time To Go (Maroon label)	1958	200.00	600.00
Vee Jay LP-1002	(M)	Goodnite, It's Time To Go (Black label) (Reproductions of Vee Jay 1002 exist.)	1961	100.00	200.00
Vee Jay LP-1024	(M)	The Spaniels	1960	100.00	200.00
Upfront UPF-131	(M)	The Hits Of The Spaniels	196?	4.00	10.00
Lost-Nite LP-137	(M)	The Spaniels	196?	10.00	25.00
Solid Smoke 8028	(M)	Greatest Hits	1984	4.00	10.00
Lost-Nite LLP-19 (10")	(M)	The Spaniels (Red vinyl)	1981	4.00	10.00
SPANKY & OUR GANG					
Mercury MG-21124	(M)	Spanky And Our Gang	1967	6.00	15.00
Mercury SR-61124	(S)	Spanky And Our Gang	1967	6.00	15.00
Mercury SR-61161	(S)	Like To Get To Know You	1968	6.00	15.00
Mercury SR-61183	(S)	Without Rhyme Or Reason	1969	6.00	15.00
Mercury SR-61227	(S)	Greatest Hits	1969	6.00	15.00
Mercury SR-61326	(S)	Live	1971	6.00	15.00
SPANN, LUCILLE					
BluesWay BLS-6070	(S)	Cry Before I Go	1974	6.00	15.00
SPANN, OTIS					
Otis Spann also recorded with Fleetwood Mac.					
Candid CJ-9001	(M)	Otis Spann Is The Blues	1960	80.00	200.00
BluesWay BL-6003	(M)	The Blues Is Where It's At	1967	10.00	25.00
BluesWay BLS-6003	(S)	The Blues Is Where It's At	1967	12.00	30.00

Label & Catalog #		Title	Year	VG+	NM
BluesWay BLS-6013	(S)	The Bottom Of The Blues	1968	10.00	25.00
Archive Of Folk Music 217	(S)	Otis Spann	1968	6.00	15.00
London PS-543	(S)	Raw Blues	1968	10.00	25.00
London PS-551	(S)	Cracked Spanner Head	1969	10.00	25.00
Prestige PRST-7719	(S)	The Blues Will Never Die	1969	8.00	20.00
Vanguard VDS-6514	(S)	Cryin' Time	1970	8.00	20.00
Blues Time 9006	(S)	Sweet Giant Of The Blues	1970	6.00	15.00
Barnaby KZ-30246	(S)	Otis Spann Is The Blues	1970	5.00	12.00
Barnaby KZ-31290	(S)	Walking The Blues	1972	5.00	12.00
BluesWay BLS-6063	(S)	Heart Loaded With Trouble	1973	6.00	15.00

SPARK PLUGS, THE
| Sutton SU-322 | (M) | The Spark Plugs | 196? | 10.00 | 25.00 |
| Sutton SSU-322 | (S) | The Spark Plugs | 196? | 12.00 | 30.00 |

SPARKS
Ron and Russel Mael, formerly of Halfnelson.
Bearsville BV-2048	(S)	Sparks	1971	6.00	15.00
		(Repackage of Halfnelson's eponymous LP.)			
Bearsville BR-2110	(S)	A Woofer In Tweeter's Clothing	1973	6.00	15.00
Columbia PC-34901	(DJ)	Introducing Sparks (Red vinyl)	1977	6.00	15.00

SPARKS, RANDY
Randy originally recorded with The Back Porch Majority.
Verve V-2103	(M)	Randy Sparks	1959	10.00	25.00
Verve V-2126	(M)	Walkin' The Low Road	1960	10.00	25.00
Verve V-2143	(M)	Randy Sparks Three	1960	8.00	20.00
Verve VS-2143	(S)	Randy Sparks Three	1960	10.00	25.00
MGM SE-4769	(S)	Hazy Sunshine	1971	4.00	10.00

SPARROWS, THE
| Elkay 3009 | (M) | That Mersey Sound | 1964 | 16.00 | 40.00 |

SPATS
| ABC-Paramount 502 | (M) | Cookin' With The Spats | 1965 | 8.00 | 20.00 |
| ABC-Paramount S-502 | (S) | Cookin' With The Spats | 1965 | 12.00 | 30.00 |

SPECTOR, PHIL
The LPs below are various artists compilations produced and compiled by Spector. Refer to The Beatles; Bobb B. Soxx & The Bluejeans; The Checkmates Ltd; The Crystals; George Harrison; John Lennon; Ramones; The Righteous Brothers; The Ronettes; The Teddy Bears; Ike & Tina Turner.
Philles PHLP-4004	(DJ)	Today's Hits (White label)	1963	400.00	800.00
Philles PHLP-4004	(M)	Today's Hits (Blue label)	1963	150.00	300.00
Philles PHLP-4004	(M)	Today's Hits (Yellow label)	1964	75.00	150.00
Philles PHLP-4005	(DJ)	A Christmas Gift For You (White label)	1963	400.00	800.00
Philles PHLP-4005	(M)	A Christmas Gift For You (Blue label)	1963	75.00	150.00
Philles PHLP-4005	(M)	A Christmas Gift For You (Yellow label)	1964	20.00	50.00
		(Reissued as "Phil Spector's Christmas Album.")			
Apple SW-3400	(M)	Phil Spector's Christmas Album	1972	12.00	30.00
		(The Apple album bears a stereo prefix but plays mono.)			
Warner/Spector 9103	(S)	Phil Spector's Christmas Album	1975	8.00	20.00
		(The Warner album claims to be mono but plays stereo.)			
Warner/Spector 9104	(M)	Phil Spector's 20 Greatest Hits (2 LPs)	1977	12.00	30.00
		("Spanish Harlem, "River Deep-Mountain High" and "He's Sure The Boy I Love" are in stereo.)			
Pavillion PZ-37686	(S)	Phil Spector's Christmas Album	1981	8.00	20.00
Passport PB-3604	(S)	Phil Spector's Christmas Album	1984	6.00	15.00

SPECTOR, RONNIE
Ronnie was formerly a member of The Ronettes.
| Polish PRG-808 | (S) | Siren | 1980 | 4.00 | 10.00 |

SPELLBINDERS, THE
| Columbia CL-2514 | (M) | The Magic Of The Spellbinders | 1966 | 6.00 | 15.00 |
| Columbia CS-9314 | (S) | The Magic Of The Spellbinders | 1966 | 8.00 | 20.00 |

SPENCE, ALEXANDER "SKIP"
Mr. Spence was formerly a member of The Jefferson Airplane; Moby Grape.
| Columbia CS-9831 | (S) | Oar | 1969 | 20.00 | 50.00 |

Label & Catalog #		Title	Year	VG+	NM

SPENCER, JEREMY
Jeremy was formerly a member of Fleetwood Mac.

Columbia KC-31990	(S)	Jeremy Spencer And The Children	1971	8.00	20.00
Atlantic SD-19236	(S)	Flee	1979	4.00	10.00

SPIDER-MAN

Lifesong 6001	(S)	Rock Reflections Of A Superhero	1976	10.00	25.00

SPIDERS, THE

Imperial LP-9140	(M)	I Didn't Wanna Do It	1961	300.00	600.00

SPIDERS FROM MARS, THE
The Spiders were formerly David Bowie's band.

Pye 12125	(S)	The Spiders From Mars	1976	6.00	15.00

SPIFFYS, THE

R.I. 2597	(M)	The Spiffys	1968	70.00	175.00

SPINNERS, THE

Time 52092	(M)	Party-My Pad After Surfin'	1963	10.00	25.00
Time S-2092	(S)	Party-My Pad After Surfin'	1963	12.00	30.00

SPINNERS, THE

Motown M-639	(M)	The Original Spinners	1967	10.00	25.00
Motown MS-639	(S)	The Original Spinners	1967	12.00	30.00
		("That's What Girls Are Made For" is rechanneled on this album.)			
V.I.P. 405	(S)	The Second Time Around	1970	10.00	25.00
Motown M-769	(S)	The Best Of The Spinners	1973	4.00	10.00
Atlantic QD-7256	(Q)	The Spinners	1973	6.00	15.00
Atlantic QD-18118	(Q)	The New And Improved Spinners	1974	6.00	15.00

SPIRAL STARECASE, THE
The Starecase was produced by Gary Usher.

Columbia CS-9852	(S)	More Today Than Yesterday	1969	6.00	15.00

SPIRIT

Ode Z12-44004	(S)	Spirit	1968	8.00	20.00
Ode Z12-44014	(S)	The Family That Plays Together	1968	8.00	20.00
Ode Z12-44016	(S)	Clear Spirit	1969	8.00	20.00
Epic KE-30267	(S)	Twelve Dreams Of Dr. Sardonicus	1970	6.00	15.00
Epic KE-31175	(S)	Feedback	1972	6.00	15.00
Epic KEG-31457	(S)	Spirit	1972	6.00	15.00
Epic KE-31461	(S)	The Family That Plays Together	1972	6.00	15.00
		— Original Epic albums above have yellow labels.—			
Nautilus NR-58	(S)	Potatoland	198?	Unreleased	

SPIRIT & WORM

A&M SP-4229	(S)	Spirit And Worm	1969	150.00	300.00

SPIRIT IN FLESH

Metromedia 1041	(S)	Spirit In Flesh	1971	5.00	12.00

SPIVEY, VICTORIA
The Three Kings are Lonnie Johnson, Roosevelt Sykes and Big Joe Williams. Both albums feature Bob Dylan on harmonica on two tracks. Ms Spivey also recorded with Lonnie Johnson.

Spivey LP-1004	(M)	Three Kings And A Queen	1964	12.00	30.00
Spivey LP-1014	(M)	Three Kings And A Queen, Volume 2	1964	12.00	30.00

SPLIT LEVEL, THE

Dot DLP-25836	(S)	The Split Level	1968	5.00	12.00

SPOELSTRA, MARK

Verve/Folkways FV-9018	(M)	The Time I've Had	1965	6.00	15.00
Verve/Folkways FVS-9018	(S)	The Time I've Had	1965	8.00	20.00

SPOKESMEN, THE

Decca DL-4712	(M)	Dawn Of Correction	1965	12.00	30.00
Decca DL-74712	(S)	Dawn Of Correction	1965	16.00	40.00

Label & Catalog #		Title	Year	VG+	NM

SPOOKY TOOTH
Spooky Tooth features Mike Patto.

Bell 6019	(S)	Spooky Tooth	1968	10.00	25.00
A&M SP-4194	(S)	Spooky Two	1969	6.00	15.00
A&M SP-4225	(S)	Ceremony	1970	6.00	15.00
A&M SP-4266	(S)	The Last Puff	1970	6.00	15.00
A&M SP-4300	(S)	Tobacco Road	1971	6.00	15.00
A&M SP-4349	(S)	Spooky Tooth	1970	6.00	15.00
A&M SP-4385	(S)	You Broke My Heart, So I Busted Your Jaw	1973	4.00	10.00
A&M SP-3528	(S)	That Was Only Yesterday (2 LPs)	1973	5.00	12.00

SPOONER

Mountain Rail. 8005	(S)	Every Corner Dance	1982	5.00	12.00
Boat 1004	(S)	Wildest Dreams	1984	4.00	10.00

SPRING
Spring is Marilyn and Diane Rovell of The Honeys. Production by Brian Wilson, more or less.

United Arts. 5571	(S)	Spring (With insert)	1972	10.00	25.00

SPRING, ROGER

Verve/Folkways FV-9037	(M)	Grassy Licks	1965	6.00	15.00
Verve/Folkways FVS-9037	(S)	Grassy Licks	1965	8.00	20.00

SPRINGFIELD, DUSTY
Ms. Springfield was originally a member of The Springfields. Refer to Led Zeppelin / Dusty Springfield.

Philips PHM-200-133	(M)	Stay Awhile	1964	10.00	25.00
Philips PHS-600-133	(P)	Stay Awhile	1964	14.00	35.00
Philips PHM-200-156	(M)	Dusty	1964	10.00	25.00
Philips PHS-600-156	(P)	Dusty	1964	14.00	35.00
Philips PHM-200-174	(M)	Oooooo Weeee!!!	1965	10.00	25.00
Philips PHS-600-174	(S)	Oooooo Weeee!!!	1965	14.00	35.00
Philips PHM-200-210	(M)	You Don't Have To Say You Love Me	1966	10.00	25.00
Philips PHS-600-210	(S)	You Don't Have To Say You Love Me	1966	14.00	35.00
Philips PHM-200-220	(M)	Dusty Springfield's Golden Hits	1966	8.00	20.00
Philips PHS-600-220	(P)	Dusty Springfield's Golden Hits	1966	10.00	25.00
		(Originally issued with "Goin' Back.")			
Philips PHM-200-220	(M)	Dusty Springfield's Golden Hits	1967	6.00	15.00
Philips PHS-600-220	(P)	Dusty Springfield's Golden Hits	1967	8.00	20.00
		(Reissued without "Goin' Back.")			
Philips PHM-200-256	(M)	The Look Of Love	1967	8.00	20.00
Philips PHS-600-256	(S)	The Look Of Love	1967	10.00	25.00
Philips PHM-200-303	(M)	Everything's Coming Up Dusty	1967	8.00	20.00
Philips PHS-600-303	(S)	Everything's Coming Up Dusty	1967	10.00	25.00
Colgems COMO-5005	(M)	Casino Royale (Soundtrack)	1967	12.00	30.00
Colgems COSO-5005	(S)	Casino Royale (Soundtrack)	1967	40.00	100.00
United Arts. UAL-4158	(M)	The Corrupt Ones (Soundtrack)	1967	20.00	50.00
United Arts. UAS-5158	(S)	The Corrupt Ones (Soundtrack)	1967	30.00	75.00
20th Century TFS-4198	(S)	The Sweet Ride (Soundtrack)	1968	8.00	20.00
Atlantic SD-8214	(S)	Dusty In Memphis	1969	8.00	20.00
Atlantic SD-8249	(S)	A Brand New Me	1970	6.00	15.00
Dunhill DSX-50128	(S)	Cameo	1973	6.00	15.00
United Arts. LA791	(S)	It Begins Again	1978	6.00	15.00
United Arts. LA936	(S)	Living Without Your Love	1979	6.00	15.00
Casablanca 7271	(S)	White Heat	1982	5.00	12.00

SPRINGFIELDS, THE
Tom and Dusty Springfield.

Philips PHM-200-052	(M)	Silver Threads And Golden Needles	1962	12.00	30.00
Philips PHS-600-052	(S)	Silver Threads And Golden Needles	1962	16.00	40.00
Philips PHM-200-076	(M)	Folksongs From The Hills	1963	12.00	30.00
Philips PHS-600-076	(S)	Folksongs From The Hills	1963	16.00	40.00

SPRINGSTEEN, BRUCE (& THE E STREET BAND)

Columbia KC-31903	(DJ)	Greetings From Asbury Park	1973	*See note below*	
Columbia KC-31903	(S)	Greetings From Asbury Park	1973	6.00	15.00
Columbia KC-32432	(DJ)	Wild, The Innocent & The E Street Shuffle	1973	*See note below*	
		(White label promos for Columbia 31903 and 32432 do not exist.)			
Columbia KC-32432	(S)	Wild, The Innocent & The E Street Shuffle	1973	6.00	15.00
		(The title on the cover is in yellow print.)			

Even Bruce's best, Born To Run *and* Darkness On The Edge Of Town, *could not make the CBS Mastersound Half-Speed mastered series a success with audiophile oriented consumers. Using poor quality vinyl and plating and compromised masters, the discs simply did not live up to the levels of quality that market demanded. . .*

Label & Catalog #		Title	Year	VG+	NM
Columbia PC-33795	(DJ)	**Born To Run** (White label)	1975	500.00	1,000.00
		(Promotional copy with the title in script print on the cover Issued in a special mailing envelope with a letter of introduction from CBS and an orange patch, which are included in the price. Should any of these be missing the price drops dramatically and would carry a suggested Near Mint value of $300-600.)			
Columbia PC-33795	(DJ)	**Born To Run** (White label)	1975	16.00	40.00
Columbia PC-33795	(S)	**Born To Run**	1975	8.00	20.00
		(Jon Landau's name is misspelled as "John" on the back cover.)			
Columbia PC-33795	(S)	**Born To Run**	1975	6.00	15.00
		(A strip with Landau's name is added to the back cover.)			
Columbia PAL-35318	(DJ)	**Darkness On The Edge Of Town**	1978	40.00	100.00
		(Picture disc)			
Columbia JC-35318	(DJ)	**Darkness On The Edge Of Town**	1978	12.00	30.00
		(White label)			
Columbia HC-33795	(S)	**Born To Run** (Half-speed master)	1980	13.00	40.00
Columbia HC-43795	(S)	**Born To Run** (Half-speed master)	1981	10.00	30.00
Columbia HC-45318	(S)	**Darkness On The Edge Of Town**	1981	13.00	40.00
		(Half-speed master)			
Columbia AS-978	(DJ)	**As Requested Around The World**	1981	20.00	50.00
Columbia FC-36854	(DJ)	**The River** (2 LPs. White label with letter)	1984	20.00	50.00
Columbia FC-36854	(DJ)	**The River** (2 LPs. White label without letter)	1984	14.00	35.00
Columbia AS-1957	(DJ)	**Born In The U.S.A.** (5 song mini-LP)	1985	14.00	35.00
Columbia AS-1957	(DJ)	**Born In The U.S.A.** (5 song mini-LP)	1987	8.00	20.00
		(Second pressings note so on the label.)			

SPUR

Cinema CSLP-1500	(M)	**Spur Of The Moment**	1969	24.00	60.00

SPYRO GYRA

Nautilus NR-9	(S)	**Morning Dance**	197?	10.00	30.00

SQUIDDLY DIDDLY

HBR HLP-2043	(M)	**Squiddly Diddly's Surfin' Surfari** (TV)	1965	20.00	50.00
HBR HST-2043	(S)	**Squiddly Diddly's Surfin' Surfari** (TV)	1965	30.00	75.00

SRC

Capitol ST-2991	(S)	**SRC**	1968	16.00	40.00
Capitol ST-134	(S)	**Milestones**	1969	12.00	30.00
Capitol SKAO-273	(S)	**Travellers Tale**	1970	12.00	30.00

STACK

Charisma CRS-303	(S)	**Above All**	1966	660.00	1,000.00

STAFFORD, JO
Refer to Gordon MacRae; Frank Sinatra; The Reprise Repertory Theatre.

Capitol H-75 (10")	(M)	**American Folk Songs**	1950	20.00	50.00
Capitol H-157 (10")	(M)	**Kiss Me Kate** (Studio Cast)	1950	30.00	75.00
Capitol H-9014 (10")	(M)	**Songs Of Faith**	1950	20.00	50.00
Capitol H-197 (10")	(M)	**Autumn In New York**	1950	20.00	50.00
Capitol H-247 (10")	(M)	**Songs For Sunday Evening**	1950	20.00	50.00
Capitol H-435 (10")	(M)	**Starring Jo Stafford**	1953	20.00	50.00
Capitol T-197	(M)	**Autumn In New York**	1955	16.00	40.00
Capitol T-435	(M)	**Starring Jo Stafford**	1955	16.00	40.00
— Original Capitol albums above have turquoise labels.—					
Columbia CL-6210 (10")	(M)	**As You Desire Me**	1952	20.00	50.00
Columbia CL-6238 (10")	(M)	**Broadway's Best**	1953	20.00	50.00
Columbia CL-6274 (10")	(M)	**My Heart's In The Highland**	1954	20.00	50.00
Columbia CL-6286 (10")	(M)	**Garden Of Prayer**	1954	20.00	50.00
Columbia CL-2501 (10")	(M)	**Soft And Sentimental**	1955	20.00	50.00
Columbia CL-2591 (10")	(M)	**A Gal Named Jo**	1956	20.00	50.00
Columbia CL-2597 (10")	(M)	**My Fair Lady** (Studio Cast)	1956	30.00	75.00
Columbia CL-584	(M)	**Broadway's Best**	1954	16.00	40.00
Columbia CL-691	(M)	**Happy Holiday**	1955	16.00	40.00
Columbia CL-910	(M)	**Ski Trails**	1956	16.00	40.00
Columbia CL-968	(M)	**Once Over Lightly**	1957	16.00	40.00
Columbia CL-1043	(M)	**Songs Of Scotland**	1957	16.00	40.00
Columbia CL-1124	(M)	**Swingin' Down Broadway**	1958	14.00	35.00
Columbia CL-1228	(M)	**Jo Stafford's Greatest Hits**	1959	12.00	30.00

Label & Catalog #		Title	Year	VG+	NM
Columbia CL-1280	(M)	I'll Be Seeing You	1959	12.00	30.00
Columbia CS-8080	(S)	I'll Be Seeing You	1959	16.00	40.00
Columbia CL-1339	(M)	Ballad Of The Blues	1959	12.00	30.00
Columbia CS-8139	(S)	Ballad Of The Blues	1959	16.00	40.00
Columbia CL-1561	(M)	Jo + Jazz	1960	16.00	40.00
Columbia CS-8361	(S)	Jo + Jazz	1960	20.00	50.00
		— Original Columbia albums above have three white "eye" logos on each side of the spindle hole.—			
Capitol T-1653	(M)	American Folk Songs	1962	8.00	20.00
Capitol ST-1653	(S)	American Folk Songs	1962	10.00	25.00
Capitol T-1921	(M)	The Hits Of Jo Stafford	1963	8.00	20.00
Capitol ST-1921	(S)	The Hits Of Jo Stafford	1963	10.00	25.00
Capitol T-2069	(M)	Sweet Hour Of Prayer	1964	8.00	20.00
Capitol ST-2069	(S)	Sweet Hour Of Prayer	1964	10.00	25.00
Capitol T-2166	(M)	Joyful Season	1964	8.00	20.00
Capitol ST-2166	(S)	Joyful Season	1964	10.00	25.00
Reprise R-6090	(M)	Getting Sentimental Over Tommy Dorsey	1963	8.00	20.00
Reprise R-96090	(S)	Getting Sentimental Over Tommy Dorsey	1963	10.00	25.00
Dot DLP-3673	(M)	Do I Hear A Waltz?	1966	6.00	15.00
Dot DLP-25673	(S)	Do I Hear A Waltz?	1966	8.00	20.00
Dot DLP-3745	(M)	This Is Jo Stafford	1966	6.00	15.00
Dot DLP-25745	(S)	This Is Jo Stafford	1966	8.00	20.00

STAFFORD, JO, & FRANKIE LAINE

Columbia CL-6268 (10")	(M)	New Orleans	1954	20.00	50.00
Columbia CL-2567 (10")	(M)	Guys And Dolls (Soundtrack)	1955	40.00	100.00
Columbia CL-2598 (10")	(M)	Mosy Happy Fella	1956	20.00	50.00
Columbia CL-578	(M)	New Orleans	1954	16.00	40.00

STAFFORD, JO, & GORDON MacRAE

Capitol T-423	(M)	Memory Songs	1954	16.00	40.00
Capitol T-1696	(M)	Whispering Hope	1962	8.00	20.00
Capitol ST-1696	(S)	Whispering Hope	1962	10.00	25.00
Capitol T-1916	(M)	Peace In The Valley	1963	8.00	20.00
Capitol ST-1916	(S)	Peace In The Valley	1963	10.00	25.00

STAFFORD, TERRY

Crusader CLP-1001	(M)	Suspicion!	1964	16.00	40.00
Crusader CLP-1001S	(P)	Suspicion!	1964	20.00	50.00

STAINED GLASS

Capitol ST-154	(S)	Crazy Horse Roads	1969	8.00	20.00
Capitol ST-242	(S)	Aurora	1969	8.00	20.00

STAIRSTEPS, THE: *Refer to* **THE FIVE STAIRSTEPS**

STALLINGS, MARY: *Refer to* **GOLDMINE'S PRICE GUIDE TO COLLECTIBLE JAZZ ALBUMS**

STANDELLS, THE
The Standells feature Dick Dodd.

Liberty LRP-3384	(M)	The Standells In Person At P.J.'s	1964	20.00	50.00
Liberty LST-7384	(S)	The Standells In Person At P.J.'s	1964	30.00	75.00
Sunset SUM-1136	(M)	Live And Out Of Sight	1966	10.00	25.00
Sunset SUS-5136	(S)	Live And Out Of Sight	1966	12.00	30.00
		(The Sunset album is a reissue of the Liberty album.)			
Tower T-5027	(M)	Dirty Water	1966	16.00	40.00
Tower ST-5027	(P)	Dirty Water	1966	20.00	50.00
Tower T-5044	(M)	Why Pick On Me	1966	16.00	40.00
Tower ST-5044	(S)	Why Pick On Me	1966	20.00	50.00
Tower T-5049	(M)	Hot Ones	1966	16.00	40.00
Tower ST-5049	(S)	Hot Ones	1966	20.00	50.00
Tower T-5098	(M)	Try It	1967	16.00	40.00
Tower ST-5098	(S)	Try It	1967	20.00	50.00

STANDLEY, JOHNNY

Capitol T-732	(M)	Comedy Caravan	1956	10.00	25.00

STANLEY, PAUL: *Refer to* **KISS**

Label & Catalog #		Title	Year	VG+	NM
STANLEY BROTHERS, THE					
Mercury MG-20349	(M)	**Country Pickin' And Singin'**	1958	30.00	75.00
Starday SLP-106	(M)	**Mountain Song Favorites**	1959	20.00	50.00
Starday SLP-122	(M)	**Sacred Songs Of The Hills**	1960	20.00	50.00
King 615	(M)	**The Stanley Brothers**	1959	20.00	50.00
King 645	(M)	**Hymns And Sacred Songs**	1960	20.00	50.00
King 690	(M)	**Everybody's Country Favorites**	1961	20.00	50.00
King 698	(M)	**For The Good People**	1961	20.00	50.00
King 719	(M)	**The Stanleys In Person**	1961	20.00	50.00
King 750	(M)	**Old Time Camp Meeting**	1961	20.00	50.00
King 772	(M)	**The Songs They Like Best**	1961	20.00	50.00
King 791	(M)	**Award Winners**	1962	20.00	50.00
King 805	(M)	**Good Old Camp Meeting Songs**	1962	20.00	50.00
Vintage 002	(M)	**Live At Antioch College**	1961	20.00	50.00
Mercury MG-20884	(M)	**Hard Times**	1963	8.00	20.00
Mercury SR-60884	(S)	**Hard Times**	1963	10.00	25.00
Cabin Creek 203	(M)	**Bluegrass Gospel Favorites**	1966	16.00	40.00
STAPLE SINGERS, THE					
Vee Jay LP-5008	(M)	**Will The Circle Be Unbroken**	196?	10.00	25.00
Vee Jay LPS-5008	(S)	**Will The Circle Be Unbroken**	196?	12.00	30.00
Vee Jay LP-5030	(M)	**Swing Low Sweet Chariot**	196?	10.00	25.00
Vee Jay LPS-5030	(S)	**Swing Low Sweet Chariot**	196?	12.00	30.00
Epic LN-246332	(M)	**For What It's Worth**	1967	6.00	15.00
Epic BN-26332	(S)	**For What It's Worth**	1967	6.00	15.00
Stax STS-2004	(S)	**Soul Folk In Action**	1968	12.00	30.00
Buddah BDS-2009	(S)	**The Best Of The Staple Singers**	1969	6.00	15.00
Buddah BDS-7508	(S)	**Will The Circle Be Unbroken**	1969	6.00	15.00
United Arts. UAS-5209	(S)	**The Landlord** (Soundtrack)	1970	6.00	15.00
Atlantic SD-7207	(S)	**Soul To Soul** (Soundtrack)	1971	6.00	15.00
Epic EG-30635	(S)	**The Staple Singers Make You Happy** (2 LPs)	1971	6.00	15.00
STARCASTLE					
Epic PE-34935	(DJ)	**Citadel** (Picture disc)	1979	8.00	20.00
STARDRIVE					
Elektra EQ-5058	(Q)	**Intergalactic Trot**	1973	6.00	15.00
STARFIRE					
Crimson S-4476/7	(S)	**Starfire**	1974	100.00	250.00
STARFIRES, THE					
Ohio Recording Serv. 34	(M)	**The Starfires Play**	1964	20.00	50.00
La Brea LS-8018	(M)	**Teenbeat A-Go-Go**	1965	20.00	50.00
STARK NAKED					
RCA Victor LSP-4592	(S)	**Stark Naked**	1971	10.00	25.00
STARLITES, THE: *Refer to* THE KODAKS / THE STARLITES					
STARR, EDWIN					
Gordy GS-931	(S)	**Soul Master**	1969	10.00	25.00
		("Agent Double-O Soul" is rechanneled on this album.)			
Gordy GS-940	(S)	**25 Miles**	1969	8.00	20.00
Gordy GS-948	(S)	**War And Peace**	1970	6.00	15.00
Gordy GS-956	(S)	**Involved**	1971	6.00	15.00
Motown 802	(S)	**Hell Up In Harlem**	1973	5.00	12.00
STARR, KAY					
Capitol H-211 (10")	(M)	**Songs By Starr**	1950	30.00	75.00
Capitol H-363 (10")	(M)	**Kay Starr Style**	1953	30.00	75.00
Capitol H-415 (10")	(M)	**The Hits Of Kay Starr**	1953	30.00	75.00
Capitol T-211	(M)	**Songs By Starr**	1955	20.00	50.00
Capitol T-363	(M)	**Kay Starr Style**	1955	20.00	50.00
Capitol T-415	(M)	**The Hits Of Kay Starr**	1955	20.00	50.00
Capitol T-580	(M)	**In A Blue Mood**	1955	20.00	50.00
— Original Capitol albums above have turquoise labels. —					
Liberty LRP-9001	(M)	**Swingin' With The Starr**	1956	20.00	50.00
Modern MLP-1203	(M)	**Singin' Kay Starr, Swingin' Erroll Garner**	1956	20.00	50.00

Label & Catalog #		Title	Year	VG+	NM
Rondo-Lette 3	(M)	Them There Eyes	1958	20.00	50.00
RCA Victor LPM-1149	(M)	The One And Only Kay Starr	1955	20.00	50.00
RCA Victor LPM-1549	(M)	Blue Starr	1957	20.00	50.00
RCA Victor LPM-1720	(M)	Rockin' With Kay	1958	30.00	75.00
RCA Victor LPM-2055	(M)	I Hear The Word	1959	14.00	35.00
RCA Victor LSP-2055	(S)	I Hear The Word	1959	20.00	50.00

— Original RCA mono albums above have "black labels with Long Play" on the bottom; stereo albums have have black labels with "Living Stereo" on the bottom.—

Capitol T-1254	(M)	Movin'	1959	8.00	20.00
Capitol ST-1254	(S)	Movin'	1959	12.00	30.00
Capitol T-1303	(M)	Losers, Weepers	1960	8.00	20.00
Capitol ST-1303	(S)	Losers, Weepers	1960	12.00	30.00
Capitol T-1358	(M)	One More Time	1960	8.00	20.00
Capitol ST-1358	(S)	One More Time	1960	12.00	30.00
Capitol T-1374	(M)	Movin' On Broadway	1960	8.00	20.00
Capitol ST-1374	(S)	Movin' On Broadway	1960	12.00	30.00
Capitol T-1438	(M)	Jazz Singer	1960	8.00	20.00
Capitol ST-1438	(S)	Jazz Singer	1960	12.00	30.00
Capitol T-1468	(M)	All Starr Hits	1961	8.00	20.00
Capitol ST-1468	(S)	All Starr Hits	1961	10.00	25.00
Capitol T-1681	(M)	I Cry By Night	1962	8.00	20.00
Capitol ST-1681	(S)	I Cry By Night	1962	10.00	25.00

— Original Capitol albums above have black labels with the logo on the left side.—

Capitol T-1795	(M)	Just Plain Country	1962	6.00	15.00
Capitol ST-1795	(S)	Just Plain Country	1962	8.00	20.00
Capitol T-2106	(M)	Fabulous Favorites	1964	4.00	10.00
Capitol ST-2106	(S)	Fabulous Favorites	1964	5.00	12.00
Capitol T-2550	(M)	Tears And Heartaches	1966	4.00	10.00
Capitol ST-2550	(S)	Tears And Heartaches	1966	5.00	12.00

— Original Capitol albums above have black labels with the logo on top.—

ABC S-631	(S)	When The Lights Go On Again	1968	4.00	10.00
Paramount 5001	(S)	How About This (With Count Basie)	1969	4.00	10.00

STARR, RINGO / PETER SELLERS / TERRY SOUTHERN

Commonwealth Un. 1761	(DJ)	"The Magic Christian" Interview	1969	60.00	150.00
		(One-sided, open-end interview with script.)			

STARR, RINGO
Refer to Badfinger; TheBeatles; Leon Russell; Doris Troy.

Apple SW-3365	(S)	Sentimental Journey	1970	8.00	20.00
Apple SMAS-3368	(S)	Beaucoups Of Blues	1970	8.00	20.00
Apple SWAL-3413	(S)	Ringo	1973	8.00	20.00
		(First pressings covers erroneously identify "Hold On" as "Have You Seen My Baby.")			
Apple SWAL-3413	(S)	Ringo	1973	6.00	15.00
		(Later covers correctly list "Hold On.")			
Apple SWAL-3413	(S)	Ringo	1973	80.00	200.00
		(Some early pressings with a cut-out hole in the cover contain a longer, 5:26 version of "Six O' Clock." Must be listened to for identification)			
Apple SW-3417	(S)	Goodnight Vienna	1974	6.00	15.00
Apple SW-3422	(S)	Blast From Your Past	1975	6.00	15.00
Atlantic SD-18193	(DJ)	Ringo's Rotogravure	1978	12.00	30.00
		(Standard copy with "DJ only" etched in trail-off vinyl.)			
Atlantic SD-18193	(S)	Ringo's Rotogravure	1978	3.50	8.00
Atlantic SD-19108	(DJ)	Ringo The 4th	1978	12.00	30.00
		(Standard copy with "DJ only" etched in trail-off vinyl.)			
Atlantic SD-19108	(S)	Ringo The 4th	1978	3.50	8.00
Portrait JR-35378	(DJ)	Bad Boy	1978	24.00	60.00
		(White label with "Advance Promotion" issued in a plain white cover.)			
Portrait JR-35378	(DJ)	Bad Boy	1978	10.00	25.00
		(White label with "Demonstration" issued in regular cover.)			
Portrait JR-35378	(S)	Bad Boy	1978	3.50	8.00
Capitol SW-3365	(S)	Sentimental Journey	197?	12.00	30.00
Capitol SN-16218	(S)	Sentimental Journey	197?	8.00	20.00
Capitol SN-16235	(S)	Beaucoups Of Blues	197?	6.00	15.00
Rykodisc RALP-0190	(S)	Ringo & His All-Star Band (Clear vinyl)	1990	10.00	25.00
		(Limited live edition sequentially numbered through #5000.)			

Originally a quintet (sort of), Steely dan quickly devolved into a duo of Walter Becker and Donald Fagen, with producer Gary Katz, and sundry L.A. session musicians. Their dedication to state-of-the-art sound made their albums obvious choices for the audiophile series of both Mobile Fidelity and MCA. After a contract dispute, Mobile Fidelity pulled Katy Lied and a collectible. was born. . .

Label & Catalog #		Title	Year	VG+	NM
STARZ					
Capitol ST-11539	(S)	**Starz**	1976	5.00	12.00
Capitol ST-11617	(DJ)	**Violation** (Yellow vinyl)	1977	8.00	20.00
Capitol ST-11617	(S)	**Violation**	1977	5.00	12.00
Capitol ST-11730	(S)	**Attention Shoppers**	1978	5.00	12.00
Capitol ST-11861	(S)	**Coliseum Rock**	1978	5.00	12.00
Capitol SPRO-8857/58	(DJ)	**Live In Louisville**	1978	12.00	30.00
STATLER BROTHERS, THE					
Columbia CL-2449	(M)	**Flowers On The Wall**	1966	10.00	25.00
Columbia CS-9249	(S)	**Flowers On The Wall**	1966	12.00	30.00
Columbia CL-2719	(M)	**The Big Hits**	1967	8.00	20.00
Columbia CS-9519	(S)	**The Big Hits**	1967	10.00	25.00
Columbia CS-9878	(S)	**Oh Happy Day**	1969	8.00	20.00
STATON, DAKOTA: Refer to GOLDMINE'S PRICE GUIDE TO COLLECTIBLE JAZZ ALBUMS					
STATUS QUO, THE					
Cadet Concept LPS-315	(E)	**Messages From The Status Quo**	1968	20.00	50.00
Janus JLS-3018	(S)	**Ma Kelly's Greasy Spoon**	1971	6.00	15.00
Pye 3301	(S)	**Dog Of Two Heads**	1972	6.00	15.00
STEAM					
Mercury SR-61254	(S)	**Steam**	1969	6.00	15.00
STEAMHAMMER					
Epic BN-26490	(S)	**Reflection**	1969	5.00	12.00
Epic BN-26552	(S)	**Steamhammer**	1970	5.00	12.00
STEAMPACKET					
Springboard SPB-4063	(S)	**Rod Stewart And Steampacket**	1972	6.00	15.00
STEELE, TOMMY					
London LL-1770	(M)	**Rock Around The World**	195?	20.00	50.00
STEELEYE SPAN					
Big Tree BTS-2004	(S)	**Please To See The King**	1971	12.00	30.00
		(The matrix numbers are stamped in the trail-off vinyl of originals; counterfeits have those numbers hand-etched.)			
Chrysalis CHR-1008	(S)	**Below The Salt**	1972	5.00	12.00
Chrysalis CHR-1046	(S)	**Parcel Of Rogues**	1973	5.00	12.00
Chrysalis CHR-1053	(S)	**Now We Are Six**	1974	5.00	12.00
Chrysalis CHR-1071	(S)	**Commoners Crown**	1975	5.00	12.00
Chrysalis CHR-1091	(S)	**All Around My Hat**	1975	5.00	12.00
Chrysalis CHR-1120	(S)	**Hark The Village Wait**	1976	5.00	12.00
Chrysalis CHR-1119	(S)	**Please To See The King**	1976	5.00	12.00
Chrysalis CHR-1121	(S)	**Ten Man Mop**	1976	5.00	12.00
Chrysalis CHR-1123	(S)	**Rocket Cottage**	1976	5.00	12.00
Chrysalis CHR-2-1136	(S)	**The Steeleye Span Story** (2 LPs)	1977	6.00	15.00
Chrysalis CHR-1151	(S)	**Storm Force Ten**	1978	4.00	10.00
Chrysalis CHR-1199	(S)	**Live At Last**	1978	4.00	10.00
Mobile Fidelity MFSL-027	(S)	**All Around My Hat**	1978	7.00	20.00
STEELY DAN					
Command QD-40009	(Q)	**Can't Buy A Thrill**	1974	6.00	15.00
Command QD-40010	(Q)	**Countdown To Ecstasy**	1974	6.00	15.00
Command QD-40015	(Q)	**Pretzel Logic**	1974	6.00	15.00
Mobile Fidelity MFSL-007	(S)	**Katy Lied**	1978	25.00	75.00
Mobile Fidelity MFSL-033	(S)	**Aja**	1979	13.00	40.00
MCA 16009	(S)	**Gaucho** (Half-speed master)	1980	16.00	40.00
STEPHEN & THE FARM BAND: Refer to THE FARM BAND					
STEPHENS, LEIGH					
Stevens was formerly a member of Blue Cheer.					
Phillips PHS-600-294	(S)	**Red Weather**	1969	20.00	50.00

Label & Catalog #		Title	Year	VG+	NM

STEPPENWOLF [JOHN KAY & STEPPENWOLF]

Label & Catalog #		Title	Year	VG+	NM
Dunhill D-50029	(M)	Steppenwolf	1968	40.00	100.00
Dunhill DS-50029	(S)	Steppenwolf	1968	10.00	25.00

— Original Dunhill albums above read "A Subsidiary of ABC Records" on the bottom of the label.—

Dunhill D-50037	(M)	The Second	1968	40.00	100.00
Dunhill DS-50037	(S)	The Second (Chrome border cover)	1968	8.00	20.00
Dunhill DS-50037	(S)	The Second (White border cover)	196?	12.00	30.00
ABC S-OC-9	(S)	Candy (Soundtrack)	1968	6.00	15.00
Dunhill DSX-50053	(S)	At Your Birthday Party	1969	5.00	12.00
Dunhill DSX-50060	(S)	Early Steppenwolf	1969	6.00	15.00
Dunhill DSX-50066	(S)	Monster	1969	5.00	12.00
Dunhill DSD-50075	(S)	Steppenwolf Live (2 LPs)	1970	5.00	12.00
Dunhill DSX-50090	(S)	Steppenwolf 7	1970	4.00	10.00
Dunhill DSX-50099	(S)	Gold/Their Greatest Hits	1970	4.00	10.00
Dunhill DSX-50110	(S)	For Ladies Only	1971	4.00	10.00

— Original Dunhill albums above have black labels with "Dunhill/ABC" on top and "Dunhill Records is a subsidiary" on the bottom.—

Nautilus NR-53	(S)	Wolftracks	198?	10.00	30.00

STEVENS, APRIL
Refer to Nino Tempo & April Stevens.

Audio Lab AL-1534	(M)	Torrid Tunes	1959	60.00	150.00
Imperial LP-9118	(M)	Teach Me Tiger	1960	20.00	50.00
Imperial LP-12055	(P)	Teach Me Tiger	1960	30.00	75.00

STEVENS, BOBBY: *Refer to* **THE CHECKMATES LTD.**

STEVENS, CAROL

Atlantic 1256	(M)	That Satin Doll	1957	14.00	35.00

STEVENS, CAT

Deram DE-18005	(M)	Matthew And Son	1967	8.00	20.00
Deram DES-18005	(P)	Matthew And Son	1967	10.00	25.00
Deram DES-18010	(S)	New Masters	1968	6.00	15.00
Deram DES-18005/10	(P)	Matthew And Son/New Masters (2 LPs)	1971	6.00	15.00
Deram DES-18061	(E)	Very Young And Early Songs	1971	5.00	12.00
London LC-5000	(S)	Cat's Cradle	1977	4.00	10.00
A&M SP-4260	(S)	Mona Bone Jakon	1969	6.00	15.00
A&M SP-4280	(S)	Tea For The Tillerman	1970	6.00	15.00
A&M SP-4313	(S)	Teaser And The Firecat	1970	6.00	15.00
A&M SP-4365	(S)	Catch Bull At Four	1972	6.00	15.00

— Original A&M albums above have brown labels.—

A&M QU-54280	(Q)	Tea For The Tillerman	1974	10.00	25.00
A&M QU-54313	(Q)	Teaser And The Firecat	1974	10.00	25.00
A&M QU-54365	(Q)	Catch Bull At Four	1974	10.00	25.00
A&M QU-54391	(Q)	Foreigner	1974	10.00	25.00
A&M QU-53623	(Q)	Buddha And The Chocolate Box	1974	10.00	25.00
A&M QU-54519	(Q)	Greatest Hits	1975	10.00	25.00
Mobile Fidelity MFSL-035	(S)	Tea For The Tillerman	1979	10.00	30.00
Mobile Fidelity MFQR-035	(S)	Tea For The Tillerman	1984	25.00	75.00
		(Ultra High Quality Recording in a box.)			

STEVENS, CONNIE

Warner Bros. W-1208	(M)	Conchetta	1958	20.00	50.00
Warner Bros. W-1335	(M)	Hawaiian Eye (TV Soundtrack)	1959	20.00	50.00
Warner Bros. WS-1335	(S)	Hawaiian Eye (TV Soundtrack)	1959	30.00	75.00
Warner Bros. W-1382	(M)	Connie Stevens From "Hawaiian Eye"	1960	10.00	25.00
Warner Bros. WS-1382	(S)	Connie Stevens From "Hawaiian Eye"	1960	12.00	30.00
Warner Bros. W-1431	(M)	From Me To You	1962	10.00	25.00
Warner Bros. WS-1431	(S)	From Me To You	1962	12.00	30.00
Warner Bros. W-1432	(M)	Connie	1962	10.00	25.00
Warner Bros. WS-1432	(S)	Connie	1962	12.00	30.00
Warner Bros. W-1460	(M)	The Hank Williams Songbook	1962	10.00	25.00
Warner Bros. WS-1460	(S)	The Hank Williams Songbook	1962	12.00	30.00
Warner Bros. W-1519	(M)	Palm Springs Weekend (Soundtrack)	1963	20.00	50.00
Warner Bros. WS-1519	(S)	Palm Springs Weekend (Soundtrack)	1963	30.00	75.00

— Original Warner albums above have grey labels.—

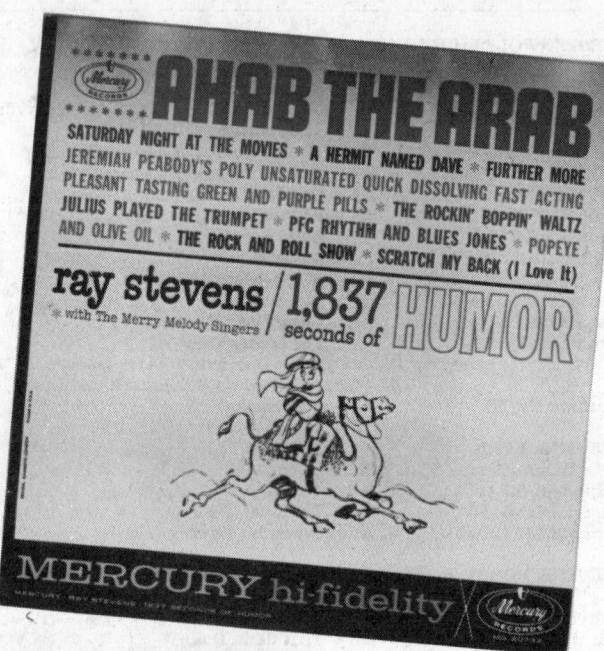

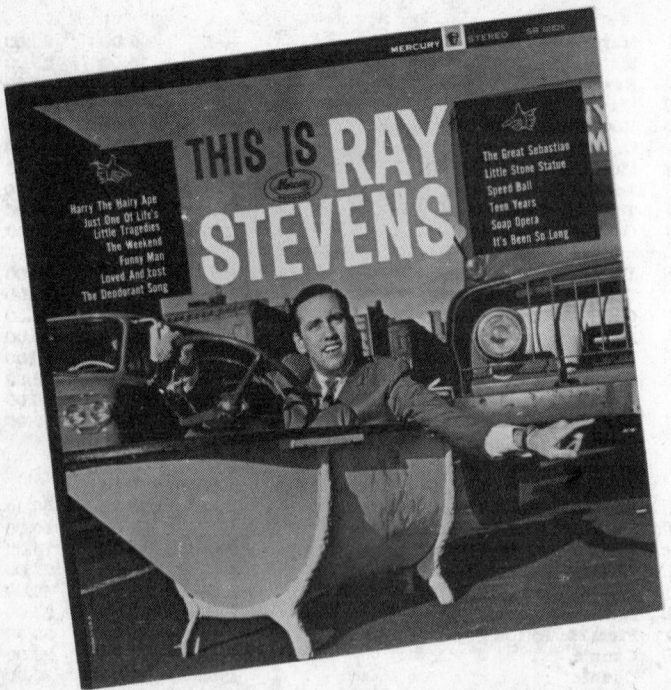

Of Ray Stevens' seven charting singles for Mercury, seven can be found on these, his first two albums. Only 1962's seasonal hit, "Santa Claus Is Watching You," remains uncollected. Ray's career has also included successful stints with Monument, Barnaby and Warner Bros.

Label & Catalog #		Title	Year	VG+	NM
STEVENS, DODIE					
Dot DLP-3212	(M)	**Dodie Stevens**	*1960*	10.00	25.00
Dot DLP-25212	(S)	**Dodie Stevens**	*1960*	14.00	35.00
Dot DLP-3323	(M)	**Over The Rainbow**	*1960*	10.00	25.00
Dot DLP-25323	(S)	**Over The Rainbow**	*1960*	14.00	35.00
Dot DLP-3371	(M)	**Pink Shoelaces**	*1961*	10.00	25.00
Dot DLP-25371	(S)	**Pink Shoelaces**	*1961*	14.00	35.00
STEVENS, RAY					
Ray also recorded as Baby Ray.					
Mercury MG-20732	(M)	**1,837 Seconds Of Humor/Ahab The Arab**	*1962*	16.00	40.00
Mercury SR-60732	(S)	**1,837 Seconds Of Humor/Ahab The Arab**	*1962*	20.00	50.00
Mercury MG-20828	(M)	**This Is Ray Stevens**	*1963*	10.00	25.00
Mercury SR-60828	(S)	**This Is Ray Stevens**	*1963*	12.00	30.00
Wing MGW-12377	(S)	**The Best Of Ray Stevens**	*1968*	5.00	12.00
Wing SRW-16377	(S)	**The Best Of Ray Stevens**	*1968*	6.00	15.00
Monument SLP-18102	(S)	**Even Stevens**	*1968*	6.00	15.00
Monument SLP-18115	(S)	**Gitarzan**	*1969*	6.00	15.00
Monument SLP-18134	(S)	**Have A Little Talk With Myself**	*1969*	6.00	15.00
STEVENS, RAY / HAL WINTERS					
Crown CLP-5333	(M)	**Ray Stevens And Hal Winters**	*1963*	8.00	20.00
Crown CST-333	(E)	**Ray Stevens And Hal Winters**	*1963*	4.00	10.00
STEWART, AL					
Epic BN-26564	(S)	**Love Chronicles**	*1970*	6.00	15.00
Arista SP-40	(DJ)	**The Live Radio Concert**	*1980*	16.00	40.00
Mobile Fidelity MFSL-009	(S)	**Year Of The Cat**	*1979*	10.00	30.00
●Mobile Fidelity MFSL-082	(S)	**Time Passages**	*1981*	7.00	20.00
Nautilus NR-34	(S)	**24 Carrots**	*198?*	5.00	15.00
STEWART, BILLY					
Chess LP-1496	(M)	**I Do Love You**	*1965*	20.00	50.00
Chess LPS-1496	(S)	**I Do Love You**	*1965*	30.00	75.00
		(Original covers are red with a black wheel design.)			
Chess LP-1496	(M)	**I Do Love You**	*1965*	12.00	30.00
Chess LPS-1496	(S)	**I Do Love You**	*1965*	16.00	40.00
		(Later pressings have a green cover with a woman at the bottom.)			
Chess LP-1499	(M)	**Unbelievable**	*1965*	12.00	30.00
Chess LPS-1499	(S)	**Unbelievable**	*1965*	16.00	40.00
Chess LP-1513	(M)	**Teaches Old Standards New Tricks**	*1967*	10.00	25.00
Chess LPS-1513	(S)	**Teaches Old Standards New Tricks**	*1967*	12.00	30.00
Chess LPS-1547	(S)	**Billy Stewart Remembered**	*1968*	12.00	30.00

STEWART, HELEYNE: *Refer to* GOLDMINE'S PRICE GUIDE TO COLLECTIBLE JAZZ ALBUMS

Label & Catalog #		Title	Year	VG+	NM
STEWART, JOHN					
Stewart was formerly a member of The Cumberland Three; The Kingston Trio.					
Capitol T-2975	(M)	**Signals Through The Glass**	*1968*	12.00	30.00
Capitol ST-2975	(S)	**Signals Through The Glass**	*1968*	6.00	15.00
Capitol ST-203	(S)	**California Bloodlines**	*1969*	6.00	15.00
		— Original Capitol albums above have black rainbow labels labels.—			
Capitol ST-540	(S)	**Willard** *(Green label)*	*1970*	6.00	15.00
Warner Bros. WS-1948	(S)	**Lonesome Picker Rides Again**	*1971*	5.00	12.00
Warner Bros. BS-2611	(S)	**Sunstorm**	*1972*	5.00	12.00
STEWART, RED					
Audio Lab AL-1528	(M)	**Favorite Old Songs**	*1959*	40.00	100.00
STEWART, ROD					
Refer to Steampacket; The Jeff Beck Group; The Small Faces.					
Mercury SR-61237	(S)	**The Rod Stewart Album**	*1969*	10.00	25.00
		(Original gatefold covers are yellow/gold with a black border.)			
Mercury SR-61264	(S)	**Gasoline Alley**	*1970*	6.00	15.00
		(Original gatefold covers are textured, especially on the pebbles.)			
Mercury SRM-1-609	(S)	**Every Picture Tells A Story**	*1971*	4.00	10.00
		(Original gatefold cover opens out into a tri-fold poster.)			
Mercury SRM-1-646	(S)	**Never A Dull Moment** *(Gatefold cover)*	*1972*	4.00	10.00
		—Mercury albums above have red labels with twelve logos around the perimeter.—			

Label & Catalog #		Title	Year	VG+	NM
Mercury SRM-1-697	(S)	Coast To Coast/Overture And Beginners	1974	5.00	12.00
Mercury SRM-1-1017	(S)	Smiler	1974	5.00	12.00
Warner Bros. BSP-3276	(S)	Blondes Have More Fun (Picture disc)	1979	4.00	10.00
Warner Bros. 1-23473	(DJ)	Absolutely Live (2 LPs. Quiex II vinyl)	1982	8.00	20.00
Mobile Fidelity MFSL-054	(S)	Blondes Have More Fun	1981	7.00	20.00

STEWART, WYNN (& THE TOURISTS)

Wrangler W-1006	(M)	Wynn Stewart	1962	10.00	25.00
Wrangler WS-1006	(S)	Wynn Stewart	1962	12.00	30.00
Capitol T-2332	(M)	The Songs Of Wynn Stewart	1965	10.00	25.00
Capitol ST-2332	(S)	The Songs Of Wynn Stewart	1965	12.00	30.00
Capitol T-2737	(M)	It's Such A Pretty World Today	1967	8.00	20.00
Capitol ST-2737	(S)	It's Such A Pretty World Today	1967	10.00	25.00
Capitol T-2849	(M)	Love's Gonna Happen To Me	1968	10.00	25.00
Capitol ST-2849	(S)	Love's Gonna Happen To Me	1968	8.00	20.00
Capitol ST-2921	(S)	Something Pretty	1968	8.00	20.00

STEWART, WYNN, & JAN HOWARD

Challenge CHL-611	(M)	Sweethearts Of Country Music	1961	24.00	60.00

STIDHAM, ARBEE

Bluesville BVLP-1021	(M)	Tired Of Wandering	1961	20.00	50.00

STING

Mobile Fidelity MFSL-185	(S)	Dream Of The Blue Turtles	198?	7.00	20.00

STITES, GARY

Carlton LP-120	(M)	Lonely For You	1960	20.00	50.00
Carlton STLP-120	(S)	Lonely For You	1960	30.00	75.00

STONE, CLIFFIE [CLIFFIE STONE'S HOMBRES]

Capitol H-4009 (10")	(M)	Square Dances	1958	20.00	50.00
Capitol T-1080	(M)	The Party's On Me	1958	20.00	50.00
Capitol T-1230	(M)	Cool Cowboy	1959	12.00	30.00
Capitol ST-1230	(S)	Cool Cowboy	1959	16.00	40.00
Capitol T-1286	(M)	Square Dance Promenade	1960	8.00	20.00
Capitol ST-1286	(S)	Square Dance Promenade	1960	12.00	30.00
Capitol KAO-1555	(M)	Original Cowboy Sing-A-Long	1961	8.00	20.00
Capitol SKAO-1555	(S)	Original Cowboy Sing-A-Long	1961	12.00	30.00
—Original Capitol albums above have black labels with the logo on the left side.—					
Tower T-5073	(M)	Together Again	1967	6.00	15.00
Tower ST-5073	(S)	Together Again	1967	8.00	20.00

STONE, ROLAND

Ace LP-1018	(M)	Just A Moment	1961	40.00	100.00

STONE CIRCUS, THE

Mainstream S-6119	(S)	The Stone Circus	1969	6.00	15.00

STONE COUNTRY

RCA Victor LSP-3958	(S)	Stone Country	1968	20.00	50.00

STONE HARBOUR

Stone Harbour 398	(S)	Stone Harbour Emerges	1974	360.00	600.00

STONE PONEYS: Refer to LINDA RONSTADT & THE STONE PONEYS

STONE THE CROWS

Polydor 24-4019	(S)	Stone The Crows	1970	8.00	20.00
Polydor 24-5020	(S)	Teenage Licks	1972	6.00	15.00
Polydor 24-5037	(S)	Continuous Performance	1972	6.00	15.00

STONEGROUND

Stoneground features Sal Valentino of The Beau Brummels.

Warner Bros. WS-1895	(S)	Stoneground	1971	8.00	20.00
Warner Bros. 2ZS-1956	(S)	Family Album (2 LPs)	1971	10.00	25.00
...rner Bros. BS-2645	(S)	Stoneground 3	1972	6.00	15.00
Out 101	(S)	Flat Out	1976	8.00	20.00
...al Clear	(S)	Play It Loud	198?	6.00	15.00

Label & Catalog #		Title	Year	VG+	NM
STONEHILL, RANDY					
One Way JC-31252	(S)	**Born Twice**	1972	20.00	50.00
Solid Rock SRA-2002	(S)	**Welcome To Paradise**	1976	6.00	15.00
Solid Rock SRA-2005	(S)	**The Sky Is Falling**	1980	8.00	20.00
Myrrh MSB-6679	(S)	**Between The Glory And The Flame**	1981	6.00	15.00
STONEMANS, THE [THE STONEMAN FAMILY]					
World Pacific WP-1828	(M)	**Big Ball In Monterey**	1964	10.00	25.00
World Pacific ST-1828	(S)	**Big Ball In Monterey**	1964	12.00	30.00
Starday SLP-393	(M)	**White Lightning**	1965	12.00	30.00
MGM E-4363	(M)	**Those Singin,' Swingin,' Stompin,' Sensational Stonemans**	1966	6.00	15.00
MGM SE-4363	(S)	**Those Singin,' Swingin,' Stompin,' Sensational Stonemans**	1966	8.00	20.00
MGM E-4453	(M)	**Stoneman's Country**	1967	6.00	15.00
MGM SE-4453	(S)	**Stoneman's Country**	1967	8.00	20.00
MGM E-4511	(M)	**All In The Family**	1967	6.00	15.00
MGM SE-4511	(S)	**All In The Family**	1967	8.00	20.00
MGM E-4578	(M)	**The Great Stonemans**	1968	6.00	15.00
MGM SE-4578	(S)	**The Great Stonemans**	1968	6.00	15.00
MGM SE-4588	(S)	**Pop Stoneman Memorial Album**	1969	6.00	15.00
MGM SE-4613	(S)	**A Stoneman Christmas**	1968	6.00	15.00
MGM GAS-125	(S)	**The Stonemans**	1970	4.00	15.00
STONEY & MEAT LOAF					
Rare Earth R-5281	(S)	**Stoney And Meatloaf**	1971	6.00	15.00
STOOGES, THE					
The Stooges feature Iggy Pop.					
Elektra EKS-74051	(S)	**The Stooges** (Red label)	1969	20.00	50.00
Elektra EKS-74101	(S)	**Fun House** (Red label)	1970	20.00	50.00
		— Original Elektra albums above have red labels.—			
Elektra EKS-74051	(S)	**The Stooges** (Butterfly label)	197?	8.00	20.00
Elektra EKS-74101	(S)	**Fun House** (Butterfly label)	197?	8.00	20.00
		— Elektra albums above have butterfly labels.—			
Columbia KC-32111	(S)	**Raw Power** (With inner sleeve)	1973	20.00	50.00
STOOKEY, PAUL					
Refer to Peter, Paul And Mary.					
Warner Bros. WS-1912	(S)	**Paul And**	1971	4.00	10.00
Warner Bros. BS-2674	(S)	**Noel**	1973	4.00	10.00
STORIES					
Stories features Michael Brown of The Left Banke.					
Kama Sutra KSBS-2068	(S)	**About Us** (Without "Brother Louie")	1973	5.00	12.00
Kama Sutra KSBS-2051	(S)	**About Us** (With "Brother Louie")	1973	6.00	15.00
Kama Sutra KSBS-2051	(S)	**Stories**	197?	4.00	10.00
Kama Sutra KSBS-2078	(S)	**Travelling Underground**	19??	4.00	10.00
STORCH, LARRY					
Prestige PRST-7683	(S)	**Phillip Roth's "Epstein" Read By Larry Storch**	1968	10.00	25.00
STORM, BILLY (& THE VALIANTS)					
Buena Vista BV-3315	(M)	**Billy Storm**	1963 1969	30.00 100.00	75.00 250.00
Famous F-504	(M)	**This Is The Night**			
		(Famous 504 conto... m's early vocal group recordings.)			
STORM, GALE					
Dot DLP-3011	(M)	**Gale Storm**	1956 1956	30.00	50.00
Dot DLP-3017	(M)	**Sentimental...ly**	1958	30.00	50.00
Dot DLP-3098	(M)	**Gale Storm...rly**	1959	16.00	40.00
Dot DLP-3197	(M)	**Softly A...gs**	1959	12.00	30.00
Dot DLP-25197	(S)	**Softly ...ings**	1959	16.00	40.00
Dot DLP-3209	(M)	**Gal...**	1959	12.00	30.00
Dot DLP-25209	(S)	**G... ...waways**		16.00	40.00
STOWAWAYS, THE					
Justice SLP-	(...		196?	150.00	300.00

Label & Catalog #		Title	Year	VG+	NM

STRACKE, WIN

Label & Catalog #		Title	Year	VG+	NM
Bally 12013	(M)	Americana	195?	10.00	25.00
Golden GLP-31	(M)	Golden Treasury Of Songs	195?	10.00	25.00

STRANGE

Label & Catalog #		Title	Year	VG+	NM
Outer Galaxie 1000	(S)	Translucent World	1973	12.00	30.00
Outer Galaxie 1001	(S)	Raw Power	1976	20.00	50.00
Star People 0013	(S)	High Flyer (Colored vinyl)	1981	8.00	20.00

(Five different colors are known for Star People 0013.)

STRANGE, BILLY

Label & Catalog #		Title	Year	VG+	NM
Coliseum CM-1001	(M)	Limbo Rock			
Crescendo GNP-94	(M)	Twelve String Guitar	1962	20.00	50.00
Crescendo GNPS-94	(S)	Twelve String Guitar	1963	6.00	15.00
Crescendo GNP-97	(M)	Mr. Guitar	1963	8.00	20.00
Crescendo GNPS-97	(S)	Mr. Guitar	1964	6.00	15.00
Crescendo GNP-2004	(M)	James Bond Theme And Others	1964	8.00	20.00
Crescendo GNPS-2004	(S)	James Bond Theme And Others	1964	6.00	15.00
Crescendo GNP2006	(M)	Goldfinger	1964	8.00	20.00
Crescendo GNPS-2006	(S)	Goldfinger	1965	6.00	15.00
Crescendo GNP-2009	(M)	English Hits Of '65	1965	8.00	20.00
Crescendo GNPS-2009	(S)	English Hits Of '65	1965	6.00	15.00
Crescendo GNP-2012	(M)	Billy Strange Plays The Hits	1965	8.00	20.00
Crescendo GNPS-2012	(S)	Billy Strange Plays The Hits	1965	6.00	15.00
Crescendo GNP-2016	(M)	Folk-Rock Hits	1965	8.00	20.00
Crescendo GNPS-2016	(S)	Folk-Rock Hits	1965	6.00	15.00
Crescendo GNP-2019	(M)	Secret Agent File	1965	8.00	20.00
Crescendo GNPS-2019	(S)	Secret Agent File	1965	6.00	15.00
Surrey S-1001	(M)	The Best Of Billy Strange	1965	8.00	20.00
Surrey SS-1001	(S)	The Best Of Billy Strange	1965	6.00	15.00
Crescendo GNP-2022	(M)	In The Mexican Bag	1966	8.00	20.00
Crescendo GNPS-2022	(S)	In The Mexican Bag	1966	6.00	15.00
Crescendo GNP-2024	(M)	King Of The Road	1966	8.00	20.00
Crescendo GNPS-2024	(S)	King Of The Road	1966	6.00	15.00
Crescendo GNP-2037	(M)	The Best Of Billy Strange	1967	8.00	20.00
Crescendo GNPS-2037	(S)	The Best Of Billy Strange	1967	6.00	15.00
Crescendo GNPS-2041	(S)	Railroad Man	1968	8.00	20.00
Tower ST-5170	(S)	De Sade (Soundtrack)	1969	16.00	40.00

STRANGELOVES, THE

Label & Catalog #		Title	Year	VG+	NM
Bang BLP-211	(M)	I Want Candy	1965	30.00	75.00
Bang BLPS-211	(S)	I Want Candy	1965	40.00	100.00

STRAWBERRY ALARM CLOCK, THE

Refer to The Wh / The Strawberry Alarm Clock.

Label & Catalog #		Title	Year	VG+	NM
Uni 3014	(M)	Incense And Peppermints	1967	12.00	30.00
Uni 73014	(S)	Incense And Peppermints	1967	16.00	40.00
Uni 3025	(M)	Wake Up It's Tomorrow	1967	10.00	25.00
Uni 73025	(S)	Wake Up It's Tomorrow	1967	12.00	30.00
Uni 73035	(S)	The World In A Sea Shell	1968	12.00	30.00
Uni 73054	(S)	Good Morning Starshine	1969	12.00	30.00
Uni 73074	(S)	The Best Of The Strawberry Alarm Clock	1970	10.00	25.00
20th Century TFS-4211	(S)	Beyond The Valley Of The Dolls (Sdtk)	1970	20.00	50.00
Vocalion 73915	(S)	[...]nges	1971	10.00	25.00

STRAY

Label & Catalog #		Title	Year	VG+	NM
Transatlantic TRA-216	(S)	Stra[y]	197?	12.00	30.00
Mercury SRM-1-611	(S)	Suic[ide]	1971	6.00	15.00
Mercury SRM-1-624	(S)	Saturd[ay Morn]ing Pictures	1971	6.00	15.00

STRAYWINDS

Label & Catalog #		Title	Year	VG+	NM
Shamyn-Alexus 413504	(S)	Straywinds	1973	30.00	75.00

STREET

Label & Catalog #		Title	Year	VG+	NM
Verve/Forecast FTS-3057	(S)	Street	1968	8.00	20.00

STREISAND, BARBRA

Label & Catalog #		Title	Year	VG+	NM
Columbia KOL-5780	(M)	I Can Get It For You Wh[olesale] (Soundtrack)	1962	10.00	25.00
Columbia KOS-2180	(S)	I Can Get It For You Wh[olesale] (Soundtrack)	1962	12.00	30.00

Label & Catalog #		Title	Year	VG+	NM
Columbia OL-5810	(M)	Pins And Needles (Soundtrack)	1962	10.00	25.00
Columbia OS-2210	(S)	Pins And Needles (Soundtrack)	1962	12.00	30.00
Columbia CL-2007	(M)	The Barbra Streisand Album	1963	8.00	20.00
Columbia CS-8807	(S)	The Barbra Streisand Album	1963	10.00	25.00
Columbia CL-2054	(DJ)	The Second Barbra Streisand Album (Blue vinyl)	1963	30.00	75.00
Columbia CS-8854	(DJ)	The Second Barbra Streisand Album (Blue vinyl)	1963	40.00	100.00
Columbia CL-2054	(M)	The Second Barbra Streisand Album	1963	8.00	20.00
Columbia CS-8854	(S)	The Second Barbra Streisand Album	1963	10.00	25.00
Columbia CL-2154	(M)	The Third Barbra Streisand Album	1964	8.00	20.00
Columbia CS-8954	(S)	The Third Barbra Streisand Album	1964	10.00	25.00
Capitol VAS-2059	(M)	Funny Girl (Soundtrack)	1964	8.00	20.00
Capitol SVAS-2059	(S)	Funny Girl (Soundtrack)	1964	10.00	25.00
Columbia CL-2215	(M)	People	1964	8.00	20.00
Columbia CS-9015	(S)	People	1964	10.00	25.00
Columbia CL-2336	(M)	My Name Is Barbra	1965	8.00	20.00
Columbia CS-9136	(S)	My Name Is Barbra	1965	10.00	25.00

— Original Columbia mono labels above read "Guaranteed High Fidelity" on the bottom; stereo albums read "360 Sound Stereo" in black .—

Label & Catalog #		Title	Year	VG+	NM
Columbia CL-2007	(M)	The Barbra Streisand Album	1965	5.00	12.00
Columbia CS-8807	(S)	The Barbra Streisand Album	1965	6.00	15.00
Columbia CL-2054	(M)	The Second Barbra Streisand Album	1965	5.00	12.00
Columbia CS-8854	(S)	The Second Barbra Streisand Album	1965	6.00	15.00
Columbia CL-2154	(M)	The Third Barbra Streisand Album	1965	5.00	12.00
Columbia CS-8954	(S)	The Third Barbra Streisand Album	1965	6.00	15.00
Columbia CL-2215	(M)	People	1965	5.00	12.00
Columbia CS-9015	(S)	People	1965	6.00	15.00
Columbia CL-2336	(M)	My Name Is Barbra	1965	5.00	12.00
Columbia CS-9136	(S)	My Name Is Barbra	1965	6.00	15.00
Columbia CL-2409	(M)	My Name Is Barbra, Two. . .	1965	5.00	12.00
Columbia CS-9209	(S)	My Name Is Barbra, Two. . .	1965	6.00	15.00
Columbia CL-2478	(DJ)	Color Me Barbra (Red vinyl)	1966	30.00	75.00
Columbia CS-9278	(DJ)	Color Me Barbra (Red vinyl)	1966	40.00	100.00
Columbia CL-2478	(M)	Color Me Barbra	1966	5.00	12.00
Columbia CS-9278	(S)	Color Me Barbra	1966	6.00	15.00
Columbia CL-2547	(M)	Je M'appelle Barbra	1966	5.00	12.00
Columbia CS-9347	(S)	Je M'appelle Barbra	1966	6.00	15.00
Columbia CL-2682	(M)	Simply Streisand	1967	8.00	20.00
Columbia CS-9482	(S)	Simply Streisand	1967	5.00	12.00
Columbia CL-2757	(M)	Barbra's Christmas Album	1967	8.00	20.00
Columbia CS-9557	(S)	Barbra's Christmas Album	1967	5.00	12.00
Columbia BOS-3220	(S)	Funny Girl (Soundtrack)	1968	6.00	15.00
Columbia CS-9710	(S)	A Happening In Central Park	1968	5.00	12.00
Columbia CS-9816	(S)	What About Today?	1969	5.00	12.00
Columbia CS-9968	(S)	Barbra Streisand's Greatest Hits	1970	6.00	15.00

— Original Columbia albums above have "360 Sound" in white on the bottom of the label.—

Label & Catalog #		Title	Year	VG+	NM
20th Century DTCS-5103	(S)	Hello Dolly! (Soundtrack)	1969	5.00	12.00
Columbia S-30410	(S)	The Owl And The Pussycat (Soundtrack)	1970	5.00	12.00
Columbia PCQ-30378	(Q)	Stoney End	1971	8.00	20.00
Columbia PCQ-30792	(Q)	Barbra Joan Streisand	1971	8.00	20.00
Columbia SQ-30992	(Q)	Funny Girl (Soundtrack)	1972	8.00	20.00
Columbia PCQ-31760	(Q)	Live In Concert At The Forum	1972	8.00	20.00
Columbia PCQ-32801	(Q)	The Way We Were	1974	8.00	20.00
Columbia PCQ-33005	(Q)	Butterfly	1974	8.00	20.00
Columbia PCQ-33815	(Q)	Lazy Afternoon	1975	8.00	20.00
Arista AQ-9004	(Q)	Funny Lady (Soundtrack)	1975	8.00	20.00
Columbia HC-42801	(S)	The Way We Were (Half-speed master)	1982	20.00	60.00
Columbia HC-45679	(S)	Greatest Hits, Vol. 2 (Half-speed master)	1982	10.00	30.00
Columbia HC-46750	(S)	Guilty (Half-speed master)	1982	7.00	20.00
Columbia HC-47678	(S)	Memories (Half-speed master)	1982	20.00	60.00
Columbia AS-1779	(DJ)	The Legend Of Barbra Streisand (2 LPs) (Interview with music promoting "Yentl.")	1983	12.00	30.00
Columbia AS-99-1891	(DJ)	Yentl (Picture disc)	1983	6.00	15.00
Columbia 9C9-39909	(S)	Emotion (Picture disc)	1985	4.00	10.00

STRIDER

Label & Catalog #		Title	Year	VG+	NM
Warner Bros. BS-2722	(S)	Exposed	1973	6.00	15.00

Label & Catalog #		Title	Year	VG+	NM
STRIDERS, THE					
Apollo 480	(M)	**Hesitating Fool**	1955	100.00	250.00
STRING-A-LONGS, THE					
Warwick W-2036	(M)	**Pick-A-Hit Featuring "Wheels"**	1961	20.00	50.00
Warwick W-2036ST	(S)	**Pick-A-Hit Featuring "Wheels"**	1961	40.00	100.00
STRINGBEAN					
Starday SLP-142	(M)	**Old Time Pickin' And Singin'**	1961	20.00	50.00
Starday SLP-179	(M)	**Stringbean**	1962	16.00	40.00
Starday SLP-215	(M)	**A Salute To Uncle Dave Macon**	1963	16.00	40.00
Starday SLP-260	(M)	**Way Back In The Hills Of Old Kentucky**	1964	16.00	40.00
STROKE BAND, THE					
Abacus 78-095	(S)	**Green And Yellow**	1978	60.00	150.00
STRONG, NOLAN, & THE DIABLOS					
Fortune LP-8010	(M)	**Fortune Of Hits**	1961	60.00	150.00
Fortune LP-8012	(M)	**Fortune Of Hits, Volume 2**	1962	60.00	150.00
Fortune LP-8015	(M)	**Mind Over Matter**	1963	80.00	200.00
		— Original Fortune albums above have purple labels on thick vinyl.—			
Fortune LP-8010	(M)	**Fortune Of Hits**	196?	20.00	50.00
Fortune LP-8012	(M)	**Fortune Of Hits, Volume 2**	196?	20.00	50.00
Fortune LP-8015	(M)	**Mind Over Matter**	196?	30.00	75.00
		— Fortune albums above have yellow labels on thick vinyl.—			
Fortune LP-8010	(M)	**Fortune Of Hits**	198?	6.00	15.00
Fortune LP-8012	(M)	**Fortune Of Hits, Volume 2**	198?	6.00	15.00
Fortune LP-8015	(M)	**Mind Over Matter**	198?	8.00	20.00
		— Fortune albums above have bluish purple labels on thin vinyl.—			
STRYPER					
Enigma E-1064	(S)	**The Yellow And Black Attack** *(Yellow vinyl)*	1984	16.00	40.00
Enigma 72077	(S)	**Soldiers Under Command** *(White vinyl)*	1985	5.00	12.00
Capitol SEAX-73277	(S)	**To Hell With The Devil** *(Picture disc)*	1986	6.00	15.00
Enigma PENVLP-501	(S)	**In God We Trust** *(Picture disc)*	1988	8.00	20.00
STYLISTICS, THE					
Avco Embassy 33023	(S)	**The Stylistics**	1971	5.00	12.00
Avco Embassy 11006	(S)	**Round 2**	1972	5.00	12.00
Avco Embassy 11010	(S)	**Rockin' Roll Baby**	1973	5.00	12.00
Avco Embassy 69001	(S)	**Let's Put It All Together**	1974	5.00	12.00
Avco Embassy 69004	(S)	**Heavy**	1974	4.00	10.00
Avco Embassy 69008	(S)	**Thank You Baby**	1975	4.00	10.00
Avco Embassy 69010	(S)	**You Are Beautiful**	1975	4.00	10.00
STYX					
A&M SP-8431	(DJ)	**The Styx Radio Special** *(2 LPs)*	1977	10.00	25.00
A&M SP-17053	(DJ)	**The Styx Radio Special** *(3 LP box)*	1978	16.00	40.00
A&M SP-17222	(DJ)	**The Styx Radio Sampler** *(2 LPs)*	1978	10.00	25.00
Mobile Fidelity MFSL-026	(S)	**The Grand Illusion**	1978	8.00	25.00
Nautilus NR-15	(S)	**Pieces Of Eight**	198?	5.00	15.00
Nautilus NR-45	(S)	**Paradise Theatre**	198?	5.00	15.00
Nautilus NR-27	(S)	**Cornerstone**	198?	5.00	15.00
SUB-ZERO BAND, THE					
Sub-Zero 1172	(S)	**The Sub-Zero Band**	197?	100.00	250.00
SUGAR BEARS, THE					
The Bears feature Kim Carnes.					
Big Tree BTS-2009	(S)	**Introducing The Sugar Bears**	1971	10.00	25.00
SUGARLOAF					
Sugarloaf features Jerry Corbetta, later of The Four Seasons.					
Liberty LST-7640	(S)	**Sugarloaf**	1970	8.00	20.00
rty LST-11010	(S)	**Spaceship Earth**	1971	6.00	15.00
006	(S)	**I Got A Song**	1973	6.00	15.00
L-1000	(S)	**Don't Call Us**	1975	10.00	25.00

MAXINE: *Refer to* GOLDMINE'S PRICE GUIDE TO COLLECTIBLE JAZZ ALBUMS

Label & Catalog #		Title	Year	VG+	NM

SULLIVAN, ROCKY
Both albums feature John Cippolina on guitar. Refer to Quicksilver Messenger Service.

Label & Catalog #		Title	Year	VG+	NM
Jupiter 2006	(S)	Illegal Entry	1980	10.00	25.00
Rag Baby 1021	(S)	Caught In The Crossfire	1984	6.00	15.00

SUMAC, YMA

Capitol H-299 (10")	(M)	Legend Of The Sun Virgin	1951	40.00	100.00
Capitol T-299	(M)	Legend Of The Sun Virgin	1954	24.00	60.00
Capitol T-564	(M)	Mambo!	1954	24.00	60.00
Capitol T-580	(M)	In A Blue Mood	1955	24.00	60.00
Capitol W-684	(M)	Voice Of The Ixtabay And Inca Tacqui	1956	24.00	60.00

SUMMER, DONNA

Casablanca OCLP-5003	(S)	Love To Love You, Baby *(With poster)*	1979	6.00	15.00
Casablanca 7119	(S)	Best Of "Live & More" *(Picture disc)*	1979	4.00	10.00
Geffen GHS-24040	(DJ)	Cats Without Claws *(Quiex II vinyl)*	1984	5.00	12.00

SUMMER SOUNDS

Laurel 90973	(S)	Up And Down	196?	500.00	800.00

SUNDAY FUNNIES, THE

Rare Earth RS-526	(S)	Sunday Funnies	1971	6.00	15.00
Rare Earth RS-538	(S)	Benediction	1972	6.00	15.00

SUNDOG SUMMIT

(No label)	(S)	On Summit Hill	1976	40.00	100.00

SUNDOWNERS, THE

Liberty LRP-3269	(M)	Folk Songs For The Rich	1962	6.00	15.00
Liberty LST-7269	(S)	Folk Songs For The Rich	1962	8.00	20.00
Decca DL-75036	(S)	Captain Nemo	1968	6.00	15.00

SUNGLOWS, THE

Sunglow SLP-103	(M)	The Original Peanuts	1965	20.00	50.00

SUNNY & THE SUNLINERS

Tear Drop 2000	(M)	Talk To Me/Rags To Riches	1963	30.00	75.00
Tear Drop 2019	(M)	All Night Worker	1964	20.00	50.00

SUNNYLAND SLIM

Bluesville BVLP-1016	(M)	Slim's Shout	1961	20.00	50.00
Prestige PRST-7723	(S)	Slim's Shout	1969	6.00	15.00
		(Prestige 7723 is a reissue of Bluesville 1015.)			
World Pacific WPS-21890	(S)	Slim's Got His Thing Goin' On	1969	8.00	20.00
Blue Horizon BM-4608	(M)	Blues Masters, Volume 8	197?	6.00	15.00
BluesWay BLS-6068	(S)	Ragtime Blues	1973	6.00	15.00
Jewel 5010	(S)	Sad And Lonesome	1973	4.00	10.00

SUNRAYS, THE

Tower T-5017	(M)	Andrea	1966	14.00	35.00
Tower ST-5017	(S)	Andrea	1966	20.00	50.00

SUUNSET DRAGSTERS, THE

Palace M-775	(M)	Hot Rod Rally	196?	5.00	12.00
Palace PST-775	(S)	Hot Rod Rally	196?	6.00	15.00

SUNSET STRINGS, THE

Liberty LRP-3395	(M)	The Sunset Strings Play Roy Orbison	1964	5.00	12.00
Liberty LST-7395	(S)	The Sunset Strings Play Roy Orbison	1964	6.00	15.00

SUNSET SURF, THE

Capitol T-1915	(M)	The Sunset Surf	1963		15.00
Capitol ST-1915	(S)	The Sunset Surf	1963		20.00

SUNSETS, THE

Palace M-752	(M)	Surfing With The Sunsets		6.00	15.00
Palace PST-752	(S)	Surfing With The Sunsets		8.00	20.00

Label & Catalog #		Title	Year	VG+	NM
SUNSHINE COMPANY, THE					
Imperial LP-9359	(M)	Happy Is The Sunshine Company	1967	6.00	15.00
Imperial LP-12359	(S)	Happy Is The Sunshine Company	1967	8.00	20.00
Imperial LP-9368	(M)	The Sunshine Company	1968	6.00	15.00
Imperial LP-12368	(S)	The Sunshine Company	1968	8.00	20.00
Imperial LP-12399	(S)	Sunshine And Shadows	1968	8.00	20.00
SUPERFINE DANDELION					
Mainstream 56102	(M)	Superfine Dandelion	1967	8.00	20.00
Mainstream S-6102	(S)	Superfine Dandelion	1967	10.00	25.00
SUPERMAN					
Reggae 15001	(S)	Reggae Beat	1970	6.00	15.00
SUPERSTOCKS, THE					
The Superstocks are a creation of Gary Usher & Co.					
Capitol T-1997	(M)	Hot Rod Rally	1963	16.00	40.00
Capitol ST-1997	(S)	Hot Rod Rally	1963	20.00	50.00
		(While this is actually a various artists compilation, half of the album consists of The Superstocks' earliest recordings.)			
Capitol T-2060	(M)	Thunder Road	1964	40.00	100.00
Capitol ST-2060	(S)	Thunder Road	1964	60.00	150.00
Capitol T-2113	(M)	Surf Route 101	1964	50.00	125.00
Capitol ST-2113	(S)	Surf Route 101	1964	70.00	175.00
		(Issued with a bonus single by Mr. Gasser & The Weirdos in a pocket on the cover.)			
Capitol T-2113	(M)	Surf Route 101 *(Without the single)*	1964	40.00	100.00
Capitol ST-2113	(S)	Surf Route 101 *(Without the single)*	1964	60.00	150.00
Capitol T-2190	(M)	School Is A Drag	1964	40.00	100.00
Capitol ST-2190	(S)	School Is A Drag	1964	60.00	150.00
SUPERSISTER					
Dwarf PDLP-2001	(S)	Supersister	197?	8.00	20.00
SUPERTRAMP					
A&M SP-3730	(S)	Breakfast In America *(Picture disc)*	1979	150.00	300.00
Mobile Fidelity MFSL-005	(S)	Crime Of The Century	1979	13.00	40.00
Mobile Fidelity MFSL-045	(S)	Breakfast In America	1980	8.00	25.00
Mobile Fidelity MFQR-005	(S)	Crime Of The Century	1983	35.00	100.00
		(Ultra High Quality Recording in a box.)			
Sweet Thunder 5	(S)	Even In The Quietest Moments	198?	12.00	35.00
SUPREMES, THE [DIANA ROSS & THE SUPREMES]					
Original members include Florence Ballard, Diana Ross and Mary Wilson.					
Motown M-606	(M)	Meet The Supremes	1963	300.00	500.00
		(The cover features the group seated on stools.)			
Motown M-606	(M)	Meet The Supremes	1964	10.00	25.00
Motown S-606	(S)	Meet The Supremes	1964	12.00	30.00
		(The cover features a close-up of the group.)			
Motown M-610	(M)	The Supremes Sing Ballas And Blues	1963	*Unreleased*	
Motown S-610	(S)	The Supremes Sing Ballas And Blues	1963	*Unreleased*	
Motown M-621	(M)	Where Did Our Love Go	1964	10.00	25.00
Motown S-621	(S)	Where Did Our Love Go	1964	12.00	30.00
Motown M-623	(M)	A Bit Of Liverpool	1964	16.00	40.00
Motown S-623	(S)	A Bit Of Liverpool	1964	20.00	50.00
Motown M-625	(M)	Country, Western And Pop	1965	12.00	30.00
Motown S-625	(S)	Country, Western And Pop	1965	16.00	40.00
Motown M-626	(M)	The Supremes Live! Live! Live!	1965	*Unreleased*	
Motown S-626	(S)	The Supremes Live! Live! Live!	1965	*Unreleased*	
Motown M-627	(M)	More Hits By The Supremes	1965	8.00	20.00
Motown 627	(S)	More Hits By The Supremes	1965	10.00	25.00
Motown 28	(M)	There's A Place For Us	1965	*Unreleased*	
Motown M	(S)	There's A Place For Us	1965	*Unreleased*	
Motown S-	(M)	We Remember Sam Cooke	1965	10.00	25.00
Motown M-6	(S)	We Remember Sam Cooke	1965	12.00	30.00
Motown S-63	(M)	The Supremes At The Copa	1965	8.00	20.00
Motown M-637	(S)	The Supremes At The Copa	1965	12.00	30.00
Motown S-637	(M)	A Tribute To The Girls	1965	*Unreleased*	
	(S)	A Tribute To The Girls	1965	*Unreleased*	

Label & Catalog #		Title	Year	VG+	NM
Motown M-638	(M)	Merry Christmas	1965	10.00	25.00
Motown S-638	(S)	Merry Christmas	1965	12.00	30.00
Motown M-643	(M)	I Hear A Symphony	1966	8.00	20.00
Motown S-643	(S)	I Hear A Symphony	1966	10.00	25.00
Motown M-648	(M)	Pure Gold	1965	Unreleased	
Motown S-648	(S)	Pure Gold	1965	Unreleased	
Motown M-649	(M)	Supremes A' Go-Go	1966	8.00	20.00
Motown S-649	(S)	Supremes A' Go-Go	1966	10.00	25.00
Motown M-650	(M)	Holland-Dozier-Holland	1967	10.00	25.00
Motown S-650	(S)	Holland-Dozier-Holland	1967	12.00	30.00
Motown M-659	(M)	The Supremes Sing Rodgers And Hart	1967	10.00	25.00
Motown S-659	(S)	The Supremes Sing Rodgers And Hart	1967	12.00	30.00
Motown M-663	(M)	Greatest Hits (2 LPs with poster)	1967	14.00	35.00
Motown S-663	(S)	Greatest Hits (2 LPs with poster)	1967	16.00	40.00
Motown M-663	(M)	Greatest Hits (2 LPs without poster)	1967	8.00	20.00
Motown S-663	(S)	Greatest Hits (2 LPs without poster)	1967	10.00	25.00
Motown M-665	(M)	Reflections	1968	12.00	30.00
Motown S-665	(S)	Reflections	1968	6.00	15.00
Motown S-676	(S)	Live At London's Talk Of The Town	1968	6.00	15.00
Motown S-672	(S)	Funny Girl	1968	6.00	15.00
Motown S-670	(S)	Love Child	1968	6.00	15.00
Motown S-682	(S)	TCB	1968	6.00	15.00
Motown S-689	(S)	Let The Sunshine In	1969	6.00	15.00
Motown S-694	(S)	Cream Of The Crop	1969	6.00	15.00

— *Original Motown albums above have the company's Detroit, MI, address on the bottom of the label.* —

Label & Catalog #		Title	Year	VG+	NM
Motown S-702	(S)	Diana Ross & The Supremes' Greatest Hits, Volume 3	1970	5.00	12.00
Motown S-708	(S)	Farewell (2 LPs)	1970	5.00	12.00
Motown S-705	(S)	Right On	1970	4.00	10.00
Motown S-720	(S)	New Ways But Love Stays	1970	4.00	10.00
Motown S-737	(S)	Touch	1971	4.00	10.00
Doral	(S)	Doral Presents Diana Ross & The Supremes	1971	20.00	50.00

(Promotional compilation of previously released material.)

Motown PR-102	(DJ)	Touch Interview	1971	10.00	25.00
Motown S-746	(S)	Promises Kept	1972	Unreleased	
Motown S-751	(S)	Floy Joy	1972	4.00	10.00
Motown S-756	(S)	The Supremes Produced And Arranged By Jimmy Webb	1972	4.00	10.00
Motown S-794	(DJ)	Anthology 1962-1969 (3 LPs)	1974	16.00	40.00
Motown S-794	(S)	Anthology 1962-1969 (3 LPs)	1974	5.00	12.00
Motown S-828	(S)	The Supremes	1975	4.00	10.00
Motown S-863	(S)	High Energy	1976	4.00	10.00
Motown S-873	(S)	Mary, Scherrie And Susaye	1976	4.00	10.00
Motown M7-904	(S)	The Supremes At Their Best	197?	4.00	10.00

SUPREMES, THE, & THE FOUR TOPS

Motown S-717	(S)	The Magnificent Seven	1970	4.00	10.00
Motown S-736	(S)	The Return Of The Magnificent Seven	1971	4.00	10.00
Motown S-745	(S)	Dynamite	1972	4.00	10.00

SUPREMES, THE, & THE TEMPTATIONS

Motown S-679	(S)	Diana Ross & The Supremes Join The Temptations	1968	6.00	15.00
Motown S-692	(S)	Together	1969	6.00	15.00
Motown S-699	(S)	On Broadway	1969	6.00	15.00

SURF RIDERS, THE

Vault LP-105	(M)	Surfbeat, Volume 2	1963	10.00	25.00
Vault VS-105	(S)	Surfbeat, Volume	1963	12.00	30.00

SURF SIDE FIVE, THE

Intermountain 153	(M)	Recorded Li	196?	60.00	150.00

SURF STOMPERS, THE

Del-Fi DFLP-1236	(M)	The O...	1963	30.00	75.00
Del-Fi DFST-1236	(S)	The ...	1963	40.00	100.00

...urfer Stomp
...urfer Stomp
(reissue of The Bruce Johnston Surfing Band album.)

The original Surfaris consisted of Bob Berryhill, Pa... ...ly, Jim Fuller, Jim Pash and Ron Wilson; their recordings appear on the Dot album. After signin... ...ecca in 1963 they found themselves basically a touring band while "their" albums were recorded... Usher and crew, often using Wilson as the vocalist. The covers of these two albums capture the honey... he period's West Coast [white] youth—rods, boards, woodies and bikes. (Hey, where are the honey...

Label & Catalog #		Title	Year	VG+	NM

SURF SYMPHONY, THE

Capitol ST-329	(S)	Song Of Summer	1969	6.00	15.00

SURF TEENS, THE

Sutton SU-339	(M)	Surf Mania	196?	12.00	30.00
Sutton SSU-339	(S)	Surf Mania	196?	16.00	40.00

SURFARIS, THE

On the Dot album only "Wipe Out" and "Surfer Joe" are by The Surfaris; the other tracks were cut by The Challengers. The final two Decca albums are essentially Gary Usher & Co. with vocalist Ron Wilson.

Dot DLP-3535	(M)	Wipe Out	1963	20.00	50.00
Dot DLP-25535	(P)	Wipe Out	1963	24.00	60.00
		(The back cover of first pressings has a photo with five members.)			
Dot DLP-3535	(M)	Wipe Out	1963	16.00	40.00
Dot DLP-25535	(P)	Wipe Out	1963	20.00	50.00
		(The back cover has a photo with four members.)			
Dot DLP-3535	(M)	Wipe Out	1963	12.00	30.00
Dot DLP-25535	(P)	Wipe Out	1963	16.00	40.00
		(The back cover does not have a photo of the group at all.)			
Decca DL-4470	(M)	The Surfaris Play Wipe Out	1963	16.00	40.00
Decca DL-74470	(S)	The Surfaris Play Wipe Out	1963	20.00	50.00
Decca DL-4487	(M)	Hit City '64	1964	16.00	40.00
Decca DL-74487	(S)	Hit City '64	1964	20.00	50.00
Decca DL-4560	(M)	Fun City, U.S.A.	1964	20.00	50.00
Decca DL-74560	(S)	Fun City, U.S.A.	1964	30.00	75.00
Decca DL-4614	(M)	Hit City '65	1965	20.00	50.00
Decca DL-74614	(S)	Hit City '65	1965	30.00	75.00
Decca DL-4683	(M)	It Ain't Me, Babe	1965	16.00	40.00
Decca DL-74683	(S)	It Ain't Me, Babe	1965	20.00	50.00

SURFERS, THE

Hi Fidelity 408	(M)	On The Rocks	1959	6.00	15.00
Hi Fidelity SR-408	(S)	On The Rocks	1959	8.00	20.00
Hi Fidelity 411	(M)	High Tide	1959	6.00	15.00
Hi Fidelity SR-411	(S)	High Tide	1959	8.00	20.00
Hi Fidelity 417	(M)	Tahiti	1959	6.00	15.00
Hi Fidelity SR-417	(S)	Tahiti	1959	8.00	20.00
Hi Fidelity 427	(M)	The Islands Call	1961	6.00	15.00
Hi Fidelity SR-427	(S)	The Islands Call	1961	8.00	20.00
Warner Bros. W-1493	(M)	Hit Movie Songs From Exotic Islands	1963	5.00	12.00
Warner Bros. WS-1493	(S)	Hit Movie Songs From Exotic Islands	1963	6.00	15.00
Decca DL-75038	(S)	Misty Rainbow	1969	5.00	12.00

SURFSIDERS, THE

Design DLP-208	(M)	The Beach Boy's Songbook	1965	8.00	20.00
Design DLPS-208	(S)	The Beach Boy's Songbook	1965	10.00	25.00

SURPRISE

(No label)

	(S)	Assault On Merryland *(With booklet)*	197?	40.00	100.00

SURPRISE PACKAGE

L.H.I. S-12005	(S)	Free Up	1968	10.00	25.00

SUZUKI, PAT

Vik LX-1127	(M)	The Many Sides Of Pat Suzuki	1958	10.00	25.00
Vik LX-1147	(M)	Pat Suzuki	1958	10.00	25.00
RCA Victor LPM-1965	(M)	Pat Suzuki's Broadway '59	1959	6.00	15.00
RCA Victor LSP-1965	(S)	Pat Suzuki's Broadway '59	1959	8.00	20.00
RCA Victor LPM-2030	(M)	Pat Suzuki	1959	6.00	15.00
RCA Victor LSP-2030	(S)	Pat Suzuki	1959	8.00	20.00
RCA Victor LPM-2186	(M)	Looking At You	1960	6.00	15.00
RCA Victor LSP-2186	(S)	Looking At You	1960	8.00	20.00

SWAMP DOGG

Canyon LP-7706	(S)	Total Destruction To Your Mind	1970	10.00	25.00
Elektra EKS-74089	(S)	Rat On	1971	6.00	15.00
Cream 9009	(S)	Cuffed, Collared And Tagged	1972	5.00	12.00
Musicor MUS-2504	(S)	Finally Caught Up With Myself	197?	5.00	12.00
Wizard 1306	(S)	Swamp Dogg	1978	4.00	10.00

Label & Catalog #		Title	Year	VG+	NM

SWAMPWATER

| King 1122 | (S) | Swampwater | 1970 | 6.00 | 15.00 |
| RCA Victor LSP-4572 | (S) | Swampwater | 1971 | 5.00 | 12.00 |

SWANN, BETTYE

Money 1103	(M)	Make Me Yours	1967	6.00	15.00
Money S-1103	(S)	Make Me Yours	1967	8.00	20.00
Capitol ST-190	(S)	The Soul View Now	1969	4.00	10.00
Capitol ST-270	(S)	Don't You Ever Get Tired Of Hurting Me	1969	4.00	10.00
Abet 405	(S)	Make Me Yours	1972	4.00	10.00

SWEAT BAND

Sweat Band features William "Bootsy" Collins and Maceo Parker.

| Uncle Jam 36857 | (S) | Sweat Band | 1980 | 5.00 | 12.00 |

SWEET, THE

Bell ST-1124	(S)	Sweet	1973	10.00	25.00
Capitol ST-11395	(S)	Desolation Boulevard	1975	6.00	15.00
Capitol ST-11496	(S)	Give Us A Wink	1976	6.00	15.00
Capitol SKAO-11636	(S)	Off The Record	1977	6.00	15.00
Capitol SKAO-11744	(S)	Level Headed	1978	6.00	15.00
Capitol SPRO-8849	(DJ)	Short And Sweet	1978	12.00	30.00
Capitol PRO-11929	(DJ)	Cut Above The Rest	1979	20.00	50.00
		(Box contains LP, cassette, 8-track, photo and biography.)			
Capitol ST-12106	(S)	Sweet VI	1980	4.00	10.00
Capitol ST-16118	(S)	Cut Above The Rest	1980	4.00	10.00

SWEET CHARLES

| People PE-6603 | (S) | For Sweet People (Prod. by James Brown) | 1974 | 6.00 | 15.00 |

SWEET INSPIRATIONS, THE

Atlantic 8155	(M)	The Sweet Inspirations	1968	12.00	30.00
Atlantic SD-8155	(S)	The Sweet Inspirations	1968	8.00	20.00
Atlantic SD-8201	(S)	What The World Needs Now Is Love	1969	8.00	20.00
Atlantic SD-8225	(S)	Sweets For My Sweet	1969	8.00	20.00
Atlantic SD-8253	(S)	Sweet, Sweet Soul	1970	8.00	20.00
Stax STS-3017	(S)	Estelle, Myrna And Sylvia	1973	6.00	15.00
RSO 1-3058	(S)	Hot Butterfly	1979	4.00	10.00

SWEET PANTS

| Barkley LP-1141 | (S) | Fat Peter Presents Sweet Pants | 1972 | 80.00 | 200.00 |

SWEET SUE & HER SOCIETY SYNCOPATERS

The Society Syncopaters were the group featuring Marilyn Monroe from the film "Some Like It Hot."

| United Arts. UAL-3029 | (M) | Some Like It Hot (Soundtrack) | 1959 | 40.00 | 100.00 |
| United Arts. UAS-6029 | (S) | Some Like It Hot (Soundtrack) | 1959 | 60.00 | 150.00 |

SWEET THURSDAY

| Great Western 32039 | (S) | Sweet Thursday | 1969 | 6.00 | 15.00 |
| Tetragrammaton T-112 | (S) | Sweet Thursday | 1969 | 6.00 | 15.00 |

SWEET TOOTHE

| Dominion NR-7360 | (S) | Testing | 1974 | 80.00 | 200.00 |

SWINGIN' MEDALLIONS, THE

Smash MGS-27083	(M)	Double Shot	1966	16.00	40.00
Smash SRS-67083	(S)	Double Shot	1966	20.00	50.00
		(Includes an unedited version of "Double Shot.")			
Smash MGS-27083	(M)	Double Shot	1966	12.00	30.00
Smash SRS-67083	(S)	Double Shot	1966	16.00	40.00
		(Includes the edited, single version of "Double Shot.")			

SWINGING BLUE JEANS, THE

| Imperial LP-9261 | (M) | Hippy Hippy Shake | 1964 | 50.00 | 125.00 |
| Imperial LP-12261 | (E) | Hippy Hippy Shake | 1964 | 30.00 | 75.00 |

Label & Catalog #		Title	Year	VG+	NM

SYKES, ROOSEVELT
Refer to Victoria Spivey.

Bluesville BVLP-1006	(M)	The Return Of Roosevelt Sykes	1960	20.00	50.00
Bluesville BVLP-1014	(M)	The Honeydripper	1961	20.00	50.00
Crown CLP-5287	(M)	Roosevelt Sykes Sings The Blues	1962	10.00	25.00
Crown CST-287	(E)	Roosevelt Sykes Sings The Blues	1962	4.00	10.00
United 7792	(M)	Roosevelt Sykes Sings The Blues	1969	4.00	10.00
Prestige PRST-7722	(S)	The Blues Of Roosevelt Sykes	1969	6.00	15.00
		(Prestige 7722 is a reissue of Bluesville material.)			
Delmark 616	(S)	In Europe	1969	6.00	15.00
Delmark 632	(S)	Feel Like Blowing My Horn	1973	6.00	15.00
BluesWay BLS-6077	(S)	Double Dirty Mother	1973	6.00	15.00

SYLVESTER, TERRY
Refer to The Hollies.

Epic KE-33076	(S)	Terry Sylvester	1974	4.00	10.00

SYNDICATE OF SOUND, THE

Bell LP-6001	(M)	Little Girl	1966	14.00	35.00
Bell SLP-6001	(S)	Little Girl	1966	20.00	50.00

SYMS, SYLVIA: *Refer to* GOLDMINE'S PRICE GUIDE TO COLLECTIBLE JAZZ ALBUMS

T

T-BONES, THE

Liberty LRP-3346	(M)	Boss Drag	1963	16.00	40.00
Liberty LST-7346	(S)	Boss Drag	1963	20.00	50.00
Liberty LRP-3363	(M)	Boss Drag At The Beach	1964	16.00	40.00
Liberty LST-7363	(S)	Boss Drag At The Beach	1964	20.00	50.00
Liberty LRP-3404	(M)	Doin' The Jerk	1965	8.00	20.00
Liberty LST-7404	(S)	Doin' The Jerk	1965	10.00	25.00
Liberty LRP-3439	(M)	No Matter What Shape	1966	8.00	20.00
Liberty LST-7439	(S)	No Matter What Shape	1966	10.00	25.00
Liberty LRP-3446	(M)	Sippin' And Chippin'	1966	8.00	20.00
Liberty LST-7446	(S)	Sippin' And Chippin'	1966	10.00	25.00
Liberty LRP-3471	(M)	Everyone's Gone To The Moon	1966	8.00	20.00
Liberty LST-7471	(S)	Everyone's Gone To The Moon	1966	10.00	25.00
Sunset SUM-1119	(M)	Shapin' Things Up	196?	5.00	12.00
Sunset SUS-5119	(S)	Shapin' Things Up	196?	6.00	15.00

T. C. ATLANTIC

Dove LP-4459	(M)	T. C. Atlantic	1966	50.00	125.00

T. I. M. E. [TRUST IN MEN EVERYWHERE]

Liberty LST-7558	(S)	T. I. M. E.	1968	10.00	25.00
Liberty LST-7605	(S)	Smooth Ball	1969	10.00	25.00

T-REX [TYRANNOSAURUS REX]
T-Rex features Marc Bolan.

Blue Thumb BTS-7	(S)	Unicorn	1969	10.00	25.00
Blue Thumb BTS-18	(S)	A Beard Of Stars	1970	10.00	25.00
Reprise PRO-511	(DJ)	Interview With Marc Bolan	1971	60.00	150.00
Reprise RS-6440	(S)	T-Rex	1971	6.00	15.00
Reprise RS-6466	(S)	Electric Warrior	1971	6.00	15.00

Label & Catalog #		Title	Year	VG+	NM
Reprise MS-2095	(S)	The Slider	1972	6.00	15.00
Reprise MS-2132	(S)	Tanx	1973	6.00	15.00
A&M SP-3514	(S)	Tyrannosaurus Rex / A Beginning (2 LPs)	1972	6.00	15.00
MFSB 5274	(S)	Ride A White Swan	1974	10.00	25.00
Casablanca NBLP-9006	(S)	Light Of Love	1974	6.00	15.00

T.V. & THE TRIBESMEN

HBR HLP-9507	(M)	Barefootin'	1966	6.00	15.00
HBR HST-9507	(S)	Barefootin'	1966	8.00	20.00

TALISMEN, THE

Blue Star M-6323	(M)	Treasury Of American Railroad Songs And Ballads	1964	6.00	15.00
Blue Star MS-6323	(S)	Treasury Of American Railroad Songs And Ballads	1964	8.00	20.00
Prestige PRLP-7406	(M)	Folk Swingers Extraordinaire	1965	6.00	15.00
Prestige PRST-7406	(S)	Folk Swingers Extraordinaire	1965	8.00	20.00

TALKING HEADS, THE

Warner Bros. PRO-	(DJ)	Live At The Roxy (Counterfeits exist)	1979	16.00	40.00
Sire 23771	(S)	Speaking In Tongues (Clear vinyl)	1983	12.00	30.00

(Issued in a clear plastic box with artwork by Robert Rauschenberg.)

TAMPA RED

Bluesville BVLP-1030	(M)	Don't Tampa With The Blues	1961	30.00	75.00
Bluesville BVLP-1043	(M)	Don't Jive With Me	1962	30.00	75.00

TAMS, THE

ABC-Paramount 481	(M)	Presenting The Tams	1964	12.00	30.00
ABC-Paramount S-481	(E)	Presenting The Tams	1964	8.00	20.00
ABC-Paramount 499	(M)	Hey Girl, Don't Bother Me	1964	10.00	25.00
ABC-Paramount S-499	(S)	Hey Girl, Don't Bother Me	1964	12.00	30.00
ABC 596	(M)	Time For The Tams	1967	6.00	15.00
ABCS-596	(S)	Time For The Tams	1967	8.00	20.00
ABC S-673	(S)	A Portrait Of The Tams	1969	6.00	15.00
"1-2-3" 567	(S)	The Best Of The Tams	1970	6.00	15.00
Sounds South SO-16010	(S)	The Mighty, Mighty Tams	1977	4.00	10.00
Capitol SM-11839	(S)	The Best Of The Tams	1979	4.00	10.00

TANEGA, NORMA

New Voice NV-2001	(M)	Walkin' My Cat Named Dog	1966	12.00	30.00
New Voice NVS-2002	(S)	Walkin' My Cat Named Dog	1966	20.00	50.00

TANGERINE

Stephen Prod. SPST-001	(S)	The Peeling Of Tangerine	197?	40.00	100.00

TANGERINE DREAM

Virgin 13-108	(S)	Phaedra	1974	4.00	10.00
Virgin V-2025	(S)	Rubycon	1975	4.00	10.00
Virgin V-2044	(S)	Ricochet	1975	4.00	10.00
Virgin PZ-34427	(S)	Stratosfear	1976	4.00	10.00
Virgin PZG-35014	(S)	Encore (2 LPs)	1977	5.00	12.00
MCA 2277	(S)	Sorcerer (Soundtrack)	1977	4.00	10.00
Virgin VI-211	(S)	Force Majeure (Soundtrack)	1978	4.00	10.00
Elektra 5E-521	(S)	Thief (Soundtrack)	1981	4.00	10.00
Elektra SE-557	(S)	Exit	1981	4.00	10.00

TANGERINE ZOO

Mainstream S-6107	(S)	Tangerine Zoo	1968	12.00	30.00
Mainstream S-6116	(S)	Outside Looking In	1968	12.00	30.00

TAR BABY

New South NR-4500	(S)	February (Issued without a cover)	197?	70.00	175.00

TARGAL, JEM

Sheavy	(M)	Lucky Guy	196?	50.00	125.00

Label & Catalog #		Title	Year	VG+	NM

TARRIERS, THE
Members include Alan Arkin, Erik Darling and Bob Carey.

Label & Catalog #		Title	Year	VG+	NM
Glory 1200	(M)	The Tarriers	1959	20.00	50.00
United Arts. UAL-4033	(M)	Hard Travelin'	1959	14.00	35.00
United Arts. UAS-5033	(S)	Hard Travelin'	1959	20.00	50.00
Atlantic 8042	(M)	Tell The World About This	1960	10.00	25.00
Atlantic SD-8042	(S)	Tell The World About This	1960	14.00	35.00
Decca DL-4342	(M)	The Tarriers	1962	6.00	15.00
Decca DL-74342	(S)	The Tarriers	1962	8.00	20.00
Kapp KL-1349	(M)	The Original Tarriers	1963	6.00	15.00
Kapp KS-3349	(S)	The Original Tarriers	1963	8.00	20.00
Decca DL-4538	(M)	Gather 'Round	1964	6.00	15.00
Decca DL-74538	(S)	Gather 'Round	1964	8.00	20.00

TASTE

Atco SD-33-296	(S)	Taste	1969	8.00	20.00
Atco SD-33-322	(S)	On The Boards	1970	8.00	20.00

TATE, BABY

Bluesville BVLP-1072	(M)	See What You Done	1963	16.00	40.00

TATE, HOWARD

Verve V6-5022	(S)	Get It While You Can	1968	6.00	15.00
Atlantic SD-8303	(S)	Howard Tate	1969	6.00	15.00
Turntable 5002	(S)	Reaction	197?	4.00	10.00

TAUPIN, BERNIE
Bernie Taupin was Elton John's lyricist throughout John's '70's heyday.

Elektra EKS-75020	(S)	Bernie Taupin	1972	6.00	15.00
Asylum 6E-263	(S)	He Who Rides The Tiger	1980	4.00	10.00

TAVENER, JOHN

Apple SMAS-3369	(S)	The Whale	1972	6.00	15.00

TAYLOR, BOBBY, & THE VANCOUVERS

Gordy GS-930	(S)	Bobby Taylor And The Vancouvers	1968	12.00	30.00
Gordy GS-942	(S)	Taylor Made Soul	1968	8.00	20.00

TAYLOR, EARL (& THE STONEY MOUNTAIN BOYS)

United Arts. UAL-3049	(M)	Folk Songs From The Bluegrass	1960	14.00	35.00
United Arts. UAS-6049	(S)	Folk Songs From The Bluegrass	1960	20.00	50.00
Capitol T-2090	(M)	Bluegrass Taylor Made	1963	14.00	35.00
Capitol ST-2090	(S)	Bluegrass Taylor Made	1963	20.00	50.00

TAYLOR, JAMES

Apple SKAO-3352	(S)	James Taylor	1969	12.00	30.00
Trip TLP-9513	(S)	Rainy Day Man (With The Flying Machine)	197?	6.00	15.00
Warner Bros. BS4-2866	(Q)	Gorilla	1975	6.00	15.00
Columbia HC-47009	(S)	Dad Loves His Work (Half-speed master)	1983	13.00	40.00
Nautilus NR-29	(S)	Gorilla	1981	8.00	25.00

TAYLOR, JOHNNIE
Johnnie Taylor originally recorded with The Soul Stirrers.

Stax ST-715	(M)	Wanted: One Soul Singer	1967	10.00	25.00
Stax STS-715	(S)	Wanted: One Soul Singer	1967	12.00	30.00
Stax STS-2005	(S)	Who's Making Love?	1968	10.00	25.00
Stax STS-2008	(S)	Raw Blues	1969	8.00	20.00
Stax STS-2012	(S)	Rare Stamps	1969	8.00	20.00
		("I Had A Dream" is rechanneled on this album.)			
Stax STS-2023	(S)	The Philosophy Continues	1969	8.00	20.00
Stax STS-2030	(S)	One Step Beyond	1970	8.00	20.00
Stax STS-2032	(S)	Greatest Hits	1970	6.00	15.00
Stax STS-3014	(S)	Taylored In Silk	1973	6.00	15.00
Stax STS-5509	(S)	Super Taylor	1974	6.00	15.00
Stax STS-5522	(S)	The Best Of Johnnie Taylor	1975	6.00	15.00
Stax 88001	(S)	Chronicle (2 LPs)	1977	6.00	15.00
Columbia PCQ-33951	(Q)	Eargasm	1976	6.00	15.00
Columbia PCQ-34401	(Q)	Rated Extraordinaire	1977	6.00	15.00

Label & Catalog #		Title	Year	VG+	NM
TAYLOR, LITTLE JOHNNY					
Galaxy 203	(M)	Little Johnny Taylor	1963	12.00	30.00
Galaxy 8203	(S)	Little Johnny Taylor	1963	16.00	40.00
Galaxy 207	(M)	Little Johnny Taylor's Greatest Hits	1964	10.00	25.00
Galaxy 8207	(S)	Little Johnny Taylor's Greatest Hits	1964	14.00	35.00
Ronn LPS-7530	(S)	Everybody Knows About My Good Thing	1972	4.00	10.00
Ronn LPS-7532	(S)	Open House At My House	1973	4.00	10.00
Ronn LPS-7535	(S)	L.J.T.	1979	4.00	10.00
TAYLOR, LITTLE JOHNNY, & TED TAYLOR					
Ronn LPS-7533	(S)	The Super Taylors	1973	4.00	10.00
TAYLOR, KINGSIZE, & THE DOMINOS					
Midnight HLP-2101	(M)	Real Gonk Man	196?	12.00	30.00
Midnight HST-2101	(S)	Real Gonk Man	196?	14.00	35.00
TAYLOR, KOKO					
Chess LPS-1532	(S)	Koko Taylor	1968	10.00	25.00
Chess CHS-50018	(S)	Basic Soul	1972	6.00	15.00
Alligator AL-4706	(S)	I Got What It Takes	1976	4.00	10.00
Alligator AL-4711	(S)	The Earthshaker	1978	4.00	10.00
Alligator AL-4724	(S)	From The Heart Of A Woman	1981	4.00	10.00
TAYLOR, MEL, & THE MAGICS					
Warner Bros. W-1624	(M)	Mel Taylor In Action	1966	6.00	15.00
Warner Bros. WS-1624	(S)	Mel Taylor In Action	1966	8.00	20.00
TAYLOR, MICK					
Mick Taylor was formerly a member of John Mayall's Bluesbreakers; The Rolling Stones.					
Columbia JC-35076	(S)	Mick Taylor	1979	6.00	15.00
TAYLOR, R. DEAN					
Rare Earth 522	(S)	I Think, Therefore I Am	1970	6.00	15.00
TAYLOR, TED					
Refer to Little Johnny Taylor & Ted Taylor.					
OKeh OKM-12104	(M)	Be Ever Wonderful	1963	8.00	20.00
OKeh OKS-14104	(S)	Be Ever Wonderful	1963	10.00	25.00
OKeh OKM-12109	(M)	Blues And Soul	1965	8.00	20.00
OKeh OKS-14109	(S)	Blues And Soul	1965	10.00	25.00
OKeh OKM-12113	(M)	Greatest Hits	1966	8.00	20.00
OKeh OKS-14113	(S)	Greatest Hits	1966	10.00	25.00
Ronn LPS-7528	(S)	Shades Of Blue	1969	6.00	15.00
Ronn KPS-7529	(S)	You Can Dig It	1970	6.00	15.00
Ronn LPS-7531	(S)	Taylor Made	1972	6.00	15.00
TEA COMPANY, THE					
Smash SRS-67105	(S)	Come And Have Some Tea	1968	12.00	30.00
TEDDY & THE PANDAS					
Tower ST-5125	(S)	Basic Magnetism	1968	6.00	15.00
TEDDY BEARS, THE					
Imperial LP-9067	(M)	The Teddy Bears Sing!	1959	150.00	300.00
Imperial LPS-12067	(S)	The Teddy Bears Sing!	1959	500.00	1,000.00
TEDESCO, TOM					
Imperial LP-9263	(M)	The Electric 12 String Guitar	1964	6.00	15.00
Imperial LP-12263	(S)	The Electric 12 String Guitar	1964	8.00	20.00
TEE SET, THE					
Colossus CCS-1001	(S)	Ma Belle Amie	1970	4.00	10.00
TEEGARDEN & VAN WINKLE					
Atco SD-33-272	(S)	An Evening At Home	1968	6.00	15.00
Westbound 2003	(S)	But, Anyhow	1969	6.00	15.00
Westbound 2010	(S)	On Our Way	1972	6.00	15.00

Label & Catalog #		Title	Year	VG+	NM
TEEMATES, THE					
Audio Fidelity DF-7042	(M)	Jet Set Dance Discotheque	1964	5.00	12.00
Audio Fidelity DFS-7042	(S)	Jet Set Dance Discotheque	1964	6.00	15.00
TEEN QUEENS, THE					
Crown CLP-5022	(M)	Eddie, My Love	1956	80.00	200.00
Crown CLP-5373	(M)	The Teen Queens	1963	20.00	50.00
Crown CST-373	(E)	The Teen Queens	1963	8.00	20.00
TEENAGERS, THE: *Refer to* **FRANKIE LYMON & THE TEENAGERS**					
TELEVISION					
Television features Tom Verlaine and Richard Lloyd, who later recorded as Richerd Hell.					
Elektra 7E-1098	(S)	Marquee Moon	1977	6.00	15.00
Elektra 6E-133	(S)	Adventure	1978	6.00	15.00
TEMPEST					
Earth 0378	(S)	Tempest	1976	40.00	100.00
TEMPESTS, THE					
Smash MGS-27098	(M)	Would You Believe?	1966	5.00	12.00
Smash SRS-67098	(S)	Would You Believe?	1966	6.00	15.00
TEMPLE, SHIRLEY					
20th Century TCF-103	(M)	Complete Shirley Temple Songbook (2 LPs)	1961	14.00	35.00
20th Century TFM-3045	(M)	More Little Miss Wonderful	1961	10.00	25.00
20th Century TFM-3102	(M)	The Best Of Shirley Temple	1963	10.00	25.00
Movietone 1001	(M)	On The Good Ship Lollipop	1956	8.00	20.00
Movietone 71001	(E)	Shirley Temple	1956	6.00	15.00
Movietone 71012	(E)	Curtain Call	1968	6.00	15.00
20th Century T-906	(E)	Remember Shirley (2 LPs)	1973	6.00	15.00
		(20th Century 906 is a reissue of Movietone 1002 and 1012.)			
TEMPO, NICK					
Liberty LRP-3023	(M)	Rock 'N Roll Beach Party	1958	30.00	75.00
TEMPO, NINO, & APRIL STEVENS					
Atco 33-156	(M)	Deep Purple	1963	12.00	30.00
Atco SD-33-156	(S)	Deep Purple	1963	16.00	40.00
Atco 33-162	(M)	Sing The Great Songs	1964	10.00	25.00
Atco SD-33-162	(S)	Sing The Great Songs	1964	12.00	30.00
Atco 33-180	(M)	Hey Baby	1966	10.00	25.00
Atco SD-33-180	(S)	Hey Baby	1966	12.00	30.00
White Whale WW-113	(M)	All Strung Out	1967	8.00	20.00
White Whale WWS-7113	(S)	All Strung Out	1967	10.00	25.00
TEMPOS, THE					
Justice JLP-104	(M)	Speaking Of The Tempos	1966	200.00	400.00
TEMPTATIONS, THE					
Gordy G-911	(M)	Meet The Temptations	1964	12.00	30.00
Gordy GS-911	(S)	Meet The Temptations	1964	16.00	40.00
Gordy G-912	(M)	The Temptations Sing Smokey	1965	12.00	30.00
Gordy GS-912	(S)	The Temptations Sing Smokey	1965	16.00	40.00
Gordy G-914	(M)	Temptin' Temptations	1965	8.00	20.00
Gordy GS-914	(S)	Temptin' Temptations	1965	10.00	25.00
		("Since I Lost My Baby" is rechanneled on this album.)			
Gordy G-918	(M)	Gettin' Ready	1966	8.00	20.00
Gordy GS-918	(S)	Gettin' Ready	1966	10.00	25.00
Gordy G-919	(M)	The Temptations' Greatest Hits	1966	8.00	20.00
Gordy GS-919	(S)	The Temptations' Greatest Hits	1966	10.00	25.00
		("Since I Lost My Baby" is rechanneled on this album.)			
Gordy G-921	(M)	The Temptations Live	1967	8.00	20.00
Gordy GS-921	(S)	The Temptations Live	1967	10.00	25.00
		— Original Gordy albums above have "Gordy" in yellow script at the top of the label.—			
Gordy G-922	(M)	With A Lot O' Soul	1967	8.00	20.00
Gordy GS-922	(S)	With A Lot O' Soul	1967	10.00	25.00
Gordy G-924	(M)	In A Mellow Mood	1967	8.00	20.00
Gordy GS-924	(S)	In A Mellow Mood	1967	10.00	25.00

Label & Catalog #		Title	Year	VG+	NM
Gordy GS-927	(S)	The Temptations Wish It Would Rain	1968	8.00	20.00
Gordy GS-933	(S)	The Temptations Show	1969	8.00	20.00
Gordy GS-938	(S)	Live At The Copa	1969	8.00	20.00
Gordy GS-939	(S)	Cloud Nine	1969	6.00	15.00
Gordy GS-947	(S)	Psychedelic Shack	1970	6.00	15.00
Gordy GS-949	(S)	Puzzle People	1969	6.00	15.00
Gordy GS-951	(S)	The Temptations' Christmas Card	1969	8.00	20.00
Gordy GS-953	(S)	Live At London's Talk Of The Town	1970	5.00	12.00
Gordy GS-954	(S)	The Temptations' Greatest Hits, Volume 2	1970	5.00	12.00
Gordy GS-957	(S)	Sky's The Limit	1971	5.00	12.00
Gordy GS-961	(S)	Solid Rock	1972	4.00	10.00
Gordy GS-962	(S)	All Directions	1972	4.00	10.00
Gordy GS-965	(S)	Masterpiece	1973	4.00	10.00
Motown M-782	(S)	Anthology (3 LPs)	1973	8.00	20.00

TEMPTATIONS, THE / STEVIE WONDER

Gordy PR-101	(DJ)	The Sky's The Limit / Where I'm Coming From (Sampler)	1971	8.00	20.00

TEN YEARS AFTER
For more information refer to The Rolling Stones.

Deram DES-18009	(S)	Ten Years After	1968	8.00	20.00
Deram DES-18016	(S)	Undead	1968	6.00	15.00
Deram DES-18021	(S)	Stonedhenge	1969	6.00	15.00
Deram DES-18029	(S)	Ssssh	1969	6.00	15.00
Deram DES-18038	(S)	Cricklewood Green	1970	6.00	15.00
Deram DES-18050	(S)	Watt	1970	6.00	15.00
Columbia CQ-30801	(Q)	A Space In Time	1972	6.00	15.00

TENNESSEE FARM BAND, THE: Refer to THE FARM BAND

TERRELL, TAMMI
Ms. Terrell also recorded with Marvin Gaye; Chuck Jackson.

Motown 652	(M)	Irresistible Tammi	1967	10.00	25.00
Motown MS-652	(S)	Irresistible Tammi	1967	12.00	30.00

TERRY, DEWEY
Refer to Don & Dewey.

Tumbleweed TWS-104	(S)	Chief	197?	6.00	15.00

TERRY, DON

Columbia CL-6288 (10")	(M)	Teen-Age Dance Session	1955	20.00	50.00

TEX, JOE

Checker LP-2993	(M)	Hold On	1964	30.00	75.00
King 935	(M)	The Best Of Joe Tex	1965	20.00	50.00
King KS-935	(E)	The Best Of Joe Tex	1965	16.00	40.00
Parrot PA-61002	(M)	The Best Of Joe Tex	1965	10.00	25.00
Parrot PAS-71002	(E)	The Best Of Joe Tex	1965	8.00	20.00
Atlantic 8106	(S)	Hold On To What You've Got	1965	8.00	20.00
Atlantic SD-8106	(S)	Hold On To What You've Got	1965	10.00	25.00
		("Hold On To What You've Got" is rechanneled on this album.)			
Atlantic 8115	(M)	The New Boss	1965	8.00	20.00
Atlantic SD-8115	(S)	The New Boss	1965	10.00	25.00
Atlantic 8124	(M)	The Love You Save	1966	8.00	20.00
Atlantic SD-8124	(S)	The Love You Save	1966	10.00	25.00
Atlantic 8133	(M)	I've Got To Do A Little Better	1966	8.00	20.00
Atlantic SD-8133	(S)	I've Got To Do A Little Better	1966	10.00	25.00
Atlantic 8144	(M)	The Best Of Joe Tex	1967	8.00	20.00
Atlantic SD-8144	(S)	The Best Of Joe Tex	1967	10.00	25.00
		("Hold On To What You've Got" is rechanneled on this album.)			
Atlantic SD-8156	(S)	Live And Lively	1968	8.00	20.00
Atlantic SD-8187	(S)	Soul Country	1968	8.00	20.00
Atlantic SD-8211	(S)	Happy Soul	1969	6.00	15.00
Atlantic SD-8231	(S)	Buying A Book	1969	6.00	15.00
Atlantic SD-8254	(S)	With Strings And Things	1970	6.00	15.00
Atlantic SD-8292	(S)	From The Roots Came The Rapper	1972	6.00	15.00
Dial DL-6002	(S)	I Gotcha	1972	6.00	15.00
Dial DL-6004	(S)	Spills The Beans	1973	6.00	15.00

Label & Catalog #		Title	Year	VG+	NM

TEXAS RUBY
Ms. Ruby also recorded with Curly Fox.

King 840	(M)	Favorite Songs Of Texas Ruby	1964	20.00	50.00

THAXTON, LLOYD

Decca DL-4594	(M)	Lloyd Thaxton Presents	1964	8.00	20.00
Decca DL-74594	(S)	Lloyd Thaxton Presents	1964	10.00	25.00

THEE IMAGE

Manticore MA6-50451	(S)	Thee Image	1975	5.00	12.00
Manticore MA6-50651	(S)	Inside The Triangle	1975	5.00	12.00

THEE MIDNIGHTERS

Chattahoochee CS-1001	(S)	Thee Midniters	1965	16.00	40.00
Whittier WS-5000	(S)	Bring You Love Special Delivery	1966	16.00	40.00
Whittier WS-5001	(S)	Unlimited	1966	16.00	40.00
Whittier WS-5002	(S)	The Giants	1967	16.00	40.00

THEE MUFFINS

(No label)	(M)	Thee Muffins Pop Up! (Fan club issue)	1967	60.00	150.00

THEE PEDDLERS

Epic BN-26458	(S)	Three In A Sell	1969	6.00	15.00
Epic BN-26529	(S)	Birthday	1970	6.00	15.00

THEE PROPHETS

Kapp KS-3596	(S)	Playgirl	1969	8.00	20.00

THEM
The Parrot recordings feature vocalist Van Morrison.

Parrot PA-61005	(M)	Them Featuring "Here Comes The Night"	1965	30.00	75.00
Parrot PAS-71005	(E)	Them Featuring "Here Comes The Night"	1965	24.00	60.00
Parrot PA-61005	(M)	Them Featuring "Gloria"	1965	20.00	50.00
Parrot PAS-71005	(E)	Them Featuring "Gloria"	1965	16.00	40.00
Parrot PA-61008	(M)	Them Again	1966	20.00	50.00
Parrot PAS-71008	(E)	Them Again	1966	16.00	40.00
Tower T-5104	(M)	Now And Them	1968	20.00	50.00
Tower ST-5104	(S)	Now And Them	1968	24.00	60.00
Tower T-5116	(M)	Time Out! Time In For Them	1968	24.00	60.00
Tower ST-5116	(S)	Time Out! Time In For Them	1968	30.00	75.00
Happy Tiger 1004	(S)	Them	1969	16.00	40.00
Happy Tiger 1012	(S)	Them In Reality	1971	30.00	75.00
Parrot BP-71053	(E)	Them Featuring Van Morrison (2 LPs)	1972	6.00	15.00
		(An abridged repackage of the first two albums with "Gloria," "Here Comes The Night," "One More Time," "If Only You And I Could Be As Two" and "One Two Brown Eyes" in stereo.)			
London PS-639	(P)	Backtrackin'	1974	6.00	15.00
		(Outtakes, etc., from the Morrison-led band.)			

THIN LIZZY

London PS-594	(S)	Thin Lizzy	1971	16.00	40.00
London PS-636	(S)	Vagabonds Of The Western World	1974	12.00	30.00
Vertigo 2002	(S)	Night Life	1974	6.00	15.00
Vertigo 2005	(S)	Fighting	1975	6.00	15.00
Mercury SRM-1-1081	(S)	Jailbreak	1976	4.00	10.00
Mercury SRM-1-1107	(S)	Night Life	1976	4.00	10.00
Mercury SRM-1-1108	(S)	Fighting	1976	4.00	10.00
Mercury SRM-1-1119	(S)	Johnny The Fox	1976	4.00	10.00
Mercury SRM-1-1186	(S)	Bad Reputation	1977	4.00	10.00

THINGS TO COME

Century 45333	(S)	Things To Come (Recorded in the late '60s)	1978	660.00	1,000.00

THIRD EAR BAND, THE

Harvest ST-376	(S)	Alchemy	1969	6.00	15.00

THIRD ESTATE, THE

3rd Estate PPE-LP1000	(S)	Years Before The Wine	197?	150.00	300.00

Label & Catalog #		Title	Year	VG+	NM

THIRD POWER, THE

| Vanguard VSD-6554 | (S) | The Third Power Believe | 1970 | 10.00 | 25.00 |

THIRD QUADRANT, THE

| Rock Cottage | (S) | Seeing Yourself As You Really Are | 1989 | 60.00 | 150.00 |
| | | *(Issued in a paper sleeve with a lyric sheet.)* | | | |

THIRD RAIL, THE

| Epic LN-24327 | (M) | Id Music | 1967 | 12.00 | 30.00 |
| Epic BN-26327 | (S) | Id Music | 1967 | 14.00 | 35.00 |

THIRTEENTH FLOOR ELEVATORS, THE
The Elevators feature Roky Erikson.

International Art. 1	(M)	Psychedelic Sounds	1967	100.00	250.00
		— Original Int. Art. album above has a green & yellow labels.—			
International Art. 1	(M)	Psychedelic Sounds	1967	40.00	100.00
International Art. 1	(S)	Psychedelic Sounds	1967	30.00	75.00
		("You're Gonna Miss Me" is rechanneled on this album.)			
International Art. 5	(M)	Easter Everywhere	1967	50.00	125.00
International Art. 5	(S)	Easter Everywhere	1967	30.00	75.00
International Art. 8	(S)	Thirteenth Floor Elevators Live	1968	20.00	50.00
International Art. 9	(S)	Bull Of The Woods	1968	20.00	50.00
		— Original Int. Art. albums above copies were pressed on thick vinyl.—			
International Art. 1	(S)	Psychedelic Sounds	1979	8.00	20.00
International Art. 5	(S)	Easter Everywhere	1979	8.00	20.00
International Art. 8	(S)	Thirteenth Floor Elevators Live	1979	8.00	20.00
International Art. 9	(S)	Bull Of The Woods	1979	8.00	20.00
		— Int. Art. reissues above are on thinner vinyl with "Masterfonics" stamped in the trail-off vinyl.—			

31 FLAVORS, THE

| Crown CST-592 | (S) | Hair | 1968 | 20.00 | 50.00 |

31ST OF FEBRUARY, THE

| Vanguard VSD-6503 | (S) | The 31st Of February | 1969 | 10.00 | 25.00 |

THOMAS, B. J.

Pacemaker PLP-3001	(M)	B. J. Thomas & The Triumphs	1965	20.00	50.00
Hickory LP-133	(M)	The Very Best Of B. J. Thomas	1966	8.00	20.00
Hickory LPS-133	(S)	The Very Best Of B. J. Thomas	1966	10.00	25.00
Scepter SP-535	(M)	I'm So Lonesome I Could Cry	1966	8.00	20.00
Scepter SPS-535	(S)	I'm So Lonesome I Could Cry	1966	10.00	25.00
Scepter SP-556	(M)	Tomorrow Never Comes	1966	6.00	15.00
Scepter SPS-556	(S)	Tomorrow Never Comes	1966	8.00	20.00
Scepter SP-561	(M)	For Lovers And Losers	1967	6.00	15.00
Scepter SPS-561	(S)	For Lovers And Losers	1967	8.00	20.00
Scepter SPS-570	(S)	On My Way	1968	6.00	15.00
Scepter SPS-576	(S)	Young And In Love	1969	6.00	15.00
Scepter SPS-578	(S)	B. J. Thomas' Greatest Hits	1969	6.00	15.00
Scepter SPS-580	(S)	Raindrops Keep Fallin' On My Head	1969	6.00	15.00
Doral	(S)	Doral Presents B. J. Thomas	1971	8.00	20.00
		(Promotional compilation of previously released material.)			

THOMAS, CARLA
Ms. Thomas also recorded with Otis Redding; Rufus Thomas.

Atlantic 8057	(M)	Gee Whiz	1961	30.00	75.00
Stax ST-706	(M)	Comfort Me	1966	14.00	35.00
Stax STS-706	(S)	Comfort Me	1966	20.00	50.00
		("Comfort Me" and "No Time To Lose" are rechanneled on this LP.)			
Stax ST-709	(M)	Carla	1966	14.00	35.00
Stax STS-709	(S)	Carla	1966	20.00	50.00
Stax ST-718	(M)	The Queen Alone	1967	10.00	25.00
Stax STS-718	(S)	The Queen Alone	1967	14.00	35.00
Atlantic SD-8232	(P)	The Best Of Carla Thomas	1969	10.00	25.00
Stax STS-2019	(S)	Memphis Queen	1969	8.00	20.00
Stax STS-2044	(S)	Love Means Carla Thomas	1971	8.00	20.00

THOMAS, IRMA

| Imperial LP-9266 | (M) | Wish Someone Would Care | 1964 | 12.00 | 30.00 |
| Imperial LP-12266 | (S) | Wish Someone Would Care | 1964 | 16.00 | 40.00 |

Label & Catalog #		Title	Year	VG+	NM
Imperial 9302	(M)	Take A Look	1966	10.00	25.00
Imperial LP-12302	(S)	Take A Look	1966	14.00	35.00
Fungus FB-25150	(S)	In Between Tears	1973	6.00	15.00

THOMAS, JEANNE

Strand SL-1030	(M)	Jeanne Thomas Sings For The Boys	1961	8.00	20.00
Strand SLS-1030	(S)	Jeanne Thomas Sings For The Boys	1961	12.00	30.00

THOMAS, JOE, & BILL ELLIOTT

Sue 1025	(S)	Speak Your Piece	1964	10.00	25.00

THOMAS, JON

ABC-Paramount 351	(M)	Heartbreak	1960	10.00	25.00
ABC-Paramount S-351	(S)	Heartbreak	1960	14.00	35.00

("Heartbreak" and "Buffalo Blues" are rechanneled on this album.)

THOMAS, RAY
Thomas is a member of The Moody Blues.

Threshold THS-016	(S)	From Mighty Oaks	1975	4.00	10.00
Threshold THS-017	(S)	Hopes, Wishes And Dreams	1976	8.00	20.00
Threshold THSX-102	(DJ)	Ray Thomas Discusses The Recording Of His First Solo Album	1975	16.00	40.00

THOMAS, RUFUS

Stax ST-704	(M)	Walking The Dog	1963	30.00	75.00
Stax STS-2022	(S)	May I Have Your Ticket Please	1969	8.00	20.00
Stax STS-2028	(S)	Do The Funky Chicken	1970	8.00	20.00
Stax STS-2039	(S)	Doing The Push And Pull Live At P.J.'s	1971	8.00	20.00
Stax STS-3004	(S)	Did You Heard Me	1972	8.00	20.00
Stax STS-3008	(S)	Crown Prince Of Dance	1973	8.00	20.00
A.V.I. 6015	(S)	If There Were No Music	1977	6.00	15.00
A.V.I. 6046	(S)	I Ain't Gettin' Older, I'm Gettin' Better	1978	6.00	15.00

THOMAS, RUFUS & CARLA

Stax 4124	(S)	Chronicle	1979	4.00	10.00

THOMAS, TERRY

London 5764	(M)	Strictly It	1963	8.00	20.00
Warner Bros. W-1558	(M)	Terry Thomas Discovers America	1964	6.00	15.00
Warner Bros. WS-1558	(S)	Terry Thomas Discovers America	1964	8.00	20.00

THOMPSON, HANK (& THE BRAZOS VALLEY BOYS)

Capitol H-418 (10")	(M)	Songs Of The Brazos Valley	1953	40.00	100.00
Capitol H-618 (10")	(M)	North Of The Rio Grande	1953	40.00	100.00
Capitol H-729 (10")	(M)	New Recordings Of Hank's All-Time Hits	1953	40.00	100.00
Capitol H-911 (10")	(M)	Hank Thompson Favorites	1953	40.00	100.00
Capitol T-418	(M)	Songs Of The Brazos Valley	1956	30.00	75.00
Capitol T-618	(M)	North Of The Rio Grande	1956	30.00	75.00
Capitol T-729	(M)	New Recordings Of Hank's All-Time Hits	1956	30.00	75.00
Capitol T-826	(M)	Hank!	1957	30.00	75.00
Capitol T-911	(M)	Hank Thompson Favorites	1957	30.00	75.00
Capitol T-975	(M)	Hank Thompson's Dance Ranch	1958	30.00	75.00

— Original Capitol albums above have turquoise labels.—

Capitol T-1111	(M)	Favorite Waltzes	1959	30.00	75.00
Capitol T-1246	(M)	Songs For Rounders	1959	12.00	30.00
Capitol ST-1246	(S)	Songs For Rounders	1959	16.00	40.00
Capitol T-1360	(M)	Most Of All	1960	10.00	25.00
Capitol ST-1360	(S)	Most Of All	1960	12.00	30.00
Capitol T-1469	(M)	This Broken Heart Of Mine	1960	10.00	25.00
Capitol ST-1469	(S)	This Broken Heart Of Mine	1960	12.00	30.00
Capitol T-1544	(M)	An Old Love Affair	1961	10.00	25.00
Capitol ST-1544	(S)	An Old Love Affair	1961	12.00	30.00
Capitol T-1632	(M)	At The Golden Nugget	1961	10.00	25.00
Capitol ST-1632	(S)	At The Golden Nugget	1961	12.00	30.00
Capitol T-1741	(M)	The #1 Country & Western Band	1962	12.00	30.00
Capitol DT-1741	(E)	The #1 Country & Western Band	1962	8.00	20.00

— Original Capitol albums above have black labels with the logo on the left side.—

Capitol T-1775	(M)	Cheyenne Frontier Days	1962	8.00	20.00
Capitol ST-1775	(S)	Cheyenne Frontier Days	1962	10.00	25.00

Label & Catalog #		Title	Year	VG+	NM
Capitol T-1878	(M)	The Best Of Hank Thompson	1963	8.00	20.00
Capitol ST-1878	(P)	The Best Of Hank Thompson	1963	10.00	25.00
Capitol T-1955	(M)	At The State Fair Of Texas	1963	10.00	25.00
Capitol DT-1955	(E)	At The State Fair Of Texas	1963	6.00	15.00
Capitol T-2089	(M)	Golden Country Hits	1964	6.00	15.00
Capitol ST-2089	(S)	Golden Country Hits	1964	8.00	20.00
Capitol T-2154	(M)	It's Christmas Time	1964	6.00	15.00
Capitol ST-2154	(S)	It's Christmas Time	1964	8.00	20.00
Capitol T-2274	(M)	Breakin' In Another Heart	1965	6.00	15.00
Capitol ST-2274	(S)	Breakin' In Another Heart	1965	8.00	20.00
Capitol T-2342	(M)	The Luckiest Heartache In Town	1965	6.00	15.00
Capitol ST-2342	(S)	The Luckiest Heartache In Town	1965	8.00	20.00
Capitol T-2460	(M)	A Six Pack To Go	1966	8.00	20.00
Capitol DT-2460	(E)	A Six Pack To Go	1966	6.00	15.00
Capitol T-2575	(M)	Breakin' The Rules	1966	6.00	15.00
Capitol ST-2575	(S)	Breakin' The Rules	1966	8.00	20.00
Capitol T-2661	(M)	The Best Of Hank Thompson, Volume 2	1967	6.00	15.00
Capitol ST-2661	(S)	The Best Of Hank Thompson, Volume 2	1967	8.00	20.00
Capitol T-2826	(M)	Just An Old Flame	1967	6.00	15.00
Capitol ST-2826	(S)	Just An Old Flame	1967	8.00	20.00
		— Original Capitol albums above have black labels with the logo on top.—			
Tower T-5120	(M)	Country Blues	1968	8.00	20.00
Tower DT-5120	(E)	Country Blues	1968	6.00	15.00
Dot DLP-25864	(S)	The Gold Standards	1968	6.00	15.00
Dot DLP-25894	(S)	On Tap, In The Can Or In The Bottle	1968	6.00	15.00
Dot DLP-25932	(S)	Smokey The Bar	1969	6.00	15.00
Dot DLP-25971	(S)	Hank Thompson Salutes Oklahoma	1969	6.00	15.00
Dot DOS-25991	(S)	Next Time I Fall In Love, I Won't	1971	4.00	10.00
Dot DOS-25996	(S)	Cab Driver-A Salute To The Mills Brothers	1972	4.00	10.00
Dot DOS2-2000	(S)	25th Anniversary Album (2 LPs)	1972	4.00	10.00
Dot DOS-26004	(S)	Hank Thompson's Greatest Hits	1972	4.00	10.00
Dot DOS-26015	(S)	Kindly Keep It Country	1973	4.00	10.00

THOMPSON, HAYDEN

Label & Catalog #		Title	Year	VG+	NM
Kapp KL-1507	(M)	Here's Hayden Thompson	1966	12.00	30.00
Kapp KS-3507	(S)	Here's Hayden Thompson	1966	16.00	40.00

THOMPSON, KAY

Label & Catalog #		Title	Year	VG+	NM
MGM E-3146	(M)	Kay Thompson	1954	10.00	25.00

THOMPSON, MAYO

Label & Catalog #		Title	Year	VG+	NM
Texas Revolution	(S)	Corky's Debt To His Father	1969	40.00	100.00

THOMPSON, RICHARD

Label & Catalog #		Title	Year	VG+	NM
Reprise MS-2112	(S)	Henry The Human Fly	1972	6.00	15.00

THOMPSON, SONNY
For additional listings refer to Freddie King & Lula Reed & Sonny Thompson.

Label & Catalog #		Title	Year	VG+	NM
King 568	(M)	Moody Blues	1956	100.00	250.00
King 655	(M)	Mellow Blues For The Late Hours	1959	50.00	125.00

THOMPSON, SUE

Label & Catalog #		Title	Year	VG+	NM
Hickory LPM-104	(M)	Meet Sue Thompson	1962	12.00	30.00
Hickory LPS-104	(S)	Meet Sue Thompson	1962	16.00	40.00
Hickory LPM-107	(M)	Two Of A Kind	1962	12.00	30.00
Hickory LPS-107	(S)	Two Of A Kind	1962	16.00	40.00
Hickory LPM-111	(M)	Sue Thompson's Golden Hits	1963	12.00	30.00
Hickory LPS-111	(S)	Sue Thompson's Golden Hits	1963	16.00	40.00
Wing MGW-12317	(M)	The Country Side Of Sue Thompson	1964	8.00	20.00
Wing SRW-16317	(S)	The Country Side Of Sue Thompson	1964	12.00	30.00
Hickory LPM-121	(M)	Paper Tiger	1965	8.00	20.00
Hickory LPS-121	(S)	Paper Tiger	1965	12.00	30.00
Hickory LPM-130	(M)	Sue Thompson With Strings Attached	1966	8.00	20.00
Hickory LPS-130	(S)	Sue Thompson With Strings Attached	1966	12.00	30.00
Hickory LPS-148	(S)	This Is Sue Thompson	1969	8.00	20.00
Hickory H3F-4511	(S)	Sweet Memories	1974	6.00	15.00
Hickory H3G-4515	(S)	...And Love Me	1974	6.00	15.00

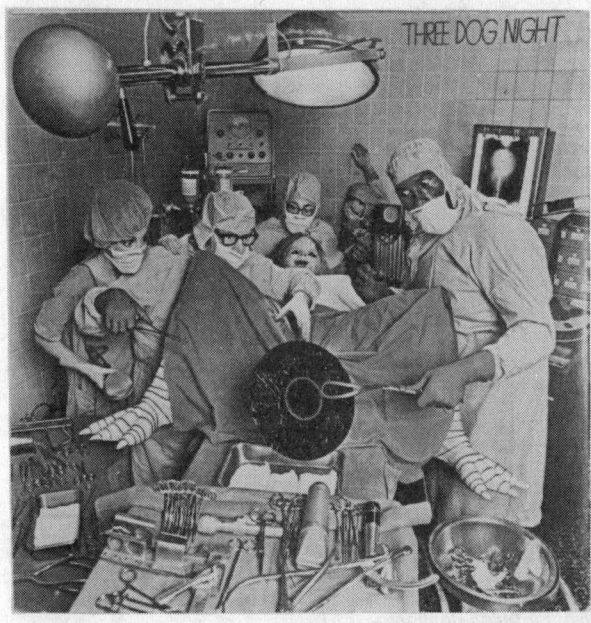

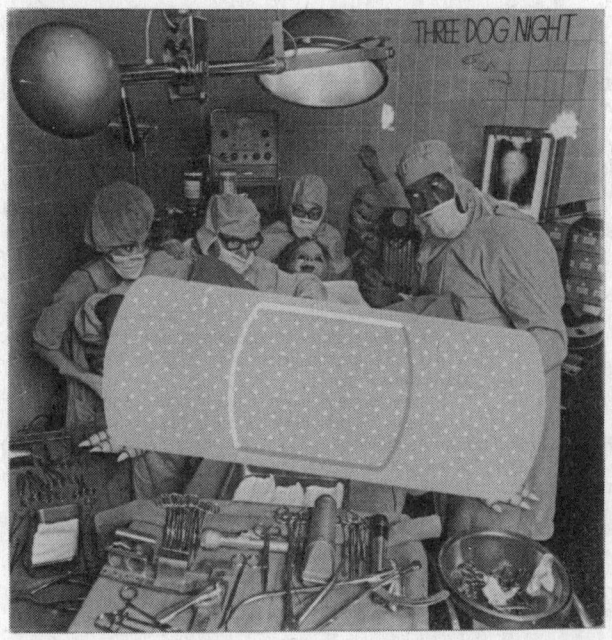

Who'da guessed that good ol' Three Dog Night—arguably the most successful group of their time with
twelve charting albums for Dunhill and twelve Gold Records from the RIAA—would be the only group to
have two albums recalled for objectionable cover art? While It Ain't Easy was issued initially with TDN
posing sans clothing, Hard Labor's original delivery scene was amended with a huge band-aid, fi
affixed to the cover (above) and, on subsequent pressings, with it printed into the art.

Label & Catalog #		Title	Year	VG+	NM

THOMPSON'S BRAZOS VALLEY BOYS, HANK

Warner Bros. W-1664	(M)	Where Is The Circus	1966	8.00	20.00
Warner Bros. WS-1664	(S)	Where Is The Circus	1966	10.00	25.00
Warner Bros. W-1679	(M)	The Countrypolitan Sound	1967	8.00	20.00
Warner Bros. WS-1679	(S)	The Countrypolitan Sound	1967	10.00	25.00
Warner Bros. W-1686	(M)	The Gold Standard Collection	1967	8.00	20.00
Warner Bros. WS-1686	(S)	The Gold Standard Collection	1967	10.00	25.00
Dot DLP-25978	(S)	The Instrumental Sound	1970	6.00	15.00

THORINSHIELD

Philips PHS-600-251	(S)	Thorinshield	1968	10.00	25.00

THORNTON, BIG MAMA

Arhoolie F-1028	(M)	Big Mama Thornton In Europe	1966	8.00	20.00
Arhoolie F-1032	(M)	The Queen At Monterey	1967	8.00	20.00
Arhoolie F-1039	(M)	Ball And Chain	1967	8.00	20.00
Mercury SRM-1-61225	(S)	Stronger Than Dirt	1969	8.00	20.00
Mercury SRM-1-61249	(S)	The Way It Is	1970	8.00	20.00
Roulette SR-42050	(S)	Maybe	1970	6.00	15.00
Back Beat BLP-68	(E)	She's Back	1970	6.00	15.00
Pentagram PE-10,005	(S)	Saved	1971	6.00	15.00
Vanguard VSD-79351	(S)	Jail	1974	6.00	15.00
Vanguard VSD-79354	(S)	Sassy Mama	1975	6.00	15.00

THORNTON, TERI: Refer to GOLDMINE'S PRICE GUIDE TO COLLECTIBLE JAZZ ALBUMS

THREE CHUCKLES, THE
The Three Chuckles feature Teddy Randazzo.

Vik LX-1067	(M)	The Three Chuckles	1956	60.00	150.00

THREE D'S, THE

Capitol T-2171	(M)	New Dimensions In Folk Songs	1964	6.00	15.00
Capitol ST-2171	(S)	New Dimensions In Folk Songs	1964	8.00	20.00

THREE DOG NIGHT
Three Dog Night features Danny Hutton, Cory Wells and Chuck Negron.

Dunhill DS-50048	(S)	Three Dog Night	1968	6.00	15.00
Dunhill DS-50058	(S)	Suitable For Framing	1969	6.00	15.00
Dunhill DS-50068	(S)	Captured Live At The Forum	1969	6.00	15.00
Dunhill DS-50078	(S)	It Ain't Easy	1970	30.00	75.00
		(Original covers have the group posing in the buff.)			
Dunhill DSD-50168	(S)	Hard Labor	1974	12.00	30.00
		("First-state delivery cover." Original covers depict a hospital delivery with a female creature giving birth to a record album.)			
Dunhill DSD-50168	(S)	Hard Labor	1974	6.00	15.00
		("Second-state delivery cover." In a pique of embarrassment, Dunhill recalled the album and rather cleverly had a huge band aid affixed to the jacket covering the "offending" scene.)			
Dunhill DSD-50168	(S)	Hard Labor	197?	1.60	8.00
		("Third-state delivery cover." Later covers have the band-aid printed on the cover as part of the artwork.)			
— *Original Dunhill albums above have "A Subsidiary of ABC" on the bottom."—*					
Command QD-40014	(Q)	Hard Labor	1974	6.00	15.00
Command QD-40018	(Q)	Coming Down Your Way	1975	6.00	15.00

THREE FACES WEST

Outpost 1000	(S)	Three Faces West	197?	8.00	20.00

THREE FLAMES, THE

Mercury MG-20239	(M)	At The Bon Soir	1957	20.00	50.00

THREE MAN ARMY

Sutra SKBS-2044	(S)	A Third Of A Lifetime	1971	12.00	30.00
		(Pink label in a gatefold cover with die-cut holes.)			
SKBS-2044	(S)	A Third Of A Lifetime *(Single cover)*	1971	8.00	20.00
150	(S)	Three Man Army	1973	10.00	25.00
82	(S)	Three Man Army Two	1974	10.00	25.00

Label & Catalog #		Title	Year	VG+	NM

THREE STOOGES, THE
The Stooges are Moe, Larry, Curly, Shemp and Curly Joe. The Stooges also recorded with Yogi Bear.

Coral CRL-57289	(M)	The Nonsense Songbook	1959	20.00	50.00
Coral CRL-757289	(S)	The Nonsense Songbook	1959	30.00	75.00
Golden GLP-43	(M)	Madcap Musical Nonsense	1959	30.00	75.00
Columbia CL-1650	(M)	Snow White & The Three Stooges (Sdtk)	1961	20.00	50.00
Columbia CS-8450	(S)	Snow White & The Three Stooges (Sdtk)	1961	30.00	75.00
Vocalion VL-73823	(S)	The Three Stooges Sing For Kids	1968	10.00	25.00
		(Vocalion 73823 is a repackage of Coral 757289.)			

THREE SUNS, THE

Varsity VLP-6001 (10")	(M)	Twilight Time	1950	20.00	50.00
Varsity VLP-6048 (10")	(M)	Midnight Time	1950	20.00	50.00
Royale 1 (10")	(M)	Twilight Time	1951	20.00	50.00
Royale 29 (10")	(M)	Midnight Time	1950	20.00	50.00
RCA Victor LPM-3 (10")	(M)	Three-Quarter Time	1951	20.00	50.00
RCA Victor LPM-20 (10")	(M)	Hands Across The Table	1951	20.00	50.00
RCA Victor LPM-52 (10")	(M)	Christmas Favorites	1951	20.00	50.00
RCA Victor LPM-3012 (10")	(M)	Twilight Moods	1952	20.00	50.00
RCA Victor LPM-3034 (10")	(M)	The Three Suns Present	1952	20.00	50.00
RCA Victor LPM-3040 (10")	(M)	Busy Fingers	1952	20.00	50.00
RCA Victor LPM-3056 (10")	(M)	Christmas Party	1952	20.00	50.00
RCA Victor LPM-3075 (10")	(M)	Slumbertime	1952	20.00	50.00
RCA Victor LPM-3113 (10")	(M)	Pop Concert Favorites	1953	20.00	50.00
RCA Victor LPM-3125 (10")	(M)	Mods	1953	20.00	50.00
RCA Victor LPM-3130 (10")	(M)	Top Pops	1953	20.00	50.00
RCA Victor LPM-3146 (10")	(M)	Polka Time	1953	20.00	50.00
RCA Victor LPM-3174 (10")	(M)	Sacred Hymns	1953	20.00	50.00
RCA Victor LPM-1041	(M)	Soft And Sweet	1955	12.00	30.00
RCA Victor LPM-1132	(M)	Sounds Of Christmas	1955	12.00	30.00
RCA Victor LPM-1171	(M)	Twilight Time	1956	12.00	30.00
RCA Victor LPM-1173	(M)	My Reverie	1956	12.00	30.00
RCA Victor LPM-1220	(M)	Malaguena	1956	12.00	30.00
RCA Victor LPM-1249	(M)	High Fi And Wide	1956	12.00	30.00
RCA Victor LPM-1316	(M)	Easy Listening	1956	12.00	30.00
RCA Victor LPM-1333	(M)	Midnight For Two	1957	12.00	30.00

THRILLINGTON, PERCY "THRILLS"
Thrills Thrillington is a pseudonym for Paul McCartney.

Capitol ST-11642	(S)	Thrillington	1977	60.00	150.00

THUNDER, JOHNNY

Diamond D-5001	(M)	Loop De Loop	1963	20.00	50.00
Diamond SD-5001	(S)	Loop De Loop	1963	30.00	75.00
Real Records RR1	(S)	So Alone	196?	4.00	10.00

THUNDERBIRDS, THE

Red Feather TH-1	(M)	Meet The Fabulous Thunderbirds	196?	80.00	200.00

THUNDERCLAP NEWMAN

Track SD-8264	(S)	Hollywood Dream	1970	8.00	20.00
		(Produced by Pete Townshend.)			
Track PR-A-160	(DJ)	Special Interview With Pete Townshend			
		& Thunderclap Newman (One-sided)	1970	30.00	75.00
MCA/Track 354	(S)	Hollywood Dream	1973	4.00	10.00

THUNDERPUSSY

M.R.T. RL-31748	(S)	Document Of Captivity	1973	60.00	150.00

TIDE, THE

Mouth 7237	(S)	Almost Live	196?	20.00	50.00

TIDES, THE

Mercury MG-20714	(M)	Limbo Rock	1962	5.00	12.00
Mercury SR-60714	(S)	Limbo Rock	1962	6.00	15.00
Wing MGW-12248	(M)	The Best Of Bossa Nova	1963	4.00	10.00
Wing SRW-16248	(S)	The Best Of Bossa Nova	1963	5.00	12.00
Wing MGW-12265	(M)	Surf City And Other Surfin' Favorites	1963	8.00	20.00
Wing SRW-16265	(S)	Surf City And Other Surfin' Favorites	1963	10.00	25.00

Label & Catalog #		Title	Year	VG+	NM
TIEKIN, FREDDIE, & THE ROCKERS					
I.T. 2301	(M)	By Popular Demand	1957	20.00	50.00
I.T. 2304	(M)	Freddie Tieken & The Rockers	1958	20.00	50.00
TIFFANY SHADE					
Mainstream 56105	(S)	Tiffany Shade	1969	10.00	25.00
TIJUANA BEATLES, THE					
Alshire 5165	(S)	The Tijuana Beatles	1969	6.00	15.00
TIKIS, THE					
Minaret TLP-7001	(M)	The Tikis	196?	20.00	50.00
Philips PHM-200-043	(M)	The Tikis	1962	8.00	20.00
Philips PHS-600-043	(S)	The Tikis	1962	12.00	30.00
TIL, SONNY, & THE ORIOLES					
RCA Victor LSP-4451	(S)	Sonny Til Returns	1970	6.00	15.00
RCA Victor LSP-4538	(S)	Old Gold / New Gold	1970	6.00	15.00
Dobre 1026	(S)	Back To The Chapel	1978	4.00	10.00
TILLIS, MEL (& THE STATESIDERS)					
Mel also recorded with Nancy Sinatra.					
Columbia CL-1724	(M)	Heart Over Mind	1962	12.00	30.00
Columbia CS-8524	(S)	Heart Over Mind	1962	16.00	40.00
— *Original Columbia albums above have six white-on-black "eye" logos around the perimeter of the label.* —					
Kapp KL-1492	(M)	Stateside	1966	6.00	15.00
Kapp KS-3492	(S)	Stateside	1966	8.00	20.00
Kapp KL-1514	(M)	Life Turned Her That Way	1967	6.00	15.00
Kapp KS-3514	(S)	Life Turned Her That Way	1967	8.00	20.00
Kapp KL-1514	(M)	Life's That Way	1967	6.00	15.00
Kapp KS-3514	(S)	Life's That Way	1967	8.00	20.00
Kapp KL-1535	(M)	Mr. Mel	1967	6.00	15.00
Kapp KS-3535	(S)	Mr. Mel	1967	8.00	20.00
Kapp KS-3543	(S)	Let Me Talk To You	1968	6.00	15.00
Kapp KS-3570	(S)	Something Special	1968	6.00	15.00
Kapp KS-3589	(S)	Mel Tillis' Greatest Hits	1969	6.00	15.00
Kapp KS-3594	(S)	Who's Julie?	1969	6.00	15.00
Kapp KS-3609	(S)	Old Faithful	1969	6.00	15.00
Kapp KS-3630	(S)	She'll Be Hanging 'Round Somewhere	1970	6.00	15.00
Kapp KS-3653	(S)	Mel Tillis' Greatest Hits, Volume 2	1971	4.00	10.00
TILLMAN, FLOYD					
RCA Victor LPM-1686	(M)	Floyd Tillman's Best	1958	20.00	50.00
Sims 110	(M)	Slippin' Around	196?	20.00	50.00
Harmony HL-7316	(M)	Floyd Tillman's Best	196?	10.00	25.00
Starday SLP-310	(M)	Let's Make Memories	196?	8.00	20.00
Mus. MM-2136	(M)	Floyd Tillman's Country	196?	12.00	30.00
TILLOTSON, JOHNNY					
Cadence CLP-3052	(M)	Johnny Tillotson's Best	1961	10.00	25.00
Cadence CLP-25052	(S)	Johnny Tillotson's Best	1961	16.00	40.00
		("Dreamy Eyes," "True, True Happiness," and "Without You" are rechanneled on this album.)			
Cadence CLP-3058	(M)	It Keeps Right On A-Hurtin'	1962	10.00	25.00
Cadence CLP-25058	(S)	It Keeps Right On A-Hurtin'	1962	16.00	40.00
Cadence CLP-3067	(M)	You Can Never Stop Me Loving You	1963	8.00	20.00
Cadence CLP-25067	(S)	You Can Never Stop Me Loving You	1963	12.00	30.00
		("Lonesome Town," "Donna," "I Got A Feelin'," "Where Is She?," "Venus" and "Come Softly To Me" are rechanneled on this album.)			
MGM E-4188	(M)	Talk Back Trembling Lips	1964	6.00	15.00
MGM SE-4188	(S)	Talk Back Trembling Lips	1964	8.00	20.00
MGM E-4224	(M)	The Tillotson Touch	1964	6.00	15.00
MGM SE-4224	(S)	The Tillotson Touch	1964	8.00	20.00
MGM E-4270	(M)	She Understands Me	1964	6.00	15.00
MGM SE-4270	(S)	She Understands Me	1964	8.00	20.00
MGM E-4302	(M)	That's My Style	1965	6.00	15.00
MGM SE-4302	(S)	That's My Style	1965	8.00	20.00
MGM E-4328	(M)	Our World	1965	6.00	15.00
MGM SE-4328	(S)	Our World	1965	8.00	20.00

Label & Catalog #		Title	Year	VG+	NM
MGM E-4395	(M)	No Love At All	1966	6.00	15.00
MGM SE-4395	(S)	No Love At All	1966	8.00	20.00
MGM E-4402	(M)	The Christmas Touch	1966	6.00	15.00
MGM SE-4402	(S)	The Christmas Touch	1966	8.00	20.00
MGM E-4452	(M)	Here I Am	1967	8.00	20.00
MGM SE-4452	(S)	Here I Am	1967	8.00	20.00
		— *Original MGM albums above have black labels.*—			
Metro M-561	(M)	Johnny Tillotson Sings Tillotson	1967	4.00	10.00
Metro MS-561	(S)	Johnny Tillotson Sings Tillotson	1967	5.00	12.00
MGM SE-4532	(S)	The Best Of Johnny Tillotson	1968	6.00	15.00
MGM SE-4814	(S)	The Very Best Of Johnny Tillotson	1971	4.00	10.00
Amos 7006	(S)	Tears On My Pillow	1969	6.00	15.00
Buddah BDS-5112	(S)	Johnny Tillotson	1972	6.00	15.00
TIMBER CREEK					
Renegade JAH-95014	(S)	Hellbound Highway	1975	60.00	150.00
TIMOTHY					
Pear	(S)	Strange But True	1972	80.00	200.00
TIN HOUSE					
Tin House features Rick Derringer.					
Epic E-30511	(S)	Tin House	1971	6.00	15.00
TIN TIN					
Atco SD-33-350	(P)	Tin Tin	1970	5.00	12.00
Atco SD-33-370	(S)	Astral Taxi	1971	4.00	10.00
TINGLING MOTHER'S CIRCUS					
Musicor MS-3167	(S)	A Circus Of The Mind	1968	8.00	20.00
TINO & THE REVLONS					
Dearborn 1004	(M)	By Request At The Sway-Zee	1966	100.00	250.00
TIR NA NOG					
Chrysalis CHR-1006	(S)	A Tear And A Smile	1972	5.00	12.00
Chrysalis CHR-1047	(S)	Strong In The Sun	1973	5.00	12.00
TITANS, THE					
MGM E-3992	(M)	Today's Teen Beat	1961	10.00	25.00
MGM SE-3992	(S)	Today's Teen Beat	1961	12.00	30.00
TITUS OATES					
(No label)	(S)	Jungle Lady	197?	60.00	150.00
TOAD					
Hallelujah	(S)	Toad	1968	80.00	200.00
TOAD HALL					
Liberty LST-7580	(S)	Toad Hall	1968	8.00	20.00
TOADS, THE					
Wiggins 64021	(M)	The Toads	1964	80.00	200.00
TOADS, THE					
Rite	(M)	The Toads	196?	40.00	100.00
TOE FAT					
Rare Earth RS-511	(S)	Toe Fat	1970	6.00	15.00
Rare Earth RS-525	(S)	Toe Fat Two	1971	6.00	15.00
TOKENS, THE					
RCA Victor LPM-2514	(M)	The Lion Sleeps Tonight	1961	30.00	75.00
RCA Victor LSP-2514	(S)	The Lion Sleeps Tonight	1961	40.00	100.00
RCA Victor LPM-2631	(M)	We, The Tokens, Sing Folk	1962	16.00	40.00
RCA Victor LSP-2631	(S)	We, The Tokens, Sing Folk	1962	20.00	50.00

— *Original RCA mono albums above have "Long Play" on the bottom of the label; stereo albums have "Living Stereo" on the bottom.*—

The original Tokens of the mid '50s were a white doo wop group featuring Hank Medress and a pre-Julliard Neil Sedaka. By 1961 the group consisted of Medress with Jay Siegel and the Margo brothers, Mitch and Phil. "The Lion Sleeps Tonight," was a highly stylized pop arrangement of a traditional South African chant of the Zulu tribe previously a favorite in the folkie community. The Wheels album (below) is highly sought-after by collectors of vocal car songs, automotive buffs and, of course, The Tokens' fans. . .

			Year	VG+	NM
RCA Victor LPM-2886	(M)	Wheels	1964	20.00	50.00
RCA Victor LST-2886	(S)	Wheels	1964	30.00	75.00
RCA Victor LPM-3685	(M)	The Tokens Again	1966	10.00	25.00
RCA Victor LSP-3685	(S)	The Tokens Again	1966	12.00	30.00
Diplomat D-2308	(M)	Kings Of The Hot Rods	196?	10.00	25.00
Diplomat DS-2308	(S)	Kings Of The Hot Rods	196?	12.00	30.00
B.T. Puppy BTP-1000	(M)	I Hear Trumpets Blow	1966	8.00	20.00
B.T. Puppy BTPS-1000	(P)	I Hear Trumpets Blow	1966	10.00	25.00
B.T. Puppy BTPS-1006	(S)	Tokens Of Gold	1969	10.00	25.00
B.T. Puppy BTPS-1012	(S)	Greatest Moments	1970	10.00	25.00
B.T. Puppy BTPS-1014	(S)	December 5th	1971	10.00	25.00
B.T. Puppy BTPS-10??	(S)	Intercourse	1971	See note below	
		(Extremely rare with no way to reasonably suggest a value.)			
Buddah BDS-5059	(S)	Both Sides Now	1971	6.00	15.00

TOKENS, THE / THE HAPPENINGS
B.T. Puppy BTP-1002	(M)	Back To Back	1967	5.00	12.00
B.T. Puppy BTPS-1002	(S)	Back To Back	1967	6.00	15.00

TOM & JERRY
Charlie Tomlinson and Jerry Kennedy.
Mercury MG-20626	(M)	Guitar's Greatest Hits	1961	8.00	20.00
Mercury SR-60626	(S)	Guitar's Greatest Hits	1961	10.00	25.00
Mercury MG-20671	(M)	Guitars Play The Sound Of Ray Charles	1962	8.00	20.00
Mercury SR-60671	(S)	Guitars Play The Sound Of Ray Charles	1962	10.00	25.00
Mercury MG-20756	(M)	Guitar's Greatest Hits, Volume 2	1962	8.00	20.00
Mercury SR-60756	(S)	Guitar's Greatest Hits, Volume 2	1962	10.00	25.00
Mercury MG-20842	(M)	Surfin' Hootenanny	1963	10.00	25.00
Mercury SR-60842	(S)	Surfin' Hootenanny	1963	12.00	30.00

TOM & SANDY
United Arts. UAL-3195	(M)	Tom And Sandy In Folkland	1963	5.00	12.00
United Arts. UAS-6195	(S)	Tom And Sandy In Folkland	1963	6.00	15.00

TOMORROW
Tomorrow features Steve Howe; Twink.
Sire SES-97912	(S)	Tomorrow	1968	16.00	40.00
		("My White Bicycle" and "Revolution" are rechanneled.)			

TONEY, OSCAR, JR.
Bell 6006	(M)	For Your Precious Love	1967	8.00	20.00
Bell S-6006	(S)	For Your Precious Love	1967	10.00	25.00

TONGUE
Hemisphere HIS-101	(S)	Tongue	197?	30.00	75.00

TONGUE & GROOVE (FEATURING LYNN HUGHES)
Fontana SRF-67593	(S)	Tongue & Groove	1968	10.00	25.00

TONTO'S EXPANDING HEAD BAND
Embryo SD-732	(S)	Zero Time	1971	10.00	25.00

TOODY, OFFICER GUNTHER
Gunther Toody is a pseudonym for Joe. E. Ross.
Golden LP-91	(M)	Tells Toody Tales	1963	14.00	35.00

TOP DRAWER
Wish Bone 721207	(S)	Solid Oak	197?	175.00	350.00

TOPSIDERS, THE
Josie J-4000	(M)	Rock Goes Folk	1963	6.00	15.00
Josie JS-4000	(S)	Rock Goes Folk	1963	8.00	20.00

TORME, MEL: *Refer to* GOLDMINE'S PRICE GUIDE TO COLLECTIBLE JAZZ ALBUMS

TORMENTORS, THE
Royal RLP-111	(M)	Hanging Around	196?	80.00	200.00

Label & Catalog #		Title	Year	VG+	NM
TORNADOES, THE [THE HOLLYWOOD TORNADOES]					
Josie J-4005	(M)	Bustin' Surfboards	1963	50.00	125.00
Josie JS-4005	(S)	Bustin' Surfboards	1963	70.00	175.00
TORNADOS, THE					
London LL-3279	(M)	Telstar	1962	30.00	75.00
London LL-3293	(M)	The Sounds Of The Tornados	1963	See note below	
		(The existence of this album is in doubt.)			
TORQUES, THE					
Wiggins 64010	(M)	Zoom!	1967	60.00	150.00
Lemco 604	(M)	The Torques Live	1968	40.00	100.00
TOSSI, AARON					
Prestige Int. PRLP-13027	(M)	Folk Songs And Ballads	1962	12.00	30.00
TOTO					
Columbia PJC-35317	(S)	Toto (Picture disc)	1979	6.00	15.00
Columbia PD-36813	(DJ)	Turn Back (Picture disc)	1979	6.00	15.00
Columbia PJC-37928	(DJ)	Toto IV (Picture disc)	1979	6.00	15.00
Columbia HC-47928	(DJ)	Toto IV (Half-speed master)	1981	7.00	20.00
Columbia 9C9-39911	(S)	Isolation (Picture disc)	1984	4.00	10.00
TOTTY					
Our First BT-205	(S)	Totty	197?	50.00	125.00
Our First OFRO-2	(S)	Totty Too	1981	12.00	30.00
TOUCH					
Mainline PS-70-116-7	(S)	Street Suite	197?	500.00	800.00
TOUCH, THE					
Coliseum DS-51004	(S)	The Touch	1968	8.00	20.00
TOUCHSTONE					
Touchstone features Tom Constanten of The Grateful Dead.					
United Arts. UAS-5563	(S)	Tarot	1972	12.00	30.00
TOUCHSTONE					
(No label)	(S)	Touchstone	1979	150.00	300.00
TOUSSAINT, ALLEN					
RCA Victor LPM-1767	(M)	The Wild Sound Of New Orleans	1958	60.00	150.00
Scepter 24003	(S)	Toussaint	1971	6.00	15.00
Reprise MS-2062	(S)	Life, Love And Faith	1972	6.00	15.00
TOURISTS, THE					
The Tourists feature Annie Lennox and Dave Stewart, later The Eurythmics.					
Epic NJE-36386	(S)	Reality Effect	1979	6.00	15.00
Epic NJE-36757	(S)	Luminous Basement	1980	6.00	15.00
Epic PE-39318	(S)	Should Have Been Greatest Hits	1984	4.00	10.00
TOWER, THE					
Other World OUR-1001	(S)	The Tower	1975	16.00	40.00
TOWER OF POWER					
San Francisco 204	(S)	East Bay Grease	1971	20.00	50.00
Direct Disk SD-16601	(S)	Back To Oakland	198?	7.00	20.00
Sheffield Lab	(S)	Direct!	198?	6.00	15.00
TOWNSEND, ED					
Capitol T-1140	(M)	New In Town	1959	6.00	15.00
Capitol ST-1140	(S)	New In Town	1959	8.00	20.00
Capitol T-1214	(M)	Glad To Be Here	1959	6.00	15.00
Capitol ST-1214	(S)	Glad To Be Here	1959	8.00	20.00
TOWNSEND, HENRY					
...esville BVLP-1041	(M)	Tired Of Bein' Mistreated	1962	16.00	40.00

TOWNSHEND, PETE
Townshend is a member of The Who. Refer to Thunderclap Newman.

Track 79189	(S)	Who Came First	1972	10.00	25.00

TOWNSHEND, PETE, & RONNIE LANE

MCA 2295	(S)	Rough Mix	1977	6.00	15.00

TOYS, THE

DynoVoice 9002	(M)	A Lovers Concerto/Attack	1966	16.00	40.00
DynoVoice 9002-S	(S)	A Lovers Concerto/Attack	1966	20.00	50.00

("A Lover's Concerto," "Attack," "I Got A Man"
and "This Night" are rechanneled.)

TRADER HORNE

Janus 3012	(S)	Morning Way	1970	5.00	12.00

TRADEWINDS, THE
The Tradewinds were Pete Anders and Vinnie Poncia.

Kama Sutra KLP-8057	(M)	Excursions	1967	10.00	25.00
Kama Sutra KLPS-8057	(S)	Excursions	1967	12.00	30.00

TRAFFIC
Traffic was origianlly Steve Winwood with Jim Capaldi, Dave Mason and Chris Wood.

United Arts. UAS-6651	(S)	Heaven Is In Your Mind	1969	20.00	50.00
United Arts. UAS-6651	(S)	Mr. Fantasy	1969	14.00	35.00

("Mr. Fantasy" is a reissue of "Heaven Is In Your Mind."
First pressing reissues have the original back covers
with "Heaven Is In Your Mind " across the top.)

United Arts. UAS-6651	(S)	Mr. Fantasy	1969	10.00	25.00

(Second pressing reissues have a green strip across
the top of the back cover listing the album's songs.)
— Original U.A. albums above have black labels.—

United Arts. UAS-6651	(S)	Mr. Fantasy	1969	6.00	15.00
United Arts. UAS-6676	(S)	Traffic	1968	6.00	15.00
United Arts. UAS-6702	(S)	Last Exit	1969	6.00	15.00

— U.A. albums above have orange & purple labels.—

United Arts. UAS-5500	(S)	The Best Of Traffic	1970	5.00	12.00
United Arts. UAS-5504	(S)	John Barleycorn Must Die	1970	5.00	12.00
United Arts. UAS-5507	(S)	Live Traffic	1971	5.00	12.00

— U.A. albums above have black & orange & labels.—

TRAMLINE

A&M SP-4208	(S)	Somewhere Down The Line	197?	10.00	25.00

TRAMMELL, BOBBY LEE

Atlanta 1503	(M)	Arkansas Twist	1962	150.00	350.00
Souncot SC-1102	(S)	I Dare America To Be Great	1971	4.00	10.00
Souncot SC-1141	(S)	Love Isn't Love Till You Give It Away	1972	4.00	10.00

TRANSIENTS, THE

Horizon T-1633	(M)	Funky Twelve String	1963	6.00	15.00
Horizon ST-1633	(S)	Funky Twelve String	1963	8.00	20.00

TRASHMEN, THE

Garrett GA-200	(M)	Surfin' Bird	1964	60.00	150.00
Garrett GAS-200	(E)	Surfin' Bird	1964	150.00	300.00

TRASK, DIANA

Columbia CL-1601	(M)	Diana Trask	1961	6.00	15.00
Columbia CS-8401	(S)	Diana Trask	1961	8.00	20.00
Columbia CL-1705	(M)	Diana Trask On TV	1961	6.00	15.00
Columbia CS-8505	(S)	Diana Trask On TV	1961	8.00	20.00

TRAVEL AGENCY, THE

Viva V-36017	(S)	Viva	1969	8.00	20.00

TRAVELLERS, THE

Kapp KL-1051	(M)	Journey With The Travellers	1960	6.00	15.00
Kapp KS-3051	(S)	Journey With The Travellers	1960	8.00	20.00

Label & Catalog #		Title	Year	VG+	NM
Epic LN-124013	(M)	Introducing The Travellers	1962	5.00	12.00
Epic BN-26013	(S)	Introducing The Travellers	1962	8.00	20.00
TRAVELERS THREE, THE					
Elektra EKL-216	(M)	The Travelers Three	1962	6.00	15.00
Elektra EKS-7216	(S)	The Travelers Three	1962	8.00	20.00
Elektra EKL-226	(M)	Open House	1962	6.00	15.00
Elektra EKS-7226	(S)	Open House	1962	8.00	20.00
Elektra EKL-236	(M)	The Travelers Three Live, Live, Live	1963	6.00	15.00
Elektra EKS-7236	(S)	The Travelers Three Live, Live, Live	1963	8.00	20.00
TRAVERS, MARY					
Refer to Peter, Paul & Mary.					
Warner Bros. B-1907	(S)	Mary	1971	4.00	10.00
Warner Bros. B-2609	(S)	Morning Glory	1972	4.00	10.00
Warner Bros. B-2677	(S)	All My Choices	1973	4.00	10.00
Warner Bros. B-2795	(S)	Circles	1974	4.00	10.00
TRAVIS, MERLE					
Capitol T-650	(M)	The Merle Travis Guitar *(Turquoise label)*	1956	40.00	100.00
Capitol T-891	(M)	Back Home *(Gray label)*	1957	30.00	75.00
Capitol T-1391	(M)	Walkin' The Strings	1960	30.00	75.00
Capitol T-1664	(M)	Travis	1962	14.00	35.00
Capitol ST-1664	(S)	Travis	1962	20.00	50.00
— Original Capitol albums above have black labels with the logo on the left side.—					
Capitol T-1956	(M)	Songs Of The Coal Mines	1963	12.00	30.00
Capitol T-1956	(S)	Songs Of The Coal Mines	1963	16.00	40.00
Capitol T-2662	(M)	The Best Of Merle Travis	1967	10.00	25.00
Capitol ST-2662	(P)	The Best Of Merle Travis	1967	12.00	30.00
Capitol ST-2938	(S)	Strictly Guitar	1969	12.00	30.00
— Original Capitol albums above have black labels with the logo on top.—					
TRAVIS, MERLE, & JOE MAPHIS					
Capitol T-2102	(M)	Merle Travis And Joe Maphis	1964	16.00	40.00
Capitol ST-2102	(S)	Merle Travis And Joe Maphis	1964	20.00	50.00
TRAVIS, MERLE, & JOHNNY BOND					
Capitol ST-249	(S)	Great Songs Of The Delmore Brothers	1969	10.00	25.00
TREMELOES, THE					
Refer to Brian Poole & the Tremeloes.					
Epic LN-24310	(M)	Here Comes My Baby	1967	10.00	25.00
Epic BN-26310	(E)	Here Comes My Baby	1967	8.00	20.00
Epic LN-24326	(M)	Even The Bad Times Are Good	1967	8.00	20.00
Epic BN-26326	(P)	Even The Bad Times Are Good	1967	10.00	25.00
Epic LN-24363	(M)	Suddenly You Love Me	1968	10.00	25.00
Epic BN-26363	(E)	Suddenly You Love Me	1968	8.00	20.00
Epic BN-26388	(S)	World Explosion '58/'68	1968	10.00	25.00
TRENIERS, THE					
Epic LG-3125	(M)	The Treniers On TV	1955	60.00	150.00
Dot DLP-3257	(M)	Souvenir Album	1960	40.00	100.00
Heritage H-1002	(M)	After Hours	196?	20.00	50.00
Heritage HS-1002	(S)	After Hours	196?	30.00	75.00
TREVOR, JEANNIE: *Refer to* GOLDMINE'S PRICE GUIDE TO COLLECTIBLE JAZZ ALBUMS					
TRIMBLE, BOBB					
Vengeance BT-8458	(S)	Iraon Curtain Dream	1980	660.00	1,000.00
(No label)	(S)	Harvest Of Dreams	1982	60.00	150.00
TRIGGER, VIC					
Sanctuary 12103	(S)	Electronic Wizzard	1977	40.00	100.00
TRIPSICHORD MUSIC BOX, THE					
Janus JLS-3016	(S)	The Tripsichord Music Box	1971	40.00	100.00

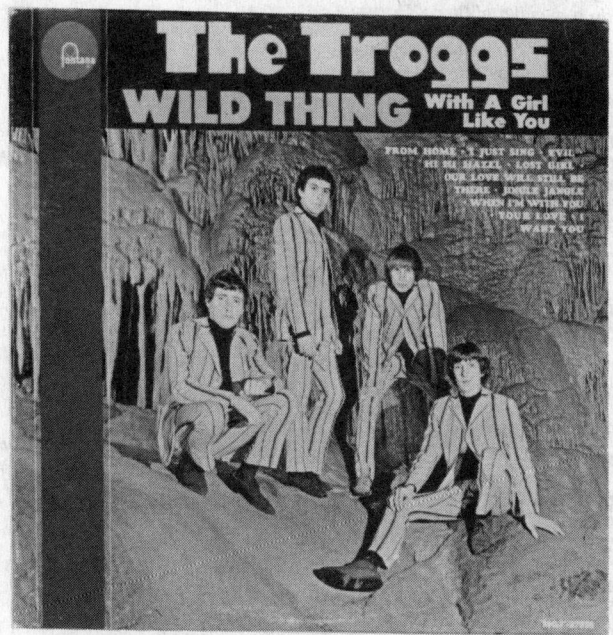

Many albums have been issued with slightly different covers or labels, usually attracting little interest from collectors (excepting Elvis and The Beatles). Fontana's pressing of The Troggs is an example: The titles of the two hits, "Wild Thing" and "With A Girl Like You," are in very different print on the two illustrations. Thus far, there has been no need to differentiate one from the other in this book's listings. . .

TRINITY RIVER BOYS, THE
The River Boys feature Michael Murphey And Michael Nesmith.   1964   *See note below*
Prospector 1   (M)   **The Trinity River Boys**
                                          (While this album was recorded, it may not have been released.).

TRIZO-50   197?   150.00   300.00
Cavern Custom 740142   (S)   **Cavern-50**

TROGGS, THE   1966   20.00   50.00
Atco 33-193   (M)   **Wild Thing**   1966   16.00   40.00
Atco SD-33-193   (E)   **Wild Thing**   1966   14.00   35.00
Fontana SR-27556   (M)   **The Troggs**   1966   12.00   30.00
Fontana SRF-67556   (E)   **The Troggs**
                                          (Atco 193 and Fontana 2/57556 are the same album.)
Fontana SRF-67576   (E)   **Love Ia All Around**   1968   10.00   25.00
Pye 12112   (S)   **The Troggs**   1975   4.00   10.00
Private Stock PS-2008   (S)   **The Trogg Tapes**   1976   4.00   10.00
Sire SASH-3714-2   (M)   **Vintage Years** *(2 LPs)*   1976   6.00   15.00

TROLL   1969   10.00   25.00
Smash SRS-67114   (S)   **Animated Music**

TROMBONES, THE   1969   8.00   20.00
Chartmaker 1105   (S)   **The Trombones**

TROUP, BOBBY: *Refer to* GOLDMINE'S PRICE GUIDE TO COLLECTIBLE JAZZ ALBUMS

TROUT   1968   6.00   15.00
MGM SE-4592   (S)   **The Trout**

TROWER, ROBIN
Trower was formerly a member of Procol Harum.
Chrysalis CHR-1039   (S)   **Twice Removed From Yesterday**   1973   4.00   10.00
Chrysalis CHR-1057   (S)   **Bridge Of Sighs**   1974   4.00   10.00
Chrysalis CHR-1073   (S)   **For Earth Below**   1975   4.00   10.00
Chrysalis CHR-1089   (S)   **Live**   1976   4.00   10.00
Chrysalis CHR-1148   (S)   **In City Dreams**   1977   4.00   10.00
Chrysalis CHR-1107   (S)   **Long Misty Days**   1976   4.00   10.00
Chrysalis CHR-1189   (S)   **Caravan To Midnight**   1978   4.00   10.00
Chrysalis CHR-1215   (S)   **Victims Of Fury**   1980   4.00   10.00
Chrysalis CHR-1324   (S)   **B.L.T.**   1981   4.00   10.00
Chrysalis CHR-1352   (S)   **Truce**   1982   4.00   10.00

TROY, BO   196?   6.00   15.00
Diplomat D-2304   (M)   **Wild Hot Rod Wails**   196?   8.00   20.00
Diplomat DS-2304   (S)   **Wild Hot Rod Wails**

TROY, DORIS   1964   14.00   35.00
Atlantic 8088   (M)   **Just One Look**   1964   20.00   50.00
Atlantic SD-8088   (S)   **Just One Look**
                                          ("Just One Look" is rechanneled on this album.)
Apple ST-3371   (S)   **Doris Troy**   1970   6.00   15.00
                                          (Features George Harrison, guitar, and Ringo, drums.)

TRUE ENDEAVOR JUG BAND, THE   1964   8.00   20.00
Folklore FRLP-14022   (M)   **The Art Of The Jug band**   1964   10.00   25.00
Folklore FRST-14022   (S)   **The Art Of The Jug band**

TRUMAN, MARGARET   1951   16.00   40.00
RCA Victor LPM-57 (10")   (M)   **American Songs**

TRUMPETEERS, THE   1956   80.00   200.00
Score SLP-4021   (M)   **Milky White Way**   195?   40.00   100.00
Grand 7701   (M)   **The Last Supper**

TRUTH & JANEY   197?   30.00   75.00
Montrose   (S)   **No Rest For The Wicked**   197?   16.00   40.00
Bee Bee 711X98   (S)   **Just A Little Bit Of Magic**

T2

Label & Catalog #		Title	Year	VG+	NM
London PS-583	(S)	It'll All Work Out In Boomland	1971	20.00	50.00

TUBB, ERNEST (& THE TEXAS TROUBADORS)
Refer to Red Foley.

Label & Catalog #		Title	Year	VG+	NM
Decca DL-5301 (10")	(M)	Ernest Tubb Favorites	1951	40.00	100.00
Decca DL-5334 (10")	(M)	Old Rugged Cross	1951	40.00	100.00
Decca DL-5336 (10")	(M)	Jimmie Rodgers Songs	1951	40.00	100.00
Decca DL-5497 (10")	(M)	Sing A Song Of Christmas	1954	40.00	100.00
Decca DL-8291	(M)	Ernest Tubb Favorites	1956	20.00	50.00
Decca DL-8553	(M)	The Daddy Of 'Em All	1956	20.00	50.00
Decca DL-8834	(M)	The Importance Of Being Ernest	1959	16.00	40.00
Decca DL-78834	(S)	The Importance Of Being Ernest	1959	20.00	50.00
		— Original Decca albums above have black & silver labels.—			
Decca DL-4042	(M)	Record Shop	1960	12.00	30.00
Decca DL-74042	(S)	Record Shop	1960	16.00	40.00
Decca DL-4046	(M)	All Time Hits	1961	10.00	25.00
Decca DL-74046	(S)	All Time Hits	1961	12.00	30.00
Decca DL-4118	(M)	Ernest Tubb's Golden Favorites	1961	10.00	25.00
Decca DL-74118	(S)	Ernest Tubb's Golden Favorites	1961	12.00	30.00
Decca DL-4321	(M)	On Tour	1962	12.00	30.00
Decca DL-74321	(S)	On Tour	1962	16.00	40.00
Decca DL-4385	(M)	Just Call Me Lonesome	1963	10.00	25.00
Decca DL-74385	(S)	Just Call Me Lonesome	1963	12.00	30.00
Decca DL-4397	(M)	The Family Bible	1964	8.00	20.00
Decca DL-74397	(S)	The Family Bible	1964	10.00	25.00
Decca DL-4514	(M)	Thanks A Lot	1964	8.00	20.00
Decca DL-74514	(S)	Thanks A Lot	1964	10.00	25.00
Decca DL-4518	(M)	Blue Christmas	1964	8.00	20.00
Decca DL-74518	(S)	Blue Christmas	1964	10.00	25.00
Decca DXA-159	(M)	The Ernest Tubb Story (2 LPs with booklet)	196?	12.00	30.00
Decca DXSA-7159	(E)	The Ernest Tubb Story (2 LPs with booklet)	196?	10.00	25.00
Decca DL-4640	(M)	My Pick Of The Hits	1965	8.00	20.00
Decca DL-74640	(S)	My Pick Of The Hits	1965	10.00	25.00
Decca DL-4681	(M)	Hittin' The Road	1965	8.00	20.00
Decca DL-74681	(S)	Hittin' The Road	1965	10.00	25.00
Decca DL-4746	(M)	By Request	1966	8.00	20.00
Decca DL-74746	(S)	By Request	1966	10.00	25.00
Decca DL-4772	(M)	Country Hits, Old And New	1966	8.00	20.00
Decca DL-74772	(S)	Country Hits, Old And New	1966	10.00	25.00
		— Original Decca albums above have black labels with "Mfrd by Decca" beneath the rainbow.—			
Decca DL-4867	(M)	Another Story	1967	8.00	20.00
Decca DL-74867	(S)	Another Story	1967	8.00	20.00
Decca DL-74957	(S)	Ernest Tubb Sings Hank Williams	1968	8.00	20.00
Decca DL-75006	(S)	Ernest Tubb's Greatest Hits	1968	8.00	20.00
Decca DL-75072	(S)	Country Hit Time	1968	8.00	20.00
Decca DL-75114	(S)	Let's Turn Back The Years	1969	6.00	15.00
Decca DL-75122	(S)	Saturday Satan, Sunday Saint	1969	6.00	15.00
Decca DL-75222	(S)	A Good Year For The Wine	1970	6.00	15.00
Decca DL-75252	(S)	Ernest Tubb's Greatest Hits, Volume 2	1970	6.00	15.00
Decca DL-75301	(S)	One Sweet Hello	1971	6.00	15.00
Decca DL-75345	(S)	Say Something Nice To Sarah	1972	6.00	15.00
Decca DL-75388	(S)	Baby, It's So Hard To Be Good	1972	6.00	15.00

TUBB, ERNEST, & LORETTA LYNN

Label & Catalog #		Title	Year	VG+	NM
Decca DL-4639	(M)	Mr. And Mrs. Used To Be	1965	8.00	20.00
Decca DL-74639	(S)	Mr. And Mrs. Used To Be	1965	10.00	25.00
		— Original Decca albums above have black labels with "Mfrd by Decca" beneath the rainbow.—			
Decca DL-4872	(M)	Singin' Again	1967	8.00	20.00
Decca DL-74872	(S)	Singin' Again	1967	8.00	20.00
Decca DL-75115	(S)	If We Put Our Heads Together	1969	6.00	15.00

TUBB, JUSTIN

Label & Catalog #		Title	Year	VG+	NM
Decca DL-8644	(M)	Country Boy In Love	1957	20.00	50.00
Starday SLP-160	(M)	Star Of The Grand Ole Opry	1962	12.00	30.00
Starday SLP-198	(M)	The Modern Country Music Sound	1962	12.00	30.00
Starday SLP-334	(M)	The Best Of Justin Tubb	1965	10.00	25.00
RCA Victor LPM-3339	(M)	Where You're Concerned	1965	8.00	20.00
RCA Victor LSP-3339	(S)	Where You're Concerned	1965	10.00	25.00

Label & Catalog #		Title	Year	VG+	NM
RCA Victor LPM-3591	(M)	Together And Alone *(With Lorene Mann)*	1966	8.00	20.00
RCA Victor LSP-3591	(S)	Together And Alone *(With Lorene Mann)*	1966	10.00	25.00
Dot DLP-25922	(S)	Things I Still Remember Very Well	1969	6.00	15.00

TUBB'S TEXAS TROUBADORS, ERNEST

Decca DL-4459	(M)	The Texas Troubadors	1964	12.00	30.00
Decca DL-74459	(S)	The Texas Troubadors	1964	16.00	40.00
Decca DL-4644	(M)	Country Dance Time	1965	12.00	30.00
Decca DL-74644	(S)	Country Dance Time	1965	16.00	40.00
Decca DL-4745	(M)	Ernest Tubb's Fabulous Texas Troubadors	1966	6.00	15.00
Decca DL-74745	(S)	Ernest Tubb's Fabulous Texas Troubadors	1966	8.00	20.00
Decca DL-75017	(S)	The Terrific Texas Troubadors	1968	6.00	15.00

TUCKER, TOMMY

Checker LP-2990	(M)	Hi Heel Sneakers	1964	20.00	50.00

TUCKY BUZZARD

Capitol ST-787	(S)	Tucky Buzzard	1971	5.00	12.00
Capitol ST-864	(S)	Warm Slash	1971	5.00	12.00
Passport 97001	(S)	Alright In The Night	1973	8.00	20.00
Passport 98002	(S)	Tucky Buzzard	1974	4.00	10.00

TUNETOPPERS, THE

Amy A-1	(M)	At The Madison Dance Party	1960	14.00	35.00
Amy AS-1	(S)	At The Madison Dance Party	1960	20.00	50.00
		("The Madison" is rechanneled on this album.)			

TURNER, IKE

Crown CLP-5367	(M)	Ike Turner Rocks The Blues	1963	60.00	150.00
Crown CST-367	(E)	Ike Turner Rocks The Blues	1963	12.00	30.00
Pompeii SD-6003	(S)	A Black Man's Soul	1969	6.00	15.00
United Artists UAS-5576	(S)	Blues Roots	1972	6.00	15.00
United Artists LA087	(S)	Bad Dreams	1973	6.00	15.00
Fantasy F-9597	(S)	The Edge	1980	4.00	10.00

TURNER, IKE & TINA

Sue LP-2001	(M)	The Soul Of Ike And Tina Turner	1961	100.00	300.00
Sue LP-2003	(M)	Ike And Tina Turner's Kings Of Rhythm Dance	1962	100.00	300.00
Sue LP-2004	(M)	Dynamite	1963	100.00	300.00
Sue LP-2005	(M)	Don't Play Me Cheap	1963	100.00	300.00
Sue LP-2007	(M)	It's Gonna Work Out Fine	1963	100.00	300.00
Sue LP-1038	(M)	Ike And Tina Turner's Greatest Hits	1965	80.00	200.00
Kent K-519	(M)	The Soul Of Ike And Tina	1961	8.00	20.00
Kent KST-519	(S)	The Soul Of Ike And Tina	1961	12.00	30.00
Kent K-538	(M)	Festival Of Live Performances	1962	8.00	20.00
Kent KST-538	(S)	Festival Of Live Performances	1962	12.00	30.00
Kent K-550	(M)	Please Please Please	1962	8.00	20.00
Kent KST-550	(S)	Please Please Please	1962	12.00	30.00
Kent K-5014	(M)	The Ike And Tina Turner Revue Live	1964	8.00	20.00
Kent KST-5014	(S)	The Ike And Tina Turner Revue Live	1964	12.00	30.00
Warner Bros. W-1579	(M)	The Ike And Tina Turner Show Live	1965	8.00	20.00
Warner Bros. WS-1579	(S)	The Ike And Tina Turner Show Live	1965	12.00	30.00
Warner Bros. WS-1810	(S)	Ike And Tina Turner's Greatest Hits	1969	6.00	15.00
Loma 5904	(M)	Live/The Ike And Tina Show	1966	12.00	30.00
Loma 5904	(S)	Live/The Ike And Tina Show	1966	16.00	40.00
Philles PHLP-4011	(M)	River Deep-Mountain High	1966		*See note below*
		(Manufactured and pressed in minute quantities, most of which were destroyed shortly afterward. No covers are known to have been completed for Philles 4011. Suggested Near Mint value for the record without the cover $5,000-10,000.)			
Pompeii SD-6000	(S)	So Fine	1968	8.00	20.00
Pompeii SD-6004	(S)	Cussin,' Cryin' And Carryin' On	1969	8.00	20.00
Pompeii SD-6006	(S)	Get It Together	1969	8.00	20.00
A&M SP-4178	(S)	River Deep-Mountain High *(Brown label)*	1969	8.00	20.00
		(A&M 4178 is the official release of Philles 4011.)			
Sunset SUS-5265	(E)	The Fantastic Ike And Tina Turner	1969	6.00	15.00
Sunset SUS-5286	(E)	Ike And Tina Turner's Greatest Hits	1969	6.00	15.00
Harmony HS-11360	(S)	Ooh Poo Pah Doo	1969	6.00	15.00

Label & Catalog #		Title	Year	VG+	NM
Capitol ST-571	(E)	Her Man, His Woman	1969	6.00	15.00
Blue Thumb BTS-5	(S)	Outta Season	1969	6.00	15.00
Blue Thumb BTS-11	(S)	The Hunter	1969	6.00	15.00
Liberty LST-7637	(S)	Come Together	1970	6.00	15.00
Liberty LST-7650	(S)	Workin' Together	1970	6.00	15.00
ABC X-4014	(S)	16 Great Performances	1971	6.00	15.00
Atlantic SD-7207	(S)	Soul To Soul (Soundtrack)	1971	4.00	10.00
Decca DL7-9181	(S)	Taking Off (Soundtrack)	1971	4.00	10.00
United Arts. UAS-9953	(S)	What You Hear Is What You Get (2 LPs)	1971	8.00	20.00
United Arts. UAS-5530	(S)	Nuff Said	1971	6.00	15.00
United Arts. UAS-5598	(S)	Feel Good	1972	6.00	15.00
United Arts. UAS-5660	(S)	Let Me Touch Your Mind	1972	6.00	15.00
United Arts. UAS-5667	(S)	Ike And Tina Turner's Greatest Hits	1973	6.00	15.00
United Arts. LA064	(S)	The World Of Ike And Tina Live	1973	6.00	15.00
United Arts. LA180	(S)	Nutbush City Limits	1973	6.00	15.00
Blue Thumb BTS-49	(S)	The Best Of Ike And Tina Turner	1973	4.00	10.00
TURNER, "BIG" JOE					
Decca DL-8044	(M)	Kansas City Jazz	1953	100.00	250.00
Atlantic 1234	(M)	Joe Turner Sings Kansas City Jazz / Boss Of The Blues	1956	60.00	150.00
Atlantic SD-1234	(S)	Joe Turner Sings Kansas City Jazz / Boss Of The Blues	195?	80.00	200.00
Atlantic 8005	(M)	Joe Turner	1957	60.00	150.00
Atlantic 8023	(M)	Rockin' The Blues	1958	60.00	150.00
Atlantic 8033	(M)	Big Joe Is Here	1959	60.00	150.00
— Original Atlantic mono albums above have black labels; stereo albums have green labels.—					
Atlantic 8005	(M)	Joe Turner	1960	30.00	75.00
Atlantic 8023	(M)	Rockin' The Blues	1960	30.00	75.00
Atlantic 8033	(M)	Big Joe Is Here	1960	30.00	75.00
Atlantic 1332	(M)	Big Joe Rides Again	1960	30.00	75.00
Atlantic 8081	(M)	The Best Of Joe Turner	1963	20.00	50.00
—Atlantic albums above have orange & purple labels.—					
Savoy MG-14012	(M)	Joe Turner And The Blues	1958	50.00	125.00
Savoy MG-14106	(M)	Careless Love	1963	30.00	75.00
BluesWay BL-6006	(M)	Singing The Blues	1967	8.00	20.00
BluesWay BLS-6006	(S)	Singing The Blues	1967	10.00	25.00
BluesWay BLS-6060	(S)	Roll 'Em	1973	6.00	15.00
Atco SD-33-376	(P)	His Greatest Recordings	1971	6.00	15.00
Savoy SJL-2223	(M)	Have No Fear, Big Joe Turner Is Here	1977	6.00	15.00
TURNER, "BIG" JOE, & PETE JOHNSON					
EmArcy 36014	(M)	Joe Turner And Pete Johnson	1955	60.00	150.00
TURNER, MICKEY					
Edmar E-1040	(M)	The Mickey Turner Show	1966	10.00	25.00
TURNER, SAMMY					
Big Top 12-1301	(M)	Lavender Blue Mods	1962	60.00	150.00
Big Top S-12-1301	(S)	Lavender Blue Mods	1962	250.00	500.00
TURNER, SPYDER					
MGM E-4450	(M)	Stand By Me	1967	8.00	20.00
MGM SE-4450	(S)	Stand By Me	1967	10.00	25.00
TURNER, TINA					
United Arts. LA200	(S)	Turns The Country On	1972	6.00	15.00
United Arts. LA495	(S)	Acid Queen	1975	6.00	15.00
United Arts. LA919	(S)	Rough	1978	6.00	15.00
TURNER, TITUS					
Jamie JLP-70-3018	(M)	Sound Off	1961	8.00	20.00
Jamie JLP-3018	(S)	Sound Off	1961	10.00	25.00
TURNER, ZEB					
Audio Lab AL-1537	(M)	Country Music In The Turner Style	195?	30.00	75.00

Label & Catalog #		Title	Year	VG+	NM

TURTLES, THE
The Turtles feature Howard Kaylan and Mark Volman, who also recorded as Flo & Eddie.

White Whale WW-111	(M)	It Ain't Me Babe	1965	12.00	30.00
White Whale WWS-7111	(S)	It Ain't Me Babe	1965	16.00	40.00
White Whale WW-112	(M)	You Baby	1966	12.00	30.00
White Whale WWS-7112	(S)	You Baby	1966	16.00	40.00
White Whale WW-114	(M)	Happy Together	1967	8.00	20.00
White Whale WWS-7114	(S)	Happy Together	1967	10.00	25.00
White Whale WW-115	(M)	The Turtles' Golden Hits	1967	6.00	15.00
White Whale WWS-7115	(S)	The Turtles' Golden Hits	1967	8.00	20.00
White Whale WWS-7118	(S)	The Battle Of The Bands	1968	8.00	20.00
White Whale WWS-7124	(S)	Turtle Soup	1969	8.00	20.00
White Whale WWS-7127	(S)	More Golden Hits	1970	6.00	15.00
White Whale WWS-7133	(S)	Wooden Head	1971	6.00	15.00
Sire SASH-3703	(S)	Happy Together Again (2 LPs)	1974	10.00	25.00

TWEETY PIE
Bugs and most of the other WB characters were done by Mel Blanc.

Capitol J-3261	(M)	Tweety Pie And Other Favorites	1962	20.00	50.00

TWENTIETH CENTURY ZOO

Vault 122	(S)	Thunder On A Clear Day	1968	16.00	40.00

TWIGGY

MGM 1SE-32	(S)	The Boy Friend (Soundtrack)	1971	6.00	15.00
Mercury SRM-1-1038	(S)	Please Get My Name Right	1977	6.00	15.00
Mercury SRM-1-1093	(S)	Twiggy	1977	6.00	15.00

TWINK
Refer to The Pretty Things; Tomorrow.

Sire SES-97022	(S)	Think Pink	1970	30.00	75.00

TWINN CONNEXION

Decca DL-75020	(S)	Twinn Connexion	1968	6.00	15.00

TWINS, THE

RCA Victor LPM-1708	(M)	Teenagers Love The Twins	1958	20.00	50.00

TWISTERS, THE

Treasure TLP-890	(M)	Doin' The Twist	1962	12.00	30.00

TWISTIN' KINGS, THE

Motown MLP-601	(M)	Twistin' The World Around	1960	60.00	150.00

TWITTY, CONWAY

MGM E-3744	(M)	Conway Twitty Sings	1959	30.00	75.00
MGM SE-3744	(S)	Conway Twitty Sings	1959	50.00	125.00
MGM E-3786	(M)	Saturday Night With Conway Twitty	1959	30.00	75.00
MGM SE-3786	(S)	Saturday Night With Conway Twitty	1959	50.00	125.00
MGM E-3818	(M)	Lonely Blue Boy	1960	30.00	75.00
MGM SE-3818	(S)	Lonely Blue Boy	1960	50.00	125.00
—Original MGM albums above have yellow labels—					
MGM E-3744	(M)	Conway Twitty Sings	196?	16.00	40.00
MGM SE-3744	(S)	Conway Twitty Sings	196?	20.00	50.00
MGM E-3786	(M)	Saturday Night With Conway Twitty	1959	20.00	50.00
MGM SE-3786	(S)	Saturday Night With Conway Twitty	1959	30.00	75.00
MGM E-3818	(M)	Lonely Blue Boy	1960	16.00	40.00
MGM SE-3818	(S)	Lonely Blue Boy	1960	20.00	50.00
MGM E-3849	(M)	Conway Twitty's Greatest Hits	1960	16.00	40.00
MGM SE-3849	(P)	Conway Twitty's Greatest Hits	1960	20.00	50.00
		(Issued with a fold-open poster, priced separately below.)			
		Conway Twitty's Greatest Hits Poster	1960	10.00	25.00
MGM E-3907	(M)	The Rock And Roll Story	1961	20.00	50.00
MGM SE-3907	(S)	The Rock And Roll Story	1961	30.00	75.00
MGM E-3943	(M)	The Conway Twitty Touch	1961	20.00	50.00
MGM SE-3943	(S)	The Conway Twitty Touch	1961	30.00	75.00
MGM E-4019	(M)	Portrait Of A Fool And Others	1962	16.00	40.00
MGM SE-4019	(S)	Portrait Of A Fool And Others	1962	20.00	50.00

Label & Catalog #		Title	Year	VG+	NM
MGM E-4089	(M)	R&B '63	1963	16.00	40.00
MGM SE-4089	(S)	R&B '63	1963	20.00	50.00
MGM E-4217	(M)	Hit The Road	1964	10.00	25.00
MGM SE-4217	(S)	Hit The Road	1964	12.00	30.00
—Original MGM albums above have black labels—					
Metro M-512	(M)	It's Only Make Believe	1965	6.00	15.00
Metro MS-512	(S)	It's Only Make Believe	1965	8.00	20.00
Decca DL-4724	(M)	Conway Twitty Sings	1966	8.00	20.00
Decca DL-74724	(S)	Conway Twitty Sings	1966	10.00	25.00
Decca DL-4828	(M)	Look Into My Teardrops	1966	8.00	20.00
Decca DL-74828	(S)	Look Into My Teardrops	1966	10.00	25.00
—Original Decca albums aove have black labels with "Mfrd. by Decca" beneath the rainbow.—					
Decca DL-4913	(M)	Conway Twitty Country	1967	6.00	15.00
Decca DL-74913	(S)	Conway Twitty Country	1967	6.00	15.00
Decca DL-74990	(S)	Here's Conway Twitty And His Lonely Blue Boys	1968	6.00	15.00
Decca DL-75062	(S)	Next In Line	1968	6.00	15.00
Decca DL-75105	(S)	Darling, You Know I Wouldn't Lie	1969	6.00	15.00
Decca DL-75131	(S)	I Love You More Today	1969	6.00	15.00
Decca DL-75172	(S)	To See My Angel Cry	1970	6.00	15.00
Decca DL-75209	(S)	Hello Darlin'	1970	6.00	15.00
Decca DL-75248	(S)	Fifteen Years Ago	1970	6.00	15.00
MGM GAS-110	(S)	Conway Twitty	1970	8.00	20.00
Decca DL-75252	(S)	Conway Twitty's Greatest Hits, Volume 1	1971	5.00	12.00
Decca DL-75276	(S)	How Much More Can She Stand	1971	5.00	12.00
Decca DL-75292	(S)	I Wonder What She'll Think About Me Leaving	1971	5.00	12.00
MGM SE-4799	(S)	Conway Twitty Hits	1971	5.00	12.00
Decca DL-75335	(S)	I Can't See Me Without You	1972	5.00	12.00
Decca DL-75361	(S)	Conway Twitty	1972	5.00	12.00
MGM SE-4837	(S)	Conway Twitty Sings The Blues	1972	5.00	12.00
MGM SE-4884	(P)	Twenty Great Hits	1973	5.00	12.00
Opryland 12636	(S)	Then And Now *(radio program)*	197?	50.00	100.00
MCA 376	(S)	Clinging To A Saving Hand/Steal Away	1973	10.00	25.00

TWITTY, CONWAY, & LORETTA LYNN

Label & Catalog #		Title	Year	VG+	NM
Decca DL-75251	(S)	We Only Make Believe	1971	5.00	12.00
Decca DL-75326	(S)	Lead Me On	1972	5.00	12.00

TYLER, RED, & THE GYROS

Label & Catalog #		Title	Year	VG+	NM
Ace LP-1006	(M)	Rockin' And Rollin'	1960	40.00	100.00

TYLER, T. TEXAS

Label & Catalog #		Title	Year	VG+	NM
Sound 607	(M)	Deck Of Cards	1958	20.00	50.00
King 664	(M)	T. Texas Tyler	1959	30.00	75.00
King 689	(M)	The Great Texan	1960	30.00	75.00
King 721	(M)	T. Texas Tyler	1961	20.00	50.00
King 734	(M)	Songs Along The Way	1961	20.00	50.00
Wrangler 1002	(M)	T. Tyler Texas	1962	14.00	35.00
Capitol T-1662	(M)	Salvation	1962	10.00	25.00
Capitol ST-1662	(S)	Salvation	1962	14.00	35.00
Capitol T-2344	(M)	The Hits Of T. Texas Tyler	1965	8.00	20.00
Capitol ST-2344	(S)	The Hits Of T. Texas Tyler	1965	10.00	25.00
Starday SLP-379	(M)	The Man With A Million Friends	1966	10.00	25.00

TYMES, THE

Label & Catalog #		Title	Year	VG+	NM
Parkway P-7032	(M)	So Much In Love *(Group cover)*	1963	60.00	150.00
Parkway P-7032	(M)	So Much In Love *(Title cover)*	1963	16.00	40.00
Parkway P-7038	(M)	The Sound Of Wonderful Tymes	1963	12.00	30.00
Parkway P-7039	(M)	Somewhere	1964	12.00	30.00
Parkway P-7048	(M)	18 Greatest Hits	1964	12.00	30.00
Columbia CS-9778	(S)	People	1969	6.00	15.00
Abkco 4228	(S)	The Best Of Tymes	1974	4.00	10.00
RCA Victor APL1-0727	(S)	Trustmaker	1974	4.00	10.00
RCA Victor APL1-1835	(S)	Turning Point	1976	4.00	10.00
RCA Victor APL1-2406	(S)	Diggin' Their Roots	1977	4.00	10.00

U. F. O.					
Rare Earth RS-524	(S)	U. F. O.	1971	10.00	25.00
ULTIMATE SPINACH					
MGM E-4518	(M)	Ultimate Spinach	1968	8.00	20.00
MGM SE-4518	(S)	Ultimate Spinach	1968	8.00	20.00
MGM SE-4570	(S)	Behold And See	1968	8.00	20.00
MGM SE-4600	(S)	Ultimate Spinach	1969	8.00	20.00
UNBEATABLES, THE					
Dawn LP-5050	(M)	Live At Palisades Park	1964	40.00	100.00
UNCLE JOSH & COUSIN JAKE					
Cotton Town 101	(M)	Just Joshing	196?	30.00	75.00
UNDERGROUND SUNSHINE					
Intrepid IT-4003	(S)	Let There Be Light	1969	12.00	30.00
UNDERGROUNDS, THE					
Mercury MG-16337	(M)	Psychedelic Visions	1967	10.00	25.00
Mercury SR-16337	(S)	Psychedelic Visions	1967	12.00	30.00
UNDISPUTED TRUTH					
Gorty G-955L	(S)	Undisputed Truth	1971	10.00	25.00
Gordy GS-959	(S)	Face To Face With The Truth	1971	6.00	15.00
Gordy GS-963	(S)	Law Of The Land	1973	6.00	15.00
Gordy GS-968	(S)	Down To Earth	1974	6.00	15.00
Gordy GS-970	(S)	Cosmic Truth	1975	6.00	15.00
UNFOLDING, THE					
Audio Fidelity AFS-6184	(S)	How To Blow Your Mind And Have A Freakout Party	1967	20.00	50.00
UNIFICS, THE					
Kapp KS-3582	(S)	Sittin' In At The Court Of Love	1968	8.00	20.00

UNION, GAP, THE: *Refer to* GARY PUCKETT (& THE UNION GAP)

UNIQUES (FEATURING JOE STAMPLEY), THE					
Paula LP-2190	(M)	Uniquely Yours	1966	10.00	25.00
Paula LPS-2190	(P)	Uniquely Yours	1966	12.00	30.00
Paula LP-2194	(M)	Happening Now	1967	10.00	25.00
Paula LPS-2194	(S)	Happening Now	1967	12.00	30.00
Paula LP-2199	(M)	Playtime	1968	10.00	25.00
Paula LPS-2199	(S)	Playtime	1968	10.00	25.00
Paula LPS-2204	(S)	The Uniques	1969	10.00	25.00
Paula LPS-2208	(P)	Golden Hits	1970	10.00	25.00
UNIT 4 + 2					
London LL-3427	(M)	Unit 4 + 2 #1	1965	16.00	40.00
London PS-427	(P)	Unit 4 + 2 #1	1965	20.00	50.00

(Half of this album is rechanneled including "Concrete And Clay.")

UNITED STATES DOUBLE QUARTET, THE
The U.S.D.Q. is The Tokens with The Kirby Stone Four.

B.T. Puppy BTS-1005	(S)	Life Is Groovy	1969	20.00	50.00

Label & Catalog #		Title	Year	VG+	NM
UNITED STATES OF AMERICA, THE					
Columbia CS-9616	(S)	The United States Of America (Originally issued in a bag.)	1968	20.00	50.00
Columbia CS-9616	(S)	The United States Of America (Without bag)	1968	16.00	40.00
UNSPOKEN WORD, THE					
Ascot AS-16028	(S)	Tuesday, April 19th	1968	8.00	20.00
Atco SD-33-335	(S)	The Unspoken Word	1970	6.00	15.00
UNUSUAL WE					
Pulsar 10608	(S)	Unusual We	1969	10.00	25.00
UPCHURCH, PHIL					
Boyd B-398	(M)	You Can't Sit Down	1961	20.00	50.00
Boyd BS-398	(S)	You Can't Sit Down	1961	30.00	75.00
United Arts. UAL-3162	(M)	You Can't Sit Down, Part 2	1961	10.00	25.00
United Arts. UAS-6162	(S)	You Can't Sit Down, Part 2	1961	12.00	30.00
United Arts. UAL-3175	(M)	Big Hits Dances	1962	10.00	25.00
United Arts. UAS-6175	(S)	Big Hits Dances	1962	12.00	30.00
URSA MAJOR					
RCA Victor LSP-4777	(S)	Ursa Major	1972	10.00	25.00

USHER, GARY

Gary Usher was one of the most creative producers of the '60s. For his work as a producer refer to Keith Allison; The Beatles; Curt Boetcher; The Byrds; Chad & Jeremy; Danny Cox; Andy Goldmark; Bruce Johnston; Millenium; The Peanut Butter Conspiracy; Sagittarius; Ship; Spiral Starecase; and Alan Watts. He also recorded and produced albums under a variety of pseudonyms. For these "Gary Usher Creations" refer to The Competitors; The Ghouls; The Hondells; The Kickstands; The Knights; Mr. Gasser; The Revells; The Road Runners; The Silly Surfers; The Super Stocks; The Surfaris; and The Weird-Ohs.

U2

Warner Bros. WBMS-117	(DJ)	Two Sides Live	1981	40.00	100.00

VALE, RICKY, & HIS SURFERS					
Strand SL-1104	(M)	Everybody's Surfin'	1963	8.00	20.00
Strand SLS-1104	(S)	Everybody's Surfin'	1963	10.00	25.00
VALENS, RITCHIE					
Del Fi DFLP-1201	(M)	Ritchie Valens	1959	60.00	150.00
Del Fi DFLP-1206	(M)	Ritchie	1959	60.00	150.00
Del Fi DFLP-1214	(M)	In Concert At Pacoima Jr. High	1960	80.00	250.00
Del Fi DFLP-1225	(M)	His Greatest Hits (Black cover)	1963	100.00	100.00
Del Fi DFLP-1225	(M)	His Greatest Hits (White cover)	1963		100.00
Del Fi DFLP-1247	(M)	Ritchie Valens: His Greatest Hits, Volume 2	1965		
		—Original Del Fi albums above have black labels with a blue logo on top.			
Guest Star GS-1469	(M)	The Original Ritchie Valens	196	12.00	30.00
Guest Star GSS-1469	(E)	The Original Ritchie Valens	196	6.00	15.00
Guest Star GS-1484	(M)	The Original La Bamba		12.00	30.00
Guest Star GSS-1484	(E)	The Original La Bamba			15.00
MGM GAS-117	(E)	Ritchie Valens			30.00

Label & Catalog #		Title	Year	VG+	NM

VALENS, RITCHIE, & JERRY KOLE
Jerry Kole alos recorded as both Cole and Kole.

Crown CLP-5336	(M)	Ritchie Valens And Jerry Kole	1963	12.00	30.00
Crown CST-336	(E)	Ritchie Valens And Jerry Kole	1963	6.00	15.00

VALENTE, DINO
Dino Valenti co-founded Quicksilver Messenger Service, got busted prior and then rejoined in 1971.

Epic LN-24335	(M)	Dino Valente	1967	8.00	20.00
Epic BN-26335	(S)	Dino Valente	1967	10.00	25.00

VALENTE, CATERINA

Decca DL-8203	(M)	The Hi-Fi Nightingale	1956	10.00	25.00
Decca DL-8436	(M)	Ole Caterina	1957	10.00	25.00
Decca DL-8440	(M)	Plenty Valente!	1957	10.00	25.00
RCA Victor LPM-2119	(M)	Classics With A Chaser	1960	8.00	20.00

VALENTINE, HILTON
Valentine was formerly a member of The Animals.

Capitol ST-330	(S)	All In Your Head	1969	10.00	25.00

VALENTINO, MARK

Swan LP-508	(M)	Mark Valentino	1963	20.00	50.00

VALHALLA

United Arts. UAS-6730	(S)	Valhalla	1969	6.00	15.00

VALLEE, RUDY

RCA Victor LPM-2507	(M)	Young Rudy Vallee	1961	12.00	30.00
RCA Victor LSP-2507	(E)	Young Rudy Vallee	1961	8.00	20.00
Decca DL-4242	(M)	Stein Songs	1962	6.00	15.00
Decca DL7-4242	(S)	Stein Songs	1962	8.00	20.00
Jubilee J-2051	(M)	The Funny Side Of Rudy Vallee	1964	6.00	15.00
Viva 6005	(M)	Ho Ho, Everybody	1966	5.00	12.00
Viva 16005	(S)	Ho Ho, Everybody	1966	6.00	15.00
RCA Victor LPM-3816	(M)	The Best Of Rudy Vallee	1967	5.00	12.00
RCA Victor LSP-3816	(S)	The Best Of Rudy Vallee	1967	6.00	15.00

VALLEY, JIM
Valley was formerly a member of Paul Revere's Raiders.

Panorama 104	(S)	Harpo (With Don & The Goodtimes)	1969	16.00	40.00
Light LS-5564	(S)	Family	197?	6.00	15.00

VALLI, FRANKI
Refer to The Four Lovers; The Four Seasons.

Phillips PHM-200-247	(M)	Solo	1967	8.00	20.00
Phillips PHS-600-247	(S)	Solo	1967	10.00	25.00
Phillips PHS-600-274	(S)	Timeless	1968	6.00	15.00
Motown M6-852	(S)	Inside You	1975	5.00	12.00

VAMPIRES, THE

United Arts. UAL-3378	(M)	At The Monster Ball	1964	8.00	20.00
United Arts. UAS-6378	(S)	At The Monster Ball	1964	10.00	25.00

VAN DER GRAAF GENERATOR

Mercury SR-61238	(S)	The Aerosol Grey Machine	1969	8.00	20.00
Pr[?]e 4515	(S)	The Least We Can Do Is Wave	1970	8.00	20.00
Du[?]ill DS-50097	(S)	H To He Who Am The Only One	1970	6.00	15.00
Mer[?] SRM-1-1069	(S)	Godbluff	1976	4.00	10.00
Merc SRM-1-1096	(S)	Still Life	1976	4.00	10.00
[?]RM-1-1116	(S)	World Record	1976	4.00	10.00

VAN D[?]

Motown [?]RL	(M)	The Motown Sound	1965	8.00	20.00
Motown [?]	(S)	The Motown Sound	1965	10.00	25.00
Soul SS-7[?]	(S)	The Earl Of Funk	1970	6.00	15.00

VAN DYKE, [?]

Mercury MG[?]	(M)	Walk On By	1962	8.00	20.00
Mercury SR-6[?]	(S)	Walk On By	1962	10.00	25.00

Label & Catalog #		Title	Year	VG+	NM
Mercury MG-20716	(M)	Movin' Van Dyke	1963	8.00	20.00
Mercury SR-60716	(S)	Movin' Van Dyke	1963	10.00	25.00
Mercury MG-20802	(M)	LeRoy Van Dyke's Greatest Hits	1963	8.00	20.00
Mercury SR-60802	(S)	LeRoy Van Dyke's Greatest Hits	1963	10.00	25.00
Mercury MG-20922	(M)	Songs For Mon And Dad	1964	8.00	20.00
Mercury SR-60922	(S)	Songs For Mon And Dad	1964	10.00	25.00
Warner Bros. W-1618	(M)	The LeRoy Van Dyke Show	1965	6.00	15.00
Warner Bros. WS-1618	(S)	The LeRoy Van Dyke Show	1965	8.00	20.00
Warner Bros. W-1652	(M)	Country Hits	1966	6.00	15.00
Warner Bros. WS-1652	(S)	Country Hits	1966	8.00	20.00
MGM E-4506	(M)	What Am I Bid? (Soundtrack)	1967	8.00	20.00
MGM SE-4506	(S)	What Am I Bid? (Soundtrack)	1967	10.00	25.00
Kapp KS-3571	(S)	Lonesome Is	1968	6.00	15.00
Kapp KS-3605	(S)	LeRoy Van Dyke's Greatest Hits	1969	6.00	15.00
Kapp KS-3607	(S)	Just A Closer Walk With Thee	1969	6.00	15.00

VAN DYKES, THE

Label & Catalog #		Title	Year	VG+	NM
Sutton SU-307	(M)	A Hootin' Hootenanny	196?	6.00	15.00
Sutton SSU-307	(S)	A Hootin' Hootenanny	196?	8.00	20.00

VAN DYKES, THE

Label & Catalog #		Title	Year	VG+	NM
Bell 6004	(M)	Tellin' It Like It Is	1967	10.00	25.00
Bell 6004	(S)	Tellin' It Like It Is	1967	12.00	30.00

VAN EATON, LON & FERREK

Label & Catalog #		Title	Year	VG+	NM
Apple SMAS-3390	(S)	Brother (With insert)	1972	6.00	15.00

VAN HALEN

Label & Catalog #		Title	Year	VG+	NM
Warner Bros.	(DJ)	1984 (Quiex II vinyl)	1984	6.00	15.00

VAN RONK, DAVE

Label & Catalog #		Title	Year	VG+	NM
Folkways FA-23??	(M)	Dave Van Ronk Sings	1959	16.00	40.00
Folkways FA-2383	(M)	Earthy Ballads & Blues	1959	16.00	40.00
Folkways FA-3818	(M)	Ballads, Blues & Spirituals	1959	16.00	40.00
Folkways FT-31020	(M)	Black Mountain Blues	1959	12.00	30.00
Folkways FTS-31020	(S)	Black Mountain Blues	1959	16.00	40.00
Folklore FRLP-14001	(M)	In The Tradition	1963	10.00	25.00
Folklore FRST-14001	(S)	In The Tradition	1963	12.00	30.00
Folklore FRLP-14012	(M)	Dave Van Ronk, Folksinger	1963	10.00	25.00
Folklore FRST-14012	(S)	Dave Van Ronk, Folksinger	1963	12.00	30.00
Folklore FRLP-14025	(M)	Inside Dave Van Ronk	1964	10.00	25.00
Folklore FRST-14025	(S)	Inside Dave Van Ronk	1964	12.00	30.00
Mercury MG-20908	(M)	Just Dave Van Ronk	1964	8.00	20.00
Mercury SR-60908	(S)	Just Dave Van Ronk	1964	10.00	25.00
Verve/Folkways FV-9006	(M)	Dave Van Ronk Sings The Blues	1965	8.00	20.00
Verve/Folkways FVS-9006	(S)	Dave Van Ronk Sings The Blues	1965	10.00	25.00
Verve/Folkways FV-9017	(M)	Gambler's Blues	1965	8.00	20.00
Verve/Folkways FVS-9017	(S)	Gambler's Blues	1965	10.00	25.00
Verve/Folkways FT-3009	(M)	No Dirty Names	1966	8.00	20.00
Verve/Folkways FTS-3009	(S)	No Dirty Names	1966	10.00	25.00
Verve/Forecast FVS-3027	(S)	Dave Van Ronk	1967		Unreleased
Verve/Forecast FVS-3041	(S)	Dave Van Ronk & The Hudson Dusters	1968	10.00	25.00
Verve/Forecast FVS-3065	(S)	Dave Van Ronk	1968		Unreleased
Prestige PRST-7527	(S)	Dave Van Ronk, Folksinger	1968	6.00	15.00
		(Prestige 7527 is a reissue of Folklore 14012.)			
Prestige PRST-7716	(S)	Inside Dave Van Ronk	1969	6.00	15.00
		(Prestige 7716 is a reissue of Folklore 14025.)			
Prestige PRST-7800	(S)	In The Tradition	1969	6.00	15.00
		(Prestige 7800 is a reissue of Folklore 14001.)			
Polydor 24-4052	(S)	Van Ronk	1971		15.00
Fantasy 24170	(S)	Dave Van Ronk (2 LPs)	1972		15.00
		(Fantasy 24170 is a reissue of Prestige 7527 and ...00			15.00
Philo 1036	(S)	Sunday Street	1976		

VAN ZANDT, TOWNES

Label & Catalog #		Title	Year	VG+	NM
				10.00	
Poppy PYS-40001	(S)	For The Sake Of A Song		6.00	25.00
Poppy PYS-40004	(S)	Our Mother The Mountain		6.00	15.00
Poppy PYS-40007	(S)	Townes Van Zandt		6.00	15.00
Poppy PYS-40012	(S)	Delta Momma Blues			15.00

Label & Catalog #		Title	Year	VG+	NM
Poppy PYS-5700	(S)	High, Low And In Between	1971	6.00	15.00
Poppy LAOO-F4	(S)	The Late Great Townes Van Zandt	1972	6.00	15.00
Tomato 2-7001	(S)	Live At The Old Quarter, Houston, Texas	1977	4.00	10.00
Tomato 7011	(S)	The Late Great Townes Van Zandt	1978	4.00	10.00
Tomato 7012	(S)	High, Low And In Between	1978	4.00	10.00
Tomato 7013	(S)	Delta Momma Blues	197?	4.00	10.00
Tomato 7014	(S)	Townes Van Zandt	197?	4.00	10.00
Tomato 7015	(S)	Our Mother, The Mountain	197?	4.00	10.00
Tomato 7017	(S)	Flyin' Shoes	197?	4.00	10.00

VANDROSS, LUTHER

Epic HE-47451	(S)	Never Too Much (Half-speed master)	1981	7.00	20.00

VANGELIS

RCA Victor DJL1-1849	(DJ)	The Vangelis Radio Special	1976	80.00	200.00

(Issued in a jacket for RCA LPL1-5110, "Heaven And Hell" with a sticker that reads "Radio Special Self-Portrait.)

VANILLA FUDGE
The Fudge were Carmine Appice, Tim Bogert, Vince Martell and Mark Stein. Refer to Beck, Bogert & Appice; Cream / Vanilla Fudge.

Atco 33-224	(M)	Vanilla Fudge	1967	10.00	25.00
Atco SD-33-224	(S)	Vanilla Fudge	1967	8.00	20.00
Atco SD-33-237	(S)	The Beat Goes On	1968	8.00	20.00
Atco SD-33-244	(S)	Renaissance	1968	8.00	20.00

— Original Atco stereo albums above have purple & brown labels.—

Atco SD-33-224	(S)	Vanilla Fudge	1969	5.00	12.00
Atco SD-33-237	(S)	The Beat Goes On	1969	5.00	12.00
Atco SD-33-244	(S)	Renaissance	1969	5.00	12.00
Atco SD-33-278	(S)	Near The Beginning	1969	5.00	12.00
Atco SD-33-303	(S)	Rock 'N' Roll	1969	5.00	12.00

— Atco albums above yellow labels with "Atlantic Recording Co." on the bottom.—

VANITY FARE

Page One 2502	(S)	Early In The Morning	1970	12.00	30.00

(Mispressing plays one side from the unreleased Sandy Coast album. Mispressed albums have less tracks than the label credits.)

Page One 2502	(S)	Early In The Morning	1970	8.00	20.00

VANNELLI, GINO

Mobile Fidelity MFSL-041	(S)	Powerful People	198?	7.00	20.00
Nautilus NR-35	(S)	Brother To Brother	198?	5.00	15.00

VAUGHAN, SARAH: *Refer to GOLDMINE'S PRICE GUIDE TO COLLECTIBLE JAZZ ALBUMS*

VAUGHAN, STEVIE RAY

Epic 8E8-39609	(S)	Couldn't Stand The Weather (Picture disc)	1984	8.00	20.00

VAUGHN, ROBERT

MGM E-4488	(M)	Readings From Hamlet	1962	8.00	20.00
MGM SE-4488	(S)	Readings From Hamlet	1962	10.00	25.00

VAUGHT, BOB, & THE RENEGAIDS

Crescendo GNP-83	(M)	Surf Crazy	1963	8.00	20.00
Crescendo GNPS-83	(S)	Surf Crazy	1963	10.00	25.00

VEE, BOBBY

Liberty LRP-3165	(M)	Bobby Vee Sings Your Favorites	1960	14.00	35.00
Liberty LST-7165	(S)	Bobby Vee Sings Your Favorites	1960	20.00	50.00
Liberty LRP-3181	(M)	Bobby Vee	1961	12.00	30.00
Liberty LST-7181	(S)	Bobby Vee	1961	16.00	40.00
Liberty LRP-3186	(M)	Bobby Vee With Strings And Things	1961	12.00	30.00
Liberty LST-7186	(S)	Bobby Vee With Strings And Things	1961	16.00	40.00
Liberty LRP-3211	(M)	Bobby Vee Sings Hits Of The Rockin' 50's	1961	12.00	30.00
Liberty LST-7211	(S)	Bobby Vee Sings Hits Of The Rockin' 50's	1961	16.00	40.00
Liberty LRP-3228	(M)	Take Good Care Of My Baby	1961	12.00	30.00
Liberty LST-7228	(S)	Take Good Care Of My Baby	1961	16.00	40.00
Liberty LRP	(M)	Bobby Vee Meets The Crickets	1962	16.00	40.00
Liberty LST	(S)	Bobby Vee Meets The Crickets	1962	20.00	50.00

Label & Catalog #		Title	Year	VG+	NM
Liberty LRP-3232	(M)	A Bobby Vee Recording Session	1962	10.00	25.00
Liberty LST-7232	(S)	A Bobby Vee Recording Session	1962	12.00	30.00
Liberty LRP-3245	(M)	Bobby Vee's Golden Greats	1962	8.00	20.00
Liberty LST-7245	(S)	Bobby Vee's Golden Greats	1962	10.00	25.00
		("Suzie Baby" is rechanneled on this album.)			
Liberty LRP-3267	(M)	Merry Christmas From Bobby Vee	1962	10.00	25.00
Liberty LST-7267	(S)	Merry Christmas From Bobby Vee	1962	12.00	30.00
Liberty LRP-3285	(M)	The Night Has A Thousand Eyes	1963	10.00	25.00
Liberty LST-7285	(S)	The Night Has A Thousand Eyes	1963	12.00	30.00
Liberty LRP-3289	(M)	Bobby Vee Meets The Ventures	1963	10.00	25.00
Liberty LST-7289	(S)	Bobby Vee Meets The Ventures	1963	12.00	30.00
Liberty LRP-3336	(M)	I Remember Buddy Holly	1963	16.00	40.00
Liberty LST-7336	(S)	I Remember Buddy Holly	1963	20.00	50.00
Liberty LRP-3352	(M)	The New Sound From England!	1964	10.00	25.00
Liberty LST-7352	(S)	The New Sound From England!	1964	12.00	30.00
Liberty LRP-3385	(M)	30 Big Hits From The 60's	1964	10.00	25.00
Liberty LST-7385	(S)	30 Big Hits From The 60's	1964	12.00	30.00
Liberty LRP-3393	(M)	Bobby Vee Live On Tour	1965	10.00	25.00
Liberty LST-7393	(S)	Bobby Vee Live On Tour	1965	12.00	30.00
		— Original Liberty albums above have black labels with a gold logo on the left side.—			
Liberty LRP-3464	(M)	Bobby Vee's Golden Greats, Volume 2	1966	8.00	20.00
Liberty LST-7464	(S)	Bobby Vee's Golden Greats, Volume 2	1966	10.00	25.00
Liberty LRP-3480	(M)	Look At Me Girl	1966	8.00	20.00
Liberty LST-7480	(S)	Look At Me Girl	1966	10.00	25.00
Liberty LRP-3534	(M)	Come Back When You Grow Up	1967	6.00	15.00
Liberty LST-7534	(S)	Come Back When You Grow Up	1967	8.00	20.00
Liberty LST-7554	(S)	Just Today	1968	6.00	15.00
Liberty LST-7592	(S)	Do What You Gotta Do	1968	6.00	15.00
Liberty LST-7612	(S)	Gates, Grills And Railings	1969	6.00	15.00
United Arts. LA025	(S)	Legendary Masters (2 LPs)	1973	12.00	30.00
		("Suzie Baby" is rechanneled on this album.)			
United Arts. LA085	(S)	Robert Thomas Velline	1973	8.00	20.00

VEGAS, PAT & LOLLY

Mercury MG-21059	(M)	At The Haunted House	1966	12.00	30.00
Mercury SR-61059	(S)	At The Haunted House	1966	16.00	40.00

VELASCO, VI

Colpix CP-438	(M)	Cantando Bossa Nova	1963	8.00	20.00

VELEZ, MARTHA

Sire SES-97008	(S)	Fiends And Angels (Features Jimi Hendrix)	1969	12.00	30.00
Sire SES-7409	(S)	Matinee Weepers	1974	5.00	12.00

VELVET, JIMMY

Velvetone 101	(S)	A Touch Of Velvet	1968	8.00	20.00
United Arts. UAS-6653	(S)	A Touch Of Velvet	1968	6.00	15.00

VELVET NIGHT

Metromedia 1026	(S)	Velvet Night	1970	5.00	12.00

VELVET UNDERGROUND, THE

The VU was Lou Reed, Sterling Morrison, Maureen Tucker and John Cale, replaced by Doug Yule in 1968.

Verve V-5008	(DJ)	The Velvet Underground & Nico	1967	150.00	300.00
Verve V-5008	(M)	The Velvet Underground & Nico	1967	100.00	250.00
Verve V6-5008	(S)	The Velvet Underground & Nico	1967	80.00	200.00

(First pressing: the cover has a yellow, peel-off banana over the pink banana printed on the cover. The photo of the group on the back cover is framed by a male torso. The price here is for ~~~es with the banana sticker completely intact on the cover.)

Verve V-5008	(M)	The Velvet Underground & Nico	1967	.00	125.00
Verve V6-5008	(S)	The Velvet Underground & Nico	1967	peeled off)	100.00

(The price here is for a first pressing with the br~~~ 80.00

Verve V-5008	(M)	The Velvet Underground & Nico	19~~	60.00	200.00
Verve V6-5008	(S)	The Velvet Underground & Nico		80.00	150.00

(Second pressing covers have the yellow~~~ banana over the pink banana but the photo on the ~~~vered with a sticker, hiding the torso. The price here is fo~~~with the banana sticker completely intact on the cover!)

The Ventures are [...] f the biggest success stories to emerge from the dampened Northwest, ranking as
the most success[...] instrumental group of the rock era with over three dozen charting albums and
three RIAA Gold R[...] The original group was Bob Boyle, Nokie Edwards, Don Wilson and Howie
Johnson, replaced b[...]ylor in 1963. While their first album, Walk-Don't Run, holds the general
collectors interest, (Th[...]es In Space also attracts automotive enthusiasts.

Label & Catalog #		Title	Year	VG+	NM
Verve V-5008	(M)	The Velvet Underground & Nico	1967	40.00	100.00
Verve V6-5008	(S)	The Velvet Underground & Nico	1967	30.00	75.00
		(The price here is for a second pressing with the banana peeled off!)			
Verve V-5008	(M)	The Velvet Underground & Nico	1967	60.00	150.00
Verve V6-5008	(S)	The Velvet Underground & Nico	1967	40.00	100.00
		(Third pressing covers have the yellow, peel-off banana over the pink banana but the torso on the back has been air-brushed out. The price here is for copies with the banana sticker completely intact on the cover!)			
Verve V-5008	(M)	The Velvet Underground & Nico	1967	30.00	75.00
Verve V6-5008	(S)	The Velvet Underground & Nico	1967	20.00	50.00
		(The price here is for a third pressing with the banana peeled off!)			
Verve V-5046	(DJ)	White Light/White Heat *(White label)*	1967	30.00	175.00
Verve V-5046	(M)	White Light/White Heat	1967	30.00	75.00
Verve V6-5046	(DJ)	White Light/White Heat *(Yellow label)*	1967	60.00	150.00
Verve V6-5046	(S)	White Light/White Heat	1967	20.00	50.00
		(Blue label. A black-on-black skull is visible in lower left corner of the front cover when viewed at an angle.)			
Verve V-5057	(M)	Velvet Underground	1966	Unreleased	
Verve V6-5057	(S)	Velvet Underground	1966	Unreleased	
MGM SE-4617	(DJ)	The Velvet Underground *(Yellow label)*	1969	60.00	150.00
MGM SE-4617	(S)	The Velvet Underground	1969	20.00	50.00
MGM GAS-131	(S)	The Velvet Underground	1970	10.00	25.00
Cotillion SD-9034	(S)	Loaded *(Light blue label)*	1970	8.00	20.00
Cotillion SD-9500	(DJ)	Live At Max's Kansas City *(White label)*	1972	20.00	50.00
Cotillion SD-9500	(S)	Live At Max's Kansas City	1972	8.00	20.00
Mercury SRM-2-7504	(M)	Live 1969 *(Gatefold cover)*	1972	6.00	15.00
VENTURAS, THE					
Drum Boy DBM-1003	(M)	Here They Are	1964	30.00	75.00
Drum Boy DFS-1003	(S)	Here They Are	1964	50.00	125.00
VENTURES, THE					
The Ventures also recorded with Bobby Vee.					
Dolton BLP-2003	(M)	Walk, Don't Run	1960	16.00	40.00
Dolton BST-8003	(S)	Walk, Don't Run	1960	20.00	50.00
		("Home" and "Walk, Don't Run" are rechanneled on this album.)			
Dolton BLP-2004	(M)	The Ventures	1961	16.00	40.00
Dolton BST-8004	(S)	The Ventures	1961	20.00	50.00
Dolton BLP-2006	(M)	Another Smash!!!	1961	16.00	40.00
Dolton BST-8006	(S)	Another Smash!!!	1961	20.00	50.00
Dolton BLP-2008	(M)	The Colorful Ventures	1961	16.00	40.00
Dolton BST-8008	(S)	The Colorful Ventures	1961	20.00	50.00
Dolton BLP-2010	(M)	Twist With The Ventures	1962	16.00	40.00
Dolton BST-8010	(S)	Twist With The Ventures	1962	20.00	50.00
Dolton BLP-2014	(M)	The Ventures' Twist Party	1962	16.00	40.00
Dolton BST-8014	(S)	The Ventures' Twist Party	1962	20.00	50.00
		— Original Dolton albums above have light blue labels with the fish logo above the spindle hole.—			
Dolton BLP-2003	(M)	Walk-Don't Run	1963	10.00	25.00
Dolton BST-8003	(S)	Walk-Don't Run	1963	12.00	30.00
Dolton BLP-2004	(M)	The Ventures	1963	10.00	25.00
Dolton BST-8004	(S)	The Ventures	1963	12.00	30.00
Dolton BLP-2006	(M)	Another Smash!!!	1963	10.00	25.00
Dolton BST-8006	(S)	Another Smash!!!	1963	12.00	30.00
Dolton BLP-2008	(M)	The Colorful Ventures	1963	10.00	25.00
Dolton BST-8008	(S)	The Colorful Ventures	1963	12.00	30.00
Dolton BLP-2010	(M)	Dance!	1963	10.00	25.00
Dolton BST-8010	(S)	Dance!	1963	12.00	30.00
		("Dance!" is a repackage of "Twist With The Ventures.")			
Dolton BLP-2014	(M)	Dance With The Ventures	1963	10.00	25.00
Dolton BST-8014	(S)	Dance With The Ventures	1963	12.00	30.00
		("Dance With The Ventures" is a repackage of "Twist Party.")			
Dolton BLP-2016	(M)	Mashed Potatoes And Gravy	1962	12.00	30.00
Dolton BST-8016	(S)	Mashed Potatoes And Gravy	1962	12.00	30.00
Dolton BLP-2016	(M)	Beach Party	196?	10.00	25.00
Dolton BST-8016	(S)	Beach Party	196?	12.00	30.00
		("Beach Party" is a repackage of "Mashed Potatoes.")			
Dolton BLP-2017	(M)	Going To The Ventures' Dance Party!	1962	10.00	25.00
Dolton BST-8017	(S)	Going To The Ventures' Dance Party!	1962	12.00	30.00

Label & Catalog #		Title	Year	VG+	NM
Dolton BLP-2019	(M)	Telstar, The Lonely Bull	1963	10.00	25.00
Dolton BST-8019	(S)	Telstar, The Lonely Bull	1963	12.00	30.00
Dolton BLP-2022	(M)	Surfing	1963	10.00	25.00
Dolton BST-8022	(S)	Surfing	1963	12.00	30.00
Dolton BLP-2023	(M)	Ventures Play The Country Classics	1963	10.00	25.00
Dolton BST-8023	(S)	Ventures Play The Country Classics	1963	12.00	30.00
Dolton BLP-2024	(M)	Let's Go!	1963	10.00	25.00
Dolton BST-8024	(S)	Let's Go!	1963	12.00	30.00
Dolton BLP-2027	(M)	(The) Ventures In Space	1964	12.00	30.00
Dolton BST-8027	(S)	(The) Ventures In Space	1964	14.00	35.00
Dolton BLP-2029	(M)	The Fabulous Ventures	1964	10.00	25.00
Dolton BST-8029	(S)	The Fabulous Ventures	1964	12.00	30.00
Dolton BLP-2031	(M)	Walk, Don't Run, Volume 2	1964	10.00	25.00
Dolton BST-8031	(S)	Walk, Don't Run, Volume 2	1964	12.00	30.00
Dolton BLP-2033	(M)	The Ventures Knock Me Out!	1965	10.00	25.00
Dolton BST-8033	(S)	The Ventures Knock Me Out!	1965	12.00	30.00
Dolton BLP-2035	(M)	The Ventures On Stage	1965	10.00	25.00
Dolton BST-8035	(S)	The Ventures On Stage	1965	12.00	30.00
—Dolton albums above have dark blue labels with a color logo on the left side.—					
Dolton BLP-16501	(M)	Play Guitar With The Ventures	1965	8.00	20.00
Dolton BST-17501	(S)	Play Guitar With The Ventures	1965	10.00	25.00
Dolton BLP-16502	(M)	Play Guitar With The Ventures, Volume 2	1965	8.00	20.00
Dolton BST-17502	(S)	Play Guitar With The Ventures, Volume 2	1965	10.00	25.00
Dolton BLP-16503	(M)	Play Guitar With The Ventures, Volume 3	1965	8.00	20.00
Dolton BST-17503	(S)	Play Guitar With The Ventures, Volume 3	1965	10.00	25.00
Dolton BLP-16504	(M)	Play Guitar With The Ventures, Volume 4	1965	8.00	20.00
Dolton BST-17504	(S)	Play Guitar With The Ventures, Volume 4	1965	10.00	25.00
Dolton BLP-2037	(M)	The Ventures A Go-Go	1965	8.00	20.00
Dolton BST-8037	(S)	The Ventures A Go-Go	1965	10.00	25.00
Dolton BLP-2038	(M)	The Ventures' Christmas Album	1965	10.00	25.00
Dolton BST-8038	(S)	The Ventures' Christmas Album	1965	10.00	25.00
Dolton BLP-2040	(M)	Where The Action Is!	1966	8.00	20.00
Dolton BST-8040	(S)	Where The Action Is!	1966	10.00	25.00
Dolton BLP-2042	(M)	Batman Theme	1966	10.00	25.00
Dolton BST-8042	(S)	Batman Theme	1966	12.00	30.00
Dolton BLP-2045	(M)	Go With The Ventures!	1966	8.00	20.00
Dolton BST-8045	(S)	Go With The Ventures!	1966	10.00	25.00
Dolton BLP-2047	(M)	Wild Things!	1966	8.00	20.00
Dolton BST-8047	(S)	Wild Things!	1966	10.00	25.00
Dolton BLP-2050	(M)	Guitar Freakout	1967	8.00	20.00
Dolton BST-8050	(S)	Guitar Freakout	1967	10.00	25.00
Liberty LRP-4052	(M)	Super Psychedelics	1967	6.00	15.00
Liberty LST-8052	(S)	Super Psychedelics	1967	8.00	20.00
Liberty LRP-4053	(M)	Golden Greats By The Ventures	1967	8.00	20.00
Liberty LST-8053	(S)	Golden Greats By The Ventures	1967	8.00	20.00
Liberty LRP-4054	(M)	$1,000,000.00 Weekend	1967	8.00	20.00
Liberty LST-8054	(S)	$1,000,000.00 Weekend	1967	8.00	20.00
Liberty LST-8055	(S)	Flights Of Fantasy	1968	8.00	20.00
Liberty LST-8057	(S)	The Horse	1968	8.00	20.00
Liberty LST-8059	(S)	Underground Fire	1969	8.00	20.00
Liberty LST-8060	(S)	More Golden Greats	1970	8.00	20.00
Liberty LST-8061	(S)	Hawaii Five-O	1969	8.00	20.00
Liberty LST-8062	(S)	Swamp Rock	1969	8.00	20.00
Liberty LST-35000	(S)	The Ventures' 10th Anniversary Album	1970	8.00	20.00
Liberty SCR-5	(S)	The Versatile Ventures (Record Club)	196?	6.00	15.00
United Arts. UXS-80	(S)	The Ventures (2 LPs)	1971	6.00	15.00
United Arts. UAS-5547	(S)	Theme From Shaft	1972	5.00	12.00
United Arts. UAS-5575	(S)	Joy/The Ventures Play The Classics	1972	5.00	12.00
United Arts. UAS-5649	(S)	Rock And Roll Forever	1972	5.00	12.00
United Arts. UAS-6796	(S)	New Testament	1971	5.00	12.00
United Arts. LA147	(S)	Only Hits (2 LPs)	1973	6.00	15.00
United Arts. LA217	(S)	The Jim Croce Songbook	1974	5.00	12.00
United Arts. LA331	(S)	The Very Best Of The Ventures	1975	5.00	12.00
United Arts. LA586	(S)	Rocky Road	1976	5.00	12.00
United Arts. LA717	(S)	TV Themes	1977	5.00	12.00

VERA, BILLY
Refer to Judy Clay & Billy Vera.

| Atlantic SD-8197 | (S) | With Pen In Hand | 1968 | 10.00 | 25.00 |

Label & Catalog #		Title	Year	VG+	NM
VERDON, GWEN					
RCA Victor LPM-1152	(M)	The Girl I Left Home For	1956	10.00	25.00
VERITY BAND, JOHN					
Dunhill DSX-500170	(S)	The John Verity Band	1974	8.00	20.00
VERNE, LARRY					
Era 104	(M)	Mister Larry Verne	196?	20.00	50.00
VERNON, MILLI					
Storyville 910	(M)	Introducing Milli Verdon	1956	12.00	30.00
VERSATONES, THE					
RCA Victor LPM-1538	(M)	The Versatones	1957	20.00	50.00
VESTICH BROTHERS, THE					
Eclipse W11779VB	(S)	Live At Woofendale's	1979	30.00	75.00
VETTES, THE					
The Vettes feature Bruce Johnston.					
MGM E-4193	(M)	Rev-Up	1963	30.00	75.00
MGM SE-4193	(S)	Rev-Up	1963	40.00	100.00
VIBRATIONS, THE					
Checker 2978	(M)	Watusi	1961	40.00	100.00
OKeh OKM-4111	(M)	Shout	1965	12.00	30.00
OKeh OKS-14111	(S)	Shout	1965	16.00	40.00
OKeh OKM-4112	(M)	Misty	1966	10.00	25.00
OKeh OKS-14112	(S)	Misty	1966	12.00	30.00
OKeh OKS-14129	(S)	The Vibrations' Greatest Hits	1969	16.00	40.00
Mandate 3006	(S)	Taking A New Step	1972	6.00	15.00
VICEROYS, THE					
Bolo BLP-8000	(M)	The Viceroys At Granny's Pad	1963	16.00	40.00
VICTIMS OF CHANCE, THE					
Crestview CRS-3052	(S)	The Victims Of Chance	197?	24.00	60.00
VICTORIA					
San Francisco 201	(S)	Secret Of The Bloom	1970	5.00	12.00
San Francisco 206	(S)	Victoria	1971	5.00	12.00
VIGRASS & OSBORNE					
Uni 73129	(S)	Queues	1971	8.00	20.00
Epic KE-33077	(S)	Steppin' Out	1975	4.00	10.00
VILLAGE PEOPLE, THE					
Casablanca 7064	(S)	Village People (Picture disc)	1978	4.00	10.00
Casablanca 7096	(S)	Macho Man (Picture disc)	1978	4.00	10.00
Casablanca 7118	(S)	Cruisin' (Picture disc)	1978	4.00	10.00
VILLAGE STOMPERS, THE					
Epic LN-24078	(M)	Washington Square	1964	5.00	12.00
Epic BN-26078	(S)	Washington Square	1964	6.00	15.00
Epic LN-24090	(M)	More Sounds Of Washington Square	1964	5.00	12.0
Epic BN-26090	(S)	More Sounds Of Washington Square	1964	6.00	15.0
Epic LN-24109	(M)	Around The World	1964	5.00	.00
Epic BN-26109	(S)	Around The World	1964	6.00	2.00
Epic LN-24129	(M)	New Beat On Broadway	1965	5.0	12.00
Epic BN-26129	(S)	New Beat On Broadway	1965		15.00
Epic LN-24161	(M)	Some Folk, A Bit Of Country And A Whole Lot Of Dixie	1965		12.00
Epic BN-26161	(S)	Some Folk, A Bit Of Country And A Whole Lot Of Dixie	19	.00 5.00	15.00
Epic LN-24180	(M)	A Taste Of Honey And Other Goodies		6.00 5.00	12.00 15.00
Epic BN-26180	(S)	A Taste Of Honey And Other Goodies		6.00	12.00
Epic LN-24318	(M)	The Village Stompers' Greatest Hits			15.00
Epic BN-26318	(S)	The Village Stompers' Greatest Hits			

Label & Catalog #		Title	Year	VG+	NM

VINCENT, GENE

Label & Catalog #		Title	Year	VG+	NM
Capitol T-764	(M)	Bluejean Bop!	1957	100.00	300.00
Capitol T-811	(M)	Gene Vincent & The Blue Caps	1957	100.00	300.00
Capitol T-970	(M)	Gene Vincent Rocks! & The Blue Caps Roll	1958	100.00	300.00
Capitol T-985	(M)	Hot Rod Gang (Soundtrack)	1958	See note below	
		(While a "Hot Rod Gang" EP does exist, an LP does not.)			
Capitol T-1059	(M)	A Gene Vincent Record Date	1958	100.00	300.00
Capitol T-1207	(M)	Sounds Like Gene Vincent	1959	100.00	300.00
Capitol T-1342	(M)	Crazy Times	1960	100.00	300.00
Capitol ST-1342	(S)	Crazy Times	1960	250.00	500.00
Capitol DKAO-380	(E)	Gene Vincent's Greatest (Green label)	1969	12.00	30.00
Dandelion 9-102	(S)	I'm Back And I'm Proud	1970	10.00	25.00
Kama Sutra 2019	(S)	If Only You Could See Me Today	1970	10.00	25.00
Kama Sutra 2027	(S)	The Day The World Turned Blue	1971	10.00	25.00

VINSON, EDDIE "CLEANHEAD"
Refer to Roy Brown; Jimmy Witherspoon.

Label & Catalog #		Title	Year	VG+	NM
Riverside 3502	(M)	Backdoor Blues	195?	20.00	50.00
Bethlehem BCP-5005	(M)	Eddie "Cleanhead" Vinson Sings	195?	20.00	50.00
Aamco 312	(M)	Eddie "Cleanhead" Vinson Sings	195?	8.00	20.00
BluesWay BL-6007	(M)	Cherry Red	1967	6.00	15.00
BluesWay BLS-6007	(S)	Cherry Red	1967	8.00	20.00
King 1087	(M)	Cherry Red	1969	8.00	20.00
Bethlehem 6036	(S)	Back In Town	1978	6.00	15.00
Muse 5116	(S)	Clean Machine	1978	4.00	10.00

VINTON, BOBBY

Label & Catalog #		Title	Year	VG+	NM
Epic BN-3727	(M)	Dancing At The Hop	1961	14.00	35.00
Epic LN-579	(S)	Dancing At The Hop	1961	20.00	50.00
Epic BN-3780	(M)	Young Man With A Big Band	1961	14.00	35.00
Epic LN-597	(S)	Young Man With A Big Band	1961	20.00	50.00
Epic LN-24020	(M)	Roses Are Red	1962	10.00	23.00
Epic BN-26020	(S)	Roses Are Red	1962	14.00	35.00
Epic LN-24035	(M)	Bobby Vinton Sings The Big Ones	1963	10.00	25.00
Epic BN-26035	(S)	Bobby Vinton Sings The Big Ones	1963	14.00	35.00
Epic LN-24049	(M)	The Greatest Hits Of The Greatest Groups	1963	10.00	25.00
Epic BN-26049	(S)	The Greatest Hits Of The Greatest Groups	1963	14.00	35.00
— Original Epic albums above have yellow labels with the Epic logo along the perimeter.—					
Epic LN-24068	(DJ)	Blue On Blue (Blue vinyl)	1963	40.00	100.00
Epic LN-24068	(M)	Blue On Blue	1963	8.00	20.00
Epic BN-26068	(S)	Blue On Blue	1963	10.00	25.00
Epic LN-24068	(M)	Blue Velvet	1963	6.00	15.00
Epic BN-26068	(S)	Blue Velvet	1963	8.00	20.00
("Blue Velvet" is a repackage of "Blue On Blue.")					
Epic LN-24081	(M)	There! I've Said It Again	1964	6.00	15.00
Epic BN-26081	(S)	There! I've Said It Again	1964	8.00	20.00
Epic LN-24098	(M)	Bobby Vinton's Greatest Hits	1964	6.00	15.00
Epic BN-26098	(S)	Bobby Vinton's Greatest Hits	1964	8.00	20.00
Epic LN-24113	(M)	Tell Me Why	1964	6.00	15.00
Epic BN-26113	(S)	Tell Me Why	1964	8.00	20.00
Epic LN-24122	(M)	A Very Merry Christmas	1964	6.00	15.00
Epic BN-26122	(S)	A Very Merry Christmas	1964	8.00	20.00
Epic LN-24136	(M)	Mr. Lonely	1965	6.00	15.00
Epic BN-26136	(S)	Mr. Lonely	1965	8.00	20.00
Epic LN-24154	(M)	Bobby Vinton Sings For Lonely Nights	1965	6.00	15.00
Epic BN-26154	(S)	Bobby Vinton Sings For Lonely Nights	1965	8.00	20.00
Epic LN-24170	(M)	Drive-In Movie Time	1965	6.00	15.00
Epic BN-26170	(S)	Drive-In Movie Time	1965	8.00	20.00
Epic LN-24182	(M)	Satin Pillows	1966	6.00	15.00
Epic BN-26182	(S)	Satin Pillows	1966	8.00	20.00
Epic LN-24187	(M)	More Of Bobby Vinton's Greatest Hits	1966	6.00	15.00
Epic BN-26187	(S)	More Of Bobby Vinton's Greatest Hits	1966	8.00	20.00
Epic LN-24	(M)	Country Boy	1966	6.00	15.00
Epic BN-26	(S)	Country Boy	1966	8.00	20.00
Epic LN-242	(M)	Live At The Copa	1966	6.00	15.00
Epic BN-262	(S)	Live At The Copa	1966	8.00	20.00
Epic LN-242	(M)	Bobby Vinton Sings The Newest Hits	1967	6.00	15.00
Epic BN-2624	(S)	Bobby Vinton Sings The Newest Hits	1967	8.00	20.00

Label & Catalog #		Title	Year	VG+	NM
Epic LN-24341	(M)	Please Love Me Forever	1967	6.00	15.00
Epic BN-26341	(S)	Please Love Me Forever	1967	8.00	20.00
Epic BN-26382	(S)	Take Good Care Of Her	1968	6.00	15.00
Epic BN-26437	(S)	I Love How You Love Me	1969	6.00	15.00

— Original Epic albums above have yellow labels with Epic on top.—

VIOLINAIRES, THE

Checker 2CK-10065	(M)	Please Answer This Prayer (2 LPs)	197?	6.00	15.00

VIRGIN INSANITY

Funky 71411	(S)	Illusions Of The Maintenance Man	1970	80.00	200.00

VIRGINIANS, THE

United Arts. UAL-3293	(M)	The Wonderful World Of Bluegrass Music	1963	6.00	15.00
United Arts. UAS-6293	(S)	The Wonderful World Of Bluegrass Music	1963	8.00	20.00
Monument MLP-8031	(M)	Ballads And Bluegrass	1965	6.00	15.00
Monument SLP-18031	(S)	Ballads And Bluegrass	1965	8.00	20.00

VIRTUE, FRANK, & THE VIRTUES

Fayette 1816	(M)	Frank Virtue & The Virtues (Blue cover)	196?	30.00	75.00
Fayette 1816	(M)	Frank Virtue & The Virtues (White cover)	196?	20.00	50.00

VIRTUES, THE

Wynne WLP-111	(M)	Guitar Boogie Shuffle	1960	30.00	75.00
Strand L-1061	(M)	Guitar Boogie Shuffle	1960	14.00	35.00
Strand SL-1061	(S)	Guitar Boogie Shuffle	1960	20.00	50.00

VISCOUNTS, THE

Madison 1001	(M)	The Viscounts	1960	50.00	125.00
Amy 8008	(M)	Harlem Nocturne	1965	12.00	30.00
Amy S-8008	(S)	Harlem Nocturne	1965	16.00	40.00

("Harlem Nocturne" is rechanneled on this album.)

VISION OF SUNSHINE

Avco Embassy 33007	(S)	Vision Of Sunshine	1970	6.00	15.00

VISITORS, THE

Cobblestone 9010	(S)	Neptune	1972	5.00	12.00
Muse 5094	(S)	Motherland	1976	4.00	10.00
Montage ST-72000	(S)	The Visitors	1981	3.00	8.00

VOGUES, THE

Co&Ce 1229	(M)	Meet The Vogues	1965	12.00	30.00
Co&Ce 1229	(S)	Meet The Vogues	1965	16.00	40.00
Co&Ce 1230	(M)	Five O' Clock World	1966	12.00	30.00
Co&Ce 1230	(S)	Five O' Clock World	1966	16.00	40.00
Reprise RS-6314	(S)	Turn Around, Look At Me	1968	6.00	15.00
Reprise RS-6326	(S)	Till	1969	6.00	15.00
Reprise RS-6347	(S)	Memories	1969	6.00	15.00
Reprise RS-6371	(S)	The Vogues' Greatest Hits	1969	6.00	15.00
Reprise RS-6395	(S)	The Vogues Sing The Good Old Songs	1970	6.00	15.00

— Reprise albums above have brown & orange labels with a steamboat on top.—

VON SCHMIDT, ERIC

Folklore FRLP-14005	(M)	Folk Blues	1964	12.00	30.00
Folklore FRST-14005	(S)	Folk Blues	1964	14.00	35.00
Prestige PRLP-7384	(M)	Eric Sings Von Schmidt	1966	8.00	20.00
Prestige PRST-7384	(S)	Eric Sings Von Schmidt	1966	10.00	25.00
Prestige PRST-7717	(S)	The Folk Blues Of Eric Von Schmidt	1969	6.00	15.00

(Prestige 7717 is a reissue of Folklore 14005.)

Smash SRS-67124	(S)	Who Knocked The Brains Out Of The Sky	1969	6.00	15.00

VOYAGER

Camwood	(S)	Sound Barriers	1981	8.00	20.00

VULCAN

13th Records	(S)	Vulcan	1985	80.00	200.00

WABASH RESURRECTION, THE

Pepperland 76294	(S)	Get It Off!	197?	50.00	125.00

WADDLSESWORTH

Martin MLM-38	(S)	The Trials Of Mary L.	1968	6.00	15.00

WADE, ADAM

Coed LPC-902	(M)	And Then Came Adam	1960	16.00	40.00
Coed LPC-903	(M)	Adam And Evening	1961	16.00	40.00
Coed LPCS-903	(S)	Adam And Evening	1961	24.00	60.00
Epic LN-24019	(M)	Adam Wade's Greatest Hits	1962	8.00	20.00
Epic BN-26019	(S)	Adam Wade's Greatest Hits	1962	10.00	25.00
Epic LN-24026	(M)	One Is A Lonely Number	1962	8.00	20.00
Epic BN-26026	(S)	One Is A Lonely Number	1962	10.00	25.00
Epic LN-24044	(M)	What Kind Of Fool Am I?	1963	8.00	20.00
Epic BN-26044	(S)	What Kind Of Fool Am I?	1963	10.00	25.00
Epic LN-24056	(M)	A Very Good Year For Girls	1963	8.00	20.00
Epic BN-26056	(S)	A Very Good Year For Girls	1963	10.00	25.00

— Original Epic albums above have yellow labels.—

WAGONER, PORTER (& THE WAGONMASTERS)

Refer to Hank Snow / Hank Lochlin / Porter Wagoner.

RCA Victor LPM-1358	(M)	A Satisfied Mind	1956	80.00	200.00
RCA Victor LPM-2447	(M)	A Slice Of Life-Songs Happy 'N' Sad	1962	12.00	30.00
RCA Victor LSP-2447	(S)	A Slice Of Life-Songs Happy 'N' Sad	1962	16.00	40.00
RCA Victor LPM-2650	(M)	The Porter Wagoner Show	1963	10.00	25.00
RCA Victor LSP-2650	(S)	The Porter Wagoner Show	1963	14.00	35.00
RCA Victor LPM-2706	(M)	Y'All Come	1963	10.00	25.00
RCA Victor LSP-2706	(S)	Y'All Come	1963	14.00	35.00

— Original RCA mono albums above have "Long Play" on the bottom of the label;
stereo albums have "Living Stereo" on the bottom.—

RCA Victor LPM-2960	(M)	The Bluegrass Story	1964	10.00	25.00
RCA Victor LSP-2960	(S)	The Bluegrass Story	1964	12.00	30.00
RCA Victor LPM-3389	(M)	The Thin Man From West Plains	1965	10.00	25.00
RCA Victor LSP-3389	(S)	The Thin Man From West Plains	1965	12.00	30.00
RCA Victor LPM-3488	(M)	Grand Old Gospel	1966	10.00	25.00
RCA Victor LSP-3488	(S)	Grand Old Gospel	1966	12.00	30.00
RCA Victor LPM-3560	(M)	The Best Of Porter Wagoner	1966	10.00	25.00
RCA Victor LSP-3560	(S)	The Best Of Porter Wagoner	1966	12.00	30.00
RCA Victor LPM-3593	(M)	Confessions Of A Broken Man	1966	10.00	25.00
RCA Victor LSP-3593	(S)	Confessions Of A Broken Man	1966	12.00	30.00
RCA Victor LPM-3683	(M)	Soul Of A Convict	1967	12.00	30.00
RCA Victor LSP-3683	(S)	Soul Of A Convict	1967	10.00	25.00
RCA Victor LPM-3797	(M)	The Cold Hard Facts Of Life	1967	12.00	30.00
RCA Victor LSP-3797	(S)	The Cold Hard Facts Of Life	1967	10.00	25.00
RCA Victor LPM-3855	(M)	More Grand Old Gospel	1967	12.00	30.00
RCA Victor LSP-3855	(S)	More Grand Old Gospel	1967	10.00	25.00
RCA Victor LPM-3968	(M)	The Bottom Of The Bottle	1968	40.00	100.00
RCA Victor LSP-3968	(S)	The Bottom Of The Bottle	1968	10.00	25.00
RCA Victor LSP-4034	(S)	Gospel Country	1968	10.00	25.00

— Original RCA albums above have black labels with Nipper on top.—

RCA Victor LSP-4116	(S)	The Carroll County Accident	1969	8.00	20.00
RCA Victor LSP-4181	(S)	Me And My Boys	1969	8.00	20.00
RCA Victor LSP-4286	(S)	You Got Ta Have A License	1970	8.00	20.00
RCA Victor LSP-4321	(S)	The Best Of Porter Wagoner, Volume 2	1970	8.00	20.00
RCA Victor LSP-4386	(S)	Skidrow Joe/Down In The Alley	1970	8.00	20.00

— Original RCA albums above have orange labels on non-flexible vinyl.—

WAGONER, PORTER, & SKEETER DAVIS

Label & Catalog #		Title	Year	VG+	NM
RCA Victor LPM-2529	(M)	Duets	1962	10.00	25.00
RCA Victor LSP-2529	(S)	Duets	1962	14.00	35.00

— *Original RCA mono albums above have "Long Play" on the bottom of the label;*
stereo albums have "Living Stereo" on the bottom. —

WAGONER, PORTER, & NORMA JEAN

RCA Victor LPM-2840	(M)	In Person	1964	8.00	20.00
RCA Victor LSP-2840	(S)	In Person	1964	10.00	25.00
RCA Victor LPM-3509	(M)	Live On The Road	1966	8.00	20.00
RCA Victor LSP-3509	(S)	Live On The Road	1966	10.00	25.00

— *Original RCA albums above have black labels with Nipper on top.* —

WAGONER, PORTER, & DOLLY PARTON

RCA Victor LPM-3926	(M)	Just Between You And Me	1968	40.00	100.00
RCA Victor LSP-3926	(S)	Just Between You And Me	1968	10.00	25.00

— *Original RCA albums above have black labels with Nipper on top.* —

RCA Victor LSP-4039	(S)	Just The Two Of Us	1968	8.00	20.00
RCA Victor LSP-4186	(S)	Always, Always	1969	8.00	20.00
RCA Victor LSP-4305	(S)	Porter Wayne And Dolly Rebecca	1970	8.00	20.00
RCA Victor LSP-4388	(S)	Once More	1970	8.00	20.00

— *Original RCA albums above have orange labels on non-flexible vinyl.* —

RCA Victor LSP-4490	(S)	Two Of A Kind	1971	6.00	15.00
RCA Victor LSP-4556	(S)	The Best Of Porter Wagoner & Dolly Parton	1971	6.00	15.00
RCA Victor LSP-4628	(S)	The Right Combination	1972	6.00	15.00
RCA Victor LSP-4761	(S)	Together Always	1972	6.00	15.00
RCA Victor LSP-4841	(S)	We Found It	1973	6.00	15.00

— *Original RCA albums above have orange labels.* —

WAILERS, THE

Refer to The Sonics.

Golden Crest CR-3075	(M)	Fabulous Wailers	1959	60.00	150.00

(*Original pressings have the cover photo in full color.*)

Golden Crest CR-3075	(M)	Fabulous Wailers	196?	30.00	75.00

(*Second pressings have a black & white cover with the title in blue.*)

Golden Crest CR-3075	(M)	Fabulous Wailers	196?	20.00	50.00

(*Later pressings replace the photo with a title cover.*)

Etiquette ALB-01	(M)	Wailers At The Castle	1962	20.00	50.00
Etiquette ALB-022	(M)	Wailers & Company	1963	20.00	50.00
Imperial LP-9262	(M)	Tall Cool One	1964	14.00	35.00
Imperial LP-12262	(S)	Tall Cool One	1964	20.00	50.00
Etiquette ALB-023	(M)	Wailers, Wailers, Everywhere	1965	20.00	50.00
Etiquette ALB-026	(M)	Out Of Our Tree	1966	20.00	50.00
United Arts. UAL-3557	(M)	Outburst!	1966	12.00	30.00
United Arts. UAS-6557	(S)	Outburst!	1966	16.00	40.00

(*"Out Of Our Tree" is rechanneled and "It's You Alone" is mono.*)

Bell 6016	(M)	Walk Thru The People	1968	8.00	20.00

WAKEFIELD SUN

MGM SE-4626	(S)	Wakefield Sun	1969	6.00	15.00

WAKELY, JIMMY

Wakely was formerly a member of Gene Autry's traveling band.

Capitol H-9004 (10")	(M)	Christmas On The Range	1950	40.00	100.00
Capitol H-4008 (10")	(M)	Songs Of The West	1950	40.00	100.00
Decca DL-8409	(M)	Santa Fe Trail	1956	20.00	50.00
Decca DL-8680	(M)	Enter And Rest And Pray	1957	20.00	50.00

— *Original Decca albums above have black & silver labels.* —

Shasta SHLP-501	(M)	Country Million Sellers	1959	10.00	25.00
Shasta SHLP-502	(M)	Merry Christmas	1959	10.00	25.00
Shasta SHLP-505	(M)	Jimmy Wakely Sings	1960	10.00	25.00
Dot DLP-3711	(M)	Slippin' Around	1966	6.00	15.00
Dot DLP-25711	(S)	Slippin' Around	1966	8.00	20.00
Dot DLP-3754	(M)	Christmas With Jimmy Wakely	1966	6.00	15.00
Dot DLP-25754	(S)	Christmas With Jimmy Wakely	1966	8.00	20.00
Decca DL-75077	(S)	Heartaches	1969	6.00	15.00
Decca DL-75192	(S)	Now And Then	1970	6.00	15.00

Label & Catalog #		Title	Year	VG+	NM

WAKEMAN, RICK
Wakeman was formerly a member of Yes.

A&M QU-54361	(Q)	The Six Wives Of Henry The VIII	1973	8.00	20.00
A&M QU-53621	(Q)	Journey To The Center Of The Earth	1975	8.00	20.00
A&M QU-54515	(Q)	The Myths And Legends Of King Arthur	1975	8.00	20.00
Sweet Thunder 1	(S)	Journey To The Center Of The Earth	1974	13.00	40.00

WALKER, BILLY

Columbia CL-1624	(M)	Everybody's Hits But Mine	1961	8.00	20.00
Columbia CS-8424	(S)	Everybody's Hits But Mine	1961	12.00	30.00

— *Original Columbia album above has three white "eye" logos on each side of the spindle hole.* —

Columbia CL-1935	(M)	Billy Walker's Greatest Hits	1963	6.00	15.00
Columbia CS-8735	(S)	Billy Walker's Greatest Hits	1963	8.00	20.00
Columbia CL-2206	(M)	Thank You For Calling	1964	6.00	15.00
Columbia CS-9006	(S)	Thank You For Calling	1964	8.00	20.00
Columbia CL-2331	(M)	The Gun, The Gold And The Girl	1965	6.00	15.00
Columbia CS-9131	(S)	The Gun, The Gold And The Girl	1965	8.00	20.00

WALKER, CHARLIE

Columbia CL-1691	(M)	Charlie Walker's Greatest Hits	1961	8.00	20.00
Columbia CS-8491	(S)	Charlie Walker's Greatest Hits	1961	12.00	30.00

— *Original Columbia album above has three white "eye" logos on each side of the spindle hole.* —

WALKER, CINDY

Monument MLP-8020	(M)	Words And Music By Cindy Walker	1964	10.00	25.00
Monument SLP-18020	(S)	Words And Music By Cindy Walker	1964	14.00	35.00

WALKER, CLINT

Warner Bros. W-1343	(M)	Inspiration	1959	10.00	25.00
Warner Bros. WS-1343	(S)	Inspiration	1959	12.00	30.00

WALKER, DAVIS T.

Revue 7207	(S)	Sidewalk	1968	6.00	15.00
Revue 7211	(S)	Going Up	1969	6.00	15.00

WALKER, JERRY JEFF
Jerry Jeff originally recorded with Circus Maximus.

Atco SD-33-259	(S)	Mr. Bojangles	1968	8.00	20.00
Atco SD-33-297	(S)	Five Years Gone	1969	12.00	30.00
Atco SD-33-336	(S)	Bein' Free	1970	8.00	20.00
Vanguard VSD-6521	(S)	Driftin' Way Of Life (Black label)	1969	8.00	20.00
Decca DL-75384	(S)	Jerry Jeff Walker	1972	6.00	15.00

WALKER, JUNIOR (& THE ALL STARS)

Soul 701	(M)	Shotgun	1965	8.00	20.00
Soul SS-701	(S)	Shotgun	1965	12.00	30.00
Soul 702	(M)	Soul Session	1966	6.00	15.00
Soul SS-702	(S)	Soul Session	1966	8.00	20.00
Soul 703	(M)	Road Runner	1966	6.00	15.00
Soul SS-703	(S)	Road Runner	1966	8.00	20.00
Soul 705	(M)	Junior Walker & The All Stars Live	1967	6.00	15.00
Soul SS-705	(S)	Junior Walker & The All Stars Live	1967	8.00	20.00
Soul 710	(S)	Home Cookin'	1969	6.00	15.00
Soul SS-718	(S)	Greatest Hits	1969	6.00	15.00
Soul SS-721	(S)	Gotta Hold On To This Feeling	1969	6.00	15.00
Soul SS-721	(S)	What Does It Take To Win Your Love	1969	5.00	12.00
		(Repackage of "Gotta Hold On To This Feeling.")			
Soul SS-725	(S)	Junior Walker & The All Stars Live	1970	5.00	12.00
Soul SS-726	(S)	A Gasssss	1970	5.00	12.00
Soul SS-732	(S)	Rainbow Funk	1971	5.00	12.00
Soul SS-733	(S)	Moody Jr.	1971	5.00	12.00
Soul SS-738	(S)	Peace And Understanding Is Hard To Find	1973	5.00	12.00
Soul SS-742	(S)	Junior Walker & The All Stars	1973	*Unreleased*	
Soul S6-745	(S)	Hot Shot	1976	4.00	10.00
Soul S6-747	(S)	Sax Appeal	1976	4.00	10.00
Soul S6-748	(S)	Whopper Bopper Show Stopper	1976	4.00	10.00
Soul S7-750	(S)	Smooth	1978	4.00	10.00
Motown MS-786	(S)	Anthology (2 LPs)	1979	8.00	20.00
Whitfield K-3331	(S)	Back Street Boogie	1979	4.00	10.00

Label & Catalog #		Title	Year	VG+	NM

WALKER, LOU

| Sims LP-114 | (M) | Swing Western Style | 1964 | 40.00 | 100.00 |

WALKER, LUCILLE

| Checker LP-1428 | (M) | The Best Of Lucille Walker | 1957 | 50.00 | 150.00 |

WALKER, OLIVE

| RCA Victor LPB-3001 | (M) | Folk Songs Of Trinidad And Tobago | 1962 | 6.00 | 15.00 |

WALKER, SCOTT
Scott Walker is a pseudonym for Scott Engel. Refer to Scott Engel & John Stewart; The Walker Brothers.

Smash SRS-67099	(S)	Aloner	1968	8.00	20.00
Smash SRS-67106	(S)	Scott, Volume 2	1968	8.00	20.00
Smash SRS-67121	(S)	Scott Walker 3	1969	8.00	20.00

WALKER, AARON "T-BONE"

Capitol H-370 (10")	(M)	Classics In Jazz	1953	300.00	500.00
Capitol T-370	(M)	Classics In Jazz	1953	100.00	250.00
Atlantic 8020	(M)	T-Bone Blues (Black label)	1959	50.00	125.00
Atlantic 8020	(M)	T-Bone Blues (Purple & orange label)	196?	30.00	75.00
Atlantic SD-8256	(S)	T-Bone Blues	1970	8.00	20.00
Imperial LP-9098	(M)	Sings The Blues	1959	30.00	75.00
Imperial LP-9116	(M)	Singing The Blues	1960	30.00	75.00
Imperial LP-9146	(M)	I Get So Weary	1961	30.00	75.00
Capitol T-1958	(M)	Great Blues Vocals And Guitar	1963		See note below

> (Should copies of this album exist on the black rainbow label
> they would carry a suggested Near Mint value of $300-500.)

| Capitol T-1958 | (M) | Great Blues Vocals And Guitar | 1963 | 30.00 | 75.00 |

> (Black "Starline" label.)

Delmark D-633	(M)	I Want A Little Girl	1967	8.00	20.00
Delmark DS-633	(S)	I Want A Little Girl	1967	10.00	25.00
Wet Soul 1002	(M)	Stormy Monday Blues	1967	8.00	20.00
Wet Soul 1002	(S)	Stormy Monday Blues	1967	10.00	25.00
Brunswick BL-754126	(S)	The Truth	1968	8.00	20.00
Bluestime 29010	(S)	Blue Rocks	1968	8.00	20.00
BluesWay BLS-6014	(S)	Funky Town	1968	8.00	20.00
BluesWay BLS-6061	(S)	Blues Classics	1973	6.00	15.00
BluesWay BLS-6058	(S)	Dirty Mistreater	1973	6.00	15.00
Polydor PD-5521	(S)	Fly Walker Airlines	1973	6.00	15.00
Reprise 2XS-6483	(S)	Very Rare (2 LPs)	1973	8.00	20.00
Blue Note BNLA-533	(S)	T-Bone Walker	197?	6.00	15.00

WALKER BROTHERS, THE
Features Scott Engel, Gary Leeds and John Maus a.k.a. John Stewart as Scott, Gary and John Walker.

Smash MGS-27076	(M)	Introducing The Walker Brothers	1966	16.00	40.00
Smash SRS-67076	(E)	Introducing The Walker Brothers	1966	12.00	30.00
Smash MGS-27082	(M)	The Sun Ain't Gonna Shine Anymore	1967	12.00	30.00
Smash SRS-67082	(S)	The Sun Ain't Gonna Shine Anymore	1967	16.00	40.00

> ("The Sun Ain't Gonna Shine (Anymore)" and
> "After The Lights Go Out" are rechanneled.)

WALLACE, JERRY

Challenge CHL-606	(M)	Just Jerry	1959	30.00	75.00
Challenge CHL-612	(M)	There She Goes	1961	10.00	25.00
Challenge CHS-612	(S)	There She Goes	1961	14.00	35.00
Challenge CHL-616	(M)	Shutters And Boards	1962	8.00	20.00
Challenge CHS-616	(S)	Shutters And Boards	1962	10.00	25.00
Challenge CHL-619	(M)	In The Misty Moonlight	1964	6.00	15.00
Challenge CHS-619	(S)	In The Misty Moonlight	1964	8.00	20.00
Mercury MG-21072	(M)	The Best Of Jerry Wallace	1966	5.00	12.00
Mercury SR-61072	(S)	The Best Of Jerry Wallace	1966	6.00	15.00

WALLACE BROTHERS, THE

| Sims 128 | (M) | Soul, Soul And More Soul | 1965 | 40.00 | 100.00 |
| Sims 128 | (S) | Soul, Soul And More Soul | 1965 | 60.00 | 150.00 |

WALLER, GORDON
Gordon was formerly a member of Peter & Gordon.

| ABC X-749 | (S) | And Gordon | 1972 | 6.00 | 15.00 |

Label & Catalog #		Title	Year	VG+	NM
WALLER, JIM, & THE DELTAS					
Arvee A-432	(M)	Surfin' Wild	1963	20.00	50.00
Arvee AS-432	(S)	Surfin' Wild	1963	30.00	75.00
WALNUT BAND, THE					
Appaloosa CSL452	(S)	The Walnut Band Goes Nuts!	197?	50.00	125.00
WALSH, JOE					
Walsh was formerly a member of The James Gang; The Eagles.					
Command QD-40016	(Q)	The Smoker You Drink, The Player You Get	1974	6.00	15.00
Command QD-40017	(Q)	So What	1975	6.00	15.00
WALTON, MERCY DEE					
Bluesville BVLP-1039	(M)	Pity And Shame	1961	16.00	40.00
WALTON, WADE					
Bluesville BVLP-1060	(M)	Shake 'Em On Down	1962	16.00	40.00
WALTONS, THE					
Columbia KC-33193	(S)	The Waltons' Christmas Album	1975	6.00	15.00
WAMMACK, TRAVIS					
Fame 1801	(S)	Travis Wammack	1972	5.00	12.00
Capricorn 0162	(S)	Not For Sale	1975	4.00	10.00
WANDERIN' FIVE, THE					
Somerset SF-8600	(M)	Pickin' And Singin' Folk Songs	1963	5.00	12.00
Somerset SF-18600	(S)	Pickin' And Singin' Folk Songs	1963	6.00	15.00
Somerset SF-9900	(M)	Hootenanny At The Limelight	1963	5.00	12.00
Somerset SF-19900	(S)	Hootenanny At The Limelight	1963	6.00	15.00
WAR					
War also recorded with Eric Burdon.					
United Arts. UAS-5508	(S)	War	1971	6.00	15.00
United Arts. UAS-5546	(S)	All Day Music	1971	6.00	15.00
United Arts. UAS-5652	(S)	The World Is A Ghetto	1972	6.00	15.00
United Arts. LA128	(S)	Deliver The Word	1973	6.00	15.00
United Arts. LA193	(S)	War Live	1974	6.00	15.00
United Arts. SP-103	(DJ)	Radio Free War *(Blue vinyl)*	1974	8.00	20.00
United Arts. LA441	(S)	Why Can't We Be Friends	1975	5.00	12.00
United Arts. LA648	(S)	Greatest Hits	1976	4.00	10.00
United Arts. LA904	(S)	Youngblood *(Soundtrack)*	1978	4.00	10.00
WARD, BILLY, & THE DOMINOES					
Federal 295-94 (10")	(M)	Billy Ward & His Dominoes	1955	*See note below*	
		(Rare and generally sold in VG condition for $500-750. Suggested values for VG+ are $1,500-3,000 and NM, $5,000-10,000.)			
Federal 395-548	(M)	Billy Ward & His Dominoes	1956	600.00	1,200.00
Federal 395-559	(M)	Clyde McPhatter With Billy Ward & His Dominoes	1957	600.00	1,200.00
King LP-548	(M)	Billy Ward & His Dominoes	1958	300.00	600.00
King LP-559	(M)	Clyde McPhatter With Billy Ward & His Dominoes	1958	300.00	600.00
King LP-733	(M)	Billy Ward & His Dominoes Featuring Clyde McPhatter And Jackie Wilson	1960	300.00	600.00
Decca DL-8621	(M)	Billy Ward & His Dominoes	1958	80.00	200.00
Liberty LRP-3056	(M)	Sea Of Glass	1957	30.00	75.00
Liberty LST-7056	(S)	Sea Of Glass	1957	40.00	100.00
Liberty LRP-3083	(M)	Yours Forever	1958	30.00	75.00
Liberty LST-7083	(S)	Yours Forever	1958	40.00	100.00
Liberty LRP-3113	(M)	Pagan Love Song	1959	30.00	75.00
Liberty LST-7113	(S)	Pagan Love Song	1959	40.00	100.00
King LP-952	(M)	Twenty Four Songs *(Ccrownless label)*	1966	20.00	50.00

WARD, HELEN: *Refer to* GOLDMINE'S PRICE GUIDE TO COLLECTIBLE JAZZ ALBUMS

WARD, ROBIN					
Dot DLP-3555	(M)	Wonderful Summer	1963	80.00	200.00
Dot DLP-25555	(S)	Wonderful Summer	1963	150.00	300.00

Label & Catalog #		Title	Year	VG+	NM
WARREN, FRAN					
RCA Victor LM-61 (10")	(M)	Mr. Imperium (Soundtrack)	1951	40.00	100.00
MGM E-3394	(M)	Mood Indigo	1956	14.00	35.00
Tops L-1585	(M)	Here's Fran Warren	1958	8.00	20.00
Venise 7019	(M)	Come Rain Or Come Shine	195?	8.00	20.00
Venise 10019	(S)	Come Rain Or Come Shine	195?	12.00	30.00
Warwick T-2012	(M)	Something's Coming	1960	8.00	20.00
Warwick ST-2012	(S)	Something's Coming	1960	12.00	30.00
WARWICK, DEE DEE					
Mercury MG-21100	(M)	I Want To Be With You	1967	8.00	20.00
Mercury SR-61100	(S)	I Want To Be With You	1967	10.00	25.00
		("I Want To Be With You" is rechanneled on this album.)			
Mercury SR-61221	(S)	Foolish Fool ("Alfie" is rechanneled)	1969	10.00	25.00
Atco SD-33-337	(S)	Turnin' Around	1970	6.00	15.00
WARWICK, DIONNE					
Scepter S-508	(M)	Presenting Dionne Warwick	1963	6.00	15.00
Scepter SS-508	(S)	Presenting Dionne Warwick	1963	8.00	20.00
Scepter S-517	(M)	Anyone Who Had A Heart	1964	6.00	15.00
Scepter SS-517	(S)	Anyone Who Had A Heart	1964	8.00	20.00
Scepter S-523	(M)	Make Way For Dionne Warwick	1964	6.00	15.00
Scepter SS-523	(S)	Make Way For Dionne Warwick	1964	8.00	20.00
Scepter S-528	(M)	The Sensitive Sound Of Dionne Warwick	1965	6.00	15.00
Scepter SS-528	(S)	The Sensitive Sound Of Dionne Warwick	1965	8.00	20.00
United Arts. UAL-4128	(M)	What's New, Pussycat? (Soundtrack)	1965	6.00	15.00
United Arts. UAS-5128	(S)	What's New, Pussycat? (Soundtrack)	1965	8.00	20.00
Scepter S-531	(M)	Here I Am	1966	6.00	15.00
Scepter SS-531	(S)	Here I Am	1966	8.00	20.00
Scepter S-534	(M)	Dionne Warwick In Paris	1966	6.00	15.00
Scepter SS-534	(S)	Dionne Warwick In Paris	1966	8.00	20.00
Scepter S-555	(M)	Here Where There Is Love	1966	6.00	15.00
Scepter SS-555	(S)	Here Where There Is Love	1966	8.00	20.00
Scepter S-559	(M)	On Stage And In The Movies	1967	6.00	15.00
Scepter SS-559	(S)	On Stage And In The Movies	1967	8.00	20.00
Scepter S-563	(M)	The Windows Of The World	1967	6.00	15.00
Scepter SS-563	(S)	The Windows Of The World	1967	8.00	20.00
Scepter S-565	(M)	Dionne Warwick's Golden Hits, Part One	1967	6.00	15.00
Scepter SS-565	(S)	Dionne Warwick's Golden Hits, Part One	1967	8.00	20.00
Scepter SS-573	(S)	Soulful	1969	6.00	15.00
		— Original Scepter albums above have orange labels.—			
Mobile Fidelity MFSL-098	(S)	Hot! Live And Otherwise (2 LPs)	1980	8.00	25.00
WASHBOARD SAM					
Washboard Sam is a pseudonym for Robert Brown.					
RCA Victor LPV-577	(M)	Feeling Lowdown	1965	10.00	25.00
WASHINGTON, BABY					
Sue LP-1014	(M)	That's How Heartaches Are Made	1963	40.00	100.00
Sue LP-1042	(M)	Only Those In Love	1965	20.00	50.00
Sue LPS-1042	(S)	Only Those In Love	1965	30.00	75.00
Veep 16528	(S)	With You In Mind	1968	10.00	25.00
Trip 8009	(S)	The One And Only Baby Washington	1971	6.00	15.00
A.V.I. 6038	(S)	I Wanna Dance	1978	4.00	10.00
WASHINGTON, DINAH					
Refer to Brook Benton; Sarah Vaughan.					
Mercury MG-25060 (10")	(M)	Dinah Washington Songs	1950	40.00	100.00
Mercury MG-25138 (10")	(M)	Dynamic Dinah	1951	40.00	100.00
Mercury MG-25140 (10")	(M)	Blazing Ballads	1951	40.00	100.00
EmArcy 26032 (10")	(M)	After Hours With Miss D	1954	40.00	100.00
EmArcy MG-36000	(M)	Dinah Jams	1954	30.00	75.00
EmArcy MG-36011	(M)	For Those In Love	1955	30.00	75.00
EmArcy MG-36028	(M)	After Hours With Miss D	1955	20.00	50.00
EmArcy MG-36065	(M)	Dinah	1956	16.00	40.00
EmArcy MG-36073	(M)	In The Land Of Hi Fi	1956	16.00	40.00
EmArcy MG-36104	(M)	The Swingin' Miss D	1956	16.00	40.00
EmArcy MG-36119	(M)	Dinah Washington Sings Fats Waller	1957	16.00	40.00
EmArcy MG-36130	(M)	Dinah Washington Sings Bessie Smith	1958	16.00	40.00

Label & Catalog #		Title	Year	VG+	NM
EmArcy MG-36141	(M)	Newport '58	1958	16.00	40.00
Mercury MG-20119	(M)	Music For A First Love	1957	16.00	40.00
Mercury MG-20120	(M)	Music For Late Hours	1957	16.00	40.00
Mercury MG-20247	(M)	The Best In Blues	1957	16.00	40.00
Mercury MG-20439	(M)	The Queen	1959	12.00	30.00
Mercury SR-60111	(S)	The Queen	1959	16.00	40.00
Mercury MG-20479	(M)	What A Diff'rence A Day Makes	1959	12.00	30.00
Mercury SR-60158	(S)	What A Diff'rence A Day Makes	1959	16.00	40.00
Mercury MG-20523	(M)	Newport '58	1959	12.00	30.00
Mercury SR-60200	(S)	Newport '58	1959	16.00	40.00
Mercury MG-20525	(M)	Dinah Washington Sings Fats Waller	1959	12.00	30.00
Mercury SR-60202	(S)	Dinah Washington Sings Fats Waller	1959	16.00	40.00
Mercury MG-20572	(M)	Unforgettable	1960	10.00	25.00
Mercury SR-60232	(S)	Unforgettable	1960	12.00	30.00
Mercury MG-20604	(M)	I Concentrate On You	1961	10.00	25.00
Mercury SR-60604	(S)	I Concentrate On You	1961	12.00	30.00
Mercury MG-20614	(M)	For Lonely Lovers	1961	10.00	25.00
Mercury SR-60614	(S)	For Lonely Lovers	1961	12.00	30.00
Mercury MG-20638	(M)	September In The Rain	1961	10.00	25.00
Mercury SR-60638	(S)	September In The Rain	1961	12.00	30.00
Mercury MG-20661	(M)	Tears And Laughter	1962	10.00	25.00
Mercury SR-60661	(S)	Tears And Laughter	1962	12.00	30.00
Mercury MG-20729	(M)	I Wanna Be Loved	1962	10.00	25.00
Mercury SR-60729	(S)	I Wanna Be Loved	1962	12.00	30.00
Mercury MG-20788	(M)	This Is My Story, Volume 1	1963	10.00	25.00
Mercury SR-60788	(S)	This Is My Story, Volume 1	1963	12.00	30.00
Mercury MG-20789	(M)	This Is My Story, Volume 2	1963	10.00	25.00
Mercury SR-60789	(S)	This Is My Story, Volume 2	1963	12.00	30.00
Mercury MG-20829	(M)	The Good Old Days	1963	10.00	25.00
Mercury SR-60829	(E)	The Good Old Days	1963	6.00	15.00
— *Original Mercury albums above have black labels with silver print.* —					
Roulette R-25170	(M)	Dinah '62 *(White label)*	1962	8.00	20.00
Roulette SR-25170	(S)	Dinah '62 *(White label)*	1962	10.00	25.00
Roulette R-25180	(M)	In Love	1962	8.00	20.00
Roulette SR-25180	(S)	In Love	1962	10.00	25.00
Roulette R-25183	(M)	Drinking Again	1962	8.00	20.00
Roulette SR-25183	(S)	Drinking Again	1962	10.00	25.00
Roulette R-25189	(M)	Back To The Blues	1962	8.00	20.00
Roulette SR-25189	(S)	Back To The Blues	1962	10.00	25.00
Roulette R-25220	(M)	Dinah '63	1963	8.00	20.00
Roulette SR-25220	(S)	Dinah '63	1963	10.00	25.00
— *Original Roulette albums above have orange & pink labels.* —					
Roulette R-25244	(M)	In Tribute	1963	6.00	15.00
Roulette SR-25244	(S)	In Tribute	1963	8.00	20.00
Roulette R-25253	(M)	Stranger On Earth	1964	6.00	15.00
Roulette SR-25253	(S)	Stranger On Earth	1964	8.00	20.00
Roulette R-25269	(M)	Dinah Washington	1964	6.00	15.00
Roulette SR-25269	(S)	Dinah Washington	1964	8.00	20.00
Roulette R-25289	(M)	The Best Of Dinah Washington	1965	6.00	15.00
Roulette SR-25289	(S)	The Best Of Dinah Washington	1965	8.00	20.00
Mercury R-60928	(M)	The Queen And Quincy	1965	6.00	15.00
Mercury SR-60928	(S)	The Queen And Quincy	1965	8.00	20.00
Mercury MG-21119	(M)	Dinah Discovered	1967	6.00	15.00
Mercury SR-61119	(S)	Dinah Discovered	1967	8.00	20.00
Mercury PKW-2-121	(S)	The Original Queen Of Soul	1969	6.00	15.00
Mercury SRM-2-603	(S)	This Is My Story *(2 LPs)*	197?	6.00	15.00

WASHINGTON, ELLA

Sound Stage-7 15007	(S)	Ella Washington	1969	6.00	15.00

WASHINGTON, GINO

Kapp KL-1415	(M)	Ram Jam Band	1965	6.00	15.00
Kapp KS-3415	(S)	Ram Jam Band	1965	8.00	20.00

WATERFORD, CROWN PRINCE: *Refer to* AMOS MILBURN

WATERS, ETHEL

Remington LP-1025 (10")	(M)	Ethel Waters	1950	20.00	50.00
Jay 3010 (10")	(M)	Ethel Waters Singing Her Best	195?	20.00	50.00

Label & Catalog #		Title	Year	VG+	NM
"X" 1009	(M)	Ethel Waters	195?	14.00	35.00
Continental 16008	(M)	Ethel Waters Sings	195?	14.00	35.00

WATSON, DOC (& MERLE WATSON)
Doc also recorded with Jean Ritchie.

Folkways FA-2366	(M)	Doc Watson And Family	1963	10.00	25.00
Vanguard VRS-9152	(M)	Doc Watson	1964	8.00	20.00
Vanguard VSD-79152	(S)	Doc Watson	1964	10.00	25.00
Vanguard VRS-9170	(M)	Doc Watson And Son	1965	8.00	20.00
Vanguard VSD-79170	(S)	Doc Watson And Son	1965	10.00	25.00
Vanguard VRS-9213	(M)	Southbound	1966	6.00	15.00
Vanguard VSD-79213	(S)	Southbound	1966	8.00	20.00
Vanguard VRS-9239	(M)	Home Again	1967	6.00	15.00
Vanguard VSD-79239	(S)	Home Again	1967	8.00	20.00
Vanguard VSD-79276	(S)	Good Deal	1968	6.00	15.00
Poppy PYS-5703	(S)	The Elementary Doc Watson	1972	6.00	15.00
Poppy LA022	(S)	Then And Now	1973	6.00	15.00
Poppy LA210	(S)	Two Days In November	1974	6.00	15.00

WATSON, JOHNNY "GUITAR"
Refer to Bobby Bland / Jimmy Soul / Johnny Watson.

King LP-857	(M)	Johnny Guitar Watson	1963	75.00	200.00
Chess LP-1490	(M)	Blues Soul	1965	20.00	50.00
Chess LPS-1490	(S)	Blues Soul	1965	30.00	75.00
OKeh OKM-4118	(M)	Bad	1967	10.00	25.00
OKeh OKS-14118	(S)	Bad	1967	14.00	35.00
OKeh OKM-4124	(M)	In The Fats Bag	1967	10.00	25.00
OKeh OKS-14124	(S)	In The Fats Bag	1967	12.00	30.00
Cadet LP-4056	(M)	I Cried For You	1967	10.00	25.00
Cadet LPS-4056	(S)	I Cried For You	1967	12.00	30.00

WATSON, JOHNNY "GUITAR", & LARRY WILLIAMS

OKeh OKM-4122	(M)	Two For The Price Of One	1967	16.00	40.00
OKeh OKS-14122	(S)	Two For The Price Of One	1967	20.00	50.00

WATTS, ALAN

Warner Bros. WS-1923	(S)	The Sounds Of Hinduism	1968	10.00	25.00
Together	(S)	Dhyana: Of The Art Of Meditation	1970	12.00	30.00
Ascension	(S)	Dhyana: Of The Art Of Meditation, Vol. 2	1970	12.00	30.00
		(Both "Dhyana" albums produced by Gary Usher.)			
Electronic Universe '73	(S)	The Essential Alan Watts	1974	50.00	125.00
Ascension 2000	(S)	Dhyana: Of The Art Of Meditation	1977	8.00	20.00

WAVECRESTS, THE

Viking VKS-6606	(M)	Surftime U.S.A.	1963	12.00	30.00

WAYFARERS, THE

RCA Victor LPM-1213	(M)	The Wayfarers	1956	20.00	50.00
RCA Victor LPM-2666	(M)	Come Along With The Wayfarers	1963	6.00	15.00
RCA Victor LSP-2666	(S)	Come Along With The Wayfarers	1963	8.00	20.00
RCA Victor LPM-2735	(M)	The Wayfarers At The Hungry i	1963	6.00	15.00
RCA Victor LSP-2735	(S)	The Wayfarers At The Hungry i	1963	8.00	20.00
		— Original RCA mono albums above have "Long Play" on the bottom of the label; stereo albums have "Living Stereo" on the bottom.—			
RCA Victor LPM-2946	(M)	The Wayfarers At The World's Fair	1964	5.00	12.00
RCA Victor LSP-2946	(S)	The Wayfarers At The World's Fair	1964	6.00	15.00

WAYFARERS TRIO, THE

Mercury MG-20634	(M)	Songs Of The Blue And Grey	1961	5.00	12.00
Mercury SR-60634	(S)	Songs Of The Blue And Grey	1961	6.00	15.00

WAYNE, FRANCES

Coral CRL-56091 (10")	(M)	Frances Wayne	1954	20.00	50.00
Epic LN-3222	(M)	Songs For My Man	1956	14.00	35.00
Atlantic 1263	(M)	The Warm Sound Of Frances Wayne	1957	14.00	35.00
Brunswick BL-54022	(M)	Frances Wayne	1957	14.00	35.00

WAYNE, JOHN

RCA Victor LSP-4828	(S)	America, Why I Love Her	1972	6.00	15.00

Label & Catalog #		Title	Year	VG+	NM

WAYNE, "WEE" WILLIE

Imperial LP-9144	(M)	Travelin' Mood	1961	100.00	300.00

WE FIVE, THE

A&M LP-111	(M)	You Were On My Mind	1965	6.00	15.00
A&M SP-4111	(S)	You Were On My Mind	1965	8.00	20.00
A&M LP-138	(M)	Make Someone Happy	1967	6.00	15.00
A&M SP-4138	(S)	Make Someone Happy	1967	6.00	15.00
A&M SP-4168	(S)	The Return Of We Five	1969	6.00	15.00
Vault 136	(S)	Catch The Wind	1970	6.00	15.00

WEASELS, THE

Wing MGW-12282	(M)	The Liverpool Beat	1964	10.00	25.00
Wing SRW-16282	(S)	The Liverpool Beat	1964	12.00	30.00

WEAVERS, THE
The Weavers feature Pete Seeger.

Decca DL-5285 (10")	(M)	The Weavers	1951	20.00	50.00
Decca DL-5373 (10")	(M)	We Wish You A Merry Christmas	1952	20.00	50.00
Decca DL-8893	(M)	Best Of The Weavers	1959	12.00	30.00
Decca DL-8909	(M)	Folk Songs Around The World	1959	12.00	30.00
Decca DXB-173	(M)	Best Of The Weavers (2 LPs)	1965	8.00	20.00
Decca DXSB-7173	(E)	Best Of The Weavers (2 LPs)	1965	10.00	25.00
Vanguard VRS-9010	(M)	The Weavers At Carnegie Hall	1957	12.00	30.00
Vanguard VRS-9013	(M)	The Weavers On Tour	1957	12.00	30.00
Vanguard VRS-9022	(M)	Travelling On With The Weavers	1961	10.00	25.00
Vanguard VSD-2022	(S)	Travelling On With The Weavers	1961	12.00	30.00
Vanguard VRS-9024	(M)	The Weavers At Home	1962	10.00	25.00
Vanguard VSD-2024	(S)	The Weavers At Home	1962	12.00	30.00
Vanguard VRS-9043	(M)	Travelling On	1962	10.00	25.00
Vanguard VSD-2043	(S)	Travelling On	1962	12.00	30.00
Vanguard VRS-9075	(M)	The Weavers At Carnegie Hall, Volume 2	1962	10.00	25.00
Vanguard VSD-2075	(S)	The Weavers At Carnegie Hall, Volume 2	1962	12.00	30.00
Vanguard VRS-9101	(M)	Almanac	1963	10.00	25.00
Vanguard VSD-2101	(S)	Almanac	1963	12.00	30.00
Vanguard VRS-9150	(M)	Reunion At Carnegie Hall	1964	8.00	20.00
Vanguard VSD-2150	(S)	Reunion At Carnegie Hall	1964	10.00	25.00
Vanguard VRS-9161	(M)	Reunion At Carnegie Hall	1965	8.00	20.00
Vanguard VSD-79161	(S)	Reunion At Carnegie Hall	1965	10.00	25.00
Vanguard VRS-3001	(M)	Song Bag	1967	8.00	20.00
Vanguard VSD-73001	(S)	Song Bag	1967	10.00	25.00
Vanguard VSD-76533	(S)	The Weavers At Carnegie Hall	1970	6.00	15.00
Vanguard VSD-6537	(S)	The Weavers On Tour	1970	6.00	15.00
Vanguard VSD-15	(S)	The Weavers' Greatest Hits (2 LPs)	1971	6.00	15.00
Decca DL-74277	(S)	Weaver's Gold	1971	6.00	15.00

WEB, THE

Deram DES-18018	(S)	Fully Interlocking	1968	10.00	25.00

WEBB, JACK

RCA Victor LPM-1126	(M)	Pete Kelly's Blues (Soundtrack)	1955	20.00	50.00
Warner Bros. W-1207	(M)	You're My Girl	1958	12.00	30.00
Warner Bros. WS-1207	(S)	You're My Girl	1958	16.00	40.00

WEDGE [ORANGE WEDGE]

(No label)	(S)	Wedge	1974	100.00	250.00
Wedge	(S)	No One But Me	1975	80.00	200.00
		("No One But Me" credits Orange Wedge.)			

WEDGES, THE

Time T-2090	(M)	Hang Ten (For Surfers Only)	1963	8.00	20.00
Time ST-2090	(S)	Hang Ten (For Surfers Only)	1963	10.00	25.00

WEIGHT

International 104	(S)	Music Is The Message	1970	8.00	20.00

WEIR, BOB
Refer to Bobby & The Midnites; The Grateful Dead.

Warner Bros. BS-2627	(S)	Ace (Green label)	1972	16.00	40.00

Label & Catalog #		Title	Year	VG+	NM

WEIRD-OHS, THE
The Wierd-Ohs are a creation of Gary Usher & Co. Refer to The Silly Surfers / The Weird-Ohs.

| Mercury MG-20976 | (M) | **The Sounds Of The Weird-Ohs** | 1964 | See note below | |
| Mercury SR-60976 | (S) | **The Sounds Of The Weird-Ohs** | 1964 | See note below | |

(Although a single claims to have been taken from this album, the existence of Mercury 2/60976 is unverfied.)

WEISBERG, TIM
Weisberg aslo recorded with Dan Fogelberg.

| Nautilus NR-7 | (S) | **The Tip Of The Weisberg** | 198? | 5.00 | 15.00 |

WELCH, BOB
Welch was formerly a member of Fleetwood Mac.

| Capitol ST-11663 | (DJ) | **French Kiss** *(Picture disc)* | 1979 | 6.00 | 15.00 |

WELCH, LENNY

Cadence CLP-5068	(M)	**Since I Fell For You**	1963	14.00	35.00
Cadence CLP-25068	(S)	**Since I Fell For You**	1963	20.00	50.00
Columbia CL-2430	(M)	**Since I Fell For You**	1965	8.00	20.00
Columbia CS-9230	(S)	**Since I Fell For You**	1965	12.00	30.00

("360 Sound" label. The Columbia album is a reissue of the Cadence.)

Kapp KL-1457	(M)	**Two Different Worlds**	1965	6.00	15.00
Kapp KS-3457	(S)	**Two Different Worlds**	1965	8.00	20.00
Kapp KL-1481	(M)	**Rags To Riches**	1966	6.00	15.00
Kapp KS-3481	(S)	**Rags To Riches**	1966	8.00	20.00
Kapp KL-1517	(M)	**Lenny**	1967	6.00	15.00
Kapp KS-3517	(S)	**Lenny**	1967	8.00	20.00

WELLER, FREDDY
Weller was formerly a member of Paul Revere's Raiders.

| Columbia CS-9904 | (S) | **Games People Play** *("360 Sound" label)* | 1969 | 6.00 | 15.00 |

WELLS, JUNIOR

Delmark DL-612	(M)	**Hoodoo Man Blues**	1966	16.00	40.00
Delmark DS-612	(S)	**Hoodoo Man Blues**	1966	16.00	40.00
Vanguard VRS-9231	(M)	**It's My Life Baby**	1966	8.00	20.00
Vanguard VSD-79231	(S)	**It's My Life Baby**	1966	10.00	25.00
Delmark DLS-628	(S)	**Southside Blues Jam**	1967	8.00	20.00
Vanguard VSD-79262	(S)	**Comin' At You**	1968	8.00	20.00
Blue Rock 64002	(S)	**You're Tuff Enough**	1968	6.00	15.00
Delmark DLS-640	(S)	**Blues Hit Big Town**	1969	6.00	15.00

WELLS, KITTY

Decca DL-8293	(M)	**Country Hit Parade**	1956	20.00	50.00
Decca DL-8552	(M)	**Winner Of Your Heart**	1956	20.00	50.00
Decca DL-8858	(M)	**Dust On The Bible**	1959	20.00	50.00
Decca DL-8888	(M)	**After Dark**	1959	16.00	40.00
Decca DL-8979	(M)	**Kitty's Choice**	1960	12.00	30.00
Decca DL-78979	(S)	**Kitty's Choice**	1960	16.00	40.00

—Original Decca albums above have black & silver labels.—

Decca DL-8293	(M)	**Country Hit Parade**	1960	10.00	25.00
Decca DL-78293	(E)	**Country Hit Parade**	1960	6.00	15.00
Decca DL-8552	(M)	**Winner Of Your Heart**	1960	10.00	25.00
Decca DL-78552	(E)	**Winner Of Your Heart**	1960	6.00	15.00
Decca DL-8858	(M)	**Dust On The Bible**	1960	10.00	25.00
Decca DL-78858	(E)	**Dust On The Bible**	1960	6.00	15.00
Decca DL-8888	(M)	**After Dark**	1960	10.00	25.00
Decca DL-78888	(E)	**After Dark**	1960	6.00	15.00
Decca DL-4075	(M)	**Seasons Of My Heart**	1960	10.00	25.00
Decca DL-74075	(S)	**Seasons Of My Heart**	1960	12.00	30.00
Decca DL-4108	(M)	**Kitty Wells' Golden Favorites**	1961	10.00	25.00
Decca DL-74108	(E)	**Kitty Wells' Golden Favorites**	1961	6.00	15.00
Decca DL-4141	(M)	**Heartbreak U.S.A.**	1961	10.00	25.00
Decca DL-74141	(S)	**Heartbreak U.S.A.**	1961	12.00	30.00
Decca DL-4197	(M)	**Queen Of Country Music**	1962	10.00	25.00
Decca DL-74197	(S)	**Queen Of Country Music**	1962	12.00	30.00
Decca DL-4270	(M)	**Singing On Sunday**	1962	10.00	25.00
Decca DL-74270	(S)	**Singing On Sunday**	1962	12.00	30.00

Label & Catalog #		Title	Year	VG+	NM
Decca DL-4349	(M)	Christmas With Kitty Wells	1962	10.00	25.00
Decca DL-74349	(S)	Christmas With Kitty Wells	1962	12.00	30.00
Decca DXB-174	(M)	The Kitty Wells Story (2 LPs)	1963	8.00	20.00
Decca DXSB-7174	(P)	The Kitty Wells Story (2 LPs)	1963	10.00	25.00
Decca DL-4493	(M)	Especially For You	1964	8.00	20.00
Decca DL-74493	(S)	Especially For You	1964	10.00	25.00
Decca DL-4554	(M)	Country Music Time	1964	8.00	20.00
Decca DL-74554	(S)	Country Music Time	1964	10.00	25.00
Decca DL-4612	(M)	Burning Memories	1965	8.00	20.00
Decca DL-74612	(S)	Burning Memories	1965	10.00	25.00
Decca DL-4658	(M)	Lonesome, Sad And Blue	1965	8.00	20.00
Decca DL-74658	(S)	Lonesome, Sad And Blue	1965	10.00	25.00
Decca DL-4679	(M)	Family Gospel Sing	1965	8.00	20.00
Decca DL-74679	(S)	Family Gospel Sing	1965	10.00	25.00
Decca DL-4741	(M)	Songs Made Famous By Jim Reeves	1966	8.00	20.00
Decca DL-74741	(S)	Songs Made Famous By Jim Reeves	1966	10.00	25.00
Decca DL-4776	(M)	Country All The Way	1966	8.00	20.00
Decca DL-74776	(S)	Country All The Way	1966	10.00	25.00
Decca DL-4831	(M)	The Kitty Wells Show	1966	8.00	20.00
Decca DL-74831	(S)	The Kitty Wells Show	1966	10.00	25.00
— Original Decca albums above have black labels with "Mfrd by Decca" beneath the rainbow.—					
Decca DL-4857	(M)	Love Makes The World Go Around	1967	6.00	15.00
Decca DL-74857	(S)	Love Makes The World Go Around	1967	8.00	20.00
Decca DL-4929	(M)	Queen Of Honky Tonk Street	1967	6.00	15.00
Decca DL-74929	(S)	Queen Of Honky Tonk Street	1967	8.00	20.00
Decca DL-74961	(S)	Showcase	1968	8.00	20.00
Decca DL-75001	(S)	Kitty Wells' Greatest Hits	1968	8.00	20.00
Decca DL-75067	(S)	Cream Of Country Hits	1968	8.00	20.00
Decca DL-75098	(S)	Guilty Street	1968	8.00	20.00
Decca DL-75164	(S)	Bouquet Of Country Hits	1969	6.00	15.00
Decca DL-75221	(S)	Singin' 'Em Country	1970	6.00	15.00
Decca DL-75245	(S)	Your Love Is The Way	1970	6.00	15.00
Decca DL-75277	(S)	They're Stepping All Over My Heart	1971	6.00	15.00
Decca DL-75313	(S)	Pledging My Love	1971	6.00	15.00
Decca DL-75350	(S)	Sincerely	1972	6.00	15.00
Decca DL-75382	(S)	I've Got Yesterday	1972	6.00	15.00
WELLS, KITTY, & RED FOLEY					
Decca DL-4906	(M)	Together Again	1967	6.00	15.00
Decca DL-74906	(S)	Together Again	1967	8.00	20.00
WELLS, KITTY, & JOHNNY WRIGHT					
Decca DL-75026	(S)	We'll Stick Together	1968	8.00	20.00
Decca DL-75325	(S)	Heartwarming Gospel Songs	1972	6.00	15.00
WELLS, MARY					
Motown 600	(M)	Bye, Bye Baby, I Don't Want To Take A Chance (White label)	1961	150.00	300.00
Motown 600	(M)	Bye, Bye Baby, I Don't Want To Take A Chance	1961	60.00	150.00
Motown 605	(M)	The One Who Really Loves You	1962	60.00	150.00
Motown 607	(M)	Two Lovers	1963	40.00	100.00
Motown 611	(M)	Live On Stage	1963	30.00	75.00
— Original Motown albums above have the company address above the spindle hole on the label.—					
Motown 612	(M)	Second Time Around	1963	Unreleased	
Motown 616	(M)	Mary Wells' Greatest Hits	1964	10.00	25.00
Motown 617	(M)	My Guy	1964	14.00	35.00
Motown 653	(M)	Vintage Stock	1966	10.00	25.00
Motown 653	(S)	Vintage Stock	1966	12.00	30.00
20th Century TFM-3171	(M)	Mary Wells	1965	16.00	40.00
20th Century TFS-4171	(S)	Mary Wells	1965	20.00	50.00
20th Century TFM-3178	(M)	Love Songs To The Beatles	1965	20.00	50.00
20th Century TFS-4178	(S)	Love Songs To The Beatles	1965	30.00	75.00
Movietone 71010	(M)	Ooh	1966	10.00	25.00
Movietone 72010	(S)	Ooh	1966	12.00	30.00
Atco 33-199	(M)	Two Sides Of Mary Wells	1966	10.00	25.00
Atco SD-33-199	(S)	Two Sides Of Mary Wells	1966	12.00	30.00
Jubilee JGS-8018	(S)	Servin' Up Some Soul	1968	10.00	25.00
EPK ARE-37540	(S)	In And Out Of Love	1981	6.00	15.00

Label & Catalog #		Title	Year	VG+	NM

WELZ, JOEY
Welz was formerly a member of Bill Haley's Comets.

Palmer 13401	(S)	Vintage Ballads To Remember Her By	1970	6.00	15.00
Palmer 13402	(S)	Rock Revival	1970	6.00	15.00
Music City 5005	(S)	Kosmik City Blues And Mellow Dreams	1978	4.00	10.00

WENDI & BONNI

Skye SK-1006D	(S)	Genesis	197?	20.00	50.00

WESLEY, FRED, & THE JB'S [FRED & THE NEW JB'S]
The JB's are James Brown's backing group and were produced by JB. Refer to The JB's.

People PE-5603	(S)	Doing It To Death	1973	6.00	15.00
People PE-6602	(S)	Damn Right I Am Somebody	1974	6.00	15.00
People PE-6604	(S)	Breakin' Bread	1974	6.00	15.00

WESLEY, FRED [THE FRED WESLEY HORNS]
Fred Wesley is a member of the Parliament/Funkadelic community.

Atlantic 18214	(S)	A Blow For Me, A Toot For You	1977	6.00	15.00

WEST

Epic BN-26380	(S)	West	1968	8.00	20.00
Epic BN-26433	(S)	Bridges	1969	8.00	20.00

WEST, ADAM, & BURT WARD: *Refer to* NELSON RIDDLE

WESS, JIM, & THE UPSETTERS

ABC S-651	(S)	We Remember Otis	1968	6.00	15.00

WEST, DOTTIE

Starday SLP-302	(M)	Country Girl Singing Sensation	1964	10.00	25.00
Starday SLP-352	(M)	Queens Of Country Music	1965	10.00	25.00
RCA Victor LPM-3368	(M)	Here Comes My Baby	1965	6.00	15.00
RCA Victor LSP-3368	(S)	Here Comes My Baby	1965	8.00	20.00
RCA Victor LPM-3490	(M)	Dottie West Sings	1966	6.00	15.00
RCA Victor LSP-3490	(S)	Dottie West Sings	1966	8.00	20.00
RCA Victor LPM-3587	(M)	Suffer Time	1966	6.00	15.00
RCA Victor LSP-3587	(S)	Suffer Time	1966	8.00	20.00
RCA Victor LPM-3693	(M)	With All My Heart And Soul	1967	8.00	20.00
RCA Victor LSP-3693	(S)	With All My Heart And Soul	1967	8.00	20.00
RCA Victor LPM-3784	(M)	Dottie West Sings Sacred Ballads	1967	8.00	20.00
RCA Victor LSP-3784	(S)	Dottie West Sings Sacred Ballads	1967	8.00	20.00
RCA Victor LPM-3830	(M)	I'll Help You Forget Her	1967	8.00	20.00
RCA Victor LSP-3830	(S)	I'll Help You Forget Her	1967	8.00	20.00
RCA Victor LPM-3932	(M)	What I'm Cut Out To Be	1968	12.00	30.00
RCA Victor LSP-3932	(S)	What I'm Cut Out To Be	1968	6.00	15.00
RCA Victor LSP-4004	(S)	Country Girl	1968	6.00	15.00
— Original RCA albums above have black labels with Nipper on top.—					
RCA Victor APD1-0151	(Q)	Dottie West	1973	6.00	15.00
RCA Victor APD1-0543	(Q)	House Of Love	1974	6.00	15.00

WEST, JEAN

Prestige Int. PRLP-13038	(M)	Roamin' The Blue Ridge	1962	12.00	30.00
Prestige Int. PRLP-13049	(M)	Country Bluegrass	1962	12.00	30.00

WEST, MAE

Decca DL-9016	(M)	The Fabulous Mae West	1955	30.00	75.00
— Decca albums above have black & silver labels.—					
Decca DL-9016	(M)	The Fabulous Mae West	196?	10.00	25.00
Decca DL-79016	(E)	The Fabulous Mae West	196?	6.00	15.00
— Decca albums above have black rainbow labels.—					
Tower T-5028	(M)	Way Out West	1966	10.00	25.00
Tower ST-5028	(S)	Way Out West	1966	12.00	30.00
Dragonet D-64	(M)	Wild Christmas	196?	6.00	15.00
Decca DL-79176	(P)	Original Voice Tracks From Her Greatest Movies *(With poster)*	1970	8.00	20.00
MGM SE-4869	(S)	Great Balls Of Fire	1972	6.00	15.00

Label & Catalog #		Title	Year	VG+	NM

WEST, SPEEDY, & JIMMY BRYANT

Capitol H-520 (10")	(M)	Two Guitars Country Style	1954	80.00	200.00
Capitol T-520	(M)	Two Guitars Country Style	1956	40.00	100.00

WEST, SPEEDY

Capitol T-956	(M)	West Of Hawaii	1958	30.00	75.00
Capitol T-1341	(M)	Steel Guitar	1960	16.00	40.00
Capitol ST-1341	(S)	Steel Guitar	1960	20.00	50.00
Capitol T-1835	(M)	Guitar Spectacular	1962	14.00	35.00
Capitol ST-1835	(S)	Guitar Spectacular	1962	16.00	40.00

WEST, BRUCE & LAING

Columbia CQ-31929	(Q)	Why Dontcha'	1973	6.00	15.00
Columbia CQ-32216	(Q)	Whatever Turns You On	1973	6.00	15.00

WEST COAST POP ART EXPERIMENTAL BAND, THE
The WCPAEB features Dan Harris, Shaun Harris and Bob Markley.

Fifo M101	(M)	West Coast Pop Art Experimental Band	1966	1,000.00	2,000.00
		(The price includes a regular cover.)			
Fifo M101	(M)	West Coast Pop Art Experimental Band	1966	300.00	500.00
		(The price is for the album in a plain cardboard jacket.)			
Razzberry Sawfly 800	(M)	West Coast Pop Art Experimental Band	1980	50.00	125.00
		(Razzberry Sawfly 800 is a reissue of Fifo 101.)			
Reprise R-6247	(M)	Part One	1967	12.00	30.00
Reprise RS-6247	(S)	Part One	1967	16.00	40.00
Reprise R-6270	(M)	Volume 2	1967	12.00	30.00
Reprise RS-6270	(S)	Volume 2	1967	16.00	40.00
Reprise RS-6298	(S)	A Child's Guide To Good And Evil	1968	12.00	30.00
Amos AAS-7004	(S)	Where's My Daddy	1969	16.00	40.00

WESTFAUSTER

Nasco 9008	(S)	In A King's Dream	1971	24.00	60.00

WESTON, KIM
Ms. Weston also recorded with Marvin Gaye.

MGM E-4477	(M)	For The First Time	1967	10.00	25.00
MGM SE-4477	(S)	For The First Time	1967	12.00	30.00
Volt VOS-6014	(S)	Kim Kim Kim	1971	8.00	20.00

WET WILLIE

Epic PRO-428	(DJ)	Manorisms/Live Concert Series	1978	8.00	20.00

WHALE FEATHERS

Nasco 9003	(S)	Whalefeathers Declare	1969	20.00	50.00
Nasco 9005	(S)	Whalefeathers	1970	20.00	50.00

WHATNAUTS, THE

Stang 1005	(S)	Introducing The Whatnauts	1970	6.00	15.00
Stang 1012	(S)	Reaching For The Stars	1971	6.00	15.00

WHEELS, BURT, & THE SPEEDSTERS

Coronet CX-216	(M)	Sounds Of The Big Racers	196?	10.00	25.00

WHEELS, THE

Montgomery Ward 10	(S)	Sounds Of The Hot Rods	196?	24.00	60.00

WHITCOMB, IAN

Tower T-5004	(M)	You Turn Me On	1965	12.00	30.00
Tower DT-5004	(E)	You Turn Me On	1965	10.00	25.00
Tower T-5042	(M)	Mod, Mod, Music Hall	1966	8.00	20.00
Tower ST-5042	(S)	Mod, Mod, Music Hall	1966	10.00	25.00
Tower T-5071	(M)	Yellow Underground	1967	8.00	20.00
Tower ST-5071	(S)	Yellow Underground	1967	10.00	25.00
Tower ST-5100	(S)	Sock Me Some Rock	1968	10.00	25.00

WHITE, BUKKA

Blue Horizon 4604	(M)	Blues Master, Volume 4	196?	10.00	25.00
Herwin 201	(M)	Sic'em Dogs	1969	6.00	15.00
Takoma 1001	(M)	Mississippi Blues	1969	6.00	15.00

Label & Catalog #		Title	Year	VG+	NM
Arhoolie 1019	(M)	Sky Songs, Volume 1	1975	6.00	15.00
Arhoolie 1020	(M)	Sky Songs, Volume 2	1975	6.00	15.00

WHITE, JOSH
Refer to Leadbelly.

Mercury MG-25015 (10")	(M)	Josh White Sings	1949	60.00	150.00
Decca DL-5082 (10")	(M)	Ballads	1950	40.00	100.00
Stinson 14 (10")	(M)	Blues	1950	40.00	100.00
Stinson 15 (10")	(M)	Folk Songs	1950	40.00	100.00
London LL-338 (10")	(M)	Josh White	1951	40.00	100.00
London LL-341 (10")	(M)	Josh White Program	1951	40.00	100.00
Decca DL-5247 (10")	(M)	Ballads, Volume 2	1952	40.00	100.00
EmArcy MG-26010 (10")	(M)	Strange Fruit	1954	40.00	100.00
Elektra 701 (10")	(M)	The Story Of John Henry	1955	30.00	75.00
Period 1115 (10")	(M)	Josh White Comes A-Visiting	1956	30.00	75.00
London LL-1341	(M)	A Josh White Program	1956	16.00	40.00
ABC-Paramount 124	(M)	The Josh White Stories	1956	20.00	50.00
ABC-Paramount 166	(M)	The Josh White Stories, Volume 2	1957	20.00	50.00
Mercury MG-20203	(M)	Josh White's Blues	1957	20.00	50.00
Elektra EKL-102	(M)	Josh At Midnight	1956	12.00	30.00
Elektra EKL-114	(M)	Josh	1957	12.00	30.00
Elektra EKL-123	(M)	25th Anniversary Album	1957	12.00	30.00
Elektra EKL-158	(M)	Chain Gang Songs	1958	12.00	30.00
Decca DL-8665	(M)	Josh White	1958	12.00	30.00
Mercury MG-20821	(M)	The Beginning	1963	10.00	25.00
Mercury SR-60821	(S)	The Beginning	1963	12.00	30.00

WHITE, JOSH, & BIG BILL BROONZY

Period 1209	(M)	Josh White & Big Bill Broonzy	1956	30.00	75.00

WHITE, KITTY

EmArcy MG-36020	(M)	A New Voice In Jazz	1955	20.00	50.00
EmArcy MG-36068	(M)	Kitty White	1955	20.00	50.00
Pacifica PL-802 (10")	(M)	Kitty White	1955	20.00	50.00
Pacifica 2002	(M)	A Moment Of Love	1956	16.00	40.00
Mercury MG-20183	(M)	Folk Songs	1957	16.00	40.00
World Pacific WP-1406	(M)	Intimate	195?	10.00	25.00
Roulette R-25020	(M)	Sweet Talk	1960	8.00	20.00
Roulette RS-25020	(S)	Sweet Talk	1960	12.00	30.00

WHITE, TONY JOE

Monument SLP-18114	(S)	Black And White	1969	6.00	15.00
Monument SLP-18133	(S)	Tony Joe White Continued	1969	6.00	15.00
Monument SLP-18142	(S)	Tony Joe	1970	6.00	15.00
Warner Bros. BS-1900	(S)	Tony Joe White	1971	4.00	10.00
Warner Bros. BS-2580	(S)	The Train I'm On	1972	4.00	10.00
Warner Bros. BS-2708	(S)	Homemade Ice Cream	1973	4.00	10.00
20th Century 523	(S)	Eyes	1977	4.00	10.00

WHITE BOY & THE AVERAGE RAT BAND

Tradewind MM-11761	(S)	White Boy & The Average Rat Band	1975	50.00	125.00

WHITE DUCK

Uni 73140	(S)	In Season	1972	6.00	15.00
Uni 73122	(S)	White Duck	1971	6.00	15.00

WHITE ELEPHANT

Just Sunshine 3000	(S)	White Elephant	1973	6.00	15.00

WHITE LIGHT

Century 39955	(S)	White Light (With "Heartbreak Hotel")	1968	50.00	125.00
Century 39955	(S)	White Light (Without "Heartbreak Hotel")	1969	60.00	150.00

WHITE LIGHTNIN'

ABC 690	(S)	File Under Rock	1969	6.00	15.00

WHITE PLAINS

Deram DES-18045	(S)	My Baby Loves Loving	1970	6.00	15.00

Label & Catalog #		Title	Year	VG+	NM
WHITE SUMMER					
(No label)	(S)	White Summer	197?	80.00	200.00
WHITE WITCH					
Capricorn CPN-0107	(S)	White Witch	1973	6.00	15.00
Capricorn CPN-0129	(S)	A Spiritual Greeting	1974	5.00	12.00
WHITEHEAD, CHARLIE, & THE SWAMP DOGG BAND					
Fungus FB-25145	(S)	Charlie Whitehead	197?	6.00	15.00
WHITING, MARGARET					
Ms. Whiting also recorded with Mel Torme.					
Capitol H-163 (10")	(M)	South Pacific	1950	20.00	50.00
Capitol H-209 (10")	(M)	Margaret Whiting Sings Rodgers & Hart	1950	20.00	50.00
Capitol H-234 (10")	(M)	Songs	1950	20.00	50.00
Capitol T-410	(M)	Love Songs	1955	14.00	35.00
Capitol T-685	(M)	For The Starry-Eyed	1955	14.00	35.00
Dot DLP-3072	(M)	Goin' Places	1957	10.00	25.00
Dot DLP-3113	(M)	Margaret	1958	6.00	15.00
Dot DLP-25113	(S)	Margaret	1958	8.00	20.00
Dot DLP-3176	(M)	Margaret Whiting Great Hits	1959	6.00	15.00
Dot DLP-25176	(S)	Margaret Whiting Great Hits	1959	8.00	20.00
Dot DLP-3235	(M)	Ten Top Hits	1960	6.00	15.00
Dot DLP-25235	(S)	Ten Top Hits	1960	8.00	20.00
Dot DLP-3337	(M)	Just A Dream	1960	6.00	15.00
Dot DLP-25337	(S)	Just A Dream	1960	8.00	20.00
Verve V-4038	(M)	The Jerome Kern Song Book	1960	6.00	15.00
Verve V6-4038	(S)	The Jerome Kern Song Book	1960	8.00	20.00
MGM E-4006	(M)	Past Midnight	1961	6.00	15.00
MGM SE-4006	(S)	Past Midnight	1961	8.00	20.00
WHITMAN, SLIM					
RCA Victor LPM-3217 (10")	(M)	Slim Whitman Sings And Yodels	1954	80.00	200.00
Imperial LP-3004 (10")	(M)	America's Favorite Folk Artist	1954	150.00	300.00
Imperial LP-9003	(M)	Favorites	1956	20.00	50.00
Imperial LP-9026	(M)	Slim Whitman Sings	1957	20.00	50.00
Imperial LP-9056	(M)	Slim Whitman Sings	1958	20.00	50.00
Imperial LP-9064	(M)	Slim Whitman Sings	1959	20.00	50.00
— Original Imperial albums above have maroon labels.—					
Imperial LP-9003	(M)	Favorites	1958	12.00	30.00
Imperial LP-9026	(M)	Slim Whitman Sings	195?	12.00	30.00
Imperial LP-9056	(M)	Slim Whitman Sings	195?	12.00	30.00
Imperial LP-9064	(M)	Slim Whitman Sings	195?	12.00	30.00
Imperial LP-9077	(M)	Annie Laurie	1959	12.00	30.00
Imperial LP-9088	(M)	I'll Walk With God	1960	12.00	30.00
Imperial LP-12032	(E)	I'll Walk With God	196?	5.00	12.00
Imperial LP-9100	(M)	Country Hits, Volume 1	1966	6.00	15.00
Imperial LP-9102	(M)	Million Record Hits	1960	12.00	30.00
Imperial LP-9102	(M)	Song Of The Old Waterwheel	1966	6.00	15.00
Imperial LP-9104	(M)	Country Hits, Volume 2	1966	6.00	15.00
Imperial LP-9105	(M)	My Best To You	1966	6.00	15.00
Imperial LP-9106	(M)	Country Favorites	1966	6.00	15.00
Imperial LP-9135	(M)	First Visit To Britain	1960	10.00	25.00
Imperial LP-9137	(M)	Just Call Me Lonesome	1961	10.00	25.00
Imperial LP-9156	(M)	Once In A Lifetime	1961	10.00	25.00
Imperial LP-9171	(M)	Forever	1966	6.00	15.00
Imperial LP-9194	(M)	Slim Whitman Sings	1962	10.00	25.00
Imperial LP-12194	(S)	Slim Whitman Sings	1962	12.00	30.00
Imperial LP-9209	(M)	Heart Songs And Love Songs	1962	10.00	25.00
Imperial LP-9226	(M)	I'm A Lonely Wanderer	1963	10.00	25.00
Imperial LP-9235	(M)	Yodeling	1963	10.00	25.00
Imperial LP-9245	(M)	Irish Songs, The Whitman Way	1963	10.00	25.00
Imperial LP-9252	(M)	All Time Favorites	1964	10.00	25.00
— Original Imperial albums above have black labels with stars on top.—					
Imperial LP-9268	(M)	Country Songs/City Hits	1964	6.00	15.00
Imperial LP-12268	(S)	Country Songs/City Hits	1964	8.00	20.00
Imperial LP-9277	(M)	Love Song Of The Waterfall	1964	6.00	15.00
Imperial LP-12277	(S)	Love Song Of The Waterfall	1964	8.00	20.00

Label & Catalog #		Title	Year	VG+	NM
Imperial LP-9288	(M)	Reminiscing	1965	6.00	15.00
Imperial LP-12288	(S)	Reminiscing	1965	8.00	20.00
Imperial LP-9303	(M)	More Than Yesterday	1965	6.00	15.00
Imperial LP-12303	(S)	More Than Yesterday	1965	8.00	20.00
Camden CAL-954	(M)	Birmingham Jail	1966	8.00	20.00
Camden CAS-954	(E)	Birmingham Jail	1966	5.00	12.00
		(Camden 954 is a repackage of RCA 3217.)			
Imperial LP-9308	(M)	God's Hand In Mine	1966	5.00	12.00
Imperial LP-9313	(M)	A Travelin' Man	1966	5.00	12.00
Imperial LP-12313	(S)	A Travelin' Man	1966	6.00	15.00
Imperial LP-9333	(M)	A Time For Love	1966	5.00	12.00
Imperial LP-12333	(S)	A Time For Love	1966	6.00	15.00
Imperial LP-9342	(M)	15th Anniversary	1967	5.00	12.00
Imperial LP-12342	(S)	15th Anniversary	1967	6.00	15.00
Imperial LP-9356	(M)	Country Memories	1967	5.00	12.00
Imperial LP-12356	(S)	Country Memories	1967	6.00	15.00
Imperial LP-12375	(S)	In Love, The Whitman Way	1968	6.00	15.00
Imperial LP-12411	(S)	Happy Street	1969	6.00	15.00
Imperial LP-12436	(S)	Slim	1969	6.00	15.00
Imperial LP-12448	(S)	The Slim Whitman Christmas Album	1969	6.00	15.00

WHITNEY, MARVA

Label & Catalog #		Title	Year	VG+	NM
King KS-1053	(S)	I Sing Soul	1969	12.00	30.00
King KS-1062	(S)	It's My Thing	1969	12.00	30.00
King KS-1079	(S)	Live And Lowdown At The Apollo	1969	12.00	30.00
		(King 1053, 1062 and 1079 were produced by James Brown.)			

WHO, THE

The Who are Roger Daltrey, John Entwhistle, Keith Moon and Pete Townshend. Moon died in 1978 and was replaced by Kenny Jones of The Faces.

Label & Catalog #		Title	Year	VG+	NM
Decca DL-4664	(M)	The Who Sing My Generation	1966	40.00	100.00
Decca DL-74664	(E)	The Who Sing My Generation	1966	24.00	60.00
Decca DL-4892	(M)	Happy Jack	1967	20.00	50.00
Decca DL-74892	(S)	Happy Jack	1967	20.00	50.00
		("Happy Jack" and "Don't Look Away" are rechanneled.)			
Decca DL-4950	(DJ)	The Who Sell Out *(White label)*	1967	80.00	200.00
		(Special promo with all of the "commercials" on one side.)			
Decca DL-4950	(M)	The Who Sell Out	1967	30.00	75.00
Decca DL-74950	(S)	The Who Sell Out	1967	20.00	50.00
Decca DL-5064	(DJ)	Magic Bus/The Who On Tour	1968	60.00	150.00
		(White label. Mono.)			
Decca DL-75064	(E)	Magic Bus/The Who On Tour	1968	20.00	50.00
		("Magic Bus," "I Can't Reach You" and "Tatoo" are stereo on this LP.)			
Decca DXW-7205	(DJ)	Tommy *(White label. Mono)*	1969	80.00	200.00
Decca DXSW-7205	(S)	Tommy *(2 LPs with booklet)*	1969	16.00	40.00
Decca DL-79175	(DJ)	Live At Leeds *(White label)*	1970	40.00	100.00
Decca DL-79175	(S)	Live At Leeds	1970	16.00	40.00
		(Fold-open jacket includes twelve different inserts and photos including reproductions of old contracts.)			
Decca DL-79182	(S)	Who's Next	1971	8.00	20.00
Track 2408-102	(S)	Who's Next	1971	40.00	100.00
		(Black Track label reads "Made in USA" on the bottom. Manufactured for export and issued in a regular UK cover.)			
Decca DL-79184	(S)	Meaty, Beaty, Big & Bouncy	1971	8.00	20.00
		("I Can't Explain," "Anyway, Anyhow, Anywhere," "Substitute," "My Generation," "Pictures Of Lily" and an alternate take of "Magic Bus" are rechanneled on this album.)			
MCA 10004	(S)	Quadrophenia *(2 LPs)*	1973	6.00	15.00
Track 2126	(S)	Odds And Sods	1974	6.00	15.00
Track 2-4067	(P)	A Quick One / The Who Sell Out *(2 LPs)*	1974	6.00	15.00
Track 2-4068	(P)	Magic Bus / My Generation *(2 LPs)*	1974	6.00	15.00
MCA 2044	(E)	The Who Sing My Generation	1974	16.00	40.00
MCA 2045	(P)	Happy Jack	1974	16.00	40.00
MCA 2161	(P)	The Who By Numbers	1975	3.50	8.00
MCA 3050	(DJ)	Who Are You *(White label)*	1978	10.00	25.00
MCA 3050	(S)	Who Are You	1978	3.50	8.00
MCAP-14950	(S)	Who Are You *(Picture disc)*	1979	6.00	15.00
Direct Disc SD-16610	(S)	Who Are You	1979	8.00	25.00
MCA 11005	(P)	The Kids Are Alright *(2 LPs)*	1979	4.00	10.00

Label & Catalog #		Title	Year	VG+	NM
Warner Bros. WBMS-116	(DJ)	**Filling In The Gaps** (2 LPs)	1981	30.00	75.00
Warner Bros. 23731	(DJ)	**It's Hard** (Quiex II vinyl)	1982	8.00	20.00
Mobile Fidelity MFSL-115	(S)	**Face Dances**	1984	5.00	15.00

WHO, THE / THE STRAWBERRY ALARM CLOCK
Decca DL-734568	(S)	**The Who / The Strawberry Alarm Clock**	1969	60.00	150.00
		(Available briefly in 1969 through Philco Electronics stores.)			

WICHITA FALLS
Imperial LP-12417	(S)	**Life Is But A Dream**	1968	6.00	15.00

WICHITA TRAIN WHISTLE, THE
The Whistle features Michael Nesmith.
Dot DLP-25861	(S)	**The Wichita Train Whistle Sings**	1968	16.00	40.00

WIERD-OHS, THE: Refer to THE WEIRD-OHS

WIGGINS, LITTLE ROY
Starday SLP-188	(M)	**Mister Steel Guitar**	195?	16.00	40.00
Starday SLP-259	(M)	**The Fabulous Steel Guitar Artistry**	196?	12.00	30.00
Starday SLP-392	(M)	**Nashville Steel Guitar**	196?	10.00	25.00

WIGWAM
Forecast FTS-3089	(S)	**Tombstone Valentine** (2 LPs)	1971	8.00	20.00

WILBURN BROTHERS, THE
Decca DL-8576	(M)	**The Wilburn Brothers**	1957	20.00	50.00
Decca DL-8774	(M)	**Side By Side**	1958	14.00	35.00
Decca DL-78774	(S)	**Side By Side**	1958	20.00	50.00
Decca DL-8959	(M)	**Livin' In God's Country**	1959	14.00	35.00
Decca DL-78959	(S)	**Livin' In God's Country**	1959	20.00	50.00
		—Original Decca albums above have black & silver labels.—			
Decca DL-4058	(M)	**The Big Heartbreak**	1960	8.00	20.00
Decca DL-74058	(S)	**The Big Heartbreak**	1960	12.00	30.00
Decca DL-4122	(M)	**City Limits**	1961	8.00	20.00
Decca DL-74122	(S)	**City Limits**	1961	12.00	30.00
Decca DL-4142	(M)	**The Wilburn Brothers Sing**	1961	8.00	20.00
Decca DL-74142	(S)	**The Wilburn Brothers Sing**	1961	12.00	30.00
King 746	(M)	**The Wonderful Wilburn Brothers**	1961	30.00	75.00
Decca DL-4225	(M)	**Folk Songs**	1962	6.00	15.00
Decca DL-74225	(S)	**Folk Songs**	1962	8.00	20.00
Decca DL-4391	(M)	**Trouble's Back In Town**	1963	6.00	15.00
Decca DL-74391	(S)	**Trouble's Back In Town**	1963	8.00	20.00
Decca DL-4464	(M)	**Take Up Thy Cross**	1964	6.00	15.00
Decca DL-74464	(S)	**Take Up Thy Cross**	1964	8.00	20.00
Decca DL-4544	(M)	**Never Alone**	1964	6.00	15.00
Decca DL-74544	(S)	**Never Alone**	1964	8.00	20.00
Decca DL-4615	(M)	**Country Gold**	1965	6.00	15.00
Decca DL-74615	(S)	**Country Gold**	1965	8.00	20.00
Decca DL-4645	(M)	**I'm Gonna Tie One On Tonight**	1965	6.00	15.00
Decca DL-74645	(S)	**I'm Gonna Tie One On Tonight**	1965	8.00	20.00
Decca DL-4721	(M)	**The Wilburn Brothers Show**	1966	14.00	35.00
Decca DL-74721	(S)	**The Wilburn Brothers Show**	1966	16.00	40.00
Decca DL-4764	(M)	**Let's Go Country**	1966	6.00	15.00
Decca DL-74764	(S)	**Let's Go Country**	1966	8.00	20.00
Decca DL-4824	(M)	**Two For The Show**	1967	6.00	15.00
Decca DL-74824	(S)	**Two For The Show**	1967	8.00	20.00
Decca DL-4871	(M)	**Cool Country**	1967	6.00	15.00
Decca DL-74871	(S)	**Cool Country**	1967	6.00	15.00
Decca DL-74954	(S)	**It's Another World**	1968	6.00	15.00
Decca DL-75002	(S)	**The Wilburn Brothers' Greatest Hits**	1968	6.00	15.00
Decca DL-75087	(S)	**We Need A Lot More Happiness**	1969	6.00	15.00
Decca DL-75123	(S)	**It Looks Like The Sun's Gonna Shine**	1969	6.00	15.00
Decca DL-75173	(S)	**Little Johnny From Down The Street**	1970	6.00	15.00
Decca DL-75214	(S)	**Sing Your Heart Out, Country Boy**	1970	6.00	15.00
Decca DL-75291	(S)	**That She's Leaving Feeling**	1971	6.00	15.00

WILD COUNTRY: Refer to ALABAMA

Label & Catalog #		Title	Year	VG+	NM

WILD ONES, THE

| United Arts. UAL-6450 | (M) | The Arthur Sound | 1965 | 10.00 | 25.00 |
| United Arts. UAS-6450 | (S) | The Arthur Sound | 1965 | 12.00 | 30.00 |

WILD TCHOUPITOULAS
Wild Tchoupitoulas is a pseudonym for The Neville Brothers.

| Island 9360 | (S) | Wild Tchoupitoulas | 1976 | 6.00 | 15.00 |

WILD THING

| Elektra EKS-74059 | (S) | Partyin' | 1969 | 6.00 | 15.00 |

WILDCATS, THE

| United Arts. UAL-3031 | (M) | Bandstand Record Hop | 1958 | 20.00 | 50.00 |

WILDE, MARTY

| Epic LN-3686 | (M) | Bad Boy | 1960 | 30.00 | 75.00 |
| Epic LN-3711 | (M) | Wilde About Marty | 1960 | 24.00 | 60.00 |

WILDWEEDS, THE
Wildweeds features Al Anderson, later of NRBQ.

| Vanguard VSD-6552 | (S) | Wildweeds | 1970 | 12.00 | 30.00 |

WILEY, LEE: *Refer to* GOLDMINE'S PRICE GUIDE TO COLLECTIBLE JAZZ ALBUMS

WILKINSON TRI-CYCLE

| Date TES-4016 | (S) | Wilkinson Tri-cycle | 1969 | 6.00 | 15.00 |

WILLETT, SLIM

| Audio Lab AL-1542 | (M) | Slim Willett | 195? | 40.00 | 100.00 |

WILLIAMS, ANDY

Cadence CLP-3030	(M)	Lonely Street	1960	8.00	20.00
Cadence CLP-25030	(S)	Lonely Street	1960	10.00	25.00
Cadence CLP-3054	(M)	Andy Williams' Best	1962	8.00	20.00
Cadence CLP-25054	(S)	Andy Williams' Best	1962	10.00	25.00
Cadence CLP-3061	(M)	Million Seller Songs	1962	8.00	20.00
Cadence CLP-25061	(S)	Million Seller Songs	1962	10.00	25.00

WILLIAMS, BILLY
Mr. Williams was formerly a member of The Charioteers.

Coral CRL-57184	(M)	Billy Williams	1957	20.00	50.00
MGM E-3400	(M)	The Billy Williams Quartet	1957	20.00	50.00
Mercury MG-20317	(M)	Billy Williams Singing Oh Yeah	1958	20.00	50.00
Wing MGW-12131	(M)	Vote For Billy Williams	1959	16.00	40.00
Coral CRL-57251	(M)	Half Sweet, Half Beat	1959	20.00	50.00
Coral CRL-757251	(S)	Half Sweet, Half Beat	1959	30.00	75.00
Coral CRL-57343	(M)	The Billy Williams Revue	1960	20.00	50.00
Coral CRL-757343	(S)	The Billy Williams Revue	1960	30.00	75.00

WILLIAMS, DENIECE

| Columbia HC-47952 | (S) | Niecy *(Half-speed master)* | 198? | 12.00 | 35.00 |

WILLIAMS, DON

| ABC SPPD-44 | (DJ) | Expression *(Picture disc)* | 1978 | 6.00 | 15.00 |

WILLIAMS, HANK [LUKE THE DRIFTER]
On several albums, MGM addded strings and choruses to the original recordings; in some cases the mono albums do not have the sweetening but the stereos do. On the "Hank With Strings" albums, the sweetening is on both the mono and stereo versions; the stereo albums have Hank's original mono tracks with the sweetening in stereo. Most albums with the strings are avoided by all but the completist.

MGM E-107 (10")	(M)	Hank Williams Sings	1952	100.00	250.00
MGM E-168 (10")	(M)	Moanin' The Blues	1952	100.00	250.00
MGM E-202 (10")	(M)	Hank Williams Memorial Album	1953	100.00	250.00
MGM E-203 (10")	(M)	Hank Williams As Luke The Drifter	1953	100.00	250.00
MGM E-242 (10")	(M)	Honky Tonkin'	1954	100.00	250.00
MGM E-243 (10")	(M)	I Saw The Light	1954	100.00	250.00
MGM E-291 (10")	(M)	Ramblin' Man	1954	100.00	250.00
MGM E-3219	(M)	Ramblin' Man	1955	50.00	125.00
MGM E-3267	(M)	Hank Williams As Luke The Drifter	1955	50.00	125.00

Label & Catalog #		Title	Year	VG+	NM
MGM E-3272	(M)	Hank Williams Memorial Album	1955	50.00	125.00
MGM E-3330	(M)	Moanin' The Blues	1956	50.00	125.00
MGM E-3331	(M)	I Saw The Light *(Yellow label. Green cover)*	1956	70.00	175.00
MGM E-3331	(M)	I Saw The Light *(Yellow label. Church cover)*	1959	50.00	125.00
MGM E-3412	(M)	Honky Tonkin'	1957	50.00	125.00
MGM E-3560	(M)	Sing Me A Blue Song	1957	50.00	125.00
MGM E-3605	(M)	The Immortal Hank Williams	1958	50.00	125.00
MGM 3E-2	(M)	36 Of Hank Williams' Greatest Hits *(3 LPs)*	195?	80.00	200.00
MGM 3E-4	(M)	36 More Greatest Hits *(3 LPs)*	195?	80.00	200.00
MGM E-3733	(M)	The Unforgettable Hank Williams	1959	50.00	125.00
		— Original MGM albums above have yellow labels.—			
MGM E-3219	(M)	Ramblin' Man	1960	12.00	30.00
MGM E-3267	(M)	Hank Williams As Luke The Drifter	1960	12.00	30.00
MGM E-3272	(M)	Hank Williams Memorial Album	1960	12.00	30.00
MGM E-3330	(M)	Moanin' The Blues	1960	12.00	30.00
MGM E-3331	(M)	I Saw The Light	1960	12.00	30.00
MGM E-3412	(M)	Honky Tonkin'	1960	12.00	30.00
MGM E-3560	(M)	Sing Me A Blue Song	1960	12.00	30.00
MGM E-3605	(M)	The Immortal Hank Williams	1960	12.00	30.00
MGM E-3733	(M)	The Unforgettable Hank Williams	1960	12.00	30.00
MGM 3E-2	(M)	36 Of Hank Williams' Greatest Hits *(3 LPs)*	1960	40.00	100.00
MGM 3E-4	(M)	36 More Greatest Hits *(3 LPs)*	1960	40.00	100.00
MGM E-3803	(M)	The Lonesome Sound Of Hank Williams	1960	12.00	30.00
MGM E-3850	(M)	Wait For The Light To Shine	1960	16.00	40.00
MGM E-3918	(M)	Hank Williams' Greatest Hits	1961	12.00	30.00
MGM E-3923	(M)	Hank Williams Lives Again	1961	12.00	30.00
MGM E-3924	(M)	Sing Me A Blue Song	1961	12.00	30.00
MGM E-3925	(M)	Wanderin' Around	1961	12.00	30.00
MGM E-3926	(M)	I'm Blue Inside	1961	12.00	30.00
MGM E-3928	(M)	First, Last And Always, Hank Williams	1961	12.00	30.00
		(MGM 3928 is a repackage of 3605.)			
MGM E-3955	(M)	The Spirit Of Hank Williams	1961	12.00	30.00
MGM E-3999	(M)	On Stage! Hank Williams Recorded Live	1962	12.00	30.00
MGM SE-3999	(E)	Hank Williams On Stage Recorded Live	1962	6.00	15.00
MGM E-4040	(M)	14 More Greatest Hits, Volume 2	1962	10.00	25.00
MGM E-4109	(M)	Hank Williams On Stage, Volume 2	1963	10.00	25.00
MGM SE-4109	(E)	Hank Williams On Stage, Volume 2	1963	6.00	15.00
MGM E-4138	(M)	Beyond The Sunset	1963	12.00	30.00
MGM SE-4138	(E)	Beyond The Sunset	196?	6.00	15.00
MGM E-4140	(M)	14 More Greatest Hits, Volume 3	1963	10.00	25.00
MGM E-4168	(M)	The Very Best Of Hank Williams	1963	8.00	20.00
MGM SE-4168	(E)	The Very Best Of Hank Williams	1963	6.00	15.00
MGM E-4227	(M)	The Very Best Of Hank Williams, Volume 2	1964	8.00	20.00
MGM SE-4227	(E)	The Very Best Of Hank Williams, Volume 2	1964	6.00	15.00
MGM E-4254	(M)	Lost Highway (And Other Folk Ballads)	1964	12.00	30.00
MGM E-4267	(M)	The Hank Williams Story *(4 LP box.)*	1965	20.00	50.00
MGM E-4300	(M)	Kaw-Liga And Other Humorous Songs	1965	10.00	25.00
MGM SE-4300	(E)	Kaw-Liga And Other Humorous Songs	1965	6.00	15.00
MGM E-4377	(M)	The Legend Lives Anew			
		(Hank Williams With Strings)	1966	8.00	20.00
MGM SE-4377	(S)	The Legend Lives Ane			
		(Hank Williams With Strings)	1966	8.00	20.00
MGM E-4380	(M)	Luke The Drifter	1966	8.00	20.00
MGM SE-4380	(E)	Luke The Drifter	1966	6.00	15.00
MGM E-4429	(M)	More Hank Williams And Strings	1966	8.00	20.00
MGM SE-4429	(S)	More Hank Williams And Strings	1966	8.00	20.00
MGM E-4481	(M)	I Won't Be Home No More	1967	8.00	20.00
MGM SE-4481	(E)	I Won't Be Home No More	1967	6.00	15.00
		— MGM albums above have black labels.—			
MGM SE-4529	(S)	Hank Williams And Strings, Volume 3	1968	8.00	20.00
MGM E-4576	(M)	Hank Williams In The Beginning	1968	12.00	30.00
MGM SE-4576	(E)	Hank Williams In The Beginning	1968	6.00	15.00
MGM SE-4651	(E)	The Essential Hank Williams	1969	6.00	15.00
MGM SE-4680	(E)	Life To Legend	1970	6.00	15.00
MGM SE-4755	(E)	24 Of Hank Williams' Greatest Hits *(2 LPs)*	1970	8.00	20.00
MGM SE-240	(E)	24 Karat Hits *(2 LPs)*	1970	10.00	25.00
MGM 1SE-33ST	(E)	The Last Picture Show *(Soundtrack)*	1971	12.00	30.00
		— MGM albums above have blue & gold labels.—			

Label & Catalog #		Title	Year	VG+	NM
MGM PRO-912	(DJ)	**Reflections Of Those Who Loved Him**	1975	80.00	200.00
		(Promotional 3 LP boxed set of various artists eulogizing Hank.)			
Metro M-509	(M)	**Hank Williams**	1965	8.00	20.00
Metro MS-509	(E)	**Hank Williams**	1965	5.00	12.00
Metro M-547	(M)	**Mr. And Mrs. Hank Williams**	1965	8.00	20.00
Metro MS-547	(E)	**Mr. And Mrs. Hank Williams**	1965	5.00	12.00
Metro M-602	(M)	**The Immortal Hank Williams**	1966	8.00	20.00
Metro MS-602	(E)	**The Immortal Hank Williams**	1966	5.00	12.00
Columbia P4S-5616	(E)	**The Hank Williams Treasury** *(4 LP box)*	197?	12.00	30.00

WILLIAMS, HANK, & HANK WILLIAMS, JR.

MGM E-4276	(M)	**Hank Williams, Sr., & Hank Williams. Jr.**	1965	6.00	15.00
MGM SE-4276	(S)	**Hank Williams, Sr., & Hank Williams. Jr.**	1965	8.00	20.00
MGM E-4378	(M)	**Again**	1966	6.00	15.00
MGM SE-4378	(S)	**Again**	1966	8.00	20.00
		— Original MGM albums above have black labels.—			

WILLIAMS, HANK, JR. (& THE CHEATIN' HEARTS)
Hank Jr. also recorded with Connie Francis.

MGM E-4213	(M)	**Songs Of Hank Williams**	1963	6.00	15.00
MGM SE-4213	(S)	**Songs Of Hank Williams**	1963	8.00	20.00
MGM E-4260	(M)	**Your Cheatin' Heart** *(Soundtrack)*	1964	6.00	15.00
MGM SE-4260	(S)	**Your Cheatin' Heart** *(Soundtrack)*	1964	8.00	20.00
MGM E-4316	(M)	**Ballads Of The Hills And Plains**	1965	6.00	15.00
MGM SE-4316	(S)	**Ballads Of The Hills And Plains**	1965	8.00	20.00
MGM E-4344	(M)	**Blue's My Name**	1966	6.00	15.00
MGM SE-4344	(S)	**Blue's My Name**	1966	8.00	20.00
MGM E-4391	(M)	**Country Shadows**	1966	6.00	15.00
MGM SE-4391	(S)	**Country Shadows**	1966	8.00	20.00
MGM E-4428	(M)	**In My Own Way**	1967	6.00	15.00
MGM SE-4428	(S)	**In My Own Way**	1967	8.00	20.00
MGM E-4513	(M)	**The Best Of Hank Williams, Jr.**	1967	6.00	15.00
MGM SE-4513	(S)	**The Best Of Hank Williams, Jr.**	1967	8.00	20.00
		— Original MGM albums above have black labels.—			
MGM SE-4527	(S)	**My Songs**	1968	6.00	15.00
MGM SE-4540	(S)	**Time To Sing** *(Soundtrack)*	1968	6.00	15.00
MGM SE-4559	(S)	**Luke The Drifter, Jr.**	1968	6.00	15.00
MGM SE-4621	(S)	**Songs My Father Left Me**	1969	6.00	15.00
MGM SE-4632	(S)	**Luke The Drifter, Jr., Volume 2**	1969	6.00	15.00
MGM SE-4644	(S)	**Live at Cobo Hall**	1969	6.00	15.00
MGM SE-4656	(S)	**Hank Williams, Jr.'s Greatest Hits**	1970	6.00	15.00
MGM SE-4657	(S)	**Sunday Morning**	1970	6.00	15.00
MGM SE-4673	(S)	**Luke The Drifter, Jr., Volume 3**	1970	6.00	15.00
MGM SE-4675	(S)	**Singing My Songs**	1970	6.00	15.00
MGM SE-4721	(S)	**Removing The Shadow**	1970	6.00	15.00
MGM SE-4750	(S)	**All For The Love Of Sunshine**	1970	6.00	15.00
MGM GAS-119	(S)	**Hank Williams, Jr.**	1970	6.00	15.00

WILLIAMS, JOE: *Refer to* GOLDMINE'S PRICE GUIDE TO COLLECTIBLE JAZZ ALBUMS

WILLIAMS, "BIG" JOE
Big Joe also recorded with Victoria Spivey.

Folkways F-3820	(M)	**Mississippi's Big Joe Williams**	1962	12.00	30.00
Folkways FS-3820	(S)	**Mississippi's Big Joe Williams**	1962	16.00	40.00
Delmark DL-604	(M)	**Blues On Highway 49**	1962	16.00	40.00
Bluesville BVLP-1056	(M)	**Blues For Nine Strings**	1962	16.00	40.00
Bluesville BVLP-1067	(M)	**Big Joe Williams At Folk City**	1963	16.00	40.00
Bluesville BVLP-1083	(M)	**Studio Blues**	1964	16.00	40.00
Delmark DL-609	(M)	**Starvin' Chain Blues**	1966	10.00	25.00
Delmark SD-609	(S)	**Starvin' Chain Blues**	1966	12.00	30.00
Milestone 3001	(M)	**Classic Delta Blues**	1966	10.00	25.00
Folkways 31004	(M)	**Hell Bound And Heaven Sent**	1967	10.00	25.00
World Pacific WPS-21897	(S)	**Big Joe Williams**	1969	6.00	15.00

WILLIAMS, LARRY
Larry also recorded with Johnny Watson.

Specialty SP-2109	(M)	**Here's Larry Williams** *(Black & gold label)*	1959	780.00	200.00
Chess LP-1457	(M)	**Larry Williams**	1961	60.00	150.00

Label & Catalog #		Title	Year	VG+	NM
OKeh OKM-2123	(M)	Larry Williams' Greatest Hits	1967	10.00	25.00
OKeh OKS-12123	(S)	Larry Williams' Greatest Hits	1967	12.00	30.00

WILLIAMS, MASON

Warner Bros. WS-1729	(S)	The Mason Williams Phonograph Record	1968	6.00	15.00
Warner Bros. WS-1776	(S)	Ear Show	1968	6.00	15.00
Warner Bros. WS-1788	(S)	Music By Mason William	1969	6.00	15.00
Warner Bros. WS-1838	(S)	Hand Made	1969	6.00	15.00
Warner Bros. WS-1941	(S)	Sharepickers	1971	6.00	15.00

WILLIAMS, MAURICE, & THE ZODIACS

Herald HLP-1014	(M)	Stay	1961	150.00	350.00
Sphere Sound SR-7007	(M)	Stay	1965	40.00	100.00
Sphere Sound SSR-7007	(E)	Stay	1965	20.00	50.00
		(Sphere Sound 7007 is a reissue of Herald 1014.)			
Snyder 5586	(M)	At The Beach	196?	30.00	75.00
Relic 5017	(M)	Greatest Hits	197?	8.00	20.00

WILLIAMS, MEL, & JOHNNY OTIS

Dig 103	(M)	All Through The Night	1955	250.00	600.00

WILLIAMS, OTIS, & THE CHARMS

Deluxe 750	(M)	Their All Time Hits	1957	350.00	750.00
King 570	(M)	Their All Time Hits	1957	150.00	300.00
King 614	(M)	This Is Otis Williams & The Charms	1959	80.00	200.00

WILLIAMS, OTIS, & THE MIDNIGHT COWBOYS

Stop STLP-1022	(S)	Otis Williams & The Midnight Cowboys	1971	6.00	15.00

WILLIAMS, ROBERT PETE

Bluesvillle BVLP-1026	(M)	Free Again	1961	16.00	40.00
Prestige PRST-7808	(E)	Free Again	1969	6.00	15.00
		(Prestige 7808 is a reisue of Bluesville 1026.)			

WILLIAMS, TEX

Decca DL-5565 (10")	(M)	Dance-O-Rama #5	1955	100.00	250.00
Camden CAL-363	(M)	Tex Williams' Best	1958	10.00	25.00
Capitol T-1463	(M)	Smoke! Smoke! Smoke!	1960	12.00	30.00
Capitol ST-1463	(S)	Smoke! Smoke! Smoke!	1960	16.00	40.00
Decca DL-4295	(M)	Country Music Time	1962	8.00	20.00
Decca DL-74295	(S)	Country Music Time	1962	10.00	25.00
Liberty LRP-3304	(M)	Tex Williams In Las Vegas	1963	6.00	15.00
Liberty LST-7304	(S)	Tex Williams In Las Vegas	1963	8.00	20.00
Imperial LP-9309	(M)	The Voice Of Authority	1966	6.00	15.00
Imperial LP-12309	(S)	The Voice Of Authority	1966	8.00	20.00

WILLIAMS, TONY

Tony Williams was formerly the lead singer for The Platters.

Mercury MG-20454	(M)	A Girl Is A Girl Is A Girl	1959	12.00	30.00
Mercury SR-60138	(S)	A Girl Is A Girl Is A Girl	1959	16.00	40.00
Reprise R-6006	(M)	His Greatest Hits	1961	10.00	25.00
Reprise R-96006	(S)	His Greatest Hits	1961	12.00	30.00
Phillips PHM-200-051	(M)	Magic Touch Of Tony	1962	10.00	25.00
Phillips PHS-600-051	(S)	Magic Touch Of Tony	1962	12.00	30.00

WILLIAMSON, CRIS

Ampex 10134	(S)	Cris Williamson	1971	6.00	15.00

WILLIAMSON, JOHN LEE "SONNY BOY (#1)"

Blues Classics BC-3	(M)	Sonny Boy Williamson, Volume 1	1964	6.00	15.00
Blues Classics BC-20	(M)	Sonny Boy Williamson, Volume 2	1964	6.00	15.00
Blues Classics BC-24	(M)	Sonny Boy Williamson, Volume 3	1964	6.00	15.00

WILLIAMSON, ALEC RICE "SONNY BOY (#2)"

Chess LP-1437	(M)	Down And Out Blues (Black label)	1959	80.00	200.00
Chess LP-1503	(M)	The Real Folk Blues	1966	20.00	50.00
Chess LP-1509	(M)	More Real Folk Blues	1966	20.00	50.00
Chess LPS-1536	(S)	Bummer Road	1969	10.00	25.00
		— Original Chess albums above have blue labels.—			

Label & Catalog #		Title	Year	VG+	NM
Chess 2CH-50027	(S)	This Is My Story (2 LPs)	1972	6.00	15.00
Chess 2CH-206	(S)	Sonny Boy Williamson (2 LPs)	1976	6.00	15.00

WILLIAMSON, SONNY BOY (#2), & THE YARDBIRDS

Mercury MG-21071	(M)	Sonny Boy Williamson & The Yardbirds	1966	20.00	50.00
Mercury SR-61071	(E)	Sonny Boy Williamson & The Yardbirds	1966	14.00	35.00

WILLIE & THE RED RUBBER BAND

RCA Victor LSP-4074	(S)	Willie And The Red Rubber Band	1968	6.00	15.00
RCA Victor LSP-4193	(S)	We're Comin' Up	1969	6.00	15.00

WILLING, FOY, & THE RIDERS OF THE PURPLE SAGE

Varsity VLP-6032 (10")	(M)	Riders Of The Purple Sage	1950	30.00	75.00
Royale 6032 (10")	(M)	Riders Of The Purple Sage	1952	30.00	75.00
Roulette R-25035	(M)	Cowboy	1958	16.00	40.00
Jubilee JL-5028	(M)	The New Sound Of American Folk	1962	8.00	20.00
Jubilee JLS-5028	(S)	The New Sound Of American Folk	1962	10.00	25.00

WILLIS, CHUCK

Epic LN-3425	(M)	Chuck Willis Wails The Blues	1958	150.00	300.00
Epic LN-3728	(M)	A Tribute To Chuck Willis	1960	100.00	250.00
Atlantic 8018	(M)	The King Of The Stroll (Black label)	1958	100.00	250.00
Atlantic 8018	(M)	The King Of The Stroll (Orange & purple label.)	1960	40.00	100.00
Atlantic 8079	(M)	I Remember Chuck Willis	1963	30.00	75.00
Atlantic SD-8079	(P)	I Remember Chuck Willis	1963	40.00	100.00

WILLS, BOB (& HIS TEXAS PLAYBOYS)

Columbia HL-9003 (10")	(M)	Bob Wills Round-Up	1949	100.00	250.00
Antones LP-6000 (10")	(M)	Old Time Favorites (Fan club issue)	195?	200.00	400.00
Antones LP-6010 (10")	(M)	Old Time Favorites (Fan club issue)	195?	200.00	400.00
MGM E-91 (10")	(M)	Ranch House Favorites	1951	100.00	250.00
Decca DL-5562 (10")	(M)	Dance-O-Rama #2	1955	100.00	250.00
MGM E-3352	(M)	Ranch House Favorites	1956	50.00	125.00
Decca DL-8727	(M)	Bob Wills And His Texas Playboys	1957	30.00	75.00
Harmony HL-7036	(M)	Bob Wills Special (Maroon label)	1957	14.00	35.00
Harmony HL-7304	(M)	The Best Of Bob Wills (Blue label)	1963	10.00	25.00
Harmony HL-7345	(M)	The Great Bob Wills (Blue label)	1965	8.00	20.00
Liberty LRP-3182	(M)	Living Legend	1961	12.00	30.00
Liberty LST-7182	(S)	Living Legend	1961	16.00	40.00
Liberty LRP-3194	(M)	Mr. Words And Music	1961	12.00	30.00
Liberty LST-7194	(S)	Mr. Words And Music	1961	16.00	40.00
Liberty LRP-3303	(M)	Bob Wills Sings And Plays	1963	12.00	30.00
Liberty LST-7303	(S)	Bob Wills Sings And Plays	1963	16.00	40.00
Starday SLP-375	(M)	San Antonio Rose	1965	10.00	25.00
Longhorn LP-001	(M)	Keepsake Album #1	1965	20.00	50.00
Vocalion VL-3735	(M)	Western Swing Band	1965	8.00	20.00
Vocalion VL-73735	(E)	Western Swing Band	1965	5.00	12.00
Vocalion VL-3922	(M)	San Antonio Rose	1971	6.00	15.00
Metro M-594	(M)	Bob Wills	1967	6.00	15.00
Metro MS-594	(S)	Bob Wills	1967	4.00	10.00
Kapp KL-1506	(M)	From The Heart Of Texas	1967	6.00	15.00
Kapp KS-3506	(S)	From The Heart Of Texas	1967	8.00	20.00
Kapp KL-1523	(M)	King Of Western Swing	1967	6.00	15.00
Kapp KS-3523	(S)	King Of Western Swing	1967	8.00	20.00
Kapp KS-3542	(S)	Here's That Man Again	1968	8.00	20.00
Kapp KS-3587	(S)	The Living Legend	1969	8.00	20.00
Kapp KS-3601	(S)	The Greatest String Band Hits	1969	8.00	20.00
Kapp KS-3569	(S)	Time Changes Everything	1969	8.00	20.00
Kapp KS-3639	(S)	Bob Wills In Person	1970	8.00	20.00
Kapp KS-3641	(S)	The Best Of Bob Wills	1971	6.00	15.00
Sunset SUS-5248	(S)	A Country Walk	1969	6.00	15.00
Harmony HS-11358	(E)	Bob Wills Special	1969	6.00	15.00
Starday SLP-469	(S)	The Bob Wills Story	1970	6.00	15.00
Vocalion VL7-3922	(E)	San Antonio Rose	1971	8.00	20.00
United Arts. UAS-9962	(P)	Legendary Masters (2 LPs)	1971	10.00	25.00
MGM GAS-141	(S)	A Tribute To Bob Wills	1971	8.00	20.00
MGM E-4866	(S)	The History Of Bob Wills & His Texas Playboys	1973	4.00	10.00

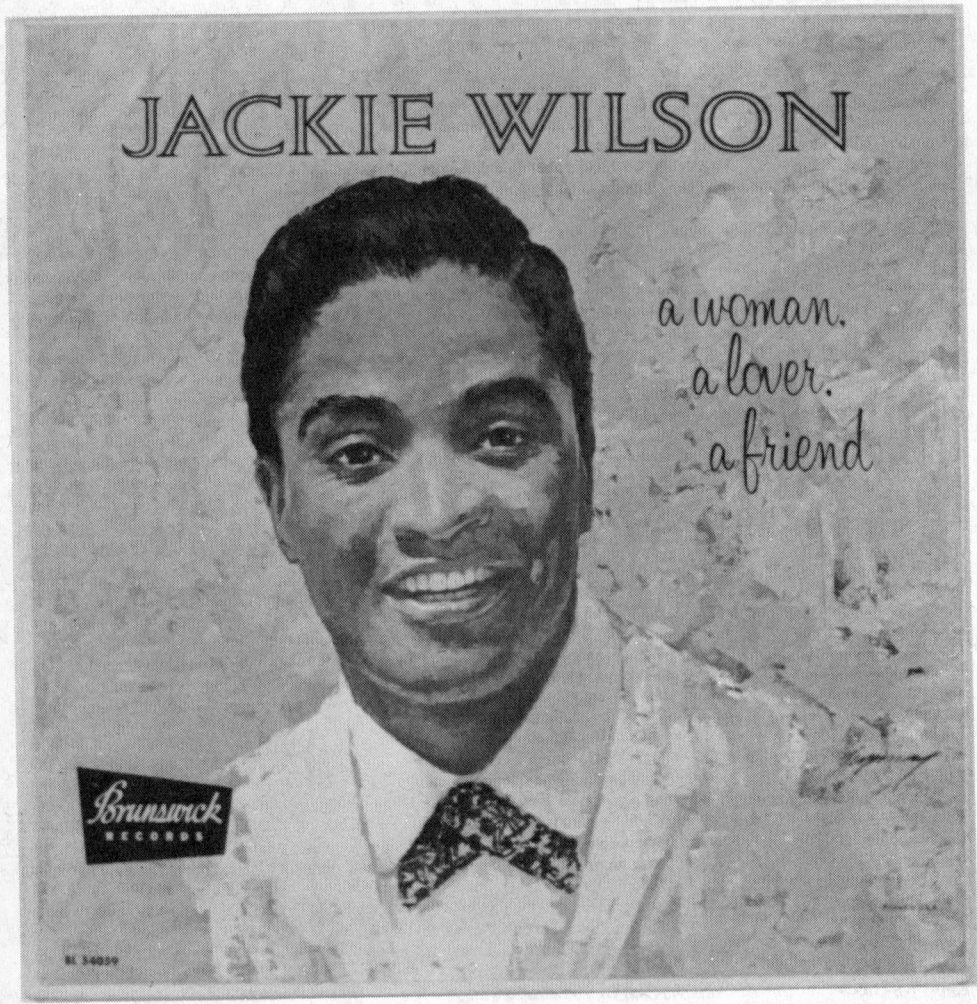

The late, great Jackie Wilson has often been referred to as the "black Elvis." Aside from the more obvious similarities (good looks, the lithe sexy movements of their early careers and the malleable voices that could seemingly sing anything), there are other comparisons: Both singers were highly successful in the '50s but suffered through a series of misguided—and mismanaged—decisions in the '60s that took them out of the milieu in which they best operated and "expanded" their horizons by assigning them MOR projects that watered down their drive as it made their images more palatable to the mainstream. Both artists were able to resurrect their careers with remarkable comebacks in the late '60s, striding masterfully through the early '70s only to have it all come to unexpected—and tragic—endings.

Label & Catalog #		Title	Year	VG+	NM
Columbia KG-32416	(M)	Bob Wills Anthology (2 LPs)	1973	4.00	10.00
United Arts. LA216	(S)	For The Last Time (2 LPs with book)	1974	4.00	10.00
Columbia P-12924	(S)	The Legendary Bob Wills (2 LPs)	1975	4.00	10.00

WILLS, BOB, & TOMMY DUNCAN

Liberty LRX-1912	(M)	Bob Wills And Tommy Duncan	195?	10.00	25.00
Liberty LSX-1912	(S)	Bob Wills And Tommy Duncan	195?	12.00	30.00
Liberty LRP-3173	(M)	Together Again	1960	10.00	25.00
Liberty LST-7173	(S)	Together Again	1960	12.00	30.00
Sunset SUM-1108	(M)	Together Again	1966	5.00	12.00
Sunset SUS-5108	(S)	Together Again	1966	6.00	15.00

WILLS, JOHNNY LEE

Sims 101	(M)	Where There's A Wills, There's A Way	1962	24.00	60.00
Sims 108	(M)	At The Tulsa Stampede	1963	24.00	60.00

WILMER & THE DUKES

Aphrodisiac 6001	(S)	Wilmer And The Dukes	1969	10.00	25.00

WILSON, AL

Soul City SCS-92006	(S)	Searching For The Dolphins	1969	10.00	25.00
Rocky Road RR-3601	(S)	Show And Tell	1973	6.00	15.00
Rocky Road 3600	(S)	Weighing In	1973	6.00	15.00
Rocky Road 3700	(S)	La La Peace Song	1974	6.00	15.00
Playboy 410	(S)	I've Got A Feeling	1976	6.00	15.00

WILSON, BRIAN
Brian Wilson was The Beach Boys... in the '60s. Refer to Spring.

Crawdaddy	(DJ)	The Crawdaddy Brian Wilson Interview	1977	60.00	150.00
Sire PRO-3248	(DJ)	Words And Music (Interview)	1988	8.00	20.00
Sire 25669	(S)	Brian Wilson	1988	4.00	10.00

WILSON, CARL
Carl Wilson is member of The Beach Boys.

Caribou JZ-37010	(S)	Carl Wilson	1981	4.00	10.00
Caribou ARZ-37970	(S)	Youngblood	1982	4.00	10.00

WILSON, DENNIS
Dennis Wilson was a member of The Beach Boys.

Caribou PZ-35354	(S)	Pacific Ocean Blue	1977	6.00	15.00

WILSON, J. FRANK, & THE CAVALIERS

Josie JM-4006	(M)	Last Kiss	1964	14.00	35.00
Josie JS-4006	(S)	Last Kiss	1964	20.00	50.00

WILSON, JACKIE
Mr. Wilson was formerly the lead singer for Billy Ward & The Dominoes.

Sesac	(M)	Jackie Wilson	1958	250.00	500.00
Brunswick BL-54042	(M)	He's So Fine	1959	40.00	100.00
Brunswick BL-54045	(M)	Lonely Teardrops	1959	40.00	100.00
Brunswick BL-54050	(M)	So Much	1960	30.00	75.00
Brunswick BL-754050	(S)	So Much	1960	40.00	100.00
Brunswick BL-54055	(M)	Jackie Sings The Blues	1960	30.00	75.00
Brunswick BL-754055	(S)	Jackie Sings The Blues	1960	40.00	100.00
Brunswick BL-54058	(M)	My Golden Favorites	1960	20.00	50.00
Brunswick BL-54059	(M)	A Woman, A Lover, A Friend	1961	16.00	40.00
Brunswick BL-754059	(S)	A Woman, A Lover, A Friend	1961	20.00	50.00
Brunswick BL-54100	(M)	You Ain't Heard Nothin' Yet	1961	16.00	40.00
Brunswick BL-754100	(S)	You Ain't Heard Nothin' Yet	1961	20.00	50.00
Brunswick BL-54101	(M)	By Special Request	1961	16.00	40.00
Brunswick BL-754101	(S)	By Special Request	1961	20.00	50.00
Brunswick BL-54105	(M)	Body And Soul	1962	16.00	40.00
Brunswick BL-754105	(S)	Body And Soul	1962	20.00	50.00
Brunswick BL-54106	(M)	The World's Greatest Melodies	1962	16.00	40.00
Brunswick BL-754106	(S)	The World's Greatest Melodies	1962	20.00	50.00
Brunswick BL-54108	(M)	Jackie Wilson At The Copa	1962	16.00	40.00
Brunswick BL-754108	(S)	Jackie Wilson At The Copa	1962	20.00	50.00

— Original Brunswick albums above have black & silver labels.—

Label & Catalog #		Title	Year	VG+	NM
Brunswick BL-54110	(M)	Baby Workout	1963	12.00	30.00
Brunswick BL-754110	(S)	Baby Workout	1963	16.00	40.00
Brunswick BL-54112	(M)	Merry Christmas From Jackie Wilson	1963	12.00	30.00
Brunswick BL-754112	(S)	Merry Christmas From Jackie Wilson	1963	16.00	40.00
Brunswick BL-54113	(M)	Shake A Hand	1963	10.00	25.00
Brunswick BL-754113	(S)	Shake A Hand	1963	12.00	30.00
Brunswick BL-54115	(M)	My Golden Favorites, Volume 2	1964	10.00	25.00
Brunswick BL-754115	(S)	My Golden Favorites, Volume 2	1964	12.00	30.00
Brunswick BL-54117	(M)	Somethin' Else	1964	10.00	25.00
Brunswick BL-754117	(S)	Somethin' Else	1964	12.00	30.00
Brunswick BL-54118	(M)	Soul Time	1965	10.00	25.00
Brunswick BL-754118	(S)	Soul Time	1965	12.00	30.00
Brunswick BL-54119	(M)	Spotlight On Jackie Wilson	1965	10.00	25.00
Brunswick BL-754119	(S)	Spotlight On Jackie Wilson	1965	12.00	30.00
Brunswick BL-54120	(M)	Soul Galore	1966	10.00	25.00
Brunswick BL-754120	(S)	Soul Galore	1966	12.00	30.00
Brunswick BL-54112	(M)	Whispers	1967	8.00	20.00
Brunswick BL-754112	(S)	Whispers	1967	10.00	25.00
Brunswick BL-54130	(M)	Higher And Higher	1967	8.00	20.00
Brunswick BL-754130	(S)	Higher And Higher	1967	10.00	25.00
Brunswick BL-754138	(S)	I Get The Sweetest Feeling	1968	8.00	20.00
Brunswick BL-754134	(S)	Manufacturers Of Soul	1968	8.00	20.00
— Original Brunswick albums above have black labels with a "Division of Decca Records" on the left side.—					
Brunswick BL-754140	(S)	Jackie Wilson's Greatest Hits	1969	6.00	15.00
Brunswick BL-754154	(S)	Do Your Thing	1969	6.00	15.00
Brunswick BL-754158	(S)	It's All Part Of Love	1970	6.00	15.00
Brunswick BL-754167	(S)	This Love Is Real	1971	6.00	15.00
Brunswick BL-754172	(S)	You Got Me Walking	1971	6.00	15.00
Brunswick BL-754189	(S)	Beautiful Day	1973	4.00	10.00
Brunswick BL-754199	(S)	Nowstalgia	1974	4.00	10.00
Brunswick BL-754212	(S)	Nobody But You	1977	4.00	10.00

WILSON, JULIE

Label & Catalog #		Title	Year	VG+	NM
Dolphin 6	(M)	Love	1956	14.00	35.00
Vik LX-1095	(M)	My Old Flame	1957	12.00	30.00
Vik LX-1118	(M)	Julie Wilson At The St. Regis	1958	12.00	30.00
Cameo C-1021	(M)	Meet Julie Wilson	1962	10.00	25.00
Cameo SC-1021	(S)	Meet Julie Wilson	1962	16.00	40.00

WILSON, MARY

Ms. Wilson was formerly a member of The Supremes.

Label & Catalog #		Title	Year	VG+	NM
Motown M7-927	(S)	Red Hot	1979	4.00	10.00

WILSON, MURRY

The father of Brian, Dennis and Carl Wilson of The Beach Boys. Refer to The Sunrays.

Label & Catalog #		Title	Year	VG+	NM
Capitol T-2819	(M)	The Many Moods Of Murry Wilson	1967	8.00	20.00
Capitol ST-2819	(S)	The Many Moods Of Murry Wilson	1967	10.00	25.00

WILSON, STAN

Label & Catalog #		Title	Year	VG+	NM
Clef MGC-163 (10")	(M)	An Evening With Stan Wilson	1954	20.00	50.00
Clef MGC-672	(M)	A Stan Wilson Recital	1955	16.00	40.00
Verve MGV-2019	(M)	Ballads And Calypso	1956	12.00	30.00
		(Verve 2019 is a reissue of Clef 672.)			
Verve MGV-2051	(M)	Calypso	1957	12.00	30.00
Verve MGV-2076	(M)	Folk Songs	1957	12.00	30.00
Verve MGV-2122	(M)	Stan Wilson At The Ash Grove	1959	12.00	30.00
Verve MGV-2139	(M)	Stan Wilson	1960	12.00	30.00
Verve MGV-2140	(M)	Leisure Time	1960	12.00	30.00

WINCHESTER, JESSE

Label & Catalog #		Title	Year	VG+	NM
Ampex A-10104	(S)	Jesse Winchester	1970	8.00	20.00
Bearsville PRO-693	(DJ)	Live At The Bijou Cafe Plus A Live Interview At Media College In Montreal (2 LPs)	1975	30.00	75.00

WIND

Label & Catalog #		Title	Year	VG+	NM
Life LLPS-2000	(S)	Make Believe	1969	6.00	15.00

WIND IN THE WILLOWS, THE
W.I.T.W. features Debbie Harry, later of Blondie.

Label & Catalog #		Title	Year	VG+	NM
Capitol SKAO-2956	(S)	The Wind In The Willows	1968	16.00	40.00

WINGS

Dunhill DS-50046	(S)	Wings	1968	6.00	15.00

WINGS: *Refer to* PAUL McCARTNEY (& WINGS)

WINNERS, THE

Crown CLP-5394	(M)	Checkered Flag	1963	8.00	20.00
Crown CST-394	(S)	Checkered Flag	1963	10.00	25.00

WINTER, EDGAR (& WHITE TRASH)

Epic EQ-31584	(Q)	They Only Come Out At Night	1973	6.00	15.00
Epic PEQ-32461	(Q)	Shock Treatment	1974	6.00	15.00
Blue Sky PZQ-33483	(Q)	Jasmine Nightdreams	1975	6.00	15.00
Blue Sky PZQ-33798	(Q)	The Edgar Winter Group With Rick Derringer	1975	6.00	15.00
Blue Sky ASZ-242	(DJ)	Johnny And Edgar Discuss "Together"	1976	8.00	20.00

WINTER, JOHNNY

Sonobeat RS-1002	(DJ)	Progressive Blues Experiment	1968	200.00	400.00
		(Issued in a plain cardboard jacket.)			
Imperial 12431	(S)	Progressive Blues Experiment	1969	14.00	35.00
		(Imperial 12431 is a reissue of Sonobeat 1002.)			
GRT 10010	(S)	The Johnny Winter Story	1969	6.00	15.00
Buddah BDS-7513	(S)	First Winter	1969	6.00	15.00
Columbia CS-9826	(S)	Johnny Winter	1969	8.00	20.00
Columbia CS-9947	(S)	Second Winter *(2 LPs)*	1969	10.00	25.00
Columbia KC-30221	(S)	Johnny Winter And	1970	8.00	20.00
— Original Columbia albums above have "360 Sound Stereo" on the bottom of the label.—					
Janus 3008	(S)	About Blues	1970	6.00	15.00
Janus 3023	(S)	Early Times	1970	6.00	15.00
Janus 3056	(S)	Before The Storm	1970	6.00	15.00
Columbia CQ-32188	(Q)	Still Alive And Well	1973	8.00	20.00
Columbia CQ-32715	(Q)	Saints And Sinners	1974	8.00	20.00
Blue Sky PZQ-33292	(Q)	John Dawson Winter III	1974	8.00	20.00
Crazy Cajun 1009	(S)	Early Winter	197?	5.00	12.00

WINTERS, JONATHAN

MGV-15009	(M)	The Wonderful World Of Jonathan Winters	1960	10.00	25.00
MGV-15011	(M)	Down To Earth	1960	10.00	25.00
MGV-15025	(M)	Here's Jonathan (In Concert)	1961	10.00	25.00
MGV-15027	(M)	A Personal Appearance	1961	10.00	25.00
— Original Verve albums above have black labels with "Verve Records, Inc." on the bottom.—					
V6-15025	(S)	Here's Jonathan (In Concert)	1962	8.00	20.00
V-15032	(M)	Another Day, Another World	1962	6.00	15.00
V6-15032	(S)	Another Day, Another World	1962	8.00	20.00
V-15035	(M)	Humor Seen Through The Eyes			
		Of Jonathan Winters	1962	6.00	15.00
V6-15035	(S)	Humor Seen Through The Eyes			
		Of Jonathan Winters	1962	8.00	20.00
V-15037	(M)	Whistle Stopping	1963	6.00	15.00
V6-15037	(S)	Whistle Stopping	1963	8.00	20.00
V-15041	(M)	Jonathan Winters' Mad... Mad World	1963	6.00	15.00
V6-15041	(S)	Jonathan Winters' Mad... Mad World	1963	8.00	20.00
V-15047	(M)	Great Moments	1964	6.00	15.00
V6-15047	(S)	Great Moments	1964	8.00	20.00
V-15057	(M)	Movies Are Better Than Ever	1964	6.00	15.00
V6-15057	(S)	Movies Are Better Than Ever	1964	8.00	20.00

WINTERS, JONATHAN / SHELLY BERMAN / MORT SAHL

MGV-15022	(M)	The Wit Of America *(3 LPs)*	195?	16.00	40.00
		(Black labels with "Verve Records, Inc." on the bottom.)			

WINWOOD, STEVE
Steve was formerly a member of the Spencer Davis Group; Traffic; Blind Faith.

United Arts. UAS-9950	(S)	Winwood *(2 LPs with a bound-in booklet)*	1971	10.00	25.00
United Arts. UAS-9950	(S)	Winwood *(2 LPs without the booklet)*	1971	6.00	15.00

Label & Catalog #		Title	Year	VG+	NM

WISE, CHUBBY

Starday SLP-154	(M)	The Tennessee Fiddler	1961	12.00	30.00

WISEMAN, MAC
Refer to Lester Flatt.

Dot DLP-3084	(M)	Tis Sweet To Be Remembered	1958	16.00	40.00
Dot DLP-25084	(E)	Tis Sweet To Be Remembered	196?	6.00	15.00
Dot DLP-3135	(M)	Beside The Still Waters	1959	12.00	30.00
Dot DLP-25135	(S)	Beside The Still Waters	1959	16.00	40.00
Dot DLP-3213	(M)	Great Folk Ballads	1959	12.00	30.00
Dot DLP-25213	(S)	Great Folk Ballads	1959	16.00	40.00
Dot DLP-3313	(M)	12 Great Hits	1960	12.00	30.00
Dot DLP-25313	(S)	12 Great Hits	1960	16.00	40.00
Dot DLP-3336	(M)	Keep On The Sunnyside	1960	16.00	40.00
Dot DLP-25336	(E)	Keep On The Sunnyside	196?	6.00	15.00
Dot DLP-3373	(M)	Best Loved Gospel Hymns	1961	8.00	20.00
Dot DLP-25373	(S)	Best Loved Gospel Hymns	1961	12.00	30.00
Dot DLP-3408	(M)	Fireball Mail	1961	12.00	30.00
Dot DLP-25408	(E)	Fireball Mail	196?	6.00	15.00
Capitol T-1800	(M)	Bluegrass Favorites	1962	12.00	30.00
Capitol ST-1800	(S)	Bluegrass Favorites	1962	16.00	40.00
Hamilton HLP-12130	(M)	Sincerely	1964	8.00	20.00
Hamilton HLP-12167	(M)	Songs Of The Dear Old Days	1966	8.00	20.00
Dot DLP-3697	(M)	This Is Mac Wiseman	1966	8.00	20.00
Dot DLP-25697	(S)	This Is Mac Wiseman	1966	10.00	25.00
Dot DLP-3730	(M)	A Master At Work	1966	8.00	20.00
Dot DLP-25730	(S)	A Master At Work	1966	10.00	25.00
Dot DLP-3731	(M)	Bluegrass	1966	8.00	20.00
Dot DLP-25731	(S)	Bluegrass	1966	10.00	25.00
Dot DLP-25896	(S)	Golden Hits Of Mac Wiseman	1968	8.00	20.00

WISHBONE ASH

Decca DL-75249	(S)	Wishbone Ash	1971	6.00	15.00
Decca DL-75295	(S)	Pilgrimage	1971	6.00	15.00
Decca DL-75437	(S)	Argus	1971	6.00	15.00
Decca DL-71919	(DJ)	An Evening Program With Wishbone Ash	1972	12.00	30.00
Decca DL-71922	(DJ)	Live From Memphis	1972	20.00	50.00

WITHERS, BILL

Sussex 7006	(S)	Just As I Am	1971	8.00	20.00
Sussex 7011	(S)	Man And Boy (Soundtrack)	1971	8.00	20.00
Sussex 7014	(S)	Still Bill	1972	8.00	20.00
Sussex 7025-2	(S)	Live At Carnegie Hall (2 LPs)	1973	8.00	20.00
Sussex 8032	(S)	Add'justments	1974	6.00	15.00
Sussex 8037	(S)	The Best Of Bill Withers	1975	6.00	15.00

WITHERSPOON, JIMMY
Jimmy Witherspoon also recorded with Eric Burdon.

Atlantic 1266	(M)	New Orleans Blues (Black label)	1956	80.00	200.00
RCA Victor LPM-1639	(M)	Goin' To Kansas City Blues	1958	40.00	100.00
Hifijazz J-421	(M)	At The Monterey Jazz Festival	1959	20.00	50.00
Hifijazz J-422	(M)	Feelin' The Spirit	1959	20.00	50.00
Hifijazz J-426	(M)	Jimmy Witherspoon At The Renaissance	1959	20.00	50.00
Crown CLP-5156	(M)	Jimmy Witherspoon	1959	12.00	30.00
Crown CLP-5192	(M)	Jimmy Witherspoon Sings The Blues	1960	12.00	30.00
Crown CSt-215	(E)	Jimmy Witherspoon Sings The Blues (Red vinyl)	1960	20.00	50.00
World Pacific WP-1267	(M)	Singin' The Blues	1959	20.00	50.00
World Pacific WP-1402	(M)	There's Good Rockin' Tonight	1961	20.00	50.00
Reprise R-2008	(M)	Spoon	1961	12.00	30.00
Reprise R9-2008	(S)	Spoon	1961	16.00	40.00
Reprise R-6012	(M)	Hey, Mrs. Jones	1962	12.00	30.00
Reprise R9-6012	(S)	Hey, Mrs. Jones	1962	16.00	40.00
Reprise R-6059	(M)	Roots	1962	12.00	30.00
Reprise R9-6059	(S)	Roots	1962	16.00	40.00
Prestige PRLP-7290	(M)	Baby, Baby, Baby	1963	10.00	25.00
Prestige PRST-7290	(S)	Baby, Baby, Baby	1963	12.00	30.00
Prestige PRLP-7300	(M)	Evenin' Blues	1964	10.00	25.00
Prestige PRST-7300	(S)	Evenin' Blues	1964	12.00	30.00

Label & Catalog #		Title	Year	VG+	NM
Prestige PRLP-7314	(M)	Goin' To Chicago Blues	1964	10.00	25.00
Prestige PRST-7314	(S)	Goin' To Chicago Blues	1964	12.00	30.00
Prestige PRLP-7327	(M)	Blue Spoon	1964	10.00	25.00
Prestige PRST-7327	(S)	Blue Spoon	1964	12.00	30.00
Prestige PRLP-7356	(M)	Some Of My Best Friends Are The Blues	1964	10.00	25.00
Prestige PRST-7356	(S)	Some Of My Best Friends Are The Blues	1964	12.00	30.00
Constellation M-1422	(M)	Take This Hammer	1964	12.00	30.00
Surrey S-1106	(M)	Blues For Spoon And Groove	1965	6.00	15.00
Surrey SS-1106	(S)	Blues For Spoon And Groove	1965	8.00	20.00
Prestige PR-7418	(M)	Spoon In London	1965	6.00	15.00
Prestige PRS-7418	(S)	Spoon In London	1965	8.00	20.00
Verve V-5007	(M)	Blue Point Of View	1967	10.00	25.00
Verve V6-5007	(S)	Blue Point Of View	1967	8.00	20.00
Verve V-5030	(SM	The Blues Is Now (With Jack McDuff)	1967	8.00	20.00
Verve V6-5030	(S)	The Blues Is Now (With Jack McDuff)	1967	8.00	20.00
Verve V-5050	(M)	A Spoonful Of Soul	1968	8.00	20.00
Verve V6-5050	(S)	A Spoonful Of Soul	1968	8.00	20.00
Prestige PRLP-7475	(M)	Blues For Easy Livers	1967	8.00	20.00
Prestige PRST-7475	(S)	Blues For Easy Livers	1967	6.00	15.00
Prestige PRST-7713	(S)	The Best Of Jimmy Witherspoon	1969	6.00	15.00
Verve V6-5050	(S)	A Spoonful Of Soul	1968	6.00	15.00
ABC S-717	(S)	Handbags And Gladrags	1970	6.00	15.00
BluesWay BLS-6026	(S)	Blues Singer	1970	6.00	15.00

WITHERSPOON, JIMMY / EDDIE VINSON

King 634	(M)	Battle Of The Blues, Volume 3	1959	500.00	800.00

WIZARD

Peon 1069	(S)	Original Wizard	1971	60.00	150.00

WIZARDS FROM KANSAS, THE

Mercury SR-61309	(S)	The Wizards From Kansas	1970	30.00	75.00

WOMACK, BOBBY

Minit LP-24014	(S)	Fly Me To The Moon	1968	8.00	20.00
Minit LP-24027	(S)	My Prescription	1969	8.00	20.00

WOMB

Dot DLP-25933	(S)	Womb	1969	8.00	20.00
Dot DLP-25959	(S)	Overdub	1969	8.00	20.00

WOMENFOLK, THE

RCA Victor LPM-2821	(M)	We Give A Hoot	1963	6.00	15.00
RCA Victor LSP-2821	(S)	We Give A Hoot	1963	8.00	20.00
RCA Victor LPM-2832	(M)	The Womenfolk	1964	6.00	15.00
RCA Victor LSP-2832	(S)	The Womenfolk	1964	8.00	20.00
RCA Victor LPM-2919	(M)	Never Underestimate The Power	1964	6.00	15.00
RCA Victor LSP-2919	(S)	Never Underestimate The Power	1964	8.00	20.00
RCA Victor LPM-2991	(M)	The Womenfolk At The Hungry i	1965	6.00	15.00
RCA Victor LSP-2991	(S)	The Womenfolk At The Hungry i	1965	8.00	20.00
RCA Victor LPM-3527	(M)	Man, Oh Man	1966	6.00	15.00
RCA Victor LSP-3527	(S)	Man, Oh Man	1966	8.00	20.00

WONDER, STEVIE
For additional listings refer to The Temptations / Stevie Wonder.

Tamla TS-232	(M)	A Tribute To Uncle Ray	1963	60.00	150.00
Tamla TS-233	(M)	The Jazz Soul Of Stevie Wonder	1963	60.00	150.00
— Original Tamla albums above have a disc over-lapping a globe at the top of the label.—					
Tamla TS-240	(M)	Recorded Live-The 12 Year Old Genius	1963	30.00	75.00
Tamla TS-248	(M)	Workout Stevie, Workout	1963	*Unreleased*	
Tamla T-250	(M)	With A Song In My Heart	1964	20.00	50.00
Tamla T-255	(M)	Stevie At The Beach	1964	16.00	40.00
Tamla TS-255	(S)	Stevie At The Beach	1964	20.00	50.00
Tamla T-268	(M)	Up-Tight (Everything's Alright)	1966	10.00	25.00
Tamla TS-268	(S)	Up-Tight (Everything's Alright)	1966	12.00	30.00
Tamla 272	(M)	Down To Earth	1966	8.00	20.00
Tamla TS-272	(S)	Down To Earth	1966	10.00	25.00
Tamla 279	(M)	I Was Made To Love Her	1967	8.00	20.00
Tamla TS-279	(S)	I Was Made To Love Her	1967	10.00	25.00

Label & Catalog #		Title	Year	VG+	NM
Tamla T-281	(M)	Someday At Christmas	1967	12.00	30.00
Tamla TS-281	(S)	Someday At Christmas	1967	14.00	35.00
Gordy GS-932	(S)	Eivets Rednow	1968	8.00	20.00
Tamla TS-282	(P)	Stevie Wonder's Greatest Hits	1968	6.00	15.00
Tamla TS-291	(S)	For Once In My Life	1968	6.00	15.00
Tamla TS-296	(S)	My Cherie Amour	1969	6.00	15.00
Tamla TS-298	(S)	Stevie Wonder 'Live!'	1970	6.00	15.00
Tamla TS-304	(S)	Signed, Sealed And Delivered	1970	5.00	12.00
Tamla TS-308	(S)	Where I'm Coming From	1971	5.00	12.00
Tamla TS-313	(S)	Stevie Wonder's Greatest Hits, Volume 2	1971	4.00	10.00
Tamla TS-314	(S)	Music Of My Mind	1972	4.00	10.00
Tamla TS-319	(S)	Talking Book (With braille note on cover)	1972	8.00	20.00
Tamla TS-319	(S)	Talking Book (Plain cover)	1972	4.00	10.00
Tamla TS-326	(S)	Innervisions (Textured cover)	1973	4.00	10.00
Tamla PR-61	(DJ)	Journey Through The Secret Life Of Plants	1979	6.00	15.00

WOOD, BRENTON

Double Shot 1002	(M)	Oogum Boogum	1967	10.00	25.00
Double Shot 5002	(S)	Oogum Boogum	1967	12.00	30.00
Double Shot 1003	(M)	Baby You Got It	1967	10.00	25.00
Double Shot 5003	(S)	Baby You Got It	1967	12.00	30.00
Double Shot 5003	(S)	Baby You Got It (Multi-color vinyl)	1967	80.00	200.00
Cream 1006	(S)	Come Softly	1977	6.00	15.00

WOOD, RON
Currently a Rolling Stone, Ron was formerly a member of The Jeff Beck Group and The Small Faces.

Warner Bros. BS-2819	(S)	I've Got My Own Album To Do	1974	5.00	12.00
Warner Bros. BS-2872	(S)	New Look (With Keith Richards)	1975	5.00	12.00
Atco SD-36126	(S)	Mahoney's Last Stand	1976	5.00	12.00
Columbia JC-35702	(S)	Gimme Some Neck	1979	4.00	10.00

WOODPECKER, WOODY
The early Woodys were done by Mel Blanc.

Capitol JAO-3251	(M)	Woody Woodpecker And His Talent Show	1961	20.00	50.00
Capitol J-3263	(M)	Woody Woodpecker's Picnic	1962	20.00	50.00

WOODS, BILL

Country Town CTR-24803	(M)	Bill Woods From Bakersfield	196?	40.00	100.00

WOODY'S TRUCK STOP

Smash SRS-67111	(S)	Woody's Truck Stop	1969	12.00	30.00

WOOFERS, THE

Wyncote W-9011	(M)	Dragsville	1964	16.00	40.00
Wyncote SW-9001	(S)	Dragsville	1964	20.00	50.00

WOOL

ABC S-676	(S)	Wool	1969	8.00	20.00

WOOLEY, SHEB
Sheb Wooley is a pseudonym for Ben Colder.

MGM E-3299	(M)	Sheb Wooley	1956	40.00	100.00
MGM E-4026	(M)	That's My Ma And That's My Pa	1962	8.00	20.00
MGM SE-4026	(S)	That's My Ma And That's My Pa	1962	10.00	25.00
MGM E-4136	(M)	Tales Of How The West Was Won	1963	8.00	20.00
MGM SE-4136	(S)	Tales Of How The West Was Won	1963	10.00	25.00
MGM E-4275	(M)	The Very Best Of Sheb Wooley	1965	8.00	20.00
MGM SE-4275	(S)	The Very Best Of Sheb Wooley	1965	10.00	25.00
MGM E-4325	(M)	It's A Big Land	1965	8.00	20.00
MGM SE-4325	(S)	It's A Big Land	1965	10.00	25.00

WOOLIES, THE

Spirit 9645-2001	(S)	Basic Rock	1970	16.00	40.00
Spirit 9645-2005	(S)	Live At Lizards	1973	12.00	30.00

WOOLY BEAR

Stereo Lab Sound NR-5057	(S)	Wouldya?	1974	24.00	60.00

Label & Catalog #		Title	Year	VG+	NM

WORLD OF OZ, THE

| Deram DES-18022 | (S) | The World Of Oz | 1969 | 12.00 | 30.00 |

WRAY, LINK (& HIS WRAYMEN)
Wray also recorded with Robert Gordon.

Epic LN-3661	(M)	Link Wray And The Wraymen	1960	60.00	150.00
Swan SLP-510	(M)	Jack The Ripper	1963	60.00	150.00
Vermillion 1924	(M)	Great Guitar Hits	1963	60.00	150.00
Vermillion 1925	(M)	Link Wray Sings And Plays Guitar	1964	60.00	150.00
Record Factory 1929	(S)	Yesterday And Today	197?	20.00	50.00
Polydor PD-24-4064	(S)	Link Wray	1971	6.00	15.00
Polydor PD-5047	(S)	Be What You Want To	1973	6.00	15.00
Polydor PD-6025	(S)	The Link Wray Rumble	1974	6.00	15.00

WRAY, VERNON

| Vermillion 1972 | (S) | Wasted (With Link Wray) | 196? | 12.00 | 30.00 |

WRIGHT, BETTY

| Atco SD-33-260 | (S) | My First Time Around | 1968 | 10.00 | 25.00 |

WRIGHT, CHARLES, & THE WATTS 103RD STREET RHYTHM BAND

Warner Bros. WS-1741	(S)	The Watts 103rd St. Rhythm Band	1968	8.00	20.00
Warner Bros. WS-1761	(S)	Together	1968	8.00	20.00
Warner Bros. WS-1801	(S)	In The Jungle, Babe	1969	8.00	20.00
Warner Bros. WS-1864	(S)	Express Yourself	1970	6.00	15.00
Warner Bros. WS-1904	(S)	You're So Beautiful	1971	6.00	15.00
Warner Bros. BS-2620	(S)	Rhythm And Poetry	1972	6.00	15.00
Dunhill DS-30162	(S)	Doing What Comes Naturally (2 LPs)	1973	6.00	15.00
Dunhill DS-50187	(S)	Ninety Day Cycle People	1974	4.00	10.00
ABC ABCD-887	(S)	Lil' Encouragement	1975	4.00	10.00

WRIGHT, JOHNNY
Johnny also recorded with Kitty Wells.

Decca DL-4698	(M)	Hello Viet Nam	1965	6.00	15.00
Decca DL-74698	(S)	Hello Viet Nam	1965	8.00	20.00
Decca DL-4770	(M)	Country Music Special	1966	6.00	15.00
Decca DL-74770	(S)	Country Music Special	1966	8.00	20.00
Decca DL-4846	(M)	Country, The Wright Way	1967	6.00	15.00
Decca DL-74846	(S)	Country, The Wright Way	1967	8.00	20.00
Decca DL-75019	(S)	Country Favorites	1968	6.00	15.00

WRIGHT, NAT: *Refer to GOLDMINE'S PRICE GUIDE TO COLLECTIBLE JAZZ ALBUMS*

WRIGHT, O. V.

Back Beat 61	(M)	If It's Only For Tonight	1965	12.00	30.00
Back Beat 61	(S)	If It's Only For Tonight	1965	16.00	40.00
Back Beat 67	(S)	Nucleus Of Soul	1969	12.00	30.00
Back Beat 70	(S)	A Nickle And A Nail And Ace Of Spades	1972	10.00	25.00
Hi 6008	(S)	Bottom Line	1978	6.00	15.00
Hi 6011	(S)	We're Still Together	1979	6.00	15.00

WUNDERLICH, FRITZ

| Verve/Folkways FV-9023 | (M) | Granada & Other Favorite Songs | 1965 | 5.00 | 12.00 |
| Verve/Folkways FVS-9023 | (S) | Granada & Other Favorite Songs | 1965 | 6.00 | 15.00 |

WYMAN, BILL
Mr. Wyman is a member of The Rolling Stones. Refer to The End; John Hammond; Sons Of Heroes.

Roll. Stones COC-79100	(S)	Monkey Grip	1974	6.00	15.00
Roll. Stones QD-79100	(Q)	Monkey Grip	1974	10.00	25.00
Roll. Stones COC-79103	(S)	Stone Alone	1976	6.00	15.00
Roll. Stones QD-79103	(Q)	Stone Alone	1976	10.00	25.00
Ripple (No number)	(S)	Digital Dreams (Soundtrack)	1983	60.00	150.00

WYNETTE, TAMMY

Epic LN-24305	(M)	Your Good Girl's Gonna Go Bad	1967	6.00	15.00
Epic BN-26305	(S)	Your Good Girl's Gonna Go Bad	1967	8.00	20.00
Epic BN-26353	(S)	Take Me To Your World	1968	8.00	20.00
Epic BN-26392	(S)	D-I-V-O-R-C-E	1968	8.00	20.00
Epic BN-26423	(S)	Inspiration	1969	6.00	15.00

Label & Catalog #		Title	Year	VG+	NM
Epic BN-26451	(S)	Stand By Your Man	1969	5.00	12.00
Epic BN-26474	(S)	Run, Angel, Run (Soundtrack)	1969	6.00	15.00
Epic BN-26486	(S)	Tammy's Greatest Hits	1969	5.00	12.00
Epic BN-26519	(S)	The Ways To Love A Man	1970	5.00	12.00
Epic BN-26549	(S)	Tammy's Touch	1970	5.00	12.00
		— Original Epic albums above have yellow labels.—			
Epic KE-30456	(P)	Five Easy Pieces (Soundtrack)	1971	6.00	15.00
Epic EQ-30658	(Q)	We Sure Can Love Each Other	1971	6.00	15.00
Columbia P6S-5856	(S)	The Very Best Of Tammy Wynette (5 LPs)	1973	14.00	35.00

WYNN, ED

Riverside RLP-1417	(M)	Grandpa Magic's Sports Car Race	195?	16.00	40.00

WYNNE, PHILIPPE
Philippe Wynne is a member of the Parliament/Funkadelic community.

Uncle Jam 36843	(S)	Wynne Jammin'	1980	4.00	10.00

X

Slash 104	(S)	Los Angeles	1980	6.00	15.00
Slash 107	(S)	Wild Gift	1981	6.00	15.00

XIT

Rare Earth R-536	(S)	Plight Of The Redman	1972	8.00	20.00
Rare Earth R-545	(S)	Silent Warrior	1973	6.00	15.00

XTC

Virgin 13134	(S)	Drums And Wires	1979	6.00	15.00
Virgin 13147	(S)	Black Sea	1980	6.00	15.00

XXX

No label	(S)	Live First Legal Bootleg Album	1973	30.00	75.00

YAMA & THE KARMA DUSTERS

Manhole 1	(S)	Up From The Sewers (With insert)	197?	30.00	75.00

YANCEY, JIMMY: *Refer to* GOLDMINE'S PRICE GUIDE TO COLLECTIBLE JAZZ ALBUMS

Another late '60s album with a vague psych connection on a major label that was a virtual give-away a short time ago, The Yankee Dollar on Dot has been selling for $50 or more for the past few years and will probably continue to rise in value with some sense of speed.

Label & Catalog #		Title	Year	VG+	NM

YANCEY, MAMA, & ART RODES

Verve/Folkways FV-9015	(M)	Blues	1965	8.00	20.00
Verve/Folkways FVS-9015	(S)	Blues	1965	10.00	25.00

YANCY DERRINGER

Hemisphere H-15104	(S)	Openers	1975	24.00	60.00

YANKEE DOLLAR, THE

Dot DLP-3874	(M)	The Yankee Dollar	1968	16.00	40.00
Dot DLP-25874	(S)	The Yankee Dollar	1968	24.00	60.00

YANOVSKY, ZALMAN
Zallie was formerly a member of The Mugwumps; The Lovin' Spoonful.

Buddah BDS-5019	(S)	Alive And Well In Argentina	1968	12.00	30.00
Kama Sutra KSBS-2030	(S)	Alive And Well In Argentina	1971	8.00	20.00

YARBROUGH, GLENN
Glenn was formerly a member of The Limeliters.

Elektra EKL-135	(M)	Here We Go, Baby	1957	16.00	40.00
Tradition 1019	(M)	Come Sit By My Side	19??	8.00	20.00
RCA Victor LPM-2905	(M)	One More Sound	1964	6.00	15.00
RCA Victor LSP-2905	(S)	One More Sound	1964	8.00	20.00
RCA Victor LPM-3301	(M)	Come Share My Life	1965	6.00	15.00
RCA Victor LSP-3301	(S)	Come Share My Life	1965	8.00	20.00
RCA Victor LPM-3422	(M)	Baby, The Rain Must Fall	1965	8.00	20.00
RCA Victor LSP-3422	(S)	Baby, The Rain Must Fall	1965	8.00	20.00
RCA Victor LPM-3472	(M)	It's Gonna Be Fine	1965	6.00	15.00
RCA Victor LSP-3472	(S)	It's Gonna Be Fine	1965	8.00	20.00
RCA Victor LPM-3539	(M)	The Lonely Things	1966	6.00	15.00
RCA Victor LSP-3539	(S)	The Lonely Things	1966	8.00	20.00
RCA Victor LPM-3661	(M)	Live At The Hungry i	1966	6.00	15.00
RCA Victor LSP-3661	(S)	Live At The Hungry i	1966	8.00	20.00
RCA Victor LPM-3801	(M)	For Emily, Whenever I May Find Her	1967	8.00	20.00
RCA Victor LSP-3801	(S)	For Emily, Whenever I May Find Her	1967	6.00	15.00
RCA Victor LPM-3860	(M)	Honey And Wine	1967	8.00	20.00
RCA Victor LSP-3860	(S)	Honey And Wine	1967	6.00	15.00
		— Original RCA albums above have black labels.—			
Warner Bros. WS-1736	(S)	Each Of Us Alone	1968	5.00	12.00

YARBROUGH, GELNN, & MARILYN CHILD

Elektra EKL-143	(M)	English And American Folk Songs	1957	16.00	40.00

YARDBIRDS, THE
Members were Chris Dreja, Jim McCarty, Keith Relf, Paul Samwell-Smith and Eric Clapton. Later members were Jeff Beck and Jimmy Page. Refer to Armageddon; Renaissance; Sonny Boy Williamson.

Epic LN-24167	(DJ)	For Your Love (White label)	1965	80.00	200.00
Epic LN-24167	(M)	For Your Love	1965	30.00	75.00
Epic BN-26167	(S)	For Your Love	1965	30.00	75.00
		("Sweet Music" is rechanneled on this album.)			
Epic LN-24177	(DJ)	Having A Rave Up (White label)	1965	80.00	200.00
Epic LN-24177	(M)	Having A Rave Up	1965	30.00	75.00
Epic BN-26177	(E)	Having A Rave Up	1965	20.00	50.00
Epic LN-24210	(DJ)	Over Under Sideways Down (White label)	1966	100.00	200.00
Epic LN-24210	(M)	Over Under Sideways Down	1966	24.00	60.00
Epic BN-26210	(S)	Over Under Sideways Down	1966	30.00	75.00
		("Over Under Sideways Down" is rechanneled on this album.)			
Epic LN-24246	(DJ)	The Yardbirds' Greatest Hits	1966	80.00	200.00
Epic LN-24246	(M)	The Yardbirds' Greatest Hits	1966	20.00	50.00
Epic BN-26246	(E)	The Yardbirds' Greatest Hits	1966	12.00	30.00
MGM E-4447	(M)	Blow-Up (Soundtrack)	1967	12.00	30.00
MGM SE-4447	(S)	Blow-Up (Soundtrack)	1967	16.00	40.00
Epic LN-24313	(DJ)	Little Games (White label)	1967	80.00	200.00
Epic LN-24313	(M)	Little Games	1967	30.00	75.00
Epic BN-26313	(S)	Little Games	1967	30.00	75.00
Epic EG-30135	(P)	The Yardbirds (2 LPs)	1970	20.00	50.00
Epic KE-30615	(S)	Live Yardbirds Featuring Jimmy Page	1972	30.00	75.00
		(Originals have a full-color cover; counterfeits are black & white.)			
Columbia P-13311	(S)	Live Yardbirds Featuring Jimmy Page	1972	24.00	60.00

This privately pressed album featured one side by The Yetti-Men (which included a rather young Tom Rapp) and another side by The Uppa Trio. Both sides of the cover are shown above.

Label & Catalog #		Title	Year	VG+	NM
Sprinboard SPB-4036	(E)	Eric Clapton & The Yardbirds	1972	6.00	15.00
Sprinboard SPB-4039	(E)	Shapes Of Things	1972	6.00	15.00
Epic HE-38455	(S)	The Yardbirds (Half-speed master)	1983	30.00	90.00
		(Epic 33455 is a reissue of 26210 plus two extra tracks.)			

YARROW, PETER
Refer to Peter, Paul & Mary.

Warner Bros. B-2599	(S)	Peter	1972	4.00	10.00
Warner Bros. B-2730	(S)	That's Enough For Me	1973	4.00	10.00
Warner Bros. B-2860	(S)	Hard Times	1975	4.00	10.00
Warner Bros. B-2891	(S)	Peter Yarrow	1975	4.00	10.00

YEAGER, ATLEE
Atlee Yeager also recorded with Damon.

Dunhill DS-50084	(S)	Atlee	1969	6.00	15.00
Chelsea BCL1-0366	(S)	Plant Me Now And Dig Me Later	197?	6.00	15.00

YEAR ONE

(No label)	(S)	Year One (2 LPs)	197?	20.00	50.00

YELLOW BALLOON, THE

Canterbury CLPM-1502	(M)	The Yellow Balloon	1967	12.00	30.00
Canterbury CLPS-1502	(S)	The Yellow Balloon	1967	16.00	40.00

YELLOW PAYGES, THE

Uni 73045	(S)	The Yellow Payges, Volume 1	1969	10.00	25.00

YES
Jon Anderson, Bill Bruford, Steve Howe, Tony Kaye, Chris Squire and Rick Wakeman.

Atlantic 2-908	(DJ)	Tales From Topographic Oceans (2 LPs)	1974	10.00	25.00
		(Promo copies are banded for air play.)			
Mobile Fidelity MFSL-077	(S)	Close To The Edge	1982	15.00	45.00

YESTERDAY'S CHILDREN

Map 3012	(S)	Yesterday's Children	196?	8.00	20.00

YESTERDAY'S FOLK

Buddah BDS-5035	(S)	U. S. 69	1969	6.00	15.00

YETTI-MEN, THE / THE UPPA-TRIO
The Yetti-Men feature Tom Rapp, later of Perals Before Swine.

Kal KB-4348	(S)	The Yetti-Men / The Uppa-Trio	1967	360.00	600.00

YOKOHAMA KNIGHTS, THE

GRT 10002	(S)	Yokohama Knights	197?	6.00	15.00

YORK BROTHERS, THE

King 586	(M)	The York Brothers	1958	20.00	50.00
King 581	(M)	The York Brothers, Volume 2	1958	20.00	50.00
King 820	(M)	16 Great Country & Western Hits	1963	12.00	30.00

YOU KNOW WHO GROUP, THE

Inter. Allied 420	(M)	The You Know Who Group	1965	16.00	40.00

YOUNG, CATHY

Mainstream S-6121	(S)	A Spoonful Of Cathy Young	196?	12.00	30.00

YOUNG, CATHY, & THE INNOCENTS
The Innocents recorded independently of Ms. Young.

Indigo 504	(M)	The Sound Of Cathy Young	1961	80.00	200.00

YOUNG, FARON

Capitol T-778	(M)	Sweethearts Or Strangers	1957	24.00	60.00
Capitol T-1004	(M)	The Object Of My Affection	1958	20.00	50.00
Capitol T-1096	(M)	This Is Faron Young	1959	20.00	50.00
		— Original Capitol albums above have turquoise labels.—			
Capitol T-1185	(M)	My Garden Of Prayer	1959	12.00	30.00
Capitol T-1245	(M)	Talk About Hits	1959	12.00	30.00
Capitol ST-1245	(S)	Talk About Hits	1959	16.00	40.00

Label & Catalog #		Title	Year	VG+	NM
Capitol T-1450	(M)	The Best Of Faron Young	1960	8.00	20.00
Capitol ST-1450	(P)	The Best Of Faron Young	1960	12.00	30.00
Capitol T-1528	(M)	Hello, Walls	1961	8.00	20.00
Capitol ST-1528	(S)	Hello, Walls	1961	12.00	30.00
Capitol T-1634	(M)	The Young Approach	1961	8.00	20.00
Capitol ST-1634	(S)	The Young Approach	1961	12.00	30.00
— Original Capitol albums above have black labels with the logo on the left side.—					
Capitol T-1876	(M)	The All-Time Great Hits of Faron Young	1963	8.00	20.00
Capitol T-2037	(M)	Memory Lane	1965	6.00	15.00
Capitol DT-2037	(E)	Memory Lane	1965	6.00	15.00
Capitol T-2307	(M)	Falling In Love	1965	8.00	20.00
Capitol DT-2307	(E)	Falling In Love	1965	6.00	15.00
Capitol T-2536	(M)	If You Ain't Lovin,' You Ain't Livin'	1966	8.00	20.00
Capitol DT-2536	(E)	If You Ain't Lovin,' You Ain't Livin'	1966	6.00	15.00
SeSac	(M)	Church Songs	195?	24.00	60.00
Mary Carter 1000	(DJ)	On Stage For Mary Carter Paints	196?	16.00	40.00
Mercury MG-20785	(M)	This Is Faron	1963	8.00	20.00
Mercury SR-60785	(S)	This Is Faron	1963	8.00	20.00
Mercury MG-20840	(M)	Faron Young Aims At The West	1963	6.00	15.00
Mercury SR-60840	(S)	Faron Young Aims At The West	1963	8.00	20.00
Mercury MG-20896	(M)	Story Songs For Country Fans	1964	6.00	15.00
Mercury SR-60896	(S)	Story Songs For Country Fans	1964	8.00	20.00
Mercury MG-20931	(M)	Country Dance Favorites	1964	6.00	15.00
Mercury SR-60931	(S)	Country Dance Favorites	1964	8.00	20.00
Mercury MG-20971	(M)	Story Songs Of Mountains And Valleys	1964	6.00	15.00
Mercury SR-60971	(S)	Story Songs Of Mountains And Valleys	1964	8.00	20.00
Mercury MG-21007	(M)	Pen And Paper	1965	6.00	15.00
Mercury SR-61007	(S)	Pen And Paper	1965	8.00	20.00
Mercury MG-21047	(M)	Faron Young's Greatest Hits	1965	5.00	12.00
Mercury SR-61047	(S)	Faron Young's Greatest Hits	1965	6.00	15.00
Mercury MG-21058	(M)	Faron Young Sings The Best Of Jim Reeves	1966	6.00	15.00
Mercury SR-61058	(S)	Faron Young Sings The Best Of Jim Reeves	1966	8.00	20.00
Mercury MG-21110	(M)	Unmitigated Gall	1967	6.00	15.00
Mercury SR-61110	(S)	Unmitigated Gall	1967	6.00	15.00
Tower DT-5121	(E)	The World Of Faron Young	1968	6.00	15.00

YOUNG, JESSE COLIN
Both Capitol and Mercury reissued JCY's solo albums and attempted to capitalize on the popularity of his group, The Youngbloods, even though the group does not appear on either of the albums.

Capitol T-2070	(M)	Soul Of A City Boy	1964	20.00	50.00
Mercury MG-21005	(M)	Young Blood (With John Sebastian)	1965	12.00	30.00
Mercury SR-61005	(S)	Young Blood (With John Sebastian)	1965	16.00	40.00
Capitol T-2070	(M)	Jesse Colin Young & The Youngbloods	1967	10.00	25.00
Capitol ST-2070	(E)	Jesse Colin Young & The Youngbloods	1967	6.00	15.00
		(This is a repackage of "Soul Of A City Boy.")			
Mercury SR-61005	(S)	Jesse Colin Young & The Youngbloods	1969	8.00	20.00
		(This is a repackage of "Young Blood.")			
Mercury SR-61273	(S)	Two Trips (Gold bordered cover)	1970	12.00	30.00
Mercury SR-61273	(S)	Two Trips (Red bordered cover)	1970	10.00	25.00
		(Side 1 contains The Youngbloods' pre-RCA recordings while side 2 comprises the best of the "Young Blood" album above.)			

YOUNG, NEIL (& CRAZY HORSE)
Crazy Horse backs Young up on 6349, 2221, 2242. Refer to The Buffalo Springfield; Crosby, Stills, Nash & Young; The Stills-Young Band.

Reprise RS-6317	(S)	Neil Young	1968	40.00	100.00
		(First pressings have brown & orange labels and Young's name does not appear on the front cover.)			
Reprise RS-6317	(S)	Neil Young	1969	20.00	50.00
		(Second pressings with four remixed tracks have brown & orange labels and "RE 1" is etched in the trail-off vinyl. Young's name does not appear on the front cover.)			
Reprise RS-6317	(S)	Neil Young	197?	6.00	15.00
		(Third pressings have brown labels with "Neil Young" across the top of the front cover.)			
Reprise RS-6349	(DJ)	Everybody Knows This Is Nowhere	1969	20.00	50.00
		(White label promo.)			
Reprise RS-6349	(S)	Everybody Knows This Is Nowhere	1969	8.00	20.00
		(Brown & orange label.)			

Label & Catalog #		Title	Year	VG+	NM
Reprise RS-6383	(DJ)	**After The Gold Rush** (White label)	1970	20.00	50.00
Reprise RS-6383	(S)	**After The Gold Rush**	1970	12.00	30.00
		(Brown & orange label. A photo of Marc Bolan was erroneously printed on the inside cover.)			
Reprise RS-6383	(S)	**After The Gold Rush**	1970	12.00	30.00
		(Brown & orange label. A photo of Neil was erroneously printed upside down on the inside cover.)			
Reprise RS-6383	(S)	**After The Gold Rush**	1970	8.00	20.00
		(Brown & orange label with all photos correct.)			
Reprise RS-6383	(S)	**After The Gold Rush**	1978	16.00	40.00
		(Includes a remixed, extended version of "When You Dance I Can Really Love." Brown label with RE 2" is etched in the trail-off vinyl and the title on the cover is in red print.)			
Reprise MS-2032	(S)	**Harvest**	1972	6.00	15.00
		(The jacket and the lyric sheet are printed on textured paper.)			
Reprise 2XS-6480	(DJ)	**Journey Through The Past** (2 LPs)	1972	16.00	40.00
		(White label promo. The cover bears a sticker that reads "Album must be played prior to airing; this album may contain words offensive to the public.")			
Reprise 2XS-6480	(S)	**Journey Through The Past** (2 LPs)	1972	6.00	15.00
		(First pressing covers are die-cut with special inner sleeves.)			
Reprise M-2151	(DJ)	**Time Fades Away** (White label. Mono)	1973	20.00	50.00
Reprise MS-2151	(DJ)	**Time Fades Away** (White label. Stereo)	1973	8.00	20.00
Reprise 3RS-2257	(DJ)	**Decade** (3 LPs. Test pressing)	1976	150.00	300.00
		("Campaigner" contains a verse deleted from the official version.)			
Reprise MSK-2266	(DJ)	**Give To The Wind**	1978	150.00	300.00
		(MSK-2266 was originally titled "Ode To The Wind" and eventually released as "Comes A Time." Issued in a plain jacket with inserts.)			
Warner Bros. WBMS-107	(DJ)	**The Warner Bros. Music Show** (Interview)	1979	16.00	40.00
Geffen GHS-2018	(DJ)	**Trans** (Quiex II vinyl)	1982	6.00	15.00
Geffen GHS-4013	(DJ)	**Everybody's Rockin'** (Quiex II vinyl)	1983	6.00	15.00
Nautilus NR-44	(S)	**Harvest** (SuperDisc)	1982	40.00	120.00

YOUNG RASCALS, THE: Refer to THE RASCALS

YOUNGBLOODS, THE
Original members were Lowell "Banana" Levinger, Joe Bauer, Jerry Corbitt and Jesse Colin Young. Refer to Banana & The Bunch.

RCA Victor LPM-3724	(M)	**The Youngbloods**	1967	12.00	30.00
RCA Victor LSP-3724	(S)	**The Youngbloods**	1967	10.00	25.00
RCA Victor LPM-3865	(M)	**Earth Music**	1968	20.00	50.00
RCA Victor LSP-3865	(S)	**Earth Music**	1968	10.00	25.00
		— Original RCA albums above have black labels with Nipper on top.—			
RCA Victor LSP-3724	(S)	**Get Together**	1969	6.00	15.00
		(This is a repackage of "The Youngbloods.")			
RCA Victor LSP-3865	(S)	**Earth Music**	1969	6.00	15.00
RCA Victor LSP-4150	(S)	**Elephant Mountain**	1969	8.00	20.00
RCA Victor LSP-4399	(S)	**The Best Of The Youngbloods**	1970	6.00	15.00
		— RCA albums above have orange labels on non-flexible vinyl.—			
RCA Victor LSP-4561	(S)	**Sunlight**	1971	5.00	12.00
RCA Victor VPS-6051	(S)	**This Is The Youngbloods** (2 LPs)	1972	6.00	15.00
		— RCA albums above have orange labels.—			
Warner/Racoon WS-1878	(S)	**Rock Festival**	1970	4.00	10.00
Warner/Racoon BS-2563	(S)	**Ride The Wind**	1971	4.00	10.00
Warner/Racoon BS-2566	(S)	**Good And Dusty**	1971	4.00	10.00
Warner/Racoon BS-2653	(S)	**High On A Ridgetop**	1972	4.00	10.00

YOUNGMAN, HENNY

Urania UR-9014	(M)	**The Horse And Auto Race Game**	195?	16.00	40.00

YOUR GANG

Mercury MG-21094	(M)	**If You Want To Buy 'Em**	1966	5.00	12.00
Mercury SR-61094	(S)	**If You Want To Buy 'Em**	1966	6.00	15.00

YUM YUM KIDS, THE

MGM E-4396	(M)	**Yummy In Your Tummy**	1966	6.00	15.00
MGM SE-4396	(S)	**Yummy In Your Tummy**	1966	8.00	20.00

Label & Catalog #		Title	Year	VG+	NM
YURO, TIMI					
Liberty LRP-3208	(M)	Hurt	1961	12.00	30.00
Liberty LST-7208	(S)	Hurt	1961	16.00	40.00
Liberty LRP-3212	(M)	Soul	1962	6.00	15.00
Liberty LST-7212	(S)	Soul	1962	8.00	20.00
Liberty LRP-3234	(M)	Let Me Call You Sweetheart	1962	5.00	12.00
Liberty LST-7234	(S)	Let Me Call You Sweetheart	1962	6.00	15.00
Liberty LRP-3263	(M)	What's A Matter, Baby?	1962	6.00	15.00
Liberty LST-7263	(S)	What's A Matter, Baby?	1962	8.00	20.00
Liberty LRP-3286	(M)	The Best Of Timi Yuro	1963	5.00	12.00
Liberty LST-7286	(S)	The Best Of Timi Yuro	1963	6.00	15.00
Liberty LRP-3319	(M)	Make The World Go Away	1963	5.00	12.00
Liberty LST-7319	(S)	Make The World Go Away	1963	6.00	15.00
Mercury MG-20963	(M)	The Amazing Timi Yuro	1964	5.00	12.00
Mercury SR-60963	(S)	The Amazing Timi Yuro	1964	6.00	15.00
Sunset SUM-1107	(M)	Timi Yuro	1966	4.00	10.00
Sunset SUS-5107	(S)	Timi Yuro	1966	5.00	12.00
Colgems COS-5007	(S)	Interlude (Soundtrack)	1968	10.00	25.00
Liberty LST-7594	(S)	Something Bad On My Mind	1968	5.00	12.00

ZABACH, FLORIAN					
Decca DL-5367 (10")	(M)	The Hot Canary	1951	16.00	40.00
ZACHERLEY, JOHN					
Elektra EKL-7190	(M)	Spook Along With Zacherley	1960	16.00	40.00
Elektra EKS-7190	(S)	Spook Along With Zacherley	1960	20.00	50.00
Parkway P-7018	(M)	Monster Mash	1962	16.00	40.00
Parkway P-7023	(M)	Scary Tales	1963	16.00	40.00
Crestview CR-803	(M)	Zacherley's Monster Gallery	1963	14.00	35.00
Crestview CRS7-803	(S)	Zacherley's Monster Gallery	1963	16.00	40.00
ZAGER & EVANS					
White Whale WW-7123	(S)	The Early Writings Of Zager And Evans	1969	5.00	12.00
RCA Victor LSP-4214	(S)	In The Year 2525	1969	6.00	15.00
RCA Victor LSP-4302	(S)	Zager And Evans	1970	5.00	12.00
ZANIES, THE					
Dore 321	(S)	The Zanies	1969	10.00	25.00
Dore 337	(S)	The Zanies (Dore 387 is a reissue of 321)	1979	6.00	15.00

ZAPPA, FRANK [THE MOTHERS OF INVENTION]
While Zappa is always in charge, the Verve albums and an occasional later album credit The Mothers Of Invention or simply The Mothers. The original group (1964-1969) was Zappa with Jimmy Carl Black, Ray Collins, Roy Estrada and Elliott Ingber. The second group (1970-72), consists of Zappa and Underwood with George Duke, Aynsley Dunbar, Jim Pons and former Turtles Howard Kaylan and Mark Volman. Refer to The Animals; Captain Beefheart; Wild Man Fischer; G.T.O.'s; Sandy Hurvitz; Jean Luc Ponty; Ruben & The Jets; and L. Shankar.

Verve V-5005-2	(DJ)	Freak Out! (2 LPs. White label)	1966	100.00	250.00
Verve V-5005-2	(M)	Freak Out! (2 LPs)	1966	40.00	100.00
Verve V6-5005-2	(DJ)	Freak Out! (2 LPs. Yellow label)	1966	60.00	150.00
Verve V6-5005-2	(S)	Freak Out! (2 LPs)	1966	20.00	50.00
		(Issued with a mail-order coupon for a map, priced separately below.)			

Label & Catalog #		Title	Year	VG+	NM
Verve 5005		**Freak Out! Coupon**	1966	10.00	25.00
		(Mail-order coupon for the map below.)			
Verve 5005		**Freak Out! Map**	1966	40.00	100.00
		(A map of "freak out hot spots" in L.A. available through the mail .)			
Verve V-5006	(M)	**Freak Out!**	1966	Unreleased	
Verve V6-5006	(S)	**Freak Out!**	1966	Unreleased	
		(Apparently a single album version of this title was scheduled			
		for release, assigned a catalog number and cancelled.)			
Verve V6-5013	(DJ)	**Absolutely Free**	1967	60.00	150.00
Verve V-5013	(M)	**Absolutely Free**	1967	40.00	100.00
Verve V6-5013	(S)	**Absolutely Free**	1967	20.00	50.00
Verve V6-5045	(DJ)	**We're Only In It For The Money**	1968	60.00	150.00
Verve V-5045	(M)	**We're Only In It For The Money**	1968	40.00	100.00
Verve V6-5045	(S)	**We're Only In It For The Money**	1968	30.00	75.00
		(Issued with a "Sgt Pepper" parody insert.)			
Verve V6-5045	(S)	**We're Only In It For The Money**	1968	80.00	200.00
		(Late edited version: in the song "Who Needs The Peace Corps?"			
		the line "I will love the police as they kick the shit out of me" has			
		been deleted. Must be listened to for identification.)			
Verve V6-8741	(DJ)	**Lumpy Gravy**	1968	60.00	150.00
Verve V6-8741	(S)	**Lumpy Gravy**	1968	20.00	50.00
Verve V6-5055	(DJ)	**Cruising With Ruben & The Jets**	1968	60.00	150.00
Verve V6-5055	(S)	**Cruising With Ruben & The Jets**	1968	30.00	75.00
		(Issued with a set of bonuses, priced separately below.)			
Verve V6-5055		**Cruising With Ruben & The Jets Insert #1**	1968	20.00	50.00
		(Paper insert titled "The Story Of Ruben & The Jets.")			
Verve V6-5055		**Cruising With Ruben & The Jets Insert #2**	1968	20.00	50.00
		(Paper insert titled "How To Comb & Set A Jellyroll.")			
Verve V6-5055		**Cruising With Ruben & The Jets Insert #3**	1968	20.00	50.00
		(Paper insert guide on how to do the "bop.")			
Verve V6-5068	(DJ)	**Mothermania**	1969	40.00	100.00
Verve V6-5068	(S)	**Mothermania**	1969	30.00	75.00
Verve V6-5074	(DJ)	**The XXXX Of The Mothers Of Invention**	1969	40.00	100.00
Verve V6-5074	(S)	**The XXXX Of The Mothers Of Invention**	1969	20.00	50.00
MGM GAS-112	(DJ)	**The Mothers Of Invention**	1970	30.00	75.00
MGM GAS-112	(S)	**The Mothers Of Invention**	1970	16.00	40.00
MGM SE-4754	(DJ)	**The Worst Of The Mothers**	1971	30.00	75.00
MGM SE-4754	(S)	**The Worst Of The Mothers**	1971	20.00	50.00
Warner Bros. PRO-368	(DJ)	**Zapped** *(Collage cover)*	1969	16.00	40.00
Warner Bros. PRO-368	(DJ)	**Zapped** *(Zappa cover)*	1969	8.00	20.00
		(Various artists sampler for Zappa's Bizarre/Straight labels.			
		First pressing covers have a black & white photo collage;			
		second pressings have a black & white close-up of Frank.)			
Bizarre MS-2024	(S)	**Uncle Meat** *(2 LPs wth booklet)*	1969	16.00	40.00
Bizarre RS-6356	(S)	**Hot Rats**	1969	12.00	30.00
Bizarre RS-6370	(S)	**Burnt Weenie Sandwich** *(With booklet)*	1969	12.00	30.00
Bizarre MS-2028	(S)	**Weasels Ripped My Flesh**	1970	12.00	30.00
Bizarre MS-2030	(S)	**Chunga's Revenge**	1970	12.00	30.00
Bizarre MS-2042	(S)	**Fillmore East, June 1971**	1971	12.00	30.00
Bizarre MS-2075	(S)	**Just Another Band From L.A.**	1972	12.00	30.00
Bizarre MS-2093	(S)	**The Grand Wazoo**	1972	12.00	30.00
Bizarre MS-2094	(S)	**Waka/Jawaka**	1972	12.00	30.00
— Original Bizarre albums above have blue labels.—					
Bizarre MS-2024	(S)	**Uncle Meat** *(2 LPs)*	1973	8.00	20.00
Bizarre RS-6356	(S)	**Hot Rats**	1973	6.00	15.00
Bizarre RS-6370	(S)	**Burnt Weenie Sandwich**	1973	6.00	15.00
Bizarre MS-2028	(S)	**Weasels Ripped My Flesh**	1973	6.00	15.00
Bizarre MS-2030	(S)	**Chunga's Revenge**	1973	6.00	15.00
Bizarre MS-2042	(S)	**Fillmore East, June 1971**	1973	6.00	15.00
Bizarre MS-2075	(S)	**Just Another Band From L.A.**	1973	6.00	15.00
Bizarre MS-2093	(S)	**The Grand Wazoo**	1973	6.00	15.00
Bizarre MS-2094	(S)	**Waka/Jawaka**	1973	6.00	15.00
— Bizarre albums above have brown Reprise labels.—					
DiscReet MS-2149	(S)	**Over-Nite Sensation**	1973	8.00	20.00
DiscReet MS4-2149	(Q)	**Over-Nite Sensation**	1973	16.00	40.00
DiscReet DS-2175	(S)	**Apostrophe**	1974	6.00	15.00
DiscReet DS4-2175	(Q)	**Apostrophe**	1974	14.00	35.00
DiscReet DSS-2202	(S)	**Roxy & Elsewhere**	1974	8.00	20.00
DiscReet DS-2216	(S)	**One Size Fits All**	1975	6.00	15.00

Label & Catalog #		Title	Year	VG+	NM
DiscReet DS-2234	(S)	**Bongo Fury** *(With Captain Beefheart)*	1975	6.00	15.00
Warner Bros. BS-2970	(S)	**Zoot Allures**	1976	6.00	15.00
DiscReet DSK-2288	(S)	**Over-Nite Sensation**	1977	8.00	20.00
DiscReet 2D-2290	(DJ)	**Zappa In New York Cover** *(2 LPs)*	1978	200.00	400.00
		(Test pressing with"Punky's Whips.")			
DiscReet 2D-2290	(S)	**Zappa In New York Cover** *(2 LPs)*	1978	60.00	150.00
		(Original covers erroneously list the deleted "Punky's Whips.")			
DiscReet 2D-2290	(S)	**Zappa In New York** *(2 LPs)*	1978	8.00	20.00
DiscReet DSK-2291	(S)	**Studio Tan**	1978	6.00	15.00
DiscReet DSK-2292	(S)	**Sleep Dirt**	1979	6.00	15.00
DiscReet DSK-2294	(S)	**Orchestral Favorites**	1979	6.00	15.00
Zappa	(DJ)	**Lather** *(4 LP test pressing)*	197?	*See note below*	
		(Rare with a suggested Near Mint value $500-1,000.)			
Zappa SRZ-2-1501	(S)	**Sheik Yerbouti**	1979	6.00	15.00
Zappa SRZ-1-1603	(S)	**Joe's Garage, Act I**	1979	5.00	12.00
Zappa SRZ-2-1502	(S)	**Joe's Garage, Acts II & III** *(2 LPs)*	1979	6.00	15.00
Barking Pumpkin 1115	(S)	**Baby Snakes** *(Picture disc)*	1982	6.00	15.00

ZENITHS, THE

Label & Catalog #		Title	Year	VG+	NM
Atlantic 8043	(M)	**Makin' The Scene**	1960	40.00	100.00
Atlantic SD-8043	(S)	**Makin' The Scene**	1960	60.00	150.00

ZEPHYR

Label & Catalog #		Title	Year	VG+	NM
Probe CPLP-4510	(S)	**Zephyr**	1969	16.00	40.00
Warner Bros. BS-1897	(S)	**Going Back To Colorado**	1971	10.00	25.00
Warner Bros. BS-2603	(S)	**Sunset Ride**	1972	10.00	25.00

ZERFAS

Label & Catalog #		Title	Year	VG+	NM
700 West 730710	(S)	**Zerfas**	197?	500.00	800.00

ZEVON, WARREN

Label & Catalog #		Title	Year	VG+	NM
Imperial LP-12456	(S)	**Wanted Dead Or Alive**	1970	6.00	15.00

ZIG ZAG PEOPLE

Label & Catalog #		Title	Year	VG+	NM
Decca DL-75110	(S)	**Take Bubble Gum Music Underground**	1969	8.00	20.00

ZIP CODES

Label & Catalog #		Title	Year	VG+	NM
Liberty LRP-3367	(M)	**Mustang**	1964	30.00	75.00
Liberty LST-7367	(S)	**Mustang**	1964	40.00	100.00

ZIPPER

Label & Catalog #		Title	Year	VG+	NM
Whizeagle	(S)	**Zipper**	1975	16.00	40.00

ZOMBIES

Features Rod Argent and Colin Blunstone.

Label & Catalog #		Title	Year	VG+	NM
Parrot PAR-1001	(M)	**The Zombies**	1965	20.00	50.00
Parrot PAS-71001	(E)	**The Zombies**	1965	16.00	40.00
RCA Victor LOC-1115	(M)	**Bunny Lake Is Missing** *(Soundtrack)*	1965	30.00	75.00
RCA Victor LSO-1115	(S)	**Bunny Lake Is Missing** *(Soundtrack)*	1965	40.00	100.00
Date TES-4013	(S)	**Odessey And Oracle**	1968	12.00	30.00
		(First pressing covers make no mention of "Time Of The Season." "This Will Be Our Year" is rechanneled on this album.)			
Date TES-4013	(S)	**Odessey And Oracle**	1969	8.00	20.00
		(Second pressing covers note the single "Time Of The Season." "This Will Be Our Year" is rechanneled on this album.)			
London PS-557	(S)	**Early Days**	1969	6.00	15.00
		(Features hits in stereo except "Tell Her No," which is rechanneled.)			
Epic KEG-32861	(S)	**Time Of The Zombies** *(2 LPs)*	1974	5.00	12.00
		(All the tracks on side 1 are in mono.)			

ZOO

Label & Catalog #		Title	Year	VG+	NM
Sunburst 7500	(S)	**The Zoo Presents The Chocolate Mousse**	1968	20.00	50.00

ZOO

Label & Catalog #		Title	Year	VG+	NM
Mercury SR-61300	(S)	**The Zoo**	1970	6.00	15.00

ZZ TOP

Label & Catalog #		Title	Year	VG+	NM
London PS-X-1001	(DJ)	**Takin' Texas to The People**	1976	20.00	50.00

Various Artists Compilations / Soundtracks

A complete list of various artists compilations would take up another whole volume. I have listed those titles that are rare and those most sought after by collectors. Even for its stated goals, this list far from complete. Most of these albums have a nominal value, especially given their age and the fact that as a genre these albums didn't sell in overwhelming numbers. The presence of any collectible artist on an otherwise mediocre compilation will affect its value somewhat; a track by a major artist can dramatically increase a value. For instance, Clarion 609, *Discoteque In Astrosound*, an otherwise nondescript comp, is sought-after by Beatles collectors because it contains one of the Tony Sheridan & The Beat Brothers sides.

RCA Victor issued samplers to radio stations throughout the '50s and '60s, often con-taining an Elvis track; each of these fetches three figure prices, even though the Elvis material is available elsewhere. To a lesser extent comps with tracks by The Beach Boys, Bowie, Dylan and The Stones also attract a premium from completists. It is simply not possible in this book to list each of the collectible artists who appear on the albums below, although a few special items have been singled out. (I *have* listed several of thes aforementioned Elvis items in a section following the regular RCA titles.) Finally, several albums that are, in fact, various artists compilations have been listed under individual artists for technical reasons; a note refers the reader to the artist. . .

(No label)	(DJ)	**Carnival Rock** *(Soundtrack)* *(Red vinyl issued without a cover. Near Mint copies* *have a suggested value of $1,500-2,000.)*	1955	**750.00**	*Rare*
(No label)	(DJ)	**Rock, Rock, Rock** *(Soundtrack)* *(Publisher's demo disc issued without a cover.* *Near Mint copies have a suggested value of $1,500-2,000.)*	1955	**750.00**	*Rare*
(No label)	(DJ)	**Go, Johnny, Go** *(Soundtrack)* *(Near Mint copies have a suggested value of $1,200-1,600.)*	1959	**600.00**	*Rare*
(No label)	(M)	**Psychedelic Patchwork, Vol. 1**	198?	**12.00**	**30.00**
A&M SP-8022	(DJ)	**The A&M Bootleg Album** *(2 LPs)*	1973	**10.00**	**25.00**
A&M PR-4738	(DJ)	**No Wave** *(Picture disc)*	1978	**6.00**	**15.00**
A&M PR-4876	(DJ)	**Propaganda** *(Picture disc)*	1980	**16.00**	**40.00**
A Go-Go	(M)	**Chosen Few, Volume 1**	198?	**16.00**	**40.00**
ABC-Paramount 216	(M)	**A Million Or More** *(Original pressing covers and labels credit the last track as* *Tommy Roe's "Sheila" while the disc plays Paul Anka's "Diana.")*	1958	**20.00**	**50.00**
ABC-Paramount 504	(M)	**Shindig!**	1964	**10.00**	**25.00**
ABC-Paramount S-504	(S)	**Shindig!**	1964	**12.00**	**30.00**
ABC OC-13	(S)	**Zachariah** *(Soundtrack)*	1970	**6.00**	**15.00**
Ace 1012	(M)	**Greatest 15 Hits**	1960	**30.00**	**75.00**
Ace 1019	(M)	**Let's Have A Dance Party**	1961	**30.00**	**75.00**
Ace 1020	(M)	**For Twisters Only**	1962	**30.00**	**75.00**
Acid 1	(M)	**Chocolate Soup, Volume 2**	198?	**12.00**	**30.00**
AGNC 100	(M)	**Nightmares From The Underworld, Vol. 1**	198?	**40.00**	**100.00**
Aladdin 710	(M)	**Rock & Roll With Rhythm & Blues** *(Although this album carries the company's 700 series* *designating a 10" album it is a 12 incher nonetheless.)*	195?	**250.00**	**600.00**
All God's Delerium	(M)	**Good Roots**	198?	**30.00**	**75.00**
Almor A-108	(M)	**The World Of Surfin'**	1963	**16.00**	**40.00**
Almor AS-108	(S)	**The World Of Surfin'**	1963	**20.00**	**50.00**

Label & Catalog #		Title	Year	VG+	NM
Almor A-109	(M)	Hot Rod Drag Races	1963	20.00	50.00
Almor AS-109	(S)	Hot Rod Drag Races	1963	24.00	60.00
Amazon 1007	(M)	Greatest Rhythm & Blues Hits	195?	20.00	50.00
Amazon 1008	(M)	Greatest Rhythm & Blues Hits, Volume 2	195?	20.00	50.00
Amos AAS-8002	(S)	Vanishing Point (Soundtrack)	1971	10.00	25.00
Ampex 50101	(S)	Jud (Soundtrack)	1971	6.00	15.00
Apollo 490	(M)	Jackpot Of Hits	1957	60.00	150.00
Apple SW-3377	(S)	Come Together (Soundtrack)	1971	8.00	20.00
Apple STCX-3385	(S)	The Concert For Bangla Desh: Refer to George Harrison & Friends			
Apple SW-3400	(M)	Phil Spector's Christmas Album: Refer to Phil Spector			
Argo LP-649	(DJ)	Remember The Oldies (Multi-color vinyl)	1963	60.00	150.00
Argo LP-649	(M)	Remember The Oldies	1963	20.00	50.00
Argo LP-656	(M)	Fanfare Of Hits	1963	10.00	25.00
Argo LP-4026	(M)	The Blues, Volume 1	1963	10.00	25.00
Argo LP-4027	(M)	The Blues, Volume 2	1963	10.00	25.00
Argo LP-4031	(M)	Folk Festival Of The Blues	1964	20.00	50.00
Argo LP-4041	(M)	The Blues, Volume 3	1965	10.00	25.00
Argo LP-4042	(M)	The Blues, Volume 4	1965	10.00	25.00
Arrawak 100	(M)	A Night Train Of Oldies	195?	16.00	40.00
Arvee 433	(M)	Golden Echoes	1962	10.00	25.00
Ascot ALM-13007	(M)	All Girl Million Sellers	1964	14.00	35.00
Ascot ALS-16007	(P)	All Girl Million Sellers	1964	14.00	35.00
Astra 1001	(M)	Terry Lee Presents For Lovers Only	1964	20.00	50.00
Atco 33-103	(M)	Rockin' Together	1958	30.00	75.00
Atco 33-118	(M)	The Good Old '50's	1960	20.00	50.00
Atco 33-143	(M)	The Great Group Goodies	1962	20.00	50.00
Atco 33-159	(M)	Apollo Saturday Night	1964	16.00	40.00
Atco SD-33-159	(S)	Apollo Saturday Night	1964	30.00	75.00
Atco 33-169		Ain't She Sweet: Refer to The Beatles			
Atco 33-171	(M)	Swinging The Bard	1964	5.00	12.00
Atco SD-33-171	(S)	Swinging The Bard	1964	6.00	15.00
Atco SD-33-245	(S)	The Savage Seven (Soundtrack)	1968	8.00	20.00
Atco D-33-269	(S)	Soul Christmas	1968	8.00	20.00
Atco SD-33-279	(S)	The Super Groups	1969	6.00	15.00
Atco SD-33-281	(S)	Soul Clan	1969	6.00	15.00
Atco SD-33-314	(S)	Rock Begins, Volume 1	1970	6.00	15.00
Atco SD-33-315	(S)	Rock Begins, Volume 2	1970	6.00	15.00
Atlantic 1239	(M)	Rock & Roll Forever	1956	60.00	150.00
Atlantic 8001	(M)	The Greatest Rock & Roll	1956	60.00	150.00
Atlantic 8010	(M)	Rock & Roll Forever, Volume 1	1956	40.00	100.00
Atlantic 8013	(M)	Dance The Rock & Roll	1957	40.00	100.00
Atlantic 8021	(M)	Rock & Roll Forever, Volume 2	1957	40.00	100.00
Atlantic 8037	(M)	The Rockin' '50's	1959	40.00	100.00
— Original Atlantic albums above have black labels.—					
Atlantic 8037	(M)	The Rockin' '50's (Red label)	1959	20.00	50.00
Atlantic 1347	(M)	Blue Ridge Mountain Music	1960	16.00	40.00
Atlantic SD-1347	(S)	Blue Ridge Mountain Music	1960	20.00	50.00
Atlantic 8058	(M)	The Greatest Twist Hits	1962	20.00	50.00
Atlantic 8065	(M)	The Solid Gold Groups	1962	20.00	50.00
Atlantic 8068	(M)	Hound Dog's Old Gold	1962	20.00	50.00
Atlantic 8098	(M)	Jamaica Ska	1963	8.00	20.00
Atlantic SD-8098	(S)	Jamaica Ska	1963	10.00	25.00
Atlantic 8101	(M)	Saturday Night At The Uptown	1964	10.00	25.00
Atlantic SD-8101	(S)	Saturday Night At The Uptown	1964	14.00	35.00
Atlantic 8108	(M)	Killer Joe's International Disco	1965	8.00	20.00
Atlantic SD-8108	(S)	Killer Joe's International Disco	1965	12.00	30.00

Label & Catalog #		Title	Year	VG+	NM
Atlantic 8116	(M)	Solid Gold Soul	1965	6.00	15.00
Atlantic SD-8116	(S)	Solid Gold Soul	1965	8.00	20.00
Atlantic 8137	(M)	Solid Gold Soul, Volume 2	1967	8.00	20.00
Atlantic SD-8137	(S)	Solid Gold Soul, Volume 2	1967	6.00	15.00
Atlantic 8140	(M)	Beach Beat	1967	8.00	20.00
Atlantic SD-8140	(S)	Beach Beat	1967	6.00	15.00
Atlantic SD-8161	(S)	The History Of Rhythm & Blues, Volume 1	1968	6.00	15.00
Atlantic SD-8162	(S)	The History Of Rhythm & Blues, Volume 2	1968	6.00	15.00
Atlantic SD-8163	(S)	The History Of Rhythm & Blues, Volume 3	1968	6.00	15.00
Atlantic SD-8164	(S)	The History Of Rhythm & Blues, Volume 4	1968	6.00	15.00
Atlantic SD-8167	(S)	Brazil's Super Hits	1968	6.00	15.00
Atlantic SD-8170	(S)	This Is Soul	1968	6.00	15.00
Atlantic SD-8191	(S)	Beach Beat, Volume 2	1968	6.00	15.00
Atlantic SD-501	(S)	The Super Hits	1968	6.00	15.00
Atlantic SD-8188	(S)	Super Hits, Volume 2	1968	6.00	15.00
Atlantic SD-8191	(S)	Beach Beat	1968	6.00	15.00
Atlantic SD-8193	(S)	The History Of Rhythm & Blues, Vol 5	1968	6.00	15.00
Atlantic SD-8194	(S)	The History Of Rhythm & Blues, Vol 6	1968	6.00	15.00
Atlantic SD-8203	(S)	Super Hits, Volume 3	1968	6.00	15.00
Atlantic SD-8208	(S)	The History Of Rhythm & Blues, Volume 7	1968	6.00	15.00
Atlantic SD-8209	(S)	The History Of Rhythm & Blues, Volume 8	1968	6.00	15.00
Atlantic SD-8224	(S)	Super Hits, Volume 4	1969	6.00	15.00
Atlantic SD-8274	(S)	Super Hits, Volume 5	1970	6.00	15.00
ATV Music	(DJ)	In The Beginning...	1980	8.00	20.00
Audio Fidelity AFLP-2168	(M)	Where It's At (Live At The Cheetah)	1966	60.00	150.00
Audio Lab LP-1520	(M)	Highway Of Blues	195?	40.00	100.00
Audio Lab AL-1546	(M)	Swing Billies	195?	40.00	100.00
Audio Lab AL-1563	(M)	Pierce, Rainwater & Stuart Hamblen Sing For You	195?	30.00	75.00
Audio Lab AL-1566	(M)	Swing Billies, Volume 2	195?	40.00	100.00
Audio Fidelity DF-7039	(M)	Discotheque Jet Set, Volume 1	196?	6.00	15.00
Audio Fidelity DFS-7039	(S)	Discotheque Jet Set, Volume 1	196?	6.00	15.00
Audio Fidelity DF-7040	(M)	Discotheque Jet Set, Volume 2	196?	6.00	15.00
Audio Fidelity DFS-7040	(S)	Discotheque Jet Set, Volume 2	196?	6.00	15.00
Audio Fidelity DFS-7777	(S)	Stereo Spectacular	196?	6.00	15.00
August 100	(M)	Money Music	1967	300.00	500.00
Authentic DTL-501	(M)	Rhythm & Blues Hit Vocal Groups	197?	10.00	25.00
Autumn 101	(M)	KYA's Memories Of The Cow Palace	1963	40.00	100.00
Bang 215	(M)	Golden Hits From The Gang At Bang	1966	5.00	12.00
Bang LPS-215	(P)	Golden Hits From The Gang At Bang	1966	6.00	15.00
Bang LPS-220	(S)	Bang And Shout Super Hits	196?	6.00	15.00
Bell 6009	(S)	More For You Money	1969	8.00	20.00
Bell 6035	(S)	Summer Souvenirs	1969	10.00	25.00
Bell 1206	(S)	On Any Sunday	197?	6.00	15.00
Beta 1414S	(M)	Gathering At The Depot	196?	16.00	40.00
Belvedere TY 8-7100	(M)	Michigan Brand Nuggets (2 LPs)	198?	16.00	40.00
Bethlehem BLP-6071	(M)	Blues 'N' Folk	195?	40.00	100.00
B. F. 20183	(M)	Son Of The Gathering Of The Tribe	198?	20.00	50.00
B. F. D. 5016	(M)	Pebbles, Vol. 1 (Original cover)	198?	40.00	100.00
Blast 6803	(M)	Blasts From The Past With Clay Cole	196?	20.00	50.00
Blast 6805	(M)	16 Goodies: Blasts From The Past	196?	20.00	50.00
Blue Mold LP-101	(M)	Tobacco A-Go-Go	198?	6.00	15.00
Blue Mold LP-103	(M)	Tobacco A-Go-Go, Volume 2	198?	6.00	15.00

Label & Catalog #		Title	Year	VG+	NM
Bluesville BVLP-1009	(M)	Soul Jazz, Volume 1	1969	14.00	35.00
Bluesville BVLP-1010	(M)	Soul Jazz, Volume	1960	14.00	35.00
Bluesville BVLP-1052	(M)	Blues We Taught Your Mother	1962	14.00	35.00
Bluesville BVLP-1055	(M)	Bawdy Blues	1962	14.00	35.00
Bluesville BVLP-1066	(M)	The New Gospel Keys	1963	12.00	30.00
BluesWay BSL-6061	(M)	Classic Blues, Volume 1	196?	6.00	15.00
BluesWay BSL-6062	(M)	Classic Blues, Volume 2	196?	6.00	15.00
Bolo 8002	(M)	Bolo Bash	1964	16.00	40.00
Bona Fide 5913-330001	(M)	Gathering Of The Tribe	198?	20.00	50.00
Bona Fide BFR-16274-66	(M)	Return Of The Young Pennsylvanians	198?	16.00	40.00
Bona Fide BFR-NJ 6601	(M)	Attack Of The Jersey Teens	198?	16.00	40.00
Bonded 777	(M)	20 Original R&B Goodies	196?	20.00	50.00
Bone 101	(M)	Oil Stanes, Volume 2	198?	20.00	50.00
Broadside BR-301	(S)	Broadside Ballads, Volume 1	1964	12.00	30.00
Broadside BR-3??	(S)	Broadside Ballads, Volume 2	1964	10.00	25.00
Broadside BR-3??	(S)	Broadside Ballads, Volume 3	1964	10.00	25.00
Broadside BR-3??	(S)	Broadside Ballads, Volume 4	1964	10.00	25.00
Broadside BR-315	(S)	Broadside Ballads, Volume 6	1964	10.00	25.00
Brooklyn 301	(M)	Murray The K's Greatest Holiday Show	196?	10.00	25.00
Brooklyn S-301	(S)	Murray The K's Greatest Holiday Show	196?	10.00	25.00
Brooklyn 302	(M)	Murray The K Presents	196?	10.00	25.00
Brooklyn S-302	(S)	Murray The K Presents	196?	10.00	25.00
Brunswick 5900 (10")	(M)	Mountain Frolic	195?	30.00	75.00
Brunswick 54001 (10")	(M)	Listen To Our Story	1958	30.00	75.00
Bud Jet 301	(M)	Country Western Hits (Volume 1)	1968	12.00	30.00
Bud Jet 302	(M)	Country Western Hits (Volume 2)	1968	12.00	30.00
Bud Jet 303	(M)	Country Western Hits (Volume 3)	1968	12.00	30.00
Bud Jet 311	(M)	Top Teen Bands (Volume 1)	1968	20.00	50.00
Bud Jet 312	(M)	Top Teen Bands (Volume 2)	1968	20.00	50.00
Bud Jet 313	(M)	Top Teen Bands (Volume 3)	1968	24.00	60.00
Buddah Vol. 1 No. 1	(P)	Current Audio Magazine	1972	10.00	25.00
Cadence CLP-3041	(M)	Rock-A-Ballads	1960	20.00	50.00
Cadence CLP-3042	(M)	Rock-A-Hits	1960	20.00	50.00
Cadence CLP-3043	(M)	Golden Encores	1960	20.00	50.00
Calico PSY-101	(M)	Psychedelic Unknowns	198?	10.00	25.00
California Recording 101	(M)	Battle Of The Beat (Yellow label)	1964	150.00	300.00
Camay C-3001	(M)	Country & Western Bonanza	1962	6.00	15.00
Camay CS-3001	(S)	Country & Western Bonanza	1962	10.00	25.00
Camden CAL-371	(M)	Rhythm & Blues	195?	20.00	50.00
Camden CAL-435	(M)	RCA Camden Rockers	195?	20.00	50.00
Camden CAL-740	(M)	Original Rhythm & Blues Hits By Rhythm & Blues Stars	1963	20.00	50.00
Camden CAL-820	(M)	Special Delivery	1964	10.00	25.00
Camden CAS-820e	(E)	Special Delivery	1964	6.00	15.00
Capitol T-9030 (10")	(M)	Merry Christmas To You	1955	12.00	30.00
Capitol H-9101 (10")	(M)	Today's Top Hits, Volume 1	1955	12.00	30.00
Capitol H-9102 (10")	(M)	Today's Top Hits, Volume 2	1955	12.00	30.00
Capitol H-9103 (10")	(M)	Today's Top Hits, Volume 3	1955	12.00	30.00
Capitol H-9104 (10")	(M)	Today's Top Hits, Volume 4	1955	12.00	30.00
Capitol H-9105 (10")	(M)	Today's Top Hits, Volume 5	1955	12.00	30.00
Capitol H-9106 (10")	(M)	Today's Top Hits, Volume 6	1955	12.00	30.00
Capitol H-9107 (10")	(M)	Today's Top Hits, Volume 7	1955	12.00	30.00

Capitol was the major label for '60s surf music. Aside from Brian Wilson's Beach Boys, they had Dick "King of the Surf Guitar" Dale and Gary Usher. Big Surfing Sounds is a promo sampler shipped to radio stations for air-play while My Son The Surf Nut plays on both the surfing phenomenon and the successful shtick of comedian Allan Sherman. Note that the latter includes a cartoon cover of "Murf the Surf" from the pen of the late, great Rick Griffin.

Label & Catalog #		Title	Year	VG+	NM
Capitol H-9108 (10")	(M)	Today's Top Hits, Volume 8	1955	12.00	30.00
Capitol H-9109 (10")	(M)	Today's Top Hits, Volume 9	1955	12.00	30.00
Capitol H-9110 (10")	(M)	Today's Top Hits, Volume 10	1955	12.00	30.00
Capitol H-9116 (10")	(M)	Today's Top Hits, Volume 11	1955	12.00	30.00
Capitol L-9117 (10")	(M)	Top Hits Of '54, Volume 1	1955	12.00	30.00
Capitol L-9119 (10")	(M)	Top Hits Of '54, Volume 2	1955	12.00	30.00
Capitol T-9124 (10")	(M)	Today's Top Hits, Volume 12	1955	12.00	30.00
Capitol T-9127 (10")	(M)	Today's Top Hits, Volume 13	1955	12.00	30.00
Capitol T-9130 (10")	(M)	Today's Top Hits, Volume 14	1955	12.00	30.00
Capitol T-732	(M)	Comedy Caravan	1951	20.00	50.00
Capitol T-308	(M)	Top Banana	1951	20.00	50.00
Capitol T-830	(M)	Gold Record	1957	20.00	50.00
Capitol T-1009	(M)	Teenage Rock	1958	20.00	50.00
Capitol T-1025	(M)	Everybody Rocks	1958	20.00	50.00
Capitol T-1179	(S)	The Country's Best	1959	12.00	30.00
Capitol T-1414	(M)	Those Good Old Memories	1950	20.00	50.00
Capitol KAO-1555	(M)	The Original Country Sing-A-Long	1961	8.00	20.00
Capitol SKAO-1555	(S)	The Original Country Sing-A-Long	1961	10.00	25.00
Capitol T-1561	(M)	Golden Gassers	1961	10.00	25.00
Capitol ST-1561	(S)	Golden Gassers	1961	12.00	30.00
Capitol TBO-1572	(M)	Shake It And Break It (2 LPs)	1961	14.00	35.00
Capitol T-1654	(M)	The Best Of The Best	1961	6.00	15.00
Capitol ST-1654	(S)	The Best Of The Best	1961	8.00	20.00
Capitol T-1656	(M)	Romantic Country Strings	1961	6.00	15.00
Capitol ST-1656	(S)	Romantic Country Strings	1961	8.00	20.00
Capitol T-1718	(M)	The Great Ones	1961	6.00	15.00
Capitol ST-1718	(S)	The Great Ones	1961	8.00	20.00
Capitol T-1837	(M)	Chartbusters	1963	8.00	20.00
Capitol DT-1837	(E)	Chartbusters	1963	6.00	15.00
Capitol T-1912	(M)	Country Hits By Country Stars	1963	6.00	15.00
Capitol ST-1912	(S)	Country Hits By Country Stars	1963	8.00	20.00
Capitol T-1918	(M)	Shut Down	1963	12.00	30.00
Capitol ST-1918	(P)	Shut Down	1963	16.00	40.00
Capitol T-1939	(M)	My Son, The Surf Nut	1963	12.00	30.00
Capitol ST-1939	(S)	My Son, The Surf Nut	1963	16.00	40.00
Capitol T-1945	(M)	Chartbusters, Volume 2	1963	8.00	20.00
Capitol DT-1945	(E)	Chartbusters, Volume 2	1963	6.00	15.00
Capitol T-1981	(M)	Shut Down	1963	8.00	20.00
Capitol ST-1981	(S)	Shut Down	1963	8.00	20.00
Capitol T-1995	(M)	Surfing's Greatest Hits	1963	6.00	15.00
Capitol ST-1995	(P)	Surfing's Greatest Hits	1963	8.00	20.00
Capitol T/ST-1997		Hot Rod Rally: Refer to The Superstocks			
Capitol T-90088	(M)	Shower Of Stars (Capitol Record Club)	1964	6.00	15.00
Capitol T-2006	(M)	Chartbusters, Volume 3	1963	10.00	25.00
Capitol DT-2006	(E)	Chartbusters, Volume 3	1963	10.00	25.00
Capitol T-2009	(M)	Country Music Hootenanny	1963	12.00	30.00
Capitol ST-2009	(S)	Country Music Hootenanny	1963	16.00	40.00
Capitol T-2024	(M)	Big Hit Rod Hits	1963	16.00	40.00
Capitol ST-2024	(P)	Big Hit Rod Hits	1963	20.00	50.00
Capitol T-2094	(M)	Chartbusters, Volume 4	1964	20.00	50.00
Capitol ST-2094	(P)	Chartbusters, Volume 4	1964	30.00	75.00
Capitol T-2125	(M)	The Big Hits From England & U.S.A.	1964	16.00	40.00
Capitol DT-2125	(E)	The Big Hits From England & U.S.A.	1964	12.00	30.00
Capitol T-2538	(M)	Who's Who Of Country Music	1966	6.00	15.00
Capitol ST-2538	(S)	Who's Who Of Country Music	1966	8.00	20.00
Capitol T-2565	(M)	Super Oldies, Volume 2	1966	6.00	15.00
Capitol ST-2565	(S)	Super Oldies, Volume 2	1966	8.00	20.00
Capitol NPB-5	(M)	The World Of Country Music (2 LPs)	1964	8.00	20.00
Capitol SNPB-5	(S)	The World Of Country Music (2 LPs)	1964	10.00	25.00
Capitol T-2544	(M)	Liverpool Today	1966	8.00	20.00
Capitol ST-2544	(S)	Liverpool Today	1966	12.00	30.00
Capitol STBB-585	(P)	Peace On Earth	1970	6.00	15.00
Capitol SABB-12248	(S)	Concert For Bangla Desh: Refer to George Harrison & Friends			

—Special/Promotional Albums—

| Capitol PRO-325 | (M) | New Album Preview (2 LPs) | 1957 | 80.00 | 200.00 |

Label & Catalog #		Title	Year	VG+	NM
Capitol PRO-326	(M)	New Album Preview (2 LPs)	1957	80.00	200.00
Capitol PRO-329	(M)	Merchandising Campaign (2 LPs)	1957	40.00	100.00
Capitol PRO-696	(M)	Preview Of New Sept. Albums (2 LPs)	1958	40.00	100.00
Capitol PRO-2376	(M)	Balanced For Broadcast	1963	16.00	40.00
Capitol PRO-2378	(M)	Salesmen's Demonstration Record	1963	20.00	50.00
Capitol PRO-2396	(M)	Big Surfin' Sounds	1963	30.00	75.00
Capitol PRO-2464	(M)	Salesmen's Demonstration Record	1963	20.00	50.00
Capitol PRO-2480	(M)	Hot Rod Music On Capitol	1963	80.00	200.00
Capitol PRO-2494	(M)	Salesmen's Demonstration Record	1963	20.00	50.00
Capitol PRO-2538	(M)	Great New Releases From The Sound Capitol Of The World	1964	40.00	100.00
Capitol PRO-2556	(M)	Balanced For Broadcast	1963	20.00	50.00
Capitol PRO-2556	(M)	Balanced For Broadcast	1963	20.00	50.00
Capitol PRO-2658	(M)	Big Surfin' Sounds	1964	30.00	75.00
Capitol PRO-2685	(M)	Balanced For Broadcast	1964	20.00	50.00
Capitol PRO-2744	(M)	Programming Aids From Capitol	1964	60.00	150.00
Capitol PRO-2744	(DJ)	Programming Aids From Capitol	1964	100.00	250.00
		(Cntains The Beach Boys' "Auld Lang Syne" without a voice-over.)			
Capitol PRO-3123	(DJ)	Silver Platter Service From Hollywood	1965	100.00	250.00
		(Features Brian introducing selections from The Hollyridge Strings' "Beach Boys Songbook.")			
Capitol PRO-3265	(M)	Silver Platter Service	1967	80.00	200.00
		(Features Brian Wilson briefly discussing the scrapping of "Smile.")			
Capitol PRO-4411	(M)	Capitol's 25th Anniversary Celebration	1967	12.00	30.00
Capitol SPRO-4673	(M)	Capitol Disc Jockey Album	1969	12.00	30.00
Capitol SPRO-4724	(M)	Capitol Hits Through The Years	1969	16.00	40.00
Capitol SPRO-5003	(M)	Listen In Good Health	1970	12.00	30.00
Capitol SPRO-8511	(M)	The Greatest Music Ever Sold	1976	12.00	30.00
Capitol SPRO-9864	(P)	Hits On Board	1982	6.00	15.00
Capitol SPRO-9867	(P)	Capitol In-Store Sampler	1982	6.00	15.00
Caribou CABPU	(DJ)	Caribou Fall Releaes (Picture disc)	1977	6.00	15.00
Carlton 121	(M)	One Dozen Goldies	1958	20.00	50.00
CBS Songs	(DJ)	Radio's Million Performance Songs	1984	20.00	50.00
Celebrity 1000	(M)	World Famous Rhythm And Blues	195?	500.00	1,500.00
Century 23214	(M)	Milwaukee Sentinal: Young America Rock 'n' Roll Songs	1966	150.00	300.00
Chainsaw Sound CSR-001	(M)	Everywhere Chainsaw Sound	198?	30.00	75.00
Chainsaw Sound CSR-002	(M)	Everywhere Interferences	198?	30.00	75.00
Chancellor CHL-50??	(M)	Wild, Wild Twist Recorded Live!	1961	10.00	25.00
Chancellor CHLS-50??	(S)	Wild, Wild Twist Recorded Live!	1961	20.00	50.00
Chancellor CHL-5009	(M)	The Hit Makers	1961	10.00	25.00
Chancellor CHL-5017	(M)	Wild Wildwood	1961	10.00	25.00
Chancellor CHS-5017	(S)	Wild Wildwood	1961	20.00	50.00
Chancellor CHL-5028	(M)	Dance On The Wild Side	1962	10.00	25.00
Checker LP-2973	(DJ)	Love Those Goodies (Multi-colored vinyl)	1959	60.00	150.00
Checker LP-2973	(M)	Love Those Goodies	1959	20.00	50.00
Checker LP-2975	(M)	Hits That Jumped	1959	20.00	50.00
Checker LP-2998	(M)	Sing A Song Of Soul	196?	20.00	50.00
Checker LPS-2998	(S)	Sing A Song Of Soul	196?	30.00	75.00
Chess LP-1425	(M)	Rock, Rock, Rock (Soundtrack)	1958	80.00	200.00
Chess LP-1439	(DJ)	Oldies In Hi Fi (Multi-colored vinyl)	1959	300.00	500.00
Chess LP-1439	(M)	Oldies In Hi Fi	1959	50.00	125.00
Chess LP-1441	(DJ)	Bunch Of Goodies (Multi-colored vinyl)	1960	300.00	500.00
Chess LP-1441	(M)	Bunch Of Goodies	1960	50.00	125.00
Chess LP-1446	(M)	Walking By Mtself	1960	20.00	50.00
Chess LP-145?	(M)	Murray The K's Golden Gassers	1961	20.00	50.00
Chess LP-1458	(M)	KYA's Golden Gate Greats	1961	50.00	125.00
Chess LP-1461	(M)	Murray The K's Blasts From The Past	1961	20.00	50.00
Chess LP-1470	(M)	Murray The K's Gassers			

Label & Catalog #		Title	Year	VG+	NM
		For Submarine Race Watchers	1963	16.00	40.00
Chess LP-1474	(M)	**Treasure Tunes From The Vault**	1963	12.00	30.00
Chess LP-1476	(M)	**Dance Tunes From The Vault**	1964	12.00	30.00
Chess LP-1478	(M)	**Group Of Goodies**	1964	20.00	50.00
Chess LP-1491	(M)	**Group Of Goodies, Vol. 2**	1966	20.00	50.00
		— Original Chess albums above have black labels with silver print.—			
Chess LPS-1520	(S)	**Petal Pushers**	1968	10.00	25.00
Chess LPS-1544	(P)	**Pop Origins**	1969	10.00	25.00
Chess LPS-1546	(P)	**Souled Out**	1969	20.00	50.00
Chess	(DJ)	**LP Sampler**	1972	4.00	10.00
Chess 2CH-50030	(M)	**Golden Age Of Rhythm & Blues** *(2 LPs)*	1972	12.00	30.00
Chevrolet SL-6658	(S)	**On The Move**	196?	6.00	15.00
Clarion 609	(M)	**Discoteque In Astrosound**	1966	50.00	125.00
Clarion SD-609	(S)	**Discoteque In Astrosound**	1966	80.00	200.00
Class 5004	(M)	**Gone But Not Forgotten**	1959	30.00	75.00
Collectables 1/2-2500	(P)	**History Of Rock & Roll** *(2 LP picture disc)*	1982	12.00	30.00
Collector's Edition 505	(P)	**All-Time Christmas Favorites** *(5 LP box)*	1978	80.00	200.00
Colpix CP-444	(M)	**Teenage Triangle**	1964	16.00	40.00
Colpix SCP-444	(E)	**Teenage Triangle**	1964	20.00	50.00
Colpix CP-466	(M)	**Groovy Goodies**	1964	30.00	75.00
Colpix SCP-466	(P)	**Groovy Goodies**	1964	40.00	100.00
Colpix CP-468	(M)	**More Teenage Triangle**	1964	16.00	40.00
Colpix SCP-468	(P)	**More Teenage Triangle**	1964	30.00	75.00
Columbia CL-6057 (10")	(M)	**Popular Favorites**	1949	30.00	50.00
Columbia CL-6119 (10")	(M)	**Popular Favorites**	1950	30.00	50.00
Columbia CL-6150 (10")	(M)	**Popular Favorites**	1950	30.00	50.00
Columbia HL-9008 (10")	(M)	**Current Country Hits #1**	195?	30.00	50.00
Columbia HL-9011 (10")	(M)	**Current Country Hits #2**	195?	30.00	50.00
Columbia HL-9016 (10")	(M)	**Current Country Hits #3**	195?	30.00	50.00
Columbia CL-2600 (10")	(M)	**Hall Of Fame**	1955	16.00	40.00
Columbia CL-613	(M)	**Treasure Chest Of Song Hits**	195?	10.00	25.00
Columbia CL-894	(M)	**Country Spectacular**	1957	12.00	30.00
Columbia CL-937	(M)	**Top Twelve**	195?	10.00	25.00
Columbia CL-944	(M)	**Top Twelve, Volume 2**	195?	10.00	25.00
Columbia CL-1048	(M)	**Phillip Morris Country Music Show**	1958	10.00	25.00
Columbia CL-1072	(M)	**Town Hall Party**	1958	20.00	50.00
Columbia XLP-42371	(DJ)	**Going Places On Columbia**	1958	40.00	100.00
Columbia CL-1239	(M)	**Pop Hit Party**	1959	10.00	25.00
Columbia CL-1257	(M)	**Greatest Western Hits**	1959	10.00	25.00
Columbia CL-1308	(M)	**Hall Of Fame Hits**	1959	6.00	15.00
Columbia CL-1353	(M)	**Big Hits**	1959	6.00	15.00
Columbia CS-8161	(S)	**Big Hits**	1959	8.00	20.00
Columbia CL-1408	(M)	**The Greatest Western Hits**	195?	10.00	25.00
Columbia CL-1462	(M)	**Golden Dozen**	1960	6.00	15.00
Columbia CL-1485	(M)	**Hitmakers**	1960	5.00	12.00
Columbia CS-8276	(P)	**Hitmakers**	1960	6.00	15.00
Columbia CL-1583	(M)	**Evolution Of The Blues Song**	1960	10.00	25.00
Columbia CS-8383	(E)	**Evolution Of The Blues Song**	1960	6.00	15.00
Columbia CL-1617	(M)	**Twelve Big Hits**	1961	5.00	12.00
Columbia CS-8417	(S)	**Twelve Big Hits**	1961	6.00	15.00
Columbia CL-1618	(M)	**Stars Are Singing**	1961	6.00	15.00
Columbia CL-1618	(M)	**Stars Are Singing**	1961	6.00	15.00
		— Original Columbia albums above have three white "eye" logos on each side of the spindle hole.—			
Columbia CL-1897	(M)	**Popular Favorites**	1962	6.00	15.00
Columbia CS-8697	(M)	**Popular Favorites**	1962	6.00	15.00
Columbia CL-1976	(M)	**Greatest Western Hits, Volume 1**	1963	5.00	12.00
Columbia CS-8776	(S)	**Greatest Western Hits, Volume 1**	1963	6.00	15.00
Columbia CL-2172	(M)	**The Exciting New Liverpool Sound**	1964	6.00	15.00
Columbia CS-8972	(S)	**The Exciting New Liverpool Sound**	1964	8.00	20.00
Columbia CL-2534	(M)	**Hot Canaries**	1966	6.00	15.00
Columbia CS-9334	(M)	**Hot Canaries**	1966	6.00	15.00

Label & Catalog #		Title	Year	VG+	NM
Columbia CL-2574	(M)	**Big Hits**	1966	6.00	15.00
Columbia CS-9374	(M)	**Big Hits**	1966	6.00	15.00
Columbia CL-2600	(M)	**Hall Of Fame**	1967	6.00	15.00
Columbia CS-9400	(M)	**Hall Of Fame**	1967	6.00	15.00
Columbia CL-2667	(M)	**18 King Size R&B Hits**	1967	6.00	15.00
Columbia CS-9467	(E)	**18 King Size R&B Hits**	1967	8.00	20.00
Columbia OS-3240	(S)	**You Are What You Eat** (Soundtrack)	1968	6.00	15.00
		— Original Columbia albums above have "360 Sound" on the bottom of the label.—			
Columbia P-14439	(P)	**Surf And Drag**	197?	10.00	25.00
Columbia KC-31171	(S)	**A Tribute To Woody Guthrie, Part 1**	1972	5.00	12.00
		(Part 2 was issued was Warner Bros. 46144.)			
		— Special/Promotional Albums—			
Columbia (No number)	(S)	**Great Folk Ballads, Country & Western**	1962	10.00	25.00
		(4 LP box prepared for Zenith.)			
Columbia CLP-128	(M)	**Hootenanny '64**	1964	4.00	10.00
Columbia CSP-128	(S)	**Hootenanny '64**	1964	5.00	12.00
Columbia CLP-149	(M)	**All-Star Hootenanny**	1964	4.00	10.00
Columbia CSP-149	(S)	**All-Star Hootenanny**	1964	5.00	12.00
Columbia CLP-156	(M)	**Songs Of The "Combat" Years**	1964	6.00	15.00
Columbia CSP-156	(S)	**Songs Of The "Combat" Years**	1964	8.00	20.00
Columbia CLP-176	(M)	**The Swingers**	1964	4.00	10.00
Columbia CSP-176	(P)	**The Swingers**	1964	5.00	12.00
Columbia CLP-205	(M)	**Folk Jamboree**	1964	4.00	10.00
Columbia CSP-205	(S)	**Folk Jamboree**	1964	5.00	12.00
Columbia CLP-216	(M)	**Zenith Presents A Hootenanny Special**	1964	4.00	10.00
Columbia CSP-216	(S)	**Zenith Presents A Hootenanny Special**	1964	5.00	12.00
Columbia CLP-251	(M)	**Power Train '66**	1966	4.00	10.00
Columbia CSP-251	(S)	**Power Train '66**	1966	5.00	12.00
Columbia CLP-270	(M)	**The Great Entertainers: The Folk Sound**	1966	4.00	10.00
Columbia CSP-270	(S)	**The Great Entertainers: The Folk Sound**	1966	5.00	12.00
Columbia CLP-293	(M)	**When We're Together With The Folk Sound**	1966	4.00	10.00
Columbia CSP-293	(S)	**When We're Together With The Folk Sound**	1966	5.00	12.00
Columbia CLP-299	(M)	**The Folk Sound**	1966	4.00	10.00
Columbia CSP-299	(S)	**The Folk Sound**	1966	5.00	12.00
Columbia CLP-301	(M)	**London Really Swings**	1966	5.00	12.00
Columbia CSP-301	(S)	**London Really Swings**	1966	5.00	12.00
Columbia CLP-314	(M)	**Sounds Of Mod Contact**	1966	4.00	10.00
Columbia CSP-314	(P)	**Sounds Of Mod Contact**	1966	5.00	12.00
Columbia CLP-333	(M)	**It's Happenin' Here**	1966	4.00	10.00
Columbia CSP-333	(S)	**It's Happenin' Here**	1966	5.00	12.00
Columbia CLP-344	(M)	**Just Plain Folk**	1966	4.00	10.00
Columbia CSP-344	(S)	**Just Plain Folk**	1966	5.00	12.00
Columbia CSM-387	(M)	**The Exciting Years**	1966	4.00	10.00
Columbia CSS-387	(P)	**The Exciting Years**	1966	5.00	12.00
Columbia CLP-389	(M)	**A Slice Of Lemon**	1966	4.00	10.00
Columbia CSP-389	(S)	**A Slice Of Lemon**	1966	5.00	12.00
Columbia CSP-523	(M)	**Zenith Salutes The Teen Sound**	1966	4.00	10.00
Columbia CSS-523	(P)	**Zenith Salutes The Teen Sound**	1966	5.00	12.00
Columbia CLP-526	(M)	**Zenith Salutes The Folk Singers**	1966	4.00	10.00
Columbia CSP-526	(S)	**Zenith Salutes The Folk Singers**	1966	5.00	12.00
Columbia CSP-731	(M)	**Groovy Sounds**	1966	4.00	10.00
Columbia CSS-731	(P)	**Groovy Sounds**	1966	5.00	12.00
Columbia D-81	(M)	**Disco Teen '65**	1965	4.00	10.00
Columbia DS-81	(S)	**Disco Teen '65**	1965	5.00	12.00
Columbia D-127	(M)	**Top Pop Song Hits, Volume 2**	1966	4.00	10.00
Columbia DS-127	(S)	**Top Pop Song Hits, Volume 2**	1966	5.00	12.00
Columbia D-155	(M)	**Disco Teen '66**	1966	4.00	10.00
Columbia DS-155	(S)	**Disco Teen '66**	1966	20.00	50.00
		(Includes an alternate stereo mix of Dylan's "Positively 4th Street.")			
Columbia DS-486	(M)	**The Columbia Sound**	1968	4.00	10.00
Columbia CL-2122	(M)	**All-Star Hootenanny**	1964	4.00	10.00
Columbia CS-8922	(S)	**All-Star Hootenanny**	1964	5.00	12.00
Columbia CSM-563	(M)	**A Very Merry Christmas**	1966	5.00	12.00
Columbia CSS-563	(S)	**A Very Merry Christmas**	1966	6.00	15.00
		(Includes Simon & Garfunkel's "The Star Carol.")			
Columbia A2S-174	(DJ)	**The Heavyweights** (2 LPs)	1975	16.00	40.00
Columbia A2S-890	(DJ)	**Hitline '80** (2 LPs)	1980	12.00	30.00

Label & Catalog #		Title	Year	VG+	NM
Columbia AS-902	(S)	**Highlights From CBS Mastersound** *(Issued with a booklet.)*	1981	20.00	50.00
Combo 400	(M)	**Rockin' At The Drive In**	195?	80.00	200.00
Coral CRL-57269	(M)	**Hitsville**	1959	30.00	75.00
Coral CRL-757269	(S)	**Hitsville**	1959	40.00	100.00
Coral CRL-57310	(M)	**Million Airs**	1959	12.00	30.00
Coral CRL-757310	(S)	**Million Airs**	1959	20.00	50.00
Coral CRL-57431	(M)	**Teenage Goodies**	1963	12.00	30.00
Coral CRL-757431	(S)	**Teenage Goodies**	1963	20.00	50.00
Cotillion SD-9037	(S)	**Homer** *(Soundtrack)*	1970	6.00	15.00
Cotillion CT3-500	(S)	**Woodstock** *(3 LPs. Soundtrack)*	1970	10.00	25.00
Cotillion CT2-400	(S)	**Woodstock, Volume 2** *(2 LPs)*	1971	8.00	20.00

— *Original Cotillion albums above have grey labels with an 1841 Broadway address.*—

Label & Catalog #		Title	Year	VG+	NM
Crescendo GNP-84	(M)	**Original Surfin' Hits** *(With bonus photos)*	1963	12.00	30.00
Crescendo GNPS-84	(P)	**Original Surfin' Hits** *(With bonus photos)*	1963	14.00	35.00
Crescendo GNP-84	(M)	**Original Surfin' Hits** *(Without the photos)*	1963	8.00	20.00
Crescendo GNPS-84	(P)	**Original Surfin' Hits** *(Without the photos)*	1963	8.00	20.00
Crescendo GNP-85	(M)	**Winners Of The 18 Band Surf Battle**	1963	8.00	20.00
Crescendo GNPS-85	(S)	**Winners Of The 18 Band Surf Battle**	1963	10.00	25.00
Crown CLP-5001	(M)	**Rock & Roll Dance Party**	1958	12.00	30.00
Crown CLP-5011	(M)	**Hollywood Rock 'N Roll Record Shop**	1958	12.00	30.00
Crown CLP-5013	(M)	**Gigantic Stars Of Rock & Roll**	1958	12.00	30.00
Crown CLP-5144	(M)	**Best Of The Oldies & Goodies**	1959	8.00	20.00
Crown CLP-5144	(M)	**The Best Of Oldies And Goodies**	1960	10.00	25.00
Crown CLP-5202	(M)	**More Of The Oldies And Goodies**	1961	10.00	25.00
Crown CLP-5238	(M)	**Blues Oldies And Goodies**	1961	10.00	25.00
Crown CLP-5241	(M)	**Oldies And Goodies**	1961	10.00	25.00
Crypt RR-66	(M)	**Back From The Grave, Vol. 1** *(First edition)*	198?	12.00	30.00
"DB" 101	(M)	**Oil Stains**	198?	16.00	40.00
"DB" 102	(M)	**Relics**	198?	16.00	40.00
Dawn DLP-119	(M)	**Rock And Roll Spectacular**	195?	40.00	100.00
Decca DL-38008	(DJ)	**Fill The Air With Music**	195?	40.00	100.00
Decca DL-738241	(DJ)	**Admiral Stereophonic Demo**	195?	40.00	100.00
Decca DL-8349	(M)	**The Wild One**	1958	20.00	50.00
Decca DL-8655	(M)	**Let's Have A Party**	1958	40.00	100.00
Decca DL-8860	(M)	**Top Pops**	1959	16.00	40.00

— *Original Decca albums above have black labels with silver print.*—

Label & Catalog #		Title	Year	VG+	NM
Decca DL-4004	(M)	**The Early Fifties**	1960	20.00	50.00
Decca DL-4005	(M)	**The Late Fifties**	1960	20.00	50.00
Decca DL-4009	(M)	**The Fifties**	1960	20.00	50.00
Decca DL-4011	(M)	**Rhythm, Blues & Boogie Woogie**	1960	20.00	50.00
Decca DL-4036	(M)	**Golden Oldies**	1960	20.00	50.00
Decca DL-4045	(M)	**Midnight Jamboree**	1960	12.00	30.00
Decca DL-74045	(S)	**Midnight Jamboree**	1960	16.00	40.00
Decca DL-4057	(M)	**Country Music Time**	1960	12.00	30.00
Decca DL-74057	(S)	**Country Music Time**	1960	16.00	40.00
Decca DL-4172	(M)	**Country Jubilee**	1962	10.00	25.00
Decca DL-74172	(S)	**Country Jubilee**	1962	12.00	30.00
Decca DL-4434	(M)	**Out Came The Blues**	1964	16.00	40.00
Decca DL-74434	(E)	**Out Came The Blues**	1964	12.00	30.00
Decca DL-4484	(M)	**All Time Hootenanny Folk Favorites**	1964	6.00	15.00
Decca DL-74484	(S)	**All Time Hootenanny Folk Favorites**	1964	8.00	20.00
Decca DL-9119	(M)	**The Lively Set** *(Soundtrack)*	1964	20.00	50.00
Decca DL-79119	(S)	**The Lively Set** *(Soundtrack)*	1964	30.00	75.00
Decca DL-4671	(M)	**Saturday Night At The Grand Ole Opry**	1966	6.00	15.00
Decca DL-74671	(S)	**Saturday Night At The Grand Ole Opry**	1966	8.00	20.00
Decca DL-4699	(M)	**Wild, Wild Winter** *(Soundtrack)*	1966	8.00	20.00
Decca DL-74699	(S)	**Wild, Wild Winter** *(Soundtrack)*	1966	12.00	30.00

Label & Catalog #		Title	Year	VG+	NM
Decca DL-4751	(M)	**Out Of Sight** (Soundtrack)	1966	12.00	30.00
Decca DL-74751	(S)	**Out Of Sight** (Soundtrack)	1966	16.00	40.00
Decca DL-75181	(S)	**Rock 'N' Roll Survival**	1970	5.00	12.00
Decca DL-75515	(S)	**The Wild One** (Reissue of 8349)	197?	4.00	10.00
Del-Fi (No number)	(DJ)	**Del-Fi Album Sampler** (Green vinyl)	1959	200.00	400.00
Del-Fi DFLP-1210	(M)	**Del-Fi Record Hop**	1960	30.00	75.00
Del-Fi DFLP-1219	(M)	**Barrel Of Oldies**	1961	20.00	50.00
Del-Fi DFLP-1227	(M)	**Very Best Of The Oldies**	1963	20.00	50.00
Del-Fi DFLP-1235	(M)	**KYA's Battle Of The Surfing Bands**	1964	20.00	50.00
Del-Fi DFST-1235	(S)	**KYA's Battle Of The Surfing Bands**	1964	30.00	75.00
Del-Fi DFLP-1249	(M)	**Big Surf Hits**	1964	20.00	50.00
Del-Fi DFST-1249	(S)	**Big Surf Hits**	1964	30.00	75.00
Design DLP-611	(M)	**Tennessee**	1964	10.00	25.00
Design SDLP-611	(E)	**Tennessee**	1964	6.00	15.00
Diplomat D-2308	(M)	**Kings Of The Hot Rods**	1963	8.00	20.00
Diplomat DS-2308	(E)	**Kings Of The Hot Rods**	1963	4.00	10.00
Diplomat D-2430	(M)	**Four Seasons / Tommy Roe /**			
		Johnny Rivers / Tony Banon	1964	8.00	20.00
Diplomat DS-2430	(E)	**Four Seasons / Tommy Roe /**			
		Johnny Rivers / Tony Banon	1964	4.00	10.00
DMG 1	(DJ)	**Songs Of Paul Simon:**			
		A Collection Of Hits	1975	8.00	20.00
DMG 2	(DJ)	**Songs Of Paul Simon:**			
		An Easy Listening Collection	1975	8.00	20.00
Do It Now LP-5000	(P)	**First Vibration**	1969	8.00	20.00
Domain 102	(M)	**Rosko's Evergreens**	1963	20.00	50.00
Dooto DTL-203	(M)	**Rock & Roll Vs. Rhythm & Blues**	195?	20.00	50.00
Dooto DTL-204	(M)	**Best In Rhythm 'N Blues:** Refer to The Penguins			
Dooto LP-224	(M)	**Best Vocal Groups In Rhythm & Blues**	1958	20.00	50.00
Dooto LP-855	(M)	**Oldies**	196?	6.00	15.00
Dot DLP-3049	(M)	**Great Hits On Dot**	1957	16.00	40.00
Dot DLP-3183	(M)	**Young Love**	1959	16.00	40.00
Dot DLP-3425	(M)	**Million Dollar Music**	1962	8.00	20.00
Dot DLP-3820	(M)	**Golden Instrumentals**	1966	6.00	15.00
Dot DLP-25820	(S)	**Golden Instrumentals**	1966	8.00	20.00
Double-L DL-2302	(M)	**Washington Committee**	1963	20.00	50.00
Double-L DDS-2302	(P)	**Washington Committee**	1963	30.00	75.00
Duke DLP-73	(M)	**Like 'Em Red Hot** (Yellow & purple label)	1965	60.00	150.00
Duke DLP-82	(M)	**Blues That Gave America Soul**	1966	6.00	15.00
Duke DLPS-82	(M)	**Blues That Gave America Soul**	1966	8.00	20.00
Dunhill DS-50057	(S)	**A Treasury Of Great Contemporary Hits**	1969	6.00	15.00
Dunhill DS-50063	(S)	**Easy Rider** (Soundtrack)	1969	10.00	25.00
Dunhill DS-50070	(S)	**The Original Hits Of Right Now**	196?	6.00	15.00
Dunhill DS-50085	(S)	**The Big Hits Now**	1970	6.00	15.00
Dunhill DSX-50100	(S)	**Monterey International Pop Festival**	197?	6.00	15.00
Economic Consultants	(M)	**Country & Western Classics 1955**	1973	12.00	30.00
Economic Consultants	(M)	**Country & Western Classics 1956**	1973	6.00	15.00
Economic Consultants	(M)	**Country & Western Classics 1957**	1973	12.00	30.00
Economic Consultants	(M)	**Country & Western Classics 1958**	1973	12.00	30.00
Economic Consultants	(M)	**Country & Western Classics 1959**	1973	6.00	15.00
Economic Consultants	(M)	**Country & Western Classics 1960**	1973	6.00	15.00
Economic Consultants	(M)	**Country & Western Classics 1961**	1973	6.00	15.00
Economic Consultants	(M)	**Country & Western Classics 1962**	1973	6.00	15.00
Economic Consultants	(M)	**Country & Western Classics 1963**	1973	6.00	15.00
Economic Consultants	(M)	**Country & Western Classics 1964**	1973	6.00	15.00
Economic Consultants	(M)	**Country & Western Classics 1965**	1973	6.00	15.00

Label & Catalog #		Title	Year	VG+	NM
Economic Consultants	(M)	Country & Western Classics 1966	1973	6.00	15.00
Economic Consultants	(M)	Country & Western Classics 1967	1973	6.00	15.00
Economic Consultants	(M)	Country & Western Classics 1968	1973	6.00	15.00
Economic Consultants	(M)	Country & Western Classics 1969	1973	6.00	15.00
Economic Consultants	(M)	A Journey Into Yesterday 1956	1973	12.00	30.00
Economic Consultants	(M)	A Journey Into Yesterday 1957	1973	6.00	15.00
Economic Consultants	(M)	A Journey Into Yesterday 1958	1973	6.00	15.00
Economic Consultants	(M)	A Journey Into Yesterday 1959	1973	6.00	15.00
Economic Consultants	(M)	A Journey Into Yesterday 1960	1973	6.00	15.00
Economic Consultants	(M)	A Journey Into Yesterday 1961	1973	6.00	15.00
Economic Consultants	(M)	A Journey Into Yesterday 1962	1973	6.00	15.00
Economic Consultants	(M)	A Journey Into Yesterday 1963	1973	6.00	15.00
Economic Consultants	(M)	A Journey Into Yesterday 1964	1973	6.00	15.00
Economic Consultants	(M)	A Journey Into Yesterday 1965	1973	6.00	15.00
Economic Consultants	(M)	A Journey Into Yesterday 1966	1973	6.00	15.00
Economic Consultants	(M)	A Journey Into Yesterday 1967	1973	6.00	15.00
Economic Consultants	(M)	A Journey Into Yesterday 1968	1973	6.00	15.00
Economic Consultants	(M)	A Journey Into Yesterday 1969	1973	12.00	30.00
Economic Consultants	(M)	Old & Heavy Gold 1956	1973	12.00	30.00
Economic Consultants	(M)	Old & Heavy Gold 1957	1973	12.00	30.00
Economic Consultants	(M)	Old & Heavy Gold 1958	1973	12.00	30.00
Economic Consultants	(M)	Old & Heavy Gold 1959	1973	6.00	15.00
Economic Consultants	(M)	Old & Heavy Gold 1960	1973	12.00	30.00
Economic Consultants	(M)	Old & Heavy Gold 1961	1973	12.00	30.00
Economic Consultants	(M)	Old & Heavy Gold 1962	1973	12.00	30.00
Economic Consultants	(M)	Old & Heavy Gold 1963	1973	6.00	15.00
Economic Consultants	(M)	Old & Heavy Gold 1964	1973	6.00	15.00
Economic Consultants	(M)	Old & Heavy Gold 1965	1973	6.00	15.00
Economic Consultants	(M)	Old & Heavy Gold 1966	1973	6.00	15.00
Economic Consultants	(M)	Old & Heavy Gold 1967	1973	6.00	15.00
Economic Consultants	(M)	Old & Heavy Gold 1968	1973	6.00	15.00
Economic Consultants	(M)	Old & Heavy Gold 1969	1973	6.00	15.00
Elektra EKL-264	(M)	The Blues Project	1964	8.00	20.00
Elektra EKLS-7264	(S)	The Blues Project	1964	12.00	30.00
Elektra EKL-299	(M)	Singer Songwriter Project	1965	8.00	20.00
Elektra EKS-7299	(S)	Singer Songwriter Project	1965	12.00	30.00
Elektra EKL-4002	(M)	What's Shakin' (With booklet)	1966	16.00	40.00
Elektra EKS-74002	(S)	What's Shakin' (With booklet)	1966	18.00	45.00
Elektra EKL-4002	(M)	What's Shakin' (Without booklet)	1966	10.00	25.00
Elektra EKS-74002	(S)	What's Shakin' (Without booklet)	1966	12.00	30.00
Elektra 7E-2006	(P)	Nuggets (2 LPs)	1972	12.00	30.00
Elektra S3-10	(S)	Garden Of Earthly Delights (3 LPs)	197?	6.00	15.00
EMI SPRO-9303	(DJ)	A Rocking Christmas Stocking	1984	5.00	12.00
EMR Ent. RH-8	(DJ)	The Age Of Rock	1969	60.00	150.00
End LP-302	(M)	Having A Ball (Groups cover)	1959	300.00	600.00
End LP-302	(M)	Rock & Roll Jamboree (Puppet cover)	1959	50.00	125.00
End LP-305	(M)	Battle Of The Groups	1960	30.00	75.00
End LP-309	(M)	Battle Of The Groups, Volume 2	1960	30.00	75.00
End LP-310	(M)	12 + 3 + 15 Hits	1960	30.00	75.00
End LP-313	(M)	Alan Freed's Golden Picks	1961	16.00	40.00
End LP-314	(M)	Alan Freed's Top 15	1962	16.00	40.00
End LP-315	(M)	Alan Freed's Top 15	1962	16.00	40.00

— Original End albums above have grey labels with dogs on top.—

Label & Catalog #		Title	Year	VG+	NM
Epic LN-3701	(M)	Cream Of The Crop	1959	20.00	50.00
Epic LN-3702	(M)	Please Say You Want Me	1959	20.00	50.00
Epic LN-24040	(M)	Great Golden Grooves	1963	12.00	30.00
Epic AS-537	(DJ)	Epic Records Sampler (Picture disc)	1978	6.00	15.00
Era BU-5870	(M)	Freewheelin'	196?	8.00	20.00
ESP-Disk' 1034	(M)	East Village Other: Electric Newspaper	1967	40.00	100.00
Etiquette ETLB-028	(P)	The Northwest Collection (6 LP box)	197?	60.00	150.00

Label & Catalog #		Title	Year	VG+	NM
Evatone 106811	(M)	The Magic Cube	198?	30.00	75.00
		(10" flexidisc with cardboard "magic cube.")			
Everlast 201	(M)	Our Best To You	196?	30.00	75.00
Excello 8001	(M)	Tunes To Be Remembered	1960	60.00	150.00
Excello 8011	(M)	The Real Blues	1969	10.00	25.00
Excello 8021	(M)	Blues Live In Baton Rouge	1971	10.00	25.00
Excello 8025	(M)	The Excello Story *(2 LPs)*	1972	10.00	25.00
Excello 8029	(M)	American Folk Blues Festival	1972	6.00	15.00
Famous 501	(M)	Rockin' Slumber Party	196?	12.00	30.00
Felsted 7503	(M)	Night At The Boulevard	196?	20.00	50.00
Fifth Pipe Dream 11680	(S)	San Francisco Sound *(Black & white cover)*	1969	60.00	150.00
Fifth Pipe Dream 11680	(S)	San Francisco Sound *(Color cover)*	1969	40.00	100.00
Fillmore 31390	(S)	The Last Days Of The Fillmore	1972	14.00	35.00
		(2 LP box with poster, booklet and bonus single.)			
Fire FLP-100	(M)	Memory Lane Hits By The Original Groups	1960	150.00	300.00
Fire FLP-100	(M)	Here Are The Hits	196?	80.00	200.00
Flashback 1001	(M)	Flashback, Vol. 1	198?	30.00	75.00
Flashback 1002	(M)	Flashback, Vol. 2	198?	30.00	75.00
Flashback 1003	(M)	Flashback, Vol. 3	198?	30.00	75.00
Flashback 1004	(M)	Flashback, Vol. 4: Fuzz Tone	198?	30.00	75.00
Flashback 1005	(M)	Great Texas Flashbacks (Vol. 5)	198?	30.00	75.00
Flashback 1006	(M)	Great Texas Flashbacks (Vol. 6)	198?	30.00	75.00
		(Original copies of Flashback 1001-6 have "Limited number of 200 copies" on the back cover.)			
Flip 1001	(M)	Twelve Flip Hits	196?	150.00	350.00
Flip 1002	(M)	Original Recordings By The Artists Who Made Them Hits	196?	250.00	500.00
Folklore FRLP-14020	(M)	Hootenanny	1964	8.00	20.00
Folklore FRST-14020	(S)	Hootenanny	1964	10.00	25.00
Folklore FRLP-14023	(M)	Folklore Jamboree	1964	8.00	20.00
Folklore FRST-14023	(S)	Folklore Jamboree	1964	10.00	25.00
Folklore FRLP-14030	(M)	Old Time Fiddlin' At Union Grove, NC	1964	8.00	20.00
Folklore FRST-14030	(S)	Old Time Fiddlin' At Union Grove, NC	1964	10.00	25.00
Folkways FR-5592	(S)	We Shall Overcome	1964	10.00	25.00
Fontana MGF-18030	(M)	To Sir With Love *(Soundtrack)*	1967	8.00	20.00
Fontana SRF-67569	(S)	To Sir With Love *(Soundtrack)*	1967	10.00	25.00
Fortune 8011	(M)	Treasure Chest Of Musty Dusties, Vol. 1	196?	30.00	75.00
Fortune 8017	(M)	Treasure Chest Of Musty Dusties, Vol. 2	196?	16.00	40.00
Frantic 555/777	(M)	Psychedelic Disaster Whirl	198?	10.00	25.00
Frog Death GLP-101	(M)	Open Up Your Door, Volume 1	198?	10.00	25.00
Frog Death GLP-1012	(M)	Open Up Your Door, Volume 2	198?	10.00	25.00
G.S.P. 6901	(M)	Beach Party	196?	40.00	100.00
Garrett 1243	(M)	Top Teen Bands	1968	30.00	75.00
Gateway 9004	(M)	1964 In Review	1965	16.00	40.00
Gee GLP-702	(M)	Teenage Party *(Red label)*	1958	40.00	100.00
Gee GLP-702	(M)	Teenage Party *(Gray label)*	196?	10.00	25.00

Label & Catalog #		Title	Year	VG+	NM
Golden Era 123	(M)	Golden Era *(3 LPs)*	196?	20.00	50.00
Goodman Group PRO-1	(DJ)	Just Let Me Hear Some Of That Rock 'N' Roll Muic	1979	16.00	40.00
Gordy GS-935	(S)	Motown's Winner's Circle, Volume 1	1969	6.00	15.00
Gordy GS-936	(S)	Motown's Winner's Circle, Volume 2	1969	6.00	15.00
Gordy GS-943	(S)	Motown's Winner's Circle, Volume 3	1969	6.00	15.00
Gordy GS-946	(S)	Motown's Winner's Circle, Volume 4	1969	6.00	15.00
Gordy GS-950	(S)	Motown's Winner's Circle, Volume 5	1970	6.00	15.00
Gott 3	(M)	Valley Of The Son Of Gathering Of The Tribe	198?	16.00	40.00
Grand Award 33-343	(M)	Rock & Roll	196?	8.00	20.00
Groovemaster BR-140	(M)	Beat Battle Of The World	1964	16.00	40.00
Groovemaster GR-140	(E)	Beat Battle Of The World	1964	10.00	25.00
Guest Star 1GS-406	(M)	Rock & Roll Party	1964	8.00	20.00
Guest Star 1GS-406	(E)	Rock & Roll Party	1964	4.00	10.00
Guest Star GS-1432	(M)	Earth Angel	1964	8.00	20.00
Guest Star GS-1432	(E)	Earth Angel	1964	4.00	10.00
Guest Star GS- 1433	(M)	Surf Kings	1964	8.00	20.00
Guest Star GS- 1433	(E)	Surf Kings	1964	4.00	10.00
Guest Star GS-1474	(M)	Ten Million Sellers	1964	8.00	20.00
Guest Star GSS-1474	(E)	Ten Million Sellers	1964	4.00	10.00
Happy Tiger 1017	(P)	Early Chicago	1969	20.00	50.00
Harmony HS-30023	(S)	Chartbusters *(Includes both sides of Neil Diamond's first single,* *"Clown Town" and "I've Never Been The Same.")*	1981	6.00	15.00
HBR HLP-8500	(M)	A Swingin' Summer *(Soundtrack)*	1966	12.00	30.00
HBR HST-8500	(S)	A Swingin' Summer *(Soundtrack)*	1966	16.00	40.00
Herald 1010	(M)	Herald Of The Beat	1960	40.00	100.00
Herald 1015	(M)	Pot Of Golden Goodies	1960	40.00	100.00
Hi SHLD-1	(DJ)	Hi Records Special DJ LP	1969	6.00	15.00
Hideout	(M)	Best Of The Hideouts	1969	100.00	250.00
Hollywood 30	(M)	Rhythm & Blues In The Night	196?	30.00	75.00
Hollywood 501	(M)	Merry Christmas, Baby	196?	12.00	30.00
Hollywood 503	(M)	R&B Hits	196?	40.00	100.00
Hull 1002	(M)	Your Favorite Singing Groups	195?	500.00	800.00
I.G.L. 103	(M)	Roof Garden Jamboree	1967	40.00	200.00
Impact LP-2	(M)	Shake, Shout And Soul	196?	40.00	200.00
Imperial DJLP-1 (10")	(DJ)	Imperial Sampler	195?	40.00	100.00
Imperial LM-94000	(M)	Goin' Up The Country	196?	10.00	25.00
Imperial LM-94001	(M)	Saturday Night Function	196?	10.00	25.00
Imperial LM-94002	(M)	Blues Uptown	196?	10.00	25.00
Imperial LM-94003	(M)	The End Of An Era	196?	10.00	25.00
Imperial LM-94004	(M)	New Orleans Bounce	196?	10.00	25.00
Imperial LM-94005	(M)	Sweet And Greasy	196?	10.00	25.00
Imperial LP-9021	(M)	A Tribute To James Dean *(Maroon label)*	1957	40.00	100.00
Imperial LP-9021	(M)	A Tribute To James Dean *(Black label)*	1957	20.00	50.00
Imperial LP-9084	(M)	Hitsville U.S.A., Volume 1	1960	16.00	40.00
Imperial LP-9099	(M)	Hitsville U.S.A., Volume 2	1960	16.00	40.00
Imperial LP-9210	(M)	A World Of Blues	1963	16.00	40.00
Imperial LP-9214	(M)	Hillbilly House Party	1963	8.00	20.00
Imperial LP-9230	(M)	Solid Gold Hits	1964	10.00	25.00

Label & Catalog #		Title	Year	VG+	NM
Imperial LP-9257	(M)	Best Of The Blues, Volume 1	1964	10.00	25.00
Imperial LP-12257	(E)	Best Of The Blues, Volume 1	1964	8.00	20.00
Imperial LP-9259	(M)	Best Of The Blues, Volume 2	1964	10.00	25.00
Imperial LP-12259	(E)	Best Of The Blues, Volume 2	1964	8.00	20.00
Imperial LP-9260	(M)	New Orleans, Our Home Town	1964	10.00	25.00
Imperial LP-12260	(E)	New Orleans, Our Home Town	1964	8.00	20.00
Imperial LP-9271	(M)	Giant Instrumental R&B Hits	1964	10.00	25.00
Imperial LP-12271	(E)	Giant Instrumental R&B Hits	1964	8.00	20.00
		— Original Imperial mono albums above have black labels with stars on top;			
		stereo albums have black labels with silver print.—			
Imperial MM-423	(DJ)	Special Programmer Selection From 1965	1965	10.00	25.00
Increase	(M)	Cruisin' 1955	1970	8.00	20.00
Increase	(M)	Cruisin' 1956	1970	8.00	20.00
Increase	(M)	Cruisin' 1957	1970	8.00	20.00
Increase	(M)	Cruisin' 1958	1970	8.00	20.00
Increase	(M)	Cruisin' 1959	1970	8.00	20.00
Increase	(M)	Cruisin' 1960	1970	8.00	20.00
Increase	(M)	Cruisin' 1961	1970	8.00	20.00
Increase	(M)	Cruisin' 1962	1970	8.00	20.00
Increase	(M)	Cruisin' 1963	1973	8.00	20.00
Increase	(M)	Cruisin' 1964	1973	8.00	20.00
Increase	(M)	Cruisin' 1965	1973	8.00	20.00
Increase	(M)	Cruisin' 1966	1973	8.00	20.00
Increase	(M)	Cruisin' 1967	1973	8.00	20.00
Increase	(DJ)	Cruisin' (Radio sampler)	1973	12.00	30.00
		(Original pressings copyrighted 1970 or 1973 on the back cover			
		and the album was centered around the presentation of a popular			
		disc jockey of the album's period; later reissues drop this format.)			
Instant 7100	(M)	All These Things	196?	16.00	40.00
International Art. 13	(S)	Epitaph For A Legend (2 LPs)	1979	20.00	50.00
Jamie LPS-3031	(E)	Old 'N Golden	196?	8.00	20.00
JAS JAS-5001	(P)	San Francisco Roots (Photo cover)	1976	16.00	40.00
JAS JAS-5001	(P)	San Francisco Roots (Titles cover)	1976	8.00	20.00
		(JAS 5001 is a reissue of Vault 119.)			
Jerden JRL-7001	(M)	Original Great Northwest Hits, Volume 1	1965	20.00	50.00
Jerden JRL-7002	(M)	Original Great Northwest Hits, Volume 2	1965	20.00	50.00
Jerden JRL-7005	(M)	Hitmakers	1966	20.00	50.00
Jin 4002	(M)	Rockin' Date With The			
		South Louisiana Stars	196?	16.00	40.00
Jobete PRO-1	(DJ)	The Top 10 Story In Sound (2 LPs)	1972	16.00	40.00
Jobete PRO-2	(DJ)	The Songs Of Smokey Robinson	1972	12.00	30.00
Jobete PRO-3	(DJ)	The Songs Of Ashford & Simpson	1974	12.00	30.00
Jobete PRO-4	(DJ)	The Songs Of Holland-Dozier-Holland	1974	12.00	30.00
Jobete PRO-5	(DJ)	The Songs Of Stevie Wonder	1974	12.00	30.00
Jobete PRO-6	(DJ)	The Songs Of Marvin Gaye	1974	12.00	30.00
Jobete PRO-7	(DJ)	The Songs Of Norman Whitfield	1976	12.00	30.00
Jobete PRO-8	(DJ)	The Songs Of Johnny Bristol / Frank Wilson /			
		Mickey Stevenson / Freddie Perren	1977	12.00	30.00
Jobete PRO-9	(DJ)	Holland-Dozier-Holland:			
		Yesterday, Today & Forever (3 LPs)	1977	16.00	40.00
Jobete PRO-9	(DJ)	Pure Magic: The Songs			
		Of Pam Sawyer & Marilyn McLeod	1978	12.00	30.00
		(Each of the Jobete albums above are publisher's demo with			
		snippets of recordings of the writers' material.)			
Josie JOZ-4002	(M)	Original Goldies From The Fabulous '50's,			
		Volume 1	1962	30.00	75.00
Josie JOZ-4003	(M)	Original Goldies From The Fabulous '50's			
		Volume 2	1962	30.00	75.00

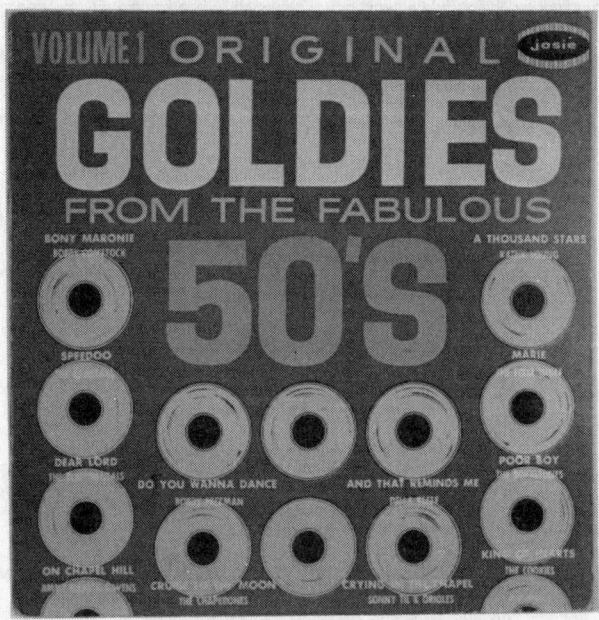

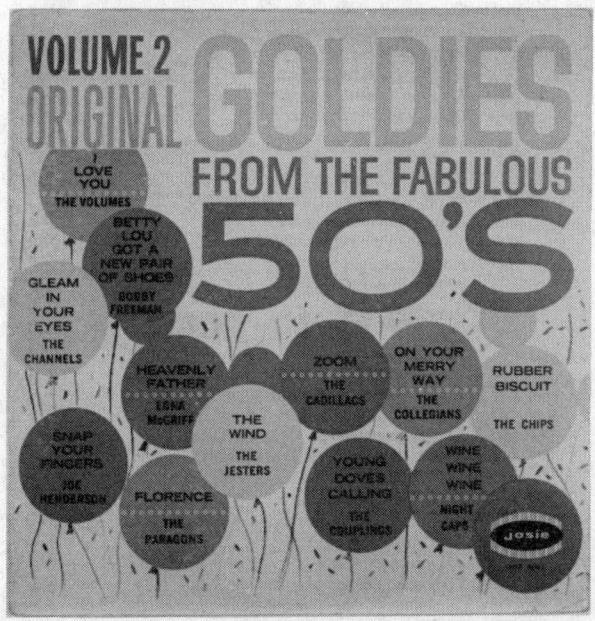

The two volumes of Josie's Original Goldies *sport fairly typical cover designs for such comps: The graphics are simple but the browser immediately notes the artist and the titles awaiting within.*

Label & Catalog #		Title	Year	VG+	NM
Jubilee J-1014	(M)	The Best of Rhythm And Blues	195?	40.00	100.00
Jubilee J-1014	(M)	The Best of Rhythm And Blues (Red vinyl)	195?	80.00	200.00
Jubilee J-1107	(M)	Surprise Party (Vol. 1)	196?	40.00	100.00
Jubilee J-1114	(M)	Rumble	195?	40.00	100.00
Jubilee J-1118	(M)	Boppin'	195?	40.00	100.00
Jubilee J-1119	(M)	Whoppers	195?	40.00	100.00
Kama Sutra KLPS-2015	(S)	Rock 'N' Roll Revival	1970	6.00	15.00
Killdozer KILL-001	(M)	Scum Of The Earth, Part 1	198?	30.00	75.00
Killdozer KILL-002	(M)	Scum Of The Earth, Part 2	198?	30.00	75.00
King 395-513	(M)	All Star Rock And Roll Revue	1958	80.00	200.00
King 395-528	(M)	After Hours	1958	150.00	300.00
King 395-536	(M)	Rock & Roll Dance Party	1958	80.00	200.00
King 395-537	(M)	All Time Country & Western Hits	1958	30.00	75.00
King 395-540	(M)	Piano Variations	1958	30.00	75.00
King 395-556	(M)	Sacred Songs	1958	30.00	75.00
King 395-562	(M)	Square Dance Music	1958	30.00	75.00
King 395-576	(M)	Spirituals, Volume 5	1958	30.00	75.00
King 395-607	(M)	Battle Of The Blues Vol. 1: Refer to Roy Brown / Wynonie Harris			
King 395-627	(M)	Battle Of The Blues Vol. 2: Refer to Roy Brown / Wynonie Harris			
King 395-634	(M)	Battle Of The Blues Vol. 3: Refer to Jimmy Witherspoon / Eddie Vinson			
King 395-638	(M)	Rock & Roll Revue	1959	40.00	100.00
King 654	(M)	Rock & Roll Revue, Volume 2	1959	40.00	100.00
King 668	(M)	Battle Of The Blues, Vol. 4: Refer to Roy Brown / Wynonie Harris			
King 680	(M)	Merry Christmas	1959	50.00	100.00
King 697	(M)	Country & Western Jamboree	1960	30.00	75.00
King 710	(M)	All Time Country & Western Hits	1960	30.00	75.00
King 725	(M)	25 Years Of Rhythm And Blues Hits	1960	30.00	75.00
King 726	(M)	Homespun Humor	1960	30.00	75.00
King 737	(M)	Hit Makers And Record Breakers	1960	30.00	75.00
King 745	(M)	Solo Spotlights	1961	30.00	75.00
King 749	(M)	25 Years Of R&B Hits	1961	30.00	75.00
King 753	(M)	Bumper Crop Of All Stars	1961	30.00	75.00
King 792	(M)	Forgotten Million Sellers	1962	30.00	75.00
King 807	(M)	All Star Country & Western	1962	20.00	50.00
King 811	(M)	Country Christmas	1962	20.00	50.00
King 813	(M)	Nashville Bandstand	1962	20.00	50.00
King 819	(M)	A Carnival Of Songs	1963	30.00	75.00
King 837	(M)	Organ Jazz Giants	1963	14.00	35.00
King 847	(M)	Nashville Bandstand, Volume 2	1963	16.00	40.00
King 855	(M)	Surfin' On Wave Nine	1963	16.00	40.00
King 859	(M)	Turning Back The Clock Blue	1963	16.00	40.00
King 862	(M)	Hootenanny	1963	16.00	40.00
King 866	(M)	Truck Driver Songs	1963	16.00	40.00
King 869	(M)	Railroad Songs	1963	16.00	40.00
King 871	(M)	Songs Of Rivers, Oceans And Seas	1963	16.00	40.00
King 875	(M)	Everybody's Favorite Blues	1964	16.00	40.00
King 876	(M)	Western Swing	1964	16.00	40.00
King 882	(M)	Look Who's Surfin' Now	1964	20.00	50.00
King 884	(M)	Top R&B Artists Sing Country	1964	16.00	40.00
King 890	(M)	14 Great All Time C&W Waltzes	1964	16.00	40.00
King 893	(M)	14 Hit Flashbacks From The Group Era	1964	16.00	40.00
King K-951	(M)	Spirituals (Re-issue of #576)	1966	10.00	25.00
King K-965	(M)	24 Scared Songs	1966	10.00	25.00
King K-994	(M)	5 String Banjo Pickin' And Singin'	1966	10.00	25.00
King K-1004	(M)	25 Years Of R&B Hits	1966	10.00	25.00
King K-1006	(M)	25 Years Of C&W	1966	10.00	25.00
King K-1008	(M)	25 Years Of Popular Music	1966	10.00	25.00
— Original King albums above have crownless black labels. —					
King KS-1023	(M)	All Time Sacred Hits	1968	6.00	15.00
King KS-1026	(M)	18 All Time R&B Hits	1968	6.00	15.00
King KS-1027	(M)	18 All Time C&W Hits	1968	6.00	15.00
King KS-1050	(E)	Radar Blues	1969	6.00	15.00
King KS-1133	(S)	Risky Blues	1971	6.00	15.00
Kramden 101	(M)	Hipsville 29 B.C.	198?	20.00	50.00

Label & Catalog #		Title	Year	VG+	NM
Laurie LLP-2010	(M)	Great Groups Great Records	1961	10.00	25.00
Laurie LLP-2014	(M)	Greatest Golden Goodies	1963	6.00	15.00
Laurie LLP-2021	(M)	Pick Hits Of The Radio Good Guys	1963	6.00	15.00
Laurie LLP-2026	(M)	Pick Hits Of The Radio Good Guys, Vol. 2	1964	6.00	15.00
Laurie LLP-2028	(M)	Radio Smash Flashbacks/Drive Time	1965	6.00	15.00
Laurie LLP-2029	(M)	Radio Smash Flashbacks/Prime Time	1965	6.00	15.00
Laurie LLP-2041	(M)	Laurie Golden Goodies	1967	6.00	15.00
Laurie LLP-2044	(M)	Rock & Roll: Evolution Or Revolution?	1968	6.00	15.00
Laurie LLP-2051	(M)	Collector's Records Of The '50's And '60's	1970	4.00	10.00
Liberty LST-101	(DJ)	This Is Stereo (Red vinyl)	1960	40.00	100.00
Liberty LRP-5503	(M)	Teensville	1962	16.00	40.00
Liberty LRP-5505	(M)	Golden Teen Hits	1962	16.00	40.00
Liberty MM-412	(DJ)	Explosive!	1962	20.00	50.00
Liberty MM-417	(DJ)	Spin Time With Liberty	1962	20.00	50.00
Liberty LRP-3048	(M)	Hot Rod Rumble	1957	14.00	35.00
Liberty LRP-3178	(M)	Original Hits, Volume 1	1961	8.00	20.00
Liberty LST-7178	(P)	Original Hits, Volume 1	1961	10.00	25.00
Liberty LRP-3180	(M)	Original Hits, Volume 2	1961	8.00	20.00
Liberty LST-7180	(P)	Original Hits, Volume 2	1961	10.00	25.00
Liberty LRP-3187	(M)	Original Hits, Volume 3	1961	8.00	20.00
Liberty LST-7187	(P)	Original Hits, Volume 3	1961	10.00	25.00
Liberty LRP-3200	(M)	Original Hits, Volume 4	1962	8.00	20.00
Liberty LST-7200	(P)	Original Hits, Volume 4	1962	10.00	25.00
Liberty LRP-3235	(M)	15 Hits, Volume 5	1962	8.00	20.00
Liberty LST-7235	(P)	15 Hits, Volume 5	1962	10.00	25.00
Liberty LRP-3260	(M)	Original Hits, Volume 6	1962	6.00	15.00
Liberty LST-7260	(P)	Original Hits, Volume 6	1962	8.00	20.00
Liberty LRP-3274	(M)	Original Hits, Volume 7	1962	6.00	15.00
Liberty LST-7274	(P)	Original Hits, Volume 7	1962	8.00	20.00
Liberty LRP-3288	(M)	Original Hits, Volume 8	1963	6.00	15.00
Liberty LST-7288	(P)	Original Hits, Volume 8	1963	8.00	20.00
Liberty LRP-3325	(M)	Original Hits, Volume 9	1963	6.00	15.00
Liberty LST-7325	(P)	Original Hits, Volume 9	1963	8.00	20.00
Liberty LRP-3344	(M)	Original Hits, Volume 10	1964	6.00	15.00
Liberty LST-7344	(P)	Original Hits, Volume 10	1964	8.00	20.00
Liberty LRP-3366	(M)	Shut Downs And Hill Climbs	1964	16.00	40.00
Liberty LST-7366	(P)	Shut Downs And Hill Climbs	1964	20.00	50.00
Liberty LRP-3381	(M)	Original Rhythm & Blues Hits, Vol. 1	1964	6.00	15.00
Liberty LRP-3382	(M)	Original Country Hits #3	1964	6.00	15.00
Liberty LRP-3418	(M)	#1 Hits, Volume 11	1964	6.00	15.00
Liberty LST-7418	(P)	#1 Hits, Volume 11	1964	8.00	20.00
Liberty LRP-3430	(M)	C'mon Let's Live A Little (Soundtrack)	1966	6.00	15.00
Liberty LST-7430	(S)	C'mon Let's Live A Little (Soundtrack)	1966	8.00	20.00
Liberty LRP-3500	(M)	The Original Golden Greats	1967	6.00	15.00
Liberty LST-7500	(S)	The Original Golden Greats	1967	6.00	15.00
Lion 70108	(M)	Celebrities	1960	10.00	25.00
London LL-3034	(M)	Music For Hand-Jiving	196?	6.00	15.00
London LL-3430	(M)	England's Greatest Hits	1964	10.00	25.00
London PS-430	(E)	England's Greatest Hits	1964	6.00	15.00
Lost-Nite LP-10?	(M)	Jerry Blavat Presents For Lovers Only, Volume 1	1965	8.00	20.00
Lost-Nite LPS-10?	(S)	Jerry Blavat Presents For Lovers Only, Volume 1	1965	10.00	25.00
Lost-Nite LP-107	(M)	Jerry Blavat Presents For Lovers Only, Volume 2	1965	8.00	20.00
Lost-Nite LPS-107	(S)	Jerry Blavat Presents For Lovers Only, Volume 2	1965	10.00	25.00
Lost-Nite LP-114	(M)	Gary Stevens' 22 Good Guy Oldies	1965	10.00	25.00
Magistral 2000	(M)	Changes	198?	20.00	50.00
Magna 71014	(M)	Northland Battle Of The Bands	1967	360.00	600.00

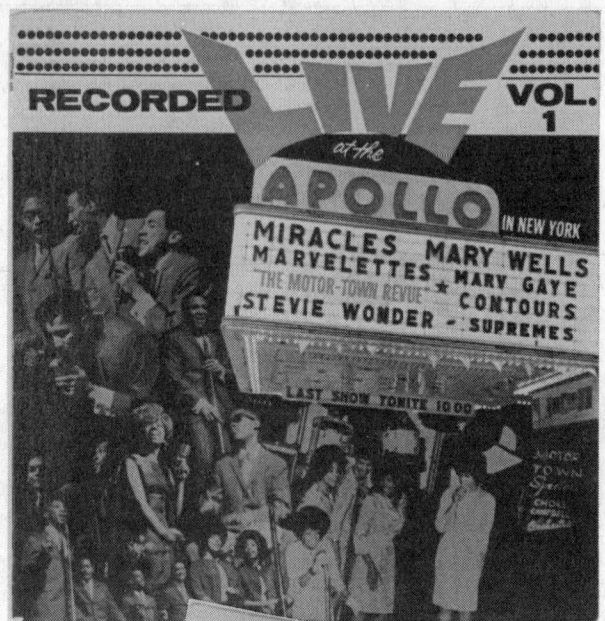

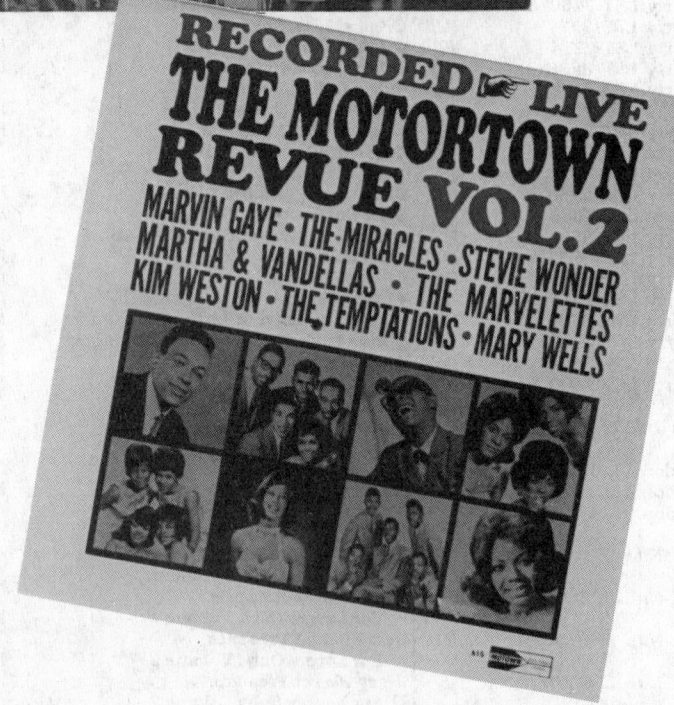

Note the vast differences in the cover designs between the two volumes of these early Motown sets: The first volume, subtitled Recorded Live At The Apollo, is a rather hectic collage that captures some of the excitement that a rhythm 'n blues show was expected to have (especially at the Apollo). Volume two has a staid, almost sedate, layout, perhaps reflecting the direction that Berry Gordy was grooming his stars towards by its 1964 release.

Label & Catalog #		Title	Year	VG+	NM
Mainstream 56100	(M)	A Pot Of Flowers	1967	10.00	25.00
Mainstream S-6100	(S)	A Pot Of Flowers	1967	12.00	30.00
Mark-56 MLP-510	(M)	Mr. Faruki's Suzuki	196?	20.00	50.00
Mark-56 MLP-511	(M)	Golden Oldies	196?	20.00	50.00
MCA	(DJ)	More American Graffiti (Picture disc)	1976	10.00	25.00
Memphis (No number)	(M)	Rebirth Of Beale Street	1984	16.00	40.00
Mercury MG-25164 (10")	(M)	Hit Parade	195?	20.00	50.00
Mercury MG-25166 (10")	(M)	Hit Parade	195?	20.00	50.00
Mercury MG-25205 (10")	(M)	Hit Parade	195?	20.00	50.00
Mercury MG-20213	(M)	A Collection Of Golden Hits	195?	20.00	50.00
Mercury MG-20282	(M)	Hillbilly Hit Parade, Volume 1	1958	20.00	50.00
Mercury MG-20328	(M)	Hillbilly Hit Parade, Volume 2	1958	20.00	50.00
Mercury MG-20350	(M)	Opry Stars Jamboree	1958	16.00	40.00
Mercury MG-20360	(M)	A Night At The Louisiana Hayride	1958	16.00	40.00
Mercury MG	(M)	Rock All Night (Soundtrack)	195?	100.00	250.00
Mercury MG-20493	(M)	14 Newies But Goodies	195?	20.00	50.00
Mercury MG-20511	(M)	Golden Goodies	195?	16.00	40.00
Mercury SR-60217	(S)	Golden Goodies	195?	20.00	50.00
Mercury MG-20581	(M)	14 More Newies But Goodies	195?	20.00	50.00
Mercury MG-20687	(M)	Twist With The Stars	1962	20.00	50.00
Mercury MG-20809	(M)	Original Golden Hits Of The Great Groups	1963	20.00	50.00
Mercury MG-20826	(M)	The Great Blues Singers	1964	12.00	30.00
Mercury MG-20857	(M)	Hootenanny Bluegrass Style	1964	8.00	20.00
Mercury SRD-2-29	(S)	Zig Zag Festival	1970	16.00	40.00
Mercury SRP-2-605	(S)	The Big Country (2 LPs)	1970	6.00	15.00
Mercury SRM1-605	(S)	Joe (Soundtrack)	1970	4.00	10.00
Mercury MK2-2-121	(DJ)	The Ultimate Radio Bootleg, Vol. 3	1976	10.00	25.00
Metro M/MS-563		This Is Where It Started: Refer to The Beatles			
MGM DJ-5	(DJ)	MGM Sounds Of 1959	1959	20.00	50.00
MGM E-3814	(M)	MGM Top Hits	1963	8.00	20.00
MGM SE-3814	(P)	MGM Top Hits	1963	10.00	25.00
MGM E-3826	(M)	MGM Hits With A Beat	1963	8.00	20.00
MGM SE-3826	(P)	MGM Hits With A Beat	1963	10.00	25.00
MGM E-3912	(M)	We Wrote 'Em And We Sing 'Em	1964	8.00	20.00
MGM SE-3912	(S)	We Wrote 'Em And We Sing 'Em	1964	12.00	30.00
MGM E-4078	(M)	MGM Parade Of Hits	1964	8.00	20.00
MGM SE-4078	(P)	MGM Parade Of Hits	1964	10.00	25.00
MGM E-4273	(M)	Get Yourself A College Girl (Soundtrack)	1964	6.00	15.00
MGM SE-4273	(S)	Get Yourself A College Girl (Soundtrack)	1964	8.00	20.00
MGM E-4306	(M)	Mickie Most Presents British Go-Go	1964	4.00	10.00
MGM SE-4306	(S)	Mickie Most Presents British Go-Go	1964	6.00	15.00
MGM E-4312	(M)	Solid Gold	1965	8.00	20.00
MGM SE-4312	(P)	Solid Gold	1965	8.00	20.00
MGM E-4334	(M)	When The Boys Meet The Girls (Sdtk)	1965	8.00	20.00
MGM SE-4334	(S)	When The Boys Meet The Girls (Sdtk)	1965	10.00	25.00
MGM E-4352	(M)	Solid Gold	1966	6.00	15.00
MGM SE-4352	(S)	Solid Gold	1966	8.00	20.00
MGM SE-4468	(S)	Zabriskie Point (Soundtrack)	1970	6.00	15.00
MGM SE-4506	(S)	What Am I Bid? (Soundtrack)	1971	8.00	20.00
MGM 1SE-11	(S)	Grand Prix (Soundtrack)	1971	6.00	15.00
MGM 2SE-14	(S)	The Strawberry Statement (2 LPs. Sdtk)	1971	8.00	20.00
MGM 1SE-21	(S)	Zigzag (Soundtrack)	1971	6.00	15.00
Minit LP-0001	(M)	New Orleans: Home Of The Blues	1961	20.00	50.00
Minit LP-0003	(M)	We Sing The Blues	1962	20.00	50.00
Minit LP-0004	(M)	New Orleans: Home Of The Blues, Volume 2	1962	20.00	50.00
Mobile Fidelity MFSL-200	(S)	Woodstock (5 LP box)	198?	50.00	150.00
Modern LMP-1210	(M)	Rock & Roll Dance Party	195?	40.00	100.00
Modern LMP-1211	(M)	Rock & Roll Record Hop	195?	40.00	100.00

Label & Catalog #		Title	Year	VG+	NM
Monsters 1002	(M)	Monsters Of The Midwest, Volume 2	198?	10.00	25.00
Monsters 1003	(M)	Monsters Of The Midwest, Volume 3	198?	10.00	25.00
Monsters 1004	(M)	Monsters Of The Midwest, Volume 4	198?	10.00	25.00
Monument MLP-8010	(M)	Demand Performances	1963	10.00	25.00
Monument SLP-18010	(S)	Demand Performances	1963	12.00	30.00
Motown MLP-603	(M)	Motown Hits, Volume 1	1962	12.00	30.00
Motown MLP-609	(M)	Recorded Live At The Apollo:			
		The Motortown Revue, Volume 1	1963	12.00	30.00
Motown MLP-614	(M)	A Package Of 16 Big Hits	1963	12.00	30.00
		(Original covers have a postal package motif.)			
Motown MLP-614	(M)	A Package Of 16 Big Hits	1967	8.00	20.00
Motown MS-614	(P)	A Package Of 16 Big Hits	1967	12.00	30.00
		(Later pressings have the standard "Big Hits" style cover.)			
Motown MLP-615	(M)	Recorded Live: The Motortown Revue, Vol. 2	1964	12.00	30.00
Motown MLP-624	(M)	16 Original Big Hits, Volume 3	1964	8.00	20.00
Motown MS-624	(S)	16 Original Big Hits, Volume 3	1964	10.00	25.00
Motown MLP-630	(M)	Nothing But A Man (Soundtrack)	1965	20.00	50.00
Motown MS-630	(S)	Nothing But A Man (Soundtrack)	1965	30.00	75.00
Motown MLP-633	(M)	16 Original Big Hits, Volume 4	1965	8.00	20.00
Motown MS-633	(S)	16 Original Big Hits, Volume 4	1965	10.00	25.00
Motown M-642	(M)	In Loving Memory	1968	40.00	100.00
Motown MS-642	(S)	In Loving Memory	1968	40.00	100.00
Motown MS-651	(S)	16 Original Big Hits, Volume 5	1968	6.00	15.00
Motown MS-655	(S)	16 Original Big Hits, Volume 6	1968	8.00	20.00
Motown MS-661	(S)	16 Original Big Hits, Volume 7	1968	6.00	15.00
Motown MS-666	(S)	16 Original Big Hits, Volume 8	1968	6.00	15.00
Motown MS-668	(S)	16 Original Big Hits, Volume 9	1968	6.00	15.00
Motown MS-681	(M)	Merry Christmas From Motown	1968	12.00	30.00
Motown MS-684	(S)	16 Original Big Hits, Volume 10	1969	6.00	15.00
Motown MS-688	(S)	The Motortown Revue Recorded Live!	1969	10.00	25.00
— Original Motown albums above have a Detroit, MI, address on the label.—					
Motown MS-693	(S)	16 Original Big Hits, Volume 11	1969	4.00	10.00
Motown MS-701	(S)	Shades Of Gospel Soul	1970	4.00	10.00
Motown MS-703	(S)	Motown At The Hollywood Palace	1970	4.00	10.00
Motown MS-707	(S)	Motown Chartbusters, Volume 1	1970	4.00	10.00
Motown MS-715	(S)	Motown Chartbusters, Volume 2	1970	4.00	10.00
Motown MS-725	(S)	Christmas Gift Wrap (Re-issue of #681)	1970	4.00	10.00
Motown MS-5-726	(S)	The Motown Story (5 LPs)	1971	10.00	25.00
Motown MS-727	(S)	The Motown Story, Volume 1	1971	4.00	10.00
Motown MS-728	(S)	The Motown Story, Volume 2	1971	4.00	10.00
Motown MS-729	(S)	The Motown Story, Volume 3	1971	4.00	10.00
Motown MS-730	(S)	The Motown Story, Volume 4	1971	4.00	10.00
Motown MS-731	(S)	The Motown Story, Volume 5	1971	4.00	10.00
Motown MS-732	(S)	Motown Chartbusters, Volume 3	1971	4.00	10.00
Motown MS-734	(S)	Motown Chartbusters, Volume 4	1971	4.00	10.00
Motown M-739L	(DJ)	1971 Sterling Ball Benefit	1971	40.00	100.00
Motown	(DJ)	The Motown Story	1983	100.00	250.00
		(3 LPs on white labels)			
Motown 121	(DJ)	The Motown Story, Volume 1	1983	20.00	50.00
Motown 121	(DJ)	The Motown Story, Volume 2	1983	20.00	50.00
Moulty MLP-101	(M)	New England Teen Scene	198?	20.00	50.00
Moulty MLP-103	(M)	New England Teen Scene, Vol. 2	198?	8.00	20.00
Mt. Vernon MUM-109	(M)	Hitsville	196?	12.00	30.00
Muse 500	(M)	Carload Of Hits	196?	80.00	200.00
Muziek Expres ME-66	(M)	Searching In The Wilderness	198?	10.00	25.00
Myst 001	(M)	Gathering Of The Tribe 4	198?	8.00	20.00
N.A.P.R.A. 2	(S)	Get Off It [BB]	1975	10.00	25.00
Nashville NLP-2052	(M)	Truck Stop	197?	6.00	15.00
Nashville NLP-2082	(M)	Truck Drivin' Son Of A Gun	197?	6.00	15.00

Label & Catalog #		Title	Year	VG+	NM
New World 207	(P)	**Country Music In The Modern Era**	1976	60.00	150.00
		(Originals have a small border along the bottom front cover.)			
New World 207	(P)	**Country Music In The Modern Era**	1978	20.00	50.00
		(Later pressings have a wider border along the bottom front cover.)			
Northridge 101	(M)	**Surf's Up At Banzai Pipeline**	1963	16.00	40.00
Numero Uno *(No number)*	(M)	**Mexican Rock 'n Roll Favorites**	197?	8.00	20.00
Ode SP-99001	(DJ)	**Tommy** *(2 LP boxed soundtrack)*	1970	20.00	50.00
Ode SP-99001	(S)	**Tommy** *(2 LP boxed soundtrack)*	1970	6.00	15.00
Ode SQ-99001	(Q)	**Tommy** *(2 LP boxed soundtrack)*	1970	20.00	50.00
Old Town 101	(M)	**Rock & Roll On The Old Town**	196?	30.00	75.00
Oldies-33 OL-8001	(M)	**Oldies Dance Party, Volume 1**	1964	8.00	20.00
Oldies-33 OL-8002	(M)	**Oldies Dance Party, Volume 2**	1964	8.00	20.00
Oldies-33 OL-8004	(M)	**We Like Boys**	1964	10.00	25.00
Omega Sales	(M)	**Country Super Sounds 1955**	1973	12.00	30.00
Omega Sales	(M)	**Country Super Sounds 1956**	1973	12.00	30.00
Omega Sales	(M)	**Country Super Sounds 1957**	1973	12.00	30.00
Omega Sales	(M)	**Country Super Sounds 1958**	1973	12.00	30.00
Omega Sales	(M)	**Country Super Sounds 1959**	1973	6.00	15.00
Omega Sales	(M)	**Country Super Sounds 1960**	1973	6.00	15.00
Omega Sales	(M)	**Country Super Sounds 1961**	1973	6.00	15.00
Omega Sales	(M)	**Country Super Sounds 1962**	1973	6.00	15.00
Omega Sales	(M)	**Country Super Sounds 1963**	1973	6.00	15.00
Omega Sales	(M)	**Country Super Sounds 1964**	1973	6.00	15.00
Omega Sales	(M)	**Country Super Sounds 1965**	1973	6.00	15.00
Omega Sales	(M)	**Country Super Sounds 1966**	1973	6.00	15.00
Omega Sales	(M)	**Country Super Sounds 1967**	1973	6.00	15.00
Omega Sales	(M)	**Country Super Sounds 1968**	1973	6.00	15.00
Omega Sales	(M)	**Country Super Sounds 1969**	1973	6.00	15.00
Original Sound LPM-5001	(M)	**Oldies But Goodies**	1959	16.00	60.00
Original Sound LPM-5002	(M)	**Oldies But Goodies, Volume 2**	1960	16.00	40.00
Original Sound LPM-5003	(M)	**Oldies But Goodies, Volume 3**	196?	16.00	40.00
Original Sound LPM-5004	(M)	**Oldies But Goodies, Volume 4**	196?	12.00	30.00
Original Sound LPM-5005	(M)	**Oldies But Goodies, Volume 5**	196?	12.00	30.00
Original Sound LPM-5006	(M)	**Oldies But Goodies, Volume 6**	196?	12.00	30.00
Original Sound LPM-5007	(M)	**Oldies But Goodies, Volume 7**	196?	10.00	25.00
Original Sound LPM-5008	(M)	**Oldies But Goodies, Volume 8**	196?	10.00	25.00
Original Sound LPM-5009	(M)	**Oldies But Goodies, Volume 9**	196?	10.00	25.00
Original Sound LPM-5010	(M)	**Oldies But Goodies, Volume 10**	196?	10.00	25.00
		(Originals advertise the next volume only on the back cover.)			
Original Sound OSR-11	(S)	**Rock Rock Rock**	1972	20.00	50.00
Original Sound OSR-11	(M)	**All Star Rock, Volume 2**	1972	16.00	40.00
		("All Star Rock" is a reissue of "Rock Rock Rock.")			
Panorama 103	(M)	**Battle Of The Bands**	1966	12.00	30.00
Parade 208	(M)	**Top Tune Time**	196?	6.00	15.00
Paramount PAS-6005	(S)	**The Hard Ride** *(Soundtrack)*	197?	6.00	15.00
Parkway P-7011	(M)	**Don't Knock The Twist** *(Soundtrack)*	1962	12.00	30.00
Parkway P-7013	(M)	**All The Hits By All The Stars**	1962	12.00	30.00
Parkway P-7028	(M)	**Million Seller Dance Hits**	1963	10.00	25.00
Parkway P-7031	(M)	**12 Greatest Golden Oldies In The Whole World Ever**	1963	10.00	25.00
Parkway P-7033	(M)	**All The Stars-Biggest Hits**	1963	14.00	35.00
Parkway P-7034	(M)	**All The Stars-Biggest Hits, Volume 2**	1963	14.00	35.00
		(Both Parkway 7033 and 7034 were issued with "Pull Off Pix" of the six artists on the album. The price is for the record and the jacket with the pix intact.)			
Parkway P-7035	(M)	**Everybody's Goin' Surfin'**	1963	12.00	30.00

Label & Catalog #		Title	Year	VG+	NM
Parrot PA-61010	(M)	The Greatest Hits From England	1964	8.00	20.00
Parrot PAS-71010	(P)	The Greatest Hits From England	1964	8.00	20.00
Parrot PA-61017	(M)	The Greatest Hits From England, Volume 2	1964	8.00	20.00
Parrot PAS-71017	(P)	The Greatest Hits From England, Volume 2	1964	8.00	20.00
Parrot PA-61023	(M)	All American Hits	1964	8.00	20.00
Parrot PAS-71023	(P)	All American Hits	1964	8.00	20.00
Passport PB-3604	(S)	Phil Spector's Christmas Album: *Refer to Phil Spector*			
Pavillion PZ-37686	(S)	Phil Spector's Christmas Album: *Refer to Phil Spector*			
Paul Winley Prod. 1001	(M)	New York City's Greatest Oldies	196?	40.00	100.00
Phantom PRS-1001	(M)	A Journey To Tyme, Vol. 1	198?	14.00	35.00
Phantom PRS-1002	(M)	A Journey To Tyme, Vol. 2	198?	14.00	35.00
Phantom PRS-1003	(M)	A Journey To Tyme, Vol. 3	198?	14.00	35.00
Phantom PLP-1004	(M)	Sound Of The 60s: San Francisco, Part 1	198?	14.00	35.00
Phantom PLP-1005	(M)	Sound Of The 60s: San Francisco, Part 2	198?	14.00	35.00
Phantom PRS-1006	(M)	A Journey To Tyme, Vol. 4	198?	14.00	35.00
Phantom PRS-1007	(M)	A Journey To Tyme, Vol. 5	198?	14.00	35.00
Philles PHLP-4004	(M)	Today's Hits: *Refer to Phil Spector*			
Philles PHLP-4005	(M)	A Christmas Gift For You: *Refer to Phil Spector*			
Pickwick PTP-2060	(M)	Rockin' Originals	196?	6.00	15.00
Pickwick SPC-3280	(S)	Rock 'N' Roll Revival	1971	4.00	10.00
Pickwick CL-001	(S)	Moving Ahead With Music	197?	12.00	30.00
Playboy 7473	(S)	The Playboy Music Hall Of Fame Winners	1978	20.00	50.00
Prestige PR-7539	(S)	Take A Trip With Psychedelic Hits	196?	20.00	50.00
Pricewise 4004	(M)	Best Of The Girl Groups	196?	10.00	25.00
Prism 1966	(M)	WONE-The Daytona Scene	1966	150.00	300.00
Psycho 1	(M)	Endless Journey, Phase 1	198?	10.00	25.00
Psycho 3	(M)	Endless Journey, Phase 2	198?	10.00	25.00
Psycho 6	(M)	The Perfumed Garden	198?	20.00	50.00
Psycho 15	(M)	The Perfumed Garden II	198?	20.00	50.00
Psycho 19	(M)	Endless Journey, Phase 3	198?	16.00	40.00
Ralph	(DJ)	10th Anniversary Radio Special *(2 LPs)*	1981	12.00	30.00
Psychotic Moose PMS-101	(M)	Psychotic Moose & The Soul Searchers	198?	20.00	50.00
Rampart LP-3303	(M)	East Side Revue	196?	40.00	100.00
Rampart LP-3305	(M)	East Side Revue, Volume 2 *(With poster)*	196?	50.00	125.00
Rampart LP-3305	(M)	East Side Revue, Volume 2 *(Without poster)*	196?	40.00	100.00
		(Both the Rampart albums are on multi-colored vinyl.)			
RCA Victor LPM-3182 (10")	(M)	The Honor Roll Of Hits 1940-41	1954	20.00	50.00
RCA Victor LPM-3183 (10")	(M)	The Honor Roll Of Hits 1942-43	1954	20.00	50.00
RCA Victor LPM-3184 (10")	(M)	The Honor Roll Of Hits 1944-45	1954	20.00	50.00
RCA Victor LPM-3192 (10")	(M)	Tennessee Jamboree	1954	30.00	75.00
RCA Victor LPM-3220 (10")	(M)	Country And Western Caravan	1954	30.00	75.00
RCA Victor LPM-3282 (10")	(M)	Top Pops	1954	30.00	75.00
RCA Victor LPM-1540	(M)	Teenagers Dance	1957	14.00	35.00
RCA Victor LPM-1802	(M)	TV Record Hop	1958	10.00	25.00
RCA Victor LPM-2210	(M)	Goodies For LP Fans	1960	8.00	20.00
RCA Victor LSP-2210	(P)	Goodies For LP Fans	1960	10.00	25.00
RCA Victor LPM-2314	(M)	High Time *(Soundtrack)*	1960	8.00	20.00
RCA Victor LSP-2314	(S)	High Time *(Soundtrack)*	1960	12.00	30.00
RCA Victor LPM-2332	(M)	Twelve Big Ones	1960	6.00	15.00
RCA Victor LSP-2332	(P)	Twelve Big Ones	1960	8.00	20.00

— *Original RCA mono albums above have black labels with "Long Play" on the bottom; stereo albums have "Living Stereo" on the bottom.* —

Label & Catalog #		Title	Year	VG+	NM
RCA Victor LPM-2740	(M)	Old 'n' Golden Goodies	1963	8.00	20.00
RCA Victor LSP-2740	(P)	Old 'n' Golden Goodies	1963	12.00	30.00
RCA Victor LPM-3441	(M)	Wild On The Beach (Soundtrack)	1965	8.00	20.00
RCA Victor LSP-3441	(S)	Wild On The Beach (Soundtrack)	1965	12.00	30.00
RCA Victor LPM-3632	(M)	The Best Of The Best Of	1966	8.00	20.00
RCA Victor LSP-3632	(P)	The Best Of The Best Of	1966	10.00	25.00
RCA Victor LPM-3641	(M)	Old 'n' Golden Goodies, Volume 2	1966	8.00	20.00
RCA Victor LSP-3641	(P)	Old 'n' Golden Goodies, Volume 2	1966	12.00	30.00
RCA Victor LPM-6015	(M)	Stars Of The Grand Ole Opry (2 LP box)	1967	16.00	40.00
RCA Victor LPM-6015	(M)	Stars Of The Grand Ole Opry (2 LPs)	1967	6.00	15.00
RCA Victor PRM-167	(M)	Oldsmobile Presents The New Stars	196?	5.00	12.00
RCA Victor PRS-167	(S)	Oldsmobile Presents The New Stars	196?	6.00	15.00
RCA Victor SP-33204	(M)	Buick Presents The Sound Of Tomorrow	196?	5.00	12.00
RCA Victor SPS-33204	(S)	Buick Presents The Sound Of Tomorrow	196?	6.00	15.00

— Original RCA albums above have black labels.—

— RCA Promotional Albums issued in plain cardboard jackets .—

RCA Victor F70P-9681	(DJ)	E-Z Pop Programming #5	1955	360.00	600.00
RCA Victor G70L-0108	(DJ)	E-Z Country Programming #2	1955	360.00	600.00
RCA Victor G70L-0197	(DJ)	E-Z Pop Programming #6	1956	300.00	500.00
RCA Victor G70L-0199	(DJ)	E-Z Country Programming #3	1956	300.00	500.00
RCA Victor SP-33-4	(DJ)	"Untitled Sampler"	1956	300.00	500.00
RCA Victor SP-33-10P	(DJ)	"Untitled Sampler"	1958	150.00	300.00
RCA Victor SP-33-59-7	(DJ)	February Sampler 59-7	1959	150.00	300.00
RCA Victor SP-33-66	(DJ)	Christmas Programming From RCA Victor	1959	300.00	500.00

(Issued in a paper sleeve, priced separately below.)

RCA Victor SP-33-66	(DJ)	Christmas Programming From RCA Victor	1959	500.00	1,000.00

(White paper sleeve with a full-color cartoon of Santa and photos of the artists. Counterfeits are obvious black & white photocopies.)

RCA Victor SPS-33-27	(DJ)	August '59 Sampler	1959	150.00	300.00
RCA Victor SPS-33-54	(DJ)	October Christmas Sampler	1959	150.00	300.00
RCA Victor SPS-33-96	(DJ)	October '60 Popular Stereo Sampler	1963	60.00	150.00
RCA Victor SPS-33-141	(DJ)	October '61 Pop Sampler	1963	60.00	150.00
RCA Victor SPS-33-191	(DJ)	October '63 Pop Sampler	1963	60.00	150.00
RCA Victor SPS-33-247	(DJ)	December '63 Pop Sampler	1963	60.00	150.00
RCA Victor SPS-33-272	(DJ)	April '64 Pop Sampler	1965	60.00	150.00
RCA Victor SPS-33-331	(DJ)	April '65 Pop Sampler	1965	60.00	150.00
RCA Victor SPS-33-347	(DJ)	August '65 Pop Sampler	1965	60.00	150.00
RCA Victor SPS-33-403	(DJ)	April '66 Pop Sampler	1966	60.00	150.00
RCA Victor RWS-0001	(DJ)	Robert W. Sarnoff-25 Years Of Leadership	1973	80.00	200.00
RCA Victor (No number)	(DJ)	WRCA Plays The Hits For Your Customers	1976	60.00	150.00

— Each promo album above features at least one song by Elvis Presley.—

Red Bird RB-20-102	(M)	Red Bird Goldies	196?	16.00	40.00
Regent MG-6015	(M)	Rock & Roll	195?	16.00	40.00
Regent MG-6042	(M)	Rock & Roll Party	195?	16.00	40.00
Relics CSFD-3	(M)	Chocolate Soup, Volume 3	198?	16.00	40.00
Relics LSD-1	(M)	Chocolate Soup, Volume 1	198?	16.00	40.00
Ren-Vell 317	(M)	Battle Of The Bands, Volume 1	1967	150.00	300.00
Reprise R-6094	(M)	Surf's Up At Banzai Pipeline	1963	14.00	35.00
Reprise RS-6094	(P)	Surf's Up At Banzai Pipeline	1963	20.00	50.00
Reprise 2MS-2031	(DJ)	The Strawberry Statement (2 LPs. Sdtk)	1970	30.00	75.00

(Issued in a plain jacket with a "Rush release" sticker.)

Roadside RBF-20	(M)	Roots: Rhythm & Blues	196?	12.00	30.00
Ronco LP-1001	(P)	Do It Now! (Yellow label)	1970	12.00	30.00
Ronco LP-1001	(P)	Do It Now! (Green label)	1970	6.00	15.00
Roulette R-25021	(M)	Pajama Party (Black label)	195?	16.00	40.00
Roulette R-25059	(M)	Rock & Roll Record Hop	1959	12.00	30.00
Roulette R-25093	(M)	Rock & Roll Bandstand	1959	12.00	30.00
Roulette R-25106	(M)	Original Hit Records	1962	10.00	25.00
Roulette SR-25106	(S)	Original Hit Records	1962	12.00	30.00

Label & Catalog #		Title	Year	VG+	NM
Roulette R-25159	(M)	Murray The K's Sing Along			
		With The Original Golden Gassers	1962	8.00	20.00
Roulette SR-25159	(S)	Murray The K's Sing Along			
		With The Original Golden Gassers	1962	10.00	25.00
Roulette R-25191	(M)	Murray & Jockey The K's Golden Gassers	1963	8.00	20.00
Roulette SR-25191	(S)	Murray & Jockey The K's Golden Gassers	1963	10.00	25.00
Roulette RE-114	(M)	Echoes Of The Rock Era: The Groups (2 LPs)	196?	8.00	20.00
Roulette RE-115	(M)	Echoes Of The Rock Era (2 LPs)	196?	6.00	15.00
Roxey	(M)	Acid Dreams	198?	16.00	40.00
RPM 3001	(M)	Rock & Roll Dance Party	195?	20.00	50.00
San Francisco SD-158	(S)	San Francisco	196?	8.00	20.00
San Fran. Sound 11680	(S)	Fifth Pipe Dream (Black & white cover)	1968	60.00	150.00
San Fran. Sound 11680	(S)	Fifth Pipe Dream (Color cover)	1968	40.00	100.00
Santo Presents	(M)	Mexican Rock 'n Roll Rumble	197?	8.00	20.00
		(Photocopied cover)			
Satan SR-666	(M)	Signed D. C.	198?	10.00	25.00
Satan SR-1003	(M)	Riot City	198?	10.00	25.00
Satan SR-1313	(M)	What A Way To Die	198?	6.00	15.00
Savoy MG-15008 (10")	(M)	Rhythm & Blues	195?	80.00	200.00
Savoy MG-15008	(M)	Rhythm & Blues	195?	16.00	40.00
Scepter SP-510	(M)	Murray The K's 1962 Golden Gassers	1963	8.00	20.00
Scepter SPS-510	(P)	Murray The K's 1962 Golden Gassers	1963	10.00	25.00
Scepter SP-518	(M)	The Group's Are The Greatest	1963	8.00	20.00
Scepter SPS-518	(P)	The Group's Are The Greatest	1963	10.00	25.00
Scepter SP-524	(M)	The Fifth Beatle Gives You			
		Their Golden Gassers	1964	8.00	20.00
Scepter SPS-524	(P)	The Fifth Beatle Gives You			
		Their Golden Gassers	1964	10.00	25.00
Score LP-4002	(M)	I Dig Rock & Roll	1957	80.00	200.00
Score LP-4018	(M)	Rock & Roll Sock Hop	1958	80.00	200.00
Screen Gems/Colgems	(DJ)	212 Hits (2 LPs)	196?	10.00	25.00
Screen Gems/Colgems	(DJ)	More Solid Gold Programming (2 LPs)	196?	12.00	30.00
Screen Gems/Columbia	(DJ)	Solid Gold-Gerry Goffin And Carole King	196?	10.00	25.00
Shelby Singleton Music 1	(DJ)	Songs For The Seventies (2 LPs)	1969	60.00	150.00
Shepherd 1300	(M)	Surf War	1963	14.00	35.00
Sidewalk T-5901	(M)	Freakout U.S.A.	1967	12.00	30.00
Sidewalk ST-5901	(E)	Freakout U.S.A.	1967	8.00	20.00
Sidewalk T-5911	(M)	Mary Jane (Soundtrack)	1968	12.00	30.00
Sidewalk DT-5911	(P)	Mary Jane (Soundtrack)	1968	8.00	20.00
Sidewalk ST-5913	(S)	Psych-Out (Soundtrack)	1968	16.00	40.00
Sire SASH-3716	(P)	Nuggets (2 LP reissue of Elektra 2006)	1976	8.00	20.00
Smash MGS-27038	(M)	Group Oldies But Goodies	1964	12.00	30.00
Smash SRS-67038	(P)	Group Oldies But Goodies	1964	16.00	40.00
Solar S-1000	(M)	Echoes In Time, Vol. 1	198?	14.00	35.00
Solar S-2000	(M)	Echoes In Time, Vol. 2	198?	14.00	35.00
Soma MG-1243	(M)	Big Hits Of Mid America	1968	30.00	75.00
Soma MG-1246	(M)	Big Hits Of Mid America, Volume 2	1968	30.00	75.00
Somerset P-1300	(M)	Rock 'N' Roll Dance Party	1954	30.00	75.00

Label & Catalog #		Title	Year	VG+	NM
Sounds Int. 005	(M)	The Boston Incest Album	197?	6.00	15.00
Sounds Of Hawaii 5014	(M)	Waikiki Surf Battle, Volume 1	1964	80.00	200.00
Sounds Of Hawaii 5014	(M)	Waikiki Surf Battle, Volume 2	1964	80.00	200.00
Specialty SP-2112	(M)	Our Significant Hits (Black & gold label)	1963	30.00	75.00
Specialty SP-2114	(M)	Doo Wop	1970	6.00	15.00
Specialty SP-2115	(M)	Ain't That Good News	1970	6.00	15.00
Specialty SP-2117	(M)	This Is How It All Began, Volume 1	1970	6.00	15.00
Specialty SP-2118	(M)	This Is How It All Began, Volume 2	1970	6.00	15.00
Specialty SP-2129	(M)	Original Rock Oldies, Volume 1	1970	6.00	15.00
Specialty SP-2130	(M)	Original Rock Oldies, Volume 2	1970	6.00	15.00
Specialty SP-2144	(M)	Gospel Gems, Volume 1	1971	6.00	15.00
Specialty SP-2145	(M)	Gospel Gems, Volume 2	1971	6.00	15.00
Specialty SP-2149	(M)	Dark Muddy Bottom Blues	1971	6.00	15.00
Specialty SP-2151	(M)	In Loving Memory Of Brother Joe May	1971	6.00	15.00
Specialty SP-2152	(M)	To Mother (Gosp)	1971	6.00	15.00
Specialty SP-2153	(M)	Gospel Stars In Concert	1971	6.00	15.00
Soul SS-720	(S)	Switched On Blues	1967	8.00	20.00
Star SRM-101	(M)	Battle Of The Bands	1964	60.00	150.00
Starday SLP-115	(M)	The Bluegrass Special	196?	16.00	40.00
Starday SLP-138	(M)	Nashville Steel Guitar	1961	20.00	50.00
Starday SLP-164	(M)	Country Music Hall Of fame	1962	16.00	40.00
Starday SLP-176	(M)	Tennessee Guitar	1962	16.00	40.00
Starday SLP-233	(M)	Steel Guitar Hall Of Fame	1963	16.00	40.00
Starday SLP-250	(M)	Diesel Smoke, Dangerous Curves & Others	1963	10.00	25.00
Starday SLP-277	(M)	Unforgettable Country Instrumentals	1963	12.00	30.00
Starday SLP-293	(M)	Steel Guitar And Dobro Spectacular	1964	10.00	35.00
Starday SLP-306	(M)	Let's Hit The Road	1964	10.00	25.00
Starday SLP-324	(M)	Country Hitmaker #1	1964	16.00	40.00
Starday SLP-345	(M)	Spectacular C&W Instrumentals	1965	12.00	30.00
Starday SLP-346	(S)	Gone But Not Forgotten	1965	16.00	40.00
Starday SLP-350	(M)	Stars Of The Steel Guitar	1965	14.00	35.00
Starday SLP-357	(M)	That's Truck Drivin'	1965	10.00	25.00
Starday SLP-352	(M)	Queens Of Country Music	1965	16.00	40.00
Starday SLP-386	(M)	Thunder On The Road	197?	10.00	25.00
Starday SLP-454	(M)	Best Of The Truck Driver Songs	197?	10.00	25.00
Starday SLP-7001	(M)	All-Star Country & Western Jamboree	197?	10.00	25.00
Starla LPM-1960	(M)	Art Laboe's Memories Of El Monte	1960	30.00	75.00
Stax 710	(M)	Memphis Gold (Blue label)	1966	6.00	15.00
Stax S-710	(P)	Memphis Gold (Blue label)	1966	8.00	20.00
Stax/Volt 11	(DJ)	Stay In School, Don't Be A Dropout	1967	300.00	600.00
Stax 721	(M)	The Stax/Volt Revue: Vol. 1, Live In London	1967	8.00	20.00
Stax S-721	(S)	The Stax/Volt Revue: Vol. 1, Live In London	1967	12.00	30.00
Stax 722	(M)	The Stax/Volt Revue: Vol. 2, Live In Paris	1967	8.00	20.00
Stax S-722	(S)	The Stax/Volt Revue: Vol. 2, Live In Paris	1967	12.00	30.00
Stax 726	(M)	Memphis Gold, Volume 2	1967	8.00	20.00
Stax SS-726	(S)	Memphis Gold, Volume 2	1967	10.00	25.00
Stax 2024	(S)	Boy Meets Girl	197?	6.00	15.00
Stax 3021	(S)	Filet Of Soul	197?	6.00	15.00
Stax 3023	(S)	Memphis Millions	197?	6.00	15.00
Stone Age SA-661	(M)	Garage Punk Unknowns, Volume 1	198?	8.00	20.00
Stone Age SA-662	(M)	Garage Punk Unknowns, Volume 2	198?	8.00	20.00
Stone Age SA-663	(M)	Garage Punk Unknowns, Volume 3	198?	8.00	20.00
Stone Age SA-664	(M)	Garage Punk Unknowns, Volume 4	198?	8.00	20.00
Stone Age SA-665	(M)	Garage Punk Unknowns, Volume 5	198?	8.00	20.00
Stone Age SA-666	(M)	Garage Punk Unknowns, Volume 6	198?	8.00	20.00
Stone Age SA-667	(M)	Garage Punk Unknowns, Volume 7	198?	8.00	20.00

(Original copies of Stone Age 661-667 have plain cardboard jackets
with omnibus cover pasted onto the front. Later pressings have
the art printed onto the cover with feature liner notes on the back
and are worth 40-50% of the originals.)

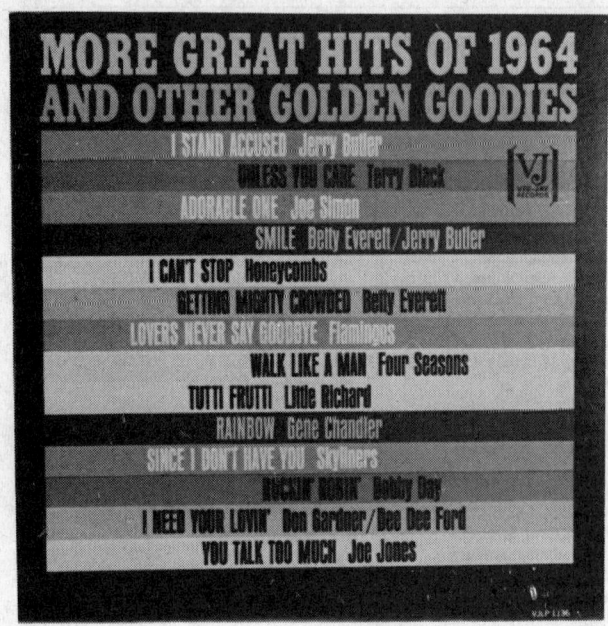

Vee Jay's Teen Delights *captures a typical teen moment of the '50s and early '60s perfectly: Even though the artists on the record are black, the cute couple in the neat car are not. Perhaps more interesting is the fact that the company did not include any of the four charting sides by The Beatles on their "Hits of 1964" compilations. . .*

Label & Catalog #		Title	Year	VG+	NM
Straight STS-1056	(S)	**Naked Angels** *(Soundtrack)*	*1969*	12.00	30.00
Sue LP-1021	(M)	**The Sue Story** *(Black cover)*	*196?*	40.00	100.00
Sue LP-1021	(M)	**The Sue Story** *(Orange cover)*	*196?*	30.00	75.00
Sue LP-1021	(M)	**Old Goodies**	*196?*	30.00	75.00
Sun LP-1250	(M)	**Sun's Gold Hits**	*1961*	40.00	100.00
Sutton SU-321	(M)	**Jumpin'**	*1961*	16.00	40.00
Sutton SSU-321	(S)	**Jumpin'**	*1961*	20.00	50.00
Sutton SU-323	(M)	**Current Craze**	*1961*	16.00	40.00
Sutton SSU-323	(S)	**Current Craze**	*1961*	20.00	50.00
Sutton SU-325	(M)	**Great Popular Oldies, Volume 2**	*1961*	16.00	40.00
Sutton SSU-325	(S)	**Great Popular Oldies, Volume 2**	*1961*	20.00	50.00
Swan LP-501	(M)	**Treasure Chest Of Hits**	*1960*	30.00	75.00
Swan LP-506	(M)	**Twistin' All Night Long**	*1961*	14.00	35.00
Swan LP-512	(M)	**Hits I Forgot To Buy**	*1963*	20.00	50.00
T.V.A.A.	(M)	**The Magic Carpet Ride**	*198?*	20.00	50.00
Tamla TM-222	(M)	**The Great Gospel Stars**	*1961*	*See note below*	
		(Suggested values in collectible condition are $1,000-3,000.)			
Tamla TM-224	(M)	**Tamla Special #1**	*1962*	30.00	75.00
Tamla TM-244	(M)	**Recorded Live At The Regal**	*1963*	*Unreleased*	
Tamla TM-256	(M)	**A Collection Of 16 Original Big Hits, Vol. 2**	*1964*	8.00	20.00
Tamla TS-256	(S)	**A Collection Of 16 Original Big Hits, Vol. 2**	*1967*	16.00	40.00
Teem 5002	(M)	**Guaranteed To Please**	*196?*	12.00	30.00
Teem 5003	(M)	**Greatest Teenage Hits Of All Time**	*196?*	14.00	35.00
Teem 5004	(M)	**Approved By 10,000,000**	*196?*	14.00	35.00
Teem 5005	(M)	**Kings Sing The Blues**	*196?*	12.00	30.00
Tempo Two T-2	(M)	**A New High** *(With poster)*	*196?*	40.00	100.00
Time Tunnel 12174-25	(M)	**Pennsylvania Unknowns**	*198?*	20.00	50.00
Together ST-1014	(S)	**Early L.A.**	*1971*	12.00	30.00
Tops LP-941 (10")	(M)	**Western Favorites**	*195?*	20.00	50.00
Tower T-5007	(M)	**Three At The Top** *(Soundtrack)*	*1965*	10.00	25.00
Tower DT-5007	(E)	**Three At The Top** *(Soundtrack)*	*1965*	8.00	20.00
Tower T-5065	(M)	**Riot On Sunset Strip** *(Soundtrack)*	*1967*	16.00	40.00
Tower DT-5065	(E)	**Riot On Sunset Strip** *(Soundtrack)*	*1967*	12.00	30.00
Tower DT-5148	(E)	**Best Of The Soundtracks**	*1969*	10.00	25.00
Tower DT-5157	(P)	**Instant Replay**	*1969*	12.00	30.00
Tradition 2062	(M)	**British Folk Artist Concert**	*1964*	6.00	15.00
Trash 0001	(M)	**Ear Piercing Punk**	*198?*	20.00	50.00
20th Century TFM-3131	(M)	**Surf Party** *(Soundtrack)*	*1964*	12.00	30.00
20th Century TFS-4131	(S)	**Surf Party** *(Soundtrack)*	*1964*	16.00	40.00
Underworld 1205	(M)	**Nightmares From The Underworld, Volume 2**	*198?*	16.00	40.00
Uni 73091	(S)	**Angels Die Hard** *(Soundtrack)*	*196?*	6.00	15.00
Unique LP-109	(M)	**Music James Dean Lived By**	*196?*	14.00	35.00
United Arts. UAL-3196	(M)	**Yesterday's Goodies**	*1961*	6.00	15.00
United Arts. UAS-6196	(S)	**Yesterday's Goodies**	*1961*	8.00	20.00
United Arts. UAL-3314	(M)	**Golden Treasure Chest**	*1963*	6.00	15.00
United Arts. UAS-6314	(S)	**Golden Treasure Chest**	*1963*	8.00	20.00
United Arts. UAL-3317	(M)	**Golden Souvenirs**	*1963*	6.00	15.00
United Arts. UAS-6317	(S)	**Golden Souvenirs**	*1963*	8.00	20.00

These two comps from Wand are interesting in that while the label could legitimately compile an rhythm 'n blues album from their roster (which included the ever-underrated Chuck Jackson), the selection of country 'n western hits below is rather dubious.

Label & Catalog #		Title	Year	VG+	NM
United Arts. UAL-4128	(M)	What's New, Pussycat? *(Soundtrack)*	1965	5.00	12.00
United Arts. UAS-5128	(S)	What's New, Pussycat? *(Soundtrack)*	1965	6.00	15.00
United Arts. UAS-5175	(S)	Here We Go 'Round			
		The Mulberry Bush *(Soundtrack)*	1968	6.00	15.00
United Arts. UAS-5185	(S)	Revolution *(Soundtrack)*	1968	6.00	15.00
United Arts. UAS-5213	(S)	Ned Kelly *(Soundtrack)*	1970	6.00	15.00
		("Wild Colonial Boy" is rechanneled on this album.)			
United Arts. SP-70	(DJ)	N. A. P. R. A. 72 Vote	1972	16.00	40.00
Unlimited Prod LP-003	(M)	Dirty Water	198?	10.00	25.00
Unlimited Prod. LP-1001	(M)	Midwest Vs. The Rest	198?	16.00	40.00
Unlimited Prod. LP-1002	(M)	Midwest Vs. Canada	198?	16.00	40.00
Vanguard VRS-9144	(M)	Newport Broadside	1964	10.00	25.00
Vanguard VSD-79144	(E)	Newport Broadside	1964	8.00	20.00
Vanguard VRS-9148	(M)	Evening Concerts At Newport, Volume 1	1964	10.00	25.00
Vanguard VSD-79148	(E)	Evening Concerts At Newport, Volume 1	1964	8.00	20.00
Vanguard VRS-9149	(M)	Evening Concerts At Newport, Volume 2	1964	10.00	25.00
Vanguard VSD-79149	(E)	Evening Concerts At Newport, Volume 2	1964	8.00	20.00
Vault LP-103	(M)	Oldies, Goodies And Woodies	1964	16.00	40.00
Vault VS-103	(S)	Oldies, Goodies And Woodies	1964	20.00	50.00
Vault LP-104	(M)	Hot Rod City	1964	20.00	50.00
Vault VS-104	(S)	Hot Rod City	1964	30.00	75.00
Vault LP-113	(M)	West Coast Love-In	1967	12.00	30.00
Vault VS-113	(S)	West Coast Love-In	1967	16.00	40.00
Vault VS-119	(P)	San Francisco Roots	1968	20.00	50.00
		(Vault 119 was reissued as JAS 5001.)			
Vee Jay LP-1020	(M)	The Blues	1962	16.00	40.00
Vee Jay LP-1021	(M)	Teen Delights	1962	16.00	40.00
Vee Jay LP-1036	(M)	Teen Delights, Volume 2	1962	16.00	40.00
Vee Jay LP-1042	(M)	Tomorrow's Hits	1962	16.00	40.00
Vee Jay LP-1051	(M)	Unavailable	1962	16.00	40.00
Vee Jay LP-1112	(M)	Great Hits Of 1964	1964	12.00	30.00
Vee Jay SR-1112	(P)	Great Hits Of 1964	1964	20.00	50.00
Vee Jay LP-1136	(M)	More Great Hits Of 1964			
		& Other Golden Goodies	1965	12.00	30.00
Vee Jay SR-1136	(P)	More Great Hits Of 1964			
		& Other Golden Goodies	1965	20.00	50.00
Vernon 521	(M)	Chart Busters	196?	16.00	40.00
Verve V-2083	(M)	Teen Time: *Refer to Rick Nelson*			
Verve V6-653	(M)	24 Karat Gold			
		From The Underground *(2 LPs)*	1968	10.00	25.00
Verve/Folkways FV-9011	(M)	Fold Au Go Go	1965	6.00	15.00
Verve/Folkways FVS-9011	(S)	Fold Au Go Go	1965	8.00	20.00
Verve/Folkways FT-3010	(M)	Living Legends	1966	6.00	15.00
Verve/Folkways FTS-3010	(S)	Living Legends	1966	8.00	20.00
Verve/Folkways FT-3011	(M)	Blues Box *(3 LPs)*	1966	10.00	25.00
Verve/Folkways FTS-3011	(S)	Blues Box *(3 LPs)*	1966	12.00	30.00
Wand WDM-651	(M)	Rocket To The Stars	1961	20.00	50.00
Wand WDM-652	(M)	Show Stoppers	1961	16.00	40.00
Wand WDM-660	(M)	The Greatest Sing Their Soul Favorites	1964	16.00	40.00
Wand WDM-671	(M)	How To Stuff A Wild Bikini *(Soundtrack)*	1965	8.00	20.00
Wand WDS-671	(S)	How To Stuff A Wild Bikini *(Soundtrack)*	1965	12.00	30.00
Wand WDM-677	(M)	Greatest Hits From The Soul Of Texas	1966	12.00	30.00
Wand WDS-677	(S)	Greatest Hits From The Soul Of Texas	1966	16.00	40.00
Warner Bros. *(No #)*	(DJ)	Jamboree *(Soundtrack)*	1955	*See note below*	
		(Suggested values in collectible condition are $1,000-3,000.)			
Warner Bros. X-1307	(M)	You Ain't Heard Nothin' Yet!	1959	12.00	30.00
Warner Bros. SX-1307	(S)	You Ain't Heard Nothin' Yet!	1959	16.00	40.00
Warner Bros. W-1448	(M)	Hits Of The Hops	1962	8.00	20.00
Warner Bros. WS-1448	(M)	Hits Of The Hops	1962	10.00	25.00

Label & Catalog #		Title	Year	VG+	NM
Warner Bros. W-1511	(M)	**Hoot Tonight**	1963	8.00	20.00
Warner Bros. WS-1511	(S)	**Hoot Tonight**	1963	10.00	25.00
Warner Bros. W-1519	(M)	**Palm Springs Weekend** (Soundtrack)	1963	10.00	25.00
Warner Bros. WS-1519	(S)	**Palm Springs Weekend** (Soundtrack)	1963	14.00	35.00
Warner Bros. W-1725	(M)	**Original Golden Instrumental Hits**	1965	6.00	15.00
Warner Bros. WS-1725	(S)	**Original Golden Instrumental Hits**	1965	8.00	20.00
Warner Bros. BS-1846	(S)	**Performance** (Soundtrack)	1970	10.00	25.00
Warner Bros. BS-2554	(S)	**Performance** (Soundtrack)	1972	5.00	12.00
Warner Bros. BS-2565	(S)	**Medicine Ball Caravan** (Soundtrack)	1971	5.00	12.00
Warner Bros. BS-2662	(S)	**Steel Yard Blues** (Soundtrack)	1972	4.00	10.00
Warner Bros. K-46144	(S)	**A Tribute To Woody Guthrie, Part 2**	1972	4.00	10.00
		(Part 1 was issued as Columbia 31171.)			
		—Special/Promotional Releases—			
Warner Bros. (10")	(DJ)	**Woodstock** (Radio spots)	1970	200.00	400.00
Warner Bros. PRO-368	(DJ)	**Zapped** (Collage cover)	1969	16.00	40.00
		(Original covers feature a black & white collage.)			
Warner Bros. PRO-368	(DJ)	**Zapped** (Photo cover)	1969	10.00	25.00
		(Later covers have a black & white photo of Frank Zappa.)			
Warner Bros. PRO-450	(DJ)	**Days Of Wine And Vinyl**	1972	4.00	10.00
Warner Bros. PRO-534	(DJ)	**Voter Registration Spots**	1972	20.00	50.00
Warner Bros. PRO-290	(M)	**Some Of Our Best Friends Are...**	1977	60.00	150.00
Warner Bros. PRO-2896	(DJ)	**Yulesville**	1987	6.00	15.00
Warner Bros. PRO-3328	(DJ)	**Winter Warnerland**	1988	10.00	25.00
		(2 LPs on colored vinyl)			
Warner/Spector 9103	(S)	**Phil Spector's Christmas Album:** Refer to Phil Spector			
Warner/Spector 9104	(P)	**Phil Spector's 20 Greatest Hits:** Refer to Phil Spector			
Warwick W-2025	(M)	**The Best Of The R&B Groups**	1962	30.00	75.00
Welk Music (No number)	(M)	**Blue Christmas**	1984	20.00	50.00
Wellington 1004	(M)	**Glimpses, Vol. 4**	198?	8.00	20.00
Wellington 201085	(M)	**Glimpses, Vol. 1**	198?	20.00	50.00
Wellington 201086	(M)	**Glimpses, Vol. 2**	198?	14.00	35.00
Wellington 201087	(M)	**Glimpses, Vol. 3**	198?	14.00	35.00
Westchester 1005	(M)	**Friday At The Cage A Go Go**	196?	50.00	125.00
White Rabbit LP-001	(M)	**Mind Blowers**	198?	20.00	50.00
White Whale WWS-7125	(S)	**Footprints In Time**	1970	10.00	25.00
White Whale WWS-7129	(S)	**Super Groups From Holland**	1970	10.00	25.00
White Whale WWS-7130	(S)	**Dutch Explosion**	1970	12.00	30.00
Winley 6001	(M)	**Everybody Digs The Boss Record Hop**	195?	20.00	50.00
Wing MGW-12371	(M)	**Scrapbook Of Golden Hits**	196?	6.00	15.00
Wing SRW-16371	(S)	**Scrapbook Of Golden Hits**	196?	6.00	15.00
World Pacific WPS-21898	(S)	**Bluegrass Special**	196?	12.00	30.00
Wreckord Wrack 1025	(M)	**Off The Wall, Vol. 1**	198?	30.00	75.00
Wreckord Wrack 1301	(M)	**Off The Wall, Vol. 2**	198?	30.00	75.00
Zephyr ZP-12010H	(M)	**Premiere**	195?	12.00	30.00

Late Additions

ACES COMBO, THE

Justice JLP-134	(S)	Introducing The Aces Combo	196?	300.00	500.00

BERRY, CHUCK

Chess LPS-1480	(E)	Chuck Berry On Stage	1966	12.00	30.00
Chess LPS-1485	(E)	Chuck Berry's Greatest Hits	1966	12.00	30.00

— *Chess albums above have black labels with a gold logo on top.*—

BIG BEN BANJO BAND, THE

Capitol T-2642	(M)	Happy Banjo Plays The Beatles	1967	6.00	15.00
Capitol ST-2642	(S)	Happy Banjo Plays The Beatles	1967	8.00	20.00

BLANC, MEL

MBA *(No number)*	(DJ)	Mel Blanc Takes A Humorous Look At Commercials... *(With insert)*	1966	40.00	100.00

BONNE VILLES, THE

Justice JLP-146	(S)	Bringing It Home	196?	360.00	600.00

BREW

ABC 672	(S)	Very Strange Brew	1969	8.00	20.00

CHERRY PEOPLE, THE

Heritage HTS-35,000	(S)	The Cherry People	1968	6.00	15.00

COBERT, ROBERT

Philips PHS-600-314	(S)	Dark Shadows *(TV Soundtrack)*	1969	16.00	40.00

CITY FOLK

20th Century TF-4153	(M)	Here Come The City Folk	1964	5.00	12.00
20th Century TFS-4153	(S)	Here Come The City Folk	1964	6.00	15.00

CLARK, DEE

Vee Jay LP-2000	(M)	Dee Clark	196?	*See note below*

(This is a Vee Jay reissue of the original Abner release with the Abner catalog number.. The copy found was in the Abner jacket.)

DIDDLEY, BO

Checker LP-2987	(M)	Surfin' With Bo Diddley	196?	*See note below*

(A copy of this album was found with a gold version of the original Checker label. . .)

Checker LPS-2992	(E)	Hey! Good Lookin'	1966	12.00	30.00
Checker LPS-2996	(E)	500% More Man	1966	12.00	30.00

— *Checker albums above have blue labels with checkers on top.*—

DIDDLEY, BO, & CHUCK BERRY

Checker LPS-2991	(E)	Two Great Guitars	1966	12.00	30.00

— *Checker albums above have blue labels with checkers on top.*—

DOORS, THE

Elektra 60345	(DJ)	The Best Of The Doors *(2 LPs)*	1985	10.00	25.00

(Promo pressed on "high quality audiophile vinyl.")

FORD, MARY

Refer to Les Paul & Mary Ford.

Challenge CHS-623	(S)	A Brand New Ford	1966	12.00	30.00

(This appears to have been manufactured for Ford distributors.)

JOPLIN, JANIS

Columbia Sp. Prod. 13792	(S)	The Greatest Hits Of Janis Joplin *(2 LPs)*	1977	8.00	20.00
Columbia PC-37569	(DJ)	A Farewell Song *(Banded for air-play)*	1982	10.00	25.00
Columbia AS-1377	(DJ)	A Collection *(Sampler)*	1982	8.00	20.00

Label & Catalog #		Title	Year	VG+	NM

LAINE, FRANKIE

Mercury MG-5363 (10")	(M)	Wild Goose/Black Lace	1949	40.00	100.00
Wing MGW-12110	(M)	His All Time Favorites	1963	8.00	20.00
Wing SRW-16110	(E)	His All Time Favorites	1963	5.00	12.00

LITTLE JOE [RITCHIE]
The record credits Little Joe Ritchie, a pseudonym for Joe Pesci.

Brunswick BL-54135	(M)	Sure Can Sing!	1967	16.00	40.00
Brunswick BL-754135	(S)	Sure Can Sing!	1967	20.00	50.00

MALVIN, ARTIE, & THE ROCK 'N ROLL RHYTHM ROCKETS

Waldorf Music 33-149 (10") (M)		Rock And Roll	1955	40.00	100.00

MARX, GROUCHO

Mark-56 758	(M)	Groucho	1978	8.00	20.00
A&M PR-3515	(DJ)	An Evening With Groucho *(Picture disc)*	1972	12.00	30.00

MILES, BUDDY

Columbia CQ-34694	(Q)	Booger Bear	1974	8.00	20.00

ODYSSEY

Trip T-1000	(S)	Setting Forth	198?	10.00	25.00
		(Reissue of the original— and rare— pressing on Organic.)			

PACIIFIC, GAS & ELECTRIC

Bright Orange 701	(S)	Get It On	1968	10.00	25.00

PINK GRASS

(No label)	(S)	Rhubarb's Revenge	197?	300.00	500.00

RAINBOW PRESS

Mr. G 9003	(S)	There's A War On	1968	12.00	30.00
Mr. G 9004	(S)	Sunday Funnies	1969	16.00	40.00

RAPP, TOM
Refer to The Yetti-Men; Pearls Before Swine.

Reprise MS-2069	(S)	Tom Rapp	1972	6.00	15.00
Blue Thumb BTS-44	(S)	Stardancer	1972	6.00	15.00
Blue Thumb BTS-56	(S)	Sunforest	1973	6.00	15.00

ROSS, DR. ISAIAH

Testament 2206	(M)	Call The Doctor	196?	30.00	75.00

SCALLYWAGS, THE

Justice JLP-	(S)	The Scallywags	196?	300.00	500.00

WALKER, CHARLIE

Epic LN-24137	(M)	Close All The Honky Tonks	1965	6.00	15.00
Epic BN-26137	(S)	Close All The Honky Tonks	1965	8.00	20.00
Epic LN-24153	(M)	Born To Lose	1965	6.00	15.00
Epic BN-26153	(S)	Born To Lose	1965	8.00	20.00
Epic LN-24209	(M)	Wine, Women And Walker	1966	6.00	15.00
Epic BN-26209	(S)	Wine, Women And Walker	1966	8.00	20.00
Epic LN-24328	(M)	Don't Squeeze My Charmin	1967	6.00	15.00
Epic BN-26328	(S)	Don't Squeeze My Charmin	1967	8.00	20.00
Epic LN-24343	(M)	Charlie Walker's Greatest Hits	1968	8.00	20.00
Epic BN-26343	(S)	Charlie Walker's Greatest Hits	1968	6.00	15.00
Epic BN-26483	(S)	Recorded Live In Dallas, Texas	1969	6.00	15.00
Epic BN-26424	(S)	He Is My Everything	1969	6.00	15.00
Epic E-30660	(S)	Honky Tonkin' With Charlie Walker	1970	6.00	15.00

Selling Your Albums

By Perry Cox

Collectors and dealers all over the world keep a watchful eye on current market trends to see how their investments are doing, as well as what they can expect to pay for items that remain on their want lists. The burning questions, then, are: "How does one realistically go about selling their records? Sure, the guide says it's worth X dollar amount, but how do I market my item(s) anywhere near its value estimate?" There are several answers, all of which depend on the seller's situation and needs.

The "set-sale" method is probably the only way to achieve near, at, or above market value in a relatively short period of time. At the point you wish to market your item(s), the sale may take no longer than a phone call to complete. Of course, this method involves plenty of prior invested time and interaction with others. As a collector among collectors, it is ideal to socialize, share one's finds, interact for feedback and advice, and keep on the lookout for other collectors' wants. By acquiring a current list of items your friends and colleagues are looking for, you will be better able to determine what you can sell and for how much.

This is not only an ideal way to obtain maximum return from collectibles you have to sell, but this also allows you a keen advantage in terms of trading for items to fill your own collection. As well, many will appreciate your servicing their wants. The longer you are involved, the larger your customer/friendship base grows. This is, *if* you have kept the required high standards of dealing ethics which is absolutely essential in building a solid relationship with other collectors.

Ethics between buyer and seller *must* be given preference over all other factors. Your records and money mean little if your code of conduct allows for dissatisfaction with the other party, especially if you do not promptly remedy the problem to their satisfaction. Universal dealing principals equate to honestly and fairly grading the items. Since most prospective buyers are unable to personally inspect the items prior to the sale, it is good policy to institute a full "money back, satisfaction guarantee" coupled with a reasonable time limit for recourse (usually a couple of weeks is sufficient).

It is very important to formulate your selling prices *before* you contact prospective buyers. It is not wise to gauge your pricing on the customers level of desire or by pitting one customer against another. These tactics spawn little more than frustration and discontent for everyone. If you agree to a set price, do not raise that price if you later realize another party expresses interest in it. (As well, if you agree to buy an item for a certain price, nit picking at minor, flaws in hopes of getting a discount is not wise.) In short, each must live by his own set of standards and always give great respect to another's valid concerns. Remember, if you get in the habit of making undesirable transaction, many will learn not to contact you the next time you have records to sell or trade.

Set Sale & Auctions In Trade Publications

The term "set sale" means to list your items at fixed prices; i.e., the items *are not* being auctioned. The advantage with this method is that your market potential is far greater due to the mass attention your items receive. The *actual* level of exposure depends on what publications you choose. If you have several "high ticket" items or a large amount of quality merchandise to sell, ads in several publications at once is certainly a viable option. This method is a bit more time consuming: ad preparation, distribution of the publication, and mail transactions involve time.

Preparing your ad needs special planning and considerations; you will need to figure the total number of lines each typewritten page gives you (normally between 50 and 60), the cost per ad, then the cost per line. Collectors tend to gravitate to the excellent condition items, so concentrate on listing in-demand items in quality shape. If you list thirty $10 items that take up half your full page ad space, you have only covered your ad cost, *if you sell them all.*

Keep in mind that a full page ad in these types of publications usually run about $300. Smaller space ads are considerably cheaper. The "Showcase" ad section in the back of *Goldmine* is very effective in presenting select items. The inexpensive rates include typesetting and placement among other eye appealing ads. This is often the first section viewed by readers.

When preparing your ad, by all means grade your items very conservatively (refer to the article on grading in this book.) Conservative, accurate grading provides a healthy, happy collecting environment for everyone. Also, you must be prepared to pack your items well with proper, snug packing and padding (2-3" of padding around the item is a good minimum). Always insure the items you are mailing; it is well worth the extra expense.

When dealing with mail-order, the buyers may notify you of their intent to reserve any particular item(s) they are interested in. Normally this is done by telephone (many buyers prefer to talk to the people they are dealing with, since it gives an added sense of security and provides an immediate response as to the availability of the item) or mail. The response you may receive from this type of advertising is an excellent way to broaden your list of other collectors.

If one has the time, this method has the potential of being the most rewarding in terms of highest yield plus it is a good way to learn just how much customers are willing to spend at any given time on any given item. With the mail-order auction, the seller sets a bid deadline; normally an auction runs for one month from the beginning of the issue's publication date. At the deadline all bids are evaluated and the highest bidders then notified.

In some cases, auctions have yielded sales substantially over the going set value; in other cases the results can be most disappointing. The factors involved in determining the final results are far too numerous to detail but the general spending mood of the public is probably the most important factor. When a given artist is focused on in the media, sales tend to surge accordingly. The death of a major star such as Elvis Presley or John Lennon is one example; the hoopla surrounding Madonna's or The Rolling Stones' last big tours is another.

Reputable auction establishments such as Sothebys, Christies and Phillips are alternative auction methods. They can, however, take the longest time in that they only hold their auctions a few times a year. Exposure to collectors is also limited but the spending frenzy sometimes associated with these houses can often play a favorable role for the seller. One thing is certain: auctions do take the longest period of time on average to sell your items. From start to completion, a mail-order auction consumes an average of two months. This is not the way to go if one wishes to liquidate in a hurry.

Selling Your Items To A Dealer

The quickest manner to sell your items once you have exhausted retail sales to personal contacts is to sell them wholesale to a dealer. If you need cash and you need it right away, selling this way can be quite convenient. Your first responsibility is to contact a *reputable* dealer who is interested in mutual satisfaction between his interests and your own. One must keep in mind that a dealer is not in a position to pay top market dollar for your items. Like any commodity, the record dealer has to buy at a modest percentage of full value in order to make enough profit to stay in business.

As a rule, it is safe to say that the more significantly rare and valuable your item is, the more the dealer will be probably willing to pay, especially if they have a ready buyer. Although the dealer takes into consideration many factors when evaluating, the bottom line is usually this: "How long will one have to keep his money tied up before one actually sells the goods and recovers their money?" Some very rare and valuable items have been known to fetch as much as 60-65% of market retail. A good average for slow movers is about 30-40% of the dealer's opinion of the market value. If the period is lengthy or if the dealer has several copies of the item you are trying to sell, he'll be less generous in his offer or may not express any interest at all! If you intend to solicit offers from various dealers, please advise each dealer of this prior to negotiations to avoid hard feelings. This eliminates the impression the dealer may have in thinking he has an exclusive on your items.

Some dealers will agree to place items obtained from the owner on consignment. That is, he will not pay the owner until the item sells. Usually this method is not entertained unless the dealer feels the item is significant enough to yield a handsome return within a reasonable time. The retail value is mutually agreed upon, while the dealer assumes responsibility for the custody and sale of the item. The final say in retail value usually goes to the dealer who knows his area and market potential best. The average consignment fee is anywhere from 15% to 30% to the dealer, certainly better than the 40-50% usually obtained in a straight sale to the dealer. Compared with some of the others, this selling method can be quite time consuming without guaranteed sales, a factor that must be considered before locking your item(s) in a consignment agreement (which is, in effect, a contract).

Mr. Cox is one of the most well-known collectors and dealers in Beatles records in the country. He is also the co-author of The Beatles Price Guide For American Records, from which this [abridged] article was taken.

The Uncommon Stereo Beatles

By John Christensen

Ever wonder why "I Want To Hold Your Hand" sounded so lousy on *Meet The Beatles?* Or why "I Feel Fine" sounded like it was recorded in a trash can? Or the crummy sound of every Beatles track on United Artists' *A Hard Day's Night?* Fact is, they were presented in rechanneled, or fake, stereo. If the record company didn't have the stereo version by release date, they simply used whatever version they could get their hands on. If it sounded awful. . . so what? Who'd ever know?

Which brings me to the purpose of this article: helping you, the Fab Four fanatic, find those uncommon stereo versions of all too many Beatles songs long neglected and difficult to find on American vinyl. I can guarantee the accuracy of the listings below; I personally listened to all of them (the lone exception being the insanely rare 1963 stereo version(s) of *Introducing The Beatles*). Many of these tracks *are* fairly common outside the U.S., but this article was intended for the American collector and is based on domestic releases. Only when a stereo version is not known on the original label U.S. LP release (like "This Boy" or "She's A Woman") have I listed an alternate source.

By the way, even though Capitol supplied U.S. Beatle fans with *most* songs in stereo, on earlier LPs they often remixed the original multi-tracks, adding reverb, echo and other obnoxious post-production alterations. A good example is *The Beatles' Second Album*. Both the Parlophone and Mobile Fidelity reissues and some later Capitol compilations (such as the remixed *Rock 'n' Roll Music*) offer much better stereo mixes for many of the more common tracks.

In 1987 Capitol finally issued these EMI/Parlophone versions, but the first four titles—*Please Please Me, With The Beatles, A Hard Day's Night* and *Beatles For Sale*—were in mono. The 1988 double-album, *Past Masters, Volumes 1 & 2*, released as two seperate CDs, collects those tracks—mostly single sides—that did not appear on the original EMI albums. The first volume contains stereo versions of "I Want To Hold Your Hand" and "I Feel Fine," plus the U.S. stereo debuts of "This Boy," "She's A Woman," and "Yes It Is," while the second contains "The Inner Light" in its American stereo debut.

Now, a few quick notes on how to use this article: Each song listed below is followed by the title of a domestically issued album (in bold print) where that track can be found in stereo. Titles followed by an asterisk (*) indicate the original EMI/Parlophone version of the album. These were reissued by Mobile Fidelity as part of their "Original Master Recording" series in their stereo format. Therefore, an asterisk refers the reader to either the import version or the "OMR."

These tracks are followed by notes of explanation leading the reader to other sources where possible. Six tracks—both sides of two early singles, "Love Me Do" / "P. S. I Love You" and "She Loves You" / "I'll Get You," along with two latter day recordings, "You Know My Name (Look Up The Number)" and "Only A Northern Song"—apparently cannot be found in stereo on any album anywhere!

9-62   Love Me Do .... *Unavailable in stereo*
9-62   P. S. I Love You .... *Unavailable in stereo*
         "Love Me Do" / "P. S. I Love You" was released as The Beatles' first single, eventually issued
         in this country by Vee Jay 18 months later. Both sides appeared on the first version of
         Vee Jay SR-1062, Introducing The Beatles, *in mono (although they are rechanneled on*
         the Parlophone/Mobile Fidelity Please Please Me*).*
2-63   Misery.. **Please, Please Me*; Introducing The Beatles; The Beatles Rarities**
2-63   There's A Place .... **Please, Please Me*; Introducing The Beatles; The Beatles Rarities**
         Although "Misery" and "There's A Place" did appear in stereo on Introducing The Beatles,
         as stereo copies of this album are as rare as hen's teeth, they are included here.
3-63   From Me To You .... **The Beatles 1962-1966**
3-63   Thank You Girl .... **The Beatles' Second Album**
         "From Me To You" and "Thank You Girl" are available on Past Masters, Vol. 1, *but in mono.*
7-63   She Loves You .... *Unavailable in stereo*
7-63   I'll Get You .... *Unavailable in stereo*
         "She Loves You" / "I'll Get You" was released as the group's fourth Parlophone single
         and their third US single (on Swan).
10-63   I Want To Hold Your Hand .... **20 Greatest Hits; Past Masters, Volumes 1 & 2**
         "I Want To Hold Your Hand" made its American stereo debut in 1964 on the Capitol
         various artists compilation Chartbusters, Volume 4.
10-63   This Boy .... **Past Masters, Volumes 1 & 2**
1-64   Sie Liebt Dich .... **The Beatles Rarities***
         "Sie Liebt Dich" was issued by Capitol on the album of the same title (SN-12009) but was
         withdrawn prior to general release. Note: This was not released by Mobile Fidelity.
2-64   Can't Buy Me Love .... **A Hard Day's Night*; Hey Jude; The Beatles 1962-1966**
2-64   You Can't Do That .... **A Hard Day's Night*; Rock 'n' Roll Music**
4-64   A Hard Day's Night .... **A Hard Day's Night*; Rock 'n' Roll Music**
4-64   I Should Have Known Better .... **A Hard Day's Night*; Hey Jude**
10-64   I Feel Fine .... **20 Greatest Hits; Past Masters, Volumes 1 & 2**
10-64   She's A Woman .... **Past Masters, Volumes 1 & 2**
2-65   Ticket To Ride .... **Help!*; Reel Music**
2-65   Yes It Is .... **Past Masters, Volumes 1 & 2**
6-66   I'm Only Sleeping .... **Revolver***
6-66   Dr. Robert .... **Revolver***
6-66   And Your Bird Can Sing .... **Revolver***
12-66   Penny Lane .... **20 Greatest Hits**
12-66   Penny Lane *(Alternate version with trumpet ending)* .... **The Beatles Rarities**
?-67   You Know My Name (Look Up The Number) .... *Unavailable in stereo*
         "You Know My Name (Look Up The Number)" was recorded in 1967 but first appeared
         in 1970 as the B-side of "Let It Be" and eventually showed up on Rarities *in mono.*
5-67   Baby, You're A Rich Man .... *See below*
         The original stereo mix of "Baby, You're A Rich Man" is unavailable in the U.S. although
         this track can be found on copies of Magical Mystery Tour *from Germany (both the Hor Zu*
         original and the Apple reissue) and France (Apple). The CD of Magical Mystery Tour *does*
         contain this song in stereo, but it has been drastically remixed.
6-67   All You Need Is Love .... **Yellow Submarine; The Beatles 1967-1970; 20 Greatest Hits**
2-68   The Inner Light .... **Past Masters, Volumes 1 & 2**
2-68   Only A Northern Song .... *Unavailable in stereo*
         "Only A Northern Song" appears in rechanneled stereo on all known pressings of
         Yellow Submarine. *One can only assume that the multi-tracks have been misplaced. . .*

What follows is a list of The Beatles albums as originally released by Vee Jay, Capitol and United Artists in the United States. All tracks should be assumed stereo except for the specific notations accompanying each title. On the 1963 version of Vee Jay SR-1062, *Introducing The Beatles*, both "Love Me Do" and "P. S. I Love You" are in mono. The 1964 reissue of *Introducing* (with "Please Please Me" and "Ask Me Why") is entirely in stereo. Similarly, both "From Me To You" and "Thank You Girl" appear in mono on Vee Jay LPS-1085, *The Beatles & Frank Ifield On Stage*.

The group's first album for Capitol, ST-2047, *Meet The Beatles*, contains both sides of their fifth Parlophone single, "I Want To Hold Your Hand" and "This Boy," in rechanneled stereo. On Capitol ST-2080, *The Beatles' Second Album*, both sides of their fourth Parlophone single, "I'll Get You" and "She Loves You," along with "You Can't Do That," are rechanneled.

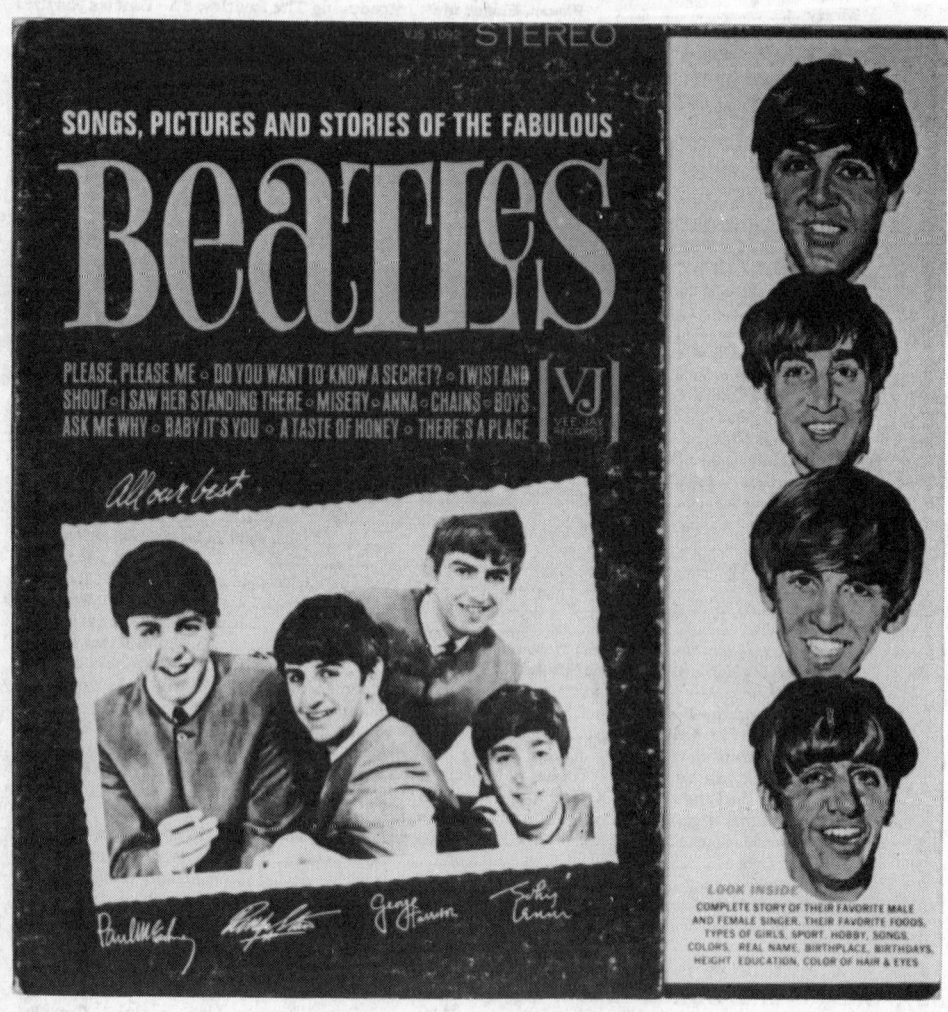

When Capitol turned down their option to handle The Beatles in the United States, the band's material was farmed out to several smaller labels willing to take a chance on the British beat group. Vee Jay, a rhythm 'n blues label having success with The Four Seasons, ended up with the rights to fourteen early Beatles' tracks. From this they managed to release four singles, an EP and four differently titled LPs. Each of the Vee Jay stereo albums are on the record collector's endangered species list, especially in Near Mint condition; each finds its way onto the top 100 list. For this reason they were not recommended in this article for those searching for stereo Beatles. Original copies of Songs, Pictures And Stories Of The Fabulous Beatles were issued with a gatefold cover. Counterfeits of this album simply copied the cover as shown above and printed the art onto a single pocket jacket.

When the Mop Tops recorded the material for their first feature length motion picture, a total of seven new songs were included. They also cut an additional four during these sessions. These eleven new recordings were combined with both sides of their previous single and issued as their third Parlophone album, *A Hard Day's Night*. In the States, these tracks were used to compile two completely different albums. . . United Artists held the rights to the soundtrack and subsequently issued an album of the eight songs that appeared in the film along with four tracks of incidental music from the George Martin Orchestra.

The problem with United Artists UAS-6366, *A Hard Day's Night*, is that all the Beatles tracks—"A Hard Day's Night," "Tell Me Why," "I'll Cry Instead," "I'm Happy Just To Dance With You," "I Should Have Known Better," "If I Fell," "And I Love Her" and "Can't Buy Me Love"—are rechanneled, although the incidental music by George Martin is stereo. Note that "I'll Cry Instead" at 2:06 is the longest released version (others clock in at 1:45) and "And I Love Her" features a single track lead vocal instead of the normal double-tracked lead.

Since Capitol *also* had the rights to the material, they followed the U.A. soundtrack with a new album in a matter of weeks. Capitol ST-2108, *Something New*, is completely in stereo and includes "Tell Me Why," "I'm Happy Just To Dance With You," "If I Fell" and the the double-tracked lead vocal version of "And I Love Her" along with the 1:45 version of "I'll Cry Instead." (The four other songs from the soundtrack sessions are also gathered on this album.)

Capitol ST-2228, *Beatles '65*, contains rechanneled versions of both sides of the group's latest double-sided hit, "I Feel Fine" and "She's A Woman," while Capitol ST-2358, *Beatles VI*, features a rechanneled "Yes It Is," originally issued as the B-side of "Ticket To Ride." In between these two Capitol reissued the Vee Jay material from *Introducing The Beatles* as ST-2309, *The Early Beatles*, with rechanneled versions of "Love Me Do" and "P. S. I Love You."

For the Fabs' second film, Capitol handled the soundtrack and followed U.A.'s lead by compiling a selection of seven tracks from the film along with five pieces by George Martin. SMAS-2386, *Help!*, contains the hit "Ticket To Ride" in rechanneled stereo. Elsewhere, EMI issued the seven movie songs with seven new recordings, all in stereo. It is this version of *Help!* that Mobile Fidelity released as an "Original Master Recording."

Both Capitol ST-2442, *Rubber Soul*, and ST-2576, *Revolver*, are in stereo, although the versions issued here are dramatically different from the Parlophone versions. Four of *Rubber Soul's* fourteen tracks were dropped and replaced by a couple of *Help!* left-overs while *Revolver* features only eleven of the Parlophone fourteen. The other three tracks make up one of the more fascinating anecdotes of the Beatles' recording career. . .

Capitol used the remaining tracks from Parlophone's *Help!* and *Rubber Soul* as the basis for ST-2553, *"Yesterday" ...And Today*. They also scooped their UK counterparts when Lennon's not-quite-completed masters for "I'm Only Sleeping," "Dr. Robert," and "And Your Bird Can Sing" were inadvertently *(sic)* shipped to Capitol. As only the mono tapes were sent, Cap's engineers were forced to Duophonticate them into rechanneled stereo. It is rumored that some later Apple and Capitol pressings contain the correct stereo masters, although that could not be verified for this article. The Parlophone *Revolver*, where these songs were intended, features all the tracks in stereo; it is from these tapes that the Mobile Fidelity "Original Master Recording" was taken.

Capitol issued two albums in 1967: SMAS-2653, *Sgt. Pepper's Lonely Hearts Club Band*, was identical in content to the Parlophone album, a first, but the second was unique. The *Magical Mystery Tour* soundtrack material was issued in the UK as a double-EP but as thsat format had been deleted in the States, Capitol added five single sides (rechanneling three from the single tapes) to the six soundtrack songs and compiled the album released only in America in 1967, although it eventually saw worldwide release. Capitol SMAL-2835, *Magical Mystery Tour* presented the American listener with rechanneled versions of "Penny Lane," "Baby, You're A Rich Man," and "All You Need Is Love." "Strawberry Fields Forever" on this album is dramatically different (i.e., burdened with echo, lack of separation, etc.) from the true stereo version on the German and French *Magical Mystery Tour*. Unfortunately, the Parlophone and Mobile Fidelity issues used the Capitol tapes and are subsequently flawed.

With the formation of their own Apple Records label, the group issued their new album in time for the 1968 Christmas season. Apple SWBO-101, *The Beatles* (a.k.a. "The White Album"), was identical in content to the Parlophone release (and all stereo). They followed this up two months later with the *Yellow Submarine* compilation (Apple SW-153), featuring the newly recorded "Only A Northern Song" in rechanneled stereo and the first stereo appearance of "All You Need Is Love." All issues of *Yellow Submarine* were taken from the same master tape.

The Beatles' final two studio albums, Apple AR-34001, *Let It Be* (recorded in January 1969) and SO-383, *Abbey Road*, were in stereo. The 1970 American only *Hey Jude* compilation (Apple SO or SW-385), featured the American stereo debuts of "Can't Buy Me Love" and "I Should Have Known Better." 1970 also saw the fan-club only release of Apple SBC-100, *The Beatles Christmas Album*, gathering the seven recorded messages the group sent out to fan club members in their original mono. Of interest is the fact that none other than Tiny Tim appears as a guest singing "Nowhere Man" on the '68 message.

When a series of bogus hits packages surfaced in ads in 1973, Apple compiled a pair of two-record sets over-viewing the group's career: Apple SKBO-3403, *The Beatles 1962-1966*, features "She Loves You," "A Hard Day's Night," "I Feel Fine" and "Ticket To Ride" in mono while "Love Me Do" and "I Want To Hold Your Hand" are rechanneled. The rest of the album is stereo including "Can't Buy Me Love" and the American stereo debut of "From Me To You." Apple SKBO-3404, *The Beatles 1967-1970*, contains mono versions of "Hello Goodbye" and "Penny Lane" while the rest of the album is stereo, including "All You Need Is Love."

1976 witnessed the release Capitol SKBO-11537, *Rock 'n' Roll Music*, a double-album collection of uptempo tracks. All four sides are in stereo, several remixed, including the American stereo debut of "You Can't Do That." This was followed in 1977 by yet another double compilation: Capitol SKBL-11711, *Love Songs*, containing rechanneled versions of "P. S. I Love You" and "Yes It Is." All other tracks are stereo including "And I Love Her" and "If I Fell."

Capitol SN-12009, *The Beatles "Rarities"*, was included as a bonus with the boxed set *The Beatles Collection*. This box offered the American public its first chance to purchase the original Parlophone versions of the albums (as the group intended them to be heard) in a limited edition, heavily hyped package. This *"Rarities"* included "Sie Liebt Dich" in stereo for the first time on an American LP. The original mix of "Across The Universe" appears here in stereo; it had previously been available on the import-only *No One's Gonna Change Our World* various artists compilation for the World Wildlife Fund. After someone with their head out of the sand determined that most of the tracks on this album were not "rare" by U.S./Capitol standards, it was pulled from proposed release and eventually replaced by. . .

Capitol SHAL-12080, *Rarities*, includes alternate mono takes of "Love Me Do," "Help," "Helter Skelter" and "Don't Pass Me By" along with "The Inner Light" and "You Know My Name (Look Up The Number)" in mono. "Misery," "There's A Place," the trumpet-ending version of "Penny Lane" and the original mix of "Across The Universe" appear here in stereo.

Later vinyl releases from Capitol include SV-12199, *Reel Music*, which includes stereo versions of "A Hard Day's Night" and "Ticket To Ride." On SV-12245, *20 Greatest Hits*, "She Loves You" and "Love Me Do" are rechanneled; the rest of the album is stereo including "I Want To Hold Your Hand," "I Feel Fine," "All You Need Is Love" and "Penny Lane."

Except for *Magical Mystery Tour* (taken from Capitol tapes), the Mobile Fidelity "Original Master Recordings" are taken from the Parlophone masters and share the same stereo content. All tracks on these audiophile pressings are stereo except "Love Me Do" and "P. S. I Love You," rechanneled on *Please, Please Me*, and "Only A Northern Song," rechanneled on *Yellow Submarine*.

In closing, special thanks to Brian Guiberson for catching some typically dumb errors and Steve Andrews for alerting me to the remixes on the *Magical Mystery Tour* compact disc. I would also like to acknowledge Mike Callahan's thorough "The Beatles On LP" article from the first edition of Perry Cox's *The Complete Beatles U.S. Record Price Guide* (O'Sullivan Woodside, 1983). I credit Mike with getting me interested in stereo collecting in the late '70s with his series of articles in the O'Sullivan Woodside price guides.

Mr. Christensen is a collector specializing in pop, '60s hits in stereo, soundtracks, and audiophile pressings. He is also the photographer responsible for most of the photos in this book. Additions, correction or suggestions should be addressed to John Christensen, Box 40116, Bellevue, WA 98015.

Collecting Country 'n Western Albums

By Joe Goldmark

What could be better than collecting records that are still relatively affordable, have the absolute best covers, feature an uniquely American music that tells real-life stories? Well, folks, the correct answer is s-e-x, but not by much. *(Editor's note: Mr. Goldmark speaks solely for himself here.)* The combination of the wonderful cover art of the '50s and '60s, the classic sounds, and the appreciating monetary value combine to create the soul, or should we say the gestalt, of the record. This is what addicts collectors and old country 'n western albums have this in spades. As the mania for country/western music continues into the '90s, collectors are zeroing in on the really rare pieces in the genre.

Did you know that contemporary country's ever-popular Alabama origi-nally recorded as Wild Country, releasing two albums for Texas' L.S.I. label and that collectors lucky enough to own a copy are being offered $1,000 a piece for them? That means we now have four figure country 'n western albums from the '70s! But you can still purchase *most* collectible country 'n western albums for under $20, especially if you go to swap meets, flea markets, garage sales and thrift stores. However, older albums in collectible condition are getting harder to find. Even a relatively popular title like *Buck Owens' Carnegie Hall Concert*, (Capitol 2556 and issued in 1966), which used to show up everywhere, is scarce now and you might have to pay $20 for a NM copy.

This is still a *lot* cheaper than an original Beatles or Stones album from the same time *and* there's also less competition. Country collectors are a distinct minority in the record collecting hobby; I would guess that at a record swap less than five out of 100 buyers are looking for country 'n western. It was not very long ago that a country collector could have carte blanche, that is, if anyone bothered to bring country records to sell. In fact, usually the response was "Why should I lug 'em out when nobody buys 'em?" Nowadays, you will see a lot more country 'n western although the prices will generally be higher.

Let's look at some of the tougher country 'n western albums: *Jim Reeves Sings*, Abbott 5001, 1956, is probably the rarest, selling for an easy $1,000 (and I've never *seen* a copy). A close second is George Jones' first, *The Grand Ole Opry's New Star* (Starday 101, 1958), which can bring $1,000 for a NM copy in an open auction, five times what it was listed for in the 2nd edition of this guide. Moon Mullican's *Moon Over Mullican*, Coral 57235, 1958, can be had for a cool $500, provided you can find a seller. Porter Wagoner, a country mainstay for the past few decades, saw his first album issued in 1956 (*A Satisfied Mind*, RCA Victor 1358, and worth every bit of $200); he had to wait until 1962 for his next LP.

Ten-inch LPs continue to rise in value, most worth at least a C-note. My own favorites are the Decca "Dance-O-Rama" titles, seven volumes of hot western swing issued in 1955, one each by Milton Brown, Bob Wills, Spade Cooley, Adolph Hofner, Tex Williams, Grady Martin and Billy Gray (Decca 5561-67, respectively). These are super rare and worth an easy $200-300 each. (and there are also two EPs released from each LP; good luck finding *them*. . .) There are also five Bob Wills' ten-inchers, each bringing $200-400, with the rarest being the two *Old*

Time Favorites on Antones, available to fan club members only. And of course, Marty Robbins' *Rock 'n Rollin' Robbins*, Columbia 2601, 1956, is $800 because the rock 'n roll collectors want it, too.

Why are these albums becoming so expensive? For one thing, CDs have supplanted phonograph records and many collectors and dealers are buying up whatever rare vinyl they can find. Then there are speculators who realize that records are vintage collectibles and could skyrocket in value like baseball cards did a few years ago. Perhaps the biggest factor is that overseas collectors, primarily the Japanese and Europeans, love original American records and, as they simply can't buy them in Tokyo or Frankfort, they have to bid high in American auctions *or* travel to the States to get what they want. So, on one hand it's getting more difficult and costlier to acquire the good records you may need, but on the other hand ("there's a golden band. . ." oops, that's a Randy Travis tune), your collection is becoming more valuable with the passage of time.

Modern country makes use of traditional instruments such as the dobro, mandolin, fiddle and acoustic guitar with strong lead and sweet harmony voices; there's still lots of honky-tonk twang in the guitar and the steel. Some of the tunes are quite good and they're always well played and recorded. But. . . there is a rather smug attitude emanating from Nashville that is disturbing. The powers-that-be from Tennessee control the radio stations and it is nigh on impossible these days to record anywhere else in the U. S. of A. and have it reach the charts (Dwight Yoakam in L. A. is the lone exception that crosses my mind). This is no accident and the result is a very homogenized sound. The program directors for the radio stations may be the worst part of the problem: They act as though George Strait and Reba McIntire invented country music in 1987; prior to that the dinosaurs roamed the earth (and ruled the airwaves).

So let's check out a little of this prehistoric past: Country 'n western music went through a period in the late '50s that aficionados lovingly call "hard country." This music, played primarily in road houses, was noted for its twin fiddles, shuffles, two beats, "Nudie" suits and "take off" guitar, songs about the hard road, hard whiskey and even harder women. Ray Price singing "City Lights" or George Jones belting "Why Baby Why." This is the glory! Hard country remains prime material, but far from the only field of collector interest.

There are the special moments, like Johnny Bush crooning "I'll Be There" (from *The Best Of Johnny Bush*, Million 1001, released in 1972). Or the brilliant ideas and execution of Buddy Emmons' *Steel Guitar Jazz*, Mercury 60843 (1963), supposedly recorded in New York under relatively adverse conditions when Buddy was still in his teens. Or the pretty funky "Home In My Hand" and "Ain't Nothin' Shakin' But The Leaves" from Dallas Frazier's *Tell It Like It Is*, Capitol 2764 (1967) and the smooth, classic bluegrass of Jim & Jesse's *Bluegrass Special*, Epic 26031 (1963); *George Jones Salutes Hank Williams*, Mercury 60257 (1960), which adequately displays why George is the best since Hank; Red Simpson's *Truck Drivin' Fool*, Capitol 2691 (1967), with its memorable trucker tunes; *Ernest Tubb Presents The Texas Troubadours*, Decca 74459 (1964), with Jack Green and Cal Smith; Porter Wagoner's *The Cold Hard Facts Of Life*, RCA Victor 3797 (1967) a great collection of cheatin' songs with classic cover art (and no one tells a story better than Porter); Lou Walker's *Swing Western Style*, Sims 114, classic hard country including some great instrumentals; or *Charlie Walker Recorded Live In Dallas Texas*, Epic 26483 (1969), a good live mix of Texas country 'n western with a border feel.

Capitol has a long history of recording and releasing solid country albums with attention to detail, including cover art. Both Tommy Collins and Merle Travis benefited by being with a major label that paid so much attention to their country stars...even during the height of the '60s rock phenomenon.

Capitol, Columbia, Decca, RCA Victor and, to a lesser extent, Imperial, Mercury and MGM, were the major country labels from 1950 through 1980. Most of the desirable LPs from these labels issued in the '50s and early '60s go for a steady $30-60 each while the bulk of the later releases from the mid '60s through the early '70s fetch $10-30 each. All original yellow label Starday albums sell for at least $20 with some now in the $60-75 range. This from a label that used to clog the cut-out bins!

King Records out of Cincinnati, mainly thought of by collectors as a strong rhythm 'n blues label with James Brown, Little Willie John, Bill Doggett, etc., also had a lot of great bluegrass and country, and just about everything on their Audio Lab subsidiary is hot. The Stanley Brothers, Reno & Smiley, the Delmore Brothers, T. Tyler Texas and Moon Mullican all released very collectible albums on King. Slim Whitman, who sold a ton of records for Imperial, is an interesting artist who owned the country charts in the early '50s and then, for the next thirty odd years, became an international pop star.

In the old days all of the majors had at least one budget line: Columbia had Harmony; RCA Victor, Camden; MGM had Metro; Decca had Vocalion; and Mercury filled the budget bins with Cumberland and Wing. Many of these labels existed to repackage older recordings, often taken from 78s. The majors didn't want to release old sounding stuff next to the new product but they did realize there was some demand for what was. As this music was culled from their vaults, they had no new recording or production fees, the royalty rates were lower, so they were able to sell the records cheaply. I also believe King and Capitol used their budget line (Audio Lab and Tower, respectively) as a sort of proving ground for some of their lesser (sic) artists.

Then there are the "labels that collectors love to hate:" Crown, Design, Guest Star, Hilltop, Pickwick, Sears, Spin-O-Rama, Sunset, Tops, Wyncote, etc. These were the budget labels, selling for a mere $1.98 when the list price of a regular catalogue album was $3.98. For your two bucks you got seemingly ripped-off recordings pressed on poor quality vinyl presented with lousy cover art. However, some of these labels are collected and a few of the titles are worth something, notably Chris Hillman's first recordings with The Scottsville Squirrel Barkers, Crown 346 (1963).

Sims, Cuca, Shasta and Longhorn are some of the more collectible small labels; they all had rosters of decent regional artists but they suffered from a lack of national distribution and the resulting inability to break national hits. However, for us, the lack of commercial success just means that fewer were pressed and that the records are more desirable now.

Challenge, Cimarron, Paula, Sage, and Sun are collectible minor labels that feature some great music. Chart, Hickory, Kapp, Liberty, Monument, Musicor, SeSac, Stop, and United Artists were the larger independent labels of the '60s and '70s while C.M.H., Flying Fish, Midland, Old Homestead, Rounder, Sierra and Sugar Hill were some of the indies offering country in the past two decades. The '80s also saw the rise of excellent European based reissue labels like ACE, Bear Family, Castle, Cattle, Charly, Danny, See-For-Miles, and Stetson. They usually license the music for Europe and then export the records back to the States.

There are many specialists among country collectors. It seems that most collectors are completists; country music feeds this obsession well, since successful artists traditionally have long careers. Some fans strive for everything recorded by a single artist, including promo items, radio shows, bootlegs and guest appearances on other artists' records. It's always been a country tradition for a singer to carry a hot band on the road; a lot of these bands recorded albums on their own. Ernest Tubb's Texas Troubadours, Buck Owens' Buckaroos and Merle Haggard's Strangers were the most successful and remain the most sought after, but there are many more that are fun to collect. Some folks are hard core bluegrass collectors while others just collect rockabilly. I specialize in guitar, dobro and steel guitar albums.

Finally, while I've mainly discussed older albums, I think that even recent records will become collectible now that CDs have taken over. You might want to get all the early albums by artists that you think will be the stars of the future and records by the more obscure contemporary artists that you like. Remember, the most important aspect of collecting should be to derive some pleasure from the hobby. . . without alienating your family!

Mr. Goldmark is a collector of country/western records—especially steel guitar—a picker himself with several albums to his credit, and a restauranteur. He is also the author of the "International Steel Guitar Discography." Additions, corrections or suggestions—including inquiries on his book—should be addressed to Joe Goldmark, 2259 14th Avenue, San Francisco, CA 94116.

Are You Ready For Glam. . . Yet?

By Dave Thompson

Between 1971 and 1975 a musical movement erupted which was to shatter the pop/rock continuum more thoroughly than ever it had been before. Brought on by Rock's growing obsessions with its own social, political and historical worth, it was to pay not the slightest attention to these pretensions. Both precious and precocious, it represented little more than a return to the frivolous basics for which rock 'n roll had been condemned when it first appeared. Glam brought British Pop to its most invigorating high in a decade.

For the collector, it is also one of the most confusing periods. Nowhere are the guidelines etched in stone, nowhere is it said that this record is Glam while that one isn't. Do you kick off with "Ride A White Swan," which was Marc Bolan's first hit and the key which unlocked the UK chart floodgates for Glam? Or with "The Road I'm On," the recently discovered '60s folk song which launched Bolan's career in the first place? Does the Glam fan care about the In Betweens' French releases or Sweet guitarist Andy Scott's early days with the Elastic Band? Should one simply stick with the long and glorious shower of "greatest hits" compilations which are these bands' proudest legacy? (If you did, you'd miss a lot of great music. . .)

One can speculate endlessly about why America never caught the Glam bug, but at the end of the day, U.S.A. 1972-1975 simply wasn't ready for a music which could so readily embrace, horror, homosexuality and ham, intellectualism and idiocy, creativity and crassness. Neither introspective nor insurrectionist, Glam was a frivolous explosion of pure physical escapism, a precursor of Punk in its insistence that life did not need to be gray and drab. It could be a star burst of sequins, glitter and ridiculous trousers, too!

The breakthrough acts in Britain were, deservedly, those who had been paying their dues in obscurity for years. Bolan, David Bowie, Sweet and Slade traced and tinted roots which reached back into the middle of the previous decade, while Gary Glitter had released records earlier, albeit under a series of salubrious pseudonyms, such as Paul Monday or, ahem, Rubber Bucket. As Shane Fenton, Alvin Stardust's career predated even the Beatles!

By 1973, however, new names had emerged to fight it out at the top of the pops:Mud, Roxy Music, David Essex, Cockney Rebel, Queen and even Americans Suzi Quatro and Sparks, all tarred (or tarted) themselves with the Glam brush. Other, already established, names followed, gratefully sprinkling stardust in their hair and on their cheeks and bringing whole, if not wholly welcome, new directions to their careers. This included the Rolling Stones (can anyone forget the video for "Angie?"), Rod Stewart, Elton John. . . even Roy bloody Wood donned a psychedelic wig and face paint! That almost each of these late bloomers eventually tired of the flippancy is obvious from their subsequent careers. What, though, of the one-shot wonders, those who were presented even in Britain as nothing more than a few pretty faces with a neat line in primal back beat?

In the United States, there is little to say. Although Bell, Big Tree and Jonathan King's UK label maintained a steady stream of [now scarce] singles, barely a handful of albums made it through American cultural barriers. So we treasure a pre-Ultravox Midge Ure in Scottish teenybop try-outs Slik *(Slik)*; the savagely futuristic Doctors Of Madness, bridging the gulf between dying Glam and nascent Punk with two UK albums packaged here as an eponymous two-fer *(Doctors Of Madness)*; and a solitary release by Gary Glitter's backing group, the Glitter Band, cut just as they made the transition from their old boss' brand of shuddering pop towards more mature *(sic)* progressive rock *(The Glitter Band Makes You Blind)*.

Of the more established Glam rockers, Gary Glitter waited eleven years for a U.S. successor to his 1972 debut. Released in 1983, *The Leader*, compiled many of his greatest UK hits onto one disc, paving the way for Rhino's 1992 *Rock 'n' Roll* collection. And while Slade, Sweet and T. Rex all enjoyed fairly full American release schedules, the emphasis of their albums seldom corresponded to the sheer exuberance of their UK hits. Thus it is easy to see how these might slip through the commercial cracks of the American market.

If any one artist epitomizes American Glam it is Jobriath (Boone), a Pennsylvania behemoth whose manager introduced him to the world by comparing him to David Bowie (of course). They both danced, they both sang. . . Two albums by Jobriath were issued on Elektra with the second featuring guests John Paul Jones, Peter Frampton and Peggy Nestor; both hit the cut-out bins like the proverbial hurricane. And, while Glam was by nature the most disposable of fun, that really was taking things too far. . .

Mr. Thompson is a record collector and a writer specializing in rock and pop music from his native England.. He is a contributor to Goldmine magazine and the author of several books in the field, including "Beyond The Velvet Underground" and the upcoming "True Men Don't Kill Coyotes," the unauthorized story of the Red Hot Chili Peppers from St. Martin's Press. Additions, corrections or suggestions should be addressed to Dave Thompson, Box 40116, Bellevue, WA 98015.

Acetates & Test Pressings

By Christopher Chatman

Many times I have been asked "What *are* acetates and test pressings?" followed closely by "Why do they cost so much?" Record collectors are continually in search of the "rarest records," the "best pressings." This has much to do with the demand for promotional records: they are usually much rarer than the stock copies and, because of their limited press runs, better sounding. However, promotional copies— and even test pressings— pale in comparison to acetates, both in terms of sound quality and particularly in rarity.

Acetates are the first step in the transfer of music from an electronic signal to the actual pressed record. They allow the musicians and producers to hear what the finished record will sound like without going through the time and expense of the plating and pressing. After all, they may decide that they don't like a particular version of a song and change it *or* not release it at all.

Acetates, also known as masters or reference discs, are usually black and 7" to 12" in diameter. While most records are made of vinyl, acetates are made out of aluminum coated with cellulose acetate. Thus, while they look like records, they weigh approximately five times as much. The cellulose acetate for these lacquers is made at a very high level of quality control. Acetates are very expensive to manufacture, therefore record companies normally make only five copies of any one record. Recently, with the sharp reduction of vinyl records, the number of acetates made has dropped dramatically.

After a recording has been taped, edited and equalized, an uncut acetate, or "blank," is sent to the mastering lab where it is placed on the turntable of an electronic lathe system. The master tape is played through a lathe system and electronically transmitted to the cutting needle so that the music literally cuts microscopic wiggles analogous to the sound waves that they represent directly into the acetate coating. Because of this direct cutting from the master tape and the high quality of the cellulose, the sound is substantially better than a record.

An acetate which has received approval is called a master lacquer. After a lacquer has been cut it is sent to a factory to be electroplated with nickel. A label from either the mastering lab or the record company is usually glued to the disc; reference discs *may* have no label at all and master lacquers rarely do. Although acetates are normally packaged in plain paper sleeves, in recent years many are shipped in special boxes with covers; this extra packaging tends to enhance the desirability of the acetate. After the music on a reference disc has been reviewed and the record pressed, the acetate is then discarded, having served its purpose.

Acetates should be treated even more carefully than records. Due to the brittleness of the cellulose, the action of playing an acetate with a phonograph needle is quite damaging to the disc's surface. After five plays, the needle begins to cut away at the finer microscopic grooves which produce the high frequencies. It is therefore advisable top play an acetate *once*, record it on tape, and then carefully store it away. Also, acetates chip easily; handle with care.

The nickel plating is then peeled away, which results in a negative metal print of the lacquer commonly referred to as a "mother." The first pressings to be run off the mother are test pressings; the final stop before the record is actually manufactured for mass consumption. Test pressings are vinyl facsimiles of the actual album; that is, they are 12" records pressed in extremely limited runs, usually at a plant that specializes in test pressings. It is not feasible for the large companies to turn on their enormous machines to print a handful of records.

These records allow the people involved to actually hear what the record will sound like as an LP. They may have special labels or they may be blank. Test pressings are checked for sound quality and technical defects; if they are satisfactory, then promotional copies are pressed, generally for distribution to radio stations. Finally, the commercial, or stock, copies are pressed for sale in your favorite endangered record store.

Since the value of an acetate depends primarily on the collectibility of the artist, they range in value from a few dollars to thousands of dollars. Acetates of released material are lowest on the value pyramid. Next are takes of released tracks prior to any sweetening being added, such as strings, horns, and background singers. Above that would be alternate takes of released material; unreleased live material would probably settle in between this level and the previous. The most valuable acetates are obviously those of unreleased material, regardless of the material's aesthetic qualities.

Acetates of albums by Elvis Presley and The Beatles have regularly sold for $500 and more; those by artists who are not quite as collectible have still sold for comparable prices. Hot new artists such as Depeche Mode and The Smiths are attracting serious bids when offered in auction. It is for this reason that some acetates have been bootlegged; be *sure* to check the reputation of the seller before spending heavy money on an acetate. It is important to note that the value increases dramatically when the material on the acetate is different from the released version of the record. However, whether or not the material is different, acetates are extremely rare and highly prized by collectors interested in owning the supposedly unattainable.

Test pressings are always worth several times the listed value of the stock copy. The most desirable are those of either unreleased albums such as Fats Domino's second album for Reprise, *Fats,* scheduled for release in 1971 and then withdrawn, or test pressings with different versions or mixes than the released album, such as the original version of Bob Dylan's *Blood On The Tracks.* Recorded with Eric Weisberg's group, Dylan pulled five of the tracks after hearing the test pressing and recorded them with another group of musicians to change the record's total mood. While the *Fats* album sells for three figures, *Blood On The Tracks* is one of the most valuable albums in the hobby. (See "The 100 Most Valuable U.S. Albums" in the front of this book.)

A recent variation to the usual type of acetate is the direct metal master, or DMM. Instead of being made of aluminum coated with cellulose acetate, they are made of stainless steel coated with polished copper. The signal from the master tape is cut directly into the copper. This technology, designed to improve the sound quality of records, was designed just as the dominance of compact discs was forcing records into relative obscurity. This, combined with the fact that DMM is very expensive to convert has resulted in few mastering labs investing in this new method. Therefore, DMM acetates are very rare and, because of their beauty, highly prized by collectors.

Finally, collectors with test pressings that differ even slightly from the released version of the album should consider dropping a line with the information, including matrix numbers from the trail-off vinyl, to Neal Umphred, Box 40116, Bellevue, WA 98015. . .

Christopher Chatman, proprietor of Beyond Records, Los Angeles, CA, is a collector and dealer of rare records, acetates, RIAA Gold and Platinum Record awards and rock 'n roll memorabilia and a regular advertiser in Goldmine.

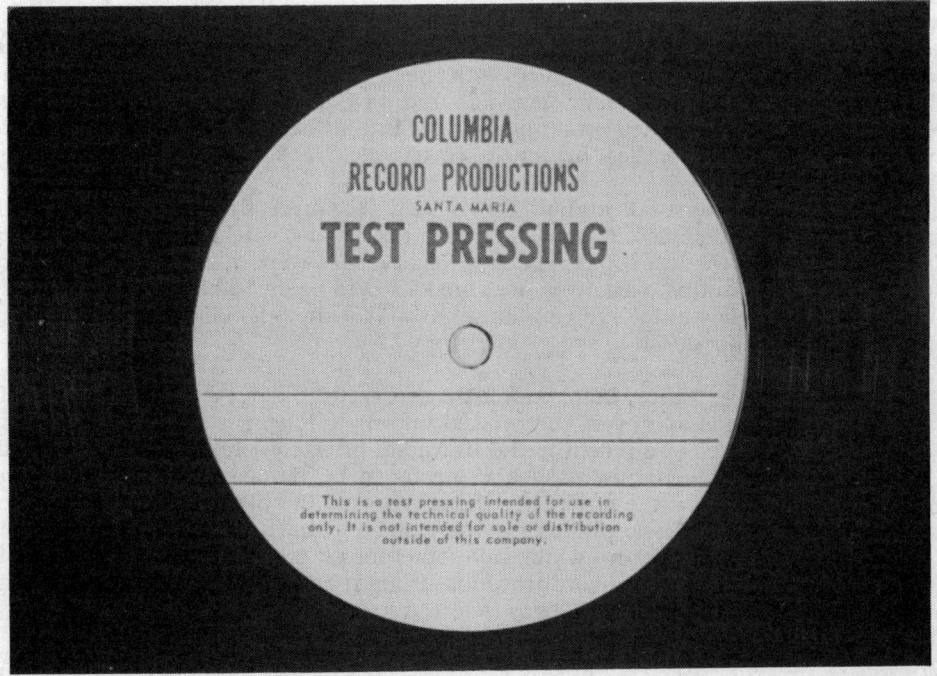

This is an example of a test pressing from Columbia Record Productions. In this case, there has been no data written onto the blank label. These discs are often packaged in plain cardboard jackets with a sheet of paper with all the pertinent information—artist, title, catalog number, song titles—taped to the front.

Collectible Artwork for Album, 45, Cassette and CD Covers

By Christopher Chatman

Artwork for album, single, cassette and compact disk covers is growing in collectibility. Though collected by a relatively small number of people, the demand is increasing. Artwork in its various forms has been sold privately or auctioned for years, but with recent listings for unreleased artwork increasing so rapidly, according to various price guides, collector interest is becoming more intense.

One of the most compelling things about collecting cover art is its rarity. There is only one original photo, perhaps a couple sets of negatives, one mock-up, a few sets of four-color separations at the most, and if you are lucky, a handful of proofs of the cover. This cover art is generated only as a byproduct of the production of covers. The number of copies made of any type of cover art is very small -- usually one and rarely more than five. In terms of rarity and even function, cover art is to the production of covers what acetates are to the production of records. The primary purpose of this appendix is to introduce the reader to the types of cover art seen most often.

1) Original Drawing, Painting or Picture. In the case of a cover that is a drawing or painting, everything starts with the original. Paintings that make up the basic designs for famous album covers do and have sold for a lot of money. Sometimes the cover art is based on a photograph. In that case, the negative or slide of the picture is the very earliest art for the cover.

2) Negatives of Finished Cover Art. Negatives that are shot after all mock-up work is completed are usually the exact same size as the format being printed. Through the late '60s, negatives for cover art were in each of the primary colors used for printing. Negatives are considered to be desirable especially if they are for a collectible album, such as the negatives for the original Beatles "Yesterday and Today" Butcher cover.

3) Black & White/Color Mock-Up or Paste-Up Art. After the basic painting or photograph is approved, the printed information (consisting of the lettering, code numbers and, more recently, the universal price code information) is added. The basic photograph or painting also needs to be reduced or enlarged to the dimensions needed for the cover. For these reasons, the black and white or color mock-up is created. First, photos for the front and back covers are taken. This image is usually in black and white, but sometimes it is in color. The new photo is then glued to a large piece of cardboard for strength and support. Then all lettering, code numbers, record company logos (referred to as "type") are added.

Sometimes type is taped or pasted directly onto the new photo, but often the type is glued onto a piece of clear acetate that is usually fastened above the new photo. After that, a piece of tracing paper is fastened over the new photo and the clear acetate with the type now glued to it. Any final instructions are written on the tracing paper.

Because of the different layers partially obscuring the cover image, mock-up art is often not as desirable as original art or four-color separations. However, as a development stage in the production of cover art, it is critical and therefore very collectible.

4) Four-Color Separations. Four-color separations are four pieces of translucent acetate sheeting, each having a basic color of the final image for the cover. The four basic colors are black, magenta, cyan and yellow. All four sheets are usually taped to a piece of heavy white paper so the four-color separations show the complete image of the cover. When displayed in this manner, four-color separations are very attractive, possessing color resolution that is usually far superior to the final printed cover.

5) Proofs. A proof is a print usually made from the negatives of the finished cover art. These usually have color or black and white graduated registration bars beneath or above the image of the cover. Proofs are often high gloss, high resolution prints on paper stock and are usually superior to the final produced covers.

6) Slicks. A slick is a print that is usually made from the same paper stock as the final covers being produced.

7) Cover. The cover is the final product. Sometimes test covers are made from basic art and/or type to get an idea of how the cover will look. Sometimes these early ideas for covers are discarded, becoming the most valued type of artwork at this time -- called "unreleased covers."

Unreleased and Alternate Artwork

The most desirable and valuable artwork is art that is never used in production. The more the artwork differs from the produced version, the more it is valued. This is called "unreleased" or "alternate" artwork. The closer an alternate idea gets to production, the more valuable it becomes. The most valuable unreleased artwork is an unreleased cover, but unreleased original art, photos, mock-ups, four-color separations and slicks are also obviously highly sought-after items. The unreleased slick for The Rolling Stones' *Beggars' Banquet* album cover is a prime example. The original art was a photograph of a bathroom wall with song titles and credits written like graphite all over the walls. But this original art was banned and replaced with a plain off-white cover with only the words "The Rolling Stones Beggars' Banquet R.S.V.P." written in script on the cover. This script cover recently sold in the neighborhood of $2,000. Be very careful in trying to acquire one because this item has been bootlegged.

Another good example of unreleased covers are the Beatles' "Hey Jude" alternate covers. These items are listed and pictured in *The Beatles Price Guide For America Records*, 3rd Edition, published in 1990 by Perry Cox and Joe Lindsay. The Cox guide listed both of these rare covers as being worth $3,500 each in 1990. Two years later, in the revised 3rd edition of the same book, these two covers are listed at $5,000. In this edition of *Goldmine's Price Guide to Collectible Record Albums*, Neal Umphred lists these rare covers as being worth $7,500 each. Please bear in mind that these are fully constructed unreleased covers.

Unreleased covers are extremely rare because all of the artwork goes through all the developmental stages before it is finally stopped. In the case of the "Hey Jude" covers, less than five of each are known to exist. The rapid escalation of the estimated prices of the "Hey Jude" covers would suggest that unreleased covers, from the Beatles in particular, are enjoying increased recognition as valuable collectibles. Obviously, unreleased art of any collectible artist has the potential to become a wise investment for the future as well as being fun to own.

Christopher Chatman, proprietor of Beyond Records, Los Angeles, CA, is a collector and dealer of rare records, RIAA Gold and Platinum Record awards and rock 'n roll memorabilia and is a regular advertiser in Goldmine.

While Glen Campbell's first two albums seem to present the young singer as a folksy country neophyte, he had already established himself as one of the premier guitar players in American with his astounding session work with sundry Los Angeles recording studios. Big Bluegrass Special, *often credited to The Green River Boys, is among the hottest and most collectible of all bluegrass albums.*

Collecting Gold & Platinum Record Awards: An Updated Primer

By Christopher Chatman

Collecting gold and platinum record awards has progressed and evolved into a specialized field of music memorabilia. Aside from the collectors, there are now investors, museums—even restaurants—contributing to the rising popularity and escalating prices for key awards. Unfortunately, this increased interest and demand has also caused increased incidents of fraud *along* with a broad based abuse of the system by which the awards themselves are ordered. Still, gold and platinum awards *are* great investments if you spend your money on an artist who will maintain collectors' interest over the years. A wise purchase in the present has the potential to grow into a healthy investment for the future. Besides giving the reader a general introduction to this field, this article will serve as an update on the current market scene as well as include tips on avoiding bad purchases, which, needless to say, can be very expensive.

The *primary* purpose of this article is to give the reader a general acquaintance with the terms and descriptions commonly used and the different types, or formats, of the various awards. This is best achieved by providing an illustration, examine it section by section, and define each term. Our example will be a nearly mint white matte RIAA Gold Record Award to Mick Jagger for The Rolling Stones' album *Through The Past, Darkly.* There are seven basic aspects that are crucial in determining the collectibility, or value, of a given award: 1) the artist, 2) the record's title, 3) the organization recognizing the sales achievement, 4) the award designation, 5) the formatting of the award, 6) the individual or group to whom the award was presented, and, finally, 7) the condition of the award.

1) Artist. The artist is probably the most important factor in determining the value of an award. A recent award for a Beatles record would probably sell quicker and for a much higher value than a vintage award for an Isaac Hayes title, simply because they are so much more collectible. Current trends indicate even greater interest and emphasis is being placed on major artists. Nevertheless, since virtually all artists are collected to one extent or another, it is important to state that the tastes of the individual collector gauge desirability.

2) Title. The title of the record greatly affects the desirability of an award. Recently an original RIAA Gold Record for *Sgt. Pepper's Lonely Heart's Club Band* presented to The Beatles sold for more than $20,000 at auction. Yet a few months later in an auction from the same house, an original RIAA Gold Record for *Rubber Soul* presented to The Beatles fetched under $10,000. While part of the reason for the staggering difference in the prices was condition (the *Pepper* award was graded higher), another was title, as *Sgt. Pepper* is one of the classic titles to own.

While different collectors will have differing opinions on what *is* "classic" and therefore desirable, certain constants do exist, such as an artist's first gold record, which most collectors place a certain premium on. The individual's personal preference is a good thought to keep in mind as you read on, as this is a report on general trends, not absolute facts.

3) Organization Recognizing the Sales Achievement. Most collectors in the United States prefer awards certified by the Record Industry Association of America, or RIAA, the membership of which includes most, but not all, of the major labels in the country. Formed in 1952 as a trade organization representing the interests of the country's major record manufacturers, the organization introduced its "official" Gold Record Award in January 1958 primarily to standardize the recognition of sales.[1] Record companies could, at their own expense, open their books to an independent auditor who would then verify the sales figures and authenticate the award later presented, often with some degree of formality, by the RIAA to the artist and the company. Of course, companies did not have to join nor open their books; subsequently, many major sellers have never been certified as gold records, notably the Motown hits of the '60s.

The RIAA has many other functions but the main one which concerns us here is that it acts as *an unbiased accounting firm to verify the actual number of units sold.* It is for this reason that many award collectors give RIAA certification so much importance. However, it is important to note that there are awards certified by the record company itself with outside certification by an umbrella organization. These are commonly referred to as "in-house" awards. These awards are produced by major record companies that belong to the RIAA *as well* as labels that do not. Major labels will often make in-house awards to avoid having to pay the RIAA their accounting and certification fee.

Or a label may choose an in-house award to create an award or plaque with design specifications that do not include the RIAA seal, making some in-house awards far more attractive than the regulation RIAA design. In certain situations, these awards were made for records that were never RIAA certified. In-house awards are increasing in collectibility, the most obvious example being early awards from Berry Gordy's aforementioned Motown conglomeration. . .

Gold record awards from other countries are also collected, with awards from the United Kingdom and Japan highly prized. The official organization certifying sales achievement in the U.K. is British Phonographics Industry, or BPI. Because of the blue, red and black felt backgrounds of these awards they are particularly nice to add to a collection. And, while awards from Japan tend to be in-house, they, too, are especially beautiful.

4) RIAA Award Designation. Qualification for RIAA awards have varied over the years. The original standards were based on one million as gold: 1,000,000 copies of a single and $1,000,000 at the manufacturer's wholesale price for an album, which generally meant *at least* 500,000 copies.[2] Extended Play albums (EPs), which generally consisted of two tracks per side, required half of a single's sales, 500,000 units, to qualify.

---

[1] *Recognizing outstanding sales levels as "Gold" had been a part of the industry for decades. While a variety of presentations had been made, one of the first of the awards today recognized as a Gold Record was made to Glenn Miller in 1942 for sales in excess of 1,000,000 copies of "Chattanooga Choo Choo." Unfortunately, as the promotional impact of such an award became apparent, companies began awarding them willy nilly. By the mid '50s, the accuracy of the awards were held in contempt even by the industry itself. — Ye Olde Editor*

[2] *By 1974 the increased cost of albums at the wholesale level had made it possible to qualify with approximately 450,000 sales. In 1975 the rules were altered so that an LP must sell both the $1,000,000 and the half-million units to qualify. This was followed in 1976 with the establishment of the RIAA Platinum Record Award: 2,000,000 for a single and 1,000,000 copies (i.e., $2,000,000) for an LP. The redundant (and self-explanatory) Multi-Platinum Award was introduced in 1984. — Ye Olde Editor*

In 1970 the sales of tapes were included in the tallies for an album's certification. While the sales of reel-to-reels were negligible, the inclusion of the then popular eight-tracks had a noticeable affect on sales levels, similar to what would follow when the cassette was introduced as the industry standard years later. The chart below illustrates the other changes:

1958-1974

45	Gold Award	1,000,000 unit sales
EP	Gold Award	500,000 unit sales
LP	Gold Award	$1,000,000

1975-1988

45	Gold Award	1,000,000 unit sales
45	Platinum Award	2,000,000 unit sales
EP	Gold Award	500,000 unit sales
EP	Platinum Award	1,000,000 unit sales
LP	Gold Award	$1,000,000 (at least 500,000 unit sales)
LP	Platinum Award	$2,000,000 (at least 1,000,000 unit sales)

1989-1993

45	Gold Award	500,000 unit sales
45	Platinum Award	1,000,000 unit sales
EP	Gold Award	250,000 unit sales
EP	Platinum Award	500,000 unit sales
LP	Gold Award	$1,000,000 (at least 500,000 unit sales)
LP	Platinum Award	$2,000,000 (at least 1,000,000 unit sales)

The recent change in levels of unit sales in order to attain gold or platinum status reflect changing levels of difficulty in accruing these sales amounts.[3] Dates are worth knowing as the minimum requirement for RIAA certification is useful in spotting fakes. It is important to remember that platinum status was recognized by individual record companies years before "official" recognition by the RIAA. Therefore, platinum in-house awards prior to 1976 can be just as valid as an RIAA gold award presented at the same time.

5) Award Format. Over the years the RIAA has varied the formats, or style, in which the award is presented. Through 1989, the RIAA kept very strict control over the specifications that were used to construct each award. These standards are helpful in identifying the different formats as the rigid standards can make visual differences slight.

---

[3]*With the sales of vinyl dropping to all but non-existent and the industries decision to phase out vinyl, Gold Record Awards to singles plummeted: in 1980 there were 42 Gold Awards for singles; by 1986 it was seven. The introduction of the cassette single (or cassingle) in 1987 didn't help much so the RIAA made a radical amendment to its standards: Beginning in 1989, the level of sales for qualification for a single would be halved from 1,000,000 and 500,000 to qualify for Gold and from 2,000,000 to 1,000,000 for Platinum. And, in a complete reversal of previous policies, the standards applied retroactively. . . opening a Pandora's box of possibilities—and complications.*

Gold singles surged to 72, which included thirty older titles that hadn't qualified under the levels extant at the time of their release. For the now historical August 16, 1992 presentation of Gold and Platinum Records to the estate of Elvis Presley, the king of rock 'n roll received 21 retroactive Gold Records for singles and an additional 14 Awards for EPs that did not sell the amount required for those awards during his life. The presentation, which combined Gold, Platinum and Multi-Platinum certifications, totaled over 100 "new" awards, raising Elvis' total to 180 RIAA Awards. It was certainly an attention-getter and will comfortably place Presley way ahead of the pack in the next Guinness Book Of Records. — Ye Olde Editor

A. *White matte (1964-1975)*. Manufactured exclusively by New York Picture & Frame Company, the plaque was an off-white linen material in an unpainted, finished wood frame. This linen material will often turn a reddish-brown with age. The dedication on the plate was engraved with the RIAA seal usually etched in. In the case of LPs, the mini-cover was mounted separately from the plate. Because of their unique looks and the difficulty in counterfeiting them, white matte awards are the most desirable and collectible style (as recent sales trends and auction results bear out). Many collectors pursue this style alone.

B. *Floater (1975-1981)*. The award's background was dark, usually black, enclosed in a wood frame painted either gold or white. The disc and plate appear to be "floating" between the background and the plexiglas. In the case of LPs, the mini-cover (also floating) was mounted separately from the plate.

C. *Strip-plate (1982-1984)*. The award's background was dark. Unlike previous awards, for LPs the plate containing the dedication and the mini-cover appeared on the same strip of metal. This was also the first format to include a gold or silver plated cassette, acknowledging the ever increasing contribution of the tapes to unit sales. These cassettes were located either directly beneath the album disc or resting atop the lower LP lip.

D. *Hologram (1984-1989)*. The award's background is dark. In the case of LPs, the dedication and the mini-cover appear on the same strip of metal. The RIAA logo on the plate is in a rainbow-like hologram to avoid unauthorized duplication. Most, if not all, of these awards have a gold or silver plated cassette's top shell beneath the album disc or resting atop the lower LP lip. Some include a gold or silver plated compact disc.

E. *"R"-Hologram (1980 to present)*. For this new format the traditional RIAA logo was replaced with a large "R" in a hologram pattern. All size and style restrictions were relaxed, giving the record companies more freedom in choosing a design for a particular award. Thus one can see a multitude of styles during these years with only the "R"-hologram logo remaining constant. (Both the hologram and the "R"-hologram award can be found in a new "format," the compact disc award. These feature either a gold or silver plated compact disc with the dedication plate with or without the picture from the CD's jewel box.)

6. Recipient. Presentation has become increasingly important in the last few years. . . and with good reason. The more closely identifiable an award is with the artist, the more desirable the award. In descending order, the desirability of an award based on the recipient is a) the artist who recorded the record, b) the record company who released the record, c) either an individual or organization closely connected with the production of the record, such as anyone listed on the album's credits, d) the production company, e) a radio station, or, finally, f) a record company executive otherwise unknown in the collecting community.

Because of the increased popularity of collecting awards, many award recipients and record company executives have acquired extra awards to sell to the collectors market, either duplicates of presented awards or new (sic) awards signifying a higher level of sales achievement. There is presently a practice running rampant across the country called "ordering," when a licensed manufacturer accepts orders from anyone other than a record company executive to have an RIAA certified award made. This has led to an explosion of hologram and "R" hologram awards being produced that threaten the collectibility, value and, most importantly, the merit of these two formats.

This unfortunate turn of events has led to the gradual lessening of the prestige of owning awards in general with the latter two hologram styles taking the biggest fall in popularity. While many dealers defend ordering awards as a practice, it devalues the awards. I therefore recommend that, when purchasing an award, the prospective buyer should ask the seller if the award was ordered for the purpose of resale or was it obtained from a "legitimate" recipient. You should always deal with a seller who *will* tell you the truth as there is virtually no difference between the ordered awards and the presented awards *because they were made in the same place!*

The RIAA is presently taking steps to reduce illegitimate orders: Soon all RIAA hologram awards will carry a serial number which will assist in keeping track of all awards made in the future. In the meantime, they have assigned a representative to assist both sellers and buyers in determining whether or not a given award *was certified* at a certain level. Interested parties can write Angela Corio at 1020 Nineteenth Street, Suite 200, Washington, D.C. 20036 or phone 202-775-0101. Keep in mind that she is only able to assist in verifying certification, *not authenticity.* For that you must turn to a knowledgeable, and trusted, expert. . .

7. Condition. The condition of the award is vital: *Everybody* wants *everything* mint and award collectors are no exception. White matte collectors are particularly fussy, sometimes wanting only items that have never been repaired, even if the matte is yellowing. Personally, I would rather have an item that has been restored and looks beautiful than one that is original but looks terrible. (It is best *not* to attempt to repair an award unless you are qualified.)

When buying any award be sure the award is the original format (i.e., the style of the award offered for sale is consistent with the style of the period in which it was presented). The original format containing the original label of the record being certified will usually be the most collectible. Another point to remember is that record companies have been known to reframe awards in a style other than the prevailing format. This was often done to replace damaged frames or the requisite frame was unavailable at the time. Before 1989, when formats were still under strict control, this practice was not met with favor by the RIAA and generally discouraged.

From a collecting point of view it is better to buy an award in its original frame whenever possible. When white mattes are found with different frames the diligent collector will often replace the frame with an original from that period, especially if it is a highly desirable title. As a matter of fact, serious collectors have been known to use parts of a white matte of a less desirable artist to restore an award of an artist of greater value.

There *are* framed gold records that do not indicate any type of music organization recognizing the sales achievement. These are not awards produced by any framing store, trophy and plaque shop, or RIAA certified manufacturers. They are made by specialist establishments for one purpose, resale. The popularity of award collecting and the desire to own a trophy has caused the manufacture of these wall-hangings to escalate. These gold records are usually identifiable by the lack of any music industry seal on the plaque. The most widely distributed of these are the [admittedly beautiful] plaques produced by California Gold Records, now located in New Jersey. This company has produced a gold record for almost every title in The Beatles' catalog. However, as of this writing the company has discontinued all framed gold records of Beatles' records with the exception of a numbered "collectible" for John Lennon's "Imagine" single.

As the hobby develops, new and unusual awards are uncovered. Recently discovered was an award produced by a band and presented to the radio station disc jockey responsible for "breaking" their first certified gold single. Since this item is neither RIAA nor in-house, it represents a new classification where the "organization" recognizing the sales achievement is the artist itself!

Finally, when purchasing an award, compare prices which may vary widely. Consider all the factors mentioned above and be certain to consider the seller's reputation. A good price is a bad buy if you receive a bogus award (or, worse, no award at all). Currently, awards sell for as little as $10 to as much as $20,000. Remember, white mattes appear to be the best investment; while later awards can be enjoyable to own, because of the large amounts legitimately ordered and manufactured it is still uncertain as to the investment potential of awards since the strip plate format. My parting advice is to purchase the best awards you can afford but don't forget that collecting is *supposed* to be fun. Sometimes the best thing to own is simply the title you like the most. . .

Christopher Chatman, proprietor of Beyond Records, Los Angeles, CA, is a collector and dealer of rare records, acetates, RIAA Gold and Platinum Record awards and rock 'n roll memorabilia and a regular advertiser in Goldmine.

Bibliography

The following books and publications helped in one way or another in making this book what it is. . . Also, each issue of *Goldmine* was perused for articles and discographies that would assist this project. Finally, those books with Pierian Press as publisher are all currently available from Popular Culture, Ink.

Aeppli, Felix
Heart Of Stone: The Definitive Rolling Stones Discography, 1962-1983
Pierian Press, 1985

Beecher, John, & Malcolm Jones
The Buddy Holly Story:
A Pictorial Account Of His Life & Music
MCA/Coral, Great Britain, 1980

Blair, John
The Illustrated Discography Of Surf Music
Pierian Press, 1985

Blair, John, & Steve McParland
The Illustrated Discography Of Hot Rod Music
Popular Culture, Ink., 1990

Brown, James, & Bruce Tucker
James Brown: The Godfather Of Soul
MacMillan, 1986

Burt, Rob
Surf City/Drag City
Blandford Press, UK 1986

Castleman, Harry, & Walter Fodrazik
All Together Now;
The First Complete Beatles Discography
Ballantine, 1975

Christgau, Robert
Rock Albums Of The '70s
Ticknor & Fields, 1981

Cotten, Lee
Jailhouse Rock:\The Bootleg Records
Of Elvis Presley, 1970-1983
Pierian Press, 1983

Cox, Perry, & Joe Lindsay
Beatles Price Guide For American Records;
Cox Ent./BIOdisc, 1992

Dalley, Robert
Surfin' Guitars:
Instrumental Surf Bands Of The Sixties
Surf Publications, 1988

DeWitt, Howard
Chuck Berry: Rock 'N' Roll Music
Pierian Press, 1985

Docks, L.R.
American Premium Record Guide
Books Americana, 1986

Elliott, Brad
Surf's Up!
The Beach Boys On Record, 1961-1981
Pierian Press, 1982

Erlewine, Michael, & Scott Bultman
All Music Guide:
The Best CDs, Albums & Tapes
Miller Freeman, 1992

Ferguson, Charles, & H. Johnson
Mainstream Jazz Reference & Price Guide
O'Sullivan Woodside, 1984

Francis, Connie
Who's Sorry Now?
St. Martin's Press, 1984

Goldmark, Joe
International Steel Guitar Directory
Privately printed, 1988

Grafman, Howard, & B.T. Manning
Folk Music USA
Citadel Press, 1962

Guralnick, Peter
The Listener's Guide To The Blues
Facts-On-File, 1982

Haley, John, & John von Hoelle
Sound & Glory:
The Incredible Story Of Bill Haley
Dyne-American, 1990

Heggeness, Fred
The Rarest Of The Rare, Volumes 1-4
FH Publishing

Heggeness, Fred
Country & Western Price Guide
FH Publishing, 1991

Hibbert, Tom
Rare Records: Wax Trash & Vinyl Treasures
Proteus Books, 1982

Hounsome, Terry
Rock Record, 1st-3rd Editions
Blandford, 1987

Hudgeons, Thomas
Official Price Guide To Records, Volumes 1-7
House Of Collectibles

Joynson, Vernon
Acid Trip:
A Complete Guide To Psychedelic Music
Babylon Books, 1984

Krogsgard, Michael
Positively Bob Dylan
Popular Culture Ink, 1991

Lazel, Larry, & Dafydd Rees & Luke Crampton
Rock Movers & Shakers
Billboard Publications Inc., 1989

Lifton, Sarah
The Listener's Guide To Folk Music
Facts-On-File, 1983

Lindsay, Joe
Picture Discs Of The World Price Guide
BIOdisc, 1990

Malone, Bill
Country Music USA
University Of Texas, 1968

Morthland, John
The Best Of Country Music
Dolphin & Company Inc., 1984

O' Brien, Ed, & Scott P. Sayers, Jr.
Sinatra: The Man And His Music
Private pressing, 1992

Osborne, Jerry
Country Music
Osborne Ent, 1984

Pareles, Jon, & Patricia Romanowski
The Rolling Stone Encyclopedia Of Rock & Roll
Rolling Stone/Summit, 1983

Parkyn, Geoff
Genesis: Turn It On Again
Omnibus, 1984

Peace, Warren
Peace Record Price Guide
Privately printed, 1979

Raymond, Jack
Show Music On Record
Frederick Ungar Publishing Co., 1982

Reinhardt, Charles
You Can't Do That;
Beatles Bootlegs & Novelty Records
Contemporary Books Inc., 1981

Rogers, Don
Dance Halls, Armories & Teen Fairs:
A History & Discography Of
Pacific Northwest Rock
Music Archives, 1988

Ruppli, Michael
The Clef/Verve Labels: A Discography
Greenwood Press, 1986

Savage, Jon
The Kinks
Faber & Faber, 1984

Sawyer, Charles
The Arrival Of B. B. King
Doubleday, 1980

Shaw, Arnold
Sinatra: The Entertainer
Delilah, 1982

Shelton, Robert, & Burt Goldblatt
The Country Music Story
Castle Books, 1966

Shestack, Melvin
Country Music Encyclopedia
Thomas Crowell Co., 1974

Tosches, Nick
Unsung Heroes Of Rock 'n' Roll
Charles Scribner's Sons, 1984

Umphred, Neal
1985-86 Rock Record Album Price Guide
O'Sullivan Woodside, 1985.

Umphred, Neal
A Touch Of Gold
White Dragon Press, 1990

Waller, Don
The Motown Story
Charles Scribner's Sons, 1985

Walters, David
The Children Of Nuggets
Popular Culture Ink, 1990

Wenner, Jann, & the editors of *Rolling Stone*
The Rolling Stone Record Review
Pocket Books, 1971

Wenner, Jann, & the editors of *Rolling Stone*
The Rolling Stone Record Review, Volume II
Pocket Books, 1974

Whitburn, Joe
Top Pop Albums 1955-1985
Record Research, 1985

Williams, Roger
Sing A Sad Song: The Life Of Hank Williams
Ballantine, 1973

And The Outro: The Author's Bio (Sort of)

I discovered the magic of the "elpee" in 1964 when I found that the big-record-with-the-little-hole played several songs before I had to get up and turn it over. Wow! My first two albums were *Elvis' Golden Records* and *Elvis' Gold Records, Vol. 2* (logical, if predictable, choices). Over the course of the next few years my nascent collection grew in rather odd directions: As both my brother, Charles, and my Aunt Judy were members of mail order record clubs, through cast-offs and trades I acquired such essentials as Gary Lewis & The Playboys' *Golden Greats* (still a favorite; Jerry's kid may not have had the world's greatest pipes but he had some of this planet's finest talents supporting him), The Dave Clark Five's *Coast To Coast* (which poses the burning question "Can an LP be less than twelve minutes per side and still be worth the money?" and leaves it unanswered) and Nancy "Yeah, Frank's m'dad zbut I love 'im anyway" Sinatra's *How Does That Grab You, Darlin'?*

I gradually learned to love an awfully broad spectrum of rock and pop music. (Although, as a pseudo-intellectual acne-ed white teenager I could not for the life of me figure out what alla those black people were moanin' n' groanin', wailin' n' railin', screechin' n' beseechin' about. Like *real* country music, that took a little maturation to make sense. . .) When the British Invasion hit I somehow managed to avoid the charm of The Beatles and The Stones. Don't ask me how; I was, how shall I put it, oh, headstrong? While my contemporaries were wearing the grooves out of The Beatles and The Stones— and, let's never forget Herman's Hermits— I stuck to the "old" stuff: Elvis, Chuck, Little Richard, the Everlys . . .

In the summer of '65 everything changed: I realized that there was a potential for rock music to be something else, something *other*, than the first generation of rockers had imagined. Call it what you like, but most of us, diehard collectors or merely casual listeners, remain inextricably bound to the sounds that first opened our ears and hearts to the possibilities of music. For some it was jazz, Duke Ellington's orchestra and "Take The A-Train;" for another it was rockabilly, Scotty Moore's guitar and "Mystery Train." For me it was folk-rock, Jim McGuinn's 12-string and "Mr. Tambourine Man."

I became an avid reader of Paul Williams' *Crawdaddy*, which, more than anything else, helped shape my opinions on Rock-with-a-capitol-R. I had discovered *Pet Sounds*, the album that has remained #1 in my heart for more than two decades. Still, I religiously purchased each new [cheesy] Elvis soundtrack, but the necessity of taking them home in brown paper bags (so my friends wouldn't see) woke me up. At a Christmas party in 1967 some noise blurted out of the speakers that had me entranced: "Why don't we sing this song all together, open our heads let the pictures come. . ." I figured it might be time for me to renege on my vow never to buy a record with Mick Jagger on it.

Through the past two decades I have grown rather detached from the merchandising aspect of the biz, constantly reminding myself that it was to get away from alla the Mad Ave bullschidt that allowed rock 'n roll to occur. Still, albums such as *Born To Run*, *Armed Forces*, *Remain In Light*, *Dream Of Life* and *Skylarking* keep my hopes up.

Through an odd series of events, in 1984 I was interviewed for the position of editor of O' Sullivan Woodside's line of record collectors price guides and was responsible for the sixth edition of their *Rock & Roll Record Albums Price Guide* (1985) and the third edition of the *Elvis Presley Record Price Guide* (1986). This led to my association with *Goldmine*. . . I am also associated with White Dragon Press, having produced *A Touch Of Gold: The Elvis Presley Record & Memorabilia Price Guide* in 1990 and their forthcoming *Rhythm & Blues Records 1948-1963: A Discography & Price Guide*, and Tower Records & Books's *Pulse!* magazine, where I pen the monthly "Avid Collector" column.

Now, being the "price guide guy," I run into some rather, y'know *odd* conversations with collectors and dealers. A typical conversation that I have at shows that I attend around the country might go something like this: "Are you sure about the prices in your book?" More or less. Certainly there are errors but each edition gets bigger and better. "Well, what about [fill in the blank]?" Okay, what about it? "Well, you say here that it's worth $100." Um, yep. I do. Why? Is that too high or too low? "Well, it seems awfully high to me." Well, have you seen a nearly mint copy for sale in recent memory? "Sure. I saw one for half that four years ago." I hope you bought it. "Oh, I did." Tell you what, I'll give you $100 for it. "No way. I'd never sell it for that!"

Current faveraves include but are not limited to hiking the mountains of the Pacific Northwest; pizza from Arcaro & Jenell's in Old Forge, PA; *Cerebus the Aardvark*; books on mind-expanding substances; Cary Grant movies; Jack Daniels on the rocks at 2 AM with headphones listening to *Music From Big Pink*; slow dancing by candlelight to Coltrane; tall women who work out; Picasso's joyously erotic lithographs; ranting at right wing propagandists; and wondering why *everyone* isn't a conspiratorialist. Finally, I am the amazed father of a gloriously four year old daughter (currently single for all you [female] price guide groupies out there). I remain an unregenerate iconoclast and anti-authoritarian whose views have been summed up by a friend—who prefers dialectical materialism—as mystically liberal. . .

Neal Umphred
March 1, 1993

Goldmine's 1993 Price Guide Survey

What do you think? In our efforts to continue to improve on our *Price Guide to Collectible Records,* we are actively encouraging you to provide us with your thoughts. Please take a few moments now to fill out this brief survey and return it to us. We've incorporated ideas from readers in the past, so your input is valuable. Thanks in advance!

1. **Check all that apply:** Which of the following *Goldmine* books have you purchased?
   - ❏ *Goldmine's Price Guide to Collectible Record Albums,* 3rd Edition (this book)
   - ❏ *Goldmine's Price Guide to Collectible Record Albums,* 2nd Edition
   - ❏ *Goldmine's Price Guide to Collectible Record Albums,* 1st Edition
   - ❏ *Goldmine's Rock 'n Roll 45 RPM Record Price Guide,* 2nd Edition
   - ❏ *Goldmine's Rock 'n Roll 45 RPM Record Price Guide,* 1st Edition
   - ❏ *Goldmine's Price Guide to Collectible Jazz Records,* 1st Edition
   - ❏ *Doo-Wop: The Forgotten Third of Rock 'n Roll*

2. Other than those listed in question #1, what other music <u>price guides</u> do you use?

   a._____

   b._____

3. How often would you like us to update our album price guide?
   - ❏ Every six months
   - ❏ Every 12 months
   - ❏ Every 18 months
   - ❏ Every 24 months
   - ❏ Every 36 months
   - ❏ Other: _____

4. How would you describe the pricing of the items in this book?
   - ❏ Most of the listed prices are too high
   - ❏ Most of the listed prices are too low
   - ❏ Listed prices are just right
   - ❏ Other: _____
   - ❏ No opinion

5. Is the 3rd Edition of *Goldmine's Price Guide to Collectible Record Albums* comprehensive enough for you, that is, does it cover the artists, eras, and records that you are interested in?
   - ❏ Yes   ❏ No

6. If this book is not comprehensive enough for you, how can we improve on it? _____

   _____

   _____

7. **Choose <u>only one</u>:** Do you want *all* albums included in this price guide or just "collectible" albums?
   - ❏ All albums   ❏ Just collectible albums   ❏ Other: _____

8. Have you ever purchased anything from the advertisers in our *Goldmine* **books**?
   - ❏ Yes   ❏ No   ❏ I don't know

9. Are you a current subscriber to *Goldmine* magazine?
   - ❏ Yes, I am a subscriber
   - ❏ No, I do not subscribe, but I buy it from a retail outlet
   - ❏ No, I do not subscribe, and I do not buy it

10. Would you purchase a hard-cover edition of this price guide, or any other *Goldmine* price guides, knowing that they would cost about $5.00 more?
    - ❏ Yes   ❏ No   ❏ I don't know

11. How much did you spend on your music collecting hobby the past twelve months?
    - ❏ I didn't spend anything
    - ❏ $1 - $249
    - ❏ $250 - $499
    - ❏ $500 - $999
    - ❏ $1,000 - $1,999
    - ❏ $2,000 - $2,999
    - ❏ $3,000 - $3,999
    - ❏ $4,000 - $4,999
    - ❏ $5,000 - $5,999
    - ❏ $6,000 - $9,999
    - ❏ $10,000 - $15,999
    - ❏ $16,000 or more

12. What is the estimated approximate value of your music collection?
    - ❏ I don't have a collection
    - ❏ $1 - $999
    - ❏ $1,000 - $3,999
    - ❏ $4,000 - $5,999
    - ❏ $6,000 - $9,999
    - ❏ $10,000 - $14,999
    - ❏ $15,000 - $19,999
    - ❏ $20,000 - $29,999
    - ❏ $30,000 - $39,999
    - ❏ $40,000 - $49,999
    - ❏ $50,000 - $59,999
    - ❏ $60,000 or more

13. **Check all that apply:** Which decade(s) does your favorite type of music generally come from?
    - ❏ Pre-1940s
    - ❏ 1940s
    - ❏ 1950s
    - ❏ 1960s
    - ❏ 1970s
    - ❏ 1980s
    - ❏ 1990s

(Over, please)

Please complete:

_____
name

_____
address

_____
city, state, zip

BUSINESS REPLY MAIL
FIRST-CLASS MAIL PERMIT NO. 12 IOLA, WI

POSTAGE WILL BE PAID BY ADDRESSEE

GOLDMINE
MARKETING RESEARCH DEPARTMENT
700 E STATE ST
IOLA WI 54945-9984

---

14. **Check all that apply:** Where did you get your copy of the *Goldmine* book(s) you have?
   ❑ Mail offer ❑ A record collector's club ❑ A record show I attended ❑ Other
   ❑ It was a gift ❑ An ad in *Goldmine* ❑ On sale in a record store
   ❑ A friend or relative ❑ An ad in another publication ❑ On sale in a book store

15. Where do you see yourself in five years as far as purchasing vinyl record albums?
   ❑ I will become increasingly more active in my purchases
   ❑ I will remain as active as I am now
   ❑ I will be less involved than I am right now
   ❑ I will not be purchasing vinyl albums five years from now

16. Would you be interested in seeing *Goldmine* publish a price guide to collectible compact discs?
   ❑ Definitely, yes ❑ Maybe ❑ Not interested at all

17. Are there any other price guides you would like to see us publish?_____

_____

_____

18. Are you male or female?
   ❑ Male ❑ Female

19. What is your age? _____ years old

20. Which of the following categories most closely approximates your total annual household income (before taxes)?
   ❑ $1 - $14,999 ❑ $50,000 - $74,999 ❑ $125,000 - $149,999 ❑ $200,000 - $249,999
   ❑ $15,000 - $24,999 ❑ $75,000 - $99,999 ❑ $150,000 - $174,999 ❑ $250,000 - $299,999
   ❑ $25,000 - $49,999 ❑ $100,000 - $124,999 ❑ $175,000 - $199,999 ❑ $300,000 or more

Thanks very much for completing this survey.
Simply fold the survey, tape it, and mail it with the postage-paid portion facing out.